For Reference

Not to be taken from this room

BURT FRANKLIN: BIBLIOGRAPHY & REFERENCE SERIES 232

LEXICON TO THE ENGLISH POETICAL WORKS OF JOHN MILTON

LEXICON TO THE
ENGLISH POETICAL WORKS
OF JOHN MILTON

BY

LAURA E. LOCKWOOD

BURT FRANKLIN
NEW YORK

BURT FRANKLIN, Publisher
235 East 44th St., New York 10017
Originally Published: 1907
Reprinted: 1968
Printed in the U.S.A.

Library of Congress Catalog Card No.: 68-56596
Burt Franklin Bibliography & Reference Series 232

TO

PROFESSOR ALBERT S. COOK

IN HONOUR OF SCHOLARSHIP AND IN GRATITUDE

FOR INSPIRATION AND WISE COUNSEL

PREFACE.

THE purpose of the present work is to provide a means by which the student may readily find the signification of any word in the poetry of Milton. The chief aim has been that of definition, and every word in the poetry has been subjected to a careful examination. Almost every significant word in the vocabulary of Milton is filled with literal and figurative meanings that shade into each other and off into other and related senses; and each word is modified and varied in the shifting lights thrown on it by the context. This is perhaps truer of Milton than of any other English poet. The precise definition of words is, I am sure, impossible, because of their chameleonlike quality and their lack of exact correspondence to the ideas they represent. Yet I hold it wise at least to attempt, in so far as possible, to reinterpret in the medium of everyday English the lines of the poet who speaks in an even less transparent language. Since I recognize that such work must by its nature be more or less tentative, and hence lacking in finality, I do not expect to win assent to all my explanations of words; the reader will doubtless often see or feel some other shade of meaning to be dominant in a particular word. But when he disagrees with what I have written, he will often, I trust, be stimulated to search for himself the thought of the poet; and I could have no higher desire for the book than that it should be an incentive to the closer reading of Milton. That "no one would nowadays read *Paradise Lost* for pleasure" has to me been disproved by years spent in teaching the poetry of Milton to college classes. But for this pleasure assistance in the way of interpretation is often necessary. The annotators, from Newton and Todd down to Masson and Jerram have done much to make clear difficult passages, yet there is much that they have not attempted to explain ; besides, the student who depends upon the annotators must have about him a small library of books. In providing this one book I hope to increase the number of those who read "the one artist of the highest rank in the great style whom we have." The reception given to Schmidt's *Shakespeare Lexicon* proves that students have found it valuable, and if such a work has been shown helpful in the study of Shakespeare, a similar book will, I believe, aid in the study of Milton.

This book was begun in 1895, and the first one hundred and seventy pages were in 1898 presented to the Philosophical Faculty of Yale University as a doctoral thesis. These pages were also, during the latter year, put through the press. In 1902 the work was resumed on the book, and it is but now brought to completion. The long time intervening between the beginning and end will account for some slight differences in form and treatment between the first and last parts.

In the arrangement and classification of meanings I have chiefly followed the *New English Dictionary*. Every occurrence of each word is recorded, except in the case of certain words that appear very frequently ; these are given in all their meanings, but starred to show that not every instance under each category is noted. Recognizing the fact that a grammar of Milton is also needed, I have included some grammatical observations looking toward such a book ; but the treatment of the syntax does not pretend to be complete. I have noted the accent of words where it differs from the modern prose accent.

I have used the text of the Globe edition, retaining the modern spelling, because the book is primarily intended for those who to-day care to understand the thought of Milton. I have added the bit of translation from Ariosto,

"And, to be short, at last his guide," etc.,

found in *Of Reformation in England*; this Mr. Masson omits. The Globe text is inconsistent in punctuation, in spelling, and in the compounding of words. The punctuation of a sentence in the Globe text sometimes gives to a word a different meaning, or assigns it to a different grammatical category, from that in the original text ; for example in the word *hiss*: P. L. x. 573. Again in spelling, the text frequently follows, in the case of the same word, now the first edition and now the modern usage. The word *tuneable* is so spelled in P. L. v. 151, but *tunable* in P. R. I. 480. The former spelling is that of the first edition in both cases. The word *loath* in five instances follows the vagaries of Milton's spelling; in five others it is spelled *loth*, where the original text has *loath*: P. L. IX. 946, 1039; XII. 585; C. 177, 473. This lack of consistency with itself, or of agreement with the first edition, is greatest in the matter of joining words in compounds. I have therefore thought good to add in an appendix the list of compounds as they appear in Milton's own edition. This list is taken from Beeching's reprint of Milton's Poetical Works.

I should be very glad to express in detail my indebtedness to the lexicographers, the annotators of Milton, the makers of concordances, and the writers of kindred books, for all the help I have gained from their works, but the names are too many, and the list of books is too long for enumeration. I wish to thank the friends who have so kindly aided me in many ways, and among these in particular to record my gratitude to Miss Josephine Burnham of Wellesley College, who has read much of the proof; and to Dr. Charles G. Osgood, of Princeton University, who has, from his wide acquaintance with the classical problems in Milton, often generously given time and careful thought to the decision of doubtful points. To Professor Albert S. Cook I owe more than I can express. He suggested the undertaking of this work, and every step of the way he has shown unfailing interest. Every page is nearer what it should be because of his friendly and discerning criticism.

L. E. L.

WELLESLEY, MASSACHUSETTS,
June 1, 1907.

ABBREVIATIONS.

A.	- -	Arcades.
absol.	- -	absolute, -ly.
abstr.	- -	abstract.
acc.	- -	accusative, -s.
adj.	- -	adjective, -ly.
adv.	- -	adverb, -ially.
art.	- -	article.
attrib.	- -	attributive, -ly.
Brit.	- -	Britannia.
C.	- -	Comus.
Cam.	- -	Camden.
Cir.	- -	Upon the Circumcision.
collect.	-	collective, -ly.
comp.	- -	compound, comparative.
compl.	- -	complement.
conj.	- -	conjunction, -tive.
concr.	- -	concrete.
cos.	- -	cosmography.
dat.	- -	dative.
def.	- -	definite.
D.F.I.	- -	On the Death of a Fair Infant dying of a Cough.
demon.	-	demonstrative.
disyl.	- -	disyllabic.
ellipt.	- -	elliptical, -ly.
emphat.	- -	emphatic.
esp.	- -	especially.
Eurip.	- -	Euripides, *Supplices.*
fem.	- -	feminine.
fig.	- -	figurative, -ly.
Gr.	- -	Greek.
H.B.	- -	From the History of Britain.
Hey.	- -	Heylyn.
Hor. Epist.	-	Horace, *Epistle.*
Hor. O.	-	The Fifth Ode of Horace.
Hor. Sat.	-	Horace, *Satire.*
Il P.	- -	Il Penseroso.
indef.	- -	indefinite.
indic.	- -	indicative.
inf.	- -	infinitive.

imper.	-	imperative.
impers.	-	impersonal, -ly.
interj.	- -	interjection.
intr.	- -	intransitive.
L.	- -	Latin.
L'A.	- -	L'Allegro.
masc.	- -	masculine.
M.M.	-	Song on May Morning.
monosyl.	-	monosyllabic.
M.W.	- -	An Epitaph on the Marchioness of Winchester.
N.E.D.	-	New English Dictionary.
neut.	- -	neuter.
N.O.	- -	On the Morning of Christ's Nativity.
nom.	- -	nominative.
obj.	- -	object, -ive.
OE.	- -	Old English.
P.	- -	The Passion.
part.	- -	participle, -ial.
pentasyl.	-	pentasyllabic.
perf.	- -	perfect.
pers.	- -	person, -al.
Petr.	- -	Petrarch, *Sonnet.*
phr.	- -	phrase.
P.L.	- -	Paradise Lost.
pl.	- -	plural.
plupf.	- -	pluperfect.
poss.	- -	possessive.
P.R.	- -	Paradise Regained.
prep.	- -	preposition, -al.
pres.	-	present.
pret.	- -	preterit.
pron.	- -	pronoun.
Ps.	- -	Psalm.
refl.	- -	reflexive.
rel.	- -	relative.
R.V.	- -	Revised Version.
S.	- -	Sonnet.
S.A.	- -	Samson Agonistes.
sb.	- -	substantive.
sing.	- -	singular.

xii

ABBREVIATIONS.

S.M.	-	At a Solemn Music.	trisyl.	-	trisyllabic.
Soph.	-	Sophocles, *Electra.*	U.C.	-	On the University Carrier.
spec.	-	specific, -ally.			
subj.	-	subject, subjunctive.	vb.	-	verb.
sup.	-	superlative.	vbl.	-	verbal.
T.	-	On Time.	V.E.	-	At a Vacation Exercise in the College.
tetrasyl.	-	tetrasyllabic.			
tr.	-	transitive.	Vulg.	-	the Vulgate.
transf.	-	transferred.	W.S.	-	On Shakespeare.

* A star prefixed to a word indicates that all the meanings are given, but not all the instances of occurrence.

LEXICON TO THE ENGLISH POETICAL
WORKS OF JOHN MILTON.

*A or An, *indef. art.* (a *before con-*
sonants, **an** *before vowels or*
silent **h**), (**1**) some, any, (*a*) *before*
the name of an individual, object,
notion, etc.: P. L. I. 61; V. 66;
VI. 387; S. A. 364.

(*b*) *following the adj. in* many
a, such a, what a: P. L. I. 196,
282, 709; II. 713; P. R. I. 196;
D. F. I. 74.

(*c*) *with nouns of multitude after*
which the prep. **of** *is omitted:*
P. L. I. 796; II. 967; S. A. 144;
C. 926.

(*d*) *following the adj. when pre-*
ceded by **so, as**: P. L. II. 202,
382, 452; III. 25.

(*e*) *preceding vbl. sb.*: P. 51.

(*f*) **an** *used for* **a** *before aspir-*
ated **h**: P. L. V. 744.

(**2**) *more definitely*, one: P. L.
I. 697; XII. 264; L'A. 14; **on a**
day, a certain, a particular: P. L.
V. 579; IX. 575.

(**3**) *corruption of O.E. formative*
syllables with prep. idea still re-
maining, in the compounds, **a-field**:
L. 27; **a-maying**: L'A. 20; *of time*
in, on: P. R. III. 234.

Aaron, *sb.* the brother of Moses:
P. L. III. 598; XII. 170; P. R.
III. 15.

Abaddon, *sb.* the abyss of hell:
P. R. IV. 624.

Abandon, *vb. tr.* (*a*) to renounce,
give up: P. L. VI. 494.

(*b*) to forsake, leave, desert:
P. L. VI. 134; S.A. 120.

(*c*) *refl.* to yield oneself unrestrainedly: P. L. X. 717.

Abarim (Ábarim), *sb.* a chain of
hills east of the Dead Sea and the
lower Jordan: P. L. I. 408.

Abash, *vb. tr.* to destroy the self-
possession of, make ashamed,
discomfit: P. L. I. 331; IV. 846;
VIII. 595; IX. 1065; X. 161;

P. R. II. 224; IV. 195; Ps.
VI. 24.

Abassin (Abássin), *adj.* Abyssinian:
P. L. IV. 280.

Abate, *vb.* (**1**) *tr.* to blunt, turn the
edge of: P. R. II. 455.

(**2**) *intr.* to grow less, decrease:
P. L. XI. 841.

Abbana (Ábbana), *sb.* Abana, a river
of Damascus: P. L. I. 469.

Abdiel (*disyl.*), *sb.* a seraph: P. L.
V. 805, 896; VI. 111, 171, 369.

Abhor, *vb.* (*pres. 2d sing.* abhorr'st:
P. L. XII. 79; *pret. or past part.,*
trisyl.: P. L. II. 87, 577; P. R.
IV. 191; C. 535; L. 75; *disyl.*:
P. L. II. 659; VI. 607; F. of C. 4;
Ps. III. 22), *tr.* to loathe, abomi-
nate: P. L. II. 659; XII. 79;
P. R. IV. 172; F. of C. 4; *with*
prep. inf.: P. L. IV. 392; V. 120;
VI. 607; XI. 686.

part. adj. **abhorred**, detested,
loathed: P. L. II. 87, 577; P. R.
IV. 191; C. 535; L. 75; Ps. III.
22.

Abide, *vb.* (*only in pres. and inf.*), (**1**)
tr. (*a*) to bear, endure, undergo:
P. 20; to endure the results of,
suffer for: P. L. IV. 87; to endure
the issue of, sustain: Ps. I. 13.

(*b*) to face, encounter: P. L.
I. 385.

(**2**) *intr.* (*a*) to continue in a
place or condition, remain, rest:
P. L. III. 388; V. 609; N. O. 225.

(*b*) to dwell, reside, sojourn:
P. L. XI. 292; S. A. 922; C. 951.

(*c*) to inhere or belong as a
quality: S. A. 1136.

Ability, *sb.* power, capacity: S. A.
743.

Abject, *adj.* brought low in condition or position, low-lying, degraded, despicable: P. L. I. 312,
322; IX. 572; XI. 520; S. A. 169.

Abjure, *vb. tr.* to renounce upon

oath, disclaim solemnly : P. L.
VIII. 480 ; *absol.* : P. R. I. 474.
Able, *adj.* having the power or
means, *followed by an inf.* (*a*)
expressed : P. L. IV. 155; V. 70 ;
X. 819, 950 ; XII. 491 ; P. R. III.
365 ; S. M. 4 ; *comp.* : P. R. I.
151 ; (*b*) *understood* : P. L. III.
211.

Abode, *sb.* (*a*) dwelling-place, home:
P. L. III. 734 ; IV. 939 ; VII. 553 ;
N. O. 18 ; C. 693 ; Ps. LXXXI. 37 ;
LXXXIV. 39.

(*b*) stay, temporary continuance
in a place : D. F. I. 60.

Abolish, *vb. tr.* to annihilate, destroy,
(*a*) *objects* : P. L. II.370; III. 163.

(*b*) *persons* : P. L. II. 93 ; IX.
947.

Abominable (abómináble), *adj.* odi-
ous, execrable, detestable : P. L.
II. 626 ; X. 465 ; P. R. IV. 173 ;
S. A. 1359.

Abomination, *sb.* (*a*) detestable
thing *as in the Bible*, an idol
or things pertaining to idolatry :
P. L. I. 389.

(*b*) cause of pollution : P. R.
III. 162.

Abortive, *adj.* (*a*) arrested in development : P. L. III. 456; *hence,*
sterile, barren : S. A. 1576.

(*b*) premature : P. L. XI. 769.

(*c*) annihilative, extermina-
tive(?) : P. L. II. 441.

(*d*) *transferred epithet,* produced
prematurely, *hence,* in a confused
mass without order (?) : P. R. IV.
411.

Abound, *vb. intr.* to be plentiful, be
present in overflowing measure :
P. L. III. 312 ; VI. 502 ; XII. 478;
Ps. IV. 36 ; LXXXIV. 24.

*****About,** (1) *adv.* (*a*) on every side :
P. L. X. 420 ; Il P. 152.

(*b*) here and there, in every
direction : V. Ex. 23 ; S. A. 530,
675, 1089 ; A. 58.

(*c*) round, in revolution : S. A.
1747.

(*d*) on the point of, ready, *with*
prep. inf. : S. A. 727.

(2) *prep.* (*a*) on every side of,
round the outside of, around,
surrounding : P. L. I. 770 ; III.
60 ; VI. 765 ; VII. 197 ; P. R. IV.
16 ; N. O. 210 ; round about :
P. L. II. 653 ; III. 379 ; IV. 21,
401 ; VIII. 261, 318 ; IX. 426 ; X.
448; S. A. 1497; V. Ex. 63; Il P.
48 : Ps. III. 17 ; LXXXVIII. 67.

(*b*) near, close to, or on some
side of *in position* : P. L. IV. 340,
552; VI. 426; C. 153; near about :
C. 146.

(*c*) over the surface of, upon :
P. L. V. 619.

(*d*) round or over the parts of,
to and fro in : P. R. I. 34 ; C. 990.

(*e*) near or close to *in time* :
P. L. II. 348.

(*f*) in connection with, occupied with, concerning, in reference to : P. L. V. 769 ; P. R. I.
489 ; II. 98 ; S. A. 483 ; V. Ex.
57 ; C. 167.

(*g*) carried by, attached to,
possessed by : S. A. 1501 ; C.
647.

*****Above,** (1) *adv.* (*a*) overhead : P. L.
VIII. 318 ; Il P. 152.

(*b*) on high : C. 1003.

(*c*) in heaven, *God's dwelling-
place* : P. L. II. 351, 731, 814,
856 ; V. 363 ; VIII. 168 ; X. 549 ;
XI. 2, 232 ; S. A. 1052 ; Cir. 18 ;
L. 178.

(*d*) in a higher place : P. L.
VII. 268.

(*e*) *as sb.* God or heaven,
always preceded by from : P. L.
II. 172 : III. 56 ; IV. 860 ; VII.
118 ; XI. 138, 668 ; P. R. I. 274,
496 ; IV. 289 ; S. A. 199, 664 ;
N. O. 4.

(2) *prep.* (*a*) in or to a higher
place than, over : P. L. I. 15,
499 ; III. 58 ; VI. 71.

(*b*) higher in rank, position, or
power than : P. L. I. 39, 249 ; II.
428, 455 ; X. 149.

(*c*) higher in degree or quantity
than, beyond, more than : P. L.
III. 268, 571 ; V. 297 ; VI. 402 ;
IX. 228.

(*d*) superior to, out of the
reach of : P. L. VII. 82 ; S.A. 62.

Abraham (*disyl. except* P. L. XII.
152), *sb.* (*a*) the founder of the
Jewish nation, as an example of
faith and righteousness : P. L. XII.
152, 273, 449.

(*b*) *fig.* the faith of Abraham
and the covenant made with him :
P. R. III. 434.

Abroad, *adv.* (*a*) at large, in all
directions : P. L. II. 463 ; P. R.
IV. 414 ; S. A. 1600 ; Ps. LXXXVI.
43; LXXXVII. 10 ; CXXXVI. 5.

(*b*) out of doors, out of one's
house : S. A. 809, 919.

Abrupt, *sb.* abyss : P. L. II. 409.

Abruptly, *adv.* without warning, suddenly : P. R. II. 10.

Absence, *sb.* state of being absent or away : P. L. V. 110 ; VII. 107 ; IX. 248, 294, 861 ; P. R. II. 100 ; S. A. 806.

Absent, (1) *adj.* not present : P. L. III. 261 ; VIII. 229 ; X. 82 ; P. R. IV. 400, 440 ; S. A. 1604 ; L. 35.

(2) *vb. tr.* to keep away, detain or withhold from being present : P. L. IX. 372 ; X. 108.

Absolute, *adj.* perfect ; (*a*) complete, entire : P. L. VIII. 421.

(*b*) unconditioned, unrestricted, unlimited : P. L. II. 560 ; III. 115 ; IV. 301 ; XI. 311 ; XII. 68 ; S. A. 1405.

(*c*) faultless, free from all deficiency : P. L. VIII. 547 ; X. 483 ; P. R. II. 138.

Absolutely, *adv.* unreservedly, unconditionally : P. L. IX. 1156.

Absolve, *vb. tr.* (*a*) to set free, deliver from the penalties of sin : P. L. III. 291.

(*b*) to acquit, exonerate : P. L. X. 829.

(*c*) to accomplish, finish : P. L. VII. 94.

Abstain, *vb. intr.* (*a*) to withhold oneself, refrain, forbear : P. L. IV. 748 ; X. 993 ; P. R. III. 192 ; *with prep. inf.* : P. L. VII. 120.

(*b*) to hold oneself back, stop : P. L. X. 557.

(*c*) to refrain from food : P. L. IX. 1022 ; P. R. II. 269.

Abstemious, *adj.* abstinent, temperate : S. A. 637.

Abstinence, *sb.* abstemiousness, self-restraint : P. L. IX. 924 ; *personified* : C. 709.

Abstract, *vb. tr.* to withdraw, remove, separate : P. L. IX. 463.

part. adj. **abstract,** having the mind withdrawn from the contemplation of present objects : P. L. VIII. 462.

Abstruse, *adj.* (*a*) difficult, recondite : P. L. VIII. 40 : S. A. 1064.

(*b*) concealed, hidden, *sup.* : P. L. V. 712.

Absurd, *adj.* unreasonable, ridiculous : S. A. 1337.

Abundance, *sb.* (*a*) superfluity, copiousness, plentifulness : P. L. IV. 730 ; IX. 620 ; C. 764.

(*b*) large quantity, plentiful supply : P. L. V. 315.

Abundant, *adj.* existing in great

plenty, plentiful, abounding : P. L. V. 72 ; VII. 388.

Abundantly, *adv.* overflowingly, copiously : P. L. VIII. 220.

Abuse, (1) *sb.* (*a*) misuse, misapplication : P. L. IV. 204 ; V. 800.

(*b*) ill-usage, injury : S. A. 76.

(2) *vb. tr.* (*a*) to deceive, impose upon : P. L. I. 479 ; P. R. I. 455.

(*b*) to misuse, pervert : S. A. 1354 ; Ariosto I. 4.

Abyss, *sb.* (1) unfathomable cavity or space ; (*a*) *fig.* : P. L. X. 842 ; XII. 555.

(*b*) the hell of the Greeks, Tartarus : S. A. 501.

(2) the primal chaos ; (*a*) out of which the universe was created : P. L. I. 21 ; VII. 211, 234.

(*b*) after the creation of the universe, the space which intervened between heaven or the earth, and hell : P. L. II. 405, 910, 917, 956, 969, 1027 ; III. 83 ; IV. 936 ; X. 314, 371, 476 ; *or possibly* hell, the infernal pit (?) : P. L. I. 658 ; II. 518.

Academe, *sb.* the Academy of Plato at Athens : P. R. IV. 244.

Academic, *sb. pl.* adherent of the philosophical school of Plato : P. R. IV. 278.

Acanthus, *sb.* the plant *Acanthus spinosus* : P. L. IV. 696.

Accaron, *sb.* Ekron, a city of the Philistines, *spelled* Accaron in *Vulg.* : P. L. I. 466.

Accent, *sb.* (*a*) modulation of voice, tone : P. L. II. 118 ; IX. 321.

(*b*) verse stress : S. XIII. 3.

Accept, *vb. tr.* (*a*) to take or receive willingly or with approval *a thing offered* : P. L. II. 58 ; III. 302 ; IV. 380 ; V. 465 ; VI. 804 ; IX. 629 ; X. 758 ; XI. 37, 505 ; P. R. II. 398 ; IV. 493 ; S. A. 510, 1179, 1255, 1460.

(*b*) to take upon oneself or undertake as a responsibility : P. L. II. 425, 452.

part. adj. **accepted,** approved, chosen : P. L. XI. 46.

Acceptable (ácceptáble), *adj.* gladly received, welcome : P. L. X. 139 : S. A. 1052 ; *comp.* **more acceptable** : Seneca 2.

See **Thrice-acceptable.**

Acceptance, *sb.* act of accepting or state of being accepted : P. L. XII. 305 ; P. R. II. 388 ; a receiving with approbation, favour-

able reception : P. L. v. 531;
VIII. 435 ; x. 972; XI. 457 ; Ps.
VI. 19.

Access, (accéss ; *doubtful* : P. L.
IV. 137 ; IX. 310), *sb. (a)* way
or means of approach : P. L.
I. 761 ; II. 130 ; IV. 137 : IX. 511,
810 ; XII. 239 ; P. R. I. 492 ; Ps.
LXXXVI. 23.

(*b*) increase, growth : P. L. IX.
310.

Accessible, *adj.* affording entrance :
P. L. IV. 546.

Accessory (áccessóry), *sb.* adherent,
helper : P. L. x. 520.

Accident, *sb. (a)* unfortunate event,
disaster : P. R. II. 39 ; S. A.
1519, 1552.

(*b*) attribute, property : S. A.
612.

(*c*) *having the double meaning of*
casualty or mishap, and logical
attribute : V. Ex. 74.

Acclaim, *sb.* acclamation, applause,
preceded by loud : P. L. II. 520 ;
III. 397 ; x. 455 ; P. R. II.
235.

Acclamation, *sb.* shout of applause :
P. L. VI. 23 ; VII. 558 ; Ps.
LXXXI. 4.

Accompany, *vb. tr.* to escort, attend,
go along with : P. L. IV. 600 ;
v. 352 ; VIII. 428 ; x. 88 ; *fig.*
(*with phenomena*) : P. L. x. 848 ;
(*with thoughts*) : P. R. I. 300.

Accomplish, *vb. tr. (a)* to fulfil, perform or carry out *a design or purpose* : P. L. III. 160 ; XII. 567 ;
P. R. II. 113 ; II. 452.

(*b*) to complete *a portion of
time* : P. L. VII. 550.

part. adj. **accomplished,** (*a*)
perfect in personal graces : P. L.
IV. 660.

(*b*) perfect in craftiness : S. A.
230.

Accomplishment, *sb.* fulfilment, completion : P. R. II. 207.

Accord (1) *sb. (a)* agreement, concur-
rence of will : P. L. II. 36.

(*b*) volition, choice : S. A. 1643.

(2) *vb. intr.* to agree, be in
harmony, **accord to,** agree with :
P. R. III. 9 ; *or possibly a noun
in sense (a)* (?) : P. L. II. 503.

According, *adv.* **according to,** in a
manner agreeing with, consistent
with, answering to : P. L. VI.
816 ; x. 517, 806 ; C. 766 ; Ps.
VII. 32, 62.

Accost, *vb. tr.* to address, speak to :

P. L. III. 653 ; IV. 822 ; P. R.
III. 6.

Account, (1) *sb. (a)* estimation, consideration : P. L. IV. 622 ; P. R.
II. 193.

(*b*) explanation answering for
conduct : P. L. IV. 841 ; S. XIX. 6.

(*c*) narration, report, description : P. L. IV. 235 ; x. 501.

(2) *vb. tr.* to consider, regard,
with two acc. : P. L. III. 238 ; VI.
726.

Accountable, *adj.* answerable, re-
sponsible : P. L. II. 255 ; x. 29.

Accurse, *vb. used only in past part.*
put under a curse, doomed to
misery or perdition : P. L. II.
1055 ; IV. 69 ; v. 877 ; x. 168,
175, 465, 723 ; XII. 413 ; S. A.
930 ; P. R. IV. 179 ; *absol.* **the
accursed,** the rebel angels under
the curse of God : P. L. VI. 850.

Accusation, *sb.* act of accusing,
arraignment : P. L. IX. 1187.

Accuse, *vb. tr.* to charge with a
crime or fault, blame, censure :
P. L. III. 112 ; IV. 67 ; VIII. 561 ;
IX. 1186 ; x. 127 ; P. R. IV. 316 ;
with acc. and of : P. L. x. 852 ;
XII. 37 ; A. 10.

part. adj. **accused,** charged with
a crime : P. L. x. 164.

Accuser, *sb.* one who accuses another
of a crime : P. L. IV. 10 ; IX.
1182.

Accustom, *vb. tr.* to familiarize by
use, habituate : P. L. XI. 285.

part. adj. **accustomed,** customary, wonted, usual : P. L. IV. 779 ;
Il P. 60.

Ache, *vb. intr.* to suffer pain : Ps.
VI. 5.

Acheron, *sb.* a river of hell : P. L.
II. 578 ; *fig.* hell : C. 604.

Achieve, *vb. tr. (a)* to accomplish,
perform : P. L. II. 21, 363, 723 ;
P. R. I. 68 ; II. 411 ; S. A. 1492.

(*b*) to gain, win : P. L. x. 368,
469 ; XI. 698, 792 ; XII. 234.

gerund, gaining : P. L. IX. 696.

Achilles, *sb.* the hero of the Iliad :
P. L. IX. 15.

Acknowledge, *vb. tr.* to own ; (*a*)
with gratitude *a gift or service
rendered* : P. L. XI. 612 ; S. A.
245 ; *with clause* : P. L. VII. 512.

(*b*) the superiority *of a person
or thing*, recognize, confess : P.
R. II. 83 ; *with two acc.* : P. L. v.
172 ; VIII. 574 ; XII. 573 ; P. R.
II. 376.

(c) the knowledge of admit as
true, *with two acc.* : S. A. 1170;
a fault or charge : P. L. x. 939;
with prep. inf. : S. A. 735; *with
clause* : S. A. 448.
part. adj. **acknowledged**, recognized : P. L. iv. 956.
Acquaint, *vb. tr.* (*a*) to familiarize,
make conversant : P. R. i. 400;
M. W. 72.
(*b*) to inform, make cognizant:
P. L. x. 395.
Acquist, *sb.* thing acquired, acquisition : S. A. 1755.
Acquit, *vb. tr.* (*a*) to declare not
guilty, exonerate : P. L. x. 827.
(*b*) *refl.* to free or deliver oneself
from a charge or an enemy : S.
A. 897.
Acquittance, *sb.* deliverance, release:
P. L. x. 53.
Act, (**1**) *sb.* (*a*) effect of the exertion
of power, thing done, deed, per-
formance : P. L. ii. 363; v. 593;
vi. 264, 377, 883; vii. 176, 601;
viii. 600; ix. 674; x. 1, 334, 390,
1026; xi. 256, 789; xii. 427, 429;
P. R. i. 216; ii. 412; iii. 24; iv.
475; S. A. 28, 231, 243, 527, 1101,
1210, 1362, 1368, 1389, 1736; P.
24; C. 465; S. viii. 6; Ps.
lxxxviii. 50.
(*b*) the doing or performing
of a thing : P. L. ii. 109; ix.
668.
(*c*) agency, operation : P. L.
iv. 94.
(*d*) actual being, actuality, activity (?) : P. L. ix. 190.
(**2**) *vb. intr.* to put forth power,
produce effects : P. L. vii. 172;
x. 807; xii. 517; S. A. 503.
Action, *sb.* (*a*) state or manner of
acting, activity : P. L. iv. 401;
viii. 602; ix. 460, 559; x. 608.
(*b*) thing done, deed : P. R. ii.
411; iii. 9, 239; iv. 215, 266;
S. A. 1440.
Active, *adj.* abounding in or exhibiting action : P. L. v. 477; ix.
96; P. R. ii. 239; given to
outward action, *opposed to contemplation* : P. R. iv. 371.
Activity, *sb.* exercise of physical
power : S. A. 1328.
Actual, *adj.* existing in act or by
influence, *opposed to bodily presence* : P. L. x. 587.
Adam, *sb.* (*a*) the first man, the progenitor of the human race : P. L.
iii. 285, 286, 734; iv. 323, 408,

610, 742; v. 3, 27, 94, 230, 299,
302, 307, 321, 358, 372, 453, 469,
561, 751; vii. 42, 45, 59, 109, 524;
viii. 1, 51, 64, 179, 296, 401, 437,
595, 644, 653; ix. 205, 226, 289,
290, 318, 342, 591, 816, 828, 831,
838, 856, 888, 960, 965, 988, 1004,
1016, 1065, 1132, 1144, 1162; x.
102, 103, 115, 124, 197, 715, 736,
845, 914, 939, 967, 1010; xi. 114,
136, 191, 212, 223, 224, 249, 251,
263, 293, 335, 370, 412, 419, 423,
448, 454, 495, 526, 596, 628, 674,
754, 868; xii. 4, 63, 270, 372, 552,
607, 624; P. R. i. 51, 102, 115;
ii. 133, 134; iv. 607, 614.
(*b*) **second Adam**, Christ the
Redeemer, *contrasted with the
first Adam through whom sin
came into the world* : P. L. xi.
383.
Adamant, *sb.* substance of surpassing hardness or impenetrability : P. L. ii. 436; vi. 110,
255; P. R. iv. 534; of surpassing
strength : P. L. x. 318.
Adamantean, *adj.* of the strength of
adamant : S. A. 134.
Adamantine, *adj.* of or like adamant : A. 66; (*a*) unbreakable :
P. L. i. 48.
(*b*) impregnable, impenetrable :
P. L. ii. 646, 853; vi. 542.
Add, *vb. tr.* (*a*) to join, unite *one
thing to another so as to increase
the number, quantity, power, or
significance* : P. L. ii. 700; iv.
36, 845, 950; v. 152; vii. 322,
484; viii. 109; ix. 821; x. 753;
xi. 138; xii. 581, 582, 583; S. A.
290, 1121, 1357; M. W. 5; Il P.
49; C. 859.
(*b*) to say further, *with object
sentence* : P. R. iv. 550; *with prep.
inf.* : P. R. iv. 113; *absol.* : P.L.
x. 909; xi. 263; P. R. i. 497.
gerund, the addition of : S. A.
1351.
Adder, *sb.* (*a*) serpent : S. A. 936.
See **Wisdom**.
(*b*) Satan, acting through the
serpent ; P. L. ix. 625.
Addicted, *part.* devoted, given up
(*to*) : P. R. iv. 213.
Addition, *sb.* enlargement, increment : P. L. v. 116; vii. 555.
Address, I. *sb.* action of making
ready, preparation : S. A. 731.
II. *vb.* (**1**) *tr.* to direct; (*a*) (*one's
way*) : P. L. ix. 496.
(*b*) (*words or praise to*) *with acc.*:

P. L. XI. 295 ; P. R. II. 301 ; C. 272 ; *with indirect object omitted,* speak : P. L. IX. 855 ; to prepare to speak : S. A. 729.

(*c*) prayers to, supplicate (*or sb.* approach to a person for a purpose) : P. L. V. 868.

(*d*) (*to a cause*) apply : P. L. IX. 672.

(2) *intr.* to prepare, make ready: P. L. VI. 296.

Ades, *sb.* Hades, the god of the lower world, *here* an attendant upon the throne of Chaos : P. L. II. 964.

Adhere, *vb. intr.* to be a close companion or follower, cleave : P. L. II. 906 ; VIII. 498.

Adherent, *sb.* follower, partizan : P. L. VI. 266 ; X. 622.

Adiabene (Ádiabéne), *sb.* the eastern district of Assyria and a province of the Parthian Empire : P. R. III. 320.

Adjoin, *vb.* (1) *tr.* to unite *one person* to another in fellowship : P. R. I. 403.

(2) *intr.* to be contiguous or adjacent to : P. L. IX. 449.

Adjourn, *vb. tr.* to defer, delay : P. L. XII. 264.

Adjudge, *vb. tr.* (*a*) to decide, determine : P. L. X. 377.

(*b*) to condemn, sentence : P. L. III. 223 ; IV. 823 ; S. A. 288.

Adjure, *vb. tr.* (*a*) to appeal to, call upon : F. of C. 5.

(*b*) to enjoin solemnly, entreat earnestly : S. A. 853.

part. adj. **adjuring,** having power to summon, exorcising : C. 858.

Admiration, *sb.* (*a*) wonder, astonishment : P. L. III. 271 ; VII. 52.

(*b*) wonder mingled with approbation or veneration : P. L. III. 672 ; P. R. II. 221 ; **to admiration,** so as to cause wonder and delight : P. L. IX. 872 ; P. R. IV. 228.

Admire, *vb.* (*pres.* 2d *sing.* admir'st: P. L. VIII. 567) (1) *intr.* to be surprised, wonder, marvel : P. L. VIII. 75 ; P. R. I. 169, 326 ; Hor. O. 8. ; *with clause* : P. L. I. 690 ; VIII. 25.

(2) *tr.* (*a*) to wonder or marvel at : P. L. II. 677 ; VI. 498.

(*b*) to regard with mingled wonder and approbation, contemplate with pleasure, think highly of : P. L. I. 681 ; VIII. 567 ; IX.

444, 542, 746 ; XI. 689 ; P. R. I. 214, 380, 482 ; II. 175 ; III. 39, 52 ; S. A. 530 ; *absol.*: P. L. I. 731 ; IX. 524 ; X. 352 ; P. R. II. 222. *gerund* : P. L. IX. 1178.

Admit, *vb. tr.* (*a*) to allow to enter the mind or heart : P. L. XI. 596 ; S. A. 605 ; into the fellowship (*of*): L'A. 38.

(*b*) to consent to the doing or existence of : P. L. VIII. 637 ; P. R. I. 95.

(*c*) to receive as valid : P. L. X. 763.

(*d*) to concede, grant, acknowledge : P. L. VIII. 115 ; *with clause* : P. L. XI. 141.

See **Re-admit.**

Admonish, *vb. tr.* (*a*) to warn, caution : P. L. IX. 1171 ; XI. 813.

(*b*) to apprise, notify : P. L. III. 647.

Admonishment, *sb.* monition, warning : P. L. VII. 77.

Adonis, *sb.* (*a*) a youth, beloved by Venus, who was killed while hunting. On account of the rivalry of Venus and Proserpina for the possession of Adonis, he was compelled to spend half of each year in the lower world and half in the upper world : P. L. IX. 440 ; C. 999. *See* **Thammuz.**

(*b*) a river rising in the mountains of Lebanon and emptying into the Mediterranean Sea, *so named because annually coloured by the blood of the youth Adonis* : P. L. I. 450.

Adopted, *part. adj.* received as one's own : P. L. V. 218.

Adoration, *sb.* (*a*) veneration, worship : P. L. III. 351 ; IV. 737 ; V. 800 ; VIII. 315.

(*b*) reverence, homage : C. 452.

Adore, *vb. tr.* (*a*) to worship, reverence as divine : P. L. I. 323, 373, 384, 475 ; III. 342 ; IV. 89, 721, 959 ; V. 805 ; VII. 514 ; VIII. 280, 360, 647 ; IX. 547 ; XI. 333 ; P. R. II. 189, 212 ; S. A. 1177 ; A. 37 ; Ps, LXXXVI. 42 ; *absol.*: P. L. V. 144.

(*b*) to regard with profound admiration or love : P. L. IX. 540.

Adorer, *sb.* worshipper : P. L. IX. 143 ; P. R. I. 451.

Adorn, (1) *adj.* ornate, beautiful : P. L. VIII. 576.

(2) *vb. tr.* (*a*) to be an ornament to, add beauty to : P. L. V. 218 ; VII. 445 ; IX. 840.

(*b*) to embellish, decorate, enrich : P. L. XI. 280.

part. adorned, made beautiful or attractive : P. L. I. 371 ; II. 446, 1049 ; III. 550 ; IV. 634, 713 ; VI. 474 ; VII. 87, 384 ; VIII. 482 ; IX. 393, 1030 ; X. 151 ; P. R. II. 137 ; IV. 35 ; S. A. 357, 679.

Adramelec, *sb.* Adramelech, an idol of the Sepharvites, *here* identified with one of the rebel angels : P. L. VI. 365.

Adria, *sb.* the Adriatic Sea : P. L. I. 520.

Adrift, *adj.* drifting, aimlessly afloat: P. L. XI. 832.

Adulterer, *sb.* one who practises adultery : Petr. 4.

Adulterous, *adj.* given to adultery : P. L. IV. 753.

Adultery, *sb.* violation of the marriage bed : P. L. XI. 717.

Adust, *vb. tr.* to dry up with heat : P. L. VI. 514.

part. adj. adust, hot and dry, parched : P. L. XII. 635.

Advance, *vb.* (*plupf. formed with auxiliary* be : P. L. V. 744) (1) *tr.* (*a*) to lift, raise on high : P. L. I. 536 ; V. 588 ; XII. 632 ; Ps. LXXX. 44.

(*b*) to promote, exalt : P. L. IV. 90, 359 ; VII. 626 ; IX. 148 ; P. R. I. 88 ; II. 69 ; III. 144 ; C. 1004.

(*c*) to bring or move forward : P. L. II. 682 ; V. 2 ; VIII. 163 ; S. A. 136.

(*d*) to augment, enhance, magnify : P. L. V. 191 ; P. R. III. 143 ; S. A. 450.

(*e*) to improve, increase : P. L. I. 119.

(2) *intr.* to go or march forward : P. L. I. 563 ; v. 744 ; VI. 109, 234, 399, 884 ; X. 616 ; XII. 215.

Advantage, (1) *sb.* (*a*) position, state, or circumstance favourable to success ; that which aids one in getting the better of another : P. L. II. 35 ; VI. 401 ; IX. 718 ; S. A. 1118, 1401 ; *esp.* favourable opportunity, chance : P. L. I. 327 ; IX. 258 ; P. R. II. 234.

(*b*) resulting benefit, gain, or profit : P. L. II. 987 ; VIII. 122 ; XII. 510 ; S. A. 1259.

(2) *vb. tr.* to give superiority to, benefit : P. R. IV. 208 ; *absol.* : S. A. 255.

Advantageous, *adj.* useful, opportune : P. L. II. 363.

Adventure, *sb.* hazardous enterprise,

bold undertaking : P. L. II. 474, 571 ; X. 468 ; S. A. 1740.

Adventurer, *sb.* one who engages in a hazardous enterprise : P. L. X. 440.

Adventurous, *adj.* (*a*) daring, bold : P. L. I. 13 ; II. 615 ; IX. 921.

(*b*) full of peril, dangerous, hazardous : P. L. VI. 66 ; X. 255 ; C. 79.

Adversary, (1) *sb.* opponent, antagonist : P. L. X. 906 ; P. R. IV. 527 ; *esp. of* Satan, *preceded by def. art. or poss. pron.* : P. L. II. 629 ; III. 81, 156 ; VI. 282 ; IX. 947 ; P. R. I. 33.

(2) *adj.* hostile, inimical : P. L. XII. 312.

Adverse (ádverse : P. L. I. 103 ; II. 77 ; VI. 206 ; X. 701 ; advérse : P. L. II. 259 ; X. 289 ; XI. 364 ; P. R. III. 189 ; S. A. 192 ; *doubtful* : P. L. VI. 490 ; VII. 239 ; S. A. 1040), (1) *adj.* (*a*) opposing, antagonistic, hostile : P. L. I. 103 ; VI. 206, 490 ; VII. 239 ; contrary to one's nature : P. L. II. 77

(*b*) acting or blowing in or from an opposite direction : P. L. X. 701.

(*c*) disastrous, unfortunate, unfavourable : P. L. II. 259 ; XI. 364 ; P. R. III. 189 ; S. A. 192, 1040.

(2) *adv.* in or from opposite directions : P. L. X. 289.

Adversity, *sb.* misfortune : P. R. IV. 479.

Advice, *sb.* counsel : P. L. II. 197 ; V. 889 ; P. R. I. 394 ; III. 364 ; *personified* : C. 108.

Advise, *vb.* (1) *tr.* (*a*) to counsel, admonish, suggest : P. L. II. 283, 292 ; V. 523 ; P. R. IV. 211 ; C. 755 ; Eurip. 2 ; *with clause* : P. L. II. 376 ; S. XVII. 7 ; *absol.* : P. L. II. 42 ; V. 888 ; IX. 212 ; P. R. II. 152.

(*b*) to inform, instruct : P. L. V. 234 ; *absol.* : P. L. XII. 611.

(2) *intr. by omission of refl. pron.* to consider, deliberate, take counsel : P. L. V. 729 ; *with clause* : S. A. 328 ; to take heed, have regard, *with prep. inf.* : Ps. LXXXI. 55.

past part. used as adv. advisedly, purposely : P. L. VI. 674.

Advocate, *sb.* intercessor : P. L. XI. 33.

Ægean (Ǽgean(?)), *adj.* of the Ægean Sea : P. L. I. 746 ; P. R. IV. 238.

Æmilian, *adj.* Æmilian (*road*), the Via Æmilia, the Roman highway in northern Italy : P. R. IV. 69.

Ænon, *sb.* a town in Samaria near Salem: P. R. II. 21. *See* **Salem.**

Æolian, *adj.* pertaining to the Æolians, *esp.* of Æolic poetry as cultivated in the island of Lesbos : P. R. IV. 257.

Aerial, *adj.* (*a*) of or pertaining to the air or atmosphere: P. L. VII. 422; X. 667.

(*b*) airy, light: P. L. III. 445.

(*c*) ethereal, heavenly: P. L. V. 548; C. 3.

Aery or **Airy, (1)** *adj.* of, through, or resembling air in some manner ; (*a*) of the atmosphere : P. L. VII. 246; N. O. 103.

(*b*) formed of the atmosphere : P. R. IV. 57.

(*c*) high in the air, lofty, towering : P. L. II. 407; III. 741 ; XI. 185; P. R. IV. 402; S. A. 974.

(*d*) elastic as air, light in movement : P. L. I. 775 ; IV. 568 ; V. 481.

(*e*) formed or fitted to travel through the air : P. L. VII. 428.

(*f*) making no more impression than air, empty, vain : P. L. VI. 283.

(*g*) having no real existence, unsubstantial, visionary : P. L. V. 105 ; II P. 148 ; C. 208.

(*h*) phantom-like, spectral: P. L. II. 536.

(*i*) spiritual: P. L. I. 430.

(*j*) **airy shell,** the vault of heaven(?): C. 231.

(**2**) *adv.* **aery light,** light as air, *fig. of sleep* : P. L. V. 4.

Ætna, *sb.* the volcano in Sicily : P. L. I. 233 ; III. 470.

Afer, *sb.* the west-southwest wind : P. L. X. 702.

Affable, *adj.* courteous, kind : P. L. VII. 41 ; VIII. 648.

Affair, *sb.* what has to be done, business, concern : P. L. X. 408 ; P. R. I. 50, 132 ; IV. 462.

See **State-affair.**

Affect, *vb. tr.* (*a*) to aim at, aspire to : P. L. III. 206; VI. 421; P. R. III. 45 ; *with prep. inf.* : P. L. XII. 81.

(*b*) to adopt by preference, choose, prefer : P. R. III. 22 ; S. A. 1030 ; C. 386.

(*c*) to assume, arrogate: P. L. V. 763.

(*d*) to act upon, influence: P. L. V. 97 ; X. 653.

Affection, *sb.* love : S. A. 739.

Affirm, *vb. tr.* to maintain or assert strongly: P. L. V. 107 ; VIII. 117; *with two acc.* : P. R. I. 253 ; *with clause* : U. C. II. 13.

Afflict, *vb. tr.* to give bodily or mental pain to, grieve, distress, torment : P. L. VI. 852 ; X. 863 ; XI. 315; P. R. I. 425; II. 93 ; S. A. 114, 195, 914, 1252 ; Ps. LXXXVIII. 61.

part. adj. (*a*) **afflicting,** grievously painful, tormenting : P. L. II. 166.

(*b*) **afflicted,** distressed, tormented : P. L. I. 186 ; IV. 939 ; *absol.* **the afflicted,** a distressed person : S. A. 660.

Affliction, *sb.* (*a*) calamity, disaster : P. L. I. 57.

(*b*) misery, distress, grief : P. R. II. 92 ; S. A. 113, 457, 503, 1257 ; Ps. LXXXVIII. 37.

Afford, *vb. tr.* to give, yield, offer, grant. *with acc. and dat.* : P. L. IV. 46 ; V. 316 ; X. 271 ; S. A. 910, 1109 ; *with acc. and* to : N. O. 16 ; Ps. LXXXV. 27 ; LXXXVI. 19, 61 ; to furnish, supply : P. L. IX. 968 ; to manage to give, spare : P. L. IX. 912.

Affright, (1) *sb.* fear, terror : C. 356.

(**2**) *vb. tr.* to frighten, terrify : P. L. VI. 869; N. O. 194 ; C. 148.

Affront, (1) *sb.* (*a*) hostile encounter, attack : S. A. 531.

(*b*) insult, wrong: P. L. IX. 302; P. R. III. 161 ; IV. 144.

(**2**) *vb. tr.* (*a*) to insult openly, treat with indignity: P. L. IX. 328.

(*b*) to face in defiance, confront : P. L. I. 391.

A-field, *adv.* into the field : L. 27.

Afloat, *adj.* borne on the water : P. L. I. 305.

Afraid, *adj.* full of fear, alarmed : P. L. II. 759; *with* of : P. L. X. 117; *of omitted before clause* : P. L. XII. 493.

Afresh, *adv.* anew : P. L. II. 801.

Afric, *adj.* of Africa : P. L. I. 585 ; P. R. II. 347.

Africa, *sb.* the continent : P. R. II. 199 ; C. 606.

African, *sb.* (*a*) Hannibal, the Carthaginian general : S. XVII. 4.

(*b*) the elder Scipio Africanus : P. R. III. 101.

*After, (1) *adv.* (*a*) in the rear, behind : S. A. 337.

(*b*) at a later time, subsequently : P. L. III. 520 ; VIII. 555 ; P. R. IV. 7 ; S. XII. 7 ; XXI. 6 ; **long after** : P. L. I. 80, 383 ; III. 497 ; V. 387, 762 ; **soon after** : P. L. II. 1023.

(2) *prep.* (*a*) behind, following : P. L. I. 476 ; II. 1026 ; VII. 298 ; IX. 48 ; XII. 131 ; P. R. III. 335 ; S. A. 1651.

(*b*) following with intent to overtake, in pursuit of : P. L. I. 172 ; VI. 866; X. 363 ; N. O. 236.

(*c*) later in time than, subsequent to, at the close of : P. L. I. 319, 797 ; II. 128, 290 ; III. 336 ; IV. 327, 646, 653 ; V. 248, 562 ; VII. 131 ; IX. 87, 102, 918, 1028.

(*d*) in succession to *in time, order, or importance* : P. L. II. 228 ; III. 196 ; V. 336 ; P. R. II. 151.

(*e*) subsequent to and notwithstanding : P. L. I. 631 ; III. 552 ; X. 828 ; P. R. II. 41 ; M. W. 49, 64.

(*f*) in obedience to, in harmony with : P. L. II. 692 ; III. 161 ; V. 710 ; P. R. II. 162 ; A. 72.

(*g*) according to the nature of, conformably to : P. L. VII. 311, 394 ; VIII. 343.

(3) *adj.* later, subsequent : S. XIII. 7.

After-bands, *sb.* bands or fetters imposed after release : P. L. IX. 761.

Afternoon, *sb.* time from the meridian to sunset : P. L. IX. 403.

After-times, *sb.* succeeding ages : P. L. III. 529.

*Again, *adv.* (*a*) another time, once more, anew : P. L. II. 83, 173 ; III. 365 ; S. A. 1128 ; **once again** : P. L. VI. 618 ; P. R. II. 17 ; S. A. 1174.

(*b*) back to a former state or position : S. A. 1355.

*Against, *sometimes* ágainst : P. L. VI. 813 ; X. 1045), *prep.* (*a*) directly opposite to, in front of : P. L. III. 526.

(*b*) toward and into contact with : P. L. IV. 542 ; P. R. IV. 18.

(*c*) in the direction of, toward : C. 99.

(*d*) in hostility or active opposition to : P. L. I. 42, 470, 667 ; P. R. II. 90 ; *with object omitted* : P. L. IV. 942.

(*e*) contrary to, not in conformity with : P. L. IV. 71 ; VII. 614 ; IX. 350.

(*f*) in resistance to, in protection from : P. L. II. 28 ; VIII. 533 ; IX. 299 ; X. 882 ; P. R. IV. 533.

(*g*) in provision for, in preparation for, in anticipation of : P. L. IV. 817 ; VII. 202 ; X. 275 ; P. R. I. 317.

See '**Gainst.**

Agape, *adv.* with open mouth of wonder : P. L. V. 357.

Agate, *sb.* the precious stone: C. 893.

Age, *sb.* (*a*) latter part of life : S. A. 69, 336, 580 ; V. Ex. 69 ; Il P. 167 ; *personified* : C. 109 ; **old age** : P. L. XI. 538 ; S. A. 572, 700, 925, 1487, 1488.

(*b*) period of life at which one has arrived : P. L. XI. 665 ; P. R. I. 209 ; IV. 380 ; S. A. 1489 ; C. 40, 59.

(*c*) long but indefinite space of time, period, epoch : P. L. II. 186 ; III. 328 ; VII. 191 ; IX. 44 ; X. 647, 733 ; XI. 326, 767 ; XII. 549 ; **the age of gold** : N. O. 135.

(*d*) period of time contemporary with the life of any one : P. L. IX. 44 ; XI. 809 ; XII. 243 ; P. R. II. 209 ; Il P. 101 ; S. XI. 12 ; XII. 1.

(*e*) a lifetime as a measure of time : P. L. I. 698 ; P. R. I. 16, 48 ; II. 441 ; III. 294 ; S. A. 764, 1707 ; W. S. 2 ; Ps. LXXX. 20.

Aged, *adj.* old, *of persons* : P. R. I. 314 ; S. A. 1568 ; C. 835 ; *of things* : N. O. 160 ; L'A. 82 ; Ps. LXXXIII. 53.

Agent, *sb.* one who acts or exerts power : P. L. IX. 683.

Aggravate, *vb. tr.* to make more burdensome, make worse : P. L. III. 524 ; X. 549 ; P. R. III. 218 ; S. A. 1000.

Aggravation, *sb.* extrinsic circumstance increasing the guilt of a crime : S. A. 769.

Aggregated, *part. adj.* collected together : P. L. X. 293.

Aghast, *adj.* dismayed, terrified : P. L. II. 616 ; P. R. I. 43 ; N. O. 160 ; Ps. CXIV. 15.

Agitation, *sb.* action of moving, motion : P. L. IX. 637.

Agony, *sb.* anguish or extreme suffering of body or mind : P. L. II. 861 ; IX. 858 ; XI. 482.

Agra, *sb.* the capital of Agra, one of

the northern provinces of India :
P. L. XI.

Agreeable, *adj.* suitable, appropriate,
with **to** : S. A. 1506.

Agrican, *sb.* a king of Tartary: P. R.
III. 338.

Ah, *interj.* exclamation expressive of
sorrow, regret, or lamentation :
P. L. IV. 42, 366 ; X. 822 ; S. A.
1565 ; Dante I.

Ahab, *sb.* the seventh king of Israel :
P. R. I. 372.

Ahaz, *sb.* the eleventh king of Judah:
P. L. I. 472.

Aialon, *sb.* Ajalon, a town in Palestine
a short distance northwest of
Jerusalem : P. L. XII. 266.

Aid, (1) *sb.* assistance of any kind,
succour, help : P. L. I. 13, 38 ;
III. 232, 727 ; IV. 927 ; VI. 119,
294, 335 ; VII. 140 ; VIII. 459,
642 ; IX. 260, 308 ; X. 271, 919,
944 ; XI. 651, 800 ; XII. 542 ;
P. R. I. 393 ; II. 148 ; III. 302 ;
IV. 377, 468, 493 ; S. A. 1146 ;
V. Ex. 15 ; C. 90 ; Ps. LXXXVI.
22 ; *pl. concr.* means of assistance : P. R. III. 392.

　(2) *vb. tr.* to assist, succour, help:
P. L. I. 235 ; VI. 38 ; IX. 208 ;
C. 856 ; Ps. LXXXIII. 32.

Aidless. *adj.* unassisted, helpless :
C. 574.

Aim, I. *sb.* (*a*) design, purpose :
P. L. I. 41, 168 ; II. 128 ; IV. 808;
S. A. 1464.

　(*b*) act of directing a weapon :
P. L. II. 28, 712.

　II. *vb.* (*pres. 2d pers.* aim'st :
P. L. XI. 884) **(1)** *tr.* (*a*) to
estimate, guess, conjecture, *absol.*:
P. L. XI. 884.

　(*b*) to endeavour to obtain :
P. R. IV. 208.

　(*c*) to direct (*a stroke with a
sword*): P. L. VI. 317 ; *fig. of
revenge* : P. L. IX. 173.

　(2) *intr.* to direct attention or
aspiration, have a purpose : P. R.
II. 202 ; **aim at,** aspire to, endeavour to obtain: P. R. IV. 105,
106.

Air, *sb.* **(1)** atmosphere which surrounds the earth or the world,
which fills heaven or hell ; considered as a whole, as that which
immediately surrounds the earth,
or as a separate element : P. L. I.
516, 595 ; II. 309, 594, 1045 ; III.
76, 429, 489, 619 ; IV. 432, 558,
682, 722, 818, 940, 1000 ; V. 180 ;

VI. 349, 587 ; VII. 89, 241, 265,
560, 629; VIII. 141, 166, 370, 626;
IX. 658 ; X. 185, 212. 400, 666,
847, 1073. 1099 ; XI. 53. 183, 337 ;
XII. 76, 454, 579, 635 ; P. R. I.
44, 45, 63, 499 ; II. 74, 374 ; IV.
41, 201, 568 ; S. A. 176. 1240.
1261 ; D. F. I. 16 ; V. Ex. 41 ;
N. O. 38, 99, 164; P. 2 ; Il P. 77 ;
C. 4, 133, 154, 481, 550, 557, 757,
928 ; L. 98 : (*a*) as the free space
in which anything flies or moves :
P. L. I. 226, 545, 767 ; II. 528,
540, 663. 842 ; III. 72, 254, 564 ;
V. 79, 270, 590 ; VI. 72, 244, 304,
536, 654, 664 ; VII. 421, 431, 447,
502, 521, 533 ; VIII. 301, 341 ; X.
188 ; XI. 202 ; XII. 452 ; P. R. I.
39, 366 ; II. 117 ; IV. 542, 585 ;
C. 730.

　(*b*) as one of the four elements
which form the universe : P. L.
II. 912 ; III. 715 ; V. 417 ; P. R.
II. 124 ; IV. 201 ; Il P. 94.

　(2) element which we breathe :
P. L. IV. 153 ; VII. 14 ; VIII. 284,
348 ; IX. 446, 530 ; X. 280, 1102 :
XI. 284 ; P. R. IV. 239 ; S. A. 8 ;
C. 247, 980.

　(3) air in motion, gentle wind :
P. L. II. 400 ; IV. 264 ; VIII. 515 ;
IX. 200 ; X. 93 ; S. A. 628.

　(4) outward appearance, aspect,
manner : P. L. VIII. 476; IX. 459 ;
XI. 542.

　(5) piece of music played or
sung, song, melody : P. R. II.
362 ; P. 27 ; L'A. 136 ; S. VIII.
12 ; XIII. 8 ; XX. 12.

　See **Mid-air.**

Ake. *See* **Ache.**

Alabaster, *sb.* the mineral: P. L. IV.
544 ; P. R. IV. 548 ; C. 660.

Alack, *interj.* exclamation of regret :
D. F. I. 28.

Alacrity, *sb.* eagerness, alertness :
P. L. II. 1012.

Aladule, *sb.* the ' Mountain King '
whose realm extended from the
beginning of the Anti-Taurus
Mountains to the Tigris River :
P. L. X. 435.

Alarm, (1) *sb.* (*a*) summons to arms,
take alarm : P. L. VI. 549. *See*
Take.

　(*b*) fear of danger, apprehension :
P. L. X. 491 ; C. 364.

　(2) *vb. tr.* (*a*) to rouse to a sense
of danger, call to arms for defence : P. L. IV. 895 ; XII. 217.

　(*b*) to strike with fear or apprehension of danger: P. L. II. 103.

Alas, *interj.* exclamation of unhappiness or sorrow : P. L. x. 949 ; XI. 461 ; P. R. II. 30, 348 ; IV. 309; S. A. 162, 368 ; D. F. I. 7 ; Cir. 12 ; U. C. I. 2 ; M. W. 8 ; C. 609 ; L. 64 ; Ps. LXXXVIII. 15.

Albracca, *sb.* a city of Cathay, *so located in Boiardo's Orlando Innamorato* : P. L. III. 339.

Alcairo, *sb.* El-Kahirah, the city of victory ; Cairo, the capital of Egypt. *Here* used for the older capital, Memphis : P. L. I. 718. *See* **Memphis.**

Alcestis, *sb.* the wife of Admetus, king of Pheræ : S. XXIII. 2.

Alchemist, *sb.* one who practises the transmutation of base metals into gold : P. L. v. 440.

Alchymy, *sb.* metallic composition resembling gold, *fig.* a trumpet composed of this metal : P. L. II. 517.

Alcides, *sb.* Hercules, the famous hero ; P. L. II. 542 ; P. R. IV. 565.

Alcinous, *sb.* the King of the Phæacians on the island of Scheria, by whom Odysseus was entertained : P. L. v. 341; IX. 441; V. Ex. 49.

Ale, *sb.* the beverage : L'A. 100 ; U. C. II. 16.

Aleian, *sb.* of Ale in Lycia (or Cilicia (?)) : P. L. VII. 19.

Alexander, *sb.* the king of Macedon : P. R. IV. 252.

Algarsife, *sb.* a son of Cambuscan : Il P. 111. *See* **Cambuscan.**

Algiers, *sb.* Algeria, one of the Barbary states of northern Africa : P. L. XI. 404.

Alien, *adj.* (*a*) of a nature differing, far removed, *with* from : P. L. IV. 571.

(*b*) strange, foreign : Ps. LXXXI. 38.

Alienate, (**1**) *sb.* alien, stranger, *with* from : P. L. v. 877.

(**2**) *vb. tr.* to estrange, make hostile : P. L. IX. 9 ; x. 378.

part. adj. **alienated,** estranged : P. L. I. 457.

Alight, *vb. intr.* to descend to the ground after flight : P. L. III. 422 ; IV. 396.

Alike, (**1**) *adj.* of the same kind or nature : P. L. v. 407; **be alike,** have the same attraction, delight equally : P. L. x. 598.

(**2**) *adv.* equally, in the same manner or degree : P. L. II. 187, 453 ; III. 593 ; IV. 70, 640 ; VI. 123, 847 ; VIII. 389; x. 520, 838 ; XI. 350 ; XII. 519 ; P. R. III. 214 ; S. A. 703, 704 ; without difference, of equal interest or concern : S. A. 1074.

Alimental, *adj.* consisting of that which nourishes : P. L. v. 424.

Alive, *adj.* in life, living : P. L. XI. 818 ; S. A. 645 ; Ps. LXXXV. 24.

***All,** (**1**) *adj.* (*a*) the entire quantity, extent, or degree of the whole, *with sing. sb.* : P. L. I. 3 ; v. 399 ; VII. 92.

(*b*) the entire number of, *with collective sb.* : P. L. I. 37 ; VII. 221 ; *with pl. sb.* : P. L. I. 18, 61, 518 ; III. 390 ; *sometimes follows sb.* : Ps. v. 31 ; *distributively,* each and every one of : P. L. VIII. 63, 265, 488.

(*c*) the utmost possible : P. L. VI. 464 ; VIII. 222 ; S. A. 1316.

(*d*) any whatever : P. L. VI. 630 ; VIII. 581 ; S. A. 476 ; C. 409.

(*e*) every, *with* **kind, kinds,** *or* **sorts** : P. L. IV. 286 ; VII. 541.

(**2**) *absol. as pron. or sb.* (*a*) the whole absolutely, **all in all,** everything in one : P. L. III. 341 ; VI. 732.

(*b*) the whole relatively, entire number of any class : P. L. VI. 633 ; VII. 516 ; VIII. 366.

(*c*) the whole distributively, each and every person or thing : P. L. I. 67 ; II. 238 ; VI. 143 ; *following sup.* **least of all** : P. L. VIII. 397 ; **first of all** : P. L. VIII. 633.

(*d*) everything concerned or involved : P. L. I. 105 ; II. 112 ; VI. 821, *as antecedent of* what : P. L. IV. 107 ; IX. 569.

(*e*) **at all,** in any way, under any conditions, *used to strengthen the assertion, in negative clause* : P. L. II. 48 ; IX. 757 ; XI. 89 ; S. A. 245, 295, 381 ; *in affirmative clause* : S. A. 1082.

(**3**) *adv.* (*a*) wholly, completely, entirely, altogether : P. L. I. 236 ; II. 138 ; IV. 130, 568.

(*b*) everywhere, throughout all parts : P. L. VI. 250 ; Il P. 58.

(*c*) even, just, *intensive with prep. phrase of time or place* : P. L. I. 544 ; II. 61, 476, 609, 752 ; IV.

218 ; **all o'er**, in every part : C.
803 ; **all at once**. *See* **Once**.

All-bearing, *adj.* producing all
things : P. L. v. 338.

All-bounteous, *adj.* showing great
liberality, munificent in all things:
P. L. v. 640.

All-cheering, *adj.* gladdening all :
P. L. III. 581.

All-commanding, *adj.* ruling all :
Ps. CXXXVI. 25.

All-conquering, *adj.* overcoming all :
P. L. X. 951.

Allege, *vb. tr.* to plead as an excuse,
adduce as a reason : P. L. IV.
921 ; S. A. 1253.

Allegiance, *sb.* fidelity of subjects,
loyalty : P. L. III. 104 ; IV. 956.

Allegoric, *adj.* of the nature of an
allegory, unreal : P. R. IV. 390.

Alley, *sb.* shady walk : P. L. IV.
626 ; P. R. II. 293 ; C. 311, 990.

All-giver, *sb.* the giver of all things,
God : C. 723.

All-judging, *adj.* passing judgement
on all : L. 82.

All-knowing, *adj.* knowing everything : P. L. X. 227.

Allot, *vb. tr.* (*a*) to appoint or destine
to dwell in a certain place: P. L.
VIII. 148.
(*b*) to assign as a lot, to grant,
with of : P. R. II. 123.

Allow, *vb. tr.* to admit, concede :
P. L. VI. 158.

Allowance, *sb.* (*a*) admission or
acknowledgment of something
claimed : S. A. 770.
(*b*) restricted portion of something granted : C. 308.

All-powerful, *adj.* having all power :
P. L. II. 851.

All-ruling, *adj.* having supreme
authority over all : P. L. I. 212 ;
II. 264.

All-seeing, *adj.* seeing all things :
P. L. X. 6.

Allure, *vb. tr.* (*a*) to attract, charm,
fascinate : P. L. III. 573; XI. 718;
P. R. IV. 112 ; *absol.* P. R. I. 179.
(*b*) to entice, tempt : S. A. 546.
(*c*) to lead or draw by power of
fascination : P. L. I. 447 ; V.
709.
part. adj. **alluring** ; (*a*) tempting : P. L. IX. 588.
(*b*) attractive, charming : C.
882.

Allurement, *sb.* enticement, temptation : P. L. XI. 810 ; P. R. II.
134, 409.

Allusion, *sb.* symbolical reference,
metaphor : P. L. X. 425.

All-worshipped, *adj.* reverenced,
honoured by all : C. 719.

Almansor (Almánsor), *sb.* Al Man-
sur, the second Abbasside caliph
of Bagdad : P. L. XI. 403.

Almighty, *adj.* all-powerful, omnipotent : P. L. II. 65 ; VI. 316,
713, 883 ; VII. 112 ; *as an attribute of* God : P. L. I. 44, 144 ; II.
144, 192, 769, 915 ; III. 56, 386 ;
V. 469, 868 ; VI. 671 ; VII. 11 ;
IX. 137 ; X. 387.
absol. God, *usually preceded
by def. art.* : P. L. I. 259, 623 ;
III. 273, 344 ; IV. 566 ; V. 154,
585, 676 ; VI. 119, 294 ; VII. 174,
181, 339 ; VIII. 398 ; X. 613 ; XI.
83 ; Ps. CXIV. 4.

Almost, *adv.* very nearly, well-nigh :
P. L. VII. 620 ; VIII. 110 ; S. A.
91 ; N. O. 104 ; Ps. LXXXIV. 5 ;
LXXXVI. 3.

Alms, *sb.* largesses : S. XIV. 5.

Aloft, *adv.* (*a*) high above the earth,
on high, high in or into the air,
upward : P. L. I. 226 ; II. 938 ;
III. 357, 493 ; VI. 252, 776 ; L. 81.
(*b*) in the sky : P. L. IV. 1014.
(*c*) on the top : P. L. IX. 500.

Alone, *adj.* (*a*) by oneself, unaccompanied : P. L. II. 426, 509,
778, 975 ; III. 441, 442, 667, 699 ;
IV. 129, 340, 689, 917, 935 ; V. 50,
875 ; VI. 820 ; VII. 28 ; VIII. 365,
405, 427, 445 ; IX. 336, 457, 480,
978 ; XI. 222 ; XII. 404 ; P. R. I.
189 ; IV. 217 ; S. A. 20 ; A. 42 ;
C. 583 ; Ps. IV. 20, 42.
(*b*) only ; being the sole example ; with no one else, or no
other thing, in the same predicament, *following the sb.* : P. L. III.
684 ; IV. 202, 491 ; VI. 145, 420 ;
VIII. 57, 89, 438 ; IX. 105, 303,
766 ; P. R. I. 285 ; III. 141, 372 ;
S. A. 939 ; N. O. 107 ; T. 18 ; A.
17 ; C. 1019 ; Ps. LXXXVI. 36 ;
*preceding or separated from the
sb.* : P. L. IX. 736 ; by thyself, in
thy very nature : P. L. III. 169.

Along, (**1**) *adv.* (*a*) side by side, in
company, together with one : P.
L. I. 100 ; S. A. 1316, 1413 ; Ps.
LXXXI. 7 ; **along with** : P. L. VI.
275 ; VII. 166 ; X. 250 ; S. A. 1384.
(*b*) onward, forward : Il P. 55 ;
along with : P. L. VIII. 166.
(**2**) *prep.* through or over the
length of : P. L. II. 574 ; V. Ex.

94 ; C. 295, 844, 984 ; *following
the sb.* : Cir. 4 ; L. 174.
Aloof, (1) *adv.* at some distance from
a person, apart : P. L. I. 380 ;
P. R. I. 313 ; S. A. 135, 1611.
(2) *prep.* at a distance from,
away or apart from : P. L. III.
577.
Aloud, *adv.* in a loud voice, loudly :
P. L. I. 126 ; IV. 2, 481, 865 ; VI.
536 ; VIII. 490 ; X. 102 ; S. A.
1639 ; Ps. III. 10 ; LXXXIV. 7.
Alp, *sb.* high mountain : P. L. II.
620 ; S. A. 628.
Alpheus, *sb.* the river-god of Elis
and Arcadia, and the lover of
Arethusa : A. 30 ; as suggestive of
Arcadia, the land of pastoral song :
L. 132. *See* **Arethuse.**
Alpine, *adj.* of the Alps in Italy :
S. XVIII. 2.
Already, *adv.* by or before this time,
even now : P. L. VI. 20 ; VII.
151 ; VIII. 85, 420 ; X. 50, 716,
905, 929 ; S. A. 481, 707, 1092,
1257 ; C. 573 ; Ps. VII. 47 ;
LXXXVIII. 59.
*****Also,** *adv.* likewise, besides, too :
P. L. I. 442 ; III. 108, 623 ; V.
628 ; VIII. 220 ; P. R. I. 334 ;
S. XIX. 14.
Altar, *sb.* raised structure on which
sacrifices are offered or at which
prayers are made : P. L. I. 384,
434, 473, 493, 494 ; II. 224 ; XI.
18, 323, 432 ; XII. 354 ; P. R. I.
257, 489 ; S. A. 26 ; N. O. 28,
192 ; Il P. 48 ; Ps. LXXXIV. 13 ;
fig. of the earth : P. L. IX. 195.
Alter, *vb. tr.* to cause to be different
in some respect, change : P. L. V.
385 ; X. 171, 953.
part. adj. **altered,** changed :
P. L. IX. 1132.
Alteration, *sb.* change in form or
character : P. L. II. 1024 ; IX.
599.
Altern, *quasi-adv.* in turns, one after
the other : P. L. VII. 348.
Alternate, *vb. tr.* to perform by
turns : P. L. V. 657.
Although, *conj.* though, admitting
that, notwithstanding : P. L.
VIII. 427 ; S. A. 1338 ; C. 664.
Always, *adv.* ever, at all times :
P. L. I. 681 ; III. 517, 704 ; VI.
724, 725 ; IX. 467 ; XII. 84 ; P. R.
III. 48, 159 ; S. A. 814 ; Hor. O.
10.
Amain, *adv.* (*a*) with might, firmly,
securely : L. 111.

(*b*) in haste, without delay :
P. L. II. 1024 ; XI. 742 ; S. A.
1304.
(*c*) at full speed : P. L. II. 165 ;
X. 675.
(*d*) exceedingly, greatly : P. R.
II. 430 ; S. A. 637.
Amalthea, *sb.* (*a*) a nymph who was
the mother of Bacchus by Ammon :
P. L. IV. 278.
(*b*) a nymph (or a goat (?)), the
nurse of the infant Zeus : P. R. II.
356. *See* **Ammon.**
Amara, *sb.* Mount Amara, a legendary mountain in Abyssinia, formerly reputed to be the place
where the Emperors of Abyssinia
educated their sons in strict
seclusion : P. L. IV. 281.
Amarant, *sb.* amaranth, a fadeless
flower : P. L. III. 352.
Amaranthus, *sb.* amaranth : L. 149.
Amarantine, *adj.* of amaranth :
P. L. XI. 78.
Amaryllis, *sb.* the name of a girl,
common in pastoral poetry : L. 68.
A-Maying, *adj.* in the act of celebrating May-day ; L'A. 20.
Amaze, (1) *sb.* (*a*) extreme astonishment, wonder, bewilderment :
P. R. II. 38 ; S. A. 1645 ; N. O.
69 ; S. XV. 3.
(*b*) loss of presence of mind
through terror, panic : P. L. VI.
646.
(2) *vb.* (*past part. trisyl.* Ps.
CXXXVI. 14) *tr.* to overwhelm
with wonder, astound : P. L. XII.
496.
part. or *adj.* **amazed ;** (*a*)
stunned, stupefied : P. L. I. 281.
(*b*) bewildered, perplexed : P.
L. IX. 640.
(*c*) terrified : P. L. IV. 820 ;
S. A. 1286.
(*d*) astounded, astonished : P. L.
IV. 820 ; IX. 614, 889 ; X. 452 ; C.
565 ; Ps. CXXXVI. 14.
Amazement, *sb.* (*a*) mental stupefac-
tion : P. L. I. 313 ; P. R. IV. 562.
(*b*) astonishment, bewilderment :
P. L. II. 758 ; P. R. I. 107.
(*c*) consternation, alarm : P. L.
VI. 198 ; C. 356.
Amazonian, *adj.* of an Amazon :
P. L. IX. 1111.
Amber, (1) *sb.* a metal (or an alloy
of metal (?)) of great brilliancy :
P. L. VI. 759.
(2) *adj.* (*a*) amber-coloured, of a
clear yellowish brown colour :

P. L. III. 359 ; P. R. III. 288 ;
L'A. 61 ; C. 333.

(b) of ambergris : S. A. 720.

Amber-dropping, *adj.* being the
colour of amber with water dropping from it (?) : C. 863.

Ambient, *adj.* encompassing, surrounding : P. L. VI. 481 ; VII. 89.

Ambiguous, *adj.* (a) doubtful, of
uncertain signification : P. L. V.
703 ; VI. 568 ; P. R. I. 435.

(b) of doubtful position or classification : P. L. VII. 473.

Ambition, *sb.* (a) personal solicitation of favour or good will, can-
vassing : S. A. 247.

(b) desire of superiority, aspira-
tion for power and honour : P. L.
I. 262 ; II. 485 ; IV. 40, 61, 92 ;
IX. 168 ; XII. 38, 511 ; P. R. III. 90.

Ambitious (ámbitióus: P. L. VI. 160),
adj. (a) desirous of superiority,
aspiring to power and honour :
P. L. I. 41 ; II. 34 ; XII. 25 ; P.
R. IV. 495.

(b) strongly desirous, eager,
with of : P. R. IV. 137 ; *with
prep. inf.* : P. L. VI. 160 ; V. Ex.
11.

Ambrosia, *sb.* anointing oil of the
gods, *here* divinely fragrant perfume : P. L. V. 57.

Ambrosial, *adj.* belonging to or
worthy of the gods, immortal, of
divine excellence; (a) *of night personified* : P. L. V. 642.

(b) *of things*, belonging to
heaven or paradise, of divine excellence : P. L. IV. 219 ; V. 427 ;
XI. 279 ; P. R. IV. 589, 590 ; C.
16 ; divinely fragrant : P. L. II.
245 ; III. 135 ; VI. 475 ; IX. 852 ;
C. 840.

Ambush, *sb.* (a) act of attacking unexpectedly from a concealed position : P. L. II. 344.

(b) person lying in wait for
another : P. L. IX. 408.

See **Chamber-ambush.**

Amend, *vb. tr.* to free from faults :
Ps. VI. 4.

Amends, *sb.* (a) reparation, compensation : P. L. VIII. 491 ; X.
1032 ; S. A. 745.

(b) improvement in health,
recovery : S. A. 9.

Amerce, *vb. tr.* to deprive as a
punishment, *with* of : P. L. I. 609.

American, *sb. sing. collect.* **the American**, the Indians, natives of
America : P. L. IX. 1116.

Amiable (ámiáble : P. L. VIII. 484),
adj. exciting love or delight,
lovable, attractive : P. L. IV.
250 ; VIII. 484 ; IX. 899 ; Hor.
O. 10.

Amiably (ámiábly), *adv.* lovably,
agreeably : P. L. IV. 479.

Amice, *sb.* garment worn by the
religious orders. It consisted of
a cape, or cape and hood, and was
made of or lined with grey fur :
P. R. IV. 427.

Amid, *prep.* (a) in the midst or
middle of, surrounded by : P. L.
IV. 186, 218, 578 ; VI. 664 ; VII.
48, 262 ; VIII. 326 ; IX. 594 ; XI.
671 ; S. A. 80.

(b) into the interior of : P. L.
IX. 401.

Amidst, *adv.* in the midst of : P. L.
I. 791 ; II. 263, 896 ; III. 376 ; V.
264, 598, 903 ; VII. 132 ; IX. 502,
661 ; X. 33 ; XI. 820 ; P. R. I. 42 ;
II. 149 ; IV. 439, 570 ; S. A. 443,
683 ; A. 42 ; C. 254, 549, 777,
981 ; Ps. VII. 20 ; LXXXIII. 45.

Amiss, *adv.* in the wrong way : C.
177 ; Ps. VII. 36.

Amity, *sb.* friendship, harmony : P.
L. IV. 376 ; VIII. 426 ; X. 248.

Admiral, *sb.* ship which carries the
admiral, flag-ship : P. L. I. 294.

Ammon, *sb.* (a) one of the chief
divinities of Africa, called by the
Greek colonists Zeus Ammon, and
by the Romans Jupiter Ammon :
P. L. IV. 277.

(b) the Ammonites : Ps. LXXXIII.
25.

Ammonian, *sb.* **Ammonian Jove,**
Jupiter Ammon as the reputed
father of Alexander the Great : P.
L. IX. 508. *See* the preceding.

Ammonite, *sb. collect.* the nation of
Palestine east of the Jordan : P.
L. I. 396 ; S. A. 285.

Ammunition, *sb.* military stores : S.
A. 1277.

*****Among** (*sometimes* ámong : P.
L. VII. 623 ; IX. 547 ; P. R.
II. 68 ; IV. 73), *prep.* (a) in the
number of, in the class or company of : P. L. II. 423, 469 ; V.
102.

(b) in or into the midst of, surrounded by : P. L. I. 771 ; II. 867.

(c) with or by (*the members of a
group generally*) : P. L. I. 385 ;
P. R. I. 432.

(d) to each of, by distribution
to : P. R. IV. 87.

(e) by the reciprocal action or consent of: P. L. II. 501; VI. 628; VIII. 383.

Amongst, *prep.* among, in the midst of, surrounded by: P. L. III. 565; D. F. I. 49; C. 11, 352, 629; Ps. CXIV. 12; CXXXVI. 34.

Amorous, *adj.* (*a*) of, pertaining to, or indicating love; passionate; tender: P. L. I. 449; IV. 311, 603; VIII. 477; S. A. 393, 1007; N. O. 50; S. I. 8.

(*b*) in love, enamoured, *with* **on:** D. F. I. 5; *fig. of the nightingale*: P. L. VIII. 518.

(*c*) full of or inciting to sexual passion: P. L. IX. 1035, 1045; XI. 584, 586; P. R. II. 158, 162.

Amorrean, *adj.* of the Amorites: Ps. CXXXVI. 66.

Amour, *sb.* illicit love affair, intrigue: P. L. IV. 767.

Amphisbæna, *sb.* a fabulous serpent, having a head at each end of its body and being able to move in either direction: P. L. X. 524.

Amphitrite, *sb.* the wife of Poseidon and the goddess of the sea: C. 921.

Ample, *adj.* (*a*) large, spacious, capacious: P. L. I. 725; III. 254; IV. 413; V. 393; VI. 255; VII. 577; VIII. 258; P. R. II. 339; IV. 82.

comp. of larger capacity: P. L. IX. 876.

sup. greatest: S. A. 1011; broadest, most extensive: P. L. XI. 380.

(*b*) rich, bountiful, liberal: P. L. III. 389.

Amplitude, *sb.* (*a*) extension in space: P. L. VII. 620.

(*b*) breadth, scope (*of mind*): P. R. II. 139.

Amply, *adv.* (*a*) abundantly, liberally: P. L. VIII. 362; X. 388.

(*b*) plainly, clearly, *comp.*: P. L. XII. 544.

Amram, *sb.* the father of Moses: P. L. I. 339.

Amuse, *vb. tr.* to puzzle, bewilder, confound: P. L. VI. 581, 623.

Amymone, *sb.* a daughter of Danaus, beloved by Poseidon: P. R. II. 188.

Anak, *sb.* the progenitor of the giant-tribe of the Anakim: S. A. 528, 1080.

Anarch, *sb.* one who incites to revolt against all government, *here* Chaos, *personified*: P. L. II. 988.

Anarchy, *sb.* absence of authority and order, *of chaos*: P. L. II. 896; VI. 873; X. 283; *in character*, moral lawlessness: P. R. II. 471.

Ancestor, *sb.* progenitor, *spec.* the progenitor of mankind, Adam: P. L. IV. 659; X. 735; XI. 546; *pl. fig. of night and chaos*: P. L. II. 895.

Anchises, *sb.* the father of Æneas: C. 923.

Anchor, (1) *sb.* appliance for holding a ship at rest: P. L. I. 206.

(2) *vb. intr.* to lie at anchor: P. L. II. 289.

Ancient, *adj.* (*a*) existing or occurring in time long past; having existed from, belonging to, or associated with antiquity, *referring to date*: P. L. I. 200, 739; III. 464; XI. 10, 11; P. R. II. 435; IV. 251, 268; S. A. 653; *referring to length of existence*: P. L. II. 346, 591, 970, 986; P. R. I. 44, 305; III. 270, 281, 428; S. XII. 2; XVIII. 6; long known: C. 314.

(*b*) advanced in years, old: P. L. XI. 862.

(*c*) former: P. L. II. 394; P. R. II. 121.

(*d*) long known to fame, renowned: V. Ex. 98.

Anciently, *adv.* from ancient times: P. L. V. 723.

***And,** *conj.* (1) *connecting coordinate words, phrases, or clauses*; (*a*) *simple connective*: P. L. II. 4, 9.

(*b*) *connecting two verbs, the latter of which would logically be in the infinitive*: P. L. VIII. 372; IX. 610; S. A. 1448.

(*c*) *introducing an explanatory or amplificative clause*: P. L. I. 82; III. 555.

(*d*) *introducing a consequence*: P. L. V. 129.

(2) *introducing a sentence and continuing the narration*: P. L. I. 17; IV. 153.

Andrew, *sb.* the brother of Simon Peter and one of the apostles of Christ: P. R. II. 7.

Andromeda, *sb.* the constellation in the northern hemisphere: P. L. III. 559.

Angel, (1) *sb.* (*a*) ministering spirit, messenger of or attendant upon God, one who executes His purposes or makes them known to others: P. L. I. 620, 734; II. 68,

413, 1033 ; III. 345, 396, 511, 521,
533, 682, 694 ; IV. 59, 320, 820 ;
V. 161, 288, 465, 494, 584, 600,
633 ; VI. 92, 220, 281, 298, 336,
375, 411, 525, 594, 638, 776, 802 ;
VII. 133 ; VIII. 72 ; IX. 146, 308,
392, 548, 937, 1081 ; X. 34, 327,
442, 650, 668, 893 ; XI. 70, 213 ;
XII. 367 ; P. R. I. 129, 131, 163,
237, 243, 371, 447 ; II. 385 ; III.
63, 113, 352 ; IV. 197, 200, 474,
557, 582 ; S. A. 343 ; N. O. 224 ;
P. 4 ;' *context indicating a particular angel sent upon a special
mission* : P. L. XII. 201, 259, 364 ;
P. R. II. 274, 310 ; S. A. 24, 361,
1431 ; *spec.* Uriel : P. L. III. 622,
645 ; God or Christ : P. L. IV.
712 ; Gabriel : P. L. IV. 902, 926,
946 ; Raphael : P. L. v. 385, 404,
435, 519 ; VII. 110 ; VIII. 1, 53,
181, 560, 618, 652 ; IX. 276 ; Abdiel : P. L. v. 849 ; VI. 1, 152 ;
Michael : P. L. XI. 286, 421, 449,
598, 635, 759, 762 ; XII. 485, 574,
637 ; L. 163.

(*b*) one of the fallen spirits,
formerly an angel of God : P. L.
I. 38, 59, 301, 344 ; III. 331 ; *spec.
with adj. or def. art.*, Satan :
P. L. I. 125 ; II. 689, 991.

(*c*) guardian or attendant spirit :
C. 214, 455, 658.

(2) *attrib.* (*a*) composed of angels :
N. O. 27.

(*b*) who is an angel : P. L. IX. 1.
See **Angel-guest, Giant-angel,
Traitor-angel, Warrior-angel.**

Angel-guest, *sb.* an angel entertained
as a visitor : P. L. v. 328.

Angelic, *adj.* (*a*) of or pertaining to
angels, of the race of angels or
having the nature of an angel :
P. L. IV. 550, 977 ; v. 251, 371,
535, 650, 834 ; VI. 308, 898 ; VII.
560 ; VIII. 559 ; IX. 142 ; X. 18 ;
XI. 76 ; P. R. IV. 505, 593 ; S. A.
672 ; N. O. 132.

(*b*) like an angel in innocence
and beauty : P. L. v. 74 ; IX. 458.

Angelica, *sb.* the daughter of Gallaphrone, King of Cathay. *The
heroine of Boiardo's Orlando Innamorato* : P. R. III. 341.

Angelical, *adj.* pertaining to or resembling angels : P. L. II. 548 ;
III. 462.

Angel-trumpet, *sb.* trumpet of an
angel : S. M. 11.

Angel-wings, *sb.* wings of angels :
P. L. IX. 155.

Anger, *sb.* feeling provoked against
the agent of an injury, resentment, wrath : P. L. II. 90, 158,
211 ; III. 237, 263 ; IV. 916 ; IX.
10, 300, 1123 ; X. 114, 802, 945 ;
XI. 878 ; P. R. I. 466 ; S. A. 818,
963 ; C. 667 ; S. IX. 8 ; Ps. II. 26 ;
VI. 1 ; LXXXV. 9.

Angola, *sb.* one of the kingdoms of
Congo, or Manicongo, which included the whole of the western
part of lower Africa : P. L. XI.
401.

Angry, *adj.* feeling or showing anger,
wrathful, enraged : P. L. I. 169,
741 ; II. 152 ; X. 1095 ; XI. 330 ;
Ps. LXXX. 19 ; LXXXV. 17, 18 ;
LXXXVI. 55.

Anguish, *sb.* agony or excessive pain
either of mind or body : P. L. I.
558 ; II. 567 ; VI. 340 ; IX. 62 ; X.
1018 ; XI. 778 ; P. R. IV. 576 ;
S. A. 458, 600 ; P. 42 ; Ps. VI. 5.

Animal, (1) *sb.* beast, lower animal,
as distinguished from man : P.
L. IV. 621.

(2) *adj.* (*a*) pertaining to the
lower animals, *as distinguished
from vegetables and from man* :
P. L. v. 484.

(*b*) **animal spirits** : P. L. IV.
805. *See* **Spirit.**

Animate, *vb. tr.* to give life and
energy to, vivify : P. L. VIII. 151.
part. adj. **animate,** alive, living :
P. L. IX. 112.

Anna, *sb.* the prophetess who prophesied concerning Christ (Luke
II. 36-38) : P. R. I. 255.

Annex, *vb. tr.* to join, add : P. L.
XII. 99.

Annihilating, *vbl. sb.* annihilation,
utter destruction : P. L. VI. 347.

Announce, *vb. tr.* to make known,
proclaim : P. R. IV. 504.

Annoy, *vb. tr.* (*a*) to molest, injure,
harm : P. L. VI. 369 ; P. R. III.
365 ; S. A. 578.

(*b*) to affect injuriously : P. L.
IX. 446.

Annual, *adj.* occurring or appearing
every year, yearly : P. L. I. 447 ;
VII. 431 ; X. 576 ; S. A. 987.

Annul, *vb. tr.* (*a*) to reduce to
nothing, extinguish : S. A. 72.

(*b*) to destroy the force of, make
of no effect : P. L. XII. 428.

Anoint, *vb. tr.* to pour on oil as a
religious ceremony, consecrate to
office : P. L. III. 317 ; v. 605 ; Ps.
II. 12.

part. adj. **anointed**, set apart to a sacred office, consecrated, *always of Christ* : P. L. v. 664, 777, 870 ; vi. 676, 718 ; xii. 359.

part. absol. **anointed**, consecrated one ; (*a*) the Messiah, Christ : P. R. ii. 50.

(*b*) the Psalmist, the King, or the Children of Israel (?): Ps. lxxxiv. 32.

Anon, *adv.* (*a*) soon, presently : P. L. i. 325, 549, 710, 759 ; vi. 360, 564 ; xi. 433, 661, 861 ; xii. 150 ; P. R. ii. 285 ; L'A. 131 ; L. 169.

(*b*) at another time : P. R. i. 304.

Another, *adj.* (*a*) second, one more, one further : P. L. ii. 347, 570, 1004 ; iv. 257 ; v. 310 ; vi. 604 ; vii. 155, 617 ; ix. 828, 911 ; xi. 877 ; P. R. iii. 149 ; iv. 27 ; S. A. 330, 559, 1352 ; one more of the same kind : P. L. ii. 292 ; iv. 459 ; Petr. 5 ; H. B. 12.

(*b*) of a different kind, a different : P. L. v. 569 ; xi. 555, 637, 756 ; P. R. iv. 540 ; S. A. 507, 1063 ; V. Ex. 54 ; C. 632, 754.

absol. the sb. omitted, some one else : P. L. v. 775 ; xii. 528 ; S. A. 561 ; **in one another's,** each in the other's : P. L. iv. 506.

Answer, (1) *sb.* (*a*) that which is said in return, reply : P. L. iii. 693 ; v. 735 ; viii. 285, 436 ; ix. 226, 552 ; P. R. i. 395, 434, 467 ; ii. 172 ; iii. 181, 442 ; S. A. 1322 ; C. 276 ; L. 96.

(*b*) return, retaliation : S. A. 1236.

(2) *vb.* (*a*) to speak in reply to a question, remark, or something else said ; reply ; respond, *with the reply as object sentence* : P. L. viii. 398, 412 ; xi. 515 ; P. R. ii. 322 ; *and* to : P. L. viii. 620 ; *with the reply following* : P. L. ii. 816 ; iv. 924 ; v. 94, 876 ; vi. 150, 450, 722 ; vii. 110 ; x. 67, 115 ; *and* to : P. L. viii. 217 ; P. R. ii. 392 ; iii. 386 ; *and the dat.* : P. L. i. 127, 272 ; ii. 990 ; v. 371 ; x. 264, 383, 596 ; P. R. i. 357 ; iv. 170, 485 ; *with the dat. alone* : S. A. 1220 ; Ps. iv. 1 ; lxxxi. 29 ; *absol.* : P. L. xii. 625 ; P. R. iii. 146.

(*b*) to sing in response to : S. M. 18.

(*c*) *absol.* to make a responsive sound, echo : P. L. x. 862.

(*d*) to reply favourably to (*a petition*) : Ps. lxxxvi. 24.

(*e*) to act in response to, obey : C. 888.

(*f*) to agree with, correspond to, be in harmony with : P. L. vii. 557 ; S. A. 1090 ; N. O. 97.

(*g*) to satisfy : P. L. vii. 119.

(*h*) to repay : P. L. iv. 834.

part. adj. **answering,** corresponding : P. L. iv. 464.

Answerable (ánsweráble : P. L. ix. 20 ; S. A. 615), *adj.* (*a*) suitable, fit, proper : P. L. ix. 20.

(*b*) corresponding, similar : S. A. 615 ; *with* to : P. L. xii. 582.

Antæus, *sb.* the mighty giant. He was the son of Poseidon and Ge, and the king of Lybia : P. R. iv. 563.

Antagonist, *sb.* opponent, adversary : P. L. ii. 509 ; x. 387.

attrib. in the character of an opponent : S. A. 1628.

Antarctic, *adv.* in the direction of the south pole : P. L. ix. 79.

Anthem, *sb.* song used in divine service : P. R. iv. 594 ; N. O. 219 ; Il P. 163.

Antic, *sb.* performer who plays a ludicrous part, buffoon : S. A. 1325.

Antigonus, *sb.* the last of the Maccabean kings : P. R. iii. 367.

Antioch, *sb.* a city of Syria, situated on the Orontes River ; the capital under the Seleucidae : P. R. iii. 297.

Antiochus, *sb.* Antiochus Epiphanes, king of Syria : P. R. iii. 163.

Antiopa, *sb.* the daughter of Nykteus, king of Thebes, and the mother of Amphion and Zethus by Zeus : P. R. ii. 187.

Antipater, *sb.* the procurator of Judea and governor of Idumea : P. R. ii. 423.

Antipathy, *sb.* hostile feeling, hatred : P. L. x. 709.

Antique (ántique : L'A. 128 ; ántick Il P. 158), *adj.* having existed for a long time, or resembling those of former times : L'A. 128 ; (*or possibly* antic, fantastically ornamented (?)) : Il P. 158

Antiquity, *sing. collect.* writers of ancient times : C. 439.

Anubis, *sb.* the Egyptian god who presided over coffins, tombs, and cemeteries, and who was represented with the head of a jackal or, according to the Greeks and Romans, of a dog : N. O. 212.

Anxious, *adj.* distressing, worrying : P. L. VIII. 185 ; S. A. 659.

Any, (1) *adj.* (*a*) one—whoever or whatever it may be : P. L. II. 572; IV. 117 ; v. 212; IX. 417, P. R. II. 82 ; S. A. 4 ; D. F. I. 55 ; U. C. I. 7 ; C. 224, 273, 392, 497.
(*b*) some, of any kind : P. L. I. 185 ; P. R. IV. 558 ; Ps. LXXXVI. 26.
(2) *absol.* anyone, anybody : P. L. II. 438 ; IV. 202 ; IX. 972; S. A. 296, 1018 ; U. C. I. 17 ; C. 78.

Aonian, *adj.* of Aonia or Bœotia, **Aonian Mount**, Mount Helicon in Bœotia, the abode of the Muses : P. L. I. 15.

Apace, *adv.* at a quick pace, rapidly, with haste : P. L. XII. 17 ; C. 657 ; L. 129 ; Ps. LXXX. 39 ; Hor. Sat. I. 3.

Apart, *adv.* (*a*) at a distance from others : P. L. II. 557 ; by oneself, aside : P. R. I. 229.
(*b*) by itself, separately : S. A. 65.
(*c*) for a special purpose : Ps. IV. 14.

Apathy, *sb.* insensibility to passion : P. L. II. 564.

Ape, *sb.* the animal *Simia* : P. L. VIII. 396 ; S. XII. 4.

Apocalypse, *sb.* the revelation of the future granted to St. John on the Isle of Patmos : P. L. IV. 2.

Apollo, *sb.* the god of ancient Greece and Rome : P. R. II. 190 ; as the god of music : V. Ex. 37 ; C. 478 ; the god of prophecy : N. O. 176 ; the lover of Daphne : C. 662 ; the lover of Hyacinthus : D. F. I. 23. *See* **Phœbus**.

Apology, *sb.* frank acknowledgment of the offence and the reason for committing it, by way of justification : P. L. IX. 854.

Apostasy, *sb.* abandonment of allegiance to God : P. L. VII. 43 ; *concr.* those who have abandoned their allegiance to God, apostates, *the fallen angels* : P. R. I. 146.

Apostate (1) *sb.* one who is unfaithful to his allegiance to God *of the fallen angels* : P. L. VII. 44 ; *spec.* Satan, *with def. art.* : P. L. V. 852; VI. 100 ; *voc.* : P. L. VI. 172.
(2) *adj.* unfaithful to allegiance to God, rebellious *of the fallen angels* : P. L. I. 125 ; VII. 610.

Apostle, *sb.* messenger, one sent forth with orders ; *pl. spec.* the twelve disciples whom Jesus Christ selected and sent forth to proclaim the kingdom of God : P. L. XII. 498.

Appaid, *part.* satisfied, content : P. L. XII. 401.

Apparent, *adj.* (*a*) visible to the eye, clearly seen : P. L. IV. 608.
(*b*) capable of being perceived, evident, obvious : P. L. X. 112 ; P. R. II. 397.

Apparition (*pentasyl.* ápparítión : C. 641), *sb.* (*a*) appearance of supernatural beings : P. L. XI. 211 ; C. 641.
(*b*) a seeming to the mind, semblance : P. L. VIII. 293.

Appear, *vb.* (*pres. 2d sing.* appear'st : P. R. IV. 193) *intr.* (*a*) to come forth into view, be in sight, be visible : P. L. I. 476, 548 ; II. 643, 890 ; III. 324 ; IV. 149, 232, 461, 964 ; v. 265 ; VI. 79, 524, 556 ; VII. 8, 193, 278, 284, 285, 383, 463, 489 ; VIII. 313 ; X. 450; XI. 216, 320, 475, 478, 589, 852, 861 ; P. R. I. 98, 249 ; N. O. 83 ; L'A. 125 ; Il P. 122 ; C. 867 ; L. 25 ; S. XXII. 4 ; Ps. v. 8.
(*b*) to stand in the presence of another, present oneself : P. L. II. 418; III. 219 ; v. 586 ; IX. 817 ; XII. 437 ; P. R. II. 238 ; S. A. 1318, 1628 ; Ps. LXXXIV. 28.
(*c*) to come : P. L. XII. 540 ; Ps. II. 25 ; LXXXV. 39 ; come before the public : P. R. IV. 99.
(*d*) to have or present the appearance, seem : P. L. I. 230, 523, 592 ; II. 15, 113, 223, 533 ; III. 380, 504, 636 ; VI. 585 ; VII. 578 ; IX. 354, 1189 ; X. 106 ; XI. 306, 609 ; XII. 300 ; P. R. III. 308 ; IV. 547 ; S. A. 822, 902 ; C. 166.
(*e*) to be or become evident, be manifest : P. L. II. 257, 1035 ; III. 105, 141 ; VI. 319 ; VIII. 30 ; IX. 110, 559 ; X. 29, 885 ; P. R. IV. 193 ; S. A. 1256 ; S. II. 7.

Appearance, *sb.* (*a*) action of coming before the public : P. R. II. 41.
(*b*) manifestation of one's presence : P. L. XI. 329.
(*c*) outward look, form : P. L. IX. 413 ; S. A. 1090.
(*d*) apparent form, aspect : P. L. VIII. 82.

Appease, *vb. tr.* to pacify ; (*a*) to

assuage, allay (*anger*): P. L. III. 406.

(*b*) to satisfy the demands of or propitiate *one who is angry*: P. L. III. 186; v. 846; x. 79, 226; XI. 149, 257, 880; XII. 298.

(*c*) to calm, quiet: P. L. x. 792; S. A. 744.

Appellant, *sb.* one who challenges another to single combat: S. A. 1220.

Appertain, *vb. intr.* to belong, *with* to: P. L. XII. 230; *sing. with compound subject*: P. L. VI. 815.

Appetence, *sb.* appetite, passion: P. L. XI. 619.

Appetite, *sb.* (*a*) desire, longing, *with prep. inf.*: P. L. VIII. 308.

(*b*) craving for food: P. L. IV. 330; v. 85, 305; VII. 49, 546; IX. 580, 740; x. 565; XI. 517; P. R. II. 247, 264, 409; C. 705; *fig.* craving for knowledge: P. L. VII. 127.

(*c*) sensual appetite, carnal desire: P. L. IX. 1129.

Appian, *sb.* **Appian road**, the Via Appia, the highway which led from Rome southeast to Brundusium: P. R. IV. 68.

Applauded, *part.* greeted with applause: P. L. VI. 26.

Applause, *sb.* expression of approbation, approval, or praise: P. R. III. 63; C. 259; S. XXI. 2; shout of approbation or approval, acclamation: P. L. II. 290; v. 873; x. 505, 545.

Apple, *sb.* fruit of the forbidden tree: P. L. IX. 585; x. 487; P. R. II. 349.

Apply, *vb. tr.* (*a*) to put or place close (*to*): P. L. VI. 583.

(*b*) to add, (*or* to devote oneself with diligence to, be busy about(?)): P. L. IV. 264.

(*c*) to refer, ascribe: P. L. IX. 1019.

(*d*) to declare as fitting or applicable: P. L. x. 172.

(*e*) to make use of with reference (*to*): P. L. v. 580.

Appoint, *vb. tr.* (1) to determine authoritatively; (*a*) to establish by decree, ordain: P. L. VI. 808; *with two acc.*: P. L. v. 606.

(*b*) to allot, designate, assign: P. L. VI. 565; *with acc. and prep. inf.*: P. L. x. 421; S. A. 1197.

(*c*) to prescribe, determine: P. L. III. 720; IV. 619.

(2) to impute blame to, arraign: S. A. 373.

part. adj. **appointed**, fixed by authority, prescribed: P. L. IV. 726; VII. 167; XI. 550; Ps. LXXXI. 11.

Appointment, *sb.* direction, command: S. A. 643.

Apprehend, *vb. tr.* to seize with the mind, conceive, understand: P. L. v. 518; IX. 574; XI. 280; C. 784; S. A. 1028.

Apprehension, *sb.* (*a*) apprehensive faculty, understanding: P. L. VIII. 854.

(*b*) anticipation of what is adverse, dread of coming evil: P. L. XI. 775.

Apprehensive, *adj.* quick to receive impressions, sensitive: S. A. 624.

Approach, (1) *sb.* act of drawing near, coming, advance, arrival: P. L. III. 42; IV. 154, 624; v. 359; VI. 256; IX. 191; XI. 121; XII. 206; P. R. II. 281.

(2) *vb.* (*a*) *tr.* to draw near to: P. L. VII. 173; VIII. 546; IX. 491, 535; x. 458; P. R. I. 384, 449; II. 160.

(*b*) *intr.* to draw near: P. L. III. 382; IV. 367, 563, 874; v. 627; VI. 552; VIII. 350; x. 102, 864; XI. 225; P. R. I. 319; S. A. 951; A. 83; C. 616.

part. adj. **approaching**, drawing near: N. O. 20.

vbl. sb. **approaching**, act of drawing near: P. L. VIII. 242.

Approbation, *sb.* approval, commendation: P. R. III. 61.

Appropriate, *vb. tr.* to claim as an exclusive right or possession: P. L. XII. 518.

Approve, *vb. tr.* (*a*) to prove, confirm, establish: P. L. IX. 367, 1140.

(*b*) to receive with favour, sanction, commend: P. L. VI. 36; VIII. 509, 611; IX. 1159; x. 31; XI. 458; S. A. 421, 510; to sanction by assenting, *with prep. inf.*: P. L. IV. 880.

April, *sb. attrib.* appearing in the month of April: C. 671.

Apt, *adj.* (*a*) fit, suited, *with* for: P. 28; *comp. with prep. inf.*: P. L. IV. 672.

(*b*) suitable, appropriate: S. A. 184.

(c) fitted to learn, intelligent, quick-witted : P. R. III. 248.

(d) inclined, ready, disposed, *with prep. inf.* : P. L. VIII. 188 ; calculated, likely, *with prep. inf.* : P. R. II. 454.

Aqueduct, *sb.* structure of masonry for the conveyance of water : P. R. IV. 36.

Aquilo, *sb.* Boreas, the north wind, *personified* : D. F. I. 8.

Arabian, *adj.* of Arabia : P. L. III. 537 ; P. R. II. 364 ; III. 274 ; S. A. 1700.

Arable, *adj.* fit for tillage : P. L. XI. 430.

Araby, *sb.* Arabia : P. L. IV. 163.

Arachosia, *sb.* a province of the Parthian Empire, lying west of the Indus River : P. R. III. 316.

Araxes, *sb.* a river of Armenia, emptying into the Caspian Sea : P. R. III. 271.

Arbiter, *sb.* (a) one whose power of deciding and governing is un-limited, absolute ruler : P. L. II. 909.

(b) one who arranges the dif-ference between two persons, *fig. of Hesperus* : P. L. IX. 50.

Arbitrary, *adj.* uncontrolled by law, tyrannical : P. L. II. 334.

Arbitrate, *vb. tr.* to weigh, con-sider : C. 411.

Arbitrator, *sb.* the Supreme Judge, God : P. L. II. 359.

Arbitrement, *sb.* power to decide for oneself, free choice : P. L. VIII. 641.

Arbitress, *sb.* female spectator or witness, *fig. of the moon* : P. L. I. 785.

Arboret, *sb.* little tree, shrub : P. L. IX. 437.

Arborous, *adj.* consisting of trees : P. L. V. 137.

Arbour, *sb.* (a) bower, shady retreat : P. L. V. 378 : IX. 216.

(b) shaded walk : P. L. IV. 626.

Arc, *sb.* curved structure of stone or marble : P. R. IV. 37.

Arcadia, *sb.* the mountainous dis-trict in the Peloponnesus, as the ideal region of pastoral life : A. 95.

Arcadian, *adj.* of Arcadia : P. L. XI. 132.

Arcady, *sb.* Arcadia : A. 28 ; the home of Callisto : C. 341. *See* **Star.**

Arch, *sb.* the rainbow : P. L. VI. 759.

Archangel, *sb.* prince or leader of angels : P. L. I. 593 ; III. 325, 445, 446 ; VI. 594 ; *spec.* Satan : P. L. I. 243, 600 ; v. 660, 694 ; Uriel : P. L. III. 648 ; Michael : P. L. VI. 257 ; XI. 238, 884 ; XII. 2, 466, 626 ; Raphael : P. L. VII. 41.

attrib. of or belonging to an archangel : P. L. VI. 203.

Archangelic, *adj.* of the archangels : P. L. XI. 126.

Arch-chemic, *adj.* supreme among alchemists, *fig. of the sun* : P. L. III. 609.

Arched (*disyl.*), *part. adj.* (a) built of arches or in the form of arches : P. L. I. 726 ; S. A. 1634 ; N. O. 175.

(b) bent like an arch, curved : P. L. VII. 438.

(c) covered with an arch : Il P. 133.

See **High-arched, Over-arched.**

Arch-enemy (arch-énemy), *sb.* the chief enemy, Satan : P. L. I. 81.

Archer, *sb.* bowman : P. R. III. 330 ; S. A. 1619.

Arch-felon (arch-félon), *sb.* the chief criminal, Satan : P. L. IV. 179.

Arch-fiend (Arch-fiend : P. L. I. 209 ; Arch-fiend : P. L. I. 156 ; P. R. I. 357), *sb.* the chief fiend or leader of fiends, Satan : P. L. I. 156, 209 ; P. R. I. 357.

Arch-foe (arch-fóe), *sb.* the chief foe, Satan : P. L. VI. 259.

Archimedes, *sb.* the celebrated mathematician of Syracuse : S. XXI. 7.

Architect, *sb.* designer or maker of buildings : P. L. I. 732 ; X. 356 ; P. R. IV. 52 ; the Divine Maker, God : P. L. V. 256 ; VIII. 72.

Architrave, *sb.* lowest division of an entablature : P. L. I. 715.

Arctic, *adj.* northern : P. L. II. 710.

Ardent, *adj.* glowing with love and admiration : P. L. IX. 397.

Ardour, *sb.* (a) ardent desire, en-thusiasm, zeal, *with* to : P. L. VI. 66.

(b) heat of passion, *with prep. inf.* : P. L. IX. 1032.

(c) effulgent spirit : P. L. V. 249.

Areed, *vb. tr.* to counsel, advise : P. L. IV. 962.

Arethuse, *sb.* Arethusa, a nymph beloved by the river-god Alpheus, and changed by Diana into a stream which issued from the earth as a fountain in the island of Ortygia, Sicily : A. 31 ; *as* *suggestive of Sicily, the land of pastoral song*: L. 85.

Argent, *adj.* resembling silver: P. L. III. 460.

Argestes, *sb.* the northwest wind: P. L. X. 699.

Argo, *sb.* the ship in which Jason sailed to Colchis in quest of the golden fleece: P. L. II. 1017.

Argob, *sb.* a province of the district of Bashan. Its exact location is unknown: P. L. I. 398. *See* **Basan**.

Argue, *vb.* (1) *tr.* (*a*) to bring forward reasons concerning a matter in debate: P. R. II. 94.

(*b*) to prove, show, indicate: P. L. II. 234; IV. 830, 931, 949; VI. 238; VIII. 21; X. 1014; XII. 283; S. A. 1193; *absol.* S. A. 514.

(**2**) *intr.* (*a*) to debate, discuss: P. L. VI. 508; *with* of: P. L. II. 562; to reason or contend (*against*): S. XXII. 6.

vbl. sb. **arguing**, logical reasoning, argumentation: P. R. III. 4.

Argument, *sb.* (*a*) proof, evidence, *with* of: P. L. X. 800; P. R. III. 401.

(*b*) statement or fact advanced for the purpose of influencing the mind, reason urged in support of a proposition: P. L. V. 809; P. R. III. 46; S. A. 283, 658, 862; C. 760.

(*c*) discussion, debate: S. A. 903.

(*d*) subject of any written or other artistic representation, theme (*of poetry*): P. L. I. 24; IX. 13, 28, 42; (*of song*): P. R. I. 172; design (*on a shield*): P. L. VI. 84.

Argus, *sb.* the hundred-eyed herdsman and guardian of Io. Hermes, commissioned by Hera, put Argus to sleep by playing on the flute, and thus obtained Io: P. L. XI. 131.

Ariel, *sb.* one of the rebel angels: P. L. VI. 371.

Aries, *sb.* the zodiacal constellation: P. L. X. 329.

Aright, *adv.* rightly, in the right way or manner: P. L. VI. 470; X. 156; XI. 578; P. R. II. 475; IV. 348; S. A. 1547.

Arimaspian, *sb.* one of the Arimaspi, the one-eyed people of Scythia: P. L. II. 945.

Arioch, *sb.* one of the rebel angels: P. L. VI. 371.

Arise, *vb.* (*pret.* arose; *past part. not used*) *intr.* (*a*) to get up from a lying or sitting posture: P. L. I. 330; VIII. 644; to come up from the grave; Ps. LXXXVIII. 42.

(*b*) to begin, be ushered in, appear above the horizon, *of the day*: P. L. V. 170; VII. 449, 582.

(*c*) to come into being or action, appear, present itself or oneself: P. L. II. 767; V. 452; VII. 60; VIII. 200; XII. 531; P. R. II. 47; S. A. 467; V. Ex. 91; S. XVI. 11.

(*d*) to be engendered, originate: P. L. IV. 805.

Ark, *sb.* (*a*) The coffer containing the tables of the law, kept in the Most Holy Place of the Tabernacle: P. L. I. 458; XII. 251, 333, 340; N. O. 220.

(*b*) the vessel in which Noah and his family were preserved during the deluge: P. L. XI. 819, 823, 840, 850, 855, 861; XII. 102.

Arm, I. *sb.* (1) limb from the shoulder to the hand: P. L. V. 64; X. 512, 541; S. A. 1633, 1636; (*a*) indicative of power: P. L. I. 113; II. 318; IV. 973; VI. 239, 316; X. 634; P. R. III. 387; S. A. 639; C. 600.

(*b*) used in manifesting affection, **in one another's arms**, embracing each other: P. L. IV. 506.

(**2**) tributary of a river: V. Ex. 94.

(**3**) branch of a tree: P. L. IX. 1103; P. R. IV. 405; of a vine: P. L. V. 217.

(**4**) *pl.* defensive or offensive outfit for war, weapons, armour: P. L. I. 94, 325, 539, 564, 667; II. 63, 395, 513, 812; IV. 1008; V. 722; VI. 17, 50, 209, 302, 361, 438, 449, 454, 525, 595, 635, 639, 662, 713; XI. 240, 643, 654; XII. 644; P. R. I. 174; III. 156, 305, 388; S. A. 131, 137, 1096, 1119, 1130; C. 612; S. VIII. 1; XVII. 3; (*a*) **in arms**, armed, furnished with weapons: P. L. II. 55, 164; VI. 32, 136, 525; XI. 641; P. R. III. 20; Ps. III. 3.

(*b*) *fig.* troops bearing arms: P. L. I. 269; P. R. III. 166.

(*c*) *fig.* means of defence: P. R. IV. 235; S. A. 1038; C. 440.

(**5**) employment of arms, war: P. L. I. 49, 119; II. 124, 537, 691; VI. 123, 247, 418; XII. 222;

P. R. IV. 83, 112, 368 ; C. 33 ; S.
XV. 1 ; (a) deeds or feats of arms
in knight-errantry : L'A. 123.

(b) **man of arms,** one skilled in
the use of weapons : S. A. 1226.

(6) support, stay : P. L. XII. 431.
II. *vb.* (*past part. disyl.* : P. L.
I. 567 ; II. 130 ; VI. 47, 127, 231 ;
S. A. 1190, 1617 ; N. O. 58 ; Ps.
LXXXIII. 31 ; *monosyl. when follow-
ing the sb.*: P. L. I. 101 ; II. 757 ;
S. A. 20, 347, 1494), (1) *tr.* (a)
to furnish with weapons defen-
sive or offensive : P. L. I. 764 ; II.
173 ; IV. 779 ; VI. 110, 168, 364,
400, 430, 655, 688, 760 ; IX. 390 ;
X. 1023 ; S. A. 1134.

(b) *fig.* to furnish with anything
that adds strength or security : P.
L. I. 305, 676 ; II. 61, 447, 568,
652, 825 ; IV. 65 ; VI. 697, 737 ; IX.
533 ; X. 9, 697 ; XII. 490 ; P. R.
III. 331 ; S. A. 623, 1280 ; C. 781.

(c) *refl.* to provide oneself with
means of defence : P. L. VI. 222,
466.

(2) *intr.* to take arms : P. L.
I. 553 ; VI. 537 ; *fig.* : P. L. XI.
374.

part. adj. **armed,** weaponed :
P. L. I. 101, 567 ; II. 130, 757 ;
VI. 47, 127, 231, 802 ; S. A. 20,
347, 1190, 1494, 1617 ; N. O. 58 ;
Ps. LXXXIII. 31.

See **Heavy-armed, Light-armed.**

Armoric, *adj.* of Amorica or Brit-
tany : P. L. I. 581.

Armour, *sb.* (a) defensive covering
worn to protect the body in
battle : P. L. VI. 209, 334, 389,
656 ; *fig.* that which protects the
soul from evil : P. L. XII. 491.

(b) defensive covering of animals : P. L. VII. 409.

Armoury, *sb.* (a) place where arms
are kept, arsenal : P. L. VI. 321 ;
VII. 200 ; S. A. 1281.

(b) *sing. collect.* armour : P. L.
IV. 553.

Army, *sb.* body of men or angels
armed for war, armed force : P. L.
I. 272 ; II. 534, 594 ; IV. 953 ; VI.
44, 138, 204, 224, 778 ; VII. 295 ;
X. 276 ; XII. 76 ; P. R. IV. 606 ;
S. A. 129, 345 ; *of Samson alone* :
S. A. 346.

Arnon, *sb.* a river rising in the
mountains of Arabia, forming the
southern boundary of the Ammonites, and emptying into the
Dead Sea : P. L. I. 399.

Aroer, *sb.* a city on the Arnon
River : P. L. I. 407.

Around, *prep.* (a) on all sides of,
about : P. L. II. 900.

(b) along the circuit of : N. O.
54.

Arraign, *vb. tr.* to call upon one to
answer for himself on a criminal
charge, accuse : P. L. III. 331.

Array, (1) *sb.* (a) arrangement in
lines or ranks : P. L. I. 548 ; II.
887 ; VI. 74 ; X. 535 ; martial
order : P. L. VI. 106 ; XI. 644 ;
S. A. 345.

(b) body of troops in order of
battle, military force : P. L. VI.
356 ; P. R. III. 17 ; *fig.* P. R. II.
219.

(c) outfit, attire, dress : P. L.
VI. 801 ; XII. 627 ; V. Ex. 26.

(2) *vb. tr.* to cover, clothe,
dress, adorn : P. L. IV. 596 ; VI.
13 ; X. 223 ; P. R. II. 386 ; N. O.
111.

Arrive, *vb.* (*perf. formed with the
auxiliary* be : S. II. 6), (1) *tr.* to
come to, reach : P. L. II. 409.

(2) *intr.* (a) to come to the end
of a journey or to some definite
place or time : P. L. II. 979 ; III.
520 ; IV. 720, 792 ; V. 254 ; VI.
835 ; VII. 587 ; VIII. 112 ; X. 22,
586 ; S. A. 1075 ; S. II. 6.

(b) to reach, attain, achieve :
P. L. III. 197 ; P. R. II. 426.

See **New-Arrived.**

Arrogate, *vb. tr.* to claim or assume
that to which one is not entitled :
P. L. XII. 27 ; P. R. IV. 315.

Arrow, *sb.* slender missile shot from a
bow or made to be so shot : P. L.
II. 811 ; VI. 546, 845 ; C. 422.

Arrowy, *adj.* consisting of arrows :
P. R. III. 324.

Arsaces (Arsáces), *sb.* the founder of
the Parthian Empire : P. R. III.
295.

Arsenal, *sb.* magazine of arms : P. R.
IV. 270.

Art, *sb.* (1) skilful and systematic
arrangement or adaptation of
means for any desired end : P. L.
I. 696, 703 ; II. 272, 410 ; VI. 513 ;
X. 312 ; P. R. III. 248 ; S. A.
1399 ; C. 309 ; (a) in literary composition : P. L. IV. 236 ; W. S. 9.

(b) in human workmanship as
opposed to nature : P. L. IV. 241 ;
V. 297 ; IX. 391 ; P. R. II. 295.

(c) in the practical application
of a science : P. L. III. 602.

(*d*) in the practice of magic:
S. A. 1133, 1139 ; C. 63, 149.

(2) skilful work : Ps. VIII. 9.

(3) duplicity, artfulness, cunning : P. L. IV. 801 ; v. 770.

(4) artifice, cunning device :
P. R. II. 158 ; S. A. 748, 749.

(5) craft, business : L. 121.

(6) *pl.* learning, letters, the fine arts : P. L. XI. 610 ; P. R. IV. 83, 240, 338, 368.

Artaxata, *sb.* the capital of Armenia, situated on the Araxes River : P. R. III. 292.

Artaxerxes, *sb.* the king of Persia : P. R. IV. 271.

Artful, *adj.* (*a*) characterized by or showing skill, artistic, beautiful : C. 494 ; S. XX. 11.

(*b*) technical *as relating to musical art* : P. R. IV. 335.

Articulate, *adj.* divided into distinct parts so as to form speech : P. L. IX. 557.

Artifice, *sb.* mechanic art : P. L. IX. 39.

Artificer, *sb.* (*a*) author, originator, inventor : P. L. IV. 121.

(*b*) artist, skilled workman : P. R. IV. 59.

Artillery, *sb. fig.* heaven's artillery, lightning and thunder : P. L. II. 715.

Artist, *sb.* skilled performer, master, adept : S. A. 1324 ; adept in astronomy, **Tuscan artist,** Galileo : P. L. I. 288.

*****As,** *adv.* (1) *in principal sentence with* **as** *in relative clause,* in that degree, to such extent, no less than : P. L. III. 289 ; IV. 103; *with relative clause omitted,* **equally** : P. L. I. 705 ; II. 444, 675.

(2) *in subordinate sentence, rel. or conj. adv.* (*a*) to which degree, to what extent, *with antecedent* **as, so** : P. L. I. 59, 74, 197 ; IV. 415 ; VII. 54 ; *with antecedent omitted* : P. L. II. 670, 903 ; III. 346.

(*b*) in which way, in the way that, *with antecedent* **so** : P. L. I. 166 ; v. 334 ; VII. 179 ; *with clauses transposed* **as—so** ; **as—such** ; **as** *frequently followed by* **when** *in introducing a long comparison* : P. L. I. 338, 594 ; II. 636 ; III. 543 ; *frequently with antecedent omitted in antithetical or parallel clauses* : P. L. I. 495 ; IV. 389, 499 ; *with subordinate clause abbreviated,* after the manner of, in the char-

acter of, the same as, like : P. L. I. 62, 149, 240 ; IX. 954 ; P. R. IV. 149 ; *introducing supposition,* as though, as if : P. L. VI. 615 ; P. R. IV. 453 ; *if expressed* : P. L. III. 115 ; *introducing independent explanatory clause* : P. L. I. 205 ; II. 796 ; III. 294 ; IV. 565.

(*c*) it being the case that, inasmuch as, since : P. L. II. 120, 973 ; III. 630 ; v. 69 ; *with participial clause* : P. L. I. 161 ; VII. 593.

(*d*) at or during the time that, at the place that, when, where : P. L. II. 291, 606, 676 ; IV. 460.

(*e*) of result, **so** *or* **such—as,** in a way—that, of the kind—that : P. L. X. 1082 ; XII. 496 ; S. A. 354 ; *with prep. inf.* : P. L. IX. 236 ; XII. 118 ; *superfluous before* **that** : C. 369.

(*f*) *introducing an attributive clause, with antecedent* such, **such as,** of the kind that : P. L. I. 620; III. 510, 637 ; v. 328 ; XII. 335 ; **such** *omitted,* that : Il P. 164.

(*g*) *with advs. of time,* **as yet** : P. L. v. 577 ; IX. 818 ; x. 951 ; **as now** : P. L. v. 859 ; IX. 1138 ; *with prep.* **as for,** with reference to : P. R. III. 414 ; S. A. 521.

Ascalon, *sb.* Ashkelon or Askelon, a city of the Philistines, *spelled* Ascalon *in Vulg.* : P. L. I. 465 ; S. A. 1187.

Ascalonite, *sb.* inhabitant of Ashkelon : S. A. 138.

Ascend, *vb.* (1) *intr.* to go or come up ; (*a*) to mount up, rise in air *on wings or by other means* : P. L. II. 56, 75, 489, 930 ; v. 80, 198, 498 ; VII. 564, 574 ; x. 18 ; XI. 143 ; XII. 451 ; S. A. 25 ; Ps. LXXXVIII. 6 ; *of sounds* to rise so as to be heard : P. L. I. 499 ; S. A. 1518 ; to climb or walk : P. L. XI. 371, 376.

(*b*) to slope upward, be one above another : P. L. IV. 140.

(*c*) to proceed from the inferior to the superior : P. L. v. 512 ; VIII. 592.

(*d*) to come above the horizon : P. L. IV. 650.

(*e*) to rise by construction, be reared : P. L. III. 502.

(2) *tr.* (*a*) to go up into, mount : P. L. VI. 711 ; x. 455 ; *absol.* : P. L. VI. 762 ; *fig.* to rise toward and seem to reach : P. L. VII. 287 ;

to take possession of : P. L. XII. 369 ; P. R. IV. 101.

(b) to walk up, climb : P. L. III. 511 ; XI. 366.

part. adj. **ascending** ; (a) mounting up, rising : P. L. IV. 354.

(b) rising by process of construction : P. L. I. 722.

See **Re-ascend.**

Ascension, *sb.* ascent of Christ to heaven : P. L. X. 187.

Ascent, *sb.* (a) action of ascending, upward movement : P. L. X. 224 ; act of climbing up : P. L. IV. 172.

(b) way by which one may ascend, upward slope : P. L. II. 81 ; III. 486, 524 ; IV. 545.

(c) rising from a lower to a higher state, advancement : P. L. IX. 936.

Ascribe, *vb.* (*pres. 2d sing.* ascrib'st : P. R. I. 453) *tr.* to assign, attribute : P. L. VIII. 131 ; P. R. I. 453.

Asdod, *sb.* Ashdod, a city of the Philistines : S. A. 981. *See* **Azotus.**

Ash, *sb. pl.* remains of something after combustion : P. L. III. 334 ; X. 566 ; *fig.* : S. A. 1691 ; of the human body : S. XVIII. 10.

Ashamed, *adj.* affected by a consciousness of guilt or error, *with clause* : P. R. II. 332.

Ashore, *adv.* on shore, on land : C. 932.

Ashtaroth, *sb.* : P. R. III. 417 ; N. O. 200. *See* **Astoreth.**

Ashur, *sb.* Assyria : Ps. LXXXIII. 29.

Ashy, *adj.* consisting of ashes : S. A. 1703.

Asia, *sb.* the continent east of Europe : P. L. X. 310 ; P. R. III. 33.

Asian, *adj.* of Asia : P. R. IV. 73.

Aside, *adv.* (a) to one side, out of the way : P. L. IV. 502 ; XI. 630 ; C. 168.

(b) away from one's person, off : N. O. 12.

Ask, *vb. tr.* (a) to inquire : P. L. IV. 887, 899 ; VII. 95 ; VIII. 614 ; *with direct or indirect question* : P. L. .II. 957 ; IV. 908 ; VII. 635 ; P. R. I. 326 ; C. 575 ; S. XIX. 8 ; XXII. 9 ; *with personal object and question* : P. L. VII. 69 ; P. R. III. 67 ; L. 91 ; *absol. or intr.* : P. L. III. 217 ; IV. 832 ; VII. 121 ; VIII. 53, 66, 201 ; P. R. I. 436 ; *with*

for, to inquire after or concerning : S. A. 40 ; U. C. I. 17.

(b) to request, petition, beg : P. L. II. 111, 685 ; V. Ex. 7 ; *absol. or intr.* : Ps. II. 16 ; LXXXI. 43.

(c) to require, demand, call for : P. L. IV. 632 ; P. R. II. 253 ; S. A. 66 ; *with two acc.* : P. R. IV. 552.

Askance, *adv.* (a) sidewise, obliquely : P. L. X. 668.

(b) with a sidelong glance of jealousy : P. L. IV. 504.

(c) *quasi adj.* turned sidewise : P. L. VI. 149.

Asleep, *adv.* (a) in a state of sleep, sleeping : P. L. IV. 791 ; V. 14.

(b) into a state of sleep : P. L. V. 92 ; XII. 614 ; L'A. 116.

Aslope, *adj.* deflected from the perpendicular (*or adv.* obliquely (?)) : P. L. X. 1053.

Asmadai, *sb.* : P. L. VI. 365. *See* the following.

Asmodai, *sb.* one of the fallen angels : P. R. II. 151. *See* the following.

Asmodeus (Asmodéus), *sb.* the lustful angel mentioned in the Book of Tobit : P. L. IV. 168.

Asp, *sb.* the venomous serpent : P. L. X. 524 ; S. XI. 13.

Aspect (aspéct : P. L. III. 266 ; IV. 541 ; V. 733 ; VI. 81, 313, 450 ; VII. 379 ; VIII. 336 ; X. 454, 658 ; P. R. III. 217 ; C. 694 ; *doubtful* : P. L. II. 301), *sb.* (a) look, gaze : P. L. X. 454.

(b) a looking in a given direction : P. L. IV. 541.

(c) appearance, semblance : P. L. VI. 81.

(d) expression, countenance, air : P. L. II. 301 ; III. 266 ; V. 733 ; VI. 450 ; VIII. 336 ; P. R. III. 217 ; face, visage : C. 694.

(e) the configuration of the planets at any time : P. L. VI. 313 ; VII. 379 ; X. 658.

Asperse, *vb. tr.* to bespatter, besmirch (*the character with dishonour*) : P. L. IX. 296.

Asphaltic, *adj.* containing asphalt : P. L. X. 298 ; **the Asphaltic Pool,** the Dead Sea : P. L. I. 411.

Asphaltus, *sb.* asphalt, mineral pitch : P. L. I. 729.

Asphodel, *sb.* the daffodil, *by the poets considered an immortal flower* : P. L. IX. 1040 ; C. 838.

Aspire, *vb. intr.* to desire ambi-

tiously, seek to attain: P. L.
II. 7; IV. 62; V. 484; VI. 383,
793, 899; IX. 167, 169; XII. 64,
560; P. R. I. 215; II. 417; D. F.
I. 63; *with prep. inf.*: P. L. I. 38;
IV. 526; P. R. II. 469; C. 12.
　　part. adj. **aspiring**, ambitious:
P. L. III. 392.
　　vbl. sb. **aspiring**, aspiration:
P. L. VI. 132.
Aspirer, *sb.* one who aspires, *here*
Satan: P. L. VI. 90.
Aspramont, *sb.* a name frequently
mentioned in medieval romances,
probably the town a short dis-
tance north of Nice in Provence(?):
P. L. I. 583.
Ass, *sb.* the animal *Asinus*: P. R.
III. 242; S. A. 143, 1095, 1097,
1162; S. XII. 4.
Assail, *vb. tr.* (*a*) to assault, attack:
S. A. 1165, 1396; to dash against:
P. L. X. 417; *fig. of trouble*: Ps.
LXXXI. 25.
　　(*b*) to tempt to evil: S. A. 756;
C. 589.
Assailant, *adj.* assailing, making an
attack: S. A. 1693.
Assassinate, *vb. tr.* to injure by
treachery: S. A. 1109.
Assassin-like, *adj.* like one who kills
another by treachery: P. L. XI.
219.
Assault, (1) *sb.* (*a*) attack, onset:
P. L. I. 277; II. 343; IV. 190;
VI. 216; P. R. III. 74; *fig. of
physical forces*: P. R. IV. 19; *of
grief*: S. A. 331.
　　(*b*) temptation to evil: P. L.
IX. 256, 305; X. 882; XII. 492;
P. R. II. 195; IV. 570; S. A. 403,
845.
　　(2) *vb. tr.* (*a*) to make an onset
upon, attack: P. L. VI. 51; VII.
214; S. A. 365; C. 649; *absol.*:
P. L. XI. 657.
　　(*b*) to strike, smite: P. L. II.
953.
Assay, (1) *sb.* (*a*) attempt, endeavour:
P. L. VI. 153.
　　(*b*) trial or test of anything by
tasting it: P. L. IX. 747.
　　(*c*) trial, affliction, tribulation:
P. L. IV. 932; P. R. I. 264; IV.
478; C. 972.
　　(2) *vb. tr.* (*a*) to try, attempt,
endeavour: S. A. 1625; *with
prep. inf.*: P. L. IV. 801; S. A.
392; A. 80; *absol.*: P. L. I. 619;
X. 567.
　　(*b*) to test the fitness or strength

of, put to the proof: P. L. X. 865;
P. R. I. 143; II. 234; *with clause*:
P. L. III. 90.
Assemble, *vb.* (1) *tr.* to bring to-
gether, convene: P. L. III. 330; V.
683, 767.
　　(2) *intr.* to come together, congregate: P. L. XI. 663.
　　part. adj. **assembled**, gathered
into one place: P. L. X. 34.
　　See **Re-assemble**.
Assembly, *sb.* gathering of people:
Ps. I. 14; for deliberation, council: P. L. II. 285, 749; VI. 446;
Ps. LXXXII. 1; *for pleasure*:
P. L. XI. 722; V. Ex. 28; *for
worship*: P. R. I. 34; S. A. 1315.
Assent, (1) *sb.* consent, agreement:
P. L. II. 388.
　　(2) *vb. intr.* to consent or comply
with a request: P. L. V. 562.
Assert, *vb. tr.* (*a*) to maintain the
cause of, defend; P. L. I. 25;
S. A. 467.
　　(*b*) to vindicate a *disputed* claim
to: P. L. VI. 157.
　　(*c*) to declare formally, affirm:
P. L. V. 801.
Assessor, *sb.* one who sits beside
another, sharer of another's posi-
tion: P. L. VI. 679.
Assiduous, *adj.* unremitting, persis-
tent: P. L. XI. 310.
Assign, *vb. tr.* to appoint, apportion,
allot: P. L. VI. 817; IX. 231; X.
926; S. A. 1116, 1217; *with* in:
P. L. V. 477.
Assimilate, *vb. absol.* to absorb and
incorporate into the system: P. L.
V. 412.
Assist, *vb. tr.* to stand by, aid, help:
P. L. IX. 247; *absol. or intr*: P.
R. II. 145; S. A. 1720.
Associate, (1) *part. adj.* allied, confederate: P. L. X. 395.
　　(2) *sb.* companion, comrade:
P. L. I. 265; V. 696; VIII. 401;
IX. 227.
Assuage, *vb. tr.* (*a*) to soothe, re-
lieve: S. A. 627.
　　(*b*) to appease, pacify: Ps. VII.
22.
Assume, *vb. tr.* (*a*) to take upon
oneself, invest oneself with, put on
form or attribute: P. L. I. 424;
III. 303, 318; VI. 353; X. 214.
　　(*b*) to take to oneself, undertake
rule or authority: P. L. V. 794;
VI. 730; P. R. II. 483.
　　(*c*) to lay claim to, appropriate:
P. L. II. 450; XII. 65.

Assure, *vb. tr.* (*a*) to make sure or certain, secure, guarantee : P. L. II. 40 ; III. 263 ; P. R. II. 148 ; S. A. 739.

(*b*) to cause to feel certain, convince, give confidence to : P. L. II. 685 ; V. 553 ; VIII. 449 ; IX. 981 ; XI. 157, 872 ; S. A. 800, 1322.

part. adj. **assured**, certain : P. L. V. 262.

Assyria, *sb.* the country of Asia : P. L. I. 721 ; P. R. III. 270.

Assyrian, *adj.* of Assyria : P. L. IV. 126, 285 ; P. R. III. 436 ; C. 1002. *See* **Flood, Mount, Queen.**

Astaroth, *sb.* : S. A. 1242. *See* **Astoreth.**

Astarte, *sb.* the Greek name for Ashtoreth : P. L. I. 439. *See* **Astoreth.**

Asthma, *sb.* disease of respiration : P. L. XI. 488.

Astonish, *vb. tr.* (*a*) to stun, stupefy : P. L. I. 266.

(*b*) to amaze, strike with wonder : P. L. II. 423.

(*c*) to dismay, strike with fear and terror : P. L. VI. 838 ; Ps. LXXXVIII. 64.

Astonied, *part.* dazed : P. L. IX. 890.

Astonishment, *sb.* (*a*) mental prostration, stupor : P. L. I. 317.

(*b*) wonder, amazement : W. S. 7 ; C. 157.

Astoreth, *sb.* Ashtoreth, the principal female divinity of the Phœnician and Canaanitish nations, the moon goddess, *identified with one of the fallen angels* : P. L. I. 438 ; *pl.* **Ashtaroth**, the collective name of the different manifestations of Ashtoreth : P. R. III. 417 ; N. O. 200 ; *identified with fallen angels* : P. L. I. 422.

Astound, *vb. tr.* (*a*) to stupefy : P. L. I. 281.

(*b*) to strike with amazement, alarm : C. 210.

Astracan, *sb.* Astrakhan, a province of Russia, lying northwest of the Caspian Sea : P. L. X. 432.

Astray, *adv.* out of the right way : Il P. 69 ; Ps. I. 1.

Astrea, *sb.* the zodiacal constellation Virgo : P. L. IV. 998.

Astronomer, *sb.* one skilled in the knowledge of the heavenly bodies : P. L. III. 589.

Asunder, *adv.* (*a*) separated, not to-

gether : P. L. IX. 258 ; V. Ex. 77.

(*b*) into parts, to pieces, *fig.* : Ps. VII. 5.

*****At**, *prep.* (**1**) *of local position* ; (*a*) in proximity to, near, by : P. L. I. 494, 578, 764.

(*b*) within the limits of, in, on : P. L. I. 756 ; II. 636.

(*c*) in contact with, on, upon : P. L. III. 504.

(**2**) *of motion* ; (*a*) toward, to : P. L. II. 711 ; III. 542 ; P. R. II. 51.

(*b*) by way of, through : P. L. IV. 191, 579 ; VI. 9.

(**3**) *of relation, condition, or manner* occupied with, attendant upon, in a state of, according to : P. L. II. 868 ; V. 377 ; VIII. 371 ; Il P. 143 ; P. R. II. 238.

(**4**) *of degree or value* up to, corresponding to : P. L. I. 641 ; VIII. 191 ; S. A. 1514 ; C. 445.

(**5**) *of time* ; (*a*) upon the point or the coming of : P. L. II. 597, 774 ; III. 616 ; IX. 58.

(*b*) during the lapse of, in, through : P. L. I. 289 ; P. R. I. 210.

(**6**) *of cause or occasion* in response to, by means of, because of : P. L. I. 378, 541 ; II. 666.

Atabalipa, *sb.* Atahualpa, the last of the Inca sovereigns of Peru : P. L. XI. 409.

Atheist, (**1**) *sb.* one who denies the existence of God : S. A. 453 ; by disregard of moral obligation : P. L. I. 495 ; XI. 625.

(**2**) *adj.* godless, impious : P. L. VI. 370.

Athenian, *adj.* of Athens : D. F. I. 9 ; S. VIII. 14. *See* **Damsel.**

Athens, *sb.* the city of Greece, the home of eloquence and the arts : P. L. IX. 671 ; P. R. IV. 240.

Atheous, *adj.* atheistic, impious : P. R. I. 487.

Athwart, *prep.* across : P. L. II. 683.

Atlantean, *adj.* having the strength of Atlas, the giant who supported the heavens, and who was finally changed into a mountain by the Gorgon's head in the hands of Perseus : P. L. II. 306.

Atlantic, *adj.* (*a*) of Atlas, **Atlantic Sisters**, daughters of Atlas, who were transferred to heaven and became the group of stars known as the Pleiades : P. L. X. 674. *See* **Pleiades.**

(*b*) from Mt. Atlas : **P. R.** IV. 115. *See* **Stone.**

(*c*) of the Atlantic Ocean : P. L. III. 559 ; C. 97.

Atlas, *sb.* Mount Atlas, the mountain chain of northern Africa : P. L. IV. 987; **Atlas Mount** : P. L. XI. 402.

Atom, *sb.* smallest particle of matter : P. L. II. 900 ; VIII. 18.

Atonement, *sb.* propitiation of God by the expiation of sin : P. L. III. 234.

Atropatia, *sb.* the northern province of Media bordering on the Caspian Sea and lying south of the Araxes River : P. R. III. 319.

Atrophy, *sb.* emaciation from want of nourishment : P. L. XI. 486.

Atropos, *sb.* the goddess of fate who cut the thread of life : M. W. 28.

Attach, *vb. tr.* to attract, captivate : P. L. XI. 595.

Attack, (1) *sb.* assault, onset : P. L. VI. 248.

(**2**) *vb. tr.* **to** assault, assail : S. A. 1113.

Attain, *vb.* (1) *tr.* (*a*) to reach, achieve, gain, or acquire by effort *a purpose, personal quality, place, or position* : P. L. VIII. 34 ; IX. 689, 724, 935 ; XII. 135 ; P. R. I. 265 ; II. 468, 469 ; III. 89, 211 ; IV. 106 ; *absol.* : P. L. III. 196 ; IX. 964 ; XI. 376 ; P. R. I. 485.

(*b*) to reach mentally, comprehend, find out : P. L. VII. 115 ; VIII. 70, 412 ; XII. 575.

(**2**) *intr.* to come, get, or reach as an acquirement or achievement, *with prep. inf.* : P. L. IX. 726 ; *with* to : P. R. II. 437 ; Il P. 173.

Attempt, (1) *sb.* (*a*) trial, essay, endeavour : P. L. II. 610 ; enterprise, undertaking, experiment : P. L. I. 44, 642 ; II. 420 ; IV. 15 ; VII. 609 ; IX. 978 ; P. R. I. 113 ; III. 26 ; IV. 625 ; S. A. 1221.

(*b*) temptation, seduction : P. L. IX. 295, 481, 1149 ; P. R. IV. 180.

(**2**) *vb. tr.* to try ; (*a*) to endeavour to perform, undertake : P. L. II. 377 ; S. A. 1267 ; *absol.* : P. L. VIII. 237.

(*b*) to try with temptation, tempt : P. L. II. 357 ; IX. 369, 1180 ; X. 8 ; P. R. II. 205.

(*c*) to seek to influence : S. A. 1457.

(*d*) **to** try an attack upon the chastity of, ravish : C. 406.

gerund, obj. omitted, undertaking : P. L. II. 450.

Attempter, *sb.* one who attacks, assailant : P. R. IV. 603.

Attend, *vb.* (1) *tr.* (*a*) to listen to, heed : P. L. III. 658 ; *absol. or intr.* to be attentive, listen : P. L. V. 520 ; VIII. 247 ; XII. 12.

(*b*) to accompany, escort, follow : P. L. I. 761 ; III. 323 ; VI. 767 ; IX. 638 ; A. 81 ; *absol.* : S. A. 1731 ; *of immaterial things* : P. L. X. 239 ; C. 211 ; *sing. with comp. subject* : P. L. VIII. 223.

(*c*) to wait for, look out for, await : P. L. III. 270 ; VII. 407 ; XI. 551 ; P. R. I. 53 ; to be in store for, *of suffering, sing. with comp. subject* : P. R. IV. 387.

(*d*) to wait upon as an attendant, serve, P. L. XII. 354 ; N. O. 242 ; to show respect and duty to : C. 35.

(*e*) to watch, seek opportunity, *with pref. inf.* : S. IX. 9.

(**2**) *intr.* to serve as an attendant, *with* on : P. R. II. 386 ; *fig. of clouds* : P. L. IV. 597.

Attendance, *sb.* persons attending : C. 315 ; retinue : P. L. X. 80.

Attendant, (1) *sb.* servant, follower : P. L. VII. 547.

(**2**) *adj.* (*a*) accompanying : P. L. VIII. 149.

(*b*) waiting upon for service, ministrant, *with* on : P. L. VII. 205.

Attent, *adj.* attentive, heedful : P. R. I. 385.

Attention, *sb.* act or state of giving heed, earnest application of the mind, consideration : P. L. I. 618; II. 308 ; IX. 529, 566 ; X. 459 ; XI. 422 ; C. 258.

Attentive, (1) *adj.* giving careful consideration, heedful : P. L. V. 545 ; X. 1011.

(**2**) *adv.* attentively, heedfully : P. L. VII. 51.

Attest, (1) *sb.* witness, testimony : P. R. I. 37.

(**2**) *vb. tr.* to bear witness to, certify ; P. L. II. 495 ; IX. 369 ; P. R. I. 122.

Attic, *adj.* of or resembling that of Attica in Greece : S. XX. 10 ; the home of Philomela, who was changed into the nightingale : P. R. IV. 245 ; the home of Cephalus, beloved by Eos : Il P. 124.

Attire, (1) *sb.* dress, apparel, *fig.* :
P. L. vii. 501; V. Ex. 21; S.
xx. 7.

    (2) *vb. tr.* to crown *the head* (or
to dress, array (?)): T. 21.
    See **Well-attired.**

Attract, *vb. tr.* to draw, allure, invite, win: P. L. v. 47; x. 152;
P. R. ii. 476.

Attraction, *sb.* invisible power by
which one person influences
another or by which two persons
are drawn together, sympathy:
P. L. iv. 493; x. 263.

Attractive, *adj.* having the quality
of attracting, alluring, winning:
P. L. ii. 762; iv. 298; viii. 124,
587; P. R. ii. 176.

Attribute (áttribute), *vb. tr.* to ascribe, impute: P. L. viii. 12, 107;
ix. 320; xi. 836; P. R. iii. 69.
    gerund : P. L. viii. 565.

Attrite, *part. adj.* worn by friction:
P. L. x. 1073.

Attune, *vb. tr.* to make tuneful or
melodious : P. L. iv. 265.

Audacious, (1) *adj.* presumptuously
wicked : P. L. i. 400.

    (2) *adv.* audaciously, fearlessly,
boldly : P. L. ii. 931.

Audible, *adj.* able to be heard : P.
L. xi. 266.

Audibly, *adv.* in an audible manner,
aloud : P. L. vii. 518; P. R. i.
284.

Audience, *sb.* (*a*) auditory, assembly
of listeners : P. L. ii. 555; vii.
31, 105; x. 641.

    (*b*) attention to what is spoken:
P. L. ii. 308; v. 804; ix. 674;
xii. 12.

Auditress, *sb.* female listener : P. L.
viii. 51.

Aught, (1) *sb. or pron.* anything : P.
L. i. 159, 683, 748; ii. 447, 657,
837; iii. 121, 592; iv. 419; v.
207, 905; vi. 121, 545; vii. 640;
viii. 30, 358, 583, 596, 636; ix.
115, 347, 573, 969; x. 962; xi.
143; xii. 4; P. R. i. 333; ii. 456;
iii. 88, 100, 399; iv. 345, 369,
382, 592; S. A. 274, 376, 743, 888,
1387; Il P. 116; L. 120.

    (2) *adv.* to any extent : P. R. i.
402; S. A. 1420.

Augment, *vb. tr.* to increase, enlarge:
P. L. ii. 386, 605; vii. 367; x.
964; P. R. iii. 38.

    part. adj. **augmented,** increased,
intensified : P. L. vi. 280; ix.
985.

Auran, *sb.* Hauran, the eastern province of the district of Bashan,
spelled Auran *in Vulg.* : P. L.
iv. 211. *See* **Basan.**

Aurora, *sb.* the goddess of the morning : P. L. v. 6; L'A. 19.

Ausonian, *adj.* of Ausonia, the
poetical name for Italy : P. L. i.
739.

Austere, *adj.* (*a*) severe, rigid, stern:
S. A. 815.

    (*b*) grave, serious : P. L. ix. 272.

Austerely, *adv.* rigorously, absti-
nently : P. L. iv. 744.

Austerity, *sb.* moral purity : C. 450.

Authentic, *adj.* (*a*) of acknowledged
authority : P. L. iii. 656.

    (*b*) belonging to himself, own :
P. L. iv. 719.

Author, *sb.* **(1)** person to whom anything owes its origin or existence;
(*a*) originator, creator, instigator :
P. L. ii. 381; iii. 122; vi. 262;
x. 356; S. A. 376; the Creator,
God : P. L. iii. 374; v. 73, 188;
vii. 591; viii. 317, 360.

    (*b*) one who begets, father, an-
cestor : P. L. v. 397; x. 236; one
who is the source of another's
being : P. L. ii. 864; iv. 635.

    (2) person on whose authority a
statement is made, informant :
P. L. ix. 771.

Authority, *sb.* (*a*) power to command,
rule, or enforce obedience : P. L.
iv. 295; xii. 66; P. R. ii. 418.

    (*b*) power to influence action or
belief : P. L. viii. 554; P. R. i.
289; S. A. 868.

    (*c*) authoritative statement, tes-
timony : P. R. ii. 5.

Autumn, *sb.* the season between
summer and winter : P. L. iv.
557; v. 394; *fig.* fruits of autumn:
P. L. v. 394.

Autumnal, *adj.* of autumn : P. L. i.
302; P. R. iv. 619.

Auxiliar, *adj.* auxiliary, affording
aid : P. L. i. 579.

Avail, *vb.* **(1)** *intr.* to be of use and
advantage, be effectual : P. R. i.
153; vi. 456, 789; xi. 312; S. A.
558.

    (2) *tr.* to be of use to, profit,
benefit : P. L. i. 748; vii. 85;
P. R. ii. 66; *refl.* to benefit oneself, *with* of : P. L. xii. 515.

Avarice, *sb.* covetousness, *personified* : S. xv. 14.

Avaunt, *interj.* begone, away : P. L.
iv. 962.

Avenge, *vb. tr.* to avenge, take satisfaction for, execute justice on behalf of *an injured person or a violated right*: P. L. x. 374; xi. 458; P. R. iv. 606; S. xviii. 1; *with* on *or* upon: P. L. iv. 718; vi. 676.

part. adj. **avenging,** that takes vengeance: P. L. vi. 278; vii. 184.

Avenger, *sb.* he who takes vengeance on or punishes *an offender*: P. L. x. 241; Ps. viii. 7.

Aver, *vb. tr.* to assert, allege, *with clause*: S. A. 323.

Averse, *adj.* (*a*) lying on the opposite side: P. L. viii, 138; ix. 67.

(*b*) turned away in mind, disinclined, unwilling: P. L. ii. 763; S. A. 1461.

Aversion, *sb.* averted state of mind, dislike: P. R. ii. 457.

Avert, *vb. tr.* (*a*) to turn away: P. L. xii. 108.

(*b*) to ward off, prevent the occurrence of: P. L. ix. 302; S. A. 519.

Avoid, *vb. tr.* (*a*) to keep away from, leave alone: S. A. 495; C. 363.

(*b*) to keep off, escape, shun: P. L. i. 505; ix. 294, 364; x. 691; S. A. 505.

Avon, *sb.* the river of England rising in Wiltshire and emptying into the Severn (?): V. Ex. 97.

Avow, *vb. tr.* to declare, assert: S. A. 115!.

Await, *vb. tr.* (*a*) to lie in wait for, waylay: S. A. 1197.

(*b*) to wait for: P. L. i. 566; ii. 418; iv. 550, 864; P. R. ii. 108.

(*c*) to be in store for: P. L. xi. 193, 710; S. xv. 9.

Awake, I. *vb.* (*pret. and past part.* awaked), (1) *intr.* to rouse oneself; (*a*) from sleep, cease to sleep: P. L. iv. 450; v. 17, 20; C. 275.

(*b*) from a state resembling sleep, from stupor: P. L. i. 330.

(2) *tr.* (*a*) to rouse from sleep; P. R. ii. 272; *fig.* to cause to stir: A. 57.

(*b*) to rouse into activity, excite, stir up: P. L. ii. 171; vi. 59; S. A. 330; Ps. lxxx. 11.

II. *adj.* roused from sleep: P. L. i. 334; v. 40; viii. 464.

Awaken, *vb. tr.* (*a*) to rouse from sleep: P. L. v. 672.

(*b*) to rouse into activity: P. R. i. 197.

Aware, *adj.* (*a*) cognizant (*of*): P. L. iv. 119.

(*b*) watchful, vigilant: P. L. vi. 547.

Away, *adv.* (*a*) from a place, to a distance: P. R. iii. 366; L. 118, 155.

(*b*) from or out of one's personal possession: P. L. vi. 639.

(*c*) from one's immediate presence: U. C. i. 16.

(*d*) from existence, to an end, to nothing: N. O. 139; *joined to vbs. with which it implies the idea of destroying by the action,* **wipe away**: D. F. I. 12; **drive away**: D. F. I. 68; U. C. ii. 15.

Awe, (1) *sb.* (*a*) fear, terror, dread: P. L. iv. 705, 860; x. 712.

(*b*) reverential fear, veneration mingled with dread: P. L. v. 135; viii. 314; P. R. i. 22; ii. 220; iv. 625; S. A. 1055; N. O. 32; C. 452.

(*c*) power to inspire fear and reverence: C. 32; as the mental and moral atmosphere surrounding a person, *with* an: P. L. viii. 558.

(2) *vb. tr.* (*a*) to inspire with fear and reverence, control or restrain by means of reverential fear: P. L. v. 358; vi. 283; ix. 703; xii. 198; Ps. iv. 19; H. B. 14.

(*b*) to influence by profound respect: S. A. 847.

Awe-strook, *adj.* affected by reverential fear: C. 301.

Awful, *adj.* (*a*) inspiring profound respect or reverential fear, solemnly impressive: P. L. i. 753; iv. 847, 960; viii. 577; ix. 537; P. R. i. 19.

(*b*) filled with awe, profoundly reverential: P. L. ii. 478; terror-stricken: N. O. 59.

Awhile. *See* **While.**

Awry, *adv.* away from the straight *position or direction*; (*a*) obliquely: P. L. iii. 488.

(*b*) out of the right course morally: S. A. 1041.

(*c*) away from the line of truth, erroneously: P. R. iv. 313.

Axe, *sb.* instrument for hewing timber; P. R. iii. 331; Il P. 136; Ps. lxxx. 66.

Axle, *sb.* (*a*) axle-tree, spindle upon which a wheel revolves, *of the chariot of the sun* : C. 96.

(*b*) imaginary line about which a heavenly body revolves, axis (*of the earth*) : P. L. II. 926 ; VIII. 165 ; (*of the sun*) : P. L. X. 670 ; (*of the heavens*) : P. L. VII. 381.

Axletree, *sb.* axle, *of the chariot of the sun* : N. O. 84.

Aye, *adv.* ever, always : S. M. 7 ; Il P. 48 ; Ps. CXIV. 16 ; CXXXVI. 3 ; **for aye** : H. B. 6.

Ay me ! *interj.* exclamation of sorrow : P. L. IV. 86 ; X. 813 ; S. A. 330 ; C. 511 ; L. 56, 154.

Azazel (Aza′zel) *sb.* one of the fallen angels : P. L. I. 534.

Azores (*trisyl.* Azo′res) *sb.* the group of islands in the Atlantic Ocean : P. L. IV. 592.

Azotus, *sb.* Ashdod, a city of the Philistines, *spelled* Azotus *in Vulg.* : P. L. I. 464. *See* Asdod.

Azure, (1) *sb.* (*a*) clear blue colour of the unclouded sky : P. L. VII. 479.

(*b*) blue vault of heaven *the abode of God* (*or* pavement of heaven, *cf.* P. L. IV. 976 ; VII. 577) : P. L. I. 297.

(2) *adj.* of the colour of the un-clouded sky : P. L. IX. 429.

Azurn, *adj.* of the colour of azure : C. 893 ; S. XIV. 11.

Azza, *sb.* Gaza, a city of the Philistines : S. A. 147.

B

Baal, *sb.* the principal male divinity of the Phœnician and Canaanitish nations : P. R. III. 417 ; *pl.* **Baalim,** the collective name of the different manifestations of Baal : N. O. 197 ; *identified with fallen angels* : P. L. I. 422.

Baal-zebub (Ba′al-ze′bub), *sb.* the fly-god, the form of Baal worshipped at Ekron : S. A. 1231.

Babble, *sb.* idle and foolish talk : C. 807.

Babe, *sb.* infant, very young child : M. W. 31 ; *spec.* the infant Christ : N. O. 151, 227, 238.

Babel, *sb.* (*a*) the tower where the confusion of tongues is said to have occurred : P. L. III. 466, 468.

(*b*) the city of Babylon : P. L. 69 Ps. LXXXVII. 13.

Babylon, *sb.* the capital of the Babylonian Empire : P. L. I. 717 ; XII. 343, 348 ; P. R. III. 280 ; IV. 336.

Babylonian, *adj.*, *fig.* of the Roman Catholic Church : S. XVIII. 14.

Baca, *sb.* Baca's vale, a valley of Canaan. Its location is uncertain : Ps. LXXXIV. 21.

Bacchus, *sb.* the son of Amalthea and Ammon, and the god of wine : P. L. IV. 279 ; VII. 33 ; as the father of Euphrosyne : L′A. 16 ; as the father of Comus : C. 46, 522.

Back (1) *sb.* (*a*) hinder part of the body of man : P. L. III. 624 ; V. 906 ; S. A. 140.

(*b*) upper part of the body of an animal : S. A. 1137.

(*c*) ridge of a mountain : P. L. VII. 286.

(2) *vb. tr.* to adjoin behind : P. R. IV. 29, 448.

(3) *adv.* (*a*) to the place of starting, to a former place or position : P. L. I. 171 ; II. 603 ; IV. 17, 914, 965 ; VI. 39, 338, 534, 606 ; IX. 172, 410, 784 ; X. 252, 814 ; XI. 313 ; XII. 172, 219, 312, 345 ; P. R. I. 153 ; III. 435 ; IV. 397 ; D. F. I. 60 ; N. O. 135 ; C. 191, 593, 607 ; S. XXIII. 14 ; Ps. LXXXV. 4 ; *morally* : Ps. LXXX. 73 ; *ellipt.* (*having come*) back : P. L. III. 397 ; *imper. for* (*go*) back : P. L. II. 699 ; C. 958.

(*b*) away from a forward position, toward what is in the rear : P. L. II. 759 ; IV. 462, 463, 480, 820 ; VI. 194, 562 ; VII. 57 ; XII. 641 ; Ps. LXXX. 73.

(*c*) in return, in requital : P. L. II. 789 ; VIII. 158 ; X. 749.

(*d*) from rapid forward motion, in a state of retardation : S. A. 336.

Backside, *sb.* outside : P. L. III. 494.

Backward, (1) *adv.* back, away from a forward position : P. L. I. 223 ; VI. 863.

(2) *adj.* said in a reverse order, reversed : C. 817.

Bactra, *sb.* the chief city of Bactria : P. R. III. 285. *See* the following.

Bactrian, *adj.* of Bactria, a province of the Persian Empire lying north-west of the Paropamisus Moun-tains and on either side of the upper Oxus River : P. L. X. 433.

Bad, *adj.* (*a*) evil, wicked, vicious *of people* : P. L. I. 344 ; II. 483,.

849 ; III. 331 ; IX. 495 ; X. 837 ;
XII. 538 ; P. R. III. 114 ; S. A. 211 ;
T. 9 ; Ps. I. 16 ; *absol.*: P. L. XI.
685 ; XII. 106, 336 ; *of condition,
position, or action,* bringing or
involving evil : P. L. II. 6 ; IV.
795 ; V. 695 ; IX. 994, 1073 ; X.
41 ; XI. 256 ; *absol.*: P. L. XI.
358.

(*b*) unfavourable, unfortunate :
P. L. IX. 1091 ; P. R. IV. 1 ; S. A.
1537.

Baffled, *part. adj.* disgraced, dishonoured : S. A. 1237.

Bait, (1) *sb.* enticement, allurement:
P. L. X. 551 ; P. R. II. 204 ; S. A.
1066 ; C. 537, 700.

(2) *vb.* (*a*) *tr.* to furnish with
that which makes a thing acceptable, render attractive : C. 162.

(*b*) *intr.* to stop at an inn for
rest and refreshment : P. L. XII.
1 ; *fig. of news* : S. A. 1538.

Balaam, *sb.* the prophet of Pethor
(Num. 22-25) : P. R. I. 491.

Balance, *sb.* (*a*) physical equipoise :
P. L. I. 349.

(*b*) swaying motion, libration :
P. L. III. 482.

Balanced, *part. adj.* poised, so
arranged with a counterpoise as
to remain in equilibrium : P. L.
IV. 1000.

See Self-balanced, Well-balanced.

Baleful, *adj.* full of malign influence,
pernicious, destructive : P. L. II.
576 ; C. 255 ; *or* full of or expressing suffering : P. L. I. 56.

Ball, *sb.* (*a*) missile projected from
an engine of war : P. L. VI. 518.

(*b*) the eye-ball : S. A. 94.

(*c*) dance : P. L. IV. 768.

Balm, *sb.* (*a*) tree or shrub yielding
balm : P. L. V. 293 ; IX. 629.

(*b*) aromatic substance exuding
from such a tree : P. L. I. 774 ;
IV. 248.

(*c*) aromatic ointment for
healing wounds : S. A. 186 ; *fig.*
that which soothes or mitigates
pain : P. L. II. 402 ; XI. 546 ;
S. A. 651.

(*d*) one of the fragrant garden
herbs : C. 674.

Balmy, *adj.* (*a*) yielding balm : P. L.
V. 23.

(*b*) fragrant : P. L. IV. 159 ; C.
991 ; *or perhaps combining senses*
(*a*), (*b*), *and* (*c*) (?): P. L. XI. 706.

(*c*) soothing, refreshing : P. L.
VIII. 255.

Balsara (Balsa′ra), *sb.* Bassora or
Basra, a city on the Persian
Gulf : P. R. III. 321.

Ban, *sb.* authoritative prohibition :
P. L. IX. 925.

Band, (1) *sb.* (*a*) that which binds
the body and takes away personal
liberty : C. 904.

(*b*) flat strip of any material
used as a support : P. L. IX. 431 ;
used to swathe the body, bandage :
N. O. 228.

(*c*) obligation by which persons
are reciprocally bound to each
other, bond, tie : S. A. 986.

(*d*) company of persons having
a common purpose, *usually* an
organized company, troop : P. L.
I. 356, 675, 758 ; II. 570, 615, 997 ;
III. 511 ; IV. 684 ; V. 287, 651 ;
XI. 208, 646 ; P. R. II. 236 ; Ps.
CXXXVI. 50.

(2) *vb.* (*a*) *tr.* to join into a
company, unite, confederate :
P. L. II. 320 ; V. 717 ; VI. 528 ;
refl. to unite themselves : S. A.
1753.

(*b*) *intr.* to join, unite : Ps.
LXXXIII. 29.

part. adj. **banded,** united, con-
federated : P. L. VI. 85.

See After-band, Close-banded.

Bandit, *sb.* outlaw, brigand : C. 426.

Bane, *sb.* (*a*) cause of destruction,
agent or instrument of woe or
ruin : P. L. I. .692 ; II. 808 ; IV.
167 ; IX. 123 ; S. A. 63, 351.

(*b*) destruction, ruin : P. L. X.
412.

Baneful, *adj.* poisonous : C. 525.

Banish, *vb. tr.* (*a*) to exile : P. L.
XII. 619.

(*b*) to drive away, expel,
dismiss : P. L. IV. 317 ; C. 413,
692.

part. adj. **banished,** expelled,
exiled : P. L. IV. 573.

See Heaven-banished.

Banishment, *sb.* exile : P. L. XI.
108.

Bank, (1) *sb.* (*a*) elevated ground,
mound : P. L. IV. 334 ; VIII. 286 ;
IX. 1037 ; P. R. IV. 587 ; S. A. 3 ;
C. 353, 543, 993.

(*b*) ridge of ground *on each side
of a walk* : P. L. IX. 438.

(*c*) ground bordering upon a
body of water : P. L. I. 468 ; II.
574 ; IV. 262, 458 ; VII. 305 ;
P. R. II. 25 ; IV. 32 ; M. W. 59 ;
A. 97 ; C. 890, 936.

(d) bench : S. A. 1610.

(2) *vb. tr.* to form a mound-like mass in or to impede navigation in *by forming such a mass* : P. L. VII. 403.

Banner, *sb.* flag, ensign : P. L. I. 545 ; V. 687.

Bannered, *part. adj.* furnished with ensigns : P. L. II. 885.

Banquet, (1) *sb.* feast : P. L. X. 688.

(2) *vb. intr.* to feast : C. 701.

Baptism, *sb.* application of water as a religious ceremony : P. R. I. 21, 273, 278 ; II. 61.

Baptist, *sb.* one who baptizes, *here* John, the forerunner of Christ, *always preceded by def. art.* : P. R. I. 25, 270 ; II. 2, 84 ; IV. 511.

Baptize, *vb. tr.* to apply water to as a religious ceremony, administer or subject to the rite of baptism : P. L. XII. 442, 500 ; P. R. I. 21, 29, 76 ; IV. 512, *absol.* : P. R. I. 184.

part. adj. (a) **baptizing,** administering baptism : P. R. I. 328.

(b) **baptized,** having been baptized, *hence,* Christian : P. L. I. 582.

See **New-baptized.**

Bar, (1) *sb.* (a) that which confines, excludes, or in other way impedes action ; barrier : P. L. IV. 585 ; VIII. 625 ; X. 417 ; closing an exit : P. L. III. 82 ; IV. 795.

(b) rod of iron used to fasten a door or gate : P. L. II. 877 ; S. A. 147.

(c) court of law : S. XXI. 4.

(2) *vb. tr.* (a) to fasten with a bar : P. L. II. 437 ; IV. 897, 967.

(b) to obstruct, make impassable : P. L. IX. 80.

(c) to debar, deprive : C. 343 ; *with* of : P. L. XII. 360.

(d) to exclude, shut off : Ps. LXXXVIII. 24.

See **Cross-barred.**

Barb, *vb. tr.* to furnish (*an arrow*) with barbs : P. L. VI. 546.

Barbaric, *adj.* in the manner of barbarians : P. L. II. 4.

Barbarous, *adj.* (a) foreign, *neither Greek nor Jewish* : P. R. III. 119.

(b) uncivilized, uncultured : P. R. IV. 86.

(c) savagely cruel : P. L. I. 353.

(d) harsh-sounding : P. L. VII. 32 ; C. 550 ; S. XII. 3.

Barber, *sb.* one whose occupation is to cut and dress the hair : S. A. 1167.

Barca, *sb.* a province of Lybia or Marmarica in northern Africa lying immediately west of Egypt. The chief city was called Barce, and was " of such accompt, that from hence the whole country had the name of Barca," Hey. *Cos.* 1657. p. 932 : P. L. II. 904.

Bard, *sb.* (a) poet and singer, minstrel, *spec.* the Druids : L. 53 ; Orpheus : P. L. VII. 34.

(b) poet : Il P. 116 ; C. 45.

Bare, *adj.* (a) open to view, unconcealed, undisguised : S. A. 902.

(b) having nothing upon it : P. L. III. 74 ; X. 317.

(c) without foliage or vegetation : P. L. III. 379, 614 ; VII. 286, 313, 314 ; XI. 834.

(d) stripped (*of virtue*) : P. L. IX. 1062.

(e) laid waste, desolate : S. VIII. 14.

(f) mere, simple, only : C. 614.

Bark, (1) *sb.* (a) rind or covering of a tree : P. L. X. 1076 ; C. 354.

(b) barque, small ship : P. L. II. 288 ; L. 100.

(2) *vb. intr.* to cry with the voice of a dog : P. L. II. 654, 658.

part. adj. **barking,** howling, roaring : C. 258.

Barn-door, *sb.* door of a barn : L'A. 51.

Baron, *sb.* nobleman : L'A. 119.

Barren, *adj.* sterile, unproductive : P. L. III. 437 ; VIII. 94 ; P. R. I. 354 ; III. 264 ; L'A. 73 ; Ps. LXXXIV. 22 ; not accompanied by fruitage : P. L. V. 219.

Barrenness, *sb.* sterility as regards offspring : P. L. X. 1042 ; S. A. 352 ; M. W. 64.

Barricado, *vb. tr.* to close with a barricade, render impassable : P. L. VIII. 241.

Basan, *sb.* Bashan, a district of Palestine east of the Sea of Galilee, *spelled* Basan *in Vulg.* : P. L. I. 398.

Base, (1) *sb.* (a) that on which anything rests or moves, lowest or supporting part, foundation (*of a serpent*) : P. L. IX. 498 ; (*of the earth*) : C. 599.

(b) lowest part in the harmony (*of the spheres*) : N. O. 130.

(c) housing of a horse (?) : P. L. IX. 36.

(2) *adj.* (*a*) low in the scale of creation, worthless, of inferior quality : P. L. IX. 150 ; *comp.* : P. L. II. 141 ; *sup.* : P. L. IX. 171.

(*b*) low in morals, mean, despicable : P. R. IV. 132 ; S. A. 415 ; C. 698, 778.

(*c*) degrading, disgraceful, befitting a person of low degree : S. A. 414.

Basis, *sb.* foundation (*of earth or heaven*) : P. L. VI. 712 : P. R. IV. 456.

Bask, *vb. tr.* to expose to a flood of warmth, lie warming : L'A. 112.

Bastard, *sb.* illegitimate child, *fig.* (*of nature*) : C. 727.

Bate, *vb. tr.* to abate, diminish : S. XXII. 7.

Bath, *sb.* building containing a series of apartments for bathing : P. R. IV. 36.

Bathe, *vb.* (1) *tr.* to immerse or wash as in a bath : VII. 437 ; *fig.* : C. 812.

(2) *intr.* to take a bath : P. L. II. 660.

Battailous (bat'tailous), *adj.* warlike : P. L. VI. 81.

Battalion, *sb.* host, army in battle array : P. L. I. 569 ; order and arrangement of the army : P. L. VI. 534.

Batten, *vb. tr.* to feed to advantage, fatten : L. 29.

Battering, *vbl. sb. attrib.* **battering engine,** an engine constructed for breaking down walls : P. L. II. 923.

See **Twice-battered.**

Battery, *sb.* (*a*) action of battering, assault, *fig. of waves* : P. R. IV. 20.

(*b*) mounted artillery : P. L. XI. 656.

See **Tongue-battery.**

Battle, *sb.* hostile encounter between opposing forces, combat : P. L. I. 43, 104, 277, 319, 436, 553 ; II. 107, 535, 550 ; IV. 12, 927, 1002 ; V. 728 ; VI. 46, 97, 108, 202, 235, 246, 386, 798, 802 ; IX. 31 ; X. 275, 377 ; XI. 644, 691, 800 ; XII. 261 ; P. R. III. 20, 73, 322, 392 ; S. A. 287, 583, 1131 ; N. O. 53 ; C. 654 ; Ps. CXXXVI. 61 ; *between the Son of God alone and the forces of Satan* : P. L. VI. 819 ; *between*

the atoms in chaos : P. L. II. 899 ; the army engaged in the combat : P. L. VI. 216.

Battlement, *sb.* indented parapet upon the wall of a building : P. R. IV. 53 ; L'A. 77 ; upon the wall of heaven : P. L. II. 1049 ; *pl.* wall : P. L. I. 742.

Baulk, *vb. tr.* to miss intentionally, omit : F. of C. 17.

Bawl, *vb. intr.* to cry loudly and roughly, bellow : S. XII. 9.

Bay, *sb.* (*a*) indentation in the shoreline of a body of water : P. L. II. 289 ; VII. 399 ; L. 191 : *with proper adj.* : P. R. II. 347 ; III. 273. *See* **Lucrine.**

(*b*) sprigs or leaves of the bay or laurel-tree : M. W. 57.

Bayona, *sb.* a sea-port town on the southeastern coast of Galicia, Spain : L. 162.

*****Be,** *vb. intr.* (*pres.* am, art, beest, is, are ; *pret.* was, wast, wert, were ; be, *indic.* : C. 12 ; *subj.* : L'A. 132 ; *see also* **Being**).

I. *as independent vb.* (**1**) to exist, possess actuality : P. L. II. 100 ; III. 264 ; IV. 6 ; VI. 218.

(**2**) to exist in a certain way specified by limiting words ; (*a*) to exist in a certain state or condition : P. L. IX. 1155 ; C. 370 ; in a certain place : P. L. III. 371 ; IX. 565 ; S. A. 647.

(*b*) to have sprung or be derived from a certain place or condition : P. L. IV. 482 ; S. A. 1078 ; A. 28.

(**3**) to be identical with : P. L. IV. 75, 468 ; X. 770.

(**4**) to come to pass, take place, happen : P. L. II. 809 ; III. 284.

II. *as simple copula* : P. L. I. 22 ; III. 659 ; VI. 366.

III. *as auxiliary* ; (**1**) *forming passive voice* : P. L. II. 855 ; III. 203, 223 ; IV. 1012.

(**2**) *forming perfect tenses. See* the verbs Advance, Arrive, Become, Cease, Come, Do, Drop, Enter, Fail, Fall, Flee, Go, Pass, Retire, Return, Rise, Sink, Spring, Wax.

(**3**) *with prep. inf. forming future of necessity, obligation, or duty* : P. L. IV. 535 ; V. 686 ; P. R. II. 407 ; IV. 525.

Beach, *sb.* (*a*) shore of the sea, strand : P. L. I. 299.

(*b*) ridge or bank of shingle : P. L. x. 299.

Bead, *sb. pl.* rosary : P. L. III. 491 ; C. 391.

Beak, *sb.* sharp and crooked bill of a bird : P. R. II. 267.

Beaked, *part. adj.* resembling a beak, pointed : P. L. XI. 746 ; L. 94.

Beam, *sb.* (*a*) long piece of timber : S. A. 1122.

(*b*) transverse bar from the ends of which the scales of a balance are suspended : P. L. IV. 1004.

(*c*) shaft of a spear : P. L. VI. 82.

(*d*) ray of light *from a radiant being* : P. L. III. 361, 378 ; N. O. 111 ; A. 16 ; *from a planet* : P. L. I. 596 ; III. 551, 616 ; IV. 37, 150, 590, 644 ; VIII. 97, 255 ; IX. 106 ; x. 1070 ; P. R. IV. 432 ; Il P. 132 ; L. 170 ; S. XIV. 10 ; *sing. collect.* : P. L. II. 493 ; III. 583 ; VIII. 139 ; C. 98 ; *from light* : P. L. VII. 363 ; *from the morn* : P. L. VI. 15 ; fig. *from the soul* : C. 460 ; **visual beam,** ray of light giving the power of seeing : S. A. 163.

(*e*) *collect.* light : P. L. II. 399 ; III. 2 ; S. A. 83.

See **Sun-beam.**

Beaming, *part. adj.* radiant, shining : P. L. III. 625.

See **Far-beaming.**

Bear, (1) *sb.* (*a*) the animal *Ursus* : P. L. IV. 344 ; C. 70.

(*b*) the constellation, Ursa Major : Il P. 87.

(2) *vb.* (*pres.* 2*d sing.* bear'st : P. L. x. 952 ; P. R. IV. 199 ; S. A. 430, 1100 ; *pret.* bore ; *past part.* borne *and* born : P. L. II. 953 ; III. 16 ; VI. 33, 544, 776 ; VII. 431 ; XI. 764 ; P. R. III. 93 ; *see also* **Born**), *tr.* (*a*) to uphold, support (*a weight, or fig. a burden of care or sorrow*) : P. L. II. 306 ; x. 835 ; S. A. 430 ; P. R. II. 465.

(*b*) to carry, convey, bring : P. L. VI. 337, 544, 646, 776 ; VIII. 166 ; IX. 104 ; P. R. III. 314 ; S. A. 146, 1303 ; N. O. 220 ; P. 39 ; C. 658, 835 ; L. 110 ; *absol.* : P. R. IV. 542 ; in flight : P. L. III. 16 ; VII. 431 ; fig. *of two constellations, used because of their relative positions* : P. L. III. 558 ; fig. *of immaterial things, either as* bearing

or borne : P. L. II. 411, 953 ; III. 652 ; IV. 591 ; v. 199 ; IX. 1175 ; S. A. 947 ; *absol.* : P. R. I. 13.

(*c*) to suffer, endure : P. L. II. 209 ; VI. 33, 34 ; x. 726, 950, 952 ; XI. 363, 764, 766, 776 ; P. R. III. 93 ; S. A. 913 ; Cir. 6, 24 ; S. XIX. 11.

(*d*) to endure without opposition, tolerate ; P. L. v. 664 ; N. O. 84 ; *absol.* : S. A. 755 ; 1353.

(*e*) to produce, yield (*plants, fruit, etc.*) : P. L. IV. 422 ; v. 368, 427 ; XI. 804 ; C. 633.

(*f*) to bring forth, give birth to (*offspring*) : P. L. IV. 473 ; IX. 509 ; P. R. I. 135 ; II. 71 ; M. W. 65 ; L'A. 16 ; Il P. 24 ; L. 58. *See* **Born.**

(*g*) to be marked with, show : P. L. v. 592 ; S. A. 190.

(*h*) to possess, have, hold : P. L. I. 528 ; VIII. 375 ; x. 155 ; XII. 241, 311 ; P. R. IV. 199 ; S. A. 57, 1100.

(*i*) to cherish or entertain *a feeling* for : P. L. x. 916.

(*j*) to admit, allow : P. R. IV. 517.

In combination with other words ; (*a*) **bear up,** raise up : P. L. VII. 470 ; keep up courage, not to succumb : S. XXII. 8.

(*b*) **bear with,** have patience with : P. L. VIII. 614.

(*c*) **bear witness,** bring testimony, give evidence, attest ; *with dat.* : S. A. 239 ; *with* to : P. R. I. 26 ; S. A. 1752.

vbl. sb. **bearing,** endurance, *with* of : S. A. 655.

See **All-bearing, Child-bearing.**

Bearded, *part. adj.* (*a*) furnished with a beard, *of animals* : C. 71.

(*b*) furnished with bristles, *of plants* : P. L. IV. 982 ; v. 342.

Bearer, *sb.* one who helps to carry a corpse to the grave : U. C. II. 20.

Bearth. *See* **Birth.**

Beast, *sb.* animal : P. L. IV. 341 ; IX. 94, 165, 521, 571, 592 ; x. 176, 217, 221 ; Ps. VIII. 20 ; *sing. collect. used for pl.* : P. L. VII. 452 ; *in combination or contrast with* man, birds, creeping things, *or* fishes, P. L. IV. 177, 704 ; VIII. 395, 397, 438, 582, 594 ; IX. 543, 556, 768, 769 ; x. 604, 710 ; XI. 187 ; XII. 30, 67 ; S. A. 37 ; C. 528 ; *sing. collect.* : P. L. IV. 600 ; VII. 503, 522 ; VIII. 341, 342, 349 ; IX. 691 ; XI. 183,

733, 822, 895 ; XII. 67 ; P. R. IV.
140, 461 ; **wild beast** : P. R. I. 310,
502 ; S. A. 127, 1403 ; Ps. LXXX.
55 ; *sing. collect.* : P. L. VII. 457 ;
beast of chase : P. L. IV. 341 ;
P. R. II. 342 ; *spec.* serpent, *always
preceded by* **subtlest** : P. L. VII.
495 ; IX. 86, 560 ; species of
animals : P. L. XI. 734.

Beat, *vb.* (*past part.* beat : P. L. II.
588 ; P. R. IV. 17 ; beaten : P.
L. II. 1026), *tr.* (*a*) to strike with
repeated blows, dash against :
P. L. II. 588 ; *of the action of feet
in the dance* : C. 143.
  (*b*) **beat off**, to drive away :
P. R. IV. 17.
  (*c*) **beat out**, to crush out,
destroy : P. L. XI. 446.
  part. adj. **beaten**, trodden, worn
hard : P. L. II. 1026.
  See **Weather-beaten**.

Beatific, *adj.* making blessed, imparting bliss : P. L. I. 684.

Beatitude, *sb.* supreme blessedness :
P. L. III. 62.

Beauteous, *adj.* beautiful : P. L. IV.
697 ; VI. 481 ; XI. 613.

Beauty, *sb.* (*a*) such combined perfection of form and charm of
colouring as excites pleasurable
emotions : P. L. IV. 490, 498, 634,
713, 845 ; V. 14, 47 ; IX. 491, 540,
607, 1029 ; XI. 539 ; P. R. II. 194 ;
S. A. 1003 ; D. F. I. 31 ; Il P.
20 ; C. 739, 745 ; L. 149 ; *personified* : P. L. VIII. 533 ; P. R. II.
212, 220.
  (*b*) *concr.* beautiful woman :
P. R. II. 186, 197 ; L'A. 79.

Because, *conj.* for the reason that,
since : P. L. III. 305, 311 ; V.
539 ; VI. 814 ; VII. 168 ; IX. 280 ;
X. 51, 175, 198 ; XI. 197 ; P. R.
I. 144 ; II. 174 ; IV. 156 ; S. A.
1265, 1402 ; F. of C. 1. ; Ps.
V. 22.

Beck, *sb.* (*a*) significant gesture of
command, **at his beck**, at the
slightest indication of his wish :
P. R. II. 238.
  (*b*) obeisance, bow : L'A. 28.

Beckoning, *part. adj.* making mute
signals of invitation to approach :
C. 207.

Become, *vb.* (bécomes : P. L. XII.
409 ; *perf. formed with the auxiliary* be : P. L. IX. 869, 1181 ; X.
120 ; XI. 84 ; S. A. 155), (1) *tr.*
to be suited to, befit : P. L. II.
445 ; P. R. I. 288.

(2) *intr.* to come to be, get to
be : P. L. II. 275, 765 ; V. 843 ;
VII. 528 ; IX. 122, 716, 869, 1181 ;
X. 120, 722 ; XI. 61, 84, 165, 420 ;
XII. 409 ; P. R. III. 103 ; S. A.
73, 155 ; **become of**, be the final
end or condition of : P. L. XII.
275.
  See **Froth-becurled**.

Bed, *sb.* (*a*) couch, resting place,
place to sleep : V. Ex. 63 ; U.
C. I. 18 ; II. 17 ; M. W. 42 ; L'A.
115, 146 ; C. 107 ; *as the place of
conjugal union* : P. L. IV. 710,
761 ; VIII. 598 ; D. F. I. 13 : S. A.
806, 1021 ; the grave : D. F. I. 31 ;
Ps. LXXXVIII. 43 ; *fig. said of the
rising sun* : N. O. 229 ; *fig.* **bed of
fire** : P. L. II. 600.
  (*b*) level plot of ground used
for raising plants, garden-plot :
P. L. IV. 242 ; L'A. 21 ; C. 998.
  (*c*) bottom of the sea : P. L. VII.
290 ; L. 168.
  (*d*) channel of a river : C. 886.
  See **Child-bed**.

Bedecked, *part. adj.* covered with
ornaments, adorned : S. A. 712.

Bedew, *vb. tr.* to besprinkle : Hor.
O. 1.

Bed-rid, *adj.* confined to the bed :
S. A. 579.

Bedrop, *vb. tr.* to wet with drops :
P. L. X. 527.

Bedward, *adv.* toward a place of
rest : P. L. IV. 352.

Bee, *sb.* the insect *Apis mellifica* :
P. L. I. 768 ; V. 24 ; VII. 490 ;
P. R. IV. 248 ; Il P. 142.

Beef, *sb.* adult bovine animal : P. L.
XI. 647.

Beëlzebub, *sb.* a prince of devils, the
one next in power to Satan : P. L.
I. 81, 271 ; II. 299, 378.

Beërsaba (Béersába), *sb.* Beersheba,
a town in the extreme southern
part of Palestine, *spelled* Bersabee
in Vulg. : P. L. III. 536.

Befall, *vb.* (*pret.* befell ; *past part.*
befallen) ; (*a*) to happen, occur,
come to pass : P. L. VI. 897 ;
VII. 43, 44 ; X. 28, 895, 896 ; *with*
to : P. L. XI. 450 ; *impers.* : P. L.
VIII. 229 ; XI. 716 ; XII. 444.
  (*b*) to happen to : P. L. II.
821 ; IV. 127 ; IX. 252, 771 ; XI.
771 ; S. A. 374, 447 ; *impers.* :
P. L. IX. 1182.

Befit, *vb. tr.* to fit, be suited to, be
appropriate for : P. L. X. 868 ;
P. 27 ; A. 92.

*Before (béfore : P. L. VIII. 464),
I. *adv.* in time preceding, in the
past: P. L. II. 703 ; v. 790 ; **long
before**: P. L. I. 748; IV. 213;
IX. 139.

II. *prep.* (1) *of motion* in front
of, in advance of : P. L. II. 535;
III. 644 ; VI. 780.

(**2**) *of position* in front of :
P. L. II. 648, 803 ; VI. 27 ; (*a*) at
the disposal of, open to : P. L.
IV. 203 ; VIII. 193 ; XII. 646.

(*b*) in the presence of, in the
sight of *the eyes or the mind* :
P. L. IV. 345 ; v. 640 ; VIII. 372 ;
P. R. II. 112.

(**3**) prior to, earlier than : P. L.
III. 8 ; v. 860 ; VII. 66.

(**4**) under the action, influence,
or power of : P. L. I. 436; IX. 53.

(**5**) in preference to, rather than :
P. L. I. 18 ; II. 256 ; VIII. 53.

III. *conj.* previous to the time
when : V. Ex. 32.

Beforehand, *adv.* in advance, in
anticipation : P. R. IV. 8, 526.

Befriend, *vb. tr.* to act as a friend
to, help: V. Ex. 59; P. 29 ; C. 135.

Beg, *vb. tr.* to ask with humility,
implore, beseech : P. L. X. 1089,
1101 ; S. A. 707 ; *with prep. inf.* :
P. L. XI. 506 ; P. R. IV. 630 ;
with acc. and simple inf. : C. 633 ;
absol. : P. L. X. 918.

    gerund : P. L. IV. 104.

Beget, *vb.* (*pret.* begot ; *past part.*
begot: P. L. v. 603; XII. 286 ;
Ps. VIII. 13 ; begotten : P. L. II.
782 ; III. 384 ; v. 835 ; VII. 163 ;
X. 983 ; Ps. II. 15), *tr.* (*a*) to pro-
create as a father : P. L. II.
794 ; VIII. 423 ; X. 728, 762, 765 ;
XI. 613 ; XII. 286 ; P. R. II. 181 ;
Ps. VIII. 13 ; *fig. of fancy* : C.
669 ; *of the relationship of the
Father, God, to the Son, Christ* :
P. L. v. 603 ; Ps. II. 15.

(*b*) to create, produce, give
rise to : P. L. IX. 95.

    part. adj. **begotten,** procreated
of Christ : P. L. III. 384 ; v. 835 ;
VII. 163 ; *absol.* offspring : P. L.
II. 782 ; X. 983.

    See **First-begot, Only-begotten,
Self-begot, Self-begotten.**

Beggary, *sb.* extreme indigence : S.
A. 69.

Begin, *vb.* (*pret.* and *past part.*
begun), (**1**) *intr.* (*a*) to take the
first step in an action or operation,
make a commencement : P. L. I.

798 ; VIII. 311 ; IX. 26 ; P. R. I.
288 ; II. 113 ; III. 179, 185 ; *with
prep. inf.*: P. L. III. 355 ; IV. 979 ;
VI. 56, 748 ; VII. 246 ; IX. 192, 1014,
1123, 1142 ; X. 213, 1064 ; XI. 21,
729 ; XII. 636 ; P. R. I. 132, 499 ;
II. 11 ; IV. 635 ; S. A. 1381 ; Cir.
13 ; Il P. 131 ; C. 206, 460, 545 ;
Ps. LXXX. 39 ; (*a*) to start to speak :
P. L. I. 83 ; II. 118, 680 ; IV. 31,
560 ; v. 152, 396, 562 ; VI. 261,
417, 679 ; IX. 204, 669, 675, 678,
794 ; X. 234, 590 ; P. R. II. 120 ;
L. 15, 17.

(*b*) to come into existence,
originate, arise : P. L. VI. 97 ;
VII. 63, 86, 636 ; VIII. 250 ; X.
706, 811 ; XI. 633, 634 ; XII. 6 ;
P. R. IV. 311 ; N. O. 167.

(**2**) *tr.* to commence, enter
upon : P. L. II. 1037 ; IV. 15,
537, 832 ; v. 144, 559 ; VI. 406 ;
VII. 93 ; VIII. 162 ; IX. 224, 531 ;
XI. 174 ; P. R. I. 186 ; III. 198,
266 ; IV. 99, 540 ; S. A. 225, 274 ;
N. O. 63 ; L'A. 41, 60 ; C. 125 ;
to commence to execute : P. L.
VI. 278.

    vbl. sb. **beginning,** commence-
ment, inception : P. L. III. 633 ;
VIII. 251 ; P. R. IV. 392 ; time
when the universe began : P. L.
I. 9 ; VII. 638 ; P. R. I. 408.

Begirt, *vb. tr.* to surround, encompass : P. L. I. 581 ; v. 868 ; P. R.
II. 213.

Beguile, *vb. tr.* to entangle with
guile, delude, deceive: P. L. I. 445;
III. 689 ; IX. 905 ; X. 162, 880 ;
P. R. II. 169 ; S. A. 759 ; P. 54.

Behalf, *sb.* (*a*) **on man's behalf,** in
man's interest : P. L. III. 218.

(*b*) **in behalf of man,** on account
of man : P. L. XI. 102.

Behemoth, *sb.* the animal described
in Job XL. 15-24, by some conjectured to be the hippopotamus :
P. L. VII. 471.

Behest, *sb.* command, injunction :
P. L. III. 533 ; v. 311 ; VI. 185 ;
VIII. 238 ; XI. 99, 251.

Behind, (**1**) *adv.* (*a*) following after
in position: P. L. I. 446 ; X. 266 ;
S. A. 721 ; *in time* : P. L. v.
119 ; P. R. III. 78, 423 ; S. A.
1300 ; S. XIV. 6 ; *in attainment
or subordination* : P. L. II. 120 ;
S. A. 858, 1375.

(*b*) at the back, in the rear :
P. L. III. 626 ; VI. 578, 864 ; IX.
277 ; S. A. 360.

(c) away from : P. R. II. 46.

(**2**) *prep.* at the back of : P. L.
I. 286, 596 ; X. 588 ; XII. 205 ; P.
R. II. 46 ; III. 323 ; IV. 193 ; S.
A. 1618.

Behold, *vb.* (*pres. 2d sing.* behold'st : P. R. III. 269 ; IV. 162 ;
pret. beheld ; *2d pers.* beheld'st : XI. 700, 819 ; *past part.*
beheld) *tr.* to look at, see, contemplate ; *sometimes with the added
idea of* to contemplate with the
mind, consider : P. L. I. 309,
323, 605, 607, 777 ; II. 959, 1046 ;
III. 64, 77, 78, 387, 554, 672 ; IV.
105, 117, 162, 358, 723, 821 ; V.
13, 45, 87, 161, 219, 308, 329, 605,
719 ; VI. 472, 550, 607, 637, 681,
810, 825 ; VII. 86, 137, 222, 255,
539 ; VIII. 284, 342, 349, 481, 529,
605 ; IX. 455, 480, 541, 576, 608,
735, 1080, 1082 ; X. 81, 326, 332,
454, 464, 724, 839, 863 ; XI. 110,
423, 429, 495, 581, 700, 711, 754,
819, 864 ; XII. 50, 142, 641 ; P.
R. I. 269, 295, 386 ; II. 31, 44,
338 ; III. 269, 293 ; IV. 26, 57,
162, 435 ; S. A. 206, 339, 708,
741, 1473, 1543, 1642 ; Il P. 67 ;
A. 40 ; C. 672, 968 ; *with clause* :
P. L. V. 866 ; P. R. I. 130 ; *absol.* :
P. L. V. 329 ; VIII. 529 ; P. R.
IV. 237 ; S. A. 1608, 1645 ; *used
as interj.* : P. L. VII. 549 ; P. R. II.
331 ; Ps. VII. 50 ; *more definitely*
to consider, regard : P. L. III.
236 ; IV. 679 ; VIII. 15 ; Ps. VIII.
9 ; LXXX. 59 ; CXXXVI. 78.

Beholder, *sb.* spectator : P. L. IX. 544.

Behoof, *sb.* advantage, benefit : P.
L. II. 982 ; D. F. I. 45.

Behove, *vb. tr.* to be necessary to :
P. L. II. 942 ; *absol.* : P. L. IV. 931.

Being, *vbl. sb.* (**1**) existence : P. L.
II. 440 ; (*a*) life, physical or conscious existence : P. L. II. 585 ;
IV. 483 ; VIII. 174, 294 ; IX. 266 ;
X. 747, 988 ; XI. 769 ; P. R. II.
114 ; C. 8 ; *of angelic or other
supernatural creatures* : P. L. I.
154 ; II. 98, 147, 865 ; V. 825,
858 ; *fig.* : P. L. XII. 85.

(*b*) existence in some particular
place : P. R. I. 62.

(*c*) manner of existence : P. L.
V. 455.

(**2**) that which exists, whatever
is : P. L. III. 374.

(**3**) essential substance or
nature : P. L. V. 487 ; C. 469.

See **Well-being.**

Belated, *part. adj.* overtaken by
the lateness or darkness of the
night : P. L. I. 783.

Belch, *vb. tr.* to eject, throw out :
P. L. I. 671 ; VI. 586 ; X. 232.

Beldam, *sb. attrib.* grandmother ;
fig. of nature : V. Ex. 48.

Belial, *sb.* one of the fallen angels :
P. L. I. 490, 502 ; II. 109, 226 ;
VI. 620 ; P. R. II. 150, 173.

Belief, *sb.* credence, acceptance,
assent : P. L. VIII. 136 ; IX. 719 ;
XI. 146 ; S. A. 117, 1535 ; P.
31.

Believe, *vb.* (*pres. 2d sing.* believ'st :
P. L. VI. 471), (**1**) *tr.* (*a*) to think,
be of opinion, be confident, *with
clause* : P. L. I. 631 ; VIII. 294 ;
P. R. I. 274 ; C. 216 ; *with two
acc.* : P. L. I. 144 ; VI. 471.

(*b*) to give credence to, have
confidence in, accept : P. L. IX.
684 ; X. 42 ; XI. 355 ; S. A. 599,
830 ; V. Ex. 12 ; C. 438 ; *absol.* :
P. L. XII. 116.

(**2**) *intr.* to have faith in God
as the creator of all things and
the bestower of salvation through
Jesus Christ : P. L. XII. 127, 407,
441 ; in Jesus Christ as the Messiah : P. R. II. 5.

Believer, *sb.* one who has faith in
Jesus Christ as the Messiah : P. L.
XII. 520.

Belike, *adv.* in all likelihood, probably : P. L. II. 156.

Bell, *sb.* (*a*) cup of a flower : L. 135.

(*b*) the instrument for giving
forth a sound when struck by a
clapper : L'A. 93.

Bellerophon, *sb.* the Greek hero who
attempted to rise to the dwelling
of the gods on Pegasus, but whose
horse threw him to earth : P. L.
VII. 18.

Bellerus, *sb. from Bellerium, the
Roman name for Land's End,
Cornwall, probably* the real or
coined name of a giant or giants(?) :
L. 160.

Bellman, *sb.* watchman, one who
cried the hours of the night and
pronounced benedictions upon
those asleep : Il P. 83.

Bellona, *sb.* the Roman goddess of
war : P. L. II. 922.

Bellow, *vb. intr.* to roar, *of
thunder* : P. L. I. 177 ; *with
pain* : P. L. VI. 362.

Belly, *sb.* (*a*) under part of the body
of an animal : P. L. X. 177, 514.

(*b*) that part of the body which receives food, stomach : L. 114.
See **Huge-bellied.**

Belong, *vb. intr.* (*always with* to) to go along with or accompany (*a*) as an attendant: P. L. v. 167.

(*b*) to be the proper accompaniment, be due, be appropriate, pertain : P. L. vi. 807 ; x. 84, 496 ; xi. 163, 166 ; P. R. iii. 135 ; C. 85 ; L. 121 ; *impers.* : P. L. iii. 111.

Belove, *vb.* (belovéd, *trisyl. when preceding the sb.* : P. L. x. 489 ; P. R. i. 32, 285), *tr.* to love, *with* of : P. L. xii. 308 ; P. R. i. 379.

part. adj. **beloved,** greatly loved: P. L. vi. 680 ; x. 70, 489 ; P. R. i. 32, 85, 285 ; iv. 513.

Below, *adv.* (*a*) in a lower place relatively to something higher : P. L. xi. 368 ; Il P. 162 ; on earth as *contrasted with heaven* : P. L. iii. 600 ; D. F. I. 49, 64 ; N. O. 90 ; in the depths of the sea : C. 734.

(*b*) lower in station or rank : V. Ex. 80.

Belus, *sb.* the national hero and divinity of several eastern nations, *here* of the Babylonians : P. L. i. 720.

Bench, *sb.* seat of justice : S. xxi. 1.

Bend, *vb.* (*past part.* bended: P. L. vi. 194 ; vii. 410 ; ix. 1105 ; Ps. vii. 46 ; bent : P. L. i. 681 ; ii. 923 ; iii. 84, 441 ; iv. 188, 568, 794 ; v. 829 ; vi. 112, 506 ; ix. 55 ; x. 885 ; xi. 190, 548, 577 ; xii. 2 ; P. R. iv. 465 ; S. A. 1486 ; S. xix. 4), (**1**) *tr.* (*a*) to bring (*a bow*) into tension : P. R. vii. 46.

(*b*) to bring into a curve : P. L. i. 616 ; iv. 981 ; x. 885 ; flex, crook (*the knee*): P. L. v. 787, 817 ; Ps. lxxxi. 40.

(*c*) to aim (*a dart*): P. L. ii. 729 ; P. R. iv. 424.

(*d*) *in various fig. senses,* to direct, turn, incline (*the eye or ear, way or course, thoughts, anger, etc.*): P. L. i. 681 ; ii. 354, 573 ; iii. 58, 573 ; iv. 794 ; vi. 826 ; x. 454 ; xi. 30, 152, 190 ; P. R. ii. 291 ; N. O. 71 ; Ps. viii. 8 ; lxxxviii. 8 ; H. B. 10 ; *with* at : P. R. iv. 465.

(*e*) *in passive,* to be intent, be determined : P. L. ix. 384 ; *with prep. inf.* : P. L. ii. 923 ; iv. 188 ; v. 829 ; xi. 577 ; S. A. 1486 ; S.

xix. 4 ; *with* on : P. L. iii. 84, 441 ; iv. 568 ; vi. 112, 506, 826 ; ix. 55 ; xii. 2 ; *with clause,* on omitted : P. L. xi. 548.

(**2**) *intr.* (*a*) to form a curve, take a curved shape : C. 899, 1015.

(*b*) to bow the body : P. L. ii. 477 ; Ps. lxxxi. 62 ; *with prep. inf. of purpose* : P. L. iv. 460, 462.

(*c*) to be directed : A. 6.

part. adj. **bended,** crooked, curved, bowed : P. L. vi. 194 ; vii. 410 ; ix. 1105.

See **Bow-bent.**

Beneath, (**1**) *adv.* below, underneath : P. L. ii. 1003 ; iii. 30, 526, 739 ; vi. 510 ; ix. 1129 ; P. R. ii. 124, 293 ; iv. 203 ; S. A. 1652 ; in hell : P. L. iv. 83 ; lower in excellence : P. R. iv. 356.

(**2**) *prep.* (*a*) lower than, below, under *in position* : P. L. i. 355 ; iv. 205, 303, 592 ; viii. 318 ; x. 687 ; N. O. 102 ; P. 18 ; L. 16, 167 ; *in the scale of creation* : P. L. viii. 382, 411 ; *in station, rank, or dignity* : P. L. i. 115.

(*b*) overborne or overwhelmed by : P. L. iii. 332.

(*c*) below the level of, *fig.* : P. L. vi. 342.

(*d*) to a greater degree than : S. A. 1469.

Benediction, *sb.* (*a*) blessing : P. L. viii. 645 ; xii. 125.

(*b*) gratitude, thanks : P. R. iii. 127.

Benefactor, *sb.* one who confers benefits : P. R. iii. 82.

Beneficence, *sb.* the doing of good, active kindness : P. R. iii. 133.

Benefit, *sb.* (*a*) act of kindness, favour, gift : P. L. xii. 426 ; P. R. iii. 137 ; S. A. 29.

(*b*) advantage, profit : P. L. viii. 90.

Benevolent, *adj.* well-wishing, kind : P. L. viii. 65.

Bengala, *sb.* Bengal, the province of India lying north of the Gulf of Bengal : P. L. ii. 638.

Benight, *vb. tr.* (*a*) to overtake by the darkness of night : C. 150.

(*b*) to involve in moral darkness : C. 384.

Benign, *adj.* favourable, kind : P. L. viii. 492 ; xi. 334 ; xii. 538.

Benison, *sb.* blessing : C. 332.

Benjamin, *sb.* the tribe of Benjamin : Ps. lxxx. 9.

Bent, *sb.* (*a*) inclination, tendency :
P. L. xi. 597.

(*b*) aim, purpose : V. Ex. 55.

Benumb, *vb. tr.* (*a*) to render torpid
(*a part of the body*) : P. L. x. 1069.

(*b*) *absol.* to stupefy mentally :
P. L. ii. 74.

part. adj. **benumbing**, stupefying, deadening : S. A. 630.

Bereave, *vb.* (*pret.* bereaved : P. L.
ix. 461 ; *past part.* bereaved : P.
L. vi. 903 ; S. A. 85, 1294 ; bereft : P. L. xi. 628 ; S. A. 48 ;
C. 277 ; S. xxii. 3), *tr.* to deprive,
rob, strip, take away, *with* of :
P. L. vi. 903 ; ix. 461 ; xi. 628 ;
W. S. 13 ; S. xxii. 3 ; *with double
object* ; *personal* (*subject of passive*)
and impersonal: S. A. 85 ; *personal omitted* : P. L. x. 810 ; *impersonal omitted* : C. 277 ; *impersonal implied* : P. L. x. 918 ; *impersonal* (*subject of passive*) *and personal or no object* : S. A. 48, 1294.

Berry, *sb.* small fruit : P. L. v. 307,
346 ; C. 55, 186 ; L. 3.

Beryl, *sb.* the precious stone : P. L.
vi. 756 ; C. 933.

Beseech, *vb.* (*pret. and past part.*
besought), *tr.* to beg earnestly
for, entreat, implore : P. L. ii.
166 ; v. 848 ; x. 912 ; xii. 238 ;
to supplicate, implore *a person* :
vii. 109 ; ix. 1135 ; P. R. iii. 421 ;
Ps. lxxxi. 43 ; *with* of : P. L. x.
1082 ; *with clause* : P. L. xii. 236 ;
absol. : P. L. v. 869 ; S. A. 751.

Beseem, *vb.* to become, befit : Il P.
18 ; *impers.* : P. L. ii. 869 ; iv.
338 ; *absol.* : P. R. ii. 335.

part. adj. **beseeming**, befitting,
proper : C. 769.

Beset, *vb. tr.* to surround, encompass, hem in (*with foes*) : P. L.
xi. 702 ; **beset round**, completely
surround : S. A. 257 ; *with difficulties*: P. L. ii. 1016 ; x. 124.

See **Hard-besetting**.

Beside, (1) *adv.* (*a*) moreover : Cir.
23 ; C. 950.

(*b*) besides, else : N. O. 224.

(2) *prep.* (*a*) by the side of : P.
L. v. 54 ; vi. 763.

(*b*) over and above, in addition
to : C. 287.

Besides, (1) *adv.* (*a*) else, other than
that mentioned : P. L. i. 32, 194 ;
ii. 504 ; vii. 125 ; viii. 25 ; xi.
527 ; P. R. ii. 408 ; iv. 150.

(*b*) moreover, in addition : P.
L. i. 298 ; ii. 20, 221 ; iii. 598 ;

vi. 626 ; xi. 300 ; P. R. ii. 481 ;
iv. 55, 202 ; S. A. 214, 845, 1361 ;
S. xvii. 9.

(2) *prep.* (*a*) in addition to,
over and above : P. L. x. 737 ;
P. R. iii. 419 ; M. W. 4, 53 ; C.
18 ; L. 128.

(*b*) other than : S. A. 441.

Besiege, *vb. tr.* to lay siege to,
assail with armed force : P. R.
iii. 339 ; D. F. I. 47 ; *absol.* : P.
L. v. 869.

Besmear, *vb. tr.* to smear over or
cover (*with*): P. L. i. 392 ; v.
356.

Besotted, *part. adj.* morally stupefied : C. 778.

Bespeak *vb.* (*only in pret.* bespake),
(1) *tr.* to speak to, address : P. L.
ii. 849 ; iv. 1005.

(2) *intr.* to speak : P. R. i. 43 ;
N. O. 76 ; L. 112.

See **Dew-besprent**.

Best, (1) *adj.* (*sup. of* good) of the
highest excellence, most appropriate or desirable, excelling all
others : P. L. i. 247 ; ii. 40, 230 ;
iv. 203 ; v. 19, 95, 333 ; viii.
550 ; ix. 249, 258, 317, 343, 402,
433, 808 ; x. 599 ; xi. 438, 603 ;
xii. 561 ; P. R. iii. 174, 224, 238 ;
iv. 262, 476, 524, 553 ; S. A. 759,
1029. 1034, 1718. 1745, 1748 ; V.
Ex. 26 ; P. 29 ; C. 171, 309, 377,
573.

absol. that which or the one
which is excellent in the highest
degree : P. L. i. 765 ; iv. 852 ;
vi. 724 ; viii. 611 ; ix. 745, 896 ;
S. A. 1264 ; C. 28 ; **his best of
man** : P. L. xi. 497. *See* **Man**.

(2) *adv.* (*sup. of* well) in the
most excellent or suitable manner
or condition, in the most eminent
degree, to the fullest extent : P.
L. i. 691 ; ii. 280, 357, 458 ; iv.
309, 398, 738, 770 ; v. 160, 574,
779 ; vi. 353 ; vii. 115 ; viii. 106,
169, 428 ; ix. 178, 201, 230, 541,
995, 1092 ; x. 82, 173, 651, 867 ;
xi. 54, 365 ; P. R. i. 105, 186,
288 ; ii. 113, 382 ; iii. 8, 177,
182, 194, 195, 250, 433 ; iv. 235,
266, 364, 381 ; S. A. 255, 314,
511, 908, 1061, 1167, 1429, 1521 ;
D. F. I. 70 ; C. 487, 908 ; S. xiii.
8, xiv. 9, xvii. 7, xix. 10, 11 ; **at
best**, under the most favourable
circumstances : Ps. lxxxiv. 36.

Bested, *vb. tr.* to support, help ; Il
P. 3.

Bestial, *adj.* (*a*) of or belonging to the lower animals : P. L. IV. 754; IX. 165.

(*b*) like that of a beast, beastlike : P. L. II. 873.

(*c*) brutish in form and spirit : P. L. I. 435.

Bestick, *vb.* (*past part.* bestuck) *tr.* to stick or pierce through : P. L. XII. 536.

Bestir, *vb. refl.* to begin to move oneself actively, move with life and vigour : P. L. I. 334; V. 337.

Bestow, *vb. tr.* to confer as a gift, grant, give : P. L. V. 317, 318; VIII. 483; Ps. LXXXV. 49; *with* on : P. L. III. 673; VIII. 537; P. R. II. 395; Ps. II. 17; to address to as a mark of honour : P. L. V. 386.

Best-resolved, *adj. absol.* one most firmly determined : S. A. 847.

Bestrew, *vb.* (*only in past part.* bestrown) *tr.* to strew or scatter about : P. L. I. 311; IV. 631.

Bestud, *vb. tr.* to set thickly as with studs : C. 734.

Betake, *vb.* (*pret.* betook ; *past part. does not occur*), *refl.* to take oneself to, have recourse to, *with dat.* : P. L. X. 610; *with* to : P. L. VI. 663; IX. 388; P. R. IV. 403; *with* whither : P. L. X. 922; C. 351.

Bethabara, *sb.* the place "beyond Jordan, where John was baptizing," *probably* Bethany, a ford on the further side of the Jordan in Perea(?) : P. R. I. 184; II. 20.

Bethel, *sb.* the town in the southern part of the kingdom of Israel : P. L. I. 485; P. R. III. 431.

Bethink, *vb.* (*pret.* bethought), *refl.* to call to one's mind, recollect oneself : C. 820; P. L. II. 73; *with* of : P. R. III. 149.

Bethlehem, *sb.* the town in Palestine : P. R. I. 243; II. 78; IV. 505; *fig.* **rays of Bethlehem**, light coming from Bethlehem as the birthplace of Christ, and, *hence*, from Christ as resplendent in his godhood : N. O. 223.

Betide, *vb.* to happen to, befall, come to : P. L. XII. 480; P. R. IV. 451.

Betimes, *adv.* soon, before it is too late : P. L. III. 186; S. XXI. 9.

Betoken, *vb. tr.* (*a*) to be an emblem of, typify : P. L. XI. 867.

(*b*) to be a sign of, presage : P. R. IV. 490.

Betray, *vb. tr.* (*a*) to deceive treacherously, deliver up by breach of trust, give over to the enemy : S. A. 33, 383, 399, 840, 946, 1109 ; C. 697 ; *absol.* : S. A. 750.

(*b*) to reveal or disclose what should be kept secret : S. A. 379 ; *with two acc.* : P. L. IV. 116.

Better, (**1**) *adj.* (*comp. of* good), of greater excellence, of superior quality, more appropriate or desirable : P. L. I. 645; II. 114; IV. 385, 939; V. 785; VI. 30; VII. 189; IX. 31, 998; X. 1011, 1068; XI. 42, 599; XII. 302; P. R. I. 248; II. 258; IV. 445; S. A. 182, 797, 1163; A. 101; C. 123; S. IX. 5, XVII. 2, XXII. 14; Ps. LXXXII. 34.

absol. thing of more excellence : P. L. IX. 102; X. 1086.

(**2**) *adv.* (*comp. of* well) in a more excellent way, in a superior degree, more fully, more appropriately : P. L. I. 688; III. 680; IV. 167, 915; VIII. 33; P. R. I. 190; II. 332; IV. 8, 357; S. A. 585; C. 775; Hor. Sat. I. 2; *in pred. after* be, *and in elliptical expressions the distinction between adj. and adv. cannot be made with certainty* : P. L. I. 263; II. 196; V. 167; IX. 365; X. 593; XI. 502, 635, 763; P. R. II. 486; III. 180, 397; S. A. 579; L. 67.

(**3**) *vb. tr.* to give advantage to : P. L. VI. 440.

Between (bétween : P. L. VII. 473), (**1**) *adv.* in an intermediate position; (*a*) *of space* : P. L. II. 726; III. 70; IV. 699; VII. 241; X. 362; P. R. III. 256; N. O. 144.

(*b*) *of place* in the midst : P. L. IX. 1107; XI. 639.

(*c*) *of time* in the interval or at intervals : P. L. V. 306, 702; VI. 162; IX. 237; XII. 207.

(**2**) *prep.* (*a*) in or at some point in the space which separates two places or objects : P. L. I. 387; V. 268; VI. 756; VII. 201, 439; XII. 197, 253; P. R. III. 361; S. A. 1630.

(*b*) in the mutual relation of : P. L. VI. 441; IX. 1151; X. 179, 497, 924.

(*c*) so as to protect from : P. R. III. 219.

(*d*) **between sea and land**, whether in the sea or on the land : P. L. VII. 473.

Betwixt, *prep.* between, *of space* : P. L. II. 593, 1018 ; IV. 252, 549, 998 ; X. 328 ; U. C. I. 8 ; L'A. 82 ; *of time* : P. L. XII. 3 ; *of likeness and difference* : P. L. III. 462.

Bevy, *sb.* company : P. L. XI. 582.

Bewail, *vb. tr.* to wail over, lament, express sorrow for : P. L. XI. 111 ; S. A. 151, 955, 1742 ; D. F. I. 7 ; *with personal object* : S. A. 182.

Beware, *vb.* (*only in inf. and imper.*), *tr.* to be wary of, guard against : P. L. IV. 559 ; VII. 42 ; *with clause without connective* : P. L. V. 237 ; *absol.* to be wary, take heed : P. L. VI. 894 ; VII. 545 ; VIII. 638.

*****Beyond** (béyond : P. L. II. 7 ; V. 159 ; X. 463, 805), (**1**) *adv.* (*a*) at a greater distance, farther away, far off, *in space* : P. L. I. 542 ; *in time* : P. L. XII. 555.

(*b*) further, in addition, more : P. L. VII. 120.

(**2**) *prep.* (*a*) farther than, more distant than, *of position* : P. L. I. 409, 781 ; II. 587.

(*b*) farther than, more than, *of quantity or amount* : P. L. IX. 1173 ; P. R. II. 230.

(*c*) superior to, surpassing, more than, *of degree* : P. L. II. 1 ; VI. 629 ; VIII. 581 ; C. 813.

(*d*) *fig.* not within the range of, out of the reach or limit of : P. L. I. 587 ; II. 318 ; III. 138, 591 ; IX. 228.

Bickering, *part. adj.* being in constant and rapid motion, *of flame* : P. L. VI. 766.

Bid, *vb.* (*pres. 2d sing.* bidd'st : P. L. IV. 635 ; *pret.* bade : C. 639 ; bid : P. L. VIII. 519 ; X. 668 ; *past part.* bid : P. L. VII. 304 ; P. R. II. 326 ; bidden : L. 118), *tr.* (*a*) to order, command : P. L. I. 246 ; II. 733 ; IV. 635 ; VI. 176 ; VII. 107 ; P. R. I. 377, 495 ; II. 326 ; *with simple inf.* : P. L. II. 514 ; IV. 748 ; VI. 202 ; XI. 590 : S. A. 967 ; A. 13 ; *in passive* : P. L. X. 672 ; P. R. II. 274 ; S. A. 1392 ; S. VIII. 10 ; *with acc. and simple inf.* : P. L. IV. 633 ; VII. 166, 304 ; VIII. 185, 519 ; IX. 353 ; X. 668. 672, 1067 ; S. A. 1310 ; N. O. 76, 124 ; Il P. 105 ; C. 93,

400, 639 ; L. 134, 149 ; S. XIV. 13 ; H. B. 4 ; *absol.* : S. A. 505.

(*b*) to pray, wish earnestly ; *with acc. and simple inf.* : L. 22 ; **bid good-morrow** : L'A. 46.

part. adj. **bidden,** invited : L. 118.

vbl. sb. **bidding,** command : P. L. III. 712 ; XI. 112, 314 ; S. XIX. 12.

Bide, *vb.* (**1**) *intr.* to abide, dwell, stay : P. L. II. 304 ; III. 321 ; X. 738 ; Ps. LXXXIV. 19 ; LXXXVI. 38.

(**2**) *tr.* to endure, bear : P. R. I. 59.

vbl. sb. **biding,** dwelling, sojourn : Ps. V. 11.

Biding-place, *sb.* dwelling-place : D. F. I. 21.

Bier, *sb.* that on which bodies are carried to the grave, *fig.* : L. 12.

Biggest, *adj.* (*sup. of* big), largest, of greatest size : P. L. VII. 471.

Bigness, *sb.* size, magnitude : P. L. I. 778 ; II. 1052.

Bill, *sb.* beak of a bird : P. L. XI. 859 ; S. I. 6.

Billow, *sb.* great wave : C. 932 ; *fig. of flame* : P. L. I. 224.

Bind (*pres. 2d sing.* bind'st : Hor. O. 3 ; *pret. and past part.* bound) *vb.* (**1**) *tr.* (*a*) to tie up, fasten together, confine, restrain, restrict ; (*a*) by a material bond, deprive of liberty : P. L. III. 256 ; IV. 171, 897 ; VI. 358, 870 ; P. R. III. 367 ; IV. 632 ; S. A. 261, 365, 438, 1184, 1209 ; N. O. 169 ; C. 816 ; *fig.* : P. L. III. 602 ; XII. 525 ; fasten up : Hor. O. 3 ; make fast : P. L. VI. 870 ; to secure with a border, *fig.* : P. L. XI. 881.

(*b*) by a non-material bond : P. L. V. 819 ; IX. 761 ; X. 297 ; XI. 265 ; S. A. 309 ; *absol.* : P. L. IX. 760.

(*c*) to encircle, wreathe : P. L. III. 361.

(*d*) to oblige or compel by obligation, *with prep. inf.* : P. L. XI. 291.

(**2**) *refl.* to oblige oneself by a covenant, pledge oneself : Ps. LXXXIII. 20.

See **Root-bound, Wedlock-bound.**

Bird, *sb.* feathered, flying animal : P. L. VI. 74 ; VII. 394 ; VIII. 351, 395 ; XI. 186 ; (*a*) *in combination or contrast with beast* : P. L. IV. 704 ; *sing. collect.* : VIII. 342, 349 ; XI. 183 ; species of birds : P. L. XI. 734.

(*b*) *esp.* one of the song birds :

P. L. II. 494 ; IV. 264, 642, 651 ;
V. 8, 197 ; VII. 433 ; VIII. 265,
515, 528 ; P. R. II. 290 ; IV. 434 ;
the nightingale : P. L. III. 38 ;
IV. 648, 655 ; V. 40 ; VIII. 518 ;
P. R. IV. 245 ; Il P. 61. *See*
Attic.

(*c*) *context indicating a particular bird*, **bird of calm**, the
Halcyon or Kingfisher, which was
fabled to brood during the seven
days preceding and the seven
following the winter solstice.
The nest floated on the water
and calms always prevailed at
sea : N. O. 68 ; **bird of hate**, the
cuckoo : S. I. 9 ; **bird of Jove**, the
eagle : P. L. XI. 185 ; the phœnix :
P. L. V. 272 ; S. A. 1699, 1707.
See **Phœnix.**

Birth, *sb.* (*a*) act of bringing forth
offspring : P. L. III. 285 ; VII.
454 ; M. W. 67 ; L'A. 14.

(*b*) act of coming into life,
nativity : P. L. XII. 360, 364 ;
P. R. I. 66, 238, 270 ; IV. 503 ;
S. A. 23, 525, 1135, 1431 ; V. Ex.
59 ; P. 3 ; M. W. 31 ; *fig.*: P. L.
IV. 15 ; VII. 102 ; XI. 768.

(*c*) that which is born or
brought forth, offspring : P. L.
IX. 111 ; XI. 687 ; P. R. II. 71 ;
Ps. VIII. 4 ; *fig. of the elements* :
P. L. V. 180 ; *of the products of
the earth* : P. L. IX. 624 ; **birth
of heaven,** angels created in heaven
and, *hence*, partaking of its nature :
P. L. V. 862.

(*d*) conditions involved in birth :
P. L. X. 207.

(*e*) parentage, lineage : P. R.
I. 141 ; II. 413 ; S. A. 171 ; M.
W. 5, 15.

Birth-day, *sb.* day of the beginning (*of
heaven and earth*) : P. L. VII. 256.

Birth-night, *sb.* night on which one
is born : P. L. IV. 506.

Birthright, *sb.* right to which one is
entitled by birth : P. L. I. 511 ;
III. 309.

Biserta, *sb.* a city of Tunis in Africa,
mentioned in medieval romance :
P. L. I. 585.

Bite, *vb.* (*pres.*) *tr.* to wound with
the teeth : A. 53.
    See **Hunger-bit.**

Bitter, *adj.* (*a*) having an acrid
taste like wormwood : P. L. X.
566 ; *fig.*: P. L. II. 808.

(*b*) causing pain or suffering,
either mental or physical : P. L.

II. 598 ; IV. 24 ; VIII. 328 ; IX.
172 ; S. A. 823 ; N. O. 152 ; C.
365 ; L. 6.

Bitterly, *adv.* in a painful manner :
S. A. 432.

Bitterness, *sb.* grievousness, painful-
ness : P. L. XI. 157.

Bituminous, *adj.* consisting of or
containing bitumen : P. L. X. 562,
XII. 41.

Bizance, *sb.* Byzantium, the ancient
Greek city on the shores of the
Bosphorus ; *here* used for Con-
stantinople, the capital of the
Ottoman Empire, which was built
on part of the site of the older
city : P. L. XI. 395.

Blab, *sb.* revealer of secrets, tattler :
S. A. 495.

Blabbing, *part. adj.* revealing what
ought to be kept secret : C. 138.

Black, (1) *adj.* (*a*) of the colour or
approaching the colour of jet :
P. L. II. 578, 670 ; VII. 238, 547 ;
XI. 738 ; XII. 41 ; S. A. 600, 622,
973 ; P. 34 ; *sup.*: P. L. VI. 515 ;
N. O. 207.

(*b*) characterized by absence of
light, dark, dusky, *of mist,
clouds, air, etc.* : P. L. II. 67,
714 ; IX. 180 ; X. 702, 847 ; C. 62,
337 ; Hor. O. 7 ; *sup.* : L'A. 2.

(*c*) characterized by a black
garb : P. L. III. 475.

(*d*) evil, malignant, foul : S. A.
1133 ; *with the added idea of* (*a*)
or (*b*) : P. L. I. 405 ; D. F. I. 67 ;
sup. : P. L. II. 136.

(**2**) *sb.* colour opposite to white,
colour of jet : Il P. 16, 17.

Blackmoor, *adj.* **Blackmoor Sea,**
that part of the Mediterranean
bordering on Mauritania : P. R.
IV. 72.

Blade, *sb.* weapon having a thin,
sharp edge : C. 651.

Blain, *sb.* blotch, blister : P. L. XII.
180.

Blame, (1) *sb.* (*a*) censure, reprehen-
sion : P. L. III. 697 ; IX. 1143 ; X.
130, 833 ; S. A. 848, 1723 ; C.
509 ; Ps. V. 34.

(*b*) thing or act worthy of
blame, fault : P. L. IV. 758 ; V.
119 ; IX. 292 ; N. O. 41 ; M. W. 27.

(**2**) *vb.* (*pres. 2d sing.* blam'st :
P. L. VIII. 612), *tr.* to censure :
P. L. X. 958, 959 ; *with acc. and
prep. inf.* : P. L. VIII. 66, 612.

Blanc, *adj.* blank or pale in colour :
P. L. X. 656.

Bland, *adj.* gentle (*words*): P. L.
IX. 855 ; balmy (*vapours*) : P. L.
v. 5 ; IX. 1047.
Blandished, *part. adj.* full of flattery: S. A. 403.
Blandishment, *sb.* flattering action :
P. L. VIII. 351.
Blank, (1) *sb.* vacant page or surface, *fig.* : P. L. III. 48.
(2) *adj.* disconcerted, helpless,
confounded : P. L. IX. 890 ;
P. R. II. 120 ; Ps. VI. 21 ; rendering powerless : C. 452.
(3) *vb. tr.* to disconcert, confound : S. A. 471.
Blaspheme (blasphéme), *vb. tr.* to
speak evil of (*God*): P. L. III.
166 ; XII. 411 ; S. A. 442 ; C. 779.
Blasphemous (blasphe'mous), *adj.*
impious, irreverent : P. L. V. 809 ;
VI. 360 ; P. R. IV. 181.
Blast, (1) *sb.* (*a*) strong gust of wind :
P. L. X. 701 ; P. R. IV. 31, 418 ;
L. 97.
(*b*) strong current of air produced artificially : P. L. I. 708.
(*c*) the blowing of a trumpet :
S. A. 972 ; the sound so produced : P. L. XI. 76 ; N. O. 161.
(*d*) blight, destructive influence : P. L. X. 693 ; C. 640,
845.
(2) *vb. tr.* to blight, wither,
shrivel ; P. L. VI. 372 ; D. F. I. 1.
part. adj. **(1) blasting,** ruinous, destructive : P. L. IV. 928 ;
blighting : A. 49.
(2) blasted ; (*a*) blighted : P. L.
I. 615.
(*b*) effected with a pernicious
influence : P. L. X. 412.
Blaze, I. *sb.* **(1)** vivid glowing flame :
P. L. IV. 818 ; *fig. of honour or
fame* : L. 74.
(2) brilliant light, brightness
from the sun or other bright object :
P. L. I. 665 ; III. 378 ; VI. 18 ;
IX. 1083 ; X. 453 ; S. A. 80 ; N. O.
9 ; A. 2 ; *fig. of fame* : P. R. III.
47.
II. *vb.* **(1)** *intr.* (*a*) to burn,
flame : P. L. IX. 639 ; Ps. LXXXIII.
56.
(*b*) to shine like flame, be resplendent : P. L. I. 194 ; VI. 306,
775 ; XII. 633.
(2) *tr.* (*a*) to shine forth, *with
cognate acc.* : P. L. X.65.
(*b*) to blow abroad or proclaim
the praise or fame of : S. A. 528 ;
A. 74 ; Ps. LXXXVI. 43 ; CXXXVI. 5.

part. adj. **blazing,** (*a*) flaming :
P. L. I. 728.
(*b*) emitting a brilliant light :
P. L. VII. 575 ; XI. 229 ; M. W. 70.
See **Far-blazing, Full-blazing.**
Bleak, *adj.* cold, chilly : P. R. II.
74 ; D. F. I. 4 ; C. 269.
Blear, *adj.* deceptive : C. 155.
Bleating, *part. adj.* crying as a
calf or sheep : P. L. II. 494 ; VII.
472 ; XI. 649 ; *contemptuously of
gods* : P. L. I. 489.
Bleed, *vb.* (*pret.* bled, *past part. not
used*), *intr.* to lose blood, shed
blood : Cir. 11 ; S. XV. 13 ; Ps.
LXXXIII. 43, 44 ; to lose that
which serves the same purpose
as blood, humour of the celestial
spirits : P. L. VI. 333.
Blemish, *sb.* stain, defect : S. XXII. 2.
Bless, *vb.* (blessed, *disyl.* : P. L. III.
136 ; V. 613 ; VI. 267 ; X. 723 ;
XI. 317 ; XII. 148 ; N. O. 25) *tr.* (*a*)
to set apart to sacred purposes :
P. L. VII. 592.
(*b*) to make happy, render fortunate : P. L. II. 847 ; D. F. I.
65 ; N. O. 126 ; *because of divine
gift or favour* : P. L. X. 723 ; XII.
126, 148, 277, 450 ; P. R. II. 68,
94 ; Ps. V. 38 ; CXXXVI. 57.
(*c*) to call down divine benedictions on : P. L. VII. 395, 530 ; X.
821.
(*d*) to protector keep from evil by
a charm : Il P. 84 ; *absol.* : A. 60.
(*e*) to bless oneself, *as an exclamation of surprise* : S. XI. 5.
part. or adj. **blest or blessed,** (*a*)
adored as holy, worthy of reverence, divine : P. L. III. 149 ; VI.
184 ; XII. 573 ; N. O. 25 ; C. 329.
(*b*) happy, fortunate : P. L. IV.
163 ; *because of the presence or
favour of God* : P. L. III. 347 ; IV.
774 ; V. 387 ; P. L. XI. 598 ; XII.
151, 553 ; N. O. 237 ; S. M. 1 ;
L. 177 ; Ps. LXXXIV. 34, 46 ; CXIV.
1 ; making fortunate : P. L. IX.
796.
(*c*) enjoying the bliss of heaven
or paradise, beatified : P. L. III.
136 ; V. 613.
(*d*) bringing blessing, blissful,
holy : P. L. VI. 267 ; XI. 317 ;
P. R. II. 56.
(*e*) bestowing prosperity by
warding off evil : C. 268.
part. absol. **the Blest,** the
angels in heaven : P. L. VIII.
640 ; XI. 67.

vbl. sb. **blessing,** favour and prospering influence : S. A. 357 ; V. Ex. 64 ; M. M. 8 ; C. 772 ; Ps. III. 24.

See **High-blest.**

Blessedness, *sb.* divine favour, felicity : P. L. VII. 59.

Blind, (1) *adj.* (*a*) destitute of the sense of sight, sightless : P. L. III. 35 ; IV. 259 ; S. A. 68, 366, 438, 563, 941, 1106, 1474, 1687 ; S. XXII. 14.

(*b*) wanting moral perception : C. 519.

(*c*) wanting mental perception, ignorant and incompetent : L. 119.

(*d*) not directed by sight : S. A. 1328.

(*e*) not governed by or proceeding from reason, acting without discrimination ; P. L. III. 452 ; L. 75 ; Ps. LXXXI. 52.

(*f*) enveloped in darkness, dark, obscure : C. 181.

absol. one who is destitute of moral perception : P. L. III. 200.

(2) *vb. tr.* (*a*) to deprive of the power of sight : N. O. 223.

(*b*) to deprive of moral perception : P. L. III. 200.

Blindness, *sb.* (*a*) want of sight : S. A. 196, 1221.

(*b*) want of moral or intellectual perception : S. A. 418, 1686.

Bliss, *sb.* (*a*) absolute felicity, highest degree of happiness, most perfect joy of heaven or earth : P. L. II. 375, 832, 867 ; IV. 359, 508, 728 ; V. 241, 517, 543 ; VI. 273, 729 ; VIII. 522 ; IX. 263, 411, 831, 879, 916, 1166 ; X. 25, 399, 503 ; XI. 43 ; XII. 462, 551 ; P. R. I. 419 ; IV. 612 ; D. F. I. 7 ; N. O. 165 ; Cir. 19 ; T. 11 ; C. 263, 741, 741, 813 ; S. XIV. 8 ; *often passing into and undistinguishable from* the place of bliss, heaven or paradise : P. L. I. 607 ; II. 86 ; III. 305, 408, 525 ; IV. 884 ; VI. 52 ; VII. 55 ; VIII. 299 ; XI. 708 ; P. R. I. 361 ; S. IX. 13 ; **the River of Bliss** : P. L. III. 358 ; the joy of nature : P. L. V. 297.

(*c*) the source of bliss, God : P. L. V. 597 ; VI. 892 ; P. R. IV. 597.

Blissful, *adj.* full of bliss, happy in the highest degree : N. O. 98 ; *of persons* : V. Ex. 35 ; C. 1010 ; *of place or condition* : P. L. I. 5 ; III. 69, 527 ; IV. 208, 690 ; V. 292 ; X. 225 ; XI. 77.

Blithe, (1) *adj.* (*a*) joyous, well-pleased : P. L. IX. 625, 886.

(*b*) gay, mirthful : P. L. XI. 615 ; L'A. 24 ; C. 55.

(*c*) *of the air* light and pure (?) ; fresh, glad, joyous (?) : P. R. IV. 585.

(2) *adv.* blithely, cheerfully : L'A. 65.

Blood, *sb.* fluid which circulates through the arteries and veins, life current, vital fluid : P. L. I. 392, 451 ; II. 664 ; IV. 805 ; X. 527 ; XI. 447, 791 ; XII. 176 ; P. R. II. 78 ; IV. 139 ; S. A. 1513, 1726 ; N. O. 57 ; P. 40 ; S. XII. 14 ; XVI. 7 ; XVIII. 10 ; shed in sacrifice : P. L. XII. 292, 293 ; kindred as connoted by blood, **Hagar's blood,** the descendants of Hagar : Ps. LXXXIII. 23 ; as the seat of passion : C. 670 ; as the seat of disposition : P. L. XI. 543 ; C. 810.

See **Life-blood.**

Bloody, *adj.* (*a*) attended with bloodshed : P. L. X. 278 ; XI. 457, 651 ; Ps. LXXXVIII. 19 ; CXXXVI. 61.

(*b*) bloodthirsty, cruel : S. XVIII. 7 ; Ps. V. 16.

Bloom, (1) *sb.* (*a*) blossom : P. L. V. 25 ; S. A. 1576 ; *sing. collect.* : P. L. III. 43 ; VIII. 45.

(*b*) freshness, beauty and innocence : C. 289.

(2) *vb.* (*a*) *intr.* to flower, put forth blossoms : P. L. III. 355.

(*b*) *tr.* to put forth, bear : P. L. IV. 219.

part. adj. **blooming,** bright, splendid : C. 394. *See* **Gold.**

Bloomy, *adj.* full of blossoms : S. I. 1.

Blossom, (1) *sb.* flower of a plant : P. L. IV. 148, 630 ; VII. 326 ; M. W. 41 ; *fig.* literary product : S. II. 4 ; freshness, innocence, and charm *of beauty* : C. 396 ; life : D. F. I. 4.

(2) *vb. intr.* to put forth blossoms, *fig. of truth* : Ps. LXXXV. 46.

Blot, (1) *sb.* (*a*) *fig.* one blot, universal darkness : C. 133.

(*b*) moral stain, disgrace : S. A. 411, 978 ; D. F. I. 12.

(2) *vb. tr.* to obliterate, annihilate, *with* out : P. L. I. 362 ; XI. 891 ; XII. 188.

Blow, I. *sb.* sudden or violent stroke

with the hand or an offensive weapon : P. L. VI. 140, 370.

II. *vb.* (*pret.* blew : P. L. XI. 73 ; *past part.* blown) (1) *tr.* (*a*) to drive or carry by means of a current of air : P. L. III. 488 ; IV. 161 ; IX. 579 ; XI. 16, 313 ; S. A. 1070.

(*b*) to direct a current of air into, fan (*a fire*) : P. L. II. 171.

(*c*) to inflate or puff *up a person with pride or vanity* : P. L. IV. 809.

(*d*) to sound (*a signal*) : P. L. II. 717.

(*e*) to give forth or cause to give forth a sound, *of wind instruments* : P. L. I. 540 ; XI. 73 ; S. M. 11.

(*f*) to announce by sounding a blast : Ps. LXXXI. 9.

(2) *intr.* (*a*) to move, flow in currents, *of the wind* : P. L. V. 192 ; L. 94 ; *with adv. indicating manner of blowing* : P. L. X. 289, 1066 ; XI. 842 ; P. R. I. 317 ; S. A. 10 ; *with complement* : Il P. 128.

(*b*) to give forth a sound, *of wind instruments* : P. L. VI. 60 ; N. O. 130 ; Il P. 161.

III. *vb.* (*not used in pret., past part.* blown), (1) *intr.* to blossom, bloom : P. L. V. 22 ; VII. 319 ; D. F. I. 1 ; L. 48.

(2) *tr.* to cause to bloom : C. 993.

part. adj. **blowing**, blossoming : P. L. IX. 629.

See **Fresh-blown.**

Blue, *adj.* (*a*) of the colour of the clear sky, *said of various things, the particular shade being indicated by context or modifying adj.* : P. L. XI. 206 ; H. 210 ; L'A. 21 ; A. 51 ; C. 894 ; L. 192.

(*b*) livid, leaden-coloured : C. 434.

Blue-haired, *adj.* having blue hair as symbolical of the sea : C. 29.

Blush, (1) *sb.* rosy glow (*of morn*) : P. L. XI. 184.

(2) *vb. intr.* (*a*) to become red in the face : P. L. VIII. 511.

(*b*) to be red : P. L. IX. 426.

Bluster, (1) *sb.* boisterous blowing : P. L. X. 665.

(2) *vb.* to blow boisterously : P. L. III. 426.

part. adj. **blustering,** tempestuous : P. L. II. 286.

Boar, *sb.* male swine : S. A. 1138 ; Ps. LXXX. 53.

Board, *sb.* table for food : P. L. V. 343.

See **Sound-board.**

Boast, I. *sb.* ostentatious speech, vaunt : P. L. IV. 87 ; P. R. II. 119 ; IV. 307 ; C. 273.

II. *vb.* (*pres. 2d sing.* boast'st : P. R. I. 409), (1) *tr.* to speak of with ostentation, brag of, vaunt : P. L. II. 483 ; IV. 1008 ; XI. 86 ; P. R. I. 409 ; S. A. 1127 ; M. M. 8 ; *with clause* : P. L. IV. 85 ; P. R. IV. 306.

(2) *refl.* to brag of oneself, *with cause of boast following* : P. L. IX. 965 ; C. 75.

(3) *intr.* to speak ostentatiously, brag : P. L. IV. 14 ; VI. 163 ; C. 662 ; *with* in : P. L. I. 693 ; *with* of : P. L. II. 52 ; P. R. I. 144 ; S. A. 1104.

part. adj. **boasted,** vaunted : P. L. I. 510 ; S. A. 470.

Boaster, *sb.* one who brags, vaunter : S. A. 1227.

Boastful, *adj.* ostentatious, self-praising : P. L. VI. 84.

Bocchus, *sb.* a king of Mauritania : P. R. IV. 72.

See **Ill-boding.**

Body, *sb.* (*a*) material frame of man *usually contrasted with* mind *or* spirit : P. L. IV. 618 ; V. 478, 497 ; VIII. 622 ; IX. 779 ; X. 587, 791 ; XI. 687 ; P. R. II. 256, 478 ; S. A. 18, 52, 159, 607 ; *fig. of the army of Satan* : P. L. IV. 953 ; material frame of a bird : S. A. 1706.

(*b*) form in which celestial beings appear : P. L. VI. 754.

(*c*) dead body : S. A. 1725 ; C. 473.

(*d*) separate mass of matter, material thing : P. L. III. 619 ; VI. 574 ; X. 1072 ; *referring to a heavenly body* planet : P. L. VII. 354 ; VIII. 28, 87.

Bog, *sb.* morass, quagmire : P. L. II. 621, 948 ; IX. 641 ; *with proper name* : P. L. II. 592.

Boggy, *adj.* swampy : P. L. II. 939.

Boil, *vb.* (1) *intr.* to bubble up through or as if through the action of heat : P. L. XII. 42 ; *fig. of that which involves the passions* : P. L. IV. 16.

(2) *tr.* to cook by boiling : P. R. II. 343.

part. adj. **boiling**; (*a*) violently agitated and fiercely hot : P. L. II. 183.

(*b*) seething : P. L. II. 1027.

(*c*) containing bubbling liquid : P. L. I. 706.

Boisterous, *adj.* (*a*) roughly violent, savage : S. A. 1273 ; D. F. I. 9.

(*b*) strong in growth, luxuriant, rank : S. A. 1164.

Bold, *adj.* (*a*) requiring or showing courage, brave : P. L. I. 763 ; II. 204, 386, 571 ; IV. 13, 854 ; X. 161 ; XI. 642 ; P. R. II. 312 ; L'A. 119 ; Il P. 110 ; C. 610 ; S. XVII. 4 ; H. B. 14 ; *comp.*: P. L. III. 13.

(*b*) presumptuous, audacious, daring : P. L. I. 82, 127, 470 ; II. 751 ; IV. 882 ; V. 66, 803, 876 ; VIII. 235 ; IX. 304, 436, 664, 921 ; X. 521 ; P. R. IV. 625 ; S. A. 138, 1152 ; C. 397 ; Ps. LXXXII. 8 ; LXXXIII. 33 ; CXXXVI. 65 ; *comp.*: P. L. IX. 523 ; XI. 93 ; P. R. IV. 180 ; *sup.*: P. L. VI. 118.

Boldly, *adv.* daringly, fearlessly : P. L. II. 968 ; IV. 891 ; C. 649.

Boldness, *sb.* presumption : P. L. IV. 908.

Bolster, *sb.* cushion to support the head : C. 353.

Bolt, (1) *sb.* (*a*) arrow : C. 445.

(*b*) thunderbolt : P. L. VI. 491.

(*c*) iron fastening for securing a gate : P. L. II. 877.

(2) *vb. tr.* (*a*) to secure or fasten with a bolt : P. L. IV. 190.

(*b*) to discharge like a bolt : S. A. 1696.

(*c*) to sift through a bolting cloth, *fig.* to refine, make subtle : C. 760.

See **Thrice-bolted.**

Bond, *sb.* (*a*) *pl.* fetters, *hence*, confinement, imprisonment : P. L. II. 207 ; VII. 465 ; S. A. 42 ; Ps. II. 7.

(*b*) uniting force, tie, attraction : P. L. IX. 956.

(*c*) obligation : S. A. 853.

Bondage, *sb.* want of freedom, captivity, servitude : P. L. I. 658 ; II. 321 ; S. A. 152, 270, 271.

Bond-slave, *sb.* an emphatic term for slave or serf : S. A. 38, 411.

Bond-woman, *sb.* female slave : P. R. II. 308.

Bone, *sb.* (1) one of the separate parts which make up the framework of the animal body : S. A. 143, 1142.

(2) bones of the body *collect.* : P. L. I. 427 ; (*a*) *hence*, the bodily frame : P. L. XI. 642 ; Ps. VI. 5.

(*b*) the remains of the dead : W. S. 1 ; L. 155 ; S. XVIII. 1.

(3) bony structure as one of the components of the body : P. L. IV. 483 ; VIII. 495 ; IX. 915.

See **Cheek-bone.**

Bonnet, *sb.* covering for the head : L. 104.

Book, *sb.* written or printed treatise or volume : P. R. IV. 321, 327 ; S. A. 653 ; W. S. 11 ; C. 391 ; S. XI. 1 ; (*a*) **Book of God,** that by which one may obtain knowledge of God : P. L. VIII. 67.

(*b*) **book of knowledge,** nature spread out before man inviting study and affording wisdom : P. L. III. 47.

(*c*) **book of life,** the record of the names of those whom God has appointed to eternal life with Himself : P. L. I. 363 ; S. XVIII. 5.

(*d*) **virtue's book,** principles of virtue : C. 367.

Boon, *adj.* (*a*) benign, bounteous : P. L. IV. 242.

(*b*) gay, convivial : P. L. IX. 793.

Boot, (1) *sb.* covering for the foot and leg : U. C. I. 16.

(2) *vb. tr.* to be of use, avail, *impers. with prep. inf.* : S. A. 560 ; L. 64.

Booty, *sb.* spoil taken from an enemy : P. L. XI. 650.

Border, (1) *sb.* (*a*) limit, boundary : P. L. II. 361 ; IV. 131.

(*b*) brink, margin *of a river* : P. L. VII. 328.

(*c*) edge (*of a veil*) : S. A. 730.

(2) *vb. intr.* to lie on the border, adjoin, *with* on : P. L. II. 959 ; III. 537.

part. adj. **bordering** ; (*a*) adjoining : P. L. II. 131 ; P. R. I. 193 ; S. A. 976.

(*b*) forming a boundary line : P. L. I. 419.

Bore, *sb.* cylindrical cavity of a piece of ordnance : P. L. VI. 485.

Boreas, *sb.* the north wind : P. L. X. 699.

Born, (*past part. of* bear (6)) (*a*) brought forth as offspring : P. L. II. 797 ; IV. 323 ; X. 584, 980 ; XII. 359 ; P. R. I. 140, 205, 245,

254, 341; II. 72; III. 152; IV. 506;
C. 1010; D. F. I. 25; S. x. 9;
Ps. LXXXVII. 16, 19, 24; *with* of :
P. L. III. 463; XI. 496; P. R. I.
65; N. O. 3; L'A. 2; C. 522;
H. B. 13; *fig.* brought forth by
the earth : P. L. VII. 471.
(*b*) brought into existence : S.
A. 11.
See **Earth - born, First - born,
Heaven-born, Heavenly-born, Hell-
born, Jove-born, New-born, Sin-
born, Sphere-born, Turchestan-
born, Twin-born, Virgin-born.**

Borrow, *vb. tr.* to obtain or derive
from another : P. L. VII. 377;
Cir. 8.
part. adj. **borrowed;** (*a*) taken
as a loan : P. L. I. 483.
(*b*) derived from another : P.
L. III. 730.
(*c*) assumed, counterfeit : P. L.
IV. 116.

Borrower, *sb.* one who takes a thing
as a loan : C. 683.

Bosky, *adj.* bushy : C. 313.

Bosom, (**1**) *sb.* breast of a human
being; (*a*) *fig. expressing the close
and intimate relation between God
and Christ* : P. L. III. 169, 239,
279; x. 225; P. R. IV. 597.
(*b*) *fig.* interior, midst : M. W.
69; depth : P. L. II. 1036.
(*c*) *fig.* surface : P. L. VII. 319;
C. 23.
(**2**) *vb. tr.* to carry or enclose in
the bosom : C. 368; *fig.* to surround : L'A. 78.
part. adj. **bosomed,** enclosed,
hidden : P. L. v. 126.
See **Rosy-bosomed.**

Bosom-snake, *sb.* snake fastening
itself on the bosom and infecting
it with poison, *fig.* : S. A. 763.

Bosporus, *sb.* the strait which con-
nects the Black Sea and the Sea
of Marmora : P. L. II. 1018.

Bossy, *adj.* swelling like a boss,
projecting in rounded form : P.
L. I. 716.

Botch, *sb.* boil, ulcer : P. L. XII.
180.

* **Both,** (**1**) *adj.* the one and the other :
P. L. I. 424; III. 382; VI. 123;
following pl. pron. : P. L. IV. 407;
XII. 606; *preceding rel. pron.* **both
which** : S. A. 1507; **both their
deeds,** the deeds of the two : P. L.
VI. 170.
absol. : P. L. I. 239; II. 845;
IV. 720.

(**2**) *adv.* or *conj.* equally; (*a*)
both—and, not only—but, as well
—as : P. L. I. 55, 489, 767.
(*b*) *following two words connected
by* **and** : P. L. III. 165; x. 96, 384.
(*c*) **both** *followed by prep. inf.*;
and *by simple inf.* : P. L. VII.
539; S. A. 1587.
(*d*) *preceding instead of following the prep. governing the clause* :
P. L. III. 316; v. 881; IX. 752;
XII. 321.
(*e*) *with more than two sbs.* : P.
L. IV. 722; S. XI. 2.

Bottom, *sb.* (**1**) lowest part of anything : P. L. VII. 213; *with* of *indicating the thing* : P. L. I. 329;
II. 882; VI. 649; L. 158; (*a*)
depth of a river : C. 883.
(*b*) base (*of a mountain*) : P.
L. VI. 649.
(*c*) *fig.* the depths of the mind
or soul : P. L. IV. 19.
(**2**) deep place on the land :
P. L. I. 236; the bed of the sea :
P. L. VII. 289.
(**3**) low ground, valley : P. R.
II. 289.
(**4**) vessel, boat : P. L. XI. 753.
attrib. of low-lying ground : C.
532.

Bottomless (bottómless (?)), *adj.*
having no bottom, *of hell* : P. L.
I. 47; VI. 866; P. R. I. 361.

Bough, *sb.* branch of a tree : P. L.
IV. 332; v. 8, 214, 326, 428; A.
50; C. 349; *of the tree of good
and evil* : P. L. IX. 579, 851, 995;
of cedar trees : P. L. IX. 1089;
of a vine : Ps. LXXX. 43. *See* **Vine.**

Bound, (**1**) *sb.* (*a*) boundary, limit, *of
material and immaterial things*;
sing. : P. L. II. 892; IV. 181; P.
R. III. 315; *pl.* : P. L. I. 466; II.
976; III. 81, 538; IV. 583, 878,
909; VI. 859; VII. 120, 167, 230;
x. 365, 380; XI. 828, 894; XII.
371; P. R. III. 270; C. 673;
S. XVII. 12.
(*b*) land within certain limits,
territory, district, *sing.* : P. L.
II. 236; *pl.* P. L. VI. 716; VIII.
338; XI. 68, 341; XII. 187; (*of
nature*) : P. L. III. 13; *with proper
name* : P. L. I. 518; S. A. 1714;
fig. : P. L. v. 478.
(*c*) leap : P. L. IV. 181.
(**2**) *vb. tr.* to confine within
bounds, limit : P. L. III. 432, 539;
v. 639; VII. 21, 608; XII. 370;
P. 23.

(3) *part. adj.* **bound,** directing
one's course, destined, *with* on *or*
for: P. L. v. 290; VIII. 230;
S. A. 715.
See **Hell-bound, Unhide-bound.**

Boundless, *adj.* without boundary
or limit: P. L. I. 177; III. 423;
VII. 168.

Bounteous, *adj.* beneficent, munifi-
cent: P. L. v. 205; VIII. 492;
M. M. 5; C. 176.
See **All-bounteous.**

Bounty, *sb.* (*a*) liberality, munifi-
cence: P. L. IV. 437; v. 431; x.
54; P. R. III. 142.
(*b*) liberal gift, favour: P. L. v.
330, 398; IX. 1033; C. 710, 987.

Bourn, *sb.* brook, small stream: C.
313.

Bout, *sb.* turn, involution *in
music*: L'A. 139.

Bow, I. *sb.* (*a*) weapon for shooting
arrows: P. L. VI. 713, 763; IX.
390; P. R. III. 305; C. 441; Ps.
VII. 46.
(*b*) rainbow: P. L. XI. 865, 897;
humid bow: P. L. IV. 151; C. 992.
II. *vb.* (*pres. 2d sing.* bow'st: S.
A. 698) (1) *intr.* to bend the body in
token of submission or reverence:
P. L. I. 111, 434; III. 321, 350,
736; v. 144, 360, 607; VI. 746;
XI. 249; P. R. I. 497; II. 171;
Ps. LXXXI. 62.
(2) *tr.* (*a*) to bend down: P. L.
IX. 524; P. R. IV. 418; Il P. 71.
(*b*) to cause to stoop, crush
as with a load, *with* down, *fig.*:
P. L. I. 436; S. A. 698.
(*c*) *refl.* to bend oneself in
token of submission: Ps. LXXXVI.
31; *absol.*: S. A. 1646.
part. adj. **bowed,** bent, curved,
arched: C. 1015.

Bow-bent, *adj.* bent into the shape
of a bow: V. Ex. 69.

Bowel, *sb. pl.* (*a*) intestines, entrails: P. L. II. 800, 863.
(*b*) *fig.* interior (*of the earth*):
P. L. I. 687.

Bower, *sb.* (*a*) abode *in heaven*:
Ps. LXXXV. 47; cottage: L'A. 87.
(*b*) inner apartment, chamber:
C. 45.
(*c*) shady recess, leafy covert:
P. L. IV. 246, 705; v. 230; VIII.
305; IX. 244, 417; x. 860; XI.
77; Il P. 27, 104; A. 45; C. 536,
921, 984; S. VIII. 9.
(*d*) place enclosed with branches
and used as a dwelling-place,

abode: P. L. III. 734; IV. 690,
738, 798; v. 300, 367, 375; VIII.
510, 653; IX. 401; XI. 280; XII.
607.

Boy, *sb.* male child, lad: Hor.
Sat. I. 2; *with proper name*: Il P.
124. *See* **Attic.**

Brace, *sb.* pair, couple *of animals*:
P. L. XI. 188.
See **Vant-brace.**

Brag, *sb.* thing boasted of, source of
pride: C. 745.

Braid, (1) *sb.* plait (*of lilies*): C.
862.
(2) *vb. tr.* to weave, intertwine: C. 105.
part. adj. **braided,** entwined,
interwoven: P. L. IV. 349.

Brain, *sb.* (*sing.* Il P. 5; *pl.* S A.
1241), mass of nervous substance
contained in the skull of man:
S. A. 1241; as the organ of
thought: Il P. 5.

Brake, *sb.* clump of bushes, thicket:
P. L. IV. 175; v. 326; VII. 458;
IX. 160; C. 147.

Branch, (1) *sb.* (*a*) shoot or limb of a
tree or plant: P. L. IV. 627; VII.
325, 433; VIII. 265; Ps. LXXX. 45,
48, 63; *of oak or fir*: P. L. VI.
575; *of the tree of good and evil*;
IX. 590, 802. *See* **Vine.**
(*b*) *fig.* child: C. 969.
(2) *vb. intr.* to bear branches,
spread in branches: P. L. IX. 1104.
part. adj. **branching**; (*a*) putting
forth or spreading in branches:
P. L. IV. 139; VI. 885; P. R. IV.
405; S. A. 1735; A. 89.
(*b*) having antlers: P. L. VII.
470.

Brand, *sb.* (*a*) mark of infamy,
stigma: S. A. 967; S. XV. 12.
(*b*) blade of a sword, *fig.* the
sword itself: P. L. XII. 643.

Brandish, *vb. tr.* to wave, shake,
flourish: P. L. II. 786; VI. 252.
part. adj. **brandished,** waved,
flourished: P. L. XII. 633; C.
651.

Brass, *sb.* alloy of copper and zinc:
P. L. II. 645; VI. 576; XI. 565;
S. A. 1120; **the horse of brass:**
Il P. 114. *See* **Horse.**

Bravery, *sb.* (*a*) bravado, boasting,
defiance: S. A. 1243.
(*b*) finery, fine clothes: S. A.
717.

Bray, *vb. tr.* to give forth in a loud
harsh manner, utter harshly: P.
L. VI. 209.

Brazen, *adj.* (*a*) made of brass:
P. L. I. 724; VI. 211; VII. 201;
X. 697; S. A. 35, 132.

(*b*) *fig.* resembling brass in
colour: P. L. VII. 496; in sound:
P. L. XI. 713.

Breach, *sb.* (*a*) broken place, gap (*in
a wall*): P. L. VI. 879.

(*b*) the breaking of a moral
obligation: P. L. IX. 6.

Bread, *sb.* food in general: P. L.
X. 205, 1055; XII. 78; P. R. I.
343, 347, 349; S. A. 573; Ps.
LXXX. 21, 22.

Breadth, *sb.* distance from side to
side of a surface, width: P. L.
II. 893: III. 561; X. 673; XI.
730; P. R. IV. 27.

Break, I. *sb.* **break of dawn,** first
appearance of light: P. L. III.
545; IX. 412.

II. *vb.* (*pret.* broke: *past part.*
broken: P. L. I. 311; II. 78,
1039; P. R. I. 61; S. A. 1335;
S. XV. 8; broke: P. L. III. 87;
IV. 918; VI. 311; VII. 465; XI.
827; P. R. IV. 611; S. A. 1189;
U. C. I. 1) *tr.* (*a*) to rend apart,
sever by violence, *said of both
material and immaterial things*:
U. C. I. 1; C. 435, 481, 651;
absol.: S. A. 1349, 1626.

(*b*) to cause to dash in pieces,
of waves, fig. : Ps. LXXXVIII.
31.

(*c*) to cause to sound discord-
antly: S. M. 21.

(*d*) to violate, fail to keep:
P. L. II. 690; III. 204; V. 612;
VI. 311; S. A. 750, 1115, 1189.

(*e*) to crush, overcome: P. L.
V. 887; P. R. I. 61; S. A. 1335;
to crush in spirit: Ps. LXXXVIII.
32; to kill: S. X. 6.

(*f*) to make or force a way
through: P. L. IV. 878; *with*
through: S. A. 1050.

(*g*) to escape by breaking
barriers: P. L. VII. 465.

(*h*) to defeat, frustrate: P. L.
IV. 611.

In combination with other words,
(*a*) **break down,** level with the
ground: Ps. LXXX. 50.

(*b*) **break forth,** burst into utterance: P. L. XI. 869.

(*c*) **break in,** interrupt, disturb: S. A. 116.

(*d*) **break loose,** escape from
confinement, get free: P. L. III.
87; IV. 889, 918.

(*e*) **break off,** hinder from proceeding: P. L. X. 1008; stop:
C. 145; rend asunder: Ps. II.
6.

(*f*) **break silence,** begin to
speak: P. L. I. 83; IX. 895; X.
353; P. R. IV. 43.

(*g*) **break up,** rend open: P. L.
XI. 827.

(*h*) **break way,** force a path or
passage: P. L. II. 134, 782.

part. adj. **broken;** (*a*) violated:
S. XV. 8.

(*b*) shattered: P. L. I. 311.

(*c*) having the ranks disarranged, routed: P. L. II. 78,
1039.

vbl. sb. **breaking,** dissolution,
with of: S. X. 5.

See **League-breaker.**

Breast, *sb.* (*a*) front of the chest,
forepart of the body (*of man or
bird*): P. L. IV. 495; V. 279;
VII. 438; P. R. III. 15; S. A.
609, 1722; C. 911.

(*b*) seat of the thoughts or
emotions, heart: P. L. II. 568;
IV. 16; V. 695; IX. 288, 730, 1131;
X. 975; XI. 154, 374; P. R. I.
185, 301; P. R. II. 63, 167; S. A.
1739; C. 246, 381.

(*c*) front of an armed force:
P. L. VI. 560, 612.

(*d*) rounded top or sides (*of a
mountain*): L'A. 73.

Breast-plate, *sb.* the decorated piece
of linen cloth worn on the breast
of the Jewish high priest: P. L.
III. 598.

Breath, *sb.* (*a*) air inhaled or exhaled in respiration: P. L. II.
170, 214; XI. 147, 312; XII. 78;
U. C. II. 25.

(*b*) life: M. W. 9; **gave them
breath,** was the author or originator of them: P. R. IV. 258;
breath of life, spirit: P. L. VII.
526; X. 784, 789. *See* **Life.**

(*c*) air in gentle motion, gentle
blowing, *as of breath exhaled from
anything and retaining its characteristic quality or odour, fig.*
breath of morn: P. L. IV. |641,
650; A. 56; **breath of heaven:**
S. A. 10; **breath of vernal air:**
S. A. 628.

(*d*) exhalation: P. L. IV. 806.

(*e*) power of breathing freely,
opposed to a state of exhaustion:
S. A. 905, 1126, 1555; **put out of
breath:** U. C. II. 12.

Breathe, *vb.* (*pres.* 2d *sing.*
breath'st: P. L. II. 697; *past
part. disyl.* : N. O. 179) (1) *intr.*
(*a*) to exhale and inhale, respire,
of both animals and plants :
P. L. IX. 194, 447; XI. 284.
(*b*) to send forth air : P. L. I.
709.
(*c*) to blow softly, *of wind* :
P. L. V. 16.
(*d*) to give forth sound, be
heard : Il P. 151.
(2) *tr.* (*a*) to exhale : P. L. XI.
313; *fig. of flowers*: P. L. V. 482;
to give out, send forth, *usually of
odours* : P. L. II. 244, 402; III.
607; IV. 265; IX. 193; L'A. 18.
(*b*) to communicate by breathing: P. L. VII. 525.
(*c*) to utter audibly, speak :
P. L. II. 697; XII. 374; to utter
in song: C. 245; to sigh : P. L. XI.
5; *fig. of the wind* : P. L. V. 193.
(*d*) to evince, display, express :
P. L. I. 554, 560; III. 267; VI. 65.
part. adj. (*a*) **breathing,** re-
spiring : A. 32.
(*b*) **breathed,** uttered in a
breath, whispered : N. O. 179.
vbl. sb. **breathing,** respiration :
U. C. II. 12.
See **Solemn-breathing.**

Breed, *vb.* (*pret. and past part.*
bred) *tr.* (*a*) to bring forth
offspring: P. L. II. 799; III.
431; Il P. 2.
(*b*) to give rise to, produce,
engender : P. L. II. 624; V. 4;
IX. 1010, 1050; XI. 414; C. 157;
S. XV. 10; *of persons*: D. F. I.
61; C. 266.
(*c*) to bring or train up, *of
plants*: P. L. XI. 276; *of persons* : P. L. XI. 618; XII. 115;
P. R. II. 300, 415; IV. 251, 509.
vbl. sb. **breeding,** training, nurture : S. A. 30.
See **Sin-bred.**

Brewed, *part. adj.* **brewed enchant-
ments,** concoction having magical
power : C. 696.
See **Sweet-briar.**

Briareos, *sb.* the son of Uranus and
Ge, who had a hundred arms and
fifty heads, and who made war
on the Olympian gods : P. L. I.
199.

Brick, *sb. sing. collect.* blocks of
baked clay : P. L. XII. 43.

Bridal, *adj.* of the bride: P. L.
VIII. 520 : S. A. 1196.

Bride, *sb.* woman newly married or
about to be married : S. A. 320,
1198; C. 1008; **Timnian bride** :
Samson's first wife : S. A. 1018.

Bridegroom, *sb.* the bridegroom of
Matt. XXV. 1; S. IX. 12.

Bridge, (1) *sb.* (*a*) structure which
spans a river : P. R. III. 334.
(*b*) structure raised over the
Abyss from hell to the world : P.
L. II. 1028; X. 301, 351, 371.
(2) *vb. tr.* to make (*a way*) by
means of a bridge : P. L. X. 310.

Bridle, *vb. tr.* to curb, restrain, *with
in* : C. 887.

Brief, I. (1) *adj.* short, concise : P.
R. IV. 264.
quasi sb. **in brief,** in few words:
P. L. VI. 171; P. R. IV. 485; S.
A. 1570.
(2) *adv.* briefly, concisely :
P. L. IV. 875; IX. 664; X. 115.

Briefly, *adv.* in few words, concisely : P. L. VI. 566; C. 512.

Brigad (bri'gad), *sb.* division of
troops : P. L. I. 675; II. 532.

Brigandine, *sb.* body armour, coat
of mail : S. A. 1120.

Bright, (1) *adj.* (*a*) emitting, reflecting, or pervaded by light;
shining; splendid; luminous, *of
the visible heaven, of God, the gods,
angels or things in heaven; often
with the added idea of* (*d*) *from
which it is sometimes indistinguish-
able* : P. L. I. 87, 272, 429, 440,
737; II. 395, 513, 812; III. 6, 362,
512, 518, 587, 591, 645, 655; IV.
361, 578, 590, 977; V. 169, 274,
587; VI. 16, 64, 334, 472, 801,
885; VII. 222, 372, 375, 385, 564;
VIII. 87, 88, 98, 367; IX. 104, 1084;
X. 63, 187, 327, 426, 615; XI. 73,
127, 215, 221, 329; XII. 254, 627;
P. R. I. 128, 252; D. F. I. 38;
N. O. 21, 84; Cir. 1; S. M. 10;
M. M. 1; M. W. 61, 69; Il P.
13; A. 18; C. 3; L. 30; S. VIII.
8; Ps. IV. 30; VIII. 10; LXXX.
5; CXXXVI. 34; *comp.*: P. L. VII.
132; X. 450; *sup.* : P. L. III. 381,
667; IV. 606; V. 644; *of day* : C.
382; *sup.*: P. R. IV. 439; *of eyes*:
L'A. 121; *fig. of honour* : A. 27.
(*b*) of splendid beauty : P. L.
II. 756; C. 966; *sup.* : C. 910.
(*c*) of vivid colour : P. L. V.
481; C. 633.
(*d*) illustrious, glorious, *with the
added idea of* splendid : P. L. IV.
44; V. 838; S. A. 1674; Ps.

LXXXIV. 42; *sup.* : P. L. III. 134.
(2) *sb.* brightness, splendour :
P. L. III. 380 ; VIII. 91.
See **Star-bright, Sun-bright.**
Brighten, *vb. tr.* to make bright,
light up (*with a smile or joy*) :
P. L. VIII. 368 ; IX. 634.
   part. adj. **brightening,** shining :
P. L. II. 399.
Bright-haired, *adj.* having shining
hair : Il P. 23.
Bright-harnessed, *adj.* having on
shining armour : N. O. 244.
Brightness, *sb.* clear light, splendour,
radiance : P. L. I. 86, 592 ; III.
376, 624 ; IV. 836 ; V. 599 ; P. R.
I. 378.
Brimmed (*disyl.*), *part. adj.* filled to
overflowing : C. 924.
Brimming, *part. adj.* that fills to
overflowing : P. L. IV. 336.
   See **Fountain-brim, Ocean-brim.**
Brimstone, *sb.* sulphur : P. L. I.
350.
Brinded, *adj.* brindled, streaked :
P. L. VII. 466 ; C. 443.
Brine, *sb.* the sea : L. 98.
Bring, *vb.* (*pres. 2d. sing.* brought'st:
P. R. I. 10 ; *pret. and past part.*
brought), *tr.* to cause to come
along with oneself, convey, carry,
conduct ; (*a*) from a more distant
place to the place where the re-
ceiver is, or the bearer is about to
be, *lit. and fig.* : P. L. I. 100, 252 ;
II. 222, 598, 639, 840, 866, 899 ; III.
190, 235, 657 ; IV. 21, 452, 470,
713, 717, 796, 875 ; V. 51, 217,
312 ; VII. 105, 537 ; VIII. 36,
343, 449, 500, 521 ; IX. 47, 49,
162, 392, 462, 475, 630 ; X. 99,
655 ; XI. 25, 302, 434, 692, 860,
895 ; XII. 504 ; P. R. I. 10, 64,
321, 335, 336 ; II. 268, 269, 394 ;
III. 244, 265, 350 ; IV. 25, 323,
325, 398, 553, 577, 638 ; S. A. 183,
519, 931, 1063, 1094, 1444 ; V. Ex.
18, 38 ; M. W. 54 ; L'A. 25 ; Il
P. 51, 132 ; A. 91, 103 ; C. 186,
305, 987 ; L. 96, 142 ; S. XXIII. 2;
Ps. V. 33 ; LXXX. 33 ; LXXXI. 6, 7,
41 ; CXXXVI. 42 ; Ariosto I. 1.
   (*b*) to cause to come by an
attractive force or by some personal characteristic : P. L. III.
666 ; IV. 908 ; S. A. 821.
   (*c*) to cause to come as a result,
cause one to have, procure : P. L.
I. 3 ; II. 981 ; VI. 267, 395 ; VIII.
216, 323 ; IX. 11, 715 ; X. 667,
734, 900, 1037 ; XI. 168, 473,

477 ; XII. 81, 355, 414 ; P. R. II.
422, 460 ; S. A. 449, 451, 453,
1536 ; N. O. 4 ; Il P. 166 ; C.
506, 967 ; S. XV. 5.
   (*d*) to cause to come or pass
from one state to another : P. R.
IV. 22 ; S. A. 269, 1585 ; to bring
into existence, create and provide
with the means of entering into
another condition : P. L. VII. 189.
   (*e*) to cause to succeed one
after another : P. L. V. 335 ; P.
R. I. 64.
   (*f*) to present to the mind,
offer for acceptance : P. L. VI.
471 ; VIII. 447 ; IX. 770.
   (*g*) to complete, finish : P. L.
X. 312.
   (*h*) to attribute, ascribe : P. L.
XI. 837.
   In combination with other words;
   (*a*) **bring about,** cause to happen :
S. A. 1747.
   (*b*) **bring back,** cause to return,
act as guide and leader to in
returning : P. L. XII. 312, 345 ;
P. R. III. 435 ; IV. 396 ; S.
XXIII. 14.
   (*c*) **bring down,** humiliate : P. L.
XI. 347 ; P. R. III. 34 ; overcome : Ps. LXXXI. 57 ; CXXXVI. 61.
   (*d*) **bring forth,** cause to arise,
work out : P. L. I. 163 ; bring to
light, manifest : P. L. I. 217 ;
bring into being, create : P. L.
III. 707 ; XII. 472 ; carry out or convey from a place of storage for
use : P. L. V. 314 ; VI. 712 ; cause
to come in the course of time :
P. L. V. 583 ; yield, produce :
P. L. VII. 315, 451 ; X. 203 ; *fig.* :
P. L. XII. 551 ; bear offspring :
P. L. X. 194 ; *fig.* : Ps. VII. 54 ;
cause one to do or to perform :
P. L. XI. 428 ; S. A. 875, 956 ;
bring to public view : S. A. 1601,
1615.
   (*e*) **bring into this world,** bear
(*offspring*) : P. L. X. 983.
   (*f*) **bring to little,** cause to be
small in amount : P. L. IX. 224.
   (*g*) **bring low,** subdue : Ps. II.
19.
   (*h*) **bring to mind** or **to one's
remembrance** : cause one to remember : P. L. IV. 38 ; S. A. 277;
C. 619.
   (*i*) **bring to nothing,** destroy :
P. R. III. 389.
   (*j*) **bring to nought,** annul, make
void : P. L. III. 158.

(*k*) **bring on**, introduce, give rise to, begin : P. L. v. 233 ; cause to come : P. L. v. 667 ; cause oneself to have as a result of action : S. A. 375.

(*l*) **bring to pass**, cause to happen : V. Ex. 72.

(*m*) **bring up**, nurture, rear : C. 58 ; cause to advance, *of an army* : S. A. 1234.

vbl. sb. **bringing forth**, act of bearing offspring : P. L. x. 1052.

Brink, *sb.* edge, margin : P. L. ii. 918 ; x. 347 ; surface : P. L. ii. 609.

Brisk, *adj.* quick and lively, active : C. 671.

Bristle, (1) *sb.* stiff hair : S. A. 1137.

(2) *vb. intr.* to be thickly set, be covered as if with bristles : P. L. vi. 82.

British, *adj.* of or belonging to Britain : P. L. i. 581 ; P. R. iv. 77 ; S. xxi. 2.

Brittle, *adj.* frail, weak : P. L. i. 427.

Broad, (1) *adj.* (*a*) extended from side to side, *frequently with little idea of direction, hence, passing to* large, ample : P. L. i. 286 ; ii. 1026 ; iv. 303 ; v. 279 ; vi. 305 ; vii. 286, 289, 577 ; ix. 1087, 1095, 1111 ; x. 298, 304, 473 ; P. R. ii. 23 ; S. A. 1120 ; C. 354 ; *sup.* : P. R. ii. 339 ; *fig.* large in number : P. L. vii. 462.

(*b*) extensive, vast : P. L. iii. 495 ; C. 979.

(*c*) spread all abroad, widely diffused : L. 80.

(*d*) *fig.* **the broad way**, the way of ease and pleasure : S. ix. 2.

(2) *adv.* widely : P. L. ix. 1104. *See* **Sail-broad**.

Broider, *vb. tr.* to adorn as with embroidery : P. L. iv. 702.

Broil, *sb. pl.* quarrels, contentions, feuds : P. L. ii. 837, 1001 ; vi. 277 ; xi. 718.

Brood, (1) *sb.* (*a*) offspring, progeny, *of human beings* : Ps. lxxxiii. 21 ; *of Titan* : P. L. i. 511 ; *of giants* : P. L. i. 576 ; S. A. 1247 ; *of animals* : P. L. vii. 418 ; *of personified abstractions* : P. L. ii. 863 ; Il P. 2.

(*b*) kind, race : D. F. I. 55 ; **the world's brood**, the crowd, people generally, those whose interests lie in the world and who are ignorant of the ways of God : Ps. iv. 27.

(2) *vb. intr.* to sit as a bird sits on eggs, hover with outspread cherishing wings : P. L. i. 21 ; N. O. 68.

part. adj. **brooding**, cherishing, incubating, *fig.* : P. L. vii. 235 ; L'A. 6 ; **brooding nest**, nest to brood in : Ps. lxxxiv. 12.

Brook, (1) *sb.* small stream of water, rivulet : P. L. i. 302, 420 ; iii. 30 ; iv. 237 ; xi. 325 ; P. R. ii. 345 ; S. A. 557 ; L'A. 76 ; Il P. 139 ; C. 119, 495 ; L. 137 ; Ps. lxxxiii. 37 ; lxxxvii. 27 ; *with proper name* : P. L. i. 11, 302 ; P. R. ii. 266. *See* **Cherith** and **Siloa**.

(2) *vb. tr.* to bear with, endure, tolerate : P. L. vi. 274 ; ix. 676, 1184 ; S. A. 1344.

Brother, *sb.* (*pl.* brothers : C. 182, 226, 288 ; V. Ex. 82 ; brethren : P. L. iii. 297 ; xi. 454, 680 ; xii. 28, 65, 169 ; P. R. iii. 374, 403 ; S. A. 332, 1413, 1445 ; V. Ex. 75 ; P. 21), (*a*) a male person having the same parents as another : P. L. iv. 757 ; xi. 454, 456, 609, 679 ; xii. 169 ; C. 182, 226, 288, 359, 407, 420, 493, 584 ; *fig.* : V. Ex. 75, 82.

(*b*) *pl.* members of the human race, fellow-men : P. L. iii. 297 ; xi. 680 ; xii. 28, 65.

(*c*) kinsman : P. R. iii. 374, 403 ; S. A. 332, 1413, 1445 ; P. 21.

Brow, (1) *sb.* (*a*) *sing.* arched projection over the eyes : P. L. viii. 560.

(*b*) forehead as the seat of the facial expression of contempt ; defiance, majesty, mercy, *etc. sing.* : P. L. iv. 885 ; ix. 537 ; xi. 880 ; P. R. i. 493 ; ii. 164, 216 ; iii. 215 ; iv. 367 ; S. A. 1073 ; Ps. viii. 7 ; lxxx. 19 ; *pl.* : P. L. i. 602 ; C. 736 ; *fig. sing. of night* : Il P. 58 ; *pl. of the foliage of trees* : C 38.

(*c*) projecting edge (*of a hill*) : P. L. iii. 546 ; (*of the wall of heaven*) : P. L. vi. 51.

(2) *vb. tr.* to form a brow to, *as hills surrounding a valley* : C. 532.

See **Low-browed**.

Brown, (1) *adj.* of a dusky colour : P. L. ix. 1088 ; P. R. ii. 293 ; Il P. 134 ; L. 2.

(2) *sb.* dusky colour shading towards red or yellow : P. R. iii. 326.

See **Nut-brown**.

Browse, *vb. intr.* to feed, graze:
Ps. LXXX. 55.

Bruise, (1) *sb.* hurt, contusion, *fig.
of the overthrow of Satan by
Christ* : P. L. x. 191, 500; XII.
383, 391.

(2) *vb. tr.* (*a*) to dent by a
heavy blow : P. L. VI. 656.

(*b*) *fig.* to crush, overwhelm,
destroy : P. L. v. 887; x. 181,
498, 499, 1031; XI. 155; XII. 149,
233, 385, 430, 433; Ps. II. 20;
LXXXVIII. 59, 61.

Brunt, *sb.* heat of an onset, violent
shock : S. A. 583.

Brush, *vb. tr.* (*a*) to sweep away,
with off : P. L. v. 429; A. 50.

(*b*) to touch with a light movement, sweep over lightly : P. L.
I. 768.

Brutal, *adj.* of or belonging to the
brutes : P. L. IX. 188, 565.

Brute, (1) *adj.* (*a*) being in the
form of a brute : P. L. I. 459.

(*b*) wanting in reason and
understanding : P. L. VII. 507;
x. 495; S. A. 673.

(*c*) without life, dead : C. 797.

(*d*) brutal, cruel, savage : P. R.
I. 219; S. A. 1273; C. 451.

(2) *sb.* (*a*) one of the lower animals as distinguished from man :
P. L. I. 371; VIII. 391, 441; IX.
96, 240, 554, 712; x. 165; C. 700.

(*b*) Brutus : C. 828. *See* **Brutus.**

Brutish, *adj.* resembling the brutes
in appearance, character, or
action : P. L. I. 481; VI. 124;
XI. 518; P. R. III. 86; IV. 128;
N. O. 211; C. 70.

Brutus, *sb.* the legendary first king
of Britain : H. B. 7.

Bubble, *sb.* small vesicle of water
filled with air : P. R. IV. 20.

Bud, (1) *sb.* unopened flower : P. L.
VIII. 45; XI. 277; C. 671; *fig.*
literary product : S. II. 4.

(2) *vb. intr.* to put forth buds,
fig. of truth : Ps. LXXXV. 46.

See **Cypress-bud.**

Budge, *adj.* wearing hoods or robes
trimmed with budge fur, lamb-
skin with the wool dressed out-
wards, *and probably with the
added idea of* solemn in demeanour, pompous, formal : C. 707.

Buffet, *sb.* blow : S. A. 1239.

Build, *vb.* (*pret.* builded : P. L. x.
373; *elsewhere* built; *past part.*
built) *tr.* to construct, erect,
frame; (*a*) *a building or some-*

thing analogous to a building :
P. L. I. 401, 443, 713, 749; III.
468; IV. 212; XI. 729, 819; XII.
43, 102; P. R. III. 276, 290; S. A.
1733; W. S. 8; L. 101; *absol.* :
P. L. I. 751; P. R. II. 170; *fig.
of immaterial things* : P. L. IV.
521; VIII. 558; XII. 527; P. R.
IV. 292; L. 11.

(*b*) *something* by a process
analogous to building : P. L. VII.
424, 491; P. R. II. 343; Ps.
LXXXIV. 12; to create : P. L. x.
373; *of the creations of God* :
P. L. VII. 270; IX. 100, 102, 152;
C. 599; *absol.* : P. L. I. 259;
VII. 92; VIII. 81, 101; *of the
human body* : P. L. IX. 485.

(*c*) to build up, establish : P. L.
II. 314.

(*d*) to base, found, *with* in :
P. L. III. 449.

See **High-built, Straw-built.**

Builder, *sb.* one who erects a building : P. L. III. 466; XII. 57.

Building, *sb.* structure, edifice :
P. L. XII. 61; S. A. 1605.

Bulk, *sb.* (*a*) size : P. L. I. 196; VII.
410; XI. 729.

(*b*) body of great size, *of man* :
S. A. 1238.

Bull, *sb.* (*a*) male of the domestic
Bostaurus : P. L. XII. 292; S. A.
1671.

(*b*) papal edict : P. L. III. 492.

(*c*) **the Bull,** the Bull Inn,
Bishopsgate Street, London :
U. C. I. 8.

Bullion-dross, *sb.* scum arising to
the surface of a melted mass of
impure gold or silver : P. L. I. 704.

Bullock, *sb.* young bull : P. L. XII.
20.

Bulwark, *sb.* powerful defence :
P. L. II. 29.

Bur, *sb.* plant producing burs :
C. 352.

Burden, (1) *sb.* load : P. L. IX. 801;
fig. (*a*) load of duty, blame, sin,
labour, etc. : P. L. IV. 57; x. 835,
961; XI. 767; P. R. II. 462; S. A.
431; S. XXI. 13; Ps. LXXXI. 21.

(*b*) that which is borne in the
womb, child : P. L. II. 767.

(2) *vb. tr.* to load heavily, overload : P. L. v. 452.

Burdenous, *adj.* being a burden to
others, useless : S. A. 567.

Burdensome, *adj.* onerous, oppressive, wearisome : P. L. IV. 53;
S. A. 54; U. C. II. 24.

Burgher, *sb.* inhabitant of a borough, citizen : P. L. IV. 189.

Burial, *sb.* interment : S. A. 104 ; M. W. 32.

Burn, *vb.* (*pret.* burnt : P. L. VI. 866 ; burned : P. L. I. 228 ; II. 708 ; S. A. 26 ; *past part.* burnt : P. L. I. 562), (**1**) *tr.* to consume with fire : P. L. I. 474 ; P. R. III. 75.

(**2**) *intr.* (*a*) to be on fire, be consumed with fire : P. L. I. 228 ; III. 334 ; S. A. 26 ; *fig. with cold* : P. L. II. 595 ; *with love, hate, desire, etc.* : P. L. IX. 467, 1015 ; Cir. 8 ; Ps. LXXXV. 12.

(*b*) to flame, blaze, shine : P. L. II. 538, 708 ; V. 713 ; VI. 866 : XII. 254 ; C. 130.

part. adj. (*a*) **burning,** on fire, blazing, flaming : P. L. I. 210, 296 ; II. 169, 436, 576 ; VI. 832 ; N. O. 207 ; glowing, shining : N. O. 84 ; S. M. 10.

(*b*) **burnt,** consumed with fire : P. L. I. 562.

See **Ever-burning.**

Burnish, *vb. tr.* to make bright and glossy : P. L. IV. 249.

part. adj. **burnished,** bright, shining : P. L. IX. 501.

Burst, I. *sb.* outbreak, explosion : S. A. 1651.

II. *vb.* (*pret.* and *past part.* burst), (**1**) *tr.* to break open, escape from by force : P. L. X. 697.

(**2**) *intr.* to be rent from within : P. L. VII. 419 ; X. 632.

In combination with advs. to exhibit some sudden and violent activity ; (*a*) **burst forth,** issue suddenly and violently : P. L. II. 800 ; *of tears* : P. L. I. 620 ; find utterance suddenly : P. R. I. 170 ; S. A. 1555.

(*b*) **burst out,** break forth (*into blaze*), *fig.* : L. 74.

part. adj. **bursting,** that cannot be restrained, uncontrollable : P. L. IX. 98.

Bury, *vb. tr.* (*a*) to deposit in the grave : S. A. 101, 103.

(*b*) to cover up, hide : P. L. VI. 652.

Bush, *sb.* thick shrub : P. L. IV. 176 ; VII. 323 ; IX. 160 ; P. R. IV. 437.

Bushing, *part.* growing in the form of a bush : P. L. IX. 426.

Bushy, *adj.* (*a*) abounding in bushes : C. 312.

(*b*) growing like a bush : P. L. IV. 696.

Business, *sb.* that which engages one's care and attention, employment, occupation : P. L. I. 150 ; IV. 943 ; P. R. II. 99 ; V. Ex. 57 ; C. 169.

Busiris, *sb.* according to Greek legend (Apollodorus 2. 1. 5) one of the sons of Ægyptus, or (Diodorus Siculus 1. 45) an Ægyptian king ; *here* the individual name of the Pharaoh who pursued the children of Israel and was drowned in the Red Sea : P. L. I. 307.

Buskined, *part. adj.* tragic, **buskined stage,** the stage on which was worn the buskin or high thick-soled boot used by the actors in ancient Athenian tragedy : Il P. 102.

See **Silver-buskined.**

Bustle, *sb.* noise, commotion : C. 379.

Busy, (**1**) *adj.* (*a*) employed, engaged : N. O. 92 ; *sup.* constantly employed, always active : P. L. XI. 490.

(*b*) that indicates activity : L'A. 118.

(**2**) *vb. intr.* to employ, occupy : P. L. IV. 876 ; IX. 518.

*But, (*a*) if not, unless, except, *after a negative and with a sb., pron., or phr.* : P. L. I. 623 ; IV. 580 ; VI. 347, 702 ; S. A. 898 ; *after universal statement with* **all, any** : P. L. IV. 156, 202, 602 ; VI. 834 ; *introducing a condition* : S. A. 45 ; C. 196 ; *preceding the conj.* **that** : P. L. X. 48.

(*b*) only, merely, solely, no more than, no otherwise than ; P. L. I. 217, 294, 649 ; III. 192 : VI. 104 ; **all** but, everything short of : P. L. I. 257 ; but now, just now : P. L. I. 777 ; cannot but, must : P. L. V. 86.

(*c*) *correlative with* **no sooner,** than : P. L. III. 344 ; S. A. 21 ; D. F. I. 1.

(*d*) *after* **else,** than : P. R. IV. 291.

(*e*) **but that,** except for the fact that : P. L. I. 211 ; II. 806 ; C. 41.

(*f*) that not, *introducing relative clause* : P. L. II. 77 ; III. 370 ; *introducing substantive clause* : P. L. IX. 1147 ; X. 788 ; **but that** : P. L. X. 239 ; P. R. IV. 284 ; *introducing* *clause of result*: S. A. 1326 ; **but that** : P. L. VI. 285 ; P. R. I. 363.

(*g*) *after* **doubt not,** that : P. L. IX. 244 ; X. 1022 ; XI. 349 ; **but that,** that : P. L. XII. 285.

(*h*) *conj. adv.* however, nevertheless, notwithstanding : P. L. I. 53, 126 ; IX. 279 ; *preceded by* **not only** : P. L. IV. 668 ; VIII. 338 ; IX. 682.

(*i*) on the contrary, on the other hand : P. L. I. 63 ; XI. 143.

Buxom, *adj.* (*a*) yielding, unresisting : P. L. II. 842 ; v. 270.

(*b*) lively, gay : L'A. 24.

Buy *vb.* (*only in past part.* bought) *tr.* to get or obtain in exchange for something else : P. L. IV. 102, 222.

part. adj. **bought,** obtained for a price, purchased : P. L. IV. 765.

* **By,** I. *prep.* (1) *of position* (*a*) at the side or edge of, close to, near : P. L. I. 207, 384, 587 ; **fast by** : P. L. II. 725 ; III. 354.

(*b*) **by itself,** apart from others, alone : P. L. XI. 89.

(2) *of motion,* alongside of, along, past : P. L. I. 12 ; in the direction of : P. L. III. 575.

(3) *of time* (*a*) not later than : P. L. III. 545 ; IV. 588, 662 ; IX. 401.

(*b*) during the time of : P. L. III. 514 ; IV. 655, 665 ; v. 53 ; VII. 347.

(4) *of ideal proximity to a standard* (*a*) according to, in harmony with : P. L. I. 150, 752 ; II. 197 ; IV. 881 ; v. 685 ; VII. 393 ; X. 806, 1026 ; XII. 226, 518.

(*b*) according to, *of measurement* : P. L. v. 582 ; XI. 730.

(*c*) *of succession of numerical groups or quantities with pl. sb.* **by turns** : P. L. VI. 7 ; **by degrees** : P. L. III. 502 ; VII. 157 ; **by thousands,** etc. : P. L. IV. 447 ; VI. 48 ; *with sb. preceding and following,* **one by one,** etc. : P. L. v. 697 ; VIII. 31, 267 ; XI. 318.

(5) *of means, instrumentality, or agency* (*a*) through the means or agency of *both personal and non-personal agents* : P. L. I. 121, 219, 455 ; II. 1030.

(*b*) because of, on account of : P. L. I. 733 ; II. 5, 45 ; III. 303.

(*c*) *after verbs of calling, knowing, perceiving* : P. L. IV. 870 ; VII. 1 ; VIII. 39, 357.

(6) *with verbs of swearing,* in the name of : P. L. v. 607.

(7) *of circumstance, condition, manner, cause* : P. L. I. 440 ; II. 1042.

(*a*) by reason of, in consequence of, in virtue of : P. L. VI. 682 ; VII. 72 ; IX. 27, 540.

(*b*) **by occasion,** as occasion offers : P. L. IX. 974.

(*c*) **by task,** in the manner of a task, as a task : P. L. v. 854.

(*d*) **by the roots,** completely, roots and all : P. L. II. 544.

II. *adv.* (1) near, close : P. L. IX. 1147 ; **fast by** : P. L. II. 1051 ; IV. 221 ; X. 333 ; **hard by** : P. L. X. 548 ; C. 531 ; L'A. 81.

(2) aside, out of use : P. L. III. 339.

C

Cabined, *part. adj.* narrow : C. 140.

Cadence, *sb.* (*a*) the rising and falling (*of the wind*) : P. L. II. 287.

(*b*) a sinking down, declination : P. L. X. 92.

Cadmus, *sb.* the builder of Thebes in Bœotia : P. L. IX. 506.

Cæcias; *sb.* the northeast wind : P. L. X. 699.

Cæsar, *sb.* the emperor of Rome : P. R. III. 385.

Calabria, *sb.* the southeastern peninsula of Italy : P. L. II. 661.

Calamitous, *adj.* fraught with or causing distress, disastrous : P. L. X. 132 ; S. A. 708, 1480.

Calamity, *sb.* grievous disaster, distressing misfortune or the misery resulting from it : P. L. I. 189 ; X. 907 ; S. A. 655, 1331.

Calculate, *vb. tr.* to ascertain the time and conditions of by computation : P. L. VIII. 80.

Cales, *sb.* a town in Campania, Italy, *noted for its wine* : P. R. IV. 117.

Calf, *sb.* idol in the form of a calf : P. L. I. 484 ; P. R. III. 416.

Calisto, *sb.* Callisto, a nymph of Artemis' train and the mother of Arcas by Zeus : P. R. II. 186. *See* **Star.**

Call, I. *sb.* summons, bidding : P. L. I. 378 ; v. 48 ; VII. 498 ; IX. 521 ; (*of trumpet*) : P. L. VII. 295 ; **at call,** when summoned : P. L. X. 858 ; Divine summons to a special work : P. R. III. 434.

II. *vb.* (*pres. 2d sing.* call'st :
P. L. II. 742, 743 ; VI. 289 ; VIII.
369 ; IX. 1146 ; P. R. III. 403),
(1) *tr.* (*a*) to give a name to,
term, designate : P. L. III. 727 ;
V. 658, 760 ; VII. 2, 132 ; X. 425 ;
XII. 140, 267 ; *with two acc.* : P. L.
I. 82, 405, 438, 740 ; II. 312, 348,
667, 669, 733, 742, 760 ; III. 495 ;
IV. 277, 474, 514 ; V. 107, 766 ;
VI. 289 ; VII. 308 ; VIII. 369 ; IX.
1020, 1146 ; X. 462, 580 ; XI. 159,
411, 690, 697 ; XII. 152, 156, 169,
310, 343, 378, 584 ; P. R. I. 136,
166, 329 ; II. 3, 27, 123 ; III. 403 ;
IV. 111, 259, 301, 516 ; S. A. 836,
1079, 1511 ; C. 6, 588, 638 ; S. I.
13 ; XI. 1 ; XIV. 4.

(*b*) to summon, request the
attendance of : P. L. I. 267,
300, 757 ; II. 92, 662 ; IV. 786 ;
V. 220, 584, 696 ; VI. 416 ;
VIII. 298, 458 ; X. 629, 654 ; XI.
67, 660 ; P. R. II. 385 ; S. A.
1678 : V. Ex. 54 ; M. W. 26 ; C.
438.

(*c*) to appoint by Divine
authority to a special work :
P. L. XII. 121, 134 ; S. A. 226.

(*d*) to ask, invite : P. L. V. 21,
36 ; XI. 172 ; *absol.* : P. L. III.
185.

(*e*) to appeal to, invoke : P. L.
VII. 5 ; N. O. 209 ; C. 131 ;
L. 134 ; Ps. LXXXVI. 10 ; to sum-
mon to come *by charms, fig.* :
S. VIII. 6.

(2) *intr.* to lift up the voice in
address or command, shout, cry :
P. L. XII. 57 ; C. 485 ; *or tr. with
the words called preceding or following* : P. L. I. 314 ; IV. 865 ; V. 307 ;
VI. 608 ; VIII. 283 ; X. 102.

In combination with other words ;
(*a*) **call forth,** summon to come
forward : P. L. X. 649.

(*b*) **call in,** summon for assistance : P. L. XI. 651.

(*c*) **call in doubt,** question : S.
A. 43.

(*d*) **call on** or **upon,** invoke :
T. 2 ; Ps. LXXX. 76 ; LXXXI. 26 ;
LXXXVI. 16, 22.

(*e*) **call to mind,** recall, recollect : P. L. X. 1030 ; XI. 898.

(*f*) **call up,** summon, command
to appear : P. L. III. 603 ; V. 179 ;
Il P. 109.

part. adj. **calling,** summoning :
C. 207.

See **Up-call, What-d'ye-call.**

Callow, *adj.* unfledged, without
feathers : P. L. VII. 420.
Calm, (1) *sb.* absence of disturbance,
quiet, serenity, tranquillity, *of
the sea* : P. L. VII. 234 ; *of the
mind or action* : P. L. IV. 120 ;
V. 210 ; **bird of calm** : N. O. 68.
See **Bird.**

(2) *adj.* free from disturbance,
not stormy, quiet, serene, *of
the elements* : P. L. III. 574 ; VII.
270 ; C. 4 ; L. 98 ; *comp.* : P. L.
II. 1042 ; *of the mind or actions* :
P. L. V. 733 ; IX. 920, 1125 ; P.
R. II. 63 ; IV. 425 ; S. A. 604,
1758 ; Il P. 45 ; C. 371 ; *of
circumstances or conditions* : P. R.
II. 81 ; *comp.* : P. R. I. 103 ;
sup. : P. L. VI. 461.

(3) *vb. tr.* to make calm, quiet,
tranquillize : S. A. 964.
Calmly, *adv.* without mental agita-
tion, tranquilly : P. R. III. 43 ;
Ps. LXXXV. 10.
Calumnious, *adj.* slanderous, de-
famatory : P. L. V. 770.
Calve, *vb. tr.* to give birth to a calf,
fig. of the earth : P. L. VII. 463.
Camball, *sb.* a son of Cambuscan : Il
P. 111. *See* **Cambuscan.**
Cambalu, *sb.* the chief city of
Cathay and the royal residence of
the Mongol rulers, now known to
have been the same city as Peking :
P. L. XI. 388.
Cambridge, *sb.* the English univer-
sity : U. C. I. 8 ; S. XI. 14.
Cambuscan (Cambúscan), *sb.* Cam-
binskan, the king of Tartary
whose story is told in the *Squieres
Tale* of Chaucer : Il P. 110.
Came, *sb.* the River Cam in Cam-
bridgeshire, England : M. W. 59.
Camel, *sb.* the animal *Camelus* : P.
R. I. 340 ; III. 335.
Camp, *sb.* (*a*) resting place of an
army : P. L. V. 651 ; P. R. III.
337 ; S. A. 1087, 1436.

(*b*) body of troops, army : P.
L. I. 677 ; XI. 217 ; S. A. 1497.
Campanian, *adj.* of Campania,
Italy : P. R. IV. 93.
Camus, *sb.* the river Cam, *personi-
fied as a god* : L. 103. *See* **Came.**
Can, I. *sb.* Khan, prince, emperor,
the title of Mongol rulers : P. L.
XI. 388.

II. *vb.* (*pres. 2d sing.* canst : P.
L. III. 281, 735 ; IV. 448 ; V. 76,
etc. ; *pret.* could ; *2d. sing.* couldst :
P. L. V. 466 ; VIII. 448 ; IX.

1149, *etc.*; *negative* cannot: P. L. I. 117; II. 100, 269, *etc.*), *as an auxiliary with simple inf.* (*a*) to be able, have the power: P. L. I. 66, 96, 138, 575; II. 113.

(*b*) to be permitted or enabled by the conditions of the case: P. L. III. 735; IV. 22, 527; X. 262.

(*c*) *ellipt. with verb to be supplied from the context*: P. L. II. 769; X. 15; S. A. 1534; *with the verbs* do, say, *etc.*, *understood*: P. L. II. 188, 553, 999; VI. 612; VIII. 630; IX. 1170; XI. 309.

(*d*) **cannot but**, must necessarily: P. L. V. 86; S. A. 735.

(*e*) **could**, *in conditional sentences*; (*a*) *in the protasis, the apodosis containing the subj.*: A. 79; *containing* could: P. L. IX. 114; should: P. L. II. 449; would: P. L. IV. 93; *ellipt.*: P. L. IV. 236.

(*b*) *in the apodosis, the protasis containing the subj.*: P. L. IX. 248; S. A. 197; *containing* should: P. L. II. 239; *ellipt.*: P. L. III. 103; *omitted*: P. R. III. 216.

(*f*) *in indirect discourse*: P. L. IV. 85.

Canaan, *sb.* the Land of Canaan: P. L. XII. 135, 156, 215, 269, 309, 315.

Canaanite, *sb.* inhabitant of Canaan: P. L. XII. 217; S. A. 380.

Canaan-land, *sb.* the Land of Canaan: Ps. CXIV. 3.

Canace, *sb.* the daughter of Cambuscan: Il P. 112. *See* **Cambuscan.**

Cancel, *vb. tr.* to strike or blot out: P. L. VI. 379.

Candaor, *sb.* Candahor, the chief city of Parapomisus, the province of Parthian Empire north of Arachosia, "giving to the whole country the name of Candahor," Hey. *Cos.* 1657, p. 826; *hence,* the province of Candahor: P. R. III. 316.

See **Rush-candle.**

Canker, *sb.* an insect that destroys the leaves and buds of plants: L. 45.

Cankered, *part. adj.* noxious, virulent, corrosive: A. 53.

Canon, *sb.*: C. 808. *See* **Law.**

Canopy, (1) *sb.* covering, overhanging shade, *of the shadow of the earth cast by the sun in its diurnal revolution*: P. L. III. 556.

(2) *vb. tr.* to cover **as with** a canopy: C. 544.

Cany, *adj.* made of cane: P. L. III. 439.

Capable, *adj.* **capable of,** able to perceive or comprehend: P. L. VIII. 49; susceptible to, affected by: P. L. IX. 283.

Capacious, *adj.* (*a*) able to hold much, spacious, roomy: P. L. VII. 290.

(*b*) *of the mind*, comprehensive: P. L. IX. 603.

Capacity, *sb.* mental ability: S. A. 1028.

Caparison, *sb.* richly ornamented cloth spread over the saddle or harness of a horse: P. L. IX. 35.

Cape, *sb.* headland, *spec.* the Cape of Good Hope: P. L. II. 641; **the Cape of Hope**: P. L. IV. 160; **green Cape,** Cape Verd: P. L. VIII. 631.

Caphtor, *sb.* the primitive seat of the Philistines. Its location is uncertain. **The sons of Caphtor,** the Philistines: S. A. 1713.

Capital, (1) *adj.* (*a*) of or relating to the head: P. L. XII. 383; *with the added idea of* (*c*): S. A. 394.

(*b*) involving the loss of life: S. A. 1225.

(*c*) chief: P. L. II. 924; XI. 343.

(2) *sb.* chief city, seat of government: P. L. I. 756.

Capitol, *sb.* the great temple at Rome: P. R. IV. 47.

Capitoline, *sb.* Jupiter Capitolinus, the reputed father of Scipio Africanus: P. L. IX. 508.

Capreæ, *sb.* Capri, a small island off the coast of Campania, Italy. The place of the retirement of the Emperor Tiberius: P. R. IV. 92.

Capricorn, *sb.* the Tropic of Capricorn: P. L. X. 677.

Captain, *sb.* military leader, commander: S. A. 1653; S. VIII. 1.

Captive, (1) *adj.* (*a*) taken prisoner: P. L. I. 458; II. 323; VI. 260; P. R. III. 414; S. A. 335, 366, 1474; **lead captive**: P. L. III. 255; P. R. III. 283, 366; **lead captivity captive**: P. L. X. 188; **make captive**: P. R. III. 77. *See* **Captivity.**

(*b*) of one taken prisoner: S. A. 1603.

(*c*) **lead captive,** charmed, sub-

dued in will and feeling: P. R.
II. 222.

(2) *sb.* prisoner: P. L. IV. 970;
P. R. I. 411; S. A. 426, 1393.

(3) *vb.* (captíved), *tr.* to take
prisoner: S. A. 33, 694.

Captivity, *sb.* the state of being a
prisoner or being held as a
prisoner in servitude: P. L. XII.
344; P. R. III. 279, 415, 420; S.
A. 108, 1744; Ps. LXXXV. 3;
(*a*) **lead captivity captive,** *abstr.
for concr.* lead into servitude a
multitude of prisoners, the enemies of Christ and His kingdom:
P. L. X. 188.

(*b*) *fig.* servitude of the reason:
V. Ex. 52.

Car, *sb.* chariot, *fig.* **car of night:**
P. L. IX. 65; **car of day,** chariot
of the sun-god, Phœbus Apollo:
C. 95; (*of a star*): N. O. 241;
(*of winter*): D. F. I. 15.

Caravan, *sb.* company of persons
travelling together for the sake of
security: P. R. I. 323; *fig. of
birds*: P. L. VII. 428.

Carbuncle, *sb.* precious stone of a
deep red colour: P. L. III. 596.

attrib. like the carbuncle in
beauty and splendour: P. L. IX.
500.

Carcase, *sb.* (*a*) dead body of man:
P. L. I. 310; XI. 654; P. R. I.
325; S. A. 693, 1097; *fig. of
death*: P. L. III. 259.

(*b*) body of man regarded as
living but as about to die: P. L.
X. 277.

Care, (1) *sb.* (*a*) grief, sorrow: P. L.
I. 601.

(*b*) anxious concern, solicitude,
anxiety: P. L. II. 48, 303; VI.
35; X. 979; XI. 776; P. R. II.
18; S. A. 805, 928; D. F. I. 18;
L'A. 135; C. 6, 506; S. XXI. 12;
personified: L'A. 31.

(*c*) watchful regard and attention: P. L. IX. 318, 799; X. 1057;
S. A. 602, 923; M. W. 36; L.
64; S. IX. 9.

(*d*) caution, pains: P. L. X. 37.

(*e*) object or matter of concern
or solicitude: P. L. IV. 575; VIII.
185; IX. 813; P. R. II. 64, 460;
IV. 96; S. A. 918; L. 116.

(*f*) charge, oversight, guardianship: P. R. I. 111; Ps. LXXXVII. 8.

(2) *vb.* (*pres. 2d sing.* car'st:
S. A. 1488), *intr.* to be anxious, be
concerned, feel interest, *with phrase*

or clause: P. L. VI. 822; S. A.
1488; *with prep. inf.*: P. L. II. 48.

Career, *sb.* (*a*) charge, encounter:
P. L. I. 766.

(*b*) a running, course implying
swift motion, *of the sun*: P. L.
IV. 353; *of night*: Il P. 121;
full career, all the speed possible:
S. II. 3.

Careering, *part. adj.* being in constant and rapid motion, darting:
P. L. VI. 756.

Careful, *adj.* showing care, attentive, provident, vigilant: P. L.
IV. 983; D. F. I. 45; performed
with care: P. L. X. 438; S. A. 327.

Careless, *adj.* (*a*) free from care or
anxiety: P. R. IV. 299.

(*b*) heedless, unconcerned: P.
R. IV. 450.

Carelessly, negligently: S. A. 118.

Caress, *sb.* fondling touch: P. L.
VIII. 56.

Carmel, *sb.* **Mount Carmel,** the mountain of Palestine: P. L. XII. 144.

Carnage, *sb.* carcases collectively,
heap of dead bodies: P. L. X. 268.

Carnal, *adj.* of or pertaining to the
body: P. L. XII. 521; as the seat
of emotion, appetite, or passion;
(*a*) fleshly, sensual: P. L. VIII.
593; XI. 212; C. 474.

(*b*) sexual: P. L. IX. 1013.

Carnation, *sb.* (*a*) crimson colour:
P. L. IX. 429.

(*b*) *attrib.* of the flower *Dianthus
Caryophyllus*: M. W. 37.

Carol, (1) *sb.* song of joy sung at
the Nativity: P. L. XII. 367.

(2) *vb. tr.* to sing of, celebrate
in song: C. 849.

Carpathian, *adj.* of the island of
Carpathus, in the Mediterranean;
Carpathian wizard, Proteus, whose
home was on this island: C. 872.
See **Proteus.**

Carpenter, *sb.* artificer in wood: P.
R. II. 414.

Carriage, *sb.* action of carrying
something from one place to another: U. C. I. 10.

Carrier, *sb.* bearer of letters, parcels, etc.: U. C. II. 20, 28.

Carry, *vb. tr.* (*a*) to bear or convey
in order to deliver it to another
person: P. L. v. 870; S. A. 385;
absol.: U. C. II. 18.

(*b*) to bear mentally, keep in
mind: P. L. XII. 621.

(*c*) to exhibit, display: S. A.
1073.

Cart, *sb.* vehicle : U. C. II. 22.

Carthaginian, *adj.* of Carthage :
P. R. III. 35.

Carved, *part. adj.* cut artistically,
sculptured : P. R. IV. 59.

Casbeen, *sb.* Casbin, a city of Media
Major, a province of Persia : P.
L. X. 436.

Casella, *sb.* the character in Dante's
Purgatorio II. 91 : S. XIII. 13.

Cash, *sb.* ready money : P. L. IV.
188.

Casius, *sb.* Mount Casius, a mountain in the extreme northeastern
part of Lower Egypt : P. L. II.
593.

Casket, *sb.* chest where valuable
things are kept, *fig.* the rock
forming the sepulchre of Christ :
P. 44.

Caspian, *sb.* the Caspian Sea : P. L.
II. 716 ; Caspian lake : P. R. III.
271.

Cassia, *sb.* the aromatic plant : P.
L. V. 293 ; C. 991.

Cast, (1) *sb.* manner, mien : Il P.
43.

(2) *vb.* (*pret. and past part.*
cast), *tr.* (*a*) to throw : P. R. IV.
575 ; L. 134 ; S. XII. 8 ; Ps. II.
7 ; *with* down : P. L. III. 351 ; P.
R. IV. 555, 605.

(*b*) to place, impute, *with* on :
P. L. II. 122 ; X. 547.

(*c*) to emit, send forth : P. L.
I. 183 ; P. R. III. 326 ; Il P. 160 ;
C. 225, 460, *with* forth : P. L. II.
889 ; *hence,* to exhibit, disclose,
reveal : P. L. I. 604.

(*d*) to direct, turn : P. L. II.
714 ; (*the eye or eyes*) : P. L. IX.
1014 ; P. R. II. 180 ; IV. 61.

(*e*) to impart, communicate,
shed, *with* on : P. L. I. 526.

(*f*) to extend by force : N. O.
170.

(*g*) to utter incidentally, make
use of as if by accident : P. L. V.
702.

(*h*) to raise by throwing up
earth : P. L. I. 678.

(*i*) to put or place with haste or
violence : P. L. I. 286 ; *fig.* : Ps.
VII. 39.

(*j*) to calculate or conjecture
as to the future : C. 360.

(*k*) to plan, contrive, devise,
with prep. inf. : P. L. III. 634 ;
XII. 43.

(*l*) to lay firmly, establish : P.
L. VI. 869 ; N. O. 123.

In combination with other words ;
(*a*) cast back, hold from forward
motion : S. A. 336.

(*b*) cast behind, get quit of, lay
aside entirely : P. R. II. 46.

(*c*) cast forth, speak : P. R. I.
228.

(*d*) cast off, discard, abandon,
disown : P. L. V. 786 ; S. A. 641.

(*e*) cast out, drive out forcibly,
expel : P. L. I. 37 ; V. 613 ; VI.
272.

Castalian, *sb.* Castalian spring, a
spring near Apollo's sacred grove
of Daphne at Antioch : P. L. IV.
274.

Casual, *adj.* (*a*) accidental, that
happens by chance : P. L. XI. 566.

(*b*) brought about without design, unpremeditated : P. L. IX.
223.

(*c*) not to be depended upon,
precarious, uncertain : P. L. IV.
767.

Cataphract, *sb.* man clad in mail
and mounted on a mailed horse :
S. A. 1619.

Cataract, *sb.* (*a*) flood-gate, sluice :
P. L. XI. 824.

(*b*) *fig.* cataracts of fire, columns
of fire resembling waterspouts :
P. L. II. 176.

Catarrh, *sb.* inflammation of a
mucous membrane : P. L. XI. 483.

Catch, *vb.* (*pret.* caught ; *past part.*
caught : P. L. II. 180 ; XI. 587 ;
P. R. II. 14 ; S. A. 932 ; L'A. 69 ;
catched : P. L. X. 544), *tr.* (*a*) to
ensnare, entrap : P. L. XI. 587 ;
S. A. 932.

(*b*) to lay hold of, capture, *with*
in : P. L. II. 180.

(*c*) to seize and keep hold of :
P. L. XII. 637.

(*d*) to seize with the eye, perceive : L'A. 69.

(*e*) to lay hold of forcibly and
take away : P. L. XII. 88.

(*f*) to take, contract (*a disease*),
fig. : P. L. X. 544.

(*g*) to come upon suddenly,
surprise : C. 953.

(*h*) catch up, raise suddenly
aloft : P. R. II. 14 ; IV. 541.

Cateress, *sb.* female caterer, *fig. of
nature* : C. 764.

Cate, *sb. pl.* dainties, delicacies : P.
R. II. 348.

Cathaian, *adj.* of Cathay, a province
of Tartary, supposed to lie northwest of China and north of India ;

now known to have been identical with China: P. L. x. 293; xi. 388.

Cattle, *sb.* domestic animals, beasts: P. L. vii. 452, 460; viii. 582; x. 176; xi. 558, 653; xii. 179.

Caucasus, *sb.* the chain of mountains extending from the Black to the Caspian Sea: P. R. iii. 318.

Cause, I. *sb.* (1) that which produces an effect; that which gives rise to an action, a phenomenon, or a condition: P. L. vi. 442; viii. 593; ix. 650, 862; Dante 1; (*a*) *referring to a person* the author: P. L. ix. 1168; x. 935, 982; S. A. 234, 376.

(*b*) *as used by Aristotelians* "the efficient cause," agency by which a thing is produced: P. L. x. 806; "the material cause," element or matter from which a thing is produced: P. L. ii. 913; iii. 707; ix. 682.

(2) ground for action, reason, motive: P. L. i. 28; iv. 14, 922; v. 702; vii. 64, 90; viii. 270, 417, 497; ix. 731, 1140; xi. 382, 461; P. R. i. 66; ii. 239; iv. 375; S. A. 157, 316, 1253, 1321, 1347, 1379, 1584, 1586, 1709; **with cause,** *adverbially,* justly, rightly: P. L. xii. 604; S. A. 472.

(3) important principle; interest, aim, or object to which the efforts of a person or party are directed: P. L. vi. 31, 67, 804; ix. 672; S. A. 1179; C. 489, 794.

(4) matter before the court for decision, action, suit: Ps. lxxxii. 10; Hor. Epist. 4.

(5) question for debate: S. A. 904.

II. *vb. tr.* to be the cause of, give rise to, make: P. L. x. 907; P. R. ii. 323; S. A. 793; *with acc. and prep. inf.*: P. L. iv. 216; v. 400; S. A. 581, 584; Ps. vii. 34; lxxx. 15, 31, 79; lxxxv. 15, 25; cxxxvi. 29.

Causeless, *adv.* without cause or reason: S. A. 701.

Causey, *sb.* highway: P. L. x. 415.

Caution, *sb.* (*a*) word of warning: P. L. v. 513, 523.

(*b*) circumspection, prudence, discretion: P. L. vii. 111.

Cautious, *adj.* wary, careful: S. A. 757; **cautious of day,** careful to be absent, or not to be seen, during the day: P. L. ix. 59.

Cautiously, *adv.* warily, prudently: P. R. iv. 377.

Cave, *sb.* cavern, hollow underground place; P. L. ii. 621, 789; iv. 257, 454; vi. 4; vii. 417; ix. 118; xi. 568; P. R. i. 307; iv. 414; L'A. 3; C. 239; L. 39; Hor. O. 2; *fig. of death*: P. L. xi. 469; **vacant interlunar cave**: S. A. 89. *See* **Interlunar.**

Cavern, *sb.* cave: C. ✿29.

Cavil, *vb. tr.* to find fault with, object to captiously: P. L. x. 759.

Cease, *vb.* (*perf. tenses formed with the auxiliary* be: P. L. xi. 780; P. R. i. 456; *with* have: P. L. i. 283; iii. 344; xi. 713; P. R. iv. 507), (1) *intr.* to leave off, stop, discontinue; P. L. i. 283; ii. 43, 159, 845, 1010; iii. 344; viii. 412; xi. 126; xii. 238, 372; P. R. ii. 235; iv. 14; D. F. I. 18; U. C. ii. 10; C. 551; Ps. vii. 34; lxxxiii. 4; lxxxv. 15; *with prep. inf.*: P. L. i. 176; iii. 27; v. 845; xi. 309, 713; P. R. ii. 222; iv. 507; D. F. I. 72; V. Ex. 86; **cease to be,** come to an end, exist no longer: P. L. ii. 100.

(2) *tr.* (*a*) to cause to stop, make an end of: N. O. 45.

(*b*) to leave off, discontinue, *with vbl. sb.*: P. L. vii. 436; x. 910; xi. 726.

See **Never-ceasing.**

Ceaseless, *adj.* without ceasing, uninterrupted, endless; P. L. ii. 795; iv. 679; v. 183; x. 573; Ps. lxxxviii. 7.

Cedar, *sb.* (*a*) the tree *Cedrus*: P. L. iv. 139; v. 260; ix. 435, 1089; P. R. i. 306; Ps. lxxx. 43.

(*b*) wood of this tree: P. L. xii. 250; P. R. iv. 60.

Cedarn, *adj.* bordered by cedar trees: C. 990.

Cedar-top, *sb.* top of a cedar tree: P. L. vii. 424.

Ceiling, *sb.* overhead covering of a room: P. L. xi. 743.

Celebrate, *vb. tr.* (*a*) to observe with solemn rites, commemorate: S. A. 435.

(*b*) to praise, extol, magnify: P. L. ii. 241; vi. 888; xi. 345; S. A. 866; A. 80.

Celestial, (1) *adj.* (*a*) of the sky, the material heaven: P. L. iv. 1011; vii. 354.

(*b*) of or pertaining to heaven,

the abode of God, the gods, or angels; godlike; heavenly, divine: P. L. I. 245, 658; II. 15; III. 51, 364; IV. 553, 682, 812; V. 249, 403, 654; VI. 44, 333, 510, 760; VII. 12, 203, 254; VIII. 455, 619; IX. 21; X. 24; XI. 239, 785; P. R. I. 170; IV. 588; S. A. 1280; N. O. 145; S. M. 27; A. 63; C. 1004.

(c) divinely beautiful: P. L. III. 638; IX. 540.

(2) *sb.* inhabitant of heaven: P. L. XI. 296.

Cell, *sb.* (a) small apartment or habitation of a monk, hermit, or other solitary: N. O. 180; L'A. 5; Il P. 169; C. 387; Ps. 41.

(b) one of the compartments in a honeycomb: P. L. VII. 491.

(c) one of the compartments of the brain supposed to be the seat of particular mental faculties: P. L. VIII. 460; *or fig. in time* (a): P. L. V. 109.

(d) hollow receptacle: P. L. I. 70, 706.

Celtic, *adj.* of the Celts: C. 60; *with sb. understood*: P. L. I. 521.

Censer, *sb.* vessel for burning incense: P. L. VII. 600; XI. 24.

Censure, *vb. tr.* to blame, find fault with, criticize adversely: S. A. 787; *absol.*: S. A. 948.

Centaur, *sb.* the southern constellation: P. L. X. 328.

Centre, (1) *sb.* (a) middle point: A. 19; of the earth: P. L. V. 579; VI. 219; VII. 242; N. O. 162; C. 382; of the universe: P. L. VIII. 123; of heaven: P. L. IX. 108; VII. 215; the earth as the centre of the universe: P. L. I. 74; the earth itself: P. L. I. 686; by **centre**, toward the centre: P. L. III. 575; **from centre to circumference**, *fig.* from beginning to end: P. L. V. 510.

(b) that about which something revolves, axis: P. R. IV. 534.

(2) *vb.* (a) *intr.* to be in the centre: P. L. IX. 108.

(b) *tr.* to place on a point which is to serve as a centre: P. L. VII. 228.

Centric, (1) *adj.* that is in the centre: P. L. X. 671.

(2) *sb.* celestial sphere having the earth as the centre about which it revolves: P. L. VIII. 83. *See* **Sphere**.

Cerastes, *sb.* horned serpent: P. L. X. 525.

Cerberean, *adj.* resembling those of Cerberus: P. L. II. 655.

Cerberus, *sb.* the many-headed dog that guarded the entrance to Hades: L'A. 2.

Ceremony, *sb.* (a) religious observance or sacred rite prescribed by the Mosaic law: P. L. XII. 297.

(b) formality, solemnity: P. L. I. 753.

Ceres, *sb.* the goddess of agriculture and the mother of Proserpina by Jove: P. L. IV. 271, 981; IX. 395.

Certain, (1) *adj.* (a) sure, assured, having no doubts: S. A. 474; *with prep. inf.*: P. L. II. 470; S. A. 1102; **for certain**, assuredly: C. 482.

(b) stated, fixed: P. L. II. 597; X. 576.

(c) inevitable, unavoidable: P. L. III. 119; X. 980.

(d) self-determined, resolved: P. L. IX. 907; *with prep. inf.*: P. L. IX. 953.

(e) particular, definite, *with sing. sb.*: C. 619; H. B. 5; *with pl. sb.*: P. L. XII. 437; C. 572.

(2) *adv.* certainly, surely, assuredly: S. A. 723; C. 266.

Certainly, *adv.* surely: P. R. II. 32.

Certainty, *sb.* surety, assurance: C. 263.

Chæronea, *sb.* a town of Bœotia in Greece, the scene of the defeat of the Greeks by Phillip of Macedon in 338 B.C.: S. X. 7.

Chafe, (1) *sb.* heat of mind, rage, fury: S. A. 1246.

(2) *vb. tr.* to inflame, make furious: S. A. 1138.

Chaff, *sb.* husk of corn separated by threshing: P. L. IV. 985.

Chain, (1) *sb.* (a) connected series of links serving the purpose of connecting or supporting *with* in: P. L. II. 1005, 1051; of confining: P. L. X. 319.

(b) *pl.* bonds, fetters, imprisonment: P. L. I. 48; II. 183, 196; III. 82; IV. 970; VI. 186, 260, 739; XII. 454; S. A. 68, 1238; C. 804; *fig.*: V. Ex. 52; L'A. 143; C. 435; S. XVI. 12.

(2) *vb.* (*past part.* ychained: N. O. 155), *tr.* to bind or fetter with a chain or something else depriving of freedom: P. L. I. 210

II. 169; IV. 965; S. A. 7; N. O. 155; C. 660.

part. adj. **chained,** *fig.* bound together as if in a chain, coming so thick and fast that they seem bound into a chain : P. L. VI. 589.

Chair, *sb.* (*a*) seat from which instruction is given : P. R. IV. 219.

(*b*) seat of authority, throne : P. L. I. 764.

(*c*) chariot, *fig.* D. F. I. 19; **cloudy chair,** clouds serving the purpose of a chariot : P. L. II. 930; C. 134.

Chaldæa, *sb.* the country of Asia bordering on the Persian Gulf and the Tigris River : P. L. XII. 130.

Challenge, *vb. tr.* (*a*) to claim : P. R. IV. 260.

(*b*) to invite to a contest, defy : S. A. 1151.

Chalybean-tempered, *adj.* tempered by the Chalybes, a people of Scythia celebrated as workers in iron and steel : S. A. 133.

Cham, *sb.* Ham, the son of Noah, *here* identified with Ammon, *spelled* Cham *in Vulg.* : P. L. IV. 276. *See* **Ammon.**

Chamber, *sb.* room or apartment in a house : P. R. II. 183; *fig.* C. 101.

Chamber-ambush, *sb.* a lying in wait for an enemy in his sleeping apartment : S. A. 1112.

Chamberlin, *sb.* waiter at an inn who has charge of the bedchambers : U. C. I. 14.

Champ, *vb. tr.* to bite upon : P. L. IV. 859.

Champaign, (**1**) *sb.* level open country : P. L. VI. 2; P. R. III. 257.

(**2**) *adj.* level and open : P. L. IV. 134.

Champion, *sb.* (*a*) brave warrior, stout fighter : P. L. II. 424; *fig. of cold, hot, etc.* : P. L. II. 898.

(*b*) one who fights on behalf of another or of a cause : P. L. I. 763; S. A. 566, 705, 1152, 1751; *fig. of conscience* : C. 212.

Chance, I. *sb.* (**1**) fortune, good or evil : P. L. II. 222, 935; P. R. I. 321; IV. 265; S. A. 1076; S. VIII. 2.

(**2**) fortuity, absence of design or assignable cause; P. L. I. 133; (*a*) *personified* as an agent, possibly with reference to the *Gr.* τύχη or

L. Fortuna : P. L. II. 233, 551; VII. 172; T. 22; C. 588; **as a** ruler in the realm of chaos : P. L. II. 910; as an attendant upon the throne of chaos : P. L. II. 965.

(*b*) **by chance,** without design, accidentally : P. L. II. 288; IV. 403.

(**3**) contingent or unexpected event : P. L. X. 108, 428; unfortunate event, mishap : S. A. 656, 918; C. 277.

(**4**) opportunity : S. A. 4.

(**5**) possibility of something happening : P. L. IV. 530.

II. *vb. intr.* to come about by chance, happen : P. L. IX. 423; *with prep. inf.* : P. L. IX. 575; P. R. IV. 559; S. A. 1295; C. 79; *with simple inf.* : P. L. II. 396, 492; IX. 452; **how chance,** how does it happen that : C. 508; **wherever chanced,** wherever an opportunity offered : S. A. 1202.

Change, I. *sb.* (**1**) alteration, variation, mutation : P. L. I. 313, 598, 625; II. 222, 820; IV. 367; VIII. 525; IX. 70, 818; X. 107, 213, 548, 692, 693; XI. 193; P. R. II. 86; III. 197; IV. 265, 442; S. A. 117, 340, 695, 753; C. 596, 841; L. 37; **mortal change,** death : P. L. X. 273; C. 10.

(**2**) substitution; (*a*) of one thing or place for another : P. L. II. 598, 599; IV. 23; V. 87, 183, 336; change of seasons : P. L. IV. 640; X. 677.

(*b*) of one condition for another, variety : P. L. V. 629.

II. *vb.* (*pres. 2d sing.* changest : S. A. 684), (**1**) *tr.* (*a*) to cause to vary, alter : P. L. I. 84, 96, 97; II. 217, 312; III. 125, 634; IV. 115, 224, 405; V. 902; VI. 613; X. 333, 541; XI. 308, 712; S. A. 684, 1406; D. F. I. 28; to turn *one thing* into another : P. L. II. 276; V. 644; VI. 824; VII. 160; IX. 5; XI. 794; C. 69.

(*b*) to substitute *one thing* for another : P. L. VIII. 347; C. 328; *with acc. and* for : P. L. I. 244; to substitute themselves for : P. L. IX. 505.

(**2**) *intr.* to become different, be altered : P. L. XI. 539; Ps. LXXXI. 18; LXXXVIII. 35.

part. adj. **changed,** altered : Hor. O. 6.

Channel, *sb.* bed of running water :
P. L. VII. 303 ; N. O. 124 ; C.
895.

Chant, *sb.* song : P. R. II. 290.

Chaos, *sb.* (1) yawning gulf, abyss :
P. L. VI. 55.

(2) the "formless void," the
confused matter ; (*a*) out of which
the universe was created : P.
L. I. 10 ; VII. 93, 220 ; *personified
as a ruler, but frequently including
also the idea of the realm* : P. L.
I. 543 ; II. 233, 895, 907, 960, 970,
1038 ; III. 18, 421 ; V. 577 ; VI.
871 ; VII. 221, 272 ; X. 416, 477 ;
C. 334.

(*b*) which intervened between
the world and hell : P. L. III.
426 ; X. 233, 283, 317, 347, 636.

Character (*possibly* charáctered : C.
530), (1) *sb.* (*a*) essential peculiar-
ity, nature : P. L. VIII. 545.

(*b*) *pl.* letters, *collect.* writing :
P. 49.

(*c*) planet denoted by a character or astrological symbol : P. R.
IV. 384.

(2) *vb. tr.* to engrave, imprint :
C. 530.

Charge, (1) *sb.* (*a*) commission, trust,
responsibility : P. L. II. 775 ; III.
628, 688 ; IV. 589, 879 ; X. 35,
421, 650.

(*b*) injunction, mandate : P. L.
IV. 421, 562, 842 ; V. 248 ; IX.
399 ; X. 123.

(*c*) load, burden, *fig.* : P. L. XI.
549.

(*d*) person intrusted to the
care of another : P. L. IX. 157.

(*e*) accusation : F. of C. 19.

In combination with other words ;
(*a*) **give in charge,** command :
P. L. IV. 787.

(*b*) **have in charge,** be commanded : P. L. VI. 566 ; VIII. 246 ;
P. R. I. 376 ; execute carefully :
P. L. XI. 99 ; have the trust laid
upon one : C. 32.

(*c*) **lay to one's charge,** accuse
one of : S. A. 849.

(*d*) **leave in charge,** leave the
commission with : P. L. XII. 439.

(2) *vb. tr.* (*a*) to accuse : C.
762.

(*b*) to command, order, enjoin :
P. L. X. 200 ; *with prep. inf.* : P.
L. VII. 46.

Chariot, (1) *sb.* (*a*) stately vehicle
for the conveyance of persons
from earth to heaven : P. L. III.

522 ; P. 36 ; *in which Sabrina
rises from the depths of the river* :
C. 892.

(*b*) car used in war : P. L. II.
887 ; VI. 17, 100, 211, 338, 390,
711, 750, 770, 829, 881 ; VII. 197,
199 ; P. R. III. 329 ; N. O. 56.

(2) *vb. tr.* to convey in a
chariot : S. A. 27.

Charioteer, *sb.* driver of a chariot :
P. L. VI. 390 ; D. F. I. 8.

Chariot-wheel, *sb.* : P. L. I. 311 ;
III. 394 ; VI. 358 ; XII. 210.

Charity, *sb.* love, affection : P. L.
III. 217 ; IV. 756 ; XII. 584.

Charlemain, *sb.* Charles the Great
of France, a prominent figure in
tales of chivalry : P. L. I. 586 ;
P. R. III. 343.

Charm, (1) *sb.* (*a*) magic spell :
P. L. II. 460, 666 ; C. 150, 613,
664, 853 ; *fig.* : S. VIII. 5.

(*b*) chanting of a verse supposed to possess magic power,
incantation : Il P. 83.

(*c*) something which exerts a
fascinating or attractive influence,
attractiveness, charmingness : P.
L. IV. 498 ; VIII. 533 ; IX. 999 ;
P. R. II. 213 ; S. A. 427, 934, 1040.

(*d*) blended singing of many
birds : P. L. IV. 642, 651.

(*e*) lyric poem : P. R. IV. 257.

(2) *vb.* (*past part. disyl.* : C. 51,
904 ; N. O. 68), *tr.* (*a*) to affect,
subdue, or control by magic
power : C. 758 ; **charm thee
strong,** make thee strong by
magic : S. A. 1134 ; to subdue by
the power of music : P. L. XI. 132.

(*b*) to allure as with a charm :
P. L. I. 561.

(*c*) to enchant, delight : P. L. I.
787 ; II. 556.

(*d*) to allay or assuage as if by
magic power : P. L. II. 566.

part. adj. (1) **charming,** en-
chanting, fascinating, delightful :
P. L. III. 368 ; V. 626 ; VIII. 2 ;
XI. 595 ; P. R. II. 363 ; C. 476.

(2) **charmed** ; (*a*) affected by a
spell so as to possess magic power :
C. 51.

(*b*) produced by magic : C. 904.

(*c*) controlled by supernatural
power : N. O. 68.

Charnel-vault, *sb.* subterranean
chamber containing dead bodies :
C. 471.

Charybdis, *sb.* the monster supposed
to dwell in the whirlpool on the

Sicilian shore of the Strait of Sicily: P. L. II. 1020; C. 259.

Chase, (1) *sb.* pursuit for the purpose of capturing or killing, hunting : P. L. XI. 191 ; **beast of chase** : P. L. IV. 341 ; P. R. II. 342.

(2) *vb. tr.* to drive away : P. L. I. 557 ; IV. 627 ; VI. 288 ; P. R. IV. 429.

Chaste, *adj.* pure, virtuous, continent : P. L. IV. 761 ; XI. 12 ; C. 146, 442, 450, 918 ; Petr. 1.

Chastening, *part. adj.* inflicting disciplinary punishment on, correcting : P. L. XI. 373.

Chastity, *sb.* sexual purity, virginity: C. 420, 425, 440, 453, 782 ; *personified* : C. 215 ; *concr. for abstr.* chaste person : C. 909.

Chat, *vb. intr.* to talk lightly and unceremoniously : N. O. 87.

Chaunt, *vb. tr.* to sing of, celebrate in song : S. A. 1672.

Chauntress, *sb.* songstress : Il P. 63.

Cheap, *adv.* with little trouble, easily : P. L. II. 472.

Cheat, *vb. tr.* to deceive, impose upon : C. 155.

Chebar, *sb. attrib.* **Chebar flood,** the stream in Chaldea where Ezekiel saw his visions : P. 37.

Check, (1) *sb.* restraint, control : P. R. I. 477.

(2) *vb. tr.* (*a*) to stay the course of, stop, repress, restrain : P. L. III. 732 ; V. 214 ; VI. 853 ; C. 761 ; Ps. LXXXIII. 28.

(*b*) to curb, rein : Il P. 59.

Cheek, *sb.* (*a*) side of the face below the eye : P. L. I. 602 ; III. 641 ; V. 10, 385 ; IX. 887 ; X. 1009 ; P. R. IV. 344 ; D. F. I. 6 ; L'A. 29 ; Il P. 107 ; C. 750 ; Ps. LXXX. 24.

(*b*) Sir John Cheke, the professor of Greek in Cambridge University, 1540-1551 : S. XI. 12.

Cheek-bone, *sb.* jaw-bone : Ps. III. 21.

Cheer, (1) *sb.* (*a*) frame of mind, mood : P. L. VI. 496.

(*b*) cheerfulness, gladness, high spirits : S. A. 1613 ; C. 955 ; Ps. LXXXIV. 26.

(2) *vb. tr.* (*a*) to make cheerful or glad, comfort, solace : P. L. IV. 165 ; V. 129 ; XII. 604 ; S. A. 545, 926.

(*b*) to brighten externally : P. R. IV. 433.

vbl. sb. **Cheering,** joy, gladness : C. 348.

See **All-cheering.**

Cheerful, *adj.* (*a*) animated by gladness, joyous, blithe: P. L. V. 123; XI. 543.

(*b*) promoting or causing gladness, cheering, gladdening, bright : P. L. II. 490; III. 46, 545; C. 388 ; S. XXI. 14 ; Ps. LXXXI. 7.

Cheerly, *adv.* cheerily, blithely : L'A. 54.

See **Arch-chemic.**

Chemos, *sb.* Chemosh, the god of the Moabites, *identified with one of the fallen angels* ; *spelled* Chamos *in Vulg.* : P. L. I. 406.

Chequered, *part. adj.* marked with alternate light and shade : L'A. 96.

Cherish, *vb. tr.* (*a*) to cheer, comfort : S. A. 958.

(*b*) to give warmth to : P. R. X. 1068.

vbl. sb. **Cherishing,** tenderness, affectionate care : P. L. VIII. 569.

Cherith, *sb.* **the brook of Cherith,** the stream upon whose bank Elijah hid from Ahab. Its location is uncertain : P. R. II. 266.

Chersonese, *sb.* the Malay Peninsula, *preceded by the adj.* golden : P. L. XI. 392 ; P. R. IV. 74.

Cherub, (*pl.* cherubim ; *sing. for pl.* : P. L. I. 324 ; VI. 771 ; VII. 198) *sb.* (*a*) the order of angels next below that of the seraphim, or a member of this order : P. L. I. 324, 665, 794 ; II. 516 ; III. 636, 666 ; IV. 778 ; VI. 102, 771 ; VII. 198, 218 ; IX. 61 ; XI. 100, 128 ; XII. 628 ; N. O. 112 ; P. 38 ; *spec.* Beëlzebub : P. L. I. 157 ; Azazel : P. L. I. 534 ; Satan *in disguise* : P. L. III. 636 ; Zephon : P. L. IV. 844 ; Zophiel : P. L. VI. 535 ; Gabriel : P. L. IV. 971 ; Contemplation : Il P. 54.

(*b*) representation of the same on the Ark of the Tabernacle : P. L. I. 387 ; XII. 254.

Cherubic, *adj.* of cherubs, angelic : P. L. V. 547 ; VI. 413, 753 ; IX. 68 ; XI. 120 ; S. M. 12.

Chest, *sb.* coffin : N. O. 217.

Chew, *vb.* to grind with the teeth, masticate : P. L. IV. 335 ; X. 566.

part. adj. **chewing,** ruminating : C. 540.

Chide, *vb.* (*pret.* chid), (1) *intr.* to utter reproof, rebuke : S. XIX. 6 ; Ps. LXXXV. 16.

(2) *tr.* to rebuke, censure : C. 258.

Chief, (1) *sb.* chieftain, commander, ruler: P. L. I. 128, 524, 566; II. 487, 527; IV. 550, 864, 920; VI. 745; X. 455, 537; *fig. of reason*: P. L. V. 102; **in chief, in command**: P. L. VI. 233.

(2) *adj.* principal, greatest, foremost: P. L. III. 168, 664; V. 684; VII. 515; IX. 29; XI. 493, 617; P. R. II. 464; S. A. 66, 457, 554, 1249; D. F. I. 3; U. C. II. 21; S. XVI. 1; *sup.*: V. Ex. 18.

absol. pl. the greatest, foremost or leading ones: P. L. I. 381; II. 469.

(3) *adv.* chiefly, principally: P. L. I. 762; III. 29; S. A. 754; *sup.*: Il P. 51.

Chiefly, *adv.* principally, particularly, especially: P. L. I. 17; II. 763; III. 663; IV. 445, 566, 790, 849; IX. 379, 878, 981; X. 401; XII. 272, 599; P. R. I. 263; III. 123; S. A. 1452.

Child, *sb.* (*pl.* children) (*a*) infant: S. A. 942; D. F. I. 71; N. O. 30.

(*b*) young person, boy or girl: P. R. I. 201; IV. 330.

(*c*) offspring, descendants in the first degree: P. L. I. 395; X. 194, 330; XI. 761, 772; S. A. 352; *fig.* expressing characteristic or relation, **Fancy's child**: L'A. 133; children of nature: C. 720, 763.

Child-bearing, *sb.* bringing forth of a child, parturition: P. L. X. 1051.

Child-bed, *sb. attrib.* pertaining to the state of a woman in labour: S. XXIII. 5.

Childhood, *sb.* time during which one is a child: P. R. IV. 220, 508.

Childish, *adj.* proper to a child: P. R. I. 201: V. Ex. 3.

Childless, *adj.* without offspring: P. L. X. 989, 1037; D. F. I. 13.

Chill, (1) *adj.* cold: N. O. 195; injuriously cold: A. 49; C. 352; *fig. of horror* as having the benumbing effect of cold: P. L. IX. 890.

(2) *vb. tr.* to benumb, *of horror*: P. L. V. 65.

part. adj. chilling, benumbing, *of sorrow*: P. L. XI. 264.

Chimæra, *sb.* the fire-breathing monster which had the head of a lion, the body of a goat, and the tail of a serpent, and which abode at the entrance of Hades: P. L. II. 628; C. 517.

Chime, *sb.* harmony, musical concord: P. L. XI. 559; *of the spheres*: N. O. 128; C. 1021; *fig. in nature*: S. M. 20.

Chiming, *part. adj.* sounding in harmony: P. R. II. 363.

Chimney, *sb.* (*a*) vent for smoke, flue: L'A. 81.

(*b*) fireplace: L'A. 111.

Chin, *sb.* part of the face below the mouth, *fig.*: N. O. 231.

Chinese, *sb. pl.* **Chineses,** natives of China: P. L. III. 438.

Chios, *sb.* an island in the Aegean Sea, noted for its wine: P. R. IV. 118.

Chivalry, *sb.* (*a*) knights equipped for battle; P. L. I. 765.

(*b*) men-at-arms, forces, troops: P. L. I. 307; P. R. III. 344.

Choaspes, *sb.* a river of Susiana emptying into the Euphrates, the modern Kerkhah: P. R. III. 288.

Choice, I. *sb.* **(1)** act of choosing, election: P. L. I. 759; II. 19, 524; III. 108, 670; IV. 434; VIII. 335, 400; IX. 214, 620; X. 978; S. A. 1030, 1743; (*a*) **at choice,** according to preference: P. L. V. 499.

(*b*) by preference, **by choice**: S. A. 311; **of choice**: P. L. IX. 992; X. 766; **with choice**: Ps. V. 7.

(*c*) **for his choice,** because that was his preference: Ps. LXXXI. 48.

(*d*) **make choice,** choose, *with prep. inf.*: S. A. 555.

(*e*) **take one's choice,** separate and take what one prefers: P. L. XI. 101.

(2) person or thing chosen: P. L. V. 327, 333; x. 904.

(3) abundance and variety to choose from: P.L. VII. 48; S.A. 3.

(4) that which is specially chosen on account of excellence, the preferable part, the pick: P. L. II. 423; P. R. III. 314.

(5) care in choosing, judgement: P. L. I. 261; II. 415.

II. *adj.* (1) select, excellent, rare: P. R. IV. 329; S. A. 633, 1654; S. XX. 9; *sup.*: P. L. V. 127, 368; IX. 840; XI. 438; P.R. I. 302; II. 334; IV. 437; S. A. 264; V. Ex. 22.

(2) careful in choosing, selective: P. L. I. 653; III. 534.

See **Marriage-choice.**

Choir, *sb.*: P. L. IV. 711. *See* Quire.

Choose, *vb.* (*pret.* chose; *past part.* chose: P. R. I. 165; Ps. IV. 13, 14; chosen: P. L. I. 8, 318; III. 183; IV. 691; P. R. I. 427; II. 45, 236; IV. 614; S. A. 368; S. IX. 6; Ps. CXXXVI. 57), (1) *tr.* to make choice of, elect: P. L. I. 318, 428; III. 123, 183; IV. 72, 406, 691; V. 333, 534; IX. 88, 221, 316, 1100, 1167; X. 1005; XI. 587; XII. 219, 225, 646; P. R. I. 165; III. 370; S. A. 368, 513, 877, 1193; N. O. 14; S. IX. 6; Ps. IV. 13, 14, 16; *with prep. inf.*: P. L. II. 60, 265; V. 787; VIII. 54; P. R. II. 397; S. A. 985, 1478; Il P. 176.

(2) *intr.* to make choice, elect: P. L. IX. 26; V. Ex. 29.

part. adj. chosen, selected, elect: P. L. I. 8; P. R. I. 427; II. 236; IV. 614; Ps. CXXXVI. 57.

part. absol. thy chosen, the Israelites: P. R. II. 45.

Choral, *adj.* (*a*) of a chorus: P. L. VII. 599.

(*b*) sung in chorus: P. L. V. 162.

Chord, *sb.* string of a harp: P. L. XI. 561.

Chorus, *sb.* song sung by a company of angels: P. L. VII. 275; by the chorus of the Greek tragedy: P. R. IV. 262.

Christ, *sb.* the Messiah: F. of C. 6.

Chrysolite, *sb.* precious stone of a green colour: P. L. III. 596.

Church, *sb.* the whole body of christians: P. L. IV. 193.

Cimmerian, *adj.* of the Cimmerii, a people said to live in perpetual darkness. Their abode was in Scythia (Herodotus IV. 12), or in Italy near Lake Avernus (Strabo V. 244): L'A. 10.

Cincture, *sb.* girdle or belt for the waist: P. L. IX. 1117.

Cinder, *sb. pl.* ashes: P. L. X. 570.

Cinnamon, *sb.* the tree *Cinnamomum zeylanicum*: C. 937.

Circe, *sb.* the sorceress who dwelt in the island of Ææa and transformed into beasts all who drank of her cup: C. 50, 153, 253, 522.

Circean, *adj.* of Circe: P. L. IX. 522.

Circle, (1) *sb.* (*a*) round, ring: P. L. VI. 305; polar circles, the arctic and antarctic circles: P. L. X. 681; in circles, in the form of rings: P. L. V. 631; in circle, in every direction round about: A. 15.

(*b*) orb of a heavenly body: P. L. IV. 578; S. VIII. 8.

(*c*) sphere of a heavenly body: P. L. VIII. 107.

(*d*) a series ending as it begins and perpetually repeated: P. L. V. 182.

(2) *vb. tr.* (*a*) to make the circuit of, move around: P. L. V. 862; IX. 65.

(*b*) to surround, encompass in the form of a ring: P. L. III. 626; V. 163; VI. 743; P. R. I. 171.

part. adj. circling, (*a*) encircling, surrounding: P. L. II. 647; IV. 146; VII. 580; S. A. 871; in the form of a circle: P. L. III. 556.

(*b*) moving in a circle, revolving: P. L. IX. 502; *fig. of time*: P. L. VI. 3; VII. 342; P. R. I. 57.

(*c*) approaching in a roundabout way: S. A. 871.

Circlet, *sb.* orb of a heavenly body, *here* of the planet Venus, *fig.* as a crown: P. L. V. 169.

Circuit, *sb.* (*a*) circumference: P. L. III. 721; V. 595.

(*b*) space enclosed within certain limits, area: P. L. II. 1048; IV. 586; V. 287; VIII. 100, 304; IX. 323; P. R. III. 254; in circuit, in extent, as far as: P. L. VII. 266.

(*c*) action of going round, circular course: P. L. IV. 784.

(*d*) roundabout course, detour: P. L. VII. 301.

Circular, *adj.* (*a*) in the form of a circle: P. L. IX. 498; N. O. 110.

Circumcised, *part. absol.* the Israelites: S. A. 975.

Circumcision, *sb.* act of circumcising: P. R. III. 425.

Circumference, *sb.* (*a*) periphery: P. L. V. 510; VII. 231.

(*b*) that which is enclosed by the periphery: P. L. I. 286; VI. 256.

(*c*) extent, bound, enclosure: P. L. II. 353.

Circumfluous, *adj.* flowing around, surrounding: P. L. VII. 270.

Circumfuse, *vb. tr.* (*a*) to surround (*with water*): P. L. VII. 624.

(*b*) to spread about, disperse: P. L. VI. 778.

Circumscribe, *vb. tr.* (*a*) to draw a line round in order to mark out the limits of: P. L. VII. 226.

(*b*) to limit, restrict: P. L. V. 825.

Circumspection, *sb.* careful looking about, caution, wariness: P. L. II. 214; IV. 537; VI. 523.

Circumstance, *sb.* particulars, details: S. A. 1557.

Circumvent, *vb. tr.* to deceive, outwit, overreach: P. L. III. 152; IX. 259; S. A. 1115.

Citadel, *sb.* stronghold: P. L. IV. 49; *fig.*: P. L. I. 773.

Cited, *part. adj.* summoned: P. L. III. 327.

Citron, *sb. attrib.* (*a*) composed of citron-trees: P. L. V. 22.

(*b*) of the wood of the citron-tree: P. R. IV. 115.

City, *sb.* large and important town, usually a walled town: P. L. I. 498; II. 533; IX. 445; XI. 386, 655; XII. 44, 51, 340; P. R. II. 22, 300; III. 74, 261; IV. 363; S. A. 1194, 1449, 1561, 1596, 1655; L'A. 117; *with proper name in immediate or close context*: P. L. X. 424; XI. 410; XII. 342; P. R. II. 21; III. 285, 311, 340; IV. 44, 238; **capital city,** chief city, seat of government: P. L. II. 924; **Holy City,** Jerusalem: P. R. IV. 545; **City of God,** Jerusalem: Ps. LXXXVII. 9; **cities of men:** P. L. XI. 640; P. R. II. 470.

attrib. belonging to the city: P. R. IV. 243.

City-gate, *sb.* gate or door leading into a city: P. L. XI. 661.

Civil, *adj.* (1) pertaining to a citizen or citizens; (*a*) pertaining to the state in general: P. R. IV. 358; S. A. 1367.

(*b*) occurring within the state or between citizens: P. L. XI. 718.

(*c*) opposed to *religious* or *ecclesiastical*: P. L. XII. 231; S. A. 853; S. XVII. 10; F. of C. 5.

(2) well-mannered, polite, gentle: P. L. VI. 667; S. A. 1467.

Civility, *sb.* good-breeding, culture, refinement: P. R. IV. 83.

Civil-suited, *adj.* clothed in sober or grave attire: Il P. 122.

Claim, (1) *sb.* demand of a supposed right: P. L. XI. 258.

(2) *vb.* (*pres. 2d sing.* claim'st: P. L. II. 817) *tr.* (*a*) to ask for or demand as a right, assert as one's own: P. L. I. 533; II. 32, 38, 817; IV. 487; V. 723; IX. 566, 1130; XII. 35, 170.

(*b*) to be entitled to: P. L. IX. 566.

(*c*) to reclaim: P. L. XII. 170.

Clamour, (1) *sb.* outcry, vociferation, loud noise: P. L. II. 862; VI. 208; VII. 36; P. R. II. 148; *of water*: P. L. XI. 853.

(2) *vb. tr.* to salute noisily: S. A. 1621.

Clamorous, *adj.* vociferous, noisy: P. L. X. 479.

Clan, *sb.* tribe, family, *fig. of atoms*: P. L. II. 901.

Clang, *sb.* (*a*) loud resonant sound of a trumpet: N. O. 157.

(*b*) the cry of birds: P. L. VII. 422; XI. 835.

Clarion, *sb.* shrill-sounding trumpet: P. L. I. 532; *fig.* crowing of a cock: P. L. VII. 443.

Clash, *vb.* (1) *intr.* to strike against each other with a confused broken metallic sound: P. L. VI. 209.

(2) *tr. with object of result*: P. L. I. 668.

Clasp, *vb. tr.* to embrace, enfold: P. L. X. 918.

part. adj. **clasping,** embracing, enfolding: P. L. IX. 217; C. 853.

See **Thunder-clasping.**

Classic, *adj.*: F. of C. 7. *See* **Hierarchy.**

Clattered, *part. adj.* struck so as to rattle: S. A. 1124.

Clay, *sb.* earth as the material of the human body: P. L. IX. 176; X. 743; N. O. 14.

attrib. made of earth: P. R. I. 501; C. 339.

Cleansing, *part. adj.* making clean, purifying: S. A. 1727.

Clear, (1) *adj.* (*a*) bright, shining, luminous: P. L. III. 595; XI. 844; L'A. 126; S. XXIII. 12.

(*b*) transparent, pellucid: P. L. III. 28; IV. 458; VII. 619; S. A. 550; C. 722; Ps. LXXXVII. 28; CXIV. 9.

(*c*) free from mist or haze, cloudless: P. L. III. 620.

(*d*) *of the eyes or the faculty of sight,* perfect: P. L. IX. 706; *comp.*: P. L. XI. 413; free (*of*): S. XXII. 1.

(*e*) *sup.* most distinct to the eye: P. L. XI. 379.

(*f*) free from sin, innocent, pure: P. L. IV. 119; C. 381, 457; L. 70.

(*g*) serene, cheerful: P. L. V. 733; VIII. 336.

(*h*) certain, evident, unmistakable: P. L. II. 770.

(*i*) sounding distinctly, ringing: Il P. 163.

(2) *adv.* clearly, plainly, distinctly: P. L. IX. 681; XII. 376; Ps. LXXXI. 1.

(3) *vb. tr.* (*a*) to free from doubt or uncertainty: P. L. V. 136; VIII. 179; from obstructions: P. L. III. 188.

(*b*) to make keen (*the eyesight*): P. L. IX. 708.

(*c*) to free from the imputation of, *with* from: S. XV. 12.

(*d*) **clear up**, make to sound distinctly, make ring: P. R. IV. 437.

Clearly, *adv.* plainly, distinctly: F. of C. 19.

Cleave, *vb.* (*pret.* cleft: P. R. III. 438; *past part.* cloven: P. L. VI. 361; L. 34; cleft: P. L. XI. 440) *tr.* to part, divide, split: P. L. VI. 361; P. R. III. 436, 438; Ps. CXXXVI. 45.

part. adj. (*a*) **cleaving**, clinging: S. A. 1039.

(*b*) **cleft** and **cloven**, divided: P. L. XI. 440; L. 34.

Cleombrotus, *sb.* a philosopher of Ambracia in Epirus: P. L. III. 473.

Clepe *vb.* (*past part.* ycelpt) *tr.* to name: L'A. 12.

Cliff, *sb.* precipitous rock, crag: P. L. IV. 547; V. 275; VII. 424; XII. 639; *with proper name*: P. L. I. 517; P. R. III. 317. *See* **Delphian.**

Climate, *sb.* region considered with reference to its atmospheric conditions: P. L. IX. 45; XI. 274.

Climb, *vb.* (*pres. 2d sing.* climb'st: P. L. V. 173; *pret.* clomb: P. L. IV. 192; *past part. not used*) (1) *intr.* (*a*) to raise oneself by the aid of hands and feet, creep up: P. L. IV. 191, 192, 193; L. 115; *with* up: P. L. X. 559.

(*b*) to ascend toward the zenith, *of the sun*: P. L. V. 173.

(*c*) to creep up by the aid of tendrils: P. L. IX. 217.

(*d*) to slope up, *with* up: P. L. XI. 119.

(*e*) to rise by continued moral effort: T. 19; C. 1020.

(2) *tr.* to ascend by means of the hands and feet: P. L. IV. 548.

See **High-climbing.**

Clime, *sb.* (*a*) climate: P. L. I. 242, 297; XII. 636.

(*b*) region, realm: P. L. II. 572;

v. 1; VII. 18; X. 678; XI. 708; A. 24; C. 977; S. VIII. 8.

Cling *vb.* (*past part.* clung) *intr.* to adhere closely: P. L. X. 512.

Clip, *vb. tr.* to cut away a part of, *fig.*: F. of C. 17.

Clod, *sb.* lump of earth, applied depreciatively to the human body: P. L. X. 786; *pl.* soil of the earth: P. L. VII. 463; lump (*of iron*): P. L. XI. 565.

Clog, *sb.* that which impedes progress, encumbrance: S. XII. 1.

Cloister, *sb.* covered walk or arcade connected with a college or cathedral: Il P. 156.

Close, I. *sb.* (1) end, termination: S. A. 651, 1748.

(2) conclusion of a musical phrase: N. O. 100; C. 548.

II. *adj. or adv.* (1) secret, hidden, secluded: P. L. I. 646, 795; II. 485; IV. 708; Il P. 139.

(2) intimate, confidential: P. L. IV. 376.

(3) shut up, having no opening, tight: C. 349; *hence*, stifling: S. A. 8.

(4) very near: P. L. II. 1053; IV. 347, 405, 800; V. 36; X. 589; P. R. II. 28.

(5) near together, in a compact group, (or possibly close to the wind (?)): P. L. II. 638.

(6) compact in texture, *fig.*: S. XI. 2.

(7) securely hidden, concealed: P. L. IX. 191.

III. *vb.* (1) *tr.* (*a*) to bring to a close, conclude: P. L. III. 144.

(*b*) to shut: P. L. V. 673; VI. 235; VIII. 459, 460; XI. 419; S. I. 5; **close up**, shut in, confine: C. 197; **close round**, enclose, encompass: P. R. IV. 481.

(2) *intr.* (*a*) to join in fight, fight hand to hand: P. L. II. 537.

(*b*) to unite, come together: P. L. IV. 863; VI. 330, 436, 875; L. 51.

Close-banded, *adj.* secretly leagued: S. A. 1113.

Close-curtained, *adj.* with curtains tightly drawn: C. 554.

Clot, *vb. intr.* to become gross or defiled: C. 467.

part. adj. **clotted**, coagulated: S. A. 1728.

Clothe, *vb.* (*pret.* clothed: P. L. X. 1059; clad: P. L. V. 278; VII. 315; X. 216; P. R. II. 65; S. XIV.

10; *past part.* clothed : P. L. I.
86; II. 226; clad : P. L. I. 410;
IV. 289, 599; X. 450; XI. 17, 240;
P. R. II. 299; III. 313; S. A.
129, 1317, 1616; D. F. I. 58; M.
W. 73; A. 92; C. 421) *tr.* (*a*) to
cover with clothing : P. L. X. 216,
219, 1059; XI. 240; P. R. II. 299;
S. A. 1317, 1616; D. F. I. 58.
(*b*) to cover or equip with
armour : P. R. III. 313; S. A.
129; *fig.* : C. 421.
(*c*) to cover as with clothing,
invest : P. L. I. 86, 410; IV. 289,
599; V. 278; VII. 315; X. 450;
XI. 17; M. W. 73; A. 92; S.
XIV. 10; XX. 7.
(*d*) to put into words, express :
P. L. II. 226; P. R. II. 65; V.
Ex. 32.
   vbl. sb. **clothing**, raiment, apparel : V. Ex. 82.
   See **Rich-clad, Sun-clad.**
Cloud, (1) *sb.* (*a*) visible mass of condensed vapour floating in the
upper air : P. L. II. 525, 637,
936; IV. 500, 544, 597; V. 86,
189, 257, 642; VI. 56; VII. 287,
422; VIII. 146; X. 449, 1073; XI.
670, 739, 841, 896; XII. 77,
545; P. R. I. 81; III. 222; IV.
410, 429, 619; Cir. 4; serving as
a guide to the Israelites : P. L.
XII. 202, 203, 208, 256; frequently
with adj. indicating some characteristic : P. L. II. 488, 714, 936;
IV. 151; VII. 247; X. 702; XI.
205, 229, 706, 865, 882; P. R. I.
41; IV. 321; N. O. 146, 159;
Il P. 72, 125; C. 221, 301, 333;
*with some degree of personifica-
tion*: N. O. 50; P. 56; L'A. 62,
74.
(*b*) anything that obscures or
overcasts, *of night* : P. L. V.
686; *of incense* : P. L. VII. 599;
of fragrance : P. L. IX. 425; that
by which God obscures his glory :
P. L. II. 264; III. 378, 385; VI.
28; X. 32; state of darkness or
obscurity : P. L. III. 45.
(*c*) anything that overshadows
with gloom or trouble : P. L. III.
262; XI. 45; S. XVI. 1.
(*d*) multitude, innumerable number (*of warriors*) : P. L. VI. 539;
P. R. III. 327; (*of locusts*) : P. L.
I. 340; XII. 185.
   (**2**) *vb. tr.* to cover as with a
cloud, overspread with gloom :
P. L. V. 122.

part. adj. **clouded** ; (*a*) overspread by a cloud : P. L. XII.
333.
(*b*) concealed or hidden by a
cloud : P. L. IV. 607.
Cloudless, *adj.* without a cloud :
S. A. 1696.
Cloudy, *adj.* (*a*) of the clouds or
composed of clouds, **cloudy
chair** : P. L. II. 930; C. 134;
cloudy red, red clouds : N. O.
230; **cloudy shrine** : P. L. VII.
360; **cloudy tabernacle** : P. L.
VII. 248; **cloudy throne** : D. F.
I. 56.
(*b*) dark : P. L. VI. 409.
(*c*) dim as a cloud, not distinctly seen : P. L. V. 266.
(*d*) dense as a cloud : P. L. VI.
107.
(*e*) gloomy (*in countenance*) :
P. L. VI. 450.
Clouted, *part. adj.* patched : C.
635.
Cloy, *vb. tr.* to surfeit, weary : Ps.
LXXXVIII. 9.
   See **Over-cloy.**
Cluster, (1) *sb.* (*a*) collection of
things of the same kind growing
closely together, bunch : P. L. V.
218; C. 296.
(*b*) number of bees gathered
together into a close body : P. L.
I. 771.
(**2**) *vb. intr.* to grow in a mass,
of hair : P. L. IV. 303; S. A.
569.
part. adj. **clustering,** (*a*) hanging in masses, *of hair* : C. 54.
(*b*) growing luxuriantly in
masses or bearing fruit in
bunches : P. L. VII. 320.
Clymene, *sb.* the wife of Merops of
Ethiopia and the mother of
Phaethon by Apollo : P. R. II.
186.
Coal, *sb.* (*a*) ignited residue of
burned wood : P. R. II. 273.
(*b*) the mineral : P. L. V. 440.
Coaly, *adj.* serving as a highway for
vessels carrying coal : V. Ex. 98.
Coarse, *adj.* rough, wanting firmness
and smoothness : C. 749.
Coast, (1) *sb.* (*a*) sea-shore, *with proper adj.* : P. L. I. 306; V. 340;
X. 293; P. R. II. 347.
(*b*) bank (*of a river*) : P. R. I.
119.
(*c*) district or region *in earth,
air, hell, or heaven* : P. L. I. 340;
II. 633; III. 487; VI. 529; X. 89;

I. 464; II. 464; III. 739; VIII. 245.

(d) border, frontier: P. L. IX. 67; (of darkness): II. 958.

(2) vb. tr. (a) to go by the side of: P. L. III. 71.

(b) to make the round of, explore: P. L. IV. 782.

(c) to sail by the coast of, skirt the shore of: C. 49.

Coat, sb. (a) defensive armour covering the upper part of the body, **adamantine coat**: P. L. VI. 542; **coat of mail**: P. R. III. 312.

(b) natural covering of fruit: P. L. V. 341; of animals: P. L. VII. 406; X. 218.

Cock, sb. full grown male of the common domestic fowl: P. L. VII. 443; L'A. 49, 114; C. 346.

Cocytus, sb. a river of hell: P. L. II. 579.

Co-eternal, adj. equally eternal: P. L. III. 2.

Coffer, sb. chest where treasures are kept, fig.: V. Ex. 31.

Cogitation, sb. reflection, meditation: P. L. III. 629.

Cohort, sb. (a) tenth part of a Roman legion: P. R. IV. 66.

(b) band of warriors: P. L. XI. 127.

Coin, sb. coined money, specie, fig.: S. A. 189, 1204; C. 739.

Cold, (1) adj. devoid of heat, not warm: P. L. I. 516; VII. 238; IX. 44, 636; X. 294, 686, 851, 1070; XI. 293; P. R. IV. 31, 403; C. 353, 802, 918; S. XVIII. 2.

(2) sb. (a) absence of heat: P. L. II. 595; X. 653, 691, 1056; XI. 544.

(b) one of the supposed qualities which in combination with another determined the nature, as 'complexion,' of a body, personified: P. L. II. 898.

Cold-kind, sb. prompted by kindness but accompanied with an absence of heat: D. F. I. 20.

Colic, adj. caused by the colic: P. L. XI. 484.

Colkitto, sb.: S. XI. 9. See **Macdonnel**.

Collateral, adj. placed side by side, concurrent: P. L. VIII. 426; X. 86.

Colleague (colléague), sb. associate, coadjutor, fig.: P. L. X. 59.

Collect, vb. tr. (a) to gather, bring together: P. R. IV. 328.

(b) to summon up, bring into action: P. L. IV. 986; P. R. III. 5.

(c) to infer, conclude, with clause: P. R. IV. 524.

part. **collected**, self-possessed, composed: P. L. VI. 581; IX. 673.

Collision, sb. act of forcibly striking together: P. L. X. 1072.

Colloquy, sb. conversation: P. L. VIII. 455.

Colonel, sb. superior officer of a regiment: S. VIII. 1.

Colour, (1) sb. (a) hue, dye: P. L. I. 546; III. 612; IV. 149; V. 24, 283; VI. 352, 759; VII. 318; IX. 577; X. 870; XI. 866; C. 300.

(b) complexion: P. R. II. 176.

(c) specious or plausible reason as serving to conceal the truth: S. A. 901.

(2) vb. tr. to mark with colour, dye: P. L. IV. 702; VII. 455; P. 32.

part. adj. **coloured**, having a colour: P. L. III. 642; XI. 879.

See **Sapphire-coloured**, **Triple-coloured**.

Columbus, sb. the discoverer of America: P. L. IX. 1116.

Column, sb. cylindrical body (of fire): S. A. 27.

Colure, sb. one of the two great circles which intersect each other at right angles at the poles, and pass, the one through the equinoctial, the other through the solstitial points of the ecliptic: P. L. IX. 66.

Comb, sb. article used for arranging the hair: C. 880.

Combat, (1) sb. single fight, duel: P. L. I. 766; S. A. 1176.

(2) vb. (a) tr. to oppose in single fight: S. A. 1152; fig. to oppose in argument: S. A. 864.

(b) intr. to fight: P. L. VI. 315; S. A. 1106.

Combatant, sb. warrior: P. L. II. 719; S. A. 344.

Combine, vb. (1) tr. to join or unite in action or relation: P. L. II. 750; VIII. 394.

(2) intr. to unite together for some end, co-operate: S. A. 1048.

part. absol. **combined**, two persons being or acting together: P. L. IX. 339.

Combustible, adj. inflammable: P L. I. 233.

Combustion, *sb.* destruction by fire, conflagration : P. L. I. 46 ; VI. 225.

Come, *vb.* (*pres.* 2*d sing.* comest : P. L. IV. 824 ; VI. 159 ; P. R. I. 410 ; III. 298 ; *pret.* came ; 2*d sing.* cam'st : P. L. IX. 563 ; S. A. 1227, 1332 ; D. F. I. 52 ; C. 497 ; *past part.* come ; *perf. tenses formed with the auxiliary* be : P. L. V. 138, 291 ; IX. 413 ; XI. 260 ; P. R. II. 43 ; III. 397 ; IV. 615 ; S. A. 205, 1088 ; N. O. 90 ; U. C. I. 12 ; II. 23 ; *with* have : P. L. IV. 923 ; XI. 344 ; S. A. 444), *intr.* (1) to move towards, approach, draw near, arrive : P. L. I. 379, 419, 438, 446, 457, 490 ; II. 508, 822, 970 ; III. 231, 232, 469, 520 ; IV. 131, 167, 469, 564, 580, 824, 869, 918, 923 ; v. 291, 372, 378 ; VI. 75, 159, 540, 610, 648 ; VIII. 295, 298 ; X. 107, 109, 276, 309, 330 ; XI. 233, 437, 719, 735 ; XII. 258, 361, 393 ; P. R. I. 22, 24, 75, 246, 273, 297, 410, 412, 484 ; III. 298 ; IV. 442 ; S. A. 326, 725, 733, 851, 1070, 1074, 1227, 1321, 1332, 1342, 1397, 1441, 1449, 1624, 1692 ; U. C. I. 12 ; D. F. I. 52 ; M. W. 19, 28 ; L'A. 45 ; C. 168, 292, 488, 497, 502, 510, 943 ; L. 75, 90, 108 ; S. XXIII. 9 ; Ps. VI. 23 ; LXXXV. 55 ; LXXXVI. 30 ; Petr. 5 ; (*a*) *with prep. inf. of purpose* : P. L. v. 770, 781 ; VII. 209 ; X. 96, 349 ; XI. 260, 344, 704 ; XII. 160, 458 ; P. R. I. 368 ; II. 375 ; S. A. 112, 180, 1076, 1088 ; N. O. 90 ; C. 35 ; L. 3.

(*b*) *with the purpose joined by* and : P. L. VIII. 372 ; IX. 610 ; S. A. 1448.

(*c*) *the accompanying action expressed by a following part.* : P. L. I. 522, 760 ; II. 663 ; IV. 555 ; V. 310 ; VI. 110, 536, 655 ; S. A. 337, 713 ; V. Ex. 62 ; N. O. 47 ; M. M. 2 ; Il P. 98.

(*d*) *of emotions, events, etc.* with the idea of movement in space merged in other ideas : P. L. I. 66 ; IX. 366, 854 ; X. 854, 858 ; XI. 528 ; P. R. I. 199 ; S. A. 704, 1404, 1566.

(*e*) *periphrastically with prep. inf.* : P. L. VIII. 79 ; C. 735.

(*f*) *imper.* as an invitation or command to approach or act : P. L. IV. 841 ; IX. 1027 ; S. A. 1229,

1395, 1708 ; L'A. 11, 33 ; Il P. 31, 37 ; C. 125, 143, 491, 599, 806, 938, 956 ; Ps. LXXX. 11 ; LXXXIII. 13.

(2) to draw near in time, arrive : P. L. V. 493, 645 ; IX. 225 ; P. R. II. 43 ; III. 397, 398 ; IV. 146 ; U. C. II. 23.

(3) to come before the public, appear publicly : P. R. I. 271 ; II. 17, 32 ; Petr. 5.

(4) to become, get to be : P. L. III. 709 ; VIII. 277 ; IX. 563.

(5) to arise, spring : P. L. III. 464.

(6) to take place in the course of events, happen : P. L. XI. 114, 357, 366, 785 ; XII. 11 ; P. R. III. 204 ; S. A. 1262.

(7) *prep. inf. attrib.* which is to come, coming, future : P. L. XI. 815 ; XII. 584 ; P. R. I. 300 ; II. 112.

In combination with other words; (*a*) **come about,** attend to : V. Ex. 57.

(*b*) **come along,** move onward with one : S. A. 1316.

(*c*) **come back,** return : P. L. X. 814 ; C. 191.

(*d*) **come down,** descend : P. L. IV. 4, 9 ; VI. 252 ; XII. 51 ; P. R. IV. 615 ; *with a part. of the action* : N. O. 47 ; fall : S. A. 1650.

(*e*) **come forth,** advance out of a place : P. L. II. 507 ; V. 138 ; VII. 203, 475 ; IX. 197, 413 ; P. R. I. 331, 502 ; IV. 427 ; L'A. 97 ; *imper.* as a command to appear : P. L. X. 108.

(*f*) **come in sight,** be seen : P. L. XI. 19.

(*g*) **come into,** enter : P. L. V. 118, 756 ; P. R. I. 409 ; yield oneself to : S. A. 258 ; **come and go into,** enter and leave : P. L. V. 118.

(*h*) **come off,** escape : S. A. 1380 ; C. 191.

(*i*) **come on,** approach, advance : P. L. IV. 598 ; VII. 583 ; VIII. 484 ; XI. 584 ; S. A. 1304 ; with hostile intent : P. L. I. 354 ; II. 715 ; VI. 609 ; be sent or offered to : P. L. XII. 600 ; *said of the descent and operation of the Holy Ghost upon the Virgin Mary* : P. R. I. 138.

(*j*) **come onward,** advance : P. L. II. 675 ; V. 298 ; VI. 768.

(*k*) **come out of,** issue from a source : P. L. XI. 454.

(*l*) **come o'er,** reach across, cover : P. L. V. 279.

(*m*) **come to hand,** be within reach : P. L. XI. 436 ; S. A. 142.

(*n*) **come to nought,** fail to succeed : P. R. I. 181.

(*o*) **come to pass,** happen, befall : P. L. X. 38 ; S. A. 444 ; V. Ex. 45.

(*p*) **come to parle,** reach an agreement, be reconciled : S. A. 785.

(*q*) **come round,** return with the revolution of time : Ps. LXXXI. 12.

(*r*) **come short,** fail, *with prep. inf.* : P. L. VIII. 414.

(*s*) **come unto** or **upon,** happen or befall to : S. A. 205, 1681 ; V. Ex. 9.

vbl. sb. **coming,** approach, arrival : P. L. XII. 405 ; *with* of : P. L. IV. 7 ; *with poss. pron.* : P. L. IV. 471 ; VI. 768 ; VIII. 46 ; IX. 647 ; X. 104 ; XI. 250 ; P. R. I. 71, 494 ; IV. 204 ; S. A. 187, 1395, 1452 ; C. 954 ; **coming-on,** approach (*of*) : P. L. IV. 646.

Comeliness, *sb.* beauty : P. L. VIII. 222 ; S. A. 1011.

Comely, *adj.* (*a*) beautiful, graceful : P. L. IX. 668 ; C. 75.

(*b*) pleasing, agreeable : S. A. 1268.

(*c*) of quiet beauty, decent, decorous : Il P. 125.

Comer, *sb.* one who comes : P. L. IX. 1097.

Comet, *sb.* blazing star : P. L. II. 708 ; XII. 634.

Comfort, (1) *sb.* that which ministers to content and enjoyment : P. L. X. 1084.

(2) *vb.* to console, solace : Ps. LXXXVI. 64.

Comfortable, (cómfórtáble) *adj.* agreeable or grateful to the senses : P. L. X. 1077.

Comforter, *sb.* the Holy Spirit : P. L. XII. 486.

Comfortless, *adj.* disconsolate, inconsolable : P. L. XI. 760.

Command, I. *sb.* (1) order, mandate, charge : P. L. I. 566 ; II. 856 ; IV. 524, 864 ; V. 691, 806 ; VI. 61, 781 ; VII. 294 ; X. 430 ; XI. 818 ; P. R. IV. 556 ; S. A. 1212, 1337, 1371, 1372, 1394, 1404, 1640 ; *of the mandate regarding the forbidden fruit* : P. L. III. 94 ; V. 551 ; VII. 47 ; VIII. 232, 329, 635 ; IX. 652.

(*a*) **at command,** ready to receive or obey orders, at one's

service : P. L. III. 650 ; VIII. 371 ; P. R. II. 149.

(*b*) **by command,** in accordance with an order : P. L. V. 685 ; XII. 210 ; **by command of** or **from,** in accordance with an order given by : P. L. I. 752 ; II. 851 ; C. 41.

(*c*) **in command,** as a mandate, as something to be absolutely followed : P. R. I. 449.

(2) sway, authority : S. A. 57.

II. *vb.* (*pres.* 2d *sing.* command'st : P. L. IX. 570), (1) *tr.* to order, enjoin : P. L. IX. 570 ; *with clause* : P. L. I. 531 ; P. R. I. 342 ; *with sentence obj.* : P. L. VI. 557 ; XII. 265 ; *with acc. and prep. inf.* : P. L. V. 768 ; IX. 1156 ; *with acc. and* to : P. L. IV. 747 ; *absol.* : P. L. V. 699 ; IX. 652 ; S. A. 852.

(2) to order to go : P. R. IV. 631.

(3) to order to appear : P. R. II. 384.

(4) to have at one's bidding, have at disposal : P. R. II. 382.

(5) to have within range of vision, overlook, *absol.* : P. L. III. 614 ; XI. 385.

part. adj. **commanding,** authoritative : Ps. VIII. 19.

See **All-commanding.**

Commander, *sb.* chief, leader : P. L. I. 358, 589.

Commandment, *sb.* command of God : P. R. IV. 176.

Commend, *vb. tr.* (*a*) to commit, entrust : C. 831.

(*b*) to praise, express approbation of : P. L. IX. 754 ; S. A. 247 ; L'A. 124.

Commerce, *vb. intr.* to hold intercourse or communication (*with*) : Il P. 39.

Commiseration, *sb.* compassion, pity : P. L. X. 940.

Commission, *sb.* command, instruction : P. L. VII. 118.

Commit, *vb. tr.* (*a*) to entrust, consign : P. L. X. 957 ; P. R. I. 111 ; II. 233 ; IV. 95 ; S. A. 47, 1000 ; C. 25.

(*b*) to be guilty of or perpetrate *an error* : P. L. VIII. 26 ; *a crime* : S. A. 1185.

(*c*) to place in hostility, join together wrongly : S. XIII. 4.

Commodiously, *adv.* conveniently, comfortably : P. L. X. 1083.

Common, *adj.* (*a*) belonging equally to more than one, shared alike

by all : P. L. VIII. 583, 597 ; S.
A. 777, 856, 1416 ; **in common,**
all together, in a body : P. L.
VII. 426.

(b) free to all, public : P. L. IV.
752 ; S. A. 6, 1161.

(c) of frequent occurrence,
usual : P. L. V. 435 ; S. A. 777.

(d) not of superior excellence,
ordinary : P. L. II. 371 ; S. A.
674.

(e) unclean : P. L. IX. 931.

Commonalty, sb. general body of the
community, common people, fig.
of ants : P. L. VII. 489.

Commotion, sb. (a) physical disturbance, tumult : P. L. IV. 992 ; VI.
310, 706.

(b) mental agitation, excitement : P. L. VIII. 531.

Commune, vb. (1) tr. to confer, consult, with clause : P. L. IX. 201.

(2) intr. to hold intercourse
with oneself, soliloquize : P. R.
II. 261.

Communicable, adj. that may be
imparted (to another) : P. L. VII.
124 ; P. R. I. 419 ; III. 125.

Communicate, vb. tr. to impart, give :
P. L. V. 72 ; VIII. 150 ; IX. 755.

Communication, sb. converse, personal intercourse : P. L. VIII.
429.

Communion, sb. fellowship : P. L. V.
637 ; VIII. 431.

Compact, part. adj. composed or
consisting (of) ; P. L. IX. 635.

Companion, sb. one who associates
with another ; (a) comrade, mate :
P. L. V. 673 ; VI. 419.

(b) sharer or partaker (of) : P.
L. I. 76 ; VI. 907 ; P. R. I. 398.

Company, sb. (a) companionship,
fellowship : P. L. VIII. 446 ; S. A.
1413 ; C. 508.

(b) collect. persons with whom
one is associated, companions :
C. 274.

Compare, (1) sb. comparison : P. L.
V. 467 ; **above compare** : P. L. VI.
705 ; S. A. 556 ; **beyond compare** :
P. L. I. 588 ; III. 138 ; IX. 228.

(2) vb. tr. to estimate by con-
sidering the relative qualities,
bring into comparison : P. L. VI.
170 ; S. A. 464 ; with to : P. L. V.
306 ; P. R. II. 348 ; S. A. 1020 ;
with with : P. L. II. 921 ; III.
592 ; V. 432 ; VIII. 18 ; P. R. I.
200 ; IV. 346, 563 ; S. A. 441.

Comparison, sb. **in comparison of,**

considered with reference to :
P. L. VIII. 92.

Compass, (1) sb. (a) instrument for
describing circles : P. L. VII. 225.

(b) instrument employed in the
guidance of a ship's course at sea :
P. L. IV. 559.

(c) space, area : P. R. IV. 51.

(d) bounds, limits, scope : V.
Ex. 56.

(e) circular course, circuit :
P. L. VIII. 33.

(2) vb. tr. (a) to encircle, surround, with round : P. L. II. 862 ;
VII. 27 ; XI. 352.

(b) to go round, make the circuit of : P. L. IX. 59.

(c) to bring round in the resolution of time : P. R. I. 58.

(d) to achieve, accomplish : P.
L. III. 342 ; S. A. 1477.

Compassion, sb. pity : P. L. III.
141 ; XI. 496.

Compeer, sb. companion, associate :
P. L. I. 127 ; IV. 974.

Compel, vb. tr. to constrain, force :
P. L. XII. 175 ; with acc. and
prep. inf. : P. L. IV. 391 ; IX. 609 ;
C. 275 ; sing. with compound sub-
ject : L. 7 ; with acc. and to :
P. L. VI. 619 ; absol. : C. 643.

Competition, sb. rivalry : S. A. 476.

Complacence, sb. (a) pleasure, delight : P. L. VIII. 433.

(b) concr. object of pleasure and
satisfaction : P. L. III. 276.

Complain, vb. intr. (a) to murmur,
with clause : P. L. II. 550 ; **complain
of,** to murmur against, express
discomfort because of : S. A. 46,
67 ; **complain on,** bewail, lament
because of : Hor. O. 6.

(b) to murmur at : S. A. 157.

Complaint, sb. lamentation : P. L. X.
131, 719 ; S. A. 662.

Complete (cómplete : C. 421), (1)
adj. (a) perfect, without defect :
P. L. V. 352 ; VIII. 548.

(b) fully equipped : P. R. IV.
283 ; S. A. 558 ; or adv. completely
(punctuation of first edition supports the former) (?) : P. L. X. 10.

(c) full, entire : M. W. 12 ; C. 421.

(2) vb. tr. to make perfect, furnish completely : P. L. XI. 618.

vbl. sb. **completing,** completion
or consummation (of) : P. L. IX.
1003.

Complexion (tetrasyl.), sb. colour
and texture of the skin of the
face : C. 749.

Compliance, *sb.* (*a*) complaisance : P. L. VIII. 603.

(*b*) acquiescence, assent : P. L. IX. 994 ; S. A. 1411.

Compliant, *adj.* yielding to physical pressure : P. L. IV. 332.

Complicated, *part. adj.* complex in form : P. L. X. 523.

Compliment, *sb.* cermonious flattery: P. R. IV. 124.

Comply, *vb. intr.* to yield, accede, consent: S. A. 1408 ; *with* with : A. 38.

Compose, *vb. tr.* (*a*) to fashion, frame : P. L. II. 111.

(*b*) to be the material of, constitute: P. L. I. 483 ; *fig.* : P. R. I. 407.

(*c*) to adjust, settle, arrange : P. L. II. 281.

(*d*) to calm, tranquillize, pacify : P. L. VI. 469 ; XII. 596 ; P. R. II. 108.

Composition, *sb.* agreement for cessation of hostilities : P. L. VI. 613 ; P. R. IV. 529.

Composure, *sb.* (*a*) agreement : P. L. VI. 560.

(*b*) tranquillity, calmness: P. L. IX. 272.

Comprehend, *vb.* (*a*) to grasp with the mind, understand : P. L. III. 705 ; VII. 114 ; P. R. IV. 224.

(*b*) to contain, include, *fig.* : P. L. V. 505.

Compulsion, *sb.* constraint, coercion: P. L. II. 80 ; IX. 474 ; A. 68.

Compute, *vb. tr.* (*a*) to calculate, reckon : P. L. VI. 685 ; VIII. 16.

(*b*) to serve to distinguish : P. L. III. 580.

Comrade (comráde), *sb.* companion, mate : S. A. 1162.

Comus, *sb.* the sorcerer : C. 58, 522.

Concave, *sb.* vault of hell : P. L. I. 542 ; II. 635.

Conceal, *vb. tr.* to hide, keep secret : P. L. I. 641 ; IV. 123, 312 ; V. 207 ; VIII. 73 ; IX. 751 ; X. 130, 136 ; P. R. II. 96 ; IV. 474; S. A. 998 ; A. 13.

part. adj. **concealed,** hidden, secret : P. L. II. 187 ; C. 142.

Conceit, *sb.* (*a*) device, scheme : Ps. LXXXI. 51.

(*b*) fanciful idea : P. L. IV. 809 ; ingenious expression: P. R. IV. 295.

Conceive, *vb.* (1) *tr.* (*a*) to receive into the womb, become pregnant with : P. L. II. 766, 796 ; P. R.

I. 239 ; *fig.* : P. L. I. 234 ; S. A. 390.

(*b*) to take or admit into the mind, become possessed with : P. L. V. 666 ; VI. 787 ; IX. 449 ; S. A. 1506, 1574.

(*c*) to think of, imagine : P. L. II. 627 ; IX. 945.

(*d*) to receive : P. R. IV. 598.

(2) *intr.* to become pregnant : P. R. II. 67 ; *fig. of the earth* : P. L. VII. 281.

vbl. sb. **conceiving,** thought, imagination : W. S. 14.

Concent, *sb.* concord or harmony in music : S. M. 6.

Concentre, *vb. tr.* to bring together at a centre : P. L. IX. 106.

Conception, *sb.* (*a*) action of conceiving or fact of being conceived, in the womb : P. L. X. 194, 987 : S. A. 1434.

(*b*) generation or formation *of minerals in the earth* : P. L. VI. 512.

Concern, *vb. tr.* (*a*) to relate to, be about : P. L. XII. 272.

(*b*) to have reference to, have a bearing upon, affect, involve : P. L. VII. 62 ; VIII. 174 ; P. R. I. 440 ; IV. 205 ; S. A. 1420, 1551 ; *absol.* : P. L. VIII. 196.

(*c*) to be of importance to, be the business of : P. L. V. 721 ; VII. 82 ; X. 170 ; XI. 144 ; XII. 599 ; P. R. I. 293 ; *impers. with phrase or clause as real subject* : P. R. III. 198 ; IV. 205 ; S. A. 1148.

Concerning, *prep.* in reference to, about : P. L. X. 199 ; P. R. I. 261 ; IV. 557.

Concernment, *sb.* matter relating to a person, affair : S. A. 969.

Conclave, *sb.* close or private assembly (possibly with a covert allusion to the assembly of cardinals for the election of a Pope (?)) : P. L. I. 795.

Conclude, *vb.* (*pres. 2d sing.* conclud'st : P. R. II. 317), *tr.* (*a*) to come to a conclusion, infer : P. R. II. 317 ; *with clause* : P. L. IX. 1142 ; XII. 292.

(*b*) to lead to a conclusion, prove, *with two acc.* : P. L. X. 839.

Concoct, *vb. tr.* (*a*) to refine by heat : P. L. VI. 514.

(*b*) to digest, *absol.* : P. L. V. 412.

Concoctive, *adj.* digestive : P. L. v.
437.
Concord, *sb.* accord, agreement or
harmony between persons : P. L.
II. 497 ; III. 371 ; XII. 29 ; S. A.
1008 ; between things : P. L. VI.
311.
Concourse (concoúrse : P. R. IV.
404 ; *doubtful* : P. L. XI. 641), *sb.*
(*a*) hostile encounter : P. L. XI.
641.
(*b*) assemblage or meeting (*of
shades*) : P. R. IV. 404.
Concubine, *sb.* kept mistress : S. A.
537.
Concupiscence, *sb.* libidinous desire,
lust : P. L. IX. 1078.
Concur, *vb. intr.* to agree, co-operate,
help, *with prep. inf.* : P. L. X. 44 ;
with to : P. L. X. 747.
part. adj. concurring, that agree:
P. L. II. 831.
Condemn, *vb. tr.* (*a*) to censure,
blame : P. L. v. 813.
(*b*) to doom to punishment,
sentence: P. L. X. 82, 823 : P. R.
III. 213 ; S. A. 1224 ; *with prep.
inf.* : P. L. I. 607 ; II. 649 ; *with*
to : P. L. II. 29, 86 ; XII. 412 ;
S. A. 500.
vbl. sb. condemning, conviction:
S. A. 844.
See Self-condemning.
Condemnation, *sb.* (*a*) strong censure : S. A. 696.
(*b*) state of being found guilty :
P. R. III. 136.
Condense, (1) *adj.* condensed, dense :
P. L. VI. 353.
(*2*) *vb. tr.* (*a*) to reduce (*vapour*)
to a more compact form : P. L.
IX. 636.
(*b*) to contract, diminish : P. L.
I. 429.
Condescend, *vb. intr.* to yield or
stoop (*to*) : S. A. 1337.
Condescension, *sb.* gracious favour :
P. L. VIII. 9,'649.
Condition (cóndítión, *tetrasyl.* : C.
685), *sb.* (*a*) stipulation, terms of
a contract, provision : P. L. X.
759 ; P. R. IV. 166, 173 ; S. A.
258 ; C. 685.
(*b*) state, situation : P. L. III.
181; VIII. 176 ; IX. 322; S. A. 928.
Condole, *vb. tr.* to grieve over, bewail : S. A. 1076.
Conduct, (1) *sb.* (*a*) guidance : P. L.
IX. 630.
(*b*) leadership, command : P. L.
I. 130 ; VI. 777 ; P. R. III. 18.

(*2*) *vb. tr.* to lead, guide : P. L.
XII. 259 ; C. 319.
Cone, *sb.* shadowy cone, conical
shadow projected into space by
the earth on the side turned from
the sun : P. L. IV. 776.
Confer, *vb. tr.* (*a*) to bestow (*on* or
upon): P. L. IV. 430; P. R. I. 278;
S. A. 993.
(*b*) to discuss, consult about :
P. L. I. 774.
Conference, *sb.* discourse, conversation : P. L. v. 454.
Confess, *vb.* (1) *tr.* (*a*) to acknowledge, own or admit *a fault or
crime* : P. L. X. 1088, 1100 ; *with
clause* : S. A. 448.
(*b*) to admit, grant, concede :
S. A. 1183 ; *with two acc.* : S. A.
829 ; *with clause* : P. L. v. 329 ;
P. R. IV. 532 ; S. A. 1467 ; *with
prep. inf.* : P. L. VIII. 523.
(*c*) to acknowledge or recognize
formally : P. L. I. 509 ; P. R. I.
431 ; *with two acc.* : P. L. v. 608,
818.
(*2*) *intr.* to own a fault, admit
sin : P. L. X. 160 ; S. A. 753.
Confide, *vb. tr.* to communicate or
reveal in confidence: P. L. XI. 235.
Confidence, *sb.* (*a*) trust, reliance :
P. L. IX. 1056.
(*b*) assurance, security, certi-
tude : P. L. VI. 651 ; IX. 1175 ;
P. R. II. 140 ; C. 583 ; *with prep.
inf.* : P. L. VI. 343 ; in confidence
of : S. A. 1174.
Confident, *adj.* full of assurance,
without fear of failure : P. R. II.
211.
Confine, I. *sb.* (*a*) boundary, border :
P. L. X. 321.
(*b*) district, territory : P. L. II.
395 ; VI. 273.
II. *vb.* (1) *intr.* to have a
common frontier, confine with,
border on : P. L. II. 977.
(*2*) *tr.* (*a*) to shut up, restrain : P. L. X. 368 ; *with* to :
P. L. v. 78 ; XI. 341 ; P. R. I. 362 ;
S. A. 94, 501, 606 ; *with* in : P. L.
II. 859 ; C. 7.
(*b*) to enclose within limits : P.
L. III. 711.
(*c*) to keep within bounds, limit,
restrict : S. A. 307 ; P. 22.
Confirm, *vb. tr.* (*a*) to make firm,
establish : P. L. II. 353 ; XI. 71 ;
Ps. LXXXIII. 30.
(*b*) to corroborate, add support
to : P. L. I. 663.

(c) to assure, make certain : P.
L. IX. 830; XI. 355.
Conflagrant, *adj.* blazing : P. L. XII.
548.
Conflict, *sb.* battle : P. L. IV. 995 ;
VI. 212.
Conflicting, *part. adj.* fighting : P.
L. VI. 245.
Conflux, *sb.* crowd, throng : P. R.
IV. 62.
Conform, *vb. tr.* to bring into har-
mony, adapt, *with* to : P. L. II.
217.
Conformity, *sb.* agreement in nature
or character : P. L. XI. 606.
Confound, *vb. tr.* (a) to defeat
utterly, destroy, ruin : P. L. I. 53;
II. 382 ; VI. 315 ; X. 908 ; XII. 455.
(b) to spoil, corrupt, pollute :
P. L. II. 136.
(c) to discomfit, abash : P. L.
IX. 1064 ; N. O. 43 ; Ps. LXXXIII.
63.
(d) to throw into confusion : P.
L. II. 996 ; VI. 871 ; to confuse
the mind, perplex : P. R. III. 2.
(e) to mingle confusedly : P. L.
X. 665.
Confuse (cónfused : P. L. II. 615),
vb. tr. (a) to discomfit, abash : S.
A. 196.
(b) to throw into disorder,
mingle indistinguishably : P. L.
II. 952 ; VI. 249 ; P. R. III. 49 ;
Ariosto I. 3.
part. adj. **confused,** disordered :
P. L. II. 615.
Confusedly, *adv.* in disorder : P. L.
II. 914.
Confusion, *sb.* (a) ruin, overthrow,
destruction : P. L. I. 220 ; II. 372,
996 ; VI. 872 ; VII. 56 ; S. A. 471,
1058.
(b) mental discomfiture, shame :
Ps. VI. 22.
(c) commotion, tumult, disorder : P. L. II. 897 ; VI. 668,
669 ; X. 472; *personified* : P. L.
III. 710 ; as an attendant upon the
throne of chaos : P. L. II. 966 ;
in confusion, in a state of disorder or commotion : P. L. XII.
343 ; S. A. 1593.
(d) the English translation of
the Hebrew word for Babel, *here*
the name of the Tower of Babel
(*cf.* Gen. XI. 9) : P. L. XII. 62.
Confute, *vb. tr.* to silence in argument : P. R. III. 3.
Congealed (cóngealed), *part. adj.*
frozen : C. 449.

Conglobe, *vb.* (1) *tr.* to gather or
form into a sphere or round mass :
P. L. VII. 239.
(2) *intr.* : P. L. VII. 292.
Congo, *sb.* the chief kingdom of
Congo, or Manicongo, which included the whole of the western
part of lower Africa : P. L. XI.
401.
Congratulant, *adj.* expressing con-
gratulation : P. L. X. 458.
Congregated, *part. adj.* collected
into one place : P. L. VII. 308.
Congregation, *sb.* assembly, **the
Mountain of the congregation,** the
Mountain where the hosts of
heaven assembled as a nation to
hear the proclamation of God,
their sovereign : P. L. V. 766.
Conjecture, (1) *sb.* (a) forecast, prognostication : P. L. II. 123 ; P. R.
IV. 524.
(b) unverified supposition : P.L.
VIII. 76 ; P. R. IV. 292.
(2) *vb. tr.* (a) to conclude or infer
from appearances : P. L. VI.
545.
(b) to surmise, guess, suppose :
P. L. X. 1033 ; *with clause* : S. A.
1071.
Conjoin, *vb. tr.* to join together,
unite : S. A. 1666.
Conjugal, *adj.* matrimonial, connubial : P. L. IV. 493 ; VIII. 56 ; IX.
263 ; S. A. 739.
Conjunction, *sb.* (a) connection,
union : P. L. X. 898.
(b) apparent proximity of two
heavenly bodies : P. R. IV. 385.
Conjure, *vb. intr.* to swear together
in a conspiracy : P. L. II. 693.
Connatural, *sb.* (a) natural, innate :
P. L. X. 246.
(b) having the same nature : P.
L. XI. 529.
Connexion, *sb.* union, harmony :
P. L. X. 359.
Connive, *vb. intr.* to remain inactive :
P. L. X. 624 ; S. A. 466.
Connubial, *adj.* pertaining to mar-
riage : P. L. IV. 743.
Conquer, *vb. tr.* (a) to gain by con-
quest : P. L. IV. 391.
(b) to vanquish, overcome by
force of arms : P. L. IV. 134 ;
S. XVI. 10 ; H. B. 14 ; *fig.* : P. R.
I. 159, 222.
part. absol. **the conquered,**
those overcome by force of arms :
P. L. XI. 797 ; S. A. 1207.
See **All-conquering.**

Conqueror, *sb.* one who overcomes an adversary, victor: P. L. II. 208; XI. 695; P. R. III. 78, 99; S. A. 244; *of God*: P. L. I. 143; *preceded by def. art.* : P. L. I. 323; II. 338; *with proper name*: P. L. I. 472; Alexander the Great: P. R. II. 196; S. VIII. 10.

attrib. of death: P. R. III. 85.

Conquest, *sb.* (*a*) action of gaining by force of arms: P. R. III. 72, 370; *fig.* the spiritual conquest of sin and death by Christ: P. R. I. 154.

(*b*) that which is gained by force of arms, conquered country: Ps. II. 18; *fig.* the world as conquered by Satan: P. R. I. 46.

(*c*) victory or triumph by force of arms: P. L. II. 339, 543; VI. 37; P. R. II. 422; S. A. 1206; *fig.* Satan's conquest of the world: P. R. IV. 609.

Conscience (*trisyl.* : C. 212), *sb.* (*a*) consciousness, internal conviction, *with* of : P. L. VIII. 502; *with prep. inf.* : S. XXII. 10.

(*b*) faculty which pronounces upon the moral quality of one's motives or actions, approving the right and condemning the wrong: P. L. IV. 23; X. 842, 849; XII. 297, 522, 529; P. R. IV. 130; S. A. 1334; S. XVI. 13; F. of C. 6; *personified*: P. L. III. 195; C. 212.

Conscious, *adj.* (*a*) inwardly sensible or aware (*of*) : P. L. II. 429.

(*b*) knowing, sharing the knowledge with another, *of night* as privy to the secrets of Satan and his allies: P. L. VI. 521.

(*c*) sensible of wrong-doing, guilty: P. L. IX. 1050.

(*d*) felt, sensible: P. L. II. 801.

Consecrated, *part. adj.* dedicated to a sacred purpose, hallowed: P. R. I. 72; S. A. 1354; N. O. 189.

Consent, (1) *sb.* (*a*) voluntary allowance or acceptance of what is done or proposed by another: P. L. I. 640; II. 24; P. R. III. 358; C. 1007.

(*b*) accord, agreement: Il P. 95.

(2) *vb. intr.* (*a*) to agree, be in harmony: P. R. II. 130.

(*b*) to agree, comply or yield to something proposed: P. L. V. 555; S. A. 846; *with prep. inf.* : P. L. V. 121.

Consequence, *sb.* (*a*) that which follows from a preceding action, result: P. L. VIII. 328.

(*b*) dependence of cause and effect: P. L. X. 364.

Consider, *vb.* (1) *tr.* (*a*) to view attentively, observe, examine: P. L. IX. 84, 604.

(*b*) to contemplate mentally, give attentive thought to: P. R. I. 197; S. A. 245; *with clause*: P. L. VIII. 90; P. R. III. 231; S. XIX. 1.

(2) *intr.* to think deliberately, reflect: S. A. 1348.

Considerate, *adj.* thoughtful, circumspect: P. L. I. 603.

Consist, *vb. intr.* (*a*) to be congruous, agree: P. L. V. 793.

(*b*) **consist in,** be comprised in, be constituted of: P. L. VIII. 589; XI. 616; S. A. 780; C. 741.

(*c*) **consist of,** be composed of: P. L. VIII. 16.

Consistence, *sb.* matter dense enough to cohere: P. L. II. 941.

Consistory (cónsistory), *sb.* meeting of councillors, assembly (possibly with a covert allusion to the Consistory, or ecclesiastical senate, of the Roman Catholic Church (?)): P. R. I. 42.

Consolation, *sb.* comfort, solace: P. L. XI. 304; XII. 620; P. R. I. 403; S. A. 183, 664, 1757; *pl.* that which affords solace: P. L. XII. 495.

Consolatory, *sb.* epistle or book designed to convey solace: S. A. 657.

Consort (consórt: P. L. VII. 529), (1) *sb.* (*a*) partner, companion, mate: P. L. II. 963; IV. 448; VIII. 392; XII. 526.

(*b*) wife: P. L. IV. 610; VII. 529; P. R. I. 51.

(*c*) accord of sound, harmony: Il P. 145; harmony of musical instruments, *fig. of the music of the spheres*: N. O. 132.

(*d*) company of musicians making music together: S. M. 27.

(2) *vb. tr.* to join company, associate: P. L. IX. 954.

part. adj. **consorted,** joined as a wife: P. L. VII. 50.

Conspicuous, *adj.* (*a*) clearly visible, easy to be seen: P. L. III. 385; IV. 545; VI. 299; VII. 63; X. 107; XI. 866; P. R. IV. 53.

(b) noteworthy, remarkable: P. L. II. 258.

Conspiracy, sb. combination to excite an insurrection : P. L. II. 751.

Conspire, vb. intr. to combine privily for an evil purpose : P. L. XI. 426 ; Ps. LXXXIII. 25 ; with prep. inf. : S. A. 892.

Constancy, sb. steadfastness, faithfulness : P. L. IX. 367 ; P. R. II. 226 ; S. A. 1032.

Constant, adj. (a) invariable, unchanging : P. L. IV. 764.

(b) steadfast, unmoved, resolute: P. L. III. 104 ; V. 552, 902 ; X. 882 ; P. R. I. 148 ; C. 731 ; sup. : S. A. 848.

Constantine, sb. the first christian emperor, the giver of the " donation " to Pope Sylvester I. : Dante 1 ; Petr. 5 ; Ariosto II. 4.

Constellation, sb. group of fixed stars : P. L. III. 577 ; VI. 312 ; VII. 562 ; X. 411 ; N. O. 121 ; as influencing human life : P. L. VIII. 512.

Constrain, vb. tr. (a) to force, compel, oblige : P. L. IX. 1066 ; P. R. I. 331 ; S. A. 836 ; with acc. and prep. inf.: S. A. 1198 ; absol.: P. L. X. 568 ; S. A. 1369.

(b) to compel to go or enter, with to, into: P. L. IX. 164 ; S. A. 1370.

Constraint, sb. (a) fl. coercion, compulsion : S. A. 1372.

(b) compulsion of circumstances, necessity : P. L. II. 972 ; X. 132 ; L. 6.

Consult (consúlt), I. sb. meeting for consultation (possibly a secret meeting for purposes of intrigue. See N. E. D.) : P. L. I. 798.

II. vb. (1) intr. (a) to take counsel together, confer, deliberate : P. L. II. 164 ; P. R. IV. 577 ; Ps. LXXXIII. 17 ; with about : P. L. V. 768.

(b) to consider maturely or deliberate (on), of one person, God, deliberating with himself : P. L. VI. 673.

(c) to ask advice, crave direction, with at : P. R. I. 438 ; with from : P. R. III. 12.

(2) tr. (a) to confer about, discuss, consider : P. L. V. 779 ; with clause : P. L. I. 187.

(b) to ask advice of, seek counsel from : S. A. 1546.

part. adj. **consulting,** in the act

of deliberating, counselling: P. L. X. 456.

Consultation, sb. conference, deliberation : P. L. II. 486 ; VI. 445.

Consume, vb. tr. (a) to destroy by fire : P. L. XI. 442 ; Ps. LXXX. 65.

(b) to destroy or waste away by disease or sorrow : P. L. XI. 545, 778 ; S. A. 575.

(c) to destroy absolutely, annihilate : P. L. II. 96.

(d) to do away with by evaporation : P. L. V. 325.

(e) to eat up, devour, fig. : T. 10.

See **Self-consumed.**

Consummate (consúmmate : P. L. VIII. 556), (1) adj. complete, perfect : P. L. V. 481 ; VII. 502 ; of the highest quality, supreme : P. R. I. 165.

(2) vb. tr. to complete, perfect : P. L. VIII. 556.

Contagion, sb. fig. (a) corrupting contact : P. L. X. 544 ; morally : C. 467.

(b) moral corruption : P. L. V. 880 ; L. 127.

Contagious, adj. exciting like emotions in others : P. L. IX. 1036.

Contain, vb. tr. (a) to comprise, enclose, hold : P. L. V. 314, 362, 409 ; VIII. 93, 473 ; XII. 559 ; P. R. III. 11 ; S. A. 1494 ; to have capacity for : P. L. VII. 128.

Contemn, vb. tr. to hold in contempt, despise, scorn : P. L. VI. 432 ; IX. 306 ; X. 1015 ; P. R. II. 390, 448 ; IV. 304, 490, 537 ; S. A. 279, 943, 1281.

Contemplate (contémplate), vb. tr. to view attentively, gaze upon : P. R. I. 380.

Contemplation (cóntemplátión, pentasyl. : Il P. 54 ; C. 377), sb. (a) action of thinking about a thing continuously, attentive consideration, with of : P. L. V. 511.

(b) thought, meditation : P. L. IV. 297 ; P. R. IV. 214.

(c) devout meditation, religious musing, personified : Il P. 54 ; C. 377.

Contemplative, adj. given to thought or meditation : P. R. II. 81 ; IV. 370.

Contempt, sb. (a) action of despising, disdain : P. L. IV. 180 ; X. 1018 ; P. R. III. 131 ; S. A. 400 ; with of : P. L. X. 763, 1013 ; S. A. 494.

(*b*) state of being despised, dishonour, disgrace : S. A. 76, 1342, 1722 ; *pl.* : P. R. III. 191.

Contemptible, *adj.* despicable, mean: S. A. 572, 1361.

Contemptibly, *adv.* in a manner deserving contempt : P. L. VIII. 374.

Contemptuous, *adj.* disdainful, insolent, scornful : P. L. IV. 885 ; V. 671 ; S. A. 1462 ; C. 781.

Contend, *vb. intr.* (*a*) to endeavour, struggle : P. L. XI. 727.

(*b*) to strive in rivalry : P. L. II. 529 ; *with prep. inf.* : L'A. 123.

(*c*) argue, dispute : P. L. X. 958.

(*d*) to combat, fight : P. L. IV. 851 ; *with* with : P. L. I. 99 ; II. 687 ; VI. 169 ; IX. 163 ; *with* against : P. L. II. 203 ; *fig. of the fight between good and evil, with* with : P. L. XI. 359 ; P. R. III. 443.

Content (contént), (**1**) *sb. pl.* that which is contained in a writing, *fig.* : P. L. VI. 622.

(**2**) *adj.* (*a*) having the desires limited to present possessions, contented, satisfied: P. L. V. 727; VI. 461 ; XI. 180 ; P. R. III. 112, 170 ; S. X. 4 ; XXII. 14 ; *with* with : P L. I. 399 ; XII. 25.

(*b*) willing, *with prep. inf.* : S. A. 1403.

(*c*) pleased, *with prep. inf.* : S. A. 1399.

(**3**) *vb.* (*a*) *tr.* to satisfy : S. A. 1322.

(*b*) *refl.* to be satisfied : P. R. II. 256.

part. adj. **contented,** satisfied, desirous of nothing more, *with* with : P. L. III. 701 ; VI. 375 ; *with clause* : P. L. VIII. 177.

Contention, *sb.* combat, fight : P. L. I. 100.

Contentment, *sb.* pleasure, delight, gratification : P. L. VIII. 366 ; X. 973.

Contest (contést) (**1**) *sb.* (*a*) strife in arms, conflict : P. L. IV. 872 ; VI. 124 ; XI. 800 ; S. A. 461.

(*b*) strife in argument, contention, dispute : P. L. IX. 1189 ; S. A. 865.

(**2**) *vb. intr.* to strive in argument, dispute : P. L. X. 756.

Contiguous, *adj.* touching, adjoining, *following the sb.* : P. L. VI. 828 ; VII. 273.

Continent, *sb.* (*a*) continuous tract of land : P. L. III. 423 ; *in hell* : P. L. II. 587 ; *in heaven* : P. L. VI. 474 ; *of hell and the world* : P. L. X. 392.

(*b*) orb of the moon : P. L. V. 422.

Continual, *adj.* constant, unremitting : P. L. IX. 814.

Continue, *vb.* (*pres. 2d sing.* continuest : P. L. V. 521), (**1**) *tr.* to carry on in space, extend : P. L. II. 1029.

(**2**) *intr.* (*a*) to remain *in a place* : P. L. II. 314 ; S. A. 588 ; *in a state* : P. L. IV. 371 ; V. 521.

(*b*) to last, endure : S. A. 592.

(*c*) to go on doing, not to cease : P. L. IX. 138 ; XI. 744 ; S. A. 1516.

part. adj. **continued,** continuous in space : P. L. IV. 175 ; in a series, successive : P. L. IX. 63.

Contract, *vb. tr.* to collect, gather : S. A. 1062.

part. adj. **Contracted,** drawn together : P. L. VIII. 560.

Contraction, *sb.* action of becoming less in size, shrinking : P. L. VI. 597.

Contradict, *vb.* (**1**) *intr.* to speak in opposition : P. R. IV. 158.

(**2**) *absol.* to be directly opposed to, go counter to : S A. 301.

Contradiction, *sb.* (*a*) opposition, gainsaying : P. L. VI. 155.

(*b*) that which denies the truth of another thing or proves another thing to be false : S. A. 898.

(*c*) self-contradictory statement : P. L. X. 799 ; U. C. II. 13.

Contrarious, *adj.* characterized by contradictory acts : S. A. 669.

Contrary (contráry : S. A. 972), (**1**) *adj.* opposite, contradicting that which preceded : S. A. 972.

(**2**) *sb.* (*a*) **the contrary,** the exact opposite of that just mentioned : S. A. 1037 ; that which is in direct opposition : P. L. I. 161.

(*b*) **contraries,** things directly opposed to each other : P. L. IX. 122.

(**3**) *adv.* (*a*) in opposite directions : P. L. VIII. 132.

(*b*) on the other hand, instead : P. L. X. 506 ; P. R. I. 126 ; IV. 382.

Contribute (cóntribúte), *vb. tr.* to supply, furnish : P. L. VIII. 155.

Contrite (contríte) *adj.* crushed in spirit by a sense of sin, extremely penitent, humble : P. L. x. 1091, 1103 ; xi. 90 ; S. A. 502.

Contrition, *sb.* penitence for sin : P. L. xi. 27.

Contrive, *vb.* (1) *tr.* to devise, invent : P. L. ii. 53 ; v.' 334 ; ix. 139 ; x. 1034 ; xi. 732 ; Ps. lxxxiii. 9 ; *with prep. inf.* : P. L. viii. 81.
(2) *intr.* to lay schemes, form devices : P. L. ii. 54.

Control, (1) *sb.* check, restraint : P. L. v. 803.
(2) *vb. tr.* to exercise power over, dominate : N. O. 228.

Controversy, *sb.* (a) action at law, lawsuit : Hor. Epist. 3.
(b) **without controversy**, beyond dispute : C. 409.

Contumacy, *sb.* stubborn perverseness : P. L. x. 1027.

Convenient, *adj.* suitable, proper : S. A. 1471.

Conversant, *adj.* concerned or occupied (*with*) : P. R. i. 131.

Conversation, *sb.* converse, familiar discourse : P. L. viii. 418 ; P. R. iv. 232.

Converse (convérse), (1) *sb.* (a) discourse, conversation : P. L. viii. 408 ; ix. 247, 909.
(b) spiritual intercourse, communion : C. 459.
(2) *vb. intr.* (a) to associate familiarly, consort : P. L. vii. 9 ; to be familiar : P. L. ii. 184 ; Ps. ii. 24.
(b) to discourse familiarly, talk : P. L. iv. 639 ; v. 230 ; viii. 252, 396 ; x. 993 ; P. R. ii. 52 ; iv. 229.
(c) to commune : P. R. i. 190.
vbl. sb. **conversing**, intercourse ; P. L. viii. 432.

Conversion, *sb.* spiritual change by which the soul is turned from sin to the love and service of God : P. L. xi. 724 ; Dante 2.

Convert, *vb. tr.* to transform (*to*) : P. L. v. 492 ; S. A. 1564.

Convex (convéx), *sb.* convex surface ; (a) **first convex**, surface of the outermost sphere of the universe, the Primum Mobile : P. L. iii. 419.
(b) **uttermost convex**, surface of the visible universe : P. L. vii. 266.
(c) vault of hell : P. L. ii. 434.

Convey, *vb. tr.* (a) to carry, transport : P. L. vi. 515 ; xii. 75.

(b) to conduct, transmit : P. L. viii. 156.

Conveyance, *sb.* (a) means of transporting : P. L. i. 707.
(b) means of communication : P. L. viii. 628 ; x. 249.

Convict, *part.* proved guilty of crime : P. L. x. 83.

Conviction, *sb.* (a) proof or declaration of guilt : P. L. x. 84, 831.
(b) confutation : P. R. iv. 308.

Convince, *vb. tr.* (a) to demonstrate or prove to, *with acc. and clause* : P. L. vi. 789.
(b) to overcome in argument, confute : P. R. iii. 3 ; C. 792.

Convolve, *vb. tr.* to contort, twist about : P. L. vi. 328.

Convoy (convóy), (1) *sb.* attendance for the purpose of protection : C. 81.
(2) *vb. tr.* to conduct, guide : P. L. vi. 752.

Convulsion, *sb.* (a) action of wrenching : S. A. 1649.
(b) *pl.* spasm, fit : P. L. xi. 483.

Cool, (1) *adj.* (a) moderately and agreeably cold : P. L. iv. 258, 329 ; v. 39, 300, 655 ; x. 95, 847 ; S. A. 546 ; C. 282, 678, 861.
(b) radiating less heat : P. L. v. 370.
(c) affording protection from heat, *fig.* : P. R. iii. 221.
(d) lacking excitement or passion, calm, deliberate : P. L. x. 95.
(2) *sb.* (a) cool place or coolness : P. L. ix. 1109.
(3) *vb. intr.* (a) to become cold, lose heat : P. L. v. 396.
(b) *fig.* to become less ardent (*in zeal*) : P. L. xi. 801.
part. adj. **cooling**, that imparts relief from fever : S. A. 626 ; from extreme heat : C. 186.

Copartner, *sb.* fellow-partner, associate : P. L. i. 265 ; ix. 821 ; P. R. i. 392.

Cope, (1) *sb.* vault or over-arching canopy (*of hell*) : P. L. i. 345 ; (*of the visible heaven*) : P. L. iv. 992 ; *fig.* **fiery cope**, flaming darts flying so as to form an over-arching canopy : P. L. vi. 215.
(2) *vb. intr.* **cope with**, meet, encounter : P. R. iv. 9.

Copious, *adj.* (a) plentiful, abundant : P. L. iii. 413 ; vii. 325 ; S. A. 1737.
(b) having abundance and free in bestowal : P. L. v. 641.

Copse, *sb.* thicket of small trees: L. 42.

Coral, *sb.* the solid secretion of marine zoophytes: P. L. VII. 405.

Coral-paven, *adj.* overlaid with coral: C. 886.

Cord, *sb.* small rope: S. A. 261.

Cordial, *adj.* (*a*) belonging to the heart: P. L. VIII. 466.

(*b*) heartfelt, sincere: P. L. V. 12.

(*c*) invigorating, cheering: C. 672.

Cormorant, *sb.* a large and voracious water-bird, *here* used as a type of voraciousness: P. L. IV. 196.

Corn, *sb.* (*a*) seed of cereals, grain, *joined with oil or wine, or both*: P. L. XII. 19; P. R. III. 259; Ps. IV. 36.

(*b*) cereal plants still containing the grain: L'A. 108.

Corner, *sb.* (*a*) **no corner**, any part, even the smallest and most remote: P. L. IV. 529; C. 717.

(*b*) region, quarter: P. L. X. 665; C. 1017.

Cornice, *sb.* uppermost member of an entablature: P. L. I. 716.

Corny, *adj.* of corn: P. L. VII. 321.

Coronet, *sb.* chaplet, wreath: P. L. III. 640.

Corporal, *adj.* (*a*) of the body, bodily: P. L. V. 496; P. R. IV. 299; S. A. 616, 1336; C. 664.

(*b*) corporeal, material: P. L. V. 573.

Corporeal (córporéal: P. L. V. 413), *adj.* of the nature of matter, material as opposed to *spiritual*: P. L. IV. 585; V. 413; VIII. 109; X. 786.

Corpse, *sb.* living body: P. L. X. 601.

Corpulence, *sb.* bulk of body: P. L. VII. 483.

Correct, *vb. tr.* to chasten: Ps. VI. 2.

Correspond, *vb. intr.* to agree, be in harmony: P. L. IX. 875; *with* with: P. L. VII. 511.

Corrosive, *adj.* gnawing or consuming (*fire*): P. L. II. 401.

Corrupt, *vb.* (**1**) *tr.* (*a*) to render unsound, infect: P. L. XI. 57.

(*b*) to render morally unsound, debase: P. L. III. 162; *absol.*: P. L. XI. 784.

(*c*) **to induce to act unfaithfully**, bribe: P. L. I. 368; S. A. 386.

(**2**) *intr.* (*a*) to become putrid: D. F. I. 30.

(*b*) to become morally unsound or debased: P. L. XI. 889.

part. adj. (*a*) infected by that which causes decay: P. L. X. 695.

(*b*) debased in character, depraved: P. L. X. 825; S. A. 268.

Corruption, *sb.* (*a*) decomposition as a consequence of death: P. L. III. 249.

(*b*) moral unsoundness, wickedness, depravity: P. L. X. 833; XI. 428.

Corse, *sb.* dead body: D. F. I. 30.

Corydon, *sb.* the name of a shepherd, common in pastoral poetry: L'A. 83.

Cost, (**1**) *sb.* expense, outlay; (*a*) **on thy cost**, at thy expense: P. R. II. 421.

(*b*) **to my cost**, to my loss or detriment: S. A. 933.

(**2**) *vb.* (*pret.* cost), to necessitate the sacrifice or expenditure of (*lives*): P. R. III. 410; (*woe or pain*), *with personal and impersonal object*: P. L. I. 414; IV. 271.

Costly, *adj.* richly adorned, *sup.*: P. L. IV. 703.

Cote, *sb.* shed for sheltering sheep: P. L. IV. 186; C. 344.

See **Sheep-cote**.

Cottage, *sb.* small house, humble dwelling-place: P. R. II. 28, 287, 288; C. 320, 693.

attrib. belonging to a cottage: L'A. 81.

Cotytto, *sb.* the goddess of licentiousness: C. 129.

Couch, I. *sb.* place for rest or repose, bed: P. L. IV. 601; IX. 1039; XI. 490; P. R. II. 282; IV. 585; C. 276; Ps. VI. 12; *fig.* **fiery couch**, burning lake of hell: P. L. I. 377.

II. *vb.* (**1**) *tr.* (*a*) to lower (*a spear*) to the position of attack: P. L. II. 536.

(*b*) to comprise, include: P. R. IV. 225.

(**2**) *intr.* (*a*) to sit or lie in a position of rest, as a beast: P. L. IV. 351; as a bird in the nest: P. R. I. 501.

(*b*) to stoop close to the ground, crouch: P. L. IV. 405, 876.

(*c*) to lie hidden: P. L. IV. 123.

See **Well-couched**.

Couchant, *adj.* carried on while stooping close to or lying on the ground: P. L. IV. 406.

Council, *sb.* (*a*) deliberative assembly or the deliberation which takes place in such an assembly : P. L. I. 755 ; II. 506 ; VI. 507 ; **to council** : P. L. VI. 416 ; XI. 661 ; P. R. I. 40 ; **in council** : P. L. II. 20 ; X. 428 ; P. R. II. 118.

(*b*) the Privy Council of England : S. X. 2.

Council-table, *sb.* table around which a council assembles : N. O. 10.

Counsel, (**1**) *sb.* (*a*) consultation, deliberation : P. L. I. 660 ; V. 681, 785.

(*b*) advice, direction : P. L. I. 636 ; II. 115, 279, 379 ; X. 920, 944, 1010 ; P. R. II. 145 ; III. 13 ; S. A. 183, 1251 ; **in counsel,** according to the advice : Ps. I. 2.

(*c*) purpose, design, scheme, plan : P. L. I. 88, 168 ; VII. 610 ; P. R. I. 127 ; Ps. V. 30 ; LXXXIII. 10.

(*d*) judgement, wisdom, prudence : P. L. II. 304 ; VI. 494 ; S. XVII. 1.

(*e*) matter of confidence, secret : S. A. 497.

(**2**) *vb. tr.* to advise, recommend : P. L. II. 160, 227 ; *absol.* to give advice : P. L. II. 125 ; IX. 1099.

Counsellor, *sb.* official adviser : S. A. 1653.

Count, *vb. tr.* (*a*) to number, enumerate : C. 347.

(*b*) to compute, measure : P. L. X. 91.

(*c*) to account, consider, regard, *with two acc.* : P. L. V. 833 ; VIII. 319 ; P. R. II. 248, 391 ; III. 71 ; S. A. 250, 949, 991 ; Ps. III. 9 ; Hor. Epist. 1.

Countenance, *sb.* (*a*) appearance, aspect : P. L. V. 708.

(*b*) face, visage : P. L. II. 756 ; C. 68 ; *esp.* as indicative of character or state of mind : P. L. I. 526 ; II. 422 ; III. 385 ; VI. 825 ; VIII. 39 ; IX. 886 ; *of animals* : P. L. X. 713 ; *of God,* equivalent to presence : P. L. XI. 317 ; equivalent to favour : S. A. 684 ; Ps. IV. 30.

(*c*) *fig.* surface of the moon : P. L. III. 730.

Counterfeit, (**1**) *adj.* (*a*) pretended, sham : P. L. IV. 117.

(*b*) spurious, forged : S. A. 189.

(**2**) *vb. tr.* (*a*) to imitate with intent to deceive : P. L. IX. 1069.

(*b*) to have the appearance of or resemble *without implying deceit* : II P. 80.

part. adj. **counterfeited,** feigned, pretended : P. L. V. 771.

Counterpoise, (**1**) *sb.* state of being balanced, equilibrium : P. L. IV. 1001.

(**2**) *vb. tr.* to balance by a weight on the opposite side, counterbalance : S. A. 770.

Counterview, *sb.* position of two persons facing each other : P. L. X. 231.

Country, *sb.* (*a*) tract of land, region : P. L. IV. 235 ; P. R. III. 73 ; C. 632.

(*b*) land of nativity or citizenship, *always with poss. pron. except in* S. A. 886 *where it is implied in the context* : P. R. III. 102, 176, 366 ; IV. 355 ; S. A. 238, 518, 851, 884, 886, 889, 891, 894, 980, 985, 994, 1208, 1213.

attrib. of a rural district, rustic : L'A. 85 ; C. 167.

Countryman, *sb.* man of one's own country, compatriot, *with poss. pron.* : S. A. 1549.

Couple, (**1**) *sb.* wedded pair : P. L. IV. 339.

(**2**) *vb. intr.* to come together sexually, pair : P. R. II. 181.

Courage, *sb.* that quality which meets danger or opposition with intrepidity, bravery, boldness, valour : P. L. I. 108, 279, 530, 603 ; II. 126 ; VI. 839 ; IX. 484 ; S. A. 524, 1381, 1716 ; C. 610.

Courageous, *adj.* brave, resolute, bold : P. L. IV. 920.

Course, *sb.* (*a*) motion forward, onward movement : P. L. I. 349 ; II. 944, 980 ; III. 573 ; IV. 164 ; VI. 406 ; X. 411 ; H. B. 11 ; in a particular path, *of heavenly bodies* : P. L. I. 786 ; IV. 661 ; V. 173 ; VII. 501 ; VIII. 126, 163 ; X. 689 ; P. R. I. 252 ; Ps. CXXXVI. 30 ; *fig.* : U. C. II. 30 ; *of a river* : C. 832.

(*b*) the path or direction of moving : P. L. III. 720 ; IV. 224.

(*c*) progress onward or through successive stages : P. L. XII. 264 ; Ps. VII. 57 ; **fatal course** : course of fate : P. L. V. 861.

(*d*) life, career : S. A. 670.

(*e*) appointed order, order of succession, *of events in nature* : P. L. XI. 900 ; *in service* : P. L. IV

561 ; v. 655 ; **by course,** by turns, in appointed order : C. 25.

(*f*) custom, practice : U. C. I. 10.

(*g*) manner of proceeding, way : P. R. IV. 445 ; C. 159.

(*h*) way of life, conduct : P. L. XI. 794.

See **Mid-course.**

Court, (1) *sb.* (*a*) residence of a sovereign, as the central seat of government and princely state : P. L. I. 497 ; P. R. II. 183, 300 ; III. 237 ; C. 325, 746 ; *of Jove* : C. 1 ; *of Satan* : P. L. I. 792.

(*b*) *pl.* the enclosures surrounding the tabernacle at Jerusalem and constituting the temple area around the sanctuary : P. R. I. 488 ; Ps. LXXXIV. 6, 33 ; *fig.* heaven, God's dwelling-place where he reveals himself and is worshipped : P. L. V. 650 ; VI. 889 ; N. O. 13.

attrib. of the court : P. L. IV. 767 ; C. 962.

(2) *vb. tr.* to woo : Hor. O. 2 ; *fig.* : S. A. 719.

Courteous, *adj.* polite, kind : C. 275.

Courtesy, *sb.* politeness, complaisance : C. 161, 322.

Courtly, *adj.* serving as a royal residence : N. O. 243.

Covenant, *sb.* (*a*) particular clause of agreement contained in a deed, *fig.* : C. 682.

(*b*) agreement or stipulation entered into by God with mankind : P. L. XII. 302 ; with Adam and Eve : P. L. XI. 116 ; as representing mankind : Cir. 21 ; with Noah : P. L. XI. 867, 892, 898 ; with Moses and Israel : P. L. XII. 252 ; with David : P. L. XII. 346.

Cover, *vb. tr.* (*a*) to overspread, overlay : P. L. VII. 234 ; XI. 749 ; to occupy the entire surface of, strew : P. L. I. 312 ; v. 430 ; VI. 16 ; C. 712 ; Ps. LXXX. 41.

(*b*) **cover round,** to envelop : P. L. II. 267 ; to serve as a covering to, clothe : P. L. IX. 1096.

(*c*) to hide, conceal, screen : P. L. I. 659 ; IX. 1088, 1120 ; X. 223 ; XI. 217 ; *absol.* : P. L. IX. 1058 ; to hide *action or emotion* ; P. L. XI. 257 ; S. A. 841.

part. adj. **covered,** roofed, closed in overhead : P. L. I. 763.

vbl. sb. **covering,** means of concealment : P. L. IX. 1113.

Covert, (1) *adj.* hidden, secret : P. L. II. 41.

(2) *sb.* (*a*) that which serves for concealment or protection, shelter : P. L. IV. 693 ; VI. 409 ; P. R. I. 305 ; II. 262 ; Il P. 139.

(*b*) thicket, grove : P. L. III. 39 ; C. 945 ; trees composing the grove : P. L. IX. 435.

Coverture, *sb.* covering for the body, clothing : P. L. X. 337.

Covet, *vb. tr.* to desire, long for : P. L. II. 35 ; X. 1020 ; *with prep. inf.* : P. L. IX. 923.

Cow (*only in pl.* kine), *sb.* female of the domestic *Bos taurus* : P. L. IX. 450 ; XI. 647.

Coward, *sb.* one who lacks courage : S. A. 347, 1237.

Cower, *vb. intr.* to bend : P. L. VIII. 350.

Cowl, *sb.* the garment with a hood worn by monks : P. L. III. 490.

Cowslip, *sb.* the plant *Primula veris* : M. M. 4 ; C. 898 ; L. 147.

Coy, *adj.* modest, shy : C. 737 ; *of actions* : P. L. IV. 310 ; L. 18.

Cozen, *vb. tr.* to deceive, beguile : C. 737.

Crab, *sb.* the zodiacal constellation : P. L. X. 675.

Crabbed, *adj.* unpalatable, bitter, *fig. of philosophy* : C. 477.

Cradle, *sb. fig.* the first stage of existence : V. Ex. 46.

Craft, *sb.* cunning, artifice : P. R. I. 432.

Craggy, *adj.* (*a*) steep and rugged : P. L. IV. 547.

(*b*) surrounded by rugged cliffs : P. L. II. 289.

Cram, *vb. intr.* to feed to satiety, stuff oneself with food : P. L. X. 632 ; C. 779.

Crane, *sb.* the wading bird *Grus cinerea* : P. L. I. 576 ; VII. 430.

Crank, *sb.* fantastic turn of speech, conceit : L'A. 27.

Crawl, *vb. intr.* to creep, trail, *of a vine* : C. 295.

Craze, *vb. tr.* (*a*) to break in pieces, shatter : P. L. XII. 210.

(*b*) to impair the health of, render infirm : S. A. 571.

Cream, *sb.* dish having the appearance or consistency of cream : P. L. V. 347.

Cream-bowl, *sb.* vessel filled with cream : L'A. 106.

Create, *vb.* (*pres. 2d sing.* creat'st :
P. L. VII. 616) *tr.* (*a*) to bring into
being, cause to exist : C. 561 ; *said
of the divine agent, God* : P. L. I.
652 ; II. 349, 916 ; III. 112, 278,
391, 679 ; IV. 107, 999 ; V. 414,
471, 838, 894 ; VII. 64, 154, 188,
209, 232, 391, 527, 535, 616, 627 ;
VIII. 28 ; IX. 146, 346, 799, 911,
942 ; X. 890 ; XI. 58, 508, 605 ;
Ps. CXXXVI. 17 ; *with two acc.* :
I. 202 ; II. 623 ; III. 100 ; IV. 43 ;
VII. 529 ; IX. 557, 618 ; *in passive* :
P. L. II. 832 ; V. 100, 373, 549 ;
VIII. 623 ; *absol.* : P. L. VII. 606,
607 ; to produce out of something
already existing : P. L. II. 260.

(*b*) to choose, appoint, *with two
acc.* : P. L. II. 19 ; X. 403.

(*c*) to give rise to, cause : P. L.
VIII. 558.

part. adj. (*a*) **creating**, that
brings into being all things : P.
L. IX. 344.

(*b*) **created**, brought into being
by the power of God : P. L. II.
679 ; III. 705 ; V. 511 ; VII. 227 ;
P. R. II. 324 ; **created man**,
the creation of man : P. L. I.
573.

part. absol. **his created**, beings
created by Him : P. L. IX. 147.

See **First-created, New-created**.

Creation, *sb.* (*a*) act of creating : P.
L. V. 857 ; VI. 690 ; X. 168, 852 ;
the creation of the universe : P. L.
VII. 223, 449, 601 ; VIII. 236 ; IX.
946 ; XII. 472.

(*b*) that which God has created,
the created world, creatures collectively : P. L. II. 365 ; III. 163,
383, 661 ; IX. 896 ; X. 852.

Creation-day, *sb.* day on which
something is created : P. L. IX.
556.

Creator, *sb.* God, the maker of all
things : P. L. I. 31, 369 ; II. 385 ;
III. 167, 673 ; IV. 684 ; VII. 91,
259, 551, 567 ; VIII. 13, 492 ; IX.
196, 938 ; X. 486, 649, 889 ; N.
O. 120.

Creature, *sb.* (*a*) created thing : P. L.
III. 442.

(*b*) created being, living being :
P. L. II. 355, 498 ; III. 230, 387 ;
IV. 287, 360, 431, 582, 616, 677,
703 ; V. 164 ; VII. 413, 455, 506,
507 ; VIII. 169, 175, 264, 276, 370,
409, 411, 546 ; IX. 84, 112, 199,
228, 612, 940 ; X. 871 ; XI. 873 ;
P. R. II. 325, 406 ; S. A. 672 ;

D. F. I. 61 ; S. M. 21 ; C. 299 ;
Ps. CXXXVI. 85 ; human being :
P. L. II. 834 ; III. 151 ; IV. 790 ;
VIII. 430, 470 ; IX. 149, 897 ; X.
943 ; P. R. II. 157 ; *voc.* : P. L.
IV. 468 ; V. 74.

Credit, *sb.* reputation, repute : P. L.
IX. 649 ; P. R. IV. 12.

Credulous, *sb.* disposed to believe,
easily deceived, over-trustful : P.
L. IX. 644 ; P. R. II. 166 ; C. 697 ;
Hor. O. 9.

Creek, *sb.* inlet of the sea : P. L.
VII. 399 ; of a river : P. R. II.
25.

Creep, *vb.* (*pret.* crept) (**1**) *intr.* (*a*)
to move with the body prone to
the ground, crawl : P. L. II. 950 ;
V. 201 ; VII. 392, 484 ; S. A. 75.

(*b*) to move stealthily, steal :
P. L. II. 656 ; L. 115.

(*c*) to move slowly : L'A. 115.

(*d*) to grow with the stems and
branches extending along the
ground or on a support : P. L. IV.
259 ; **creep forth**, to rise out of and
grow along the ground : P. L.
VII. 320.

(**2**) *tr.* to move or crawl along
(*the ground*) : P. L. VII. 475, 523.

part. adj. **creeping**, crawling :
P. L. VII. 452, 523.

See **Low-creeping**.

Cremona, *sb.* the town in Lombardy,
Italy, the home of Vida : P. 26.
See **Trump**.

Crescent, (**1**) *sb.* figure of the new or
old moon : P. L. X. 434. *See*
Horn.

(**2**) *adj.* shaped like the new or
old moon, lunulate : P. L. I. 439.

Cresset, *sb.* vessel holding material
to be burnt for light : P. L. I.
728.

Crest, (**1**) *sb.* (*a*) natural ornament
upon the serpent's head : P. L. IX.
525 ; *fig.* **brighten his crest**, raise
his spirits : P. L. IX. 634.

(*b*) helmet : P. L. IV. 988 ; VI.
188, 191.

(**2**) *vb. tr.* to furnish with a
crest : P. L. IX. 500.

part. adj. **crested** ; (*a*) having a
comb : P. L. VII. 443.

(*b*) plumed : S. A. 141.

Crest-fallen, *adj.* dispirited, dejected : S. A. 1244.

Crete, *sb.* the island in the Mediterranean Sea, the home of the
gods : P. L. I. 514 ; famous for
its wine : P. R. IV. 118.

Crew, *sb.* company of people, band, *of the followers of Mirth* : L'A. 38 ; with derogatory adj. or the derogation implied in the context, *of men* : P. L. XII. 38 ; S. A. 891 ; Ps. CXXXVI. 70 ; *of heathen gods* : N. O. 228 ; C. 805 ; *of the followers of Comus* ; C. 653 ; *of devils* : P. L. I. 51, 477, 688, 751 ; IV. 573, 952 ; V. 879 ; VI. 49, 277, 370, 806 ; P. R. I. 107 ; II. 178 ; IV. 577 ; *fig. of diseases* : P. L. XI. 474.

Cricket, *sb.* the insect *Acheta domestica* ; Il P. 82.

Crime, *sb.* (*a*) offence or sin against the laws of God : P. L. I. 214, 606 ; III. 215, 290 ; V. 881 ; VI. 268 ; IX. 971 ; X. 545, 841 ; XI. 424 ; XII. 619 ; P. R. III. 212, 419 ; S. A. 490, 842 ; against the laws of truth : U. C. II. 7.

(*b*) *sing. collect.* wrong-doing : P. L. I. 79.

(*c*) charge, accusation : P. L. X. 127.

(*d*) matter of accusation, subject of reproach : P. L. IX. 1181.

Cringe, *vb. intr.* to behave obsequiously, show servile deference : P. L. IV. 945, 959.

Crisped (*disyl.*), *part. adj.* (*a*) having the surface curled into minute waves, rippled : P. L. IV. 237.

(*b*) having the leaves curled or ruffled by the wind (?) : C. 984.

Crocodile, *sb.* the animal *Crocodilus* : P. L. VII. 474.

Crocus, *sb.* the flower *Crocus* : P. L. IV. 701.

Croft, *sb.* piece of enclosed ground used for pasture : C. 531.

Cromwell, *sb.* Oliver Cromwell, Lord Protector of England : S. XVI. 1.

Cronian, *sb.* **Cronian sea,** Arctic sea : P. L. X. 290.

Crook, *vb. tr.* to bend : P. L. X. 885.

Crooked, *adj. transf. epithet,* **with crooked age,** bowed or bent with age : V. Ex. 69.

Crop, (**1**) *sb.* harvest : P. L. 18.

(**2**) *vb. tr.* to gather, pluck : P. L. V. 68 ; M. W. 39.

Crop-full, *adj.* filled to repletion : L'A. 113.

Cross, (**1**) *sb.* the wooden structure on which Christ suffered death : P. L. XII. 413, 415 ; N. O. 152.

(**2**) *adj.* (*a*) blowing across the direct course, contrary : P. L. III. 487.

(*b*) malign, pernicious : A. 52.

(*c*) morose, churlish : U.C. II. 19.

(**3**) *vb. tr.* (*a*) to go over : P. L. II. 290 ; X. 39.

(*b*) to pass from side to side of : P. L. IX. 65.

Cross-barred, *part. adj.* secured by transverse rods : P. L. IV. 190.

Cross-flowing, *part. adj.* flowing in an opposite direction : C. 832.

Crowd, (**1**) *sb.* (*a*) large number, multitude, *of bees* : P. L. I. 775 ; *of serpents* : P. L. X. 538.

(*b*) people in general, the multitude, as distinguished from persons of position and power : P. L. V. 357 ; the fallen angels, as distinguished from their leaders : P. L. I. 380.

(**2**) *vb. tr.* to press or pack closely : P. L. X. 287.

Crown, (**1**) *sb.* (*a*) ornamental fillet, chaplet : P. L. III. 352.

(*b*) ornament or covering for the head worn as a mark of sovereignty : P. L. II. 673 ; P. R. II. 458 ; C. 26 ; sovereignty of which the crown is a symbol : P. R. III. 169 ; IV. 213.

(*c*) that which adorns as a crown, chief ornament : S. A. 1579.

(*d*) consummation, acme : P. L. IV. 728.

(*e*) reward, guerdon : C. 9, 973.

(**2**) *vb.* (*pres. 2d sing.* crown'st : P. L. V. 168 ; *past. part. disyl.* : S. XVI. 5) *tr.* (*a*) to adorn with a garland : P. L. III. 365 ; V. 636 ; N. O. 47 ; (*with a circlet*) : P. L. V. 168.

(*b*) to invest or adorn *with something material which adds beauty or dignity* : P. L. IV. 262 ; V. 260 ; VII. 326 ; IX. 117 ; C. 934 ; L. 86 ; (*with glory or radiance*) : P. L. IV. 32 ; V. 839 ; VII. 194.

(*c*) to occupy the summit of, top : P. L. IV. 133.

(*d*) to complete, finish : P. L. VII. 386.

(*e*) to honour, bless, reward : P. L. II. 542 ; IX. 841 ; XI. 781 ; S. A. 175, 1296.

(*f*) to fill to overflowing : P. L. V. 445.

part. adj. **crowned,** invested with a crown as a mark of sovereignty : S. XVI. 5 ; as a mark of dignity or honour : D. F. I. 54.

See **Ivy-crowned.**

Crow-toe, *sb.* the wild hyacinth : L. 143.

Crucify, *sb.* to nail to the cross : P. L. XII. 417.

Crude, *adj.* (*a*) not reduced to order, chaotic : P. L. II. 941 ; VI. 478, 511.

(*b*) undigested, *fig.* : C. 480.

(*c*) unripe, sour : L. 3.

(*d*) premature : S. A. 700.

(*e*) immature in mind, without knowledge or power : P. R. IV. 328.

(*f*) coarse, common : P. R. II. 349.

Cruel, *adj.* (*a*) destitute of compassion, hard-hearted, merciless, pitiless : P. L. I. 604 ; X. 927 ; P. R. IV. 139 ; S. A. 642, 784 ; C. 679.

(*b*) causing bodily or mental suffering, hard, painful, severe : P. L. II. 501 ; VI. 448 ; X. 782 ; XI. 652 ; P. R. I. 149 ; IV. 388 ; S. A. 1198.

Cruelly, *adv.* in a cruel manner, mercilessly : P. R. I. 425.

Cruelty, *sb.* mercilessness, inhumanity : S. A. 646 ; M. W. 29 ; *pl.* cruel deeds ; P. L. XII. 494.

Crumble, *vb. tr.* to reduce to fragments : C. 615.

part. adj. **crumbled** : P. L. VII. 468.

Crush, *vb. tr.* (*a*) to press so as to force out a liquid : P. L. V. 345 ; so as to force out of shape, *with* in : P. L. VI. 656.

(*b*) to force out by pressing : C. 47.

(*c*) to destroy, overcome : P. L. X. 1035 ; XII. 430.

Cry, I. *sb.* (**1**) shriek or wail of pain : P. L. I. 395.

(**2**) clamour, outcry : S. A. 1524, 1553.

(**3**) appeal or entreaty for mercy : P. L. X. 859, 933 ; XI. 310.

(**4**) barking, howling : P. L. II. 795.

(**5**) pack (*of hounds*) : P. L. II. 654.

II. *vb.* (*pret. 2d sing.* cried'st : P. L. IV. 481) (**1**) *tr.* (*a*) to exclaim, call out : P. L. II. 787 ; S. XII. 11 ; *with object sentence containing the utterance* : P. L. II. 727 ; III. 515 ; IV. 2, 481 ; VI. 536 ; XI. 449 ; S. A. 1639 ; U. C. II. 26 ; S. XI. 5.

(*b*) to announce publicly, proclaim : P. L. II. 514 ; P. R. I. 19.

(**2**) *intr.* to call in supplication : Ps. III. 10 ; LXXXVIII. 2.

Crystal, (**1**) *sb. fig.* molten crystal, pure limpid water : C. 931.

(**2**) *adj.* (*a*) composed of crystal, the clear transparent mineral : P. L. I. 742 ; VI. 757, 860 ; P. R. I. 82 ; IV. 119; or of clear glass (?) : C. 65, 673.

(*b*) clear, transparent, *of water* : P. L. IV. 263 ; V. 133 ; VII. 293 ; XII. 197.

(*c*) **crystal spheres** : N. O. 125. *See* **Sphere.**

Crystalline (crystálline : P. L. III. 482 ; VI. 772 ; S. A. 546 ; *doubtful* : VII. 271), *adj.* (*a*) composed of crystal : P. L. VI. 772.

(*b*) clear or transparent (*stream*) : S. A. 546.

(*b*) **crystalline sphere** or **ocean** : P. L. III. 482 ; VII. 271. *See* **Sphere.**

Ctesiphon, *sb.* a city of Babylonia on the Tigris River, one of the capitals of the Parthian Empire : P. R. III. 292, 300.

Cube, *sb.* body in the form of a cube : P. L. VI. 552.

Cubic, *adj.* cubical : P. L. VI. 399.

Cubit, *sb.* a unit of measure derived from the length of the forearm : P. L. XI. 730.

Cuckoo, *sb.* the bird *Cuculus* : S. I. 6 ; XII. 4.

Cuirass, *sb.* defensive armour covering the body from neck to waist : S. A. 132.

Cuirassier, *sb.* mounted soldier wearing a cuirass : P. R. III. 328.

Cull, *vb. tr.* (*a*) to pick out or select from many : V. Ex. 21 ; *with* out : C. 630.

(*b*) to gather, pluck : C. 255.

Culminate, *vb. intr.* to be vertical, reach the highest altitude : P. L. III. 617.

Cumber, *vb. tr.* to overload, burden : C. 730.

Cumbersome, *adj.* unwieldy, clumsy : P. R. III. 400.

Cumbrance, *sb.* that which hinders free activity : P. R. II. 454.

Cumbrous, *adj.* (*a*) unwieldy, heavy : P. L. I. 428 ; III. 715 ; XII. 131.

(*b*) troublesome, wearisome : P. L. XI. 549.

Cunning, *sb.* (*a*) skill, dexterity : L'A. 141.

(*b*) skilfulness in deceiving, craftiness : P. R. I. 145 ; IV. 11.
Cunningly, *adv.* craftily : S. A. 819.
Cup, *sb.* (*a*) drinking vessel : P. L. V. 444 ; P. R. IV. 119 ; *fig.* **attend on my cup**, wait upon me while eating : P. R. II. 386.
(*b*) liquor in the cup : S. A. 934 ; C. 51, 525.
(*c*) *pl.* drunken revelry : P. L. XI. 718.
(*d*) cup-shaped blossom, *of the daffodil* : L. 150.
Cupid, *sb.* the god of love as armed with bow and arrow : C. 445 ; as the lover of Psyche : C. 1004. *See* **Love**.
Curb, (**1**) *sb.* (*a*) strap or chain used for controlling horses : P. L. IV. 859 ; *fig.* : C. 825.
(*b*) check, restraint : P. L. II. 322.
(**2**) *vb. tr.* (*a*) to control with a curb : P. L. II. 531 ; XI. 643.
(*b*) to check, restrain : D. F. I. 73.
Cure, (**1**) *sb.* means of healing or relief, remedy : P. L. II. 145, 146, 460 ; IX. 776 ; X. 1079 ; S. A. 630, 912 ; C. 913.
(**2**) *vb. tr.* to heal, remedy : C. 811.
Curfew, *sb.* bell rung at night as a signal for retiring : Il P. 74.
attrib. **curfew time**, hour when the bell is rung : C. 435.
Curiosity, *sb.* inquisitiveness : S. A. 775.
Curious, *adj.* (*a*) careful, attentive : P. R. I. 319.
(*b*) nice, fastidious : C. 714.
(*c*) desirous of knowing, eager to learn, inquisitive, *with prep. inf.* : P. R. I. 333 ; IV. 42.
(*d*) skilful, well-wrought : P. L. IV. 242.
Curius, *sb.* Curius Dentatus, the Roman consul who refused the Samnite gold and the lands assigned him by the senate : P. R. II. 446.
Curl, (**1**) *sb.* ringlet of hair : P. L. III. 641 ; C. 608.
(**2**) *vb. tr.* (*a*) to coil or twist spirally (*tendrils*): P. L. IV. 307.
(*b*) to adorn with ringlets : P. L. X. 560 ; *fig.* to adorn with foliage : A. 46.
(*c*) to form by twisting or coiling : P. L. IX. 517.

Current, (**1**) *adj.* (*a*) running, flowing : P. L. VII. 67.
(*b*) in general circulation, *of money, fig.* : C. 740.
(**2**) *sb.* (*a*) stream, river : P. L. IV. 227 ; XI. 853 ; S. A. 547.
(*b*) *fig.* course or progress (*of fury*): P. L. V. 808.
Curse, (**1**) *sb.* (*a*) condemning judgement, utterance consigning to evil : P. L. II. 622 ; X. 174, 640, 732, 1053 ; XII. 103 ; L. 101.
(*b*) the evil inflicted : P. L. X. 729 ; XII. 99.
(*c*) that which brings evil, bane : P. L. X. 822.
(**2**) *vb.* (*past part. disyl.* : P. L. I. 389 ; II. 1055 ; VI. 650, 806 ; IX. 904 ; X. 984 ; XII. 406 ; C. 939) *tr.* to load with maledictions, invoke evil upon : P. L. II. 374 ; IV. 71 ; X. 201, 734, 818, 852 ; C. 609.
part. adj. **cursed**, under a curse, deserving a curse, execrable, abominable : P. L. I. 389 ; II. 1055 ; VI. 650, 806 ; IX. 904 ; X. 984 ; XII. 406 ; C. 653, 939.
Curtain, *vb. tr.* to cover as with curtains, conceal, veil : N. O. 230.
See **Close-curtained**.
Cusco, *sb.* Cuzco, the capital of the Empire of the Incas : P. L. XI. 408.
Custody, *sb.* (*a*) charge, guardianship : P. L. II. 946.
(*b*) confinement, imprisonment : P. L. II. 333 ; S. A. 802.
Custom, (**1**) *sb.* established usage, received order : P. L. I. 640 ; XI. 810.
(**2**) *vb. tr.* to accustom : P. L. V. 3.
Cut, *vb.* (*pret. and past part.* cut) *tr.* (*a*) to divide or sever with an edged tool : P. L. VI. 325.
(*b*) to make by cutting : P. L. IX. 1110.
In combination with other words;
(*a*) **cut down**, fell : Ps. LXXX. 66.
(*b*) **cut off**, shut out, debar, exclude : P. L. III. 47 ; X. 1043 ; S. A. 1157 ; destroy, kill : S. A. 764 ; Ps. LXXXIII. 13, 39.
(*c*) **cut short**, abridge in length : P. R. III. 269.
(*d*) **cut through**, wound severely in feeling : Ps. LXXXVIII. 66.
Cybele, *sb.* the Phrygian name of the goddess Rhea : A. 21.

Cyclades, *sb.* the principal islands of the Grecian Archipelago : P. L. v. 264.

Cycle, *sb.* celestial sphere : P. L. VIII. 84. *See* **Sphere.**

Cyllene, *sb.* a mountain on the north-eastern border of Arcadia, sacred to Hermes, the father of Pan : A. 98.

Cymbal, *sb.* one of a pair of instruments which produce a sharp ringing sound when struck together : N. O. 208.

Cynic, *adj.* **Cynic tub,** *fig.* Diogenes or the Cynic school of philosophy : C. 708.

Cynosure, *sb.* (*a*) the constellation of the Lesser Bear containing the pole-star by which the Phœnician mariners directed their course : C. 342.

(*b*) *fig.* object upon which all eyes are turned : L'A. 80.

Cynthia, *sb.* a name of Diana, the goddess of the moon, derived from her birthplace, Mount Cynthus in the island of Delos : N. O. 103 ; Il P. 59.

Cypress, *sb. attrib.* (*a*) of the tree *Cupressus* : C. 521.

(*b*) cypress lawn, light material resembling crape : Il P. 35.

Cypress-bud, *sb.* unexpanded blossom of the tree *Cupressus*, as a symbol of mourning : M. W. 22.

Cyrene, *sb.* a province of northern Africa lying immediately east of Tunis and west of Marmarica (Lybia); "at the present, it passeth with that last described (Marmarica) by the name of Barca, or Barca Marmarica," Hey. *Cos.* 1657, p. 932 : P. L. II. 904.

Cyriack, *sb.* Cyriack Skinner, Milton's pupil and friend : S. XXI. 1 ; XXII. 1.

Cyrus, *sb.* Cyrus the Great, the founder of the Persian Empire : P. R. III. 33, 284.

Cytherea, *sb.* a surname of Venus, probably derived from the island of Cythera, which was sacred to her worship, *here* the mother of Æneas : P. L. IX. 19.

D

Daffodil, *sb.* the flower *Narcissus pseudo-Narcissus* : C. 851.

Daffodilly, *sb.* same as above : L. 150.

Dagon, *sb.* the god of the Philistines : S. A. 13, 437, 440, 450, 462, 468, 478, 861, 1145, 1151, 1311, 1360, 1370, 1463 ; identified with one of the fallen angels : P. L. I. 462.

Daily, (1) *adj.* belonging to or occurring every day : P. L. IV. 445, 618 ; VIII. 193 ; IX. 548 ; P. R. IV. 142 ; S. A. 76, 114 ; C. 314.

(2) *adv.* every day : P. L. VIII. 601 ; IX. 565 ; S. A. 6, 919, 1261 ; C. 635 ; L. 129.

Dainty, *adj.* (*a*) delicate, lovely : C. 680.

(*b*) pleasing to the palate, delicious, *sup. fig.* : V. Ex. 14.

Dairy, *sb.* building in which milk and cream are kept, and made into butter and cheese : P. L. IX. 451.

Daisy, *sb.* the flower *Bellis perennis* : L'A. 75 ; C. 120.

Dale, *sb.* valley : N. O. 184 ; L'A. 68 ; C. 496 ; *in combination or contrast with* hill : P. L. II. 944 ; IV. 243, 538 ; VI. 641 ; VIII. 262, 275 ; X. 860 ; P. R. III. 267 ; M. M. 8 ; *with proper name* : P. L. I. 410 ; P. R. III. 318.

Dalila (Dálila ; *spelled* Dalilah : P. L. IX. 1061) *sb.* the second wife of Samson, *spelled* Dalila *in Vulg.* : P. L. IX. 1061 ; S. A. 229, 724, 1072.

Dalliance, *sb.* amorous caressing : P. L. IV. 338 ; IX. 443 ; wanton play : P. L. II. 819 ; IX. 1016.

Dally, *vb. intr.* to trifle or play (*with*) : L. 153.

Dam, (1) *sb.* female parent *of an animal* : C. 498.

(2) *vb. tr.* to confine, obstruct, *with* up : C. 336.

Damage, *sb.* loss, detriment : P. L. VII. 152.

Damasco, *sb.* the Italian form of the following : P. L. I. 584.

Damascus, *sb.* the city of Syria : P. L. I. 468.

Damask, *vb. tr.* to ornament with a variegated design : P. L. IV. 334.

Dame, *sb.* (*a*) female ruler, *of Eve* : P. L. IX. 612 ; *of Cotytto* : C. 130.

(*b*) housewife, *fig. of the hen* : L'A. 52 ; C. 347.

Damiata, *sb.* a city of Lower Egypt between the Damietta branch of the Nile and Lake Menzaleh : P. L. II. 593.

Damn, *vb.* (*past part. disyl.* : N. O. 228), *tr.* to condemn to hell, doom to eternal punishment : P. L. II. 482, 496 ; IV. 392 ; P. R. IV. 194.

part. adj. **damned**, accursed, execrable : N. O. 228 ; C. 571, 602.

part. absol. **the damned**, the fallen angels in hell : P. L. II. 597.

Damnation, *sb.* condemnation to eternal punishment : P. L. I. 215.

Damœtas, *sb.* the name of a shepherd, common in pastoral poetry : L. 36.

Damp, (1) *sb.* (*a*) exhalation of a noxious kind : P. L. X. 848 ; C. 640.

(*b*) mist, fog : P. R. IV. 406.

(*c*) stupor : P. L. XI. 293.

(*d*) loss of vitality, weakness : P. L. XI. 544.

(2) *adj.* (*a*) of the nature of a noxious exhalation : S. A. 8 ; C. 470.

(*b*) moist, humid : P. L. X. 283.

(*c*) stupefying, benumbing : P. L. V. 65.

(*d*) showing dejection of spirits : P. L. I. 523.

(3) *vb. tr.* to take away the power of, weaken, restrain : P. L. IX. 45.

Damsel, *sb.* maiden, girl : P. R. II. 359 ; C. 158, 829 ; *with proper adj.* : P. L. I. 448 ; Oreithyia, the daughter of Erechtheus, king of Athens : D. F. I. 9.

attrib. composed of maidens : S. A. 721.

Dan, *sb.* the tribe of Israel : P. L. I. 485 ; III. 431 ; S. A. 332, 976, 1436.

Danaw, *sb.* the Danube : P. L. I. 353.

Dance, (1) *sb.* (*a*) a series of rhythmical movements of the body, usually to the accompaniment of music : P. L. VII. 324 ; VIII. 243 ; as an expression of joy or praise : P. L. IV. 267 ; V. 619, 620, 630 ; VI. 615 ; N. O. 210 ; C. 176, 974 ; as an amusement : P. L. I. 786 ; IV. 768 ; XI. 584, 715 ; C. 104, 952.

(*b*) *fig.* of the motion of planets : P. L. III. 580 ; V. 178.

(2) *vb. intr.* (*a*) to move lightly and rhythmically, usually to the accompaniment of music : P. L. II. 664 ; VI. 615 ; XI. 619 ; V. Ex. 60 ; L'A. 96 ; A. 96 ; C. 883 ; L. 34 ; Ps. LXXXVII. 25 ; *fig.* of the

motion of planets or stars : P. L. VII. 374 ; VIII. 125 ; IX. 103 ; M. M. 2 ; *of spring and autumn* : P. L. V. 395 (*cf.* P. L. IV. 267).

(*c*) to quiver : C. 673.

part. adj. **dancing**, quivering : S. A. 543.

Dancer, *sb.* one who dances professionally in public : S. A. 1325.

Dandle, *vb. tr.* to move up and down playfully : P. L. IV. 344.

Danger, *sb.* peril, risk : P. L. I. 275, 636 ; II. 421, 444, 449, 1008 ; IV. 934 ; V. 239 ; VI. 418 ; VII. 27 ; IX. 267, 349, 864, 1157, 1172, 1176 ; P. R. I. 94 ; II. 460 ; IV. 479 ; S. A. 529, 1522 ; P. 11 ; C. 370 ; or mischief, harm : P. L. III. 635 ; *personified* : C. 401.

Dangerous, *adj.* full of or causing danger, perilous : P. L. II. 107, 342 ; VI. 698 ; X. 382 ; P. R. IV. 455.

Daniel, *sb.* the prophet : P. R. II. 278, 329.

Danite, *sb.* a member of the tribe of Dan, *here* Samson : P. L. IX. 1059.

Dank (1) *sb.* water : P. L. VII. 441.

(2) *adj.* moist, wet, watery, *of trees or fields* : P. L. IX. 179 ; C. 891 ; S. A. XX. 2 ; *of clothing* : Hor. O. 15.

Dante, *sb.* the Italian poet : S. XIII. 12.

Danubius, *sb.* the Danube, the river of Europe : P. R. IV. 79.

Daphne, *sb.* a nymph who was beloved by Apollo. She fled from him and was changed into the laurel-tree : P. L. IV. 273 ; P. R. II. 187 ; C. 661.

Dapper, *adj.* small and active : C. 118.

Dappled, *adj.* marked with patches of shade : L'A. 44.

Dare, *vb.* (*pres.* 2d *sing.* dar'st : P. L. II. 682 ; VI. 182 ; P. R. IV. 178 ; S. A. 1394 ; 3d *sing.* dares : P. R. III. 57 ; C. 780 ; A. 23 ; *with compound subject,* 2d *sing. and* 3d *pl.* dare : P. L. IV. 942 ; *pret.* durst ; *past part.* dared) (1) *intr.* (*a*) to have courage, be bold enough, *with prep. inf.* : P. L. IX. 922 ; XI. 703 ; P. R. IV. 172 ; C. 427 ; *with simple inf.* : P. L. I. 49, 102, 382, 385, 391 ; II. 682 ; III. 220 ; IV. 704, 829 ; VI. 155, 182 ; VIII. 237 ; IX. 1180 ; P. R. III. 57 ; IV. 178, 580, 610 ; S. A. 1110, 1113,

1130, 1254, 1255, 1256, 1394, 1628;
N. O. 225; A. 23; C. 577, 616,
780; F. of C. 5; *with inf. understood* : P. R. I. 100, 324.

(*b*) to dare to do, venture : P.
L. IV. 942.

(2) *tr.* (*a*) to challenge, defy :
P. L. III. 523.

(*b*) to have courage for, venture
upon, run the risk of meeting :
P. L. IX. 304, 305; S. A. 531.

part. adj. **daring,** bold : P. L.
VI. 129.

Darien, *sb.* the Isthmus of Darien :
P. L. IX. 81.

Dark, (1) *adj.* (*a*) absolutely or
relatively void of light, frequently
with the implication of cheerless-
ness : P. L. II. 58, 405, 464,
588, 618, 823, 891, 916, 960,
1027; III. 11, 20, 424, 498, 544;
IV. 899; VI. 482, 870; VII. 212;
X. 283, 371, 438, 594, 667; XI.
478; P.R. I. 194; III. 318; IV. 456;
S. A. 86, 154; D. F. I. 30; V.
Ex. 71; N. O. 123; P. 7; L'A.
10; C. 500; S. XIX. 2; Ps.
LXXXVIII. 52; *comp.* : P. L. II.
720; V. 646; *fig.* : P. 33.

(*b*) transmitting or reflecting
little light : C. 197; *of the clouds* :
P. L. II. 264, 718; P. R. I. 41.

(*c*) approaching black in hue :
P. L. III. 380; VI. 478; XI.
743.

(*d*) deep in colour, *sup.* : Il P.
33.

(*e*) evil, wicked : P. L. I. 213,
456; IX. 90, 162; C. 383; bringing evil : L. 101.

(*f*) gloomy, cheerless, sad : P.
L. II. 486; VIII. 478.

(*g*) obscure in meaning : P. R.
I. 434; mysterious : W. O. 219.

(*h*) secret, concealed : P. L. X.
457.

(*i*) sightless, blind : S. A. 75,
80, 81, 591; Ps. VI. 14.

(*j*) not directed by eyesight :
S. A. 2.

(*k*) void of intellectual light,
ignorant : P. L. I. 22; III. 188;
XI. 809.

(*l*) void of the light of memory :
P. L. VI. 380.

(2) *sb.* (*a*) darkness : P. L. III.
45, 611; IV. 609; V. 208; VI.
415.

(*b*) dark place : P. L. II. 953.

(3) *vb. tr.* to make dark : C.
730.

Darken, *vb. tr.* (*a*) to make dark,
deprive of light : P. L. I. 343,
501; VI. 57.

(*b*) to deprive of brightness :
P. L. I. 599.

(*c*) to deprive of intellectual or
spiritual light : P. L. IX. 1054.

part. adj. **darkened,** deprived
of light : P. L. II. 491.

Darkish, *adj.* somewhat dark in
colour : C. 631.

Darkling, *adv.* in the dark : P. L.
III. 39.

Darkness, *sb.* (1) partial or total
absence of light : P. L. I. 63, 659;
II. 220, 263, 266, 269, 377, 754,
984; V. 179; VI. 6, 11, 142, 407,
739; VII. 233, 250, 251, 255, 352;
IX. 64; XI. 204; XII. 187, 188,
207, 473; M. W. 10; C. 204, 278,
335; Ps. LXXXVIII. 27; *with a
greater or less degree of personification* : P. L. III. 421, 712; L'A.
50; C. 194; *fem. gender* : P. L.
IV. 665; VI. 10; P. R. IV. 397;
C. 132; *as a bird, masc. gender* :
L'A. 6; *neut.* : C. 252; perhaps
region characterized by absence
of light (?), *of hell or chaos* : P. L. I.
72; II. 958; III. 16, 539; V. 614;
X. 394.

(2) lack of sight, blindness : P.
L. VII. 27; S. A. 159.

(3) absence of spiritual or intellectual light : P. L. I. 391; XII.
271; Ps. LXXXII. 18; (*a*) **powers
of Darkness,** powers of evil : P.
L. III. 256. *See* **Power.**

(*b*) **Prince of Darkness,** Satan :
P. L. X. 383; P. R. IV. 441.

(*c*) **Sons of Darkness,** the rebel
angels : P. L. VI. 715. *See* **Son.**

(4) death, the grave : S. A. 99,
593; Ps. LXXXVI. 48; LXXXVIII.
49, 72.

(5) non-existence : P. L. X. 745.

Darksome, *adj.* somewhat dark : P.
L. II. 973; IV. 232; V. 225; N.
O. 14; in colour : P. L. XII. 185.

Dark-veiled, *adj.* concealed by the
darkness of night : C. 129.

Darling, (1) *sb.* one dearly loved,
favourite : P. L. II. 870.

(2) *adj.* dearly loved : P. L. II.
373.

Dart, (1) *sb.* pointed missile thrown
by the hand, spear : P. L. II. 672,
702, 729, 786, 854; VI. 213; XI.
491, 658; P. R. IV. 424; *fig.* : P.
L. VIII. 62; XII. 492, 536; P. R.
IV. 366.

(2) *vb. tr. said of the eye*, to
send forth suddenly and rapidly,
shoot : P. L. IX. 1036 ; to cast
quickly and keenly : P. L. I. 568.
See Love-darting.

Darwen, *sb. attrib.* **Darwen stream,**
the river Darwen in Lancashire,
England, near which occurred the
battle of Preston, Aug. 17, 1648 :
S. XVI. 7.

Dash, *vb. tr.* (*a*) to strike, knock :
P. R. IV. 559.

(*b*) to shatter (*to pieces*) : P. L.
VI. 488 ; P. R. IV. 19 ; (*to shivers*) :
P. R. IV. 19.

(*c*) to destroy, frustrate : P. L.
II. 114.

(*d*) to throw or thrust with violence : S. A. 1240.

(*e*) to cast down, depress : P. L.
X. 577.

(*f*) to abash, put to shame : C.
451.

Date, *sb.* (*a*) term of existence, duration : P. L. XII. 549.

(*b*) time stipulated or prescribed : P. R. IV. 392 ; C. 362.

(*c*) term of life : U. C. II. 29.

Daughter, *sb.* (*a*) female child : P. L.
III. 463 ; IV. 324 ; P. R. II. 154,
180 ; III. 342 ; S. A. 221 ; M. W.
3 ; L'A. 23 ; Il P. 25 ; C. 51, 827,
837, 922, 982 ; S. X. 1 ; *of Sin,
the child of Satan* : P. L. II. 817,
870 ; X. 353, 384 ; daughter of God
and man, Eve : P. L. IV. 660 ; IX.
291 ; daughter of Sin, Discord :
P. L. X. 708 ; daughters of Necessity, the Fates : A. 69.

(*b*) anything considered in re-
lation to its source or origin :
P. L. IX. 653 ; C. 241 ; *of trees* :
P. L. IX. 1105.

(*c*) a woman in relation to her
country or tribe : P. L. I. 453 ;
S. A. 876, 1192.

Daunt, *vb. tr.* to intimidate : Il P.
137 ; S. XV. 4.

Dauntless, *adj.* fearless : P. L. I.
603 ; IX. 694 ; C. 650.

David, *sb.* the king of Israel, as the
progenitor of Christ : P. L. XII.
326, 347, 357 ; P. R. I. 240 ; III.
153, 169, 282, 353, 357, 373, 383,
405, 408 ; IV. 108, 147, 379, 471,
500.

Dawn, (1) *sb.* (*a*) first appearance of
light, daybreak, P. L. V. 167 ;
VI. 492 ; N. O. 86 ; L'A. 44 ;
break of dawn : P. L. III. 545 ; IX.
412 ; *personified* : P. L. VII. 374.

(*b*) gleam of light : P. L. II.
1037 ; III. 24.

(2) *vb. intr.* to begin to grow
light or shine, *of morn or light* :
P. L. VI. 749 ; IX. 192.

part. adj. **dawning** ; (*a*) beginning to shine, *of light* : P. L. III.
500 ; XII. 421, 423.

(*b*) beginning to brighten with
the light of dawn : P. L. VI. 528.

vbl. sb. **dawning**, dawn, daybreak : P. L. IV. 588.

Day, *sb.* (*a*) time between the rising
and setting of the sun, or an
analogous time in heaven : P. L.
I. 50 ; IV. 613, 725 ; VI. 8 ; VII. 98,
341, 347, 350, 371 ; VIII. 136, 137,
143 ; IX. 51 ; X. 680 ; XI. 204, 898 ;
Il P. 141 ; C. 978 ; S. I. 5 ; with
special emphasis on light as a characteristic of day, *hence*, light, daylight : P. L. III. 42, 725 ; V. 168,
170, 558 ; VIII. 206 ; IX. 59 ; X.
681 ; P. R. IV. 221, 400 ; S. A. 82 ;
N. O. 78, 140 ; P. 33 ; M. M. 1 ;
382, 569 ; S. XXIII. 14 ; *fig.* the
sun : C. 95 ; everlasting day,
heaven ; N. O. 13.

(*b*) time of twenty four hours :
P. L. III. 581 ; VII. 342 ; VIII.
69.

(*c*) either of the above as a unit
of time on, or during which, something exists or takes place : P. L.
I. 449, 744 ; III. 392 ; IV. 284, 449,
564, 616, 712 ; V. 33, 53, 162, 229,
313, 579, 582, 603, 612, 618, 662 ;
VI. 87, 170, 246, 423, 424, 539,
544, 550, 592, 684, 699, 802, 809,
871 ; VII. 25, 202, 251, 252, 256,
275, 338, 386, 448, 504, 544, 568,
593, 601, 605 ; VIII. 24, 229, 329,
331 ; IX. 136, 137, 201, 209, 220,
224, 575, 705, 762, 968, 1021,
1029 ; X. 49, 53, 99, 125, 210, 278,
576, 773, 811, 854, 962, 1050 ; XI.
177, 178, 212, 272, 550, 765, 826 ;
P. L. XII. 188, 203, 257, 264 ; P.
R. I. 130, 303, 309, 352, 353 ; II.
11, 12, 243, 245, 276, 315 ; III. 234,
276, 412 ; IV. 22 ; S. A. 12, 404,
434, 1016, 1062, 1297, 1299, 1311,
1388, 1574, 1600, 1741 ; N. O. 167 ;
Cir. 26 ; S. XX. 4 ; XXI. 13 ; XXII.
1 ; Ps. I. 6 ; II. 16 ; LXXXIV. 33, 36 ;
LXXXVIII. 2, 39, 67 ; Ps. CXXXVI.
30 ; one day, on a certain day :
P. R. I. 189 ; day by day, daily :
P. L. VIII. 31 ; day and night,
continually : P. L. II. 505 ; IV.
680 ; S. A. 807.

(d) used more indefinitely, *hence*, time, period: P. L. I. 339; II. 222, 695; III. 198, 337; VI. 502; VII. 25, 26; IX. 1102; X. 178, 202, 275, 964; XI. 114, 357, 600, 689; XII. 347, 446, 539; P. R. I. 317; S. A. 145, 191, 265, 794, 1067, 1216; V. Ex. 72; S. X. 9; Ps. LXXXVI. 21; **one day**, at some future time: P. L. II. 178, 734; **many days**, for a long time: P. L. XI. 254; XII. 602; **some days**, for a short time: P. L. XI. 198; P. R. I. 183.

(e) *pl.* period of life, life: P. L. X. 1037; XI. 782; XII. 22, 465; S. A. 702, 762, 1389; L. 72; S. II. 3; XIX. 2; Ps. VI. 11; LXXXI. 54; **number of days**, length of life: M. W. 11.

(f) period of power or influence: P. L. XII. 242, 277.

See **Birth-day, Creation-day, Holy-day, Mid-day, Sabbath-day, To-day.**

Day-labour, *sb.* labour done each day: P. L. V. 232; S. XIX. 7.

Day-labourer, *sb.* labourer hired to work by the day: L'A. 109.

Daylight, *sb.* light of the day: P. R. IV. 398; L'A. 99; C. 126.

Day-spring, *sb.* daybreak: P. L. V. 139; VI. 521; S. A. 11.

Day-star, *sb.* the sun, *personified*: L. 168.

Dazzle, *vb. tr.* (a) to overpower the vision with excess of brightness: P. L. III. 381; IX. 1083.

(b) to overpower the mental faculties: P. L. VIII. 457; to surprise with splendour: P. L. IV. 798; V. 357.

part. adj. **dazzling**; (a) overpowering the eye with brilliance: P. L. I. 564

(b) having power to confuse and deceive the vision: C. 154.

(c) confounding the mental faculties: C. 791.

Dead, (1) *adj.* (a) devoid of life, lifeless: P. L. III. 477; IX. 870; XII. 190; P. R. II. 77; S. A. 79, 100, 143, 984, 1570; D. F. I. 29; S. M. 4; C. 879; L. 8, 166.

(b) devoid of sensation: Ps. LXXXVIII. 38.

(c) destitute of spiritual life: P. L. III. 233.

(d) no longer existing: P. L. VII. 16.

(2) *sb.* dead persons, *collect.*: P. L. III. 327; XII. 460, 461; Ps. LXXXVIII. 18, 41.

Deadly, (1) *adj.* (a) causing death, fatal: P. L. II. 811; III. 221; IX. 932; S. A. 19, 623; N. O. 6; C. 567; *comp.*: P. L. XII. 391; *sup.*: P. R. IV. 622.

(b) aiming to kill: P. L. II. 712; implacable: P. L. II. 577; IV. 99; *sup.*: S. A. 1262.

(2) *adv.* resembling death: P. L. XI. 446.

Deaf, *adj.* unwilling to hear, inattentive: S. A. 249, 960.

Deafening, *part. adj.* stunning with noise: P. L. II. 520.

Deal, *vb.* (*pret. and past part.* dealt) (1) *tr.* (a) to apportion, distribute: P. L. IV. 68, 70.

(b) to deliver: P. L. XI. 676; S. A. 1529.

(2) *intr.* deal with; (a) engage in conflict, contend: P. L. VI. 125; P. R. II. 133.

(b) make use of: C. 683.

(c) act towards, treat: P. L. XII. 483, 484; S. A. 283, 705; with *understood*: S. A. 707.

Dear, (1) *adj.* (a) beloved, cherished, *of persons*: P. L. III. 403; V. 673; VI. 419; IX. 228, 289, 965; X. 238, 330, 349; W. S. 5; C. 564, 902, 1005; Ps. LXXXIV. 32; LXXXV. 32, 33; *used ironically*; P. L. II. 817, 818; *comp.*: P. L. IV. 412; V. 95; *sup.*: P. 10; L. 187.

(b) highly esteemed or precious, with more or less of the idea of personal attachment, *of things, emotions, etc.*: P. L. III. 276, 297, 531; IV. 486, 756; VIII. 580; S. A. 894; C. 453, 790, 864, 879; L. 173.

(c) affectionate, fond: P. L. IX. 970; *sup.*: P. L. VIII. 426.

(d) unselfish, generous(?): P. L. III. 216.

(e) earnest, heartfelt, *sup.*: P. L. III. 226.

(f) hard, grievous: L. 6.

(2) *adv.* (a) at the cost of great suffering: P. L. IV. 101, 222; X. 742.

(b) affectionately, fondly: P. L. IX. 832; Ps. LXXXI. 47.

Dearly, *adv.* (a) at the cost of great suffering: P. L. III. 300; IV. 87; S. A. 933, 1660.

(b) affectionately, fondly: P. L. XI. 909.

Dearly-loved (loved *disyl.*), *adj.* regarded with fond affection : D. F.
I. 24.

Dearth, *sb.* (*a*) scarcity of food :
P. L. VIII. 322 ; Ps. VIII. 22.
(*b*) famine : P. L. XII. 161.

Death, *sb.* (1) act or fact of dying,
cessation of life, state of þeing
dead, frequently implying both
physical and spiritual death : P.
L. I. 555 ; III. 212, 223, 252, 299 ;
VII. 545 ; IX. 283, 685, 695, 702,
714, 827, 832, 901, 954, 969, 977,
984, 989, 993, 1167 ; X. 49, 210,
278, 774, 797, 962, 1004, 1008,
1020, 1024, 1037, 1050 ; XI. 36,
40, 157, 197, 529, 537, 547,‘601,
676 ; XII. 392, 398, 412, 424, 425,
428, 571 ; P. R. III. 98 ; IV. 305 ;
S. A. 104, 288, 485, 513, 575, 630,
1232, 1263, 1513, 1579, 1581, 1666 ;
V. Ex. 96 ; Cir. 18 ; U. C. II. 11 ;
Ps. LXXXVIII. 11 ; *used fig. of life* :
S. XIV. 3 ; (*a*) *in the abstract* :
P. L. I. 3 ; II. 621, 622, 624 ; IX.
760, 767, 775 ; X. 798, 809, 1028 ;
XI. 61, 168, 709 ; Ps. VI. 9 ; VII.
48.

(*b*) *personified,* usually as the
son of Sin and the conqueror of
all men ; often less definitely,
but always with some idea of
personality : P. L. II. 787, 789,
804, 840, 845, 854, 1024 ; III. 241,
245, 252, 259 ; VII. 547 ; IX. 12,
13, 953 ; X. 230, 234, 251, 294,
304, 407, 473, 490, 588, 591, 635,
709, 815, 852, 854, 858, 981, 989,
1001 ; XI. 252, 258, 268, 462, 466,
468, 491, 676 ; XII. 420, 431 ; P. R.
I. 159 ; III. 85 ; S. A. 1572 ; P.
20 ; T. 22 ; U. C. I. 1, 6, 9 ;
M. W. 10 ; S. XXIII. 4 ; Ps.
LXXXVIII. 24.

(*c*) with qualifying word or
words indicating the kind or
manner of death : P. L. X. 788 ;
XII. 406, 433, 434, 445 ; P. R. III.
87 ; IV. 388 ; S. A. 100, 650, 1198,
1724 ; C. 608.

(*d*) **to the death**: P. L. XII. 494 ;
P. R. I. 264.

(*e*) **to death,** *adverbially with
vbs.* : S. A. 138 ; U. C. II. 26.

(2) that which causes death :
P. L. IV. 197, 221, 425, 427, 518 ;
IX. 792, 830 ; X. 731 ; S. XIX. 3.

(3) dead things collectively :
P. L. X. 269.

(4) a skeleton as the symbol of
death : C. 562.

Deathful, *adj.* bringing death, destructive : S. A. 1513.

Deathless, *adj.* (*a*) not subject to
death, immortal : P. L. X. 798.
(*b*) everlasting, perpetual : P.
L. X. 775 ; C. 973.

Debar, *vb. tr.* to prohibit from, *with
two acc.* : P. L. IX. 236.

Debase, *vb. tr.* to lower in position,
dignity, or character : P. L. IX.
487 ; XI. 510 ; S. A. 37, 999, 1335.

Debate, (1) *sb.* (*a*) argument, discussion : P. L. II. 390 ; VI. 122 ;
P. R. I. 95.
(*b*) discussion with oneself, deliberation: P. L. IX. 87 ; S. A. 863.
(2) *vb.* (*a*) *tr.* to argue, discuss :
P. L. V. 681.
(*b*) *intr.* to engage in discussion : P. L. II. 42 ; Ps. LXXXII. 4.

Debel, *vb. tr.* to conquer, overcome :
P. R. IV. 605.

Debonair, *adj.* courteous, affable :
L'A. 24.

Debt, *sb.* that which is owed or
due *to the law* : S. A. 313 ; *to
God* : P. L. IV. 52 ; S. A. 509 ;
to death : P. L. III. 246.

Decan, *sb.* a province of India north
of Malabar, Hey. *Cos.* 1657, p.
889 : P. L. IX. 1103. *See* **Malabar.**

Decay, (1) *sb.* decline of vital energy,
loss of health : Ps. LXXXVI. 4.
(2) *vb. tr.* (*a*) to wear out : U.
C. II. 5.
(*b*) to lose the bloom of youth
and health, *fig.* : P. L. XI. 843.

Deceased, *part. absol.* dead persons :
Ps. LXXXVIII. 42.

Deceit, *sb.* deception, fraud : P. L.
V. 243 ; IX. 772 ; particular in-
stance of deception, stratagem :
P. L. X. 1035.

Deceitful, *adj.* full of deceit, false :
S. A. 202, 537.

Deceivable, *adj.* capable of being
deceived : S. A. 350, 942.

Deceive, *vb. tr.* (*a*) to betray or
beguile into sin : P. L. I. 35 ; III.
130 ; IX. 404, 998 ; X. 496, 917 ;
P. R. I. 52 ; S. A. 211.
(*b*) to cause to believe what is
false, delude, cheat : P. L. II. 189 ;
IV. 124 ; X. 6, 564 ; XI. 783 ; P. R.
II. 142 ; C. 221 ; *absol.* to use deceit : S. A. 750 ; N. O. 175.
(*c*) to cause to seem · a falsehood, make appear an untruth :
S. II. 5.
(*d*) to cheat out of : P. L. X.
990.

(*e*) to relieve the tedium of, beguile : P. L. II. 461.

See **Self-deceived.**

Deceiver, *sb.* impostor : C. 696.

Decency, *sb. pl.* seemly or becoming acts : P. L. VIII. 601.

Decent, *adj.* comely, graceful : P. L. III. 644 ; well-formed, handsome : Il P. 36.

Deception, *sb.* condition of being deceived : P. L. IX. 362.

Decide, *vb. tr.* to determine or settle *a matter in dispute* : P. L. VI. 603 ; Hor. Sat. II. 1 ; *with clause* : S. A. 1176.

Decision, *sb.* determination *of a matter in dispute* : P. L. II. 908.

Deck, *vb.* to array, adorn : P. L. IV. 710 ; V. 189, 379 ; VII. 478 ; V. Ex. 26 ; C. 120, 717.

Declare, *vb.* (*pres. 2d sing.* declar'st : P. L. VI. 728) *tr.* (*a*) to make known, relate : P. L. XI. 250.

(*b*) to manifest, show, prove : P. L. IV. 619 ; V. 158 ; VIII. 603 ; P. R. I. 445 ; Ps. LXXX. 18 ; *with clause* : P. R. II. 252 ; IV. 337 ; *with acc. and prep. inf.* : Hor. O. 14 ; *with two acc.* : P. L. IX. 968 ; to show one fitted for : P. L. IV. 300.

(*c*) to make known publicly or formally, proclaim : P. L. V. 765 ; XI. 720 ; P. R. III. 119 ; Ps. II. 14 ; *with two acc.* : P. L. IV. 746 ; V. 603 ; VI. 677, 728 ; X. 462 ; *in passive* : P. L. VII. 181 ; IX. 611, 658 ; X. 401 ; P. R. I. 385 ; II. 4 ; IV. 520.

See **New-declared.**

Decline, (1) *sb.* action of sinking, *of the sun* : P. L. IV. 792.

(2) *vb. intr.* (*a*) to bend down : S. A. 727.

(*b*) to descend, sink toward setting, *of the sun* : P. L. IV. 353 ; V. 370 ; *of day* : P. L. X. 99.

(*c*) to sink into evil, fall morally : P. L. XII. 97.

Decree, (1) *sb.* authoritative decision or edict of God : P. L. II. 198 ; III. 115, 126, 659 ; V. 602, 674, 717, 774, 814, 884 ; VI. 683 ; X. 43, 644, 772, 953 ; XI. 47, 311 ; P. R. I. 55 ; S. A. 85 ; Ps. II. 13.

(2) *vb. tr.* (*a*) to command, order, appoint, ordain : P. L. II. 160 ; IX. 151 ; P. R. III. 186 ; *with prep. inf.* : P. L. XI. 96 ; *with clause* : P. R. III. 188 ; *absol.* or *intr.* : P. L. III. 172 ; X. 68.

(*b*) to determine, resolve, decide : P. L. III. 116.

Decrepit, *adj.* old and feeble : S. A. 69 ; *fig. of winter* : P. L. X. 656.

Dee, *sb.* the river forming part of the eastern boundary of Wales and emptying into the Irish Sea : V. Ex. 98.

Deed, *sb.* (*a*) thing done, act, action : P. L. I. 130 ; II. 116, 484, 549, 722, 739 ; III. 292, 337, 454 ; IV. 26, 394, 990 ; V. 66, 113, 865 ; VI. 66, 112, 170, 237, 240, 283, 354 ; IX. 921 ; X. 142, 354 ; XI. 256, 428, 461, 659, 796 ; XII. 161, 322, 582 ; P. R. I. 14, 215, 233, 386 ; II. 139, 438 ; III. 16, 91, 103 ; IV. 99 ; S. A. 247, 248, 276, 369, 372, 638, 826, 875, 893, 898, 972, 1043, 1267, 1513 ; L. 83 ; S. VIII. 3 ; IX. 10 ; Soph. 1, 2.

(*b*) power of action : P. L. V. 549.

Deem, *vb.* (1) *tr.* to judge, think, consider, *with two acc.* : P. L. I. 205 ; VI. 429 ; XII. 534 ; P. R. IV. 44 ; *in passive* : P. L. II. 46, 748 ; III. 469 ; VII. 152 ; IX. 29, 683 ; XII. 567 ; P. R. I. 23 ; S. A. 1705.

(2) *intr.* to judge (*of*) : P. L. VIII. 599 ; P. R. III. 150.

Deep, I. *adj.* (1) of great depth ; reaching far down, back, or in : P. L. I. 28, 601 ; II. 262, 578, 591 ; III. 11 ; V. 872 ; VI. 898 ; VII. 289, 303 ; C. 1000 ; *with the depth specified* : P. L. II 934 ; *of ranks of soldiers* : P. L. VI. 356, 554 ; *sup.* : P. L. III. 678 ; V. 542 ; *fig. of emotions* : P. L. X. 844.

(2) deep-rooted in the breast, heartfelt, profound, intense : P. L. I. 126 ; II. 382 ; IV. 123 ; VI. 666 ; P. R. I. 108 ; N. O. 69 ; W. S. 12 ; Cir. 9 ; Ps. LXXXII. 11.

(3) intense, very great in degree : P. L. II. 431 ; Ps. LXXXVI. 48.

(4) loud, full-toned : P. L. II. 267 ; XI. 489 ; N. O. 130 ; Ps. LXXXI. 29.

(5) hard to comprehend : P. L. III. 707.

(6) penetrating, profound : P. L. II. 421 ; III. 629 ; IX. 83, 602 ; P. R. I. 190 ; III. 227 ; S. XXI. 5 ; *sup. of persons* : V. Ex. 22 ; profoundly absorbing the mind : P. L. VII. 52.

(7) profound in craft : P. R. III. 391 ; Ps. LXXXIII. 10.

II. *sb.* (1) abyss : P. L. II. 12 ;
(*a*) *of hell* : P. L. I. 314 ; II. 87,
392, 773 ; IV. 574 ; VI. 716 ; X.
245 ; P. R. I. 90, 361 ; IV. 631 ;
the lake of hell (?) : P. L. II. 634.
  (*b*) *of Hades* : H. B. 2.
  (*c*) *of space or chaos, usually
with def. art.* : P. L. I. 152, 177 ;
II. 79, 131, 167, 344, 829, 891,
961, 994 ; III. 586 ; VI. 862 ; VII.
103, 134, 166, 168, 216, 245 ; X.
301, 471.
  (*d*) *of eternity* : P. L. XII. 578.
  (*e*) *fig. of sorrow or affliction* :
Ps. LXXXVIII. 28 ; *of misery or
despair* : P. L. IV. 76.
  (2) sea, ocean, *with def. art.* :
P. L. VII. 413 ; XI. 826, 848 ; C.
23, 733 ; L. 50.
  (3) the underground of heaven :
P. L. VI. 482.
  (4) the midst, **in deep of night** :
P. L. IV. 674 ; A. 61.
III. *adv.* (1) deeply, far below
the surface, far down or in : P. L.
II. 302 ; IV. 99 ; V. 614 ; VI. 326,
478, 652, 869 ; X. 299, 677 ; XI. 417,
749 ; P. R. IV. 417 ; S. A. 1568 ;
N. O. 123 ; VII. 55 ; LXXX. 38 ;
LXXXVIII. 20 ; *comp.* : P. L. III.
201 ; XII. 432.
  (2) profoundly : C. 523.
  (3) very craftily : Ps. II. 4.
Deep-throated, *adj.* having a large
cavity : P. L. VI. 586.
Deep-vaulted, *adj.* having a high
arched roof : P. R. I. 116.
Deep-versed, *adj.* profoundly learned (*in*) : P. R. IV. 327.
Deface, *vb. tr.* to disfigure : P. L. IX.
901 ; XI. 522.
Defame, *vb. tr.* to attack the good
name of, calumniate : P. L. IV.
746 ; S. A. 977.
Default, *sb.* misdeed, offence : P. L.
IX. 1145 ; S. A. 45.
Defeat, (1) *sb.* overthrow, rout : P.
L. I. 135.
  (2) *vb. tr.* (*a*) to overthrow or
vanquish in battle : P. L. VI. 606 ;
fig. : P. L. XII. 431 ; P. R. I. 6.
  (*b*) to bring to nought, frustrate : P. L. VI. 138 ; S. A. 1278, 1571.
  (*c*) to disappoint or defraud
(*of*) : P. L. XI. 254.
Defect, *sb.* (*a*) deficiency, incompleteness : P. L. VIII. 419.
  (*b*) *concr.* one who is imperfect
or has many faults : P. L. X. 891.
Defective, *adj.* imperfect, incomplete : P. L. VIII. 425.

Defence, *sb.* (*a*) act of guarding or
state of being guarded from
attack, protection : P. L. II. 362 ;
V. 731 ; S. A. 560 ; C. 42, 489 ;
S. XXII. 11 ; Ps. VII. 40 ; or arms
as a means of protection (?) : P. L.
VI. 337.
  (*b*) means of protection or resistance : P. L. VI. 467 ; IX. 325 ;
S. A. 1286.
  (*c*) vindication : P. L. III. 166.
Defenceless, *adj.* without defence,
unprotected : P. L. X. 815 ; C.
414 ; S. VIII. 2.
Defend, *vb. tr.* (*a*) to prohibit, forbid : P. L. XII. 207 ; P. R. II.
370.
  (*b*) to ward off attack or injury
from, protect, guard : P. L. II.
1000 ; VII. 37 ; XII. 483 ; S. A.
1179 ; Ps. LXXXII. 13 ; *with* from :
P. R. I. 306 ; S. A. 285 ; C. 396 ;
absol. to make defence : P. L. XI.
657.
  (*c*) to vindicate : Ps. v. 35.
  part. adj. **defended,** forbidden :
P. L. XI. 86.
Defensive, *adj.* (*a*) serving for defence, protecting : S. A. 1038.
  (*b*) capable of making a defence :
P. L. VI. 393.
Defer, *vb. tr.* to delay, postpone :
S. A. 1557 ; *with prep. inf.* : P. L.
IX. 586 ; S. A. 474.
Defiance, *sb.* (*a*) challenge to combat : P. L. I. 669 ; II. 697 ; IV.
873 ; XII. 74 ; S. A. 1073.
  (*b*) **in heaven's defiance,** in open
resistance to heaven : V. Ex. 44.
Deficience, *sb.* deficiency, incompleteness : P. L. VIII. 416.
Deficient, *adj.* defective : P. L. IX.
345.
Defile, *vb. absol.* to render morally
foul, corrupt : S. A. 1368.
Defilement, *sb.* moral pollution or
corruption : C. 466.
Deflower, *vb. tr.* to rob of moral
beauty : P. L. IX. 901.
Deform, *adj.* deformed, misshapen,
hideous : P. L. II. 706 ; XI. 494.
Deformed, *part. adj.* (*a*) that mar
the appearance, disfiguring : S. A.
699.
  (*b*) unsightly, hideous : P. L. VI.
387.
  (*c*) morally ugly, base : P. R.
III. 83.
Deformity, *sb.* physical disfigurement : P. L. XI. 513 ; moral : N.
O. 44.

Defy, *vb. tr.* to challenge to combat:
P. L. I. 49, 765 ; VI. 130, 357 ;
S. A. 1175, 1222.

Degenerate, *adj.* (*a*) having lost the
qualities proper to the race or
kind, debased, degraded : P. L.
XI. 806 ; P. R. IV. 144.

(*b*) characterized by degener-
acy : C. 475.

Degenerately, *adv.* in a degenerate
manner, basely : S. A. 419.

Degrade, *vb. tr.* (*a*) to depose from a
position of honour : S. A. 687.

(*b*) to lower in estimation, bring
into contempt : P. L. VIII. 552.

(*c*) to lower both morally and
physically : P. L. XI. 501 ; to lower
morally, corrupt, debase : P. L.
III. 304 ; P. R. IV. 312.

part. adj. **degraded,** corrupt,
depraved : C. 475.

Degree, *sb.* ·(*a*) one of a flight of
steps : P. L. III. 502.

(*b*) one of a succession of steps
in progress, **by degrees,** by successive steps : P. L. VII. 157 ; C. 462.

(*c*) relative social or official
rank or order : P. L. V. 591, 707,
750, 792, 838 ; VIII. 176 ; IX. 883 ;
S. A. 414, 1607 ; relative position
in the order of creation : P. L. V.
473.

(*d*) relative extent, amount, or
intensity : P. L. V. 490 ; VIII. 417 ;
IX. 599, 934 : P. R. IV. 516.

(*e*) unit of angular measurement : P. L. X. 669.

Deify, *vb. tr.* (*a*) to exalt to the
position of a god : P. L. VIII. 431.

(*b*) to adore as a god : P. L. I.
112.

Deign, *vb.* (**1**) *intr.* to condescend,
think fit, *with prep. inf.* : P. L. V.
59, 221, 364 ; VII. 84, 569 ; XII.
281 ; P. R. II. 336 ; S. A. 1226.

(**2**) *tr.* to condescend to give or
grant, vouchsafe : P. L. VIII.
202 ; IX. 21 ; Il P. 56.

Deity, *sb.* (**1**) godhead : P. L. VI. 157 ;
S. A. 464, 899 ; D. F. I. 10 ; (*a*)
the Godhead : P. L. V. 724 ; Ps.
VII. 63 ; **by Deity,** in my Godhead :
P. L. VI. 682 ; the position or
condition in which God exists :
P. L. IX. 167 ; the glory and
splendour of the Godhead : P. L.
X. 65.

(*b*) *fig. said of a person deified* :
A. 93.

(**2**) god, divine being : P. L. I.
373 ; II. 11 ; P. R. III. 416 ; IV.

340 ; V. Ex. 35 ; C. 29 ; *fig.* person deified : A. 25.

(**3**) the Supreme Being, God :
P. L. III. 187 ; V. 806 ; VI. 750 ;
VII. 142 ; XI. 149 ; XII. 15.

Deject, *vb. tr.* to humiliate, humble : P. R. II. 219 ; *refl.* : S. A.
213.

part. adj. (*a*) **dejected,** lowered
in fortune, abased : S. A. 338.

(*b*) **deject,** downcast, disheartened : Ps. VI. 3.

Dejection, *sb.* depression, sadness,
gloom : P. L. XI. 301.

Delay, I. *sb.* procrastination, lingering : P. L. II. 60 ; IV. 311 ; IX.
675 ; S. A. 1344 ; **without delay,**
immediately : P. L. X. 163 ; S. A.
1395 ; stay, sojourn : P. L. XII.
223 ; (*a*) detention, hindrance to
progress : P. L. III. 635.

(*b*) cause or reason for lingering : P. L. IV. 163 ; XII. 615.

II. *vb.* (**1**) *tr.* (*a*) to put off,
defer : P. L. IX. 844 ; *with prep.
inf.* : P. L. X. 771 ; XI. 492.

(*b*) to cause to linger : C. 494.

(**2**) *intr.* to linger, tarry : P. L.
I. 208 ; V. 247 ; VII. 101 ; P. R. I.
56 ; II. 95.

Delectable, *adj.* delightful : P. L. V.
629 ; VII. 539.

Delia, *sb.* a surname of the goddess
Diana derived from her birthplace,
the island of Delos : P. L. IX.
387, 388.

Deliberate, *adj.* well-weighed, not
hasty or rash : P. L. I. 554.

Deliberation, *sb.* careful consideration, wisdom in advising or deciding : P. L. II. 303.

Delicacy (délicácy : P. L. V. 333 ;
P. R. II. 390), *sb.* (*a*) agreeableness
to the sense of taste, deliciousness :
P. L. V. 333.

(*b*) luxury, voluptuousness : C.
681.

(*c*) dainty, something that delights one of the senses : P. L. VIII.
526 ; the sense of taste : P. R. II.
390.

Delicious, *adj.* highly pleasing or
delightful : P. L. IV. 132, 729 ;
VII. 537 ; IX. 439 ; X. 746 ; to the
sense of taste : P. L. IV. 251, 422 ;
IX. 1028 ; S. A. 541 ; C. 704 ; to the
sense of touch : P. L. II. 400 ;
transferred epithet, bearing delicious fruit : P. L. V. 635.

Deliciously, *adv.* with delicious food :
P. L. VII. 491.

Delight, I. *sb.* (1) high degree of pleasure, joy, or gratification : P. L. III. 704 ; IV. 155, 206, 894 ; V. 400 ; VII. 330; VIII. 11, 384, 391, 477, 524, 576, 580; IX. 114, 242, 419, 449, 454, 468, 787 ; X. 272 ; XI. 533, 596 ; P. R. II. 373 ; III. 54 ; IV. 263 ; S. A. 71, 916, 1642 ; V. Ex. 20 ; L'A. 91, 151 ; C. 262, 812, 967 ; S. XXIII. 12 ; *with* in : P. L. III. 168 ; XII. 245 ; *with* of : P. L. IV. 497.

(2) that which gives pleasure, source of pleasure : P. L. I. 160 ; II. 247 ; III. 664 ; IV. 106, 286, 367, 435 ; V. 19, 431 ; VI. 727 ; X. 941 ; P. R. I. 208 ; II. 480 ; IV. 345 ; S. A. 633, 1490 ; L. 72 ; S. XX. 13.

II. *vb.* (1) *tr.* (*a*) to give great pleasure to, gratify to a high degree : P. L. I. 11 ; V. 627 ; VII. 571 ; VIII. 49, 600 ; IX. 398 ; P. R. II. 192.

(*b*) to fill (*hours*) with pleasure : P. R. IV. 331.

(2) *intr.* to take great pleasure, *with prep. inf.* : P. R. I. 481 ; C. 846.

part. adj. **delighted,** greatly pleased : P. L. V. 545.

Delightful, *adv.* highly pleasing : P. L. I. 467 ; IV. 437, 643, 652, 692 ; IX. 1023.

Delightfully, *adv.* with great delight : P. L. X. 730.

Delineate, *vb. tr.* to portray in words, describe : P. L. V. 572.

Deliver, *vb. tr.* (*a*) to set free, release : P. R. III. 380, 404 ; S. A. 39.

(*b*) to surrender, yield, give over : P. L. IV. 368 ; IX. 989 ; S. A. 437, 1184 ; Ps. LXXXVIII. 23 ; *with* up : S. A. 1158.

(*c*) to distribute (*letters*) to the proper persons : U. C. II. 33.

Deliverance, *sb.* (*a*) release from captivity or servitude, either personal or national : P. L. II. 465 ; VI. 468 ; P. R. II. 35 ; III. 374 ; S. A. 225, 246, 292, 603.

(*b*) release from sin, redemption : P. L. III. 182 ; XII. 235, 600.

Deliverer, *sb.* one who sets another free from servitude : P. L. VI. 451 ; P. R. III. 82 ; S. A. 40, 274, 279, 1214, 1270, 1289 ; from sin : P. L. XII. 149, 479.

Delivery, *sb.* release, liberation from captivity : S. A. 1505, 1575.

Dell, *sb.* small deep vale : C. 312.

Delos, *sb.* a small island in the Ægean Sea : P. L. V. 265 ; as the birthplace of Apollo : P. L. X. 296.

Delphian, *adj.* of Delphi, **Delphian cliff,** Mount Parnassus, at the foot of which was situated Delphi, the seat of the oracle of Apollo : P. L. I. 517.

Delphic, *adj.* inspired : W. S. 12.

Delphos, *sb.* Delphi : P. R. I. 458 ; **the steep of Delphos,** Mount Parnassus : N. O. 178. *See* **Delphian.**

Delude, *vb. tr.* (*a*) to disappoint the hopes of, mock : P. L. X. 557 ; S. A. 396.

(*b*) to deceive, beguile, mislead : P. L. XI. 125 ; *absol.* : P. R. I. 435.

part. adj. **deluding,** deceptive : Il P. 1.

Deluge, *sb.* (*a*) inundation : P. L. I. 68, 354.

(*b*) the waters of the great flood : P. L. XI. 843.

Delusion, *sb.* (*a*) state of being deluded, false impression, error : P. R. IV. 319.

(*b*) act of deluding, deception : P. R. I. 443.

See **Self-delusion.**

Delusive, *adj.* apt to delude, deceptive : P. L. IX. 639 ; X. 563.

See **Low-delved.**

Demand, (1) *sb.* request, petition : Ps. LXXXI. 44.

(2) *vb. tr.* to call for, request : Ps. LXXXII. 16.

Demeanour, *sb.* carriage, behaviour : P. L. IV. 129, 871 ; VIII. 59 ; XI. 162.

Demi-god, *sb.* a being of divine nature, *of angels* : P. L. I. 796 ; IX. 937.

Democraty, *sb.* government by the people : P. R. IV. 269.

Demodocus, *sb.* the famous minstrel of the Phæacians : V. Ex. 48.

Demogorgon, *sb.* the mysterious divinity who was an object of terror rather than of worship, *here* an attendant upon the throne of chaos : P. L. II. 965. *See* **Name.**

Demon, *sb.* spirit : Il P. 93.

Demoniac, *adj.* (*a*) belonging to a demon : P. R. IV. 628.

(*b*) caused by demoniacal possession : P. L. XI. 485.

Demonian, *adj.* of the nature of demons : P. R. II. 122.

Demur, (1) *sb.* hesitation : P. L. II. 431.

(2) *vb.* (*a*) *intr.* to hesitate, delay action : P. R. I. 373.

(*b*) *tr.* to hesitate about : P. L. IX. 558.

Demure, *adj.* sober, grave, modest : S. A. 1036 ; Il P. 32.

Den, *sb.* cave : P. L. I. 199 ; IX. 118 ; (*a*) *of hell* : P. R. I. 116 ; **den of shame** : P. L. II. 58 ; **den of death** : P. L. II. 621.

(*b*) lair of a beast : P. L. IV. 342 ; VII. 458 ; IX. 185.

(*c*) secret lurking-place (*of an outlaw*) : C. 399.

Denial, *sb.* refusal to grant a request : L. 18.

Denounce, *vb. tr.* (*a*) to announce, proclaim : S. A. 968 ; to declare *an event* about to take place, *of death or other punishment* as a warning against sin : P. L. IX. 695 ; X. 49, 210, 853, 962 ; XI. 106, 815.

(*b*) to presage, portend : P. L. II. 106.

Dense, *adj.* condensed, compact : P. L. II. 948.

Deny, *vb. tr.* (*a*) to declare to be untrue, refuse to admit : P. L. V. 107 ; *with prep. inf.* : P. L. XII. 173.

(*b*) to refuse to give, not to grant, withhold : S. XIX. 7 ; *with dat. and acc.* : S. A. 881 ; V. Ex. 15 ; *in passive with* to : P. L. IX. 240, 555, 767 ; L. 159 ; *fig.* : P. L. IV. 137.

(*c*) to disown, disavow : C. 559.

Depart, *vb. tr.* to go away, withdraw : P. L. VI. 40 ; VIII. 632 ; X. 430 ; XII. 192 ; Ps. VI. 16 ; *with* from : P. L. IV. 839 ; XII. 155 ; Ps. VI. 17 ; *with* hence : P. L. XI. 315 ; XII. 557 ; *with* from hence : P. L. XI. 356.

Departure, *sb.* act of going away : P. L. XI. 303.

Depend, *vb. tr.* to rely (*on*) for what is necessary : P. L. X. 406 ; XII. 564 ; P. R. IV. 312 ; V. Ex. 82.

Dependent, *adj.* having existence conditioned by the existence of something else : P. L. IX. 943.

Deplore, *vb. tr.* to lament over, bewail : P. L. VIII. 479 ; X. 939 ; A. 100.

Depopulation, *sb.* destruction of mankind at the flood : P. L. XI. 756.

Deport, *sb.* (*a*) deportment, carriage, mien : P. L. IX. 389 ; XI. 666.

Depose, *vb. tr.* to bring down from a position of honour : P. R. I. 413.

Deposit, *vb. tr.* to place for care, lodge in trust : S. A. 429.

Deprave, *vb.* (*pres. 2d sing.* deprav'st : P. L. VI. 174) *tr.* (*a*) to pervert or corrupt morally : P. L. V. 471 ; X. 825 ; XI. 806, 886 ; S. A. 1042.

(*b*) to calumniate, vilify : P. L. VI. 174.

See **Self-depraved.**

Deprecation, *sb.* prayer for the averting of disapproval or anger : P. L. VIII. 378.

Depress, *vb. tr.* (*a*) to overcome, vanquish : S. A. 1698.

(*b*) to lower in vigour or activity, render weak : P. L. IX. 46.

Deprive, *vb. tr.* to dispossess, divest, *with* of : P. L. XII. 100 ; *with two objs., in passive* : P. L. IX. 857 ; XI. 316.

(*b*) to debar, *with two objs.* : P. R. III. 23.

Depth, *sb.* (*a*) distance from the front to the rear : P. L. I. 549.

(*b*) unfathomable distance downwards, by implication, hell, *contrasted with* highth : P. L. II. 324 ; P. R. I. 13.

(*c*) profundity : P. L. I. 627 ; *contrasted with* highth : P. L. VIII. 413.

Deride, *vb. tr.* to laugh to scorn, turn to ridicule : P. L. II. 191 ; VI. 633 ; XI. 817 ; L'A. 31 ; *fig.* : P. L. IX. 211.

Derision, *sb.* (*a*) contempt manifested by laughter, scorn : P. L. VI. 608 ; XII. 52 ; **have in derision,** laugh at, deride : P. L. V. 736.

(*b*) *concr.* object of contempt or scorn : S. A. 366.

Derive, *vb.* (*pres. 2d sing.* deriv'st : P. R. II. 418) *tr.* (*a*) to draw as from a source, obtain, *with* from : P. L. IX. 837 ; XI. 427 ; XII. 36 ; P. R. I. 289 ; IV. 338 ; *with* whence : P. R. II. 418.

(*b*) to communicate by descent, *with* to : P. L. X. 965.

(*c*) to turn aside, divert, *with* on : P. L. X. 77.

Descant (déscant), **(1)** *sb.* song with variations : P. L. IV. 603.

(2) *vb. intr.* to comment, *with* on : S. A. 1228.

Descend, *vb.* (1) *intr.* (*a*) to go or come down: P. L. I. 327; III. 511; v. 363; VI. 325; VII. 1; X. 394; XI. 3, 75, 207, 670, 862; XII. 228, 588, 628; P. R. I. 31, 83, 228; IV. 273; S. A. 361, 635; *with* down: P. L. X. 90, 398; *with* down from: P. L. X. 648; XI. 576; D. F. I. 19; to move toward the horizon: P. L. IV. 541.

(*b*) **to descend into oneself**, betake oneself to deep meditation: P. R. II. 111.

(*c*) to come down in thought, touch upon a subject less abstruse: P. L. VII. 84; VIII. 198.

(*d*) to condescend, stoop, *with* to: P. L. IX. 169; *with prep. inf.*: P. L. III. 303; XII. 48; P. R. II. 213.

(*e*) to be derived, in the way of generation: Il P. 22; from a source, *with* from: P. L. V. 399; XI. 142; *with* whence: P. L. VII. 513.

(2) *tr.* to come down: P. L. XII. 606, 607.

Descent, *sb.* (*a*) downward motion: P. L. II. 76; XI. 127.

(*b*) downward slope, declivity: P. L. III. 20; L. 31.

(*c*) fall from a higher to a lower position or state, degradation: P. L. II. 14; IX. 163.

(*d*) degree lower in the order of being: P. L. VIII. 410.

(*e*) descendants collectively, offspring: P. L. X. 979; XII. 269.

(*f*) lineage, pedigree: S. A. 171.

Describe, *vb. tr.* (*a*) to portray in words, represent: P. L. VIII. 38; IX. 33; P. R. IV. 266.

(*b*) to descry, perceive, observe: P. L. IV. 567.

Descry, *vb. tr.* (*a*) to make known, reveal: C. 141.

(*b*) to get sight of, discover, espy: P. L. I. 290; II. 636; III. 501; VI. 530; VIII. 149; IX. 60; X. 325; XI. 228; P. R. I. 26; II. 280; S. A. 1301; A. 3.

Desert, (1) *sb.* (*a*) uninhabited and uncultivated region, wilderness: P. R. III. 264; as a place of wandering or seclusion: P. R. II. 271; III. 166; L'A. 10; *spec.* the wilderness in which the children of Israel wandered: P. L. XII. 139, 216; the place of Christ's temptation: P. R. I. 9, 193, 296, 501; II. 109, 241, 416; IV. 465.

(*b*) *fig.* **watery desert**, the waters of the flood: P. L. XI. 779.

(*c*) *fig.* **darksome desert**, abyss of chaos: P. L. II. 973.

(*d*) that which is due a person: S. A. 205.

(2) *adj.* (*a*) uninhabited, desolate: P. L. III. 544; VIII. 154; X. 437; C. 387; L. 39.

(*b*) barren, waste: P. L. II. 270; VII. 314; C. 209.

(3) *vb. tr.* to forsake, abandon: P. L. V. 515; VIII. 563; IX. 980; XI. 655; P. R. II. 316; S. A. 88, 275.

part. adj. **deserted**, forsaken: P. L. IV. 922.

Desertion, *sb.* the action of forsaking: S. A. 632.

Deserve, *vb.* (*past part.* trisyl.: P. L. VI. 709; D. F. I. 69), (1) *tr.* to be worthy of, merit, be entitled to, *of both good and evil*: P. L. I. 692; IV. 42; V. 446; VI. 354, 467; X. 726; XI. 171; P. R. III. 77, 106; IV. 169; S. A. 493, 1169, 1366; Eurip. 3; *with prep. inf.*: P. L. X. 16.

(2) *absol.* or *intr.* to be worthy, merit: S. A. 489.

part. adj. **deserved**, merited: P. L. VI. 709; D. F. I. 69.

vbl. sb. **deserving**, that which is due a person, desert: P. L. X. 727.

Deservedly, *adv.* justly, rightly: P. R. I. 407; IV. 133.

Design, (1) *sb.* (*a*) plan of action, scheme, project: P. L. I. 213, 646; II. 386, 630; V. 33, 737; IX. 261; P. R. II. 410.

(*b*) purpose, intention: P. L. III. 467; IV. 524; P. R. II. 203.

(2) *vb. tr.* (*a*) to designate, appoint, or select (*for*): P. L. X. 277; S. A. 32.

(*b*) to plan, devise: P. L. II. 179, 838.

(*c*) to purpose, intend: S. A. 801; *with prep. inf.*: P. L. V. 227.

part. adj. **designed**, appointed: P. L. X. 60.

Desirable, *adj.* worthy to be desired: P. L. VIII. 505; S. A. 358.

Desire, (1) *sb.* (*a*) longing, craving, wish: P. L. III. 177, 694; IV. 466, 509, 808; V. 518; VIII. 62, 451, 526; IX. 592, 741; X. 995, 997; XII. 87; P. R. II. 166, 211, 230, 467; *with* of: P. L. VI. 201; VII. 119; IX. 584, 1136; S. A. 541; *with* *prep. inf.* : P. L. II. 295 ; III. 662 ; IV. 523 ; V. 555 ; VII. 61 ; VIII. 252, 417 ; P. R. I. 383 ; S. A. 1677.

(*b*) love, affection : M. M. 6.

(*c*) passion, lust : P. L. IX. 1013.

(*d*) object of longing, thing wished for : P. L. V. 45.

(2) *vb.* (*pres. 2d sing.* desir'st : P. L. X. 837, 948) (*a*) *tr.* to wish or long for : P. L. VIII. 628 ; IX. 398 ; X. 837, 948 ; V. Ex. 22 ; Ps. VII. 24.

(*b*) *absol.* or *intr.* to wish : S. A. 980.

Desirous, *adj.* full of desire or longing, wishful, eager : P. L. V. 631 ; IX. 839 ; *with* of : P. L. X. 947 ; *with prep. inf.* : P. L. X. 749 ; S. A. 741.

Desist, *vb. intr.* to stop, cease, forbear : P. R. IV. 497 ; *with* from : P. L. VII. 552 ; *with prep. inf.* : S. A. 969.

Desolate, *adj.* (*a*) uninhabited, unpeopled : P. L. VIII. 154 ; and also lonely, dreary : P. L. IV. 936 ; deserted, abandoned : P. L. X. 420.

(*b*) cheerless, dreary : P. L. XI. 306.

(*c*) forlorn, disconsolate, wretched : P. L. X. 864.

absol. or *sb.* one who is needy and forsaken : Ps. LXXXII. 13.

Desolation, *sb.* (*a*) destruction, ruin : S. A. 1561.

(*b*) dreary barrenness and utter uninhabitableness : P. L. I. 181 ; C. 428.

Despair, (1) *sb.* utter hopelessness : P. L. I. 126, 191, 525 ; II. 6, 45, 126, 143 ; IV. 23, 74, 115, 156 ; VI. 787 ; X. 113, 1007 ; XI. 139, 301 ; S. A. 631 ; *personified* : P. L. XI. 489.

(2) *vb.* (*a*) *intr.* to be without hope, *with* of : P. L. IX. 255 ; S. A. 1171 ; *with prep. inf.* : P. R. I. 485.

(*b*) *tr.* to cease to hope for : P. L. I. 660 ; VI. 495.

Desperate, *adj.* (*a*) hopeless (*of*) : P. R. IV. 23, 445.

(*b*) prompted by the recklessness of despair : P. L. II. 107 ; III. 85.

Desperation, *sb.* despair, utter hopelessness : P. R. IV. 579.

Despicable (déspicáble), *adj.* that deserves to be despised, contemptible : P. L. I. 437 ; XI. 340.

Despise, *vb. tr.* (*a*) to look down upon, *literally* (*L.* despicere) : P. L. VII. 422.

(*b*) to look upon with contempt, contemn, scorn, disregard : P. L. II. 481 ; V. 60 ; VI. 602, 717, 812 ; IX. 878 ; P. R. II. 218 ; III. 28 ; S. A. 272, 1688 ; C. 724.

Despite, *sb.* (*a*) act of malice : P. L. VI. 906.

(*b*) anger, indignation, ill-will, malice : P. L. VI. 340 ; X. 1044 ; P. R. IV. 446 ; **son of despite** : P. L. IX. 176. *See* Son.

(*c*) **in despite of**, in defiance of : P. L. XII. 34 ; notwithstanding the opposition of : Ps. CXXXVI. 41.

Despiteful, *adj.* malicious : P. L. X. 1.

Despoil, *vb. tr.* to strip or deprive by force : S. A. 539 ; *with* of : S. A. 469 ; *of immaterial things* : P. L. III. 109 ; IX. 411, 1138 ; P. R. III. 139.

Despotic, *adj.* arbitrary, unlimited : S. A. 1054.

Destine, *vb. tr.* (*a*) to appoint by divine decree or ordain (*to*) : P. L. II. 161 ; P. R. I. 65.

(*b*) to design or intend (*to*) : P. L. II. 848.

part. adj. **destined** ; (*a*) appointed, ordained : P. L. X. 646 ; XII. 233 ; P. R. IV. 469 ; L. 20 ; appointed to become : P. L. X. 62 ; which are to be in the future : P. L. XI. 387.

(*b*) intended, designed : P. L. I. 168 ; VII. 622.

part. absol. **destined**, one set apart for a certain purpose : S. A. 634.

Destiny, *sb.* (*a*) appointed lot, fate : P. L. V. 534 ; U. C. II. 3.

(*b*) divine preordination : P. L. IV. 58.

Destitute, *adj.* entirely bereft, devoid (*of*) : P. L. IX. 1062 ; P. R. II. 305.

Destroy, *vb. tr.* (*a*) to raze, demolish : P. R. III. 80.

(*b*) to lay waste, make desolate : P. L. VI. 226 ; XI. 892 ; XII. 3.

(*c*) to ruin, overthrow : P. L. II. 85, 92 ; to ruin morally : P. L. III. 301.

(*d*) to kill, slay : P. L. II. 502 ; IX. 939 ; X. 611 ; XI. 761, 875 ; XII. 262 ; S. A. 856, 1587 ; *absol.* : P. L. II. 787 ; or perhaps in sense (*e*) (?) : P. L. III. 91 ; IX. 130.

(e) to condemn to eternal death : Ps. v. 15.

(f) to put an end to, bring to naught : P. L. II. 734; VI. 855; VII. 607; IX. 477; X. 838, 1006; XII. 394; P. R. II. 372.

vbl. sb. **destroying**, action of bringing ruin : P. L. IX. 129, 478.

Destroyer, *sb.* one who brings moral ruin : P. L. IV. 749; death : P. L. XI. 697; S. A. 985, 1678.

Destruction, *sb.* ruin, usually implying physical or moral death, or both, sometimes annihilation : P. L. I. 137; II. 84, 505; III. 208; v. 907; VI. 162, 253; VIII. 236; IX. 56, 134; X. 612, 1006; P. R. I. 376; III. 202; S. A. 764, 1514, 1658, 1681; region characterized by ruin, *of chaos* : P. L. II. 464.

See **Self-destruction**.

Detain, *vb. tr.* (a) to restrain from proceeding, stop : P. L. III. 14; VIII. 207; X. 108, *with* from : P. L. X. 367.

(b) to occupy, engage : P. R. III. 227.

Detect, *vb. tr.* to discover, find out : P. L. X. 136.

Deter, *vb. tr.* to discourage and restrain because of danger or pain, *with* from : P. L. II. 449; IX. 696.

Determine, *vb.* (*pres.* 2d *sing.* determin'st : S. A. 843) (1) *tr.* (a) to make an end of : P. L. II. 330; *absol.* or *intr.* : P. L. VI. 318.

(b) to resolve on, decide, conclude : P. L. v. 879; *with prep. inf.* : P. L. IX. 148; P. R. II. 291; **determine for**, decide *a thing* to be : S. A. 843

(2) *intr.* to make an end (*of*) : P. L. XI. 227.

Detestable, *adj.* abominable, odious : P. L. II. 745.

Detraction, *sb.* (a) act of taking away (*from the praise of another*) : A. 11.

(b) defamation, calumny : S. XVI. 2.

Detriment, *sb.* damage, loss, injury : P. L. VII. 153; X. 409.

Deucalion, *sb.* the son of Prometheus and the founder of a new race after the flood sent by Zeus : P. L. XI. 12.

Deva, *sb.* the river Dee : L. 55. *See* **Dee**.

Device, *sb.* (a) inclination, desire : Ps. LXXXI. 52.

(b) stratagem, trick : P. R. IV. 443; C. 941.

Devil, *sb.* (a) Satan, *with def. art.* : P. L. III. 613; IV. 502, 846; IX. 188; X. 878.

(b) one of the fallen angels, evil spirit : P. L. I. 373; II. 496; *by implication* Satan : P. R. IV. 129.

Devilish, *adj.* belonging to or befitting Satan : P. L. II. 379; IV. 17, 394, 801; VI. 504, 553, 589; P. R. I. 181.

Devious, *adj.* remote, distant : P. L. III. 489.

Devise, *vb. tr.* to contrive, invent, or think out *something material* : P. L. VI. 504; IX. 1091; *something immaterial* : P. L. II. 379; IV. 197; v. 780; VI. 304; C. 963; *with pref. inf.* : P. L. VIII. 207.

Devoid, *adj.* void or destitute (*of*) : P. L. II. 151.

Devolve, *vb. tr.* to cause to fall *with on* : P. L. X. 135.

Devote, *vb. tr.* to dedicate or set apart (*to*) : M. W. 60.

part. adj. **devoted**, doomed : P. L. v. 890.

part. or *adj.* **devote**, doomed (*to death* or *destruction*) : P. L. III. 208; IX. 901; XI. 821.

Devotion, *sb.* (a) reverence, veneration : A. 35.

(b) devoutness, godliness : P. L. XI. 452.

(c) act of religious worship : P. L. VII. 514; S. A. 1147.

Devour, *vb. tr.* (a) to eat up ravenously, swallow up : P. L. X. 712; P. R. IV. 573; L. 129; *fig.* : T. 4; *of death* : P. L. II. 805; X. 606, 880.

(b) to consume, destroy : P. L. II. 435; IV. 77; XII. 183, 184; Ps. CXXXVI. 53.

part. adj. **devouring**, consuming : P. L. v. 893; destroying : V. Ex. 86.

Devout, *adj.* (a) pious, reverent : P. L. XI. 14; Il P. 31.

(b) expressing piety : P. L. XI. 863; S. M. 15; Ps. LXXXVIII. 6.

Dew (1) *sb.* (a) moisture precipitated by the cooling of the atmosphere, regarded as gleaming : P. L. IV. 645, 653; **pearls of dew** ; M. W. 43; as beautiful or beneficial : P.L. I. 771; v. 212, 429, 646; XI. 135; S. A. 729; L'A. 22; Il P. 172; C. 996; L. 29; *fig.* **dew of sleep** : P. L. IV. 614; as harmful : P. R. I. 306; IV. 406; C. 352; A. 50.

(b) sweat, perspiration : C. 802.

(2) *vb. tr.* to wet as if with dew, moisten : P. L. XII. 373.

Dew-besprent, *adj.* sprinkled with dew : C. 542.

Dew-drop, *sb.* drop of dew : P. L. v. 746.

Dewy, *adj.* (*a*) abounding in dew : P. L. I. 743.

(*b*) moist with dew or as if with dew : P. L. v. 56.

(*c*) showing the dew : P. L. v. 141.

(*d*) resembling dew : P. L. VII. 333 ; thin, light(?) : P. L. XI. 865.

(*e*) refreshing : P. L. IX. 1044.

Dewy-feathered, *adj.* with moist feathers : Il P. 146.

Dextrous, *adj.* skillful, adroit : P. L. v. 741.

Dextrously, *adv.* skillfully, adroitly : P. L. XI. 884.

Diabolic, *adj.* of an evil spirit : P. L. IX. 95.

Diadem, *sb.* crown : P. L. IV. 90 ; P. R. II. 461.

Dialect, *sb.* language, speech : P. L. v. 761.

Diamond, (1) *sb.* (*a*) the most precious gem : P. L. III. 506 ; IV. 554 ; C. 732.

(*b*) vessel made of this gem : P. L. v. 634.

(*c*) adamant : P. L. VI. 364.

(2) *adj.* (*a*) containing diamonds : P. L. v. 759.

(*b*) adamantine : C. 881.

Dian, *sb.* Diana : C. 441.

Diana, *sb.* the goddess of the moon and of the chase : P. R. II. 355.

Diapason, *sb.* concord, harmony : S. M. 23.

Dictæan, *adj.* of Dicte, the mountain in Crete : P. L. x. 584. *See* **Jove.**

Dictate, (1) *sb.* authoritative rule, principle : P. R. I. 482 ; C. 767.

(2) *vb.* (*a*) *absol.* to communicate orally what is to be written down by another : P. L. IX. 23.

(*b*) *intr.* to direct or prescribe with authority : P. L. IX. 355.

Dictator, *sb.* person invested with absolute authority : P. R. I. 113.

Die, *vb.* (*pres. 2d sing.* diest : P. L. VII. 544) **(1)** *intr.* to cease to live, suffer death, expire : P. L. III. 209, 210, 246, 295, 296, 479 ; IV. 527 ; VII. 544 ; VIII. 330 ; IX. 663, 685, 713, 763, 764, 907, 928 ; x. 783, 790, 792, 974, 1005 ; XII. 163, 419, 507 ; S. A. 1579, 1661, 1706 ; N. O. 137 ; W. S. 16 ; U. C. II. 2, 16 ; *with*

for : P. L. III. 240, 409 ; W. S. 16 ; U. C. II. 22 ; *with* with : Ps. LXXXIII. 63 ; *with* of : P. L. XII. 179 ; *with* by : P. L. VI. 347 ; XI. 471 ; *with prep. inf. of purpose* : P. L. III. 299, 342 ; Ps. LXXXIV. 5 ; with adj. part. or phrase indicating manner of death or state of person dying : P. L. III. 240 ; IX. 979 ; XI. 459 ; P. R. III. 422 ; S. A. 32, 287 ; L. 142 ; Ps. LXXXII. 23, 24 ; *said of a flower* : L. 142 ; *said of life* : P. L. II. 624.

(2) *tr.* to die (*the death*) : P. L. XII. 428 ; (*a specified death*) : P. L. x. 788 ; XII. 445.

part. adj. **dying,** (*a*) indicative of death : N. O. 193.

(*b*) that on which one dies : M. W. 42.

vbl. sb. **dying,** action of dying : P. L. x. 964.

Diet, (1) *sb.* food : P. L. v. 495.

(2) *vb.* (*a*) *tr.* to feed : P. L. IX. 803.

(*b*) *intr.* to take food, eat : Il P. 46.

Differ, *vb. intr.* to be unlike, *with* in : P. L. v. 490 ; *with* from : P. L. VII. 71.

Difference, *sb.* distinction, discrimination : P. R. III. 115.

Different, *adj.* (*a*) unlike, dissimilar, not of the same kind : P. L. VIII. 130, 471 ; IX. 883 ; XI. 382, 574 ; P. R. III. 89 ; C. 145.

(*b*) differing, disagreeing : P. L. I. 636.

Difficult, *adj.* hard, not easy, arduous : P. L. IX. 593 ; P. R. II. 428 ; *with prep. inf.* : P. L. x. 992 ; hard to go over : P. L. II. 71 ; P. R. I. 298.

absol. person hard to satisfy : P. R. IV. 157.

Difficulty, *sb.* want of ease, arduousness : P. L. II. 449, 1022 ; *with* of : P. L. x. 252.

Diffidence, *sb.* distrust or doubt (*of*) : S. A. 454.

Diffident, *adj.* distrustful or doubtful *of* : P. L. VIII. 562 ; IX. 293.

Diffuse, *vb. tr.* (*a*) to pour out, scatter, spread abroad : P. L. IV. 818 ; VII. 265 ; IX. 852 ; P. R. II. 351 ; *of immaterial things* : P. L. III. 137, 639 ; VII. 190 ; S. A. 96, 1141.

(*b*) to spread out or extend *the body* : S. A. 118.

(*c*) *fig.* to be lost to sight, vanish : P. R. I. 499.

Dig, *vb.* (*pret. and past part.* digged) *tr.* (*a*) to form by removing earth, excavate : Ps. VII. 55.

(*b*) to obtain by excavation, gain by turning up the earth, *with* out : P. L. I. 690 ; *with* up : P. L. VI. 516.

Digest, *vb. absol.* to convert food into chyme in the stomach : P. L. V. 412.

Digestion, *sb.* conversion of food into chyme : P. L. V. 4.

Dight, *vb. tr.* to deck, adorn : L'A. 62 ; Il P. 159.

Dignify, *vb. tr.* to invest with honour, exalt : P. L. IX. 940 ; S. A. 682.

Dignity, *sb.* (*a*) nobleness, excellence, worth : P. L. IV. 619 ; X. 151 ; nobility of mien : P. L. VIII. 489.

(*b*) honour, position, rank : P. L. V. 827.

(*c*) honourable office, high official position : P. R. III. 30 ; or in sense (*b*) (?) : P. L. II. 25, 111.

(*d*) one holding high rank, dignitary : P. L. I. 359.

Digression, *sb.* deviation or departure from the main subject : P. L. VIII. 55.

Dilate, *vb. tr.* to make larger, increase in size, expand : P. L. I. 429 ; IV. 986 ; VI. 486.

part. adj. **dilated,** increased in capability and power : P. L. IX. 876.

Diligence, *sb.* (*a*) constant and earnest effort, assiduity : S. A. 924.

(*b*) officiousness : P. R. II. 387.

Dim, (**1**) *adj.* (*a*) faintly luminous, *of light* : Il P. 160.

(*b*) obscure from scarcity of light : P. L. I. 597 ; N. O. 198 ; C. 5.

(*c*) dusky, shadowy, *of night or darkness* : P. L. V. 685, 700 ; C. 278.

(*d*) not easily penetrated by the eye : P. L. III. 26.

(*e*) indistinct, faint : L. 105.

(*f*) not seeing clearly, *of the eye* : P. L. II. 753 ; IX. 707, 876 ; Ps. LXXXVIII. 38.

(*g*) that makes less bright and beautiful : P. L. X. 23.

(**2**) *vb. tr.* (*a*) to make less bright and beautiful, mar : P. L. IV. 114.

(*b*) to impair the sight of, hinder from seeing : P. L. XI. 212.

Dimension, *sb.* (*a*) spatial extent : P. L. II. 893 ; *spec.* length : P. L. VII. 480.

(*b*) *pl.* bulk, size : P. L. I. 793.

Dimensionless, *adj.* without physical extension : P. L. XI. 17.

Diminish, *vb. tr.* to lessen in power : P. L. VII. 612.

part. adj. **diminished,** lessened in brilliance : P. L. IV. 35.

Diminution, *sb.* (*a*) lessening, decrease : S. A. 303.

(*b*) apparent decrease in size due to distance : P. L. VII. 369.

Dimly, *adv.* not clearly : P. L. V. 157.

Dimple, *sb.* small depression in the cheek produced by the act of smiling : L'A. 30.

Dimpled, *part. adj.* broken into ripples : C. 119.

Din, *sb.* loud confused noise : P. L. II. 1040 ; X. 521 ; XII. 61 ; *of war* : P. L. I. 668 ; VI. 408 ; *of the crowing of the cock* : L'A. 49 ; *fig. of sin* : S. M. 20.

Dingle, *sb.* deep, closely wooded hollow : C. 312.

Dinner, *sb.* principal meal of the day taken at midday : P. L. V. 304, 396 ; L'A. 84.

Dint, *sb.* blow, stroke : P. L. II. 813.

Dip, *vb. tr.* (*a*) to dye : P. L. V. 283 ; XI. 244.

(*b*) to suffuse or overspread with moisture : C. 803.

Dipsas, *sb.* a serpent whose bite was fabled to produce mortal thirst : P. L. X. 526.

Dire, *adj.* fearful, dreadful, horrible : P. L. I. 94, 134, 189, 624, 625 ; II. 128, 589, 628, 820 ; IV. 15 ; VI. 211, 248, 665, 766 ; VII. 42 ; IX. 643 ; X. 524, 543 ; XI. 248, 474, 489 ; XII. 175 ; P. R. IV. 431 ; S. A. 626, 1544, 1666 ; C. 207, 517.

Direct, (**1**) *adj.* straight, not crooked : P. L. VII. 293 ; or *adv.* in sense (*a*) : P. L. VII. 576 ; coming straight from their source, *of rays of light* : P. L. VI. 719.

(**2**) *adv.* (*a*) in a straight line or course : P. L. III. 618 ; V. 301 ; XI. 190.

(*b*) without delay, at once : P. L. IV. 798 ; XII. 639.

(*c*) not by secondary means, immediately : P. L. IX. 974.

(*d*) just, exactly : P. L. III. 526 ; absolutely : C. 807.

(3) *vb. tr.* (*a*) to govern the actions of, regulate: P. R. I. 396.

(*b*) to cause (*walk or steps*) to move straight (*to*): P. L. v. 49 ; P. R. I. 119 ; to turn (*the eyes or mind to*) : P. L. VII. 514 ; to omitted : P. L. XI. 711.

(*c*) to point out a way to, guide : P. L. I. 348 ; II. 980, 981 ; III. 631 ; v. 558 ; IX. 216 : P. R. I. 247.

(*d*) to inform, instruct : P. R. IV. 393.

Directly, *adv.* (*a*) in a straight line : P. L. III. 89.

(*b*) without delay, at once : S. A. 1250.

Direful, *adj.* dreadful : C. 357.

Dire-looking, *adj.* of evil influence : A. 52.

Dirt, *sb.* earth, ground : U. C. I. 2.

Dis, *sb.* the god Pluto : P. L. IV. 270. *See* **Pluto.**

Disable, *vb. tr.* to render unable, incapacitate : S. A. 1219 ; *with prep. inf.* : P. L. XII. 392.

Disadvantage, *sb.* injury, loss : P. L. VI. 431.

Disagree, *vb. intr.* to be at variance, dispute : P. L. II. 497.

Disally, *vb. tr.* to annul or disregard the alliance of : S. A. 1022.

Disappear, *vb. intr.* to pass out of sight, be no longer seen : P. L. VI. 414 ; VIII. 478 ; XII. 640 ; P. R. I. 498 ; IV. 397.

Disapprove, *vb. tr.* to regard with disfavour, censure : S. A. 970 ; S. XXI. 12.

Disarm, *vb. tr.* to deprive or divest of arms : P. L. x. 945 ; S. A. 540 ; *with* of : P. L. III. 253 ; VI. 490 ; *fig.* (*of enmity, guile, etc.*) : P. L. IX. 465.

Disarray, *vb. tr.* to throw into disorder : P. L. III. 396.

Disastrous, *adj.* foreboding disaster, of evil omen : P. L. I. 597.

Disband, *vb. intr.* to break rank, disperse : P. L. II. 523.

Disburden, *vb.* (**1**) *tr.* to relieve of a burden, unload : P. L. IX. 624.

(**2**) *intr.* (*a*) to unload : P. L. v. 319.

(*b*) to ease the mind, be relieved : P. L. x. 719.

part. adj. **disburdened,** freed from a burden : P. L. VI. 878.

Discern, *vb. tr.* (*a*) to distinguish by the eye, see, perceive : P. L. I. 78 ; III. 407 ; IV. 867 ; v. 299,

711 ; M. W. 22 ; *with two acc.* : P. L. IV. 570.

(*b*) to discover by the intellect, perceive or distinguish mentally, recognize : P. L. I. 326 ; III. 682 ; IX. 544, 573, 681, 1149 ; x. 331 ; P. R. IV. 390, 497 ; *with two acc.* : P. L. XII. 372 ; P. R. I. 348 ; S. A. 1305 ; *with clause* : P. R. I. 164 ; *absol.* : P. L. IX. 765.

Discharge, (**1**) *sb.* (*a*) release, exemption : P. L. XI. 196.

(*b*) that which frees from obligation : S. A. 1573.

(**2**) *vb. tr.* (*a*) to release from obligation : P. L. IV. 57.

(*b*) to set free, dismiss (*from life*) : Ps. LXXXVIII. 17.

(*c*) to perform, execute : P. L. VI. 564.

Disciple, *sb. pl.* the twelve disciples who followed Christ : P. L. XII. 438.

Discipline, (**1**) *sb.* subjection to authority : P. L. IV. 954.

(**2**) *vb. tr.* to train, educate : P. L. XII. 302.

Disclose, *vb. tr.* (*a*) to open, expose to view : P. L. VI. 861.

(*b*) to set free from the egg : P. L. VII. 419.

(*c*) to reveal, make known : P. L. VIII. 607 ; *with clause* : P. L. VI. 445.

Discomfit, *sb.* defeat : S. A. 469.

Discompose, *vb. tr.* (*a*) to agitate, trouble : P. L. x. 110.

(*b*) to disarrange, disorder : P. L. v. 10.

Disconsolate, *adj.* destitute of comfort, inconsolable : P. L. XI. 113.

Discontented, *part. adj.* dissatisfied : P. L. IV. 807.

Discontinuous, *adj.* breaking continuity between parts : P. L. VI. 329.

Discord, *sb.* (*a*) want of concord, dissension, strife : P. L. VI. 897 ; VII. 217 ; IX. 1124 ; *personified*, as the daughter of Sin : P. L. x. 707 ; as an attendant upon the throne of Chaos : P. L. II. 967.

(*b*) confused noise, uproar : P. L. VI. 210.

Discountenance, *vb. tr.* to put out of countenance, put to shame, abash : P. L. VIII. 553 ; x. 110 ; P. R. II. 218.

Discourse, (**1**) *sb.* (*a*) power of reasoning from premises : P. L. v. 488.

(*b*) conversation, talk : P. L. II. 555 ; v. 233, 395 ; VIII. 48, 211, 552 ; IX. 5, 223 ; x. 343.

(c) formal speech, address : P. L. v. 803.

(2) *vb. tr.* to treat of, discuss : P. R. I. 479.

Discourtesy, *sb.* incivility, rudeness : C. 281.

Discover, *vb. tr.* (a) to lay open to view, disclose, show : P. L. I. 64, 724 ; v. 142 ; VI. 571 ; to afford a view of : P. L. III. 547.

(b) to reveal, make known : P. L. XI. 267 ; XII. 290 ; to show to be, *with two acc.*: P. R. III. 85.

(c) to find out, detect, uncover : P. L. IV. 814; x. 10 ; P. R. IV. 3 ; S. A. 998.

(d) to explore : P. L. II. 571.

Discreet, *adj.* judicious, prudent : P. R. II. 157; *sup.* : P. L. VIII. 550.

Discursive, *adj.* ratiocinative : P. L. v. 488.

Disdain, (1) *sb.* (a) contempt, scorn : P. L. I. 98 ; IV. 82, 770 ; IX. 534 ; P. R. IV. 170.

(b) indignation from a sense of offended dignity : P. L. v. 666 ; P. R. I. 466.

(2) *vb. tr.* (a) to think unworthy of oneself, treat with contempt, scorn : P. L. IV. 180 ; VI. 798 ; *with prep. inf.* : P. L. VI. 367 ; x. 213, 876 ; P. R. I. 448 ; S. A. 1106.

(b) to refuse on account of scorn or aversion : P. R. I. 492.

Disdainful, *adj.* showing contempt : P. L. II. 680.

Disdainfully, *adv.* scornfully : P. L. IV. 903.

Disease, *sb.* sickness, illness : S. A. 698 ; an illness, a malady : P. L. XI. 474; S. A. 618, 699 ; U. C. II. 21.

Diseased, *part. absol.* persons suffering from sickness : P. L. XI. 480.

Disencumber, *vb. tr.* to free from encumbrances : P. L. v. 700.

Disenthrall, *vb. tr.* to free from thraldom : Ps. IV. 4.

Disenthrone, *vb. tr.* to depose from sovereign authority : P. L. II. 229.

Disespouse, *vb. tr.* to take away after espousal : P. L. IX. 17.

Disfigure, *vb. tr.* to deform, deface : P. L. IV. 127 ; XI. 521.

Disfigurement ; *sb.* deformity, defacement : C. 74.

Disglorify, *vb. tr.* to deprive of glory : S. A. 442.

Disgorge, *vb. tr.* to discharge, pour out : P. L. II. 575 ; VI. 588 ; *absol.* : P. L. XII. 158.

Disguise, (1) *sb.* (a) **in disguise,** presenting a false appearance : P. L. x. 331; C. 571; because of altered clothing : A. 26.

(b) dress or clothing intended to conceal the form : P. L. IV. 740.

(c) masque : P. 19.

(2) *vb. tr.* to hide or conceal by a counterfeit appearance : P. L. I. 481 ; IX. 522 ; x. 330 ; C. 645 ; by altered clothing : P. L. III. 480.

Dish, *sb.* (a) cup : C. 391.

(b) food served in a dish : P. R. II. 341 ; *fig.* : V. Ex. 14.

Dishearten, *vb. tr.* to discourage, depress : P. L. v. 122 ; P. R. I. 268 ; S. A. 563.

Dishevel, *vb. tr.* to disarrange : P. L. IV. 306.

Dishonest, *adj.* disgraceful, ignominious : S. x. 6 ; dishonourable : P. L. IV. 313.

Dishonour, (1) *sb.* (a) disgrace, ignominy, indignity : P. L. IX. 267, 297, 330 ; S. A. 452 ; Ps. VII. 18.

(b) words showing dishonour, insult : S. A. 1232.

(2) *vb. tr.* to bring shame on, disgrace : S. A. 563, 1385.

Dishonourable, *adj.* showing a lack of honour, shameful, base : P. L. IV. 314 ; S. A. 1424.

Dishonourer, *sb.* one who treats another with indignity : S. A. 861.

Disinherit, *vb. tr.* (a) to deprive of an inheritance : P. L. x. 821.

(b) to dispossess : C. 334.

Disjoin, *vb.* (1) *tr.* to part, sunder : P. L. v. 106 ; IX. 884.

(2) *intr.* to separate oneself, cease, *with* from : P. L. III. 415.

Dislike, (1) *sb.* disapprobation : P. L. XI. 720.

(2) *vb. tr.* to be displeased with, regard with aversion : P. L. I. 102 ; VIII. 443.

Dislodge, *vb. intr.* (a) to go away from a place of abode : P. L. III. 433 ; VI. 7.

(b) to remove from a place of encampment or a field of battle : P. L. v. 669 ; VI. 415.

Disloyal, *adj.* untrue to one's allegiance : P. L. III. 204 ; IX. 7.

Dismal, *adj.* causing dismay, gloom, or sorrow, *said of a place or an object* : P. L. I. 60 ; II. 572, 823 ; VIII. 241 ; IX. 185 ; X. 787; XI. 469 ; Ps. LXXXVIII. 14 ; *of shade or night* : P. L. VI. 666 ; P. R. IV. 452 ; *of an event* : P. R. I. 101 ; S. A. 1519 ; V. Ex. 68 ; N. O. 210 ; *of a sound* : P. L. VI. 212 ; X. 508.

Dismay, (1) *sb.* sudden and complete loss of courage, despairing fear and apprehension : P. L. I. 57 ; II. 422 ; IX. 917 ; XI. 156 ; P. R. I. 108 ; IV. 579.

(2) *vb. tr.* to overcome with fear and apprehension, utterly dishearten : P. L. II. 792 ; IV. 861 ; X. 35 ; XI. 449 ; P. R. I. 268 ; S. A. 1060.

Dismiss, *vb. tr.* (*a*) to let go or send away *a person* : P. L. VII. 108 ; VIII. 564 ; X. 410 ; XI. 113, 507 ; XII. 195 ; P. R. II. 199 ; S. A. 1757 ; *absol.* : P. L. IX. 1159.

(*b*) to put out of mind : P. L. II. 282.

Dismission, *sb.* discharge from service : S. A. 688.

Dismount, *vb. intr.* to alight from a horse : P. L. VII. 19.

Disobedience, *sb.* refusal to obey a command or prohibition, disregard of lawful authority : P. L. I. 1; V. 541, 888 ; VI. 396, 911 ; IX. 8 ; P. R. I. 2.

Disobedient, *adj.* not submitting to lawful authority : P. L. VI. 687 ; X. 761.

Disobey, *vb.* (1) *intr.* to refuse to do what is commanded : P. L. III. 203 ; VI. 403.

(2) *tr.* to violate the commands of : P. L. V. 611, 612.

Disorder, (1) *sb.* want of order, confusion : P. L. III. 713 ; VI. 388.

(2) *vb. tr.* to disarrange : P. L. X. 911.

part. adj. **disordered,** unruly, riotous: P. L. VI. 696.

Disordinate, *adj.* not living in accordance with moral order, irregular in conduct : S. A. 701.

Disparage, *vb. tr.* (*a*) to speak contemptuously of, vilify: S. A. 1130.

(*b*) to bring reproach upon, dishonour : P. L. I. 473.

Disparity, *sb.* inequality: P. L. VIII. 386.

Dispart, *vb. tr.* to separate and assign, distribute: P. L. VII. 241.

part. adj. **disparted,** divided : P. L. X. 416.

Dispatch, (1) *sb.* (*a*) expedition, haste : P. L. V. 436.

(*b*) prompt execution: P. L. IX. 203.

(2) *vb. tr.* (*a*) to send : C. 42.

(*b*) to execute promptly, accomplish, get done : S. A. 1599 ; Ps. LXXXII. 10.

Dispatchful, *adv.* indicating haste : P. L. V. 331.

Dispel, *vb. tr.* to drive away or dissipate (*fears*): P. L. I. 530 ; (*the dark*) : v. 208.

Dispensation, *sb.* arrangement or control of events by Providence : S. A. 61.

Dispense, (1) *sb.* dispensation ; license granted by a pope, archbishop, or bishop to a person to do what is forbidden by ecclesiastical law : P. L. III. 492.

(2) *vb. tr.* (*a*) to distribute, deal out : P. L. III. 579; IV. 157 ; V. 330, 571 ; XI. 766.

(*b*) **dispense with,** to give special relief or exemption from : S. A. 314 ; to do without, forego: S. A. 1377.

See **Well-dispensed.**

Dispeople, *vb. tr.* to depopulate : P. L. VII. 151.

Disperse, *vb. tr.* (*a*) to cause to go or move in different directions : P. L. IV. 261; V. 651; XII. 45; P. R. III. 376 ; Ps. II. 20.

(*b*) to spread abroad, diffuse : P. L. X. 578.

(*c*) to make to vanish, dissipate: P. L. III. 54 ; V. 7, 208.

Displace, *vb. tr.* (*a*) **displace for,** put *something else* in the place of : P. L. I. 473.

(*b*) to take the place of, supplant : C. 560.

Display, *vb. tr.* (*a*) to unfold or spread out (*wings*) : P. L. VII. 390 ; N. O. 114.

(*b*) to make manifest, show, exhibit : P. L. II. 10 ; IX. 1012 ; P. R. I. 67 ; S. A. 819 ; Il P. 149 (?) ; S. XV. 7.

Displease, *vb. tr.* to be displeasing to, offend : P. L. VIII. 398 ; X. 22, 944 ; XII. 63 ; S. A. 1373 ; *part.* annoyed, vexed, *with clause*: P. L. IX. 535 ; *with* in : S. A. 1084.

See **Self-displeased.**

Displeasure, *sb.* dislike, disfavour, disapproval : P. L. IX. 993 ; X. 952, 1094 ; S. A. 733 ; Ps. VI. 2.

Displode, *vb. tr.* to discharge or fire off with explosive violence : P. L. VI. 605.

Disport, (1) *sb.* sport, pastime : P. L. IX. 520, 1042.

    (2) *vb. intr.* to sport, make merry, *fig. of the winds* : P. L. VIII. 518.

Disposal, *sb.* dispensation, Divine control of the course of events : S. A. 210, 506.

Dispose, (1) *sb.* (*a*) disposal, dispensation : S. A. 1746.

    (*b*) control, **at his dispose,** under his control : P. R. III. 34 ; **at dispose,** to deal with according to one's will : P. R. III. 369.

    (2) *vb. tr.* (*a*) to arrange, regulate, adjust : P. R. IV. 56.

    (*b*) to regulate, govern, control : P. L. III. 115 ; to order, command : P. L. I. 246.

    (*c*) to adapt, make suitable, or ready (*for*) : P. L. XI. 54.

    (*d*) to make inclined : P. L. XII. 349; *with* to : P. L. V. 646 ; S. A. 1382.

    (*e*) **dispose of,** do what one will with : P. L. VIII. 170 ; find a use for : P. R. II. 400.

Disposer, *sb.* one who controls another, *of God* : P. L. IV. 635 ; *of Satan* : P. R. I. 393.

Disposition, *sb.* dispensation : S. A. 373. *See* **Disposal.**

Dispossess, *vb. tr.* to deprive of possession, eject, drive out : P. L. IV. 961 ; VII. 142 ; to banish (*from*) : P. L. XII. 28.

Dispraise, (1) *sb.* blame, censure : P. L. VI. 382 ; XI. 166 ; S. A. 1723.

    (2) *vb. tr.* to blame, censure : P. R. III. 56.

Disproportioned, *part. adj.* unmetrical, unrhythmical, *hence,* inharmonious, discordant(?), *fig. of sin* : S. M. 19.

Disproportion, *sb.* want of symmetry or due relation between things : P. L. VIII. 27.

Disputant, *adj.* disputing, engaged in controversy : P. R. IV. 218.

Dispute, (1) *sb.* (*a*) contest, strife : P. L. VI. 123.

    (*b*) disputation, controversy, discussion : P. L. VIII. 55, 77, 158 ; X. 828 ; P. R. IV. 214.

    (2) *vb. tr.* (*a*) to argue about, discuss : P. L. V. 822.

    (*b*) to strive against, resist : S. A. 1395.

Disrelish, (1) *sb.* dislike, disgust : P. L. X. 569.

    (2) *vb. tr.* to destroy the relish of : P. L. V. 305.

Dissect, *vb. tr.* to cut in pieces : P. L. IX. 29.

Dissemble, *vb. intr.* to conceal one's real feeling or intention : P. R. I. 467 ; C. 805.

Dissembler, *sb.* one who dissembles, hypocrite : P. L. III. 681.

Dissension, *sb.* disagreement, discord : P. L. XII. 353.

Dissent, (1) *sb.* refusal of assent : P. L. IX. 1160.

    (2) *vb. intr.* to think differently, disagree, *with* from : P. L. VI. 146 ; to bring or hold difference of opinion or feeling(?), to be unlike(?) : P. L. V. 679.

Dissevering, *part. adj.* disuniting, freeing from that which confines : C. 817.

Dissimulation, *sb.* that by which concealment is affected, **gray dissimulation,** gray head assumed to disguise the real appearance : P. R. I. 498.

Dissipation, *sb.* dispersion, separation : P. L. VI. 598.

Dissolute, *adj.* wanton, lewd, debauched : P. L. XI. 803 ; S. A. 702 ; *sup.* : P. R. II. 150.

Dissolution, *sb.* (*a*) final destruction of the world : P. L. III. 458 ; XII. 459.

    (*b*) extinction of life, death : P. L. X. 1049 ; XI. 55, 552 ; annihilation : P. L. II. 127.

Dissolve, *vb.* (1) *tr.* (*a*) to melt by heat : P. L. XII. 546 ; to melt or disintegrate, *fig.* : S. A. 729 ; Il P. 165 ; to soften, *fig.* : P. R. II. 165.

    (*b*) to release from life : P. L. III. 457.

    (*c*) to bring to an end, destroy : P. L. IV. 955 ; P. R. II. 436.

    (*d*) to break the continuity of, disconnect : S. A. 177.

    (*e*) to break or destroy the power of (*magic spells*) : S. A. 1149.

    (2) *intr.* (*a*) to become disintegrated or dissipated : P. L. VIII. 291 ; XI. 883.

    (*b*) to break up, disperse : P. L. II. 506.

Dissonance, *sb.* discord : P. L. VII. 32 ; C. 550.

Dissonant, *adj.* discordant : S. A. 662.

Dissuade, *vb. tr.* (*a*) to give advice against, speak against : P. L. II. 188 ; IX. 293.

(*b*) to divert by reasons, render adverse : P. L. II. 122.

Distance, *sb.* (*a*) intervening space, remoteness : P. L. VII. 379 ; VIII. 21, 113 ; X. 247, 683 ; *with* from : S. A. 1550; **at distance,** with space intervening : S. A. 954.

(*b*) alienation of feeling, coldness : P. L. IX. 9.

(*c*) deferential attitude : P. L. IV. 945 ; **keep distance due,** show proper respect and reserve, *fig. of stars* : P. L. III. 578.

Distant, *adj.* (*a*) remote, far off, not near : P. L. III. 428, 501, 566, 621 ; IV. 453 ; VI. 530, 551 ; VII. 87 ; IX. 576 ; X. 362 ; P. R. II. 353 ; IV. 454.

(*b*) in distance or extent : P. L. X. 673.

Distaste, *sb.* dislike : P. L. IX. 9.

Distemper, (**1**) *sb.* (*a*) disease, malady : P. L. XI. 53 ; disease of mind : P. L. IV. 118.

(*b*) perturbation, excitement : P. L. IX. 887.

(**2**) *vb. tr.* to disorder, disturb, derange : P. L. VII. 273 ; XI. 56.

part. adj. **distempered,** out of humour, irritated : P. L. IX. 1131; mentally disordered : P. L. IV. 807.

Distend, *vb.* (**1**) *tr.* to extend : P. L. XI. 880.

(**2**) *intr.* to expand, dilate : P. L. I. 572.

Distil, *vb. tr.* (*a*) to let fall in drops, *of tears* : Cir. 7.

(*b*) to give forth in vapour : P. L. V. 56.

part. adj. **distilled,** obtained by distillation : C. 556.

Distinct, (**1**) *adj.* clear, plain, or definite to the mind : S. A. 1595; clear to the eye, or *adv.* clearly, plainly (?) : P. L. IX. 812.

(**2**) *past. part.* (*a*) marked, distinguished : P. L. VII. 536.

(*b*) decorated, adorned : P. L. VI. 846, 847.

Distinction, *sb.* mark of difference : P. L. V. 590.

Distinguish, *vb.* (**1**) *absol.* to discern, perceive : C. 149.

(**2**) *intr.* to make distinctions, discriminate : P. L. V. 892.

Distinguishable (distínguisháble : P. R. III. 424), *adj.* (*a*) capable of being perceived : P. L. II. 668.

(*b*) capable of being distinguished or discriminated from others : P. R. III. 424.

Distort, *vb. tr.* to twist out of shape, deform : P. L. II. 784.

Distract, *vb. tr.* to confound, perplex, bewilder : P. L. IV. 18 ; P. R. I. 108 ; S. A. 1286.

part. adj. **distract,** confounded, bewildered : S. A. 1556.

Distress, (**1**) *sb.* anguish, affliction, misery : P. L. X. 942 ; XII. 613 ; sore trouble or calamity : P. L. X. 920 ; Ps. LXXXII. 11 ; either of the above : Ps. IV. 3 ; LXXXVI. 21.

(**2**) *vb. tr.* to afflict, make miserable : S. A. 1330 ; C. 905.

Distrust, *sb.* (*a*) doubt, suspicion : P. R. I. 355 ; III. 193.

(*b*) discredit, loss of confidence : P. L. XI. 166.

(*c*) breach of trust : P. L. IX. 6.

Distrustfully, *adv.* in a distrustful manner, with doubt : Ps. III. 5.

Disturb, (**1**) *sb.* disturbance, disorder : P. L. VI. 549.

(**2**) *vb. tr.* (*a*) to agitate and destroy *love, peace* : P. L. VI. 266 ; IX. 262 ; to break up the quiet or tranquility of *a place* : P. L. II. 102, 971 ; IV. 994 ; VI. 225 ; *a person* : P. L. V. 226 ; C. 820 ; *sleep* : P. L. IX. 191 ; P. R. IV. 409.

(*b*) to agitate or disquiet mentally : P. L. IX. 668, 918 ; S. A. 1546.

(*c*) to interfere with, interrupt : P. L. II. 657 ; L. 7.

(*d*) to turn aside (*from*) : P. L. I. 167.

Disturbance, *sb.* (*a*) interruption of arrangement : P. L. II. 373.

(*b*) *pl.* interruption of peace, tumult : P. L. X. 897.

Ditty, *sb.* simple song : P. L. I. 449 ; XI. 584 ; L. 32.

See **Smooth-dittied.**

Diurnal. *adj.* (*a*) of or belonging to the day : P. L. VII. 22 ; X. 1069 ; **diurnal rhomb** : P. L. VIII. 34. *See* **Rhomb.**

(*b*) daily : P. L. IV. 594 ; VIII. 22 ; **diurnal sphere** : P. L. VII. 23. *See* **Sphere.**

Divan, *sb.* council (possibly with a covert allusion to the Oriental council of state presided over by the Sultan (?)) : P. L. X. 457.

Diverse (díverse), *adv.* in different directions : P. L. IV. 234 ; X. 284.

Divert, *vb. tr.* (*a*) to turn aside (*from*) : P. L. IX. 814.

(*b*) to lead astray from duty or right : P. R. II. 349.

Divide, *vb. intr.* (*a*) to separate into different parts, part : P. L. IV. 233 ; VI. 70, 570 ; XII. 157, 199 ; P. R. IV. 32 ; N. O. 50.

(*b*) to separate or disjoin *one thing from something else* : P. L. III. 419 ; VI. 381 ; VII. 251, 262, 269, 340, 352 ; C. 279.

(*c*) to take or have a portion of, share : P. L. IX. 214 ; *with* with : P. L. X. 379, 836 ; *with prep. inf.* **divide to sing with**, share in a song with : P. 4 ; to lessen by causing others to share with one : P. R. I. 401.

(*d*) to mark off (*the night*) into watches : P. L. IV. 688.

part. adj. **divided**; (*a*) distributed into shares : P. L. IV. 111.

(*b*) separated from other : P. L. VI. 230.

Dividual, *adj.* (*a*) separate *from another* : P. L. XII. 85.

(*b*) shared in common : P. L. VII. 382.

Divine (dívine : S. M. 3 ; C. 469) (1) *adj.* (*a*) partaking of the nature of God or of the gods, proceeding from God or the gods, *said of persons or what pertains to them as birth, voice, etc.*: P. L. II. 99 ; III. 44; IV. 291 ; V. 278, 458, 546; VII. 2, 72 ; VIII. 295, 314, 436 ; IX. 606, 899 ; X. 139 ; XI. 319, 354 ; P. R. I. 35, 141 ; A. 4, 30 ; D. F. I. 35 ; *sup.* : Il P. 12 ; *of command, disposal, effect, majesty, power, work, etc.* : P. L. V. 159, 256, 806 ; VI. 101, 158, 184, 780 ; VII. 195 ; IX. 865 ; X. 857, 858 ; S. A. 44, 210, 422, 526 ; C. 469 ; *of compassion, love, wrath, etc.* : P. L. III. 141, 225, 411 ; VIII. 215 ; IX. 993 ; P. R. II. 138 ; S. A. 1683 ; Ps. LXXX. 13, 29, 77 ; *of sounds* : P. L. V. 625 ; S. M. 3 ; C. 245 ; *of things* : P. L. I. 683 ; V. 67 ; IX. 776 ; XII. 9 ; *of a place* : Ps. LXXX. 58 ; **divine conformity** or **similitude**, likeness to God : P. L. XI. 512, 606 ; the latter as a synonym of Christ : P. L. III. 384 ; **divine resemblance**, resemblance to God : P. L. IV.

364 ; *possibly adv.* in a divine manner(?) : P. L. V. 734.

(*b*) excellent in the highest degree : P. L. IX. 986 ; C. 476, 630.

(*c*) dear to or watched over by the gods : Il P. 100.

(*d*) prescient or foreboding (*of*) : P. L. IX. 845.

(2) *vb.* (*a*) *tr.* to learn by intuition : P. L. X. 357.

(*b*) *intr.* to foretell, prophesy : N. O. 177.

Divinely, *adv.* (*a*) by the agency of God : P. L. VI. 761 ; VIII. 500 ; P. R. I. 26 ; IV. 357 ; S. A. 226.

(*b*) in a divine manner : P. L. X. 67.

(*c*) with more than human perfection : P. L. IX. 489.

Divinely-warbled, *adj.* modulated in a godlike manner : N. O. 96.

Divinity, *sb.* the Divine nature, Godhead : P. L. IX. 1010.

Divisible, *adj.* capable of being divided : P. L. VI. 331.

Divulge, *vb. tr.* (*a*) to proclaim : P. R. III. 62 ; *with two acc.* : S. A. 1248.

(*b*) to make known, reveal : P. L. VIII. 73 ; S. A. 201.

(*c*) to impart generally, bestow upon all : P. L. VIII. 583.

Dizzy, *adj.* (*a*) giddy, having the sensation of vertigo : P. L. II. 753.

(*b*) thoughtless, heedless : P. R. II. 420.

*** Do,** *vb.* (*pres. 2d sing.* dost : P. L. I. 17 ; VIII. 588 ; P. R. II. 417 ; III. 21, *etc.* ; *3d sing.* does : C. 223, 411, *elsewhere* doth ; *pret.* did ; *2d sing.* didst : P. L. III. 10, 393, 401 ; V. 120, 886, etc.) (1) *tr.* (*a*) to perform, effect, execute, bring to pass : P. L. I. 152 ; II. 162, 384 ; III. 105 ; IV. 475, 855, 1008 ; V. 121 ; VI. 29, 241, 600, 683, 695 ; VII. 65, 164, 506, 637 ; VIII. 203, 549, 561, 562, 636 ; IX. 375, 926 ; X. 2, 69, 141, 158, 175, 470, 826, 1086 ; XI. 256, 694, 791 ; XII. 493, 501 ; P. R. I. 15, 88, 223, 389 ; II. 259, 399, 444, 448, 456 ; III. 8, 74, 100, 180 ; IV. 168, 372, 440, 475, 489 ; S. A. 243, 478, 781, 793, 896, 1104, 1128, 1210, 1217, 1373, 1385, 1520, 1594 ; D. F. I. 76 ; C. 431 ; L. 57 ; S. XVII. 11 ; Ps. VII. 8 ; LXXXVI. 34 ; LXXXVIII. 41 ; Soph. 1 ; *with acc. and dat.* : P. L. I. 149 ; S. A. 486 ; D. F. I. 56 ; V. Ex. 10, 17 ; *absol.* : P. L. IX. 944 ; **to do good** or **ill** :

P. L. I. 159, 160; VII. 151; P. R. I. 423.

(b) to commit, perpetrate: P. L. IX. 889; XII. 475.

(c) to inflict, render, offer, show, *with acc. and to*: P. L. V. 462, 844; IX. 835; XII. 103; S. A. 1191; C. 535; *with acc. and dat.*: P. L. I. 414; P. R. I. 75, 80; IV. 487; S. A. 1178; C. 392, 611.

(d) (*only in past part.*) to complete, finish: P. L. III. 203; IX. 199; N. O. 105; L'A. 115; C. 137, 1012.

(2) *intr.* (a) to act *in a specified way*: P. L. VI. 566, 805; VIII. 588; P. R. I. 495; III. 64, 195; Ps. LXXXIII. 33, 36; *part. for inf.*: L. 67.

(b) to perform deeds, opposed to *suffer*: P. L. II. 199.

(3) *as an auxiliary*: P. L. I. 7, 17, 86, 96; II. 263; P. R. II. 417; III. 21, 44; S. A. 124, 204, 448, 674, 707, 1329; V. Ex. 53; W. S. 14, 15; M. W. 1; L. 108; S. I. 3; XXII. 9; Petr. 2; Ps. IV. 39; LXXX. 1; LXXXIV. 4; LXXXVI. 64; LXXXVIII. 22, 33.

(4) *as a substitute for a verb just used, to avoid repetition, or elliptically for the paraphrastic form*: P. L. I. 495; IV. 389; V. 409; P. R. II. 452; III. 97, 162, 165, 353; S. A. 773, 818; S. M. 19; C. 82; *tr. with object*: C. 624.

In combination with other words;

(a) do amiss, sin: Ps. VII. 36.

(b) have to do with, be concerned about or connected with: P. R. II. 389; C. 122.

vbl. sb. doing, *pl.* action: P. L. IV. 622; X. 142; XI. 720; XII. 50; P. R. I. 469; S. A. 947; U. C. II. 27; *sing. gerund*: P. L. II. 340.

Doat, *vb.* (*pres. 2d sing.* doat'st) *intr.* to love to excess or be over fond (*on*): P. R. II. 175.

Doctor, *sb.* (a) learned man: S. A. 299; C. 707.

(b) physician: U. C. II. 19.

Doctrine, *sb.* principle of belief or faith: P. L. V. 856; XII. 506; P. R. II. 474; IV. 290; S. A. 297; C. 787.

Dodge, *vb. intr.* to shift about or change places (*with*): U. C. I. 8.

Dodona, *sb.* the city of Epirus containing the oracle of Jove: P. L. I. 518.

Doer, *sb.* one who has done a deed: S. A. 248.

Doff, *vb. tr.* to take off: S. A. 1410; N. O. 33.

Dog, (1) *sb.* the domestic animal *Canis*: S. A. 694; S. XII. 4; *fig.* dogs of Hell, Sin and Death: P. L. X. 616; the dog Anubis: N. O. 212. *See* Anubis.

(2) *vb. tr.* to hunt, track, *fig.*: C. 405.

Dole, *sb.* sorrow, grief: P. L. IV. 894; S. A. 1529.

Doleful, *adj.* dismal, gloomy: P. L. I. 65.

Dolorous, *adj.* (a) dismal, cheerless: P. L. II. 619; P. R. I. 364; N. O. 140.

(b) expressing sorrow or distress; P. L. VI. 658.

Dolphin, *sb.* the animal *Delphinus delphis*: P. L. VII. 410; L. 164.

Domain, *sb.* (a) territory over which dominion is exercised: P. R. IV. 81.

(b) estate, lands held in possession: Dante 2.

Domestic, *adj.* (a) pertaining to the home: P. L. IV. 760; XI. 617; S. A. 917, 1048.

(b) attached to or fond of the home: P. L. IX. 318.

Domination, *sb.* the fourth of the nine orders of angels: P. L. III. 392; V. 601, 772, 840; X. 87, 460.

Dominic, *sb.* the Dominican order of monks: P. L. III. 479.

Dominion, *sb.* (a) sovereign authority, lordship: P. L. IV. 430; VI. 422, 887; VII. 532; VIII. 545; X. 244, 400; XII. 27, 68; P. R. II. 434; III. 296; *fig. of the sun*: P. L. IV. 33.

(b) territory over which authority is exercised: P. L. V. 751; *in chaos*: P. L. II. 978; *fig.* that lighted by the moon's rays: P. L. III. 732.

(c) domination: P. L. II. 11; III. 320. *See* Domination.

Donation, *sb.* (a) act of giving: P. L. XII. 69.

(b) gift, grant: P. R. IV. 184.

Doom, *sb.* (1) (a) judgement, decision: P. L. II. 550.

(b) sentence of punishment, condemnation: P. L. I. 53; II. 209; III. 159, 224; VI. 278, 378, 385, 692; IX. 763, 953; X. 76, 172, 344, 378, 517, 769, 841, 926, 1026; XI. 40; XII. 428; Cir. 17; place of doom, hell: P. L. IV. 840.

(c) appointed lot, fate: S. I. 10.

(d) the action of judging, trial: P. L. VI. 817.

(e) **general doom**, the last judgement: P. L. III. 328; XI. 76; **trump of doom**, trumpet calling to the last judgement: N. O. 156.

(2) *vb. tr.* (a) to pronounce sentence against: P. L. III. 401, 404; D. F. I. 33; to condemn *to a place*: P. L. IV. 890; condemn to be, *with two acc.*: P. L. X. 796.

(b) to destine to an adverse fate: L. 92.

(c) to decree, appoint, *with two acc.*: P. L. II. 316.

See **Hell-doomed.**

Door, *sb.* (a) gate, that which opens to yield entrance to a house or other enclosed place: P. L. I. 723; II. 881; IV. 189; VII. 566; XI. 17, 731, 737; P. R. I. 82, 281; S. VIII. 2; Ps. LXXXIV. 38.

(b) passage into a building or other enclosed place: P. L. I. 504; V. 299; VI. 9; X. 389, 443; S. A. 950; V. Ex. 34, 85; Il P. 84; L. 130; **within doors**, within the house: S. A. 77; **out of doors**, out of the house: L'A. 113; *fig. of the mouth*: V. Ex. 5; *of death*: Ps. LXXXVIII. 11.

See **Barn-door.**

Dorian, *adj.* belonging to or characteristic of the music or the poetry of the Dorian people: P. L. I. 550; P. R. IV. 257.

Doric, *adj.* Dorian: P. L. I. 519, 714; **Doric lay**, pastoral song: L. 189.

Dotage, *sb.* excessive fondness: S. A. 1042.

Dothan, *sb.* a place about ten miles north of the city of Samaria: P. L. XI. 217.

Double, (1) *adj.* (a) twofold: P. L. XI. 201; S. A. 593; C. 335.

(b) two together, being in pairs: P. L. V. 783; XI. 129.

(c) twice as much: P. L. IV. 102; IX. 332; X. 850; S. A. 53.

(d) equivocal: P. R. I. 435.

(2) *vb. tr.* (a) to increase by adding an equal portion: P. L. IV. 1009; VI. 602; X. 1040; C. 955; to commit twice: P. L. I. 485.

part. adj. **doubled**, united so as to form one rank: P. L. I. 616.

Double-faced, *adj.* having two faces: S. A. 971.

Double-formed, *adj.* combining the

forms of two different beings: P. L. II. 741.

Double-founted, *adj.* having two sources: P. L. XII. 144.

Double-mouthed, *adj.* having two mouths: S. A. 971.

Double-shade, *vb. tr.* to increase the darkness and gloom of: P. R. I. 500.

Doubt, I. *sb.* (a) uncertainty of mind, indecision of belief: P. L. IV. 888, 907; V. 554; VI. 630; VIII. 13, 179; XII. 473; P. R. II. 12; S. A. 454; **in doubt**, in uncertainty: P. L. IX. 615; P. R. IV. 501; **no doubt**, without question, certainly: P. L. IV. 426, 795, 890; VIII. 568; IX. 257; P. R. IV. 473; S. A. 905; **call in doubt**: S. A. 43. *See* **Call.**

(b) a question proposed for solution: P. L. VIII. 64.

(c) apprehension, suspicion, fear: P. L. I. 558; IV. 18; VII. 60; IX. 251; X. 782, 793; XI. 211; P. R. III. 193; S. A. 740; *with* of: P. L. IX. 95; **without doubt**, beyond apprehension: C. 409.

II. *vb.* (*pres. 2d sing.* doubt'st: P. R. II. 377) (1) *tr.* (a) to hesitate to believe: P. L. VI. 563; VIII. 116; IX. 270; P. R. IV. 296; *with clause without introductory word*: P. R. I. 79; II. 383; *introduced by* that: S. A. 1379; *by* how: P. R. I. 137; *by but after negative*: P. L. IX. 244; X. 1022; XI. 349; *by* but that *after negative*: P. L. XII. 285; **doubt his ways not just**, doubt whether his ways are just: S. A. 300.

(b) to distrust, call in question: S. A. 1745.

(c) to scruple, hesitate, delay: P. R. II. 377; *with prep. inf.*: P. L. II. 94; P. R. II. 368.

(d) to fear, *with clause introduced by* lest: P. L. IV. 983; to have misgivings about obtaining: S. A. 920; to fear for the stability of, consider uncertain or insecure, P. L. I. 114.

(2) *intr.* to be in uncertainty or wavering in belief: P. R. II. 11, 147.

Doubtful, *adj.* (a) admitting of doubt, uncertain, questionable: P. L. I. 527; II. 154, 203; S. A. 477.

(b) of uncertain issue or result: P. L. II. 486; V. 682; VI. 423.

(c) hesitating because of uncertainty or fear : S. A. 732.

Doubtless, *adv.* undoubtedly, certainly : P. L. II. 315; IX. 745; S. A. 1473.

See **Tongue-doughty.**

Dove, *sb.* the bird *Columba* : P. L. XI. 857 ; the form assumed by the Holy Ghost : P. R. I. 30, 83, 282.

Dove-like, *adj.* in the manner of a dove : P. L. I. 21.

Dower, *sb.* property which a woman brings to her husband at marriage, *fig.* : P. L. V. 218.

Down, (1) *sb.* (a) level tract of country used for pasturing sheep : P. L. IV. 252 ; C. 505.

(b) fine soft plumage of birds : S. A. 327 ; C. 251.

(2) adv. (a) in a descending direction, from a higher to a lower place or position : P. L. I. 46; II. 771, 935; III. 562, 574; (a) **up and down,** to and fro or hither and thither, the direction indefinite : P. L. II. 841 ; III. 441 ; X. 287.

(b) to the world : P. L. IV. 4 ; VII. 73 ; XII. 51.

(c) from the clouds to the earth : P. L. X. 1075 ; XI. 743.

(d) to or on the ground : P. L. IV. 327, 396 ; VI. 593, 839 ; IX. 893 ; X. 513.

(e) to or toward the south : P. L. X. 675 ; XI. 392.

(f) into a recumbent position on the ground or floor : P. L. IV. 457 ; V. 91 ; L'A. 110.

(g) into a sitting position : P. L. V. 433 ; VII. 587.

(h) into an overthrown or conquered condition : P. L. I. 327 ; III. 391 ; P. R. III. 34 ; U. C. I. 6.

(i) into a distressed or afflicted condition : S. A. 698.

(j) into the hand *in payment* : S. A. 1478.

(k) aside from one's self, out of one's possession : P. R. II. 482.

(l) *used for the imperative with the verb elided* : S. A. 322.

(3) prep. (a) in a descending direction through or along : P. L. III. 19 ; IV. 231, 261 ; x. 414 ; XII. 639 ; Il P. 107 ; C. 927.

(b) along the course or current of : P. L. XI. 833 ; L. 62, 63.

See **Plump-down.**

Downcast, *part. adj.* directed to the ground : P. L. I. 523.

Downfall, *sb.* fall from rank and state, ruin : P. L. I. 116.

Downward, (1) *adv.* (a) from a higher place to a lower, down : P. L. III. 722 ; IV. 591 ; VII. 237 ; IX. 79.

(b) toward the ground : P. L. I. 681.

(c) to the ground : C. 53.

(d) in the lower parts : P. L. I. 463.

(2) *adj.* directed toward the ground : Il P. 43.

Downy, *adv.* (a) **downy gold,** down the color of gold : P. L. V. 282.

(b) covered with down or soft hairs : P. L. VII. 438 ; IX. 851.

(c) like down in softness : P. L. IV. 334.

Draff, *sb.* refuse, dregs : P. L. X. 630 ; S. A. 574.

Drag, *vb. tr.* to draw or pull by main force *a convict or criminal to or by way of punishment* : P. L. IV. 965 ; VI. 260, 358 ; XII. 454 ; S. A. 1371 ; C. 608.

Dragon, *sb.* (a) huge serpent : P. L. X. 529 ; S. A. 1692.

(b) Satan, *with def. art.* : P. L. IV. 3 ; N. O. 168.

attrib. pertaining to the mythical flying serpent ; (a) of dragons : Il P. 59.

(b) like that of a dragon : C. 131.

See **River-dragon.**

Dragon-watch, *sb.* a dragon acting as a sentinel : C. 395.

Drain, *vb. tr.* (a) to draw or cause to flow off : P. L. XI. 570.

(b) to exhaust the supply : P. R. II. 346.

(c) to deprive (*of virtue*) : P. L. VI. 851.

(d) to distil : P. L. III. 605.

Draught, *sb.* (a) quantity of liquid drunk at one time : P. L. V. 306 ; C. 701.

(b) air inhaled at one breath : S. A. 9.

Draw, *vb.* (*pres. 2d sing.* draw'st : P. L. IV. 975 ; *pret.* drew; *past part.* drawn) (1) *tr.* (a) to pull along, cause to move toward the force applied : P. L. III. 522; IV. 975 ; VII. 306, 480 ; S. A. 360, 1650 ; C. 554.

(b) to shrink, contract : P. L. X. 511.

(c) to pull *something over* so as to conceal or cover : P. L. XI. 205 ; Il P. 36 ; *something round about* : P. L. XII. 379.

(d) to inhale : P. L. VII. 14 ;
VIII. 284, 348 ; S. A. 7 ; L. 126 ;
to drink, *fig. of the sun* : P. L. XI.
845 ; to smell : P. L. X. 267.

(e) to attract as a magnet : P.
R. I. 168.

(f) to cause to come by some
non-physical force : P. L. X. 629 ;
S. A. 1596 ; to induce to come, attract, allure, lead : P. L. II. 308 ;
IX. 822, 914, 956 ; X. 262 ; P. R.
II. 161 ; S. A. 804 ; A. 71 ; to entice, lead astray ; P. L. VII. 144 ;
P. R. I. 372 ; *with two acc.* : S. A.
1041 ; to convert to one's party,
induce to follow : P. L. II. 692 ;
III. 161 ; IV. 63 ; V. 710.

(g) to influence to a course of
action, persuade, *with acc. and
prep. inf.* : P. L. I. 472 ; S. A. 762.

(h) to bring together, assemble :
P. L. V. 729.

(i) to cause to follow as a consequence : S. A. 736, 1267 ; S.
XXI. 6.

(j) to cause *evil* to come or fall
(*on* or *upon*) : P. L. III. 220 ; S.
A. 1058.

(k) to take out, extract : P. L.
X. 886 ; to pull *a sword* from the
sheath : P. L. I. 664.

(l) to cause *liquid* to flow from
a vessel, *fig.* : P. L. VII. 365 ; to
cause (*tears*) to flow : L. 107.

(m) to elicit, evoke : P. L. II.
25 ; IV. 532.

(n) to represent by a picture,
delineate : P. L. III. 509.

(2) *intr.* or *absol.* (a) to pull,
exert strength in drawing : S. A.
1626.

(b) to move, advance : P. L. VI.
798.

(c) to unsheathe one's sword :
C. 487.

In combination with other words;
(a) approach, **draw hitherward** :
S. A. 1067 ; **draw near** : P. L. IX.
434, 578 ; **draw nigh** : P. L. III.
645, 646 ; IV. 861 ; V. 82 ; XI. 238 ;
S. A. 178 ; Ps. LXXXVIII. 12.

(b) **draw in**, suck in : P. L. VII.
416.

(c) **draw off**, withdraw, go away,
depart : P. L. IV. 782.

(d) **draw on**, occasion, bring on :
P. L. IX. 223 ; allure : P. L. X.
245 ; approach : P. L. IX. 739.

(e) **draw out**, lengthen, prolong :
P. L. X. 801 ; L'A. 140 ; delude, mislead : P. R. II. 166.

(f) **draw up**, raise, lift : P. L.
III. 517.

See **Up-draw.**

Dread, (1) *sb.* (a) great fear, terror,
awe : P. L. VI. 59 ; P. R. IV. 576 ;
Ps. LXXX. 8 ; fear as to a future
event : P. L. I. 555 ; IV. 82 ; XII.
14 ; P. R. I. 53.

(b) cause of fear : P. L. XI. 248;
P. R. III. 306 ; person to be feared
or held in reverence : P. L. I. 406 ;
S. A. 342, 1474 ; **living Dread**,
God : S. A. 1673.

(2) *vb. tr.* to fear greatly, regard
with awe or reverence : P. L. I.
333, 464 ; IX. 158 ; P. R. IV. 626 ;
S. A. 530, 1247, 1417 ; to look
forward to with anxiety, fear, or
terror : P. L. I. 644 ; II. 263, 293,
474 ; X. 998 ; P. R. III. 22 ; S. A.
733.

part. adj. (a) **dread**, to be great-
ly feared, held in awe, terrible,
awful : P. L. I. 589 ; II. 16, 510 ;
III. 326 ; VI. 648 ; IX. 969 ; N. O.
206 ; C. 405, 441 ; L. 132 ; **dreaded** :
P. L. II. 964 ; IV. 929 ; VI. 491 ;
IX. 1114 ; P. R. I. 58 ; N. O. 222 ;
H. B. 13.

Dreadful, *adj.* terrible, awful : P. L.
I. 130, 183, 564 ; II. 426, 672, 706 ;
III. 393 ; IV. 426, 990 ; VI. 105,
225, 828 ; VIII. 335 ; X. 121, 521,
779, 814, 848 ; XII. 236, 644 ; S.
A. 1591, 1622 ; N. O. 164 ; Ps.
LXXX. 67.

Dreadless, *adj.* fearless, intrepid :
P. L. VI. 1.

Dream, I. *sb.* (a) train of thoughts
or images passing through the
mind during sleep : P. L. IV. 803 ;
V. 93, 98, 112, 115 ; VIII. 310,
482 ; IX. 1050 ; XII. 595, 611 ; P. R.
I. 395 ; II. 283 ; IV. 408 ; Il P.
9, 147 ; C. 457, 813.

(b) object seen in a dream ; P.
L. VIII. 292.

(c) vision of the fancy : P. L.
VII. 39 ; P. R. II. 337 ; IV. 291.

II. *vb.* (*pret. and past part.*
dreamed) (1) *tr.* (a) to behold in
sleep : P. L. V. 120.

(b) to fancy, imagine : L'A. 129 ;
with clause : P. L. I. 784 ; *with
prep. inf.* : P. L. XI. 95 ; *absol.* :
P. L. III. 459.

(2) *intr.* (a) to have a train of
thoughts or images pass through
the mind during sleep : P. L. III.
514 ; *with of* : P. R. II. 264 ; P. L.
V. 31.

(b) to imagine, form visions: P.
L. II. 315; L. 56; *with* of: P. L.
VIII. 175; XII. 386.

Drear, *adj.* (a) dreary, dismal,
gloomy: N. O. 193; C. 37.

(b) dreadful, terrible: P. L. X.
525.

(c) grievous, lamentable: Il P.
119.

Dreary, *adj.* dismal, gloomy: P. L.
I. 180; II. 618.

Dreg, *sb. pl.* refuse: P. L. VII. 238.

Drench, (1) *sb.* draught: P. L. II.
73.

(2) *vb. tr.* (a) to wet thoroughly:
C. 996; *fig.* to steep in slumber:
P. L. XI. 367.

(b) *fig.* to drown (*thoughts*): S.
XXI. 5.

Dress, I. *sb.* array, fine clothes: P. L.
XI. 583.

II. *vb.* (1) *tr.* (a) to array, attire:
S. XIV. 11.

(b) to cultivate or tend (*a garden*): P. L. IX. 205.

(c) to prepare (*food*): L'A. 86.

(2) *intr.* to adorn oneself with
fine clothing: P. L. XI. 620.

vbl. sb. **dressing**, decking, adorning: M. M. 7.

Drift, *sb.* design, aim, intention:
P. R. III. 4; S. XVII. 6.

Drink, I. *sb.* liquid to be swallowed:
P. L. V. 344, 451; IX. 838; XI.
473; P. R. II. 265; III. 289; IV.
590; S. A. 541, 554, 557.

II. *vb.* (*pres. 2d sing.* drink'st:
P. L. XI. 532; *pret.* drank; *past
part.* drunk) (1) *tr.* (a) to swallow:
P. L. X. 728; XI. 532; C. 722;
Ps. LXXX. 23; **drink one's fill of**:
S. XIV. 14.

(b) to absorb: P. L. VII. 362.

(2) *absol.* to swallow water or
some other liquid: P. L. V.
637; P. R. I. 340, 352; S. A.
550; C. 527; *with* of: P. L. II.
584.

part. adj. **drunk**, intoxicated:
S. A. 1670.

Drive, *vb.* (*pres. 2d sing.* drov'st:
P. L. III. 396; *pret.* drove; *past
part.* driven) *tr.* (a) to force to
move on before or away from one:
P. L. II. 366, 367; VI. 858; X.
245; XI. 186, 646; P. R. I. 90,
360; V. Ex. 5; *with advs.* indicating direction or character of
motion: P. L. I. 260, 418; II. 772;
VI. 738; IX. 62; X. 538; P. R.
I. 153; *with* out: P. L. II. 86;

III. 677; VI. 52, 715; VII. 185;
XI. 105; *of things*: P. L. I. 223;
X. 287, 1075; *fig. of evil, etc.*: P. L.
IV. 153, 753; VII. 32, 57; D. F. I.
68; C. 456; *absol.* or *intr.* to drive
flocks: L. 27.

(b) to constrain to go: P. L.
IV. 169; X. 843.

(c) to direct the course of *a
vehicle*: P. L. III. 438; *absol.* to
act as driver: P. L. III. 396; VI.
831.

(d) to carry along, *of wind*: P.
L. X. 290; XI. 739, 842; *fig.*: S.A.
209; *of water*: P. L. XI. 853.

(e) to force, compel, *with prep.
inf.*: P. L. IV. 184.

(f) to cause (*time*) to pass: U.
C. II. 15.

Drizzling, *part. adj.* falling in fine
drops: P. L. VI. 545.

Dromedary, *sb.* light and fleet camel:
P. R. III. 335.

Drone, *sb.* (a) the male of the honey-
bee: P. L. VII. 490.

(b) *fig.* sluggard: S. A. 567.

Droop, *vb. intr.* (a) to hang or bend
down: P. L. IX. 430.

(b) to come to a close: P. L. XI.
178.

(c) to sink in exhaustion, languish: P. L. I. 328. S. A. 594.

(d) to become despondent: S.
A. 594.

part. adj. **drooping**; (a) bending
down: P. R. IV. 434.

(b) sinking down: L. 169.

(c) dejected, despondent: P. L.
VI. 496; C. 812.

Drop, I. *sb.* (a) globule of a fluid:
P. L. II. 607; VII. 292; XI. 416;
C. 912; **drop serene** (*L.* gutta
serena), the disease of the eye
called amaurosis: P. L. III. 25.

(b) tear-drop: P. L. V. 132;
fig. of rain: P. L. IX. 1002.

II. *vb.* (*perf. formed with the
auxiliary* be: L. 191) (1) *intr.* (a) to
fall, descend: P. L. I. 745; II. 933;
VI. 839; IX. 893; XI. 535; L. 191.

(b) to drip or trickle (*with*): P.
L. IX. 582; P. 16.

(2) *tr.* (a) to let fall in drops:
P. L. V. 23; C. 106, 840; *fig.*:
P. L II. 113; to shed (*tears*):
P. L. XII. 645.

(b) to let fall: P. R. I. 324.

(c) to sprinkle as if with drops:
P. L. VII. 406.

part. adj. **dropping**; (a) falling
in drops: P. L. IV. 630.

(b) letting drops fall: Hor. O. 15.
See **Amber-dropping, Dew-drop, Minute-drop.**

Dropsy, *sb.* morbid accumulation of water in the body: P. L. XI. 488.

Dross, *sb.* refuse, waste matter: P. R. III. 29; T. 6.
See **Bullion-dross.**

Drossy, *adj.* abounding with waste matter, *sup.*: P. L. V. 442.

Drouth, *sb.* (a) want of rain, dryness, aridity: C. 298.

(b) dry land, desert: P. R. III. 274.

(c) thirst: P. L. VII. 66; P. R. I. 325; C. 66.

Drove, *sb.* shoal of fish: C. 115.

Drown, *vb. tr.* (a) to overflow, inundate: P. L. XI. 894.

(b) to suffocate by submersion in water: P. L. XI. 13; *fig.*: P. L. XI. 757.

(c) to make unheard by a louder sound: P. L. VII. 36.

Drowse, *vb.* (*past part. disyl.*: P. L. VIII. 289) *intr.* to be heavy with sleep: P. L. XI. 131.

part. adj. **drowsed,** heavy with sleep: P. L. VIII. 289.

Drowsiness, *sb.* sleepiness: A. 61.

Drowsy, *adj.* (a) sleepy: V. Ex. 61.

(b) lulling, soporific: Il P. 83.

Drowsy-flighted, *adj.* flying slowly and heavily on account of drowsiness: C. 553.

Drudge, (1) *sb.* one employed in servile labour, slave: P. L. II. 732; S. A. 1338, 1393.

(2) *vb. intr.* to labour servilely: S. A. 573.

part. adj. **drudging,** toiling: L'A. 105.

Drug, (1) *sb.* (a) medicinal substance: C. 255.

(b) substance, **spicy drugs,** spices: P. L. II. 640.

(2) *vb. tr.* to nauseate: P. L. X. 568.

Druid, *sb. pl.* priests and bards of the ancient Celts: L. 53.

Drum, *sb.* the musical instrument: P. L. I. 394.

Dry, (1) *adj.* free from water or moisture, not wet: P. L. I. 227; II. 940; VII. 284, 304, 307; IX. 179; X. 294; XI. 861; XII. 197; P. R. III. 264; S. A. 582; Il P. 66; Ps. LXXXIV. 22.

(2) *adv.* so as to take away moisture and cause dryness: P. L. XI. 842.

(3) *sb.* (a) dry land: P. L. III. 652; VII. 292.

(b) one of the supposed qualities which in combination with another determined the nature or 'complexion' of a body: P. L. XI. 544; *personified*: P. L. II. 898.

(4) *vb. tr.* (a) to cause to evaporate: P. L. VIII. 256; P. R. IV. 433.

(b) to wither: D. F. I. 4.

Dryad (*pl.* dryades: C. 964), *sb.* wood-nymph: P. L. IX. 387; C. 964.

Dry-eyed, *adj.* tearless: P. L. XI. 495.

Dubious, *adj.* (a) not clear, indistinct, dim: P. L. II. 1042.

(b) of uncertain issue: P. L. I. 104.

Duck, *sb.* sudden downward movement of the head: C. 960.

Due, (1) *adj.* (a) falling by right (*to*): P. L. II. 453, 454; S. A. 1225.

(b) that should be given, morally owed, justly claimable, proper: P. L. III. 190, 191, 578, 738; IV. 48; V. 817; VIII. 11; IX. 566, 800; X. 994; XII. 12; Ps. LXXXIII. 59; or *adv.* adequately (?): C. 776; merited: P. L. X. 833; XI. 253; P. R. III. 87; S. A. 513; appropriate or fitting (*to*): P. L. XII. 399, 400.

(c) such as ought to be, proper, fitting, rightful: P. L. I. 569; IV. 180; VI. 445; VII. 149; VIII. 385; XI. 440; P. R. III. 10; S. A. 1055; C. 12; Ps. VII. 57; *of time*: P. L. XII. 152; P. R. III. 182, 440; L. 7; regular, established: P. L. XII. 264.

(d) such as is necessary, adequate, sufficient: P. L. XI. 533; C. 199.

(e) appointed or expected to come or arrive: P. L. X. 93; Il P. 155.

(2) *sb.* that which is claimed as a right, lawful claim: P. L. II. 850; III. 245; C. 137.

(3) *adv.* exactly, directly: P. L. V. 303; C. 306.

Duel, (1) *sb.* combat between two persons; P. L. XII. 387; S. A. 1102; spiritual combat: P. R. I. 174.

(2) *vb. tr.* to encounter in combat: S. A. 345.

Dulcet, *adj.* sweet to the ear, melodious: P. L. I. 712.

(b) sweet to the taste, delicious: P. L. v. 347.

Dulcimer, *sb.* the musical instrument : P. L. vii. 596.

Dull, *adj.* (a) heavy, inert : L'A. 42.
(b) stupid, doltish : C. 477, 634.

Duly, *adv.* (a) rightly, fitly : P. L. v. 145.
(b) regularly : L'A. 106.

Dumb, *adj.* (a) destitute of the power of speech : V. Ex. 5 ; C. 796.
(b) not speaking, silent : N. O. 173.
(c) not accompanied by words : P. L. ix. 527.

Dun, (1) *sb.* the Don, a river in Yorkshire, England : V. Ex. 92.
(2) *adj.* dark, dusky : P. L. iii. 72 ; C. 127.

Dunbar, *sb. attrib.* **Dunbar field,** the field of the battle of Dunbar, fought Sept. 3, 1650: S. xvi. 8.

Dungeon, *sb.* deep dark place of confinement, prison : S. A. 69, 367 ; where the winds were confined : P. L. x. 697; L. 97 ; *of hell* : P. L. i. 61 ; ii. 317, 1003 ; x. 466 ; *fig.* : *of a dense wood* : C. 349 ; *of the body deprived of the sense of sight* : S. A. 156 ; *of the soul in moral darkness* : C. 385.

Durable, *adj.* enduring, permanent : P. L. v. 581 ; x. 320.

Durance, *sb.* imprisonment : P. L. iv. 899.

See **Ever-during.**

Dusk, *adj.* dark from absence of light : P. L. xi. 741 ; dark in colour : P. R. i. 296 ; iv. 76.

Dusky, *adj.* (a) somewhat dark in colour : P. L. ii. 488 ; v. 186 ; vi. 58.
(b) deprived of or deficient in light, dim, obscure : P. L. i. 226 ; v. 667 ; C. 99.
(c) not seeing clearly (?) : N. O. 223.

Dust, *sb.* (a) fine dry particles of earth : P. L. vii. 292, 577 ; x. 178 ; xi. 460 ; S. A. 141 ; Ps. vii. 16, 17 ; as the common origin of man : P. L. iv. 416 ; v. 516 ; vii. 525 ; ix. 178 ; x. 208, 770, 1085 ; xi. 529 ; Cir. 19 ; as that to which man returns : P. L. x. 208, 748, 770, 1085 ; xi. 199, 463 ; *hence,* death : P. L. x. 805.
(b) powder : C. 165.

Duteous, *adj.* dutiful, obedient: P. L. ix. 521.

Duty, *sb.* (a) what one ought to do, an obligation : S. A. 853, 870; *with prep. inf.* : P. R. iii. 175 ; *absol.* moral obligation: P. R. iii. 172.
(b) obedience, submission : P. R. ii. 326 ; due respect, reverence ; P. L. x. 106.
(c) **on duty,** engaged in the performance of prescribed military service : P. L. i. 333.

Dwarf, *sb.* human being much below the ordinary stature : P. L. i. 779.

Dwell, *vb.* (*pres. 2d sing.* dwell'st : P. L. vii. 7 ; P. R. iv. 466 ; C. 268 ; *pret. and past part.* dwelt)
(1) *intr.* (a) to abide, remain : P. L. xii. 344.
(b) to live, exist : P. L. xii. 22.
(c) to have one's habitation : P. L. i. 47 ; ii. 86, 398, 841 ; iii. 5, 335, 570, 670 ; iv. 214, 377; v. 373, 456, 500 ; vi. 292, 380 ; vii. 7, 156, 329, 627 ; viii. 103 ; ix. 125, 322, 836 ; x. 399, 492, 587 ; xi. 43, 48, 178, 259, 348, 608, 838, 901 ; xii. 146, 248, 281, 316, 487 ; P. R. i. 116, 391 ; iv. 466, 616 ; S. A. 1673 ; Cir. 18 ; C. 268, 521 ; Ps. ii. 8 ; iv. 42 ; lxxxiii. 24 ; lxxxiv. 4, 39 ; lxxxviii. 47 ; cxxxvi. 74 : H. B. 9 ; *of the soul* : P. L. iii. 249 ; S. A. 159 ; S. xiv. 2 ; *of the Holy Spirit in the hearts of men* ; P. R. i. 462 ; *fig. of desolation, joy, liberty, peace, etc.* : P. L. i. 66, 250 ; iii. 216, 225 ; vi. 788 ; viii. 185 ; ix. 729 ; xii. 84 ; C. 428, 667, 988 ; L'A. 10 ; Il P. 5 ; Ps. lxxxv. 40.
(2) *tr.* (a) to inhabit : P. R. i. 331.
(b) *according to the punctuation of the first edition,* to cause to abide (*in*) : P. L. xii. 487.
vbl. sb. **Dwelling,** habitation, place of abode : P. L. iv. 378, 884 ; viii. 118 ; P. R. ii. 80 ; home : P. L. vii. 183, 570 ; house : P. L. xi. 747.

Dwelling-place, *sb.* place of abode : P. L. ii. 57 ; vii. 625.

Dye, (1) *sb.* colour : D. F. I. 5.
(2) *vb. tr.* to colour : P. L. x. 1009.

E

*Each, *adj.* I. every individual of a number regarded separately, *followed by a substantive* : P. L. i. 222, 704, 707 ; ii. 26 ; iii.

516, 584; IV. 114, 120, 240, 696, 697; V. 145, 326, 327, 337, 428, 479; VI. 98, 230, 231, 233, 529, 530, 885; VII. 327, 334, 391, 399; VIII. 152, 156, 223, 306, 342, 349, 351, 514, 582; IX. 179, 428; XI. 765; XII. 142, 503; P. R. I. 304, 349, 402; II. 19, 22, 155, 462; IV. 475; S. A. 397, 1599, 1607, 1655; V. Ex. 35; N. O. 100, 196, 234; T. 9; W. S. 10; C. 19, 311, 839; L. 83, 94; S. XV. 2; Ps. II. 4; VII. 25; LXXXVIII. 56; **each other**, every other: P. R. II. 406; *of two*, both, either: P. L. I. 578; II. 535; IV. 408; V. 252, 279; VI. 307, 362, 770; IX. 66; X. 288; XI. 659; P. R. III. 327; IV. 33; S. A. 1617.

absol. or pron. every one, every body; (a) *referring to a preceding sb.*: P. L. II. 421, 523, 901; III. 720; VI. 239, 498, 541, 578, 753; VII. 392; XI. 128, 587; S. A. 65; *of two*: P. L. II. 670, 711, 714; S. XVII. 10, 11; *followed by* of: P. L. X. 324.

(b) *distributing a pl. subj. or obj.*: P. L. I. 737; II. 181; VI. 782; P. R. II. 123, 240; S. A. 1289; *as antecedent of* their: P. L. V. 133, 477; VII. 453; VIII. 393; XI. 889; *of two*: P. L. IV. 1003.

(c) **each other**, one another, one the other: P. L. II. 502; IX. 220; X. 112, 235, 513, 712, 959, 961; S. A. 1087; **each to other**: P. L. IV. 683; V. 576; IX. 259; XII. 57; **each the other**: P. L. IX. 1052; **each from other**: P. L. IX. 1093.

Eager, *adj.* (a) ardent, earnest: L. 189.

(b) keenly desirous (*of*): P. L. VI. 378.

(c) keen (*appetite*): P. L. IX. 740.

Eagerly, *adv.* ardently, earnestly: P. L. II. 947.

Eagle, *sb.* the bird *Aquila*: P. L. V. 271; VII. 423; S. A. 1695. *See* **Bird**.

Eagle-winged, *adj.* having wings like those of an eagle: P. L. VI. 763.

Ear, *sb.* (1) organ of hearing: P. L. II. 920, 953; III. 647; IV. 800; V. 36, 810; VII. 177; IX. 736; X. 99, 506; P. R. I. 199; III. 390; S. A. 177, 858, 1231, 1568; V. Ex. 28; Il P. 120; C. 170,

203, 272, 570; F. of C. 17; (a) as sensitive to musical sounds: P. L. I. 787; V. 626; VIII. 606; N. O. 94, 126; Cir. 3; L'A. 148; Il P. 164; A. 73; L. 49; as sensitive regarding quantity and accent in verse set to music: S. XIII. 4; as delighting in or dreading speech of a certain character: P. L. II. 117; V. 545; VII. 70; VIII. 1, 211, 335; X. 780; XII. 236; P. R. I. 479; IV. 337; S. A. 937; as the seat of memory: L. 77.

(b) *of the ear of God* as ever willing to listen to man: P. L. X. 1060; XI. 30, 152; S. A. 1172; Ps. V. 1; LXXX. 2; LXXXIV. 30; LXXXVI. 1, 18; LXXXVIII. 8; **mine ear shall not be slow**, I shall not be slow to hear and attend: P. L. III. 193.

(c) *fig. of inanimate things* as sensitive to musical sounds: P. L. VII. 35.

(d) *fig. of the mind* as capable of understanding or appreciating lofty thoughts: P. L. VIII. 49; IX. 47; C. 458, 784, 997.

(e) **all ear**, eagerly attentive: P. L. IV. 410; C. 560; having the sense of hearing in every part of the body: P. L. VI. 350.

(f) **give ear**: P. L IX. 1067; **lend one's ear**: P. R. IV. 272; C. 706.

(2) audience: S. A. 921; *pl.* attention: P. L. V. 771.

(3) spike of grain: P. L. IV. 982; XI. 435.

Earl, *sb.* Thomas Darcy, Earl of Rivers: M. W. 3; James Ley, first Earl of Marlborough: S. X. 1.

Early, (1) *adj.* (a) belonging to the first part of the morning: P. L. IX. 799; XI. 275; M. M. 9; *sup.*: P. L. IV. 642, 651.

(b) relatively near the beginning of the year, *comp.*: L'A. 89; *sup.*: P. R. II. 365.

(c) pertaining to the first part *of youth, sup.*: S. IX. 1.

(2) *adv.* (a) in the first part of the morning: P. L. IX. 225; S. A. 1596; A. 56.

(b) near the beginning of a course of action, soon: P. L. IX. 457.

(c) in good season, before it is too late: S. XVIII. 14.

Earn, *vb. tr.* to gain by labour : P. L.
x. 592, 1054; P. R. ii. 401;
S. A. 573, 1260; L'A. 106; to
gain (*repute, rest, salvation*) : P. L.
ii. 473; xi. 375; P. R. i. 167.
Earnest, *adj.* (*a*) intent : P. L. x.
553.
(*b*) fervent, zealous : S. A. 359.
(*c*) **in earnest,** with a serious
purpose, seriously, really : P. L.
i. 458; ix. 939.
Earnestly, *adv.* eagerly, zealously,
urgently : P. L. ix. 1141; P. R.
ii. 367.
Earth, *sb.* (1) visible surface of
the earth, ground, soil : P. L. i.
710; iv. 152, 228; v. 2, 190;
vii. 332, 333, 452, 468; xi. 744;
xii. 183; Il P. 44; C. 730; S.
xx. 7; Ps. vii. 15; cxiv. 9; (*a*)
as a solid stratum : P. L. xi.
568.
(*b*) as a place of burial : N. O.
189; D. F. I. 30; M. W. 32.
(*c*) soil as productive : P. L.
iv. 645; v. 401; vii. 309, 312,
313, 335, 541; viii. 96; ix. 720;
xi. 804; P. R. iv. 30; C. 712;
Ps. lxxxv. 45.
(*d*) soil as that from which man
was formed : P. L. ix. 149; C.
244; and to which he returns at
death : P. L. x. 776.
(2) the world in which we live :
P. L. i. 365, 382; ii. 484, 502;
iii. 64, 283, 444, 451, 457, 508,
520, 528, 724; iv. 5, 341, 546,
672, 677, 733; v. 88, 141, 224,
302, 321; vi. 195; vii. 389, 398,
451, 522, 531, 581, 624; viii. 98,
99, 118, 274, 306, 338, 369, 513,
631; ix. 50, 153, 195, 813, 1011;
x. 22, 36, 72, 94, 229, 273, 325,
360, 399, 404, 653, 679, 891, 897;
xi. 22, 136, 339, 345, 384, 473, 698,
780, 825, 883, 888, 893, 896; xii.
29, 147, 281, 371, 437, 463, 528;
P. R. i. 50, 99, 125, 131, 218; ii.
44, 114, 179, 435; iii. 24, 61, 246;
iv. 45, 148, 201, 453; S. A. 165,
1272; N. O. 63; M. W. 6; C. 6,
1014; Ps. ii. 2, 19, 23; lxxxiii.
68; Ariosto i. 4; ₁H. B. 3; (*a*)
*in immediate combination or con-
trast with heaven, the heavens, hell,
or the air* : P. L. ii. 383; iii. 133,
274, 322, 335, 685; iv. 208, 940;
v. 78, 164, 329, 519, 574, 576,
649, 752; vi. 299, 374, 516, 640,
893; vii. 90, 124, 160, 328;
viii. 120, 224, 483; ix. 99, 605,

658; x. 22, 57, 69, 638, 647; xi.
66, 335, 901; xii. 549; P. R. i.
63, 237; iii. 65, 68; D. F. I. 51,
59; H. 108; P. 2, 32; S. M. 17;
conceived as resting on a foundation : P. R. iv. 456; C. 599.
(*b*) *more or less clearly personified* : P. L. i. 687; v. 338; vii.
453, 501; ix. 782, 1000, 1041; N.
O. 160; C. 797; Ps. cxiv. 15;
cxxxvi. 14; the goddess Ge : P.
L. i. 509, 778; ₁P. R. iv. 563,
566; D. F. I. 47.
(*c*) land as distinguished from
air or water : P. L. iv. 432, 540;
v. 201, 752; vii. 307, 502, 534,
629; xii. 579.
(3) the world considered as
a sphere : P. L. i. 785; ii. 927;
iii. 592, 651, 731, 739; iv.
594, 661, 1000; v. 260, 578; vi.
218; vii. 23, 242, 269, 276, 278,
345, 350; viii. 23, 32, 129, 137,
144, 161; ix. 59; x. 669, 835; xi.
379; ₁P. R. i. 365; Ps. lxxxii.
19; cxxxvi. 21; *in immediate
combination or contrast with
heaven, the heavens, or the air* :
P. L. i. 9; ii. 1004; iv. 722;
vii. 63, 90, 167, 232, 256, 560;
viii. 16, 17, 70, 89, 91, 178.
(4) the inhabitants of the earth :
P. L. iii. 146; vii. 471; S. A.
174; Ps. lxxxii. 25, 26.
(5) one of the four elements
which form the universe : P. L.
iii. 715; v. 416, 417; P. R. ii.
124.
Earth-born, *adj.* born of the goddess Ge : P. L. i. 198; iv. 360;
V. Ex. 93.
Earthly, *adj.* of or pertaining to
the earth, terrestrial, opposed to
heavenly : P. L. v. 464; vii.
14, 82, 179; viii. 120, 522; xii.
315; P. R. iv. 612; N. O. 138.
absol. : P. L. viii. 453; ix.
1083.
Earth-shaking, *adj.* making earth
tremble : C. 869.
Earthy, *adj.* dwelling on the earth :
P. L. ix. 157; characteristic of
earthly existence : P. L. iv. 583;
T. 20; S. xiv. 3.
Ease, (1) *sb.* absence of pain or
trouble, comfort : S. A. 271, 917;
(*a*) physical comfort : P. L. iv.
329; xi. 794; P. R. iv. 299; S.
A. 18.
(*b*) freedom from pain or solicitude : P. L. ii. 261; iv. 96, 893;

IX. 129; S. A. 17; Cir. II. ; C. 687 ; L. 152.

(c) absence of effort, inactivity : P. L. II. 227 ; freedom from labour, leisure : U. C. II. 21.

(d) absence of difficulty (or sence (a)(?) : P. L. I. 320.

(e) **at ease**, free from pain, anxiety, or discomfort : P. L. II. 521, 841, 868 ; VII. 407 ; IX. 1120 ; P. R. II. 201 ; **with ease**, easily, without difficulty : P. L. II. 878, 1041 ; III. 563 ; IV. 187, 632 ; V. 439 ; IX. 245 ; X. 394, 622 ; XI. 536 ; P. R. IV. 97, 378.

(2) *vb. tr.* (a) to free from care or anxiety : P. L. XII. 274.

(b) to relieve of, *in passive with prep. omitted* : P. L. IV. 739.

(c) to lighten (*a load, burden*) : P. L. V. 59 ; IX. 801.

(d) to alleviate, mitigate : P. L. II. 458 ; S. A. 72.

(e) to facilitate, make less difficult : P. L. VII. 430 ; X. 260.

See **Heart-easing.**

Easily, *adv.* (a) with little exertion or difficulty : P. L. I. 696; III. 301 ; VI. 596 ; VII. 48, 609 ; X. 31, 136 ; XI. 141; P. R. I. 471; II. 194; IV. 126, 168 ; S. A. 48, 291, 409, 943, 1005 ; P. 54.

(b) with little resistance or reluctance : P. L. III. 94 ; P. R. III. 156 ; S. A. 1466.

East, (1) *adv.* to or toward the east : P. L. IV. 178 ; VIII. 138 ; XII. 141 ; P. R. III. 272, 316.

(2) *sb.* (a) portion of the horizon or the sky near the place of the sun's rising : P. L. X. 685 ; *with def. art.* : P. L. IV. 595, 623 ; V. 142 ; VII. 30, 380, 583 ; VIII. 162 ; XI. 203 ; M. M. 2; C. 101; *with poss. pron.* : P. L. VII. 245, 370.

(b) eastern part of the world, the orient, *with def. art.* : P. L. II. 3 ; P. R. I. 250 ; II. 197.

(c) eastern side (*of*) : P. L. IV. 209.

(3) *adj.* situated toward the east : P. L. XI. 118 ; **East India** : P. L. V. 339.

See **North-east.**

Eastern, *adj.* (a) situated toward the east : P. L. III. 557; IV. 542 ; V. 1, 275 ; XI. 190 ; XII. 638, 641; N. O. 22 ; L'A. 59.

(b) dwelling in the east : P. L. XII. 362 ; C. 138.

(c) coming from the east : P. L. I. 341; S. A. 548.

Eastward, *adv.* toward the east : P. L. IV. 211 ; V. 309 ; X. 292 ; XII. 145.

Easy, (1) *adj.* (a) free from difficulty, requiring little labour or exertion : P. L. II. 81, 1031 ; III. 524 ; IV. 421, 433 ; VI. 499 ; IX. 734 ; *with prep. inf.* : P. L. IX. 569 ; S. A. 95 ; C. 286 ; *comp.* : P. L. II. 345 ; VI. 37 ; X. 978 ; *with prep. inf.* : P. L. VI. 286 ; *sup.* : P. L. IV. 47 ; P. R. III. 128 ; **with easy eye**, easily with the eye : P. R. III. 293.

(b) not difficult to cross : P. L. X. 305, 393.

(c) not difficult to obtain : P. L. VI. 437 ; *comp.* : S. A. 772.

(d) causing little pain or discomfort : P. L. II. 256 ; IV. 330 ; *comp.* : P. L. II. 573 ; IV. 943 ; *sup.* : P. L. VIII. 183.

(e) not beset with difficulties : P. R. I. 120.

(f) showing no effort, *of verse* : W. S. 10.

(2) *adv.* with little effort or difficulty : P. L. VI. 632 ; VII. 304 ; IX. 24 ; X. 58 ; S. A. 583 ; *comp.* : P. L. VIII. 626 ; IX. 699 ; *sup.* : P. L. XI. 119, 549 ; P. R. IV. 361.

Easy-hearted, *adj.* readily yielding, compliant : C. 163.

Eat, *vb.* (*pres. 2d sing.* eat'st : P. L. VII. 544 ; VIII. 329 ; XI. 532 ; *pret.* eat : P. L. IX. 781 ; P. R. I. 352 ; II. 275 ; L'A. 102 ; *past part.* eaten : P. L. IX. 764, 869 ; X. 122, 199) (1) *tr.* to masticate and swallow as food : P. L. X. 178, 204, 205, 728 ; XI. 532 ; XII. 186 ; L'A. 102 ; Ps. LXXX. 22 ; **eat death** : P. S. IX. 792 ; **eat one's fill** : P. L. IX. 595, 1005. *Absol.* : P. L. VII. 544 ; VIII. 147, 309 ; IX. 764, 781, 997 ; X. 143, 162 ; XI. 94 ; *with* of : P. L. VIII. 320, 322, 329 ; IX. 657, 660, 662, 706, 724, 762, 869 ; X. 122, 123, 199, 200, 202.

(2) *intr.* to take food : P. L. V. 637 ; P. R. I. 352 ; II. 274, 275, 314, 321, 336, 368, 377.

part. adj. eating, consuming, tormenting : L'A. 135.

Eaves, *sb.* projecting edge of a roof : Il P. 130.

Ebb, *sb.* reflux of the tide : P. L. XI. 847.

Ebbing, *part. adj.* flowing back toward the ocean : C. 19.
See **Soft-ebbing.**

Ebon, *adj.* black, dark : L'A. 8 ; C. 134.

Ebrew, (*spelled* Hebrew *when used as adj.*) *sb.* a member of the Israelitish race : S. A. 1308, 1319, 1540.
See **Hebrew.**

Ecbatan (Ecbátan), *sb.* P. L. XI. 393. *See* the following.

Ecbatana, *sb.* the capital city of Media and the summer residence of the Persian Kings : P. R. III. 286.

Eccentric, (1) *adj.* not having the same centre of revolution : P. L. v. 623.

　(2) *sb.* (*a*) **by eccentric,** away from the centre : P. L. III. 575.

　(*b*) celestial sphere not having the earth as the centre about which it revolves : P. L. VIII. 83.
See **Sphere.**

Echo, (1) *sb.* repercussion of sound : P. L. X. 861 ; N. O. 100 ; P. 53 ; L. 41 ; *personified*, the woodnymph of classical mythology : C. 230, 275.

　(2) *vb.* (*a*) *intr.* to resound: L'A. 56.

　(*b*) *tr.* to repeat in the manner of an echo : P. L. v. 873.

　part. adj. echoing, giving back sound : P. L. IV. 681 ; IX. 1107.

Eclipse, I. *sb.* (*a*) obscuration of a luminous body : P. L. X. 413 ; considered of evil omen : P. L. I. 597 ; L. 101.

　(*b*) absence of light : S. A. 81.

　II. *vb.* (1) *intr.* (*a*) to suffer an eclipse, be darkened : P. L. II. 666.

　(*b*) to grow dark : P. L. XI. 183.

　(2) *tr.* to overshadow, obscure, surpass : P. L. v. 776.

Ecliptic, *sb.* orbit of the sun : P. L. III. 740.

Ecron, *sb.* Ekron, a city of the Philistines : S. A. 981. *See* **Accaron.**

Ecstasy, *sb.* rapture, transport : Il P. 165 ; C. 625.

Ecstatic, *adj.* of the nature of a trance or mystical frenzy : P. 42.

Eden, *sb.* (*a*) the first home of Adam and Eve : P. L. I. 4 ; IV. 27, 132, 210, 223, 275, 569 ; v. 143 ; VI. 75 ; VII. 65, 582 ; VIII. 113 ; IX. 54, 77, 193, 341 ; X. 89 ; XI. 119, 342 ; XII. 40, 465, 649.

　(*b*) place of delight : P. R. I. 7.

　(*c*) state of supreme happiness : P. L. IV. 507.

　(*d*) **sons of Eden,** a tribe of people dwelling somewhere near the union of the Tigris and Euphrates rivers : P. L. IV. 213.

Edge, (1) *sb.* (*a*) cutting side of a sword : P. L. VI. 252, 323 ; *fig. of virtue* : P. R. II. 455.

　(*b*) border of a garment: L. 105.

　(*c*) extreme margin, brink, *fig.* (*of hazard*) : P. R. I. 94 ; or forefront (*of battle*) (?) : P. L. I. 276 ; VI. 108.'

　(2) *vb. tr.* to border : N. O. 185.
See **Grunsel-edge.**

Edict, *sb.* decree, command : P. L. v. 798 ; S. A. 301.

Edifice, *sb.* building, structure : P. R. IV. 55 ; S. A. 1588 ; *fig. of the world* : P. L. VIII. 104.
See **Re-edify.**

Edomite, *sb.* an inhabitant of Edom, the country south of the Dead Sea : P. R. II. 423.

Edward, *sb.* King Edward VI. of England : S. XI. 14.

Edwards, *sb.* Rev. Thomas Edwards, the author of several pamphlets against Independency and Toleration : F. of C. 12.

E'er. *See* **Ever.**

Effect, (1) *sb.* (*a*) that which is produced by an agent, consequence, result : P. L. II. 595 ; VIII. 95 ; IX. 650, 875 ; XI. 424 ; P. R. II. 215.

　(*b*) power to produce consequences, force, efficacy : P. L. III. 612 ; IX. 865 ; C. 630.

　(*c*) state of being operative : P. L. VII. 175.

　(*d*) achievement, realization : P. L. VI. 493.

　(2) *vb. tr.* to produce, bring about, achieve : P. L. I. 647 ; IX. 152 ; S. A. 681.

Effectual, *adj.* producing or having power to produce its intended effect : P. L. III. 170 ; powerful in effect, efficient : P. R. IV. 432.

Effeminacy, *sb.* unmanly weakness : S. A. 410.

Effeminate, *adj.* unmanly : P. L. XI. 634 ; proceeding from unmanly weakness : P. R. IV. 142.

Effeminately, *adv.* weakly : S. A. 562.

Efficacious, *adj.* operative, effectual : S. A. 1437.

Efficacy, *sb.* effectiveness, potency: P. L. x. 660.

Effluence, *sb.* an efflux or emanation : P. L. iii. 6.

Effulgence, *sb.* splendid radiance : P. L. iii. 388 ; v. 458 ; vi. 680.

Effusion, *sb.* copious emission (*of flame, etc.*) : P. L. vi. 765.

Egg, *sb.* that from which the young of certain animals are produced : P. L. vii. 418.

Eglantine, *sb.* the sweet-briar, *here probably* the honey suckle (?) or *possibly* the dog-rose (?) : L'A. 48.

Egress (**egréss**), *sb.* going out, departure : P. L. ii. 437.

Egypt, *sb.* the country in northern Africa : P. L. i. 421, 480, 721 ; iii. 537 ; iv. 171 ; P. R. iii. 384, 417 ; C. 676 : Ps. lxxx. 33 ; lxxxvii. 11 ; (*a*) the home of the Israelites : P. L. xii. 157, 219 ; **land of Egypt** : P. R. iii. 379 ; visited by the plagues : P. L. i. 339, 488 ; xii. 190 ; **Egypt land** ; Ps. cxxxvi. 38.

(*b*) the place to which Christ was taken when fleeing from Herod : P. R. ii. 76, 79.

Egyptian, *adj.* in or of Egypt : P. L. v. 274 ; xii. 182 ; who is a native of Egypt : P. L. ix. 443.

Egypt-land, *sb.* Ps. lxxxi. 19, 42. *See* **Egypt,** *sense* (*a*).

Eight, *sb.* the cardinal numeral next after seven : M. W. 7.

Eighth, *adj.* the ordinal of eight : P. L. ix. 67.

Either, (**1**) *adj.* (*a*) the one or the other of two : P. L. i. 424 ; xi. 363.

(*b*) each of two, both : P. L. ii. 538, 649 ; iii. 350, 487, 641 ; iv. 695 ; v. 131, 284 ; vi. 214, 221, 570, 778, 800, 844 ; x. 415 ; xii. 637 ; P. R. iv. 409 ; S. xvii. 12.

(**2**) *absol. or pron.* the one or the other : P. L. ii. 670, 721 ; viii. 388 ; *with* of : S. A. 1292.

(**3**) *conj. correlative with* or : P. L. i. 644 ; ii. 96, 229, 364 ; ix. 284, 407, 1176 ; x. 111, 126, 898 ; xi. 505 ; S. A. 1033, 1458 ; C. 483 ; S. xix. 9.

Eject, *vb. tr.* to expel, banish, thrust out : P. L. xi. 52 ; P. R. i. 414 ; S. A. 1207.

Elaborate, *adj.* executed with great nicety, highly finished : P. L. viii. 539.

Eld, *sb.* old age : D. F. I. 13.

Eldest, *adj.* (*a*) first-born, *fig.* : P. L. v. 180 ; S. xvii. 14.

(*b*) first created, most ancient : P. L. ii. 894, 962.

El Dorado, *sb.* the king of the fabulous city (Manoa) of boundless wealth supposed to exist somewhere in the northern part of South America ; the word is here used for the city itself, which is placed in Guiana : P. L. xi. 411.

Eleale (Eleále), *sb.* Elealeh, a town of Moab a short distance north of Heshbon, (*spelled* Eleale *in Vulg.*) : P. L. i. 411. *See* **Hesebon.**

Elect, (**1**) *adj.* chosen as the special object of divine favour, *of the Israelites* : P. L. xii. 214 ; *of angels* (defined in *Christian Doctrine* ix. as beloved or excellent) : P. L. iii. 136, 360 ; vi. 374 ; predestined to eternal salvation : P. L. iii. 184.

(**2**) *vb. tr.* to choose as the object of divine favour : S. A. 678.

Election, *sb.* act of choosing, choice : P. L. x. 764.

Electra, *sb.* the daughter of Agamemnon and Clytemnestra, **Electra's poet,** Euripides, the author of the tragedy *Electra* : S. viii. 13.

Elegant, *adj.* correct and delicate in taste : P. L. ix. 1018.

Element, *sb.* (*a*) one of the simple substances of which all material things are composed ; these substances being earth, water, air, and fire : P. L. ii. 925, 1015 ; iii. 715 ; iv. 993 ; v. 180, 415 ; vi. 222 ; xi. 50 ; P. R. ii. 334.

(*b*) earth, water, air, and fire as they appear separately in nature : P. R. ii. 122 ; Il. P. 96.

(*c*) the sky : P. L. ii. 490 ; or the air (?) : C. 299.

(*d*) proper and natural habitation : P. L. ii. 275 ; vii. 16 ; viii. 348.

Elephant, *sb.* the animal *Elephas* : P. L. iv. 345 ; P. R. iii. 329.

Elevate, *vb. tr.* to raise : P. L. ix. 633.

part. or *adj.* **elevate,** raised aloft : P. R. iv. 34 ; exalted (*in thought*) : P. L. ii. 558.

Elf, *sb.* diminutive spirit, **fairy** : P. L. i. 781 ; C. 118, 846.

Eli, *sb.* the Hebrew judge and high priest : P. L. i. 495.

Elijah, *sb.* the Hebrew prophet : P. R. i. 353 ; ii. 19, 268, 277.

Elixir, *sb.* substance supposed to turn baser metals into gold : P. L. III. 607.

Ellops, *sb.* a kind of serpent : P. L. X. 525.

Elm, *sb.* the tree *Ulmus* : P. L. V. 216 ; L'A. 58 ; A. 89 ; C. 354.

Elocution, *sb.* power of speaking, speech : P. L. IX. 748.

Eloquence, *sb.* the art or practice of expressing thought in lofty, fluent, and impassioned language: P. L. II. 556 ; IX. 671 ; P. R. IV. 241, 354 ; *concr.* eloquent language : P. L. V. 149 ; P. R. IV. 268.

Eloquent, *adj.* having the power of eloquence : S. X. 8.

Else, *adv.* (1) other than that mentioned ; (*a*) besides, further, more, *with prons.* : P. L. I. 96 ; VII. 639 ; VIII. 636 ; IX. 786 ; X. 1079 ; XI. 572 ; Il P. 116 ; L. 120 ; *with* all : P. L. II. 591.

(*b*) different, instead, with that exception, *with prons.* : P. L. I. 109, 683 ; II. 769 ; P. R. II. 169 ; III. 129 ; S. A. 1163, 1324 ; *followed by* but : P. L. X. 1096 ; Ps. IV. 12 ; *with sb. preceded by* all : P. L. IV. 434, 752 ; VII. 49 ; VIII. 524, 531 ; X. 805 ; XI. 305, 747 ; P. R. III. 28 ; **little else but** : P. R. IV. 291.

(2) in any other way, by other means : P. L. III. 387 ; IV. 861 ; VIII. 10 ; **how else** : S. A. 604.

(3) in any other place : P. L. VIII. 97 ; **where else** : C. 179.

(4) at another time, *preceded by* but : A. 61.

(5) otherwise, under other circumstances, if not : P. L. III. 125, 635, 725 ; IV. 392, 929 ; V. 63 ; VI. 593, 896 ; VII. 74, 129 ; VIII. 131, 135 ; IX. 975, 1117 ; X. 678, 689 ; XI. 201, 299 ; P. R. I. 12 ; III. 394 ; IV. 165 ; S. A. 315, 586 ; C. 195, 491 ; **or else,** or if it be not so, in the contrary case : P. L. II. 397 ; S. A. 694, 770 ; N. O. 91 ; U. C. I. 3 ; C. 484.

Elsewhere (elsewhere : P. L. I. 656 ; X. 959 ; P. R. I. 458), *adv.* in another place : P. L. I. 656 ; III. 599 ; X. 959 ; P. R. I. 458 ; IV. 325.

Elude, *vb. tr.* to evade (*vigilance*) : P. L. IX. 158.

Elysian, *adj.* of Elysium, in Greek mythology the abode of the blessed after this life : D. F. I. 40 ;

L'A. 147 ; C. 996 : *said of that which is in heaven* : P. L. III. 359.

Elysium, *sb.* (*a*) the abode of the blessed after this life: P. L. III. 472.

(*b*) perfect happiness : C. 257.

Emathian, *adj.* of Emathia, a district of Macedonia, *hence,* Macedonian : P. R. III. 290 ; S. VIII. 10.

Embalm, *vb. tr.* to impart fragrance to, fill with sweet odour : P. L. II. 842 ; XI. 135.

Embark, *vb. intr.* to go on board ship : P. L. XI. 753 ; S. A. 1045.

Embassy, *sb.* (*a*) body of persons sent on a mission from one government to another : P. R. IV. 67, 121.

(*b*) message entrusted to an ambassador : P. L. III. 658.

Embathe, *vb. tr.* to bathe, wash : C. 837.

Embattle, *vb. tr.* to draw up in battle array : P. L. VI. 550 ; *fig.* P. L. VII. 322.

part. adj. **embattled,** drawn up in battle array : P. L. I. 129 ; VI. 16 ; XII. 213 ; S. A. 129.

See **Re-embattled.**

Embellish, *vb. tr.* to adorn, decorate : P. L. III. 507.

Ember, *sb. pl.* live coals : Il P. 79.

Emblaze, *vb. tr.* (*a*) to light up, cause to shine : C. 73.

(*b*) to adorn with figures of heraldry : P. L. I. 538.

(*c*) to inscribe conspicuously : P. L. V. 592.

part. adj. **emblazoned,** adorned with heraldic decoration : P. L. IX. 34.

Emblazonry, *sb.* shields covered with heraldic decoration : P. L. II. 513.

Emblem, *sb.* inlay, mosaic work : P. L. IV. 703.

Embody, *vb.* (1) *tr.* to organize (*an army*) : P. L. VI. 779.

(2) *intr.* to become corporeal in character : C. 468.

part. adj. **embodied,** organized, arrayed, *of an army* : P. L. I. 574.

Embolden, *vb. tr.* to make bold, encourage : P. L. VIII. 434.

Emborder, *vb. tr.* to place as a border (*on*) : P. L. IX. 438.

Embosom, *vb. tr.* to enclose in the bosom : P. L. V. 597 ; to be enveloped (*in*) : P. L. III. 75.

Emboss, *vb. tr.* (*a*) to adorn with raised work, ornament in relief : P. R. IV. 119.

(*b*) to cover with swellings : P. L. XII. 180.

(*c*) to imbosk, conceal in a wood : S. A. 1700.

Embowed (*trisyl.*), *part. adj.* arched, vaulted : Il P. 157.

Embowel, *vb. tr.* to eviscerate, *fig. of the air* : P. L. VI. 587.

Embower, *vb.* (**1**) *tr.* to cover as with a bower : P. L. IX. 1038 ; to conceal as in a bower : C. 62.

(**2**) *intr.* to form a bower or shady covert : P. L. I. 304.

Embrace, (**1**) *sb.* a clasping in the arms, fond pressure to the bosom : P. L. IV. 322, 471 ; S. A. 389 ; D. F. L 20 ; *fig. of the boughs of trees* : P. L. V. 215 ; sexual intercourse : P. L. II. 793 ; X. 994.

(**2**) *vb. tr.* (*a*) to infold in the arms : P. L. V. 27 ; IX. 990 ; X. 912 ; S. XXIII. 13 ; *absol.* to clasp each other in the arms, join in an embrace : P. L. IV. 771 ; VIII. 626.

(*b*) to surround, encompass : P. L. VII. 90.

(*c*) to receive with willingness, accept with joy ; P. L. XII. 426.

See **Half-embracing, Violet-embroidered.**

Embroidery, *sb.* adornment, *of the markings of flowers* : L. 148.

Embroil, *vb. tr.* to throw into uproar or tumult : P. L. II. 908, 966.

Embrown. *See* **Imbrown**.

Embryo, *sb.* a being in an undeveloped state : P. L. III. 474.

Embryon, (**1**) *sb.* germ, rudiment : P. L. VII. 277.

(**2**) *adj.* embryonic, rudimental : P. L. II. 900.

Emerald, *adj.* of the colour of the emerald : C. 894.

Emergent, *adj.* rising out of the water : P. L. VII. 286.

Emims, *sb.* the prehistoric inhabitants of the land of Moab : S. A. 1080.

Eminence, *sb.* (*a*) high position, exalted station : P. L. II. 6 ; IV. 44.

(*b*) supreme degree : P. L. VIII. 624.

See **Pre-eminence.**

Eminent, *adj.* (*a*) high, elevated, towering above surrounding objects : P. L. I. 590 ; IV. 219 ; *fig.* : P. R. II. 70.

(*b*) remarkable in degree : P. R. III. 91 ; high in merit, distinguished : P. L. V. 594 ; XI. 665, 789.

See **Pre-eminent.**

Eminently, *adv.* (*a*) in an especial degree, highly : S. A. 679.

(*b*) conspicuously, in a manner to attract attention : S. IX. 3.

(*c*) clearly, indisputably : P. L. IX. 976.

Emmet, *sb.* ant : P. L. VII. 485.

Empedocles, *sb.* the Greek philosopher : P. L. III. 471.

Emperor, *sb.* sovereign, supreme ruler, *spec.* Tiberius : P. R. IV. 81, 90, 126 ; Satan : P. L. I. 378 ; II. 510 ; X. 429.

Empire, *sb.* (*a*) supreme power, sovereignty : P. L. I. 114 ; II. 327 : VI. 303 ; XII. 32.

(*b*) territory under the sway of an emperor or supreme ruler : P. L. XI. 387 : P. R. II. 435 ; III. 45, 237 ; IV. 222, 284, 369 ; *with proper name* : P. L. XI. 397 : P. R. III. 270, 296 ; the empire of God : P. L. IV. 111 ; V. 724 ; VII. 96, 555, 609 ; of Satan : P. L. II. 296, 315, 378 ; IV. 390 ; X. 592 ; P. R. I. 63 ; of Adam : P. L. IV. 145 ; XII. 581 ; of chaos and night : P. L. II. 974 ; *fig. of the air* as the empire of winter : D. F. I. 16.

(*c*) inhabitants of this territory : P. L. X. 389.

Empiric, *adj.* versed in physical experimentation : P. L. V. 440.

Employ, *vb. tr.* (*a*) to use, apply : P. L. IV. 763 ; S. M. 8 ; *with prep. inf.*: P. L. IV. 883 ; *with* in : P. L. V. 730 ; *with clause* : P. L. IX. 229 ; S. M. 3.

(*b*) to find work or occupation for, busy, engage : P. L. V. 219 ; *with* on : P. L. III. 628 ; *with* in : P. L. IV. 726.

Employment, *sb.* business, occupation : P. L. V. 125.

Empower, *vb. tr.* to give power or authority to, *with acc. and prep. inf.* : P. L. X. 369 ; *in passive* : P. R. II. 130.

Empress, *sb.* female sovereign, *of Eve* : P. L. IX. 568, 626.

Emprise, *sb.* martial prowess : P. L. XI. 642 ; daring spirit ; C. 610.

Emptiness, *sb.* worthlessness : P. L. VIII. 195.

Empty, (**1**) *adj.* (*a*) vacant, unfilled, *comp.* : P. L. II. 1045.

(b) wanting substance, shadowy: P. L. VII. 39; P. R. IV. 321.

(c) void or destitute (of): P. L. XI. 616.

(d) vain, hollow: P. L. III. 454.

(2) vb. tr. (a) to make vacant or unoccupied: P. L. I. 633; to draw off, fig. of light: P. L. III. 731.

(b) to lay aside (glory): Cir. 20; to deprive of glory: P. L. I. 714.

Empty-vaulted, adj. enclosed by the vault of heaven in which no stars are visible (?): C. 250.

Empyreal (empýreal), adj. of or partaking of the nature of the abode of God and the angels, heavenly, of angels: P. L. II. 430; v. 460, 583; of the angelic form or substance: P. L. I. 117; VI. 433; of heaven or something found in heaven; as, air, mansion, road, etc.: P. L. II. 1047; III. 699; v. 253; VI. 14; VII. 14; X. 380.

Empyrean (empýréan), (1) adj. empyreal: P. L. X. 321.

(2) sb. the abode of God and the angels, heaven: P. L. II. 771; III. 57; VI. 833; VII. 73, 633.

Emulate, vb. tr. to strive to equal, vie with: P. L. IX. 963.

Emulation, sb. rivalry: P. L. II. 298.

Emulous, adj. desirous of rivalling, with of: P. L. VI. 822.

Enamelled, part. adj. (a) bright or glossy, and variegated: P. L. IV. 149; IX. 525; L. 139.

(b) beautified with various colours: A. 84.

Enamour, vb. tr. to enflame with love, captivate: P. L. II. 765; IV. 169; v. 13, 448; P. R. II. 214.

Encamp, vb. (1) tr. to form into a camp: P. L. XII. 591.

(2) intr. to go into camp: P. L. II. 132; VI. 412; X. 276; XI. 656; Ps. III. 17.

Enchanted, part. adj. (a) laid under a spell: C. 517.

(b) endowed with magical powers: S. A. 934.

Enchanter, sb. sorcerer, magician: C. 645, 814, 907.

Enchanting, part. adj. pleasing to the mind or the senses, charming: P. L. X. 353; P. R. II. 158; S. A. 1065; C. 245; L. 59.

Enchantment, sb. incantation, spell, charm: S. A. 1133; Il P. 119; C. 640, 696.

Enclose, vb. tr. (a) to surround so as to prevent free ingress or egress: P. L. IV. 283; VIII. 304; S. A. 1117.

(b) to fence in (from): P. L. III. 420.

(c) to envelop or contain (in): P. L. VII. 486; IX. 494, 722.

(d) to hem in on all sides, of persons: P. L. VI. 101; with round: P. L. I. 617; II. 512; fig. of evils: S. A. 194.

part. adj. **enclosing,** hemming in on all sides: P. R. III. 361.

Enclosure, sb. tract of land surrounded by a wall: P. L. IV. 133; IX. 543.

Encompass, vb. tr. to surround with hymns of praise: P. L. III. 149; with a cloud: Ps. LXXXI. 30; to hem in on all sides (round): P. L. v. 876.

Encounter, (1) sb. hostile meeting, battle: S. A. 1086; fig.: P. L. II. 718.

(2) vb. tr. to meet: P. L. VI. 664.

part. adj. **encountering,** fighting, combating: P. L. VI. 220.

Encroach, vb. intr. to trench or intrude usurpingly (on): P. L. II. 1001.

See **Wide-encroaching.**

Encroachment, sb. act of encroaching upon the domain of another: P. L. XII. 72.

Encumber, vb. tr. to load or oppress (with): P. L. VI. 874; IX. 1051: C. 774.

End, I. sb. (1) extreme part of an extended surface: C. 1014; boundaries of a country: Ps. LXXXVII. 15.

(2) region, quarter: P. L. v. 586; XI. 345.

(3) one of the two extremities of the length of an object: P. L. II. 538; X. 446; P. R. IV. 410; **from end to end,** throughout the length: P. L. IX. 51.

(4) point at which continuity ceases, termination, close: P. L. II. 89, 186, 561; III. 633; VI. 172; VIII. 189; IX. 1189; X. 720, 977, 1004, 1020; XII. 330, 556; P. R. I. 241; III. 197; IV. 151, 391; S. A. 576; D. F. I. 77; U. C. I. 12; C. 136; Ps. LXXXI. 64; (a) **without end,** interminable, never ceasing: P. L. I. 67; VII. 161; without limitation, in-

finite: P. L. III. 142 ; VII. 542 ;
eternally, always : P. L. II. 870 :
V. 165, 615 ; VI. 137 ; X. 797 ;
P. R. II. 442 ; Ps. LXXXV. 17.

(b) **to the end,** to the close of
life : P. L. III. 197 ; S. A. 1720.

(c) **in the end,** at last : P. L.
VI. 731.

(d) **have end,** be finished : P.
R. II. 337 ; S. A. 461 ; A. 7.

(5) destruction, death : P. L.
II. 807 ; XI. 755 ; or ultimate condition (?) : S. A. 704, 709.

(6) completion, consummation :
P. L. VII. 79, 505, 591.

(7) that which is found at the
close, issue, result : P. L. I. 164 ;
XII. 605 ; P. R. III. 211.

(8) intended result of an action,
aim, purpose, intention : P. L.
III. 157 ; IV. 398 ; VIII. 540 ;
P. R. III. 123, 211 ; S. A. 62,
232, 1265 ; C. 160, 196 ; **to what
end,** for what purpose : P. R. III.
350 ; S. A. 522 ; C. 783.

(9) the purpose for which a
thing exists or was created : P. L.
VIII. 35 ; IX. 241 ; X. 167 ; XI.
602, 605 ; P. R. I. 205 ; II. 114 ;
S. A. 893 ; **to no end,** for no purpose : P. L. IV. 442 ; IX. 798.

II. vb. (1) tr. (a) to complete :
L'A. 109 ; to fulfil : P. L. VI.
493.

(b) to bring to a close, finish,
terminate : P. L. II. 390, 487,
514 ; III. 406, 729 ; VI. 98, 258,
296, 702, 703 ; VII. 217 ; IX. 468 ;
XI. 137 ; P. R. I. 125 ; D. F. I.
18 ; absol. to cease to speak : P.
L. II. 106, 291 ; IV. 874 ; VI. 496,
569 ; VIII. 1, 452 ; IX. 733 ; X.
641, 937, 1007 ; XI. 72, 238 ; XII.
552, 606 ; P. R. I. 106, 346.

(c) to kill, destroy, annihilate :
P. L. II. 145, 157 ; X. 797, 856 ;
XI. 300.

(2) intr. (a) to be finished, come
to a close, cease : P. L. III. 266 ;
IV. 833 ; VI. 288 ; VII. 108 ; X.
53, 725 ; XI. 246 ; XII. 6 ; P. R.
I. 309 ; II. 245 ; III. 185 ; IV. 20 ;
S. A. 1043 ; Il P. 129.

(b) to have an end or be ter-
minated (in) : P. L. II. 651 ; N.
O. 226.

(c) to die : U. C. II. 10.

(d) to cease to be : P. L. XI.
502, 786 ; P. R. I. 408.

(e) to issue or result (in) : P.
R. II. 245 ; S. A. 871, 1008.

vbl. sb. **Ending,** conclusion, close :
N. O. 239.

See **Mile-end, Never-ending.**

Endanger, vb. tr. to bring into
danger, put in hazard : P. L. I.
131 ; II. 1017 ; S. A. 1009.

Endear, vb. tr. to bind by ties of
affection, attach : S. A. 796.

part. adj. **endearing,** manifesting affection : P. L. IV. 337.

Endeavour, I. sb. effort, exertion,
labour : S. XIV. 5.

II. vb. (1) tr. to attempt to
gain, strive after : P. L. III. 192 ;
XII. 355 ; P. R. III. 399.

(2) intr. (a) to exert oneself,
strive : P. L. VIII. 260 ; P. R. III.
353.

(b) to attempt, try, with prep.
inf. : S. A. 766.

part. adj. **endeavouring,** making
an effort : V. Ex. 2.

See **Slow-endeavouring.**

Endless, (1) adj. unending, eternal :
P. L. I. 142 ; II. 30, 897 ; IV. 52 ;
X. 754, 840 ; XII. 549 ; P. R. III.
178 ; S. M. 28 ; perpetual, incessant : S. XV. 10.

(2) adv. without end, endlessly,
eternally : P. L. II. 159 ; VI. 694.

Endow, vb. tr. to furnish or enrich
(with) : P. L. IV. 715 ; IX. 149 ;
XI. 58.

Endue, vb. (pres. 3d sing. endu'th :
S. II. 8) tr. to endow, invest :
P. L. II. 356 ; with with : P. L.
V. 473, 815 ; VII. 507 ; VIII. 353.
IX. 324, 561, 871 ; XII. 500 ; P.
R. II. 437 ; IV. 98, 602 ; S. A.
1293 ; to be inherent in : S.
II. 8.

Endurance, sb. ability to endure
suffering : P. L. II. 262.

Endure, vb. (1) tr. (a) to bear, undergo, sustain : P. L. II. 206 ; IV.
925 ; VI. 431 ; IX. 269, 833 ; XI.
365 ; XII. 405 ; absol. : P. L. IV.
920.

(b) to sustain without change :
P. L. IV. 811.

(c) to bear with patience or
without opposition, submit to :
P. L. II. 1028 ; V. 783 ; VI. 111 ;
P. R. I. 476 ; IV. 174 ; to allow to
remain, with two acc. : S. A. 477.

(2) intr. (a) to persist in an
action, hold out : P. L. I. 299.

(b) to last, continue : P. L. XII.
324 ; Ps. CXXXVI. 3 ; to continue
in a certain state, the complement
omitted : P. R. II. 251.

Enemy, *sb.* foe, adversary : P. L.
IV. 825 ; X. 219 ; XII. 318, 482 ;
P. R. II. 330 ; III. 361, 392, 432 ;
S. A. 34, 68, 112, 238, 316, 380,
54C, 640, 642, 782, 856, 878,
882, 1159, 1202, 1416, 1582, 1622,
1711, 1726 ; Ps. VI. 15, 21 ;
LXXXI. 60 ; CXXXVI. 82 ; *of God,
Christ, or angels* : P. L. I. 188 ;
II. 137 ; VI. 466 ; P. R. II. 126 ;
IV. 525 ; *of Satan or his angels* :
P. L. II. 157, 822 ; V. 239 ; VI.
677, 826 ; VIII. ·234 ; IX. 274, 304,
494, 905, 1172 ; X. 625 ; XII. 390 ;
of death : P. L. II. 785 ; *fig. of
hunger* : P. R. II. 372 ; *fig. of law
and sin* : P. L. XII. 415.

  See **Arch-enemy.**

Encrve, *vb. tr.* to weaken morally :
P. R. II. 165.

Enfeeble, *vb. tr.* to weaken and deprive of courage : P. L. IX. 488.

Enforce, (1) *sb.* effort, exertion : S.
A. 1223.

  (2) *vb. tr.* to force, constrain,
oblige, *with prep. inf.* : P. L. XI.
419 ; P. R. I. 472 ; II. 75.

Engage, *vb. tr.* (*a*) to pledge,
promise : P. L. IV. 954 ; *with
prep. inf.* : P. L. IX. 400.

  (*b*) to induce, persuade : P. L.
IX. 963.

  (*c*) to enlist in an undertaking :
P. R. III. 347.

  (*d*) to allow to be drawn, at-
tracted, or involved (?) : C. 193.

Engine, *sb.* machine, instrument :
P. L. IV. 17 ; S. A. 1396 ; U. C.
II. 9 ; L. 130 ; for purposes of
war : P. L. I. 750 ; II. 65, 923 ;
VI. 484, 518, 586, 650.

Enginery, *sb.* engines of war : P. L.
VI. 553.

England, *sb.* the country : S. X. 2.

English, *adj.* of England : S. XIII. 2.

Engrave (*past part.* engraven : P.
L. II. 302), *vb. tr.* to impress
deeply or indelibly : P. L. II.
302 ; XII. 524.

Engross, *vb. tr.* to gain and keep exclusive possession of : P. L. V. 775.

Engulf, *vb. tr.* (*a*) to swallow up in
the abyss of hell : P. L. V. 614.

  (*b*) to disappear underground,
of a river : P. L. IV. 225.

Enjoin, *vb.* (*pres. 2d sing.* enjoin'st :
P. L. V. 563) *tr.* (*a*) to prescribe
authoritatively : P. L. IX. 207 ;
XI. 177 ; *with acc. and dat.* : P.
L. V. 563 ; *in past part. with dat.* :
S. A. 6 ; *with clause* : P. L. IX.

357 ; *clause represented by adv.* :
S. A. 870.

  (*b*) to force, oblige, *with prep.
inf.* : P. L. X. 575.

Enjoy, *vb.* (*pres. 2d sing.* enjoy'st :
P. L. VIII. 622 ; *pret. 2d sing.* enjoy'dst : P. L. XII. 580) *tr.* (*a*) to
possess and use with pleasure, take
delight in : P. L. I. 683 ; III. 306 ;
IV. 433, 445, 446, 472, 534 ; VIII.
366, 523, 584, 622, 623 ; IX. 264 ; X.
758 ; XI. 142, 804 ; P. R. I. 125,
364 ; II. 203 ; III. 360 ; IV. 94 ; S. A.
807, 915, 991 ; C. 382, 790 ; Hor. O.
9 ; **enjoy one's fill** : P. L. V. 503 ;
with of : P. L. IV. 507. *See* **Fill.**

  (*b*) *absol.* to live in happiness,
take pleasure : P. L. VIII. 365 ;
IX. 829.

  (*c*) to possess or obtain *something
giving pleasure* : P. L. III. 471 ;
XII. 580 ; S. A. 157.

  (*d*) to have sexual intercourse
with : P. L. IX. 1032.

Enjoyment, *sb.* (*a*) the act of deriving pleasure from an object, *with*
of : C. 742 ; pleasurable possession and use (*of*) : P. L. VI. 452.

  (*b*) a pleasure, a delight : P. L.
VIII. 531.

Enlarge, *vb. tr.* (*a*) to extend the
limits of : P. L. IV. 390.

  (*b*) to extend the scope of : P.
L. I. 415.

  (*c*) to increase the capacity of
(*the heart*) for affection : P. L.
VIII. 590.

Enlighten, *vb. tr.* (*a*) to shed light
upon, illuminate : P. L. III. 731 ;
IV. 668 ; VIII. 143.

  (*b*) to impart knowledge to,
instruct : P. L. XI. 115.

  (*c*) to revive : P. L. VI. 497.

  part. adj. **enlightened,** illuminated : P. L. VIII. 274.

  See **New-enlightened.**

Enlightener, *sb.* one who instructs :
P. L. XII. 271.

  See **New-enlivened.**

Enmity, *sb.* ill-will, hatred, hostility : P. L. I. 431 ; IX. 465,
1151 ; X. 180, 497, 925 ; S. A.
1201 ; **at** or **in enmity,** in a state
of mutual hostility : P. L. II.
500 ; V. Ex. 88.

Enna, *sb.* a town on the island of
Sicily, a seat of the worship of
Ceres : P. L. IV. 269.

Ennoble, *vb. tr.* to impart a higher
character to, dignify, elevate : P.
L. IX. 992 ; S. A. 1491 ; Il P. 102.

Enormous, *adj.* (*a*) excessive in size, huge, vast: P. L. I. 511; VII. 411.
(*b*) out of all rule, abnormal: P. L. V. 297.

Enough, (1) *adj.* sufficient, adequate: P. L. VIII. 535; C. 958; S. XIII. 6.
absol. that which is sufficient, as much as is requisite: P. L. VII. 125; VIII. 537; XI. 766, 805; S. A. 1592; C. 780.
(2) *adv.* sufficiently: P. L. IV. 124; IX. 1169; X. 959; S. A. 431, 455, 1468; Ps. LXXXI. 43.

Enow, *adj.* sufficient, *with pl. sb.*: P. L. II. 504.
absol. sufficient number (*of*): L. 114.

Enrage (*past part. trisyl.*: C. 830), *vb. tr.* (*a*) to put in a rage, make furious: P. L. I. 216; II. 698.
(*b*) to add fury to, make violent: P. L. II. 95.
part. adj. **enraged,** furious, exasperated: C. 830.

Enrich, *vb. tr.* to make rich, store with wealth: P. R. IV. 46; C. 505.

Enroll, *vb. tr.* to register, record: P. L. XII. 523; S. A. 653, 1224, 1736.

Ensanguined, *part. adj.* bloodstained: P. L. XI. 654.

Enshrine, *vb. tr.* to enclose in a shrine: P. L. I. 719; V. 273; XII. 334; *fig. of Christ in the body*: P. R. IV. 598.

Ensign, *sb.* (*a*) military standard, banner: P. L. I. 325, 536; II. 886; V. 588; VI. 356, 533, 775.
(*b*) *pl.* insignia: P. R. IV. 65.

Enslave, *vb. tr.* to deprive of liberty, reduce to slavery: P. L. II. 332; XI. 797; reduce to moral slavery: P. R. IV. 144; S. A. 1041.

Ensnare, *vb. tr.* entrap, beguile: P. L. IV. 717; S. A. 365, 860; C. 700.
part. adj. **ensnared,** entrapped: C. 900.

Ensue, *vb. intr.* (*a*) to follow, be subsequent to: P. L. XII. 331.
(*b*) to follow as a result or consequence: P. L. IV. 26, 527, 991; V. 682; VI. 456; VII. 40; IX. 827, 977, 1185; XI. 839.

Entangle, *vb. tr.* to interlace, *fig.*: S. A. 763.

Enter, *vb.* (*pret. trisyl.*: P. 17; *perf. formed with the auxiliary* be: P. L. IV. 373) (1) *tr.* (*a*) to come

or go into: P. L. III. 261; X. 623; P. R. I. 193; II. 292; S. A. 252, 463, 950, 1597; Cir. 11; P. 17; C. 646.
(*b*) to begin to engage in: P. R. I. 174.
(2) *intr.* (*a*) to come or go in: P. L. I. 731; IV. 373, 704; V. 464; VI. 10, 388; XII. 217; *with* in: P. L. IV. 563; IX. 90, 188; XI. 735; P. R. IV. 62.
(*b*) to penetrate into the substance: P. L. VI. 326.
(*c*) to make a beginning, *with prep. inf.*: P. L. XI. 630.
(*d*) **enter on,** to make a beginning of: P. L. VIII. 40; P. R. IV. 635.
(*e*) **enter into,** to take on oneself the duties or pleasures of: P. L. X. 503; XII. 456.
See **Re-enter.**

Enterprise, (1) *sb.* undertaking: S. A. 1223; *esp.* arduous or momentous undertaking: P. L. I. 89; II. 345, 465; P. R. I. 112; II. 412; III. 228; S. A. 804.
(2) *vb.* (*pres. 2d sing.*, enterprisest) *tr.* to undertake, attempt: P. L. X. 270.

Entertain, *vb. tr.* (*a*) to pass or spend (*time*) agreeably, while away: P. L. II. 526.
(*b*) to divert, gladden, please: P. L. IV. 166; L. 178.
(*c*) to receive, admit: P. L. IV. 382; VI. 611.
(*d*) to receive as a guest, show hospitality to: P. L. V. 328, 383; X. 105.
(*e*) to hold in the mind, harbour: P. L. X. 1009.

Entertainment, *sb.* reception, welcome: P. L. V. 690.

Enthrall, *vb. tr.* (*a*) to reduce to the condition of a thrall, enslave: P. L. II. 551; to take away (*freedom*): P. L. XII. 94.
(*b*) to enslave morally: P. L. III. 176; VI. 181; C. 590.
(*c*) *refl.* to enslave oneself morally: P. L. III. 125.

Enthralment, *sb.* national bondage: P. L. XII. 171.

Enthrone, *vb. tr.* to seat on a throne: P. L. II. 961; V. 536.
part. adj. **enthroned,** seated on a throne: C. 11.

Entice, *vb. tr.* to allure, attract: II P. 146; C. 940; *with acc. and pref. inf.*: P. L. I. 412.

part. adj. **enticing,** alluring, attractive : P. L. IX. 996 ; S. A. 559.

Enticement, *sb.* allurement : C. 525.

Entire, *adj.* (*a*) whole, with no part excepted : P. L. I. 671 ; V. 753 ; XII. 264.

(*b*) unimpaired, undiminished : P. L. I. 146 ; V. 502 ; X. 9.

(*c*) forming an unbroken body : P. L. VI. 399.

(*d*) pure, unmixed : P. L. III. 265 ; VI. 741.

(*e*) free (*from sin and blame*) : P. L. IX. 292.

Entirely, *adv.* wholly, perfectly : P. L. VII. 549 ; Cir. 22.

Entitle, *vb. tr.* to confer a certain title on : P. L. XI. 170.

Entomb, *vb. tr.* to enclose as in a tomb : T. 9.

Entrails, *sb.* organs enclosed in the trunk of man : P. L. XII. 76 ; S. A. 614 ; bowels : P. L. II. 783 ; VI. 346.

(*b*) *fig.* inner part *of the earth or heaven* : P. L. I. 234 ; VI. 517 ; IX. 1000 ; *of the air* : P. L. VI. 588.

Entrance, (1) *sb.* (*a*) act of entering : P. L. IV. 882 ; IX. 61 ; X. 21.

(*b*) liberty of entering, admission ; S. IX. 14.

(*c*) that by which anything is entered : P. L. IV. 180, 546 ; IX. 68 ; XI. 119, 470 ; C. 518 ; *fig.* entrance *to the mind* or *heart* : P. L. III. 50 ; IX. 734.

(2) *vb. tr.* (*a*) to throw in a trance, make insensible to present objects : P. L. I. 301 ; XI. 420.

(*b*) to overpower with delight, enrapture : C. 1005.

Entrap, *vb. tr.* to catch by artifice, ensnare : S. A. 855.

Entwine, *vb. tr.* (*a*) to interweave, interlace : P. L. IV. 174.

(*b*) to twist about, enfold : P. L. X. 512.

Envenomed, *part. adj.* poisoned : P. L. II. 543.

Envermeil, *vb. tr.* to tinge as with vermilion, give a ruddy colour to : D. F. I. 6.

Envier, *sb.* one who envies, *of Satan* : P. L. VI. 89.

Envious, *adj.* (*a*) discontented at the good fortune of another : P. L. VII. 139 ; *fig. of darkness* : C. 194 ; or full of ill-will, spiteful, *of winds* and *time* : P. L. XI. 15 ; T. 1.

(*c*) invidious, odious : P. L. IV. 524.

Environ, *vb. tr.* to surround, encompass : S. XII. 3 ; *with* round : P. L. II. 1016 ; IX. 636 ; P. R. I. 194 : IV. 423.

Envy, I. *sb.* mortification and ill-will at the sight of another's prosperity or excellence, *usually of Satan* : P. L. I. 35, 260 ; II. 26 ; III. 553 ; IV. 115, 503 ; V. 61 ; VI. 793 ; IX. 175, 264, 466, 729 ; XI. 456 ; P. R. I. 38, 397 : A. 13 ; S. XV. 2 ; *with* against : P. L. V. 662 ; *personified* : S. XIII. 6.

II. *vb.* (*pres. 2d sing.* enviest : P. L. VIII. 494) (1) *tr.* (*a*) to feel mortification and ill-will toward or on account of, *with obj. a person* : P. L. II. 27 ; VI. 813 ; S. A. 272 ; *with obj. a thing* : P. L. VI. 900 ; IX. 254. 805 ; F. of C. 4 ; *with double obj. person and thing* : S. A. 551.

(*b*) to grudge, refuse to give ; *with acc. and dat.* : P. L. IV. 517 ; *absol.* : P. L. VIII. 494.

(2) *intr.* to have envious or grudging feelings : P. L. IX. 593, 770 ; *with* at : S. A. 995.

part. adj. **envied,** regarded with ill-will : P. L. II. 244.

Enwrap, *vb. tr.* to engross, absorb : N. O. 134.

Ephraim, *sb.* (*a*) the tribe of Ephraim : S. A. 282 ; Ps. LXXX. 9.

(*b*) **Mount Ephraim,** the hill country of central Palestine west of the Jordan : S. A. 988.

Epicurean, *adj.* founded by Epicurus, the Greek philosopher : P. R. IV. 280.

Epicycle, *sb.* small circle revolving about a centre on the circumference of a cycle : P. L. VIII. 84. *See* **Cycle.**

Epidaurus, *sb.* a city of Argolis, Greece, the seat of the worship of Æsculapius : P. L. IX. 507.

Epilepsy, *sb.* the disease of the nervous system characterized by violent paroxysms : P. L. XI. 483.

Epirot, *sb.* a native of Epirus, here Pyrrhus, King of Epirus : S. XVII. 4.

Epithet, *sb.* adjective indicating some quality of the person described : P. R. IV. 343.

Equal, (1) *adj.* (*a*) identical in amount, being of the same quality, quantity, or degree :

P. L. I. 88, 91 ; II. 67 ; VI. 49 ;
VIII. 228 ; IX. 286, 882 ; X. 271 ;
P. R. III. 306 ; IV. 29 ; C. 410 ;
of the same length : P. L. X.
680.

(b) on the same level in rank,
power, or ability : P. L. IV. 296 ;
V. 791, 797 ; VI. 690 ; VIII. 407 ;
IX. 823, 881 ; X. 147 ; P. R. III. 99 ;
IV. 324 ; with to : P. L. II. 479 ;
III. 306 ; V. 726, 835 ; P. R. IV.
303 ; with with : P. L. II. 47 ; IV.
526.

(c) sufficient, adequate, fit : P.
L. VIII. 6 ; with prep. inf. : P. L.
II. 200.

(d) just, impartial : P. L. X.
748 ; Ps. LXXXII. 12.

(2) adv. equal to, equally with :
P. L. I. 654.

(3) sb. one having the same
rank or power : P. L. I. 249 ; V.
796, 820, 832, 866 ; VI. 248 ; P.
R. II. 146.

(4) vb. tr. (a) to make equal,
bring to the same level : P. L. I.
248, 488 ; III. 33, 34 ; VI. 441.

(b) to be or become equal to,
match, rival : P. L. I. 40, 719 ;
IV. 916 ; VI. 343.

(c) to compare with : P. L. I.
292.

Equality, sb. condition of having
equal dignity, power, or privileges with others : P. L. V. 763 ;
VII. 487 ; XII. 26.

Equally, adv. in the same manner
or degree : P. L. III. 306 ; IV. 68 ;
V. 97, 792 ; XI. 362.

Equator, sb. the great circle : P. L.
III. 617.

Equinoctial, adj. (a) of the celestial
equator : P. L. X. 672 ; of the
terrestrial equator : P. L. IX. 64.

(b) on or near the terrestrial
equator : P. L. II. 637.

Equipage, sb. (a) apparatus of war :
P. L. VII. 203 ; S. XVII. 9.

(b) military garb, accoutre-
ments : P. R. III. 304.

Equity, sb. justice : P. R. I. 220.

Equivalent, adj. of equal power or
excellence to : P. L. IX. 609 ;
S. A. 343.

Ercoco (Ercóco), sb. Arkeeke or
Arkiko, a seaport of Abyssinia :
P. L. XI. 398.

*Ere, (1) prep. before ; of time : P. L.
VI. 492, 521 ; VIII. 112, 204, 242,
246 ; IX. 931 ; X. 240, 987 ; XI.
204, 769 ; P. R. IV. 621 ; L'A.

107 ; C. 548, 920 ; L. 8 ; in adv.
phrase, ere long : P. L. I. 651 ;
IV. 113 ; ere now : P. L. II. 831 ;
ere then : P. L. I. 93 ; IV. 971.

(2) conj. sooner than, before ; of
time : P. L. I. 334 ; II. 409 ; III.
646 ; IV. 623 ; V. 133, 685, 699,
871 ; VI. 108, 278 ; VII. 108, 304,
335 ; VIII. 444 ; IX. 674 ; X. 53,
229 ; XI. 29, 356 ; XII. 51, 421 ;
P. R. I. 98, 158 ; III. 32, 196 ;
IV. 236, 480 ; S. A. 177, 784 ;
L'A. 114 ; A. 56 ; C. 56, 138.

Erebus, sb. hell : P. L. II. 883 ; Tartarus : C. 804.

Erect, (1) adj. (a) having an upright
posture : P. L. IV. 288, 289 ; IX.
501 ; XI. 509 ; S. A. 1639.

(b) alert, watchful : P. L. IX.
353.

(2) vb. tr. (a) to raise to an upright posture : P. L. VII. 508 ;
VIII. 432.

(b) to set up a standard : P. L.
II. 986.

(c) to establish a throne : P. L.
V. 725.

(d) to rouse, embolden : P. L.
V. 785.

part. adj. erected, high-souled,
noble : P. L. I. 679 ; P. R. III. 27.

Erelong, adv. before a great while :
P. L. XI. 626, 627. See Ere.

Eremite, sb. hermit, recluse : P. L.
III. 474 ; spec. Christ, when undergoing the temptation in the wilderness : P. R. I. 8.

Erewhile, adv. little while ago, some
time ago, formerly : P. L. I. 281 ;
VI. 334, 610 ; X. 106 ; XII. 275 ;
P. R. I. 1 ; S. A. 1442, 1702 ; P. I.

Err, vb. (pres. 2d sing. err'st : P. L.
VI. 172) intr. (a) to go astray
mentally, be mistaken : P. L. I.
747 ; VI. 172, 173, 288 ; XI. 208 :
P. R. III. 71 ; C. 223 ; of sight ;
P. L. VIII. 121 ; to be mistaken in
thinking ; with clause : P. L. VI.
288 ; to be incorrect : P. L. II.
347.

(b) to be at fault, do wrong,
sin : P. L. V. 799 ; VI. 148 ; IX.
1049, 1178 ; S. A. 211, 369.

(c) either tr. to miss, lose, or intr.
with way as the object of leading ;
but the latter construction is not
borne out by the punctuation :
P. L. X. 266.

part. adj. erring, being in the
wrong, not enlightened : P. R. I.
224 ; C. 588.

Errand, *sb.* (*a*) expedition made for a special purpose, mission : P. L. I. 152 ; II. 827 ; IV. 795 ; VII. 573 ; X. 41 ; C. 15, 506.

(*b*) message, commission : P. L. III. 652.

(*c*) purpose : S. A. 1285.

Erroneous, *adj.* (*a*) wandering, roving : P. L. VII. 20.

(*b*) under the influence of error, misled, misguided : P. L. VI. 146.

(*c*) incorrect, wrong : P. L. X. 969.

Error, *sb.* (*a*) devious or winding course : P. L. IV. 239 ; VII. 302.

(*b*) mistaken belief, false opinion : P. R. II. 474 ; IV. 235.

(*c*) wrong-doing, fault : P. L. IX. 1181 ; P. R. III. 212.

Erst, *adv.* (*a*) once, formerly : P. R. II. 145 ; S. A. 339 ; A. 9.

(*b*) not long ago, a little while since : P. L. I. 360 ; II. 470 ; VI. 187, 308 ; IX. 163, 876, 1081 ; XI. 868 ; S. A. 1543 ; Cir. 2.

Eruption, *sb.* action of breaking forth ; *of the escape of fallen angels from hell* : P. L. I. 656 ; VIII. 235.

Erymanth, *sb.* Erymanthus Mountains, the mountain range on the northern border of Arcadia, Greece, a part of which was sacred to Pan : A. 100.

Esau, *sb.* the twin brother of Jacob : P. L. III. 512.

Escape, (1) *sb.* action of fleeing from danger : P. L. II. 444.

(2) *vb.* (*a*) *intr.* to get off safely, go unhurt : P. L. XI. 777 ; *with* from : P. L. VI. 448 ; to avoid punishment : P. L. X. 339.

(*b*) *tr.* to get safely out of, effect flight from : P. L. III. 14 ; IV. 794, 824.

Eshtaol, *sb.* a town in the lowland of Judah, *Eshtaol and Zora* ; in the Bible both towns are in some places allotted to Judah, in others to Dan : S. A. 181.

Espoused (*trisyl.* : P. L. IV. 710 ; S. XXIII. 1), *part. adj.* wedded : P. L. IV. 710 ; S. XXIII. 1.

part. absol. wedded one, wife : P. L. V. 18.

Espy, *vb. tr.* to descry, discover, get sight of : P. L. IV. 477.

Essence, *sb.* (*a*) being that has existence, entity : P. L. I. 138.

(*b*) constituent substance : P. L. I. 425 ; II. 215 ; III. 6 ; IX. 166 ; Cir. 7 ; C. 462.

Essential, (1) *adj.* being such in essence or true nature : P. L. V. 841.

(2) *sb.* being, essence, substance : P. L. II. 97.

Establish, *vb. tr.* (*a*) to settle or secure *in a throne* : P. L. II. 23.

(*b*) to enact or institute *laws* : P. L. XII. 245.

Estate, *sb.* (*a*) condition, situation : P. L. XII. 351 ; S. A. 742.

(*b*) rank, dignity : S. A. 170.

Esteem, (1) *sb.* (*a*) estimate, valuation : P. R. IV. 160.

(*b*) estimation, opinion, judgement : P. L. IX. 328, 329 ; the opinion of men(?), value, valuation(?) : Il P. 17.

(*c*) high estimation, respect : P. R. IV. 207 ; F. of C. 10.

(*d*) fame, reputation ; P. L. IV. 886.

(2) *vb. tr.* (*a*) to estimate, value : P. R. II. 447 ; III. 29 ; C. 634.

(*b*) to think, consider, account ; with two *acc.* : P. R. I. 235 ; in *passive* : C. 514.

See **Self-esteem.**

Estotiland, *sb.* "the most northern region on the east side of America," Hey. *Cos.* 1666, p. 1020 ; on the map, p. 1010, it lies east of Hudson Bay : P. L. X. 686.

Estrange, *vb. tr.* to change or render different *in look* : P. L. IX. 1132.

Eternal, (1) *adj.* (*a*) infinite in past and future duration : P. L. II. 896 ; P. R. IV. 391 ; *said of God* : P. L. I. 25, 70 ; III. 374 ; V. 246 ; VI. 96, 227, 630 ; VII. 137, 517 ; X. 32, 68 ; P. R. I. 168, 236 ; N. O. 2 ; *of that which pertains to God, as, eye, house,* etc. : P. L. II. 172 ; V. 711 ; VII. 96, 226, 576 ; VIII. 413 ; *of heaven or things in heaven* : P. L. I. 610 ; III. 349 ; VII. 9 ; XII. 314 ; P. R. I. 281 ; *of night* : P. L. III. 18 ; *of spring or summer* : P. L. IV. 268 ; C. 988.

(*b*) infinite in future duration : P. L. I. 121 ; II. 161, 695 ; IV. 70 ; V. 173 ; VI. 240, 385, 424, 865, 904 ; X. 597 ; XII. 551 ; S. A. 964, 1717 ; C. 596, 1008 ; *of fallen angels* : P. L. I. 154, 155 ; II. 98 ; or perhaps in sense (*a*) : P. L. I. 318 ; *of sin and death* : P. L. X. 816.

(*c*) immutable, unalterable : P. L. III. 127.

(2) *sb.* **the Eternal**, God : P. L.
II. 46 ; III. 2 ; IV. 996.
Eternity, *sb.* (*a*) infinite duration,
both past and future : P. L. II.
148 ; III. 5 ; VIII. 406 ; opposed
to the created universe : P. L. V.
580 ; eternity in the past : P. L. III.
5 ; VII. 92 ; VIII. 406 ; in the future :
P. L. II. 248 ; XII. 556 ; T. 11.
(*b*) heaven : C. 14.
Eternize, *vb. tr.* (*a*) to give endless
duration to : P. L. XI. 60.
(*b*) to perpetuate the fame of,
immortalize : P. L. VI. 374.
Etham, *sb.* Etam, a town of Judah ;
rock of Etham, a rock near this
place to which Samson retired
after his slaughter of the Philistines : S. A. 253.
Ethereal, *adj.* (*a*) of or partaking of
the nature of heaven; *of God* : P.
L. II. 978 ; *of angels or that which
belongs to angels* : P. L. II. 311,
601 ; III. 100 ; V. 499, 863 ; VI.
330 ; VIII. 646 ; X. 27 ; XII. 577 ;
P. R. I. 163 ; II. 121 ; *of heaven
or things in heaven* : P. L. I. 45,
285 ; II. 139 ; III. 7, 716 ; VI. 60 ;
VII. 244 ; P. 1 ; *of man* ; P. R. III.
28.
(*b*) composed of ether : P. L.
III. 716 ; V. 267, 418 ; VII. 356 ;
impalpable, intangible, or in sense
(*a*) : S. A. 549.
Ethereous, *adj.* heavenly : P. L. VI.
473.
Ethiop, *adj.* of or pertaining to
Ethiopia, the country south of
Egypt : P. L. IV. 282 ; Il P. 19.
Ethiopian, *adj. absol.* according to
Hey. *Cos.* 1666, p. 931, "Africa
is bounded . . . on the South with
the Æthiopick Ocean," and likewise Mercator, *Atlas*, 1635, p.
14, "to the South it (Africa) is
washed with the Æthiopian
Ocean" : P. L. II. 641.
Etrurian, *adj.* of Etruria, the
country in Italy : P. L. I. 303.
Euboic, *adj.* Euboic sea, the sea
between the island of Eubœa and
the mainland of Greece : P. L.
II. 546.
Euclid, *sb.* the Greek geometrician ;
here used for his works or the
study of those works : S. XXI. 7.
Euphrasy, *sb.* the plant *Euphrasia
officinalis* : P. L. XI. 414.
Euphrates, *sb.* the river of Mesopotamia : P. L. I. 420 ; XII. 114 ;
P. R. III. 272, 384.

Euphrosyne, *sb.* one of the Graces :
L'A. 12.
Europe, *sb.* the continent : P. L. X.
310 ; XI. 405 ; S. XV. 1 ; XXII. 12.
Eurotas, *sb.* a river of Laconia,
Greece : D. F. I. 25.
Eurus, *sb.* the east wind : P. L. X. 705.
Eurydice, *sb.* the wife of Orpheus :
L'A. 150.
Eurynome, *sb.* a daughter of Oce-
anus, and the wife of Ophion : P.
L. X. 581. *See* **Ophion**.
Evade, *vb.* (1) *intr.* to get away,
escape : P. L. VI. 596.
(2) *tr.* to escape *penalty* : P. L.
X. 1021 ; to avoid *conviction* : P.
R. IV. 308.
Evangelize, *vb. tr.* to preach the
gospel to : P. L. XII. 499.
Evasion, *sb.* subterfuge, shift : P. L.
II. 411 ; X. 829 ; S. A. 842.
Eve, *sb.* (*a*) evening : P. L. I. 743 ;
at eve : P. L. IV. 185 ; P. R. I.
318 ; L'A. 130 ; C. 843 ; S. I. 2.
(*b*) the first woman, the wife of
Adam, the mother of the human
race : P. L. I. 364 ; IV. 324, 409,
440, 481, 610, 634, 660, 710, 742,
800 ; V. 9, 38, 74, 93, 303, 308,
321, 379, 443 ; VII. 50 ; VIII. 40,
172 ; IX. 204, 227, 270, 291, 319,
376, 404, 422, 424, 438, 456, 495,
517, 528, 550, 568, 613, 631, 644,
659, 785, 886, 889, 892, 920, 921,
960, 1005, 1013, 1016, 1017, 1036,
1065, 1067, 1133, 1143, 1164 ; X.
3, 109, 157, 159, 332, 335, 551,
863, 909, 966, 1012, 1097 ; XI. 136,
140, 141, 159, 162, 181, 192, 193,
224, 226, 265, 287, 367, 476, 519 ;
XII. 594, 607, 624 ; P. R. I. 51, 54 ;
II. 141, 349 ; IV. 5, 6, 180 ; as
possibly identified with Eurynome : P. L. X. 582 ; *second Eve*,
Mary the mother of Jesus : P. L.
V. 387 ; X. 183 ; *another Eve*, another woman bearing the same
name : P. L. IX. 828, 911.
Even, (1) *sb.* evening : P. L. III. 42 ;
IV. 555 ; VII. 435 ; *at even* : P. L.
V. 425 ; IX. 582 ; XI. 276 ; joined
to *morn* or *morning* : P. L. V.
202 ; VII. 252, 274, 338, 550 ; P.
R. II. 268 ; *personified* : C. 188.
(2) *adj.* (*a*) not hilly, plain, and
also with the idea of sense (*b*) :
P. L. XI. 348.
(*b*) on the same level, *fig.* : P. L.
III. 179.
(*c*) equable, uniform, unvary-
ing : Il P. 38.

(*d*) equally balanced, not inclining to either side : P. L. VI.
245 ; X. 47 ; *even balance* : P. L.
I. 349.

(*e*) equal towards all, just, impartial : C. 773.

(*f*) commensurate, corresponding : S. II. 10.

(**3**) *adv.* (*a*) precisely; *even now* :
C. 202.

(*b*) quite, fully ; with *to* : P. L.
I. 416 ; III. 586 ; V. 83 ; XI. 148,
418; P. R. I. 264; Cir. 20; U. C.
II. 25 ; C. 625.

(*c*) serving to emphasize word
or phrase : P. L. I. 680 ; V. 837;
IX. 1079 ; X. 191 ; C. 557, 591 ; S.
XVIII. 3 ; Ps. VI. 5 ; LXXXIV. 9,
13 ; LXXXVI. 47.

(*d*) equably, uniformly, steadily:
P. L. VIII. 165.

(*e*) straight out in front of the
body : P. L. VI. 544.

Evening, *sb.* the close of the day,
the time of sunset and later : P.
L. IV. 355, 598, 647, 654, 662,
792; V. 115, 627 ; VII. 104 ; IX.
1088 ; C. 540 ; *at evening* : P. L.
I. 289 ; L. 30 ; joined to *morn* :
P. L. V. 628 ; VII. 260, 386, 448 ;
spoken of as rising : P. L. V. 876 ;
VII. 582 ; A. 54.

attrib. pertaining to or occurring in the evening : P. L. II.
493 ; IV. 151, 543 ; VII. 450 ; IX.
278 ; X. 95 ; XII. 629 ; S. A.
1692.

See **Sabbath-evening.**

Evening-star, *sb.* the planet Venus,
called Hesperus when appearing
in the evening, as the star of love :
P. L. VIII. 519 ; XI. 588.

Evenly, *adv.* equably, uniformly :
S. A. 671.

Even-song, *sb.* song sung in the
evening : Il P. 64.

Event, *sb.* (*a*) that which happens,
occurrence : P. L. I. 118 ; IV.
1001 ; IX. 405 ; P. R. II. 104 ; S.
A. 1551, 1756 ; V. Ex. 70.

(*b*) issue, consequence, result :
P. L. I. 134, 624 ; II. 82 ; IV.
716 ; V. 740 ; IX. 334, 984 ; X.
969 ; XI. 593 ; S. A. 737 ; C. 405,
411.

Ever, *adv.* (*a*) throughout all time :
P. L. I. 210 ; II. 914 ; III. 149 ;
VI. 184 ; X. 71 ; XII. 573 ; L'A.
10 ; W. S. 48 ; T. 16.

(*b*) at all times, always : P. L.
I. 160, 228 ; II. 338 ; III. 366 ; IV.

119, 436 ; V. 405 ; VIII. 649 ; XII.
563 ; P. R. III. 240 ; IV. 22 ; S. A.
510, 761, 858, 903, 925, 1172, 1734,
1748 ; P. 5 ; C. 211, 368 ; L'A.
135 ; S. II. 14 ; XV. 5 ; Ps. I. 5 ;
V. 35.

(*c*) **for ever**, eternally : P. L. I.
250 ; C. 442 ; for all future time :
P. L. I. 330, 608 ; II. 182, 776 ;
III. 244, 249, 318, 333 ; V. 611 ;
VI. 733 ; VII. 586 ; VIII. 479 ; X.
637 ; XI. 95, 96 ; XII. 324, 429 ;
P. R. IV. 194 ; T. 21 ; L. 181 ;
S. XIV. 8 ; Ps. LXXXIII. 15, 62 ;
LXXXV. 18.

(*d*) at any time : P. L. I. 210 ;
II. 153, 744 ; IV. 322 ; V. 446,
810 ; P. R. I. 324, 438 ; S. A. 446,
1336 ; S. VIII. 3 ; at any time
before : P. L. IX. 1033.

Ever-burning, *adj.* always burning :
P. L. I. 69.

Ever-during, *adj.* always enduring,
everlasting : P. L. III. 45 ; VII.
206.

Ever-failing, *adj.* always waning :
S. A. 348.

Everlasting, *adj.* enduring forever,
eternal : P. L. II. 232 ; *of heaven
or things in heaven* : P. L. III.
395 ; VII. 565 ; N. O. 13 ; infinite
in future duration : P. L. II. 184 ;
P. R. III. 199 ; that never fails :
C. 199.

Everlastingly, *adv.* forever, eternally : S. M. 16.

Evermore, *adv.* for all future time :
M. W. 50 ; preceded by *for* : Ps.
LXXXIV. 40 ; LXXXVI. 44.

Ever-new, *adv.* always fresh : P. L.
V. 19.

Ever-threatening, *adj.* at all times
impending : P. L. III. 425.

Every, *adj.* each of an indefinite
number, expressing distributively
the sense expressed collectively
by *all*; followed by a *sb.* or a *sb.*
preceded by an *adj.* : P. L. I.
758 ; II. 877 ; III. 638 ; V. 8, 194,
410, 747, 816 ; VI. 345, 554, 848 ;
VII. 317, 336, 357, 394, 523, 534,
621 ; VIII. 321, 489 ; IX. 84, 160,
310, 521, 721 ; XI. 324, 337,
734 ; XII. 522 ; P. R. I. 295, 448 ;
II. 224, 468 ; III. 125, 348 ; S. A.
93, 97, 204, 749, 1323 ; T. 14 ;
L'A. 67 ; Il P. 171, 172 ; A.
59 ; C. 251, 269, 313, 496, 524,
621, 768 ; L. 93, 148 ; Ps. LXXX.
26 ; preceded by *poss. pron.* : P.
L. IX. 459 ; as antecedent of *pl.*

pron.: C. 64; in same construction with *each*: P. L. I. 356; C. 19, 311; *every one*, everybody: V. Ex. 76; *every day*: Ps. VII. 44.

Evidence, (1) *sb.* witness, testimony, proof: P. L. IX. 962.

(2) *vb. tr.* to make evident, show clearly: P. L. X. 361.

Evident, *adj.* apparent, manifest: P. L. IX. 1077.

Evil, (1) *adj.* (*a*) morally depraved, wicked, vicious: P. L. VI. 289; IX. 698; Ps. VII. 35; *the* or *that Evil one*, Satan: P. L. IX. 463; P. R. IV. 194.

(*b*) accusing or condemning of sin: P. L. X. 849.

(*c*) having qualities tending to injury and mischief, bad, hurtful: P. L. II. 623; A. 50; and also wicked: P. L. IV. 563; IX. 638; XII. 47; C. 432; slanderous: P. L. VII. 26.

(*d*) unfavourable: P. L. XII. 47.

(*e*) disagreeable, painful: S. A. 1538, 1567.

(*f*) unfortunate, disastrous, calamitous: P. L. I. 335, 339; VII. 25, 26; IX. 780, 1067; X. 125; P. R. III. 218; S. A. 704.

(*g*) foreboding trouble or unhappiness: S. A. 967.

(2) *sb.* (*a*) that which is morally evil, sin; *abstr. and concr.* often with the added idea of sense (*c*): P. L. III. 683; v. 98, 99, 117; VII. 262, 276; VII. 56, 615; IX. 464, 864, 1180, 1185; XII. 604; P. R. II. 371; C. 593; Ps. v. 11; contrasted with *good* or *goodness*: P. L. I. 163, 165; II. 562; IV. 110; VII. 188, 543; IX. 697, 698, 709, 723, 752, 774, 1072; XI. 85, 87, 89; XII. 470, 471, 566; considered the offspring of Satan: P. L. VI. 275.

(*b*) that which causes harm, injury, mischief: P. L. I. 216; v. 207.

(*c*) suffering, misfortune, disaster, calamity: P. L. II. 261, 281; IV. 896; v. 871; VI. 395, 437, 455, 463; IX. 1079; X. 734, 963, 978, 1080; XI. 373, 765, 772, 774; S. A. 105, 194, 374, 648, 736, 1169, 1523; C. 360; *evil store*, store of evils: P. L. IX. 1078.

(3) *adv.* unsuccessfully, unfortunately: Ps. LXXXIII. 41.

Evince, *vb. tr.* (*a*) to conquer, overcome: P. R. IV. 235.

(*b*) to make evident, show clearly: P. L. XII. 287.

Ewe, *sb.* female sheep: P. L. IX. 582; XI. 649; P. R. I. 315; C. 503; Ps. CXIV. 12.

Exact, (1) *adj.* (*a*) perfected, highly wrought: P. L. VII. 477.

(*b*) refined *of taste*: P. L. IX. 1017.

(*c*) accurate, careful, or in sense (*a*) (cf. S. A. 1027): P. L. VIII. 539.

(*d*) precise, rigorous, or *adv.* entirely, perfectly: P. L. XII. 402.

(2) *vb. tr.* to demand authoritatively, require: P. L. XII. 590; P. R. III. 120; S. A. 507, 788; S. XIX. 7.

Exactly, *adv.* precisely: P. L. VIII. 451.

Exalt, *vb. tr.* (*a*) to raise *the head* because of pride, carry loftily: Ps. LXXXIII. 8.

(*b*) to raise in rank, honour, or power: P. L. I. 736; II. 5; III. 313; IV. 525; v. 829; VI. 99; IX. 150; XII. 457; P. R. II. 46; S. A. 689.

(*c*) to elate with pride: P. L. VII. 150.

part. adj. **exalted,** lofty in character, noble: P. R. I. 36; II. 206.

Exaltation, *sb.* physical elevation: P. L. v. 90; elevation in honour: P. L. VI. 727; P. R. II. 92; III. 97.

Example, *sb.* (*a*) instance: P. L. VII. 42; X. 840; S. A. 290; given as a warning: P. L. VI. 910; VII. 42.

(*b*) conduct regarded as an object for imitation, pattern, precedent: P. L. IV. 881; v. 901; IX. 962; XI. 809; XII. 572; P. R. I. 232; S. A. 166, 765, 822.

Exasperate, *vb. tr.* (*a*) to stimulate through anger, stir up; with *acc.* and *prep. inf.*: P. L. II. 143.

(*b*) to provoke, anger, enrage: S. A. 1417.

(*c*) *absol.* to irritate, render sore: S. A. 625.

Exceed, *vb. tr.* to surpass, excel: P. L. v. 459; S. A. 817.

part. adj. **Exceeding,** extremely great, surpassing; *exceeding love*: P. L. IX. 961; Cir. 15, 16.

Excel, *vb.* (1) *intr.* (*a*) to be preëminent, surpass others : P. L. VIII. 542 ; P. R. IV. 347 ; with *in* : P. L. II. 124, 125 ; III. 133.

(*b*) to be present in a preëminent degree : P. L. IX. 897.

(2) *tr.* (*a*) to be superior to, surpass : P. L. I. 359 ; IV. 490 ; VI. 177, 822 ; X. 150 ; S. A. 74, 523 ; C. 63.

(*b*) to exceed, be beyond : P. L. II. 884 ; to be too great for, overpower : P. L. VIII. 456.

Excellence, *sb.* (*a*) possession of good qualities in an eminent degree : P. L. II. 350 ; V. 456 ; VI. 637 ; VIII. 91 ; X. 1017 ; V. Ex. 79.

(*b*) excellent quality : P. L. VI. 821.

Excellent, *adj.* preëminent, superior : P. L. VIII. 566 ; X. 1015 ; P. R. I. 381.

Except, (1) *past part.* not included ; following the *sb.*: P. L. II. 300, 678 ; IX. 545 ; XI. 808 ; P. R. IV. 85.

(2) *prep.* with the exception of, not including : P. L. II. 1032.

(3) *conj.* otherwise or elsewhere than ; followed by an *adv. phr.* : P. L. III. 684 ; X. 680.

Excepted, *part. adj.* excluded : P. L. XI. 426.

Exception, *sb.* instance to be excluded from the general rule : P. R. III. 119.

Excess, *sb.* (*a*) unrestrained manifestation of grief : P. L. XI. 498.

(*b*) violation of the law of God, transgression : P. L. III. 696, 698 ; XI. 111 ; Cir. 24.

(*c*) intemperance in eating or drinking : P. L. V. 640.

(*d*) superfluity, superabundance : P. L. IX. 648 ; C. 771 ; with *of* : P. L. I. 123, 593.

Excessive, *adj.* exceedingly great : P. L. II. 779 ; VI. 463 ; III. 380.

Excite, *vb. tr.* (*a*) to incite, instigate ; with *acc.* and *prep. inf.* : P. R. I. 397 ; with *acc.* and *to* : P. R. III. 26.

(*b*) to be the motive for doing : P. L. II. 484 ; P. R. I. 423.

(*c*) to rouse, stir up, awaken *hope, envy* : P. L. II. 567 ; IX. 264 ; *thirst* : P. L. VII. 68 ; *the mind, thoughts* : P. L. IV. 522 ; IX. 472.

Exclaim, *vb. intr.* to cry out suddenly and vehemently : P. L. X. 416.

Exclude, *vb. tr.* (*a*) to shut out, prevent from entrance : P. L. IV. 584 ;

to give no place to *hope* : P. L. IV. 105.

(*b*) to shut off, debar ; with *from* : P. L. III. 202 ; in passive with *from* omitted : S. A. 494.

(*c*) to prohibit, forbid : P. R. I. 367.

Exclusion, *sb.* state of being shut out : P. L. III. 525.

Exclusive, *adj.* having the power of shutting out or keeping apart : P. L. VIII. 625.

Excursion, *sb.* (*a*) sally, sortie : P. L. II. 396.

(*b*) journey : P. L. VIII. 231.

Excuse, (1) *sb.* (*a*) action of offering an apology : L. 18.

(*b*) apology, plea offered in extenuation : P. L. IX. 853 ; X. 764 ; S. A. 829.

(*c*) that which serves as a reason for excusing : P. L. XII. 96 ; S. A. 734 ; with *prep. inf.* : P. L. V. 447.

(2) *vb.* (*a*) *tr.* to seek to remove the blame of : P. L. IV. 394.

(*b*) *absol.* to serve as an exculpation : S. A. 831.

Execrable (éxecráble), *adj.* abominable, detestable : P. L. II. 681 ; XII. 64.

Execrably, *adv.* accursedly, abominably : S. A. 1362.

Execration, *sb.* uttered curse, imprecation : P. L. X. 737.

Execute, *vb. tr.* (*a*) to carry into effect : P. L. I. 430 ; II. 732 ; X. 772 ; S. A. 1284.

(*b*) to perform acts of *vengeance* : P. L. III. 399.

Execution, *sb.* (*a*) the carrying into effect : S. A. 506.

(*b*) action, operation : P. L. X. 853.

Exempt, (1) *adj.* or *part.* (*a*) freed *from* allegiance to : P. L. II. 318.

(*b*) freed *from care, pain,* etc. : P. L. IX. 486 ; XI. 514, 709 ; S. A. 103, 918.

(*c*) excluded from participation : P. L. III. 370.

(2) *vb. tr.* (*a*) to grant *a person* freedom or immunity *from obligation* : S. A. 310 ; *from pain* : P. L. X. 1025.

(*b*) to single out or select *from* ; sing. with compound subject : S. XIII. 5.

Exemption, *sb.* freedom from liability, immunity : P. R. III. 115.

Exercise, (1) *sb.* disciplinary suffering, trial : S. A. 1287.

(2) *vb. tr.* (*a*) to employ, bring to bear : S. A. 612.

(*b*) to train by practice, employ for the sake of acquiring spiritual strength : P. R. I. 156.

(*c*) to harass, afflict : P. L. II. 89.

(*d*) to practise or take part in *games* : P. L. IV. 551.

(*e*) to wield, possess : P. L. X. 400.

(*f*) to perform acts of *hatred, wrath* : P. L. X. 796, 927.

Exhalation, *sb.* mist, vapour : P. L. I. 711 ; v. 185, 425 ; x. 694 ; xi. 741.

Exhale, *vb.* (1) *tr.* to give forth, throw off, send out : P. L. v. 421 ; IX. 1049 ; *fig. of night* : P. L. v. 642.

(2) *intr.* to rise as vapour *from* ; *fig. of light* : P. L. VII. 255.

Exhaust, *vb. tr.* to drain a *person of strength* : P. L. VI. 852 ; *a country of resources* : P. R. IV. 136.

Exhilarating, *part. adj.* stimulating, enlivening : P. L. IX. 1047.

Exhort, *vb. tr.* to recommend earnestly, insist upon : P. L. II. 179.

Exile (exíle : P. L. I. 632 ; x. 484 ; *doubtful* : P. L. II. 207), (1) *sb.* banishment : P. L. I. 632 ; II. 207 ; x. 484.

(2) *vb.* (*part.* exíled) *tr.* to banish : P. L. IV. 106 ; *fig.* to separate *from light* : S. A. 98.

Exorbitant, *adj.* inordinate, excessive : P. L. III. 177.

Expanded, *part. adj.* spread out, extended : P. L. I. 225.

Expanse, *sb.* widely extended space or area ; *of the firmament* : P. L. VII. 264 ; *expanse of heaven* : P. L. IV. 456 ; VII. 340 ; *the expanse,* chaos : P. L. II. 1014.

Expatiate, *vb. intr.* to walk about at large : P. L. I. 774.

Expect, *vb. tr.* (*a*) to wait for, await : P. L. XII. 591 ; *absol.* : P. R. III. 192.

(*b*) to look forward to, regard as about to come or happen, anticipate : P. L. VI. 186 ; x. 439, 1048 ; XI. 226 ; XII. 384 ; S. A. 1352 ; L. 84 ; with *prep. inf.* : P. L. IV. 972 ; v. 811, 892 ; IX. 281 ; XI. 359 ; P. R. IV. 181 ; S. A. 1423 ; with *acc.* and *prep. inf.* : P. L. X. 504 ; with *clause* : P. L. IX. 382 ; or in sense (*a*) : P. R. II. 33.

(*c*) to look for as due from another : P. R. III. 126.

Expectance, *sb.* expectation : V. Ex. 54.

Expectation, *sb.* (*a*) state of looking forward to or awaiting something : P. L. II. 417 ; x. 782 ; P. R. II. 42 ; with *when* and *inf. phr.* : P. L. x. 536 ; with *of* : P. L. IX. 789 ; P. R. III. 207 ; *personified* : P. L. VI. 306.

(*b*) person expected ; *of Christ* : P. L. XII. 378.

Expedite, *vb. tr.* to facilitate, clear of difficulties : P. L. X. 474.

Expedition, *sb.* (*a*) journey or excursion made for a special purpose : P. L. II. 342 ; VII. 193 ; P. R. I. 101.

(*b*) haste, dispatch : P. L. VI. 86 ; S. A. 1283.

Expel, *vb. tr.* to drive out, banish a *person* : P. L. II. 195 ; VIII. 332 ; P. R. IV. 100, 127, 129 ; *mischief, usurpation* : P. L. II. 140, 983.

Experience, *sb.* (*a*) actual observation or practical acquaintance as a source of knowledge : P. L. I. 118 ; v. 826 ; VIII. 190 ; IX. 988 ; S. A. 188, 382 ; *personified* : P. L. IX. 807.

(*b*) knowledge gained by actual observation or trial : P. R. III. 238 ; S. A. 1756 ; Il P. 173.

Experienced, *part. adj.* skilful through experience : P. L. I. 568.

Experiment, *sb.* action of putting a thing to proof, test : P. L. X. 967.

Expert, *adj.* experienced, skilful : S. A. 1044 ; with *in* : P. R. II. 158 ; with *when* and *inf. phr.* : P. L. VI. 233.

Expiate, *vb. tr.* (*a*) to offer or serve as a propitiation for : P. L. III. 207 ; *absol.* : S. A. 736.

(*b*) to pay the penalty of : S. A. 490.

Expiation, *sb.* that by which atonement is made, *here* the sacrifices required by the Jewish law : P. L. XII. 291.

Expire, *vb. intr.* (*a*) to die : P. R. IV. 568 ; Ps. LXXXVIII. 62 ; to cease to be absolutely ; *of angels* : P. L. II. 93.

(*b*) to come to an end ; *of time* : P. R. IV. 174 ; *of power* : P. R. IV. 395.

Explain, *vb. tr.* (*a*) to give details of : S. A. 1583.

(*b*) to state the meaning of : P. L. II. 518.

Explode, *vb. tr.* to hoot or hiss away: P. L. XI. 669.
  part. adj. **exploding,** expressing contempt or scorn: P. L. X. 546.
Exploit, *sb.* heroic act, deed of renown: P. L. II. 111; III. 465; v. 565; x. 407; XI. 790; P. R. I. 102; S. A. 32, 525, 1492.
Explore, *vb. tr.* (*a*) to seek to find out *secrets*: P. L. II. 971; VII. 95; to examine *one's heart*: P. L. VI. 113.
  (*b*) to try, make proof of: P. L. II. 632.
Expose, *vb. tr.* (*a*) to turn out of doors, cast out: P. L. I. 505.
  (*b*) to leave unprotected: P. L. II. 360; III. 425; IX. 341.
  (*c*) to put in peril, endanger: P. L. II. 828; x. 957.
  (*d*) to give up, leave to the mercy of; with *to*: P. L. XII. 339; P. R. I. 142; II. 204; IV. 140; S. A. 75.
  (*e*) to render liable or subject; with *to*: P. L. x. 130; S. A. 919; with *acc.* and *prep. inf.*: P. L. II. 27.
  (*f*) to lay open or render accessible *to*: P. L. x. 407.
  (*g*) to disclose or display *to*: P. L. IV. 206.
Express, (1) *adj.* (*a*) precisely resembling, exact: P. L. VII. 528; C. 69.
  (*b*) definite, explicit: P. L. x. 926.
  (2) *vb. tr.* (*a*) to put into words, give utterance to: P. L. IX. 554; P. R. IV. 351; *absol.*: P. R. II. 332.
  (*b*) to declare in words: P. L. XI. 597; A. 12; with two *acc.*: P. L. III. 3; in *passive*: P. L. IX. 1164; with *clause*: P. L. II. 480.
  (*c*) to make known, manifest, reveal: P. L. III. 140; v. 574; VI. 720; VIII. 440, 544, 616; x. 67; XI. 354; P. R. I. 233; IV. 601.
Expression, *sb.* (*a*) action of expressing feeling: P. L. IX. 527.
  (*b*) **beyond expression,** beyond description: P. L. III. 591.
Expressly, *adv.* in direct terms, explicitly: P. L. IX. 356; P. R. II. 3; S. A. 578.
Expulsion, *sb.* action of driving out *an enemy*: P. L. VI. 880; P. R. II. 128.
Expunge, *vb. tr.* to blot out, *fig.*: P. L. III. 49.
Exquisite (éxquisítest), *adj.* choice, delicious, *sup.*: P. R. II. 346.
  See **Over-exquisite.**

Extend, *vb.* (1) *tr.* (*a*) to spread out in area, make to cover a certain space: P. L. v. 651.
  (*b*) to enlarge in area: P. L. II. 326.
  (*c*) to prolong, protract: P. L. x. 804; Ps. LXXXV. 19.
  (*d*) to hold out, reach forth: P. L. XII. 211; *fig.*: P. L. II. 493.
  (*e*) to spread abroad or diffuse *fame*: P. R. III. 65.
  (2) *intr.* (*a*) to spread or stretch out; *of the body*: P. L. I. 195.
  (*b*) to continue for a specified distance, reach: P. L. II. 1047; VII. 230; IX. 108; P. R. IV. 222.
  (*c*) to have a certain range; *of the mind*: P. R. IV. 223.
  part. adj. **extended**; (*a*) expanded, stretched out: P. L. II. 885.
  (*b*) large in area, extensive: P. L. III. 557.
Extent, *sb.* (*a*) dimensions, size: P. L. VII. 496.
  (*b*) limit: P. L. x. 808; P. R. III. 406.
Extenuate, *vb. tr.* (*a*) to lessen in honour or disparage *a person*: P. L. x. 645.
  (*b*) to underrate or treat *an offence* as of trifling magnitude: S. A. 767.
Exterior, *adj.* external: P. L. IX. 336.
External, *adj.* belonging to the world of things considered as outside the perceiving mind: P. L. v. 103.
Extinct, *adj.* (*a*) extinguished, quenched; *of light*: P. L. I. 141; *of glory*: S. A. 70.
  (*b*) dead; *of a person*: P. L. IX. 829.
Extinguish, *vb. tr.* to quench or destroy *life*: P. L. IV. 666; to take away power to act: S. A. 1688.
Extol, *vb.* (*pres. 2d sing.* extoll'st: P. R. IV. 353) *tr.* to raise high with praise, magnify: P. L. II. 479; III. 146, 398; IV. 436, 733; v. 164; P. R. II. 453; III. 50, 54. IV. 353; S. A. 654.
Extort, *vb. tr.* to wring, wrest: P. L. I. 111; P. R. I. 423.
Extract, *vb. tr.* (*a*) to draw out: P. L. v. 25.
  (*b*) to take out of something of which the thing taken was a part; with *of*: P. L. VIII. 497.

Extraordinary (éxtraórdináry), *adj.* unusual, remarkable : S. A. 1383.

Extravagant, *adj.* irregular, fantastic : P. L. VI. 616.

Extreme (éxtreme : C. 273), (1) *adj.* (*a*) last : C. 273.

(*b*) exceedingly intense : S. A. 1342.

(2) *sb.* (*a*) one of two things removed as far as possible from each other in nature : P. L. II. 599 ; VII. 272.

(*b*) *pl.* extremities, sufferings : P. L. I. 276 ; X. 976.

Extremity, *sb.* extreme need or distress : C. 643.

Exulcerate, *vb.`* *absol.* to irritate as with ulcers : S. A. 625.

Eye, I. *sb.* (*pl.* eyn, *for the sake of the rhyme* : N. O. 223) (1) organ of sight : P. L. I. 193 ; V. 131 ; VII. 496 ; IX. 500, 1122 ; XI. 620, ; L. 181 ; Ps. LXXXVIII. 44 ; (*b*) covering the body and wings of the four cherubic shapes which convoy the chariot of God : P. L. VI. 755, 846, 848.

(*c*) covering the wheels of the chariot : P. L. VI. 755, 847, 848.

(*d*) covering the bodies of the cherubim : P. L. XI. 130.

(*e*) region of the eyes : P. 16.

(*f*) *fig.* the sun as the eye of day : Il P. 141 ; C. 978 ; S. I. 5 ; as the eye of the world : P. L. V. 171.

(*g*) *fig.* the stars as the eyes of heaven : P. L. V. 44.

(2) the eye as possessing the power of vision : P. L. I. 456 ; II. 753 ; III. 23, 382, 547, 614, 700 ; IV. 117, 358 ; VI. 476 ; VIII. 307 ; IX. 777 ; XI. 212, 305, 412, 419, 423, 429 ; P. R. II. 31 ; S. A. 33, 94, 124, 459, 584, 1103, 1160, 1490, 1543, 1625, 1744 ; V. Ex. 66 ; N. O. 223 ; P. 43 ; L'A. 69 ; C. 155, 164, 342, 395, 758 ; S. XXII. 1 ; Ps. LXXXVIII. 38 ; CXXXVI. 94.

(*b*) the eye of God : P. L. II. 189 ; III. 193 ; V. 647 ; N. O. 43 ; *Eternal Eye* : P. L. V. 711.

(*c*) **all eye**, possessing the power of vision in every part of the body : P. L. VI. 350.

(*d*) attributed to the mind : P. L. III. 53 ; S. A. 1689.

(*e*) *fig.* one of the seven archangels who stand near the throne of God, and act as his chief messengers : P. L. III. 650, 660.

(*f*) *fig.* mental vision, perception : P. L. XII. 556 ; Ps. LXXXVI. 51.

(*g*) a biblical use in which the word has the ideas of both mental and spiritual perception : P. L. IX. 706, 866, 875, 985, 1053, 1070 ; also with the significance of sense (2) : P. L. XI. 598 ; XII. 274.

(3) with reference to the direction in which the eye is turned, usually equivalent to : look, glance, gaze : P. L. III. 573 ; IV. 125, 466, 492, 572 ; VII. 513 ; IX. 397, 518, 528, 1036 ; XI. 191, 385, 396, 585, 711 ; P. R. III. 293 ; IV. 61, 112 ; S. A. 1637 ; L'A. 121.

(*b*) the look of God : P. L. III. 58, 534 ; XII. 109.

(*c*) with *adjs.* expressing the character, feeling, or position of the person looking : P. L. I. 56, 568, 604 ; II. 616 ; IV. 300 ; V. 26 ; VI. 149 ; VIII. 257 ; IX. 743, 1014 ; X. 553 ; XI. 863 ; P. R. I. 319 ; II. 180, 296 ; N. O. 59 ; L'A. 80 ; Il P. 140 ; C. 753 ; *of God* : S. A. 1172 ; Ps. CXXXVI. 78 ; *of Jove* : L. 81 ; *of the sun* : P. L. III. 578.

(4) ocular perception, sight : P. L. II. 748, 803, 890 ; IV. 279 ; VI. 571 ; VIII. 310 ; X. 5 ; XI. 478 ; P. R. III. 245, 390 ; IV. 38 ; Il P. 166.

(5) range of vision, view : P. R. II. 153.

(6) attentive or observing look : P. R. II. 210 ; watchful care, attentive regard, oversight : P. R. IV. 216 ; *of God* : S. A. 636 ; S. II. 14.

(7) *pl.* look, countenance, aspect : P. L. II. 239.

(8) opinion, judgement, estimation : S. A. 690.

(9) *fig.* the seat of intelligence ; *of Athens* : P. R. IV. 240.

(10) one of the spots near the end of the tail-feathers of a peacock : P. L. VII. 446.

(11) blossom of a plant : L. 139.

II. *vb. tr.* (*a*) to look on, observe, behold : P. L. IV. 504 ; VII. 67 ; IX. 923 ; XI. 585 ; S. A. 726 ; C. 329.

(*b*) to keep an eye on, observe narrowly : P. R. IV. 507.

See **Dry-eyed, Green-eyed, Meek-eyed, Pale-eyed, Pure-eyed.**

Eyeless, *adj.* blind, sightless : S. A. 41.

Eyelid, *sb.* membrane covering the eye : P. L. IV. 616 ; v. 674 ; Il P. 150 ; *fig. of the morn* : L. 26.

Eye-sight, *sb.* sense of seeing, sight : S. A. 919, 1489, 1502, 1503, 1527.

Eye-witness, *sb.* (*a*) one who is present and sees for himself : P. L. VI. 883.

(*b*) result of actual observation, report of one who saw : S. A. 1594.

Eyrie, *sb.* nest of a bird of prey : P. L. VII. 424.

Ezekiel, *sb.* the Hebrew prophet : P. L. I. 455.

F

Fable, (1) *sb.* (*a*) legend, myth : P. L. I. 197, 580 ; II. 627 ; IV. 250 ; XI. 11 ; P. R. II. 215 ; IV. 341.

(*b*) fabled abode : L. 160.

(**2**) *vb.* (*pres. 2d sing.* fablest : P. L. VI. 292) (*a*) *tr.* to tell fictitious tales of, fabricate : P. L. VI. 292 ; P. R. II. 358 ; with *clause* : P. L. I. 741 ; x. 580.

(*b*) *intr.* to speak falsely, lie : C. 800.

part. adj. **fabled,** mythical, legendary : P. L. IX. 30.

vbl. sb. **fabling,** the making of fables, the inventing of falsehoods : P. R. IV. 295.

Fabric, *sb.* structure, building : P. L. I. 710 ; *fig. of the heavens* : P. L. VIII. 76 ; *of the earth* : P. L. x. 482.

Fabricius, *sb.* the Roman consul and general who refused the bribe of Pyrrhus : P. R. II. 446.

Fabulous, *adj.* fictitious : C. 513.

Face, *sb.* (*a*) visage, countenance : P. L. I. 600 ; III. 44 ; v. 30 ; VI. 753 ; x. 205 ; XI. 128 ; P. R. IV. 76 ; S. A. 742 ; S. XXIII. 10 ; Ps. LXXXIV. 31 ; as expressing character or emotion : P. L. II. 304 ; III. 637 ; IV. 114 ; VI. 540 ; IX. 853, 1063, 1077 ; XI. 641 ; XII. 644 ; D. F. I. 34 ; C. 530 ; S. XXIII. 12 ; Ps. LXXXIII. 60 ; *of God or Christ,* usually indicating the attitude toward man : P. L. III. 140, 262, 407 ; VI. 681, 721 ; IX. 1080 ; XI. 353 ; P. R. I. 92 ; S. A. 1749 ; Ps. LXXX. 15, 31, 79 ; LXXXVI. 57 ; LXXXVIII. 58 ; sight, presence : P. L. x. 723 ; XI. 316.

fig. face of earth : P. L. VII. 278, 316 ; P. R. IV. 433 ; *of deluge* :

P. L. XI. 843 ; *of heaven* : P. L. II. 490 ; v. 644 ; VI. 783 ; *of the moon* : P. L. VII. 377 ; *of the sky* : P. L. x. 1064.

(*b*) front of the body : P. R. III. 324.

(*c*) appearance, look, aspect : P. L. v. 43 ; VII. 636 ; XI. 712.

See **Double-faced.**

Facile, *adj.* (*a*) courteous, affable : P. L. VIII. 65.

(*b*) easily persuaded, yielding : P. L. IX. 1158 ; P. R. I. 51 ; easily moved : P. L. IV. 967.

Fact, *sb.* thing done, deed, act : P. L. IX. 928, 980 ; XI. 457 ; S. A. 493, 736 ; brave deed or feat *of arms* : P. L. II. 124.

Faction, *sb.* (*a*) adherents of a cause, party : P. L. II. 901.

(*b*) disorderly opposition to established authority, dissension : P. L. II. 32.

Factious, *adj.* dissentious : P. L. XII. 352 ; arising from factions : P. L. XI. 664.

Faculty, *sb.* (*a*) active quality of a plant : C. 628.

(*b*) inherent power of the five senses : P. L. v. 410.

(*c*) one of the powers of the mind : P. L. v. 101 ; VIII. 542.

Fade, *vb.* *tr.* to wither, decay : P. L. III. 360 ; D. F. I. 2.

part. adj. **faded;** (*a*) withered, decayed : P. L. IX. 893.

(*b*) grown dim : P. L. IV. 870 ; having lost freshness and beauty : P. L. I. 602.

(*c*) vanished, departed : P. L. II. 375, 376.

Faery or **Fairy, (1)** *sb.* (*a*) diminutive spirit : C. 118.

(*b*) evil spirit, goblin : C. 436.

(**2**) *adj.* (*a*) who is a fairy : P. L. I. 781 ; V. Ex. 60 ; *faery Mab* : L'A. 102. *See* **Mab.**

(*b*) of fairies : C. 298.

(*c*) beautiful as a fairy ; P. R. II. 359.

Fail, (1) *intr.* (*a*) to be absent or wanting : P. L. VI. 117.

(*b*) to cease to be, no longer to exist, disappear : P. L. I. 117 ; II. 931 ; IX. 942 ; P. R. IV. 612 ; U. C. I. 10 ; L'A. 99.

(*c*) to lose strength or power, decline ; *of a kingdom* : N. O. 171 ; *of the sight* : P. L. XII. 9.

(*d*) to prove deficient on trial, be wanting at need : P. L. VIII.

38 : S. A. 901 ; with *dat.* of the person : P. L. II. 205 ; with *dat.* omitted : P. L. VII. 38 ; to prove untrue : C. 597.

(*e*) to fall short, not to come up to expectation : P. R. II. 54 ; to come short of performing one's duty : P. L. VIII. 534 ; to grow weak in faith : P. L. IX. 1142.

(*f*) to fall into sin : P. L. III. 101.

(*g*) to be unsuccessful : P. L. VII. 139 ; P. R. I. 147 ; with *prep. inf.* : P. L. I. 633.

(*h*) to err, be mistaken : P. L. I. 167.

(**2**) *tr.* (*a*) to cause *one* to miss or come short *of* : P. R. III. 395.

(*b*) to omit, neglect, leave undone ; with *prep. inf.* : P. L. II. 480 ; IX. 145 ; X. 856 ; Il P. 155 ; Ps. LXXXI. 27.

part. adj. (*a*) **failing**, being at fault : P. L. IX. 404.

(*b*) **failed**, lost : P. L. IV. 357.

vbl. sb. **failing**, weakness, fault : P. L. X. 129.

See **Ever-failing.**

Fain, (**1**) *adj.* glad, well-pleased ; with *prep. inf.* : Ps. LXXXI. 61.

(**2**) *adv.* gladly, with pleasure : S. A. 1535 ; C. 783.

Faint, (**1**) *adj.* (*a*) weak-hearted, cowardly : P. L. VI. 799.

(*b*) exhausted, weak : P. L. VI. 392 ; S. XXIII. 4 ; Ps. VI. 4 ; CXIV. 10.

(*c*) indistinct, dim : C. 331.

(**2**) *vb. intr.* (*a*) to become weak in spirit, lose courage : P. L. XI. 631.

(*b*) to swoon : P. L. XI. 108 ; U. C. II. 16.

part. adj. **fainting** ; (*a*) failing : P. L. I. 530.

(*b*) losing courage, disheartened : S. A. 666.

vbl. sb. **fainting**, swooning : S. A. 631.

Fair, I. *adj.* (**1**) pleasing to the eye, beautiful ; (*a*) *of persons, also of parts of the body* : P. L. IV. 300, 339, 477, 479, 790, 820 ; IX. 538 ; V. Ex. 28 ; P. 16 ; C. 34, 969 ; ironically : P. L. II. 818 ; *comp.* : P. L. II. 110 ; *applied esp. to women* : P. L. I. 445 ; II. 650, 748, 757 ; V. 129, 380 ; VIII. 172, 471, 568, 596 ; IX. 443, 452, 545 ; X. 352, 891, 943 ; XI. 582, 614, 625 ; P. R. II. 155, 200 ; S. A.

217 ; D. F. I. 11 ; M. W. 63 ; L'A. 11, 23 ; C. 283, 442, 689, 880, 929 ; Hor. O. 13 ; *comp.* : P. L. IX. 1032 ; P. R. II. 858 ; S. A. 217 ; *sup.* : P. L. IV. 324 ; V. 381 ; VIII. 493 ; IX. 896 ; P. R. II. 154 ; III. 341.

(*b*) used in respectful address : P. L. III. 694 ; V. 58 ; VIII. 276 ; esp. to women : P. L. IV. 468, 481, 610 ; V. 74 ; X. 384 ; A. 33 ; C. 860.

(*c*) *of animals* : P. L. XI. 647 ; C. 152.

(*d*) *of places or things* : P. L. I. 468 ; IV. 268, 379 ; VIII. 338, 472, 493 ; IX. 605 ; P. R. I. 63 ; III. 257 ; IV. 55, 544 ; S. A. 934 ; D. F. I. 21 ; C. 981 ; Ps. LXXXIV. 1 ; LXXXVII. 5, 6 ; *comp.* : P. R. IV. 613 ; *of the world, a star, a cloud,* etc. : P. L. III. 554, 727 ; IV. 151, 648 ; V. 155 ; VII. 556 ; IX. 568, 720 ; X. 618 ; C. 331 ; *sup.* : P. L. V. 166 ; *of flower, fruit, plant, tree,* etc. : P. L. V. 52 ; IX. 385, 661, 731, 763, 777, 798, 972, 996 ; X. 550, 561, 1067 ; S. A. 728 ; M. W. 41 ; A. 45 ; C. 393 ; *comp.* : P. L. IV. 270 ; V. 53 ; *sup.* : P. L. IV. 147 ; VIII. 307 ; IX. 432, 851 ; D. F. I. 1.

(*e*) *of morn, light, colour* : P. L. II. 398 ; VI. 524 ; VIII. 273 ; *sup.* : P. L. IX. 577.

(*f*) *of wisdom* : P. L. IV. 491.

(*g*) *of appearance, look, resemblance,* etc. : P. L. IV. 718 ; VIII. 221 ; P. R. III. 351 ; *comp.* : P. R. II. 352 ; *sup.* : P. L. IX. 538.

(**2**) good, desirable : P. L. XI. 57 ; P. R. IV. 442 ; S. A. 1723 ; L. 73 ; ironically : P. L. X. 818.

(**3**) specious, plausible : P. R. II. 310 ; S. A. 1178 ; C. 160.

(**4**) a combination of the ideas of beauty and purity : P. L. III. 338 ; C. 831, 1009 ; S. M. 21 ; M. W. 4.

(**5**) favourable, auspicious : P. L. XI. 593 ; Ps. VI. 19 ; or gentle, benign : L. 22.

(**6**) impartial, just : P. L. X. 769 ; XII. 26 ; S. A. 688.

(**7**) bright, sunny ; *of day or morning* : P. L. V. 124 ; P. R. IV. 426, 451 ; S. A. 1062.

(**8**) promising, suitable : P. L. IV. 521.

(**9**) kind, gentle : P. L. VIII. 47.

(**10**) gracious, courteous : N. O. 37.

(11) open to view, or a *fig.* use of sense (*a*): P. L. III. 47.

II. *absol.* or *sb.* (*a*) fair one, beautiful woman: P. L. IV. 770; *sup.*: P. L. V. 18.

(*b*) fairness, beauty: P. L. IX. 608; XI. 717; P. R. I. 381.

III. *adv.*(*a*)auspiciously,favourably: P. L. XI. 630.

(*b*) civilly, courteously, kindly: P. L. VI. 611; IX. 1159.

(*c*) honourably, honestly, *sup.*: P. L. XI. 549.

(*d*) excellently; *fair appearing*, seeming excellent or desirable: P. L. IX. 354.

Fairfax, *sb.* Lord General Fairfax, the commander of the parliamentary forces during the Civil War in England: S. XV. 1.

Fairly, *adv.* (*a*) justly, honourably; used ironically: P. R. IV. 187.

(*b*) softly, gently: C. 168.

Fairy. *See* **Faery.**

Faith, *sb.* (*a*) trust, confidence: P. L. XI. 807.

(*b*) belief and trust in God: P. L. XI. 64, 141, 458; XII. 128, 154, 306, 449, 527, 529, 536, 582, 599, 603; S. XIV. 1; XVI. 3; F. of C. 9; *personified*: C. 213; S. XIV. 7, 9; faith in Christ by which the sinner is justified in the sight of God; this idea may enter also into some of the preceding citations: P. L. XII. 295, 409, 427, 488.

(*c*) allegiance, fealty: P. L. II. 690; IV. 954; VI. 143; IX. 1141; the obligation of a pledge or promise: S. A. 750, 987.

(*d*) faithfulness, fidelity, loyalty: P. L. II. 36; III. 104; IV. 520; VI. 115; VIII. 325; IX. 286, 298, 320, 335, 411, 1075; X. 129; S. A. 388; C. 88, 971; Hor. O. 6.

(*e*) integrity, honesty: S.xv. 12. *See* **Marriage-faith.**

Faithful, *adj.* (*a*) full of or characterized by trust in God: P. L. XII. 113, 152; Ps. CXIV. 1; *faithful works*: P. L. XI. 64.

(*b*) firm in fidelity or allegiance, loyal, true: P. L. I. 264, 611; IV. 933, 950, 952; V. 896; VI. 204, 271; IX. 265; S. A. 957, 1498, 1751; C. 944; L. 121; *faithful love*: P. L. IX. 983; *warfare*: P. L. VI. 803.

(*c*) that may be relied on, trustworthy: Ps. CXXXVI. 4, 96.

absol. those constant in their obedience to and trust in God: P. L. XII. 462, 481, 571.

Faithfulness, *sb.* fidelity, loyalty, constancy: P. L. IV. 951; Ps. LXXXVIII. 48.

Faithless, *adj.* without fidelity, disloyal: P. L. III. 96; S. A. 380.

absol. those who are disloyal: P. L. V. 897.

Falerne, *sb.* Falernus ager, a district in Campania, Italy, noted for its wine: P. R. IV. 117.

Fall, (1) *sb.* (*a*) action of dropping from a higher to a lower place, usually implying also the idea of sense (*b*): P. L. I. 76, 642; II. 76, 177, 549, 773; VI. 872, 898; XII. 391; *their fall*, them fallen: P. L. VI. 55.

(*b*) descent from a high estate or from moral elevation, degradation, downfall: S. A. 690; P. R. II. 88; III. 201; the lapse into sin of man or angels, and the consequent degradation: P. L. II. 16; III. 128; IV. 101; V. 241, 542, 878; IX. 941, 1069; X. 44, 451; XII. 500.

(*c*) a falling to the ground: P. R. IV. 567.

(*d*) cadence: C. 251.

(2) *vb.* (*pres. 2d sing.* fall'st: P. L. V. 174; *pret.* fell; *past part.* fallen; *perf.* formed with the auxiliary *be*: P. L. V. 541; P. R. II. 31; S. A. 169, 414, 1523, 1558) *intr.* (*a*) to drop from a higher to a lower place or level, descend: P. L. I. 740, 743; II. 925; V. 133, 191; VI. 190, 844; VII. 19; P. R. IV. 571; Ps. VII. 56, 60; with *down*: P. L. II. 935; *of the fall of Satan or his followers to hell*, often implying the idea of sense (*b*): P. L. I. 75, 174, 282, 491, 679, 748; II. 826, 1006; V. 240, 613; VI. 871; VII. 134; P. R. IV. 562, 576, 581, 620; with *down*: P. L. II. 771; X. 184; *of tears*: P. L. V. 130, 133; M. W. 45; *fig.* P. 49; *of a star*: D. F. I. 44; *fig. of the dew of sleep*: P. L. IV. 615.

(*b*) to descend from a high estate or from moral elevation: P. L. V. 540; S. A. 169, 414; *fig. knowledge falls degraded*: P. L. VIII. 551; to lapse into sin and suffer the consequent degradation, the emphasis sometimes upon the sin and sometimes upon the degradation ; *of the fall of Satan* or *his angels*: P. L. I. 84, 92 ; II. 13, 457 ; III. 102, 129 ; IV. 39, 64, 91, 905 ; V. 541 ; VI. 24, 852, 912 ; P. R. IV. 150; *of the fall of Adam and Eve or their posterity* : P. L. II. 1023 ; III. 95, 99, 130, 152, 201, 400 ; VIII. 640 ; X. 16, 62, 846 ; XI. 29 ; P. R. I. 405 ; II. 134 ; IV. 311.

(*c*) to sink down; *of the sun or other heavenly body* : P. L. IV. 591 ; V. 174 ; X. 663.

(*d*) to flow : P. L. IV. 230, 260.

(*e*) to drop from an erect posture or to the ground : P. L. I. 461 ; IV. 731 ; VI. 285 ; XI. 446 ; Ps. I. 9 ; with *down* : P. L. VI. 593 ; X. 513, 542 ; C. 53 ; to droop : P. R. II. 223.

(*f*) to be cast on the ground; *of shadows* : P. L. III. 619 ; P. R. IV. 70.

(*g*) to prostrate oneself in supplication or reverence; *fall at his feet* : P. L. VIII. 315 ; X. 912 ; *fall down* : P. R. IV. 166, 192 ; *fall prostrate before* : P. L. X. 1087, 1099.

(*h*) to be overthrown, be slain, perish : P. L. I. 586 ; VI. 796 ; P. R. I. 373 ; IV. 568 ; S. A. 55, 144, 1558, 1559, 1580, 1582 ; Ps. V. 29 ; LXXXII. 23.

(*i*) to stumble or be drawn *into, fig.* : P. L. IX. 362 ; S. A. 532, 1683.

(*j*) to rush violently *on* : P. R. IV. 415.

(*k*) to be directed *on* ; *of anger* : P. L. III. 237 ; *of a curse* : P. L. X. 174 ; to come *on* so as to control; *of horror* : P. L. X. 539 ; *of sleep* : P. L. VIII. 458.

(*l*) to strike or impinge *on* : C. 491.

(*m*) to come *on* in the course of life or circumstances : P. L. VII. 25, 26 ; S. A. 1523.

(*n*) to come by chance *on* : C. 50.

(*o*) to pass *to* or *into* a specified condition : P. L. VI. 614 ; IX. 362 ; X. 570 ; P. R. II. 31 ; *fall asleep* : P. L. V. 92 ; XII. 614.

(*p*) to become ; with *adj.* complement : P. R. I. 443.

(*q*) to enter upon an action, begin; with *prep. inf.* : P. L. XII. 118 ; with *to* and *vbl. sb.* : P. R. IV. 295.

(*r*) to pass under the sway of ; *fell to idols* : P. L. I. 445.

(*s*) to happen, come to pass : P. L. II. 203.

In combination with other words ;

(*a*) **fall off**, withdraw from allegiance : P. L. I. 30 ; P. R. III. 415 ; S. A. 456.

(*b*) **fall out**, happen, come to pass : S. A. 1265.

(*c*) **fall short**, fail to accomplish one's aim : P. L. IX. 174.

(*d*) **fall to**, apply oneself to with eagerness : P. L. IV. 331 ; V. 434.

part. adj. (*a*) **falling**, descending ; *of showers* : P. L. V. 190 ; *of heavenly bodies* : P. L. I. 745 ; C. 30.

(*b*) **fallen**, in a degraded state morally, ruined : P. L. I. 157, 330 ; III. 181 ; X. 47 ; XI. 180.

See **Crest-fallen, Heaven-fallen.**

Fallacious, *adj.* (*a*) deceitful : S. A. 320.

(*b*) deceptive, misleading : P. L. II. 568 ; P. R. III. 4 ; S. A. 533.

(*c*) mocking expectation, delusive : P. L. IX. 1046.

Fallacy, *sb.* deception : P. R. I. 155.

Fallible, *adj.* liable to error : P. L. VI. 428.

Fallow, *sb. pl.* ploughed fields left unsown : L'A. 71.

False, (1) *adj.* (*a*) contrary to what is true, erroneous : P. L. II. 565 ; V. 809 ; VI. 121 ; IX. 333 ; P. R. IV. 291 ; C. 759 ; L. 153.

(*b*) wrong, unjust : Ps. LXXXII. 6.

(*c*) deceitful, treacherous, unfaithful, disloyal : P. L. II. 700 ; III. 681 ; IV. 694 ; VI. 271 ; IX. 1068, 1070 ; X. 868 ; P. R. III. 138 ; S. A. 227, 749, 824 ; C. 690, 799, 814 ; S. XV. 7.

(*d*) deceptive, misleading : P. L. II. 522 ; III. 92 ; IX. 306 ; P. R. IV. 320, 491 ; T. 5 ; C. 156, 364 ; Ps. IV. 12.

(*e*) disappointing hopes, delusive : P. L. IX. 1011 ; XI. 413.

(*f*) not genuine, not real, sham : P. L. II. 112 ; X. 452 ; P. R. III. 69 ; that is not really such ; *false gods* : P. L. XII. 122 ; feigned, counterfeited : S. A. 901.

absol. those who are untrue to their allegiance : P. L. V. 898.

(2) *adv.* not rightly, wrongly : P. L. IX. 355 ; incorrectly : P. R. II. 179 ; S. XI. 7.

Falsehood, *sb.* (*a*) that which is contrary to truth : P. R. III. 443.

(*b*) deception, imposture : P. L. IV. 122, 811 ; C. 698.

(*c*) treachery, perfidy : P. L. x. 873 ; S. A. 955, 979 ; C. 281.

False-imagined, *adj.* supposed contrary to what is true : D. F. I. 72.

Falsity, *sb.* falsehood, or possibly counterfeit character : P. L. I. 367.

Falter, *vb. tr.* to hesitate in utterance of words : P. L. x. 115.

part. adj. **faltering** ; (*a*) hesitating : P. L. II. 989 ; speaking hesitatingly : Ps. v. 25.

(*b*) unsteady, irregular : P. L. IX. 846.

Fame, (**1**) *sb.* (*a*) rumour, report, tradition : P. L. I. 651 ; II. 346 ; IV. 938 ; x. 481 ; P. R. I. 334 ; S. A. 1248 ; *personified,* masc. gender: S. A. 971 ; less definitely *personified* : A. 8, 41 ; S. XIII. 12.

(*b*) honour, renown : P. L. I. 695 ; III. 449 ; VI. 240, 375, 384 ; XI. 386, 623, 698, 699, 793 ; XII. 47 ; P. R. II. 209 ; III. 25, 47, 65, 70, 99, 100, 101, 289 ; IV. 371 ; S. A. 1706, 1717 ; W. S. 5 ; L. 70, 78, 84 ; S. VIII. 6.

(**2**) *vb. tr.* to report; in *passive* with *prep. inf.* : S. A. 1094.

part. adj. **famed,** famous, celebrated, renowned : P. L. III. 568 ; P. R. I. 34 ; IV. 59 ; C. 1004 ; with *for* : P. L. XII. 332.

Familiar, (**1**) *adj.* well-known from association : P. L. II. 761 ; XI. 305.

(**2**) *adv.* (*a*) intimately, or *adj.* intimate : P. L. IX. 2.

(*b*) with ease and unconcern, or *adj.* well-known from experience : P. L. II. 219.

Family, *sb.* (*a*) group of persons forming a domestic household and ruled over by a father : P. L. XII. 23.

(*b*) group of persons consisting of parents and their children ; *of Adam and Eve,* as part of the family of God : P. L. x. 216.

(*c*) those descended from a common ancestor, house : P. R. III. 168.

Famine, *sb.* (*a*) want of food, hunger : P. L. x. 573, 597 ; P. R. II. 257 ; starvation : P. L. XI. 472, 778.

(*b*) fierce appetite : P. L. II. 847.

Famish, *vb.* (**1**) *tr.* to deprive of that which is necessary to life; with *acc.* and *of* : P. L. XII. 78.

(**2**) *intr.* to die of starvation : P. R. II. 311.

Famous, *adj.* renowned; *of persons* : P. R. II. 7 ; III. 68, 94 ; IV. 221, 241, 267 ; S. A. 528, 542 ; L. 53 ; *sup.* famousest *of* : S. A. 982 ; *of places* : P. L. IV. 234 ; S. A. 145 ; A. 28.

Fan, (**1**) *sb.* (*a*) instrument for winnowing grain; *fig. of wings* : P. L. v. 269.

(*b*) the wing-like organ of an insect : P. L. VII. 476.

(*c*) *fig.* **Aurora's fan,** the wind in gentle motion, or the leaves stirred by the wind : P. L. v. 6.

(**2**) *vb. tr.* (*a*) to winnow away *chaff* : Ps. I. 11.

(*b*) to cause to be dispersed by a fan-like movement : P. R. II. 364.

(*c*) to set in motion : P. L. VII. 432.

(*d*) to move like a fan : P. L. IV. 157 ; L. 44.

(*e*) to blow gently and refreshingly upon : P. L. v. 655 ; x. 94.

Fanatic, *adj.* characterized by excessive and mistaken zeal in religion : P. L. I. 480.

Fancy, (**1**) *sb.* (*a*) power of forming mental images of things not present to the senses, imagination : P. L. IV. 802 ; v. 53, 102, 110, 486 ; VIII. 188, 294, 461 ; S. A. 601 ; N. O. 134 ; P. 31 ; W. S. 13 ; C. 548 ; *personified* : L'A. 133 ; C. 669.

(*b*) fanciful image or conception of the mind : P. R. IV. 292 ; V. Ex. 32 ; Il P. 6.

(*c*) caprice, whim : P. L. v. 296.

(*d*) inclination, liking : S. A. 794.

(**2**) *vb. tr.* to imagine : P. L. IX. 789 ; with *clause*; P. L. IX. 1009.

part. adj. **fancied,** influenced or controlled by the imagination : S. XXIII. 10.

See **New-fangled.**

Fantastic, (**1**) *adj.* (*a*) quaint or grotesque in form or movement; *of the dance* : C. 144.

(*b*) making quaint or grotesque movements in the dance, or *possibly* directed by the fancy : L'A. 34.

(2) *sb.* one given to showy dress: V. Ex. 20.

Fantasy (phantasy: S. M. 5), *sb.* (*a*) fancy, imagination: S. M. 5.

(*b*) mental image: C. 205.

*Far, *adv.* (1) at or to a great distance: P. L. I. 507, 670, 792; II. 1036; III. 428, 501, 621; IV. 545; V. 213, 744; VI. 79, 415, 551; VII. 220, 272, 618; VIII. 231; IX. 576, 642; X. 233, 423; XII. 45; P. R. I. 191, 332, 340; IV. 53; S. A. 341, 1038; Il P. 81; C. 388, 824; *sup.*: P. L. XI. 401; P. R. IV. 69; C. 227; *far away*: L. 155; *far off*: P. L. II. 582, 1047; III. 88; IV. 14; VI. 768; VII. 32; VIII. 185; X. 104; XI. 121, 727; P. R. IV. 547; C. 456; *far round*: P. L. I. 666; IX. 482; *that be from thee far, far be it,* of deprecation: P. L. III. 153, 154; IV. 758; *far from,* in asserting something opposite or unlike: P. L. IV. 103; V. 828; (*b*) **far and nigh,** in every part, everywhere: P. L. VI. 295; P. R. IV. 122.

(*c*) **far and wide,** to a great distance, everywhere: P. L. II. 133, 519, 1003; III. 614; IV. 579; VI. 773; P. R. III. 72.

(2) to a great degree, greatly: P. L. XI. 783.

(3) by a great interval, widely: P. R. IV. 7; in expressing excess, defect, inequality, or unlikeness: with *vbs.*: P. L. II. 1; VII. 71; VIII. 359; X. 150; with *adjs.*: P. L. VIII. 38; P. R. III. 89; the *adjs.* in comp. or sup. degree: P. L. II. 97; III. 504; IV. 288; VII. 145; VIII. 33: X. 593; XII. 587; S. A. 1467; *far other,* widely different: P. L. I. 607; X. 862; P. R. II. 132; S. A. 875; C. 612.

(4) to a distant time: P. L. X. 211.

(5) preceded by *as, how, so, thus,* the context specifying more or less definiteness in degree or extent; (*a*) at or to a definite distance: P. L. I. 59, 73; II. 211, 321; III. 476, 609; VII. 230, 369; VIII. 102, 120, 156; IX. 79, 433; X. 281, 686; P. R. I. 322; III. 272; N. O. 170.

(*b*) to a certain extent or degree: P. L. I. 138, 587; II. 22; IV. 446; V. 457, 458; VI. 342; VIII. 177, 437; S. A. 755.

(*c*) up to a definite point of advance or time: P. L. V. 803; X. 370; P. R. II. 49.

(6) quasi-*sb.* (*a*) a great distance: P. L. II. 1007.

(*b*) **from far,** from or at a distance: P. L. III. 579; VI. 487; X. 1077; P. R. III. 303; D. F. I. 17; N. O. 22.

(*c*) **by far,** by a great interval of distance: P. L. III. 529; of measure: P. L. VII. 359: of inequality: P. L. VIII. 598.

Far-beaming, *adj.* shining to a great distance: N. O. 9.

Far-blazing, *adj.* shining brilliantly to a great distance: P. L. V. 757.

Fare, (1) *sb.* ⌐(*a*) food: P. L. V. 495; IX. 1028.

(*b*) prosperity, success: P. R. II. 202.

(2) *vb. intr.* (*a*) to go, travel, journey: P. L. II. 940; IV. 131.

(*b*) to happen, fall out; *impersonal*: P. R. III. 443.

(*c*) fare ill, experience bad fortune: P. L. X. 735.

Farewell, (1) *interj.* (*a*) expression of good wishes at parting: S. A. 959, 1413.

(*b*) expression of regret at abandoning *happy fields*: P. L. I. 249; *fear* or *hope*: P. L. IV. 108; *remorse*: P. L. IV. 109.

(2) *sb.* parting salutation, adieu: P. L. II. 492.

Far-fet, *adj.* far-fetched, brought from a distance: P. R. II. 401.

Farm, *sb.* tract of cultivated land: P. L. IX. 448.

Far-off, *adj.* distant or remote in space: Il P. 74; C. 481.

Fashion, (1) *sb.* form and nature: C. 360.

(2) *vb. tr.* to shape, form; P. L. VIII. 469.

Fast, (1) *sb.* abstinence from food; P. R. II. 247; *personified*: Il P. 46.

(2) *vb. intr.* to go without food: P. R. II. 284.

vbl. sb. **fasting,** abstinence from food: P. R. II. 243.

Fast, (1) *adj.* (*a*) firm, stable: Ps. LXXXVII. 2.

(*b*) tenacious; *get fast hold of*: P. R. IV. 480.

(*c*) **make fast,** fasten firmly: P. L. X. 319; shut or lock tightly: P. L. XI. 737.

(2) *adv.* (*a*) firmly, immovably: P. L. VIII. 640; XI. 851; Il P. 44; S. A. 1637; Ps. VII. 37; LXXXVII. 20.

(*b*) deeply, soundly: P. L. IX. 182.

(*c*) tightly, securely: P. L. IV. 171, 190, 796; VI. 543, 870; VIII. 240; XI. 587; C. 816; Ps. LXXX. 38.

(*d*) **fast by**, close to: P. L. I. 12; II. 725, 1051; III. 354; IV. 221; VI. 5; IX. 628; X. 333; S. A. 1432; P. 21.

(*e*) swiftly, quickly: P. L. II. 675; X. 542; XII. 631, 639; N. O. 211; *thick and fast*: P. L. II. 754.

Fasten, *vb. tr.* to make fast, fix, attach: P. L. X. 300; S. A. 1398.

Fat, (1) *adj.* fertile, rich: P. L. XI. 648.

(2) *sb.* fat parts of the bodies of animals: P. L. XI. 439; S. A. 1671.

Fatal, *adj.* (*a*) allotted by fate, destined: P. L. II. 104; with a blending of sense (*c*): P. L. X. 191; P. R. I. 53; IV. 525; *fatal course*, course of fate: P. L. V. 861.

(*b*) influencing or deciding destiny, fateful: P. L. II. 725, 871; IV. 349, 514; IX. 889; X. 4, 364, 480; XII. 99; S. A. 1024; L. 100.

(*c*) deadly, destructive, ruinous: P. L. II. 712, 786; P. R. I. 441; IV. 205; D. F. I. 7; S. X. 7.

Fate, *sb.* (*a*) principle, power, or agency by which events are unalterably fixed from eternity: P. L. I. 116, 133: II. 197, 393, 559, 560; III. 120; V. 527; X. 265; P. R. IV. 265, 317; or in sense (*c*) (?): P. R. IV. 383, 470; suggesting *personality* but not clearly *personified*: P. L. II. 232, 550, 610, 809; VI. 869; IX. 689, 885, 927; X. 480; XI. 181; M. W. 13; N. O. 149.

(*b*) that which is destined to happen: P. L. VII. 173.

(*c*) what a person is fated to do or suffer, appointed lot, fortune, destiny: P. L. III. 33, 113; U. C. II. 30; A. 67.

(*d*) doom, destruction, death: P. L. I. 448; II. 17; D. F. I. 22.

Father, *sb.* (1) male parent, he who has begotten a child: P. L. IV. 757; VIII. 498; XI. 760; XII. 103, 121; P. R. II. 414; S. A. 355, 373, 447, 448, 487, 602, 1248, 1432, 1459, 1485, 1506, 1717, 1733; C. 35, 57, 493, 828, 947; S. X. 10; XX. 1; *spec.*; (*b*) applied to Satan, the parent of Sin: P. L. II. 727, 730, 743, 810, 864.

(*c*) applied to the Father, God, in relation to Christ as Son: P. L. III. 139, 143, 144, 154, 227, 262, 271, 393, 398, 415; V. 663, 735, 855; VI. 710, 720, 723, 890; VII. 196, 588; X. 66, 68, 223; XI. 22; P. R. I. 31, 93, 176, 236, 283, 486; II. 85, 99, 259; III. 110, 219; IV. 603; N. O. 7; in relation to angels or mankind as offspring, the objects of His care, or owing Him reverence and obedience; frequently including also the relation to Christ: P. L. III. 56, 372, 386, 401; V. 246, 403, 596, 836, 847; VI. 96, 671, 814; VII. 11, 137, 517; X. 32, 63; XI. 20, 45; XII. 487, 546; P. R. I. 168; III. 175, 186; IV. 552, 596.

(*d*) applied to Christ, in relation to Adam and Eve, the objects of his care: P. L. X. 216.

(*e*) *fig.*: Il P. 2.

(2) ancestor, progenitor, *pl.*: P. R. I. 351; II. 33; III. 379, 439; S. A. 667; S. XVIII. 4; *sing., spec.* Adam: P. L. IV. 495; VIII. 298; X. 1097; David: P. R. III. 153, 154, 282, 353.

Fatherless, *adj. absol.* person having no father: Ps. LXXXII. 9.

Fatherly, *adv.* in the manner of a father: P. L. XII. 63.

Fathom, *sb.* the measure of length: P. L. II. 934.

Fault, *sb.* (*a*) defect in moral character: S. A. 777.

(*b*) dereliction of duty: S. A. 241; sin, transgression: P. L. I. 609; III. 118; X. 823, 938, 1089, 1101; S. A. 431, 502.

(*c*) blame of causing or doing evil, culpability: P. L. III. 96.

Faulty, *adj.* defective, imperfect: P. L. XI. 509.

Faun, *sb.* (*a*) Faunus, the Roman god: P. R. II. 191.

(*b*) one of a class of similar deities: L. 34.

Faunus, *sb.* the Roman god of woods and fields: P. L. IV. 708.

Favonius, *sb.* Zephyrus, the west wind : S. xx. 6.

Favour, (1) *sb.* (*a*) friendly regard, goodwill: P. L. v. 462; viii. 202; ix. 334; x. 1096; xi. 153; xii. 622; S. A. 273, 1357; Ps. iv. 30; v. 40; lxxxviii. 8; *by favour,* because of goodwill : P. L. vii. 72; *great in favour,* receiving exceptional marks of goodwill and friendly regard : P. L. v. 661.

(*b*) hospitality, or used by inversion instead of the adj. *favouring, i.e.* propitious : C. 184.

(*c*) object of kind regard, favourite: P. L. iii. 664.

(*d*) something conferred out of special goodwill : P. L. xii. 278; S. A. 685.

(2) *vb. tr.* (*a*) to regard with favour, treat kindly, show goodwill to : P. L. i. 654; ix. 949; S. A. 1412; L. 20; Ps. lxxxv. 1; *absol.*: S. A. 1720; *past part.* with *of*: P. L. i. 30; ii. 350; S. A. 1064; C. 78.

(*b*) to aid, support; P. R. ii. 430; Ps. lxxxii. 7.

part. adj. **favoured**, granted because of special goodwill : P. R. ii. 91.

part. absol. **favoured**, one who is honoured by special marks of goodwill : P. R. ii. 68.

See **Highly-favoured.**

Favourable, (fávoráble), *adj.* well-disposed, propitious : P. L. v. 507; xi. 169; S. A. 921.

Favourite, *sb.* (*a*) a person treated with peculiar favour: P. L. ix. 175.

(*b*) one who is unduly favoured by a prince : P. R. iv. 95.

Fawn, *sb.* young deer: P. L. iv. 404.

Fawn, *vb. intr.* (*a*) to show delight or fondness : P. L. ix. 526.

(*b*) to flatter meanly, court favour by cringing and subserviency : P. L. iv. 959.

part. adj. **fawning**, showing servile deference in order to gain favour : P. R. i. 452.

Fay, *sb.* fairy : N. O. 235.

Fealty, *sb.* (*a*) fidelity or loyalty on the part of man to God: P. L. iii. 204; ix. 262.

(*b*) recognition of superiority, paid by animals to Adam : P. L. viii. 344.

Fear, I. *sb.* (*a*) emotion aroused by threatening evil or impending danger or pain, apprehension, dread : P. L. i. 530, 558, 788; ii. 49, 627, 783; iv. 108, 822; vi. 393, 394, 397, 494; x. 813, 842, 1003; xi. 139, 212, 361; P. R. i. 66, 69, 110, 223, 422, 451; ii. 467; iii. 206; iv. 189, 195; S. A. 740, 1469; V. Ex. 67; N. O. 45; C. 355, 364, 410, 412, 511, 512, 565; F. of C. 18.

(*b*) feeling of awe and reverence towards God : P. L. vii. 305, 562; Ps. ii. 23; v. 19; with *of*: P. L. xi. 799; P. R. ii. 47; Ps. lxxxvi. 52.

(*c*) state of fearing : P. L. i. 275; with *of*: P. L. i. 598; ii. 293; ix. 326, 702, 989; x. 780; P. R. iv. 617; S. A. 1374; II P. 30; with *prep. inf.*: P. L. ii. 85; with *clause* : P. L. ix. 286.

(*d*) anxiety or solicitude *lest* : P. L. v. 396; solicitude for the safety of a person or a cause, mingled with dread of possible danger : P. R. ii. 53, 64, 70; S. A. 805; C. 355, 364, 410, 412, 511, 512.

(*e*) timidity, cowardice : P. L. iv. 854; vi. 238; xii. 218.

(*f*) cause of apprehension : P. L. ix. 285.

II. *vb.* (*pres. 2d sing.* fear'st : P. L. ix. 282; x. 838) (1) *tr.* (*a*) to regard with apprehension, be afraid of, dread : P. L. ii. 17, 82, 94, 205, 470, 678; v. 905; vi. 539; viii. 322; ix. 382, 331, 773; x. 340, 409, 838, 1000; P. R. ii. 257; iii. 385; iv. 454; S. A. 900, 939, 1065, 1234, 1526; C. 405, 446, 800; Ps. iii. 17; *fig. of inanimate or immaterial objects* : P. L. ii. 343; iv. 190; V. Ex. 27.

(*b*) to regard with awe and reverence, revere: P. L. viii. 168; ix. 701; xii. 15; P. R. iv. 304; Ps. lxxxv. 37; lxxxvi. 39.

(*c*) to hesitate through fear of the consequences; with *prep. inf.*: P. L. ii. 511, 1006; C. 328.

(*d*) to be afraid; with clause introduced by *lest*: P. L. x. 1024; S. A. 794; by *how*: P. L. i. 628; with clause without connection : P. L. vi. 490; P. R. iv. 488; parenthetically : P. L. iv. 574; v. 98; x. 51; S. A. 1250, 1719; with *prep. inf.*: P. L. v. 135; vi. 912.

(*e*) to feel anxiety about; with *prep. inf.*: P. L. x. 1084.

(2) *intr.* to be afraid : P. L. x. 119 ; xi. 234.

Fearless, *adj.* without fear, bold, intrepid : P. L. i. 131 ; iv. 14 ; v. 875 ; vi. 51, 804 ; ix. 57, 187 ; S. A. 810 ; with *of* : P. L. xi. 811 ; S. A. 529 ; with *prep. inf.*: P. L. ii. 855.

Feast, (1) *sb.* (*a*) religious festival in honour of God : P. L. i. 390 ; xii. 21 ; Ps. lxxxi. 12 ; in honour of Dagon : S. A. 12, 434, 1311, 1315, 1448, 1612, 1656 ; the feast of the Passover : P. R. i. 210.

(*b*) sumptuous meal, entertainment, banquet : P. L. v. 467 ; ix. 37 ; P. R. iv. 114, 637 ; V. Ex. 49 ; C. 746, 777 ; L. 117 ; *fig. philosophy ... a perpetual feast* : C. 479 ; in celebration of a marriage : S. A. 1194 ; M. W. 18.

(*c*) rejoicing, festivity : P. L. vi. 167 ; xi. 592, 715 ; L'A. 127 ; C. 102.

(2) *vb. tr.* to provide a feast for, regale : S. xx. 9.

See **Marriage-feast, Well-feasted.**

Feastful, *adj.* (*a*) festival : S. A. 1741.

(*b*) festive, joyful : S. ix. 12.

Feat, *sb.* (*a*) deed of valour, exploit : P. L. ii. 537 ; S. A. 1278.

(*b*) action displaying great dexterity or strength : S. A. 1083, 1304, 1602 ; L'A. 101.

Feather, *sb. pl.* plumage ; *fig. wisdom ... plumes her feathers* : C. 378.

Feathered, *part. adj.* provided with feathers : P. L. vii. 420 ; covered with feathers : P. L. v. 284 ; composed of feathers : P. L. ix. 1117.

See **Dewy-feathered.**

Feathery, *adj.* clothed with feathers : C. 347.

Feature, *sb.* (*a*) *concr.* a form or shape : P. L. x. 279.

(*b*) *pl.* the face : C. 748.

Fee, *sb.* (*a*) bribe : S. x. 3.

(*b*) an estate of inheritance in land ; *fig. held in fee*, held as one's absolute and rightful possession : S. xii. 7.

Feeble, *adj.* (*a*) having little strength, weak ; *feeble hands* : P. 45 ; *virtue* : C. 1022.

(*b*) wanting in force or vigour ; *of the mind* : S. A. 455.

Feed, I. *sb.* **at feed,** in the act of eating : P. L. ix. 597.

II. *vb.* (*pret.* and *past part.* fed)

(1) *tr.* (*a*) to supply with food : P. L. ii. 843 ; iii. 435 ; v. 415 ; vii. 490 : ix. 779 ; P. R. ii. 313, 421 ; L. 24, 125 ; God being the supplier : P. R. ii. 313 ; Ps. cxxxvi. 85 ; with *with* : P. R. i. 350 ; Ps. lxxx. 21 ; lxxxi. 65 ; *fig. of Christ*, as sustained in the wilderness by holy thoughts : P. R. ii. 110, 258.

(*b*) to supply with nourishment, support, sustain ; *of the elements, air, earth*, etc. : P. L. v. 416, 417 ; *brooks ... fed flowers* : P. L. iv. 240.

(*c*) to supply *fire with fuel* : P. L. i. 68, 728.

(2) *intr.* to take food : P. L. v. 467 ; P. R. iv. 593 ; with *on* : P. L. ii. 863 ; x. 604 ; C. 721 ; *fig., of the sun* : P. L. viii. 256 ; *of the mind* : P. L. iii. 37 ; S. A. 1562.

See **Self-fed.**

Feeder, *sb.* one who supplies food ; *of God* : C. 779.

Feel, *vb.* (*pres. 2d sing.* feel'st : P. L. x. 951 ; P. R. iv. 621 ; *pret.* and *past part.* felt) *tr.* (*a*) to perceive by the sense of touch : P. L. ii. 543 ; S. A. 1636.

(*b*) to perceive or have the sensation of *heat, hunger, pain,* etc. : P. L. i. 336 ; ii. 216, 598, 780 ; ix. 846 ; P. R. i. 308 ; with two *acc.* : P. L. x. 511, 541 ; with *clause* : P. L. ii. 77 ; P. R. ii. 252 ; *fig.* : P. L. iii. 22 ; P. R. iv. 621 ; P. 38 ; *of the earth* : P. L. ix. 782 ; *of the air* : P. L. i. 227.

(*c*) to perceive mentally, be conscious of : P. L. vi. 157 ; ix. 680, 984 ; P. R. i. 198 ; S. A. 663, 1381 ; C. 145 ; with two *acc.* : P. L. i. 153 ; ii. 101 ; ix. 1009 ; with *acc.* and *simple inf.* : P. L. ix. 913, 955 ; x. 243 ; S. A. 594 ; with *clause* : P. L. viii. 282 ; x. 361, 362 ; P. R. i. 400 ; iv. 847 ; C. 800 ; to experience : P. L. viii. 530, 608 ; ix. 120, 315, 859 ; x. 717, 1098 ; xi. 465 ; S. A. 1006 ; with two *acc.* : P. L. xi. 775.

(*d*) to have experience of, suffer, undergo : P. L. ii. 340 ; iv. 972 ; v. 892 ; vi. 872 ; ix. 51 ; x. 733 ; P. R. i. 89 ; S. A. 9, 1257.

(*e*) to know by means of experience : S. A. 1155.

vbl. sb. **Feeling**; (*a*) sense of touch : S. A. 96.

(*b*) that which one must undergo, suffering : P. R. III. 208.

See **Home-felt.**

Feign, *vb.* (*pret. 2d sing.* feign'dst : S. A. 1135) *tr.* (*a*) to relate or represent in fiction, fable : P. L. II. 627 ; IV. 706 ; V. 381 ; IX. 31, 439 ; P. R. II. 358 ; with *acc.* and *prep. inf.* : S. A. 150.

(*b*) to maintain fictitiously, allege ; with *clause* : S. A. 1135.

(*c*) to make a false show of, dissemble, counterfeit, pretend : P. L. IX. 492 ; XI. 799 ; S. A. 829 ; *absol.* to practice simulation : P. L. III. 639 ; P. R. I. 474.

(*d*) to make oneself appear, pretend ; with *prep. inf.* : P. L. XII. 517 ; P. R. IV. 397.

part. adj. **feigned,** counterfeited, pretended : P. L. IV. 96 ; S. A. 752, 872, 1116.

Felicity, *sb.* bliss, happiness : P. R. IV. 297 ; or the place of bliss, heaven : M. W. 68.

Fell, *adj.* fierce, ruthless, cruel : P. L. II. 539 ; X. 906 ; C. 259 ; Ps. II. 10 ; LXXXIII. 7 ; CXXXVI. 41.

Fell, *vb. tr.* (*a*) to strike down : P. L. VI. 250 ; to kill, slay : S. A. 263.

(*b*) to cut down *trees* : P. L. VI. 575 ; P. R. III. 332.

Fellow, *sb.* (*a*) associate, comrade : P. L. VI. 160 ; C. 485.

(*b*) sharer or partaker *of* : P. L. I. 606.

(*c*) equal, peer : P. L. II. 428.

Fellow-servant, *sb.* one who serves the same master as another : P. L. VIII. 225.

Fellowship, *sb.* (*a*) sharing or participation *in pain* : P. R. I. 401.

(*b*) companionship, society : P. L. VIII. 389, 442.

(*c*) company, band : P. L. XI. 80.

Felon, *adj.* cruel and wicked : L. 91.

See **Arch-felon.**

Felonious, *adj.* wicked, thievish : C. 196.

Female, (1) *adj.* (*a*) belonging to the sex which bears offspring ; *of women* : P. L. VII. 530 ; IX. 822 ; P. R. I. 151 ; S. A. 711 ; *absol.* : S. A. 711 ; *female bee* : P. L. VII. 490 ; *fig. female light* : P. L. VIII. 150.

(*b*) characteristic of womankind : P. L. IX. 999 ; P. R. II. 219 ; S. A. 777.

(*c*) devised or effected by women : P. L. X. 897 ; S. A. 1060.

(*d*) composed of women : P. L. XI. 614.

(2) *sb.* wife : S. A. 1055.

Feminine, (1) *adj.* (*a*) belonging to the female sex : P. L. I. 423.

(*b*) characteristic of the female sex : S. A. 403.

(*c*) like that of a woman, delicate and lovely : P. L. IX. 458.

(2) *sb.* the female sex, women : P. L. X. 893.

Fen, *sb.* marsh : P. L. II. 621 ; VII. 417 ; C. 433.

Fence, (1) *sb.* (*a*) art of fencing, *fig.* : C. 791.

(*b*) barrier, enclosure : P. L. IV. 187 ; Ps. LXXX. 50.

(2) *vb. tr.* (*a*) to cover or screen *the body* : P. L. IX. 1119.

(*b*) to surround as with a fence, fortify, protect : P. L. IV. 372 ; *fig.* : S. A. 937 ; to enclose *up* : P. L. IV. 697.

Fenceless, *adj.* defenceless : P. L. X. 303.

Fennel, *sb.* the plant *Fœniculum vulgare* : P. L. IX. 581.

Ferment, *vb.* (1) *intr.* to suffer fermentation ; *fig. of grief* : S. A. 619.

(2) *tr.* to cause fermentation in ; *fig. of the action of water on the earth* : P. L. VII. 281.

Ferry, *vb. intr.* to pass over water in a boat : P. L. II. 604.

Fertile, *adj.* (*a*) fruitful : P. L. I. 468 ; IV. 216, 645 ; VII. 454 ; P. R. III. 259.

(*b*) abundant, ample : P. L. V. 319 ; IX. 801.

Fertility, *sb.* fruitfulness : C. 729.

Fervent, *adj.* intensely earnest, ardent : P. L. V. 849.

Fervently, *adv.* earnestly, ardently : P. L. IX. 342 ; P. R. III. 121.

Fervid, *adj.* burning, glowing : P. L. V. 301 ; VII. 224.

Fesole, *sb.* a hill three miles northeast of Florence, Italy : P. L. I. 289.

Fester, *vb. intr.* to ulcerate, suppurate ; *fig. of grief* : S. A. 621.

part. adj. **festered,** ulcerated : S. A. 186.

Festival, *sb.* festive celebration : P. L. XI. 723 ; N. O. 147 ; in heaven : P. L. VI. 94 ; among shepherds :

C. 848 ; celebration in honour of
a god : S. A. 1598 ; *solemn festivals* : S. A. 983.
See **Far-fet.**

Fetch, *vb. tr.* (*a*) to go after and
bring *a person* : S. A. 921, 1731 ;
a thing : P. R. IV. 589 ; N. O.
135.

    (*b*) to make to go by constrain-
ing force : U. C. II. 18.

    (*c*) to derive or draw from a
source : C. 708.

    (*d*) to go or make *my round* :
A. 54.

    (*e*) to reach, come to : P. L.
VIII. 137.

Fetter, (1) *sb. pl.* chain, shackle :
S. A. 35 ; *fig.* : C. 819.

    (2) *vb. tr.* to chain, shackle :
S. A. 1160, 1235.

    part. adj. **fettered,** bound to
return to the grave at a certain
time : N. O. 234.

Feverish, *adj.* excited, restless :
C. 8.

Feverous, *adj.* characterized by fever :
P. L. XI. 482.

Few, *adj.* not many, small in num-
ber : P. L. VII. 31 ; XII. 13 ; P. R.
III. 59, 234 ; C. 391 ; with *of* : S.
A. 1400.

    absol. few persons : P. L. III.
496 ; VI. 148 ; XI. 777 ; XII. 480 ;
P. R. III. 20, 59 ; C. 771 ; S. IX.
3 ; XVII. 11.

    ellipt. **in few,** in few words :
P. L. X. 157.

Fez, *sb.* one of the Barbary states
of northern Africa, lying north of
Morocco (Mercator, *Atlas*, 1636,
p. 429) : P. L. XI. 403.

Fickle, *adj.* changeable, inconstant,
uncertain : P. L. II. 233 ; IX. 948 ;
S. A. 164 ; Il P. 10.

Fie, *interj.* exclamation of impatience or disapprobation : V.
Ex. 53.

Field, *sb.* (*a*) open land as opposed
to woodland, usually devoted to
pasture or tillage : P. L. II. 493 ;
IV. 186, 245, 265 ; v. 20, 136,
292 ; VII. 335, 358, 460, 495, 522 ;
VIII. 301 ; IX. 86, 417, 520, 560,
575 ; X. 176, 204 ; XI. 171, 429 ;
P. R. I. 318 ; III. 268 ; S. A. 1432 ;
S. XX. 2 ; Ps. VIII. 20 ; combined
with figurative use of sense (*d*) :
P. L. VII. 322 ; used of the Hesperian Gardens : P. L. III. 569 ;
with proper name : P. R. I. 243 ;
IV. 505 ; open land in hell : P. L.

X. 533 ; in the moon : P. L. VIII.
145.

    (*b*) *fig.* grain raised on the land :
P. L. IV. 980.

    (*c*) country, place, region : P.
L. XI. 215 ; with proper name :
P. L. I. 520 ; III. 513 ; IV. 268 ;
D. F. I. 40 ; C. 60 ; S. XVIII. 11 ;
Ps. CXIV. 3 ; *Aleian* plain : P. L.
VII. 19 ; region in the moon : P.
L. III. 460 ; in the sun : P. L. III.
606.

    (*d*) ground where war is waged,
battle-ground : P. L. I. 677 ; VI.
410 ; X. 275 ; XI. 654 ; P. R. III.
73, 326 ; S. A. 1094 ; with proper
name : S. XVI. 8 ; *fig.* where Christ
contended with Satan : P. R. I. 9.

    (*e*) open space between armies :
P. L. VI. 309.

    (*f*) battle, contest : P. L. I.
105 ; II. 292, 768.

    (*g*) open ground used for tour-
naments : P. L. I. 763 ; S. A.
1087 ; for the Pythian games :
P. L. II. 530.

    (*h*) extended surface on the out-
side of the universe : P. L. III.
430 ; expanse of the sky : C. 979.
See **A-field.**

Fiend, *sb.* (*a*) evil spirit ; *spec.* Robin
Goodfellow : L'A. 110.

    (*b*) one of the fallen angels,
devil : P. L. IV. 953 ; the Devil,
Satan ; with *def. art.* : P. L.
I. 283 ; II. 643, 677, 815, 917,
947 ; III. 430, 440, 498, 524, 588 ;
IV. 166, 285, 393, 819, 857, 924,
1005, 1013 ; IX. 412 ; X. 20, 233 ;
XI. 101 ; P. R. I. 465 ; II. 323 ;
III. 345, 441 ; IV. 195, 430, 499,
576.
See **Arch-Fiend.**

Fierce, *adj.* (1) vehement and merciless in hostility ; *of persons* : P. L.
II. 78 ; VI. 794 ; XI. 641 ; S. A.
985 ; C. 426 ; S. XVII. 4 ; *comp.* :
P. L. II. 45 ; *sup.* : P. L. II. 44 ;
of death : P. L. II. 671 ; *of personifications* : P. L. II. 898 ; *of
animals* : P. R. I. 313 ; *sup.* :
S. A. 127.

    ellipt. with *sb.* (foe or onset)
understood : P. L. IV. 927.

    or *adv.* (?) violently, furiously :
P. L. I. 667 ; VI. 220, 610.

    (2) violent in action ; (*a*) *of
natural forces* : P. L. I. 305 ; II.
219, 580, 599 ; VI. 765 ; VII. 272 ;
X. 703 ; P. R. I. 90 ; IV. 412 ;
fig. : P. L. X. 739.

(*b*) violent, impetuous, passionate; *of emotions*: P. L. IV. 509; VI. 201; IX. 462, 471; X. 709, 865; Ps. II. 11; LXXXV. 11; LXXXVIII. 65; *of the Greek nation*: P. R. IV. 269.

(*c*) grievous, hard to overcome; *fierce temptation*: P. 24.

(*d*) merciless or unrelenting *vengeance*: P. L. III. 399.

(*e*) painful, torturing; *of disease or suffering*: P. L. I. 336; X. 556; XI. 483; S. A. 612; *of remembrance*: S. A. 952.

(*f*) violent, furious; *of conflict*: P. L. I. 100; VI. 93; *comp.*: P. R. IV. 567; *sup. fig.*: P. L. VI. 314.

(*g*) carried or driven furiously: P. L. VI. 356, 829.

(3) indicating violence or fury: P. L. IV. 128, 871; C. 654.

(4) fiery, blazing: P. L. XII. 634.

Fiercely, *adv.* violently, vehemently: P. L. X. 478; XII. 593.

Fierceness, *sb.* fury, rage: P. L. IX. 462.

Fiery, *adj.* (*a*) consisting of or flaming with fire, or shining like fire; said of things in heaven or hell, or sent from heaven: P. L. I. 52, 68, 173, 184, 377; II. 180, 635; VI. 55, 80, 215, 479; XII. 208, 257; P. R. II. 16; S. A. 27; *of horses*: P. L. III. 522; VI. 17, 391; *of swords*: P. L. VI. 304; XII. 644; or fire-bearing, *of darts*: P. L. VI. 213; XII. 492; P. R. IV. 424; or of the nature of fire, *of angels*: P. L. II. 512; P. R. IV. 581; Cir. 7.

(*b*) emitting fire; *of a mountain*: P. L. II. 620; striking fire; *of flint*: Ps. CXIV. 18.

(*c*) of the colour of fire: P. L. IV. 978.

(*d*) **heaven's fiery rod**, the ray of the sun: S. A. 549.

(*e*) glowing or flashing *eyes*: P. L. IV. 402.

(*f*) ardent or vehement *virtue*: S. A. 1690.

(*g*) poisonous: P. R. I. 312.

(*h*) spirited *steeds*: P. L. II. 531.

Fiery-wheeled (wheelèd, *disyl.*), *adj.* having wheels surrounded by fire: Il P. 53.

Fifth, *adj.* the ordinal of five: P. L. VII. 448.

Fight, I. *sb.* (*a*) combat, battle: P. L. II. 20; IV. 1003; VI. 48, 87, 232, 243, 308, 403, 423, 448, 531, 537, 687, 693, 786; X. 278; P. R. III. 328; S. A. 344, 1111; Ps. LXXXVIII. 19; combat between two persons: P. L. VI. 296; XII. 385; S. A. 1175, 1222, 1253.

(*b*) *fig.* spiritual conflict of Christ and Satan: P. L. XII. 386; struggle in maintaining the cause of truth: P. L. VI. 30.

(*c*) manner of fighting: P. R. III. 307.

II. *vb.* (*pret.* fought; *past part.* fought: P. L. II. 768: VI. 29; XII. 261; foughten: P. L. VI. 410), (1) *intr.* (*a*) to contend, struggle for mastery: P. L. II. 914.

(*b*) to engage in battle, combat: P. L. I. 578; II. 45; IV. 945; VI. 220, 355, 454, 666; to engage in single combat: S. A. 1226; *fig.* to withstand the commands; *against law to fight*: P. L. XII. 289.

(2) *tr.* to carry on, wage; with *cognate acc.*: P. L. II. 768; XII. 261; *fig.* to carry on in maintaining the cause of truth: P. L. VI. 29.

part. adj. (*a*) **fighting**, warring: P. L. VI. 249; struggling for mastery; *of beasts*: P. R. IV. 140; *of the elements in chaos*: P. L. II. 1015.

(*b*) **foughten**, that has been the scene of a battle: P. L. VI. 410.

Fig-tree, *sb.* the tree *Ficus*: P. L. IX. 1101.

Figure, *sb.* (*a*) definite order or form: P. L. VII. 426.

(*b*) representation of a form in a decorative pattern: L. 105.

(*c*) **in figure**, typically: P. L. XII. 241.

File, *sb.* (*a*) line of soldiers: P. L. I. 567; IV. 797; V. 651; VI. 339, 599.

(*b*) line of persons one beside another, rank: S. XI. 6.

Filial, *adj.* (*a*) of or pertaining to a child in relation to a parent; *of Christ*, in relation to God: P. L. III. 269; P. R. I. 177; *of man*, in relation to God: P. L. IV. 294; XII. 306; S. A. 511.

(*b*) bearing the relation of a child; *of Christ*: P. L. VI. 722; VII. 175, 587.

Fill, (1) *sb.* (*a*) full supply, enough to satisfy desire; with the vbs. *drink, eat* : P. L. IX. 595, 1005 ; with *of* : S. XIV. 14 ; *of bliss, knowledge*, etc., with the vbs. *have, enjoy* : C. 548 ; in apposition to the *obj.* of the *vb.* : P. L. V. 504 ; with *of* : P. L. IV. 507 ; XII. 558.

(*b*) to *his* heart's content; *blow his fill* : II P. 128.

(2) *vb. tr.* (*a*) to make full : P. L. I. 707 : II. 129 ; X. 570 ; P. R. II. 931 ; L. 150 ; with immaterial things, as *hope, lust, scorn*, etc. : P. L. I. 495 ; III. 447 ; IV. 827 ; VII. 51, 257 ; IX. 196 ; XII. 177, 178 ; S. A. 1613 ; C. 550 ; S. I. 3 ; XV. 2 ; Ps. LXXXIII. 60 ; CXXXVI. 26 ; to pour into until no more can be received ; *fig. of light*, etc.: P. L. III. 731 ; S. IX. 10.

(*b*) to make pregnant : L'A. 23.

(*c*) to cause *sails* to fill with wind : S. A. 718.

(*d*) to make *valleys* level with the surrounding land : P. R. III. 332.

(*e*) to store abundantly : P. L. IV. 733 ; V. 389 ; VII. 397, 531 ; X. 892.

(*f*) to occupy completely, pervade : P. L. I. 350 ; VII. 88, 168 ; VIII. 104 ; Ps. LXXX. 40 ; *of fragrance, joy, sound*, etc.: P. L. II. 284 ; III. 135, 348 ; V. 286 ; VI. 200 ; X. 506 ; XI. 77, 336, 888.

(*g*) to satisfy or satiate with food *sin, death* : P. L. II. 843 ; *animals* : P. L. IV. 351 ; *the appetite* : P. L. II. 847 ; *absol.* : P. L. VIII. 214 ; *the mind* : II P. 4.

(*h*) **fill up**, close or stop up *a wound* : P. L. VIII. 468.

Film, *sb.* morbid growth upon the eye : P. L. XI. 412.

Filth, *sb.* pollution : P. L. X. 630.

Fin, *sb.* the organ of a fish : P. L. VII. 401 ; P. R. II. 345.

Final, *adj.* last, ultimate, conclusive : P. L. II. 142, 563 ; III. 458 ; VI. 798 ; IX. 88 ; X. 1085 ; XI. 62, 493 ; P. R. I. 461 ; III. 221 ; S. A. 1171.

Finally, *adv.* at last, in the end : P. L. III. 150 ; S. A. 1296.

Find, *vb.* (*pres. 2d sing.* find'st : P. L. V. 231 ; VIII. 586 ; P. R. I. 495 ; IV. 486 ; *pret.* found ; *2d*

sing. found'st : P. L. IX. 407 ; S. A. 427 ; *past part.* found) *tr.*

(*a*) to come or light upon, meet with *a person*: P. R. II. 9, 10, 59 ; V. Ex. 83 ; II P. 93 ; *a place* : P. L. III. 498 ; XII. 40 ; *a kingdom* : P. R. III. 242 ; *resting, courtesy, darkness*, etc. : P. L. I. 237 ; IX. 1176 : XII. 537 ; C. 204, 323 ; said of sleep as an agent : P. L. VIII. 288 ; to meet with in writings : P. 25.

(*b*) to come to have : P. L. II. 1011 ; to meet with, get, obtain or receive *acceptance, favour, pardon, retribution*, etc. : P. L. I. 513 ; III. 131, 145, 227, 453 ; V. 531, 848 ; VII. 31 ; VIII. 366, 435 ; IX. 333 ; X. 968 ; XI. 456, 800, 890 ; XII. 295 ; P. R. I. 495 ; II. 388 ; IV. 333 ; S. A. 1376 ; L. 73 ; *occasion, temptation* : S. A. 423, 425, 427.

(*c*) to gain or win *a lover* : M. W. 16.

(*d*) to come to the knowledge of by experience, observation, or trial ; discover ; perceive : P. L. III. 615 ; V. 494 ; VIII. 355, 416, 624 ; IX. 232 ; P. R. III. 203 ; IV. 477 ; S. A. 387, 789 ; S. IX. 8 ; with *acc.* and *prep. inf.* : P. L. VI. 453 ; IX. 874 ; P. R. II. 131 ; Ps. V. 37 ; with *clause* : P. L. I. 648 ; IX. 107 ; P. R. II. 283 ; *clause* abbreviated : P. L. IV. 849 ; V. 93.

to discover or perceive *a person* or *thing* to be ; with two *acc.* : P. L. I. 525 ; III. 591 ; IV. 450 : V. 429 ; VI. 19, 341, 433 ; VIII. 240, 309, 438, 586 ; IX. 85, 257, 370, 381, 421, 1053, 1071, 1116 ; X. 52, 420 ; XI. 137 ; XII. 273, 522, 608 ; P. R. I. 207, 459 ; II. 273 ; III. 398 ; IV. 532 ; S. A. 40 ; A. 12 ; C. 644 ; in *passive* : P. L. I. 333 ; III. 308, 310 ; V. 406, 501, 513, 742, 896 ; VI. 420 ; IX. 301, 932 ; X. 888, 969, 970 ; XI. 350, 876 ; P. R. I. 104 ; II. 154 ; III. 365 ; IV. 346 ; S. A. 20, 1746 ; C. 454 ; *1st sing.* with compound subject in *1st* and *3d sing.* : P. L. X. 816 ; with complement a phrase : P. L. I. 524 ; V. 9 ; U. C. I. 11 ; S. IX. 8.

(*e*) to discover or obtain by search or effort *an animal* or *a person* : P. L. II. 403, 424 ; III. 443, 671 ; IV. 448, 575, 796, 799, 875, 900 ; V. 48, 49, 231 ; VIII. 594 ; IX. 160, 181, 182, 414 ;

X. 1001; P. R. I. 121, 256, 471;
II. 59, 97, 131, 208; IV. 217, 373,
447; S. A. 193, 1046, 1047, 1443,
1725; C. 304, 579; *a place*: P.
L. IV. 938; XI. 223; P. R. I.
252; P. 43; C. 500, 570; Ps.
LXXXIV. 10, 14; *a way*: P. L.
II. 83; III. 228; IV. 174; 889;
VII. 298, 302; IX. 69; X. 884, 894;
S. A. 610; *a thing*: P. L. III. 24;
VI. 513; IX. 219; X. 480; XI.
566; P. R. II. 232; *enterprise,
solution, wisdom,* etc.: P. L. I.
165; II. 344; III. 213, 228, 411;
VI. 694; P. R. IV. 319; *to recover
a person lost*: P. L. VIII. 479.

(*f*) to gain, obtain, or secure
ease, joy, rest, repose, etc.: P.
L. I. 320; II. 617, 525, 802; IV.
92; V. 28; VIII. 375, 433, 523;
IX. 119, 129, 288, 407, 597; XI.
673; P. R. II. 309: S. A. 17,
619; Ps. LXXXIII. 50.

(*g*) to procure, supply; with *acc.*
and *dat.*: P. L. VI. 635; Soph. 2.

(*h*) to summon up *courage*: S.
A. 1716.

(*i*) to arrive at or reach; *found
no end*: P. L. II. 561; *nor end
wilt find of erring*: P. L. VI. 172.

(*j*) to begin to exercise or to
make effective: P. L. VIII. 97.

(*k*) to ascertain or discover by
mental effort: P. L. V. 114; S.
A. 306; Ps. VIII. 14; with *clause*:
P. R. I. 262.

(*l*) to contrive, devise, invent:
P. L. VI. 500; S. A. 1396.

(*m*) to determine and declare *a
person guilty*: Ps. V. 29.

(*n*) **find** out, discover *a person*:
P. L. X. 899; P. R. I. 101; C.
606; *a place*: L'A. 5; Il P. 168;
C. 307; *a way*: P. L. I. 621; II.
406; *tricks*: F. of C. 14; *peace*:
P. L. III. 275; to reach by
searching out: P. R. I. 334; to
unriddle: P. R. IV. 574; to detect and punish: P. R. IV. 130.
past part. absol.: P. L. V. 18.

Fine, (1) *sb.* **in fine**, to sum up,
finally: S. A. 702.

(2) *adj.* excellent in quality,
sup.: Ps. LXXXI. 66.

Finger, *sb.* digit of the hand: C.
914; L. 4; *sing.* for *pl.*: N. O.
95; *fig. morning fair with radiant
finger*: P. R. IV. 428.

Finish, *vb.* (1) *tr.* (*a*) to bring to an
end, arrive at the end of: P. L. IV.
661, 727; V. 559; S. A. 1710.

(*b*) to bring to completion: P.
L. VI. 522.

(*c*) to defeat: P. L. VI. 141.

(2) *intr.* to cease: P. L. VII.
548; to cease speaking: P. L. II.
284, 815.

Finisher, *sb.* one who completes;
finisher of hope: P. L. XII. 375.

Finite, *absol.* or *sb.* that which is ter-
minable: P. L. X. 802.

Finny, *adj.* having fins: C. 115.

Fir, *sb.* (*a*) the tree *Abies*: P. L. IV.
139; X. 1076.

(*b*) wood of this tree: P. L. VI.
574.

Fire, I. *sb.* (1) active principle
operative in combustion: P. L.
I. 395; II. 595, 937, 1013; III.
594; V. 439; IX. 392; X. 1073,
1078; Ps. VII. 21; LXXX. 65;
LXXXV. 12.

(*b*) one of the four elements
which form the universe: P. L. II.
912; III. 715; as the abode of
devils or demons: P. R. II. 124;
IV. 201; Il P. 94.

(*c*) the pure element of fire in
heaven or sent from heaven, either
lit., or *fig.* as a symbol of brilliance;
used variously in warfare: P. L.
V. 893; VI. 50, 214, 245, 485, 546,
580, 756, 849; or the essence of angels, *cherubic waving fires*, flaming cherubs: P. L. VI. 413; *camp
of fire*, horses and chariots of fire:
P. L. XI. 217; *pillar of fire*, that
which led the children of Israel:
P. L. XII. 202, 203; *shield of
fire*, strong defence: S. A. 1435;
a symbol of inspiration: N. O.
28; *fire from heaven*, fire sent
from God in token of favour: P.
L. XI. 441.

(*d*) as found in hell: P. L. I.
671, 701; a means of punishment: P. L. I. 48, 77, 151, 229,
280, 298, 346; II. 88, 170, 176,
213, 275, 401, 434, 581, 600, 603,
647; VI. 876; P. R. III. 220; a
means of warfare: P. L. II. 67,
69, 141.

(*e*) as found in Olympus; *Jove's
fire*: P. L. IV. 719.

(*f*) the essence of Comus and
crew, referring to sense (*c*): C.
111.

(*g*) **sulphurous fire**, gunpowder:
P. L. XI. 658.

(2) state of combustion; *conceive fire*: P. L. I. 234; *take fire*:
Ps. LXXXIII. 53.

(3) mass of burning fuel on the hearth : L'A. 112 ; S. xx. 3.

(4) a conflagration : P. L. XI. 472, 566 ; the fire which shall finally consume heaven and earth : P. L. XI. 900.

(5) lightning : P. L. XII. 182 ; P. R. IV. 412 ; *heaven's fire* : P. L. I. 612 ; *red fire* : N. O. 159.

(6) planet, star : P. L. IV. 667 ; V. 177, 417 ; VII. 87 ; XII. 256 ; *sing.* for *pl.* : V. Ex. 40.

(7) ignis fatuus : P. L. IX. 634 ; as surrounding an evil spirit, or in sense (*b*) : C. 433.

(8) ardour, passion : P. L. IX. 1036.

(9) **set on fire**, inflame with zeal : D. F. I. 62.

II. *vb.* (1) *tr.* (*a*) to set on fire, ignite : P. L. IV. 557.

(*b*) to inflame *with zeal* : S. A. 1419.

(2) *intr.* (*a*) to glow or shine as if on fire : P. L. II. 709.

(*b*) to discharge artillery : P. L. VI. 520.

See **Hell-fire.**

Firm, (1) *adj.* (*a*) of solid or compact structure or texture : P. L. I. 350; III. 418 ; *dry land* or *ground* : P. L. II. 589 ; III. 75 ; VI. 242 ; *of the sun* : P. L. VII. 362 ; *firm leaf* : P. L. IV. 695 ; *fig.* certain, sure : P. R. IV. 292.

(*b*) strongly fixed, immovable, stable ; *of things* : P. L. VII. 267, 586 ; X. 295 ; established, secure ; *of persons* : P. L. XI. 71.

(*c*) steady *hand* : S. XVII. 13 ; steady in motion and with compact rank and file : P. L. VI. 69, 399, 534.

(*d*) sound, vigorous : Ps. LXXX. 64.

(*e*) immutable *decree* : Ps. II. 13.

(*f*) resolute, steadfast, unshaken; *of persons* : P. L. VI. 911; IX. 359 ; P. R. IV. 534 ; *of concord, faith, love,* etc. : P. L. I. 554; II. 36, 497 ; V. 210, 502 ; IX. 286, 1160 ; P. R. I. 4 ; S. XV. 5 ; Ps. LXXXIII. 20 ; *no word is firm* : Ps. V. 26 ; determined *thoughts, comp.* : P. L. XI. 498.

(2) *adv.* (*a*) steadily : P. L. VII. 443 ; immoveably : P. L. IV. 873.

(*b*) closely, inseparably, *sup.* : S. A. 796.

(*c*) steadfastly, resolutely, unalterably : P. L. XII. 127 ; C. 588.

Firmament, *sb.* (*a*) the vaulted expanse of heaven, the sky : P. L. III. 75 ; *open firmament of heaven* : P. L. VII. 390 ; in which the stars appear : P. L. IV. 604 ; VIII. 18 ; Ps. VIII. 11 ; *firmament of heaven* : P. L. VII. 344, 349 ; where the clouds move : P. L. XI. 206 ; conceived as solid and supported by pillars : C. 598.

(*b*) over-arching vault of hell : P. L. II. 175.

(*c*) the likeness of a firmament forming a part of the chariot of God : P. L. VI. 757.

(*d*) the expanse of "elemental air" or transparent ether filling all space between the earth and the crystalline sphere : P. L. VII. 261, 264, 274 ; or in sense (*a*) : P. L. III. 574.

Firmly, *adv.* strongly, securely : P. L. VI. 430 ; *comp.* : S. A. 1398.

Firmness, *sb.* (*a*) compactness, solidity : P. L. V. 324.

(*b*) faithfulness, fidelity : P. L. IX. 279.

*First, (1) *adj.* (*a*) that is before all others, earliest in time or order : P. L. I. 1, 656 ; III. 65 ; IV. 6, 12, 192, 495, 624 ; VI. 153 ; VII. 252, 260 ; VIII. 297, 298 ; IX. 261, 412, 718 ; XI. 277, 467 ; P. R. I. 154 ; III. 277 ; S. M. 24 ; L'A. 114; original : P. L. V. 472 ; C. 469.

(*b*) foremost in position or importance : P. L. V. 659, 660.

(*c*) outermost : P. L. III. 419 ; uppermost : P. L. III. 562.

absol. (*a*) the one who is before all others : P. L. IV. 121 ; P. R. IV. 504 ; *of God* : P. L. VI. 724.

(*b*) the person first mentioned : S. A. 219.

(*c*) the beginning of creation : P. L. I. 19.

(*d*) **at first**, in or at the beginning : P. L. II. 201, 760 ; VI. 92, 164, 661 ; IX. 171, 571 ; XI. 57 ; P. R. I. 114, 399 ; S. A. 883, 1035.

(2) *adv.* (*a*) before all others in time, order, place, or position : P. L. I. 8, 376, 392, 514 ; II. 680, 690, 1002 ; III. 64, 372 ; IV. 643, 935, 999 ; V. 418 ; VI. 151, 261, 774 ; VII. 354, 484 ; X. 326 ; XI. 572 ; XII. 320, 350 ; P. R. I. 319 ; II. 328 ; N. O. 26 ; C. 46 ; at first, originally : P. L. III. 356 ; VII. 63, 86, 255, 355, 501, 636 ; C. 325 ; as the first thing to be men-

tioned or considered : P. L. II. 129, 402 ; VIII. 90.

that first moved, the Primum Mobile : P. L. III. 483. *See* **Sphere.**

(*b*) before some other specified thing or event : P. L. II. 740 ; III. 131, 634 ; IV. 528 ; V. 137 ; IX. 97 ; X. 402 ; XII. 173 ; C. 82.

(*c*) for the first time : P. L. III. 549 ; IV. 710 ; VI. 154, 327, 394 ; VIII. 284, 530 ; IX. 25, 1030 ; XII. 273.

(*d*) **first and last,** altogether, from beginning to end, at all times : P. L. II. 324 ; III. 134 ; X. 831 ; **first or last,** at one time or another : P. L. IX. 170 ; S. A. 1594.

First-begot, *adj. absol.* first begotten one : P. R. I. 89.

First-born, *adj.* first brought forth, eldest ; *fig. of light* : P. L. III. 1 ; *the first-born bloom of spring* : S. A. 1576.

absol. : P. L. I. 489, 510 ; XII. 189 ; Ps. CXXXVI. 38 ; *fig. of treason* : S. A. 391.

First-created, *adj.* first brought into being : S. A. 83.

First-fruit, *sb. pl.* fruits first gathered in a season : P. L. XI. 435 ; *fig.* : P. L. XI. 22.

Firstling, *sb. pl.* first offspring of animals : P. L. XI. 437.

First-moving, *adj.* receiving motion before and imparting motion to all others : D. F. I. 39.

Fish, *sb.* always *sing.* (*a*) animal living in the water and breathing by means of gills, *collect.* : P. L. VII. 401 ; in combination or contrast with *bird, beast. fowl* : P. L. VIII. 395 ; X. 604, 711 ; *collect.* : P. L. VII. 447, 503, 521, 533 ; VIII. 341, 346 ; XII. 677 ; kinds of fish : P. R. II. 344.

(*b*) the form of a fish : P. L. I. 463.

Fisherman, *sb.* person whose occupation is the catching of fish : P. R. II. 27.

Fishy, *adj.* characteristic of fish : P. L. IV. 168.

Fist, *sb.* clenched hand : S. A. 1235.

Fit, *sb.* sudden and transient state of feeling or emotion : P. 42 ; *fit of melancholy* : C. 546 ; *of passion* : P. L. X. 626.

Fit, I. *adj.* (*a*) adapted, suited, qualified : P. L. IX. 89 ; with *prep. inf.* : P. L. II. 306 ; VI. 303, 636 ;

VIII. 390 ; C. 700 ; *sup.* : P. L. IX. 89.

(*b*) appropriate, suitable, proper : P. L. III. 454 ; IV. 953 ; V. 148, 348, 690 ; VI. 876 ; VII. 31 ; VIII. 450 ; IX. 489 ; X. 139, 899 ; XI. 271 ; XII. 597 ; D. F. I. 46 ; V. Ex. 32 ; with *for* : P. L. V. 69 ; A. 76 ; with *prep. inf.* : P. L. V. 315 ; *comp.* : P. L. XI. 98, 262 ; *sup.* : P. R. IV. 373.

(*c*) of the right pattern, suiting : P. L. XI. 571 ; with *for* : P. L. III. 643.

(*d*) prepared or ready *for* : P. L. IV. 816.

(*e*) deserving, worthy; with *prep. inf.* : C. 792.

absol. what is suitable : P. L. VIII. 448.

II. *vb.* (**1**) *intr.* to be suitable or proper : Il P. 78 ; *impersonal* : S. A. 929, 1318.

(**2**) *tr.* (*a*) to be adapted or suited to, be proper for : P. L. X. 242 ; P. R. IV. 219 ; S. A. 1236 ; H. B. 10.

(*b*) to render competent or qualified ; with *acc.* and *prep. inf.* : P. R. I. 73.

(*c*) to adjust : P. L. VI. 543. *See* **Ill-fitted.**

Fitly, *adv.* (*a*) appropriately : P. L. VIII. 394.

(*b*) rightly : P. 49.

Five, *adj.* consisting of five : P. L. V. 104, 177 ; S. A. 1248 ; *sb.* understood : P. L. X. 657.

Fix, *vb.* (*past part. disyl.* : P. L. I. 206, 560 ; III. 669 ; Il P. 4) *intr.* (*a*) to make firm in position, place immovably, fasten : P. L. X. 295 ; with *in* : P. L. V. 176 ; C. 819 ; with *on* : P. L. XI. 851 ; *till time stand fixed,* till time ceases to be the measure of motion : P. L. XII. 555 ; to insert *in* and secure against displacement : P. L. XII. 432 ; to bring to a standstill and fasten : N. O. 241.

(*b*) to settle immovably the purpose of ; with *prep. inf.* : S. A. 1481.

(*c*) to direct steadily or fasten *eyes* : S. A. 1637 ; *eyes* or *look on* or *towards* : P. L. IV. 28, 465 ; X. 553 ; Il P. 44 ; *fixed in cogitation deep* : P. L. III. 629.

(*d*) to make motionless with strong feeling : P. L. VIII. 3 ; IX. 735 ; S. A. 726 ; *fig. of the stars* : N. O. 70.

(e) to impress, stamp, *fig.*: C. 529.

(*f*) to locate in a certain place : P. L. I. 382.

(*g*) to establish *the throne of Godhead* : P. L. VII. 586 ; *Zion* : Ps. LXXXVIII. 20.

(*h*) to appoint or ordain by edict : P. L. X. 773 ; P. R. I. 127.

(*i*) to decide upon, choose : P. L. IX. 952.

part. adj. **fixed**; (*a*) made firm in position : P. L. I. 206 ; firmly or solidly built : P. L. I. 723.

(*b*) appearing always to occupy the same position in the heavens : P. L. V. 176.

(*c*) steadfast or immovable *mind, thought*, etc. : P. L. I. 97, 560 ; IX. 1160 ; II P. 4 ; S. IX. 9.

(*d*) appointed, allotted, or established *abode, station* : P. L. III. 669 ; XII. 627 ; *fate, law* : P. L. II. 18, 560.

part. absol., **fixed**, the fixed stars : P. L. V. 621 ; *the fixed* : P. L. III. 481 ; X. 661.

Flag, *sb.* banner, standard : P. L. II. 900 ; C. 604.

Flail, *sb.* instrument for threshing grain : L'A. 108.

Flame, (1) *sb.* (*a*) burning vapour, blaze : P. L. II. 889 ; IV. 784 ; S. A. 25, 262, 1433 ; C. 129 ; Ps. LXXXIII. 55 ; in heaven : P. L. II. 754 ; VI. 58, 483, 751, 766 ; in hell : P. L. I. 62, 182, 222 ; II. 172, 214 ; X. 232 ; *Ætna flames* : P. L. III. 470 ; *flame of a sword* : P. L. XI. 120.

(*b*) torch : M. W. 20.

(*c*) the flash of lightning : P. L. X. 1075.

(*d*) the bright beams of the sun : N. O. 81 ; L'A. 61.

(*e*) condition of visible combustion : P. L. V. 891 ; VI. 584 ; IX. 637.

(*f*) *fig.* heat of emotion, passion : S. A. 1351 ; *flame of vehemence* : C. 795 ; *of zeal* : P. L. V. 807 ; *virtue roused ... into flame* : S. A. 1691.

(*g*) ambition : P. R. III. 26.

(2) *vb. intr.* (*a*) to burn with flame, emit flames, blaze : P. L. I. 45, 62 ; X. 562 ; *fig.* : P. R. I. 216.

(*b*) to shine like flame ; *of the sun* : L. 171 ; *of the diamond* : P. L. IV. 554 ; *of a liquid* : C. 673.

part. adj. **flaming**, on fire, or shining with the brilliance of fire ; *flaming arms, sword*, etc. : P. L. I. 664 ; III. 394 ; VI. 17, 213; XII. 592, 643 ; *mount* : P. L. V. 598; XI. 216 ; *of angels, cherubim, seraphim*, etc. : P. L. V. 875 ; VI. 102 ; VII. 134 ; IX. 156 ; XI. 101 ; Cir. 1 ; *of the path of the sun* : P. L. VIII. 162.

See **Hell-flame.**

Flamen, *sb.* priest devoted to the service of a particular deity : N. O. 194.

Flank, *sb.* one of the sides of an army : P. L. VI. 570.

Flaring, *part. adj.* shining brightly and fitfully : II P. 132.

Flash, *vb. tr.* to emit or send forth suddenly : P. L. VI. 751.

Flashy, *adj.* destitute of meaning, trashy : L. 123.

Flat, (1) *adj.* (*a*) horizontally level : C. 375.

(*b*) stretched at full length ; *fell flat* : P. L. I. 461.

(*c*) prostrate ; *plumes fall flat* : P. R. II. 223 ; *fig. hopes all flat* : S. A. 595 ; level with the ground, overthrown : *lays cities flat* : P. R. IV. 363.

(*d*) absolute, downright : P. L. II. 143.

(*e*) stale, insipid : P. L. IX. 987.

(2) *sb.* plot of level ground : P L. IX. 627.

Flatly, *adv.* absolutely : P. L. V. 819.

Flatter, *vb. tr.* (*a*) *absol.* to try to win favour by obsequious speech : P. R. I. 474.

(*b*) to coax or wheedle *out of* : P. L. X. 42.

part. adj. (*a*) **flattering**, fawning : P. R. I. 375 ; coaxing, wheedling : S. A. 392 ; deceitful *gales* : Hor. O. 11.

(*b*) **flattered**, deceived : P. 31.

Flattery, *sb.* adulation : P. R. IV. 125.

Flaunting, *part. adj.* waving gaily like a plume ; *flaunting honeysuckle* : C. 545.

Flavour, *sb.* aroma : S. A. 544.

Flaw, *sb.* sudden and violent windstorm : P. L. X. 698 ; P. R. IV. 454.

Fledge, *adj.* (*a*) having the wings developed for flight : P. L. VII. 420.

(*b*) furnished for flight *with wings* : P. L. III. 627.

Flee, *vb.* (*pret.* fled, *2d pers.* fledd'st:
P. L. IV. 963; *past part.* fled;
perf. formed with the auxiliary
be: P. L. XI. 841; with *have*;
P. L. VI. 868.) (1) *intr.* (*a*) to run
away from danger, seek escape or
safety by flight: P. L. I. 520; II.
165, 787, 790, 994; IV. 1014; VI.
362, 395, 531, 538; IX. 53, 58;
X. 339; S. A. 264; D. F. I. 48;
N. O. 205; with *from*: P. L. III.
512; S. A. 139; with *into*: P. R.
II. 270; *said of hell*: P. L. VI.
868; *of the sea*: Ps. CXIV. 7, 13.

(*b*) to withdraw hastily, take
oneself off: S. XIII. 14; with *to*:
M. W. 68.

(*c*) to make one's escape *from*:
P. L. IV. 963.

(*d*) to move swiftly, fly: P. L.
XI. 563.

(*e*) to disappear, vanish; *of
clouds, darkness*: P. L. III. 712;
IV. 1015; XI. 841.

(**2**) *tr.* (*a*) to run or hasten away
from *a person*: P. L. II. 613; IX.
394; X. 713; XI. 330; C. 662;
to escape *pain* by flight: P. L.
IV. 919.

(*b*) to avoid with dread, shun:
P. R. I. 312.

Fleece, *sb.* coat of wool that covers
a sheep; *fig. of the hair of the
head*: S. A. 538.

Fleeced, *part. adj.* provided with a
fleece: P. L. VII. 472.

Fleecy, *adj.* (*a*) covered with fleece:
P. L. XI. 648; *fig. fleecy star*,
Aries: P. L. III. 558.

(*b*) derived from fleeces: C.
504.

(*c*) resembling a fleece; *of a
cloud*: Il P. 72; *of mist*: P. L.
V. 187.

Fleet, *sb.* a number of ships sailing
in company: P. L. II. 636.

Fleet, (**1**) *adj.* swift, rapid: P. R.
III. 313; C. 896.

(**2**) *vb. intr.* to flit: P. L. III.
457.

part. adj. **fleeting**, quickly passing, transient: P. L. X. 741.

Flesh, *sb.* (**1**) the soft substance of
an animal body which covers the
bones and is enclosed by the skin:
P. L. I. 428; VIII. 468; XII. 180;
denoting the whole body: P. L.
VIII. 629; Ps. LXXXIV. 7.

(*b*) *fig.* susceptibility to the
drawing of divine grace: P. L.
XI. 4.

(*c*) expressing the relationship
of Eve to Adam as his wife and as
formed out of a part of his body:
P. L. IV. 441, 483; VIII. 495; IX.
914, 959; expressing the unity of
man and wife: P. L. VIII. 499.

(**2**) tissue of animals as an
article of food: P. L. III. 434.

(**3**) a human being: P. L. III.
284; *all flesh*, the human race,
mankind: P. L. XI. 888.

(**4**) **in the flesh**, in a bodily
form: P. L. XII. 505.

(**5**) sensual appetites and in-
clinations opposed to the spiritual
nature: P. L. XII. 303; P. R. I.
162.

Fleshly, *adj.* (*a*) of the material
body, opposed to *spiritual*: P. R.
III. 387; IV. 599; P. 17; Il P. 92.

(*b*) lascivious, lustful, *sup.*: P.
R. II. 152.

Flight, *sb.* (*a*) action of passing
through the air on wings; *of birds*:
P. L. VII. 430; L'A. 41; *of a
person*: P. L. V. 89; *of Satan or
his angels*: P. L. I. 225; II. 80,
407, 632, 928; III. 563, 631, 741;
V. 266; P. R. II. 241; *fig. of fame*:
S. A. 974; *of sighs*: P. L. XI. 7.

(*b*) swift movement: P. L. VII.
294; C. 579; *of the earth*: P. L.
IV. 595.

(*c*) the mounting or soaring of
imagination: P. L. III. 15.

(*d*) swift passage *of future days*:
P. L. II. 221.

(*e*) distance which a bird can
fly: P. L. VII. 4; *fig. of imagination or thought*: P. L. I. 14; VIII.
199.

(*f*) company *of angels* passing
through the air: P. R. II. 385.

(*g*) action of fleeing from danger,
justice, or an enemy: P. L. I.
555; IV. 12, 913; V. 871; VI.
152, 187, 236, 285, 367, 397, 539,
798; X. 83; XI. 190, 202; P. R.
III. 306, 325; S. A. 1118; C. 158,
832; from pain; P. L. IV. 921,
922.

(*h*) hasty departure: D. F. I.
42; N. O. 72.

See **Drowsy-flighted**.

Fling, *vb.* (*pret.* and *past part.*
flung) (**1**) *tr.* (*a*) to throw, cast,
or hurl with violence: P. L. I.
610; VI. 654.

(*b*) to emit or send forth *light*:
Il P. 131; to diffuse *odours*: P.
L. VIII. 517; C. 990.

(2) *intr.* to go hastily, rush : L'A. 113.

Flint-stone, *sb.* the hard stone that gives off sparks when struck : Ps. CXIV. 18.

Float, *vb. intr.* (*a*) to be supported or carried along by water or other liquid : P. L. I. 196 ; X. 296 ; XI. 850 ; L. 12 ; *fig.* : S. A. 1072.

(*b*) to spread in undulating form : P. L. IX. 503.

(*c*) to move gently and freely through the air : C. 249 ; to move gently to and fro ; *of the air* : P. L. VII. 432.

part. adj. **floating,** resting on the water ; P. L. I. 310 ; supported and carried along by water : P. L. XI. 745 ; moving gently and freely through the air : P. R. IV. 585.

Flock, (1) *sb.* (*a*) number of birds travelling together : P. L. X. 273.

(*b*) number of domestic animals, usually as kept together under the care of a shepherd : P. L. III. 435 ; IV. 185, 252 ; VI. 857 ; VII. 472 ; XI. 437, 648 ; L'A. 72 ; A. 103 ; C. 175, 344, 499, 531, 540, 712 ; L. 24, 29 ; Ps. LXXX. 3 ; in combination with *herds* : P. L. III. 44 ; VII. 461 ; XII. 19, 132 ; P. R. III. 260 ; Ps. VIII. 19 ; *fig.* the stars as under the guardianship of the morning-star : P. L. V. 709.

(2) *vb. intr.* to gather or assemble in crowds : P. L. I. 522 ; P. R. I. 21 ; IV. 511 ; S. A. 1450.

part. adj. **flocking,** assembling in crowds : N. O. 232.

Flood, *sb.* (*a*) a body of flowing water, stream, river : P. L. IV. 231 ; VI. 830 ; VII. 57, 295 ; P. R. III. 268 ; with proper name : P. L. I. 419 ; II. 577, 587 ; III. 535 ; P. R. I. 24 ; P. 37 ; A. 29 ; C. 831 ; L. 85 ; *Assyrian flood,* the river Euphrates : P. R. III. 436.

(*b*) the lake of fire in hell : P. L. I. 195, 239, 312, 324.

(*c*) pool of water : Ps. CXIV. 17.

(*d*) the sea : P. L. II. 640 ; C. 19 ; L. 185.

(*e*) an overflowing of a great body of water, deluge : P. L. XI. 472, 893 ; the deluge in the time of Noah : P. L. XI. 748, 831, 840 ; XII. 117 ; P. R. II. 178 ; *fig. flood of joy, sorrow, tears* : P. L. XI. 756, 757 ; T. 13.

(*f*) violent downpour of rain : C. 930 ; *fig. of fire* : P. L. I. 77.

(*g*) water as one of the four elements which form the universe : P. L. III. 715 ; the abode of devils or demons : P. R. IV. 201 ; 11 P. 94.

Floor, *sb.* **watery floor,** surface of the sea : L. 167.

Flora, *sb.* the goddess of flowers and spring : P. L. V. 16 ; P. R. II. 365.

Florid, *adj.* (*a*) abounding in flowers, flowery : P. L. VII. 90.

(*b*) bright or brilliant *hue* : P. L. VII. 445.

(*c*) ruddy : P. L. IV. 278.

Flour, *sb.* finely ground meal ; *flour of wheat* : Ps. LXXXI. 66.

Flourish, *vb. intr.* (*a*) to grow vigorously and luxuriantly : P. L. VII. 320.

(*b*) to thrive, prosper ; *of a person* : S. X. 10 ; *of eloquence* : P. L. IX. 672.

part. adj. (*a*) **flourishing,** prosperous : P. R. III. 80.

(*b*) **flourished,** luxuriant in growth : P. L. IV. 699.

Flout, *sb.* scoff, jibe : Ps. LXXX. 28.

Flow, *vb.* (*pret.* flowed ; *past part.* flown : P. L. I. 502) *intr.* (*a*) to move along in a current, stream, run ; *of fountain, river, sea* : P. L. I. 11 ; III. 31, 518 ; V. 195 ; VII. 8, 279 ; IX. 81 ; XII. 158 ; P. R. III. 255 ; S. A. 547.

(*b*) to hang loose and waving, lie in undulating folds ; *of a garment* : P. L. XI. 241 : 11 P. 34.

(*c*) to glide smoothly along ; *of speech* : P. L. IV. 410 ; *of verse* : W. S. 10.

(*d*) to issue in a stream, well forth ; *of tears* : P. L. X. 910 ; *nectarous humour issuing flowed* : P. L. VI. 332.

(*e*) to issue or proceed *from* : P. L. V. 150 ; VIII. 601 ; IX. 239.

(*f*) *past part.* swollen, in flood ; *fig. of persons,* probably with the meaning : flushed, inflamed : P. L. I. 502.

(*g*) to be poured out without stint : P. L. V. 633 ; *fig. of blessing, wrath* : Ps. III. 24 ; LXXXVIII. 65.

part. adj. **flowing** ; (*a*) hanging loosely and gracefully ; *of hair* : P. L. III. 640 ; IV. 496.

(*b*) full to overflowing, brimming : P. L. V. 444.

(c) abundant: P. R. II. 436.

vbl. sb. **flowing**; (a) action of moving in a current: P. L. XI. 846.

(b) ebb and flow *of the seas*: U. C. 31.

See **Cross-flowing**.

Flower, I. *sb.* (1) blossom, bloom: P. L. I. 771; IV. 256, 269, 334, 451; V. 212, 481, 636, 747; IX. 206, 278, 428, 437, 840, 1039; XI. 594; P. R. II. 356; S. A. 728, 987, 1742; M. W. 39, 57; C. 994; L. 47, 148; in combination with *fruit, herb*: P. ·L. IV. 644, 652, 709; V. 482; VIII. 527; X. 603; XI. 327.

(b) *spec.* iris, rose, jessamine: P. L. IV. 697; blossom of the plant Hæmony: C. 633; hyacinth: D. F. I. 27; L. 106; *May flowers*: P. L. IV. 501; *Elysian flowers*: P. L. III. 359; L'A. 147; *ambrosial flower*: P. L. II. 245; VI. 475; *vernal* or *vernant flowers*: P. L. X. 679; L. 141.

(c) used *fig. of persons*: P. L. IV. 270; IX. 432; D. F. I. 1.

(2) plant cultivated or esteemed for the sake of its blossoms: P. L. IV. 241; V. 126; VIII. 286; IX. 193, 408; XI. 273; Ps. LXXXV. 45; in combination with *fruit, herb, plant*: P. L. IV. 438; VIII. 44; IX. 206; *spec.* amaranth: P. L. III. 353.

(3) the choicest among a number of persons: P. L. I. 316; P. R. III. 314; S. A. 144, 1654.

(4) bloom or prime *of youth*: P. R. I. 67; S. A. 938.

II. *vb. intr.* to produce flowers, blossom: P. L. III. 357; VII. 317.

Floweret, *sb.* small flower: P. L. V. 379, 636; VI. 784; L. 135.

Flower-inwoven, *adj.* intertwined with flowers: N. O. 187.

Flowery, *adj.* (a) full of or abounding in flowers; *flowery herb, brook, cave, mountain, valley*, etc.: P. L. I. 410; III. 30, 569; IV. 254, 626, 772; VIII. 254; IX. 456; P. R. IV. 247, 586; C. 239; Ariosto II. 1; *month of May*: M. M. 3; *fig. lap of peace*: V. Ex. 84.

(b) in or among flowers: Il P. 143.

(c) decorated with a floral design: P. L. XI. 881.

Flowery-kirtled, *adj.* wearing a long flowing garment woven of flowers (?): C. 254.

Fluctuate, *vb. intr.* to move to and fro like a wave: P. L. IX. 668.

Fluid, *adj.* having the property of flowing; *of air*: P. L. VI. 349; *of a cloud*: P. L. XI. 882; *of the waters of chaos*: P. L. VII. 237.

Flush, *vb. intr.* to produce a heightened colour: P. L. IX. 887.

Flute, *sb.* the wind instrument: P. L. I. 551; C. 173; *oaten flute*: L. 33.

Flutter, *vb. tr.* to move in quick irregular motion; *fluttering his pennons*: P. L. II. 933; *cowls... fluttered into rags*: P. L. III. 491.

Fly, *sb.* the insect *Musca*: P. L. XII. 177; P. R. IV. 15.

Fly, *vb.* (*pres. 2d sing.* fliest: P. L. IV. 482; V. 175; *pret.* flew; *past part.* flown) (1) *intr.* (a) to pass through the air by the aid of wings; *of birds, insects*: P. L. I. 772; III. 435; V. 274; VII. 389, 429; VIII. 264; X. 276; XI. 855; *of Satan* in the form of a bird, with *up*: P. L. IV. 194; *of angels or spirits*: P. L. II. 942, 950; V. 251; VI. 536, 642; P. R. I. 39; IV. 582; D. F. I. 60; C. 976, 1013; *of sin and death*: P. L. X. 284, 422; *of a person*: P. L. V. 87; *fig. of alms, prayers*, with *up*: P. L. XI. 15; S. XIV. 11.

(b) to pass or rise quickly in or through the air, *of persons or things*: P. L. III. 494, 521; with *up*: P. L. III. 445, 717; *of darts*: P. L. VI. 213, 214; *of thoughts*: V. Ex. 28.

(c) to move or travel swiftly: P. L. V. 176; with *up*: P. L. IV. 1004; *of time*: T. 1; with *on*: S. II. 3.

(d) to hasten, rush: P. L. VI. 507; N. O. 236; *fly on*, attack with fury: S. A. 262; *fly off*, take another course: P. L. VI. 614.

(e) **fly open**, start or be thrown suddenly open: P. L. II. 879.

(f) to flee, seek escape or safety by flight: P. L. IV. 75, 859; V. 871; VI. 295; XI. 650; P. R. III. 323; IV. 629; S. A. 254; with *from*: P. R. II. 75.

(g) to hasten for safety *to*; P. L. IV. 963; P. R. III. 216; Ps. VII. 1.

(h) to go or hasten away *from*: C. 668.

(*i*) to make one's escape or get safely away *from*: P. L. IV. 22, 910.

(2) *tr*. (*a*) to fly in or through *the air*; in passive with *air* as subject: P. L. VII. 503.

(*b*) to flee or hasten away from *a person, place*: P. L. II. 612; IV. 482; V. 889; C. 829, 939.

(*c*) to go from or in an opposite direction to: P. L. V. 175.

(*d*) to escape or save oneself from: P. L. IV. 73; S. A. 1541; to escape *pain* by flight: P. L. IV. 948; to evade *death*: P. L. XI. 547.

(*e*) to shun, avoid: P. R. I. 440; S. XVIII. 14; Ps. LXXXVIII. 71.

part. adj. **flying**; (*a*) moving by the aid of wings: P. L. II. 643; VII. 17.

(*b*) made on wing; *flying march*: P. L. II. 574; V. 688.

vbl. sb. **flying**, the seeking escape by flight: P. L. IV. 913.

See **Grey-fly, Out-fly**.

Foam, *sb*. (*a*) froth, spume: P. L. VI. 512.

(*b*) the sea; *Norway foam*: P. L. I. 203.

Foaming, *part. adj*. (*a*) frothing; *of the abyss of chaos*: P. L. X. 301.

(*b*) being covered with froth; *foaming steed*: P. L. VI. 391; XI. 643.

Foe, *sb*. (*a*) an adversary in mortal combat: P. L. IX. 15; *of angels, sin, death*: P. L. II. 722; VI. 129, 363; *mortal foe*: P. L. III. 179.

(*b*) one who hates or seeks to injure another, enemy: P. L. I. 649; IX. 486; XI. 703; S. A. 109, 342, 366, 423, 424, 884, 897, 1193, 1262, 1469, 1518, 1529, 1586, 1667; V. Ex. 83; C. 449; S. XVI. 11; Ps. VII. 12, 21; VIII. 6; LXXXIII. 5; LXXXVI. 62; *of God or angels*: P. L. I. 179; II. 72, 78, 152, 202, 369, 463; D. F. I. 66; *Almighty Foe*: P. L. II. 769; *grand Foe*: P. L. I. 122; *Supreme Foe*: P. L. II. 210; *of Satan or his angels, of sin or death*: P. L. II. 504, 804; III. 258; IV. 7, 372, 373, 749; V. 724, 876; VI. 39; VII. 139; IX. 253, 280, 295, 323, 327, 361, 383, 951; X. 11, 926, 1038; XI. 155; XII. 453; P. R. I. 387; III. 120; *grand foe, Satan*: P. L. VI. 149; X. 1033;

grand foes, sin and death: P. R. I. 159; *spiritual foe*: P. R. I. 10; *of chaos*: P. L. II. 1039.

(*c*) enemy in war: P. L. I. 437; Ps. III. 1, 21; LXXX. 8, 26; LXXXI. 57; with proper name: P. L. X. 431; *of the army of God*: P. L. VI. 440, 487, 627, 688; *of the army of Satan*: P. L. III. 399, 677; V. 735; VI. 402, 530, 537, 551, 603, 688, 785, 831, 880; *fig.*: S. A. 561.

See **Arch-foe**.

Fog, *sb*. watery vapour: C. 269, 433.

Foil, *sb*. a leaf of metal placed under a jewel to increase its lustre, *fig.*: L. 79.

Foil, (1) *sb*. defeat, overthrow: P. L. X. 375; P. R. IV. 569; *receive the foil*, be defeated: Ps. CXIV. 10.

(2) *vb. tr.* (*a*) to defeat, overthrow: P. L. I. 273; II. 330; VI. 200; XII. 389; P. R. IV. 565; Ps. CXXXVI. 65; to subdue or bring under the power of an influence: P. L. VIII. 608.

(*b*) to baffle, frustrate: P. R. I. 5; IV. 13.

Fold, (1) *sb*. enclosure for sheep, pen: P. L. IV. 187; XI. 431; P. R. I. 244; C. 498, 542; *fig*. native land, home: S. XVIII. 6; the garden of Eden: P. L. IV. 192; the church: L. 115.

(2) *vb. absol.* to enclose flocks in a fold: C. 93.

part. adj. **folded**, enclosed in a pen: C. 344.

Fold, (*a*) *sb*. layer: P. L. II. 645.

(*b*) the coil of a serpent's body: P. L. II. 651; VII. 484; IX. 161, 498, 499.

(*c*) toil, snare: S. A. 1665.

(*d*) movable division of a door, leaf: P. L. I. 724.

Folded, *part. adj*. bent, coiled: N. O. 172.

See **Seven-times-folded**.

Follow, *vb*. (1) *tr*. (*a*) to move behind in the same direction, go or come after *a person*: P. L. I. 238, 467; IV. 469; VII. 222; VIII. 508; X. 533; XI. 371; P. R. IV. 523; A. 86, 90; C. 657, 1018; S. XIV. 8.

(*b*) to go forward along *a track*: P. L. II. 1025; X. 314, 367.

(*c*) to succeed in time or order: P. L. XII. 335; P. R. I. 192.

(*d*) to go along with as an attendant or companion, accompany: P. L. II. 662; VIII. 645;

XI. 291 ; as a disciple : P. L. XII. 439.

(e) *fig.* to accompany : P. L. VII. 558 ; XI. 352 ; to be consequent upon : P. L. II. 25.

(*f*) to seek to gain, strive after : P. R. I. 440.

(*g*) to take as leader or master, obey the dictates or guidance of : P. L. II. 866 ; VII. 3 ; IX. 808 ; by *zeugma* also, to return : P. R. III. 430.

(*h*) to conform to, act in accordance with : P. L. VIII. 611; P. R. I. 483.

(*i*) to pursue, occupy oneself with, engage in : P. L. IV. 437 ; P. R. I. 315.

(2) *intr.* or *absol.* (*a*) to go or come behind a person : P. L. IV. 476, 481 ; X. 589.

(*b*) to happen after something else, ensue : P. L. II. 206 ; VI. 598.

(*c*) to conform to what has preceded : P. L. IX. 133.

part. adj. **following**, ensuing : P. L. X. 278.

Follower, *sb.* (*a*) one who follows a leader, supporter : P. R. II. 419.

(*b*) one who follows in practice the conduct of another : P. L. I. 606 ; one who follows a teacher, disciple of Christ : P. L. XII. 484.

Folly, *sb.* (*a*) weakness of judgement or character, or an act springing therefrom : P. L. III. 158 ; IV. 905, 1007 ; VI. 139 ; VII. 130 ; VIII. 553 ; X. 619, 621 ; XII. 560 ; S. A. 377, 825, 1000, 1043 ; *concr.* foolish persons, or the light-minded frivolous world : Il P. 61 ; the results of a foolish act : P. L. II. 686; *personified* : Il P. 2.

(*b*) wickedness : C. 975 ; Ps. LXXXV. 35.

Foment, *vb. tr.* (*a*) to cherish with heat, in combination with *warm* : P. L. IV. 669 ; XI. 338.

(*b*) to foster or promote the spread of *fire* : P. L. X. 1071.

Fond, *adj.* (*a*) foolish, silly : P. L. III. 449 ; VI. 90 ; VIII. 195, 209 ; X. 834 ; S. A. 228, 812, 1682 ; Il P. 6 ; C. 67.

(*b*) doting, tender : P. R. II. 211. *See* **Over-fond.**

Fondly, *adv.* foolishly : P. L. III. 470 ; VII. 152 ; IX. 999 ; X. 564 ; XI. 59 ; L. 56 ; S. XIX. 8.

Fontarabbia, *sb.* the modern Fuen-terrabia, a town and fortress in the province of Guipuzcoa, Spain : P. L. I. 587.

Food, *sb.* aliment, nourishment, victuals : P. L. V. 400, 401, 407, 465 ; VII. 126, 408, 540 ; IX. 237, 573, 768 ; XI. 54 ; XII. 74 ; P. R. I. 308, 345, 353 ; II. 231, 246, 268, 320 ; S. A. 574, 1366 ; Ps. LXXX. 55 ; LXXXV. 52 ; *angels', godlike, celestial food* : P. L. V. 633 ; IX. 717 ; P. R. IV. 588 ; *fig.* mankind as devoured by Death : P. L. X. 986 ; that which sustains the mind or love : P. L. IX. 238, 240 ; lying as that by which Satan subsists : P. R. I. 429.

Fool, (1) *sb.* (*a*) one who acts or thinks stupidly : P. R. II. 453 ; S. A. 77, 203, 298, 496, 907 ; C. 477 ; Ps. V. 12 ; *vocative* : C. 662 ; as an exclamation : P. L. VI. 135 ; S. A. 201.

(*b*) vain, foolish, or idiotic persons or things ; *Paradise of Fools* : P. L. III. 496.

(*c*) buffoon : S. A. 1338.

(2) *vb. tr.* to make a fool of, dupe : P. L. X. 880.

Foolish, *adj.* wanting in judgement : S. A. 198.

Foolishness, *sb.* want of understanding : C. 706.

Foot, I. *sb.* (1) terminal part of the leg, upon which the body rests in standing : P. L. II. 949 ; III. 486 ; IV. 183 ; V. 283 ; X. 215 ; XI. 858 ; P. R. IV. 559 ; S. A. 111 ; Il P. 155 ; C. 877, 897 ; with *adjs.* denoting the kind of motion : P. L. II. 404 ; IV. 866 ; VII. 440 ; *from head to foot* : P. L. VI. 625 ; *on foot*, opposed to *flying* : P. L. II. 941 ; *set foot* : P. R. IV. 610 ; *stand on one's feet* : P. L. VI. 592 ; VIII. 261 ; XI. 759.

(*b*) put for the whole person : P. R. III. 224 ; S. A. 136, 931, 950 ; with *adjs.* indicating the character, condition, or appearance of the person : P. L. I. 238 ; III. 73 ; S. A. 336, 732 ; C. 180, 310 ; N. O. 25, 146.

(*c*) **under foot,** on the ground : P. L. IV. 700.

(*d*) **at his feet,** before him in adoration or humiliation : P. L. VIII. 315 ; X. 911, 942 ; N. O. 25.

(*e*) **under one's feet,** in subjection to one : P. L. X. 190 ; P. R. IV. 621 ; Ps. VIII. 18.

(*f*) *fig.* gentle motion of water while ebbing : P. L. XI. 848.

(2) foot-soldiers : P. R. III. 327; *horse and foot* : P. L. XI. 645; S. A. 1618.

(3) extremity of the leg of a pair of compasses : P. L. VII. 228.

(4) lower part or bottom of stairs : P. L. III. 485; base of a mountain : P. L. IX. 71 ; *pl.* : P. L. III. 31 ; P. R. III. 253.

(5) end of a bridge : P. L. X. 347.

II. *vb. intr.* to go on foot, walk, *fig.* : L. 103.

vbl. sb. **footing**, footstep : C. 146.

See **Four-footed, Harpy-footed.**

Footstep, *sb.* (*a*) step : Ps. LXXXV. 56.

(*b*) footprint : P. L. XI. 329.

(*c*) course of action : P. R. IV. 522.

*****For,** (1) *prep.* (*a*) as representative of : P. L. III. 295.

(*b*) in place of, instead of : P. L. I. 245 ; II. 66 ; III. 47, 236 ; in the place and behalf of : P. L. II. 827 ; III. 210, 240 ; in order to pay the penalty of : P. L. III. 410.

(*c*) in favour of, on the side of : P. L. II. 51, 119 ; VI. 62.

(*d*) with a view to, with the purpose of : P. L. V. 629 ; in order to engage in : P. L. VI. 296, 537 ; P. R. III. 328.

(*e*) in order to obtain : P. L. I. 111, 688 ; II. 31 ; IV. 184.

(*f*) in order to arrive at : P. L. XI. 7 ; S. A. 715.

(*g*) appropriate or adapted to, suitable to the purpose of : P. L. II. 111, 623 ; III. 643 ; IV. 298, 981 ; V. 323.

(*h*) designed to serve as : P. L. I. 366 ; VII. 341 ; designed to indicate : P. L. VII. 342.

(*i*) in the interest of, with a view to the use or benefit of : P. L. II. 465, 481 ; III. 275, 664 ; IV. 107 ; P. 12 ; in order to show or manifest : P. L. I. 260.

(*j*) as affects the condition of : P. L. III. 232.

(*k*) in the character of, as being : P. L. I. 373 ; II. 14, 224, 761 ; IV. 370.

(*l*) on account of, because of : P. L. I. 94, 394, 432, 609 ; on account of one's regard for : P. L. III. 238 ; IX. 993 ; X. 201.

(*m*) as answering or corresponding to : P. L. X. 512.

(*n*) with respect or regard to, as regards : P. L. I. 635.

(2) *conj.* for the reason that, seeing that : P. L. I. 19, 57, 139, 423 ; II. 313; followed by *that* : P. R. I. 327.

Forage, *sb.* roving search for provisions : P. L. XI. 646.

Forbear, *vb.* (*pret.* forbore ; *past part.* forborne) (1) *tr.* (*a*) to bear or have patience with : Ps. IV. 9.

(*b*) to dispense with, do without : P. L. IX. 747.

(*c*) to abstain from : P. L. IX. 1034 ; *absol.* : P. L. VIII. 490.

(2) *intr.* to abstain, refrain, cease : P. L. II. 736 ; Ps. VII. 45.

Forbearance, *sb.* a refraining from retribution : P. L. X. 53.

Forbid, *vb.* (*pret.* not used ; *past part.* forbid : P. L. IX. 356, 703 ; X. 685; forbidden : P. L. I. 2 ; II. 852 ; IV. 515 ; V. 69 ; IX. 904, 1025, 1026 ; X. 554 ; XII. 279 ; P. R. II. 369 ; S. A. 555, 1139, 1409) *tr.* (*a*) to prohibit, interdict ; with *obj.* of the thing : P. L. IX. 356, 703, 750, 758 ; P. R. I. 495 ; S. A. 13, 1320; in *passive* : P. L. IV. 515 ; V. 69 ; IX. 904, 1026 ; P. R. II. 369 ; S. A. 555, 1409 ; the *obj.* of the person preceded by *to* : P. L. IX. 1025 ; with *obj.* of both person and thing : P. L. IV. 82 ; IX. 759; with *obj.* of the person and *prep. inf.* : P. L. IV. 515 ; IX. 753, 759 ; XI. 49 ; in *passive* with *prep. inf.* : P. L. II. 852 ; *absol.* : P. L. II. 475 ; V. 62.

(*b*) to prevent, hinder ; with *prep. inf.* : P. L. V. 61 ; with *acc.* and *prep. inf.* : C. 269 ; to hinder or keep back *from* : P. L. X. 685.

part. adj. **forbidden,** prohibited : P. L. I. 2 ; X. 554 ; XII. 279 ; S. A. 1139.

vbl. sb. **forbidding,** prohibition : P. L. IX. 753.

Forbiddance, *sb.* prohibition : P. L. IX. 903.

Forbidder, *sb.* one who forbids ; *of God* : P. L. IX. 815.

Force, (1) *sb.* (*a*) physical strength or might ; *of a person* : P. L. II. 853, 1012; VI. 293; S. A. 1087, 1627 ; *by main force* : S. A. 146 ; strength or impetus *of the elements* : P. L. I. 230; VI. 222; S. A. 1647; *of a weapon* : P. L. VI. 324.

(b) military strength: P. L. I.
94, 145, 560, 574, 629.

(c) body of armed men, army:
P. L. I. 101; V. 730; P. R. I.
153; III. 337.

(d) violence or physical coercion: P. L. I. 248, 647; II. 188;
VI. 125; IX. 348; P. R. I. 97;
S. A. 1206, 1219, 1273, 1369; D.
F. I. 4; C. 590, 906; S. XXIII. 4;
personified: P. L. II. 551; *by
force*, by employing violence, by
violent means: P. L. I. 121, 649;
II. 135, 250, 358; III. 91; VI. 41,
794; XII. 412; P. R. II. 479.

(e) constraint, compulsion: P.
L. IX. 1173, 1174.

(f) moral strength: P. R. IV.
602.

(g) intellectual power, strength
of mind: V. Ex. 89.

(h) virtue, efficacy: P. L. IX.
1046; P. R. I. 347; S. A. 935.

(i) used punningly with the
double meaning of, power to convince the judgement, and strength
or impetus: P. L. VI. 622.

(j) agency, influence: P. L. X.
246.

(k) of force, of necessity, unavoidably: P. L. I. 144; IV. 813;
S. A. 1397.

(2) vb. tr. (a) to compel, con-
strain: P. L. X. 829; XII. 525;
F. of C. 6; with *acc.* and *to*: S.
A. 1451; with *acc.* and *prep. inf.*:
C. 607; in *passive*: P. L. X. 475,
991; with *acc.* and *simple inf.*: S.
A. 1096.

(b) to impose *something* forcibly
on: P. L. XII. 521.

(c) to bring about or effect *a
way* by violence: P. L. II. 62;
VI. 196.

(d) to evoke, elicit: V. Ex. 67.
part. adj. forced; (a) brought
about by violence: P. L. VI. 598.

(b) unwilling: L. 4.

(c) extorted by authority: P. L.
II. 243.

Forcible, *adj.* (a) powerful, strong:
P. L. VI. 465; IX. 955.

(b) effected by force, violent:
P. L. II. 793.

Ford, *sb.* (a) shallow place in a river;
spec. ford of Jordan: P. R. I. 328;
IV. 510; probably a ford of the
Euphrates: P. L. XII. 130.

(b) stream: P. L. II. 612.

Forecast, *vb. tr.* (a) to plan in advance: S. A. 254.

(b) to conjecture beforehand,
absol.: V. Ex. 13.

Forefather, *sb.* ancestor: P. R. III.
422; Ps. LXXXVII. 12.

Foregoing, *part. adj.* preceding in
time: P. R. IV. 483.

Forehead, *sb.* part of the face above
the eyes; *fig. forehead of the deep*:
C. 733; *of the sky*: L. 171.

Foreign, *adj.* (a) belonging to another
country: C. 265; Ps. LXXXI. 39.

(b) situated in another country:
P. L. III. 548; XII. 46; *foreign
worlds*: P. L. X. 441.

Foreknow, *vb. absol.* to know beforehand: P. L. III. 117.

vbl. sb. **foreknowing**, foreknowledge, prescience: P. L. XI. 773.

Foreknowledge, *sb.* prescience: P.
L. II. 559, 560; III. 116, 118; XI.
768.

Foreland, *sb.* headland, promontory:
P. L. IX. 514.

Forelock, *sb.* lock of hair that grows
on the fore part of the head: P.
L. IV. 302; *fig. on Occasion's forelock ... wait*, act promptly, let no
opportunity slip: P. R. III. 173.

Foremost, *adv.* first in place: P. L.
II. 28.

Forerun, *vb. tr.* (a) to go before and
prepare for: P. L. I. 677.

(b) to come before, be the pre-
cursor of: P. L. VII. 584.

Forerunner, *sb.* sign betokening
something to follow: P. L. XI.
195.

Foresee, *vb.* (*pret.* foresaw; *past
part.* foreseen) *tr.* to see or discern beforehand, foreknow: P. L.
III. 121; VI. 673; XI. 763; S. A.
737; V. Ex. 72; *absol.*: P. L. I.
627; III. 79.

Foresight, *sb.* (a) the action of looking forward: P. L. XI. 368.

(b) prudence in guarding against
an enemy: P. L. I. 119.

Fore-signify, *vb. tr.* to foretell: P.
R. IV. 464.

Foreskin, *sb. fig.* uncircumcised man:
S. A. 144.

Forest, *sb.* large tract of land
covered with trees: P. L. IX. 117;
P. R. III. 268; *spicy forest*: P. L.
V. 298; the home of the beasts:
P. L. IV. 342; VII. 458; XI. 189;
Ps. VIII. 20; the place of enchant-
ment, loneliness, or romance: P.
R. II. 359; Il P. 119; C. 423;
fig. forest of spears: P. L. I. 547.
attrib. of the forest: P. L. I. 613

Forestall, *vb. tr.* (*a*) to hinder or prevent by anticipation : P. L. X. 1024.

(*b*) to think of before the due time : C. 362.

part. adj. **forestalling**, hindering, obstructing : C. 285.

Forest-side, *sb.* edge of a forest : P. L. I. 782.

Foretasted, *part. adj.* tasted before by another : P. L. IX. 929.

Foretell, *vb.* (*pret.* and *past part.* foretold) (1) *tr.* to tell beforehand, predict, prophesy : P. L. IX. 1171 ; X. 38, 191, 482 ; XII. 543 ; P. R. I. 238, 453 ; III. 351 ; S. A. 23, 44 ; S. I. 10 ; with two *acc.*: P. R. IV. 204 ; with *acc.* and *dat.*: P. L. XI. 771 ; P. R. IV. 375, 478 ; with *acc.* and *to* : P. L. X. 1051 ; XII. 327, 328, 329 ; S. A. 1662 ; with *clause* : P. L. II. 830 ; P. R. I. 239 ; II. 87.

(2) *intr.* to prophesy *of* : P. L. XII. 242 ; P. R. IV. 502 ; S. A. 525.

Forewarn, *vb. tr.* to admonish or caution beforehand : P. L. II. 810 ; IX. 61 ; with *acc.* and *prep. inf.* : P. L. VII. 41 ; with *acc.* and *of* : P. L. VII. 73 ; with *acc.* and *clause* : P. L. IX. 378.

absol. to apprise beforehand : P. L. XII. 507.

vbl. sb. **forewarning**, premonition : P. L. X. 876.

Forfeit, (1) *sb.* penalty for trespass : N. O. 6 ; *penal forfeit* : S. A. 508.

(2) *adj.* lost by breach of conditions or by trespass : P. L. III. 176 ; with *to* : P. L. X. 304.

Forfeiture, *sb.* penalty for trespass : P. L. III. 221.

Forge, (1) *sb.* furnace in which metal is heated to be hammered into shape : P. L. XI. 564.

(2) *vb. tr.* to frame or fashion *illusions* : P. L. IV. 802.

Forgery, *sb.* (*a*) action of forging metal into shape : S. A. 131.

(*b*) deception : C. 698.

Forget, *vb.* (*pret.* and *past part.* forgot) *tr.* (*a*) to lose the remembrance of, cease to remember : P. L. II. 585, 586, 747 ; III. 32 ; IV. 512 ; IX. 474 ; C. 76 ; S. XXII. 3.

(*b*) to cease to think of, let slip out of mind, neglect, slight : P. L. XI. 807, 878 ; S. A. 479 ; S. XVIII. 5 ; with *prep. inf.*: P. L. V.

550 ; N. O. 67 ; to take no note of *time* : P. L. IV. 639 ; to cease to celebrate *praise* : P. L. III. 415.

(*c*) *refl.* to lose consciousness of oneself : Il P. 42.

Forgetful, *adj.* (*a*) causing one to forget : P. L. II. 74.

(*b*) heedless, neglectful ; *of* omitted : P. L. IV. 54.

Forgetfulness, *sb.* loss of memory : P. L. II. 608.

Forgive, *vb. tr.* (*a*) to pardon *an offence* : Ps. LXXXV. 5 ; *an offender* : S. A. 761, 954.

(*b*) to regard leniently *a weakness* : P. L. X. 956 : S. A. 787.

Forgiveness, *sb.* pardon : S. A. 909, 1376.

Forgo, *vb. tr.* (*a*) to go from, forsake, or leave *a place* : N. O. 196; *a person* : P. L. VIII. 497 ; S. A. 940.

(*b*) to give up, relinquish, or resign *material possessions* : S. A. 1483 ; *love, pleasure* : P. L. IX. 908 ; XI. 541.

Forked, *part. adj.* bifurcate *tongue* : P. L. X. 518, 519.

Forlorn, *adj.* (*a*) lost : C. 39 ; not held to any definite course : P. L. II. 615.

(*b*) desolate, dreary ; *of places* : P. L. I. 180 ; IX. 910 ; L'A. 3.

(*c*) abandoned, forsaken : P. L. IV. 374 ; or wretched, miserable (?) : Ps. LXXXVIII. 26 ; *forlorn of*, forsaken by : P. L. X. 921 ; alone, solitary ; *of a person* : P. L. VII. 20.

Form, (1) *sb.* (*a*) shape, figure, external appearance : P. L. III. 717 ; V. 473, 573 ; X. 214; *of living beings*, sometimes nearer, body considered with respect to outward appearance : P. L. I. 301, 358, 481, 591, 789 ; III. 605 ; IV. 876 ; V. 457 ; VI. 433 ; VII. 455 ; IX. 457 ; X. 543, 872 ; P. R. IV. 599; N. O. 8 ; C. 70, 605 ; *form of chastity* : C. 215.

(*b*) arrangement of ideas : S. XI. 2.

(*c*) order *of battle* : P. R. III. 322.

(*d*) ceremony, ritual : P. L. XII. 534.

(2) *vb. tr.* (*a*) to give form to, mould : P. L. VIII. 469.

(*b*) to construct, make : P. L. I. 705 ; IX. 392 ; XI. 571.

(c) to create, bring into existence *living beings* : P. L. IV. 365, 441 ; V. 824, 853 ; VI. 690 ; XI. 369; with two *acc.*: P. L. III. 124; VIII. 596 ; *man from dust* : P. L. V. 516; VII. 524 ; IX. 149; *the earth, the moon* : P. L. VII. 276, 356; *fancy ...forms imaginations* : P. L. V. 105; *be formed to thought*, be created by the imagination : P. L. IX. 898.

(d) to create and adapt *for* : P. L. IV. 297.

(e) to determine the form ,or fashion of ; *sing.* with compound subject : P. L. VIII. 223.

(f) to shape by influence, mould, train : P. R. IV. 364.

(g) to arrange themselves in the form of : P. L. II. 532.

part. adj. forming, that shapes or moulds : P. L. VIII. 470.

See **Double-formed.**

Former, *adj.* (a) previous, antecedent, prior : P. L. II. 585 ; IV. 94 ; V. 658 ; VIII. 290 ; IX. 1006 ; S. A. 231, 372, 416, 1510 ; P. 25.

(b) first mentioned of two, opposed to *latter* : P. L. II. 234 ; XII. 105.

Formidable (fórmidáble), *adj.* dreadful, terrible ; P. L. II. 649.

Formless, *adj.* without form, chaotic : P. L. III. 12, 708.

Forsake, *vb.* (*pret.* forsook ; *past part.* forsaken : P. L. V. 878 ; L. 142; forsook : S. A. 629 ; Il P. 91) *tr.* (a) to renounce allegiance to or be faithless to *God* : P. L. I. 368, 432; XII. 118.

(b) to leave, abandon, or depart from *a place* : D. F. I. 51 ; N. O. 13, 198; to leave *the flock* : C. 499 ; *of the image of God, mind, sleep*, etc., departing from *a person* : P. L. V. 875 ; XI. 516 ; S. A. 629 ; Il P. 91.

(c) to withdraw one's presence and companionship from, desert : P. L. X. 914; to withdraw one's presence and help from : Ps. LXXXVIII. 57.

past part. unnoticed, unappreciated : L. 141.

Fort, *sb.* fortified place : S. A. 278; *fig. fort of silence* : S. A. 236.

*****Forth,** (1) *adv.* (a) into motion, onward : P. L. VII. 427.

(b) away or out from a place : P. L. I. 501, 770 : V. 36, 138, 351; VII. 203 ; VIII. 44.

(c) out, into view : P. L. IV. 997 ; V. 15, 315 ; out of the mouth : P. L. XI. 313.

(d) into existence : P. L. I. 163; III. 707 ; XI. 428 ; S. A. 875.

(e) into activity : P. L. I. 217 ; VI. 853.

(2) *prep.* out of ; preceded by *from* : P. L. V. 712 ; S. A. 922.

Forth-reaching, *pres. part.* reaching out : P. L. IX. 781.

Forth-stepping, *pres. part.* stepping out : P. L. VI. 128.

Forthwith (forthwíth : P. L. III. 327 ; V. 86 ; IX. 724 ; fórthwith : P. L. I. 535, 755 ; III. 326 ; VII. 243 ; VIII. 271, 291 ; X. 1098 ; P. R. II. 236 ; (?) S. A. 329 ; *doubtful, but probably* forthwíth : P. L. II. 585, 874 ; V. 586, 630 ; VI. 335, 507, 637 ; VII. 399 ; XI. 855 ; XII. 56), *adv.* without delay, at once, immediately : P. L. I. 221, 356, 535, 755 ; II. 585, 874 ; III. 326, 327 ; V. 86, 586, 630 ; VI. 335, 507,637 ; VII. 243,399 ; VIII. 271, 291; IX. 724; X. 1098 ; XI. 855 ; XII. 56 ; P. R. II. 236 ; S. A. 329.

Fortify, *vb. intr.* to build strongly : P. L. X. 370.

Fortitude, *sb.* moral courage : P. L. IX. 31 ; XII. 570 ; S. A. 654, 1288; S. XVI. 3.

Fortunate, *adj.* favoured by fortune; *fortunate fields* : P. L. III. 569.

Fortune, *sb.* (a) chance, luck : S. A. 1093.

(b) the divinity supposed to distribute arbitrarily the lots of life: P. R. IV. 317 ; S. A. 172.

(c) good or ill that befalls a person as his lot in life : S. A. 169, 1291 ; M. W. 72.

(d) success, prosperity, *personified* : S. XVI. 5.

(e) possessions, wealth : P. R. II. 429.

Forty, *adj.* four times ten ; *forty days* : P. R. I. 303, 352, 353 ; II. 243, 276, 315, 316.

Foul, *adj.* (a) disgusting, loathsome: P. L. II. 793 ; IV. 840 ; XI. 464 ; C. 74 ; Ps. LXXXVI. 48 ; *fig.* : L. 127.

(b) impure, polluted : P. L. XI. 51.

(c) miry, muddy : U. C. I. 3.

(d) morally polluted, wicked, base, vile ; *of persons* : P. L. I. 446 ; III. 692 ; X. 986 ; XI. 124 ; S. A. 902 ; C. 645, 696 ; Hor.

Epist. 6 ; *of action, emotion, thought* : P. L. I. 33; III. 177 ; IX. 1078 ; XII. 337 ; P. R. IV. 628 ; C. 383, 464 ; and, *hence*, dimming brightness : P. L. IV. 118, 571.

(*e*) unsightly, ugly : P. L. II. 651, 748 ; VI. 388 ; N. O. 44.

(*f*) disgraceful, ignominious, shameful : P. L. I. 135, 555 ; VI. 124, 598 ; IX. 6, 163, '297, 328, 329 ; P. R. III. 161 ; S. A. 371, 410 ; D. F. I. 14 ; C. 608 ; Ps. VII. 18.

(*g*) not clear, cloudy : P. R. IV. 426.

(2) *adv*. (*a*) in a revolting manner : P. L. VI. 588.

(*b*) with disgrace or shame : P. L. IX. 331.

Found, *vb. tr. a*) to build, construct : P. L. X. 256.

(*b*) to set or place firmly *on*; *of the world* : P. L. VII. 618.

(*c*) to set up or establish *institutions* : P. L. II. 296 ; XII. 224 ; P. R. III. 295 ; Petr. 1 ; *fig.* : P. R. IV. 613.

(*d*) to base or ground *hope, love* : S. A. 1504 ; with *in* : P. L. IV. 755 ; *fig.* to ground *the earth in righteousness*, etc. : P. L. XII. 550.

Found, *vb. tr.* (*a*) to form into shape by running molten metal in a mould, cast : P. L. I. 703 ; VI. 518.

(*b*) to blend or combine by fusion (?), to make solid *that which has been fluid* (?) : P. L. VII. 239.

Foundation, *sb.* (*a*) the base on which something rests ; *fig. of the hills* : P. L. VI. 643 ; *of the world* : N. O. 123 ; *of hell* : P. L. VI. 870 ; *of obedience, faith* : P. L. IV. 521.

(*b*) an organized society, institution : C. 808.

Founder, *vb. tr.* to sink or stick fast *in a bog* : P. L. II. 940.
See **Night-foundered.**

Fount, *sb.* natural spring or source of water, in the garden of Eden : P. L. IV. 237 ; XI. 279 ; in heaven ; *Fount of Life* : P. L. III. 357 ; P. R. IV. 590; with proper name: P. L. III. 535.
See **Double-founted.**

Fountain, *sb.* (*a*) natural spring or source of water : P. L. I. 783 ; VII. 8 ; S. A. 547, 581 ; C. 912 ; L. 24 ; Ps. LXXXVII. 28 ; CXIV. 14 ; in the garden of Eden : P. L.

IV. 229; v. 126, 195, 203 ; IX. 73, 420, 597, 628 ; X. 860 ; XI. 322; in heaven : P. L. XI. 78 ; *fountains of the deep* : P. L. XI. 826; with proper name : L. 85 ; *fig.* the sun as the source whence the stars draw light : P. L. VII. 364.

(*b*) origin, source : P. L. IV. 760 ; source of light : P. L. III. 8 ; God as the source of light, physical or spiritual : P. L. III. 375 ; P. R. IV. 289.

Fountain-brim, *sb.* edge or brink of a fountain : C. 119.

Fountainless, *adj.* having no spring of water : P. R. III. 264.

Fountain-side, *sb.* ground bordering on a fountain : P. L. IV. 326, 531 ; VII. 327 ; P. R. II. 184.

Four, *adj.* three and one : P. L. II. 516, 574, 575, 898 ; IV. 233 ; V. 192 ; VI. 753 ; XI. 128, 737 ; P. R. IV. 415 ; *four times* : P. L. IX. 65 ; P. R. II. 245 ; *four hundred* : P. R. I. 428.

absol. **the Four**, the four cherubic Shapes : P. L. VI. 827, 845.

Fourfold-visaged, *adj.* having four faces ; P. L. VI. 845.

Four-footed, *adj.* having four feet, quadruped : P. L. IV. 397.

Fourth, *adj.* the ordinal of four : P. L. VII. 386 ; S. A. 402.

Fowl, *sb.* bird ; *collect. flock of fowl* : P. L. X. 274 ; *villatic fowl* : S. A. 1695 ; in combination or contrast with *beast* or *fish* : P. L. VIII. 395 ; X. 604, 710 ; *collect.* : P. L. VII. 389, 398, 447, 503, 521, 533 ; VIII. 341 ; XII. 67 ; Ps. VIII. 21 ; *fowl of game* : P. R. II. 342 ; *pl.* : P. L. V. 271 ; P. R. I. 501 ; S. A. 694.

Fragile, *adj.* easily broken : P. R. III. 388.

Fragrance, *sb.* sweetness of smell, agreeable odour : P. L. IV. 653 ; VIII. 266 ; IX. 425 ; *ambrosial, heavenly fragrance* : P. L. III. 135 ; V. 286.

Fragrant, *adj.* sweet-smelling; *of the earth* : P. L. IV. 645 ; *fragrant leaf* : P. L. IV. 695 ; *smell* : P. L. V. 379 ; P. R. II. 351 ; *syrups* : C. 674.

Frail, *adj.* (*a*) perishable ; *of the world* : P. L. II. 1030.

(*b*) transient ; *frail happiness* : P. L. IX. 340.

(*c*) weak, feeble; *frail thoughts* : L. 153.

(d) physically or morally weak; *of man* : P. L. II. 375 ; III. 180, 404 ; IV. 11 ; VI. 345 ; S. A. 656 ; Cir. 19 ; C. 8.

Frailty, *sb.* *(a)* physical weakness : P. L. XI. 302 ; *mortal frailty,* frail mortals : C. 686 ; both physical and moral weakness : P. L. X. 956.

(b) moral weakness : S. A. 369, 783.

Frame, (1) *sb.* fabric, structure; *of heaven* : P. L. III. 395 ; *of the heavens* : P. L. II. 924 ; VIII. 81 ; P. R. IV. 455 ; *of the world* : P. L. V. 154 ; VII. 273 ; VIII. 15.

(2) *vb. tr.* *(a)* to construct, make : P. L. XII. 249 ; *of God,* as building a structure : P. L. V. 256 ; as forming the sun or the world : P. L. IV. 691 ; VII. 355 ; *fig. of reason* : P. L. V. 106.

(b) to put oneself in the posture of ; with *prep. inf.* : Ps. LXXXVI. 30.

(c) to adapt *speech to* : P. L. V. 460.

Franciscan, *adj.* characteristic of the order of St. Francis : P. L. III. 480.

Fraternal, *adj.* appropriate to brothers : P. L. XII. 26.

Fraud, *sb.* *(a)* faithlessness, perfidy : S. XV. 13.

(b) criminal deception : P. L. IV. 121 ; IX. 55, 89, 285, 287, 1150 ; P. R. I. 97 ; S. A. 76 ; *by fraud* : P. L. I. 401, 646 ; III. 152 ; VI. 794 ; X. 485 ; deceitfulness ; *thy inward fraud* : P. L. X. 871.

(c) an act of deception, stratagem, trick : P. L. V. 880 ; VI. 555 ; IX. 904 ; P. R. IV. 3.

(d) state of being deluded; *draw* or *lead into fraud* : P. L. VII. 143 ; IX. 643 ; P. R. I. 372.

Fraudulent, *adj.* *(a)* guilty of fraud : P. L. III. 692.

(b) characterized or accomplished by fraud : P. L. IX. 531 ; P. R. IV. 609.

Fraught, (1) *sb.* freight, cargo, *fig.* : S. A. 1075.

(2) *vb.* (only in *past part.*) *tr.* to fill, store, or supply *with utensils* : P. R. III. 336 ; *persons* : P. L. XI. 207 ; *lightning, fire* : P. L. II. 715 ; VI. 876 ; *envy, joy, revenge,* etc. : P. L. II. 1054 ; V. 661 ; X. 346 ; P. R. I. 38 ; C. 355.

Fray, *sb.* fight, combat : P. L. II. 908 ; IV. 996 ; XI. 651.

Freaked, *part. adj.* flecked : L. 144.

Free, (1) *adj.* *(a)* not enslaved, not subject to another : P. L. VI. 181 ; IX. 825.

fig. not enslaved to passions : P. L. XII. 90 ; not limited by force or chance : P. L. II. 551.

(b) enjoying civil liberty, not subject to a despotic government; frequently including sense *(a)* : P. L. I. 259 ; II. 255 ; V. 791, 792, 819 ; VI. 292 ; P. R. IV. 145 ; granting freedom to its citizens ; *of Rome* : P. L. IX. 671.

(c) unrestricted, unlimited : P. L. IV. 434 ; VI. 451 ; L'A. 40 ; Ps. LXXXVI. 23.

(d) at liberty; with *prep. inf.* : P. L. III. 99 ; not restricted by necessity ; with *prep. inf.* : P. L. VII. 171.

(e) allowed or permitted *to* : P. L. IV. 747.

(f) not restrained in movement : S. A. 1235.

(g) having liberty to follow one's own choice, acting of one's own will and not under constraint ; *of persons, their will, choice,* etc. : P. L. II. 19 ; III. 103, 124 ; V. 235, 236, 527, 532, 549 ; VIII. 440, 610 ; IX. 351, 352 ; XII. 92 ; S. XVI. 13 ; having perfect liberty ; *of virtue* : C. 1019 ; **free will** : P. L. II. 560 ; IV. 66 ; V. 236 ; VIII. 636 ; IX. 1174 ; X. 9, 46. *See* **Will.**

(h) voluntary : P. L. IX. 372 ; XII. 304 ; P. R. III. 358 ; C. 1007.

(i) ready in giving, liberal : P. L. IV. 415.

(j) bounteous, abundant : P. L. IV. 68 ; Ps. LXXX. 34.

(k) generous, kind : A. 34.

(l) affable and ingenuous (?) : L'A. 11.

(m) exempt *from* : P. L. XI. 513.

(n) not subject to ; with *from* : P. L. XII. 71.

(o) **get free,** get loose, extricate : P. L. VII. 464.

(p) **set free,** release from subjection or servitude : P. R. III. 284 ; S. A. 317, 1412, 1572 ; with *from* : Ps. LXXXI. 22 ; give individual and social liberty : S. XII. 10 ; release *conscience* from the bondage of authority : F. of C. 6 ; set at liberty, not keep in confinement : L'A. 149 ; with *from* : P. L. II. 823 ; Ps. LXXXVI. 47.

(2) *adv.* freely, without restraint: P. L. VIII. 641 ; IX. 802; Eurip. 2.

(3) *vb. tr.* (*a*) to release *a person* from servitude : S. A. 1572.

(*b*) to release from the oppression of or servitude to a despotic government or a foreign nation : P. R. III. 428 ; IV. 131, 143 ; S. A. 1213 ; Ps. LXXXI. 27 ; with *from* : P. L. IX. 140 ; P. R. II. 48 ; III. 102, 175 ; IV. 102 ; Ps. CXXXVI. 81.

(*c*) to release *a person* from confinement : C. 818 ; to deliver *truth* from violence: P. R. I. 220 ; *truth and right from violence be freed* : S. XV. 11 ; to deliver *the sparrow from wrong* : Ps. LXXXIV. 9.

(*d*) to relieve *from* : P. L. VIII. 182.

(*e*) to make safe or secure *from* : P. L. X. 999.

Freeborn, *adj.* born to the privileges of citizenship : Eurip. 1.

Freedom, *sb.* (*a*) exemption from despotic control, civil liberty : P. L. V. 797 ; XI. 798 ; XII. 95 ; P. R. III. 77 ; S. A. 1715 ; or in sense (*b*) : P. R. I. 62 ; *concr.* those who possess civil liberty : P. L. VI. 169.

(*b*) liberty of action or thought: P. L. IV. 294 ; IX. 762 ; C. 663 ; S. XII. 9 : or in sense (*a*) : P. L. XI. 580.

(*c*) the quality of being free from the control of necessity : P. L. III. 109, 128.

(*d*) openness, frankness : P. L. VIII. 434.

Freely, *adv.* (*a*) willingly, readily, gladly : P. L. III. 240 ; IV. 381 ; VI. 565 ; P. 12.

(*b*) with freedom of will or choice : P. L. III. 102 ; IV. 72 ; V. 538 ; S. A. 1373.

(*c*) unreservedly, openly : P. L. VIII. 443 ; Eurip. 2.

(*d*) without restriction : P. L. VII. 540 ; without restraint or interference : S. A. 7.

(*e*) without stint, abundantly, plentifully : P. L. III. 175 ; VIII. 322 ; IX. 732, 988 ; P. R. III. 126.

Freeze, *vb.* (*pret.* freezed :- C. 449 ; *past part.* frozen, *also part. adj.* frore, q. v.), *tr.* to harden *to stone* : C. 449.

part. adj. **freezing,** intensely cold : D. F. I. 16.

frozen, (*a*) surrounded by ice : P. L. II. 602.

(*b*) congealed by cold, subject to severe cold : P. L. I. 352 ; II. 587, 620 ; S. XX. 7.

French, *adj. absol.* the French people, and esp. the French army : S. XXI. 8.

Frequence, *sb.* concourse, assembly ; *full frequence* : P. R. I. 128 ; II. 130.

Frequent, I. *adj.* (*a*) crowded, thronged : P. L. I. 797 ; or *adv.* (?) : in throngs : P. L. III. 504 ; VII. 534.

(*b*) common, usual : S. A. 275.

(*c*) often recurring : P. L. VII. 571.

II. *vb.* (1) *tr.* (*a*) to crowd, fill : P. L. X. 1091, 1103 ; to supply abundantly : P. L. VII. 148.

(*b*) to visit often, resort to : P. L. XI. 317, 722.

(2) *intr.* to resort : P. L. XI. 838.

Fresh, (1) *adj.* (*a*) new : S. I. 3 ; not previously exerted, made, or known : P. L. II. 1012 ; P. R. IV. 570 ; L. 193.

(*b*) newly flowing, or pure ; *of blood* : P. L. VIII. 467.

(*c*) pure and refreshing ; *of dew, water* : P. L. I. 771 ; IV. 229, 326 ; XI. 135, 845 ; S. A. 547 ; L. 29 ; *of air* : P. L. VIII. 515.

(*d*) cool and refreshing *shade* : P. L. V. 203 ; cool and delightful; *of work* : P. L. V. 125.

(*e*) unobliterated : P. L. XII. 15.

(*f*) blooming, gay, unfaded ; *of flowers, fields* : P. L. V. 20, 636 ; VI. 784 ; P. R. IV. 435 ; L. 138 ; S. XX. 7 ; *sup.* : P. L. IX. 1041 ; blooming and beautiful; *of the earth* : P. L. VIII. 274.

(*g*) pure and radiant : P. L. XII. 423.

(*h*) full of new life and vigour : P. R. IV. 567.

(*i*) young, vigorous : C. 670.

(*j*) early *morning* : P. L. IV. 623*l*

(2) *adv.* (*a*) newly, anew : S. A. 1317.

(*b*) refreshingly : S. A. 10.

Fresh-blown, *adj.* newly blossomed : L'A. 22.

Freshet, *sb.* small stream of fresh water : P. R. II. 345.

Fret, *sb.* small ridge set across the finger-board of a musical instrument: P. L. VII. 597.

Fret, *vb. tr.* irritate, chafe: S. IX. 7.

Fretted, *part. adj.* wrought into fretwork: P. L. I. 717.

Friar, *sb.* (*a*) a member of one of the mendicant order: P. L. III. 474.

(*b*) **Friar's lantern,** the ignis fatuus or will-o'-the-wisp: L'A. 104.

Friend, *sb.* one who is attached to another by feelings of personal regard and preference: P. L. X. 11; XII. 129; P. R. II. 422, 425; S. A. 180, 189, 334, 492, 605, 1196, 1263, 1415, 1730; C. 76, 949; S. IX. 12; Ps. LXXXVII. 13; LXXXVIII. 33, 69; *vocative*: S. A. 187, 193, 202; S. XXII. 10; *of angels, vocative*: P. L. IV. 866; VI. 609; perhaps rather, follower, supporter: P. L. I. 264; VI. 38; *of God, Christ, angels* in relation to man: P. L. V. 229; IX. 2; X. 60.

Friendly, *adj.* (*a*) disposed to act as a friend, kind: P. L. VIII. 651; IX. 564, 772; S. A. 1508.

(*b*) befitting a friend: P. L. IV. 36; VIII. 9; S. A. 1078; C. 160.

(*c*) not hostile, disposed to peace: P. L. VI. 22; C. 488.

(*d*) favourable, propitious, salutary: C. 282, 678; *sup.*: P. L. V. 668.

Friendship, *sb.* the relation of being a friend: P. L. XI. 796; S. A. 495.

Frieze, *sb.* that part of the entablature which is between the architrave and the cornice: P. L. I. 716.

Frieze, *sb.* coarse woollen cloth: C. 722.

Fright, *vb. tr.* to terrify: P. L. I. 543; with *adv.* or *prep.* phrase: P. L. XI. 121; Il P. 138.

part. adj. **frighted,** terrified; *of chaos*: P. L. II. 994.

Fringed (*disyl.*), *part. adj.* bordered as if with a fringe: P. L. IV. 262. *See* **Rushy-fringed.**

Frisk, *vb. intr.* to skip, gambol: P. L. IV. 340.

Frith, *sb.* arm of the sea: P. L. II. 919.

Frivolous, *adj.* of little importance: C. 445.

Frizzled, *part. adj.* curled; *fig. of foliage*: P. L. VII. 323.

Fro, *adv.* away, back; *to and fro*: P. L. I. 772; II. 605, 1031; III. 533; VI. 328, 643, 665; S. A. 1649.

Frock, *sb.* **frock of mail,** coat of mail: S. A. 133.

Frog, *sb.* the animal *Rana*: P. L. XII. 177; S. XII. 5.

Frolic, *adj.* gay, joyous, merry: L'A. 18; *frolic of*: C. 59.

*From, *prep.* (1) of place; (*a*) noting the point of departure: P. L. I. 45; VII. 1; VIII. 111; *from—to,* with repeated *sb.*: P. L. VII. 433; IX. 51, 66.

(*b*) noting the first of two boundaries given in defining an extent in space: P. L. I. 74.

(*c*) noting an object left behind by one turning away: P. L. IX. 385, 834; X. 909.

(*d*) noting an object left on one side by one turning away: P. L. X. 670, 672.

(*e*) noting a place whence action is originated: P. L. IX. 782; X. 32; XII. 227; C. 276; whence a person directs his vision: P. L. I. 289, 310; VII. 137, 210; whence something comes or is brought: P. L. IX. 990; X. 22; C. 439.

(2) of time; noting the point of departure or reckoning: P. L. I. 19, 742; III. 5; VII. 638; VIII. 331, 424; X. 93.

(3) noting distance, absence: P. L. VIII. 192; IX. 433, 590, 642; away from, out of: P. L. IX. 790.

(4) noting abstention, freedom, privation, removal, separation: P. L. I. 27, 363; II. 168; III. 397; IV. 118; VII. 250, 567, 612; VIII. 119; IX. 292; after: P. L. VIII. 213.

(5) of change, difference; noting a condition changed for another: P. L. I. 85; VIII. 433; IX. 150, 917; *differing from*: P. L. VII. 71.

(6) of source: (*a*) noting derivation, source: P. L. I. 62; III. 61; V. 479; VII. 58; VIII. 602; X. 267; C. 828.

(*b*) noting a person or thing as a source of action: P. L. I. 111, 179; VIII. 344, 647; IX. 276; X. 140; by: P. L. VIII. 609.

(7) because of, on account of, owing to: P. L. I. 98, 113; IX. 333.

(8) followed by *advs.* or *preps.* ;
by *above*: P. L. II. 172; *about*: P.
L. VI. 426; *amidst*: P. L. V. 264;
among: P. L. XI. 100; *before*: P.
L. VI. 14; *beneath*: P. L. III. 526;
behind: P. L. I. 596; *betwixt*:
L'A. 82; *far*: P. L. III. 579;
forth: P. L. V. 712; *hence*: P.L.
III. 540; *midst*: P. L. VI. 28;
off: P. L. I. 184; *out*: P. L. X.
282; *on high*: Ps. IV. 17; *round*:
Ps. LXXXIV. 15; *thence*: P. L.
III. 53; *thenceforth*: P. L. XII.
109; *under*: P. L. XI. 740; *underground*: P. L. XI. 570; *whence*:
P. L. I. 75; *where*: P. L. VII.
284; *within*: P. L. IV. 64; *without*: P. L. IV. 65.

Front, (1) *sb.* (*a*) forehead or brow
as expressive of character : P. L.
II. 302; IV. 300; VII. 509; IX.
330; S. A. 496; P. 18.

(*b*) the foremost part of an army
or division of troops : P. L. IV.
865; VI. 558, 569, 611; XII. 592;
front to front : P. L. VI. 105; *fig.
of clouds* : P. L. II. 716; line of
battle : P. L. I. 563.

(*c*) the forepart of the body,
put for the whole body : P. L. II.
683; or the whole face *fig.* :
N. O. 39.

(*d*) **in front,** in a position directly ahead : P. L. XII. 632.

(2) *vb. tr.* to stand over against,
face : C. 30.

part. adj. **fronted,** drawn up in
line, or confronted by others :
P. L. II. 532.

Frontier, (1) *sb.* confines of one
country bordering on another : P.
L. II. 998.

(2) *adj.* lying on the frontier :
P. L. I. 466.

Frontispiece, *sb.* the pediment over
a gate : P. L. III. 506.

Frore, *part. adj.* frosty, intensely
cold : P. L. II. 595.

Frost, *sb.* (*a*) freezing cold : S. A.
1577; L. 47.

(*b*) frozen dew; *hoary frost* : P.
L. XI. 899.

Froth, *sb.* spume, foam : P. R. IV.
20.

Froth-becurled (becurlèd, *trisyl.*),
adj. covered with foam resembling
curls ; *of the sea* : Ps. CXIV. 8.

Frounce, *vb. tr.* to curl or frizz the
hair : Il P. 123.

Frown, (1) *sb.* (*a*) a knitting of the
brow in anger or displeasure : C.

446, 667; *of angels or death* : P.
L. II. 713, 720; VI. 260; *fig. of
night* : P. L. III. 424.

(*b*) manifestation of disfavour ;
of God : Ps. LXXX. 59, 68.

(2) *vb. intr.* to knit the brow in
anger or displeasure : S. A. 948;
C. 666; *of angels or death* : P. L.
II. 106, 719; IV. 924.

part. adj. **frowning,** stern : Ps.
LXXXV. 19.

Frugal, *adj.* not prodigal, sparing :
P. L. V. 324; P. R. IV. 134; *fig.
of nature* : P. L. VIII. 26.

Fruit, *sb.* (*a*) edible product of a tree
or other plant; *sing., collect.* : P. L.
IV. 147, 249, 422; V. 341; VII.
325, 540; VIII. 307, 320; IX. 621,
656, 659, 788; X. 550, 565; XI.
125; Ps. I. 9; *ripe* or *cooling fruit* :
P. L. XI. 535; C. 186; *pl.* : P. L.
IV. 332; V. 304, 390, 464; VIII.
147; IX. 745; P. R. II. 369; IV.
30; Ps. LXXXV. 52.

in combination or contrast with
flower, herb, plant ; *sing.* : P. L.
IV. 644, 652; V. 482 : VI. 475;
VII. 311; XII. 184; *pl.* : P. L.
VIII. 44, 527; X. 603; XI. 327;
P. R. II. 356; with *odours, plants* :
C. 712; with *blossoms* : P. L. IV.
148.

spec. the fruit of the vine :
P. L. V. 635; fruit of the fig-
tree : P. L. IX. 1101; of the
palm-tree : P. L. VIII. 212; the
forbidden fruit of the Tree of
Knowledge : P. L. I. 1; V. 58,
67, 83; IX. 577, 588, 616, 648,
661, 686, 731, 735, 741, 763, 776,
781, 798, 851, 869, 904, 924, 929,
972, 996, 1011, 1023, 1046, 1073;
X. 4, 13, 687; XI. 86, 413. ·

ambrosial fruit : P. L. VI. 475;
the fruit of the Tree of Life in the
garden of Eden, *sing.* : P. L. IV.
219; in heaven, *pl.* : P. R. IV. 589.

fig. of joy, bliss : P. L. XII. 551;
of sighs, prayers : P. L. XI. 26;
of beauty : C. 396.

(*b*) offspring, child : M. W. 30;
fruit of thy womb : P. L. X. 1053.

(*c*) effect, consequence, or result
of joy, love, superstition, etc. : P.
L. III. 67, 451.

See **First-fruit, Supper-fruit.**

Fruitage, *sb.* fruit collectively : P.
L. V. 427; X. 561.

Fruitful, *adj.* (*a*) fertile, productive :
P. L. V. 320; VIII. 96; S. A. 181;
Ps. LXXXIV. 23.

(*b*) producing offspring in abundance, prolific: P. L. v. 388; VII. 396, 531.

(*c*) productive *of deeds*: P. L. III. 337.

Fruition, *sb.* enjoyment: P. L. III. 307; IV. 767.

Fruitless, *adj.* useless: P. L. v. 215; IX. 648; unprofitable: P. L. IX. 1188.

Fruit-tree, *sb.* tree bearing fruit: P. L. v. 213; VII. 311.

Frustrate (frústratéd: P. R. IV. 609), (1) *vb. tr.* to bring to nothing, defeat, foil: P. L. II. 193; III. 157; P. R. IV. 609; S. A. 1149.

past part. **frustrate**; (*a*) of no effect, null: S. A. 589.

(*b*) defeated, balked: P. L. IX. 944; P. R. I. 180.

(2) *adv.* so as to be ineffectual or useless: P. L. XI. 16.

Fry, *sb.* young fishes just produced from the spawn: P. L. VII. 400.

Fuel, *sb.* combustible matter used in fires: Ps. II. 27; *fig.* that which inflames anger or resentment: S. A. 1351.

Fuelled, *part. adj.* supplied with fuel: P. L. I. 234.

Fugitive, (1) *adj.* fleeing from danger or pursuit: P. L. IX. 16; P. R. II. 308.

(2) *sb.* deserter: *of Satan or his angels*: P. L. II. 57, 700; IV. 923.

Fugue, *sb.* a polyphonic composition, in which one or more themes introduced by one part are repeated and developed by the others in succession: P. L. XI. 563.

Fulfil, *vb. tr.* (*a*) to bring to consummation, render perfect: P. L. XI. 602.

(*b*) to satisfy *justice, will, request*: P. L. v. 246; VI. 729; VII. 635; *malice*: P. L. III. 157; to satisfy the demands of *law*: P. L. XII. 404.

(*c*) to carry out *a promise*: P. L. VIII. 491; *a prophecy*: P. R. III. 177; IV. 381; S. A. 45; *a purpose, counsel*: P. L. VI. 675; P. R. I. 126.

(*d*) to perform or accomplish *a work*: P. L. I. 431; IX. 230; P. R. III. 182; S. A. 1661.

(*e*) to obey or follow *law*: P. L. XII. 402.

gerund, faithfulness to *obedience to the law*: P. L. XII. 396.

vbl. sb. **fulfilling**, fulfilment, completion: N. O. 106; the carrying out of prophecy: P. R. II. 108.

Fulgent, *adj.* shining, resplendent: P. L. x. 449.

Full, (1) *adj.* (*a*) having no empty space, filled: P. L. I. 797; C. 175; abundantly loaded with fruit: P. L. IX. 802.

(*b*) abounding in; *full of pomp, doubt, pain, peace, wonder, wrath,* etc.: P. L. I. 372; II. 147, 688; v. 517; VI. 622, 826; VII. 70; IX. 62, 1126; XI. 815; XII. 473; P. R. II. 34, 201; S. A. 526, 805; Ps. LXXXVI. 15; LXXXVII. 14; CXXXVI. 18.

(*c*) not defective or partial, complete, perfect, or entire *bliss, happiness, wrath,* etc.: P. L. IX. 819; x. 503, 951; P. R. III. 383; Cir. 23; N. O. 166; *consent, assent*: P. L. II. 24, 388; *harmony*: N. O. 132; *relation*: P. L. v. 556; *resplendence*: P. L. v. 720; *right,* etc.: S. A. 310, 869; Ps. LXXXI. 44; *sight*: S. XXIII. 8; adequate or mature *counsel*: P. L. I. 660.

(*d*) complete in time: P. L. XII. 301; P. R. I. 287; U. C. I. 7.

(*e*) complete in number: P. L. III. 332; IV. 687; VIII. 232; having none of the members absent, *full frequence*: P. R. I. 128; II. 130.

(*f*) complete in extent, magnitude, or measure: P. L. v. 639, 862; P. R. I. 67, 267; III. 405; S. A. 1573; C. 925; as much as one can bear: S. A. 214; having the disc wholly illuminated; *of the moon*: P. L. VII. 377; *full age*, years of maturity and discretion, or period of life which qualifies for something: P. R. IV. 380.

(*g*) exerting the utmost force; *full career*: S. II. 3; *full sail of wing*: P. R. IV. 562.

(*h*) intense, brilliant: P. L. III. 378.

(*i*) bountiful, liberal: C. 711, 772; Ps. CXXXVI. 86.

(2) *adv.* (*a*) very, exceedingly; with *adjs.* or *advs.*: P. L. II. 655; x. 65; XI. 675; D. F. I. 10; V. Ex. 70; N. O. 88; Ps. II. 19; LXXXV. 32; LXXXVIII. 30; *full high*: P. L. I. 536; Ps. LXXXIII. 8; *full oft*: P. L. II. 763; S. A.

759; A. 42; *full soon*: P. L. II. 805; VI. 834; Ps. III. 11.

(*b*) exactly, directly: P. L. IV. 784.

(*c*) fully, completely, quite; with numeral: P. R. I. 303; with *vbs.* or *parts.*: P. L. II. 1054; VI. 720; P. R. I. 14; II. 83.

(3) *sb.* at full, fully, completely: P. L. I. 641.

Full-blazing, *adj.* shining at the height of its power: P. L. IV. 29.

Full-grown, *adj.* having attained full size: P. L. VII. 456; *full-grown age*, the age of manhood: C. 59.

Full-orbed, *adj.* having the orb complete: P. L. V. 42.

Full-voiced, *adj.* having a voice rich and complete in volume: Il P. 162.

Fully, *adv.* completely, entirely, thoroughly: P. L. VIII. 180; X. 79, 374; P. R. I. 4; S. A. 1712.

Fulmine, *vb. intr.* to thunder; *fig. of eloquence*: P. R. IV. 270.

Fulness, *sb.* (*a*) completeness, perfection: P. L. III. 225.

(*b*) **fulness of time**, the destined time: P. R. IV. 380.

Fume, (1) *sb.* (*a*) smoke: P. L. IV. 168.

(*b*) noxious exhalation rising to the brain from the stomach: P. L. IX. 1050; S. A. 552.

(*c*) something light and empty as smoke: P. L. VIII. 194.

(2) *vb. intr.* (*a*) to emit smoke: P. L. XI. 18.

(*b*) to pass off, arise; *of incense*: P. L. VII. 600.

part. adj. emitting vapour; *of foaming water*: P. L. V. 6.

Function, *sb.* the special activity of the physical, intellectual, or moral powers: S. A. 596.

Funeral, (1) *adj.* pertaining to burial: S. A. 1732.

(2) *sb.* burial, obsequies: M. W. 46.

Fur, *sb.* dressed skins of certain animals used for the ornamentation of garments, as a distinguishing characteristic of a certain class of people; *hence*, sect, school: C. 707.

Furious, *adj.* (*a*) full of fury, raging, frantic: P. L. IV. 4; VI. 357; VIII. 244; S. A. 836; Ps. LXXXIII. 5.

(*b*) raging, tempestuous; *of the wind*: P. L. VII. 213; *of water*: P. L. XI. 854.

(*c*) characterized by tempestuosity or violent energy: P. L. VI. 86.

Furlong, *sb.* eighth part of a mile: C. 946.

Furnace, *sb.* enclosed place for maintaining a hot fire: P. L. I. 62; N. O. 210.

Furnace-mouth, *sb.* opening to a furnace: P. L. II. 888.

Furniture, *sb.* outfit, equipment: P. L. IX. 34.

Furrow, *sb.* narrow trench in the earth made by a plough: C. 292.

Furrowed, *part. adj.* plowed: L'A. 64.

Further, (1) *adj.* (*a*) extending beyond: P. L. IV. 174.

(*b*) additional, more, new: P. L. X. 555; XI. 193; XII. 620; S. A. 520; C. 321; anything more: C. 580; *no further*, nothing more: P. L. X. 170, 793.

(2) *adv.* (*a*) to a greater distance: S. A. 2.

(*b*) besides, in addition: P. L. IV. 533; X. 1062; XI. 839; S. A. 1252, 1499.

(3) *vb. tr.* to promote, forward: A. 39.

Fury, *sb.* (*a*) fierce passion: P. L. V. 808; ungovernable rage, wild anger: P. L. I. 179; II. 61, 728; X. 240; Ps. VII. 22; the rage of battle, fierceness in conflict: P. L. VI. 207.

(*b*) fierce violence; *of things*: P. L. I. 235; II. 938; VI. 591.

(*c*) one of the goddesses of vengeance: P. L. II. 596, 671; P. R. IV. 422; C. 641; not definitely *personified*: P. L. VI. 859; used for Atropos, one of the Fates: L. 75; applied to Sin and Death on the earth after the transgression of man: P. L. X. 620.

Fusil, *adj.* formed by casting: P. L. XI. 573.

Future (*futúre*: P. L. X. 840), (1) *adj.* to come, that will be: P. L. II. 222; VI. 502; VII. 183; X. 345, 840; XI. 114, 357, 764, 774, 870; P. R. I. 396; V. Ex. 72.

(2) *sb.* time to come: P. L. VI. 429; VII. 486; in combination with *present, past*: P. L. V. 582; or what will happen in the future: P. L. III. 78.

G

Gabble, *sb.* noisy and incoherent talk : P. L. XII. 56.

Gabriel, *sb.* the archangel, leader of the cherubim : P. L. IV. 549, 561, 781, 865, 877, 886, 1005 ; second in command of the celestial armies: P. L. VI. 46, 355 ; IX. 54 ; the messenger to Mary : P. R. I. 129 ; IV. 504.

Gadding, *part. adj.* straggling ; *of a vine* : L. 40.

Gades, *sb.* the Latin form for Cadiz, the city and province in the southern part of Spain : P. R. IV. 77.

Gadire (Gadíre, *Gr.* Γάδειρα), *sb.* Cadiz : S. A. 716.

Gain, (**1**) *sb.* (*a*) profit, advantage : P. L. II. 1009 : opposed to *loss* : T. 8.

(*b*) riches, wealth : P. R. III. 29.

(**2**) *vb. tr.* (*a*) to secure or obtain : P. L. I. 190 ; IV. 512 ; VIII. 122, 435 ; IX. 332, 529 ; X. 373 ; XI. 768 ; XII. 223 ; P. R. I. 391 ; II. 419 ; S. A. 353 ; S. IX. 14; XX. 5 ; with *dat.* and *acc.* : S. A. 835 ; to obtain or win *dominion, a throne*, etc. : P. R. II. 434, 486 ; IV. 211 ; *gerund*: P. R. IV. 471; to secure because of position : P. L. III. 428 ; to attain ; with *prep. inf.* : P. L. IX. 933.

(*b*) to obtain the friendship or support of, win : P. L. I. 471 ; VI. 907 : P. R. I. 397.

(*c*) to obtain in marriage : P. L. X. 901, 902.

(*d*) to secure by way of increment : P. L. V. 324.

(*e*) to reach, arrive at : P. L. V. 174 ; XII. 199.

Gainsay, *vb. absol.* to speak against, oppose : P. L. IX. 1158.

'Gainst, *prep.* (*a*) in contact with : C. 354.

(*b*) in hostility to : U. C. II. 8 ; Petr. 2.

(*c*) in protection from : C. 640. *See* **Against.**

Gait, *sb.* manner of walking : P. L. IX. 389 ; Il P. 38 ; *of angels* : P. L. IV. 568, 870 ; XI. 230 ; *of animals* : P. L. VII. 411.

Galasp, *sb.* S. XI. 9. *See* **Macdonnel.**

Galaxy, *sb.* the Milky Way : P. L. VII. 579.

Gale, *sb.* breeze ; *fresh* or *gentle gale* : P. L. IV. 156 ; VIII. 515 ; P. R.

II. 364 ; *fig. flattering gales* : Hor. O. 11.

Galilean, *adj.* of Galilee : P. R. III. 233 ; *Galilean Lake*, Lake of Gennesaret : L. 109.

Galilee, *sb.* the northernmost division of Palestine : P. R. I. 135.

Galileo, *sb.* the astronomer : P. L. V. 262.

Gallaphrone, *sb.* a king of Cathay, the father of Angelica: P. R. III. 340. *See* **Angelica.**

Gallia, *sb.* Gaul : P. R. IV. 77.

Gambol, *vb. intr.* to leap or spring in sporting : P. L. IV. 345.

Game, *sb.* (*a*) sport, pastime : P. L. VI. 667 ; XI. 714.

(*b*) *pl.* athletic contests : P. L. IX. 33 ; S. A. 1312, 1602 ; *of angels* : P. L. IV. 551 ; *Olympian games* : P. L. II. 530.

(*c*) sport derived from the chase ; *fowl of game* : P. R. II. 342.

(*d*) that which is pursued in the chase, *fig.* : P. L. XII. 30.

(*e*) joke, jest ; *make a game of* : S. A. 1331.

Gamesome, *adj.* (*a*) sportive, playful : P. L. VI. 620.

(*b*) inciting to sport or play : C. 164.

Ganges, *sb.* the river of India : P. L. III. 436 ; IX. 82.

Gangrene, *vb. intr.* to become mortified : S. A. 621.

Ganymed, *sb.* the beautiful youth who was carried away by the gods to be the cup-bearer of Zeus : P. R. II. 353.

Gap, *sb.* opening, breach : P. L. VI. 861.

Gape, *vb. intr.* to open wide : P. L. VI. 577.

See **Wide-gaping.**

Garb, *sb.* dress, apparel ; *fig. reason's garb* : P. L. II. 226 ; C. 759.

Garden, (**1**) *sb.* enclosed piece of ground devoted to the cultivation of herbs, flowers, or trees, or laid out for pleasure : P. R. IV. 38 ; Il P. 50 ; *spec.* the garden of Eden, or Paradise " in the east of Eden " : P. L. III. 66 ; IV. 209, 215, 230, 285, 529, 789 ; V. 260, 368, 752 ; VII. 538 ; VIII. 299, 321, 326 ; IX. 206, 660, 662 ; X. 98, 116, 746 ; XI. 97, 118, 222, 261 ; P. R. I. 1 ; gardens of Hesperus : P. L. III. 568 ; C. 981 ; of Adonis or Alcinous : P. L. IX. 439.

(2) *vb. intr.* to cultivate a garden: P. L. IX. 203.

part. adj. **gardening,** expended or used in cultivating a garden: P. L. IV. 328; IX. 391.

Garden-mould, *sb.* rich earth suitable for a garden: P. L. IV. 226.

Garden-plot, *sb.* plot of ground used as a garden: P. L. IX. 418.

Garden-tree, *sb.* tree of a garden: P. L. IX. 657.

Garish, *adj.* glaring; *of the sun*: Il P. 141.

Garland, *sb.* wreath of flowers or leaves: P. L. III. 362; IV. 709; IX. 840, 892; XI. 594; M. W. 21.

     attrib. that is a garland: C. 850.

Garrison, *vb. tr.* to station *troops* for defence, *fig.*: S. A. 1497.

Garrulity, *sb.* loquacity, talkativeness: S. A. 491.

Gash, *sb.* deep and wide wound: P. L. VI. 331.

Gasp, *vb. intr.* to catch the breath with open mouth because of astonishment: S. XI. 11.

Gate, *sb.* (*a*) large door, either the passageway or the movable barrier, giving entrance into a building, *pl.*: P. L. I. 761: C. 667; into a city, *pl.*: P. L. XI. 640; S. A. 1597; with proper name in context, *pl.*: P. R. III. 287, 311; IV. 61; S. A. 147; Ps. LXXXVII. 5; giving entrance into Paradise: P. L. IV. 178, 542, 579; XI. 190; XII. 638, 643; into heaven: P. L. III. 515; V. 253; *pl.*: P. L. I. 171; VII. 206, 565; N. O. 148; into hell: P. L. II. 873; X. 298, 418; *pl.*: P. L. II. 436, 631, 645, 648, 684, 776, 853, 884; IV. 382, 898, 967; VIII. 231, 241; X. 230, 231; *in all her gates,* throughout all her territory: P. R. IV. 624; giving entrance into the cave of light: P. L. VI. 4.

     (*b*) *fig.*: S. A. 560; the horizon where the sun rises: L'A. 59; *death the gate of life*: P. L. XII. 571; *Wisdom's gate*: P. L. III. 687.

     See **City-gate, Heaven-gate, Hell-gate, Palace-gate.**

Gath, *sb.* a city of the Philistines: P. L. I. 465; S. A. 266, 981, 1068, 1078, 1127, 1129.

Gather, *vb. tr.* (*a*) to bring together or assemble *an army*: P. R. III. 300.

     (*b*) to bring together *things*: P. L. V. 207; to collect *sticks, pebbles*: P. R. I. 316; IV. 330: to bring together into one mass *hail, water, scum*: P. L. VII. 283; C. 595; *gather heap,* pile up into a mass: P. L. II. 590.

     (*c*) to pluck or pick *flowers, fruits, leaves*: P. L. IV. 269; V. 343; IX. 852, 1111; *fig.*: P. L. IV. 271; XI. 537.

     (*d*) to infer, deduce by reasoning: P. L. X. 344.

     (*e*) to gain; *gather ground,* advance, make progress: P. L. XII. 631.

     part. adj. **gathered,** assembled or collected into one place; *of an army*: S. A. 251; *of sand*: P. L. X. 299; *of light*: P. L. VII. 363; X. 1070.

Gaudy, *adj.* gay and showy: N. O. 33; Il P. 6; C. 851.

Gaul, *sb.* the country of Europe: H. B. 8.

Gauntlet, *sb.* a glove forming part of defensive armour: S. A. 1121.

Gay, *adj.* (*a*) brilliant in colour, bright, showy, fine: P. L. IV. 149, 942; VII. 318, 444; VIII. 274; IX. 428; XI. 866; Il P. 8; C. 299; L. 47; *sup.*: P. L. XI. 186; *fig.*: V. Ex. 21; gorgeous, magnificent: P. L. I. 372.

     (*b*) richly or showily dressed: P. L. XI. 582, 615; S. A. 712.

     (*c*) brilliant; *gay rhetoric*: C. 790.

Gaza, *sb.* a city of the Philistines: P. L. I. 466; S. A. 41, 435, 981, 1558; the inhabitants of Gaza: S. A. 1729, 1752.

Gaze, I. *sb.* (*a*) an object eagerly looked on; *of Samson*: S. A. 34, 567.

     (*b*) intent look of admiration or wonder: P. L. III. 671; N. O. 70; *at gaze,* in the act of gazing: P. L. VI. 205; *in gaze,* gazing, lost in wonder: P. L. IV. 356; IX. 524.

     II. *vb.* (1) *intr.* to look vacantly: P. L. IV. 351; to look intently and eagerly: P. L. V. 47; IX. 535, 578, 611; with *on* or *upon*: P. L. V. 57; IX. 539, 735; A. 43; C. 54, 736; *fig. of the sun*: P. L. XI. 845.

     (2) *tr.* to look at intently: P. L. III. 613; V. 272; VIII. 258; P. R. I. 414.

Gear, *sb.* affair, business: C. 167.

Gehenna, *sb.* the valley of Hinnom, called Gehenna, or the valley of lamentation, from the cries of the children who were there thrown into the arms of Moloch. Afterwards through hatred of the place, the Jews cast into this valley all kinds of refuse, even the dead bodies of animals and criminals. From the fire, either that used in sacrifice or that necessary to consume the bodies, it was called *Gehenna of Fire*; whence it became a type of hell: P. L. I. 405.

Gem, (1) *sb.* precious stone, jewel; always *pl.* : P. L. I. 538; II. 271; VI. 475; XI. 583; P. R. IV. 119; C. 22, 719; *orient gems* : P. L. III. 507; *oraculous gems* : P. R. III. 14; *fig. of stars* : P. L. IV. 649.

(2) *vb. tr.* to put forth *blossoms*: P. L. VII. 325.

General, (1) *adj.* not particular or special, but pertaining to or concerning all: P. L. I. 421; II. 773; S. A. 1524; *general doom*; P. L. III. 328; XI. 76; *general sire, mother, ancestor* : P. L. IV. 144, 492, 659; relating to all, common, public : P. L. II. 481.

(2) *sb.* leader, commander; *of Satan* : P. L. I. 337.

Generally, *adv.* usually, commonly : P. R. I. 387.

Generate, *vb. tr.* to bring into existence *mankind* : P. L. X. 894; *animals*, said of the waters: P. L. VII. 387, 393.

Generation, *sb.* (*a*) manner or way of creating : P. L. VII. 102.

(*b*) race, family : P. L. I. 653; XI. 344.

Generous, *adj.* noble-minded, magnanimous : P. R. II. 479; S. A. 1467.

Genezaret, *sb.* the Lake of Gennesaret in Palestine: P. R. II. 23.

Genial, *adj.* (*a*) pertaining to or presiding over marriage : P. L. IV. 712; VIII. 598.

(*b*) generative, contributing to propagation; *of moisture* : P. L. VII. 282.

(*c*) pertaining to innate disposition, natural : S. A. 594.

Genius, *sb.* tutelary deity *of dale, spring* : N. O. 186; *of the shore* : L. 183; *of the wood* : Il P. 154.

Gentile, *sb. pl.* people not of the Jewish nation : P. L. IV. 277; XII. 310; P. R. I. 456; III. 425; IV. 227, 229; S. A. 150, 500; Ps. II. 1.

Gentle, (1) *adj.* (*a*) noble, generous; *of persons* : C. 236; L. 92; in direct address : P. L. IV. 366; M. W. 47.

(*b*) tame, docile : P. L. IV. 404; XI. 188.

(*c*) not violent or severe ; *of the sun, wind*, etc. : P. L. III. 585; IV. 156, 806; VIII. 515; X. 93; *sup.* : P. R. II. 364.

(*d*) mild or lenient *sway* : P. L. IV. 308.

(*e*) kind, gracious; *of persons* : C. 824; L. 19; in direct address : A. 26; C. 271, 304, 900; *of angels or spirits* : P. L. VIII. 648; XI. 421; P. R. II. 375; *fig. of things* : N. O. 38; C. 337.

(*f*) loving, tender : P. L. IV. 337.

(*g*) merciful, compassionate : S. VIII. 6.

(*h*) mild or kindly in action; *gentle hand, voice, sleep*, etc. : P. L. IV. 488; V. 37, 130; VIII. 287; XII. 435, 595.

(*i*) indicating kindness or mildness; *gentle expression, looks, brow* : P. L. IX. 527; X. 919; P. R. III. 215.

(*j*) not harsh *usage* : C. 681.

(*k*) quiet, tranquil : P. 52.

(2) *adv.* gently, not harshly, *comp.* : S. A. 788.

Gentleness, *sb.* kindness : C. 843.

Gently, *adv.* (*a*) in a gentle manner, mildly, kindly, tenderly : P. L. I. 529; VII. 81; VIII. 293; IX. 431; XI. 298, 758; C. 575.

(*b*) softly, quietly : P. L. IV. 259; Il P. 60; not violently or intensely : P. L. III. 583.

German, *sb.* a native of Germany : P. R. IV. 78.

Geryon, *sb.* the fabulous monster who was king in Erytheia, an island of Spain; *Geryon's sons*, the Spanish : P. L. XI. 410.

Gesture, *sb.* action or motion of the body, as expressive of character or emotion : P. L. I. 590; IV. 128; VIII. 489; IX. 460; C. 464.

Get, *vb.* (*pret.* and *past part.* got) (1) *tr.* (*a*) to procure or obtain *friends, name*; with *acc.* and *dat.* : P. L. I. 365; XII. 45; P. R. II. 425.

(b) to gain, win, or obtain *power, riches*: P. L. x. 579; P. R. ii. 427; *evil*: P. L. ix. 1072; xi. 87.

(c) to obtain; *get hold of*: P. R. iv. 480; *get head*, obtain control: P. R. ii. 64.

(d) to gain possession of *a person*: D. F. I. 9.

(e) to meet with, suffer: S. xii. 8.

(*f*) to beget, procreate, *fig.*: P. 56.

(g) to cause or procure to be, succeed in bringing; *had got him down*: U. C. i. 6; *get into my power*: S. A. 798.

(h) *refl.* to betake oneself, go: P. R. iv. 193.

(i) to bring into a specified state; with two *acc.*: P. L. vii. 464.

(2) *intr.* (a) to succeed in going: P. L. ix. 594.

(b) **get together**, meet, assemble: P. R. ii. 28.

See **Ill-got.**

Ghastly, *adj.* shocking to look upon, horrible: P. L. vi. 368; xi. 481; C. 1611; hideous and grisly: P. L. ii. 846.

Ghost, *sb.* (a) spirit of a deceased person, as wandering over the earth at night: N. O. 234; C. 434.

(b) evil spirit, demon: P. R. iv. 422.

(c) **Holy Ghost**, third person of the Trinity: P. R. i. 139.

Giant, *sb.* a being in human form but of monstrous size: H. B. 9; in mythology, a son of Uranus and Ge: V. Ex. 93; in the Bible (cf. Gen. vi. 4): P. L. iii. 464; xi. 642, 688; S. A. 148; *spec.* Harapha: S. A. 1068, 1181.

attrib. composed of or being giants: P. L. i. 576, 778; S. A. 1247.

Giant-angel, *sb. pl.* Satan and his angels, as at war with God; doubtless with allusion to the mythical giants who made war on the gods: P. L. vii. 605.

Giantship, *sb.* a descriptive title of Harapha: S. A. 1244.

Gibeah, *sb.* a city of the tribe of Benjamin: P. L. i. 504.

Gibeon, *sb.* a city of the Hivites, lying northwest of Jerusalem: P. L. xii. 265.

Gibraltar, *sb.* the promontory on the southern coast of Spain: P. L. i. 355.

Giddy, *adj.* (a) affected with vertigo, dizzy: Ps. lxxxiii. 51.

(b) governed by mere impulse, flighty: P. R. iv. 410.

Gideon, *sb.* the leader who delivered Israel from the Midianites: S. A. 280; (cf. Judg. vi. 15) P. R. ii. 439.

Gift, *sb.* (a) action of giving, bestowal: P. L. v. 366; ix. 540; P. R. ii. 381; power of giving, or in sense (b): P. L. ix. 806.

(b) thing given or bestowed, present: P. L. v. 317; viii. 494; P. R. ii. 391; iii. 116; iv. 169; Ariosto. ii. 3; *said of the earth*: P. L. xi. 340; *of the Land of Canaan*: P. L. xii. 138; *of Eve*: P. L. v. 19; x. 138; *of sleep*: P. L. iv. 735.

(c) faculty, endowment, or power bestowed by God or the gods, grace; *of beauty, strength*, etc.: P. L. iv. 715; viii. 220; x. 153; xi. 57, 612, 636; P. R. ii. 137; S. A. 47, 59, 201, 358, 577, 589, 679, 1026, 1354, 1500; S. xix. 10; the power miraculously bestowed upon the apostles and other early Christians: P. L. xii. 500; endowment bestowed by nature: C. 754.

(d) inherent power: P. L. vi. 626.

See **Heaven-gifted.**

Gigantic, *adj.* characteristic of giants; *gigantic size*: S. A. 1249; *deeds*: P. L. xi. 659.

Gild, *vb.* (*past part.* gilded; *pret.* not used) *tr.* to make bright and shining like gold; *of the sun*: P. L. iii. 551; *of the planet Venus*: P. L. vii. 366.

part. adj. **gilded**, overlaid with gold: P. R. iv. 53; C. 95.

Gill, *sb. pl.* breathing organs of animals living in the water: P. L. vii. 415.

Gin, *sb.* snare, *fig.*: S. A. 933.

Gin, *vb.* (only in *pret.* gan) *intr.* to begin, commence; with *simple inf.* indicating the action begun: P. L. vi. 60; ix. 1016; x. 710; P. R. iv. 410.

Gird, *vb.* (*pret.* girt; *past part.* girded: P. L. ix. 1096; P. R. i. 120; girt: P. L. iv. 276; vii. 194; ix. 1116; S. A. 1415; N. O.

202 ; C. 214, 602) *tr. (a)* to bind
round or encircle *the waist* with a
girdle : P. L. v. 281 ; IX. 1113,
1116 ; *fig.* to invest, endue : P. L.
VII. 194.

(b) to fasten *weapons* to one's
person by a belt : P. L. VI. 714 ;
to secure *armour, clothing* with a
girdle : P. L. VI. 542 ; P. L. IX.
1096.

(c) to surround as with a girdle :
P. L. VIII. 82.

(d) to encircle, enclose : *of a
river* : P. L. IV. 276 ; *of a crowd
of people* : S. A. 1415; C. 602 ; *of
immaterial things* : P. R. I. 120 ;
N. O. 202 : *girt round* : S. A. 846;
or perhaps, to clothe ; *of wings* :
C. 214.
See **Sea-girt.**

Girt, *sb.* saddle-girth : U. C. I. 1.

Give, *vb.* (*pres. 2d sing.* giv'st : P.
L. IX. 810; *pret.* gave ; *2d sing.*
gav'st : P. L. II. 865; VII. 493;
x. 138 ; *past part.* given) **(1)** *tr.*
(a) to bestow *a thing* gratuitously :
P. L. IX. 805 ; P. R. II. 481 ; D.
F. I. 76 ; C. 648, 703 ; with *to* :
C. 525, 637, 676 ; with *dat.* : P. L.
VI. 322; x. 138 ; C. 638 ; with
dat. and *of* : P. L. IX. 996 ; x.
143 ; or perhaps rather, to cause
to have as one's share, apportion
or assign *a place* : P. L. IV. 381 ;
P. R. IV. 185; with *to* : P. L.
VIII. 171, 339 ; P. R. IV. 163, 164,
182, 186 ; with *dat.* : P. L. IV.
380 ; VIII. 319 ; *a thing,* with *to* :
P. L. v. 404; with *dat.* : P. L.
VII. 541.

(b) to confer, grant, or bestow
authority, power, etc. : P. L. VIII.
545 ; XII. 66 ; C. 9 ; with *to* : P.
L. VI. 887 ; P. R. IV. 104 ; S. A.
1054 ; with *dat.* : P. L. III. 318 ;
IV. 430 ; v. 740; x. 244 ; XII.
67 ; P. R. III. 251 ; IV. 104 ; with
dat. and *prep. inf.* : P. L. I. 736 ;
III. 243 ; IX. 818 ; XI. 339 ; to
bestow *being, life, strength,* etc. :
P. L. II. 153 ; IV. 1007 ; v. 485;
XI. 502 ; S. A. 359 ; C. 419 ; with
to : P. L. XII. 519 ; with *dat.* :
P. L. II. 865 ; IV. 483 ; v. 206,
858 ; S. A. 58, 378, 578, 1135,
1140.

(c) to allow, concede, or grant
pardon, peace, leave, odds, etc.,
with *to* : P. L. II. 332 ; with *dat.* :
P. L. IX. 951 ; XI. 255 ; S. A. 825;
A. 23 ; C. 26 ; S. XIII. 12.

(d) to hand over : P. L. II. 775;
give one's room, surrender one's
place : N. O. 78 ; *fig. give the
reins to,* leave without restraint :
S. A. 302, 1578.

(e) to commit or entrust *a person to* : C. 837.

(f) to restore *a person to* : S.
XXIII. 3.

(g) to inflict *a wound* ; with *dat.* :
P. L. XII. 392 : S. A. 1581.

(h) to emit or utter *a groan* : P.
L. IX. 1001.

(i) to impose and make known
in words *command, law, signal,*
etc. : P. L. I. 347, 776 ; v. 693;
x. 430 ; XII. 282, 300 ; P. R. IV.
556 ; with *to* : P. L. v. 822 ; XI.
72 ; with *dat.* : P. L. x. 123, 650;
XII. 287 ; *give one in charge* or
command : P. L. IV. 787 ; P. R.
I. 449.

(j) to deliver *verdict, judgement* : P. L. IX. 10 ; S. A. 1228.

(k) to present for acceptance
account, confidence ; with *to* : P. L.
IV. 841 ; with *dat.* : C. 584 ; to
present or show *a sign* : P. L. XI.
182 ; with *of* : P. L. VIII. 514 ;
IX. 783 ; to show *proof of* : P. L.
III. 103 ; IV. 350 ; *proof to be* :
P. L. x. 385; to set *an example* :
S. A. 822.

(l) to be the origin of *a name
to* : P. L. IX. 40.

(m) to impart *information,
knowledge,* etc. ; with *dat.* : P. L.
v. 523 ; P. R. IV. 385 ; S. A. 1593;
V. Ex. 65 ; to make known *oracles* : P. R. I. 431.

(n) to assign *a thing a name* :
P. L. VII. 493 ; XI. 277.

(o) to assign or fix *a limit* : M.
W. 14.

(p) to impose or enjoin *a charge
to* : P. L. IV. 561 ; to prescribe
law to : P. L. XI. 49.

(q) to attribute or ascribe *glory
to* : P. R. IV. 315.

(r) to yield or furnish *light* : P.
L. VII. 345; with *to* : C. 199 ; to
furnish *access, occasion* : P. L. IX.
810 ; with *dat.* : P. L. v. 454.

(s) to cause to have or receive,
or be the source of *advantage,
appearance* ; with *dat.* : P. L. VI.
402 ; S. A. 1117 ; C. 156 ; *breath,
life, speech,* etc., with *to* : P. L.
IX. 266, 748 ; S. A. 1264 ; with
dat. : P. L. IX. 686 ; P. R. IV.
258 ; U. C. II. 11 ; *delight, ease,*

wish, etc.: P. L. VIII. 386; L'A.
151; Il P. 175; with *dat.*: P. L.
II. 157; v. 119; Cir. 11; to invest with *grace*; with *to*: C. 243;
to provide means or opportunity
for; with *to*: P. L. IV. 144.

(2) *intr.* (*a*) to bestow or confer
gratuitously: P. L. v. 403; P. R.
II. 393; IV. 161.

(*b*) to yield, submit: P. L. III.
299.

In combination with other words;
(*a*) with various sbs., the idea
of the phrase being that of the
vb. corresponding to the sb.; *give
answer*: C. 276; *attest*: P. R. I.
37; *cause*: P. R. I. 66; *convoy*:
C. 81; *effect*: P. L. VII. 175; *heed*:
P. L. IV. 969; *honour*: L'A. 37;
increase: M. W. 51; *respite*: C.
553; *support*: S. A. 1634; *thanks*:
A. 101.

(*b*) **give audience**, listen: P. L.
XII. 12.

(*c*) **give ear**, listen or give heed:
P. L. IX. 1067; Ps. v. 1; LXXX.
2; LXXXIV. 30; LXXXVI. 17.

(*d*) **give over** or o'er, abandon,
surrender: S. A. 121, 629; abandon hope: P. R. IV. 23.

(*e*) **give part**, cause to share:
S. A. 1453.

(*f*) **give for**, consider or account as: P. L. II. 14; S. A.
1697.

(*g*) **give up**, yield, surrender:
P. L. X. 488; P. R. I. 369, 442;
S. A. 236, 1209, 1215; to cause to
abandon: P. L. XI. 497.

(*h*) **give utterance**, speak: P.
L. IX. 1066; make known, reveal: P. R. III. 10.

(*i*) **give way**, leave the way
clear for: P. L. v. 252.

vbl. sb. **giving**, thing given,
gift: P. L. VI. 730.

See **Life-giving, Wisdom-giving.**

Giver, *sb.* one who bestows something upon another: P. R. II.
322; *esp. of God* or *angels*: P.
L. v. 317; VIII. 493; P. R. IV.
187; C. 775.

See **All-giver.**

Glad, (1) *adj.* (*a*) rejoiced, pleased,
joyous: P. L. III. 630; VI. 258;
VIII. 322; IX. 625; XI. 20; U. C.
I. 6; S. XXIII. 3; with *of*: P. L.
IX. 528; P. R. II. 53; IV. 441;
with *clause*: P. L. II. 1011; with
prep. inf.: P. L. III. 270; XI.
507; P. R. I. 477; or *adv.* (?) with

joy or pleasure: P. L. VIII. 245;
X. 383.

(*b*) filled with or expressive of
joy, or causing joy; *glad precipitance*: P. 'L. VII. 291; *sound*: L.
35; *tidings, news*: P. L. XII. 375;
S. A. 1444; *office*: S. A. 924;
solemnity: A. 39.

(*c*) full of brightness or beauty;
of sun, morn: P. L. IV. 150; VII.
386.

(2) *adv.* with pleasure, joyfully: P. L. v. 29, 92; X. 777.

Glade, *sb.* open space in a wood: P.
L. IV. 231; IX. 1085; Il P. 27;
C. 79, 532.

Gladly, *adv.* (*a*) with pleasure, joyfully, willingly: P. L. II. 1044;
VI. 21; VIII. 226; IX. 966; X.
775; XI. 332; XII. 366; S. A.
259; C. 413; Ps. LXXX. 75;
comp.: P. L. VI. 731.

(*b*) vigorously, thrivingly, *comp.*:
P. L. VIII. 47.

Gladness, *sb.* pleasure of mind, delight: Ps. IV. 32.

Gladsome, *adj.* (*a*) characterized by
joy: Ps. LXXXIV. 26.

(*b*) filled with joy: Ps. CXXXVI.
1.

Glance, (1) *sb.* (*a*) swift movement (?):
C. 884.

(*b*) sudden movement producing
a gleam of light: P. L. VII. 405;
the flash of light, gleam: P. L.
XI. 442; *lightning glance*: S. A.
1284.

(*c*) brief or rapid look: P. L.
VIII. 533; IX. 1034.

(2) *vb. intr.* (*a*) to strike obliquely
on *one object* and turn aside and
strike *on another*: P. L. X. 1054.

(*b*) to flash, sparkle; *of water*:
Ps. LXXXVII. 27.

part. adj. **glancing**, shooting:
C. 80.

Glare, (1) *sb.* fierce piercing look; *a
lion ... with fiery glare*: P. L. IV.
402.

(2) *vb.* (*a*) *tr.* to send forth or
shoot out *lightning*: P. L. VI. 849.

(*b*) *intr.* to look with a fierce
piercing stare; *of beasts*: P. L.
X. 714; P. R. I. 313.

Glass, *sb.* (*a*) the brittle and transparent substance: Ps. CXXXVI.
49.

(*b*) objects composed of that
substance; *spec.* a drinking-vessel:
C. 65, 651; a magic mirror: Il
P. 113; a telescope: P. L. I. 288;

v. 261; the lens of a telescope:
P. R. IV. 41.

(c) *fig.* **watery glass**, surface of
the water : P. L. XI. 844.

See **Prospective-glass.**

Glassy, *adj.* resembling glass; *glassy
sea, wave, floods* : P. L. VII. 619;
C. 861; Ps. CXIV. 17.

Glaucus, *sb.* a fisherman of Anthe-
don in Bœotia, who, having eaten
of a divine herb, became immortal,
and was changed into a sea-god.
He had a peculiar power of prophesy : C. 874.

Glazed, *part. adj.* fitted with a glass
or lens : P. L. III. 590.

Gleam, *sb.* (a) **fiery gleam,** the
brilliant light of fire : P. L. XII.
257; **watery gleam,** the smooth
shining surface of water : P. L.
IV. 461.

(b) dim or subdued light : C.
225; or beam, ray; *gleam of
dawning light*: P. L. III. 499.

Gleaming, *part. adj.* shining : P. R.
III. 326.

Glebe, *sb.* soil, ground : P. R. III.
259.

Glib, *vb. tr.* to make fluent or ready
in speech : P. R. I. 375.

Glide, *vb. intr.* to move smoothly
and easily through the water ; *of
fish* : P. L. V. 200; VII. 402; over
the ground or through the air; *of a
liquid* : P. L. XI. 568; *of mist*:
P. L. XII. 629; *of angels* : P. L.
IV. 555; IX. 159; XII. 630.

Glimmering, (1) *vbl. sb.* faint and unsteady light : P. L. I. 182.

(2) *part. adj.* (a) shining with
a faint light : P. L. II. 1037; N.
O. 75.

(b) faintly illuminated : Il P.
27; penetrated by feeble and in-
termittent rays of light : P. L. III.
429.

Glimpse, *sb.* (a) ray or glimmer *of
light*: P. L. VIII. 156; *of morn*:
L'A. 107.

(b) faint and transient appearance *of glory* : P. R. I. 93; *of
joy* : P. L. I. 524.

(c) transient view, glance : P.
L. IV. 867.

See **Lightning-glimpse.**

Glister, *vb. intr.* to glitter, shine,
sparkle : P. L. IV. 645, 653; VIII.
93; IX. 643.

part. adj. **glistering,** shining,
sparkling : P. L. III. 550; XI.
247; C. 219; L. 79.

Glitter, (1) *sb.* brilliancy, splendour :
P. L. X. 452.

(2) *vb. tr.* to gleam, sparkle,
shine : P. L. III. 366.

part. adj. **glittering,** gleaming,
sparkling, shining : P. L. I. 535;
IV. 656; v. 291, 592; P. R. IV.
54; N. O. 114; A. 81.

Globe, *sb.* (a) ball : P. L. VI. 590.

(b) celestial body having the
form of a sphere : P. L. V. 259;
spec. the earth : P. L. III. 722;
VII. 280; X. 671; P. R. I. 365;
the moon : P. L. I. 291; IV. 723;
the world : P. L. III. 418, 422,
498.

(c) compact body, company or
throng *of angels*: P. L. II. 512;
P. R. IV. 581; mass *of light* : N.
O. 110.

Globose, *adj.* spherical in form; *of
the moon* : P. L. VII. 357.

absol. globe, sphere : P. L. V.
753.

Globous, *adj.* globose; *of the earth* :
P. L. V. 649.

Gloom, *sb.* (a) indefinite degree of
darkness, the result of night or
the absence of light : P. L. X.
848; Il P. 80; C. 132; in hell :
P. L. I. 244, 544; II. 400, 858;
aery gloom, the air before the
creation of light; P. L. VII. 246;
shady gloom, dusk before dawn :
N. O. 77.

Gloomy, *adj.* (because of the blending of senses, the following is
only approximately an accurate
discrimination) (a) full of gloom,
dark, obscure; *of chaos* : P. L. I.
152; II. 976; *of the grave* : Ps.
LXXXVIII. 51; *of night* : S. A.
161; *of a wood* : C. 945; *of shade,*
sup. : P. L. X. 716.

(b) affected with or productive
of gloom, cheerless : P. R. I. 42;
having dark or sullen looks;
of Christ : P. L. VI. 832; or perhaps, stern, harsh ; *of Dis.* : P.
L. IV. 270; dark and dreary; *of
death* : P. L. III. 242; dark and
spectral : C. 470.

Glorify, *vb. tr.* (a) to render glorious,
obtain glory for : P. L. VI. 725;
N. O. 154.

(b) to ascribe honour to, exalt
with praise : P. L. III. 695; VII.
116; P. R. III. 113.

Glorious, *adj.* (a) possessing glory,
entitled to brilliant and lofty
renown; *of persons* : P. R. I. 8;

S. A. 363, 705 ; *of angels*, but also with some blending of sense (*c*) : P. L. II. 16 ; V. 567, 833 ; VI. 39 ; X. 537.

(*b*) conferring glory, worthy of or bringing brilliant and lofty renown; *of war, march*, etc. : P. L. I. 89; II. 179; X. 474; P. R. III. 70 ; S. XVI. 4; with *prep. inf.* : P. R. III. 71; S. A. 855; *of trial, revenge, work*, etc. : P. L. IX. 961, 1177 ; X. 391; P. R. IV. 634; S. A. 1660 ; S. XIV. 12 ; *of strength, arms, hand* : S. A. 36, 1130, 1581.

(*c*) splendid, brilliant, shining; *of God, Christ*, or *angels* : P. L. III. 139, 622; IV. 39 ; V. 309, 362; VII. 574 ; VIII. 464; XI. 211, 213 ; P. R. I. 242 ; N. O. 8 ; *of the brightness surrounding God* : P. L. III. 376 ; supreme in majesty : P. L. IV. 292.

(*d*) of splendid beauty or magnificence ; *of the heavens, the world* : P. L. IV. 658; V. 153; VII. 370; X. 721 ; *of a building, a city* : P. L. XII. 334 ; P. R. IV. 45, 546 ; P. 40.

(*e*) brilliant *colour* : P. L. III. 612.

See **Vain-glorious.**

Gloriously, *adv.* (*a*) illustriously : P. R. IV. 127'; S. A. 1752.

(*b*) splendidly, brilliantly : P. L. III. 323, 655.

(*c*) magnificently : S. A. 200.

Glory, I. *sb.* (**1**) desire for fame, honour, or renown: P. L. II. 484 ; III. 312 ; P. R. III. 41.

(**2**) exalted praise, honour, or renown : P. L. II. 564; III. 449 ; VI. 383; XI. 694; XII. 172 ; P. R. II. 227 ; III. 25, 38, 46, 47, 59, 60, 69, 88, 100, 105, 109, 134, 144, 160 ; IV. 315, 371, 536 ; S. A. 597, 1098 ; Ps. IV. 8 ; VII. 6 ; the honour or renown of God or angels : P. L. II. 386 ; III. 853 ; V. 839 ; VI. 290, 422 ; XII. 477 ; P. R. II. 48 ; III. 110, 143, 148 ; S. A. 303, 475, 1148, 1429 ; Ps. CXIV. 6.

(*b*) the honour of God as the end of creation : P. L. III. 164 ; P. R. III. 110, 123.

(*c*) praise or honour offered in adoration of God : P. L. VII. 182, 184, 187 ; VIII. 12 ; P. R. III. 114, 117, 120, 127.

(**3**) that which brings honour and renown, distinguished honour

or ornament : P. L. I. 110 ; VI. 701, 726 ; IX. 135 ; P. R. I. 454 ; S. A. 680 ; C. 592 ; said of a person : P. L. V. 29 ; X. 722 ; S. A. 179 ; just pride or exultation : P. L. V. 738.

(**4**) splendour or brilliance *of the sun* : P. L. IV. 32 ; *of the heavens* : P. L. VII. 499 ; *of angels* : P. L. I. 141, 594, 612 ; IV. 838 ; V. 839 ; X. 451 ; P. R. II. 386 ; *of saints* : L. 180.

(*b*) the splendour or the majesty of God or Christ : P. L. II. 265 ; III. 63, 133, 239, 388 ; V. 719 ; VI. 650, 792, 815 ; VII. 208, 219 ; X. 64, 86 ; XI. 333 ; XII. 371, 460, 546 ; P. R. I. 93 ; Cir. 20 ; Ps. LXXXV. 39 ; the absolute perfection of God : P. L. I. 370.

(*c*) God : P. L. VII. 747.

(*d*) dignity or majesty *of Satan* : P. L. II. 427.

(*e*) resplendent beauty *of man* : P. L. IX. 1115.

(*f*) brilliant colour, *pl.* : N. O. 143.

(**5**) the splendour and bliss of heaven : M. W. 61 ; *esp.* that enjoyed by Christ in the immediate presence of God : P. L. VI. 891 ; X. 226 ; XII. 456.

(**6**) magnificence, majesty, or power *of a king* : P. L. I. 39 ; P. R. III. 383 ; *of a city or kingdom* : P. L. XI. 384 ; P. R. III. 236 ; IV. 89 ; *pl.* : P. L. I. 573.

(**7**) state of exaltation and power : S. A. 167.

II. *vb. intr.* to rejoice proudly, exult; with *in* : P. L. X. 386; with *prep. inf.* : P. L. I. 239.

part. adj. **gloried,** honoured : S. A. 334.

Gloss, (**1**) *sb.* explanation : P. L. V. 435.

(**2**) *vb. intr.* to comment *upon* : S. A. 948.

Glossy, *adj.* shining : P. L. I. 672.

Glow, *vb. intr.* (*a*) to shine brightly : P. L. IV. 604 ; N. O. 75.

(*b*) to exhibit a strong bright colour, be red : P. L. VIII. 618 ; IX. 427, 887.

part. adj. **glowing** ; (*a*) emitting bright light and heat : P. L. III. 594 ; Il P. 79 ; C. 96.

(*b*) having the heightened colour of excitement : P. L. V. 10.

(*c*) brilliant in colour ; *of the violet* : L. 145.

Gloze, *vb. tr.* to use flattering words :
P. L. IX. 549.
part. adj. **glozing,** flattering,
deceitful : P. L. III. 93 ; C. 161.
Glut, (1) *sb.* (*a*) a surfeit of food; *of
that which death devours* : P. L. X.
990 ; *fig. engines...disgorging their
glut* : P. L. VI. 589.
(*b*) an excessively abundant harvest : Ps. IV. 33.
(**2**) *vb. tr.* to feed to repletion;
fig. glut the grave : P. L. III. 259 ;
refl. Time ... glut thyself : T. 4.
part. adj. **glutted,** swallowed
greedily ; *of that which sin and
death devour* : P. L. X. 633.
Glutinous, *adj.* gluey, viscid ; transferred epithet (*see* Heat) : C. 917.
Gluttonous, *adj.* characterized by or
arising from gluttony : P. L. XI.
533.
Gluttony, *sb.* excess in eating, *pl.* :
P. R. IV. 114 ; *personified* : C.
776.
Gnash, *vb. intr.* to grind the teeth
together for rage : P. L. VI. 340.
Gnaw, *vb. tr.* to bite off little by
little, eat into : P. L. II. 799.
Go, *vb.* (*pret.* went; *2d sing.* went'st :
P. L. XII. 610 ; P. R. IV. 216 ;
past part. gone ; *perf.* tenses
formed with the auxiliary *be* : P.
L. V. 91, 885 ; IX. 1055 ; P. R.
II. 39, 116 ; IV. 459 ; S. A. 1244 ;
U. C. II. 33 ; C. 107 ; L. 37, 38 ;
with *have* : P. L. IV. 994 ; VI. 670;
XI. 781 ; *doubtful* because of ab-
breviation; S. A. 997, 1350 ; U. C.
I. 18) *intr.* (*a*) to move on foot,
walk, opposed to *run* : P. L. VIII.
268.
to march : S. A. 1617 ; to dance :
L'A. 33.
with *pres. part.* indicating manner of moving : P. L. X. 177 ; L. 103.
(*b*) to move along, proceed,
travel : P. L. VI. 884 ; A. 78 ; Ps.
LXXX. 51 ; *go with speed* : P. L. V.
313 ; with *acc.* of time : P. L. III.
544 ; with cognate acc., *go an
errand* : P. L. II. 826 ; *said of
steps* : Ps. v. 24.
(*c*) to take a specified course :
P. L. IV. 126 ; *go well* : P. L.
XI. 781.
(*d*) to pour along through a
channel, flow : P. L. IV. 223.
(*e*) to be pregnant : M. W. 25.
(*f*) to be current : P. L. I. 651.
(*g*) to move from a place, leave,
depart : P. L. IV. 469 ; v. 91 ;

VIII. 48 ; IX. 382, 1156 ; XII.
617 ; P. R. II. 10; S. A. 967,
997, 999, 1244, 1350 ; N. O. 76 ;
L. 108 ; the *imper.* as a command,
permission, or request to depart :
P. L. II. 456, 1008 ; V. 229 ; VI.
44, 710; VIII. 646 ; IX. 372, 373 ;
X. 409 ; XII. 594 ; S. A. 954, 1237,
1427.
(*h*) to cease to be present, be
taken away or lost : P. L. II. 49 ;
IX. 1055 ; to come to an end : P.
R. IV. 459.
(*i*) to depart from life, die : L.
37, 38.
(*j*) to fall or be thrown down
to the ground : S. VIII. 12.
(*k*) to give up or deliver to
another person : U. C. II. 33.
(*l*) to take one's way, move or
proceed to a place or in a particular direction : P. L. VI. 782 ;
VII. 588 ; S. A. 1403 ; C. 648 ;
with *to* or *into* : P. L. IV. 739 ; V.
118 ; IX. 1099 ; X. 414 ; P. R. I.
211 ; IV. 216 ; S. A. 1146 ; Ps. V.
18 ; to proceed *thither, whither* :
P. L. IV. 456 ; X. 265 ; XII. 610 ;
P. R. II. 39 ; to proceed *before
one* : P. L. XII. 201 ; Ps. LXXXV.
53 ; the purpose of going indicated
by *simple inf.* : S. A. 1725 ; by
prep. inf. : P. L. X. 71 ; P. R. I.
340 ; *gone to bed* : U. C. I. 18 ; C.
107 ; *went to sleep* : P. R. II. 284 ;
going into danger : P. L. IX. 1157.
(*m*) to extend, reach ; *of a vine* :
Ps. LXXX. 48.
In combination with other words ;
(*a*) **go about,** set to work upon :
P. R. II. 98.
(*b*) **go back from—to,** cease to
follow and revert to : Ps. LXXX. 73.
(*c*) **go by the worse,** be defeated : S. A. 904.
(*d*) **go forth,** pass out of a place :
P. L. VIII. 44, 59 ; *of morn* : P. L.
VI. 12 ; the purpose indicated by
prep. inf. : P. L. VI. 686 ; IX.
847 ; be issued ; *of a decree* : P. L.
V. 885.
(*e*) **go light,** have nothing to
carry : U. C. II. 22.
(*f*) **go on,** move forward in
position : P. L. IV. 858 ; P. R.
IV. 484 ; in time : P. L. XII. 537 ;
continue speaking : C. 779.
(*g*) **go out,** move from within ;
of morn : L. 187.
(*h*) **go round about,** surround :
Ps. LXXXVIII. 67.

(i) **go to wrack**, be ruined : P. L. IV. 994 ; VI. 670.

(j) **go up, arise** : P. L. VII. 334 ; P. R. II. 116 ; advance to battle : S. A. 1190.

(k) **go with**, accompany : P. L. XI. 290 ; XII. 615 ; *go along with* : P. L. VI. 275 ; S. A. 1384.

vbl. sb. **going**, departure : P. L. XI. 290.

Goal, *sb.* limit or mark to be reached in a race : P. L. II. 531 ; *fig.* to be reached by the sun in its course round the earth : C. 100.

Goat, *sb.* the animal *Capra* : P. L. VI. 857 ; IX. 582 ; XII. 292 ; S. A. 1671 ; C. 71.

Goblin, *sb.* an evil or mischievous spirit : C. 436 ; Robin Goodfellow : L'A. 106 ; applied to death : P. L. II. 688.

*****God**, *sb.* (a) deity : P. L. I. 384, 435 ; XI. 696 ; P. R. I. 117 ; II. 171 ; III. 430 ; IV. 56 ; S. A. 441, 529, 545 ; N. O. 224 ; A. 79 ; the *context* specifying a deity of Babylon, Chaldæa, or Syria : P. L. I. 475 ; XII. 122, 129 ; Belus : P. L. I. 720 ; of Egypt : P. L. I. 481, 489 ; N. O. 211 ; Serapis : P. L. I. 720 ; of Greece or Rome : P. L. I. 508, 509 ; P. R. IV. 342 ; Æsculapius : P. L. IX. 506 ; Hymen : M. W. 18 ; Neptune : Hor. O. 16 ; of Philistia : S. A. 859, 896, 899 ; Dagon : S. A. 1145, 1340, 1621 ; N. O. 199 ; applied to idols : P. L. XII. 120 ; to men : P. L. III. 470 ; P. R. III. 81 ; applied to men of high authority as representative of God : Ps. LXXXII. 3, 21 ; to Eve as obeyed by Adam : P. L. X. 145 ; to the sun in its apparent supremacy : P. L. III. 33.

(b) the Supreme Being, *esp.* as the Creator and Ruler of all things, the Father of Christ and of mankind, the Avenger of the rebel angels, the Rewarder of good and the Punisher of evil : P. L. I. 12, 26, 42, 73 ; II. 368, 499, 1030 ; III. 3, 10 ; IV. 152, 202 ; *the living God* : P. L. XII. 118 ; S. A. 1140 ; *the only God* : P. L. XII. 562 ; *God omnipotent* : P. L. IX. 927.

(c) Christ : N. O. 16.

(d) divine being, usually an appellation of angels, but sometimes apparently of a higher

order of beings : P. L. I. 116, 138, 240, 629 ; II. 352, 391, 868 ; III. 341 ; IV. 526 ; V. 59, 70, 71, 77, 81 ; VI. 156, 452 ; VII. 329 ; IX. 100, 164, 489, 547, 708, 710, 712, 804, 838, 866 ; X. 90, 502 ; XI. 271 ; *esp.* applied to Satan : P L. II. 478 ; VI. 99 ; P. R. IV. 192, 203, 495 ; contrasted with angels : P. L. I. 570 ; II. 108 ; VI. 301, 366 ; IX. 937.

See **Demi-god, Wood-god.**

Goddess, *sb.* female deity : P. L. XI. 615 ; P. R. II. 156 ; D. F. I. 48 ; A. 18 ; C. 267 ; *spec.* Cotytto : C. 128 ; Diana : H. B. 1 ; Euphrosyne : L'A. 11 ; Melancholy : Il P. 11, 132 ; Sabrina : C. 842, 865, 902 ; Urania : P. L. VII. 40 ; Venus : P. L. V. 381 ; applied to Eve : P. L. V. 78 ; IX. 547, 732 ; to sin : P. L. II. 757.

Goddess-like, *adj.* like that of a goddess : P. L. VIII. 59 ; IX. 389.

Godhead, *sb.* (a) divine nature, deity : S. A. 1153 ; used with reference to persons : P. L. III. 206 ; IX. 790, 877.

(b) the divine nature of God, Deity ; without *article* : P. L. VII. 586 ; with *poss. pron.* : P. L. II. 242 ; as revealed in Christ : P. L. XII. 389 ; N. O. 227 ; *filial Godhead*, Christ : P. L. VI. 722 ; VII. 125.

Godless, *adj.* not owning the authority of God : P. L. VI. 49, 811.

Godlike, *adj.* (a) resembling God ; *of angels* : P. L. I. 358 ; V. 351 ; VI. 67 ; VII. 110 ; VIII. 249 ; S. A. 29 ; *of men* : P. R. IV. 348.

(b) resembling that of God or divine beings ; *of acts*, etc. : P. L. XII. 427 ; P. R. I. 188, 386 ; P. 24 ; *of appearance* : P. L. II. 511 ; *of joy, power*, etc. : P. L. III. 307 ; VI. 301 ; P. R. III. 21 ; IV. 602 ; *of food* : P. L. IX. 717.

quasi-*adv.* after the fashion of divine beings : P. L. IV. 289.

Gold, (1) *sb.* (a) the most precious metal : P. L. I. 682, 690, 717 ; II. 271, 947 ; III. 352, 506, 541, 595 ; IV. 238, 554 ; V. 356, 442, 759 ; VI. 110, 475 ; VII. 577 ; XII. 250, 253, 363 ; P. R. I. 251 ; IV. 60 ; golden ornaments : P. L. I. 483 ; probably, gold dust : P. L. II. 4 ; *potable gold*, the aurum potabile of the alchemists : P. L. III. 608 ; *blooming gold*, the golden fruit of

the Garden of the Hesperides :
C. 394 ; *fig. of hair* : P. L. IV. 496.

(*b*) money, wealth, riches : P.
R. II. 425 ; S. A. 389, 831, 849,
958, 1114 ; S. X. 3 ; XVII. 8.

(*c*) drinking vessel made of
gold : P. L. V. 634.

(*d*) golden or shining garments:
P. L. VI. 13.

(*e*) splendour, magnificence: P.
L. I. 372.

(*f*) ideal happiness and prosperity ; *the age of gold* : N. O.
135.

(*g*) bright golden colour : P. L.
III. 642 ; V. 282 ; VII. 406, 479 ;
IX. 429, 501, 578 ; the colour at
sunrise or sunset : P. L. IV. 596 ;
V. 187 ; *vegetable gold*, the golden
fruit of the Tree of Life in the
garden of Eden : P. L. IV. 220.

(2) *adj.* (*a*) made of gold : P. R.
IV. 118.

(*b*) radiantly beautiful : Hor.
O. 9.

Golden, *adj.* (*a*) consisting of gold :
P. L. I. 715 ; C. 880, 933, 983 ; *of
altar, chain, hinges, seat*, etc. : P.
L. I. 796 ; II. 1005, 1051 ; IV.
997 ; V. 255, 713 ; VII. 207, 225,
365, 600 ; XI. 18, 24 ; P. R. IV.
548 ; *of crown, shield*, etc. : P. L.
III. 625 ; VI. 102, 527 ; P. R. II.
459 ; *of harps* : P. L. III. 365 ;
VII. 258, 597 ; S. M. 13 ; V. Ex.
38 ; *of wings* : C. 214 ; Il P. 52 ;
of key, sceptre, etc., as a symbol of
benevolence or goodwill : P. L.
II. 328 ; V. 886 ; C. 13 ; L. III. ;
S. XIV. 7 ; as exciting love : P. L.
IV. 763.

(*b*) **golden lustre**, lustre of gold :
P. L. I. 538.

(*c*) abounding in gold : P. L.
XI. 392 ; P. R. IV. 74.

(*d*) rich in magnificence or splendour : P. R. III. 277.

(*e*) resembling gold in colour
and brightness : P. L. III. 572 ;
VI. 28 ; *of flower, fruit* : P. L. IV.
148, 249 ; C. 633 ; *of hair* : P. L.
IV. 305 ; Hor. O. 4.

(*f*) most delightful, happy, or
prosperous : P. L. III. 337 ; L'A.
146.

Golden-tressed (tressèd, *disyl.*), *adj.*
having hair of the colour and
brightness of gold ; *fig. of the sun* :
Ps. CXXXVI. 29.

Golden-winged (wingèd, *disyl.*), *adj.*
having golden wings : D. F. I. 57.

Golgotha, *sb.* the place where Christ
was crucified : P. L. III. 477.

Goliath, *sb.* the famous giant of
Gath : S. A. 1249.

Gonfalon, *sb.* banner : P. L. V. 589.

Good, (1) *adj.* (*a*) excellent in its
nature and therefore well-adapted
to its ends : P. L. II. 940 ; C. 703,
704 ; T. 14 ; *esp. of what God
creates* : P. L. VII. 249, 309, 337,
353, 395, 549, 556 ; IX. 605, 606,
899 ; X. 138, 618 ; discerning or
acute *intellect* : S. XI. 4.

(*b*) an epithet of courteous address : C. 277, 307, 497, 512, 609.

(*c*) noble ; *of persons* : A. 33.

(*d*) commendable, praisewor-
thy : P. L. IX. 233.

(*e*) honourable : P. L. XII. 47.

(*f*) morally excellent ; *of persons* : P. L. I. 418 ; IV. 838 ; V.
525 ; IX. 465 ; XII. 538 ; P. R. III.
114 ; IV. 535 ; C. 703 ; S. XII. 12 ;
Ariosto II. 4 ; Hor. Epist. 1 ; upright, honourable : P. R. III. 57 ;
S. XI. ; consummately and essen-
tially upright and benevolent ; *of
God or Christ* : P. L. III. 310 ; IV.
414 ; V. 826 ; Ps. LXXX. 70 ;
LXXXVI. 13 ; applied to angels in
something of the same sense : P.
L. II. 1033 ; C. 658 ; *of actions* :
S. XIV. 5.

(*g*) kind or benevolent *to* : P. L.
VIII. 651 ; L'A. 184 ; Il P. 153.

(*h*) bringing or involving happiness : P. L. II. 848 ; *good luck* :
V. Ex. 59 ; agreeable or pleasing
news : S. A. 1538.

(*i*) advantageous, desirable,
right : P. L. II. 152 ; VIII. 445 ;
S. A. 350 ; Ps. LXXXV. 50 ; with
for : P. L. V. 491 ; fit, proper : C.
665 ; *as good*, in abbreviated
phrase, equivalent to, *it were as
good for me* : P. L. IX. 1154.

(*j*) adapted or suitable *for* :
P. L. II. 623 ; S. A. 1163.

(*k*) such as one ought to be : C.
764.

(*l*) valid or sound *reason* : P. L.
VIII. 443 ; P. R. IV. 526 ; S. A.
811 ; *proof* : P. L. IX. 967 ; just
cause : C. 489.

(*m*) fully adequate or sufficient
example : P. L. XI. 809 ; *heed,
courage* : S. A. 1230, 1381 ; *success* : S. A. 1454.

(2) *sb.* or *absol.* (*a*) that which
is excellent, admirable, or desirable in itself : P. L. V. 71 ; IX.

122, 973 ; *solid good* : P. L. VIII.
93 ; that which is excellent in
itself and also conduces to happiness : P. L. V. 153, 399.

(*b*) the state of being excellent :
P. L. V. 471.

(*c*) that which is morally excellent, frequently blended with
(*a*) (*d*) or (*e*), and difficult to distinguish from these senses ; *abstr.*
and *concr.*, contrasted with *bad*,
evil, *ill* : P. L. I. 163, 165 ; II.
562 ; IV. 109, 222 ; VII. 188, 543,
616 ; VIII. 324 ; IX. 697, 709, 723,
752, 774, 1072 ; XI. 85, 87, 89, 358 ;
XII. 336, 470, 471, 565 ; goodness,
virtue : P. L. V. 878 ; IX. 1139 ; P. R.
I. 381 ; III. 11, 125, 139 ; S. M. 24.

good or virtuous person : P. L.
XI. 685 ; *the good* : P. L. XI. 710 ;
C. 765 ; God ; *the infinitely Good* :
P. L. VII. 76 ; *the Supreme Good* :
C. 217.

(*d*) well-being, advantage, benefit : P. L. II. 30, 253 ; V. 60, 570,
827 ; IX. 754, 756, 759, 771 ;
household, *domestic good* : P. L.
IX. 233 ; S. A. 1048 ; *public good* :
P. R. I. 204 ; S. A. 867 ; the resulting advantage *of* : C. 740 ;
happiness, prosperity : P. L. IV.
895.

(*e*) that which conduces to advantage or happiness : P. L. IV.
203 ; V. 206 ; VII. 512 ; VIII. 361 ;
IX. 354 ; X. 752, 758 ; XI. 142,
493 ; XII. 476, 596, 612 ; P. R.
III. 211 ; S. A. 1537 ; Ps. IV. 26 ;
LXXXIV. 43 ; *solid good* : S. XXI.
10 ; *do good*, show kindness ; with
dat. : D. F. I. 56.

(*f*) goodness, beneficence : P.
L. III. 44, 48 ; IV. 414 ; VII. 191 ;
XI. 616 ; P. R. III. 88, 133.

(3) *adv.* **as good**, as well : P. R.
I. 437.

Goodly, *adj.* (*a*) excellent in its
nature and therefore well adapted
to its ends : P. L. VIII. 15.

(*b*) comely, graceful, beautiful :
P. L. IX. 576 ; XI. 509 ; C. 968 ;
sup. : P. L. IV. 147, 323 ; VIII.
304 ; with *of* : P. L. XI. 189 ; fair
or pleasing *prospect, valley* : P. L.
III. 548 ; Ariosto I. 2.

Good-morrow, *sb.* good-morning, a
term of salutation : L'A. 46.

Goodness, *sb.* (*a*) moral excellence :
S. A. 760 ; virtue, purity : P. L.
IV. 847 ; C. 368, 594 ; *personified* :
P. L. III. 688.

(*b*) kindness : C. 849 ; S. XXIII.
11 ; the infinite benevolence and
beneficence of God : P. L. I. 218 ;
III. 158, 165 ; IV. 734 ; V. 159 ;
VIII. 279, 647 ; XI. 353 ; XII. 469 ;
P. R. III. 1241 ; power exercised
with benevolence : P. L. VII. 171.

Good-will, *sb.* benevolence, kindness, favour : P. L. VII. 182 ; XII.
477 ; Ps. V. 40.

Gordian, *adj.* (*a*) **Gordian knot**, the
inextricable knot tied by Gordius,
king of Phrygia, *fig.* : V. Ex. 90.

(*b*) intricate, involved : P. L.
IV. 348.

Gordon, *sb.* a name, possibly that of
Lord Gordon, a Scottish officer
who served under Montrose (?) :
S. XI. 8.

Gore, *sb.* blood effused from the
body : P. L. XI. 460 ; S. A. 1728.

Gore, *vb. tr.* to pierce deeply, *fig.* :
P. L. VI. 387.

Gorge, *vb. tr.* (*a*) to stuff with food,
glut : P. L. X. 632.

(*b*) to devour greedily : P. L.
III. 434.

Gorgeous, *adj.* (*a*) adorned with rich
and brilliant colours ; *of persons* :
P. L. IX. 36 ; *of wings, throne,
arms* : P. L. V. 250 : VI. 103 ; S.
A. 1119.

(*b*) abounding in splendour or
pomp ; *of the East* : P. L. II. 3 ;
of feasts : P. R. IV. 14 ; C. 777 ;
of tragedy : Il P. 97.

Gorgon, *sb.* the common name of
three fabulous women, the sight
of whom turned beholders to stone :
P. L. II. 628 ; *spec.* Medusa : P.
L. X. 527.

attrib. **gorgon shield**, the shield
having on it the head of the gorgon Medusa, who was slain by
Perseus : C. 447.

Gorgonian, *adj.* characteristic of a
gorgon : P. L. II. 611 ; X. 297.

Gory, *adj.* covered with blood : L.
62.

Goshen, *sb.* the country occupied by
the children of Israel during their
sojourn in Egypt : P. L. I. 309.

Gospel, *sb.* that for which a person
lives, and to which he makes the
gospel of Christ subservient : S.
XVI. 14.

Gourd, *sb.* the plant bearing melons :
P. L. V. 327 ; or similar fruit : P.
L. VII. 321.

Govern, *vb.* (1) *tr.* (*a*) to rule with
authority, reign over *people*,

nations, etc. : P. L. VI. 178 ; VII.
510 ; P. R. IV. 135 ; *of God*: P. R.
III. 112 ; *of chance* : P. L. II. 910.
(b) to sway, direct, or control
war : P. L. VI. 706 ; *song, the
appetite*, etc. : P. L. VII. 30, 546 ;
P. R. II. 477.
(2) *intr.* to bear sway, rule,
reign : P. L. V. 802.
See **Well-governed.**
Government, *sb.* (a) rule, authority,
supreme power : C. 25 ; *fig.* : P.
L. XII. 88 ; direction, control : P.
L. X. 154.
(b) system of polity by which
affairs of state are administered :
P. L. XII. 225 ; *civil government* :
P. R. IV. 358.
Governor, *sb.* one who rules a nation :
S. A. 242.
Gown, *sb.* a long loose garment worn
by a civil magistrate, *pl. fig.*
statesmen : S. XVII. 3 ; garment
worn by a hermit : Il P. 169.
Grace, (1) *sb.* (a) pleasing quality,
attractiveness. loveliness, sweetness, charm ; *in persons*: P. L. III.
639 ; IV. 364, 490, 845 ; VIII. 222 ;
P. R. I. 68 ; II. 138 ; *esp. in
women* : P. L. II. 762 ; IV. 298 ;
V. 15 ; VIII. 43, 488 ; P. R. II.
176 ; C. 451 ; M. W. 15 ; *in words,
wisdom* : P. L. VIII. 215 ; P. R.
II. 34 ; *in music* : C. 243 ; *do
grace*, embellish : V. Ex. 10.
(b) *pl.* the goddesses of grace
and beauty : P. L. IV. 267 ; L'A.
15 ; C. 986.
(c) goodwill, favour: L'A. 124 ;
A. 104 ; *heaven lends us grace* :
C. 938 ; the free and unmerited
favour of God : P. L. X. 767 ;
P. R. III. 142 ; shown towards
man in pardoning sin or calling
the sinner to salvation : P. L.
I. 218 ; II. 499 ; III. 131, 145,
174, 187, 227, 302 ; X. 1081 ;
XI. 3, 23, 359 ; XII. 305, 478 ;
P. R. III. 205 ; IV. 312 ; *day of
grace*: P. L. III. 198 ; *Father of
grace* : P. L. III. 401 ; *Spirit of
Grace* : P. L. XII. 525 ; *personified* : P. L. III. 228 ; the peculiar
favour of God towards certain
men : P. L. II. 1033 ; III. 183 ;
VII. 573 ; XI. 890 ; loving-kindness
revealed in the countenance of
Christ : P. L. III. 142 ; X. 1096.
(d) a favour conferred, or in
sense (a) : P. L. III. 674 ; S. A.
360, 679.

(e) virtue, power : P. L. VI. 703.
(f) moral excellence, uprightness : S. II. 13.
(g) favour shown by granting
immunity from penalty for a
specified time : P. L. XI. 255.
(h) pardon, forgiveness : P. L.
I. 111 ; II. 238 ; IV. 94.
(2) *vb. tr.* to honour : C. 24 ;
to designate honourably ; with two
acc.: P. L. XI. 168.
Graceful, *adj.* displaying beauty in
form or action : P. L. II. 109 ;
VIII. 600 ; IX. 459 ; X. 1066 ; P.
R. II. 157.
Gracious, *adj.* (a) pleasing, agreeable,
acceptable : P. L. V. 134 ; XII.
271.
(b) characterized by kindness :
P. L. III. 144 ; VIII. 337 ; X. 1047.
(c) disposed to show kindness ;
of God, Christ : P. L. VIII. 436 ;
X. 118 ; S. A. 1173 ; Ps. LXXXVI. 1.
Graciously, *adv.* with kindness : Ps.
LXXXV. 1 ; LXXXVI. 20.
Gradual, *adj.* proceeding or marked
by degrees : P. L. V. 483 ; IX.
112.
Grain, *sb.* (a) corn in general ; *sing.
collect.*: P. L. IX. 450 ; XII. 184.
(b) small seed, possibly manna
or certainly with allusion to
manna ; *sing. collect.* : P. L. V.
430.
(c) minute particle : P. L. VIII.
17 ; small hard particle of gunpowder: P. L. IV. 817 ; VI. 515.
(d) smallest amount *of* : S. A.
408.
(e) the colour of the dye obtained from the grain-like insect
Coccus, purple or vermilion (or
merely, colour, hue (?)) : P. L. V.
285 ; Il P. 33 ; *grain of Sarra*,
Tyrian purple : P. L. XI. 242.
Grand, *adj.* (a) principal, chief : P.
L. IV. 192 ; *grand foe* : P. L. I.
122 ; P. L. VI. 149 ; X. 1033 ;
P. R. I. 159 ; prefixed to a term
of kinship ; perhaps, first, original :
P. L. I. 29.
(b) high in power or authority :
P. L. II. 507 ; *absol.* : P. L. X.
427.
Grandchild, *sb.* a child in the second
degree of descent : P. L. XII. 153,
155 ; *of death* : P. L. X. 384.
Grandeur, *sb.* magnificence, splendour : P. R. IV. 110.
Grandsire, *sb.* grandfather : S. XXI.
1.

Grange, *sb.* granary, barn : C. 175.
Grant, (1) *sb.* (*a*) assent, consent :
P. R. II. 235.
(*b*) authoritative bestowal of a
possession : Ps. II. 16.
(**2**) *vb. tr.* (*a*) to bestow or confer in answer to a request : P. L.
IV. 104 ; XII. 238 ; II P. 108 ; Ps.
LXXXI. 44 ; with *acc.* and *dat.* :
S. A. 356 ; Ps. LXXXVI. 23.
(*b*) to admit, concede ; with two
acc. : P. R. IV. 290 ; and *dat.* :
P. L. V. 831 ; with *clause* : S. A.
773 ; C. 361.
part. adj. **granted,** permitted :
P. R. II. 302.
Grape, *sb.* fruit of the vine ; *sing.
collect.* : P. L. IV. 259 ; V. 307,
344 ; C. 46 ; *pl.* : Ps. LXXX. 56 ;
juice of the grape, wine : S. A.
551.
Grapple, *sb.* close fight : P. R. IV.
567.
Grasp, (1) *sb.* grip or seizure of the
hand : P. L. IV. 989 ; *fig.* hold,
control : C. 357.
(**2**) *vb.* (graspèd, *disyl.* : P. L.
I. 667) *tr.* to seize and hold,
gripe : P. L. VI. 836.
part. adj. **grasped,** held fast :
P. L. I. 667.
Grass, *sb.* the common herbage of
the field : P. L. IV. 350 ; VII. 310,
315 ; IX. 450, 502 ; N. O. 215 ; C.
624.
See **Knot-grass.**
Grassy, *adj.* (*a*) abounding in or
covered with grass ; *of clod, sord,
turf* : P. L. V. 391 ; VII. 463 ; XI.
324, 433 ; C. 280 ; *of a couch* : P.
L. IV. 601 ; P. R. II. 282.
(*b*) consisting of grass : P. L.
IX. 186.
Grate, *vb.* (1) *intr.* to sound harshly :
L. 124.
(**2**) *tr.* to produce by a grating
movement : P. L. II. 881.
Grateful, *adj.* (*a*) pleasing, agreeable, or delightful to the mind or
the senses : P. L. IV. 331 ; VI.
407 ; VIII. 55, 606 ; S. A. 926 ; *of
appetite, smell,* etc. : P. L. IV.
165 ; IX. 197, 580 ; XI. 442 ; *of
evening, twilight,* etc. : P. L. IV.
647, 654 ; V. 645 ; VI. 8.
(*b*) thankful ; *of persons* : P. L.
IV. 55 ; VII. 512 ; XI. 864 ; full of
gratitude ; *of memory* : P. L. VIII.
650.
(*c*) denoting thankfulness : P.
L. XI. 323.

Gratefully, *adv.* with thankfulness :
P. L. VIII. 4 ; XI. 370.
Gratify, *vb. tr.* to give pleasure to :
P. L. X. 625.
Gratitude, *sb.* thankfulness : P. L.
IV. 52 ; P. R. IV. 188.
Gratulate, *vb.* (1) *tr.* (*a*) to express
joy at the coming of, welcome :
P. R. IV. 438.
(*b*) to express joy on account
of : C. 949.
(**2**) *intr.* to rejoice : P. L. IX.
472.
Gratulation, *sb.* joy or rejoicing ; *the
earth gave sign of gratulation* : P.
L. VIII. 514.
Grave, (1) *sb.* place in which a dead
body is deposited, sepulchre : P.
L. III. 247, 259 ; X. 185, 635, 786 ;
XII. 423 ; N. O. 234 ;
C. 472 ; S. XIV. 6 ; XXIII. 2 ; Ps.
VI. 10 ; LXXXVIII. 12, 20, 46 ; *fig.*
put for the person who lies in the
grave : M. W. 47 ; *of chaos,* the
grave of nature : P. L. II. 911 ;
of the throat : Ps. V. 28.
(**2**) *vb. tr.* (*a*) to shape by cutting : P. L. XI. 573.
(*b*) to engrave, carve : P. L. I.
716.
See **New-graven.**
Grave, *adj.* (*a*) having weight or
authority, eminent, venerable ; *of
persons* : P. L. XI. 662 ; P. R. IV.
261 ; *sup.* : P. R. 218.
(*b*) weighty, authoritative : S.
A. 868 ; serious and important :
V. Ex. 30.
(*c*) of reverend seriousness ; *of
persons* : P. L. XI. 585 ; serious,
earnest, or solemn *appearance,
speech* : P. L. II. 300 ; IV. 844 ;
C. 110 ; slow and dignified *pace* :
C. 870.
Gravely, *adv.* seriously : P. L. IV.
907.
Gray. *See* **Grey.**
Graze, *vb.* (grazèd, *disyl.* : P. L. I.
486) (1) *intr.* to feed on grass :
P. L. XI. 558 ; C. 152 ; L. 46.
(**2**) *tr.* to feed on : P. L. IV. 253 ;
VII. 404 ; IX. 571 ; X. 711.
part. adj. **grazed,** provided with
grass for food : P. L. I. 486.
Great, I. *adj.* (1) large in size or
extent ; *of animals* : P. L. VII.
391 ; *sup.* : P. L. X. 528 ; *of
buildings* : P. L. I. 62, 294 ; *of
heaven, the world, a river,* etc. :
P. L. V. 171, 560 ; VI. 303 ; VII.
267, 307, 346, 381 ; IX. 195 ; XI.

833 ; XII. 141 ; *comp.* : P. L. VII. 347 ; VIII. 29, 87 ; *sup.* : C. 28 ; *of the sun*, with some blending of senses (**4**) or (**5**) : P. L. III. 576 ; VII. 98, 363 ; L'A. 60.

(**2**) large *number, part, share*, etc. : P. L. II. 452 ; XII. 503 ; *comp.* : P. L. VII. 145, 359 ; IX. 621 ; XII. 533 ; *sup.* : P. L. I. 367 ; II. 29 ; large or ample *means* : P. R. II. 412 ; munificent *gift* : P. R. IV. 169.

(**3**) unusual in degree ; *of joy, sorrow, triumph*, etc. : P. L. VII. 180 ; IX. 843 ; X. 350 ; XI. 720 ; Ps. LXXXVIII. 37 ; *comp.* : P. L. VI. 199 ; *of power, strength* : P. L. X. 284 ; P. R. III. 299 ; S. A. 1439 ; *comp.* : P. L. X. 515 ; S. A. 1644 ; *of grace, mercy* : Ps. LXXXVI. 45 ; *comp.* : A. 104 ; *of advantage, peril*, etc. : P. L. IX. 922 ; X. 469 ; XI. 450 ; P. R. I. 145 ; S. A. 1118 ; *of laughter* : P. L. XII. 59.

(*b*) surpassing : P. L. IX. 745.

(*c*) noteworthy, remarkable : P. R. II. 86.

(*d*) very wicked, heinous : S. A. 1356 ; *comp.* : S. A. 1357.

(**4**) of more than ordinary consequence or significance, important, weighty, momentous, famous, or renowned : P. L. XI. 226 ; XII. 612 ; P. R. I. 21 ; S. A. 1500 ; L. 161 ; *great year* : P. L. V. 583 ; *great acts, deeds, events, work*, etc. : P. L. I. 118 ; II. 392 ; VII. 70 ; P. R. II. 112, 412, 426 ; S. A. 28, 243, 680, 1389, 1499, 1537, 1756 ; *comp.* : P. L. VII. 607 ; *sup.* : P. R. I. 69 ; II. 139, 208 ; III. 239 ; *expedition, war*, etc. : P. L. VI. 702 ; VII. 193 ; P. R. I. 158, 174 ; III. 73 ; *argument, cause, conference, result*, etc. : P. L. I. 24, 798 ; II. 515 ; V. 454 ; IX. 669, 672 ; S. A. 1638 ; Hor. Sat. II. 1 ; Hor. Epist. 3 ; *charge, command* : P. L. III. 628 ; V. 311 ; VII. 294 ; VIII. 635 ; XI. 314 ; S. A. 83 ; *covenant, redemption*, etc. : P. L. XII. 600 ; N. O. 4 ; Cir. 21 ; *intent, purpose* : P. L. VI. 675 ; P. R. II. 95, 101 ; *will* : P. L. III. 656.

(*b*) in combination or contrast with *small* : P. L. II. 258 ; XII. 567 ; *sup.* : P. R. IV. 564 ; perhaps with something of sense (**1**) : P. L. II. 922 ; VI. 311 ; X. 306.

(*c*) chief *feast* : P. R. I. 210.

(*d*) magnificent or splendid : P. L. V. 769 ; S. A. 436, 1315.

(*e*) glorious *reign* : P. L. V. 609.

(*f*) illustrious or carrying weight or authority ; *of a name* : P. L. V. 706 ; S. A. 467, 1430 ; *sup.* : S. A. 974.

(*g*) bringing renown : P. L. II. 722 ; XI. 795 ; S. A. 32.

(*h*) applied to a standard as a symbol of power : P. L. V.

(*i*) applied to cities or an assembly with blending of sense (**1**) : P. L. I. 718 ; IV. 212 ; XI. 410 ; XII. 225 ; P. R. III. 73, 291 ; IV. 45 ; *sup.* : P. L. I. 695.

(*j*) universal : P. L. VIII. 151.

(*k*) last, final : P. L. XII. 467.

(**5**) of eminent rank, power, or position : P. L. II. 722 ; XI. 695 ; P. R. I. 18, 70 ; II. 16, 51 ; IV. 81 ; S. A. 40, 279, 1474 ; A. 33, 36 ; S. VIII. 10 ; XXIII. 3 ; *comp.* : P. R. II. 27 ; *sup.* : S. A. 1131 ; *of God, Christ, or angels* : P. L. II. 137, 202, 385 ; III. 167, 271, 311, 673, 696 ; IV. 684 ; V. 184, 188, 663, 691 ; VI. 95, 257, 799 ; VII. 135, 500, 567, 588 ; VIII. 72, 278 ; IX. 815 ; XI. 19, 225, 231 ; XII. 149, 244, 378 ; P. R. I. 240 ; III. 110 ; N. O. 34, 120 ; S. M. 22 ; S. II. 14 ; *comp.* : P. L. I. 4, 258 ; VII. 604 ; XII. 242 ; *fig.* more brilliant : N. O. 83 ; *of Satan or his angels* : P. L. I. 348, 358, 378, 794 ; II. 527 ; IV. 62, 63 ; V. 706, 760, 833 ; X. 236, 440, 456 ; P. R. I. 113 ; prefixed to proper names ; *great Alexander* : P. R. IV. 252 ; *Arsaces* : P. R. III. 295 ; *Comus* : C. 522 ; *Hermes* : Il P. 88 ; *Julius* : P. R. III. 39 ; *Oceanus* : C. 868 ; part of a title ; *Great Mogul* : P. L. XI. 391.

comp. absol. master, superior ; with *poss. pron.* : P. L. V. 172 ; P. R. I. 279.

(**6**) extraordinary *in hopes* : S. A. 523 ; eminent *in power and favour* : P. L. V. 660 ; *in renown* : P. R. I. 136 ; extraordinary in achievement : Il P. 116 ; eminent in genius : W. S. 5 ; eminent in moral attainment, or in sense (**5**), *sup.* : P. R. II. 228 ; lofty *idea* : P. L. VII. 557.

(**7**) eminently entitled to the designation : P. R. III. 82.

(**8**) prefixed to terms of kinship ; *great sire* : P. L. V. 350 ; or in

sense (5); *great progenitor*: P. L.
v. 544; XI. 346; or in sense (1);
great mother: P. L. VII. 281.
II. *sb.* largeness of size: P. L.
VIII. 90.
III. *adv.* magnanimously, honourably, *comp.*: P. R. II. 482.

Greatly, *adv.* in a high degree, much,
very: P. L. x. 193; XI. 869; XII.
557, 558.

Greatness, *sb.* (*a*) dignity, power,
might: P. L. II. 257; III. 165;
P. R. II. 418.
(*b*) superior excellence, eminence: P. L. VIII. 557.

Greave, *sb.* armour for the leg below
the knee: S. A. 1121.

Grecian, *adj.* of Greece: P. L. IV.
212.

Greece, *sb.* the country in Europe:
P. L. I. 739; x. 307; as the home
of oratory, philosophy, poetry,
etc.: P. R. IV. 240, 270, 338, 360;
C. 439.

Greedily, *adv.* eagerly, ravenously:
P. L. IX. 791; x. 560.

Greedy, *adj.* (*a*) ravenous, voracious: *fig. of fire*: Ps. LXXXIII. 55;
of time: T. 10.
(*b*) avaricious, *comp.*: P. R. IV.
141.
(*c*) eager *hope*: P. L. IX. 257.

Greek, (1) *sb.* (*a*) **the Greek,** Ulysses:
P. L. IX. 19.
(*b*) the Greek language: S. XI.
14.
(2) *adj.* of the Greeks: P. R.
III. 118.

Green, (1) *adj.* (*a*) of the colour of
growing herbage; *of stalk, stem,*
etc.: P. L. v. 480; VII. 337; P.
R. IV. 435; C. 716; L. 140; *of
laurel, olive, hazel*: S. A. 1735;
N. O. 47; L. 42: *of a wave*: P.
L. VII. 402.
(*b*) abounding in or covered
with foliage: P. L. IV. 133, 458,
626; VII. 460; VIII. 286; XI. 858;
P. R. II. 185; IV. 587; M. M. 3;
L'A. 58; C. 232, 294, 311, 1014;
Ariosto II. 1; *green Cape*, Cape
Verd: P. L. VIII. 631; *fig. the
green way*, the way full of
pleasures: S. IX. 2.
(*c*) made by growing foliage; *of
shade*: Ps. LXXX. 41.
(*d*) young and tender: P. L.
XI. 435; growing: P. L. XII. 186.
(2) *sb.* (*a*) green colour: P. L.
VII. 316, 479; *emerald green*: C.
894.

(*b*) grassy plot of ground: P.
L. IV. 325; II P. 66; A. 84; *spec.
Memphian green*: N. O. 214.
(*c*) part of a proper name: S.
XI. 7. *See* **Mile-End.**

Green-eyed, *adj.* an epithet of Neptune: V. Ex. 43.

Greet, *vb. tr.* (*a*) to salute, hail, or
welcome: N. O. 26; *with a song*:
P. R. II. 281; *with a kiss*: T. 11.
(*b*) to congratulate; with *acc.*
and *of*: M. W. 24.
(*c*) to meet: N. O. 94.
vbl. sb. **greeting,** salutation:
P. L. VI. 188.
See **Ill-greeting.**

Grey or **Gray,** *adj.* (*a*) of a colour
between black and white, ash-coloured; *grey hair*: C. 392; *hill,
lake*, etc.: P. L. v. 186; XII. 227;
L'A. 71; *grey dawn, evening,
morn*, usually personified and
wearing a grey garment: P. L.
IV. 598; VII. 373; P. R. IV. 427;
A. 54; L. 187; *grey dissimulation*: P. R. I. 498. *See* **Dissimulation.**
absol. the grey hair and deadness of colour characteristic of old
age: P. L. XI. 540.
(*b*) characterized by a grey
garb: P. L. III. 475.

Grey-headed, *adj.* having grey hair:
P. L. XI. 662.

Grey-hooded, *adj.* wearing a grey
hood; *fig. of even*: C. 188.

Grey-fly, *sb.* the trumpet-fly: L. 28.

Griding, *part. adj.* piercing: P. L.
VI. 329.

Grief, *sb.* (*a*) regretful or remorseful
sorrow: P. L. IV. 358; IX. 97;
P. R. I. 110; IV. 574; S. A. 72,
330, 617, 659, 1562, 1578; P. 29,
45, 54; C. 362, 565; Ps. VI. 14;
contrasted with *joy*: P. L. II. 586;
XII. 373.
(*b*) cause of sorrow: S. A. 179.
See **Heart-grief.**

Grieve, *vb.* (*pres. 2d sing.* griev'st:
P. R. I. 407; *past part. disyl.*: P.
L. IV. 28) (1) *tr.* to afflict, distress: P. L. I. 167; XI. 887; Ps.
LXXXV. 7.
(2) *intr.* to feel grief, sorrow
deeply: P. R. I. 407; with *prep.
inf.*: P. L. XI. 754.
part. adj. **grieved,** distressed:
P. L. IV. 28.

Grievous, *adj.* (*a*) heavy or severe
degradation: S. A. 691.
(*b*) acute *pain*: P. L. x. 501.

(c) causing both mental and physical suffering; *of calamity* : P. L. XI. 776.

Grim, *adj.* (a) fierce or cruel *Aquilo* : D. F. I. 8; *wolf* : L. 128; *idol* : P. L. I. 396; *fire* : P. L. II. 170.

(b) furious *war* : P. L. VI. 236.

(c) of forbidding or terrible aspect; *of death* : P. L. II. 682, 804; X. 279; *of the cave of death* : P. L. XI. 469; *of countenance, aspect* : P. L. X. 713; C. 694.

Grin, *vb. tr.* to draw back the lips from the teeth; with *cognate acc.* : P. L. II. 846.

Grind, *vb.* (only in *pres.*) (1) *tr.* to reduce *air to fire* by friction : P. L. X. 1072.

(2) *intr.* to turn a mill : S. A. 35, 1161.

vbl. sb. **grinding,** act of one who grinds a mill : S. A. 415.

Gripe, (1) *sb.* grasp or control *of sorrow* : P. L. XI. 264.

(2) *vb. tr.* to seize and hold firmly : P. L. IV. 408; VI. 543.

Grisamber-steamed, *adj.* steamed with ambergris : P. R. II. 344.

Grisly, *adj.* fear-inspiring, horrible; *of death* : P. L. II. 704; *of Satan, his angels* : P. L. IV. 821; C. 603; *of Moloch* : N. O. 209; *of spectres* : P. R. IV. 430; *a hill, whose grisly top* : P. L. I. 670.

Groan, (1) *sb.* low mournful sound uttered in pain or sorrow : P. L. II. 184; VI. 658; XI. 489; S. A. 1511; S. XVIII. 6; the groan of nature in sorrow for sin : P. L. IX. 1001.

(2) *vb.* (a) *intr.* to utter a low mournful sound expressive of pain or sorrow : P. L. IV. 88; *said of the world* : XII. 539.

(b) quasi-*tr.* **groan out one's soul,** breathe out one's soul in groaning : P. L. XI. 447.

Groom, *sb.* servant having charge of horses : P. L. V. 356.

Gross, *sb.* (a) great, large : P. L. VI. 552.

(b) dense and coarse, contrasted with *air, spiritual substance,* etc. : P. L. VI. 661; XI. 51, 53; XII. 76; *comp.* : P. L. V. 416.

(c) compact *band of angels* : P. L. II. 570.

(d) heavy and troubled *sleep, comp.* : P. L. IX. 1049.

(e) lacking in delicacy of perception; *of the ear* : C. 458; A. 73.

(f) coarse in a moral sense : P. L. I. 491.

Grossness, *sb.* materiality : T. 20.

Grot, *sb.* grotto; *grots and caves* : P. L. IV. 257; *grots and caverns* : C. 429.

Grotesque, *adj.* picturesquely irregular : P. L. IV. 136.

Ground, I. *sb.* (1) foundation *of safety* : P. R. III. 349.

(2) cause, reason : P. L. IX. 1151.

(3) surface of the earth : P. L. IV. 702, 731; V. 348; IX. 304, 334, 422, 456, 475, 481, 523; IX. 497; X. 850, 851, 1054, 1090, 1102; XI. 202; XII. 186, 628; C. 143, 652, 1001; L. 141; without the art. *from ground* : P. L. IX. 590; *on ground* : P. L. VII. 442; *under ground* : P. L. VI. 196; XII. 42.

(b) the corresponding surface in heaven : P. L. III. 350; V. 429; VI. 71, 388; *firm ground* : P. L. VI. 242; *heavenly* : P. L. VII. 210; *under* : P. L. VI. 478; in hell : P. L. I. 705, 767; II. 929.

(c) **under ground,** in hell : N. O. 168.

(d) *fig.* **go to the ground,** be destroyed : S. VIII. 12.

(e) *fig.* **on even ground,** having equal advantage and disadvantage : P. L. III. 179.

(f) the ground as a place of burial : P. L. X. 206; as the place whence man was taken when formed of dust : P. L. VII. 525; X. 207; also *in* sense (9) : P. L. XI. 98, 262.

(g) the part of the earth's surface on which a person walks : P. L. IX. 526.

(4) land contrasted with water : P. L. XI. 850, 858; *dry ground* : P. L. XI. 861.

(5) area or distance; *gather ground* : P. L. XII. 631.

(6) an area having a specified character; *dry ground* : S. A. 582; Ps. LXXXIV. 22; *rising* : Il P. 73; *even ground,* with a blending of sense (3) (e) : P. L. XI. 348; *hallowed* : P. L. XI. 106; A. 55; *holy* : C. 943; *hostile* : S. A. 531.

(7) territory; *Syrian ground* : P. L. I. 421.

(8) the particular space or area occupied or possessed : P. L. IV. 406; V. 367; C. 146.

(9) soil : P. L. IV. 216 ; VII. 332 ; IX. 1104 ; X. 201.

II. *vb. tr.* to base *courage, self-esteem on* : P. L. II. 126 ; VIII. 572. *part. adj.* **grounded,** established : S. A. 865.

See **Meadow-ground. Ground-nest,** *sb.* nest built on the ground : P. R. II. 280.

Grove, *sb.* small wood : P. L. IV. 248, 265 ; V. 126 ; IX. 388 ; X. 548 ; P. R. II. 184 ; IV. 38 ; P. 52 ; M. M. 7 ; A. 46 ; L. 174 ; S. I. 10 ; *tuft of grove* : P. L. IX. 418 ; *tufted grove* : C. 225 ; *shady, delicious, pleasant, twilight* : P. L. III. 28 ; VII. 537 ; P. R. II. 289 ; Il P. 133 ; the trees specified, *citron grove* : P. L. V. 22 ; *groves of myrrh, cinnamon* : P. L. V. 292 ; C. 937 ; *spec. of Daphne* (*see* Castalian) : P. L. IV. 272 ; *Ida's grove* : Il P. 29 ; *Memphian* : N. O. 214 ; *of Moloch* (but *see N. E. D.*) : P. L. I. 403, 416 ; used of the Hesperian gardens (*see* Hesperian) : P. L. III. 569 ; *fig.* applied to corn : P. L. IV. 982 ; to coral : P. L. VII. 404.

See **Olive-grove.**

Grovel, *vb. intr.* to lie or move with the face downwards ; *of angels, men* : P. L. I. 280 ; S. A. 140 ; *of the serpent* : P. L. X. 177.

part. adj. **grovelling,** prone ; *of swine* : C. 53.

Grow, *vb.* (*pret.* grew ; *past part.* grown ; *perf.* tenses formed with auxiliary *be* : P. L. XII. 116 ; with *have* : P. L. IX. 807, 1154) *intr.* (*a*) to have life and increase in size : P. L. IV. 671 ; to have vegetative life, exist as a living plant ; *of flower, leaf, tree,* etc. : P. L. III. 356 ; IV. 195, 221, 425, 694 ; VIII. 321 ; IX. 617, 618 ; XI. 274.

(*b*) to be fixed or attached : P. L. IX. 1154.

(*c*) to spring up, be produced ; *of fruit, plant, tree,* etc. : P. L. III. 356 ; IV. 216 ; VI. 477 ; VII. 336 ; IX. 776, 807, 1105 ; X. 551, 561 ; C. 891 ; L. 78 ; *of flesh* : P. L. XI. 5 ; *of wings* : P. L. X. 244 ; *fig. of persons* : S. XVIII. 12 ; *of riches* : P. L. I. 691.

(*d*) to come into existence, arise ; *of sin* : P. L. XII. 400 ; *of reconcilement, persuasion* : P. L. IV. 98 ; XI. 152.

(*e*) to increase gradually in size ; *of plants* : P. L. VIII. 47 ; *of wings* : C. 378 ; *of persons,* **full grown,** having attained majority : P. R. II. 83 ; to take shape, be formed : P. L. VIII. 470.

(*f*) to increase in magnitude : P. L. IX. 208 ; to increase *in years* : P. R. III. 40 ; *in wealth* : P. L. XII. 351.

(*g*) to become by degrees ; with adjs. *dark, high, fruitful,* etc. : P. L. II. 720, 779, 784 ; V. 72, 319 ; VI. 661 ; S. A. 1612 ; C. 467, 670, 735, 956, 968 ; S. XI. 10 ; *ambitious, corrupt, mature,* etc. : P. L. IX. 742, 803 ; XII. 116, 164 ; P. R. IV. 137 ; S. A. 268 ; *friendly, dreadful, mild,* etc. : P. L. II. 220, 705, 761 ; IX. 564 ; XII. 352 ; P. R. I. 310 ; with prep. phrase ; *into a nation* : P. L. XII. 164 ; *to perfection* : P. R. I. 208 ; with *sb.* : P. L. X. 529.

(*h*) **grow up,** advance to or toward maturity ; *of persons* : S. A. 637, 676 ; *of strength* : S. A. 1496 ; increase in number : P. L. IX. 623 ; come into existence : P. L. II. 3.

part. adj. **growing,** increasing in size or extent : P. L. II. 315, 767 ; IV. 438 ; in degree or magnitude : P. L. IX. 202 ; X. 715 ; S. IX. 7 ; in scope : P. R. I. 227.

See **Full-grown, Up-grow.**

Growth, *sb.* (*a*) natural increase of animal or vegetable bodies : P. L. IX. 113, 211 ; P. R. I. 67.

(*b*) size or stature attained by growing : P. L. I. 614 ; IV. 629 ; C. 270.

(*c*) that which has grown, product : P. L. V. 319, 635.

Grudging, *part. adj.* showing covetousness and ill-will : C. 725.

Grunsel-edge, *sb.* edge of the door-sill or threshold : P. L. I. 460.

Gryphon, *sb.* one of the fabulous animals conceived of as having the head and wings of an eagle and the body of a lion. They were supposed to guard the gold of the north of Europe : P. L. II. 943.

Guard, (1) *sb.* (*a*) position of watching to prevent attack : P. L. VI. 412 ; *stand upon our guard* : C. 487.

(*b*) body of men engaged in escorting a prisoner : S. A. 1617 ;

of angels in protecting a person or place : P. L. IV. 550, 862 ; VIII. 559 ; X. 18 ; XII. 590.

(c) defence, protection : C. 42, 394.

(2) vb. tr. to watch over in order to keep from injury or attack, protect, defend : P, L. II. 611 ; IV. 280 ; IX. 269 ; S. VIII. 4 ; of God : P. L. II. 1033 ; of mercy : C. 695 ; of a sword : P. L. XI. 122.

part. adj. guarded ; (a) watched : P. L. II. 947.

(b) fortified : L. 161.

Guardian, sb. one who watches over or cares for another ; of angels : P. L. III. 512 ; XI. 215 ; C. 219.

Guendolen, sb. the daughter of Corineus and the wife of Locrine : C. 830. See **Locrine.**

Guerdon, sb. reward, recompense : L. 73.

Guess, (1) sb. conjecture, surmise : C. 310.

(2) vb. tr. to conclude on merely probable grounds, conjecture, surmise : P. L. VIII. 85 ; with two acc. : P. L. V. 290 ; with clause : C. 577 ; absol. in parenthetic clause : S. A. 1540 ; C. 201.

Guest, sb. one who is entertained by another : P. L. VII. 14 ; XII. 166, 167 ; P. R. II. 278 ; S. A. 1196 ; L. 118 ; of angels : P. L. V. 313, 351, 383, 507 ; VII. 69, 109 ; VIII. 646 ; IX. 1.

See **Angel-guest.**

Guiana, sb. the country in South America : P. L. XI. 410.

Guide, (1) sb. (a) one who directs or leads another in a way or course : P. L. II. 975 ; P. R. I. 336 ; S. A. 1630 ; C. 279, 994 ; of God or angels : P. L. V. 91 ; VIII. 298, 312 ; XI. 371, 674, 785 ; of the serpent : P. L. IX. 646 ; fig. of providence : P. L. XII. 647 ; love : P. L. VIII. 613 ; the ear : C. 171.

(b) one who directs another in conduct : P. L. IV. 442 ; X. 146 ; of God : S. A. 1428 ; S. XXII. 14 ; fig. of conscience : P. L. III. 194 ; of experience : P. L. IX. 808.

(2) vb. tr. (a) to go with or before for the purpose of leading the way ; of God : P. L. VII. 15 ; VIII. 486 ; XII. 204 ; of the ear : C. 570 ; a star : P. L. V. 708 ; XII. 392 ; P. R. I. 250 ; providence, instinct, reason : S. A. 1547.

(b) to direct the course of a vehicle : P. L. VI. 711 ; II P. 53.

(c) to direct in conduct or action : P. L. XII. 482 ; P. R. II. 473 ; C. 32 ; of the Holy Spirit : P. L. XII. 490 ; guided by faith and fortitude : S. XVI. 3.

part. adj. **guiding,** directing the way : S. A. 1.

See **Heavenly-guided.**

Guile, sb. (a) insidious cunning, duplicity, treachery : P. L. I. 34, 121, 646 ; II. 41, 188 ; IV. 349 ; IX. 306, 466, 733, 772 ; X. 114 ; P. R. I. 123 ; II. 237 ; S. A. 989.

(b) wile, stratagem : P. L. III. 92 ; pl. : P. R. II. 391.

Guileful, adj. deceitful, treacherous : P. L. IX. 567 ; X. 334 ; C. 537 ; Ps. v. 16.

Guilefully, adv. deceitfully : P. L. IX. 655.

Guilt, sb. state of moral pollution resulting from conscious wrongdoing, criminality : P. L. IX. 971, 1043, 1114 ; X. 112, 166 ; XII. 443 ; P. R. III. 147 ; S. A. 902 ; C. 456.

Guiltless, adj. (a) free from guilt, innocent : P. L. X. 823, 824 ; C. 829 ; guiltless blood : P. 40.

(b) having no knowledge or knowledge of : P. L. IX. 392.

Guilty, adj. (a) liable to punishment by reason of a violation of moral law : P. L. III. 290 ; IX. 785 ; X. 340 ; Ps. v. 29 ; guilty front : N. O. 39.

(b) chargeable with the crime of : V. Ex. 96.

(c) arising from a sense of guilt ; of shame : P. L. IV. 313 ; IX. 1058.

Guise, sb. (a) manner, mode, fashion : C. 962.

(b) manner of acting, behaviour : P. L. XI. 576.

(c) external appearance, semblance : P. L. I. 564.

Gulf, sb. (1) the Persian Gulf : P. L. XI. 833.

(2) a deep hollow : (a) the burning lake of hell : P. L. I. 329 ; fiery gulf : P. L. I. 52 ; a deep hollow filled with snow and ice : P. L. II. 592.

(b) underground bed of a river : P. L. IX. 72.

(c) abyss, esp. the abyss of chaos : P. L. III. 70 ; X. 39 ; abortive, boiling, darksome gulf : P. L. II. 441, 1027 ; V. 225 ; impassable, unvoyageable : P. L. X. 253, 366 ;

a yawning abyss; *gulf of Tartarus* : P. L. VI. 53 ; lowest part, depth (?) : P. L. II. 12.

Gulfy, *adj.* overflowing its banks and inundating the land ("marshdrowning," Drayton *Polyolbion* S. XXVIII. 451) : V. Ex. 92.

Gum, *sb.* the exuded sap of trees or shrubs : P. L. IV. 630 ; *odorous gums* : P. L. IV. 248 ; the mass resulting from the drying of this substance : C. 917 ; used as incense ; *sweet-smelling gums* : P. L. XI. 327.

Gummy, *adj.* covered with gum : P. L. X. 1076.

Gurge, *sb.* whirlpool : P. L. XII. 41.

Gush, *vb. intr.* to issue with force : Ps. CXIV. 18.

part. adj. **gushing**, flowing with force and volume ; *of water* : L. 137 ; issuing in a copious stream ; *of blood* : P. L. XI. 447.

Gust, *sb.* sudden blast of wind : P. L. X. 698 ; Il P. 128 ; L. 93.

Gust, *sb.* keen relish : P. L. X. 565.

Gymnic, *adj.* **Gymnic artist**, person skilled in the art of gymnastics : S. A. 1324.

Gyve, *sb. pl.* shackels for the legs : S. A. 1093.

H

Habergeon (habérgeon), *sb.* a sleeveless coat of mail : S. A. 1120.

Habit, *sb.* dress, garb : P. L. III. 643 ; P. R. IV. 601 ; S. A. 122, 1073, 1305 ; *pl.* : P. R. IV. 68 ; C. 157 ; the dress of a religious order : P. L. III. 490.

Habitable (hábitáble) *adj. absol.* the habitable globe : P. L. VIII. 157.

Habitant, *sb.* inhabitant, resident : P. L. II. 367 ; III. 460 ; VIII. 99 ; X. 588 ; C. 459.

Habitation, *sb.* (*a*) occupancy : P. L. VII. 622.

(*b*) place of abode : P. L. II. 573 ; XII. 49 ; *of heaven* : P. L. VII. 186 ; *of hell* : P. L. VI. 876 ; P. R. I. 47 ; house ; *clay habitation* : C. 339.

Habitual, *adj.* constant *habitant* : P. L. X. 588.

Habor, *sb.* the modern Kabur, a river of Mesopotamia emptying into the Euphrates ; *in Habor*, in the country through which the Habor flows : P. R. III. 376.

Hæmony, *sb.* the name given by Milton to a supposed plant of miraculous power ; possibly suggested by Hæmonia, a poetical name of Thessaly, the land of magic : C. 638.

Hag, *sb.* witch : C. 434.
   See **Night-hag**.

Hagar, *sb.* the concubine of Abraham : Ps. LXXXIII. 23.

Hail, *sb.* frozen rain-drops : P. L. II. 589 ; X. 698, 1063 ; XII. 181, 182 ; *fig. sulphurous hail* : P. L. I. 171 ; balls shot from cannon : P. L. VI. 589.

Hail, (1) *sb.* an exclamation of "hail" : P. L. V. 385.

(2) *interj.* exclamation of salutation : P. L. I. 250 ; *esp.* respectful or reverential salutation : P. L. III. 1, 412 ; IV. 750 ; V. 205, 388 ; XII. 379 ; P. R. II. 68 ; IV. 633 ; V. Ex. 1 ; M. M. 5 ; Il P. 11, 12 ; C. 128, 265 ; with *to* : P. L. XI. 158.

(3) *vb. tr.* to give greeting to, salute ; with two *acc.* : S. A. 354.

Hair, *sb.* (*a*) one of the filaments growing from the skin : S. A. 1138 ; *pl. fig. grey hairs*, a person in old age : C. 392.

(*b*) *sing. collect.* natural covering of the head : P. L. V. 131 ; S. A. 59, 1135, 1355, 1496 ; *amber-dropping hair* : C. 863 ; *flowing* : P. L. III. 640 ; *golden* : Hor. O. 4 ; *Neæra's hair* : L. 69 ; *fig.* foliage, leaves ; *frizzled hair* : P. L. VII. 323 ; the tail of a comet ; *horrid hair* : P. L. II. 710.
   See **Blue-haired**, **Bright-haired**, **Smooth-haired**.

Hairy, *adj.* (*a*) covered with hair : L'A. 112 ; *fig.* covered with that which resembles hair : L. 104 ; covered with foliage : P. L. IV. 135.

(*b*) consisting of hair : P. L. VII. 497 ; made of hair, or coarse and shaggy : Il P. 169.

Hale, *vb. tr.* to drag by force : P. L. II. 596.

Half, (1) *sb.* one of the two corresponding or equal parts into which a thing is or may be divided : P. L. IV. 112, 488, 785 ; V. 95, 560 ; VI. 770 ; VII. 21 ; A. 12 ; *in half*, into two parts : P. L. VI. 325.

(2) *adj.* being one of two equal parts ; followed by *def. art.* : P. L.

I. 598; IX. 141; by *demon.*, *poss.*, or *rel. pron.*: P. L. I. 649; IV. 495, 782; V. 229, 559; VI. 853; IX. 545; C. 724; S. XIX. 2.

(3) *adv.* to the degree or extent of a half, in part; qualifying an *adj.*: S. A. 79, 100; U. C. I. 6; an *adv.*: P. L. I. 617; S. A. 1606; N. O. 170; an *adv. phrase*: P. L. II. 941; a *part.* or *vb.*: P. L. II. 941, 975; IV. 820, 903; V. 12; VI. 198; VII. 463; VIII. 595; IX. 426; S. A. 79; V. Ex. 4.

Half-embracing, *adj.* partly enfolding in the arms: P. L. IV. 494.

Half-moon, *sb.* crescent-shaped line of battle: P. R. III. 309.

Half-regained, *adj.* partly brought back into one's possession: L'A. 150.

Half-rounding, *adj.* going half way round a circle: P. L. IV. 862.

Half-spied, *adj.* not wholly or clearly seen: P. L. IX. 426.

Half-starved, *adj.* not having sufficient food; *of death*: P. L. X. 595.

Half-sunk, *adj.* half submerged: P. L. VI. 198.

Half-told, *adj.* half narrated: Il P. 109.

Half-way, *adv.* at half the distance: P. L. IV. 777; VI. 128.

Hall, *sb.* (*a*) palace: C. 649; the cave of Nereus at the bottom of the sea: C. 835; *fig. aerial hall,* the sky: P. L. X. 667.

(*b*) any large room used as the main living-room or as a reception-room: P. L. IX. 38; C. 45, 324.

(*c*) the large room where Satan holds his court: P. L. I. 762, 791; X. 444, 522.

See **Palace-hall.**

Halleluiah, *sb.* song of praise to God: P. L. II. 243; VI. 744; VII. 634; X. 642.

Hallo (hállo), (1) *sb.* call uttered to attract attention: C. 481, 490.

(2) *vb. intr.* to call with a loud voice: C. 226, 487.

Hallow, *vb. tr.* to set apart as sacred to God: P. L. VII. 592.

part. adj. **hallowed,** consecrated or sacred *limits, ground, haunt,* etc.: P. L. III. 31; IV. 964; V. 321; XI. 106; Il P. 138; A. 55; *hallowed Dee*: V. Ex. 98; *fire*: N. O. 128; *reliques*: W. S. 3; *gift, pledge*: P. R. III. 116; S. A. 535.

Halt, *sb.* temporary stoppage on a march: P. L. VI. 532; XI. 210.

Hamath, *sb.* a city and district on the northern frontier of Palestine, at the foot of Mt. Hermon: P. L. XII. 139.

Hamlet, *sb.* small village: L'A. 92.

Hammered, *part. adj.* forged with a hammer: S. A. 132.

Hammon, *sb.* the god Ammon represented in the form of a ram, or in the form of a human body with a ram's head: N. O. 206. *See* **Ammon.**

Hamper, *vb. tr.* to bind, fetter: S. A. 1397.

Hand, *sb.* (1) end of the arm from the wrist outward: P. L. I. 459; II. 949; V. 17; VIII. 300; IX. 385, 1037; XI. 421, 863; S. A. 951; C. 143; Ps. LXXXVIII. 40.

(*b*) as used for grasping, holding, or retaining: P. L. VI. 579, 646; VII. 224; IX. 385, 850, 892; XI. 248; XII. 637; P. R. IV. 557; S. A. 1302; *right hand*: P. L. VI. 835; L'A. 35.

(*c*) used to denote custody: P. L. II. 775; possession: P. R. II. 429; power, disposal: P. R. I. 969; S. A. 259, 438, 1105, 1185; Ps. LXXXII. 14; authority, command: P. R. II. 449.

(*d*) used to denote strength, power: P. L. VI. 458; P. R. II. 144; military power: P. R. III. 168; Ps. LXXXIII. 31.

the activity or power of God or Christ shown in creating, providing, or punishing: P. L. II. 174; IV. 365, 417; V. 854; VI. 683; VII. 500; VIII. 362; X. 772; XI. 372; P. R. III. 187; S. A. 668, 684; N. O. 222; S. XXII. 7; Ps. LXXXVIII. 49; CXXXVI. 37; *copious, full hand*: P. L. V. 641; Ps. CXXXVI. 86; *creating*: P. L. IX. 344; *good*: Ps. LXXX. 75; *repenting*: P. L. II. 369; *solemn*: S. A. 359; *solitary*: P. L. VI. 139; the activity of a goddess: C. 903; the activity of nature: P. L. III. 455; VIII. 27; C. 711.

(*e*) as indicating direction, nearness, or intimate relation; *right hand*: P. L. II. 869; III. 279; V. 606; VI. 747, 762, 892; XII. 457; Ps. LXXX. 69.

side: P. L. I. 222; V. 252; VI. 307, 770, 800; XI. 659; Ps. LXXXII. 3; *left hand*: P. L. X. 322; *right*: P. L. II. 633; X. 64.

(*f*) used in adjuration: C. 875.

(*g*) as performing some action : P. L. IV. 629 ; v. 214 ; VI. 3 ; VIII. 469, 47 ; IX. 203, 244 ; x. 458, 1002, 1058 ; XI. 28 ; S. A. 1, 1233, 1299 ; *right hand* : P. L. v. 864 ; VI. 154 ; *fatal, gentle, rash,* etc. : P. L. II. 712 ; IV. 488 ; IX. 780 ; XI. 93, 276, 609 ; C. 397 ; *impious, glorious, unweeting, just* : P. L. I. 688 ; S. A. 1581 ; D. F. I. 23 ; C. 13 ; *rich, unsparing, liberal* : P. L. II. 3 ; v. 344 ; IX. 997 ; skilled in music, joined to *voice* : P. R. I. 171 ; IV. 256 ; A. 77 ; regarded as the agent : P. L. II. 727, 738 ; S. A. 1230.

(**2**) as representing the person, sometimes the person who does something with his hands (often difficult to distinguish from sense (*g*), where perhaps some of the following belong) : P. L. I. 699 ; VI. 231, 508, 807 ; IX. 207, 246, 623 ; x. 140, 373 ; P. R. III. 155 ; S. A. 507, 1260, 1270, 1526, 1584 ; P. 45 ; S. xv. 9 ; XVII. 13 ; *learned hands* : V. Ex. 90 ; *Parthian hands* : P. R. III. 290.

(**3**) mode of using the hand, skill : P. L. I. 732.

(**4**) handiwork, workmanship : P. L. IX. 438 ; P. R. IV. 59.

In combination with other words ; (*a*) **at hand**, near by in position : P. L. II. 674 ; VI. 537 ; VII. 202 ; VIII. 199 ; P. R. II. 238 ; S. A. 1306 ; *nigh* or *near at hand* : P. L. IV. 552 ; IX. 256 ; L'A. 63 ; near in time : P. R. II. 35 ; Ps. LXXXV. 38 ; *nigh at hand* : P. R. I. 20 ; S. A. 593.

(*b*) **hand in hand**, with hands mutually clasped : P. L. IV. 321, 689 ; v. 395 ; XII. 648 ; Ps. LXXXV. 44.

(*c*) **come to hand** : P. L. XI. 436 ; S. A. 142. *See* Come.

(*d*) **take in hand** : Ps. I. 10. *See* Take.

See Neat-handed, Nigh-hand, Two-handed, White-handed.

Handed, *adj.* joined hand in hand : P. L. IV. 739.

Handle, *vb. tr.* to touch with the hand : P. R. I. 489.

Handmaid, *sb.* female servant ; *fig.* of *faith, love* : S. XIV. 10 ; one who worships and obeys God : Ps. LXXXVI. 60.

attrib. belonging to an attendant : N. O. 242.

Hang, *vb.* (*pret.* and *past part.* hung) (**1**) *tr.* (*a*) to suspend : Hor. O. 14 ; Il P. 118 ; *fig., stars* : C. 198 ; *the world* : P. L. II. 1005 ; VII. 242 ; *the world on hinges* : N. O. 122 ; *fig.* hang *in*, to make to depend upon, cause to be conditioned by : S. A. 59.

(*b*) to let droop or bend downward : M. W. 41 ; L. 147.

(*c*) to furnish with that which is suspended : P. L. VII. 325 ; S. A. 1736.

(**2**) *intr.* (*a*) to remain suspended from above, depend : P. L. III. 367 ; *of armour* : P. L. IV. 554 ; VI. 763 ; XI. 247 ; *of fruit* : P. L. IV. 250 ; v. 323 ; VIII. 307 ; IX. 594, 622, 798 ; *of hair* : P. L. I. 287 ; IV. 302 ; *fig. of the world* : P. L. II. 1051.

(*b*) to hover, impend : P. L. I. 342 ; to rest or float *in the clouds* : P. L. II. 637.

(*c*) to bend downward : P. L. IX. 430 ; to lean *over* : P. L. v. 13.

(*d*) to cling : L'A. 29.

(*e*) not to let go, pursue closely : P. L. II. 78.

(*f*) to remain with suspended motion : P. L. VI. 190.

(*g*) to be decreed or determined : U. C. II. 3.

(*h*) **hang forth**, suspend in open view : P. L. IV. 997.

(*i*) **hang in even scale**, be undecided or not determined : P. L. VI. 246.

Hap, (**1**) *sb.* chance, fortune : P. L. IX. 160, 421 ; V. Ex. 83 ; *dismal hap* : V. Ex. 68.

(**2**) *vb. intr.* to happen, chance : P. L. IX. 56 ; with *prep. inf.* : P. L. II. 837.

Hapless, *adj.* unhappy, unfortunate ; *of persons* : P. L. v. 879 ; VI. 785 ; IX. 404 ; x. 342, 965 ; M. W. 31 ; C. 350, 566 ; L. 164 ; Hor. O. 12 ; *of an event* : P. L. II. 549.

Haply, *adv.* by chance, perhaps : P. L. I. 203 ; IV. 8, 378 ; VI. 501 ; VIII. 200 ; XI. 196 ; S. A. 62.

Happen, *vb. intr.* to come to pass, take place : P. L. IX. 1147 ; P. R. I. 334 ; S. A. 1423 ; *impers.* : V. Ex. 13.

Happiness, *sb.* (*a*) enjoyment, pleasure : C. 343.

(*b*) pleasurable content of mind, felicity : P. L. I. 55 ; II. 563 ; III. 450 ; IV. 417 ; v. 235, 504 ; VI.

741, 903 ; VII. 632 ; VIII. 365, 399, 405, 621 ; IX. 254, 340, 819 ; X. 725 ; XI. 58; P. R. I. 417; C. 789.

Happy, (1) *adj.* (*a*) fortunate or blessed, with a blending of sense (*c*); *of persons* : P. L. III. 532, 570, 679 ; VII. 625, 631 ; X. 485 ; P. R. IV. 362; S. A. 354; Cir. 3; *comp.*: P. L. II. 97; VIII. 282 ; XI. 88 ; *sup.*: P. L. IV. 774.

(*b*) characterized by or involving happiness, blessed, fortunate, propitious, favourable : P. L. III. 232; *sup.* : P. R. III. 225 ; S. A. 1718; *happy clime, field, isle, place, walk*, etc.: P. L. I. 85, 249 ; II. 347, 410; III. 66, 567, 570, 632; IV. 247, 562 ; V. 143, 364 ; VI. 226 ; XI. 270, 303; XII. 642; P. R. I. 1, 360, 416 ; S. A. 1049; C. 977 ; *comp.* : P. L. IV. 507 ; X. 237 ; XII. 464 ; *constellation*: P. L. VIII. 512 ; *light* : P. L. VIII. 285 ; *lot, life* : P. L. II. 224 ; *comp.* : P. L. IV. 446 ; IX. 697 ; *sup.*: P. L. IV. 317 ; *state* : P. L. I. 29, 141 ; IV. 519 ; V. 234, 504, 536, 830 ; VIII. 331 ; IX. 337, 347 ; *comp.*: P. L. II. 24 ; IV. 775 ; *league, union* : P. L. IV. 339 ; *comp.* : N. O. 108 ; *reign, comp.* : P. R. III. 179 ; *choice, sup.* : P. L. X. 904 ; *end* : P. L. XII. 605 ; *trial* : P. L. IX. 975 ; C. 592 ; *interview* : P. L. XI. 593 ; *hour, day, morn* : P. L. III. 417 ; XI. 782; N. O. 1, 167; *comp.* : P. L. XII. 465.

(*c*) having the feeling of happiness or felicity : P. L. IV. 60, 128, 370, 534, 727 ; V. 74, 75, 520, 611 ; VIII. 621 ; IX. 326, 1138 ; X. 720, 874 ; *comp.* : P. L. V. 76 ; VII. 117 ; XII. 587.

(*d*) felicitous, *sup.* : S. XIII. 11.

(*e*) appropriate, fitting, *sup.* : P. L. IV. 638.

(2) *adv.* happily : P. L. VIII. 633.

Happy-making, *adj.* conferring felicity : T. 18.

Harald. *See* **Herald.**

Haran, *sb.* a town in the northwestern part of Mesopotamia : P. L. XII. 131.

Harangue, *sb.* public address : P. L. XI. 633.

Harapha (Hárapha), *sb.* the giant; the name is probably a modification of Arapha. *See* the Vulgate, Regum, lib. sec. XXI. 16, 18, 20, 22 : S. A. 1068, 1079.

Harass, *sb.* the laying waste *of* : S. A. 257.

Harbinger, *sb.* one who goes before and announces the coming of another person : P. R. I. 71, 277 ; S. A. 721 ; *fig. of misery* : P. L. IX. 13 ; *of a star* : P. L. XI. 589 ; M. M. 1 ; *of peace, righteousness, personified* : N. O. 49 ; Ps. LXXXV. 54.

Harbour, (1) *sb.* (*a*) lodging, entertainment, *fig.* : P. L. IX. 288.

(*b*) port, haven, *fig.* : P. R. III. 210.

(2) *vb.* (*a*) *tr.* to provide a lodging for, give shelter to, protect : P. R. I. 307 ; V. Ex. 88 ; *fig. of sleep* : S. A. 459.

(*b*) *intr.* to lodge, dwell ; *fig. of evil* : P. L. V. 99 ; *of rest* : P. L. I. 185.

Hard, (1) *adj.* (*a*) compact in substance, solid : P. R. I. 343 ; *sup.* : P. R. II. 168.

(*b*) used punningly with the double meaning of, hard to understand and solid in substance : P. L. VI. 622.

(*c*) difficult to accomplish, full of obstacles, arduous, fatiguing ; *hard assay* : P. L. IV. 932 ; P. R. I. 264 ; IV. 478 ; C. 972 ; *escape, adventure* : P. L. II. 444 ; X. 468 ; *task*, etc. : P. L. V. 495, 564 ; S. A. 1528 ; P. 14 ; *way, descent* : P. L. II. 433 ; III. 21 ; difficult, not easy ; with *prep. inf.* : P. L. III. 575 ; IV. 584 ; VII. 452 ; VIII. 251 ; X. 992 ; XI. 146 ; S. A. 1013 ; S. XVII. 6 ; *comp.* : S. A. 1014.

(*d*) difficult to pronounce, *comp.* : S. XI. 8.

(*e*) difficult to bear, oppressive, rigorous, cruel ; *hard liberty, captivity* : P. L. II. 256 ; Ps. LXXXV. 3 ; *mishap* : L. 92 ; *service, terms*, etc. : P. L. IV. 45, 432 ; X. 751 ; P. R. III. 132.

(*f*) rigorous *season* : S. XX. 5.

(*g*) involving great effort : P. L. II. 1021 ; S. A. 865.

absol. one who is obdurate : P. L. III. 200.

(2) *adv.* (*a*) harshly, severely : P. R. I. 469.

(*b*) **hard beset**, surrounded with great difficulties or dangers, *comp.* : P. L. II. 1016.

(*c*) **hard by**, very near to : P. L. I. 417 ; near, close by : P. L. X. 548 ; L'A. 81 ; C. 531.

Hard-besetting, *adj.* surrounding with great difficulties and dangers: C. 857.

Harden, *vb.* (1) *tr.* (*a*) to make firm and solid : P. L. XII. 194.

(*b*) to make obdurate : P. L. III. 200 ; VI. 791.

(2) *intr.* to become obdurate : P. L. I. 572.

Hardihood, *sb.* boldness : C. 650.

Hardly, *adv.* (*a*) with difficulty : P. R. I. 279.

(*b*) scarcely : P. L. IX. 304.

Hardship, *sb.* extreme want or suffering : P. R. I. 341.

Hardy, *adj.* (*a*) daring, bold : P. L. II. 425.

(*b*) strong, enduring : P. L. IV. 920 ; S. A. 1274.

See **Over-hardy**.

Harlot, *sb.* prostitute : P. L. IV. 766 ; P. R. IV. 344.

Harlot-lap, *sb.* lap of a woman who is a prostitute : P. L. IX. 1060.

Harm, (1) *sb.* injury, hurt, damage, or wrong, either physical or moral : P. L. IV. 791, 843, 901 ; VI. 656 ; VII. 150 ; IX. 251, 326, 327, 350 ; X. 1055 ; P. R. II. 257 ; IV. 486 ; S. A. 486, 1187 ; Il P. 84 ; C. 591 ; an injury, *pl.* : A. 51 ; S. VIII. 4.

(2) *vb. tr.* to hurt, injure : P. L. IX. 1152 ; P. R. I. 311 ; II. 407.

Harmless, *adj.* free from power to harm : P. R. IV. 458 ; free from disposition to harm : P. L. IV. 388 ; C. 166.

Harmonic, *adj.* harmonious ; *harmonic number* : P. L. IV. 687.

Harmonious, *adj.* concordant or symphonious ; *harmonious airs* : P. R. II. 362 ; *numbers* : P. L. III. 38 ; *sound* : P. L. VII. 206 ; VIII. 606 ; *harmonious sisters*, *Voice and Verse* : S. M. 2.

Harmony, *sb.* (*a*) concord of musical sounds, melody, music : P. L. II. 552 ; VI. 65 ; VII. 560 ; P. R. IV. 255 ; V. Ex. 51 ; N. O. 107 ; A. 63 ; C. 243 ; *personified* : P. L. V. 625 ; the music of the spheres ; *ninefold harmony* : N. O. 131 ; probably the combination of simultaneous notes in chords, *personified* : L'A. 144.

(*b*) accord in action and feeling, agreement : P. L. VIII. 384, 605 ; X. 358.

Harness, *vb. tr.* to equip with armour : P. L. VII. 202.

See **Bright-harnessed**.

Harp, (1) *sb.* the stringed musical instrument : P. L. II. 548 ; III. 366, 414 ; V. 151 ; VII. 37, 559, 594 ; XI. 560, 583 ; P. 9 ; *golden harp* : P. L. III. 365 ; VII. 258 ; *immortal* : S. M. 13 ; the music played on the harp : P. R. IV. 336 ; *evening harp* : P. L. VII. 450.

(2) *vb. intr.* to play on the harp : N. O. 115.

Harpy, *sb.* the ravenous and loathsome monster having the face and body of a woman and the wings and claws of a bird of prey : P. R. II. 403 ; C. 605.

Harpy-footed, *adj.* having feet like those of a harpy : P. L. II. 596.

Harrow, *vb. tr.* to torment, harass : C. 565.

Harry, *sb.* a form of Henry, the Christian name of Lawes, a composer of music, and a member of the King's band of musicians : S. XIII. 1.

Harsh, *adj.* (*a*) disagreeable to the taste, acrid, sour : P. L. IX. 987 ; L. 3.

(*b*) discordant to the ear, grating, jarring ; *harsh din* : S. M. 20 ; *thunder* : P. L. II. 882 ; *tune* : S. A. 662 ; *philosophy* : C. 477.

(*c*) hard, unfeeling : S. A. 1461.

Harshly, *adv.* in a harsh manner, roughly : P. L. XI. 537 ; C. 683.

Hart, *sb.* male deer : P. L. XI. 189.

Harvest, *sb.* (*a*) time of reaping and gathering grain : P. L. XI. 899.

(*b*) the reaping and gathering of grain : P. L. IV. 981.

(*c*) growth, crop ; *fig. of hair* : S. A. 1024.

Harvest-queen, *sb.* the name given to an image, probably representing Ceres, carried about by the reapers at the festival of the harvest-home ; or to a young woman chosen from the reapers for special honours on this occasion : P. L. IX. 842.

Haste, (1) *sb.* (*a*) speed, expedition : P. L. V. 777 ; VII. 294 ; C. 568 ; *in haste*, speedily, quickly, hurriedly : P. L. III. 500 ; IV. 560 ; V. 331 ; X. 17, 456 ; XI. 449 ; P. R. III. 303 ; S. A. 1441, 1678 ; L'A. 87 ; Ps. VI. 23 ; Petr. 5 ; *make haste*, hasten ; with *prep. inf.* : P. L. X. 29.

(*b*) hurry, precipitancy : S. A. 1027.

(2) *vb.* (*a*) *refl.* to cause oneself to move rapidly; *imper. haste thee* : P. L. XI. 104; V. Ex. 17; L'A. 25.

(*b*) *intr.* to come or go quickly, act with expedition : P. L. I. 357; III. 714; IV. 353, 867; V. 136, 308, 326, 686; VII. 105, 291; IX. 853; XI. 81; XII. 366; P. R. III. 223, 437; IV. 64; N. O. 23, 212; A. 58; C. 956; with *on* : P. L. V. 211; VI. 85; with *prep. inf.* : P. L. II. 838; VI. 254; VIII. 519; C. 920; Ps. VII. 5.

part. adj. **hasting**, coming and going quickly : S. II. 3.

Hasten, *vb.* **(1)** *tr.* to cause to haste, urge on, expedite : S. A. 576; *hasten on*, bring on, cause to come before the due time : U. C. II. 14.

(2) *intr.* to haste, move or act quickly : P. L. I. 675; III. 329; with *prep. inf.* : P. L. V. 846; X. 857.

part. adj. (*a*) **hastening**, hurrying : P. L. XII. 637; coming soon, approaching : M. W. 46.

(*b*) **hastened**, caused to come before the due time : S. A. 958.

Hasty, *adj.* in a hurry : P. L. I. 730.

Hatch, *vb. tr.* (*a*) to bring forth *a* brood from the egg : P. L. VII. 418.

(*b*) to contrive, devise : P. L. II. 378.

Hate, (1) *sb.* (*a*) intense dislike or aversion, detestation : P. L. I. 58, 417; II. 120, 336; IV. 69; V. 738; VII. 54; IX. 466, 471, 475, 491, 492, 1123; X. 114; XI. 601; P. R. IV. 386; S. A. 400, 790, 839, 966, 1266; *deadly hate* : P. L. II. 577; IV. 99; *hellish* : P. L. III. 298, 300; *immortal* : P. L. I. 107; *bird of hate* : S. I. 9. *See* **Bird.**

(*b*) an object of hatred : P. L. X. 906.

(2) *vb.* (*pres. 2d sing.* hat'st : P. L. VI. 734; Ps. v. 14) *tr.* to regard with intense aversion, detest : P. L. II. 249; IV. 37; XI. 553, 702; XII. 411; P. R. IV. 97; S. A. 939; C. 760; S. XI. 13; Ps. LXXXI. 61; LXXXIII. 7; *of God, Christ, or angels* : P. L. II. 857; VI. 559, 734; Ps. v. 14.

part. adj. **hated**, regarded with aversion, detested : P. R. I. 47; D. F. I. 51.

Hateful, *adj.* (*a*) full of hate, malignant : P. L. X. 869; Ps. LXXXIII. 26.

(*b*) exciting hate, odious, detestable ; P. L. I. 626; II. 859; IV. 505; VI. 264; IX. 121; C. 92; *sup.* : P. L. X. 569.

Hatred, *sb.* hate, detestation : P. L. I. 308; II. 500; X. 928; S. A. 772.

Haughty, *adj.* (*a*) arrogantly proud, disdainful : P. L. IV. 858; or *adv.* : P. L. V. 852.

(*b*) indicating arrogant pride ; *haughty look* : S. A. 1069; *stride* : P. L. VI. 109.

(*c*) eminent or lofty *nation* : C. 33; bold *of courage* : P. L. IX. 484.

Haunt, (1) *sb.* place where men or animals frequently resort : P. L. IV. 184; XI. 835; C. 388; where gods or nymphs resort : P. L. XI. 271; P. R. II. 191, 296; Il P. 138; C. 536.

(2) *vb. tr.* to resort to frequently or habitually; *of the gods* : P. L. VII. 330; *of the Muses* : P. L. III. 27; *of nymphs and fauns* : P. L. IV. 708.

part. adj. frequented by water-nymphs : N. O. 184; L'A. 130.

Haut, *adj.* haughty or arrogant *nation* : Ps. LXXX. 35.

*Have, *vb.* (*pres. 2d sing.* hast : P. L. II. 747; III. 164, 171; *3d sing. usually* hath : P. L. I. 89, 136, 169; *rarely* has : U. C. I. 18; C. 32, 381; *pret.* had; *2d sing.* had'st : P. L. IV. 66, 886) **(1)** *tr.* (*a*) to be in possession or control of, possess, own : P. L. II. 98; III. 668; V. 558; S. A. 1323; C. 821; with *clause obj.* : P. L. V. 281; with *adv.* or *adv. phrase* expressing qualification or condition : P. L. I. 608; V. 392; VIII. 118; IX. 1174; S. A. 1367.

(*b*) to possess as an attribute, faculty, function, right, etc. : P. L. II. 667; IV. 881; VI. 640; VII. 347, 590; IX. 374; X. 790; P. R. IV. 175; S. A. 196; as a part of the body : P. L. VI. 754.

(*c*) to be affected by, experience, enjoy or suffer : P. L. II. 413, 819; III. 168; VIII. 8; IX. 584; XII. 245; P. R. II. 247, 319; S. A. 214, 845; C. 394; S. XXIII. 7.

(*d*) to hold as something to be done; with *acc.* and *prep. inf.* : P.

L. I. 567; XI. 415; P. R. IV. 2;
to be obliged or necessitated; with
prep. inf.: P. L. II. 920; VI. 125;
XI. 415; P. R. II. 389; C. 122;
with *inf.* understood: P. L. II.
1007.

(*e*) to hold *me in his keeping*:
Ps. VI. 20.

(*f*) to entertain *hope*: P. L. XI.
271, 779; S. A. 1453.

(*g*) to show *mercy*: Ps. LXXXVI.
58; to exert *influence*: P. L. III.
118.

(*h*) to hold in estimation or regard as *in derision, scorn*: P. L.
V. 736; S. A. 442; Ps. IV. 8.

(*i*) to become possessed of, re-
ceive, obtain, get: P. L. II. 283;
VIII. 232; X. 501, 652; XII. 558;
P. R. I. 446; III. 298; S. A. 837;
M. W. 32; C. 749; to receive as
fulfilled, realize *one's wish*: P. L.
VI. 818.

*See also for use in phrases the
words* Charge, On, Regard, Remembrance, Thought, Show,
View, Will, Work.

(2) as auxiliary forming com-
pound tenses; (*a*) *perf. tense*: P.
L. II. 747; III. 308; IV. 62; P.
R. III. 236.

forming *perf. inf.* for the *pres.*:
P. L. I. 40; III. 99; V. 447, 467;
VII. 143; XI. 88; S. A. 848, 994;
preceded by *would*: S. A. 908; by
had thought: P. L. VI. 21; C.
756.

(*b*) *plupf. tense*: P. L. I. 37, 211;
II. 723; III. 224; IX. 1148; X.
156; *plupf.* for *pret.*: A. 24; after
thought, had been = were: P. L.
VI. 164.

(*c*) *part.* having (—): P. L. V.
754; IX. 917; X. 157.

Haven, *sb.* port; *Balsara's haven*:
P. R. III. 321.

Havoc, (1) *sb.* relentless destruction,
indiscriminate slaughter: P. L.
II. 1009; IX. 30; *hew to havoc*:
P. L. VI. 449. *See* **Hew.**

(2) *vb. tr.* to devastate: P. L.
X. 617.

Hawthorn, *sb.* the shrub *Cratægus
oxjacantha*: L'A. 68.

Haycock, *sb.* conical heap of hay in
the field: L'A. 90.

Hazard, (1) *sb.* (*a*) exposure to loss
or harm, risk, peril: P. L. I. 89;
II. 453, 455; X. 491; *huge hazard*:
P. L. II. 473; *edge of*: P. R. I.
9; *to the hazard of*: S. A. 1241.

(*b*) undertaking full of risk: P.
L. V. 729.

(2) *vb. tr.* to expose to loss,
risk, imperil: P. L. IV. 933.

Hazardous, *adj.* perilous: P. R. III.
228.

Hazel, *sb. attrib.* composed of hazel-
trees: L. 42.

***He,** (1) *pers. pron.* (*dat.* and *acc.*
him) (*a*) referring to a male person previously mentioned: P. L.
I. 34, 54, 149, 221, 414; II. 473,
511; not previously mentioned
but understood from the context:
P. L. I. 93; P. R. IV. 299; in
parallel construction with *whom*:
P. L. V. 470.

(*b*) referring to a bird or beast:
P. L. I. 203; V. 274; VII. 445,
457; IX. 87, 182; XI. 186, 856.

(*c*) referring to various things
with more or less personification;
to chaos: P. L. II. 909, 961, 1010;
death: P. L. X. 1001; U. C. I. 6;
hot, cold, etc.: P. L. II. 907;
shame: P. L. IX. 1058; the sun:
P. L. IV. 643; VII. 100, 374; VIII.
125, 162; IX. 48; N. O. 83; a
tree: P. L. V. 216; winter: D.
F. I. 5, 10.

(*d*) that one, that person; as
antecedent of *rel. pron.*: P. L. I.
84, 87; II. 454; III. 469, 471; IV.
1; VI. 179; followed by explanatory participial phrase: P. L. VI.
294; P. R. II. 199.

(*e*) any person: P. L. II. 125;
IV. 203; VI. 178; as antecedent of
rel. pron.: P. L. II. 124; VI. 177,
464; IX. 296; XI. 313; P. R. II.
466; IV. 288; C. 381, 527; any
male person: P. L. X. 898, 901.

(2) *refl. pron., arm him*: P. L.
VI. 222; *betake*: P. R. IV. 403;
C. 61; *bethink*: P. R. III. 149;
lie: P. 21; L'A. 110; *repent*: P.
R. I. 306; *return*: P. L. IV. 906;
sit: P. L. VII. 587; *turn*: IV.
410; *withdraw*: P. R. II. 55;
writhe: P. L. VI. 328.

Head, *sb.* (1) that part of the body
of an animal which contains the
brain and the organs of special
sense; in man or supernatural
beings: P. L. I. 193, 211; II. 672,
711, 730, 754, 758, 949; III. 626;
VI. 346, 757; S. A. 197, 535, 609,
727, 1024, 1125, 1636, 1639; L'A.
145; Ps. LXXXIII. 8; or possibly
in sense (2) (*d*): C. 934; *helmed,
fulgent, regal head*: P. L. VI. 840;

x. 449 ; P. 15 ; *languished, unpillowed, lank* : S. A. 119 ; C. 355,
836 ; *nectared, rosy* : D. F. I. 49 ;
C. 885 ; *from head to foot* : P. L.
VI. 625 ; *head and hands* : P. L.
I. 459 ; *head or heel* : P. L. XII.
388 ; *at one's head* : P. L. VIII.
292 ; P. R. IV. 407 ; *at the head
of* : P. L. IV. 826 ; *on* or *upon
one's head* : P. L. II. 178 ; v. 893 ;
VI. 653 ; P. R. I. 82 ; S. A. 1589,
1652, 1696.

in animals : P. L. IX. 499 ;
branching head : P. L. VII. 470 ;
head and tail : P. L. X. 523 ;
Hydra head, fig. : S. XV. 7.

fig. in the sun, moon, or star :
P. L. IV. 35 ; N. O. 80 ; Il P. 71 ;
L. 169 ; in the sea : Ps. CXIV. 8.

(*b*) as the seat of the mind : S.
A. 552 ; C. 108 ; as the seat of
brute sense : P. L. IX. 184, 189.

(*c*) **all head,** having the special
functions of the head performed
by all parts of the body : P. L.
VI. 350.

(**2**) put for the whole person :
P. L. I. 435 ; x. 735, 934 ; S. A.
192, 677 ; L. 51 ; Ps. III. 9 ; *false
head* : C. 799 ; *sacred, sheltered* :
P. R. IV. 406 ; L. 102 ; *sleeping* :
V. Ex. 64 ; used with reference
to Satan as overcome by Christ :
P. L. x. 1035 ; XII. 432 ; P. R. I.
60 ; *bruise one's head* : P. L. x.
181, 499, 1032 ; XII. 150, 430.

(**3**) something resembling the
head in form or position ; (*a*)
flower, blossom : P. L. IV. 699 ;
IX. 428 ; M. W. 41 ; C. 744, 898 ;
pensive head : L. 147.

(*b*) summit *of a building* : P. R.
IV. 48 ; top *of a vine* : Ps. LXXX.
44.

(*c*) upper or highest part *of a
wilderness* : P. L. IV. 134.

(*d*) source of a river ; *Nilus'
head* : P. L. IV. 283 ; *fig.* source
of mankind : P. L. III. 286.

(**4**) chief, commander, ruler :
P. L. I. 357 ; IV. 953 ; S. A. 242 ;
of Christ : P. L. III. 319 ; v. 606,
830, 842 ; VI. 779 ; *of Adam* : P.
L. IV. 443 ; VIII. 574 ; IX. 1155.

In combination with other words ;
(*a*) **at head,** in front of an army :
P. L. VI. 556.

(*b*) **get head,** gain ascendency :
P. R. II. 64.

(*c*) **in the head of,** as the ruler
of : P. R. I. 98.

(*d*) **make head against,** resist
successfully : P. L. II. 992.

(*e*) **on** or **upon one's head,** said
of a curse, fear, mischief, etc., as
falling upon a person : P. L. III.
86, 220 ; x. 133, 732, 815, 955,
1040 ; P. R. I. 55, 267 ; Ps. VIII.
58.

(*f*) **over one's head,** in the air
or sky : P. L. XI. 864 ; P. R. IV.
463 ; said of time : P. L. XI. 534.

See **Grey-headed, Oughly-headed,
Snaky-headed.**

Headlong, (**1**) *adv.* (*a*) head foremost : P. L. I. 45, 750 ; II. 374,
772 ; VI. 864 ; P. R. IV. 575.

(*b*) without delay, hastily : P.
R. III. 430.

(**2**) *adj.* (*a*) rushing forward impetuously : C. 887.

(*b*) precipitate or rash ; *headlong haste* : C. 568 ; *joy* : P. 5.

Headstrong, *adj.* intractable, ungovernable : P. R. II. 470.

Heal, *vb.* (**1**) *tr.* (*a*) to make whole,
restore to soundness : P. L. VI.
436 ; both physically and spiritually : Ps. VI. 4.

(*b*) to restore to soundness *a
wound* : P. L. VIII. 468 ; *a scar* :
P. L. II. 401.

(*c*) to remedy, remove, repair :
A. 51 ; C. 847.

(**2**) *intr.* to become whole or
sound : P. L. VI. 344.

part. adj. **healing** ; (*a*) curative
herb : C. 621.

(*b*) soothing or comforting *words* :
P. L. IX. 290 ; S. A. 605.

Health, *sb.* (*a*) soundness of body :
S. A. 554.

(*b*) spiritual soundness : Ps.
LXXXV. 13, 27.

Healthful, *adj.* conducing to bodily
health : P. L. XI. 523.

Heap, (**1**) *sb.* (*a*) collection of things
laid or thrown together in a mass :
P. L. IV. 815 ; S. A. 1530 ; C.
398 ; *came to a heap* : P. L. III.
709 ; *lay on a heap* : P. L. VI.
389 ; *shattered into heaps* : C. 799 ;
gathers heap : P. L. II. 590.

(*b*) crowd, throng : P. L. x.
558.

(**2**) *vb. tr.* (*a*) to pile *on* : P. L.
III. 83 ; v. 344 ; to amass *treasure* :
P. R. II. 427.

(*b*) to add so as to increase the
mass ; *fig. faults heaped* : P. L.
XII. 338 ; *confusion heaped upon
confusion* : P. L. VI. 668.

(c) to form a heap on, fill to overflowing : P. L. v. 391.

(d) to deal or bestow in large quantities : C. 771 ; *fig. heap damnation on* : P. L. I. 215 ; *ingratitude on* : S. A. 276.

part. adj. **heaped,** piled up : L'A. 147.

Hear, *vb.* (*pres. 2d sing.* hear'st : P. L. III. 7 ; v. 224 ; *pret.* heard, *2d sing.* heard'st : P. L. VII. 561 ; *past part.* heard) (1) *tr.* (*a*) to perceive by the ear *applause, song, sound, voice, words,* etc. : P. L. I. 274, 275 ; II. 65, 290, 477, 580 ; IV. 866 ; v. 659 ; VI. 28, 208, 782 ; VII. 68 ; VIII. 242, 452 ; IX. 518 ; x. 97, 116, 119, 163, 506, 731 ; XI. 74, 322, 560 ; XII. 61 ; P. R. I. 33, 84, 198, 284 ; II. 235, 362, 403 ; IV. 452 ; S. A. 176, 1515, 1524 ; D. F. I. 37 ; N. O. 54, 101, 183 ; Cir. 3 ; L'A. 147 ; Il P. 64, 137 ; A. 72 ; C. 91, 227, 343, 458 ; L. 87, 176 ; S. I. 6 ; Ps. LXXXI. 20 ; with *acc.* and *part.* : P. L. VI. 557 ; VII. 181 ; VIII. 203 ; P. R. IV. 513 ; S. A. 110 ; C. 792 ; S. xx. 11 ; *voices singing* : P. L. IV. 681 ; *carol sung* : P. L. XII. 367 ; *whom called* : P. R. II. 3 ; with *part.* only, *foretold of* : P. R. IV. 502 ; with *acc.* and *simple inf.* : P. L. III. 185 ; IV. 2, 410 ; VII. 101 ; VIII. 204 ; IX. 966 ; S. A. 215 ; V. Ex. 65 ; L'A. 41 ; Il P. 47, 74 ; C. 480 ; in *passive* with *prep. inf.* : C. 533 ; *inf.* omitted : P. L. x. 729 ; *absol.* or *intr.* : P. L. I. 331 ; II. 993 ; VI. 567 ; VII. 561 ; VIII. 3 ; x. 99 ; P. R. I. 330 ; L. 27 ; Ps. LXXXI. 3.

said of personifications : *of abyss* : P. L. II. 519 ; *of chaos* : P. L. VII. 221 ; *of confusion* : P. L. III. 710 ; *of hell* : P. L. VI. 867 ; *of the sun* : P. L. VII. 100.

be louder heard, speak with a louder voice and be heard above another : P. L. x. 954.

(*b*) to give ear to, listen or attend to *a person* : P. L. VIII. 500 ; XII. 529 ; P. R. I. 211, 848 ; S. A. 766 ; C. 252 ; V. Ex. 68 ; *imper.* without obj. : P. R. IV. 500 ; Ps. LXXXI. 33 ; *absol.* : Ps. LXXXI. 45 ; to listen to *conscience* : P. L. III. 195.

(*c*) to listen to with more or less attention *decree, song, story, words,* etc. : P. L. v. 546, 555, 557,

600, 602, 810 ; VII. 51 ; VIII. 10 ; IX. 213 ; XI. 266, 663 ; XII. 103 ; P. R. I. 259, 481 ; II. 33, 107 ; III. 349 ; IV. 123 ; S. A. 845, 1232 ; C. 44 ; L. 36, 176 ; *wisdom* : P. R. I. 385 ; *power of harmony* : P. R. IV. 254 ; *the will heard not her lore* : P. L. IX. 1128 ; *the brook to hear his madrigal* : C. 495 ; used punningly with the twofold meaning of (*a*) and (*c*) : P. L. VI. 618.

(*d*) to listen to with assent, grant the request of *a person, sighs, voice,* etc. : P. L. XI. 31, 153 ; S. A. 649 ; Ps. III. 12 ; IV. 18 ; v. 3, 6 ; VI. 18 ; LXXXV. 21 ; LXXXVI. 2 ; to grant *a prayer* : P. L. XI. 252 ; Ps. IV. 6 ; VI. 18 ; LXXXIV. 29.

(*e*) to learn by hearing, receive information about, be told : P. L. III. 701 ; v. 224 ; VIII. 205 ; IX. 862 ; XII. 598 ; *hear business* : C. 169 ; *news* : P. R. I. 333 ; S. A. 1423, 1449, 1553 ; *reward, trespass, good* : P. L. VI. 909 ; IX. 888 ; XI. 359 ; or in sense (*a*) : P. L. VI. 769 ; with *clause* : P. L. II. 846 ; IX. 281 ; x. 27 ; P. R. II. 182 ; *absol.* : P. L. x. 23 ; P. R. IV. 116 ; to feel because of what is heard : C. 264.

(*f*) **hear rather,** prefer to be addressed or called : P. L. III. 7.

(2) *intr.* (*a*) to have the sensation of sound : P. L. v. 411.

(*b*) to listen, give heed : P. L. VIII. 208 ; x. 1047 ; XII. 624 ; Ps. LXXXI. 45.

(*c*) to be informed, learn : S. A. 1456 ; with *from* : S. A. 1631 ; with *of* : P. L. VII. 52, 296 ; P. R. I. 270 ; S. A. 1082 ; parenthetically : P. R. II. 83.

vbl. sb. **hearing** ; (*a*) perception by the ear : P. L. VII. 18.

(*b*) audience : Ps. LXXXVI. 20.

Hearer, *sb.* one who hears what is said by another : U. C. II. 19.

Hearken, *vb. intr.* (*a*) to listen : C. 169 ; *hearken to ecstasy* : C. 625.

(*b*) to give heed *to* : P. L. III. 93 ; IX. 1134 ; x. 198 ; P. R. II. 428 ; Ps. LXXXI. 46 ; *imper.* : Ps. LXXXI. 33.

Hearse, *sb.* wooden platform used as a bier : M. W. 58 ; L. 151.

Heart, *sb.* (1) principal organ of the vascular system : P. L. IV. 484 ; VI. 346 ; S. A. 609 ; *all heart,* having the special functions of the heart performed by all parts of the body : P. L. VI. 350.

(2) the seat of feeling, understanding, and thought (because of the blending of senses accurate discrimination is sometimes impossible) ; (a) the mind in general as the seat of thoughts, passions, desires, purposes, affections : P. L. I. 400, 444 ; VII. 160 ; IX. 550, 734, 876 ; P. R. I. 216, 222 ; II. 169, 410 ; III. 10 ; W. S. 10 ; *hearts of men* : D. F. I. 62 ; *to thy heart's desire* : P. L. VIII. 451 ; as divining what is in the future : P. L. IX. 845 ; X. 357 ; as joined to another by the bond of nature : P. L. IX. 955 ; X. 358 ; *esp.* the mind or soul as the seat of the moral life, as wrought upon by God or as choosing the right or wrong : P. L. VII 513 ; XI. 27, 150 ; XII. 489, 524 ; Ps. LXXXIV. 7, 26 ; LXXXVI. 39, 43 ; *contrite heart* : P. L. X. 1091, 1103 ; *feeble* : S. A. 455 ; *pious* : P. R. I. 463 ; *stony* : P. L. III. 89 ; *remove the stony from* : P. L. XI. 4 ; *upright* : P. L. I. 18 ; Ps. VII. 42 ; *variable* : P. L. XI. 92 ; as speaking : Ps. VIII. 11 ; as spoken to : Ps. IV. 20.

(b) inmost being ; *unlocked my heart* : S. A. 407.

(c) the will : P. L. V. 532 ; XII. 193 ; S. A. 1368 ; desire ; *set thy heart on* : P. L. XI. 288.

(d) disposition, character : P. L. XII. 25 ; Ps. IV. 15

(e) the mind or soul as affected by delight, fear, loss, pain, pride, etc. : P. L. I. 571, 788 ; IV. 154 ; VIII. 266, 475 ; IX. 913 ; X. 973, 1061 ; XI. 448, 595, 868 ; XII. 613 ; Cir. 28 ; Ps. IV. 31 ; *glad heart* : P. L. VIII. 322 ; *heart of rock* : P. L. XI. 494 ; *grieved at his heart* : P. L. XI. 887 ; as affected by music : P. L. XI. 595 ; N. O. 94 ; as affected by what is eaten or drunk : S. A. 545, 1613, 1669.

(f) as the seat of affection or love : P. L. V. 448 ; X. 915, 940 ; S. A. 792 ; P. R. II. 162 ; S. I. 3 ; *one heart*, the union of man and wife in oneness of affection : P. L. VIII. 499 ; IX. 967.

(g) as the seat of courage ; *undaunted heart* : P. L. VI. 113 ; courage, spirit : P. L. IV. 861 ; X. 966 ; S. XXII. 8.

(h) as the seat of the mental faculty, intellect, understanding, mind : P. L. VII. 60 ; VIII. 590 ; XII. 274 ; P. R. II. 103 ; *heart of man* : P. L. VII. 114 ; *heart of the fool* : S. A. 298 ; the mind of God : P. L. X. 6 ; the understanding of the ant : P. L. VII. 486 ; as the seat of brute sense : P. L. IX. 189.

(3) inmost part ; *heart of hell* : P. L. I. 151.

See Easy-hearted.

Heart-easing, *adj.* affording relief to the heart : L'A. 13.

Hearten, *vb. tr.* to inspirit, animate : S. A. 1317.

Heart-grief, *sb.* profound grief : S. A. 1339.

Hearth, *sb.* (a) the floor of a fireplace : Il P. 82.

(b) as typical of the home ; *on the hearth*, by the fireside, in one's home : S. A. 566 ; V. Ex. 60 ; *the holy hearth*, the lararium, the part of a house in which the tutelary deities were placed : N. O. 190.

Heart-sick, *adj.* caused by heart-sickness : P. L. XI. 482.

Heart-strook, *part. adj.* overwhelmed with anguish or dismay : P. L. XI. 264.

Heat, *sb.* (a) high temperature or warmth issuing from fire : P. L. II. 219 ; X. 1077 ; from the stars : P. L. IV. 668 ; from a sword : P. L. XII. 634.

(b) hot condition of the atmosphere : P. L. IX. 1108 ; X. 653, 691, 1057 ; *meridian, summer's, harvest heat* : P. L. V. 369 ; X. 656 ; XI. 899 ; *heat of noon* : P. L. V. 231.

(c) heat of the body, vital warmth : P. L. V. 437.

(d) vehemence, ardour : P. L. X. 616.

(e) sexual desire, passion : P. L. I. 453 ; C. 358 ; *in heat* : P. L. XI. 589 ; *gums of glutinous heat*, glutinous gums producing the heat of passion : C. 917.

Heath, *sb.* uncultivated or desert land : P. L. I. 615 ; C. 423.

Heathen, (1) *adj.* pagan : P. L. I. 375 ; to a pagan nation : P. R. III. 176.

(2) *sb.* one who, or a nation which, does not acknowledge the God of the Bible : P. R. III. 418 ; S. A. 693 ; the Greeks : P. L. X.

579; *collect.*, the Gentile nations :
S. A. 451, 1430; Ps. II. 18; the
Roman nation : P. R. II. 443.
Heathenish, *adj.* befitting a pagan,
savage, barbarous : P. R. III.
419.
Heave, *vb.* (*pret.* and *past part.*
heaved; the latter *disyl.* : Il P.
136) **(1)** *tr.* (*a*) to raise or lift *the
head* : P. L. I. 211; S. A. 197;
L'A. 145; C. 885; *absol.* to lift
with effort something heavy : S.
A. 1626.
(*b*) to cause to increase in volume, swell : P. L. XI. 827.
(2) *intr.* to rise above the general level, swell up : P. L. VII.
288.
part. adj. **heaved,** lifted *stroke* :
Il P. 136.
***Heaven,** *sb.* **(1)** vaulted expanse of
the sky : P. L. VII. 232; VIII.
257; IX. 604; XII. 618; *bear up
heaven* : S. A. 150; *pillared frame
of* : P. R. IV. 455; *either end of* :
P. L. II. 538; as an arch meeting
earth and ocean : P. L. IV. 539;
as varied and rich in colour : P.
L. V. 283; *painted heavens* : Ps.
CXXXVI. 18.
(*b*) *esp.* the expanse in which
appear the sun, moon, and stars :
P. L. III. 716; IV. 355, 997; XII.
361; P. R. I. 249; *heaven's high
road* : P. L. VII. 373; *pathless
way* : Il. P. 70; *cope, zone, expanse, top of* : P. L. IV. 993; V.
560; VII. 340; C. 94; the region
of the stars which influence or
reveal the fate of men : P. L.
VIII. 511; P. R. IV. 382, 383; the
region of the music of the spheres :
N. O. 130; C. 243; in combination or contrast with *earth, air,
sky* : P. L. VIII. 16, 70, 92, 120;
IV. 722; with *def. art.* : P. L. VII.
358; N. O. 19; *pl.* : P. L. III.
19; VII. 562; VIII. 76; X. 692;
personified (?) : P. L. II. 490; N.
O. 240; *masc. gen.* : P. L. V. 44;
in sense **(3)** as well as (*b*); antecedent of both *sing.* and *pl. pron.* :
P. L. VII. 499.
(*c*) **heaven and earth,** the universe : P. L. II. 1004; VII. 63,
167, 256; N. O. 108; *pl.* : P. L.
I. 9; the new universe which
shall arise after the burning of
the world : P. L. III. 335; X.
638, 647; XI. 901; *pl.* : P. L. XII.
549.

(2) the region of the atmosphere
where clouds float and storms
gather : P. L. I. 612; II. 715; XI.
879; P. R. II. 312; *breath of
heaven* : S. A. 10; *both ends of* :
P. R. IV. 410; *cataracts of* : P. L.
XI. 825; *heaven his windows shut* :
P. L. XI. 849.
(3) heavenly bodies or the
spheres with which they revolve,
pl. : P. L. V. 156, 578; VIII.
115.
(4) region above the universe
which is the seat of an order of
things eternal and consummately
perfect, where God and the angels
dwell : P. L. I. 37, 73, 680; II.
137, 328; III. 136, 257; IV. 2; V.
163, 635, 816; *circumference, ends,
bounds,* etc. *of* : P. L. II. 190, 236,
353; V. 586; VI. 716; VII. 215;
*pavement, plains, precipice, towers,
walls,* etc. *of* : P. L. I. 104, 174,
321, 682; II. 62, 1035; III. 71,
427, 484, 515; IV. 976; V. 254;
VI. 51, 228, 474, 865; *king, lord,*
etc. *of* : P. L. II. 229, 264, 316,
751, 851; IV. 111, 960; VI. 425;
IX. 125; *tyranny, laws of* : P. L.
I. 124; II. 18; *deity, spirit,* etc.
of : P. L. I. 316; II. 11, 696; III.
60; IV. 552; V. 824; VII. 162;
light, year, day of : P. L. II. 137,
398; V. 583; VI. 685; XII. 347;
peace, joy of : P. L. VI. 267; S.
M. 1; in combination or contrast
with *earth, hell* : P. L. III. 133,
274, 323; VI. 705; VII. 124; VIII.
483; X. 57; as an agent : P. L.
VII. 205; P. R. I. 30, 281; *voc.* :
P. L. VII. 566; with *def. art.* : P.
L. VI. 11; usually *fem. gen.* : P.
L. VI. 272; VII. 574; P. R. I. 81;
but sometimes *masc.* : P. L. VI.
783; as an exclamation : P. L. VI.
114; X. 125.
(*b*) the peculiar dwelling-place
of God; *heaven of heavens* : P.
L. III. 390; VII. 13, 553; XII.
451; P. R. I. 366, 410; *highest
heaven* : P. L. III. 657; VI. 13;
heaven's top : P. L. VII. 585.
(*c*) used with reference to that
which partakes of the heavenly
nature; *birth of heaven* : P. L. V.
863; *offspring of* : P. L. II. 310;
III. 1; IX. 273; *progeny of* : P. L.
II. 430; *race of* : P. L. II. 194;
heaven's ray : P. L. VI. 480; *son
of* : P. L. I. 654; II. 692; V. 519,
790; P. R. II. 121.

(5) inhabitants of heaven, the angels: P. L. III. 146, 272, 381; V. 765; God and the angels: P. L. II. 9, 457, 509; VI. 563; God as the source of authority and power: P. L. I. 212; II. 319, 1025; III. 205; IV. 68, 620, 688, 1009; VI. 62; IX. 8, 334; N. O. 116; C. 417, 600; S. II. 12.

(6) perfection resembling that of heaven; *heaven of mildness*: P. L. IX. 534; beauty and innocence: P. L. VIII. 488.

(7) place or state of such supreme felicity that it may be compared to heaven: P. L. I. 255; IV. 78, 208, 371; VII. 617; VIII. 210; IX. 103.

(8) habitation of the gods: P. L. I. 517, 741; L'A. 12.

(9) the gods of Olympus: V. Ex. 44; N. O. 210; Uranus: P. L. I. 509, 510.

See **Mid-heaven.**

Heaven-banished, *adj.* exiled or expelled from heaven: P. L. X. 437.

Heaven-born, *adj.* begotten by God; *of Christ*: N. O. 30.

Heaven-fallen, *adj.* having fallen from heaven: P. L. X. 535.

Heaven-gate, *sb.* the portal of heaven: P. L. I. 326; II. 996; III. 541; V. 198; VII. 619; X. 22, 88.

Heaven-gifted, *adj.* given or bestowed by God: S. A. 36.

Heaven-loved, *adj.* beloved by heaven: D. F. I. 65.

Heavenly, (1) *adj.* (*a*) of the firmament, celestial: P. L. XII. 256; A. 72.

(*b*) of, from, or in heaven; celestial; divine: P. L. I. 361; VIII. 356, 485; IX. 151, 730, 1082; X. 641; XI. 207, 871; P. R. I. 28; IV. 637; S. A. 635; P. 3; C. 459; *heavenly essences, powers, spirits*, etc.: P. L. I. 138; III. 213; IV. 361; VI. 723, 788; VIII. 379, 615; *band, host, brood*: P. L. II. 824; XI. 208, 230; D. F. I. 55; *choir*: P. L. III. 217; IV. 711; *muse*: P. L. I. 6; III. 19; VII. 39; N. O. 15; C. 515; *stranger, guest*: P. L. V. 316, 397; VII. 69; VIII. 646; *mind, soul*: P. L. IV. 118; VI. 165; *Paradise, ground*, etc.: P. L. V. 500; VII. 210; XI. 17; Ps. LXXXV. 47; of God: S. A. 373; *grace, love, truth*: P. L. II. 499; III. 298; S. IX. 4.

(*c*) characteristic of heaven: P. L. IV. 686; V. 286; VIII. 592; P. R. IV. 594.

(*d*) having the excellence or beauty of heaven: P. L. IX. 607; X. 624; S. A. 1035; *heavenly form*: P. L. IX. 457; X. 872; or in sense (*c*): N. O. 100.

(*e*) worthy of heaven, godlike: P. R. I. 221.

absol. divine nature: P. L. VIII. 453.

(2) *adv.* divinely: P. L. II. 757, 813; VIII. 217.

Heavenly-born, *adj.* born in or of heaven: P. L. II. 860; VII. 7.

Heavenly-guided, *adj.* guided by God or angels: T. 19.

Heaven-tower, *sb. pl.* the battlements of the sky: P. L. XII. 52.

Heaven-warring, *adj.* engaging in war against God: P. L. II. 424.

Heaviness, *sb.* sadness, grief: U. C. II. 22.

Heavy, *adj.* (*a*) having great weight: T. 3; *comp.*: P. L. IV. 972; *fig. of sin, blame*: P. L. X. 741; *comp.*: P. L. X. 835, 836.

(*b*) hard to bear or endure, grievous, severe; *heavy curse, persecution, change*, etc.: P. L. XII. 103, 531; L. 37; *comp.*: P. L. III. 159; IV. 101; *sup.*: P. L. VI. 265; S. A. 445; P. 13.

(*c*) slow *pace*: P. L. VI. 551.

absol. that which is grievous: P. L. IX. 57.

Heavy(-armed) (last member of the compound understood from *light-armed*, which precedes), *adj.* wearing heavy armour: P. L. II. 902.

Hebe, *sb.* the goddess of youth and the cupbearer of the gods: V. Ex. 38; L'A. 29; C. 290.

Hebrew, *adj.* of or belonging to the Israelitish race: P. R. IV. 336; Ps. CXXXVI. 50. *See* **Ebrew.**

Hebrides, *sb.* the group of islands west of Scotland: L. 156.

Hebron, *sb.* the city of Judah: S. A. 148.

Hebrus, *sb.* a river of Thrace emptying into the Ægean Sea: L. 63.

Hecate, *sb.* the goddess of the lower world and of sorcery: C. 135, 535.

Hecatompylos, *sb.* a city south of the Caspian, the capital of the Parthian Empire under the Arsacidæ: P. R. III. 287.

Hedge, *sb.* barrier or fence formed by bushes or small trees growing close together: Ps. LXXX. 49.

Hedger, *sb.* one who repairs hedges: C. 293.

Hedgerow, *adj.* hedgerow elms, elms growing among the bushes forming a hedge: L'A. 58.

Heed, *sb.* careful attention, care: P. L. X. 1030; L'A. 141; *give heed*: P. L. IV. 969; *take heed*: P. L. VIII. 635; S. A. 1230.

Heel, *sb.* part of the foot below and behind the ankle: P. L. V. 284; *head or heel*: P. L. XII. 388; at one's heel, close behind one, *sing.*: P. L. XII. 631; *pl.*: P. L. II. 135; P. R. II. 420.

(*b*) put for the whole foot: S. A. 1235; *cloven heel*: L. 34; as a symbol of power or might: S. A. 140.

(*c*) put for the whole person, used with reference to the injury done by Satan to Christ or mankind; *bruise his heel*: P. L. X. 181, 498; *bruise the victor's heel*: P. L. XII. 385, 433.

Height. *See* Highth.

Heighten. *See* Highthen.

Heinous, *adj.* highly or odiously wicked: P. L. IX. 929; X. 1; S. A. 493, 991.

Heir, *sb.* one who succeeds or is entitled to succeed to a possession: C. 501; applied to Christ as succeeding to the power and authority of God: P. L. V. 720; VI. 707, 708, 887; P. R. IV. 633; N. O. 116; as succeeding to the throne of David: P. R. III. 405; used of a woman: M. W. 3; *fig. Shakespeare ... heir of fame*: W. S. 5.

Helena, *sb.* Helen, the wife of Menelaus: C. 676.

Helicon, *sb.* the mountain in Bœotia, the abode of the Muses: M. W. 56.

*Hell, *sb.* (*a*) the abode of departed spirits, Hades: C. 518; Sheol: Ps. LXXXVI. 47.

(*b*) the gods of Hades: Il P. 108.

(*c*) infernal regions, habitation of Satan and his angels and of the souls of the wicked after death: ·P. L. I. 666; II. 49, 268, 671, 1002; III. 160; IV. 508; X. 39; P. R. I. 46; *cope, deep, pit*, etc. *of*: P. L. I. 315, 345, 381, 542; II. 176, 918; X. 288, 299, 594,

636; XII. 42; P. R. I. 116; *bars, gates of*: P. L. II. 631; III. 82; IV. 795, 967; VIII. 231; X. 230; *emperor, prince of*: P. L. II. 313, 510; IV. 871; X. 621; *deepest, profoundest, utmost*: P. L. I. 251; III. 678; V. 542; N. O. 218; in combination or contrast with *earth, heaven, paradise*: P. L. II. 383; VI. 705; X. 57, 598; *fem. gen.*: P. L. III. 332; IV. 381; X. 365; *personified*: P. L. II. 788; VI. 867.

(*d*) inhabitants of hell, devils: P. L. II. 135, 554; III. 255; IV. 918; C. 581; as an exclamation: P. L. IV. 358.

(*e*) state of such extreme mental suffering that it may be compared to hell: P. L. I. 255; IV. 20, 21, 75, 78; P. R. I. 420; *hot hell*: P. L. IX. 467; *lover's hell*: P. L. V. 450.

Hell-born, *adj.* born in hell: P. L. II. 687.

Hell-bound, *sb. pl.* border or confines of hell: P. L. II. 644.

Hell-doomed, *adj.* condemned to hell: P. L. II. 697.

Hellespont, *sb.* the Strait of Dardanelles: P. L. X. 309.

Hell-fire, *sb.* fire of hell: P. L. II. 364.

Hell-flame, *sb. pl.* flames of hell: P. L. II. 61.

Hell-gate, *sb.* gate of hell: P. L. II. 725, 746; X. 415; *pl.*: P. L. X. 282, 369.

Hell-hound, *sb.* dog of hell: P. L. II. 654; *fig. of sin and death*: P. L. X. 630.

Hellish, *adj.* (*a*) of or from hell, infernal; *hellish foe, pest*, etc.: P. L. II. 504, 735; X. 585; P. R. IV. 422; *hate, rancour*, etc.: P. L. III. 298, 300; IX. 409; P. R. I. 175; C. 613.

(*b*) worthy of hell, diabolical; *hellish mischief, falsehood*: P. L. VI. 636; X. 873.

Helm, *sb.* rudder, tiller: S. A. 1045; *fig. helm of Rome*: S. XVII. 3.

Helm, *sb.* helmet: P. L. IV. 553; VI. 543, 840; XI. 245; *fig.* men wearing helmets: P. L. I. 547.

Helmed, (*disyl.*) *part. adj.* armed with helmets: P. L. VI. 840; N. O. 112.

Helmet, *sb.* defensive armour for the head: P. L. VI. 83; S. A. 141, 1119.

Help, (1) *sb.* (*a*) assistance, aid : P.
L. IV. 727; IX. 336; P. R. IV.
103; S. A. 1625; Ps. III. 6, 23;
LXXXII. 16.

   (*b*) relief, succour : S. A. 1266.

   (*c*) helpmate; *of Eve* : P. L.
VIII. 450; X. **137**; **XI. 165.**

   (2) *vb. tr.* (*a*) to assist, aid : Ps.
LXXXVI. 64; with *simple inf.* : S.
XX. 4; with *prep. inf.* : P. L. IX.
624; with *acc.* and *simple inf.* : C.
304; with *acc.* and *prep. inf.* : S.
XVI. 13.

   (*b*) to bring succour to, relieve,
rescue : C. 909.

   (*c*) to assist in bringing about,
further : P. L. VI. 656.

   (*d*) to remove wholly or in part,
remedy : P. L. VIII. 418; C. 845.

Helpful, *adj.* useful *service* : A. 38.

Helpless, *adj.* unable to help oneself, needing aid : S. A. 644;
helpless child, maiden, virgin : S.
A. 943; C. 402, 583.

Hem, (1) *sb.* border; *vesture's hem* :
A. 83.

   (2) *vb. tr.* to enclose or encompass *round* : P. L. IV. 979.

Hemisphere, *sb.* half of the sphere
of earth : P. L. III. 725; XI. 379;
of the sphere of the universe :
P. L. VII. 250; that half of the
heavens seen above the horizon :
P. L. VII. 384; *fig. night's hemisphere* : P. L. IX. 52.

*Hence, *adv.* (*a*) from this place : P.
L. I. 260; IV. 872; VI. 288; X.
260; XI. 315; XII. 557, 617; P.
R. I. 336; II. 56; S. A. 1229,
1572, 1731; *from hence* : P. L.
III. 540, 723; V. 257; VIII. 332;
IX. 617; X. 304; XI. 356; A. 3;
C. 824.

   (*b*) with ellipsis of vb. of motion;
hence, go hence, as a command to
depart : P. L. VI. 275; L'A. 1;
Il P. 1; *hence with,* take away :
C. 696; L. 18.

   (*c*) from this source : P. L. III.
731; VII. 366.

   (*d*) for this cause or reason,
therefore : P. L. IV. 522; S. A.
15; C. 441.

   (*e*) from this circumstance : S.
A. 224; from these data : P. R.
II. 317.

Henceforth (hénceforth : P. L. I.
187; IV. 966; VII. 569; X. 379;
P. R. I. 142, 456; hencefórth : P.
L. III. 414; V. 77, 881; IX. 799,
1140; XI. 176; P. R. I. 462; IV.

610; *doubtful* : P. L. I. 643; IV.
378, 486; IX. 1081; X. 872; XI.
547, 771; XII. 11, 561; S. A. 970;
L. 183), *adv.* from this time forward, from now on : P. L. I. 187,
643; III. 414; IV. 378, 486, 966;
V. 77, 881; VII. 569; IX. 799,
1081, 1140; X. 379, 872; XI. 176,
547, 771; XII. 11, 561; P. R. I.
142, 456, 462; IV. 610; S. A. 970;
L. 183.

*Her, I. *pers. pron. See* **She.**

   II. *poss. pron.,* of or belonging
to her; (1) referring to a female
person; with *sb.* : P. L. I. 443; II.
653; IV. 495; *obj. gen.* : P. L.
VIII. 480; D. F. I. 72; without
sb., her own : P. L. VIII. 549.

   (2) referring to a bird or insect :
P. L. VII. 431; S. A. 1703; Il P.
143; C. 318; L. 28; *spec.* to the
nightingale : P. L. III. 40; IV.
603.

   (3) referring to various things,
usually without personification;
(*a*) to a city, country, nation : P.
L. I. 352, 397, 480, 489; II. 4; P.
R. III. 170, 270; S. A. 1558; to
chaos : P. L. II. 1039; earth : P.
L. VII. 241; Eden : P. L. IV. 210;
hell : P. L. II. 175; heaven : P.
L. VI. 273; Paradise : P. L. IV.
133; the world : P. L. III. 334.

   (*b*) to a flower or plant : P. L.
IV. 259; VII. 311; M. W. 37; C.
622.

   (*c*) to the moon or other
heavenly bodies : P. L. I. 291,
786; III. 727; IV. 608; V. 621;
N. O. 240.

   (*d*) to air : P. L. II. 402;
beauty : P. R. II. 195; a building : P. L. I. 723; a cloud :
C. 224; darkness : P. L. IV. 666;
faith : S. XIV. 7; fancy : P. L. V.
103; the firmament : P. L. VIII.
19; form : P. L. I. 592; gloom :
N. O. 78; grace : P. L. III. 228;
harmony : P. L. V. 626; justice :
P. L. X. 859; knowledge : P. L.
VII. 127; light : P. L. VII. 242;
the mind : P. L. III. 52; May :
M. M. 3; morn : P. L. IV. 641;
nature : P. L. II. 911; night : P.
L. IV. 648; peace : S XVI. 10;
reason : P. L. V. 109; religion :
S. XVII. 14; a river : P. L. II.
584; a ship : P. L. IX. 515; Sin :
P. L. IX. 12; silence : C. 559;
soil : P. L. II. 271; the soul : P.
L. V. 487; strength : S. A. 173;

suspicion : P. L. III. 688 ; a table :
P. L. V. 393 ; truth : P. L. X.
856; twilight: P. L. IV. 599; the
understanding : P. L. IX. 1128 ;
verse : S. XIII. 9 ; vice : C. 760 ;
virtue : P. R. I. 483 ; war : S.
XVII. 8 ; wisdom : C. 378.

Herald, (*spelled* harald : P. L. I. 752;
II. 518 ; XI. 660) *sb.* (*a*) one who
has official authority to announce
a formal message or proclamation : P. L. II. 518 ; XI. 660 ;
winged haralds : P. L. I. 752 ;
herald of the sea, Triton : L. 89.
   (*b*) harbinger ; *attrib.* herald
lark : P. R. II. 279.

Heraldry, *sb.* pomp, ceremony : Cir.
10.

Herb, *sb.* any plant of which the
stem does not become woody, but
dies to the ground after flowering : P. L. VII. 310, 317 ; X. 204,
711 ; L'A. 85; Il P. 172 ; *flowery,
grassy, tender, trodden herb* : P. L.
IV. 253 ; VIII. 254 ; IX. 186, 572 ;
*cooling, cleansing, potent, savoury
herb* : S. A. 626, 1727 ; C. 255, 541 ;
in combination or contrast with
flower, fruit, plant, tree : P. L.
IV. 644, 652, 709 ; VII. 336 ; VIII.
527 ; IX. 111, 206 ; X. 603 ; XII.
184 ; C. 621.

Herculean, *adj.* resembling Hercules
in strength : P. L. IX. 1060.

Herd, *sb.* (*a*) a number of animals
together : P. L. VII. 462 ; P. R.
II. 287, 288 ; C. 731, 844 ; *haunt of
men and herds* : C. 388 ; *bleating,
pasturing, weanling herds* : P. L.
II. 494 ; IX. 1109 ; L. 46 ; *sportful, bestial* : P. L. IV. 396, 754 ;
herd of goats, beeves, cattle, swine :
P. L. VI. 856 ; XI. 557, 647 ; P.
R. IV. 630 ; in combination or
contrast with *flock* : P. L. III. 44;
XII. 19, 132 ; P. R. III. 260 ; said
of men changed into beasts : P. L.
IX. 522 ; C. 152.
   (*b*) used disparagingly of people,
the multitude, the rabble : P. L.
XII. 481 ; P. R. III. 49.   •

Herdman, *sb.* herdsman : L. 121.

Herdsman, *sb.* one who tends a herd,
keeper : P. L. IX. 1108.

*Here, *adv.* (*a*) in or at this place :
P. L. I. 71, 142 ; II. 458, 694 ; III.
430, 613 ; IV. 416 ; V. 294, 373 ;
after the name of a person to
whose presence attention is called :
P. L. II. 818 ; in pointing to a
place : P. L. XII. 144 ; P. R. III.

269 ; in reaching something to a
person : P. L. V. 74 ; opposed to
there : P. L. VI. 12 ; VIII. 157 ;
IX. 1149 ; X. 375 ; *here and there* :
P. R. III. 263 ; C. 936 ; *here below,* on earth : P. L. III. 600 ;
D. F. I. 49.
   (*b*) at this point in action,
speech, or thought : P. L. III.
266 ; IV. 235 ; VII. 548 ; VIII. 311,
528 ; XI. 502 ; XII. 270 ; N. O.
239.
   (*c*) in this case : P. L. VIII.
530 ; P. R. II. 143 ; IV. 6 ; in this
event or circumstance: S. A. 1721.

Hereafter, *adv.* at a later time, in
time to come, in future : P. L.
III. 444 ; VII. 488 ; VIII. 79 ; XII.
156 ; P. R. I. 164 ; IV. 625.

Hereby (herebý : S. A. 106 ; héreby :
P. L. IV. 672), *adv.* by this
means : P. L. IV. 672 ; by this
fact : S. A. 106.

Hereditary, *adj.* passing by inheritance from father to son ; *of the
throne of God* : P. L. XII. 370.

Herein (hérein : P. R. IV. 356), *adv.*
in this thing or matter : P. R. IV.
356 ; S. A. 61.

Hereof, *adv.* of this : S. A. 1145.

Heretic, *sb.* one who holds opinions
differing from the accepted faith :
F. of C. 11.

Hermes, *sb.* (*a*) the messenger of the
gods : P. L. IV. 717 ; C. 637 ; as
a musician : P. L. XI. 133.

   used for the metal mercury :
P. L. III. 603.
   (*b*) **thrice great Hermes,** Hermes
Trismegistus, the name given by
Neo-platonists to the Egyptian
god Thoth, reputed to be the
author of many books on art,
science, alchemy, magic, and religion : Il P. 88.

Hermione, *sb.* Harmonia, the wife of
Cadmus : P. L. IX. 506.

Hermit, *sb.* one who from religious
motives has retired into solitary
life : C. 390.

Hermitage, *sb.* habitation of a hermit : Il P. 168.

Hermon, *sb.* the mountain on the
northeastern border of Palestine :
P. L. XII. 141, 142.

Hero, *sb.* a man distinguished for
strength and valour : S. A. 1131 ;
heroes old : P. L. I. 552 ; XI. 243 ;
V. Ex. 47 ; applied to Christ, evidently in comparison with Hercules : P. 13.

Herod, *sb.* Herod the Great : P. R. II. 424.

Heroic. *adj.* (*a*) having the character of a hero ; *of persons* : S. A. 125, 318 ; of or characteristic of a hero ; *heroic act, deed, life* : P. L. II. 549 ; P. R. I. 15, 216 ; S. A. 527, 1711 ; *ardour, virtue,* etc. : P. L. VI. 66 ; IX. 32 ; XI. 690 ; S. A. 1279 ; *games, name* : P. L. IV. 551 ; IX. 40 ; like a hero in size : P. L. IX. 485.

(*b*) of the heroes of antiquity ; *heroic race* : P. L. I. 577.

(*c*) describing the deeds of heroes ; *heroic argument, song* : P. L. IX. 14, 25, 29.

Heroically, *adv.* courageously : S. A. 1710.

Hers, *poss. pron.* referring to a preceding *sb.* : P. L. X. 151 ; antecedent of rel. pron. : P. L. IX. 47.

Herself, *pron.* (1) *emphatic* ; (*a*) in apposition with a *sb.* : P. L. VIII. 506 ; L. 58, 57.

(*b*) taking the place of the nominative *pron.* : P L. IV. 270 ; as subject of the vb. *be* : C. 857 ; following *than* : P. L. VIII. 34 ; following *but* : P. L. II. 875.

(2) *refl.* : P. L. IV. 575 ; with a *prep.* : P. L. V. 380 ; VIII. 548 ; IX. 744, 794, 1185 ; referring to earth : P. L. VIII. 137 ; to fruit : P. L. VII. 312; to nature : S. A. 596 ; *prep.* omitted : P. L. IX. 432.

Hesebon, *sb.* Heshbon, the capital city of Sihon, king of the Amorites, (spelled Hesebon in Vulg.) : P. L. I. 408.

Hesperian, *adj.* (*a*) **Hesperian fields,** the country of Italy or Spain : P. L. I. 520.

(*b*) of the Hesperides, *Hesperian tree* : C. 393 ; *fables* : P. L. IV. 250 ; *Hesperian gardens,* apparently identified with Elysium and the Islands of the Blest : P. L. III. 568 ; *adv.* westward ; but certainly also with the meaning : of the Hesperides : P. L. VIII. 632.

Hesperides, *sb.* the daughters of Hesperus and the guardians of the golden apples ; *here* the garden in which the apples grew : P. R. II. 357.

Hesperus, *sb.* (*a*) the evening star : P. L. IV. 605; *the star of Hesperus* : P. L. IX. 49.

(*b*) the father of the Hesperides : C. 982.

Hew, *vb. tr.* (*a*) to cut down : P. L. I. 293 ; XI. 728.

(*b*) **hew to havoc,** cut all to pieces : P. L. VI. 449.

(*c*) to cut out *from* : P. L. V. 759.

Hide, *vb.* (*pret.* hid ; *past part.* hid : P. L. I. 673, 688 ; III. 39, 624 ; IV. 497 ; VI. 896 ; VIII. 126, 167 ; IX. 76, 408, 436 ; X. 100, 716 ; XI. 316, 579, 699 ; S. A. 89 ; D. F. I. 32 ; W. S. 3 ; C. 239 ; hidden, always *adj.* : P. L. II. 271 ; VI. 442, 516 ; C. 248, 415, 416, 418 ; L'A. 144.) *tr.* (1) to put or keep out of sight, conceal from discovery, secrete : P. L. I. 27, 673, 688 ; III. 39, 624 ; VII. 600 ; *a person or part of the body* : P. L. IV. 278, 497 ; IX. 76, 408, 436, 1090, 1092 ; X. 716 ; XI. 316 ; D. F. I. 32 ; Il P. 141 ; C. 239, 571 ; *stars, the moon* : P. L. VIII. 126 ; S. A. 89 ; *fraud, guilt, shame,* etc. : P. L. VI. 555 ; IX. 90, 1113 ; XI. 111 ; Ps. LXXXV. 8.

(*b*) **hide one's head** or **front,** cover or keep out of sight because of fear or shame ; *of nature* : N. O. 39 ; *of the sea* : Ps. CXIV. 8 ; *of the sun* : N. O. 80 ; *of stars* : P. L. IV. 35 ; conceal oneself from heaven or the gods : D. F. I. 49.

(*c*) to protect, keep in safety : Ps. LXXXIII. 12.

(*d*) to turn away *the face* as a sign of indifference or displeasure : S. A. 1749 ; Ps. LXXXVIII. 58.

(2) to conceal from the knowledge of others, keep secret *cause, judgement, talent, thought,* etc. : P. L. III. 707 ; VI. 896 ; VIII. 167 ; X. 974 ; XI. 68, 579, 699 ; P. R. III. 21 ; C. 383 ; S. XIX. 3.

(3) *refl.* to conceal oneself from sight : P. L. IX. 162 ; X. 100, 117, 723 ; P. R. IV. 630.

part. adj. **hidden,** concealed from sight or knowledge : P. L. II. 271 ; VI. 516 ; C. 248 ; *hidden cause* : P. L. VI. 442 ; *strength* : C. 415, 416, 418 ; *soul of harmony* : L'A. 144.

Hideous, (1) *adj.* (*a*) frightful, dreadful, horrible ; *hideous orifice, place,* etc. : P. L. VI. 577 ; P. R. I. 362 ; C. 520 ; Ps. LXXXVIII. 24 ; *peal, outcry,* etc. : P. L. II. 656, 726 ; XII. 56 ; S. A. 1509 ; N. O. 174 ; L. 61 ; *ruin, change, fall* : P. L. I. 46, 313 ; II. 717 ; *name* : P. L. II. 788.

(*b*) terrible on account of size; *hideous length* : P. L. VI. 107.

(2) *adv.* horribly: P. L. VI. 206.

Hie, *vb. intr.* to go in haste : P. L. II. 1055; *to thee my prayer doth hie* : Ps. LXXXVIII. 55.

Hierarch, *sb.* chief or leader of angels : P. L. V. 468, 587 ; XI. 220.

Hierarchal, *adj.* of a hierarchy : P. L. V. 701.

Hierarchy, *sb.* (*a*) each of the three divisions into which the nine orders of angels are divided in the system of the Pseudo-Dionysius the Areopagite: P. L. I. 737; V. 591, 692 ; the collective body of angels : P. L. VII. 192. *See* **Order.**

(*b*) **classic hierarchy,** the body of ecclesiastical rulers composing a classis or presbytery in the Presbyterian Church : F. of C. 7.

High, I. *adj.* (1) having great or considerable upward extent; *high hill, mountain* : P. L. IV. 284 ; VIII. 303; XI. 575, 851 ; P. R. II. 286 ; III. 252, 265; IV. 26; L. 54; Ps. LXXXVII. 1; CXIV. 11 ; *comp.*: P. L. XI. 381; *sup.* : P. L. XI. 378, 829; *tree, wood,* etc. : P. L. IV. 395 ; VII. 326 ; L'A. 56 ; A. 58 ; Ps. LXXX. 43; *sup.* : P. L. IV. 195 ; X. 1086 ; *temple, tower, wall,* etc. : P. L. I. 463, 733, 749 ; II. 62, 343 ; III. 503; IV. 546; VII. 141 ; X. 308, 445; XII. 342 ; P. R. IV. 51 ; Il P. 86 ; *sup.* : P. L. IV. 182 ; P. R. IV. 549; *God's high throne* : P. L. III. 655; *high mount of God* : P. L. V. 643 ; *high temple* : P. L. VII. 148 ; *palace-hall* : N. O. 148; *high Olympus* : P. L. X. 583; perhaps with a blending of sense (6) : P. L. II. 756 ; VII. 373.

(*b*) **high place,** eminence used as a place of worship; *of God's throne* : P. L. V. 732.

(2) situated far above some surface, having a lofty position : P. L. III. 77 ; IV. 371 ; V. 90; VII. 553 ; VIII. 121, 126 ; *high sphere, orb* : D. F. I. 39 ; *comp.* : P. L. V. 422 ; *high heaven* : P. L. VI. 228 ; VIII. 172 ; IX. 811, 812 ; *sup.* : P. L. I. 517 ; III. 657; VI. 13 ; VIII. 178 ; X. 889 ; *lawns* : L. 25 ; *pitch* : P. L. VIII. 198.

(*b*) having the rule of Olympus : C. 20. *See* **Jove.**

(3) exalted in position, station, or rank : P. L. III. 311; *comp.* : P. R. IV. 521 ; *high arbitrator, king, creator,* etc. : P. L. II. 359, 909 ; V. 220 ; VIII. 12 ; *sup.* : P. L. IX. 164, 683 ; XI. 297 ; *high Jove* : C. 78 ; *High God* : Ps. LXXXVII. 20; *high in salvation* : P. L. XI. 708 ; *high in the love of* : P. L. XII. 380; *high birth, degree, estate, office,* etc. : P. L. V. 707 ; X. 86 ; XII. 240 ; S. A. 170 ; M. W. 15 ; S. II. 11 ; *comp.* : P. L. IV. 50 ; *sup.* : P. L. II. 27 ; IV. 51 ; powerful; *higher foe* : P. L. II. 72.

(4) of exalted quality or character, of lofty or elevated kind, of great consequence or importance : P. L. III. 369 ; V. 543 ; VIII. 101; S. A. 47 ; C. 785; *comp.* : P. L. VIII. 358, 598; P. R. IV. 198 ; L. 87 ; *sup.* : P. L. III. 305 ; S. A. 685 ; *high deed, exploit, triumph, victory,* etc. : P. L. II. 111 ; III. 254 ; VII. 53 ; P. R. II. 114, 410, 411 ; III. 26, 228 ; V. 266 ; S. A. 525, 1221, 1492, 1740 ; L'A. 120 ; *sup.* : P. L. *comp.* : P. R. II. 203 ; II. 630; V. 865 ; VI. 112 ; XII. 570; P. R. I. 69 ; II. 438 ; *feast, service, solemnity* : P. L. V. 467 ; Il P. 163 ; C. 746 ; *decree, behest, summons,* etc. : P. L. III. 126, 533; V. 289, 290, 717 ; VIII. 238 ; X. 13, 953 ; XI. 72, 81, 251 ; *power, supremacy,* etc. : P. L. I. 132; II. 319 ; III. 205 ; V. 458 ; *sup.* : P. R. III. 30 ; *permission, will,* etc. : P. L. I. 161, 212, 366 ; *example,* etc. : P. L. IX. 962 ; X. 385 ; P. R. I. 37 ; *esteem, praise, renown, worth,* etc. : P. L. II. 472 ; VI. 745 ; X. 259 ; XI. 688 ; P. R. I. 370 ; II. 66 ; IV. 160 : A. 8 ; F. of C. 10 ; Eurip. 3 ; *comp.* : S. A. 685 ; *sup.* : P. L. II. 429 ; S. A. 175 ; *knowledge, thought, wisdom,* etc. : P. L. III. 116 ; V. 563 ; P. R. I. 229, 232 ; *comp.* : P. L. VIII. 551 ; IX. 42, 483 ; XII. 576 ; *sup.* : P. L. VII. 83 ; S. A. 1747 ; *verse* : C. 516 ; *hope, affliction* : P. R. II. 30, 92.

(*b*) of or from God : P. R. I. 142 ; S. A. 506 ; *sup.* : S. A. 61 ; high justice : P. L. XII. 401.

(*c*) above the physical nature : P. L. IX. 574 ; *comp.* : P. L. VIII. 586.

(*d*) trustworthy *authority* : P. R. II. 5.

(e) indicating high rank or position; *high title*: P. L. XI. 793; renowned; *highest name*: S. A. 1101.

(5) hard to comprehend, abstruse: P. L. VIII. 50, 55; IX. 602.

(6) chief; *highstreet*: S. A. 1458, 1599; *council-table*: N. O. 10.

(7) rich *fare*: P. R. II. 202.

(8) great in amount or degree: P. L. IX. 789, 1123; *comp.*: P. L. IX. 934; *sup.*: P. L. XI. 693; *high applause*: P. L. X. 505; *cheer*: S. A. 1613; strong *wind*: P. L. IX. 1122; violent *menace*: C. 654; great *advantage*: P. L. VI. 401.

(9) fully come; *high noon*: P. L. V. 174; S. A. 1612; *fig. sup.* highest point of ascension: Il P. 68.

(10) lofty, proud: P. L. I. 98, 528; IV. 95, 809.

(11) relatively acute in pitch, opposed to *low*: P. L. XI. 562.

absol. or *sb.* (a) **on high**, in heaven: Ps. LXXXIV. 45; CXXXVI. 93; in the mount of God: P. L. VI. 891; **from on high**, from heaven: P. L. II. 826; VI. 60; Ps. IV. 17.

(b) **the Most High**, God: P. L. I. 40; V. 699; VI. 906; VII. 182; X. 31; XI. 705; XII. 120, 369; P. R. I. 128; IV. 633; Ps. VII. 64; LXXXIII. 67; *God Most High*: P. L. XII. 382.

(c) **the Highest**, God: P. L. I. 667; II. 479, 693; VI. 114, 205; X. 1027; P. R. I. 139; *Highest*: P. L. VI. 724.

(d) the highest place: P. R. IV. 553.

(e) that which is greatest or most exalted: P. R. IV. 106.

II. *adv.* (a) at or to a great distance or extent upward: P. L. I. 304, 536; II. 1, 635, 644, 874; III. 58, 556; IV. 30, 90, 181, 219, 226, 554, 699, 944; V. 588, 757; VI. 71, 99, 189, 544; VII. 87, 288, 340, 428; IX. 170, 590, 1107; XII. 632; P. R. II. 280; IV. 417, 545; S. A. 1606; N. O. 55; L'A. 78; C. 798, 956; *comp.*: P. L. IV. 142, 146, 694; P. R. IV. 546; C. 1021; Ps. LXXXIII. 55; *sup.*: P. R. IV. 553; so as to protect the head: P. L. VI. 544.

(b) at, to, or in an elevated position or rank :. P. L. II. 7, 8;

IV. 49, 359; V. 812; VI. 899; IX. 940; XII. 457; S. A. 689; M. W. 61; to heaven: L. 172; *comp.*: P. L. IX. 174, 690; S. XIII. 12; from noble parentage, *comp.*: Il P. 22.

(c) to a great degree, eminently: P. L. II. 456; III. 146; VI. 26; *advance his praises high*: S. A. 450.

(d) abstrusely, profoundly: P. L. II. 558.

(e) proudly, loftily: Ps. LXXXIII. 8.

(f) in a noble manner, *comp.*: P. R. IV. 258.

High-arched, *adj.* having a high arch: P. L. X. 301.

High-blest, *adj.* supremely happy: P. L. XI. 145.

High-built, *adj.* of lofty structure: S. A. 1069.

High-climbing, *adj.* rising a great distance upwards, lofty: P. L. III. 546.

Highly, *adv.* in a great degree, very much, exceedingly: P. L. I. 666; S. A. 1148, 1333; *highly favoured*: P. L. I. 30; P. R. II. 68; *beloved*: P. L. XII. 308; *pleased*: P. L. II. 387, 845; *entitle highly*, honour with a high title: P. L. XI. 170.

Highly-favoured, *adj.* given very great blessings: M. W. 65.

High-raised, *adj.* exalted; *high-raised phantasy*; S. M. 5.

High-roofed, *adj.* having the covering composed of the interwoven branches of trees high above the ground: P. R. II. 293.

High-seated, *adj.* situated on high, lofty: P. L. VII. 585.

Highth (*spelled* height: A. 74), *sb.* (a) distance above some natural or assumed base, altitude: P. L. I. 282, 723; II. 893; XI. 730; *above all highth*: P. L. III. 58; *fig. highth of this argument*: P. L. I. 24; *of thy eternal ways*: P. L. VIII. 413; *to highth*, to full stature: P. L. IX. 677; immeasurable distance upward, by implication heaven, contrasted with *depth*: P. L. II. 324; P. R. I. 13.

(b) high or exalted rank, state, or degree: P. L. IV. 95; VI. 793; VIII. 430; IX. 167; P. R. I. 231; II. 45; A. 75.

(c) high point or position: P. L. I. 92.

(*d*) top, summit: P. L. II. 190;
P. R. IV. 39; *fig. of a person*: P.
L. IX. 510.

(*e*) highest degree or point;
*highth of aspiring, happiness,
wealth*, etc.: P. L. I. 552; VI.
132, 300; X. 724; P. R. II. 436;
S. A. 384, 683; *to the highth*:
P. L. II. 95; VIII. 454; S. A.
1349; *at highth of noon*, just at
noon: P. L. IV. 564; *in highth*,
at the highest point of passion
and the central point of the subject: P. L. IX. 675.

(*f*) something that is high; *of
heaven*: P. L. VII. 215; *of shade*:
P. L. IV. 138.

Highthen (*spelled* heighten: P. L.
IX. 793) *vb. tr.* to exalt *in thoughts*:
P. L. VI. 629; to elate, excite:
P. L. IX. 793.

High-throned, *adj.* seated on a high
throne: Cir. 19.

High-towered, *adj.* having lofty
towers: P. R. III. 261.

Hill, *sb.* natural elevation of the
earth's surface of indefinite height;
used of a single peak, of a range
of peaks, and of what in other
places is termed a mountain: P.
L. I. 231, 670, 689; II. 540, 557;
III. 435; IV. 182; V. 186, 261,
757; VI. 639, 664; VII. 8, 300;
VIII. 514; XI. 187, 210, 229, 367,
377, 381, 740, 829, 852; XII. 591,
606, 626; P. R. II. 285; III. 260,
333; IV. 29; C. 295; L. 23, 190;
Ps. LXXX. 42; CXIV. 12; *neighboring hill*: P. L. V. 547; VI. 663;
XI. 575; *high-climbing, slope,
tumid*: P. L. III. 546; IV. 261;
VII. 288; *hoar, snowy*: L'A. 55;
C. 927; *sunny*: P. L. III. 28; P.
R. IV. 447; *seated, uprooted*: P.
L. VI. 644, 781; *savage, shaggy*:
P. L. IV. 172, 224; *dawning*: P.
L. VI. 528; *echoing*: P. L. IV.
681; *infamous*: C. 424; in combination or contrast with *dale,
vale, valley*: P. L. II. 495, 944;
IV. 243, 538; V. 203; VI. 69, 641,
784; VII. 326; VIII. 262, 275; IX.
116; P. R. I. 303; III. 267, 332;
M. M. 8; S. XXIII. 9; *spec.* with
proper *adj.* or *sb.*: P. L. I. 10,
293; VII. 3; XII. 146; P. R. IV.
247; S. A. 148; Ps. II. 13; the
hill on which was situated the
throne of God: P. L. V. 732; VI.
57; *holy, sacred hill*: P. L. **V.**
604, 619; VI. 25; one of the

seven hills on which Rome was
built: P. R. IV. 35; the southern
summit of the Mount of Olives;
hill of scandal: P. L. I. 416; *opprobrious hill*: P. L. I. 403.

fig. hills of snow: V. Ex. 42;
hill of truth: S. IX. 4; *virtue's
hill*: P. R. II. 21.

See **Up-hill.**

Hillock, *sb.* small hill: P. L. VII.
469; L'A. 58; joined to *dale,
valley*: P. L. IV. 254; X. 860.

Hill-top, *sb.* summit of a hill, *fig.*:
P. L. VIII. 520.

Hilly, *adj.* abounding in hills: C.
531.

Him. *See* **He.**

*****Himself,** *pron.* (1) *emphatic*; (*a*) in
apposition with a *sb.*: P. L. X.
62, 799, 879; N. O. 70; referring
to the sun: N. O. 79; in apposition with a *pron.*: P. L. VIII. 251;
XII. 228; P. R. I. 76; III. 144;
L. 11.

(*b*) taking the place of the
nominative *pron.*: P. L. IV. 397;
P. R. II. 471; S. A. 42, 346; as
subject of the vb. *be*: C. 385;
following *but*: S. A. 299.

(2) *refl.*: P. L. I. 39; III. 409;
V. 665; VI. 341; XII. 76; P. R.
II. 98; S. A. 347; N. O. 154;
with a *prep.*: P. L. I. 79, 215;
III. 234; IV. 22; VI. 238; IX. 57;
X. 510; P. R. II. 237; S. A. 121;
S. X. 4.

Hind, *sb.* female of the red deer:
P. L. XI. 189.

Hind, *sb.* peasant, rustic: C. 174; S.
XII. 5.

Hinder, *adj.* posterior *parts*: P. L.
VII. 465.

Hinder, *vb.* (1) *tr.* to keep back, prevent; with *prep. inf.*: Hor. Sat. I.
2; with *simple* and *prep. inf.*: P.
L. IX. 778; with *acc.* and *prep.
inf.*: P. L. X. 8.

(2) *intr.* or *absol.* to stand in
the way, frustrate action: S. A.
1533.

Hindmost, *adj.* furthest in the rear:
C. 190.

Hinge, *sb.* (*a*) artificial moveable
joint: P. L. II. 881; *golden hinges*:
P. L. V. 255; VII. 207.

(*b*) one of the two poles about
which the earth revolves: N. O.
122.

(*c*) one of the four cardinal
points; *four hinges of the world*:
P. R. IV. 415.

Hinnom, *sb.* **valley of Hinnon**, the narrow ravine southwest of Jerusalem : P. L. I. 404. *See* **Gehenna.**

Hippogrif, *sb.* a fabulous creature having the fore parts of a griffin and the body and hind parts of a horse : P. R. IV. 542.

Hippotades, *sb.* Æolus, god of the winds, a son of Hippotas : L. 96.

Hire, *vb. tr.* to induce by the payment of money, bribe : S. A. 1114.

Hireling, (1) *sb.* one who acts only with a view to wages or reward : P. L. IV. 193.

(2) *adj.* serving for wages, mercenary : S. XVI. 14.

*His, *poss. pron.* of or belonging to him ; (1) referring to a male person; with *sb.* : P. L. I. 31, 51, 95 ; *his own* : P. L. I. 513 ; II. 370 ; *obj. gen.* : P. L. VII. 102 ; without *sb.*, *his own* : P. L. VI. 773 ; VIII. 103 ; X. 766.

(2) referring to bird, beast : P. L. I. 207 ; III. 437 ; XI. 185 ; to the nightingale, elsewhere regarded as feminine : P. L. V. 41.

(3) referring to various things, usually without personification ; (*a*) to the sun or other heavenly bodies : P. L. III. 578, 581, 616, 720 ; IV. 30, 543, 644 ; V. 141, 301, 424, 559 ; VII. 370 ; VIII. 97, 520.

(*b*) to a building : P. R. IV. 48; chaos : P. L. II. 960 ; a comet : P. L. II. 710 ; darkness : L'A. 6 ; day : C. 978 ; error : P. R. IV. 235 ; fame : S. A. 973 ; fate : P. L. V. 862 ; gluttony : C. 777 ; heaven : P. L. V. 44 ; a hill : P. L. VI. 782 ; hot, cold, etc. : P. L. II. 901 ; julep : C. 673 ; laughter : L'A. 32 ; leisure : Il P. 50 ; love : P. L. VIII. 590 ; a mountain : P. L. VI. 197 ; a plain : P. R. III. 255 ; a river : P. L. IV. 224, 232 ; the sea, the deep : P. L. XI. 849, 894 ; shame : P. L. IX. 1058 ; sleep : P. L. VII. 107 ; a spell : C. 919 ; Tartarus : P. L. VI. 52 ; time : S. II. 2 ; torment : S. A. 612 ; a tree : P. L. V. 219.

Hispahan, *sb.* Ispahan, the capital of Persia under the Sufawi Dynasty : P. L. XI. 394.

Hiss, *sb.* the cry of a serpent : P. L. X. 509, 518, 543, 546, 573 ; a similar sound ; *hiss of rustling wings* : P. L. I. 768 ; *of fiery darts* : P. L. VI. 212.

Hissing, *vbl. sb.* the sibilation of serpents : P. L. X. 522.

Hist, *vb. tr.* to summon in silence or without noise, *imper.* : Il P. 55.

Historian, *sb.* narrator of history ; *of Raphael* : P. L. VIII. 7.

Hit, *vb.* (*pret.* not used ; *past part.* hit) *tr.* (*a*) to strike : P. L. VI. 592.

(*b*) to be perceptible to ; *hit the sense of sight* : Il P. 14 ; *hitting thy aged ear* : S. A. 1568.

(*c*) to reach in execution, produce : P. L. IV. 255 ; A. 77.

(*d*) to light upon, come at, guess : S. A. 1014 ; C. 286.

Hither, (1) *adv.* to this place : P. L. II. 857 ; III. 445, 457, 463, 698 ; IV. 796, 908 ; V. 308 ; VII. 195, 364 ; VIII. 313, 347 ; IX. 475, 647 ; XI. 344 ; P. R. I. 335, 494 ; III. 350 ; S. A. 335, 821, 1070, 1445, 1536, 1539 ; L. 134, 139 ; Ps. LXXXI. 6.

(2) *adj.* on the side of the person speaking : P. L. III. 722 ; XI. 574.

Hitherto, *adv.* to this time, until now : P. L. IX. 28, 797 ; S. A. 1640.

Hitherward, *adv.* toward this place, this way : P. L. IV. 794 ; S. A. 1067.

Hive, *sb.* beehive : P. L. I. 770.

Hoar, *adj.* (*a*) gray from absence of foliage (?) : L'A. 55.

(*b*) old, ancient : A. 98.

Hoard, *vb. tr.* to treasure up, store : C. 739.

Hoarse, *adj.* (*a*) deep and rough to the ear : P. L. V. 873 ; *fig.* : P. L. VII. 25.

(*b*) having a hoarse voice : P. L. XII. 58 ; *fig. of the sea* : P. L. II. 661 ; *of the wind* : P. L. II. 287.

Hoary, *adj.* (*a*) white *frost* : P. L. XI. 899 ; or greyish white ; *of the deep of chaos* : P. L. II. 891.

(*b*) grey with age : C. 871.

Hobson, *sb.* Thomas Hobson, the carrier of letters and parcels between Cambridge and London : U. C. I. 1, 18.

Hog, *sb.* swine : C. 71 ; S. XII. 8.

Hold, I. *sb.* (*a*) possession, keeping : P. L. X. 406.

(*b*) grasp ; *fig. get hold of a sceptre* : P. R. IV. 480 ; *whom the grave hath hold on* : Ps. LXXXVIII. 46 ; *lay hold on occasion* : S. A. 1716 ; *the spell hath lost his hold* : C. 919.

(c) fortified place; *strong hold* :
P. L. VI. 228 ; *Bayona's hold* : L.
162.

(d) keeping, custody : S. A. 802.

(e) habitation : P. R. IV. 628.

II. *vb.* (*pres. 2d sing.* hold'st :
P. R. IV. 623 ; *pret.* and *past
part.* held) (1) *tr.* (a) to keep fast,
grasp : L'A. 32.

(b) to support in the arms : C.
1005.

(c) to hold in the hands so as
to manage or control : L. 119 ;
A. 65 ; *fig.* : S. XVII. 2 ; so as to
keep in a particular position : P.
L. III. 643 ; so as to present or
offer to another person : P. L. V.
82, 83 ; *fig.* : P. L. IV. 263.

(d) to contain : P. L. V. 347 ;
to be capable of containing, have
capacity for : P. L. II. 541 ; to
serve as a habitation for : P. L.
I. 200 ; III. 461 ; Il P. 90 ; A. 24.

(e) to have, possess, or occupy
a place : P. L. I. 734 ; II. 362 ;
S. A. 1081 ; *dominion, office,
power,* etc. : P. L. I. 124 ; IV.
111 ; V. 103 ; VII. 382, 532 ; XII.
68 ; P. R. III. 33 ; IV. 168, 494 ;
to remain in *a state* : P. L. V. 537 ;
to occupy or be in ; *star ... the top
of heaven doth hold* : C. 94.

(f) to retain ownership or control of : P. L. V. 723 ; X. 751 ;
XI. 635 ; P. R. II. 125.

(g) to keep or not to let go *a
person* : P. L. III. 84 ; to keep the
attention of *their ears* : P. L. V.
771.

(h) to keep in a specified place,
state, or relation : P. L. I. 657 ;
II. 12 ; X. 365 ; P. R. III. 296 ; S.
A. 796 ; V. Ex. 51 ; N. O. 108 ;
Il P. 41 : with two *acc.* : P. L. I.
618 ; S. A. 410 ; *held his look suspense* : P. L. II. 417 ; *he ... held
suspense in heaven* : P. L. VII. 100.

(i) to convoke and preside over
a council : P. L. I. 755.

(j) to celebrate or solemnize *a
feast* : S. A. 12, 1194 ; *triumphs* :
L'A. 120.

(k) to carry on or prosecute : P.
L. II. 895 ; to have *discourse, con-
versation,* etc. : P. L. V. 395 ;
VIII. 408 ; IX. 443 ; P. R. IV. 232 ;
S. A. 863.

(l) to maintain *concord* : P. L.
II. 497.

(m) to observe or obey *a law* :
Ps. LXXXI. 15.

(n) to believe : C. 588.

(o) to consider, judge to be ;
with two *acc.* : P. L. I. 508 ; III.
690 ; IV. 860, 887, 907 ; V. 441 ;
X. 800 ; XI. 693 ; P. R. I. 221 ;
IV. 10 ; D. F. I. 14 ; Il P. 26 ;
with *acc.* and *for* : P. L. II. 761.

(p) to entertain a specified feeling for ; *held in high esteem* : F. of
C. 10.

(q) to make for, direct one's
course toward : P. L. II. 1043.

(2) *intr.* (a) to continue, last,
remain : P. L. V. 537.

(b) to remain unbroken, *fig.* :
S. A. 1349.

(c) to be valid : S. A. 1369.

In combination with other words:
(a) **hold one's course** or **way**, keep
on going, proceed : P. L. VI. 2 ;
X. 411 ; XI. 900.

(b) **hold in fee** : S. XII. 7. *See*
Fee.

(c) **hold on**, continue, keep up :
P. L. IX. 180 ; *intr.* : P. L. XI.
633.

(d) **hold one's peace**, refrain
from speaking : P. L. X. 135 ;
Ps. LXXXIII. 2 ; Eurip. 4.

(e) **hold them play** : S. A. 719.
See Play.

(f) **hold up**, keep raised : C.
834.

Hole, *sb.* opening, aperture : C. 338.
See Key-hole, Loop-hole.

Holiday, *sb.* day of recreation and
amusement ; *sunshine holiday* :
L'A. 98 ; C. 959.

Hollow, *adj.* (a) having an empty
space or a cavity within : P. L. I.
707 ; II. 285 ; VI. 484, 552 ; VII.
289 ; *hollow abyss* : P. L. II. 518 ;
deep of hell : P. L. I. 314 ; *orb* :
P. L. VII. 257 ; *round of Cynthia's
seat* : N. O. 102 ; *hollow dark* :
P. L. II. 953.

(b) sunken *eyes* : Ps. LXXXVIII.
44.

(c) as if reverberated from a
cavity ; *hollow shriek* : N. O. 178.

(d) not sincere, false, deceitful : P. L. II. 112 ; VI. 578 ; P. R.
IV. 124 ; S. XVII. 6.

Hollowed, *part. adj.* excavated : P.
L. VI. 574.

Holocaust, *sb.* sacrifice wholly consumed by fire ; *fig. of the phœnix* :
S. A. 1702.

Holy. *adj.* (1) consecrated to a god ;
tapers' holy shine : N. O. 202 ; *holy
hearth* : N. O. 190. *See* Hearth.

(2) of, pertaining to, or in some way connected with God; (a) worthy of veneration, reverend, sacred; *memorials* : P. L. v. 593; *salutation* : P. L. v. 386; *secret* : S. A. 497; *rest* : P. L. vi. 272; vii. 91; *dictate of temperance* : C. 767; divine or sacred; *holy eyes* : P. L. xii. 109; *holier ground, ground less unholy* : C. 943.

(b) set apart for the use or service of God : P. L. i. 683; S. A. 1358; *holy day* : P. L. vii. 594; *hill* : P. L. v. 604; *mount* : P. L. v. 712; vi. 743; vii. 584; set apart for the worship of God; *holy ark*, etc. : P. L. xii. 340; P. R. i. 489; *rites* : P. L. i. 390; *mountain* : Ps. lxxxvii. 1; *Holy City* : P. R. iv. 545.

(c) concerned with God; *holy meditations* : P. R. i. 195; *sup.* : P. R. ii. 110; *holy psalms, song* : S. M. 15; N. O. 133; revealing God; *holy vision* : P. 41.

(d) setting apart or dedicating to the service of God; *holy nurture* : S. A. 362.

(e) of divine quality or character : C. 246; *holy light* : P. L. iii. 1.

(f) **Holy Land**, the Land of Canaan : P. L. iii. 536.

(g) **Holy Writ**, the New Testament Scriptures : P. R. ii. 8.

(3) conformed to the will of God; (a) of great moral purity and spiritual excellence : P. L. vii. 631; ix. 899; xi. 606; *holy sages* : N. O. 5; *holy goddess* : Il P. 11.

(b) of absolute moral purity; *of God* : P. R. i. 486; *the Holy One* : P. L. vi. 359; xii. 248; S. A. 1427; *the Holy Ghost* : P. R. i. 139.

absol. Holiest : P. L. vi. 724; *Holiest of Holies* : P. R. iv. 349.

(c) sinless; *holy rapture, passion* : P. L. v. 147; Il P. 41.

Holy-day, *sb.* day of a religious festival : S. A. 1421.

Homage, *sb.* dutiful respect, reverence : P. R. ii. 376.

Home, (1) *sb.* place or country in which one's fixed abode is located; *keep home* : C. 748; used of hell : P. L. ii. 458.

(b) **at home**, in one's own town, neighbourhood, or country : P. R. ii. 415; iii. 233; iv. 281; used of hell : P. L. ii. 457; in one's own house : S. A. 529, 805, 810, 917, 1458; U. C. i. 11.

(c) **native home**, one's own country : C. 76; applied to dust as the material out of which Adam and Eve were created : P. L. x. 1085.

(2) *adv.* (a) to one's own dwelling-place : P. R. iv. 639; S A. 1733; Ps. lxxxiv. 15; *fig. home to my breast* : P. L. xi. 154.

(b) to one's own country : P. L. xi. 692; P. R. ii. 79; S. xv. 6; *home to thy country* : S. A. 518.

(c) to the mark aimed at, effectively : P. L. vi. 622.

Home-felt, *adj.* felt in one's own heart : C. 262.

Homely, *adj.* (a) simple or humble *trade* : L. 65; common or ordinary *morsel* : P. L. x. 605.

(b) uncomely *features* : C. 748.

Homer, *sb.* the poet : P. R. iv. 259.

Homeward, *adv.* (a) toward one's abode : P. L. v. 688; xii. 632.

(b) toward one's country : L. 163.

Homicide, *sb.* manslayer : P. L. i. 417.

Honest, *adj.* faithful, genuine : S. A. 1366.

Honest-offered, *adj.* offered with sincerity and candour : C. 322.

Honesty, *sb.* integrity, uprightness : C. 691.

Honey, *sb.* the sweet substance gathered by the bees : P. L. vii. 492; Ps. lxxxi. 68.

Honeyed, *adj.* (a) covered with honey; *honeyed thigh* : Il P. 142.

(b) sweet *showers* : L. 140.

(c) flattering *words* : S. A. 1066.

Honeysuckle, *sb.* the plant *Lonicera caprifolium* : C. 545.

Honour, I. *sb.* (1) high respect, esteem, or reverence; (a) as rendered or shown : P. L. iii. 738; Ps. viii. 16; *do honour to* : P. L. v. 844; P. R. i. 75; S. A. 1178; *give, yield thee honour due* : L'A. 37; Ps. lxxxiii. 59; *treat, name with honour* : P. R. ii. 336; iii. 95.

(b) as enjoyed, gained, or received : P. R. ii. 422, 464; iv. 122, 207; *honour's sake of former deeds* : S. A. 372; *public marks of honour* : S. A. 992; *have the honour to* : N. O. 26; *woman's domestic honour* : P. L. xi. 617; opposed to *dishonour* : P. L. ix. 332.

(2) nice sense of and strict allegiance to what is right or due : P. L. IV. 314 ; VIII. 58, 508, 577 ; IX. 1057, 1074 ; *bright honour* : A. 27 ; *native honour* : P. L. IV. 289 ; *a blot to honour* : S. A. 412.

(*b*) sense of what is right according to the standard of conduct in war : S. A. 1166.

(*c*) **deed of honour,** act prompted by this sense of right : S. VIII. 3.

(3) purity, chastity : C. 220 ; *for dear honour's sake* : C. 864.

(4) high rank or position, dignity, distinction : P. L. I. 533 ; II. 453 ; III. 660 ; S. A. 1101, 1715 ; or in sense (1) : P. L. IV. 390 ; VI. 422 ; P. R. II. 86, 202, 227 ; IV. 368.

(5) mark or token of esteem or reverence ; *this* or *that honour* : P. L. V. 462, 817 ; P. R. II. 66 ; S. A. 449 ; *pl.* : P. L. V. 780 ; or position or title of rank, *pl.* : P. R. IV. 536.

(*b*) **in honour to,** as a mark of reverence or respect for, for the sake of honouring : P. L. V. 188, 289 ; S. A. 1360 ; A. 35 ; Ps. LXXXI. 40.

(6) that which confers honour on one ; *fairest flower ... summer's honour* : D. F. I. 3.

II. *vb.* (*pres. 2d sing.* honour'st : S. XIII. 9) *tr.* (*a*) to do honour to, pay respect to : P. L. II. 456 ; V. 315 ; P. R. I. 251, 329.

(*b*) to hold in honour, respect or revere ; *thy condescension shall be honoured* : P. L. VIII. 649 ; *honour truth* : S. A. 1276 ; to regard or treat *a person* with honour : S. A. 939.

(*c*) to confer honour upon *a person* : P. L. V. 663 ; VI. 676, 816 ; VIII. 227 ; S. XIII. 9 ; *a feast* : S. A. 1315 ; *thou honour'st verse* : S. XIII. 10 ; to raise in dignity, ennoble : P. L. V. 73.

part. adj. **honoured** respected, revered ; *of persons* : M. W. 2 ; C. 564 ; S. X. 14 ; *honoured bones* : W. S. 1 ; *honoured flood* : L. 85.

vbl. sb. **honouring,** respect : P. L. VIII. 569.

Honourable (hónouráble : S. A. 1108), *adj.* (*a*) of distinguished rank ; or, ironically, actuated by principles of honour : S. A. 1108.

(*b*) consistent with integrity, upright : S. A. 855.

Hood, *sb.* the covering for the head worn by monks : P. L. III. 490.

See **Grey-hooded.**

Hook, *sb.* shepherd's crook : C. 872.

See **Proteus.**

See **Sheep-hook.**

Hooked (*disyl.*), *adj.* armed with hooks or scythes : N. O. 56.

Hope, I. *sb.* (*a*) expectation of something desired, desire combined with expectation : P. L. I. 66, 275 ; IV. 60, 105, 108 ; IX. 424, 633 ; X. 1043 ; P. R. II. 30 ; III. 206 ; S. A. 460, 472, 1455, 1535 ; C. 410, 412 ; S. I. 3 ; *successful hope* : P. L. I. 120 ; *languished* : P. L. VI. 497 ; *voluptuous* : P. R. II. 165 ; *false, fallacious, vain* : P. L. II. 522, 568 ; IV. 808 ; *final, utmost* : P. L. II. 142 ; XII. 376 ; *out of, without, past* : P. L. VIII. 481 ; X. 995 ; S. A. 120 ; *uplifted, successful beyond hope* : P. L. II. 7 ; X. 463 ; *heart or hope* : S. XXII. 8 ; combined or contrasted with *despair* : P. L. I. 190 ; II. 7, 142 ; VI. 787 ; XI. 138 ; followed by *in* : P. L. I. 88 ; by *of* : P. L. II. 89, 498 ; VIII. 209 ; IX. 422, 475 ; X. 838 ; XI. 599 ; P. R. I. 105 ; III. 204 ; S. A. 82 ; with *prep. inf.* : P. L. III. 630 ; IV. 938, 960 ; IX. 476 ; XI. 271 ; P. R. II. 58 ; S. A. 1453, 1571 ; with *clause* : P. L. V. 119 ; XI. 779 ; or rather, feeling of trust or confidence : P. L. II. 416 ; S. IX. 11 ; Petr. 3.

pl. : P. L. IV. 808 ; IX. 985 ; X. 1011 ; S. A. 595, 1504 ; *great in hopes* : S. A. 523 ; *hopes of glory* : P. L. III. 449.

personified : C. 213.

(*b*) ground or reason for hope : P. L. II. 221 ; something giving hope : P. R. II. 417 ; object of hope, thing desired : P. L. VI. 131 ; XI. 493 ; P. R. II. 57 ; IV. 3 ; M. W. 25 ; *pl.* : P. L. I. 637.

II. *vb.* (1) *tr.* (*a*) to expect with desire, desire with expectation of obtaining : P. L. II. 234 ; XII. 576 ; S. A. 838 ; with two *acc.* : Hor. O. 11 ; with *prep. inf.* : P. L. II. 232, 811 ; IV. 892 ; VI. 258, 287 ; IX. 493 ; P. R. II. 341 ; X. 308 ; P. R. III. 359 ; L. 73 ; F. of C. 13 ; with *clause* : P. R. III. 216 ; C. 400.

(*b*) to hope to know or find out : P. L. VII. 121.

(2) *intr.* to trust confidently that good will come: S. A. 647. *part. adj.* hoped, confidently expected; *hoped success*: P. L. III. 740; P. R. IV. 578.

Hopeful, *adj.* (*a*) full of hope, desiring with confident expectation: P. L. XI. 543; with *of*: S. A. 1575; with *prep. inf.*: P. L. X. 972.

(*b*) exciting hope; *hopeful sheaves*: P. L. IV. 984.

Hopeless, *adj.* (*a*) destitute of hope; with *prep. inf.*: P. L. IX. 259.

(*b*) affording no hope: S. A. 648; S. I. 10.

(*c*) unhoped-for; *ages of hopeless end*: P. L. II. 186.

Horizon, *sb.* (*a*) the line at which the earth and sky appear to meet: P. L. III. 560; *the horizon round invested*: P. L. VII. 371; *veiled the horizon round*: P. L. IX. 52; *rounded still the horizon*: P. L. X. 684; a similar line in heaven: P. L. VI. 79.

(*b*) *fig.* the limit of one's effort: P. 23.

Horizontal, *adj.* of the horizon: P. L. I. 595.

Horn, *sb.* (1) the excrescent growth upon the head; (*a*) the horns of Astarte, who, as the goddess of the moon, was represented with a crescent moon on her head, or with horns resembling those of the moon: P. L. I. 439.

(*b*) the horn of the god Ammon: N. O. 203. *See* Hammon.

(*c*) Amalthea's horn, the horn of plenty, the cornucopia, which yielded either food or drink as its possessor wished: P. R. II. 356.

(*d*) as a symbol of power; *lift thy horn*: Petr. 3.

(2) anything in the shape of a horn or in some way resembling a horn; (*a*) each of the extremities of the planet Venus when waning or waxing: P. L. VII. 366.

(*b*) sharpening in mooned horns their phalanx, bringing the wings of the phalanx into the shape of the waning or waxing moon: P. L. IV. 978.

(*c*) the horns of Turkish crescent, the figure of the new or old moon upon the Turkish standard, *fig.* the Turkish power: P. L. X. 433.

(*d*) each of the two wings of an army: P. R. III. 327.

(3) wind instrument; *hounds and horn*: L'A. 53; *tasselled horn*: A. 57; *fig.*: L. 28.

Horned (*disyl.*: P. L. XI. 831; Ps. CXXXVI. 33), *adj.* (*a*) having horns: P. L. X. 525.

(*b*) having what resembles horns; *the horned moon*, the moon as it appears in the first and last quarter: Ps. CXXXVI. 33; *the horned flood*, a body of water divided into two streams resembling horns in shape: P. L. XI. 831.

Hornet, *sb.* the insect *Vespa*: S. A. 20.

Horny, *adj.* consisting of horn; *horny beaks*: P. R. II. 267.

Horonaim, *sb.* a town of Moab: P. L. I. 409.

Horrent, *adj.* bristling *arms*: P. L. II. 513.

Horrible, (1) *adj.* exciting horror, dreadful, terrible, hideous: P. L. I. 61; XI. 465; *horrible destruction*: P. L. I. 137; *horrible discord, confusion, convulsion*: P. L. VI. 210; X. 472; S. A. 1649.

(2) *adv.* horribly; *grinned horrible*: P. L. II. 846.

Horribly, *adv.* dreadfully *loud*: S. A. 1510.

Horrid, *adj.* (*a*) bristling, shaggy, rough; *horrid front of battle*: P. L. I. 563; *arms*: P. L. II. 63; *hair*: P. L. II. 710; *shade*: P. R. I. 296; C. 429; savage, wild (?): P. L. IX. 185; jagged, or in sense (*b*): P. R. IV. 411.

(*b*) exciting horror, dreadful, terrible, detestable: P. L. I. 51, 83, 224, 392; II. 644, 676; IV. 996; VI. 207, 252, 305, 668; X. 540, 789; XI. 465; P. R. IV. 94; S. A. 501, 1542; L'A. 4; N. O. 157.

Horror, *sb.* (*a*) painful emotion of fear or loathing: P. L. II. 220, 703; IV. 18; VI. 863; X. 539; *chill horror*: P. L. IX. 890; *damp horror chilled*: P. L. V. 65; *shuddering horror*: P. L. II. 616; *abyss of horrors*: P. L. X. 843; *stood in horror*: P. L. VI. 307; *personified*: P. L. IV. 989.

(*b*) that which excites horror: P. L. II. 67; S. A. 1550; N. O. 172; C. 38; *pl.*: P. L. I. 250; II. 177.

Horse, *sb.* (1) the animal *Equus*: P. L. V. 356; P. R. III. 313.

(b) **pale horse**, the horse on which death rides (cf. Rev. VI. 8) : P. L. X. 590.

(c) **the horse of brass**, the horse described in Chaucer's Squieres Tale, which could bear its rider wherever he wished in the space of a day : Il P. 114.

(2) horsemen, cavalry : P. L. II. 887 ; P. R. IV. 66 ; *horse and foot* : P. L. XI. 645 ; S. A. 1618. *See* **River-horse.**

Horseman, *sb.* mounted soldier : P. R. III. 307.

Hosanna, (1) *interj.* as an ascription of praise to God ; *Hosanna to the Highest* : P. L. VI. 205.

(2) *sb.* shout of praise : P. L. III. 348.

Hospitable (hóspitáble), *adj.* extending a generous welcome to strangers ; *hospitable thoughts* : P. L. V. 332 ; *door* : P. L. I. 504 ; *Athens* : P. R. IV. 242 ; *covert, woods* : P. R. II. 262 ; C. 187.

Host, *sb.* (*a*) armed company of men or angels, army : P. L. I. 754 ; II. 885 ; IV. 922 ; VI. 104, 214, 231, 392, 527, 590, 633, 647, 800 ; XII. 196, 209 ; P. R. III. 300 ; S. A. 262.

(*b*) great multitude (some of the following possibly belong in (*a*)) : P. L. VI. 830 ; multitude of angels : P. L. I. 37, 136, 541 ; II. 993 ; VI. 38 ; X. 437 ; *infinite host* : P. L. V. 874 ; *angelic host, host of angels* : P. L. V. 535, 583 ; VII. 132 ; *host of heaven, heaven's host, heavenly host* : P. L. I. 635 ; II. 759, 824 ; V. 710 ; XI. 230 ; P. R. I. 416 ; *cherubic* : S. M. 12 ; *golden-winged* : D. F. I. 57 ; *God of Hosts* : Ps. LXXX. 17, 30, 57, 78 ; LXXXIV. 2, 13, 29, 45 ; preceded by *an* : P. L. V. 744.

(*c*) multitude of stars ; *starry host* : P. L. IV. 606 ; *spangled* : N. O. 21.

Host, *sb.* one who lodges and entertains another in his own house : P. L. IX. 441.

Hostile, *adj.* (*a*) of or pertaining to an enemy ; *hostile arms, sword* : P. L. VI. 50 ; S. A. 692 ; *snare* : P. L. XII. 31 ; *ground* : S. A. 531 ; *city* : S. A. 1561 ; *blood* : N. O. 57 ; *acts, deeds* : P. L. XI. 796 ; S. A. 893, 1210 ; of warfare ; *hostile din* : P. L. II. 1040.

(*b*) showing enmity ; *hostile*

scorn, frown : P. L. V. 904 ; VI. 260.

Hostility, *sb.* (*a*) inimical feeling, antagonism : P. L. II. 336.

(*b*) open opposition by war or other means : S. A. 1203.

Hosting, *sb.* hostile encounter : P. L. VI. 93.

Hot, (1) *adj.* (*a*) of a high temperature ; *hot vapour*, etc. : P. L. X. 694.

(*b*) intense, violent ; *hot displeasure* : Ps. VI. 2 ; *hell* : P. L. IX. 467.

(2) *sb.* one of the supposed qualities which in combination with another determined the nature or 'complexion' of a body, *personified* : P. L. II. 898.

(3) *adv.* with great heat : P. L. XI. 845 ; at a high temperature : P. L. XI. 568.

Hound, *sb.* dog used in the chase : L'A. 53. *See* **Hell-hound.**

Hour, *sb.* (*a*) the time of sixty minutes : P. L. VIII. 69 ; X. 923 ; or *pl.* the seasons, with reference to sense (*f*) : P. R. I. 57.

(*b*) used indefinitely for a short time : S. A. 1056 ; *in an hour* : P. L. I. 697 ; S. A. 364 ; *each hour*, all the time : P. L. X. 440.

(*c*) definite time of day : P. L. VII. 444 ; *dusky hour* : P. L. V. 667 ; *meridian hour* : P. L. IV. 581 ; *midnight* : Il P. 85 ; *morning* : C. 920 ; *hour of night* : P. L. IV. 610 ; P. R. II. 260 ; *hour of noon* : P. L. IX. 769 ; *hour of prime* : P. L. V. 170 ; *hour of repast, supper* : P. L. VIII. 213 ; IX. 225.

(*d*) definite time in general ; *cheerful, happy*, etc. : S. XXI. 14 ; *pl.* : P. L. II. 527 ; III. 417 ; IX. 1188 ; *private hours* : P. R. IV. 331.

(*e*) particular or appointed time at which something occurs : P. L. II. 934 ; IV. 779, 963 ; VI. 396 ; VIII. 512 ; IX. 406, 596 ; XI. 202 ; XII. 589 ; P. R. IV. 522 ; *her, their hour* : P. L. V. 303 ; VI. 10 ; X. 93 ; *cursed, evil, torturing* : P. L. II. 91, 1055 ; IX. 780, 1067 ; *hour of revenge* : P. L. VI. 150 ; *good, welcome hour* : P. L. II. 848 ; X. 771.

(*f*) *pl.* the Horæ, goddesses of the seasons : P. L. IV. 267 ; VI. 3 ; T. 2 ; C. 986 ; S. I. 4. *See* **Mid-hour, Morning-hour.**

Hourly, *adv.* every hour : P. L. II.
796.
House, I. *sb.* (1) building for human
habitation : P. L. IX. 446 ; XII.
121 ; P. R. IV. 639 ; S. A. 1112,
1491, 1733 ; *house of Pindarus* :
S. VIII. 11 ; *of Socrates*: P. R. IV.
273 ; *houses of gods* : P. R. IV.
56 ; applied to a jail ; *house of
liberty* : S. A. 949.
   (2) *fig.* (*a*) **God's house,** the
throne of God : P. L. VII. 576.
   (*b*) **house of pain** or **woe,** hell :
P. L. II. 823 ; VI. 877 ; X. 465.
   (*c*) **death's house,** the grave :
Ps. LXXXVIII. 24.
   (*d*) **house of mortal clay,** the
human body : N. O. 14.
   (*e*) the nest of a bird : Ps.
LXXXIV. 10.
   (3) building devoted to the worship of God : S. A. 518 ; Ps. v.
19 ; LXXXIV. 17.
   (*b*) **thy Father's house,** the
Temple in Jerusalem : P. R. IV.
552.
   (*c*) **the house of God,** God's
house : P. L. I. 470 ; the Tabernacle in Shiloh : P. L. I. 496 ;
the Temple in Jerusalem : P. L.
XII. 349 ; *pl.* habitations : Ps.
LXXXIII. 47.
   (4) family, household : S. A.
1049 ; C. 85 ; Hor. Epist. 5.
   (5) family, race : P. R. III.
282 ; S. A. 447, 1717 ; M. W. 54 ;
thy Father's house, the Israelitish
nation as the chosen people of
God : P. R. III. 175.
   II. *vb. intr.* to take up one's
abode *with death* : M. W. 10.
   See **Lazar-house, Prison-house,
Senate-house.**
Household, (1) *sb.* family : P. L. XI.
820.
   (2) *adj.* pertaining to the family,
domestic : P. L. IX. 233 ; X. 908 ;
S. A. 566.
Hover, *vb. intr.* to hang in the air
with fluttering wings ; *of angels,
spirits*: P. L. I. 345 ; X. 285 ;
D. F. I. 38 ; *fig. of clouds* : P. L.
II. 717 ; *of fire* : P. L. IX. 639 ; *of
the sun* : P. L. v. 140.
   part. adj. **hovering,** hanging
poised in air ; *hovering angel* : C.
214 ; *fig. hovering dreams* : Il P.
9.
   See **Wide-hovering.**
*****How,** I. *adv.* (1) in direct ques-
tions ; in what way or manner (?),

P. L. v. 531, 564 ; VIII. 359, 408 ;
IX. 326 ; X. 120 ; XII. 284 ; P. R.
II. 319 ; S. A. 838 ; C. 616.
   (2) in direct exclamations ; in
what a way ! to what an extent
or degree !, P. L. IV. 94, 680 ; v.
92 ; VI. 266 ; IX. 900, 1114 ; XI.
754 ; S. A. 944.
   (3) (*a*) in dependent questions
and exclamations ; in what way,
by what means ; qualifying a
vb. and depending on a vb. :
P. L. I. 187, 217, 611 ; IV. 236 ;
VII. 62 ; IX. 201 ; P. R. I. 137 ;
with ellipsis of the rest of the
clause : S. A. 1547 ; qualifying a
vb. and depending on an adj. :
P. L. II. 153 ; P. R. IV. 311 ;
followed by an inf. : P. L. v.
822 ; P. R. II. 113 ; C. 274 ; L.
119 ; S. XIII. 2.
   (*b*) =that : S. XIX. 1.
   (*c*) to what extent or degree ;
qualifying an adj. or adv. : P. L.
III. 276 ; IV. 39, 87, 366 ; v. 826 ;
VI. 148 ; IX. 138 ; S. A. 189.
   (4) introducing a relative clause ;
(*a*) however ; qualifying an adv. :
P. L. XI. 554.
   (*b*) to what extent or degree ;
correlative to *so*, which is omitted,
the rarer ... by how much : S. A.
167.
   (*c*) in some way ; *how else* :
S. A. 604.
   II. *sb.* the way (in which) ; *the
how* : P. R. IV. 472.
However, *adv.* (*a*) in whatever manner, by whatever means ; qualifying an adj. or part. : P. L. v. 258 ;
IX. 683 ; X. 134 ; XI. 373 ; S. II.
11.
   (*b*) for all that, nevertheless ;
qualifying a clause or sentence :
P. L. IV. 911 ; VI. 292, 563 ; IX.
95 ; X. 578 ; P. R. II. 135 ; IV.
321 ; S. A. 601.
Howl, *vb. intr.* to cry as a dog or
wolf : P. L. II. 658, 799 ; C. 533 ;
ghosts and furies ... howled : P. R.
IV. 423.
Hubbub, *sb.* confused noise of many
voices or sounds : P. L. II. 951 ;
XII. 60.
Huddling, *part. adj.* hurrying : C.
495.
Hue, *sb.* (*a*) appearance, look : P.
L. I. 527.
   (*b*) colour : P. L. I. 230 ; IV.
256, 698 ; XI. 557 ; P. R. II. 352 ;
N. O. 207 ; C. 994 ; *golden hue* :

P. L. IV. 148; *red, love's proper hue*: P. L. VIII. 619; *black, staid wisdom's hue*: Il P. 16; *hue of rainbows*: P. L. VII. 445.

Hug, *vb. tr. fig.* hug **him into snares**, allure him into snares by means of acts of courtesy or tokens of affection: C. 164.

Huge, *adj.* (*a*) very large, immense, enormous, vast: P. L. I. 196, 209, 547, 710; II. 434, 709, 874; VI. 193, 364, 552; VII. 285, 410, 496; X. 531; XI. 729; P. R. III. 261; IV. 51; N. O. 226; C. 423; *sup.*: P. L. I. 202; VII. 413; very great in number: P. L. VI. 873.

(*b*) powerful, mighty: P. L. VI. 251.

(*c*) very great; *huge affliction, hazard, labour*, etc.: P. L. I. 57; II. 473; S. A. 65; Cir. 27; P. 14.

Huge-bellied, *adj. fig.*, high and rounded; *of mountains*: Ps. CXIV. 11.

Hull, *vb. intr.* to drift or float on the water: P. L. XI. 840.

Hum, *sb.* the low confused noise of distant voices: N. O. 174; *busy hum of men*: L'A. 118.

Human, (1) *adj.* (*a*) of, belonging to, or characteristic of man: P. L. VIII. 392, 587; P. R. II. 137; S. A. 792; D. F. I. 58; *human breath, ears, face, voice,* etc.: P. L. III. 44; VII. 177, 368; IX. 561, 871; XI. 147; P. R. I. 298; S. A. 690; C. 68, 297; Il P. 14; N. O. 126; *form, mould*: P. L. I. 359, 482; P. R. IV. 599; A. 73; *human sense*: P. L. IV. 206; V. 565, 572; VIII. 119; IX. 554, 871; XII. 10; *power, strength, weakness,* etc.: P. L. V. 459; VII. 640; X. 793; P. R. III. 402; S. A. 1313; *human nature*: P. R. III. 231; *life*: P. L. VIII. 250; IX. 241; X. 908; P. R. IV. 265; *food*: P. R. I. 308; II. 246; *human desire, glory, knowledge,* etc.: P. L. V. 518; VI. 300; VII. 75; VIII. 414; XI. 694.

(*b*) that is a man, consisting of men; *human kind, race, offspring,* etc.: P. L. III. 462; IV. 475, 751; VI. 896; P. 14; *human pair*: P. L. V. 227; IX. 197; *sacrifice*: P. L. I. 393.

(2) *sb.* (*a*) human being: P. L. IX. 712; XII. 71.

(*b*) human nature: P. L. IX. 714.

Humane, *adj.* (*a*) gentle in demeanour: P. L. IX. 732.

(*b*) worthy of man, kind, benevolent: P. R. I. 221.

(*c*) polite, elegant: P. L. II. 109.

Humber, *sb.* the river of England: V. Ex. 99.

Humble, (1) *adj.* (*a*) lowly, meek: P. L. II. 240; X. 912; *humble deprecation*: P. L. VIII. 378; *submission*: S. A. 511; *words*: P. L. XI. 295.

(*b*) modest, unassuming: N. O. 24.

(*c*) lowly in condition; *humble state*: P. R. III. 189; *poverty*: Petr. 1; low-growing *shrub*: P. L. VII. 322.

(2) *vb. tr.* (*a*) to make *the heart* meek and submissive: P. L. XI. 150; XII. 193.

(*b*) to abase *pride*: P. L. VI. 342.

(*c*) *refl.* to make oneself meek and submissive: P. R. III. 421; S. A. 965.

vbl. sb. **humbling**, abasement: P. L. X. 576.

See **Much-humbled.**

Humbly, *adv.* meekly: P. L. X. 1089, 1101.

Humid, *adj.* damp, moist; *humid exhalations*: P. L. V. 425; *flowers*: P. L. IX. 193; *rivers ... draw their humid train*: P. L. VII. 306; *humid bow*, the rainbow: P. L. IV. 151; C. 992.

Humiliation, *sb.* abasement: P. L. III. 313; X. 1092, 1104; P. R. I. 160.

Humming, *part. adj.* buzzing *sound*: P. R. IV. 17.

Humour, (1) *sb.* (*a*) moisture: P. L. III. 610; VII. 280.

(*b*) **black humour**, black bile or melancholy, one of the four chief fluids of the body; these were supposed to determine, by their conditions and proportions, a person's physical and mental qualities and disposition: S. A. 600.

(*c*) the vital fluid of celestial spirits: P. L. VI. 332.

(2) *vb. tr.* to comply with the peculiar nature of: S. XIII. 8.

Hundred, (1) *sb.* ten times ten: P. L. I. 760.

(2) *adj.* consisting of a hundred: P. R. III. 287; A. 22; *four hundred*: P. L. I. 428.

Hundredfold, *sb.* a hundred times as many : S. XVIII. 13.

Hunger, (1) *sb.* pain or uneasiness from want of food : P. L. IV. 184; V. 437; P. R. I. 308; II. 252, 255, 306, 319, 373, 389, 406; C. 358; joined to *thirst, droughth* : P. L. VIII. 213; IX. 586; X. 556, 568; P. R. II. 325; IV. 592.

(2) *vb. intr.* (*a*) to feel or suffer hunger : P. R. I. 309; II. 231, 244, 333 ; joined to *thirst* : P. R. IV. 121.

(*b*) to have an eager desire; with *prep. inf.* : P. R. II. 259.

Hunger-bit, *adj.* perishing of hunger : P. R. II. 416.

Hungry, *adj.* feeling pain or uneasiness from want of food : P. R. IV. 403 ; L. 125.

Hunt, *vb.* (1) *tr.* to pursue *with war* : P. L. XII. 30.

(2) *intr.* to follow the chase : Il P. 124.

Hunter, *sb.* one who engages in the chase, huntsman : P. L. XII. 33 ; applied to a beast : P. L. XI. 188.

Huntress, *sb.* a woman who hunts, *spec.* Diana : C. 441 ; H. B. 1.

Hurdled, *part. adj.* constructed of hurdles or movable frames made of interwoven twigs or sticks : P. L. IV. 186.

Hurl, *vb. tr.* (*a*) to throw or cast with violence *persons* : P. L. I. 45 ; II. 374; X. 636; *things* : P. L. VI. 665; C. 153 ; to cast or dash by the action of wind or waves : P. L. II. 180; L. 155.

(*b*) to utter with vehemence : P. L. I. 669.

Hurry, *vb. tr.* to cause to go or move with excessive haste : P. L. II. 603, 937 ; P. R. IV. 402 ; P. 50.

part. adj. **hurried,** brought about with haste and confusion : P. L. V. 778.

Hurt, *vb.* (*pret.* hurt : S. A. 1676 ; *past part.* not used) *tr.* to harm, injure, do mischief to : P. L. IX. 700, 727; XII. 418; S. A. 1676; C. 589.

Hurtful, *adj.* tending to injury, causing harm, injurious : P. L. II. 259; *hurtful power* : C. 437 ; noxious *worm* : A. 53.

Husband, *sb.* a man joined to a woman in marriage : P. L. IX. 234, 268 ; S. A. 755; applied to Adam : P. L. VIII. 52 ; IX. 204,

385, 482; X. 4, 195, 336; XI. 291; to Samson : S. A. 883, 940; to Admetus : S. XXIII. 3.

attrib. fig. the bee ...*feeds her husband drone* : P. L. VII. 490.

Hush, *vb. tr.* to make silent *the woods* : C. 88.

Husk, *sb.* rind or hull of seeds : P. L. V. 342.

Huswife, *sb.* housewife : C. 751.

Hutch, *vb. tr.* to hoard or lay up in a chest : C. 719.

Hyacinth, *sb.* (*a*) the beautiful youth whom Apollo loved, and whom he accidentally killed during a game of discus : D. F. I. 25, 26.

(*b*) the flower *Hyacinthus* : P. L. IV. 701; IX. 1041 ; C. 998.

Hyacinthine, *adj.* of the colour of the hyacinth, evidently *here* dark brown or black (cf. *Odyssey* VI. 231 ; Theocritus X. 28) : P. L. IV. 301.

Hyæna, *sb. fig.* used by Samson in addressing Dalila, as a term of aversion and hatred : S. A. 748.

Hyaline, *sb.* glassy sea (θάλασσα ὑαλίνη, Rev. IV. 6 ; XV. 2) : P. L. VII. 619.

Hydaspes, *sb.* the modern Jhelum, a river of the Punjab, India : P. L. III. 436.

Hydra, *sb.* the many-headed snake of the marshes of Lerna, which was slain by Heracles : P. L. II. 628 ; C. 605.

attrib. fig. with allusion to the fact that for every head cut off by Heracles two grew in its place : S. XV. 7.

Hydrus, *sb.* a fabulous sea-snake : P. L. X. 525.

Hylas, *sb.* a beautiful youth beloved by Heracles : P. R. II. 353.

Hymen, *sb.* the god of marriage : P. L. XI. 591 ; L'A. 125.

Hymenæan, *sb.* marriage-song : P. L. IV. 711.

Hymettus, *sb.* the mountain southeast of Athens, celebrated for its honey : P. R. IV. 247.

Hymn, (1) *sb.* song of praise to God : P. L. II. 242 ; III. 148 ; V. 656 ; VI. 745 ; P. R. I. 169 ; IV. 335 ; N. O. 17; S. M. 15; S. XIII. 11 ; song of praise in honour of a god : P. R. IV. 341.

(2) *vb.* (*a*) *tr.* to celebrate or worship in song *the Father* : P. L. VI. 96; *hymn his throne* : P. L. IV. 944.

(b) *intr.* to sing songs of praise: P. L. VII. 258.

vbl. sb. **hymning,** the singing of songs of praise: P. L. III. 417.

Hypocrisy, *sb.* the assuming of a false appearance of piety or virtue: P. L. III. 683 ; *smooth hypocrisy* : S. A. 872.

Hypocrite, *sb.* one one pretends to piety or virtue, dissembler : P. L. IV. 744 ; P. R. I. 487 ; *voc.* : P. L. IV. 957.

Hyrcanian, *adj.* of Hyrcania, the province of the Parthian Empire lying south and east of the Caspian Sea : P. R. III. 317.

Hyrcanus, *sb.* Hyrcanus II., the uncle of Antigonus and the next to the last of the Maccabean kings : P. R. III. 367.

I

*I, *pers. pron.* (*dat.* and *acc.* me) : P. L. I. 96, 134 ; II. 119, 122, 466 ; IX. 41, 688 ; X. 721 ; P. R. I. 277 ; II. 382 ; S. A. 820 ; C. 404 ; in the epics referring to the poet himself : P. L. I. 12, 22, 25 ; III. 3, 13, 18, 21, 27, 32, 33, 34, 41, 46, 49, 54 ; IV. 741, 758 ; VI. 373 ; VII. 3, 5, 13, 16, 19, 24 ; IX. 5, 20, 23, 26, 41 ; P. R. I. 1 ; II. 6 ; in exclamations ; *me miserable !* : P. L. IV. 73 ; *ay me !* : P. L. IV. 86 ; dative of reference : C. 630.

refl. with a *vb.* ; *betake me* : P. L. X. 922 ; *bethink* : C. 820 ; *content* : P. R. II. 256 ; *hide* : P. L. IX. 162 ; *laid* : P. L. IV. 457 ; *persuade* : D. F. I. 29 ; *repent* : P. L. XII. 474 ; *sat* : P. L. VIII. 287 ; *wind* : C. 163 ; with a *prep.* : P. L. IX. 599.

Iambic, *sb.* dialogue in iambic metre : P. R. IV. 262.

Iberian, *adj.* (*a*) of Iberia in Europe, the peninsula comprising the modern Spain and Portugal : P. R. II. 200 ; C. 60.

(b) of Iberia in Asia, the province of Parthian Empire lying between Armenia and the Caucasus Mountains : P. R. III. 318.

Ice, *sb.* frozen water : P. L. II. 591 ; X. 1063 ; XII. 193 ; *to starve in ice* : P. L. II. 600 ; *armed with ice* : P. L. X. 697 ; *mountains of ice* : P. L. X. 291.

Icy-pearled (pearlèd, *disyl.*), *adj.*

covered with sparkling drops of ice : D. F. I. 15.

Ida, *sb.* (*a*) the mountain in Crete : P. L. I. 515 ; Il P. 29.

(b) the mountain in Mysia, Asia Minor : P. L. v. 382.

Idea, *sb.* plan, design : P. L. VII. 557.

Idiot, *sb.* an imbecile: P. L. III. 474.

Idle, *adj.* (*a*) not occupied, doing nothing : P. L. IV. 617 ; S. A. 566, 579, 1500 ; Il P. 5.

(b) serving no useful purpose, useless : P. L. VI. 839 ; VII. 279 ; *idle orbs*, eyes which have lost the power of sight : S. XXII. 4.

(c) remaining unused : N. O. 55.

Idleness, *sb.* absence of employment : P. L. X. 1055.

Idly, *adv.* without working, indolently : P. L. X. 236 ; XI. 645.

Idol, *sb.* (*a*) image of a god to which worship is offered : P. L. I. 375, 446 ; P. R. II. 329 ; III. 426, 432 ; S. A. 441, 456, 1358 ; *spec.* the image of Dagon : S. A. 1297, 1672 ; of Moloch : P. L. I. 396 ; N. O. 207.

(b) counterpart, imitation : P. L. VI. 101.

See **Sea-idol.**

Idolatress, *sb.* female worshipper of idols : P. L. I. 445.

Idolatrous, *adj.* (*a*) used in the worship of idols : S. A. 1378.

(b) given to the worship of idols : P. R. I. 144 ; S. A. 443, 1364.

Idolatry, *sb.* (*a*) worship of idols : S. A. 1670 ; *pl.* : P. L. I. 456 ; XII. 337.

(b) idolatrous objects : P. R. III. 418.

Idolism, *sb.* false motion, fallacy : P. R. IV. 234.

Idolist, *sb.* worshipper of idols : S. A. 453.

Idol-worship, *sb.* worship of idols : P. L. XII. 115 ; S. A. 1365.

*If, *conj.* (1) on condition that, in case that, supposing that ; (*a*) with protasis in pres. indic. ; apodosis in pres. or perf. indic. : P. L. II. 977 ; VIII. 75 ; S. A. 504 ; in future indic. : P. L. I. 274 ; v. 788 ; XII. 479 ; in pret. subj. : C. 302 ; in imper. : P. L. IV. 898 ; VIII. 277 ; S. A. 817 ; apodosis with *may, should* : P. L. I. 167 ; P. R. II. 394 ; apodosis ellipt. : P. L. IV. 851.

(*b*) with protasis in pret. or
plupf. indic.; apodosis in pres.
indic.: P. R. IV. 519; in plupf.
indic.: S. A. 1218; apodosis with
should, would: P. L. II. 120,
657; construction not clear: P.
R. IV. 467.

(*c*) with protasis in future in-
dic.; apodosis in pres. indic.: P.
R. IV. 166; in future indic.: P. L.
III. 195; P. R. III. 381; Il P. 77.

(*d*) with protasis in pres. or
perf. subj.; apodosis in pres. indic.: P. L. I. 10; II. 99, 492,
1007; VIII. 563; IX. 340, 728,
760; P. R. II. 249; S. A. 296;
in pret. indic.: C. 170; in future
indic.: P. L. II. 214; IV. 586;
S. A. 1387; in imper.: P. L. II.
73; V. 206; X. 992; P. R. III.
171; C. 238; apodosis with *may,
could, should*: P. L. V. 501; IX.
46, 247; S. A. 369; apodosis ellipt.: P. L. IV. 577; V. 574;
apodosis omitted: P. L. I. 84;
V. 513.

(*e*) with protasis in pret. subj.;
apodosis in pres. indic.: P. L. IX.
311; in pret. or plupf. indic.:
P. L. II. 202; S. A. 1471; V. Ex.
29; apodosis with *would*: P. R.
II. 320; apodosis ellipt.: P. L.
II. 174.

(*f*) protasis with *could*; apodosis *should, could, would*: P. L. II.
447; IX. 115; X. 952; protasis
with *should*; apodosis *might*: P.
L. VI. 502.

(*g*) protasis ellipt.: P. L. I.
191; II. 105; III. 595; IV. 251;
V. 32; VI. 293; VII. 299; VIII.
614; IX. 650; S. A. 490; protasis expressed by part. phrase:
P. L. II. 93.

(*h*) as if, with clause containing pret. or plupf. subj.: P. L.
II. 503; VI. 195; X. 626; S. A.
1512; ll P. 71; *if it be so that*:
D. F. I. 37.

(*i*) *if* omitted: P. L. II. 82;
IV. 439; S. A. 197.

(2) granted that: P. L. II.230;
III. 117; even if: P. L. I. 655.

(3) whether: P. L. I. 636; II.
376; XII. 4; P. R. II. 287; S. A.
337, 1090; C. 575.

Ignoble, *adj.* not honourable, mean
in character, base, unworthy: P.
L. II. 227; S. A. 416.

absol. persons of ignoble character: P. L. XII. 221.

Ignobly, *adv.* dishonourably, basely:
P. L. XI. 624.

Ignominious, (1) *adj.* disgraceful,
shameful: S. A. 417.

(2) *adv.* with ignominy or dishonour: P. L. VI. 395.

Ignominy, *sb.* dishonour, disgrace:
P. L. II. 207; VI. 383; P. R. III.
136; a disgrace; *an ignominy*: P.
L. I. 115.

Ignorance, *sb.* (*a*) want of knowledge: P. L. IV. 519; IX. 809;
with *of*: P. L. IX. 774.

(*b*) those who lack knowledge:
C. 514.

Ignorant, *adj.* destitute of knowledge, uninformed: P. L. IX.
704; with *of*: P. L. XI. 764; P.
R. IV. 310.

Ilissus, *sb.* a river of Attica, Greece,
flowing just southeast of Athens:
P. R. IV. 249.

Ilium, *sb.* the seat of the ten years'
war between the Greeks and Tro-
jans: P. L. I. 578.

Ill, (1) *adj.* (*a*) wicked, malevolent:
C. 217.

(*b*) not upright; *ill borrower*:
C. 683.

(*c*) wretched, miserable, disastrous, unfortunate: P. L. IV. 48;
VI. 150; IX. 845; *ill chance, lot*:
P. L. II. 224, 935; P. R. I. 321;
success: P. L. IV. 932.

(*d*) of bad import; *ill news*: P.
R. I. 64.

(*e*) **ill mansion**, hell, as full of
evil and suffering: P. L. II. 462;
VI. 738.

(2) *sb.* (*a*) moral evil, wickedness: P. L. III. 689; IV. 222;
VIII. 324; IX. 1055; Dante I.;
author of ill: P. L. II. 381; *think,
suspect no ill*: P. L. III. 688; IV.
320; X. 140; wicked act; *do ill*:
P. L. I. 160; P. R. I. 423.

(*b*) harm, injury: P. L. IX.
1152; A. 48.

(*c*) misfortune, calamity, disaster: P. R. IV. 464.

(3) *adv.* (*a*) not well, imperfectly, badly, poorly, hardly: P.
L. II. 445; IV. 370, 372; V. 113;
X. 950, 952; P. R. I. 200; II.
469; IV. 135, 339, 419; S. A. 209,
1504; C. 271.

(*b*) unfortunately, disastrously:
P. L. IX. 1147; X. 735; XI.
763.

Illaudable, *adj.* unworthy of commendation: P. L. VI. 382.

Ill-boding *adj.* of evil omen : P. R. iv. 490.

Ill-fitted, *adj.* not well adapted in size : S. A. 122.

Ill-got, *adj.* wrongly obtained : Petr. 4.

Ill-greeting, *adj.* accosting for an evil purpose : C. 406.

Illimitable (illímitáble), *adj.* without bound, having no determinate limits : P. L. ii. 892.

Ill-joined, *adj.* who should not be united in marriage: P. L. iii. 463.

Ill-luck, *sb. attrib.* of evil or misfortune : C. 845.

Ill-managed, *adj.* uncontrolled : C. 172.

Ill-mated, *adj.* wrongfully united in marriage : P. L. xi. 684.

Ill-meaning, *adj.* intending evil or injury : S. A. 1195.

Illuminate, *vb. tr. (a)* to give light to : P. L. vii. 350.

(*b*) to enlighten intellectually : S. A. 1689.

Illumine, *vb. tr. (a)* to light up : P. L. i. 666.

(*b*) to enlighten spiritually or intellectually : P. L. i. 23.

Illusion, *sb. (a)* condition of being deceived by appearances ; *fell into ... illusion* : P. L. x. 571.

(*b*) something that deceives the mind : P. L. iv. 803 ; that deceives the eye : C. 155.

Illustrate (illústrate), *vb. tr. (a)* to make illustrious, confer honour upon : P. L. v. 739.

(*b*) to make clear or evident : P. R. i. 370 ; to show *them fully satisfied* : P. L. x. 78.

Illustrious, *adj. (a)* luminous, bright, shining : P. L. iii. 627 ; vi. 773.

(*b*) famous, renowned, eminent; *of persons* : P. L. v. 842 ; vii. 109 ; S. A. 957, 1318 ; *illustrious evidence* : P. L. ix. 962 ; *illustrious track* : P. L. x. 367.

Ill-worthy, *adj.* not at all worthy : P. L. xi. 163.

Illyria, *sb.* the country east of the Adriatic Sea : P. L. ix. 505.

Image, *sb. (a)* representation of the form of a person or animal as an object of worship : P. L. i. 440 ; *brute image* : P. L. i. 459 ; *image of a brute* : P. L. i. 371.

(*b*) counterpart, copy : P. L. iv. 472 ; viii. 424 ; *perfect image* : P. L. ii. 764 ; *smooth watery image* : P. L. iv. 480 ; *image of*

myself : P. L. v. 95 ; applied to Christ as the counterpart of God : P. L. iii. 63 ; v. 784 ; vi. 736 ; P. R. iv. 596 ; applied similarly to man : P. L. iv. 567.

(*c*) the physical and spiritual likeness of God seen in or imparted to man : P. L. iv. 292 ; viii. 221, 441, 544 ; xi. 508, 514, 515, 518, 525 ; *in his* or *our image* : P. L. vii. 519, 526, 627 ; *in the image of God* : P. L. vii. 527.

(*d*) embodiment *of strength* : S. A. 706.

Imagination, *sb. (a)* faculty of the mind by which it conceives and forms images of things not present to the senses : P. L. vi. 300.

(*b*) product of this faculty, mental image, fancy : P. L. v. 105 ; S. A. 1544.

(*c*) inward reasoning, thoughts : P. L. ii. 10.

Imagine, *vb. tr. (a)* to create by the imagination : P. L. iii. 599.

(*b*) to think, suppose, believe; with two *acc.* : P. L. x. 553, 881 ; *absol.* : C. 415.

part. adj. **imagined,** created by the imagination, fancied : P. L. v. 263 ; x. 291.

See **False-imagined.**

Imaus, *sb.* the great mountain range of Central Asia, "which beginning near the shores of the Northern Ocean, runneth directly towards the South ; dividing the Greater Asia into East and West, and crossing Mount Taurus in right angles, in or about the Longitude of 140," Hey. *Cos.* 1657, bk. iii. p. 640 ; cf. Mercator *Atlas*, 1636, map at p. 402 : P. L. iii. 431.

Imbalm. *See* **Embalm.**

Imbark. *See* **Embark.**

Imbathe. *See* **Embathe.**

Imbattle. *See* **Embattle.**

Imbellish. *See* **Embellish.**

Imblaze. *See* **Emblaze.**

Imblazonry. *See* **Emblazonry.**

Imbody. *See* **Embody.**

Imborder. *See* **Emborder.**

Imbosom. *See* **Embosom.**

Imbower. *See* **Embower.**

Imbroil. *See* **Embroil.**

Imbrown, *vb. tr.* to make dark or obscure : P. L. iv. 246.

Imbrue, *vb. tr.* to stain *with blood* : S. xvi. 7.

Imbrute, *vb.* (1) *tr.* to degrade to the level of a brute : P. L. ix. 166.

(2) *intr.* to sink to the level of a brute : C. 468.

Imbue, *vb. tr.* to pervade *with grace divine* : P. L. VIII. 216.

Imitate, *vb. tr.* (*a*) to make a copy of, reproduce : P. L. II. 270 ; P. R. IV. 339.

(*b*) to act in the manner of, pattern after : P. L. V. 111 ; C. 112.

part. adj. **imitated,** copied : P. L. II. 511.

Immanacle, *vb. tr.* to bind as with fetters : C. 665.

Immature, *adj.* not complete in development ; *of the earth* : P. L. VII. 277.

Immeasurable (imméasuráble : S. A. 206), *adj.* incapable of measurement, limitless ; *immeasurable abyss* : P. L. VII. 211 ; *depth* : P. L. I. 549 ; *strength* : S. A. 206.

Immeasurably, *adv.* beyond all measure ; *immeasurably fed and filled* : P. L. II. 844.

Immediate, (1) *adj.* (*a*) involving actual contact : P. L. VIII. 617.

(*b*) without lapse time, instant : P. L. II. 121 ; X. 52, 1049; *immediate are the acts of God* : P. L. VII. 176.

(2) *adv.* instantly : P. L. VI. 584.

Immediately, *adv.* without delay, instantly : P. L. VII. 285 ; XI. 477 ; XII. 87 ; S. A. 1614.

Immedicable, *adj.* incurable *wounds* : S. A. 620.

Immense, *adj.* (always follows the *sb.*) (*a*) immeasurable, limitless ; *amplitude almost immense* : P. L. VII. 620 ; *void immense* : P. L. II. 829.

(*b*) vast in size or extent : P. L. I. 790 ; V. 88 ; X. 300.

(*c*) very great in degree or quantity ; *debt immense* : P. L. IV. 52; *grace, love, goodness*, etc. : P. L. VI. 704 ; VII. 196 ; XII. 469.

Imminent, *adj.* (*a*) hanging over and about to fall ; *arm uplifted imminent* : P. L. VI. 317.

(*b*) dangerous and close at hand; *rancour imminent* : P. L. IX. 409; impending ; *judgements imminent* : P. L. XI. 725.

Immix, *vb. tr.* to mix in *with* : S. A. 1657.

Immortal, *adj.* (*a*) not subject to death; *of persons* : P. L. IX. 291 ; C. 463 ; U. C. II. 28 ; *of God* : P.

L. III. 373 ; *of angels* : P. L. I. 53 ; *immortal minds*: P. L. I. 559; Il P. 91 ; *spirits* : P. L. I. 622 ; II. 553 ; *vigour* : P. L. II. 13 ; *shapes* : C. 2 ; *life* : P. L. XII. 435 ; not liable to decay ; *immortal elements* : P. L. XI. 50 ; *immortal change,* change to immortality : C. 841.

(*b*) heavenly, divine ; *immortal fruits, nectar* : P. L. XI. 285 ; V. Ex. 39; *harps*: S. M. 13 ; *streams*: S. XIV. 14.

(*c*) everlasting, imperishable ; *immortal amarant* : P. L. III. 353 ; *verse, notes* : L'A. 137 ; C. 516 ; S. XX. 12 ; *thanks, praise* : P. L. VII. 77 ; A. 75 ; *hate, love, bliss* : P. L. I. 107 ; III. 67, 267 ; IX. 1166.

Immortality, *sb.* exemption from death, eternal life: P. L. IV. 201; XI. 59 ; the bliss of immortality ; *quaff immortality and joy* : P. L. V. 638.

Immovable, *adj.* (*a*) firmly fixed, fast : P. L. II. 602; X. 303.

(*b*) unalterable : P. L. X. 938.

Immure, *vb. tr.* to wall *round* ; *fig. of fire* : P. L. II. 435 ; to shut in *in cypress shades* : C. 521.

Immutable, *adj.* not susceptible of change : P. L. V. 524; IX. 1165 ; *of God* : P. L. III. 373.

Immutably, *adv.* unchangeably, unalterably : P. L. III. 121 ; VII. 79.

Imp, (1) *sb.* evil spirit : P. L. IX. 89.

(2) *vb. tr.* to mend *wings* by supplying with feathers: S. XV. 8.

Impair, *vb. tr.* to make worse, weaken, or injure *a person* : P. L. VI. 691 ; P. R. IV. 592 ; *human sense* : P. L. XII. 10 ; *wings* : C. 380 ; *lustre* : P. L. IV. 850 ; to lessen in dignity, honour, or power : P. L. V. 73, 665 ; VII. 608 ; to diminish *numbers* : P. L. IX. 144.

Impale, *vb. tr.* to surround, inclose : P. L. II. 647 ; VI. 553.

Imparadise, *vb. tr.* to make supremely happy : P. L. IV. 506.

Impart, *vb. tr.* (*a*) to make another a partaker of, bestow, communicate : P. L. IX. 728 ; with *to* : P. L. VIII. 441 ; *impart what (food) to thy need* : P. R. II. 397 ; *light* : P. L. V. 423 ; *happiness, good, strength* : P. R. I. 417 ; III. 124 ; S. A. 1438.

(b) to communicate, make known, tell : P. L. VII. 81 ; with *to* : P. L. V. 677.

Impartial, *adj.* not favouring one more than another : S. A. 827.

Impassable, *adj.* that cannot be crossed : P. L. X. 254.

Impassioned, *part. adj.* inflamed with passion : P. L. IX. 678.

Impassive, *adj.* not susceptible of pain or suffering : P. L. VI. 455.

Impatience, *sb.* want of composure in trial and suffering : P. L. X. 1044.

Impearl, *vb. tr.* to form into pearl-like drops : P. L. V. 747.

Impediment, *sb.* baggage of an army : P. L. VI. 548.

Impendent, *adj.* imminent, threatening ; *impendent horrors* : P. L. II. 177 ; *wrath* : P. L. V. 891.

Impenetrable, *adj.* that cannot be pierced ; *impenetrable rock* : P. L. II. 647 ; *woods* : P. L. IX. 1086.

Impenetrably (impénetrábly), *adv.* in an impenetrable manner ; *impenetrably armed* : P. L. VI. 400.

Impenitence, *sb.* want of repentance, obduracy : P. L. XI. 816.

Impenitent, *adj.* not repenting of sin : P. R. III. 423.

Imperfect, *adj.* defective : P. L. IX. 338, 345 ; *imperfect law* : P. L. XII. 300 ; incomplete *words* : V. Ex. 3.

Imperfection, *sb.* incompleteness : P. L. VIII. 423.

Imperial, *adj.* (a) of or belonging to a supreme ruler : P. R. IV. 51 ; the supreme ruler being God or angels ; *imperial throne* : P. L. VII. 585 ; *titles* : P. L. V. 801 ; *summons* : P. L. V. 584 ; Satan ; *imperial ensign* : P. L. I. 536 ; *sovereignty* : P. L. II 446 ; Jove ; *imperial rule* : C. 21.

(b) being the seat of empire : P. R. IV. 33.

(c) supreme in authority, ruling : P. L. II. 310.

Imperious, *adj.* (a) domineering, dictatorial : P. L. VI. 287.

(b) imperative *message* : S. A. 1352.

Imperishable (impérisháble), *adj.* ex·mpt from destruction : P. L. VI. 435.

Impertinence, *sb.* irrelevance : P. L. VIII. 195.

Impervious, *adj.* that cannot be passed through : P. L. X. 254.

Impetuous, (ímpetuóus), *adj.* (a) violent ; *impetuous winds, rain* : P. L. IV. 560 ; XI. 744 ; *recoil* : P. L. II. 880.

(b) vehement, passionate ; *of persons* : S. A. 1422 ; *impetuous rage, fury* : P. L. I. 175 ; VI. 591.

Impious, *adj.* lacking veneration for God or his authority, sinful, profane ; *of persons* : P. L. I. 342 ; VI. 831 ; *impious hands, crest* : P. L. I. 686 ; VI. 188 ; S. A. 891 ; *impious war* : P. L I. 43 ; *obloquy, rage* : P. L. V. 813, 845 ; *condition* : P. R. IV. 173.

Impiously, *adv.* wickedly : P. L. VII. 611 ; S. A. 498.

Implacable, *adj.* (a) not to be appeased, inexorable : S. A. 960.

(b) not to be relieved : P. L. VI. 658.

Implanted, *part. adj.* set in the ground ; *fig. implanted grace* : P. L. XI. 23.

Implement, *sb.* instrument : P. L. VI. 488.

Implicit, *adj.* entangled : P. L. VII. 323.

Implore, *vb. tr.* (a) to beg or pray for : C. 903 ; *pardon, mercy* : S. A. 512, 521 ; *leave of speech* : P. L. VIII. 377.

(b) to call upon in supplication, beseech : P. L. VII. 38.

Imply, *vb. tr.* to import, signify : P. L. IV. 307, 901 ; X. 1017.

Import, *vb.* (1) *tr.* to betoken, indicate : P. L. IX. 731.

(2) *intr.* to be of consequence or importance : C. 287 ; with *clause* as subject : P. L. VIII. 71.

Important, *adj.* of much import, weighty, momentous : P. L. XI. 9 ; S. A. 1379.

Importune (impórtune : P. L. X. 933 ; P. R. II. 404 ; S. A. 799, 1680 ; ímportúne : P. L. IX. 610 ; S. A. 775), (1) *adj.* pertinacious : P. R. II. 404 ; with *of* : S. A. 775.

(2) *adv.* inopportunely, unseasonably : P. L. IX. 610.

(3) *vb. tr.* to beset with petitions ; with *acc.* and *clause* : P. L. X. 933 ; with *acc.* and *prep. inf.* : S. A. 1680.

vbl. sb. **importuning,** importunity : S. A. 797.

Importunity, *sb.* pertinacity in solicitation : P. R. IV. 24 ; S. A. 51, 397, 779.

Impose, *vb. tr.* to lay on or enforce as something to be borne or endured ; *impose affliction* : S. A. 1258 ; *command, laws, message* : P. L. I. 567 ; II. 241 ; V. 679 ; XI. 227 ; with *on* : S. A. 1343; *death is the penalty imposed* : P. L. VII. 545 ; *impose truce* : P. L. VI. 407 ; *labour, work* : P. L. IX. 235; XI. 172 ; S. A. 565, 1640 ; *revolution on* : P. L. VIII. 30.

Imposition, *sb.* the laying on or enforcing *of laws* : P. L. XII. 304.

Impossible, *adj.* beyond the reach of power to obtain or accomplish : P. L. II. 250 ; VI. 501 ; with *to* : P. L. X. 800 ; with *prep. inf.* : P. L. IV. 548 ; VII. 58.

Impossibly, *adv.* **not impossibly**, perhaps : P. L. IX. 360.

Impostor, *sb.* one who deceives by a fictitious character: P. L. III. 692; *voc.* : C. 762.

Impotence, *sb.* weakness, inability : P. L. II. 156 ; *impotence of mind* : S. A. 52.

Impotent, *adj.* powerless : P. R. II. 433.

Impower. *See* **Empower.**

Impregn *vb. tr.* (*a*) to impregnate ; *fig.* he (Jupiter) *impregns the clouds* : P. L. IV. 500.

(*b*) to fill or imbue *with reason* : P. L. IX. 737.

Impregnable, *adj.* not to be taken by assault, resisting any attack : P. L. II. 131 ; P. R. IV. 50.

Impress, *sb.* device, emblem : P. L. IX. 35.

Impress, *vb. tr.* (*a*) to imprint, stamp ; *on which* (blossoms and fruit-) *the sun .. impress'd his beams* : P. L. IV. 150.

fig. Nature first gave signs impressed on bird, etc. : P. L. XI. 182 ; *on thee impressed the effulgence ... abides* : P. L. III. 388 ; to impose, enjoin ; *such flight the command impressed on the floods* : P. L. VII. 294.

(*b*) to exert pressure upon ; *vapours impress the air* : P. L. IV. 558.

Impression, *sb.* effect produced upon the mind or heart : P. R. I. 106 ; W. S. 12.

Imprison, *vb. tr.* to shut up or confine *the air* : S. A. 8 ; *the soul* : S. A. 158.

Imprisonment, *sb.* state of being imprisoned, *fig.* : S. A. 155.

Improve, *vb. tr.* to make better *the body* : P. L. V. 498 ; *Satan ... improved ... in fraud* : P. L. IX. 54 ; to increase *knowledge* : P. R. I. 213.

Imprudence, *sb.* indiscretion : P. L. XI. 686.

Impudence, *sb.* shameless effrontery: S. A. 398.

Impudent, *adj.* shameless, brazen : P. R. IV. 154 ; Petr. 3.

Impulse (impúlse), *sb.* (*a*) force communicated suddenly, push : P. L. IX. 530.

(*b*) incitement to action : P. L. III. 120 ; X. 45 ; S. A. 223.

Impulsion, *sb.* incitement, instigation : S. A. 422.

Impure, *adj.* not pure morally, defiled by sin ; *of persons* : P. L. III. 630 ; X. 735 ; *of actions* : P. L. IV. 746 ; S. A. 1424.

absol. the angels who were defiled by sin : P. L. VI. 742.

Impurple, *vb. tr.* to make purple or brilliant in colour : P. L. III. 364.

Impute, *vb.* (*pres. 2d sing.* imput'st : P. L. IX. 1145) *tr.* (*a*) to lay to the charge of ; with *to* : P. L. X. 620 ; to attribute as owing *to* : P. L. IX. 1145 ; P. R. I. 422 ; II. 248.

(*b*) to attribute vicariously *to* : P. L. III. 291 ; XII. 295, 409.

*****In**, I. *prep.* (1) of position ; (*a*) within the limits or bounds of : P. L. I. 85, 321, 767 ; II. 150, 289, 535, 930; III. 66 ; IV. 261 ; VI. 100 ; C. 150; *in one's eyes, face*, etc. : P. L. II. 304, 388; III. 140 ; VI. 540 ; VIII. 1 ; C. 203.

the article omitted : P. L. I. 43 ; V. 200 ; IX. 38, 1109.

with proper names of cities, countries, etc. : P. L. I. 80, 290, 303 ; V. 340 ; X. 329.

(*b*) = on : P. L. II. 23 ; IV. 151 ; VI. 772.

(*c*) = at : P. R. I. 98.

(*d*) defining the part affected : P. L. I 206 ; VI. 837.

(*e*) surrounded by, enveloped in : P. L. I. 151 ; II. 600, 928 ; III. 4 ; V. 341.

(*f*) clothed in, wearing : P. L. VI. 13, 110, 364 ; VII. 501.

(*g*) within ; *in heavenly records* : P. L. I. 361 ; *in your notes* : P. L. V. 199 ; *in books* : S. A. 653.

(*h*) belonging to, in the membership of : P. L. II. 901 ; V. 166 ; VII. 488.

(*i*) within *the soul, heart, thoughts,* etc.: P. L. v. 100, 448; vi. 629; within *me, him, us,* etc. : P. L. i. 22; iii. 174; v. 681; viii. 507.

(2) of situation ; *in chains,* etc.: P. L. i. 48, 658 ; ii. 183; *in darkness, light,* etc.: P. L. i. 72; ii. 377; iii. 611; P. R. i. 116; *in view, sight,* etc.: P. L. i. 563; ii. 240, 394, 748; iii. 265, 655; v. 46; vii. 618.

(3) of condition or state ; *in ruin, destruction* : P. L. i. 91, 137; *in glory, rage, joy, fear,* etc.: P. L. i. 39, 95, 123, 275; iv. 97, 888 ; C. 356; *in solitude* : P. L. iii. 69; *in sweat* : P. L. viii. 255.

(4) of occupation ; *in battle, worship, flight,* etc.: P. L. i. 436; ii. 248; iii. 15; iv. 726; v. 511, 619; viii. 552; with *vbl. sb.* : P. L. ii. 340; ix. 129, 478, 1178; xi. 300; S. A. 237.

(*b*) in the act of: P. L. vii. 604; *in gaze*; P. L. ix. 524; in the process of and on account of : P. L. vi. 872; ix. 941.

(5) of manner, form, arrangement : P. L. i. 172, 224, 349, 548; ii. 507, 887; iii. 641; iv. 242, 687; vii. 402, 461.

(*b*) of manner of speech or writing : P. L. i. 16, 449, 580; v. 761; vi. 568, 628; C. 516.

(6) by, by means of : P. L. i. 130; ii. 20, 1005, 1051; v. 740, 817.

(*b*) through : P. L. vi. 728; x. 1034.

(*c*) represented by : P. L. iv. 299; vii. 208; xii. 201.

(7) of material : P. L. v. 634.

(8) of degree, extent, measure, number : P. L. i. 196, 209; iii. 561, 580; v. 490; x. 26.

(9) of object, purpose : P. L. v. 194, 731; vii. 514, 628; viii. 315, 459; ix. 552; x. 1103; C. 626; L. 90.

(10) in reference or regard to, in the case of ; following an *adj.*: P. L. i. 378, 506; ii. 47, 109, 120, 350, 415; iv. 92; vi. 32; following a *sb.*: P. L. vi. 231; ix. 310; following a *vb.*: P. L. i. 230, 778.

trust in : P. L. vi. 119; *glory in* : P. L. x. 386; *excel in* : P. L. iii. 132; *join in* : P. L. x. 661; *proceeded in her plaint* : P. L. x. 913; *consists in* : C. 741.

(11) of time ; (*a*), during the time of, within the limits of : P. L. i. 9, 544, 769; iv. 557; v. 295; *in life* : P. L. iii. 450; viii. 193; *in his way* : P. L. iii. 437; *in mid-volley* : P. L. vi. 854.

(*b*) in the course of : P. L. i. 697; ix. 140.

(*c*) = on : P. L. vii. 544; ix. 705.

(*d*) = during : P. L. v. 110.

(12) according to, after the nature of: P. L. i. 261; vii. 451.

(13) belonging to, inherent in : P. L. iv. 295; viii. 597.

(14) in the power of : P. L. vi. 239.

(15) apart from connexion with others ; *in itself, myself, himself,* etc.: P. L. i. 254; iii. 244; v. 353; x. 141.

(16) in mystical or spiritual union with : P. L. iii. 287, 293; vi. 732.

(17) in the person or case of : P. L. iii. 302, 311; v. 228, 474; viii. 524; ix. 91, 233; x. 803, 817.

(18) = into : P. L. vii. 525; x. 476; L. 168.

(19) = over : P. L. i. 737.

(20) with *sb.* forming adv. phrase ; *in vain, haste,* etc.: P. L. iii. 23, 457, 500; iv. 180, 356, 560, 670, 902; v. 672; x. 17.

II. *adv.* (*a*) so as to pass into a certain place : P. L. iv. 563; xi. 735; S. A. 561; C. 834, 840; *in at* : P. L. ix. 188; *in through* : P. L. xi. 16; *in to* : C. 466; *in with* : P. L. ix. 74.

(*b*) *bridle, break, crush, take in.* *See* the verbs.

Inabstinence, *sb.* indulgence of appetite : P. L. xi. 476.

Inaccessible, *adj.* that cannot be reached ; *of God* or *His throne* : P. L. ii. 104; iii. 377; vii. 141; that cannot be entered or crossed : P. R. iii. 274.

Inbreathed, *part. adj.* communicated by inspiration : S. M. 4.

Inbred, *part. adj.* begotten within one's own body : P. L. ii. 785.

Incapable, *adj.* not capable of receiving ; with *of* : P. L. ii. 140; v. 505; vi. 434.

Incarnate, (1) *adj.* embodied in flesh : P. L. iii. 315.

(2) *vb. tr.* to embody in flesh : P. L. ix. 166.

Incense, (1) *sb.* (*a*) mixture of fragrant gums producing a sweet odour when burned : P. L. XII. 363; burned as an offering to God : P. L. XI. 25, 439 ; P. R. I. 251.

(*b*) fragrant fumes arising from incense burned in sacrifice : P. L. VII. 599; XI. 18 ; *fig.* the fragrance of flowers : P. L. IX. 194.

(2) *vb.* (incensèd, *disyl.* : P. L. III. 187 ; v. 847) *tr.* (*a*) to inflame *the ire of God* : P. L. II. 94 ; IX. 692.

(*b*) to enrage or make angry : P. L. IX. 1162 ; to incense *Satan* : P. L. II. 707 ; VI. 130; *God* : P. L. VIII. 235 ; XII. 338.

part. adj. **incensed,** wrathful ; *of God* or *Christ* : P. L. III. 187 ; v. 847.

Incentive, *adj.* having the property of setting on fire : P. L. VI. 519.

Incessant, *adj.* ceaseless; *incessant toil* : P. L. I. 698 ; *prayer* : P. L. XI. 308; Ps. LXXXVI. 19; numberless ; *incessant armies* : P. L. VI. 138.

Incessantly, *adv.* continually : P. R. IV. 323.

Incestuous, *adj.* guilty of incest : P. L. X. 602 ; S. A. 833.

Incident, *adj.* naturally appertaining *to* : S. A. 656, 774.

Incite, *vb. tr.* to move to action : P. L. VIII. 125.

Inclement, *adj.* not mild, severe ; *inclement seasons* : P. L. X. 1063 ; stormy or tempestuous; *inclement sky* : P. L. III. 426.

Inclinable, *adj.* disposed ; with *prep. inf.* : P. L. IX. 742.

Inclination, *sb.* bent of the will or desires towards a particular object : P. L. II. 524 ; x. 265.

Incline, *vb.* **(1)** *tr.* (*a*) to cause to bend down or close *our eyelids* : P. L. IV. 615.

(*b*) to bend or dispose *his will* : P. L. XI. 145.

(2) *intr.* (*a*) to bend down, stoop : S. XXIII. 13 ; to bow, bend : P. L. XI. 250 ; S. A. 1636.

(*b*) to be disposed : P. L. II. 314 ; with *to* or *prep. inf.* : P. L. III. 402, 405 ; x. 1061 ; XI. 596 ; P. R. IV. 212 ; C. 412.

vbl. sb. **inclining,** propensity : P. L. x. 46.

Inclose. *See* **Enclose.**

Included, *part. adj.* comprised ; *the whole included race* : P. L. IX. 416.

Incomposed, *adj.* disordered or disturbed ; *visage incomposed* : P. L. II. 989.

Incomprehensible, *adj.* boundless, infinite : P. L. VIII. 20.

Inconsiderable (inconsíderáble), *adj.* unimportant, insignificant : P. R. IV. 457.

Incontinence, *sb.* licentiousness, *personified* : C. 397.

Inconvenient, *adj.* unsuitable : P. L. v. 495.

Incorporate, (1) *adj.* united in one body : P. L. x. 816.

(2) *vb. intr.* to grow one with ; *thy soul ... to incorporate with gloomy night* : S. A. 161.

Incorporeal (incórporéal : P. L. v. 413), *adj.* (*a*) immaterial : P. L. I. 789 ; v. 413.

(*b*) characteristic of immaterial beings ; *incorporeal speed* : P. L. VIII. 37.

Incorrupt, *adj.* not affected by corruption or decay : P. L. XI. 56.

Incorruptible, *adj.* (*a*) incapable of corruption or decay : P. L. IX. 622 ; immortal ; *of God* : P. L. II. 138.

(*b*) not corruptible morally : P. L. IX. 298.

Increase (incréase), I. *sb.* (*a*) augmentation : Ps. IV. 36 ; *give the world increase* : M. W. 51.

(*b*) source or means of prosperity : U. C. II. 32.

II. *vb.* **(1)** *tr.* (*a*) to augment *wonder* : P. L. x. 486 ; to multiply *curses* : P. L. x. 731.

(*b*) to make greater or enrich *with twelve sons* : P. L. XII. 155.

(2) *intr.* (*a*) to become greater in number or degree; *of days* : P. R. II. 12 ; *of joy, doubt* : P. L. x. 351 ; P. R. II. 12.

(*b*) to bring forth offspring, be fruitful : P. L. IV. 748 ; x. 730.

Increate, *adj.* uncreated ; *of light* : P. L. III. 6.

Incredible, *adj.* beyond or difficult of belief, inconceivable : P. L. IV. 593 ; S. A. 1084, 1532, 1627.

Incubus, *sb.* a devil who was supposed to consort with women in their sleep : P. R. II. 152.

Incumbent, *adj.* lying or resting *on* : P. L. I. 226.

Incumber. *See* **Encumber.**

Incur, *vb.* (*pres. 2d sing.* incurr'st : P. L. IV. 913) *tr.* to become liable to or bring upon oneself *wrath,* *displeasure, penalty* : P. L. IV. 913; IX. 992; X. 15; *absol.* : P. L. VIII. 336.

Incurable, *adj.* remediless : S. A. 1234.

Incursion, *sb.* hostile inroad or invasion : P. R. III. 301.

Ind, *sb.* India : P. L. II. 2; C. 606.

Indamage, *vb. tr.* to harm, injure : P. R. IV. 206.

Indebted, *part. adj.* (*a*) under obligation to God because of the unfulfilled requirements of His law : P. L. III. 235.

(*b*) under obligation for favours received : P. L. IV. 57.

Indecent, *adj.* disgraceful; *indecent overthrow* : P. L. VI. 601.

Indeed, *adv.* (*a*) really, in fact, in truth : P. L. II. 99; IX. 1071; X. 152; S. A. 527; placed for emphasis after the *adj.* : P. L. I. 114; III. 702; V. 706; IX. 650; after the *sb.* : P. L. VIII. 524; S. A. 1036; P. R. IV. 354; S. A. 1515, 1571.

(*b*) in reality, opposed to what is merely apparent : S. A. 158, 1347; emphasizing the real fact in opposition to what is false : P. R. I. 410.

(*c*) as a matter of fact; used to confirm or amplify a previous statement : P. L. IV. 444; P. R. II. 316.

(*d*) it is true; denoting a concession, followed by an adversative clause : P. L. IV. 477; P. R. III. 165; S. A. 291; Cir. 16.

(*e*) as an interjection, expressing incredulity : P. L. IX. 656.

Indefatigable (indefátigáble), *adj.* unwearied, untiring : P. L. II. 408.

Indented, *part. adj.* (*a*) deeply cut along the margin : V. Ex. 94.

(*b*) having a zigzag course : P. L. IX. 496.

India, *sb.* the country of Asia : P. L. V. 339; P. R. IV. 74.

Indian, (**1**) *adj.* of or pertaining to India : P. L. I. 781; III. 436; IX. 1108; P. R. IV. 75; C. 139.

(**2**) *sb. pl.* the inhabitants of India : P. L. IX. 1102.

Indignant, *adj.* moved by anger and scorn; *fig. indignant waves* : P. L. X. 311.

Indignation, *sb.* anger excited by what is unworthy, unjust, or wrongful; *of God* : P. L. VI. 811;

with *toward* : Ps. LXXXV. 15; *of Satan*; P. L. II. 707; with *at* : P. L. IX. 666; *of chaos* : P. L. X. 418.

Indignity, *sb.* (*a*) disgraceful act; *O indignity!* : S. A. 411.

(*b*) contemptuous or insolent usage, insult, *pl.* : S. A. 371, 1168, 1341; *O indignity!* : P. L. IX. 154.

Indirect, *adj.* devious; *paths indirect, fig.* : P. L. XI. 631.

Indissolubly, *adv.* inseparably : P. L. VI. 69.

Indite, *vb. tr.* to describe *wars* in literary composition : P. L. IX. 27.

Individual, *adj.* indivisible, inseparable; *individual solace* : P. L. IV. 486; *one individual soul* : P. L. V. 610; *an individual kiss* : T. 12.

Indorse, *vb. tr.* to load the back of; *elephants indorsed with towers* : P. R. III. 329.

Induce, *vb. tr.* (*a*) to bring on *darkness* : P. L. VI. 407.

(*b*) to move, influence, prevail upon; with *acc.* and *prep. inf.*, or *to* and *sb.* : P. L. II. 503; with *acc.*, the *inf.* omitted : P. L. VIII. 253; with *inf.* only : P. R. I. 105.

Inducement, *sb.* that which influences conduct, incentive : P. L. IX. 934; S. A. 1445.

Inductive, *adj.* leading *to* : P. L. XI. 519.

Indulgence, *adj.* (*a*) gratification of another's desire : P. L. IX. 1186.

(*b*) the yielding *to their fears or grief* : P. R. I. 110.

(*c*) in the Roman Catholic Church, remission of the punishment which is still due to sin after sacramental absolution : P. L. III. 492.

Indulgent, *adj.* showing favour or leniency : P. L. V. 883; *indulgent laws* : P. L. IX. 3.

Indus, *sb.* the river of India : P. L. IX. 82; P. R. III. 272.

Industrious, *adj.* (*a*) zealous, painstaking, attentive; *his thoughts were low—to vice industrious* : P. L. II. 116; *force of violent men, industrious to support tyrannic power* : S. A. 1274.

(*b*) sedulous, diligent : P. L. I. 751; *of the earth* : P. L. VIII. 137.

(*c*) showing industry or diligence : P. R. IV. 248.

Ineffable, *adj.* unspeakable, inexpressible : P. L. III. 137 ; v. 734.

Ineffably, *adv.* inexpressibly : P. L. VI. 721.

Ineffectual, *adj.* not producing the desired effect: P. L. IX. 301.

Inelegant, *adj.* not answering to the correct standards of refinement : P. L. V. 335.

Ineloquent, *adj.* wanting the power of speaking eloquently ; *of the tongue* : P. L. VIII. 219.

Inevitable (inévitáble): *adj.* not to be escaped or evaded, unavoidable ; *inevitable fate, curb, cause* : P. L. II. 197, 322 ; S. A. 1586. '

Inevitably (inévitábly), *adv.* unavoidably : P. L. VIII. 330 ; S. A. 1657.

Inexorable (inéxoráble), *adj.* rigidly severe, relentless ; *inexorable pardon* : S. A. 827.

Inexorably (inéxorábly), *adv.* relentlessly : P. L. II. 91.

Inexperience, *sb.* want of knowledge gained by experience : P. L. IV. 931.

Inexpert, *adj.* wanting knowledge derived from experience: P. L. XII. 218.

Inexpiable (inéxpiáble), *adj.* implacable ; *inexpiable hate* : S. A. 839.

Inexplicable (inéxplicáble), *adj.* inscrutable ; *inexplicable thy justice* : P. L. X. 754.

Inexpressible, *adj.* that cannot be expressed in words ; *orbs of circuit inexpressible* : P. L. V. 595 ; *distance inexpressible by numbers* : P. L. VIII. 113.

Inextinguishable (inextínguisháble), *adj.* unquenchable ; *inextinguishable rage* : P. L. VI. 217.

Inextricable (inéxtricáble), *adj.* that cannot be escaped from ; *fate inextricable* : P. L. V. 528.

Infallible, *adj.* exempt from liability to error : P. L. XII. 530 ; P. R. III. 16.

Infame, *vb. tr.* to spread an ill report of, defame : P. L. IX. 797.

Infamous (infámous : D. F. I. 12 ; probably also : C. 424), *adj.* (*a*) of ill fame ; *infamous hills* : C. 424.

(*b*) utterly detestable : S. A. 417 ; D. F. I. 12.

Infamy, *sb.* extreme baseness, shameful vileness : P. L. VI. 384 ; S. A. 968.

Infancy, *sb.* early childhood of Christ : P. R. IV. 508 ; N. O. 151 ; Cir. 14.

Infant, (1) *sb.* young child: S. XVIII. 8 ; *of Christ* : N. O. 222 ; P. 3.

(2) *attrib.* or *adj.* (*a*) who is an infant ; *infant God* : N. O. 16 ; *males* : P. L. XII. 168.

(*b*) of or belonging to an infant ; *infant blood* : P. L. II. 664 ; P. R. II. 78 ; *lips* : V. Ex. 4.

Infantry, *sb.* body of foot-soldiers ; *that small infantry,* the Pygmies, a fabulous race of dwarfs, said to have been destroyed by cranes : P. L. I. 575.

Infect, *vb. tr.* (*a*) to taint with moral corruption : P. L. X. 608.

(*b*) to affect ; *the love-tale infected Sion's daughters with like heat* : P. L. I. 453.

Infection, *sb.* (*a*) moral contamination : P. L. I. 483.

(*b*) the diffusive influence of example or sympathy in communicating feelings ; *the infection of my sorrows loud* : P. 55.

Infer, *vb. tr.* (*a*) to cause to be ; with two *acc.* : P. L. VII. 116.

(*b*) *absol.* to draw an inference : C. 408.

(*c*) to involve as a consequence, imply : P. L. VIII. 91 ; IX. 285, 754.

Inferior, (1) *adj.* lower in rank, importance, or quality ; *of persons* : P. L. VIII. 541 ; IX. 825; with *to* : P. R. II. 135 ; S. A. 73 ; in comparison with heavenly beings : P. L. IV. 362 ; VIII. 410; *inferior angel* : P. L. IV. 59 ; *of animals* : P. L. VIII. 382 ; S. A. 672 ; *of places* or *things* : P. L. III. 420 ; X. 468; N. O. 81; A. 77.

(2) *sb.* person of a lower station : P. L. II. 26.

Infernal, *adj.* (*a*) of the realms of the dead : N. O. 233.

(*b*) of or pertaining to hell ; *infernal world, court* : P. L. I. 251, 792; *infernal pit* : P. L. I. 657 ; II. 850 ; IV. 965 ; X. 464; *rivers, vale, doors* : P. L. II. 575, 742, 881 ; *thunder* : P. L. II. 66 ; *infernal states, peers, powers,* etc. : P. L. II. 387, 507 ; IX. 136 ; X. 259, 389 ; P. R. I. 107 ; *spirit, ghosts* : P. L. IV. 793 ; P. R. IV. 422 ; *serpent* : P. L. I. 34 ; P. R. IV. 618.

(*c*) like that of hell ; *infernal*

flame, noise, dregs: P. L. VI. 483, 667; VII. 238.

Infest, *vb. tr.* to harass: S. A. 423.

Infidel, *sb.* (*a*) one who is not a Christian, *here* a Saracen: P. L. I. 582.

(*b*) one who is not of the Jewish faith: S. A. 221.

Infinite (infínite: P. L. V. 874), (**1**) *adj.* (*a*) boundless, unlimited, innumerable; *of God*: P. L. III. 373; V. 596; VIII. 420; XI. 794; X. 167; *infinite goodness, sorrow, wisdom, wrath*, etc.: P. L. I. 218; II. 797; III. 706; IV. 74, 415, 734, 916; VII. 602; X. 907; XII. 469; *deeds, ages, descents*: P. L. VI. 241; VII. 191; VIII. 410; *infinite host*: P. L. V. 874; *infinite abyss, chaos*: P. L. II. 405.

(*b*) very great; *infinite manslaughter*: P. L. XI. 692.

(**2**) *absol.* or *sb.* that which has no limit: P. L. X. 802; *the void and formless infinite*, chaos: P. L. III. 12.

Infinitely, *adv.* boundlessly: P. L. IV. 414; VII. 76.

Infinitude, *sb.* illimitable space: P. L. III. 711; VII. 169.

Infirm, *adj.* weak, irresolute; *thought infirm*: P. L. V. 384; *comp. infirmer sex*: P. L. X. 956.

Infirmity, *sb.* weakness of character: S. A. 776; a weakness or defect in character: L. 71.

Infix, *vb. tr.* to implant firmly: P. L. II. 602; *in their souls infixed plagues*: P. L. VI. 837; *of constancy no root infixed*: S. A. 1032.

Inflame (inflamèd, *trisyl.*: P. L. I. 300), *vb.* (**1**) *tr.* (*a*) to fill with flames: P. L. IV. 818.

(*b*) to fire with passion or strong feeling: P. L. VI. 261; *inflame their breasts to valour*: S. A. 1739; *inflame with lust, rage, ardour, glory*: P. L. II. 791; IV. 9; IX. 1031; P. R. III. 40; *carnal desire inflaming*: P. L. IX. 1013; *thoughts inflamed of highest design*: P. L. II. 630.

(*c*) to exaggerate, make worse: P. R. I. 418.

(**2**) *intr.* to be on fire, burn: P. L. II. 581.

part. adj. **inflamed,** filled with flames, on fire: P. L. I. 300.

Inflammation, *sb.* the morbid condition characterized by pain, swelling, and redness: S. A. 626.

Inflexible, *adj.* unyielding in temper: S. A. 816.

Inflict, *vb. tr.* to lay on, impose, cause to be suffered: P. L. I. 96; X. 341; S. A. 1291; *punishment, death, wound inflicted*: P. L. II. 335; X. 51; P. R. I. 54; *slaveries*: S. A. 485; *indignities, evils*: S. A. 1170.

Infliction, *sb.* that which is inflicted, suffering: P. R. I. 428.

Influence (ínfluénce: P. L. II. 1034; IV. 669; V. 695; VII. 375; VIII. 513; IX. 107; X. 662; C. 336; L'A. 122; N. O. 71), *sb.* (**1**) the power or 'virtue' exerted by celestial bodies; *Pleiades ... shedding sweet influence*: P. L. VII. 375; *exerted on the earth or on man*; *heat of various influence foment and warm*: P. L. IV. 669; *sacred, precious influence*: P. L. IX. 107; N. O. 71; *selectest influence*: P. L. VIII. 513; *influence malignant*: P. L. X. 662; *if your influence be quite damned up*: C. 336.

(*b*) *transf.* power exerted by light; *sacred influence of light*: P. L. II. 1034.

(*c*) *fig.* *bright eyes rain influence*: L'A. 122.

(**2**) the power which is infused; *infused bad influence into the unwary breast*: P. L. V. 695.

(**3**) unseen operation of some cause, outgoing energy producing effects: P. L. III. 118; IX. 309.

Infolded, *part. adj.* enclosed one within another: A. 64.

Inform, *vb. tr.* (*a*) to determine the essential character of: P. L. III. 593.

(*b*) to enlighten, teach, instruct: P. L. VII. 639; XII. 232; P. R. III. 247; S. A. 1229.

(*c*) to guide or direct *feet*: S. A. 335; or, possibly, to obtain guidance for: C. 180.

(*d*) to acquaint, apprise, tell: P. L. IX. 275.

Informidable (infórmidáble), *adj.* not to be dreaded: P. L. IX. 486.

Infringe, *vb. tr.* to destroy; *our power to be infringed*: P. R. I. 62.

Infuriate, *adj.* excited to fury; *fig. of things*: P. L. VI. 486.

Infuse, *vb. tr.* to introduce as by pouring, instil: P. L. IX. 836; *infused bad influence*: P. L. V. 694; *vital virtue and vital warmth*:

P. L. VII. 236 ; *sweetness into my heart*: P. L. VIII. 474.

Ingender, *vb. tr.* (*a*) to beget *on* ; *fig. of the sun*: P. L. X. 530.

(*b*) *absol.* to have sexual intercourse *with* : P. L. II. 794.

(*c*) to give rise to *pride*: P. L. IV. 809.

Inglorious, *adj.* (*a*) without fame or renown : P. L. III. 253 ; P. R. III. 42 ; S. A. 580 ; D. F. I. 22.

(*b*) dishonourable, disgraceful, ignominious ; *inglorious strife, servitude*: P. L. I. 624 ; IX. 141 ; *life*: P. L. XII. 220 ; *likeness of a beast* : C. 528.

Ingorged, *vb. intr.* to feed to excess: P. L. IX. 791.

Ingraft, *vb. tr.* to superadd ; *all his works on me ... ingraft* : P. L. XI. 35.

Ingrate, (1) *adj.* unthankful : P. R. III. 138.

(2) *sb.* an unthankful person : P. L. III. 97 ; V. 811.

Ingrateful, *adj.* (*a*) disagreeable ; *no ingrateful food*: P. L. V. 407.

(*b*) ungrateful, unthankful : P. L. IX. 1164 ; S. A. 282, 696.

Ingratitude, *sb.* unthankfulness : S. A. 276 ; C. 778.

Ingredient, *sb.* that which enters into a compound : P. L. XI. 417.

Ingulf. *See* **Engulf.**

Inhabit, *vb.* (1) *tr.* to dwell in, occupy as a place of abode : P. L. X. 690.

(2) *intr.* to dwell, live : P. L. II. 355 ; VII. 162.

Inhabitant, *sb.* resident, dweller ; *inhabitants on earth* : P. L. IV. 5 ; *if land be there* (in the moon), *fields and inhabitants* : P. L. VIII. 145 ; *inhabitant of heaven* : P. L. II. 860 ; in direct address ; *Inhabitant with God* : P. L. V. 461.

Inhabitation, *sb.* inhabitants collectively, population : S. A. 1512.

Inherit, *vb. tr.* to have or hold : S. A. 1012.

Inheritance, *sb.* (*a*) possession or property received by right of succession : P. R. III. 382 ; S. A. 1476.

(*b*) possession received by gift or grant : P. L. II. 38.

Inhospitable (inhóspitáble), *adj.* (*a*) unfriendly to strangers ; *inhospitable guile* : S. A. 989.

(*b*) barren and cheerless : P. L. XI. 306.

Inhospitably (inhóspitábly), *adv.* in violation of hospitality : P. L. XII. 168.

Inhuman, *adj.* (*a*) cruel, unfeeling ; *inhuman foes* : S. A. 109.

(*b*) not of the ordinary human type; *inhuman pains* : P. L. XI. 511.

Inhumanly, *adv.* cruelly, mercilessly : P. L. XI. 677.

Inimitable (inímitáble), *adj.* surpassing imitation : P. L. III. 508 ; A. 78.

Iniquity, *sb.* wickedness, sin : Ps. v. 13 ; VI. 16 ; LXXXV. 5 ; *pl.* unrighteous deeds, sins : P. L. XII. 107.

Injunction, *sb.* command, order : P. L. X. 13.

Injure, *vb. tr.* to hurt, harm : P. L. X. 1057.

part. adj. **injured** ; (*a*) wronged ; *injured lover's hell* : P. L. V. 450.

(*b*) impaired ; *sense of injured merit* : P. L. I. 98.

Injurious, *adj.* inflicting harm or suffering : S. A. 1003.

Injury, *sb.* (*a*) suffering or mischief inflicted : P. L. I. 500 ; *pl.* the wrongs suffered : P. L. X. 925 ; P. R. III. 190 ; IV. 387.

(*b*) hurt, damage : P. L. VI. 434.

Inland, *sb.* interior part of hell : P. L. X. 423.

Inlay, (1) *sb.* ornamental design produced by inlaying one material in another ; *violet, crocus, and hyacinth, with rich inlay broidered the ground* : P. L. IV. 701.

(2) *vb. tr.* to ornament, with inserted material : P. L. VII. 758 ; *fig. sea-girt isles ... inlay the unadorned bosom of the deep* : C. 22.

Inlet, *sb.* place of ingress ; *inlet of each sense* : C. 839.

Inly, *adv.* inwardly : P. L. XI. 444 ; P. R. I. 228, 466 ; III. 203.

Inmate, *sb.* one who is an associate in occupancy : P. L. IX. 495.

attrib. dwelling in the same place : P. L. XII. 166.

Inmost, *adj.* (*a*) furthest within ; *earth's inmost womb*: P. L. V. 302 ; *inmost bower, grove* : P. L. IV. 738 ; Il P. 29 ; C. 536 ; with blending of sense (*b*) ; *inmost seat of mental sight, mind* : P. L. XI. 418 ; S. A. 611.

(*b*) deepest, most vital ; *inmost counsels, powers* : P. L. I. 168 ; IX. 1048.

Inn, *sb.* a house of entertainment for travellers : P. R. I. 248 ; U. C. I. 13.

Inner, *adj.* inward ; *the inner man*, the mind or soul : P. R. II. 477.

Innocence, *sb.* (*a*) the state of being untainted with, or unacquainted with, evil ; moral purity : P. L. IV. 318, 388, 745 ; V. 445 ; VI. 401 ; VIII. 501 ; IX. 373, 411, 1054, 1075 ; XI. 30 ; D. F. I. 65 ; *betrayed my credulous innocence* : C. 697 ; put for the person ; *commended her fair innocence to the flood* : C. 831.

   (*b*) guilelessness, artlessness : P. L. IX. 459.

Innocent, *adj.* (*a*) pure, sinless : P. L. IV. 11 ; V. 209 ; C. 574 ; *fig.* spotless ; *innocent snow* : N. O. 39.

   (*b*) not guilty ; *innocent nature* : C. 762.

Innumerable (innúmeráble, except in P. L. V. 585), *adj.* not to be counted, numberless ; (*a*) with sing. sb. ; *innumerable force, host, race* : P. L. I. 101 ; V. 585, 745 ; VII. 156 ; *prey* : P. L. X. 268 ; *fry, spawn* : P. L. VII. 400 ; C. 713 ; *sound* : P. L. III. 147.

   (*b*) with pl. sb. : P. L. I. 338 ; III. 565 ; V. 898 ; VI. 508 ; IX. 1089 ; X. 507, 896 ; following the sb. : P. L. I. 699 ; VI. 82 ; VII. 88 ; VIII. 297 ; S. A. 608.

Innumerous, *adj.* numberless ; *innumerous living creatures* : P. L. VII. 455 ; *boughs* : C. 349.

Inoffensive, *adj.* (*a*) free from obstacles : P. L. X. 305 ; not stumbling or striking against any obstacle : P. L. VIII. 164.

   (*b*) not causing one to offend, not intoxicating : P. L. V. 345.

Inordinate, *adj.* immoderate ; *inordinate desires* : P. L. IV. 808 ; XII. 87.

Inquire, *vb.* (1) *tr.* (*a*) to seek knowledge concerning : P. L. XII. 362 ; with *clause* : P. L. III. 571.

   (*b*) to question, interrogate : P. R. I. 458.

   (2) *intr.* to make search or investigation : P. R. IV. 42 ; with *into* : P. L. VIII. 225.

Inquisition, *sb.* investigation, inquiry : P. R. III. 200.

Inquisitive, *adj.* unduly curious, prying : S. A. 775.

Inroad, *sb.* incursion : P. L. II. 103 ; VI. 387 ; *fig. the inroad of darkness old* : P. L. III. 421.

Inroll. *See* **Enroll.**

Insatiable (insátiáble), *adj.* not to be satisfied ; with *of* : P. R. III. 148.

Insatiate, *adj.* insatiable : P. L. IX. 536 ; with *prep. inf.* : P. L. II. 8.

Inscribe, *vb. tr.* to mark with words or characters ; *our Psalms with artful terms inscribed* : P. R. IV. 335 ; *that sanguine flower inscribed with woe* : L. 106.

Insect, *sb.* the small invertebrate animal ; in combination with *bird, beast,* or *worm* : P. L. IV. 704 ; *sing. collect.* for *pl.* : P. L. VII. 476 ; species of insects : P. L. XI. 734.

Insensate, *adj.* lacking understanding, foolish : P. L. VI. 787 ; S. A. 1685.

Insensible, *adj.* without the power of sensation : P. L. VIII. 291 ; X. 777.

Insensibly, *adv.* imperceptibly : P. L. VI. 692 ; VIII. 130.

Inseparable (inséparáble), *adj.* not to be parted : P. L. X. 250.

Inseparably (inséparábly), *adv.* (*a*) so as not to be separated : P. L. IV. 473.

   (*b*) indivisibly : S. A. 154.

Inshrine. *See* **Enshrine.**

Inside, *sb.* (*a*) interior of a building : P. R. IV. 58.

   (*b*) inward nature, mind or heart : Hor. Epist. 6.

Insinuate, *vb. intr.* to make one's way tortuously : P. L. IV. 348.

Insist, *vb. tr.* (*a*) to continue steadfastly, persist ; with *prep. inf.* : S. A. 913.

   (*b*) to dwell with emphasis *on* : P. R. I. 468.

Insolence, *sb.* pride or arrogance exhibited in contemptuous or insulting treatment of others : S. A. 1236 ; *flown with insolence* : P. L. I. 502 ; *swilled insolence* : C. 178.

Insolent, *adj.* arrogant, overbearing : S. A. 1422.

Inspection, *sb.* critical examination, careful survey : P. L. IX. 83.

Insphere, *vb. tr.* to place in a celestial sphere : C. 3.

Inspire, *vb. tr.* (*a*) to breathe into ; *inspiring venom* : P. L. IV. 804 ; *that pure breath of life, the spirit of man which God inspired* : P. L. X. 785 ; to breathe the breath of life into ; *earth's hallowed mould, of God inspired* : P. L. V. 322.

(*b*) to actuate ; *his brutal sense
... inspired with act intelligential* :
P. L. IX. 189 ; to animate *with
contradiction* : P. L. VI. 155 ; *with
machination* : P. L. VI. 503.

(*c*) to guide or control by divine
influence : P. L. I. 7 ; P. R. I.
492 ; N. O. 180 ; *from God inspired* : P. R. IV. 350.

(*d*) to communicate by divine
agency : P. L. IX. 23 ; P. R. I.
11 ; IV. 275.

(*e*) to arouse, awaken ; *May,
that dost inspire mirth* : M. M. 5 ;
to the heart inspires vernal delight :
P. L. IV. 154 ; *inspired the spirit
of love* : P. L. VIII. 476 ; *sighs ...
which the Spirit of prayer inspired* :
P. L. XI. 7.

part. adj. **inspired,** having the
power of prophecy : P. L. IV. 273.
Instant, (1) *adj.* immediate, without
delay : P. L. X. 210, 345.

(2) *adv.* instantly : P. L. VI.
549.
Instantly, *adv.* immediately, without delay : P. L. VIII. 458.
Instead, *adv.* in place of it or him :
P. L. III. 45 ; IV. 316 ; X. 538,
1040 ; XI. 5 ; XII. 54 ; P. R. III.
131 ; C. 529 ; *instead of,* in place
of : P. L. I. 553 ; IV. 105 ; VII.
188 ; X. 565.
Instil, *vb. tr.* (*a*) to pour in by
drops : P. L. XI. 416.

(*b*) to infuse or insinuate gradually : P. L. VI. 269.
Instinct (instínct), (1) *sb.* innate impulse : P. L. X. 263 ; *divine instinct* : S. A. 526 ; *instinct of
nature* : S. A. 1545.

(2) *past part.* (*a*) impelled or
moved *with* : P. L. II. 937 ; VI.
752.

(*b*) animated, inspired, or *possibly,* adv. with unconscious dexterity : P. L. XI. 562.
Instinctive, *adj.* prompted by instinct : P. L. VIII. 259.
Instruct, *vb. tr.* to furnish with
knowledge, teach : P. L. I. 19 ;
XII. 557 ; with *acc.* and *prep. inf.* :
P. L. V. 320 ; X. 1081 ; with
clause : P. L. XII. 239 ; *fig. so
well instructed are my tears* : P. 48.

part. adj. (*a*) **instructed,** trained :
S. A. 757.

(*b*) **instruct,** taught ; with *prep.
inf.* : P. R. I. 439.
Instruction, *sb.* education, enlighten-
ment : P. L. VII. 81.

Instructor, *sb.* teacher ; vocative,
Divine instructor : P. L. V. 546 ;
Heavenly instructor : P. L. XI. 871.
Instrument, *sb.* (*a*) that through
which something is done : P. L.
II. 872 ; X. 166.

(*b*) implement, weapon : P. L.
VI. 505 ; *collect.* apparatus ; *instrument of war* : P. R. III. 388.

(*c*) a contrivance for producing
musical sounds : P. L. XI. 559.
Instrumental, *adj.* made by musical
instruments : P. L. IV. 686 ; VI.
65.
Insufferably (insúfferábly), *adv.* to
an intolerable degree ; *insufferably
bright* : P. L. IX. 1084.
Insult, (1) *sb.* affront, indignity : P.
R. III. 190.

(2) *vb. absol.* to behave with insolent triumph, exult contemptuously : P. L. II. 79 ; S. A. 113,
944.

part. adj. **insulting,** triumphing
insolently : P. L. IV. 926 ; causing
one to offer insults to others : P.
R. IV. 138.
Insuperable (insúperáble), *adj.* that
cannot be surmounted : P. L. IV.
138.
Insupportable, *adj.* unbearable, insufferable : P. L. X. 134.
Insupportably, *adv.* irresistibly : S.
A. 136.
Insurrection, *sb.* seditious rising,
rebellion : P. L. II. 136.
Integrity, *sb.* entire uprightness of
character : P. L. V. 704 ; IX. 329.
Intellect, *sb.* (*a*) a person of great
intellect : S. XI. 4.

(*b*) *all intellect,* having the
special functions of the intellect
performed by all parts of the
body : P. L. VI. 351.
Intellectual, (1) *adj.* (*a*) having intellectual capacity : P. L. II. 147.

(*b*) giving intellectual capacity :
P. L. V. 485 ; conferring the
power of understanding : P. L.
IX. 768.

(2) *sb.* intellect, mind : P. L.
IX. 483.
Intelligence, *sb.* an intelligent
being ; *how fully hast thou satisfied
me, pure Intelligence of Heaven* :
P. L. VIII. 181.
Intelligent, *adj.* (*a*) having a high
degree of understanding : P. R.
III. 58.

(*b*) having knowledge *of* : P. L.
VII. 427.

Intelligential, *adj.* (*a*) directed by intelligence : P. L. IX. 190.

(*b*) possessing absolute intelligence ; *of angels* : P. L. V. 408.

Intemperance, *sb.* lack of moderation ; *intemperance more in meats and drinks* : P. L. XI. 472 ; *sensual folly and intemperance* : C. 975.

Intemperate, *adj.* immoderate : C. 67.

Intend, *vb. tr.* (*a*) to occupy oneself with, attend to : P. L. II. 457.

(*b*) to have in mind, purpose, design : P. L. IX. 295 ; S. A. 911 ; S. XXI. 8 ; Ps. VII. 47 ; *if he intends our stay* : P. L. IV. 898 ; with *prep. inf.* : P. L. I. 652 ; V. 693, 725, 867 ; P. R. I. 61 ; with two *acc.* : P. L. X. 58 ; with *acc.* and *dat.* : P. L. VIII. 447 ; *fig.* said *of the hand* : P. L. II. 713, 727, 740 ; *to God his tower intends siege* : P. L. XII. 73 ; *my ... song intends ... to soar* : P. L. I. 14.

to purpose to obtain : S. A. 1259.

(*c*) to design, plan, model : P. L. VIII. 555.

part. adj. **intended,** (*a*) extended ; *intended wing, fig.* : P. L. IX. 45.

(*b*) designed : P. L. X. 689.

Intense, *adj.* (*a*) tense, stretched ; *fig.* of keen perception and noble understanding : P. L. VIII. 387.

(*b*) existing in a high degree, violent : S. A. 615.

Intent, (1) *adj.* assiduously engaged : P. L. IV. 810 ; with *on* : P. L. I. 787 ; V. 332 ; VI. 503 ; IX. 786 ; P. R. II. 195.

(2) *sb.* intention, purpose : R. IV. 528 ; *sincere, friendly, free, pure intent* : P. L. III. 192 ; S. A. 1078 ; A. 34 ; F. of C. 9 ; *dark, fierce, amorous* : P. L. IX. 162, 462, 1035 ; *great, uncontrollable* : P. R. II. 95 ; S. A. 1754 ; *to what intent* : P. R. I. 291.

Inter, *vb. tr.* to enclose the corpse of : M. W. 1.

Intercede, *vb. intr.* to make intercession, mediate : P. L. XI. 21, with *to* : S. A. 920.

Intercept, *vb. tr.* (*a*) to seize on the way, cut off from the destination aimed at : P. L. V. 871 ; X. 429 ; *his shield such ruin intercept* : P. L. VI. 193.

(*b*) to cut off *thy way* : P. L. IX. 410.

Intercession, *sb.* entreaty in behalf of another : P. L. X. 228.

Intercessor, *sb.* one who intercedes with God for man : P. L. III. 219 ; *of Christ* : P. L. X. 96 ; XI. 19.

Interchange, *sb.* alternate succession ; *sweet interchange of hill and valley* : P. L. IX. 115.

Intercourse, *sb.* (*a*) communication between places : P. L. II. 1031 ; VII. 571 ; X. 260.

(*b*) interchange ; *intercourse of looks and smiles* : P. L. IX. 238.

Interdict, *sb.* authoritative prohibition : P. R. II. 369.

Interdicted, *part. adj.* forbidden, prohibited : P. L. V. 52 ; VII. 46.

Interdiction, *sb.* interdict, prohibition : P. L. VIII. 334.

Interfuse, *vb. tr.* to cause to spread throughout ; *the ambient air wide interfused* : P. L. VII. 89.

Interlunar, *sb.* **interlunar cave,** the place where the moon was supposed to hide during the interval between the disappearance of the old and the appearance of the new moon : S. A. 89.

Interminable (intérmináble), *adj.* *absol.* the *Interminable*, God : S. A. 307.

Intermission, *sb.* temporary cessation, respite : P. L. II. 802 ; IV. 102 ; *for intermission sake* : S. A. 1629.

Intermit, *vb. tr.* (*a*) to suspend, interrupt, delay : P. L. IX. 223, 1133.

(*b*) to omit, neglect : P. L. II. 462.

part. adj. **intermitted,** suspended : P. L. II. 173.

Intermix, *vb. tr.* to intermingle ; *spring of roses intermixed with myrtle* : P. L. IX. 218 ; *soft tunings intermixed with voice* : P. L. VII. 598 ; *intermix grateful digressions* : P. L. VIII. 54 ; *intermix my covenant in the woman's seed* : P. L. XI. 115.

Internal, *adj.* pertaining to the mind or soul ; *internal man* : P. L. IX. 711 ; *sight* : P. L. VIII. 461 ; *peace* : S. A. 1334 ; *blindness internal* : S. A. 1686.

Interpose, *vb.* (*pres. 2d sing.* interposest* : P. L. II. 738) (1) *tr.* (*a*) to place between : P. L. IV. 253 ; P. R. IV. 39.

(*b*) to present, bring, or thrust in for intervention or relief ;

death ... interpose his dart : P. L.
II. 854; *interpose aid, defence,
ease, delights* : P. L. III. 728; VI.
336; L. 152; S. XX. 14.

(2) *intr.* or *absol.* (*a*) to come
between, stand in the way : P. L.
V. 258; X. 323.

(*b*) to speak by way of interruption : P. L. II. 738; XII. 4,
270.

Interposition, *sb.* that which is interposed for relief : P. R. III. 222.

Interpret, *vb.* (*pres. 2d sing.* interpret'st : S. A. 790) (1) *tr.* (*a*) to
expound by means of translation :
P. L. V. 762.

(*b*) to construe or understand
as ; with two *acc.* : S. A. 790.

(2) *intr.* to act as interpreter ;
of Christ : P. L. XI. 33.

Interpreter, *sb.* (*a*) one who explains ; *of Raphael* : P. L. VII. 72.

(*b*) one who makes known the
will or commands of another ;
*Uriel ... interpreter through high-
est heaven* : P. L. III. 657.

Interrupt, *vb. tr.* (*a*) to break off,
cause to cease or stop : *interrupt
their public peace* : P. L. XII. 317;
His joy : P. L. II. 371; *the sweet
of life* : P. L. VIII. 184.

(*b*) to break in upon *a person*
while speaking : P. L. XI. 286.

(*c*) to break in upon action : P.
L. IX. 512.

past part. **interrupt,** thrown
between so as to form an interval
or gap between hell and the
world : P. L. III. 84.

Intertwine, *vb. tr.* to interweave,
interlace : P. L. IV. 405.

Interval, *sb.* open space, gap : P. L.
VI. 105.

Interveined, *adj.* intersected as if
with veins ; *fair champaign, with
less rivers interveined* : P. R. III.
257.

Intervene, *vb. intr.* to come in as
something extraneous; *looks intervene and smiles* : P. L. IX. 222.

Interview, *sb.* (*a*) meeting : P. L.
II. 593.

(*b*) *at interview,* face to face,
viewing each other : P. L. VI.
555.

Intervolved, *part. adj.* wound one
with another : P. L. V. 623.

Interweave (*past part.* interwove :
P. L. I. 621; C. 544; interwoven :
P. R. II. 263), *vb. tr.* (*a*) to weave
together, interlace ; *of trees thick*

interwoven : P. R. II. 263; *a bank
... interwove with flaunting honeysuckle* : C. 544.

(*b*) to intermingle ; *words interwove with sighs* : P. L. I. 621.

Intestine, *adj.* (*a*) domestic, civil ;
intestine broils, war : P. L. II.
1001; VI. 259.

(*b*) internal with regard to the
body : S. A. 1038; intestinal ;
intestine stone and ulcer : P. L. XI.
484.

Inthrall. *See* **Enthrall.**

Intimate, *adj.* existing in one's
inner thoughts, inmost : S. A. 223.

*Into (usually accented on the first
syllable, but sometimes on the
second, as in : P. L. I. 3, 689; V.
117), *prep.* (*a*) to the interior of,
to a point within the limits of :
P. L. I. 3; II. 133; III. 470; IV.
187; V. 292; IX. 1100; P. R.
I. 9.

inquire ... into the ways of God :
P. L. VIII. 226; *fallen into wrath
divine* : S. A. 1683.

(*b*) into the possession of : P.
L. IV. 359; VIII. 148; P. R. I.
369; S. A. 259.

(*c*) of state or condition ; *into
woe, fraud,* etc. : P. L. V. 543;
VI. 614; VII. 143; IX. 362; X.
503.

(*d*) of action ; *into hymns burst
forth* : P. R. I. 169; *sprung into
swift flight* : C. 579.

(*e*) of the substance or form into
which a thing turns or is changed :
P. L. II. 63, 278; IV. 455; V.
420; VI. 291; P. R. I. 499; S. A.
729; C. 53.

(*f*) of the result of action : P.
L. II. 171; III. 491; V. 891; C.
258, 799.

(*g*) indicating the parts produced by division : P. L. IV. 233.

(*h*) of direction ; *look into* : P.
L. II. 917; IV. 458; *gave prospect
large into* : P. L. IV. 145.

(*i*) of the part penetrated ;
smote him into the midriff : P. L.
XI. 445.

Intoxicate, *vb. tr.* to make drunk,
inebriate : P. L. IX. 1008.

part. adj. **intoxicate,** excited in
mind as if with an intoxicant : P.
R. IV. 328.

Intrance. *See* **Entrance.**

Intrench, *vb. tr.* to furrow ; *his face
deep scars of thunder had in-
trenched* : P. L. I. 601.

Intricacy (íntricácy), *sb.* perplexity, *pl.*: P. L. VIII. 182.

Intricate, *adj.* perplexingly involved, complicated: P. L. II. 877; V. 622; interwinding in a complicated manner; *of paths*: P. L. IX. 632.

Introduce, *vb. tr.* (*a*) to bring in; *sin ... death introduced*: P. L. X. 709.

(*b*) to institute *law and edict on us*: P. L. V. 797.

(*c*) to bring forward with preliminary matter: P. L. III. 368.

(*d*) to make known by acting as a type of: P. L. XII. 241.

Introduction, *sb.* that which leads to the knowledge of something else: P. R. III. 247.

Intrude, *vb. intr.* to thrust oneself in without warrant or invitation: L. 115.

Intrusion, *sb.* unbidden and unwelcome entrance: P. L. XII. 178.

See **New-intrusted.**

Intuitive, *adj.* acting by immediate apprehension and without ratiocination: P. L. V. 488.

Inundation, *sb.* an overflow of water, a flood: P. L. XI. 828.

Inure, *vb. tr.* (*a*) to put into practice; *to inure our prompt obedience*: P. L. VIII. 239.

(*b*) to accustom, habituate: P. L. II. 216; with *prep. inf.*: P. L. XI. 362: P. R. II. 102; with *to*; *to thirst inured*: P. R. I. 339; *to blood*: P. R. IV. 139; *inured to light*: C. 735.

Inutterable (inútteráble), *adj.* indescribable: P. L. II. 626.

Invade, *vb. tr.* (*a*) to make an inroad into: P. L. II. 342.

(*b*) to seize upon, take possession of: P. L. XI. 102; Ps. LXXXIII. 47; *fig. of night*: P. L. III. 726.

(*c*) to make an attack upon *a person*: P. L. VI. 603; P. R. II. 127.

part. adj. **invading,** making an inroad: Ps. CXXXVI. 82.

Invader, *sb.* one who makes an inroad into a country: P. L. XI. 801.

Invalid, *adj.* not valid, of no force: P. L. VIII. 116.

Invasion, *sb.* hostile inroad: P. R. III. 365.

Inveigle, *vb. tr.* to lead astray by blinding to the truth, beguile, entrap: C. 538.

Invent, *vb. tr.* to contrive, devise: P. L. VI. 464; *for us alone was death invented*: P. L. IX. 767; *envious commands, invented with design to keep them low*: P. L. IV. 524; *whate'er his cruel malice could invent*: P. R. I. 149.

part. adj. **invented,** devised; *invented torments*: P. L. II. 70.

Invention, *sb.* (*a*) an original contrivance: P. L. VI. 498, 631.

(*b*) intellectual device, *pl.*: P. L. VII. 121.

Inventor, *sb.* one who devises something new: P. L. VI. 499; XI. 610.

Invert, *vb. tr.* to change to the contrary, reverse: C. 682.

Invest, *vb. tr.* to cover or surround; *such majesty invests him*: P. L. XI. 233; *night invests the sea*: P. L. I. 208; *thou* (light) ... *didst invest the rising world of waters*: P. L. III. 10; *horizon ... invested with bright rays*: P. L. VII. 372.

Invincible, *adj.* not to be overcome, unconquerable; *of persons*: P. L. VI. 47; S. A. 341; *invincible spirit, grace, temperance, might*: P. L. I. 140; IV. 846; P. R. II. 408; S. A. 1271.

Invincibly, *adj.* unconquerably: P. L. VI. 806.

Inviolable (invíoláble), *adj.* (*a*) free from violence or profanation: P. L. IV. 843.

(*b*) not yielding to force or violence: P. L. VI. 398.

Invisible (invisíble: P. L. III. 586), *adj.* that cannot be seen: P. L. III. 55; VIII. 135; V. Ex. 66; *of God* or *his throne*: P. L. III. 375; V. 157, 599; VI. 681; VII. 122, 589; *of Satan*: P. L. X. 444; *invisible glory, virtue, evil*: P. L. I. 369; III. 586, 684; *exploits*: P. L. V. 565.

Invisibly, *adv.* so that the person leading cannot be seen: P. L. IV. 476.

Invitation, *sb.* solicitation to take part: P. R. II. 367.

Invite, *vb.* (1) *tr.* (*a*) to ask or solicit *a person*: P. L. XII. 169; P. R. I. 72; with *acc.* and *prep. inf.*: P. L. VIII. 208; P. R. II. 314; *absol.*: P. L. III. 188.

(*b*) unintentionally to bring on; *their own ruin on themselves to invite*: S. A. 1684.

(*c*) to present incitement to; *invite noontide repast*: P. L. IX.

402 ; *guileful spells ... invite the unwary sense* : C. 538; with *prep. inf.* : P. L. v. 374.

(2) *intr.* or *absol.* (*a*) to offer inducement ; *all things invite to peaceful counsels* : P. L. II. 278.

(*b*) to offer attractions, allure : L'A. 92 ; with *to* : P. R. IV. 248.

part. adj. inviting, alluring *to* : P. L. IX. 777.

Invocate, *vb. tr.* to implore *aid* : S. A. 1146.

See Oft-invocated.

Invoke, *vb. tr.* (*a*) to call on in prayer : P. L. XI. 492, 590, 591 ; XII. 112 ; P. R. IV. 203 ; C. 854.

(*b*) to call for or implore *aid* : P. L. I. 13.

vbl. sb. invoking, supplication : M. W. 19.

Involve, *vb. tr.* (*a*) to enwrap, enfold, envelop : P. L. VII. 277 ; *involved with stench* : P. L. I. 236 ; *in mist* : P. L. IX. 75 ; *within thick clouds ... involved* : P. R. I. 41 ; *earth with hell to mingle and involve* : P. L. II. 384.

(*b*) to entwine ; *involved their snaky folds* : P. L. VII. 483 ; *fig. his end with mine involved* : P. L. II. 807.

(*c*) to beset with difficulties : S. A. 304.

(*d*) to implicate *in this fraud* : P. L. v. 879.

Invulnerable (invúlneráble), *adj.* incapable of being wounded : P. L. II. 812 ; VI. 400.

Inward, (1) *adj.* (*a*) internal, interior : P. L. III. 584.

(*b*) of, in, or pertaining to the mind or soul : P. L. VIII. 539 ; IX. 1125 ; P. R. IV. 145 ; *inward faculties, powers,* etc. : P. L. VIII. 542 ; IX. 600 ; C. 466 ; S. A. 1026 ; *oracle, light, eyes* : P. R. I. 463 ; S. A. 162, 1689 ; *apparition* : P. L. VIII. 293 ; *silence* : P. L. IX. 895 ; *freedom, liberty, ripeness* : P. L. IX. 762 ; XII. 101 ; S. VII. 7 ; *grief* : P. L. IX. 97 ; S. A. 330 ; *passion* : S. 1006 ; *consolation* : P. L. XII. 495 ; *nakedness, fraud* : P. L. x. 221, 871.

(2) *sb. pl.* inner parts of an animal, entrails : P. L. XI. 439.

(3) *adv.* (*a*) towards the interior : P. L. VI. 861.

(*b*) into or within the mind or soul : P. L. III. 52 ; VIII. 221, 608 ; P. R. IV. 145.

Inwardly, *adv.* in the mind or soul : P. L. IV. 88 ; L. 127.

Inweave, *vb.* (*past part.* inwove : P. L. III. 352 ; inwoven : P. L. IV. 693) *tr.* to form by weaving ; *inwove with amaranth and gold* : P. L. III. 352.

part. adj. inwoven, intertwined : P. L. IV. 693.

See Flower-inwoven.

Inwork. *See* Inwrought.

Inwreathe, *vb. tr.* to surround as with a wreath : P. L. III. 361.

Inwrought, *past part.* having a decorative pattern worked in it, *fig.* : L. 105.

Ionian, *adj.* of Ionia, *here* put for Greece in general ; hence, of Greece : P. L. I. 508.

Irassa, *sb.* a town or region in Lybia, Africa : P. R. IV. 564.

Ire, *sb.* anger, wrath ; the anger of God : P. L. II. 95, 155 ; VI. 843 ; IX. 692 ; x. 936 ; XI. 885 ; P. R. III. 219, 220 ; S. A. 520 ; Ps. LXXX. 67 ; LXXXVIII, 64 ; *vengeful* or *avenging ire* : P. L. I. 148 ; VII. 184 ; x. 1023 ; *frowning ire* : Ps. LXXXV. 19 ; of Satan : P. L. IV. 115 ; *Neptune's ire* : P. L. IX. 18.

Iris, *sb.* (*a*) the goddess who was the messenger of the gods, the personification of the rainbow : P. L. XI. 244 ; C. 83, 992.

(*b*) the plant *Iris* : P. L. IV. 698.

Irksome, *adj.* wearisome, burdensome ; *irksome hours, night, toil* : P. L. II. 527 ; v. 35 ; IX. 242.

Iron, (1) *sb.* (*a*) the metal : P. L. III. 594 ; *bar of massy iron* : P. L. II. 878 ; *massy clods of iron* : P. L. XI. 565 ; *magnetic hardest iron* : P. R. II. 168.

(*b*) armour : S. A. 129, 1124.

(*c*) arms, weapons : S. XVII. 8.

(*d*) glistening with weapons : P. R. III. 326.

(*e*) *in irons*, in fetters : S. A. 1243.

(2) *adj.* (*a*) made of iron : P. L. II. 646 ; IV. 859, 898 ; VI. 576 ; C. 491 ; *hail of iron globes* : P. L. VI. 590.

(*b*) as a symbol of hardness, sternness, or severity; *iron sceptre* : P. L. II. 327 ; Ps. II. 20 ; *iron rod to bruise* : P. L. v. 887 ; *the iron* (key) *shuts amain* : L. 111 ; *iron tears* : Il P. 107.

Irradiance, *sb.* splendour : P. L.
VIII. 617.

Irradiate, *vb. tr.* to illuminate with
spiritual and intellectual light :
P. L. III. 53.

Irrational, *adj.* without the faculty
of reason : P. L. IX. 766 ; S. A.
673 ; *sb.* omitted ; *the irrational*,
the lower animals : P. L. X. 708.

Irreconcilable, *adj.* implacably hostile *to* : P. L. I. 122.

Irrecoverably (írrecóverábly), *adv.*
irretrievably : S. A. 81.

Irregular, *adj.* not regular in form :
P. L. V. 624.

Irreligious, *adj.* godless : S. A. 860.

Irreparable (irréparáble), *adj.* that
cannot be made good ; *irreparable
loss* : P. L. II. 331 ; S. A. 644.

Irresistible, *adj.* that cannot be
withstood ; *union irresistible* : P.
L. VI. 63 ; *irresistible Samson* :
S. A. 126.

Irresolute, *adj.* undecided as to a
course of action : P. R. III. 243 ;
irresolute of thoughts : P. L. IX.
87.

Irreverent, *adj.* wanting in veneration : P. L. XII. 101.

Irrevocable (irrévocáble), *adj.* not to
be recalled : P. L. XII. 323.

Irriguous, *adj.* well-watered : P. L.
IV. 255.

Irruption, *sb.* a bursting in : S. A.
1567.

Isaac, *sb.* the son of Abraham and
Sarah : P. L. XII. 268.

Ishmael, *sb.* the son of Abraham
and Hagar ; *the brood ... of
Ishmael*, the Ishmaelites : Ps.
LXXXIII. 22.

Isis, *sb.* the chief female deity of
the Egyptians, the sister and wife
of Osiris and the mother of
Horus ; sometimes represented
with the head, or only the horns,
of a cow : P. L. I. 478 ; N. O. 212.

Island, *sb.* a tract of land surrounded by water : P. L. I. 205 ;
the island formed from the Mount
of Paradise after its removal by
the flood : P. L. XI. 834 ; *Circe's
island*, the island of Aeaea off the
west coast of Italy ; by the
Romans identified with the promontory of Circeii, the modern
Monte Circeo : C. 50.

Isle, *sb.* island ; *the ocean isles* : P.
L. IV. 354 ; *verdant isles* : P. L.
VIII. 631 ; *isles and woody shores* :
P. L. IX. 1118 ; *sea-girt* : C. 21 ;

enchanted : C. 517 ; with proper
name : P. L. I. 746 ; II. 638 ; IV.
275 ; X. 527 ; P. R. IV. 71, 75 ;
S. A. 715 ; *happy isles*, the Islands
of the Blest : P. L. III. 567, 570.

(*b*) *utmost isles*, the British
Isles : P. L. I. 521 ; *this isle*, Great
Britain ; C. 27.

(*c*) *fig. happy isle*, the earth :
P. L. II. 410.

Ismenian, *adj.* of the river Ismenus
near Thebes, poetical for Theban ;
Ismenean steep, Mount Phicium,
the hill of the Sphinx : P. R. IV.
575.

Israel, *sb.* (*a*) the patriarch Jacob ;
the race of Israel, the twelve
tribes : P. L. I. 432 ; P. R. II.
311 ; *stock of Israel* : Ps. LXXXI.
35.

(*b*) the Hebrew or Jewish
nation : P. L. I. 413, 482 ; XII.
267 ; P. R. I. 217, 254 ; II. 36, 42,
89, 442 ; III. 279, 378, 406, 408,
410, 413, 441 ; IV. 480 ; S. A. 39,
179, 225, 233, 240, 242, 285, 342,
454, 1150, 1177, 1428, 1527, 1663,
1714 ; Ps. LXXX. 1 ; LXXXI. 14,
47, 55 ; LXXXIII. 15 ; CXIV. 5, 6 ;
CXXXVI. 42, 73.

Israelite, *sb.* a descendant of Israel,
a Hebrew : P. R. III. 411 ; S. A.
1560.

Issue, (1) *sb.* offspring : P. L. IV.
280 ; descendants : P. L. I. 508.

(2) *vb. intr.* (*a*) to go or come
out ; *sound of waters issued from
a cave* : P. L. IV. 454 ; with
forth : P. L. IV. 779 ; VIII. 233 ;
IX. 447 ; X. 533, 537 ; P. R. IV.
62 ; *he* (death) *forth issued* : P. L.
II. 786 ; *in what martial equipage
they issue forth* : P. R. III. 305 ;
light issues forth : P. L. VI. 9.

to run or flow out ; *nectarous
humour issuing flowed* : P. L. VI.
332 ; *fig. from whose mouth issued
forth mellifluous streams* : P. R.
IV. 276.

(*b*) to come forth as from a
source : P. L. X. 405.

*It, *pers. pron.* (*dat.* and *acc.* it)
(*a*) referring to a *sb.* previously
mentioned : P. L. I. 15, 22, 179 ;
V. 37 ; IX. 74, 462 ; X. 120 ; XI.
883 ; S. A. 379 ; referring to a
statement : P. L. I. 153, 245 ; IX.
720 ; X. 762, 769 ; XI. 783 ; P. R.
IV. 474 ; S. A. 1183.

(*b*) as subject of impersonal *vbs.*,
or in impersonal statements : P.

L. II. 790; VI. 428, 499; IX.
1182; *so fares it*: P. R. III. 443;
it recks me not: C. 404; *it pleases
him*: S. A. 311; in statements of
time: P. L. IX. 857; P. R. II.
260; N. O. 29.

(c) taking the place of the
logical subject of the *vb.*, which
is a clause or sentence: P. L. X.
58; P. R. I. 347; S. A. 91; U. C.
I. 17; which is an infinitive
phrase: P. L. IV. 860; VIII. 641;
IX. 569; X. 747; XI. 88; P. R. I.
221.

(d) with an *intr. vb.*; *trip it*:
L'A. 33.

(e) as antecedent of *rel. pron.*:
P. L. I. 228; II. 667; X. 789; S.
A. 849, 1010; L. 100; the *pron.*
clause omitted: P. L. IX. 729.

Italian, *adj.* of Italy: S. XVIII. 11.

Iterate, *vb. tr.* to repeat: P. L. IX.
1005.

Ithuriel, *sb.* a cherub: P. L. IV.
788, 810.

Its, *pers. pron.* of or belonging to
it; *her reign had here its last fulfilling*: N. O. 106; *the mind is
its own place*: P. L. I. 254; *falsehood... returns of force to its own
likeness*: P. L. IV. 813.

Itself, *pron.* (1) *emphat.* in apposition with a *sb.*: P. L. I. 388, 526;
II. 68; VI. 291, 834; IX. 295,
702; X. 189; XII. 356, 525; S. A.
91; N. O. 139; C. 1023.

(2) *refl.* (a) direct object: C.
474.

(b) with a *prep.*: P. L. I. 254,
492; II. 612; VIII. 95; IX. 43,
172; X. 141; XI. 89; P. R. III.
213; S. A. 769; W. S. 13; C.
261, 593, 595, 742.

Ivory, (1) *sb.* the hard substance derived from the tusks of certain
animals: P. R. IV. 60.

(2) *adj.* consisting of ivory: P.
L. IV. 778.

Ivy, *sb.* the plant *Hedera*: P. L. IX.
217; C. 544; L. 2.

attrib. of the ivy: C. 55.

Ivy-crowned (crownèd, *disyl.*), *adj.*
adorned with a crown made of
ivy: L'A. 16.

J

Jabin, *sb.* a king of Hazor, a city in
the northern part of Canaan near
the Waters of Merom: Ps.
LXXXIII. 36.

Jacob, *sb.* the brother of Esau, and
the progenitor of the Israelites:
P. L. III. 510; XI. 214; P. R. III.
377; Ps. LXXXI. 3, 15; LXXXIV.
30; LXXXV. 4; LXXXVII. 7.

Jaculation, *sb.* the action of throwing: P. L. VI. 665.

Jael, *sb.* the wife of Heber, the
Kenite: S. A. 989.

Jail (gaol: S. A. 949), *sb.* prison: S.
A. 949; *fig. the flocking shadows
pale troop to the infernal jail*: N.
O. 232.

Jangling, *part. adj.* discordant: P.
L. XII. 55.

Janus, *sb.* the Roman god with two
faces. He was regarded as the
doorkeeper of heaven, as the protector of doors and gates, and as
the god of the beginnings of
things: P. L. XI. 129.

Japhet, *sb.* the son of Noah, identified with Iapetus, one of the
Titans and the father of Epimetheus and Prometheus: P. L. IV.
717.

Jar, *vb. intr.* (a) to strike *against*
with a grating sound, *fig.*: S. M.
20.

(b) to be at variance, conflict:
P. L. V. 793.

part. adj. **jarring**; (a) grating,
discordant: P. L. II. 880.

(b) clashing: P. L. VI. 315.

Jasper, *sb.* the precious stone; used
of that which resembles jasper;
sea of jasper: P. L. III. 363, 519;
sky of jasper: P. L. XI. 209.

Jaunt, *sb.* a fatiguing journey: P.
R. IV. 402.

Javan, *sb.* a son of Japheth, identified with Ion, the progenitor of
the Ionians and, by extension, of
the whole Greek race; *Javan's
issue*, the Greeks: P. L. I. 508;
isles of Javan, isles of Greece: S.
A. 716.

Javelin, *sb.* spear: P. L. XI. 658.

Jaw, *sb.* (a) jaw-bone: S. A. 143,
1095.

(b) *pl.* the bones and associated
structures of the mouth: P. L. X.
569.

(c) *pl.* mouth; *fig. the mouth of
hell ... his ravenous jaws*: P. L. X.
637.

Jealous, *adj.* (a) anxiously watchful, suspiciously vigilant; *night
and chaos...jealous of their secrets*:
P. L. X. 478; *darkness spreads
his jealous wings*: L'A. 6.

(b) envious, suspicious: S. XV.
3; showing envy: P. L. IV. 503.

Jealousy, *sb.* (a) fear of successful
rivalry in love: P. L. V. 449; S.
A. 791.

(b) *pl.* words intended to arouse
suspicion, or fear of loss through
rivalry: P. L. V. 703.

(c) the love of God which permits no rivalry: S. A. 1375.

Jehovah, *sb.* God: P. L. I. 386, 487;
VII. 602; Ps. I. 5; II. 24; III. 11;
IV. 17, 24; V. 1, 5, 37; VII. 19,
29, 61, 64; VIII. 1, 23; LXXXIII.
66; CXIV. 5.

Jephthah, *sb.* the leader of the
Gileadites (cf. Judg. XI. 1-3; XII.
1-3): P. R. II. 439; S. A. 283.

Jericho, *sb.* the city of Palestine: P.
R. II. 20.

Jerusalem, *sb.* the capital of Palestine: P. R. III. 234, 283; IV. 544.

Jessamine, *sb.* the plant *Jasminum*:
P. L. IV. 698; L. 143.

Jest, *sb.* jesting, merriment: L'A.
26.

Jester, *sb.* buffoon: S. A. 1338.

Jesus, *sb.* (a) the Greek form of
Joshua, the successor of Moses as
leader of the Israelites: P. L. XII.
310.

(b) the personal name of Christ:
P. L. X. 183; P. R. II. 4, 317,
322, 378, 432; IV. 560.

Jet, *sb.* the colour of jet, black: L.
144.

Jew, *sb.* Hebrew: P. R. III. 359.
attrib. Jewish, Hebrew: P. R.
III. 118.

Jig, *sb.* a lively irregular dance: C.
952.

Job, *sb.* the hero of the Book of
Job: P. R. I. 147, 389, 425; III.
64, 67, 95.

Jocund, *adj.* merry, gay, blithe: P.
L. IX. 793; *their hearts were
jocund*: S. A. 1669; *of the sun*:
P. L. VII. 372; *jocund spring*: C.
985; *jocund music*: P. L. I. 787;
said of musical instruments which
produce lively music; *jocund
rebeck, flute*: L'A. 94; C. 173.

Jog, *vb. intr.* to move *on* at a heavy
pace: U. C. II. 4.

John, *sb.* (a) a Christian name: S.
XI. 12. *See* **Cheek.**

(b) the forerunner of Christ:
P. R. I. 184; *John the Baptist*:
P. R. II. 84.

(c) Saint John: P. L. III. 623.

Join, *vb.* (1) *tr.* (a) to connect;

Europe with Asia joined: P. L.
X. 310.

past part. together, in the
same place, opposed to *asunder*:
P. L. IX. 259.

(b) to unite or combine: P. L.
V. 106; VI. 494; XII. 516; S. A.
1342; *join voices*: P. L. V. 197;
in full harmonic number joined:
P. L. IV. 687; *man ... joined with
his own folly*: P. L. III. 152;
their nature to thy nature join: P.
L. III. 282; *all angelic nature
joined in one*: P. L. V. 834; *manhood to Godhead*: P. L. XII. 388;
tastes not well joined: P. L. V.
335; *virtue joined with riches*: P.
R. IV. 298; *delight to reason joined*:
P. L. IX. 243.

(c) to add: P. L. IX. 198; P.
R. III. 258; IV. 284; N. O. 27;
that caution joined: P. L. V. 513;
join him ... to thy aid: P. L. VI.
294.

(d) to bring into one body;
in squadron joined: P. L. IV. 863;
in mighty quadrate: P. L. VI. 62;
in ... tribes: P. L. VII. 488.

(e) to link or unite *persons* in
close relationship: P. L. VIII. 58;
IX. 882, 909; X. 359; *joined in
injuries*: P. L. X. 925; *in ruin*:
P. L. I. 90; *God with idols in
their worship joined*: P. R. III.
426; to unite in marriage: S. A.
1037.

(f) to unite, associate, or ally
with: P. L. I. 90; XII. 38; *join
with thee ... spare Fast*: Il P. 45;
*night and shades how are ye joined
with hell*: C. 581; to unite *with*
for warfare: P. L. I. 577.

(g) to take part in, engage in;
join melodious part: P. L. III.
370; *joining ... one enmity*: P. L.
X. 924; *join encounter, shock,
grapple*: P. L. II. 718; VI. 206;
P. R. IV. 567.

(2) *intr.* (a) to be in contact or
adjoin *to*: P. L. X. 302.

(b) to attach oneself; *join with
idols*: S. A. 456.

(c) to combine in action or purpose: S. A. 1368; *the other five
(planets) ... when to join in synod*;
P. L. X. 660; with *prep. inf.*: P.
L. V. 164.

to enter into marriage: P. L.
XI. 686.

to take part in a battle: S. A.
265.

(*d*) to come together and begin a battle ; *the squadrons join* : P. L. XI. 652 ; said of the battle ; *edge of battle ere it joined* : P. L. VI. 108.

See Ill-joined.

Join, *vb. tr.* to enjoin or impose *on* : S. A. 1342.

Joint, (1) *sb.* articulation of bones : P. L. VIII. 269 ; IX. 891 ; *joint or limb* ; P. L. I. 426 ; II. 668 ; VIII. 625 ; *joints and limbs* : S. A. 614 ; *joints and bones* : S. A. 1142 ; *unthread thy joints* : C. 614 ; *tear thee joint by joint* : S. A. 953.

(2) *adj.* combined, acting or moving together ; *joint hands, vigour, power, pace* : P. L. IX. 244 ; X. 405, 408 ; S. A. 110.

Jointed, *adj.* having joints ; *jointed armour* : P. L. VII. 409.

Joint-racking, *adj.* causing great pain in the joints : P. L. XI. 488.

Joking, *vbl. sb.* the action of jesting : Hor. Sat. II. 1.

Jollity, *sb.* (*a*) exuberant mirth, gaiety : L'A. 26.

(*b*) merrymaking, revelry : P. L. XI. 714 ; C. 104.

Jolly, *adj.* joyous : S. I. 4.

Jonson, *sb.* Ben Jonson, the dramatist : L'A. 132.

Jordan, *sb.* the river of Palestine : P. L. III. 535 ; XII. 145 ; P. R. I. 119 ; II. 25 ; as the place where John baptized : P. R. I. 24, 329 ; II. 2, 62 ; IV. 510 ; as divided to allow the Israelites to pass over : P. R. III. 438 ; Ps. CXIV. 9, 14.

Joseph, *sb.* (*a*) the father of Ephraim and Manasseh : P. R. III. 377 ; M. W. 65 ; Ps. LXXXI. 8.

(*b*) the reputed father of Jesus : P. R. I. 23.

Joshua, *sb.* the leader of the Israelites into the land of Canaan : P. L. XII. 310.

Josiah, *sb.* the King of Judah : P. L. I. 418.

Jostle. *See* Justle.

Jot, *sb.* an iota ; *bate a jot of heart or hope* : S. XXII. 7.

Journey, (1) *sb.* (*a*) the daily course of the sun through the heavens : P. L. V. 559 ; *heaven such journeys run* : P. L. VIII. 88.

(*b*) passage from place to place, travel : P. L. II. 985 ; III. 633 ; X. 479 ; XII. 1, 204 ; C. 303 ; *day's journey* : P. L. IV. 282 ; P. R. III. 276 ; *journey of a Sabbath*

day : S. A. 149 ; *fig.* passage through life : U. C. I. 12.

(*c*) the distance passed over : P. L. VIII. 36.

(2) *vb. tr.* to go from place to place, travel : P. L. XII. 258 ; with *on* : P. L. IV. 173 ; *fig. they journey on from strength to strength* : Ps. LXXXIV. 25 ; said of light : P. L. VII. 246.

Joust, (1) *sb.* tournament, tilt : P. L. IX. 37.

(2) *vb. intr.* to engage in a tournament, tilt : P. L. I. 583.

Jove, *sb.* the supreme deity of the ancients : P. L. I. 198, 512, 741 ; IX. 396 ; P. R. II. 215 ; III. 84 ; IV. 565 ; Il P. 30 ; A. 44 ; C. 803, 1011 ; L. 16 ; S. I. 7 ; XXIII. 3 ; *sovran, high, all-judging, careful Jove* : C. 41, 78 ; L. 82 ; D. F. I. 45 ; *Jove's altar, court* : Il P. 48 ; C. 1 ; *Jove's authentic fire* : P. L. IV. 719 ; identified with one of the fallen angels : P. L. I. 514.

(*b*) with proper adj. ; *Ammonian Jove,* Jupiter Ammon, the name of Jove as worshipped in Africa : P. L. IX. 508 ; *Lybian Jove,* the same : P. L. IV. 277 ; *Dictæan Jove,* so called because born and reared on Mt. Dicte in Crete : P. L. X. 584.

(*c*) *bird of Jove,* the eagle : P. L. XI. 185.

(*d*) *high and nether Jove,* Zeus, the ruler of heaven, and Hades, the ruler of the lower world : C. 20.

Jove-born, *adj.* being the daughter of Jove : C. 676.

Joy, (1) *sb.* (*a*) lively emotion of pleasure, delight, happiness ; sometimes the perfect joy of heaven : P. L. I. 123, 250, 524 ; II. 387, 495 ; III. 68, 137, 265, 347, 417 ; IV. 92, 155, 369 ; V. 641 ; VI. 774 ; IX. 478, 770, 843 ; X. 103, 345, 350, 351, 457 ; XI. 628, 869 ; XII. 22, 468, 504 ; P. R. II. 37, 119 ; III. 437 ; IV. 439, 638 ; Cir. 4 ; T. 13 ; S. M. 1 ; C. 677 ; S. XIV. 8 ; Ps. II. 24 ; V. 34 ; in combination or contrast with *love* : P. L. III. 67, 338 ; IV. 509 ; VI. 94 ; IX. 882 ; L. 177 ; with *hope, rapture, happiness, gladness, cheer* : P. L. IX. 633, 1081 ; P. R. I. 417 ; Ps. IV. 31 ; LXXXIV. 26 ; with *fear, grief, sorrow* : P. L. I. 788 ; II. 586 ; XI. 139, 361 ; XII. 372 ; S. A.

1564 ; *joy and eternal bliss* : P. L.
XII. 551 ; *joy and union* : P. L.
VII. 161 ; *fragrance and joy* : P.
L. VIII. 266 ; *joy and feast* : C.
102 ; *joy and acclamation, shout* :
P. L. VI. 23, 200 ; VII. 256 ; *dwell
in joy and bliss* : P. L. XI. 43 ;
they sat in fellowships of joy : P. L.
XI. 80 ; *swim in joy* : P. L. XI.
625 ; *quaff immortality and joy* :
P. L. V. 638 ; *joy thou took'st
with me* : P. L. II. 765 ; *headlong
joy* : P. 5 ; *windy joy* : S. A. 1574 ;
joy in, of, for, thereon : P. L. II.
371, 372 ; VI. 617 ; X. 577 ; S. A.
1505 ; *for joy* : P. L. IX. 990.
a joy : S. A. 1531 ; *pl. joys* :
P. L. II. 819 ; IV. 411 ; IX. 985 ;
X. 741 ; N. O. 66.
personified : Il P. 1 ; C. 1011.
(*b*) that which causes gladness
or delight, source of happiness :
P. L. X. 1052 ; P. R. II. 9, 57 ;
C. 501.
(2) *vb.* (*a*) *intr.* to feel joy, be
glad, rejoice ; with *in* : P. L. V.
46 ; VIII. 170 ; IX. 115.
(*b*) *tr.* to enjoy, delight in possessing : P. L. IX. 1166.

Joyfully, *adv.* gladly : Ps. LXXXV.
42.

Joyless, *adj.* (*a*) sad, cheerless : P.
L. IV. 766.
(*b*) affording no pleasure : P. R.
IV. 578.

Joyous, *adj.* (*a*) glad, blithe ; *joyous
the birds* : P. L. VIII. 515 ; *joyous
leaves* : L. 44.
(*b*) causing gladness : P. 3.

Jubilant, *adj.* rejoicing with songs
and acclamations : P. L. VII. 564.

Jubilee, *sb.* joyful shouting : P. L.
III. 348 ; VI. 884 ; *saintly shout
and solemn jubilee* : S. M. 9.

Judah, *sb.* the most powerful of the
twelve tribes of Israel : P. L. I.
457 ; P. R. III. 282 ; S. A. 256,
265, 976 ; hence, the Jewish
nation : P. R. II. 424, 440 ; N. O.
221.

Judea, *sb.* the southern division of
Palestine : P. R. III. 157 ; S. A.
252.

Judge, I. *sb.* (*a*) public officer invested with authority to hear and
determine causes : Ps. II. 23.
(*b*) God, as supreme arbiter : P.
L. III. 154 ; X. 96, 118, 126, 160,
209 ; XI. 167 ; N. O. 164 ; S. XIV.
13 ; Ps. VII. 43.
(*c*) the chief magistrate of

Israel before the time of the
kings : P. L. XII. 320.
II. *vb.* (*pres. 2d sing.* judgest :
P. L. III. 155) (1) *tr.* (*a*) to pronounce sentence upon : P. L. XII.
412 ; said of God or Christ : P. L.
III. 295, 330 ; X. 55, 62, 71, 209,
338, 494, 1087, 1099 ; XI. 705 ;
XII. 460, 461 ; Ps. VII. 29, 31 ;
LXXXII. 25 ; *ere thus was ... judged
on earth* : P. L. X. 229.
absol. or *intr.* : P. L. III. 155 ;
X. 73, 1047, 1059.
(*b*) to give sentence concerning,
decide, determine : P. L. II. 233,
448.
(*c*) to award by judgement :
L'A. 122.
(*d*) to declare authoritatively ;
I was judged to have shown : S. A.
994 ; *now am judged an enemy* :
S. A. 884.
(*e*) to form or give an opinion
upon : P. L. III. 123 ; XI. 603 ;
to believe, consider, think, hold :
P. L. V. 850 ; with two *acc.* : P.
L. IV. 910 ; VI. 37 ; X. 992 ; in
passive : P. L. VI. 426 ; X. 173 ;
P. R. IV. 215 ; with *acc.* and *prep.
inf.* : S. X. 13 ; *absol.* : P. L. IV.
912.
(2) *intr.* (*a*) to form an opinion
or judgement : P. L. II. 390 ; U.
C. II. 21 ; with *of* : P. L. IV. 904 ;
VIII. 448 ; S. XX. 13.
(*b*) to act as judge : Hor. Epist.
3 ; said of God : Ps. LXXXII. 4.
See **Ill-judging.**

Judgement, *sb.* (*a*) the act of Christ
in judging man : P. L. X. 81, 164,
932 ; the business of judging man :
P. L. X. 57.
(*b*) a judicial decision : Ps.
LXXXII. 6.
(*c*) the sentence or decision of
God or Christ in punishing sin :
P. L. IX. 10 ; X. 197 ; XI. 69,
725 ; XII. 14, 92, 175.
(*d*) a disaster or affliction regarded as a divine punishment
for sin : P. L. XI. 668.
(*e*) the faculty of judging, discernment : P. L. VIII. 636 ; P. R.
III. 37 ; IV. 324 ; S. A. 1027 ; C.
758.

Judicious, *adj.* discerning, wise ;
love ... is judicious : P. L. VIII.
591 ; *and palate call judicious* :
P. L. IX. 1020.

Juggler, *sb.* (*a*) one who plays tricks
by sleight of hand : S. A. 1325.

(b) one who deceives by trickery, cheat : C. 757.

Juice, sb. water : S. A. 550.

Juicy, adj. full of juice, succulent, sup.: P. L. v. 327.

Julep, sb. sweet drink : C. 672.

Julius, sb. Caius Julius Caesar : P. R. III. 39.

Juniper, sb. the evergreen shrub Juniperus : P. R. II. 272.

Junket, sb sweetmeat, confection : L'A. 102 ; Hor. Sat. I. 3.

Juno, sb. the supreme goddess of the ancients, the wife of Jove : P. L. IV. 500 ; IX. 18 ; A. 23 ; C. 701.

Jupiter, sb. Jove : P. L. IV. 499 ; P. R. II. 190. See **Jove.**

Jurisdiction, sb. controlling authority : P. L. II. 319.

Just, (1) adj. (a) keeping the commands of God, righteous, upright, pure : P. L. III. 98, 215 ; IV. 755 ; VII. 570, 631 ; XI. 577, 681, 703, 818, 876, 890 ; P. R. III. 62 ; S. A. 1269 ; C. 13, 768 ; S. XIV. 2 ; Ps. I. 14 ; v. 38 ; just Abraham : P. L. XII. 273 ; just spirits : S. M. 14 ; just Simeon : P. R. I. 255 ; just blood, sword : P. L. XII. 294 ; C. 601.

absol. righteous person : S. A. 703 : preceded by the def. art.: P. L. VII. 186 ; XI. 455 : Ps. I. 15 ; VII. 37 ; LXXXVI. 6 ; as resurrected to everlasting life with God : P. L. III. 335 ; XI. 65, 901 ; XII. 540.

(b) upright and impartial in one's dealings ; of God : P. L. IX. 700, 701 ; x. 7 ; Ps. VII. 38, 41, 43 ; justice divine ... to be just ; P. L. x. 857 ; of the Roman nation : P. R. IV. 133.

(c) that just maid, Astræa, the goddess of justice : D. F. I. 50.

(d) conforming to the principles of justice, righteous, equitable, fair : P. L. III. 294 ; VI. 121, 265, 726 ; XI. 526 ; XII. 16 ; S. A. 854 ; just command, decree, judgement : P. L. v. 552, 814 ; XII. 92 ; just law ; Cir. 15, 16 : Ps. LXXXII. 12 ; just trial : P. R. III. 196 ; just avenging ire : P. L. VII. 184 ; of the ways of God : P. L. x. 643 ; S. A. 293, 300 ; Ps. LXXXIV. 44 ; such as ought to be ; just event : P. L. x. 969 ; fitting ; just object of his ire : P. L. x. 936 ; deserved, merited : P. L. IX. 10.

(e) grounded in right, lawful, rightful ; just right : P. L. II. 18 P. R. II. 325 ; inheritance : P. L. II. 38 ; pretences : P. L. II. 825 ; equality : P. L. VII. 487 ; obedience : P. L. VI. 740 ; yoke ; P. L. x. 1045 ; occasion : S. A. 237 ; extent : P. R. III. 406 ; public reason just : P. L. IV. 389.

(f) well-founded ; just fear : P. R. I. 66 ; F. of C. 18 ; confidence : P. L. IX. 1056 ; cause : S. A. 316.

(g) right in amount, extent, quality, or character ; proper ; correct : P. L. VII. 231 ; x. 535, 888 ; S. A. 770 ; Ps. IV. 23 ; to span words with just note : S. XIV. 3.

(h) in accordance with reason and right : P. L. IV. 443 ; right and proper : P. L. IX. 698.

(i) justness, righteousness : P. R. III. 11.

(j) justice : P. L. VI. 381 ; VIII. 572.

(2) adv. (a) exactly, precisely ; of position : P. L. III. 527 ; IV. 460 ; of time : P. L. IX. 278 ; P. R. III. 298.

(b) but now : P. L. IV. 863.

See **Over-just.**

Justice, sb. (1) conformity to the laws and principles of right-dealing, just conduct, rectitude ; used chiefly with reference to God : P. L. II. 733 ; v. 247 ; x. 755 ; XI. 667, 807 ; XII. 99 ; Ps. VII. 62 ; LXXXVIII. 51 ; mercy and justice : P. L. III. 132, 407 ; mercy colleague with justice : P. L. x. 59 ; temper justice with mercy : P. L. x. 78 ; die he or Justice must : P. L. III. 210 ; justice shall not return ... scorned : P. L. x. 54 ; high justice : P. L. XII. 401 ; vengeful justice : Cir. 24.

(b) Eternal Justice, God : P. L. I. 70.

(c) personified : N. O. 141 ; Ps. LXXXV. 47 ; Justice divine : P. L. x. 857, 858.

(2) administration of law ; civil justice : P. L. XII. 231.

Justifiable, adj. that can be shown to be just ; S. A. 294.

Justification, sb. the condition of being freed from the penalty of sin, and accounted righteous in the sight of God : P. L. XII. 296.

Justify, *vb. tr.* (*a*) to show the justice of ; *justify the ways of God to men* : P. L. I. 26.

(*b*) to make right or proper ; *her doing seemed to justify the deed* : P. L. X. 142.

Justle, *vb. intr.* to push or strike against each other ; *the clouds justling* : P. L. X. 1074.

part. adj. **justling**, clashing together : P. L. II. 1018.

Justly, *adj.* in accordance with reason or justice, equitably, rightly : P. L. III. 112, 677 ; IV. 72 ; V. 736 ; IX. 40, 100 ; X. 168, 768 ; XI. 288 ; XII. 79 ; P. R. I. 442, 443 ; IV. 84 ; S. A. 375, 1171 ; A. 10.

K

Keen, (**1**) *adj.* (*a*) eager ; *keen dispatch of real hunger* : P. L. V. 436.

(*b*) having a sharp point ; *arrows keen* : C. 422.

(*c*) biting, piercing ; *keen wind* : P. L. X. 1066 ; XI. 842 ; P. R. I. 317.

absol. that which has a sharp edge : P. L. VI. 322.

(**2**) *adv.* keenly ; *hunger and thirst ... urged me so keen* : P. L. IX. 588.

Keep, *vb.* (*pret.* and *past part.* kept) *tr.* (*a*) to observe, perform, or fulfil *charge, command, word, counsel* : P. L. IV. 420 ; VIII. 634 ; X. 856 ; S. A. 497.

(*b*) to solemnize *the sabbath* : P. L. VII. 594, 634 ; to celebrate *wakes and pastimes* : C. 121.

(*c*) to guard, protect : C. 486 ; Ps. LXXX. 1 ; LXXXIII. 12 ; LXXXVIII. 1 ; Hor. Epist. 2.

(*d*) to have charge of *a door* : Ps. LXXXIV. 38.

(*e*) to preserve in proper order : P. L. VIII. 320.

(*f*) to preserve in being, continue to hold, maintain ; *that distance keeps* : P. L. VII. 379 ; *keep ... thy state* : Il P. 37 ; *keep his trot* : U. C. II. 4 ; *consort ... keep* : Il P. 145.

(*g*) to preserve, maintain, or cause to continue in some specified state, condition, or place ; with two *acc.*, *acc.* and phrase, or *adv.* : P. L. III. 578 ; V. 128 ; X. 619 ; P. R. IV. 362 ; S. A. 49, 429 ; S. XXIII. 3 ; Ps. IV. 39 ; *keep these gates shut* : P. L. II. 775 ; *odds of*

knowledge in my power : P. L. IX. 820 ; *keep this place inviolable* : P. L. IV. 842 ; *keep them* or *ye low* : P. L. IV. 525 ; IX. 704 ; *thoughts so busy keep* : N. O. 92 ; *keep unsteady nature to her law* : A. 70 ; *keep my life ... unassailed* : C. 220.

(*h*) to hold back or restrain *from* : P. L. IX. 245.

(*i*) to continue to have, hold, or possess : P. L. II. 725, 852 ; XI. 550 ; V. Ex. 99 ; C. 639, 913; *his loyalty he kept* : P. L. V. 900 ; *kept ... station* : P. L. VII. 145 ; P. R. I. 360 ; *to gain dominion or to keep it* : P. R. II. 434 ; *confidence* : C. 584.

(*j*) to withhold *from* : P. L. IX. 746.

(*k*) to continue to follow ; *waves their ... channel keep* : N. O. 124 ; *fig., his mischief that due course doth keep* : Ps. VII. 57.

(**2**) *intr.* (*a*) to stay *together* : S. A. 1521.

(*b*) to continue or remain ; *keep in compass of thy predicament* : V. Ex. 56 ; *keep in tune* ; S. M. 26.

In combination with other words ;.

(*a*) **keep home**, stay at home : C. 748 ; *keep residence*, reside : P. L. II. 999.

(*b*) **keep out**, hinder from entering ; P. L. IV. 372.

(*c*) **keep under**, hold in subjection : V. Ex. 78.

(*d*) **keep up**, maintain : C. 8 ; cause to be busy *about* : C. 167.

(*e*) **keep watch**, act as sentinel : P. L. IV. 685 ; XII. 365 ; N. O. 21 ; *keep their watch* : P. L. IX. 62 ; X. 427 ; be vigilant : P. L. IX. 363.

vbl. sb. **keeping** ; (*a*) guardian care : Ps. VI. 20.

(*b*) maintenance, support : S. A. 1260.

Ken, (**1**) *sb.* range of vision or sight ; *within* or *in ken* : P. L. III. 622 ; XI. 379.

(**2**) *vb. tr.* to see, descry : P. L. V. 265 ; XI. 396 ; P. R. II. 286 ; *absol.* : P. L. I. 59.

Kennel, *vb. intr.* to lodge as in a kennel : P. L. II. 658.

Kerchief, *vb. tr.* to attire as with a kerchief ; *Morn ... kerchieft in a comely cloud* : Il P. 125.

Kernel, *sb.* edible substance of a nut : P. L. V. 346.

Key, *sb.* (*a*) the instrument for opening or fastening a lock ; the key to the gates of heaven : P. L. III. 485 ; *golden key* : C. 13 ; *massy keys* : L. 110 ; the key to the gates of hell : P. L. II. 850 ; *fatal, powerful key* : P. L. II. 725, 774, 871.

(*b*) *fig.*, *thy key of strength* : S. A. 799.

Key-hole, *sb.* aperture in a lock for receiving the key : P. L. II. 876.

Kick, *vb. tr.* to strike with violent impact ; *kicked the beam* : P. L. IV. 1004.

Kid, *sb.* young goat : P. L. IV. 344 ; S. A. 128 ; C. 498 ; *lamb or kid* : P. L. III. 434 ; IX. 583 ; XII. 20.

Kill, *vb. tr.* to deprive of life, slay : P. L. X. 402 ; XII. 168 ; S. X. 8 ; *absol.* : D. F. I. 7.

part. adj. Killing, deadly : L. 45.
See Self-killed.

Kind, (1) *sb.* (*a*) essential character, nature : P. L. V. 490 ; X. 248 ; S. A. 786.

(*b*) race ; *angelical and human kind* : P. L. III. 462 ; *total kind of birds* : P. L. VI. 73 ; *serpent kind* : P. L. VII. 482 ; IX. 504 ; *brutal kind* : P. L. IX. 565.

(*c*) class, genus, species ; *of living things* : P. L. V. 479 ; VII. 393, 451 ; *of birds* or *beasts* : P. L. IV. 397 ; VII. 394, 453 ; VIII. 343, 393 ; *of trees* : P. L. IV. 217 ; VII. 311 ; IX. 1101 ; *absol.* species of living things : P. L. IV. 671 ; IX. 721 ; X. 612 ; XI. 337 ; species of animals : P. L. VIII. 597.

In vaguer sense : sort, variety ; *all kind of living creatures* : P. L. IV. 286 ; *fruit of all kinds* : P. L. V. 341 ; *the massy ore ... each kind* : P. L. I. 704 ; *kind of interposition, tempest, answer, sea* : P. R. III. 221 ; S. A. 1063, 1236 ; Ps. VI. 12 ; *maladies ... all feverous kinds* : P. L. XI. 482.

(*d*) essential character, nature : P. L. V. 490 ; X. 248.

(2) *adj.* (*a*) friendly, benevolent : Ps. CXXXVI. 2 ; *kind, hospitable woods* : C. 187.

(*b*) marked by kindness ; *kind office* : U. C. I. 14.
See Cold-kind.

Kindle, *vb. tr.* (*a*) to set on fire or ignite *fire* ; P. L. II. 170 ; IX. 637 ; *kindles the ... bark of fir* : P. L. X. 1076.

(*b*) to inflame ; *kindle ... spirits ... to vehemence* : C. 794.

Kindly, (1) *adj.* natural, characteristic ; *kindly thirst, heat, rupture* : P. L. IV. 228, 668 ; VII. 419 ; natural, not artificial ; *sup.*, *kindliest change* : P. L. V. 336.

(2) *adv.* with benevolence : N. O. 90.
See Loving-kindness.

Kindred, *sb.* relatives collectively : P. L. XII. 122 ; S. A. 1730.

Kine. *See* Cow.

King, *sb.* (1) monarch, sovereign : P. L. XI. 243 ; XII. 262, 329, 348 ; P. R. II. 44, 82, 449, 463, 467 ; III. 12, 289 ; IV. 87, 364 ; V. Ex. 47 ; N. O. 59 ; W. S. 16 ; S. XV. 4 ; Seneca 3 ; *spec.* Ahaz : P. L. I. 471 ; *pl.* Antigonus and Hyrcanus : P. R. III. 366 ; Antiochus Epiphanes : P. R. III. 167 ; David : P. L. XII. 326 ; Herod the Great : P. R. II. 76 ; Jeroboam : P. L. I. 484 ; Mithridates : P. R. III. 36; Moloch, whose name, properly Molech, signifies *King* ; *horrid, sceptred, furious, grisly king* : P. L. I. 392 ; II. 43 ; VI. 357 ; N. O. 209 ; Pharaoh : P. L. XII. 165, 205 ; Solomon ; *uxorious, sapient king* : P. L. I. 444 ; IX. 442 ; *Abassin kings* : P. L. IV. 280 ; *Asian* : P. R. IV. 73 ; *Grecian* : P. L. IV. 212 ; *Memphian* : P. L. I. 694 ; *Sinæan* : P. L. XI. 390 ; *Parthian king* : P. R. III. 299 ; *Tartar king* : Il P. 115 ; *Syrian king* : P. L. XI. 218 ; *kings of Babylon or Alcairo* : P. L. I. 721; *of Antioch* : P. R. III. 297 ; *of Madian* : S. A. 281 ; *of the east* : P. L. II. 4.

(*b*) applied to God ; *Heaven's King* : P. L. I. 131 ; II. 751, 851, 992 ; IV. 41, 111, 973 ; V. 220 ; P. R. I. 421 ; N. O. 2 ; *King of Heaven* : P. L. II. 229, 316 ; *King of kings* : P. R. IV. 185 ; *King of Glory* : P. L. VII. 208 ; *supreme, sole, mighty,* etc. : P. L. I. 735 ; II. 325 ; VII. 608 ; VIII. 239 ; X. 387 ; *Eternal* : P. L. III. 374 ; VI. 227 ; P. R. I. 236 ; *Ethereal* : P. L. II. 978 ; *invisible* : P. L. VII. 122 ; *all-bounteous* : P. L. V. 640.

(*c*) applied to Christ : P. L. V. 690, 769 ; VI. 42, 708 ; P. R. I. 75, 99 ; III. 226 ; IV. 283 ; *anointed King* : P. L. V. 664, 777, 870 ; VI.

718 ; XII. 359 ; *universal, rightful, victorious* ; P. L. III. 317 ; V. 818 ; VI. 886 ; *King of Israel* : P. R. I. 254 ; *Israel's true King* : P. R. III. 441.

(*d*) applied to Satan or his angels : P. L. IV. 383 ; P. R. I. 117 ; *grisly King* : P. L. IV. 821.

(*e*) applied to death : P. L. II. 698, 699.

(*f*) applied *fig.* to Substance : V. Ex. 75.

(*g*) as a title ; *King Ahab* : P. R. I. 372 ; *King Edward* : S. XI. 14.

(2) kingdom : P. L. XI. 398.

Kingdom, *sb.* (*a*) supreme rule, sovereignty : P. R. III. 171 ; IV. 369 ; *the kingdom shall to Israel be restored* : P. R. II. 36 ; the sovereignty of God ; P. L. VI. 815.

(*b*) the spiritual sovereignty of Christ or God : P. R. I. 241, 265 ; III. 199 ; IV. 151 ; *Heaven's kingdom* : P. R. I. 20.

(*c*) the country subject to a king : P. L. XII. 262 ; P. R. II. 481 ; III. 242 ; IV. 363, 536 ; *the kingdoms of the world* : P. R. IV. 89, 163, 182, 210 ; *earth's kingdoms* : P. L. XI. 384 ; *kingdoms of Almansor*, etc.: P. L. XI. 403 ; subject to Christ as king : P. R. III. 152, 351 ; IV. 282, 389 ; subject to God as king : P. L. II. 325, 361 ; *Heaven to Earth, one kingdom* : P. L. VII. 161 ; subject to Satan as king ; *of hell* : P. L. VI. 183 ; *of the world* : P. L. X. 406 ; N. O. 171.

(*d*) *fig.* realm ; *blest kingdoms ... of joy and love* : L. 177.

Kingly, *adj.* (*a*) of or belonging to a king, royal ; *kingly crown, palace-gate* : P. L. II. 673 ; III. 505 ; befitting a king : P. R. II. 476 ; S. XIX. 12.

(*b*) kinglike, majestic : P. L. XI. 249 ; V. Ex. 39.

Kiriathaim (Kíriatháim), *sb.* Shaveh Kiriathaim, the plain adjacent to Kiriathaim, a town of Moab : S. A. 1081.

See **Flowery-kirtled.**

Kishon, *sb.* a river rising at the foot of Mt. Gilboa, flowing through the plain of Esdraelon, and emptying into the Mediterranean : Ps. LXXXIII. 37.

Kiss, I. *sb.* salute or caress given by

touching the lips : P. L. IV. 502 ; T. 12.

II. *vb.* (1) *tr.* to touch with the lips in reverence or love : P. L. V. 134 ; A. 83 ; Ps. II. 25 ; *absol.* : D. F. I. 6.

(2) *intr.* (*a*) to salute mutually with the lips ; *Peace and Righteousness have kissed* : Ps. LXXXV. 43.

(*b*) to touch each other ; *smoothly the waters kissed* : N. O. 65.

Knack, *sb.* toy : Hor. Sat. I. 3.

Knee, *sb.* the joint in which the leg and thigh meet : P. L. VI. 194 ; as bent, bowed, or clasped in supplication or reverence : P. L. I. 112 ; III. 321 ; V. 608, 788, 817 : Ps. LXXXI. 40 ; *suppliant I beg, and clasp thy knees* : P. L. X. 918.

Kneel, *vb.* (*pret.* kneeled) *intr.* to go down on the knees in supplication : P. L. XI. 150.

Knee-tribute, *sb.* personal acknowledgment of submission, obedience, and reverence, evidenced by kneeling : P. L. V. 782.

Knight, *sb.* (*a*) a person of noble birth trained to arms and chivalry : L'A. 119 ; *gorgeous, prowest knights* : P. L. IX. 36 ; P. R. III. 342 ; *aery* : P. L. II. 536 ; *fabled* : P. L. IX. 30 ; *British and Armoric knights* : P. L. I. 581 ; *knights of Logres or of Lyones* ; P. R. II. 360.

(*b*) one holding a title of honour next below that of baronet : S. VIII. 1.

Knit, *vb.* (used only in *pres.*) *tr.* (*a*) to join closely, clasp ; *knit hands* : C. 143.

(*b*) to weave, braid : P. L. IV. 267 ; C. 862.

Knock, *vb.* (1) *intr.* to rap for exit : V. Ex. 24.

(2) *tr.* to strike, beat : S. A. 1722.

Knot, *sb.* (*a*) the interlacement of the parts of a cord for the sake of strength ; *Gordian knot, fig.* : V. Ex. 90. *See* **Gordian.**

(*b*) bond of association, close union, tie : C. 581 ; Ps. LXXXIII. 30.

(*c*) a flower-bed laid out in a fanciful design : P. L. IV. 242.

Knot-grass, *sb.* the plant *Polygonum aviculare* : C. 542.

Know, *vb.* (*pres. 2d sing.* know'st : P. L. I. 19 ; II. 730 ; III. 276 ; IV.

426, etc.; *pret.* knew; *2d sing.* knew'st : P. L. XII. 577 ; S. A. 878) *tr.* (1) to recognize ; (*a*) *a person* : P. L. III. 647 ; IV. 827, 828, 836 ; V. 287 ; VIII. 280 ; P. R. I. 275 ; S. A. 1081 ; C. 645 ; *not knew by sight* : P. R. I. 271 ; *I know him by his stride* : S. A. 1067 ; *I know thee, stranger, who thou art* : P. L. II. 990 ; *absol.* : P. L. IV. 831.

(*b*) *a thing* ; *the fiend ... knew his mounted scale* : P. L. IV. 1013.

(2) to be acquainted or familiar with by experience or through report ; (*a*) *a person* : P. L. I. 80, 374, 376, 515 ; II. 744 ; IV. 757, 830 ; V. 789 ; VIII. 406 ; XI. 307 ; XII. 174 ; P. R. I. 89 ; II. 7 ; III. 68 ; S. A. 641, 1082 ; C. 50, 311 ; *the Father knows the son* : P. R. I. 176 ; *such as come well known from heaven* : P. L. IV. 581 ; *his hand was known in heaven* : P. L. I. 732.

(*b*) *a place or thing* : P. L. IX. ·1102 ; XI. 307 ; C. 724 ; S. XIV. 9 ; *that halloa I should know* : C. 490 ; *I know thy trains ... thy gins* : S. A. 932 ; *know force, might, strength* : P. L. I. 93, 643 ; IV. 1006.

(3) to have personal experience of *repulse, charity, good, trouble, pain,* etc. : P. L. I. 630 ; IV. 895 ; V. 35, 461 ; VI. 327, 432 ; IX. 1023 ; X. 948 ; C. 788 ; *to have known the days* : S. X. 9 ; *that self-begotten bird, that no second knows* : S. A. 1701 ; *the low sun ... not known east or west* : P. L. X. 684 ; *whom their place knows here no more* : P. L. VII. 144 ; *elements that know no gross ... mixture foul* : P. L. XI. 50.

(4) to have cognizance or knowledge of through observation, inquiry, or information : P. L. IV. 637 ; VI. 20 ; VII. 127 ; IX. 368, 976 ; X. 5, 12, 169, 170, 793 ; S. A. 1075, 1401, 1508, 1592 ; C. 580 ; *know the works or acts of God* : P. L. III. 662, 694, 703 ; IV. 565 ; VII. 85, 97 ; XI. 578 ; *who himself beginning knew* : P. L. VIII. 251 ; *thy answer ... as good not known* : P. R. I. 437 ; *his providence to thee not known* : P. R. I. 446 ; *what know to fear* : P. L. IX. 773 ; *if truth were known* : U. C. I. 5 ; *to all truth requisite for men to know* : P. R. I. 464 ;

ends above my reach to know : S. A. 62 ; *my sorrows are too dark for day to know* : P. 33 ; *what may concern her faith to know* : P. L. XII. 599.

(*b*) *absol.* : P. L. IV. 588 ; C. 316.

(*c*) *make known,* reveal : P. L. IX. 817 ; S. A. 778.

(*d*) to be aware or conscious of : P. L. V. 859, 860 ; *if they know their happiness* : P. L. VII. 631 ; *no ground of enmity between us known* : P. L. IX. 1151.

(5) to be conversant with or skilled in : P. R. IV. 286, 287 ; *know'st thou not their language* : P. L. VIII. 372 ; *each to know his part* : P. R. II. ·240 ; *I know no spells* : S. A. 1139 ; *he knows the charms* : S. VIII. 5.

(6) to have a clear and distinct perception or apprehension of : P. L. VII. 125, 493, 622 ; VIII. 106, 192, 548 ; IX. 804 ; X. 207 ; P. R. I. 262, 494 ; III. 433 ; IV. 288, 294 ; *hadst thou known thyself aright* : P. L. X. 156 ; *to know this only that he nothing knew* : P. R. IV. 294.

know good or *evil,* a blending of the senses : to apprehend and to know by experience : P. L. IX. 699, 709, 1071 ; XI. 85, 88.

absol. or *intr.* to have knowledge or understanding, usually understanding of truth or right : P. L. I. 19 ; IV. 517, 523 ; VI. 148 ; VIII. 373 ; IX. 726, 758, 765, 1073 ; P. R. II. 475 ; IV. 227 ; Ps. LXXXII. 17.

(7) to be cognizant of, have learned, apprehend, understand ; (*a*) with clause without connective : P. L. II. 821, 839 ; IV. 426, 926 ; V. 414 ; VI. 689 ; VIII. 103, 328 ; X. 72 ; XI. 356 ; XII. 82 ; P. R. I. 150, 234 ; II. 231 ; III. 347 ; IV. 146, 492 ; S. A. 850, 1319 ; V. Ex. 10, 55 ; N. O. 60, 107 ; A. 34, 44 ; Ps. IV. 13.

(*b*) with clause introduced by *that* : P. L. II. 316, 807 ; V. 100 ; VII. 131 ; IX. 705 ; X. 629 ; XI. 199 ; P. R. III. 201 ; IV. 159 ; S. A. 221, 803 ; by *what* = that which : P. L. VII. 61 ; P. R. III. 7.

(*c*) with clause introduced by *but* ; *who knows but might as ill have happened* : P. L. IX. 1146 ;

who knows but I shall die: P. L.
x. 787 ; *who knows but God hath
set before us*: S. A. 516.

(*d*) with dependent question
(the question sometimes elliptical)
introduced by *who*: P. L. v. 895;
VIII. 271 ; P. R. I. 356; introduced by *what*: P. L. II. 740;
VIII. 173, 508; IX. 252; XI. 199,
475, 504 ; P. R. I. 203; III. 52,
53, 193; IV. 153, 538; S. A.
1556 ; S. XVII. 9 ; XXI. 9 ; introduced by *how*: P. L. III. 180,
276 ; IV. 86 ; V. 826 ; IX. 138 ; X.
27, 967 ; XI. 92 ; P. R. I. 47 ; S.
A. 1350, 1418, 1547 ; introduced
by *whether*: P. L. II. 151; V. 741;
by *whither*: P. L. VIII. 283 ; by
whence: P. L. v. 856 ; IX. 1137 ;
XII. 610 ; by *where*: Ps. LXXXV.
8 ; by *when*: P. R. IV. 471.

(*e*) the clause or phrase omitted : P. L. II. 730; VI. 163; VII.
639 ; XII. 127 ; P. R. I. 292; S.
A. 222, 395, 1091, 1554; *I am
happier than I know*: P. L. VIII.
282; the clause represented by
as: P. L. IV. 113; by *so*: C. 572;
this as object in place of the
clause: P. L. IV. 103; V. 243,
402 ; P. R. IV. 294 ; S. A. 381.

(*f*) with *prep. inf.* ; *know to
know no more*: P. L. IV. 775 ; *he
knew himself to sing*: L. 10;
knows to still the woods: C. 87;
*now known in arms not to be over-
powered*: P. L. VI. 418; *nor knew
I not to be created free*: P. L. v.
548; *knows to yield his fruit*: Ps.
I. 8; *so little knows any ... to value
right the good*: P. L. IV. 201;
know how to hold a sheep-hook: L.
119.

(*g*) with two *acc.*: P. L. II.
806; IV. 584; VIII. 445, 620; IX.
561; XI. 335; P. R. I. 254, 286,
384 ; IV. 394; S. A. 1313, 1549,
1560 ; in *passive*: P. L. XII. 544;
P. R. II. 414; or in sense (6): P.
L. v. 789; with a *part.; knew not
eating death*: P. L. IX. 792;
*knowing, as needs I must, by thee
betrayed*: S. A. 840.

(*h*) parenthetically: P. L. II.
206; VII. 536; VIII. 54; P. R. II.
305; S. A. 1534.

(8) **know of,** to be conversant
with : P. L. VIII. 573; to learn :
P. L. v. 454; to have apprehension or understanding : P. L.
VIII. 191, 438; to be informed of :

P. L. X. 19 ; P. R. IV. 504 ; S. A.
742 ; L. 95.

part. adj. **known,** familiar,
recognized ; *known virtue, offence,
rules*: P. L. IX. 110 ; S. A. 1218;
S. XII. 2.

vbl. sb. **knowing,** knowledge ;
concerned our knowing, important
for us to know : P. L. VII. 83;
gerund ; *by, from knowing ill* : P.
L. IV. 222 ; IX. 1055.

See **All-knowing, Self-knowing.**

Knowledge, *sb.* (*a*) acquaintance
with facts, state of being informed : P. L. I. 628 ; IX. 998;
P. R. I. 293.

(*b*) intellectual perception of
fact or truth : P. L. v. 509 ; VIII.
353, 551; P. R. I. 213; IV. 224;
the knowledge gained from
eating the fruit of the forbidden
tree ; *knowledge* is often a blending of sense (*b*) and acquaintance
or familiarity gained by experience : P. L. VII. 515, 525 ; v. 60;
IX. 687, 727, 790, 804, 820, 1073;
XII. 279; *knowledge of good* or
evil: P. L. IV. 222; VII. 543;
VIII. 324; IX. 697, 723; XI. 87;
tree of knowledge: P. L. IV. 221,
424, 514; v. 52; IX. 752, 849;
with allusion to the fruit of this
tree : P. R. II. 371.

(*c*) the faculty of understanding ; *human knowledge could not
reach* : P. L. VII. 75.

(*d*) that which is known or
made known ; *desire of, thirst of* :
P. L. VII. 120; VIII. 8; *fill of* :
P. L. XII. 559; *deeds answerable
to thy knowledge*: P. L. XII. 582.

(*e*) the sum of what is known :
P. L. IV. 638; v. 108; VII. 126;
P. R. IV. 225; *book of knowledge*:
P. L. III. 47.

Ksar, *sb.* emperor ; *Russian Ksar*:
P. L. XI. 394.

L

Laborious, *adj.* (*a*) toilsome, wearisome ; *laborious flight, work*: P.
L. II. 80; XI. 178; S. A. 14.

(*b*) filled with toil; *laborious
days*: L. 72.

Labour, I. *sb.* (*a*) exertion of body
or mind, physical or mental toil :
P. L. VIII. 213; IX. 208, 236; x.
1054, 1056; XI. 172, 375; *labour
honest and lawful*: S. A. 1365;
gardening, pleasant labour : P. L.

IV. 328, 625; *labour and rest*: P.
L. IV. 613; *labour of a beast*: S.
A. 37; *labour of my thoughts*: C.
192; the labour of God or angels:
P. L. IX. 944; X. 670; of Satan
or his angels: P. L. I. 164; II.
262, 1021, 1022; VI. 492; X. 491;
P. R. I. 132; *fig., save the sun his
labour*: P. L. VIII. 133.

pl.: S. A. 709, 1259; *rural
labours*: P. L. IX. 841.

(*b*) task or work performed or
to be performed, *pl.*: P. L. IX.
214; P. R. IV. 486; *Psyche...
after her wandering labours*: C.
1006; *Hero* (Christ) *... tried in ...
labours huge and hard*: P. 14.

(*c*) the result of toil; *the labour
of an age in piled stone*: W. S. 2.

II. *vb.* (1) *intr.* (*a*) to work
hard, toil: P. L. XI. 565; *his
mind ... labouring*: P. L. X. 1012;
with *prep. inf.*; *labour to dress
this garden*: P. L. IX. 205.

(*b*) to strive; *such affront I
labour to avert*: P. L. IX. 302.

(*c*) to travel slowly and with
difficulty *up, fig.*: S. IX. 4.

(2) *tr.* (*a*) to till, cultivate: P.
L. XII. 18.

(*b*) to impose labour upon: S.
A. 1298.

part. adj. (1) labouring; (*a*)
toiling: P. R. III. 330; *fig., of the
clouds*: L'A. 72.

(*b*) eclipsed; *the labouring moon*:
P. L. II. 665.

(2) laboured, wearied with labour: C. 291.

See Day-labour, Love-laboured;
Over-laboured.

Labourer, *sb.* one who performs
physical labour: P. L. XII. 631.
See Day-labourer.

Labyrinth, *sb.* maze; *fig., Lethe ...
rolls her watery labyrinth*: P. L.
II. 584; *the serpent ... in labyrinth
of many a round self-rolled*: P.
L. IX. 183; *leafy labyrinth*: C.
278.

Lack, *sb.* want; *lack of breath*: S.
A. 905; *of load*: U. C. II. 24.

Lackey, *vb. tr.* to attend, serve;
angels lackey her: C. 455.

Lad, *sb.* youth; *shepherd lad*: C.
619; David: P. R. II. 439.

Lade, *vb.* (*past part.* laden) *tr.* to
load *with fruit*: P. L. X. 550; C.
394.

Ladon, *sb.* a river of Arcadia,
Greece: A. 97.

Lady, *sb.* (*a*) a woman who rules
over subjects: A. 105.

(*b*) the wife of a man of rank,
correlative of *lord*: S. A. 1653.

(*c*) a woman of superior social
position, of noble birth and refinement: L'A. 121; vocative; *gentle
Lady*: M. W. 47; applied to *The
Lady* in *Comus*, which part was
taken by the daughter of the Earl
of Bridgewater: C. 507, 574, 618,
818; vocative: C. 283, 319, 659,
666, 737, 938; *good, brightest
Lady*: C. 277, 910; possibly
merely a courteous title without
reference to birth: S. IX. 1.

fairy ladies: V. Ex. 60; *ladies
of the Hesperides*: P. R. II. 357.

(*b*) as a title: C. 966.

Laertes, *sb.* the father of Odysseus:
P. L. IX. 441.

Lag, *vb. intr.* to hang back or linger
behind: P. L. X. 266; *mine
(feet) ... came lagging after*: S. A.
337.

part. adj. lagging, lingering;
lagging rear of winter's frost: S.
A. 1577.

Lahor, *sb.* the capital of the Panjab,
India: P. L. XI. 391.

Lair, *sb.* den: P. L. VII. 457.

Lake, *sb.* (1) body of water sur-
rounded by land: P. L. II. 621;
IV. 261, 459; *steaming lake*: P. L.
V. 186; *seas and lakes*: P. L. VII.
397; *silver lakes and rivers*: P. L.
VII. 437; *lake or moorish fen*: C.
433; *spec., lake Genezaret*: P. R.
II. 23; *Galilean Lake*: L. 109;
Caspian lake: P. R. III. 271; *that
bituminous lake*, the Dead Sea:
P. L. X. 562.

(*b*) the burning lake of hell: P.
L. I. 229, 702; *lake of fire*: P. L.
I. 280; *burning lake*: P. L. I. 210;
II. 169, 576; *forgetful*: P. L. II.
74.

(*c*) applied to the waters of the
great flood; *standing lake*: P. L.
XI. 847.

(*d*) *fig.* the crystalline sphere:
P. L. III. 521.

(2) river; *silver lake*, the river
Severn: C. 865.

Lamb, *sb.* young of sheep: P. L. IX.
583; XI. 649; XII. 20; Ps. CXIV.
12; *flesh of lambs*: P. L. III. 434.

Lament, (1) *sb.* the expression of
grief or sorrow; *loud lament*: P.
L. VIII. 244; N. O. 183; *audible*:
P. L. XI. 266.

(2) *vb.* (*a*) *tr.* to deplore : S. A. 1242 ; to mourn for the loss of *a person* : L. 60 ; *lament his fate* : P. L. I. 448; *her loss*: D. F. I. 72.

(*b*) *intr.* to express sorrow, mourn, wail : P. L. v. 894 ; x. 845 ; XI. 287, 675 ; with *for*: P. L. XI. 874.

Lamentable (lámentáble), *adj.* to be lamented, grievous, pitiable: P. L. II. 617.

Lamentation, *sb.* the expression of sorrow, mourning : P. L. II. 579 ; S. A. 1708, 1713.

Lamp, *sb.* (*a*) vessel containing oil and a wick for the purpose of illumination : Il P. 85 ; *starry lamps* : P. L. I. 728 ; the lamps burning before God : P. L. v. 713 ; the seven lamps of the Jewish tabernacle : P. L. XII. 255 ; *fig.* : S. IX. 10.

(*b*) the torch of Love ; *Love... here lights his constant lamp* : P. L. IV. 764.

(*c*) used *fig.* of the sun ; *sovran, vital lamp* ; P. L. III. 22; *all-cheering*: P. L. III. 581; *glorious*: P. L. VII. 370; of the stars; *bear their bright officious lamps* : P. L. IX. 104; *the evening star ... to light the bridal lamp* : P. L. VIII. 520 ; *nature...filled their lamps with everlasting oil*: C. 198; *handmaid lamp* : N. O. 242.

Lance, *sb.* spear : P. L. I. 766.

Lancelot, *sb.* the knight of Arthur's Round Table : P. R. II. 361.

Land, I. *sb.* (1) solid portion of the earth's surface ; in combination or contrast with *sea* : P. L. III. 75, 653 ; VII. 473; IX. 76, 117 ; X. 693 ; XI. 337 ; S. A. 710 ; N. O. 52 ; S. XIX. 13 ; *dry land* : P. L. II. 940; VII. 284, 307; XII. 197.

(*b*) solid portion of the surface of the moon : P. L. VIII. 144 ; of the surface of hell : P. L. I. 228 ; *dry, firm land* : P. L. I. 227 ; II. 589; the outside of the hard shell of the universe; *windy sea of land*: P. L. III. 440.

(*c*) tract of land : P. L. VII. 415.

(2) ground, soil : L'A. 64 ; Ps. LXXXV. 51.

(3) country, region : P. L. IV. 643, 652, 662; XII. 127 ; P. R. III. 94 ; H. B. 4 ; *foreign land* : P. L. III. 548; XII. 46 ; in combination with *seas* : P. L. VII. 429 ; S. VIII. 7.

(*b*) *spec.* the Land of Canaan: P. L. XII. 122, 134, 138, 172, 259, 339 ; P. R. III. 437; Ps. LXXXVII. 7 ; *the Promised Land* : P. L. III. 531 ; P. R. III. 157, 439; *Holy Land*: P. L. III. 536 ; the territory of Judah: S. A. 257 ; Judea: N. O. 221 ; Egypt: P. L. XII. 156, 159, 178; P. R. III. 379; Ps. CXXXVI. 37 ; Assyria : P. R. III. 420; *land of Nile* : P. L. I. 343 ; India : P. L. IX. 81; *Doric, Ausonian, Spartan land* : P. L. I. 519, 739; D. F. I. 26; England: S. XV. 14; H. B. 8.

(*c*) region in the moon : P. L. I. 290 ; v. 263.

(*d*) *fig.* realm ; *land of darkness*: S. A. 99 ; *land of oblivion*, the grave: Ps. LXXXVIII. 51.

II. *vb. tr.* to come to land : P. L. III. 588 ; x. 316.

See **Canaan-land, Egypt-land.**

Landmark, *sb.* an object marking a locality : P. L. XI. 432.

Land-pilot, *sb.* a guide on a journey by land : C. 309.

Landskip, *sb.* view or prospect of scenery : P. L. II. 491 ; IV. 153 ; v. 142 ; L'A. 70.

Lane, *sb.* a narrow path in the woods : C. 311.

Language, *sb.* (*a*) peculiar tongue of a nation ; *native language* : P. L. XII. 54 ; P. R. IV. 333 ; vocative ; *Hail, Native Language*: V. Ex. 1 ; inarticulate sounds of animals : P. L. VIII. 373.

(*b*) uttered expression, human speech : P. L. IX. 553.

Languish, *vb. intr.* to pine *with desire* : P. L. x. 995, 996.

part. adj. **languished**; (*a*) grown faint ; *languished hope* : P. L. VI. 497; grown feeble because of disease, or possibly *tr.* reduced to feebleness ; *the languished mother's womb*: M. W. 33.

(*b*) drooping ; *languished head*: S. A. 119 ; *a rose ... with languished head* : C. 744.

Lank, *adj.* drooping : C. 836.

Lantern (lanthorn : L'A. 104), *sb.* transparent case for a light ; *fig.*, *Night ... in thy dark lantern* : C. 197 ; *Friar's lantern* : L'A. 104. *See* **Friar.**

Lap, (1) *sb.* front part of the body from the waist to the knees of a person seated : P. L. x. 778 ; *lascivious lap* : S. A. 536.

fig., thy mother's (earth's) *lap*:
P. L. XI. 536 ; *earth's freshest,
softest lap*: P. L. IX. 1041 ; *flowery
lap of some ... ralley* : P. L. IV.
254 ; *ye valleys ... on whose lap* :
L. 138 ; *flowery May who from her
green lap* : M. M. 3 ; *peace shall
lull him in her flowery lap* : V.
Ex. 84.

(2) *vb. tr.* to enfold, surround :
lap me in soft Lydian airs : L'A.
136 ; *the ... soul and lap it in
Elysium* : C. 257.
See **Harlot-lap.**

Lapland, *attrib.* of the country in
the extreme north of Europe, the
fabled home of witches: P. L. II.
665.

Lapse, (1) *sb.* (*a*) a flowing ; *liquid
lapse of murmuring streams* : P.
L. VIII. 263.

(*b*) fall into sin : P. L. XII. 83.

(2) *vb.* (lapsèd, *disyl.* : P. L. III.
176), *intr.* to fall into sin : P. L.
X. 572.

part. adj. **lapsed,** weakened
through sin : P. L. III. 176.

Larboard, *sb.* that side of a ship on
the left hand of a person facing
the bow : P. L. II. 1019.

Large, (1) *adj.* (*a*) ample in quantity,
abundant : P. L. V. 343 ; XII. 21 ;
we have yet large day : P. L. V. 585.

(*b*) ample in size or dimensions ;
large place, field, edifice, etc. : P.
L. IV. 730 ; VI. 309 ; VIII. 104,
375 ; P. R. III. 73 ; *large and
round* : P. L. I. 285 ; *large and
broad* : P. L. III. 495 ; *large front
and eye sublime* : P. L. IV. 300 ;
comp. : P. L. X. 529.

fig. capacious, with unusual
breadth of comprehension ; *large
heart* : P. L. I. 444 ; P. R. III. 10 ;
said of the ant : P. L. VII. 486.

(*c*) broad, wide : P. L. III. 530 ;
IV. 223 ; *long and large* : P. L. I.
195.

(*d*) comprehensive; *large grace* :
P. L. XII. 305 ; ample ; *large
recompense* : L. 184.

(*e*) extensive *prospect* : P. L.
IV. 144 ; P. R. III. 262 ; *dominion* :
P. L. X. 244.

(*f*) having few limitations or
restrictions ; *large liberty* : P. R.
I. 365 ; *leave* : P. L. IV. 434.

(2) *adv.* (*a*) amply, abundantly :
P. L. XI. 732.

(*b*) liberally : P. L. V. 317, 318 ;
Ps. LXXXI. 43.

(*c*) in full : F. of C. 20.

(3) *sb.* **at large** ; (*a*) at liberty,
without restraint : P. L. I. 213,
790 ; III. 430 ; Ps. IV. 5.

(*b*) in a general way : P. L.
VIII. 191 ; in the literal sense of
the word : P. L. XI. 626.

Large-limbed, *adj.* having limbs of
great size : Ps. CXXXVI. 69.

Largely, *adv.* abundantly : P. L.
VIII. 7 ; IX. 1043 ; XI. 845.

Lark, *sb.* the bird *Alauda ; low-
roosted lark* : C. 317 ; *herald* : P.
R. II. 279 ; *hear the lark begin his
flight* : L'A. 41.

Lars, *sb.* (*pl.* lars) in Roman mythology, the tutelary deities of a
house ; after their death the distinguished members of a family
became its Lares : N. O. 191.
See **Lemur.**

Lascivious, *adj.* lewd, lustful : P. L.
IX. 1014 ; P. R. IV. 91 ; S. A. 536.

Last, (1) *adj.* (*a*) coming after all
others in time or place : P. L. V.
19, 166 ; IX. 379, 896 ; XI. 872 ;
T. 10.

(*b*) beyond which or whom
there is no more; *last day, breath* :
P. L. VII. 449 ; U. C. II. 25 ;
visitation : P. L. XI. 275 ; *prey,
wound* : P. L. X. 609 ; P. R. IV.
622 ; *hope* : P. L. II. 416 ; *affront* :
P. R. IV. 444 ; *world's last end,
session* : D. F. I. 77 ; N. O. 163 ;
of kings the last : P. L. XII. 330 ;
of my days the last : S. A. 1389.

(*c*) next before the present; *last
evening's talk* : P. L. V. 115.

(*d*) remaining after others have
disappeared ; *fame ... last infirmity
of noble minds* : L. 71.

(*e*) final ; *her reign had here its
last fulfilling* : N. O. 106.

(*f*) utmost, extreme ; *shame ...
the last of evils* : P. L. IX. 1079.

absol. (*a*) the last-mentioned
person ; *this last* : S. A. 1023.

(*b*) end ; *the last of me* : S. A.
1426.

(*c*) **at last,** at or in the end,
finally : P. L. I. 620 ; II. 426, 643,
781, 927, 1034 ; III. 499, 545 ; IV.
79 ; V. 497 ; VI. 78, 874; X. 171,
190, 449, 635, 890, 981, 985 ; XI.
664, 759, 778 ; XII. 106, 356 ; P.
R. I. 309 ; S. A. 24, 275, 1566,
1639 ; N. O. 109, 165 ; Il P. 167 ;
C. 61, 555, 594, 735 ; L. 192 ;
Ps. VII. 42 ; LXXX. 40 ; Ariosto
I. 1.

(2) *adv.* (*a*) after all others : P.
L. I. 376, 490 ; III. 259, 278 ; V.
165 ; VII. 323 ; IX. 377 ; X. 197 ;
XI. 545, 579, 736 ; P. R. I. 35 ;
IV. 300 ; V. Ex. 14 ; L. 108 ; Ps.
LXXXVII. 18.

(*b*) very lately : P. L. XI. 787.

(*c*) in the last place, lastly : P.
L. I. 571 ; V. 481, 568 ; XII. 189 ;
P. R. IV. 509 ; V. Ex. 47.

(*d*) in the end, finally : P. L.
VI. 797 ; VIII. 302 ; IX. 377 ; XI.
545 ; XII. 545, 552, 574 ; P. R. I.
283 ; S. A. 944.

(*e*) *first and last* : P. L. II. 324 ;
III. 134 ; X. 831 ; *first or last* : P.
L. IX. 571 ; S. A. 1594. *See* **First.**

Last, *vb. intr.* to continue, endure ;
had his doings lasted as they were :
U. C. II. 27 ; *of Him that ... aye
shall last* : Ps. CXIV. 16 ; *they
needs must last endless* : P. L. VI.
693 ; *last to perpetuity* : P. L. X.
812.

part. adj. **lasting,** enduring,
permanent ; *lasting seat* : H. B.
11 ; continuing ; *lasting fame* : P.
L. III. 449 ; *favour* : Ps. V. 40 ;
woes : P. L. X. 742 ; perhaps,
everlasting ; *lasting pain* ; P. L.
I. 55.

Lastly, *adv.* (*a*) in the last place :
P. L. XI. 280 ; P. R. IV. 388.

(*b*) in the end, finally : P. L.
III. 240 ; X. 402 ; *lastly overstrong
against thyself* : S. A. 1590.

(*c*) conclusively ; *as he pronounces lastly on each deed* : L. 83.

Late, *adj.* (*a*) coming after the due
time : S. A. 746 ; coming after the
favourable or auspicious time ; *an
age too late* : P. L. IX. 44.

(*b*) deferred beyond the due
time ; *late spring* : S. II. 4.

(*c*) keeping late hours ; *late
wassailers* : C. 179.

(*d*) recent in date : P. L. V. 113 ;
comp., later fame : P. R. III. 289 ;
age : Il P. 101 ; belonging to a
recent period ; *of persons* : V. Ex.
20 ; *sup.* : Ps. VIII. 4.

(*e*) *sup.* coming after all others,
last : P. L. IV. 567 ; P. 22 ; final :
U. C. I. 13.

(*f*) quasi-*adv. my latest found* :
P. L. V. 18.

absol. **of late,** lately, recently :
P. L. II. 77, 991 ; IX. 1115 ; P. R.
III. 364 ; D. F. I. 47 ; S. XI. 1.

(2) *adv.* (*a*) after the due time :
P. L. IX. 26 ; *too late* : P. L. VI.

147 ; IX. 884 ; X. 755, 904 ; P. R.
III. 42 ; S. A. 228 ; S. I. 11.

(*b*) at a late hour : C. 540.

(*c*) recently, not long since, but
now : P. L. I. 113 ; III. 151 ; V.
240 ; IX. 53 ; X. 861, 1073 ; XI.
70, 653, 886 ; XII. 195 ; P. R. I.
65, 133, 327 ; *so late* : P. L. V.
675 ; VII. 92 ; IX. 982 ; X. 941 ;
P. R. II. 3 ; qualifying a *part. adj.*,
late heaven-banished : P. L. X.
436 ; *espoused* : S. XXIII. 1 ; recently (but no longer) : P. L. XI.
751, 752 ; S. A. 179 ; *so late* : P.
L. X. 721 ; XII. 642.

(*d*) *comp.* at a subsequent time :
P. L. I. 509 ; *sooner or later* : P.
L. X. 613 ; *though later born
than to have known the days* : S.
X. 9.

Lately, *adv.* not long since, recently :
P. L. II. 979, 1004 ; U. C. I. 11 ;
so lately : P. L. X. 38 ; XII. 542 ;
P. R. II. 9, 10.

Lateral, *adj.* proceeding from the
side : P. L. X. 705.

Latona, *sb.* the mother of Apollo
and Diana : A. 20 ; S. XII. 6.

Latter, *adj.* (*a*) belonging to sub-
quent period, later : V. Ex. 8.

(*b*) being the second of two
things considered : P. L. IV. 1004 ;
V. 489 ; *the former ... the* or *this
latter* : P. L. II. 235 ; XII. 105 ;
the first ... the latter : P. L. IX.
558.

Laugh, *vb.* (*pres. 2d sing.* laugh'st :
P. L. V. 737) *intr.* (*a*) to give vent
to laughter : P. L. XI. 626 ; Ps.
LXXX. 27 ; Hor. Sat. I. 1 ; of
Satan or his angels : P. L. II. 204 ;
X. 626.

(*b*) *laugh at*, make fun of, ridicule ; of God : P. L. II. 731 ; V.
737.

Laughter, *sb.* (*a*) the action of laugh-
ing ; said of God or angels : P. L.
VIII. 78 ; *great laughter was in
heaven* : P. L. XII. 59 ; of the
fallen angels : P. L. X. 488 ; *personified* : L'A. 32.

(*b*) a cause of merriment : P. L.
VI. 603.

Laureate, *adj.* (*a*) decked with
laurel : L. 151.

(*b*) composed of laurel : S. XVI.
9.

Laurel, *sb.* the bay-tree, *Laurus
nobilis* : P. L. IV. 694 ; as an
emblem of victory or honour : S.
A. 1735 ; L. 1.

Lave, *vb. tr.* to wash, bathe: L. 175.
  part. adj. **laving**, cleansing: P.
  R. I. 280.
Laver, *sb.* (*a*) vessel for bathing;
  nectared lavers: C. 838.
  (*b*) water used in the bath;
  lavers pure: S. A. 1727.
Lavinia, *sb.* the daughter of Latinus,
  betrothed to Turnus, but later
  married to Æneas: P. L. IX. 17.
Lavish, (1) *adj.* (*a*) unrestrained,
  wild; *lavish act of sin*: C. 465.
  (*b*) profuse, prodigal: A. 9.
  (2) *vb. tr.* to bestow with profusion: S. A. 1026.
Law, *sb.* (1) rule of action prescribed
  by the authority of a state or a
  ruler: S. A. 1225; *law of nations*:
  S. A. 890; *pl.* the body of such
  rules: S. XXI. 3; Hor. Epist. 2.
  (*b*) prescribed by God and
  recognized as binding in heaven
  or hell; *sing.*: P. L. II. 200; X.
  83; *pl.*: P. L. V. 679, 680, 693,
  819, 844; *fixed, strict, indulgent
  laws*: P. L. II. 18, 241; V. 883;
  sing. the body of rules: P. L. V.
  798, 822.
  (*c*) prescribed by God and
  recognized by man as binding:
  P. L. IX. 775; XII. 397; *God's
  universal law*: S. A. 1053; *God is
  thy law*: P. L. IV. 637; *pl.*: P. L.
  XI. 228.
  (*d*) *necessity, whose law*: S. A.
  1666.
  (2) *canon laws*, established rule:
  C. 808.
  (3) rule of action given by God
  to nature: P. L. XI. 49; *keep
  unsteady nature to her law*: A.
  70; implanted by nature in man;
  nature's law: P. L. X. 805; *law
  of nature*: P. L. XII. 29; S. A.
  809; *live according to her sober
  laws*: C. 766.
  (4) the Mosaic system of rules
  and ordinances, usually the moral
  precepts; *sing.*: P. L. XII. 287,
  289, 290, 300, 306, 309, 416; Cir.
  15, 16; Ps. I. 5, 6; *the law*: P.
  L. XII. 297, 404; P. R. II. 328;
  III. 161; *the old Law*: S. XXIII.
  6; *our law*: P. R. I. 212; IV.
  334, 364; S. A. 1320, 1386, 1409,
  1425; *Moses' law*: P. R. IV. 225;
  the law of God: P. L. XII. 402;
  pl.: P. L. XII. 226, 230, 244, 282,
  283, 304; S. A. 314; *our laws*:
  S. A. 309.
  (*b*) the books of the Bible containing the Mosaic law: P. R. I.
  207, 260.
  (5) in the Christian religion the
  law demanding faith; *the law of
  faith*: P. L. XII. 488.
  (6) rule of action or procedure;
  *law to ourselves, our reason is our
  law*: P. L. IX. 654; *reason for
  their law*: P. L. VI. 41, 42;
  spiritual laws: P. L. XII. 521,
  522.
  (*b*) *love's law*: S. A. 811;
  wedded love, mysterious law: P.
  L. IV. 750.
  See **Sword-law**.
Lawful, *adj.* allowed by law, not
  forbidden; *lawful desires, labour*:
  P. R. II. 230; S. A. 1366; *if lawful what I ask*: P. L. VIII. 614;
  secrets ... not lawful to reveal: P.
  L. V. 570; *I thought it lawful ...
  to oppress*: S. A. 231.
Lawless, *adj.* uncontrolled by law;
  lawless tyrant: P. L. XII. 173;
  passions: P. R. II. 472.
Lawn, *sb.* open space between woods:
  P. L. IV. 252; N. O. 85; L'A.
  71; C. 568, 965; *the high lawns*:
  L. 25.
Lawn, *sb.* a kind of cloth: Il P. 35.
  See **Cypress**.
Lawrence, *sb.* the son of Henry
  Laurence, President of Cromwell's
  Council: S. XX. 1.
Lax, *quasi-adv.* so as to have ample
  room: P. L. VII. 162.
Lay, *sb.* song: L. 44; *rustic lays*:
  C. 849; *Doric lay*: L. 189; the
  song of the nightingale: P. L.
  VII. 436; S. I. 8.
Lay, *vb.* (*pres. 2d sing.* lay'st: P. R.
  II. 189; S. A. 849; *pret.* and *past
  part.* laid) *tr.* (*a*) to bring down;
  fig., hath laid him in the dirt: U.
  C. I. 2.
  (*b*) to cause to subside *the fiery
  surge*: P. L. I. 172; *the winds*:
  P. R. IV. 429.
  (*c*) to place in a position of rest;
  with *on* or *upon*: P. L. XI. 438;
  Il P. 150; *fig.*: P. L. X. 1046;
  Ps. LXXX. 70; *lay my head ... in
  the ... lap*: S. A. 535; *lay it ... at
  his blessed feet*: N. O. 25; *laid in
  earth*, buried: M. W. 32.
  (*d*) to place *a person* in a recumbent position *there*: P. L. VI.
  339; *on*: P. L. VIII. 254; *wherein*:
  P. L. XI. 479; *laid ... asleep*: P.
  L. IV. 791; *hath laid her Babe to
  rest*: N. O. 238.

refl. lay me or *him down* : P. L. IV. 457 ; X. 777 ; P. R. II. 261 ; Ps. IV. 38 ; in *passive* ; *they straight side by side were laid* : P. L. IV. 741.

(*e*) to place in the proper position ; *pillars laid on wheels* : P. L. VI. 572 ; *powder laid fit for the tun* : P. L. IV. 815 ; *fig., fair foundation laid* : P. L. IV. 521.

(*f*) to bring forward as a charge or accusation, impute : P. R. II. 189 ; *as to my charge thou lay'st* : S. A. 849.

(*g*) to contrive, devise : Ps. II. 4.

In combination with other words ; (*a*) **lay by** or **aside**, put away from one's person : P. L. III. 339 ; N. O. 12.

(*b*) **lay down**, relinquish : P. L. XI. 506 ; P. R. II. 482 ; formulate definitely : P. R. I. 157.

(*c*) **lay flat** or **waste**, devastate, desolate : P. R. III. 283 ; IV. 363.

(*d*) **lay forth**, display openly : P. L. IV. 259.

(*e*) **lay hands on**, get hold of : C. 13.

(*f*) **lay hills plain**, level hills : P. R. III. 332.

(*g*) **lay hold on**, turn to advantage : S. A. 1716.

(*h*) **lay in**, place in store : P. L. XI. 732.

(*i*) **lay low**, strike down *a person* : S. A. 1237 ; beat down *hedges* : Ps. LXXX. 49 ; overthrow, conquer : P. L. I. 137.

(*j*) **lay on**, give up to, commit : P. R. II. 54.

(*k*) **lay out**, expend : S. A. 1486.

(*l*) **lay siege to**, besiege : P. L. XI. 656.

(*m*) **lay up**, store away in the memory : P. R. II. 104 ; *absol.* save money : S. A. 1485.

See **Thick-laid**.

Lazar-house, *sb.* lazaretto, leper-house : P. L. XI. 479.

Lazy, *adj.* slow-moving : T. 2.

Lea, *sb.* tract of open ground, grass-land : C. 965.

Lea, *sb.* a river of Middlesex, England : V. Ex. 97.

Lead, *vb.* (*pres. 2d sing.* lead'st, leadest : P. L. XI. 372 ; Ps. LXXX. 3 ; *pret.* led ; *2d sing.* led'st : P. R. I. 8 ; *past part.* led) I. *tr.* (1) to guide by going on in advance, accom-

pany and show the way to : P. L. VI. 26 ; XII. 309 ; A. 40 ; *led astray* : Il P. 69 ; *lead* or *led captive* : P. L. III. 255 ; X. 188 ; P. R. III. 283 ; *captive lead away* : P. R. III. 366 ; *by Friar's lantern led* : L'A. 104 ; *the bright morning star ... leads with her the flowery May* : M. M. 2 ; *the starry quire ... lead ... the months and years* : C. 114 ; *Time leads me* : S. II. 12 ; with *on* : P. R. I. 252 ; *the jolly hours lead on ... May* : S. I. 4 ; *the Hours ... led on ... the Spring* : P. L. IV. 268 ; *Love led them on* : S. XIV. 9.

(*b*) God as the leader : P. L. IV. 476 ; VIII. 485 ; *thou Spirit, who led'st* : P. R. I. 8 ; *led on* : P. R. I. 192, 299 ; *up led* : P. L. VII. 12.

(*c*) used of thought, inclination, choice, etc. : P. L. I. 455 ; II. 525 ; III. 698 ; IX. 215 ; X. 266 ; P. R. I. 290 ; S. A. 741 ; S. XXII. 13 ; *whose lustre leads us* : A. 76.

(*d*) *absol.* or *intr.* : P. L. IX. 631 ; X. 267 (*see* Err) ; *the Spirit leading* : P. R. I. 189 ; *chance may lead* : P. L. IV. 530 ; *the earlier season lead* : L'A. 89 ; *Love ... leads up to heaven* : P. L. VIII. 613 ; *lead on, imper.* : P. L. V. 375 ; XII. 614 ; C. 330, 657.

(2) to show the way to ; *I follow thee ... the path thou lead'st* : P. L. XI. 372 ; *what leads the nearest way* : S. XXI. 10 ; *he ... led ... the way* : P. L. VII. 575.

(*b*) to take the lead in a course of action ; *I led the way* : S. A. 823.

(3) to be at the head of, direct the movement of, command : P. L. I. 129 ; V. 684 ; VI. 232 ; P. R. I. 115 ; III. 295 ; with *on* : P. L. I. 678 ; IV. 797 ; with *forth* : P. L. VI. 46, 47 ; X. 463 ; *fig., Hesperus that led the starry host* : P. L. IV. 605.

(4) to conduct by holding the hand : P. L. V. 356 ; VIII. 511 ; IX. 1039 ; XII. 639 ; S. A. 365, 1623, 1629, 1635 ; L'A. 35 ; *led me up* : P. L. VIII. 302.

(5) to guide with reference to action or thought : P. L. VIII. 86 ; P. R. III. 53 ; S. A. 638 ; *lead at will* : P. R. II. 166 ; *lead captive* : P. R. II. 222 ; *lead me in thy righteousness* : Ps. v. 21, 22 ; *the Gentiles ... led by Nature's light* :

P. R. IV. 228; *thoughts whither have ye led me*: P. L. IX. 473; *reasonings ... lead me ... to my own conviction*: P. L. X. 830; *led on ... with desire*: P. L. VII. 61.

(*b*) to cause to go or act, impel, induce: P. L. IV. 100; *the ... Snake ... into fraud led Eve*: P. L. IX. 644; *led to build*: P. L. I. 401; *lead to know*: P. R. II. 474; *led the vine to wed her elm*: P. L. V. 215.

(*c*) *absol.* or *intr.*: P. L. X. 261; VIII. 269; *desire ... leads to no excess*: P. L. III. 696; *lead to greatest actions*: P. R. III. 239; *where rashness leads not on*: P. L. XII. 222.

(**6**) to go through or pass *life*: P. L. XI. 364.

II. *intr.* (*a*) to have as a consequence: P. L. IX. 696.

(*b*) or *absol.* to conduct; *of way, path, entrance*: P. L. II. 976; X. 324; XI. 468; C. 518; with *up*: P. L. II. 433; VIII. 613.

part. adj. **leading**, acting as commander: P. L. II. 991.

See **Star-led.**

Leaden, *adj.* gloomy, melancholy: Il P. 43.

Leaden-stepping, *adj.* moving with heavy slow step: T. 2.

Leader, *sb.* (*a*) guide: P. L. VI. 451.

(*b*) chief, commander: P. L. I. 357; VI. 67, 232; need of Christ: P. R. I. 99; of Satan: P. L. I. 272; II. 19; IV. 933, 949; VI. 621.

Leaf, *sb.* (*a*) one of the parts of a plant or tree which collectively form its foliage: P. L. V. 6, 480, 747; VII. 317; IX. 1095; C. 622; *autumnal leaves*: P. L. I. 302; *firm and fragrant*: P. L. IV. 695; *trembling, rustling*: P. L. IV. 266; IX. 519; Il P. 129; *slumbering*: A. 57; *spec.* the leaf of the elm-tree; *barren leaves*: P. L. V. 219; of the fig-tree: P. L. IX. 1110; of willow, hazel; *joyous leaves*: L. 44; of laurel, myrtle, ivy: L. 5; of the plant Hæmony: C. 631.

(*b*) the part of a book containing two pages: P. 34; W. S. 11.

See **Olive-leaf.**

League, (1) *sb.* a military or political compact: P. L. II. 319; P. R. III. 370, 392; IV. 529; S. XV. 8; any compact or alliance: P. L. I. 87; IV. 375; S. A. 1189; *nuptial league*: P. L. IV. 339.

(**2**) *vb. tr.* to combine or band with: P. L. X. 868; *leagued with millions in revolt*: P. R. I. 359.

League, *sb.* measure of length; *many a league*: P. L. II. 929; IV. 164; X. 274, 438; P. R. III. 269; *ten thousand leagues*: P. L. III. 488.

League-breaker, *sb.* one who breaks a compact: S. A. 1184, 1209.

Lean, *adj.* (*a*) wanting in flesh; *the lean ... abstinence*: C. 709.

(*b*) lacking in substance, poor, mean; *lean ... songs*: L. 123.

Lean, *vb.* (**1**) *intr.* (*a*) to recline or lie *on*: P. L. V. 12.

(*b*) to rest for support *on*: P. L. IV. 494; S. A. 1632; *fig.*, *on thy firm hand Religion leans*: S. XVII. 13; *lean on it* (confidence): C. 585.

(**2**) *tr.* to cause to rest; *'gainst the ... bark ... leans her unpillowed head*: C. 355.

Leap, *vb.* (*pret.* leaped; *past part.* not used) *intr.* to spring or jump *into*: P. L. III. 470, 472; *o'er*: P. L. IV. 187.

Learn, *vb.* (*pret.* and *past part.* learned and learnt; learnèd *disyl.*: V. Ex. 90; L'A. 132) (**1**) *tr.* (*a*) to acquire knowledge of or skill in: P. L. XII. 440, 575; P. R. IV. 361; S. A. 798; L. 120; *learn his seasons, hours, or days*: P. L. VIII. 68; *meaner thoughts learned in their flight*: P. L. VI. 367; *learn patience, overweening*: P. L. XI. 360; P. R. I. 146; *power of harmony*: P. R. IV. 254; *lore, doctrine, wisdom*: P. L. II. 816; V. 856; S. A. 936; *way*: S. XVIII. 13.

with clause introduced by *that*: P. L. VIII. 190; XII. 561; with dependent question introduced by *who*: P. L. V. 894; by *what*: P. R. I. 292; IV. 515; by *how*: P. L. I. 695; VI. 147; S. A. 187.

with *prep. inf.*: P. L. II. 686; VI. 717; P. R. IV. 625; D. F. I. 73; S. XVII. 11; XXI. 9.

(*b*) to become informed of, hear of, ascertain: P. L. IV. 400, 533; C. 530, 822; with clause: P. L. IX. 275; with dependent question introduced by *who*: P. R. I. 91; by *what*: P. L. II. 354.

(**2**) *intr.* to acquire knowledge, receive instruction: P. R. I. 203; Hor. Sat. I. 3.

part. adj. **learned,** characterized or showing profound knowledge ; *learned hands* : V. Ex. 90 ;
Jonson's learned sock : L'A. 132.

    vbl. sb. **learning,** erudition,
scholarship : P. R. IV. 231 ; S.
XI. 13 ; F. of C. 9.

Lease, *sb.* time allotted for possession ; *life's lease* : M. W. 52.

Least *(sup.* of little), (1) *adj.* little
in size or degree beyond all
others : P. L. III. 120; IV. 510 ;
VIII. 35 ; IX. 460 ; X. 951 ; S. A.
1058.

    absol. (*a*) the weakest in might :
P. L. IV. 855 ; VI. 221, 284.

    (*b*) the smallest thing in im-
portance : L. 120.

    (*c*) **at least,** not to say more
than is certainly true, at any rate,
at all events : P. L. I. 258 ; II.
22 ; IV. 110, 807, 994 ; VII. 139 ;
VIII. 537 ; IX. 146, 296, 555 ; XI.
39, 95 ; P. R. I. 60, 224, 380,
459, 485 ; II. 136, 371 ; III. 103 ;
IV. 494 ; S. A. 208, 218, 322, 499,
951.

    (2) *adv.* in a degree lower than
all others : P. L. I. 679 ; II. 338,
339 ; III. 277 ; VIII. 578; IX. 380;
X. 875 ; P. R. III. 109 ; IV. 11 ;
S. A. 195, 927, 1136 ; *least of all* :
P. L. V. 811 ; VIII. 397.

Leathern, *adj.* made of leather : C.
626.

Leave, *sb.* (*a*) permission, liberty
granted : P. R. I. 409 ; *leave
obtained, asked, granted* : P. L.
II. 250, 685 ; P. R. II. 302 ; *give
leave* : C. 26 ; S. XIII. 12 ; *enjoy
free leave* : P. L. IV. 434 ; *with
leave* : P. L. VIII. 377 ; S. A. 15 ;
without : P. L. VIII. 237 ; IX. 725 ;
X. 760 ; *by leave of* : P. L. XII.
348.

    (*b*) *take leave,* bid farewell : P.
L. III. 739.

Leave, *vb.* (*pres. 2d sing.* leav'st :
S. A. 692 ; *pret.* and *past part.*
left) *tr.* (1) to have remaining at
death ; *a grandchild leaves* : P. L.
XII. 153 ; *left a race behind* : P.
R. III. 423 ; *hath not left his peer* :
L. 9.

    (2) to bequeath *patrimony* : P.
L. X. 819, 820 ; to transmit to
others at death ; *left them years of
mourning* : S. A. 1712 ; *to Israel
honour hath left* : S. A. 1715 ; to
let remain at death ; *their story
written left* : P. L. XII. 506.

    (3) to let remain in any place or
condition ; (*a*) to allow to be or
remain ; with two *acc.* or *acc.*
and phrase : P. L. IV. 747, 789 ;
V. 236, 669 ; VI. 443, 851 ; VIII.
460, 534 ; IX. 142, 338, 345, 351,
621, 1074, 1185 ; X. 46 ; XII. 61,
71 ; P. R. I. 16 ; III. 256 ; S. A.
1027, 1685 ; A. 41 ; Il P. 109 ;
unfrequented left his ... altar : P.
L. I. 433 ; *no corner leave unspied* :
P. L. IV. 529 ; *his power left free
to will* : P. L. V. 235 ; *left him at
large* : P. L. I. 213 ; *left it in thy
power* : P. L. V. 526 ; *his fabric of
the heavens hath left to their dis-
putes* : P. L. VIII. 77 ; *leaves in
doubt the virtue of that fruit* : P.
L. IX. 615 ; *walls left in confusion* :
P. L. XII. 343 ; *leave me in the ...
grave* : P. L. III. 247 ; with *acc.*
and *dat.* ; *have left us this our
spirit* : P. L. I. 146 ; *with what ...
glory since his fall was left him* :
P. L. X. 452 ; *laws which none
shall find left them enrolled* : P. L.
XII. 523.

    (*b*) to let be or remain in de-
parting or withdrawing : P. L. I.
224, 236 ; V. 118 ; VI. 309 ; IX.
652 ; P. R. I. 106 ; III. 78 ; IV.
207 ; with two *acc.* or *acc.* and
phrase : P. L. VIII. 478 ; XII. 455 ;
P. R. II. 62 ; S. A. 692, 996, 1097,
1480 ; N. O. 206 ; C. 280, 283,
414 ; *them ... naked left to guilty
shame* : P. L. IX. 1057 ; *leaves all
waste* : P. L. X. 434 ; *left desert
utmost hell* : P. L. X. 437 ; *leave
cold the night* : P. L. X. 1020 ;
left him vacant : P. R. II. 116 ;
left me all helpless : S. A. 644 ; *in
Adam's ear so charming left his
voice* : P. L. VIII. 2 ; *leave them to
their own polluted ways* : P. L. XII.
110 ; *to themselves I left them* : P.
L. VI. 689 ; *on the ground leave
nothing green* : P. L. XII. 186.

    (*c*) *part.* left = unremoved, un-
taken, remaining : P. L. II. 1000 ;
III. 207 ; IV. 80, 81, 428 ; V. 730 ;
VI. 104 ; VII. 125 ; X. 534 ; XI.
304, 753 ; XII. 481, 513 ; P. R. I.
248 ; III. 206.

    (4) to commit, entrust, refer ;
with *to* : P. L. II. 361 ; VIII. 168 ;
P. R. III. 440 ; S. A. 506 ; with
prep. inf. ; *to them shall leave in
charge to teach all nations* : P. L.
XII. 439 ; with blending of sense
(5) ; *there left his Powers to seize*

possession of the Garden : P. L.
XI. 221.

(*b*) to allow ; *what their lords
shall leave them to enjoy* : P. L.
XI. 804.

(*c*) to surrender to the possession of another ; *leave her ...
mansion to the ... day* : N. O. 140.

(**5**) to depart from, quit : P. L.
IX. 1051 ; XI. 269 ; XII. 129, 339,
586 ; P. R. I. 364 ; II. 280 ; IV.
236, 396 ; N. O. 178, 236 ; L'A.
87 ; C. 188, 473 ; S. X. 4 ; *I for
his sake will leave thy bosom* : P.
L. III. 238 ; *leave not the faithful
side* : P. L. IX. 265 ; *this earth
had left behind him* (the sun)
there : P. L. IV. 595 ; or in sense
(**4**) (*b*) ; *here leave me to respire* :
S. A. 11 ; to depart from at
death ; *leaves his race* : P. L. XII.
163.

(*b*) to surrender *wealth, pleasure*,
etc. : P. R. IV. 306.

(**6**) to go away from *a person*
permanently : S. A. 794, 885.

(**7**) to desert or forsake *their
charge* : P. L. X. 421.

(**8**) to cease ; *to graze the herb
all leaving* : P. L. X. 711.

(**9**) **leave out**, omit : C. 137.
See **Self-left**.

Leavy, *adj.* abounding in leaves : C.
278.

Lebanon, *sb.* the mountain in Syria :
P. L. I. 447.

Lee, *sb. under the lee*, on that side
which is sheltered from the wind :
P. L. I. 207.

Lee, *sb. pl.* dregs : C. 809.

Leer, *sb.* glance expressive of malicious thought or intent : P. L.
IV. 503.

Left, (**1**) *adj.* being on the side
opposite to the right : P. L. II.
633 ; VIII. 465 ; *on the left side* or
hand : P. L. II. 755 ; X. 322.

(**2**) *sb.* side opposite to the
right ; *to right and left* : P. L. VI.
558, 569.

Leg, *sb.* one of the two lower limbs :
P. L. X. 512.

Legal, *adj.* warranted by law : P.
L. XII. 410 ; *legal debt*, that which
is due to the Mosaic law : S. A.
313.

Legend, *sb.* narrative, history : S. A.
1737.

Legion (*trisyl.* : C. 603), *sb.* (**1**) the
body of Roman infantry : P. R.
IV. 66.

(**2**) an armed host of angels ;
the number indefinite ; *sing.* : P.
L. VI. 230, 232 ; *squared in full
legion* : P. L. VIII. 232 ; *pl.* : P.
L. I. 301, 632 ; II. 132, 1006 ; V.
669 ; VI. 142, 206, 655 ; X. 427 ;
thickest legions : P. L. II. 537 ;
gay, bright, flaming : P. L. IV.
942 ; VI. 142 ; VII. 134.

(*b*) a great multitude of devils :
P. R. IV. 629.

(*c*) a multitude of monsters ;
*the grisly legions that troop under
the sooty flag of Acheron* : C. 603.

Leisure, *sb.* (*a*) opportunity afforded
by freedom from occupation : P.
L. X. 510 ; *at leisure to behold* :
P. L. II. 1047.

(*b*) state of having time at one's
disposal ; *at home in leisure* : S.
A. 917 ; free or unoccupied time :
U. C. II. 23 ; *personified ; on
whom his leisure will vouchsafe
an eye of fond desire* : P. R. II.
210 ; *retired Leisure that in trim
gardens takes his pleasure* : Il P.
49.

Lemnos, *sb.* the island in the Ægean
Sea : P. L. I. 746.

Lemur, *sb.* (*pl.* lemures) the spirits
of the departed, probably the
spirits of evil men ; but for a
discussion of *Lars* and *Lemures*
see Osgood, *Classical Mythology*,
p. 52 : N. O. 191.

Lend, *vb.* (*pret.* lent ; *past part.* not
used) *tr.* (*a*) to give for temporary
use on condition of return : D. F. I.
75.

(*b*) to grant, bestow : C. 680 ;
*the brute earth would lend her
nerves* : C. 797 ; with *acc.* and
dat. ; *lend them ... aid* : P. R. I.
393 ; *heaven lends us grace* : C.
938 ; with *acc.* and *to* : S. A. 1 ;
lend life, aid, power to : P. L. IV.
483 ; IX. 260 ; XII. 200.

lend ... ears to, listen to, heed :
P. R. IV. 272 ; C. 706.

Length, *sb.* (*a*) extent from end to
end : P. L. I. 209 ; II. 709, 893 ;
VI. 78 ; IX. 79 ; XI. 730 ; P. R.
III. 275 ; IV. 29 ; S. A. 348 ; L'A.
111 ; *wondrous, prodigious length* :
P. L. II. 1028 ; VII. 483 ; X. 302 ;
dreadful, hideous : P. L. I. 564 ;
VI. 107.

(*b*) extent in time ; *length of
years* : S. A. 570 ; *in length of
time*, in course of time : P. L. II.
274.

(c) the quality of being long; *peace would have crowned with length of happy days the race of man*: P. L. XI. 782.

(d) **at length**, after a long time, at last, finally: P. L. I. 648; II. 217, 951; IV. 357, 607; V. 755; VI. 249, 635, 795; VII. 158; IX. 527, 551, 598, 792, 894, 1066; XI. 719; XII. 191, 258, 504; P. R. I. 152; III. 5, 433; IV. 503, 568; S. A. 250, 535, 865, 962, 1629; V. Ex. 43; Ps. II. 22; VII. 34, 54; LXXXIII. 1; LXXXIV. 27; LXXXVI. 57.

Lengthen, *vb. tr.* to make longer in time, prolong; with *out*: P. L. X. 774.

Lenient, *adj.* softening, mitigating; with *of*: S. A. 659.

Leo, *sb.* the zodiacal constellation: P. L. X. 676.

Leopard. *See* **Libbard.**

Leper, *sb.* person affected with leprosy: P. L. I. 471.

Leprous, *adj.* infected with leprosy; *fig.*, *leprous sin*: N. O. 138.

Lesbian, *adj.* of the island of Lesbos: L. 63.

Less (*comp.* of little) (**1**) *adj.* (a) smaller in size or extent than something else: P. L. I. 779; *less compass, rivers, universe*: P. L. VIII. 33; P. R. III. 257; IV. 459; *less maritime kings*: P. L. XI. 398.

(b) of an inferior degree, of smaller quantity or amount: P. L. II. 1040, 1041; IV. 854, 919, 925; VI. 59; X. 998, 1098; P. R. I. 147; S. A. 772; C. 88; S. II. 9; *love ... less than divine*: P. L. III. 411; *less in power and excellence or splendour*: P. L. II. 349; V. 796; *less (in strength)*: P. L. II. 47; *no less desire or choice*: P. L. II. 295, 414.

(c) of lower station or condition: P. L. I. 593; II. 509; VI. 366; *all but less than he*: P. L. I. 257; *how far from thought to make us less*: P. L. V. 829.

(d) of slighter significance, of smaller import; *what remains him less than*: P. L. II. 443; P. R. IV. 169; *what can be ... less in me*: P. R. I. 383; *what could he less expect*: P. R. III. 126; in parenthetic clause; *what could or can it or they less*: P. L. II. 553; X. 15; P. R. I. 404.

(**2**) *absol.* (a) a body smaller in size; *the less*: P. L. VII. 348; VIII. 88.

(b) a smaller amount; *less than half*: A. 12.

(c) those inferior in power: P. L. II. 108; *no less than such*: P. L. I. 144; smaller extent of power or authority: P. R. IV. 105.

(d) that which is of slighter significance or smaller import: P. L. VI. 468; *nor less think we ... of thee*: P. L. VIII. 224; *thought less attributed to her faith*: P. L. IX. 320; *no less threatens*: P. R. II. 127.

(**3**) *adv.* (a) in a lower degree, to a smaller extent; qualifying an *adj.*: P. L. IV. 46, 478, 594, 920; VI. 206, 378; VII. 375; VIII. 539, 566; IX. 126; X. 107; XI. 11, 285; S. A. 1064, 1245; *nor, not, no less*: P. L. III. 626; VI. 844; IX. 14; XI. 9; S. A. 792, 1421; qualifying an *adv.*: P. L. VI. 430; qualifying a *vb.* or *part.*: P. L. II. 924; III. 429; IV. 617; V. 262; VIII. 543, 544; P. R. III. 68; IV. 171; S. A. 305, 1071; C. 327; *far less*: P. L. II. 659; IX. 381; XI. 874; *nor, not, no less*: P. L. I. 647; II. 848, 920; III. 119; V. 874; VII. 85, 126; VIII. 248; IX. 1065; X. 531; XI. 774, 784; P. R. II. 69; S. A. 620, 1142; C. 288; S. XVI. 11; *less to be fled*: P. L. IV. 919; *less to be pleased*: S. A. 900.

(b) *much less*, used with a statement: P. L. III. 220; V. 799; VI. 495; VIII. 395, 407; IX. 346, 533; P. R. III. 236; IV. 113; S. II. 7; *much* omitted: P. L. VI. 192.

(**4**) *conj.* *'less*, unless: Il P. 56.

Lessen, *vb. tr.* (a) to make less, diminish: S. A. 767, 1563.

(b) to lower the dignity of, degrade: P. L. III. 304; VII. 614.

Lesser, *adj.* (a) smaller: P. L. VII. 382.

(b) of lower rank or station: A. 79; *fig.*, *lesser faculties, that serve reason as chief*: P. L. V. 101.

Lest, *conj.* (a) for fear that, in order that not; followed by present *subjunctive*: P. L. II. 701; V. 244, 731, 890; VI. 163; VII. 17, 44, 150, 546; VIII. 635; IX. 354, 663, 883, 947; X. 133, 252, 872; XI.

93, 101, 108, 123, 883; XII. 45,
217; P. R. II. 140, 145; IV. 558,
631; S. A. 952, 1237, 1254, 1414,
1521; C. 156, 940; S. XIX. 6;
Ps. II. 25; VII. 4; followed by
might: P. L. II. 468, 836; VII.
272; VIII. 235; by *should*: P. L.
II. 483; IV. 665; X. 1056; S. A.
1451, 1567.

(*b*) that; after the vb. or sb.
fear, doubt; followed by the
present *subjunctive*: P. L. IV. 984;
V. 396; IX. 251; C. 406; followed
by *cannot*: P. L. X. 783, 784; by
will: P. L. X. 1024; by *would*:
S. A. 794.

*Let, *vb.* (*pret.* and *past part.* let)
tr. (*a*) to permit, allow; with *acc.*
and *simple inf.*: P. L. V. 130, 453,
820; VI. 163; IX. 798, 1184; X.
174; XI. 585; XII. 192, 196, 344;
P. R. II. 233; S. A. 1632; M. W.
45; C. 378, 402, 743, 814.

(*b*) to cause; *this let him know*:
P. L. V. 243; *to let thee know*: P.
L. VI. 163.

(*c*) the imperative as an auxiliary; followed by *acc.* and *simple
inf.*: P. L. I. 178, 183, 692; II.
60, 249; IV. 432; V. 125; VI.
909; VII. 339, 387; with ellipsis
of *go; let us forth*: P. L. XI. 175;
let's on: C. 599.

In combination with other words;
(*a*) let down, cause or allow to
descend: P. L. III. 523; D. F. I.
56.

(*b*) let forth, allow to pass out:
P. L. VII. 207.

(*c*) let in, allow to enter: P. L.
VII. 566; X. 620; S. A. 561.

(*d*) let loose, abandon; *to …
rage let loose the reins*: P. L. VI.
696; give way to; *let loose … his
ire*: P. L. II. 155.

(*e*) let pass, miss; *let pass occasion*: P. L. IX. 479; *advantage*:
P. R. II. 233.

(*f*) let slip, miss; *let time slip*:
C. 743.

Lethe, *sb.* the river of hell: P. L.
II. 583.

Lethean, *adj.* of the river Lethe: P.
L. II. 604.

Letter, *sb.* (*a*) alphabetical character:
P. 35.

(*b*) written message, epistle:
U. C. II. 33.

Leucothea, *sb.* Ino, a sea-goddess,
the mother of Melicertes: C. 875;
identified with Matuta, the Roman

goddess of the dawn: P. L. XI.
135.

Levant (lévant), *adj.* east *winds*:
P. L. X. 704.

Level, (1) *adj.* (*a*) having an even
surface; *level pavement, downs,
brine*: P. L. I. 726; IV. 252; L.
98.

(*b*) moving in a horizontal
plane; *shaves with level wing the
deep*: P. L. II. 624.

(2) *vb. tr.* to aim a *weapon*;
with *on*: P. L. VI. 591; *each …
levelled his deadly aim*: P. L. II.
712; to dart; *the setting sun …
against the eastern gate … levelled
his evening ray*: P. L. IV. 543.

part. adj. levelled; (*a*) held in
a horizontal position, *fig.*: C. 340.

(*b*) being in the same plane with
something else: P. L. VII. 376.

Leviathan, *sb.* the enormous marine
animal: P. L. I. 201; VII. 412.

Levity, *sb.* want of serious thought:
S. A. 880.

Levy, *vb. tr.* (*a*) to call out *troops* by
authority, *fig.*: P. L. II. 905.

(*b*) to make or undertake *war*:
P. L. II. 501; XI. 219.

Lewd, *adj.* (*a*) base, wicked: P. L.
IV. 193.

(*b*) lustful, wanton: P. L. I.
490; C. 465.

Lewdly, *adv.* basely, wickedly: P.
L. VI. 182.

Lewdly-pampered, *adj.* wickedly
indulged with whatever delights,
or ministers to ease and voluptuous living: C. 770.

Liable, *adj.* having a tendency, subject; with *to*: P. L. VI. 397;
with *prep. inf.*: S. A. 55.

Liar, *sb.* one who knowingly utters
falsehood: P. L. IV. 949; P. R. I.
428.

Libbard, *sb.* leopard: P. L. VII. 467.

Libecchio, *sb.* the Italian name for
the southwest wind: P. L. X. 706.

Liberal, *adj.* bountiful, munificent:
P. L. IV. 415; *liberal hand*: P. L.
VIII. 362; IX. 997.

Liberty, *sb.* (*a*) release from captivity or confinement: S. A. 803;
to work his liberty: S. A. 1454;
this jail I count the house of liberty:
S. A. 949; *thou hast achieved our
liberty, confined within hell-gates*:
P. L. X. 368.

(*b*) freedom from arbitrary or
despotic rule: P. R. III. 427; S.
A. 270; S. X. 7; XXII. 11; Ps.

CXIV. 2; Eurip. 1; *outward liberty*: P. L. XII. 100; *strenuous liberty*: S. A. 271; *the liberty of Greece to yoke*: P. L. X. 307; with blending of sense (c); *rational liberty*: P. L. XII. 82; *true liberty*: P. L. XII. 83; freedom from the despotic rule of God: P. L. II. 256; IV. 958; V. 793, 823; VI. 164, 420.

(c) freedom of action or thought; *license they mean when they cry liberty*: S. XII. 11; *the known rules of ancient liberty*: S. XII. 2.

personified, force the Spirit of Grace and bind his consort Liberty: P. L. XII. 526; with blending of sense (b); *the mountain-nymph, sweet Liberty*: L'A. 36.

(d) free opportunity; *liberty to round this globe*: P. R. I. 365.

Libra, *sb.* the zodiacal constellation: P. L. III. 558.

Libyan, *adj.* of or pertaining to Libya. "By the Grecians it is called most commonly Libya ... part of it taken for the whole.... But the most noted name thereof is Africa." Hey. *Cos.* 1666, p. 931. "Libya or Marmarica hath on the east, Egypt, properly so call; on the west, Cyrene." Hey. *Cos.* 1666, p. 944 (930): P. L. I. 355; XII. 635; *Libyan Jove*: P. L. IV. 277.

Libyc, *adj.* Libyan: N. O. 203.

Lice. *See* **Louse.**

License, *sb.* unrestrained liberty of action: S. XII. 11.

Lichas, *sb.* the attendant of Hercules who brought him the poisoned garment from Deianira, and who was thrown by him into the sea: P. L. II. 545.

Lick, *vb. tr.* (a) to pass over with the tongue; *licked the ground, fig.*: P. L. IX. 526.

(b) to take *up* by licking: P. L. X. 630.

Lickerish. *See* **Liquorish.**

Lictor, *sb.* one of a body of officers attending the chief Roman magistrates: P. R. IV. 65.

See **Eye-lid.**

Lie, (1) *sb.* a false statement uttered for the purpose of deception; *speak a lie*: Ps. V. 15; *brought forth a lie*: Ps. VII. 54; *pl.*: P. L. I. 367; V. 243, 709; X. 42; P. R. I. 433; IV. 124; C. 692; Ps. IV. 12; *glozing lies*: P.

L. III. 93; *glibbed with lies*: P. R. I. 375; *composed of lies from the beginning, and in lies wilt end*: P. R. I. 407, 408.

(2) *vb. intr.* to utter falsehood intentionally: P. R. I. 473.

vbl. sb. **lying,** the telling of lies: P. R. I. 429.

Lie, *vb.* (*pres. 2d sing.* liest: S. A. 1663; *3d sing.* lieth: U. C. II. 1; *pret.* lay; *2d sing.* lay'st: P. R. I. 247) *intr.* (1) to be in a recumbent or prostrate position: P. R. I. 247; S. A. 339; V. Ex. 36; N. O. 31; with a part. adj. or phrase expressing condition; *lie floating chained, vanquished, prostrate*, etc.: P. L. I. 52, 196, 209, 266, 279, 301; II. 168; VI. 390; X. 851; XII. 190; Ps. LXXXVIII. 4; *thick bestrown ... lay these*: P. L. I. 312; *the ass lay thrown*: S. A. 1097; *lay sleeping*: P. L. VIII. 463; XII. 608; *in slumber*: C. 110; *bed-rid*: S. A. 579; *lies in ... infancy*: N. O. 151; *lies at random*: S. A. 118; or merely, to remain; *under his ... power ... lie vanquished*: P. L. III. 243; *lie in this ... plight neglected*: S. A. 480.

(b) said of a dead body: S. A. 1725; U. C. I. 1; II. 1; *liest victorious among the slain*: S. A. 1663; *the ... hearse where Lycid lies*: L. 151; *to be buried*: W. S. 15; L. 53; *lie in wormy bed*: D. F. I. 31.

(c) to be in bed for the purpose of sleeping: V. Ex. 62; Ps. III. 13; IV. 40.

(2) to assume a recumbent position; with *refl. pron.*, *lies him down*: P. 21; L'A. 110.

(3) to remain in concealment; *lie hid*: P. L. IX. 76; *the ... enemy that lay in wait*: P. L. IX. 1173.

(4) to dwell, reside: L'A. 79.

(b) to take up a position in a field; *armies lie encamped*: P. L. X. 276.

(5) to be placed at rest on some surface: P. L. IV. 631; *his locks ... lay waving round*: P. L. III. 628; *bones lie scattered*: S. XVIII. 2; *fig., on his shoulders each man's burden lies*: P. R. II. 462.

(6) to be situated, have a location: P. L. II. 360, 588, 958; IV. 569; XI. 380; C. 977; H. B. 8, 9; *the coast in prospect lay*: P. L. X.

89 ; *Eden which now in his view lay
pleasant*: P. L. IV. 28; *a spacious
plain ... lay pleasant*: P. R. III.
255 ; *garden-plot more pleasant
lay*: P. L. IX. 418.

(*b*) to extend ; *of a way*: P. L.
II. 974; P. R. I. 263 ; C. 37.

(7) to be, exist, or have place:
P. L. XI. 177 ; *scattered lies with
carcases ... the field*: P. L. XI.
653 ; *bird ... lay erewhile a holocaust*: S. A. 1702 ; *surcharged my
soul doth lie*: Ps. LXXXVIII. 10 ;
to the bait of women lay exposed:
P. R. II. 204 ; *with in*: P. L.
VIII. 193 ; IX. 349 ; *in what part
my strength lay stored*: S. A. 395 ;
in such abundance lies our choice:
P. L. IX. 620 ; *such compulsion
doth in music lie*: A. 68.

(*b*) to rest or centre *in* or
within: P. L. VI. 239 ; VIII. 641 ;
IX. 349 ; X. 987 ; Ps. III. 6 ; VII.
40.

(*c*) to consist *in*, have ground
or basis *in*: P. L. IX. 725 ; L. 80.

Life, *sb.* (1) animate existence ; (*a*)
the principle of animate existence:
S. A. 91 ; *various degrees ... of
life*: P. L. V. 474 ; *gradual life of
growth, sense, reason*: P. L. IX.
112 ; *substantial life*: P. L. IV.
485 ; *extinguish life in nature and
all things*: P. L. IV. 666.

(*b*) *breath of life*, the spirit of
man, "an inspiration of some
divine virtue fitted for the exercise of life and reason, and infused
into the organic body," *C. D.*
chap. VII.: P. L. VII. 527 ; X.
784, 790.

(*c*) the continuance of animate
existence ; said of certain things
in heaven or Paradise which give
and maintain eternal life ; *fount
of life*: P. L. III. 357 ; P. R. IV.
590 ; *tree of life* in Paradise: P.
L. III. 354 ; IV. 194, 218, 424 ;
VIII. 326 ; IX. 73 ; XI. 94, 122 ;
trees or *tree of life* in heaven : P.
L. V. 427, 652 ; P. R. IV. 589 ;
waters of life: P. L. XI. 79 ; *well
of life*: P. L. XI. 416.

(*d*) the condition of a living
being as dependent on sustenance:
P. R. II. 372 ; C. 678 ; as dependent on physical conditions ;
light so necessary is to life: S. A.
90.

(*e*) the condition in which the
soul, through faith in Christ, is

raised from the death of sin and
is devoted to the love and service
of God, or the divinely implanted
power producing this condition :
P. L. III. 294 ; XII. 407, 414, 425,
429, 443 ; Ps. LXXXV. 28.

(*f*) a blessed existence devoted
to God ; *true life*: P. L. IV. 196.

(*g*) a blessed existence in heaven
with God : S. XIV. 4 ; *second
life*: P. L. XI. 64 ; *better life*: P.
L. XI. 42 ; *immortal life*: P. L.
XII. 435 ; *death, the gate of life*:
P. L. XII. 571 ; *book of life*: P. L.
I. 363. *See* Book.

(*h*) the more perfect intellectual or spiritual life conferred by
the eating of the forbidden fruit:
P. L. IX. 689, 934, 984 ; eternal
life so conferred : P. L. IX. 686.

(*i*) animate existence, viewed as
a possession to be surrendered at
death : P. L. III. 244 ; V. 485 ; X.
790, 1013, 1019 ; XI. 331, 446,
502, 506, 548, 553, 650, 823 ; XII.
220 ; P. R. II. 77 ; III. 410 ; IV.
305 ; S. A. 512, 521, 888, 1002,
1009, 1406 ; U. C. II. 11 ; C. 220 ;
Ps. III. 5 ; VII. 15 ; LXXXVI. 51 ;
LXXXVIII. 11, 17, 54 ; *human life*:
P. L. VIII. 250 ; IX. 241 ; X. 908 ;
P. R. IV. 265 ; *man's frail life*:
S. A. 656 ; *slits the thin-spun life*:
L. 76 ; *death is to me as life*: P.
L. IX. 954 ; *a life half dead*: S.
A. 100 ; *death to life is crown or
shame*: S. A. 1579 ; *earthy load of
death, called life*: S. XIV. 4 ; *she
to life was formed*: P. L. XI. 369 ;
life for life I offer: P. L. III. 236 ;
ransomed with his own dear life:
P. L. III. 297 ; *the balm of life*:
P. L. XI. 546 ; *the ... light of life* =
life : S. A. 592.

so as to save one's life ; *for thy
life*: S. A. 952.

(*j*) the source of life ; said of
the tree of life as the source of
eternal life : P. L. IV. 220, 425.

fig. as a term of endearment;
*his heart relented towards her, his
life*: P. L. X. 941.

(*k*) living human beings : P. L.
XI. 169 ; living things; *all life
dies*: P. L. II. 624 ; *infernal
dregs, adverse to life*: P. L. VII.
239.

(2) the period from birth to
death : P. L. XII. 438 ; S. A. 66,
1388, 1668 ; M. W. 14, 52 ; *long
life*: P. R. IV. 298 ; *his whole*

life : S. A. 1059 ; *days of thy life* : P. L. x. 178, 202 ; *ages of lives* : S. A. 1707.

(3) the course of human existence from birth to death : P. L. iv. 317 ; vi. 460 ; viii. 184 ; ix. 833 ; x. 128 ; xi. 198 ; S. A. 915 ; U. C. ii. 24 ; S. xxi. 9 ; *daily life* : P. L. viii. 193 ; *future life* : P. R. i. 396 ; *lead safest thy life* : P. L. xi. 365 ; *arts that polish life* : P. L. xi. 610.

(b) a particular manner or course of living : P. L. xi. 621 ; xii. 17 ; S. A. 107 ; C. 609 ; F. of C. 9 ; *private, obscured* : P. R. ii. 80 ; iii. 22, 232 ; S. A. 688 ; *contemplative* : P. R. iv. 370 ; *voluptuous* : S. A. 534 ; *wretched, inglorious, reproachful* : P. L. x. 985 ; xii. 220, 406 ; *heroic* : S. A. 1711 ; *happy, calm* : P. L. iv. 317 ; vi. 461 ; ix. 697 ; *what life the gods live* : P. L. v. 81 ; *life in captivity* : S. A. 108 ; *in tribulation* : P. L. xi. 62.

(c) the earthly state of human existence; *this life* : P. L. x. 1083.

(d) the state of existence after death ; *the other life* : P. L. iii. 450.

Life-blood, *sb.* vital blood : P. L. viii. 467.

Life-giving, *adj.* that which confers and maintains eternal life : P. L. iv. 199.

Lifeless, *adj.* (a) destitute of life, dead : P. L. iii. 443.

(b) not possessing life, inanimate : P. L. ix. 1154 ; x. 707.

Lift, *vb. tr.* (a) to raise, heave : P. L. iii. 486 ; *lift stroke, spear* : P. L. vi. 189 ; S. viii. 9 ; *sword be lifted up* : C. 601 ; *lift us up* : P. L. ii. 393.

(b) to raise in dignity or rank ; with *up* : P. L. iv. 49.

(c) to raise, elevate ; *lifting up his eyes* : P. R. ii. 338 ; *lift my soul and voice* : Ps. LXXXVI. 12 ; *lift our thoughts to heaven* : P. L. iv. 688 ; *lift human imagination* : P. L. vi. 299 ; *lift up the light ... the favour of thy countenance* : Ps. iv. 19, 20.

(d) *lift thy horn,* oppose or strive against : Petr. 2.

(e) to carry in an elevated position : P. R. iv. 48 545.

Ligea, *sb.* one of the Sirens : C. 880.

Light, I. *sb.* (1) the natural agent or influence by which it is possible to see ; (a) as the medium of visual perception, opposed to *darkness* : P. L. i. 63, 181 ; ii. 220, 1042 ; P. R. iv. 400 ; S. A. 70, 75, 90, 98, 99, 160, 591 ; C. 369, 735 ; *precincts of light* : P. L. iii. 88 ; *new world of light* : P. L. ii. 867 ; *sacred influence of light* : P. L. ii. 1035 ; as first created by God : P. L. iii. 713 ; v. 179 ; vii. 249, 352, 359 ; xii. 473 ; S. A. 84 ; *the liquid light* : P. L. vii. 362 ; *light ... from her native east to journey ... began* : P. L. vii. 243 ; *fig.* : S. A. 592.

(b) as itself an object of perception : P. L. iii. 500 ; vii. 254 ; viii. 285 ; C. 340.

(c) as residing in or emanating from the sun or other heavenly bodies : P. L. iii. 579, 594, 723, 730 ; iv. 608, 664 ; v. 42, 423 ; vii. 377, 378 ; viii. 22, 37, 140, 156, 158 ; C. 199 ; *their office ... to give light on the earth* : P. L. vii. 345 ; *the sun robed ... in amber light* : L'A. 61 ; *stars ... in their golden urns draw light* : P. L. vii. 365 ; *suns ... moons ... communicating male and female light* : P. L. viii. 150 ; *the sun ... great palace now of light* : P. L. vii. 363.

(d) as emanating from a lamp, a fire, etc. : P. L. i. 729 ; v. 714 ; ix. 639 ; *embers ... teach light to counterfeit a gloom* : Il P. 80.

(e) as coming through a window : Il P. 160.

(f) as emanating from or surrounding a person : A. 19 ; emanating from or surrounding God or angels : N. O. 8, 110 ; *fountain of light,* God : P. L. iii. 375.

(g) light in heaven as created by God or coexistent with Him : P. L. ii. 269 ; iii. 4 ; vi. 6, 9, 481 ; *that high mount of God whence light and shade spring both* : P. L. v. 643 ; *the gates of light* : P. L. vi. 4 ; *light of heaven, heaven's light* : P. L. i. 73 ; ii. 137, 398 ; *celestial light* : P. L. i. 245 ; *Hail, Holy Light* : P. L. iii. 1.

(h) applied to God as incorporeal, spotless, holy : P. R. iv. 597 ; *God is light* : P. L. iii. 3 ; applied to angels as partaking of the nature of God or heaven ; *spirits of ... light* : P. L. vi. 660 ;

progeny of light: P. L. v. 600; *sons of light*: P. L. v. 160; xi. 80.

(*i*) = heaven; *realms, coasts of light*: P. L. i. 85; viii. 245; as a state consummate and free from every imperfection; *morn of light*: S. M. 28; *the bosom bright of blazing ... light*: M. W. 70.

(*j*) the regions where light exists, opposed to *hell* or *chaos*: P. L. ii. 433, 959, 974; P. R. i. 116.

(*k*) favour, kindness: Ps. iv. 29.

(2) the light of day, daylight: P. L. iv. 624; v. 208; N. O. 20; P. 6; *dawning light*: P. L. xii. 421, 423; *morning light*: N. O. 73; *sacred light*: P. L. ix. 192; xi. 134; *that light his day*: P. L. iii. 724; *light the day ... he named*: P. L. vii. 251.

(3) the power of vision, eyesight: S. A. 584; S. xix. 1, 7; xxii. 3.

(4) a body emitting light; (*a*) used of heavenly bodies: P. L. vii. 339, 343, 346, 382; *the great light of day*: P. L. vii. 98; *thou sun ... fair light*: P. L. viii. 273; *bear their ... lamps, light above light*: P. L. ix. 105.

(*b*) an ignited candle or lamp: U. C. i. 16.

(5) *nature's light, light of nature*, the capacity of man for discerning divine truth without revelation: P. R. iv. 228, 352.

(6) the illumination of the soul by divine truth: P. L. iii. 196; S. A. 92; *inward light*: S. A. 162; *light from above*: P. R. iv. 289; divine truth and purity: P. L. i. 391; divine wisdom; *thou, Celestial Light, shine inward*: P. L. iii. 51; the saving truth embodied in Christ; *Prince of Light*: N. O. 62.

(7) purity, holiness: C. 381; *deeds of light*: S. ix. 10; *son of light*, a holy man: P. L. xi. 808; *virtue could see ... by her own radiant light*: C. 374.

II. *vb. tr.* to set burning *a lamp* or *torch*: P. L. iv. 763; xi. 590; *fig., haste the evening star ... to light the bridal lamp*: P. L. viii. 520.

Light, (1) *adj.* (*a*) of little weight, not ponderous: P. L. iii. 439; *fig.*: P. L. iv. 1012; *comp., from the root springs lighter the green*

stock: P. L. v. 480; perhaps with blending of sense (*f*); *poise their lighter wings*: P. L. ii. 906.

(*b*) easy of digestion: S. xx. 9.

(*c*) without substance and nutrition: P. L. v. 495.

(*d*) thin, poor; *light the soil*: P. R. iv. 239.

(*e*) slight, inconsiderable, *sup.*: P. L. x. 45.

(*f*) moving with ease, swift, nimble; *wood-nymph light*: P. L. ix. 386; *light fantastic toe*: L'A. 34; *comp., lighter toes*: C. 962.

(*g*) gay, lively: C. 144.

(*h*) not oppressive, easily shaken off; *sleep was ... light*: P. L. v. 4.

(2) *adv.* lightly, easily, nimbly: P. L. v. 250; vi. 643; *his cart went light*: U. C. ii. 22. *See* Go.

Light, *vb. intr.* (*a*) to descend *from his ... throne*: P. L. vi. 103.

(*b*) to descend and settle on a surface: P. L. iv. 570; *he ... lighted from his wing*: P. L. x. 316; *down from a sky of jasper lighted now in Paradise*: P. L. xi. 209; with *on*: P. L. i. 228; iii. 437, 742; v. 276; xi. 858; *down they light on the firm brimstone*: P. L. i. 349; *within lights on his feet*: P. L. iv. 183; *a spark lights on a heap of ... powder*: P. L. iv. 815.

(*c*) to fall and strike; *so it* (revenge) *light well aimed*: P. L. ix. 173; to descend or fall violently *on*; *where they* (storms) *light on man*: P. R. iv. 460.

(*d*) to fall upon or to the lot of; with *on*: P. L. x. 73, 740; xi. 767; *on me ... all the blame lights due*: P. L. x. 833; *on me the assault shall light*: P. L. ix. 305; *all the sentence ... may light on me*: P. L. x. 934.

See **Morning-light, Star-light, Well-lighted.**

Light-armed (armèd, *disyl.*: P. L. vi. 529; P. R. iii. 311), *adj.* bearing light armour: P. L. ii. 902; vi. 529; P. R. iii. 311.

Lighten, *vb. tr.* to make lighter *a burden* or *load* of *woe* or *pain*: P. L. x. 960; P. R. i. 402; to alleviate; *lighten what thou sufferest*: S. A. 744.

Lightly, *adv.* (*a*) with little pressure, gently: P. L. iv. 811.

(*b*) easily, without difficulty: P. L. v. 7.

(c) with light motion, nimbly : P. R. II. 282.

Lightning, *sb.* (*a*) the flash of light that precedes thunder : P. L. II. 66 ; XII. 229 ; P. R. IV. 412 ; *red lightning* : P. L. I. 175 ; *tine the slant lightning* : P. L. X. 1075 ; *swift as lightning* : S. A. 1284 ; *fall like lightning* : P. L. X. 184 ; P. R. IV. 620 ; *fig.*, *every eye glared lightning* : P. L. VI. 849.

(b) glory, radiance ; or, possibly, a *part.* flashing like lightning : P. L. V. 734.

Lightning-glimpse, *sb.* the transient gleam of lightning : P. L. VI. 642.

*Like,** I. *adj.* (1) having the same characteristics or qualities as some other person or thing, corresponding, similar, resembling ; (*a*) with *to* : P. L. VI. 573 ; VII. 329 ; IX. 99 ; X. 841 ; P. R. II. 156 ; *like to us, me, themselves*, etc. : P. L. II. 349 ; IV. 448 ; VIII. 407 ; P. R. III. 424 ; *like to what, that* : P. L. II. 391 ; III. 600 ; *each to other like* : P. L. V. 576 ; *sup.* : P. L. IX. 394 ; *likest to thee, himself* : P. L. II. 756 ; P. R. II. 237.

(b) with *dat.* : P. L. IV. 8 ; XII. 434 ; P. R. IV. 462 ; A. 16 ; *more like* : P. R. IV. 55 ; *much like* : S. A. 1016 ; C. 57 ; *like his* : P. L. X. 870 ; *like themselves* : P. L. I. 793 ; *like which* : P. L. I. 351 ; *sup.* : P. L. III. 572 ; VI. 301 ; Il P. 9 ; the *dat.* omitted ; *too like in sad event* : P. L. IV. 715 ; the *dat.* preceded by the *def. art.* or a *pron.* : P. L. I. 287, 296 ; III. 568 ; IV. 33, 384 ; C. 303 ; *sup.* : C. 237 ; preceded by the *indef. art.* : P. L. I. 763 ; XI. 743 ; P. R. IV. 147.

(c) attributively with a *sb.* : P. L. I. 453 ; IV. 612 ; VII. 15 ; IX. 315, 325 ; X. 457 ; P. R. I. 105 ; *our like mouths,* mouths like ours : S. XI. 10.

(d) alike ; *they ... like in punishment* : P. L. X. 544 ; *not all parts like* : P. L. III. 593.

(2) approaching in quality ; *experience do attain to something like prophetic strain* : Il P. 174.

(3) likely ; with *prep. inf.* : P. L. II. 721 ; IV. 833.

II. *adv.* (*a*) after the manner of, in the same manner or to the same extent as : P. L. I. 343, 630 ; III. 367, 445 ; V. 55 ; X. 184 ; XI. 535 ;

S. A. 1137 ; C. 534, 727 ; S. XXIII. 2 ; *like us, night-foundered* : C. 483 ; *false like thee* : S. A. 749 ; or, possibly, *adj.*, *like whom the Gentiles feign to bear up heaven* : S. A. 150 ; the *sb.* preceded by the *def. art.* : P. L. VIII. 511 ; P. 6 ; C. 393, 655 ; preceded by the *indef. art.* : P. L. I. 354 ; II. 708 ; III. 363 ; IV. 17 ; VII. 414 ; IX. 180 ; P. R. I. 452 ; IV. 619 ; S. A. 198 ; C. 422.

like to = just as : L. 106 ; Ps. II. 21 ; LXXXV. 45.

(b) equally ; *like esteemed* : C. 634 ; qualifying an *adj.* : P. L. I. 527 ; VI. 620 ; X. 673.

(c) as ; used as a conjunction, followed by a *sb.*, the rest of the clause being suppressed ; *may not please like this ... Paradise* : P. L. IV. 379 ; *no place like this can fit his punishment* : P. L. X. 241 ; *who shore me like a tame wether* : S. A. 538 ; *they shall not trail me ... like a wild beast* : S. A. 1403.

III. *absol.* or *sb.* (*a*) one who is the equal or counterpart of another ; *by conversation with his like* : P. L. VIII. 418 ; *beget like of his like* : P. L. VIII. 424.

(b) something similar ; *the like* : P. L. VII. 44 ; XII. 324.

See **Assassin-like, God-like, Goddess-like, Man-like, Nymph-like.**

Like, *vb.* (*pres. 2d sing.* likest : P. R. IV. 281) *intr.* (*a*) to be pleasing ; *impers., as likes them* : P. L. VI. 717 ; *as likes them best* : P. L. VI. 353 ; *where likes me best* : P. R. II. 382.

(b) to regard with favour, take pleasure in : P. L. IV. 738 ; V. 97 ; VI. 561 ; P. R. II. 321 ; IV. 171 ; S. A. 996 ; *absol.* : P. L. XI. 587.

to feel inclined ; the *inf.* object omitted ; *these here revolve, or, as thou likest, at home* : P. R. IV. 281.

vbl. sb. **liking,** a person liked ; *each his liking chose* : P. L. XI. 587.

Likely, I. *adj.* (1) probable ; *comp.*, *what likelier can ensue* : P. L. IV. 527.

(b) with quasi-impersonal *vb.* ; *which to avoid were better, and most likely if* : P. L. IX. 365 ; *'tis likeliest they had engaged* : C. 192 ; parenthetic ; *as likely* : P. L. IX.

935 ; *sup.*, *as was likeliest* : P. L.
VI. 688.

(*c*) with personal *vb.* followed
by *prep. inf.* : P. L. IV. 872 ;
sup. : P. L. III. 659.

(2) fit, suitable, *sup.* : C. 90.

(3) well-looking, pleasing : P.
L. III. 460.

II. *adv.* probably, *sup.* : P. L.
II. 525 ; IX. 414 ; P. R. I. 121 ;
III. 130.

Liken, *vb. tr.* to represent as like or
similar *to* : P. L. I. 486 ; V. 573 ;
VI. 299.

Likeness, *sb.* (*a*) semblance ; with
of : P. L. II. 673 ; C. 84, 528 ;
form, shape ; *in likeness of* : P. L.
X. 327 ; P. R. I. 30 ; *falsehood* ..
returns ... to its own likeness : P. L.
IV. 813.

(*b*) representation, image ; *disfiguring not God's likeness ... or if
his likeness* : P. L. XI. 521, 522 ;
one who closely resembles another ;
thy likeness : P. L. VIII. 450.

Likewise, *adv.* in the like manner :
D. F. I. 11.

Lilied, *adj.* abounding in lilies : A.
97.

Lily, *sb.* the flower *Lilium candi-
dum* : C. 862 ; S. XX. 8.

Limb, (1) *sb.* one of the extremities
of the body, arm or leg : P. L.
III. 638 ; VIII. 267 ; S. A. 1089 ;
joint or limb : P. L. I. 426 ; II.
668 ; VIII. 625 ; *pl.* : S. A. 571 ;
joints and limbs : S. A. 614.

= body, *sing.* : P. L. IX. 484 ;
pl. : P. L. IV. 772 ; X. 1069 ; C.
680.

(2) *vb. refl.* to provide oneself
with limbs : P. L. VI. 352.

Limbec, *sb.* alembic, still : P. L. III.
605.

Limbed, *adj.* having limbs : P. L.
VII. 456.

See **Large-limbed**.

Limber, *adj.* flexible, pliant : P. L.
VII. 476.

Limbo, *sb.* a region on the outside of
the universe to which are borne
from the earth things transitory
and vain, the incomplete creations of nature, and the spirits of
vain and foolish persons : P. L.
III. 495.

Lime-twig, *sb.* twig smeared with
bird-lime, *fig.* : C. 646.

Limit, (1) *sb.* (*a*) boundary : P. L.
XII. 115.

(*b*) the reach beyond which

action or continuity ceases ;
reaching beyond all limit : P. L.
VI. 140 ; *giving limit to her life* :
M. W. 14.

(*c*) *pl.* the region defined by a
boundary, district, territory : P.
L. V. 755 ; C. 316 ; *narrow, straiter
limits* : P. L. IV. 384 ; N. O. 169 ;
hallowed : P. L. IV. 964.

(2) *vb. tr.* to restrict ; *limited
their might* : P. L. VI. 229.

Limitary, *adj.* stationed on the
boundary (?) ; *proud limitary
cherub* : P. L. IV. 971.

Line, *sb.* (*a*) a mark which has
length with little appreciable
breadth : P. L. VII. 480.

(*b*) the equator ; *equinoctial
line* : P. L. IX. 64 ; *Ethiop line* :
P. L. IV. 282.

(*c*) limit, boundary : P. L. IV.
210 ; VIII. 102.

(*d*) metrical verse : W. S. 12 ;
S. XIII. 11.

(*e*) lineage, race ; *Pelops', Anchises' line* : 11 P. 99 ; C. 923.

Lineament, *sb.* a part of the body,
considered with respect to its
outline ; *six wings he wore to shade
his lineaments divine* : P. L. V.
278 ; contrasted with the *face* :
P. R. I. 92 ; applied to the parts
of insects : P. L. VII. 277.

Linger, *vb.* (*pres. 2d sing.* linger'st :
P. R. III. 227) *intr.* (*a*) to tarry,
loiter : P. L. II. 56 ; C. 472.

(*b*) to be tardy in doing or
beginning something, delay : P.
R. III. 227 ; *He* (God) *will not ...
linger* : S. A. 466.

part. adj. **lingering** ; (*a*) tarrying : P. L. XII. 638.

(*b*) painfully protracted : S. A.
618.

vbl. sb. **lingering**, the action of
tarrying ; *with a whip of scorpions
I pursue thy lingering* : P. L. II.
702.

Lining, *sb.* inner covering of a cloud ;
*did a sable cloud turn forth her
silver lining* : C. 222.

Link, (1) *sb.* (*a*) *pl.* chains, fetters :
S. A. 1410.

(*b*) bond ; *I feel the link of nature
draw me* : P. L. IX. 914.

(2) *vb.* (*part.* linkèd, *disyl.* :
P. L. I. 328 ; L'A. 140) *tr.* to
couple or join ; (*a*) two or more
things together ; *with in* ; *heaven
and earth linked in a golden chain* :
P. L. II. 1005 ; *fair couple linked*

in ... nuptial league: P. L. IV.
339 ; *us, linked in love* : P. L. IX.
970.

(*b*) one thing *to* or *with* another:
P. L. IX. 133; U. C. II. 31; S.
I. 8 ; *linked and wedlock-bound to a
fell adversary* : P. L. X. 905 ;
linked itself to: C. 474 ; *joy but
with fear yet linked* : P. L. XI.
139.

part. adj. **linked**, connected as
if by links; *fig., linked thunderbolts*: P. L. I. 328 ; *linked sweetness* : L'A. 140.

Lion, *sb.* the animal *Felis leo* : P. L.
IV. 402; VIII. 393; P. R. I. 313;
tawny lion : P. L. VII. 464 ; *the
lion ramped* : P. L. IV. 343 ; *tore
the lion as the lion tears the kid* :
S. A. 128.

attrib. lion ramp: S. A. 139.

Lioness, *sb.* the female of the lion :
P. L. VIII. 393; *brinded lioness*:
C. 443.

Lip, *sb.* (*a*) one of the two organs
forming the edges of the mouth ;
sing. for *pl.* : P. L. IV. 501 ; *the
lip of Tantalus* : P. L. II. 614;
vermeil-tinctured, rubied lip : C.
752, 915 ; used in both senses, (*a*)
and (*b*) : P. L. VIII. 56 ; *pl., unrazored lips* : C. 290.

(*b*) as one of the organs of
speech, *pl.* : P. L. V. 150, 675 ;
IX. 1144 ; *words ... slide through
my infant lips* : V. Ex. 4 ; *unlocked my lips* : C. 756 ; hence,
speech, language ; *nor are thy lips
ungraceful* : P. L. VIII. 218.

Liquid, *adj.* (*a*) not solid, flowing :
P. L. XI. 570 ; *liquid brook* : S. A.
557 ; *fire* : P. L. I. 229, 701 ;
pearl : P. L. III. 519 ; *sweet* : P.
L. V. 25 ; *odours* : Hor. O. 1 ;
*spirits that live ... in their liquid
texture* : P. L. VI. 348.

consisting of water ; *liquid
plain* : P. L. IV. 455.

(*b*) clear, transparent; *liquid
air* : P. L. VII. 264 ; C. 980 ; *to
drink the liquid light* : P. L. VII.
362.

(*c*) pure and clear in tone : S.
I. 5 ; *stream whose liquid murmur* :
P. L. VII. 68 ; *liquid lapse of mur-
muring streams* : P. L. VIII. 263.

Liquor, *sb.* (*a*) a liquid ; *medicinal
liquor* : S. A. 627 ; *with precious
vialed liquors heals* : C. 847.

(*b*) beverage, drink; *pleasant,
orient, luscious* : P. L. V. 445 ; C.

65, 652 ; intoxicating beverage ;
turbulent liquor : S. A. 552.

Liquorish, *adj.* tempting to the
appetite : C. 700.

List, *sb.* a place of combat; *Dagon ...
to enter lists with God* : S. A. 463.

List, *sb.* roll, catalogue ; *the list of
them that hope* : S. A. 647.

List, *vb. intr.* to desire, choose; with
personal subject and *prep. inf.* :
P. L. VIII. 75 ; and simple *inf.*, in
subordinate clause ; *when they
list* : P. L. II. 656, 798 ; L. 123 ;
when he lists : P. R. IV. 306 ; un-
inflected ; *as he list* : P. L. IV.
803 ; *as the winds listed* : C. 49.

List, *vb.* to listen; *imper.* : C. 480,.
737, 992 ; with *to* : Ps. LXXXI. 36.

Listed, *adj.* (*a*) arranged in bands
or stripes : P. L. XI. 866.

(*b*) enclosed for a combat : S.
A. 1087.

Listen, *vb.* (1) *tr.* to hear attentively ; *I ... listened them a while* :.
C. 551.

(2) *intr.* to attend closely with
a view of hearing, give ear : C.
860, 864, 866, 867, 889 ; *listening
where* : P. L. X. 342; *listening
how* : L'A. 53 ; *listen why* : C. 43 ;
God's own ear listens : P. L. V.
627 ; *fig., the planets listening
stood* : P. L. VII. 563 ; with *to* :
V. Ex. 37 ; A. 62 ; L. 89 ; *fig.,
sleep listening to thee* : P. L. VII.
106.

(*b*) to allow oneself to be persuaded by ; *listen not to his temptations* : P. L. VI. 908.

part. adj. **listening**, giving
attention, hearkening : C. 203 ;
fig., of the night : Cir. 5.

Lithe, *adj.* easily bent, supple : P.
L. IV. 347.

Litter, *sb.* the vehicle consisting of a
bed or couch suspended between
shafts ; *steeds that draw the litter
of close-curtained sleep* : C. 554.

Little, (1) *adj.* (*a*) small in quantity :.
P. L. X. 600.

(*b*) short in extent : P. L. X.
320 ; short in duration : S. A.
1126, 1536.

(*c*) small in degree or amount :.
P. L. X. 968; T. 7, 8 ; *little grace,
ease* : V. Ex. 10 ; L. 152 ; *cheering* : C. 348 ; *reckoning* : C. 642 ;
L. 116 ; *do thee little stead* : C.
611.

(*d*) not of great importance ;.
wield their little tridents : C. 27.

(2) *absol.* or *sb.* (*a*) only a small amount, not much : S. A. 1599 ; *so little* : P. R. IV. 6 ; *that little* : P. L. II. 1000 ; *our day's work, brought to little* : P. L. IX. 224.

(*b*) *a little* ; used *advb.*, *a little onward* : S. A. 1 ; *a little further on* : S. A. 2.

(3) *adv.* in a small degree or extent, not much : ll P. 3 ; *little else but* : P. R. IV. 291 ; qualifying an *adj.* : P. L. IV. 362 ; x. 468 ; P. R. II. 82.

before the *vb.* as an emphatic negative ; *little know, think, prevail* : P. L. IV. 86, 201, 366 ; S. A. 661 ; *full little thought they* : N. O. 88.

Liturgy, *sb.* the form of public worship contained in the Book of Common Prayer : F. of C. 2.

Live, *vb.* (*pres. 2d sing.* liv'st : P. L. XI. 553 ; C. 230) *intr.* (1) to be alive, have life : P. L. VIII. 152, 264, 276, 281, 295 ; *living or dying* : P. L. x. 974 ; S. A. 1661 ; *things that live* : P. L. v. 474 ; x. 269 ; *kind that lives* : P. L. XI. 337 ; *by thee* (Eve) *man is to live and all things live for man* : P. L. XI. 161 ; *scarce half I seem to live* : S. A. 79 ; *lives there who loves his pain* : P. L. IV. 888 ; *fig., fame lives* : L. 81.

(*b*) *fig.* to have being ; *what delight ... to live upon their tongues* : P. R. III. 55.

(2) to feed or subsist *on* or *by* : P. R. I. 339 ; *fig., whereon I live, thy gentle looks* : P. L. x. 919 ; with blending of sense (6) ; *man lives not by bread only* : P. R. I. 349.

(3) to pass life in a specified fashion ; (*a*) said of angels or gods ; with *prep.* phrase : P. L. II. 254, 500, 869 ; with *adj.* : P. L. II. 194, 318 ; VI. 461 ; with *sb.*, *live his equals* : P. L. v. 795.

(*b*) said of man or beast : with *prep.* phrase : P. R. II. 201 ; C. 727, 766 ; with *adj.* or *part.* : P. L. XI. 38 ; XII. 602 ; S. A. 945 ; S. x. 3 ; *live happy, content, secure,* etc. : P. L. VIII. 633 ; IX. 829 ; XI. 180, 802 ; XII. 351 ; *so may'st thou live* : P. L. XI. 535 ; *forlorn, savage, ignorant,* etc. : P. L. IX. 910, 1085 ; XI. 764 ; XII. 411 ; P. R. I. 287 ; III. 41 ; with *sb.*, *live the poorest* : S. A. 1479 ; *law to ourselves* : P. L. IX. 653 ;

higher degree of life : P. L. IX. 932 ; *the easiest way* : P. L. VIII. 182.

(*c*) *live well,* live virtuously : P. L. XI. 554, 629.

(*d*) *fig.* of personifications : V. Ex. 77, 85 ; *echo ... livest unseen* : C. 230.

(4) quasi-*tr.* to pass or spend *life* : P. L. IX. 833 ; XI. 553 ; S. A. 100 ; *what life the gods live* : P. L. v. 81 ; *live laborious days* : L. 72.

(5) to have life in its fulness and perfection ; said of spirits : P. L. VI. 344, 350 ; said of Christ ; *by thee* (God) *I live* : P. L. III. 244 ; *seek ... him dead who lives in heaven* : P. L. III. 477.

(6) to have spiritual life through God or Christ : P. L. III. 293 ; IV. 198 ; XII. 299.

(7) to enjoy one's life abundantly : P. L. IV. 533.

(8) to continue in life : P. L. IX. 688, 764, 908, 932, 1166 ; x. 924 ; XI. 158, 872 ; XII. 117 ; S. A. 264.

(*b*) to have eternal life ; *live for ever* : P. L. XI. 95 ; *to live with Him* (God) : S. M. 28.

(*c*) *fig.* to continue in operation ; *to make death live in us* : P. L. x. 1028 ; *life dies, death lives* : P. L. II. 624.

(9) to continue in the memory of men ; *Socrates ... lives now* : P. R. III. 98 ; *make thy name to live* : D. F. I. 77.

(10) to have one's abode, dwell : P. L. VIII. 176 ; N. O. 90 ; A. 45, 103 ; *spirits live insphered* : C. 3 ; *gay creatures ... that in the colours of the rainbow live* : C. 300 ; *things that ... live in sea or air* : P. L. VIII. 340, 341.

= to be ; *within them* (chariots) *spirit lived* : P. L. VII. 204.

fig. : L'A. 39, 152 ; Il P. 176 ; *smiles ... love to live in dimple sleek* : L'A. 30.

part. adj. **living** ; (*a*) alive ; predicatively : S. x. 11 ; following the *sb.* : P. L. IX. 539 ; XI. 160 ; S. A. 984.

(*b*) having life, animate ; *living soul* : P. L. v. 197 ; VII. 388, 392, 451, 528 ; VIII. 154 ; *wight, creature* : P. L. II. 613 ; III. 443 ; IV. 287 ; VII. 413, 455 ; VIII. 370 ; IX. 228 ; *thing* : P. L. VII. 534 ;

carcases: P. L. x. 277; tomb: M. W. 34; *his living temples*: P. L. xii. 527; *living oracle*: P. R. i. 460; *living might*, the might of the living, opposed to *death*: P. L. ii. 855.

absol. the living, those who are alive: P. L. iii. 327.

(c) possessing absolute life; said of God; *living God*: P. L. xii. 118; S. A. 1140; Ps. lxxxiv. 8; *strength*: P. L. i. 433; *Dread*: S. A. 1673.

(d) *fig.*, *living death*, life filled with the suffering of death: P. L. x. 788; S. A. 100.

(e) instinct with life; *living wheels*: P. L. vi. 846; *doors*: P. L. vii. 566.

(f) flowing; *living stream*: P. L. v. 652.

(g) brilliant, vivid: P. L. ii. 1050; iv. 605.

Livelong, *adj.* (a) an intensive of *long*; *livelong daylight*: L'A. 99.

(b) lasting, durable: W. S. 8.

Lively, (1) *adj.* (a) lifelike: Il P. 149.

(b) active, vigorous; *of a person*, *comp.*: S. A. 1442; *lively vigour*: P. L. viii. 269; *blood*: C. 670.

(c) noisy: L'A. 49.

(d) bright, vivid, *comp.*: P. L. xi. 242.

(e) forcible in effect; *liveliest pledge of hope*: P. L. i. 274.

(2) *adv.* in lifelike manner: P. L. iv. 363; viii. 311; clearly, plainly: P. 47.

Liver, *sb.* the gland which secretes the bile: P. L. vi. 346.

Liveried, *adj.* wearing a livery; *liveried angels*: C. 455.

Livery, *sb.* the distinguishing dress of servants or officials; *state livery*: S. A. 1616.

fig., *those* (insect or worm) ... *in all the liveries decked of summer's pride*: P. L. vii. 478; *the clouds in thousand liveries*: L'A. 62; *twilight gray ... in her sober livery*: P. L. iv. 599.

Livid, *adj.* of a bluish leaden colour; *livid flames*: P. L. i. 182.

Lo, *interj.* behold! observe! a word used to excite or direct attention: P. L. iii. 486; x. 1050; xi. 733; Ps. lxxxiii. 5; lxxxvii. 16.

Load, (1) *sb.* (a) burden: P. L. v. 59; U. C. ii. 24; *the seated hills, with all their load*: P. L. vi. 644.

(b) a material object which acts as a weight: P. L. iv. 972.

(c) *fig.* a burden *of pain*: P. R. i. 402; *of sorrow*: S. A. 214; *of death*: S. xiv. 3.

(2) *vb.* (*past part.* loaded: S. A. 149; loaden: P. L. iv. 147; viii. 307; ix. 577; P. R. iv. 418; S. A. 1243) *tr.* (a) to furnish with a burden: S. A. 149.

(b) to be a weight or burden upon; *tree loaden with fruit*: P. L. iv. 147; viii. 307; ix. 577.

(c) *fig.* to burden or oppress: S. xxi. 13; to weigh down; *pines ... and oaks ... loaden with stormy blasts*: P. R. iv. 418.

(d) to heap or pile *on*: S. A. 1243.

Loath, *adj.* averse, reluctant, unwilling: P. R. iii. 241; *puts me, loath, to this revenge*: P. L. iv. 386; *Eve, more loath*: P. L. x. 109; *nothing loath*: P. L. ix. 1039; with *prep. inf.*: P. L. ix. 946; xii. 585; N. O. 99; C. 177, 473.

Loathed (*disyl.*: L'A. 1), *part. adj.* hated, abhorred: P. L. xii. 178; L'A. 1.

Loathsome, *adj.* disgusting, odious: P. L. iii. 247; xi. 524; S. A. 480, 922; Ps. lxxxviii. 43.

Local, *adj.* pertaining to a particular spot: P. L. xii. 387.

Lock, *sb. pl.* the hair of the head collectively: S. A. 587, 1143, 1493; C. 105; *locks white as down*: S. A. 327; *snaky, oozy, ragged locks*: P. L. x. 599; L. 175; L'A. 9; *redundant, boisterous, clustering*: S. A. 568, 1164; C. 54; *hyacinthine, dewy*: P. L. iv. 301; v. 56; *resplendent, illustrious, alluring*: P. L. iii. 361, 626; C. 882; *mitred*: L. 112.

fig. the foliage of trees: P. L. x. 1066.

Lock, *vb. tr.* to confine with a lock; *fig.*, *drowsiness hath locked up mortal sense*: A. 62.

See **Up-lock**.

Locrine, *sb.* the son of Brutus: C. 827, 922. *See* **Brutus**.

Locust, *sb.* the insect; *cloud of locusts*: P. L. i. 341; xii. 185.

Lodge, I. *sb.* (a) dwelling-place; *shady, sylvan lodge*: P. L. iv. 720; v. 377.

(b) a small house in a forest: C. 346.

II. *vb.* (1) *tr.* (*a*) to provide with sleeping quarters or temporary habitation : C. 315 ; to place as a resident *in* : P. L. VIII. 105.

(*b*) to put, place, deposit : P. L. VII. 201 ; with *in* or *with* : P. L. XI. 823 ; *thoughts ... lodged in his breast* : P. R. I. 301 ; *gift of strength ... in what part lodged* : S. A. 48 ; *that one talent ... lodged with me* : S. XIX. 4.

(*c*) to thrown down on the ground, *fig.* : Ps. VII. 18.

(**2**) *intr.* (*a*) to encamp : P. L. VI. 531.

(*b*) to dwell temporarily *in* a place : P. R. I. 184 ; *with* a person : P. R. II. 6 : *fig.*, *a cave .. where light and darkness ... lodge and dislodge* : P. L. VI. 7.

(*c*) to have one's abode, dwell ; *fig.*, *something holy lodges in that breast* : C. 246.

(*d*) to pass the night : P. L. IV. 790 ; U. C. I. 15 ; C. 183.

Loft, *sb.* layer, stratum ; *lofts of piled thunder* : V. Ex. 42.

Lofty, *adj.* (*a*) elevated, high, towering : P. L. III. 734 ; IV. 395 ; XI. 640 ; Ps. LXXX. 44 ; possibly *fig.* : C. 934 ; *sup.* : P. L. I. 499 ; IV. 138.

(*b*) elevated in style, sublime ; *the lofty rhyme* : L. 11 ; *transf.*, *the lofty grave tragedians* : P. R. IV. 261.

(*c*) solemn, impressive ; *trumpets' lofty sound* : Ps. LXXXI. 10.

Logres, *sb.* an old name for that part of England which lies east of the river Severn : P. R. II. 360.

Loin, *sb. pl.* that part of the body lying between the false ribs and the hip-bone ; (*a*) as covered by clothing ; *leaves ... girded on our loins* : P. L. IX. 1096 ; by wings : P. L. V. 282.

(*b*) as the seat of the generative power : P. L. X. 983 ; XI. 455 ; XII. 380, 447 ; *fig.*, *a multitude like which the ... loins* : P. L. I. 352 ; *in her* (nature's) *own loins she hutched the all-worshipped ore* : C. 718.

Loneliness, *sb.* the condition of being alone, solitariness : C. 404.

Lonely, *adj.* (*a*) companionless, solitary : P. L. XI. 290 ; C. 200 ; *lonely steps* : P. L. II. 828.

(*b*) isolated ; *lonely tower* : Il P. 83.

(*c*) desolate ; *lonely mountains* : N. O. 181.

Long, (1) *adj.* (*a*) relatively great in measurement from end to end : P. L. VI. 484 ; VII. 328, 480 ; IX. 1104 ; XII. 146 ; P. R. IV. 27 ; *long and large* : P. L. I. 195 ; *long way* : P. L. II. 432 ; V. 904 ; IX. 626 ; C. 183 ; *reach* : P. L. X. 323 ; *beams, rule of light* : N. O. 111 ; C. 340.

(*b*) having a great extent from beginning to end ; *long debate* : P. L. II. 390 ; IX. 87 ; P. R. I. 95 ; S. A. 863 ; *petition* : S. A. 650 ; *retinue* : P. L. V. 355 ; *comp.*, *longer scroll* : P. L. XII. 336.

(*c*) having a great extent in duration ; *long time* : P. L. II. 297 ; VI. 245 ; XII. 23, 316 ; *sup.* : P. R. I. 56 ; *night* : P. 7 ; *eternity* : L. 11 ; *vacation* : U. C. II. 14 ; *succession, descent of birth* : P. L. XII. 331 ; S. A. 171 ; *life* : P. R. IV. 298 ; *pursuit* : P. L. VI. 538 ; *labour, toil*, etc. : P. L. VI. 492 ; X. 573 ; C. 1006 ; Ps. CXIV. 2 ; *sufferance, tribulations*, etc. : P. L. III. 198, 336 ; IV. 535 ; P. R. III. 279 ; *obedience, indulgence* : P. L. VII. 159 ; P. R. I. 110 ; *comp., longer pause* : P. L. III. 56. *fig.*, *time's long and dark prospective-glass* : V. Ex. 71.

(*d*) excessive in duration ; *long day's dying* : P. L. X. 964 ; *I ... thought it long* : P. L. IX. 857.

(*e*) lengthy, prolix : P. L. IX. 30 : tedious ; *long were to tell what* : P. L. X. 469 ; *the rest were long to tell* : P. L. I. 507 ; XII. 261 ; in elliptical phrase ; *too long*, too long to recount : P. L. III. 473 ; P. R. II. 189.

(*f*) that has continued for a long time ; *long renown* : P. R. IV. 84.

(**2**) *absol.* or *sb.* (*a*) great extent of time ; *ere long* : P. L. I. 651 ; IV. 113 ; IX. 172, 246, 598 ; S. A. 468, 1242 ; Cir. 26 ; P. 10 ; S. M. 26 ; C. 151, 562 ; Ps. LXXXV. 39 ; as one word, *erelong* : P. L. XI. 626, 627.

(*b*) continued stay : M. M. 10.

(*c*) a long syllable : S. XIII. 4.

(**3**) *adv.* (*a*) for or during a great extent of time : P. L. I. 659 ; II. 778 ; III. 14, 261, 499 ;

IV. 371; V. 113; VI. 659; VIII. 454; IX. 26, 397, 445, 949, 1064; X. 115, 189, 352, 482; XI. 494, 581; XII. 421; P. R. I. 28, 55; II. 15, 103; III. 360, 378, 389; S. A. 476, 592, 1012, 1125, 1269; D. F. I. 13, 17; N. O. 134; L'A. 140; L. 35; *not long*: P. L. III. 242; VI. 331, 582, 634; IX. 601; X. 509; P. R. IV. 107, 618; S. A. 474, 1033; M. M. 34; *so long*: P. L. III. 601; IX. 18, 844; P. R. I. 17, 125; II. 32, 304; III. 41; U. C. I. 11; *how long*: P. L. XI. 198, 554; Ps. VI. 7; LXXX. 17, 18; LXXXII. 5; *too long*: P. L. IX. 747; *thus long*: P. L. III. 378; P. R. II. 101.

comp.: P. L. V. 63; VII. 101; VIII. 252; X. 1003; XI. 48, 259; N. O. 225; C. 577; *no longer*: P. L. X. 365; XII. 594; *longer than*: P. L. XI. 91; XII. 437; P. R. II. 421; *not longer than*: P. L. IX. 140.

(*b*) at or to a point of time far distant from the time indicated; *long after*: P. L. I. 80, 383; III. 497; V. 387, 762; *long before*: P. L. I. 748; IV. 213; *how long before*: P. L. IX. 138; *long ere*: P. L. VIII. 242; *long since*: P. R. I. 399; IV. 189; S. A. 929; *long of old*: P. R. IV. 604; *long of yore*: Il. P. 23.

(*c*) in the far past, long ago: Ps. LXXX. 62.

(*d*) for the period of, throughout the length of; *all day long*: P. L. IV. 616; Ps. CXXXVI. 30; *all night long*: P. L. II. 286; IV. 603, 657; V. 657; Ps. LXXXVIII. 3; *the summer long*: P. R. IV. 246.

(**4**) *vb. intr.* to be desirous, wish: P. L. II. 55; IX. 593; with *prep. inf.*: P. L. X. 877; S. A. 1554; Ps. LXXXIV. 5.

part. adj. **longing**, showing yearning desire: P. L. IX. 743.

vbl. sb. **longing**, yearning desire: P. L. IV. 511.

Longitude, *sb.* (*a*) a plain continuous in one direction (Masson): P. L. V. 754.

(*b*) *in utmost longitude*, at the farthest distance west: P. L. IV. 539; *by ... longitude*, toward the east or west: P. L. III. 576.

(*c*) the course of the sun from east to west: P. L. VII. 373.

Long-threatened, *adj.* announced as something to be inflicted long before the infliction: P. R. I. 59.

Long-wandered, *adj.* having erred for a great extent of time: P. L. XII. 313.

Look, I. *sb.* (often impossible to determine whether a passage belongs in (**1**) (*b*) or in (**2**)) (**1**) the action of looking, glance of the eye: P. L. I. 680; II. 418; VIII. 616; IX. 222, 239, 309; X. 608; P. R. II. 216; 11 P. 39; said of death: P. L. X. 296.

(*b*) with adj. or phrase denoting the feelings expressed by the look; *ardent, gentle look*: P. L. IX. 397; X. 919; *grieved*: P. L. IV. 28; *disdainful, fallacious, unchaste*: P. L. II. 680; S. A. 533; C. 464; *looks of love*: P. L. V. 12; *of sympathy*: P. L. IV. 464.

(**2**) appearance of the countenance, visual or facial expression: P. L. II. 106, 307; *in his look defiance lours*: P. L. IV. 873; *with look composed*: P. L. VI. 469; *estranged in look*: P. L. IX. 1132; *look serene*: P. L. X. 1094; *pl.*: P. L. I. 522; V. 122; IX. 534; S. A. 1246; *dispatchful looks*: P. L. V. 331; *rigid looks of ... austerity*: C. 450; *looks aghast and sad*: P. R. I. 43; *love was not in their looks*: P. L. X. 111; said of animals; *in their looks much reason*: P. L. IX. 558.

(*b*) appearance, aspect: P. L. IX. 454; S. A. 1068, 1304; C. 871; *pl.*: P. L. IV. 291, 570, 718; VIII. 474; X. 360.

II. *vb.* (*pres. 2d sing.* look'st: P. L. IV. 33) *intr.* (**1**) to direct the eyes upon some object, use the eyes in seeing: P. L. V. 54; X. 993; XI. 556, 638, 712, 840; P. R. III. 310; *where no profaner eye may look*: 11 P. 140; *as I bent down to look*: P. L. IV. 460; *imper.*: P. R. IV. 236.

(*b*) with an *adv.*; *look homeward angel now*: L. 163; with *back*: P. L. XII. 641; with *down* or *downward*: P. L. III. 542; XI. 887; *imper.*: P. L. III. 722; with *on*: P. L. XI. 897; *thou looking on*: P. L. IX. 312; with *up*: P. L. IV. 1010, 1013; S. A. 197; *the hungry sheep look up*: L. 125.

(c) with a *prep.* ; with *into* : P. L. ii. 918 ; iv. 458 ; with *on* : P. L. iv. 462 ; *imper.* : C. 910 ; H. B. 3 ; *fig.*, *on whose fresh lap the swart star ... looks* : L. 138 ; with *through* ; *she* (the soul) *might look at will through every pore* : S. A. 97 ; *fig.*, *the sun ... looks through the ... air* : P. L. i. 595.

(d) with *adv.* and *prep.* ; *look in at* : V. Ex. 35 ; *justice ... look down on ... men* : Ps. lxxxv. 48.

(e) said of God ; *out of heaven shalt look down* : P. L. iii. 257 ; *look down from heaven* : Ps. lxxx. 57 ; *through the fiery pillar ... looking forth* : P. L. xii. 209 ; *looking on the earth* : P. R. iii. 61 ; *look so near upon* : N. O. 44.

(2) to fix the attention or regard *on* : P. L. ix. 687 ; Ps. lxxxiv. 31.

(3) behold ! see ! used to win attention : A. 1.

(4) to afford an outlook : P. L. iv. 178 ; *looks toward* : L. 162.

(5) to seem, appear; *the blasted stars looked wan* : P. L. x. 412 ; *envy to look wan* : S. xiii. 6.

In combination with other words ; (a) **look for**, expect : P. L. v. 800 ; P. R. ii. 86 ; S. A. 1065.

(b) **look like**, appear as if thou wert : P. L. iv. 33.

(c) **look round**, look about in every direction : P. L. vi. 529.

(d) **look to**, think of, consider : C. 777.

vbl. sb. **looking** ; (a) the action of looking ; with *down* : P. L. xii. 60.

(b) prospect ; with *round* : P. L. xi. 381.

See **Dire-looking**.

Loop-hole, *sb.* a small aperture made to look through : P. L. ix. 1110 ; *fig.*, *the morn ... from her cabined loop-hole peep* : C. 140.

Loose, *adj.* (a) free from restraint ; *break loose* : P. L. iii. 87 ; iv. 889, 918 ; *let loose ... his ire* : P. L. ii. 155.

(b) not tied up or secured ; *of hair* : P. L. iv. 497 ; C. 863.

(c) not tightly drawn ; *loose traces* : C. 292 ; *fig.*, *to disordered rage let loose the reins* : P. L. vi. 696.

(d) not compact in arrangement(?), detached(?) ; *loose garlands* : P. L. iii. 362.

(e) not dense ; *loose array* : P. L. ii. 887.

(f) wanton, dissolute : C. 174, 464.

(2) *adv.* carelessly, thoughtlessly : S. A. 675.

(3) *vb. tr.* to untie ; *loose this Gordian knot* : V. Ex. 90.

Loosely, *adv.* (a) not in a compact body : P. L. vii. 425.

(b) immorally : S. A. 1022.

Loosen, *vb.* to unfix, detach : P. L. vi. 643.

Lop, *vb. tr.* (a) to cut off the branches from : P. L. ix. 210.

(b) to cut off ; *to lop their* (branches) *wanton growth* : P. L. iv. 629 ; *with branches lopped* : P. L. vi. 575.

fig., *head and hands lopped off* : P. L. i. 459.

Loquacious, *adj.* talkative : P. L. x. 161.

Lord, I. *sb.* (1) master, ruler, sovereign : P. L. xi. 803 ; xii. 93, 349 ; *man over men he made not lord* : P. L. xii. 70 ; *their lords, the Philistines* : S. A. 251 ; *the herds would over-multitude their lords* : C. 731.

(b) applied to Adam and Eve, or to Adam only, as possessing the earth : P. L. i. 32 ; iv. 290 ; viii. 339 ; ix. 154, 273, 658 ; x. 401 ; applied to man ; *o'er the works of thy hands thou mad'st him lord* : Ps. viii. 17.

(c) applied to death : P. L. ii. 699.

(d) applied to the fallen angels on earth : P. L. x. 467 ; to Satan : P. R. iv. 167.

(e) applied to the Prelacy ; *your Prelate Lord* : F. of C. 1.

(2) God, the ruler of the universe : P. L. vi. 516, 943 ; v. 608 ; viii. 106 ; ix. 235 ; xi. 257 ; S. A. 477 ; *their great Lord* : S. M. 22 ; *heaven's Lord* : P. L. ii. 236 ; vi. 425 ; *universal Lord* : P. L. v. 205 ; viii. 376 ; *the Lord of all* : P. L. x. 794 ; *the Lord* : P. L. xii. 34 ; Ps. i. 15 ; ii. 5, 9, 14 ; iii. 15, 23 ; iv. 13 ; vi. 18, 20 ; lxxxi. 41, 61 ; lxxxiv. 41 ; lxxxv. 29, 49 ; lxxxvii. 5, 21 ; vocative : S. xviii. 1 ; Ps. iii. 1, 7, 19 ; iv. 28, 42 ; v. 21 ; vi. 1, 3, 7 ; vii. 1, 7, 31 ; lxxxiii. 60 ; lxxxiv. 6 ; lxxxv. 2, 25 ; lxxxvi. 1, 9, 11, 13, 17, 26, 31, 37, 41, 53, 63

LXXXVIII. 39, 53, 57 ; *the Lord thy God* : P. R. IV. 177, 561 ; Ps. LXXXI. 41 ; *Jehovah our Lord* : Ps. VIII. 1, 23 ; *Lord God, Lord God of Hosts, Lord of Hosts* : P. L. X. 163 ; Ps. LXXX. 17, 78 ; LXXXIV. 2, 13, 29, 45 ; LXXXVIII. 1.

(3) applied to the Son of God as a partner in the divine administration : P. L. V. 799 ; VI. 451, 887 ; VII. 205 ; applied to Christ as having power on earth, or as the saviour of man : P. L. XII. 502, 544 ; P. R. I. 475 ; II. 335, 376 ; N. O. 26, 60, 76, 242 ; P. 10.

(4) as a designation of official rank ; used, always in the pl., of the Philistian lords, sometimes apparently in sense (1) : S. A. 482, 920, 947, 1108, 1182, 1195, 1205, 1250, 1310, 1318, 1371, 1391, 1411, 1418, 1447, 1457, 1607, 1653 ; vocative : S. A. 1640 ; used of angels ; *the great Seraphic Lords* : P. L. I. 794.

(5) as a title, forming part of a person's customary appellation : C. 492, 966.

II. *vb. intr.* to rule tyrannically over : S. A. 267.

Lordly, (1) *adj.* (*a*) ruled by lords : Ps. LXXXII. 2.

(*b*) absolute in authority ; *fig.*, *his lordly feet* : Ps. VIII. 18.

(*c*) proud, haughty, domineering, *sup.* : S. A. 1418 ; imperious, sovereign ; *fig.*, *his* (the sun's) *lordly eye* : P. L. III. 578.

(2) *adv.* in the manner of a lord, imperiously : P. L. II. 243 ; S. A. 1353.

Lore, *sb.* (*a*) a piece of instruction, lesson : P. L. II. 815.

(*b*) teaching, doctrine ; *princely lore* : C. 34 ; *virtue ... her lore* : P. R. I. 483.

(*c*) command ; *understanding ruled not, and the will heard not her lore* : P. L. IX. 1128.

See **Love-lorn.**

Lose, *vb.* (*pret.* and *past part.* lost) *tr.* in *passive* : (*a*) to be brought to destruction or ruin : P. L. I. 312, 525 ; IX. 784 ; to perish ; *of persons* : P. L. IX. 642 ; XI. 682.

(*b*) to be ruined morally, be damned ; said of Adam or Eve, or of mankind : P. L. III. 150, 173, 223, 280 ; IX. 900, 1165 ; X. 929 ; *dead in sins and lost* : P. L. III.

233 ; *lost in death* : Cir. 18 ; said of Abdiel, who did not sin with the fallen angels ; *returned not lost* : P. L. VI. 25.

(2) to be deprived of ; (*a*) a *place, state, quality,* etc. : P. L. I. 270 ; II. 325 ; III. 206 ; V. 731 ; VIII. 332 ; XI. 288, 347 ; XII. 621 ; P. R. I. 390 ; C. 468 ; *Paradise, heaven* : P. L. I. 316 ; P. R. I. 2, 52 ; *give not heaven for lost* : P. L. II. 14 ; *lose strength* : S. A. 1502 ; *lose brightness, lustre* : P. L. I. 591 ; P. R. I. 377 ; *glory, honour* : P. L. IV. 854 ; S. A. 1103 ; *happiness, good* : P. L. IX. 1072 ; XI. 59, 87 ; *freedom, liberty* : P. L. XI. 798 ; XII. 101 ; *hope, gratitude* : P. R. III. 204 ; IV. 188 ; *virtue* : P. L. II. 483 ; XI. 798 ; P. R. IV. 352.

(*b*) *lose being* : P. L. II. 146 ; *sense* : P. R. I. 382 ; *sight, eyes* : S. A. 914, 927, 1489 ; S. XXII. 10 ; *upright shape* : C. 52.

(*c*) to be deprived of *a person* by death : P. L. IX. 959 ; by separation : P. L. I. 471 ; II. 110 ; III. 280 ; P. R. III. 377.

(*d*) to fail to maintain *resistance, courage* : P. L. VI. 838 ; S. A. 1286 ; *the spell hath lost his hold* : C. 919.

(*e*) to cease to have *pain and woe* : P. L. II. 607 ; *care* : P. L. II. 48 ; *anger* : P. L. X. 945.

(*f*) to part with ; *the air such pleasure loth to lose* : N. O. 90.

(*g*) to allow to go into another's possession ; *lose it* (sceptre) *to a stranger* : P. L. XII. 358.

(*h*) to be deprived of the power of ; with *prep. inf.* : P. R. I. 378.

(*i*) in *passive* without reference to any definite person ; *true liberty is lost* : P. L. XII. 84 ; *virtue given for lost* : S. A. 1697 ; to cease to be present ; *for ever lost from life* : P. L. XII. 429 ; to cease to exist ; *time and place are lost* : P. L. II. 895.

(*j*) *absol.* or *intr.* to suffer loss : P. L. VII. 153 ; *wisdom in discourse with her loses* : P. L. VIII. 553.

(3) to cease to know the whereabouts of *a person* : P. R. II. 97 ; C. 288, 510 ; *an animal* : C. 498.

(*b*) to fail to keep in sight ; *lost sight of* : P. L. IV. 573.

(*c*) to fail to retain in memory ; *their memory be lost* : P. L. XII.

46 ; *name ... be lost in memory* :
Ps. LXXXIII. 16.

(**4**) to spend unprofitably or in
vain ; *labour lose* : P. L. IX. 944 ;
fair event of love and youth not lost :
P. L. XI. 594 ; *ill is lost that
praise* : C. 271 ; to waste *the
prime* : P. L. V. 21.

(**5**) to fail to obtain *revenge* :
P. L. X. 1036 ; *pleasure* : P. L. IX.
1022.

(*b*) to fail to receive *reward* :
P. L. XI. 459 ; P. R. III. 104.

(**6**) to lose in a contest, *fig.* :
P. R. I. 154 ; III. 148 ; to be de-
feated in ; *the field be lost* : P. L.
I. 105 ; *absol.* to be defeated : P.
R. IV. 6.

(**7**) to cause the loss of ; *what
war hath lost* : P. L. X. 374 ; *lost
our hopes* : P. L. I. 637 ; with
dat., hath lost us heaven : P. L. I.
136.

(**8**) *refl.* to lose one's way, go
astray : P. R. II. 98; in *passive* :
P. L. II. 975 ; P. R. II. 416 ; *fig.,
thoughts ... lost* : P. L. II. 149 ; *in
wandering mazes* (of thought) *lost* :
P. L. II. 561.

part. adj. **lost** ; (*a*) ruined
morally : P. L. I. 243.

(*b*) no longer held or possessed ;
lost region, Paradise : P. L. II.
982 ; P. R. IV. 608 ; *shape* : P. L.
X. 574 ; *sight* : S. A. 152 ; *right* :
P. L. II. 231 ; *happiness, bliss,*
etc.: P. L. I. 55 ; P. R. I. 419 ;
to me is lost, has passed from my
possession : P. L. IV. 109 ; IX.
479.

(*c*) not to be found ; *of persons* :
P. R. II. 19 ; C. 350.

See **Self-lost**.

Loss, *sb.* (**1**) ruin, destruction, overthrow : P. L. I. 188, 265, 526,
631 ; II. 21, 330, 770.

(*b*) spiritual ruin ; *utter loss* :
P. L. III. 308 ; IX. 131 ; *must redeem our loss* : N. O. 153.

(**2**) the being deprived of, or
the failure to hold or keep what
one has possessed : P. L. IV. 849;
with *of* : P. L. I. 4 ; *loss of life,
sight,* etc. ; P. L. X. 1019 ; S. A.
67, 644, 1744 ; S. XII. 14 ; *utter
loss of being* : P. L. II. 440.

(*b*) the being deprived of a person by death ; with *of* : P. L. IX.
912 ; preceded by pron. in the
objective genitive : D. F. I. 72 ;
L. 49 ; by separation : P. R. II.

29 ; with *of* : P. L. IV. 904; with
obj. gen. pron. : P. L. VIII. 480 ;
A. 100 ; C. 287 ; L. 49.

(*c*) the being defeated in; *loss
of ... battle* : P. L. IV. 11.

(**3**) failure to obtain : P. L. X.
752.

(**4**) the cause of spiritual ruin :
P. L. VII. 74.

(**5**) diminution of one's possessions : V. Ex. 9 ; T. 7 ; *repair
that loss* : P. L. III. 678.

(**6**) **at a loss**, uncertain what to
say : P. R. IV. 366.

Lot, *sb.* (**1**) the casting of lots ; *by
lot* : C. 20.

(**2**) what falls to a person by
lot ; (*a*) one's turn ; *to thee thy
course by lot hath given* : P. L. IV.
561.

(*b*) that which comes to a person by fate or divine providence,
fortune, destiny : P. L. I. 608 ;
IV. 1011 ; IX. 690, 881, 952 ; P. R.
III. 57 ; S. A. 996 ; S. II. 11 ;
present lot : P. L. II. 223; C. 789;
*lamentable, favoured, happier, un-
fortunate* : P. L. II. 617 ; IV. 446;
P. R. II. 91 ; S. A. 1743 ; *each
day's lot* : P. L. XI. 765 ; *the lot of
other women* : P. R. II. 70 ; *either
of these is in thy lot* : S. A. 1292 ;
as their lot shall lead : P. L. X.
261.

by lot from Jove : A. 44.

Lot, *sb.* the son of Haran and the
nephew of Abraham : Ps. LXXXIII.
32.

Loth. *See* **Loath**.

Loud, (**1**) *adj.* (*a*) strong or powerful
in sound : P. L. II. 921 ; S. A.
1510 ; N. O. 215 ; *loud acclaim,
shout,* etc. : P. L. II. 520 ; III.
346, 348, 397 ; VI. 23 ; X. 455 ;
P. R. II. 235 ; *sup.* : P. R. I. 275;
accompanied by a loud sound ;
loud accident : S. A. 1552 ; *sup.,
loudest vehemence* : P. L. II. 954 ;
expressed with or in a loud sound
or voice ; *loud lamentation* or
lament : P. L. II. 579 ; VIII. 244 ;
N. O. 163 ; *praises, sorrows,
mirth* : S. A. 436 ; P. 55 ; C. 202;
sup., loudest oratory : P. L. XI. 8 ;
singing or crying with a loud
voice ; *loud choir* : N. O. 115 ;
Cerberean mouths full loud : P. L.
II. 655.

(*b*) making a loud sound ; *loud
timbrels, trumpets* : P. L. I. 394,
532 ; VI. 59 ; XII. 229 ; S. M. 11 ;

tempest : P. L. III. 429 ; *Argestes loud* : P. L. X. 699 ; *Humber loud* : V. Ex. 99 ; *loud misrule of chaos* : P. L. VII. 271.

(c) current ; *loud report, rumour* : S. A. 1090 ; S. XV. 4.

(2) *adv.* with a great noise or voice : P. L. I. 314 ; VI. 557, 567 ; X. 641 ; XII. 56 ; P. R. II. 290 ; IV. 488 ; P. 26 ; C. 849 ; S. XVI. 8 ; Ps. LXXXI. 2 ; *ye winds breathe soft or loud* : P. L. V. 193 ; *rocking winds are piping loud* : Il P. 126 ; *deeds ... though mute spoke loud the doer* : S. A. 248 ; *comp.*, *be louder heard* : P. L. X. 954 ; *sup.* : P. R. IV. 339 ; aloud, audibly : P. L. X. 845.

Loudly, *adv.* with a great sound : V. Ex. 24 ; L. 17.

Lour, *vb. intr.* (a) to frown, scowl : S. A. 1057 ; to be expressed by frowning ; *in his look defiance lours* : P. L. IV. 873.

(b) to look dark and threatening ; *sky loured* : P. L. IX. 1002.

part. adj. **louring,** dark and stormy ; *louring night* : P. R. IV. 398 ; dark and threatening ; *louring element* : P. L. II. 490.

Louse, *sb.* the insect *Pediculus* : P. L. XII. 177.

Love, I. *sb.* (1) warm affection, tender attachment : P. L. IV. 465 ; *a father's love* : S. A. 1506.

(b) as an abstract quality ; *the spirit of love* : P. L. VIII. 477 ; *in every gesture dignity and love* : P. L. VIII. 489 ; *love, sweetness, goodness in her person shined* : S. XXIII. 11 ; *love refines the thoughts* : P. L. VIII. 589 ; *rosy-red, love's proper hue* : P. L. VIII. 619.

(2) affection, benevolence, goodwill ; (a) as one of the elements of heaven : P. L. XII. 550 ; L. 177.

(b) the affection and benevolence of God or Christ : P. L. III. 142 ; IV. 68, 69 ; *love divine* : P. L. III. 225 ; *sapience and love immense* : P. L. VII. 195 ; the love of God or Christ towards men : P. L. III. 213, 298 ; V. 502, 515 ; XII. 380 ; S. M. 22 ; Ps. LXXX. 34 ; *immortal love to mortal men* : P. L. III. 267 ; *set on man his equal love* : P. L. VIII. 228 ; *in thee love hath abounded* : P. L. III. 312 ; *unexampled, exceeding love* : P. L. III. 410 ; C. 15, 16 ; *paternal* : P. L. XI. 353.

(c) the affection or devotion of angels towards God or each other : P. L. III. 104 ; *acts of zeal and love* : P. L. V. 593 ; *his love, his zeal* : P. L. V. 900 ; *festivals of joy and love* : P. L. VI. 94 ; the benevolence of angels to men ; *works of love or enmity* : P. L. I. 431 ; *the Tempter ... with show of zeal and love to man* : P. L. IX. 665 ; *show of love well feigned* : P. L. IX. 492.

(d) the affectionate devotion of man to God : P. L. IX. 286, 335 ; X. 111 ; XII. 489 ; *by obedience and love* : P. L. XII. 403 ; *heavenly love, such love as heavenly beings feel* : P. L. VIII. 592.

(e) the affection of man to man as prompted by religion ; *add love, by name to come called charity, the soul of all the rest* : P. L. XII. 583.

(f) *personified ; Faith and Love* : S. XIV. 1, 9 ; *Truth and Peace and Love* : T. 16 ; possibly also ; *Joy and Love* : P. L. III. 338.

(3) liking, devotion ; *the love of sacred song* : P. L. III. 29.

(4) the affection between the sexes, usually as the basis of marriage : P. L. IV. 499 ; VIII. 569, 589 ; IX. 241, 822, 991, 1163 ; X. 153, 973 ; XI. 588, 594 ; S. A. 790, 810, 813, 836, 837, 838, 863, 873, 923, 1005 ; Il P. 108 ; *woman's love* : S. A. 1012 ; *mutual love* : P. L. IV. 728 ; *equal joy as equal love* : P. L. IX. 882 ; *connubial, wedded*, etc. : P. L. IV. 743, 750 ; IX. 263, 319 ; S. A. 385 ; *cordial, tender*, etc. : P. L. V. 12 ; IX. 357, 983 ; X. 915 ; *unlibidinous* : P. L. V. 449 ; *love's embraces* : P. L. IV. 322 ; *love and spousal embraces* : S. A. 388 ; *love's due rites* : P. L. X. 994 ; *love's law* : S. A. 811 ; *love's prisoner* : S. A. 808 ; *linked in love* : P. L. IX. 970 ; *glorious or happy trial of love* : P. L. IX. 961, 975 ; *agony of, jealousy of love* : P. L. IX. 858 ; S. A. 791 ; *terror be in love* : P. L. IX. 490 ; *success in love* : S. I. 7 ; *offices of love* : P. L. X. 960 ; *joy and love* : P. L. III. 67, 68 ; *love and mutual honour* : P. L. VIII. 58 ; *collateral love and dearest amity* : P. L. VIII. 426 ; *love and sweet compliance* : P. L. VIII. 602 ; *firm faith and love* : P. L. IX. 286 ;

sweet converse and love : P. L. IX.
909 ; *smiles ... are of love the food* :
P. L. IX. 240 ; a similar emotion
aroused in Satan at the sight of
Eve : P. L. IX. 475 ; used in the
same connection of, the tender
attachment between angels : P.
L. VIII. 615 ; *without love no happiness* : P. L. VIII. 621 ; *hell ...
where neither joy nor love* : P. L.
IV. 509.

(**5**) the god of love, Cupid : C.
124 ; S. I. 13 ; *here Love his golden
shafts employs* : P. L. IV. 763 ; or,
possibly, Venus : P. L. XI. 589.

(**6**) the gratification of sexual
passion : P. L. IX. 1042.

(**7**) an object of tender attachment ; *she ... fit love for gods* : P.
L. IX. 489 ; sweetheart : N. O. 91.

II. *vb.* (*pres. 2d sing.* lov'st :
P. L. VI. 733 ; lovèd, *disyl.* : Ps.
LXXX. 4) *tr.* (**1**) to regard with
warm affection, hold dear : S. A.
939 ; C. 623 ; Ps. LXXXVIII. 71 ;
used of Satan in reference to
man : P. L. IV. 363.

(*b*) to regard with affectionate
reverence ; used of the sentiment
of angels or men towards God :
P. L. V. 550 ; VIII. 634 ; Ps. V.
36 ; *absol.* : P. L. V. 539, 540.

(*c*) to have affection and bene-
volence for ; used of the senti-
ment of God towards man : P. L.
III. 151 ; VI. 733 ; XII. 562 ; Ps.
LXXXI. 47 ; *Sion's fair gates the
Lord loves* : Ps. LXXXVII. 5.

(*d*) with reference to love between the sexes : P. L. VIII. 577,
587 ; IX. 832 ; S. A. 878.

(*e*) *absol. or intr.* : P. L. VIII. 612 ;
IX. 271 ; X. 903, 993 ; to regard
each other with warm affection :
P. L. VIII. 633 ; used in this
connection of angels ; *love not the
heavenly spirits* : P. L. VIII. 615.

(**3**) to be strongly attached to ;
love thy life : P. L. XI. 553 ; *love
nothing* : S. A. 1033 ; *groves ...
that Sylvan loves* : Il P. 134 ; or,
to delight in ; *love the high embowed roof* : Il P. 157 ; to be
unwilling to part with : C. 473.

(**4**) to take pleasure in ; *love
virtue*, etc. : P. R. I. 380 ; C.
1019 ; *courage, liberty* : C. 610 ;
S. XII. 12 ; *vice, vanity* : P. L. I.
491 ; Ps. IV. 10, 11 ; *pain,
bondage* : P. L. IV. 888 ; S. A.
270 ; *love the just* : Ps. LXXXVI. 4 ;

maidenhood she (Sabrina) *loves* :
C. 856 ; *thou, fair moon, that
wont'st to love the traveller's benison* : C. 332.

(**5**) to have great pleasure in
doing ; with *prep. inf.* : P. L. VII.
330 ; L'A. 30 ; L. 36.

part. adj. **loved** ; (*a*) regarded
with warm affection : C. 501 ; L.
51.

(*b*) regarded by God with affection and benevolence : Ps. LXXX. 4.

(*c*) greatly enjoyed, delighted
in : P. L. IX. 1007.

vbl. sb. **loving**, affectionate devotion : P. L. VIII. 588.

See **Dearly-loved, Heaven-loved,
Moon-loved, Self-love.**

Love-darting, *adj.* shooting glances
indicative of or inspiring love : C.
753.

Love-laboured, *adj.* burdened with
a tale of love : P. L. V. 41.

Loveless, *adj.* without affection : P.
L. IV. 766.

Loveliness, *sb.* the quality of exciting love, beauty and charm : P.
L. VIII. 547.

Love-lorn, *adj.* pining from love : C.
234.

Lovely, (**1**) *adj.* beautiful, charming,
attractive ; (*a*) used of persons or
animals : M. W. 24 ; *lovely Venus* :
L'A. 14 ; *Leucothea's lovely hands* :
C. 875 ; *of Eve* : P. L. IX. 714,
848 ; X. 152 ; *pleasing was his* (the
serpent's) *shape and lovely* : P. L.
IX. 504 ; *comp.* : P. L. IX. 505 ;
sup. : P. L. IV. 321.

(*b*) used of things ; *lovely landscape* : P. L. IV. 152 ; *earth* : P.
L. VII. 502 ; *dye* : D. F. I. 5.

(*c*) with reference to moral
beauty, *comp.* : P. L. IX. 232.

(**2**) *adv.* beautifully, attrac-
tively ; *lovely fair* : P. L. V. 380 ;
VIII. 471 ; *sup., build in her loveliest* : P. L. VIII. 558.

Love-quarrel, *sb.* contention of those
in love : S. A. 1008.

Lover, *sb.* (*a*) one who loves or is
kindly disposed towards another :
Ps. LXXXVIII. 69.

(*b*) one who is in love ; used
only of the man : P. L. IV. 769 ;
v. 450 ; M. W. 16 ; S. I. 3.

(*c*) one who has affection for ;
lovers of their country : P. R. IV.
355.

Love-tale, *sb.* story of tender attachment : P. L. I. 452.

Loving-kindness, *sb.* the loving care of God for his people: Ps. LXXXVIII. 45.

Low, I. *adj.* (1) of small extent upward; *low cottage*: P. R. II. 28; C. 319.

(2) being below some recognized level, deep: L. 136; *now high, now low*: P. L. VIII. 126.

comp.: P. L. IV. 76; *lower clime, world*: P. L. VII. 18; XI. 283; *lower stair*, the bottom of the stairs: P. L. III. 540; *lower flight*, used *fig.* of thought: P. L. VIII. 199.

sup.: P. L. II. 392; IV. 76; v. 418; *lowest bottom*, the lowest part of the bottom: P. L. II. 822.

(b) near the horizon: P. L. x. 92, 682.

(c) said of a bow; *low subjection*: P. L. VIII. 345; *reverence*: P. L. IX. 835; A. 37.

(3) of humble station, rank, or position: P. L. IV. 525; IX. 704; *low of parentage*: P. R. I. 235; *low of birth*: P. R. II. 413; *low ... state*: S. A. 338; wretched, miserable: Ps. LXXXII. 15.

sup. angel ... of lowest order: P. L. x. 443; *the lowest of your throng*: P. L. IV. 831; with blending of sense (2): P. L. v. 158.

(4) of inferior character, commonplace, mean: P. L. I. 23; used of the world in contrast to heaven, perhaps also with the idea of local situation: A. 71.

comp. lower faculty of sense: P. L. v. 410.

sup. lowest end of human life: P. L. IX. 241.

(5) abject, base: P. L. I. 114; *his thoughts were low*: P. L. II. 115; *abject thoughts and low*: P. L. IX. 572.

(6) dejected, dispirited: Ps. LXXXVIII. 61.

(7) *comp.* less proud and haughty: S. A. 1246.

(8) *sup.* the minimum in amount or degree; *lowest poverty*: P. R. II. 438; *lowest pitch of abject fortune*: S. A. 169.

(9) relatively grave in pitch, opposed to *high*: P. L. XI. 562.

(10) with vbs.; *bring low*: Ps. II. 19; *lay low*: P. L. I. 137; S. A. 1239; Ps. LXXX. 49; *throw low*: S. A. 689. *See the verbs.*

II. *adv.* (1) to a point or position below some recognized level: P. L. II. 81; *bow low*: P. L. III. 736; v. 360; XI. 249; P. R. I. 497; Ps. LXXXVI. 31; *fig.*: P. L. I. 435; *cowering low*: P. L. VIII. 350; *worship low*: Ps. v. 20.

comp. fig. to a lower level in thought: P. L. VII. 84.

(b) beneath the level of the earth's surface; *so high ... so low*: P. L. VII. 288.

(c) beneath the waters of the sea: L. 102; opposed to *high*: L. 172.

(2) to a low station, rank, or position; opposed to *high*: P. L. IX. 169.

comp. to a condition of wretchedness and misery; *the lower still I fall*: P. L. IV. 91; to a condition of dishonour or disgrace: S. A. 38.

(3) to a degraded condition morally: P. L. XII. 97.

Low-browed, *adj.* close overhanging: L'A. 8.

Low-creeping, *adj.* creeping on the ground: P. L. IX. 180.

Low-delved (delvèd, *disyl.*), *adj.* deeply dug: D. F. I. 32.

Lower. *See* **Lour.**

Lowing, *vbl. sb.* the bellowing cry of cattle: N. O. 215.

Lowliness, *sb.* freedom from pride, humility: P. L. VIII. 42.

Lowly, (1) *adj.* (a) humble; *lowly plight*: P. L. x. 937; *sup.*: P. L. XI. 1.

(b) poor, unpretending; *lowly roof*: P. L. v. 463; *sheds*: C. 323.

(2) *adv.* humbly: P. L. VIII. 173, 412; humbly and reverently: N. O. 25; with blending of the sense, on or near to the ground; *bow lowly*: P. L. I. 434; III. 349; v. 144; *stately tread or lowly creep*: P. L. v. 201.

Low-roofed, *adj.* having a low roof: P. R. IV. 273; *fig.*: P. 18.

Low-roosted, *adj.* having a resting-place on the ground: C. 317.

Low-thoughted, *adj.* having the thoughts fixed upon mean and unworthy things: C. 6.

Loyal, *adj.* characterized by fidelity: P. L. IV. 755; *loyal cottage*: C. 320.

Loyalty, *sb.* faithful adherence to a sovereign: P. L. v. 900.

Lubbar, *sb. attrib.* one who drudges : L'A. 110.

Lucent, *adj.* shining, luminous : P. L. III. 589.

Lucid, *adj.* (*a*) bright, shining : P. L. XI. 240.

(*b*) clear, transparent : P. L. I. 469.

Lucifer, *sb.* (*a*) the morning star : N. O. 74. *See* Star.

(*b*) Satan (cf. Isaiah XIV. 12) : P. L. v 760 ; VII. 131 ; X. 425.

Lucina, *sb.* the Latin name of the goddess who assisted women in childbirth : M. W. 26, 28.

Luck, *sb.* fortune ; *good luck befriend thee* : V. Ex. 59. *See* Ill-luck.

Lucky, *adj.* presaging or bringing good luck : L. 20.

Lucre, *sb.* gain : P. L. XII. 511.

Lucrine, *sb. Lucrine bay,* a small salt-water lake near Baiæ, Italy. It was celebrated for its oysters : P. R. II. 347.

Luggage, *sb.* baggage of an army ; *luggage of war* : P. R. III. 401.

Lull, *vb. tr.* to compose to sleep or rest by pleasing sounds : P. L. II. 287 ; *there lulled by nightingales* : P. L. IV. 771 ; *by whispering winds soon lulled asleep* : L'A. 116 ; *in pleasing slumber lull the sense* : C. 260 ; *music ... to lull the daughters of Necessity* : A. 69 ; *peace shall lull him in her flowery lap* : V. Ex. 84.

Luminary, *sb.* the sun or other heavenly body ; *the great luminary* : P. L. III. 576 ; *bright luminaries* : P. L. VII. 385 ; VIII. 98.

Luminous, *adj.* (*a*) emitting light : P. L. III. 420

(*b*) lighted, illuminated : P. L. VIII. 140.

Lure, (1) *sb.* enticement, temptation : P. R. II. 194.

(**2**) *vb. tr.* to attract ; *lure her eye* : P. L. IX. 518 ; to allure, entice ; *lured with the smell* : P. L. II. 664 ; *lured with scent* : P. L. X. 276.

Lurk *vb.* (*pres. 2d sing.* lurk'st : P. R. II. 183) *intr.* (*a*) to lie in ambush : P. L. IV. 587 ; P. R. II. 183.

(*b*) *fig.* to be concealed ; *wherever danger or dishonour lurks* : P. L. IX. 267.

part. adj. **lurking,** lying in wait : P. L. IX. 1172.

Luscious, *adj.* sweet and pleasant to the taste : C. 652.

Lust, *sb.* (*a*) desire of money, eagerness for gain : P. R. IV. 137.

(*b*) sexual appetite or its unlawful gratification : P. L. I. 417, 496 ; II. 791 ; IV. 753 ; IX. 1015 ; XI. 795 ; S. A. 837 ; C. 463 ; *pl.* : P. R. IV. 94.

Lustful, *adj.* marked by or full of sensual desire or its gratification : P. L. I. 415 ; XI. 619.

Lustre, *sb.* brightness, splendour : P. L. I. 97 ; II. 271 ; IV. 850 ; A. 76 ; *golden lustre* : P. L. I. 538 ; *regal lustre* : P. L. X. 447 ; *every stone of lustre from the brook* : P. L. XI. 325 ; *I have lost much lustre of my native brightness* : P. R. I. 378.

Lusty, *adj.* (*a*) full of life and spirits (?) : N. O. 36.

(*b*) lustful : P. R. II. 178.

Lute, *sb.* the stringed musical instrument : S. XX. 11 ; *lute or harp* : P. L. v. 151 ; *softer strings of lute or viol* : P. 28 ; *Apollo's lute* : C. 478.

Luxuriant, *adj.* growing profusely, exuberant : P. L. IV. 260.

Luxurious, *adj.* (*a*) given to luxury, voluptuous : P. L. I. 498 ; P. R. III. 297 ; IV. 141.

(*b*) characterized by a display of luxury ; *luxurious wealth* : P. L. XI. 788.

(*c*) growing profusely, exuberant : P. L. IX. 209.

Luxury, *sb.* extravagant indulgence in that which is choice or costly : P. L. I. 722 ; XI. 715, 751 ; P. R. IV. 111 ; *personified* : C. 770.

Luz, *sb.* an old name of Bethel, the town in Palestine : P. L. III. 513.

Lycæus, *sb.* a mountain in the southwestern part of Arcadia, one of haunts of Pan and the nymphs : A. 98.

Lyceum, *sb.* the gymnasium outside of Athens where Aristotle taught his philosophy : P. R. IV. 253.

Lycid, *sb.* Lycidas : L. 151.

Lycidas, *sb.* the name of a shepherd, common in pastoral poetry ; here used of Edward King : L. 8, 9, 10, 49, 51, 166, 172, 182.

Lydian, *adj.* characteristic of Lydia : L'A. 136.

Lyones, *sb.* according to tradition, the land, now submerged, between Cornwall and the Scilly

Isles. "The neighbours will tell you too, from a certain old tradition, that the land there drown'd by the incursions of the sea was call'd Lionesse." *Cam. Brit.*, 1722, vol. i. p. 11 : P. R. II. 360.

Lyre, *sb.* the stringed musical instrument ; *Orphean lyre* : P. L. III. 17.

Lyric, *adj.* meant to be sung ; *lyric odes, song* : P. R. IV. 257 ; S. A. 1737.

M

Mab, *sb.* the queen of the fairies : L'A. 102.

Macdonnel, *sb.* a name, probably that of Alexander Macdonald, a Scottish officer who served under Montrose. He was called also 'Young Colkitto' and 'Macgillespie,' from the names of his father and grandfather : S. XI. 9.

Mace, *sb.* a heavy club ; *Neptune's mace* : C. 869 ; *death with his mace petrific* : P. L. X. 294.

Macedon, *sb.* the kingdom of Alexander the Great : P. R. IV. 271.

Macedonian, *adj.* of Macedonia : P. R. III. 32.

Machabeus, *sb.* Judas Maccabeus, a leader of the Jewish nation in the war against Antiochus Epiphanes, King of Syria : P. R. III. 165.

Machærus, *sb.* a castle and fortified place in the mountainous district east of the Dead Sea : P. R. II. 22.

Machination, *sb.* intrigue, plot ; *devilish machination* : P. L. VI. 504 ; P. R. I. 181.

Mad, *adj.* (*a*) arising from frenzy, insane : S. A. 1677.

(*b*) acting rashly and without reflection : Ps. V. 12.

(*c*) proceeding from or indicating rage, prompted by fury : P. L. IV. 129; P. R. IV. 446 ; C. 829.

Madam, *sb.* formal term of address to a lady of rank : S. X. 11.

Madding, *part. adj.* moving furiously; *madding wheels* : P. L. VI. 210.

Madian (so spelled in Vulgate), *sb.* the Midianites : S. A. 281.

Madness, *sb.* (*a*) insanity, derangement of mind : P. L. XI. 486.

(*b*) extreme folly : S. A. 553.

(*c*) wild or intense emotion : C. 261.

Madrigal, *sb.* pastoral song : C. 495.

Mæander. *See* **Meander.**

Mænalus, *sb.* Mount Mænalus in the southeastern part of Arcadia, one of the haunts of Pan and the nymphs : A. 102.

Mæonides, *sb.* a surname of Homer, given him because he was believed to have been a native of Mæonia, or Lydia, or, according to others, because he was a son of Mæon : P. L. III. 35.

Mæotis, *sb.* Pool *Mæotis*, Mæotis Palus, the Sea of Azof : P. L. IX. 78.

Magazine, *sb.* warehouse for military stores : P. L. IV. 816 ; S. A. 1281.

Magellan, *sb.* the Strait of Magellan : P. L. X. 687.

Magic, *sb.* (*a*) enchantment, sorcery : P. L. I. 727.

(*b*) having the power of enchanting ; *magic dust* : C. 165.

(*c*) produced by enchantment ; *magic spells* : S. A. 1149; *chains* : C. 435; *structures* : C. 798.

Magician, *sb.* sorcerer : S. A. 1133 ; C. 602.

Magistrate, *sb.* civil officer : S. A. 850, 1183.

Magnanimity, *sb.* superiority to petty resentment : S. A. 1470.

Magnanimous, *adj.* noble in feeling or conduct, high-minded : P. L. VII. 511 ; P. R. II. 483 ; nobly ambitious; *magnanimous thoughts* : S. A. 524.

Magnetic, (1) *adj.* having the properties of the magnet ; *they* (the constellations) *turn swift their various motions or are turned by his* (the sun's) *magnetic beam* : P. L. III. 583.

(2) *sb.* magnet, loadstone : P. R. II. 168.

Magnific, *adj.* (*a*) great, glorious ; *magnific deeds* : P. L. X. 354.

(*b*) highly honorific ; *magnific titles* : P. L. V. 773.

Magnificence, *adj.* (*a*) greatness, glory : P. L. VIII. 101.

(*b*) splendour of appointments : P. R. IV. 111.

(*c*) grandeur of appearance : P. L. I. 718 ; or that which is grand in appearance : P. L. II. 273.

Magnificent, *adj.* (*a*) vast and glorious : P. L. VII. 568 ; IX. 153.

(*b*) splendidly adorned : P. L. III. 502.

Magnify, vb. tr. to extol, glorify; thee that day thy thunders magnified : P. L. VII. 606; so Dagon shall be magnified : S. A. 440; the more to magnify his works : P. L. VII. 97.

Magnitude, sb. (a) greatness; magnitude of mind : S. A. 1279.

(b) size, dimensions : P. L. II. 1053; VIII. 17; every magnitude of stars : P. L. VII. 357.

Mahanaim, sb. a city east of the river Jordan : P. L. XI. 214.

Maia, sb. the daughter of Atlas and the mother of Hermes by Zeus : P. L. V. 285.

Maid, sb. young unmarried woman : L'A. 95; the fair Iberian maid : P. R. II. 200; Tyrian maids : N. O. 204; Sara, the daughter of Raguel : P. L. V. 223; that just maid, Astræa, the goddess of justice : D. F. I. 56; the Virgin Mary; of wedded maid and virgin mother born : N. O. 3.

Maiden, (1) sb. maid : V. Ex. 96; C. 402.

(2) adj. pertaining to or befitting a maid : C. 843; maiden white : N. O. 42.

Maidenhood, sb. virginity : C. 855.

Mail, sb. armor composed of metal chains, rings, or plates; plate and mail : P. L. VI. 368; coats of mail : P. R. III. 312; frock of mail : S. A. 133; in mail their horses clad : P. R. III. 313.

fig. feathered mail : P. L. V. 284.

Maim, vb. tr. to cripple, mutilate : P. L. I. 459; to disable; by his blindness maimed for high attempts : S. A. 1221.

Main, (1) sb. (a) the physical universe : P. R. IV. 457; the whole continent of heaven : P. L. VI. 698.

(b) ocean, sea : C. 28; Ps. CXXXVI. 46.

(c) the broad expanse of chaos : P. L. X. 257.

(2) adj. (a) strong, mighty, powerful; main pillars : S. A. 1606; main wing : P. L. VI. 243; to the arched roof gave main support : S. A. 1634; war ... move by her two main nerves, iron and gold : S. XVII. 8; sin and death, his two main arms : P. L. XII. 431.

(b) sheer; main force : S. A. 146.

(c) great in numbers; both battles main : P. L. VI. 216.

(d) great in size, vast : P. L. VI. 654; or in sense (e); four main streams : P. L. IV. 233.

(e) used of a great stretch of water or space; the main abyss, chaos : P. L. III. 83; over all the face of earth main ocean flowed : P. L. VII. 279.

(f) of great weight, important, momentous : P. R. I. 112; so main to our success : P. L. VI. 471.

(g) first in importance, chief : P. L. II. 121.

Mainly, adv. chiefly, principally : P. L. XI. 519.

Maintain, vb. tr. to give support to, defend : P. L. VI. 30.

Majestic, adj. of imposing dignity or grandeur : P. L. II. 305; lowliness majestic : P. L. VIII. 42; majestic brow, pace : P. R. II. 216; C. 870.

used of things; majestic...style : P. R. IV. 359; majestic show of luxury : P. R. IV. 110; flowing with majestic train : Il P. 34.

Majesty, sb. (1) the greatness of a sovereign; blaze of majesty : A. 2.

(b) the greatness and glory of God; majesty divine : P. L. VI. 101; VII. 195; Ps. CXXXVI. 90; blaze of majesty : N. O. 9; bosom bright of blazing Majesty : M. W. 70.

(2) the magnificence befitting a sovereign; the majesty of darkness : P. L. II. 266.

(3) exalted dignity of look or appearance : P. L. IV. 290; XI. 232; C. 430; obsequious majesty : P. L. VIII. 509; virgin : P. R. II. 159; concr., the virgin majesty of Eve ... replied : P. L. IX. 270; transf., the moon rising in clouded majesty : P. L. IV. 607.

Make, vb. (pres. 2d sing. mak'st : Ps. LXXX. 25; pret. mad'st : P. L. I. 22; IV. 724; X. 137; V. Ex. 3; past part. made) tr. (1) to construct; made of oak : P. L. VI. 574; made of sphere-metal : U. C. II. 5.

(2) to create; said of God : P. L. I. 370; III. 155; IV. 413, 722, 724; V. 836; VII. 263, 336, 346, 348, 548; VIII. 409, 544, 555; IX. 138, 152; X. 760; Ps. LXXXVI. 29.

(b) with two acc. : P. L. VII. 515; was she made thy guide : P.

L. x. 146; the compl. an *adj.*:
God made thee ... his own: P. L.
x. 766; *I made him just and right*,
P. L. III. 98; *God made thee perfect*: P. L. v. 524, 525; *reason he
made right*: P. L. IX. 352; *who
made thee what thou art*: P. L. v.
823.

in *passive*: P. L. III. 110; VII.
361; *made so adorn*: P. L. VIII.
576; *dependent made*: P. L. IX.
943.

(*c*) with phrase denoting form;
let us make man in our image: P.
L. VII. 519.

(*d*) with the purpose expressed
by *prep. inf.*: P. L. x. 137, 766;
S. A. 56, 309; expressed by *for*:
P. L. III. 164; IX. 132; x. 149;
P. R. III. 111; Ps. VII. 49; *for*
omitted: P. L. II. 207; expressed
by *to*; *to delight he made us*: P.
L. IX. 243; by the *dat.*; *command
that out of these hard stones be made
thee bread*: P. R. I. 343.

(*e*) to be fitted or destined; *his
fatal dart, made to destroy*: P. L.
II. 787; *the tongue not made for
speech*: P. L. IX. 749.

(**3**) to cause to exist by some
action: C. 654, 846; *in the air
made horrid circles*: P. L. VI.
305; *murmurs made to bless*: A.
60; *music ... made*: N. O. 118;
S. M. 21.

(**4**) to produce, bring about;
makes wild work in heaven: P. L.
VI. 697; *makes a bloody fray*: P.
L. XI. 651.

(*b*) with *dat.*, *make them mirth
or sport*: P. L. IV. 346; S. A.
1328.

(*c*) *made way*: P. L. IX. 550;
S. A. 481. See **Way.**

(**5**) to give rise to, be the cause
of: P. L. VI. 7; *'tis only daylight
makes sin*: C. 126; *what between us
made the odds*: P. L. VI. 441.

(**6**) to cause persons to become:
U. C. II. 20.

(**7**) used with *of*, to designate
the action of changing what is the
object of the prep. into what is
the object of the vb.; *make a
heaven of hell*: P. L. I. 255; *make
gods of men*: P. L. v. 70; *makes
one blot of all the air*: C. 133.

(**8**) to cause to be or become;
with two *acc.*; (*a*) the compl. a
sb.: P. L. I. 403; x. 166, 391;
XII. 167; P. R. I. 208; IV. 129;

S. A. 425, 1289, 1622; D. F. I.
66; V. Ex. 76; W. S. 14; C.
1008; *make them gods*: P. L. IX.
866; *make him your thrall*: P. L.
x. 402; *make me traitor*: S. A.
401; *man over men he made not
lord*: P. L. XII. 70; *made me here
thy substitute*: P. L. VIII. 381; *his
throne now made a sty*: P. R. IV.
101; *a strife thou mak'st us*: Ps.
LXXX. 25; *my couch I make a kind
of sea*: Ps. VI. 12.

in *passive*: P. L. XI. 44; P. R.
IV. 133; *made goddess*: C. 842;
made flesh: P. L. III. 284.

(*b*) the compl. an *adj.*: P. L. I.
248, 258; v. 599; VI. 458; VII.
318; VIII. 484; x. 319, 611; P.
R. III. 363; IV. 145, 362; U. C.
II. 24; Ps. LXXX. 34, 64, 72;
LXXXVIII. 34; *make us less*: P. L.
v. 829; *make thee memorable*: S.
A. 956; *makes guilty all his sons*:
P. L. III. 290; *make others such
as I*: P. L. IX. 127; *make ease,
easy*; P. L. IV. 329; *make deathless death*: P. L. x. 798; *mad'st
it pregnant*: P. L. I. 22; *made
fast the door*: P. L. XI. 737; *made
void all his wiles*: P. R. III. 442;
made arms ridiculous: S. A. 131.

in *passive*: P. L. III. 386; v.
204, 842; x. 485, 638; P. R. III.
77, 94; S. A. 106, 1489; C. 463;
made common: P. L. VIII. 583;
IX. 931; *made apter to receive*: P.
L. IV. 672.

(*c*) the compl. **a** *part.*; *make
known my change*: P. L. IX. 817;
*make known ... wherein consisted
all my strength*: S. A. 778.

(*d*) the compl. a phrase; *make
them as a wheel*: Ps. LXXXIII. 48.

(*e*) absol. *this fruit divine .. of
virtue to make wise*: P. L. IX.
778; *ourselves ... to free ... let us
make short*: P. L. x. 1000.

(**9**) to cause, constrain, induce;
(*a*) with simple *inf.*: P. L. IX.
1049; XI. 4, 846; P. R. I. 223;
II. 170, 171; D. F. I. 4; V. Ex.
3, 31; S. XI. 11; Ps. IV. 42;
CXIV. 18; *make the worse appear
the better reason*: P. L. II. 113;
make appear their vigilance: P. L.
x. 29; *make death live*: P. L. x.
1028; *made hell grant what love
did seek*: II P. 108; *make intricate seem straight*: P. L. IX. 632;
make rejoice thy servant's soul: Ps.
LXXXVI. 10.

(b) with *prep. inf.*: Ps. VIII.
15; *make ... heaven and earth to
shake*: Ps. CXXXVI. 13; *make
noise to be heard*: C. 227; *make
thy name to live*: D. F. I. 77.

(10) joined to a sb., with which
it forms an expression approximately equivalent in sense to the
corresponding vb.; *make account
of*: P. R. II. 193; *address*: S. A.
731; *amends*: P. L. VIII. 491;
answer: P. L. V. 735; P. R. III.
442; *biding*: Ps. V. 11; *chime*:
P. L. XI. 559; *choice*: S. A. 555;
contradiction: P. L. X. 798; *a
covenant*: P. L. XI. 892; *defence*:
S. A. 560; *a grant*: Ps. II. 16;
halt: P. L. XI. 210; *haste*: P. L.
X. 29; *massacre*: P. L. XI. 680;
neglect: V. Ex. 16; *offers*: P. R.
IV. 155; *promise*: P. L. II. 238;
reckoning: C. 642; L. 116; *relation*: C. 617; *request*: P. L. V.
561; *roar*: L. 61; *a scorn or
gaze of*; P. L. VI. 632; S. A. 34;
speed: P. L. IV. 928; *vows*: P.
L. IV. 97.

In combination with other words;
(a) **make for**, be favourable to:
S. A. 803.

(b) **make a game of**, turn into
ridicule, jest at: S. A. 1331.

(c) **make head against**: P. L.
II. 992. *See* Head.

(d) **make up**, complete: N. O.
132.

vbl. sb. **making**, creation; *their,
thy making*: P. L. III. 113; V. 858.
See Happy-making, New-made.

Maker, *sb.* creator; always of God;
preceded by *def. art.* or *poss.
pron.*: P. L. I. 486; II. 915; III.
113, 676; IV. 292, 380, 748; V.
148, 184, 551, 858; VII. 116;
VIII. 101, 380, 485; IX. 177, 338,
538; X. 43; XI. 514, 515, 611;
N. O. 43; S. XIX. 5; *some great
Maker*: P. L. VIII. 278; *vocative*:
P. L. IV. 725; X. 743.

Malabar, *sb.* the extreme southwestern province of India; Heylyn, *Cos.* 1657, p. 891: P. L. IX.
1103.

Malady, *sb.* disease: P. L. XI. 480;
S. A. 608.

Malcontent. *See* Malecontent.

Male, (1) *adj.* belonging to the sex
that begets offspring: P. L. I.
422; VII. 529; applied *fig.* to
light to denote greatness or brightness: P. L. VIII. 150.

(2) *sb.* one of the male sex;
infant males: P. L. XII. 168.

Malecontent, *adj.* dissatisfied, discontented: P. R. II. 392.

Malediction, *sb.* the utterance of a
curse: S. A. 978.

Malice, *sb.* (a) active ill-will or
hatred: P. L. I. 217; III. 400;
VI. 502; IX. 55, 306; P. R. I.
149, 424; S. A. 821; *deep malice*:
P. L. IV. 123; V. 666; *threats of
malice*: C. 587; *his good ...
wrought but malice*: P. L. IV. 49;
shall he fulfil his malice: P. L.
III. 158; *how hast thou instilled
thy malice*: P. L. VI. 270; *over-
awed his malice*: P. L. IX. 461.

(b) a malicious device;* *so deep
a malice*: P. L. II. 382.

Malicious, *adv.* (a) harboring malice:
P. L. IX. 253.

(b) proceeding from malice: S.
A. 1251.

Malign, *adj.* (a) malicious; *spirit
malign*: P. L. III. 553; VII. 189.

(b) of evil influence; *two planets,
rushing from aspect malign*: P. L.
VI. 313.

Malignant, *adj.* (a) malign; *taught
the fixed* (stars) *their influence
malignant*: P. L. X. 662.

(b) showing extreme enmity;
the world ... to good malignant:
P. L. XII. 538.

Mammon, *sb.* one of the fallen
angels: P. L. I. 678; II. 228, 291.

*****Man**, *sb.* (1) a human being; with-
out the *art.*: P. L. VII. 155; VIII.
250; X. 823; *man to till the
ground none was*: P. L. VII. 332;
to mould me man: P. L. X. 744;
Redeemer ... destined man himself:
P. L. X. 62; *mere man*: P. R. IV.
535; *mortal men*: P. L. I. 51; S.
A. 1682; *man's frail life*: S. A.
656; *race of men*: P. L. VII. 156;
sons of men: P. R. I. 167; *cities
of, seats of*: P. R. II. 470; IV.
30; *track of, road of*: P. R. I.
191, 322; *affairs of, ways of*: P.
R. IV. 462; S. A. 1407; *hum of*:
L'A. 118; *sinfulness of*: P. L. XI.
360.

(b) applied to Christ; *be thyself man among men*: P. L. III.
283; *both God and man*: P. L.
III. 316; *man ... shall satisfy for
man*: P. L. III. 294; *if he be man*:
P. R. II. 136.

(c) applied to Adam and Eve,
usually as representing mankind;

difficult to distinguish from (2), where perhaps some of the following belong: P. L. III. 90, 232; IV. 113; VIII. 228; IX. 152; *when man fell*: P. L. II. 1023; *to judge man fallen*: P. L. X. 62; *man's mortal crime*: P. L. III. 215; *man ... shall find grace*: P. L. III. 131; *earth, the seat of man*: P. L. III. 724; *man, God's latest image*: P. L. IV. 566; *the ways of God with man*: P. L. VIII. 226; *this man of clay*: P. L. IX. 176; *man, sole lord of all*: P. L. X. 401; apparently also in *pl.*: P. L. VII. 625; Adam alone: P. L. VIII. 416; *first man*: P. L. VIII. 297; *one man*: P. R. I. 2.

(d) in combination or contrast with *God, the gods, angels*, etc.: P. L. II. 496; V. 493; XI. 239; *God and man*: P. L. IV. 660; IX. 291; *God or man*: P. L. V. 60, 117; *men and angels*: P. L. III. 331; *gods and men*: S. A. 545; C. 445; A. 67; *to make gods of men*: P. L. V. 70; *tongue of seraph ... heart of man*: P. L. VII. 114; *dialect of, years of, secrets of*: P. L. V. 761; P. R. I. 48; S. A. 492; in combination or contrast with *beast*, etc.: P. L. IV. 177; XII. 30; *the cheerful haunt of men and herds*: C. 388.

(e) person; *all men*: P. L. III. 287; P. R. III. 355; S. A. 354; *each man*: P. R. I. 402; II. 462; *every man*: C. 768; *most men*: P. R. I. 482; *no man*: P. L. XI. 770; P. R. IV. 471; S. A. 299.

(2) human beings collectively, mankind; without the *art.*: P. L. III. 294; VII. 347; VIII. 103; X. 607; XI. 161; *new race called man*: P. L. II. 348; *since created man*: P. L. I. 573; *since man on earth*: S. A. 165; *foe to God and man*: P. L. IV. 749; *the image of God in man*: P. L. XI. 508; *man's effeminate slackness*: P. L. XI. 634; *long-wandered man*: P. L. XII. 313; *man lives not by bread only*: P. R. I. 349.

(b) in combination or contrast ·with *beast*, etc.: P. L. IV. 177; XI. 733, 822, 895; *man, beast, plant*: P. R. IV. 461; *man or worm*: S. A. 74.

(3) *the inner man*, the mind or soul: P. R. II. 477.

(4) an adult male person: P. L.

II. 288; XI. 680; P. R. II. 447; S. A. 1186; *mortal man*: P. R. I. 234; *the just man*: P. R. III. 62.

(b) a particular man or men; *a man*: P. R. II. 298; S. A. 1224; *the man*: S. A. 340; *one man*: P. L. XI. 219; *that meek man*: P. L. XI. 451; *that just man*: P. L. XI. 681; *one faithful man*: P. L. XII. 113; *that old man*: S. X. 8; *the first man*: P. R. I. 154; Christ: P. R. I. 122, 140; *one greater man*: P. L. I. 4; *this perfect man*: P. R. I. 166.

(c) with special reference to sex: P. L. VIII. 445, 585; *man or woman*: S. A. 844; *woman is her name, of man extracted*: P. L. VIII. 496; *fill the world ... with men ... without feminine*: P. L. X. 893.

(d) with special reference to adult age: *full grown to man*: P. R. II. 83; *childhood shows the man*: P. R. IV. 220.

(5) manliness, courage; *his best of man*: P. L. XI. 497.

(6) husband; *man and wife*: P. L. X. 101; *gave to the man despotic power over his female*: S. A. 1054.

(7) the form of a man: P. L. I. 462.

Manacle, (1) *sb.* shackle, fetter: S. A. 1309.

(2) *vb. tr.* to shackle, fetter: P. L. I. 426.

Manage, *vb. tr.* to control, govern: P. L. VIII. 573.

See **Ill-managed.**

Management, *sb.* conduct, administration: P. R. I. 112.

Manasseh, *sb.* the tribe of Manasseh: Ps. LXXX. 10.

Mane, *sb.* the hair growing on the neck of a lion; *brinded mane*: P. L. VII. 466; on the neck of the serpent; *hairy mane*: P. L. VII. 97.

Manger, *sb.* the feeding-trough for beasts in which Christ was laid: P. R. I. 247; II. 75; N. O. 31.

Mangle, *vb. tr.* to lacerate: P. L. VI. 368; *fig., of thoughts*: S. A. 624.

Manhood, *sb.* (a) the state of being a man, opposed to *godhead*: P. L. III. 314; XII. 389.

(b) period of mature age, opposed to *youth*: P. R. IV. 509; S. II. 6; *prime in manhood where youth ended*: P. L. XI. 246.

(c) manliness, honour, resolution : P. L. x. 148 ; *a grain of manhood* : S. A. 408.

Manifest, (1) *adj.* evident, apparent : S. A. 997.

(2) *adv.* clearly, plainly : P. L. x. 66.

(3) *vb. tr.* to make appear, show plainly, reveal : P. L. VIII. 422 ; *to manifest the more thy might* : P. L. VII. 615 ; with two *acc.* : P. L. VI. 707.

Manifold, *adj.* (a) of many kinds, diverse : P. L. IV. 435 ; VIII. 29.

(b) characterized by a variety of forms ; *manifold in sin* : P. L. x. 16.

Mankind (usually accented mankínd, but mánkind : P. L. I. 368 ; II. 383 ; III. 66, 275 ; VIII. 358 ; IX. 415 ; XI. 13, 38, 69, 500, 696), *sb.* the human race, or Adam and Eve as representing the human race : P. L. I. 36, 368 ; III. 275 ; IV. 10, 107, 718 ; VII. 530 ; VIII. 358, 579, 650 ; IX. 494, 950 ; x. 498, 646 ; XI. 38, 69, 500, 696, 752, 891 ; XII. 276 ; P. R. I. 114, 187, 266 ; III. 82 ; IV. 635 ; *race of mankind* : P. L. II. 383 ; III. 161 ; XI. 13 ; *all mankind* : P. L. III. 222, 286 ; IV. 315 ; v. 228 ; x. 822 ; XII. 276, 417, 601 ; P. R. I. 3, 388 ; *to generate mankind* : P. L. x. 895 ; *mother of mankind* : P. L. v. 388 ; *mother of all mankind* : P. L. XI. 159 ; *the patriarch of mankind* : P. L. v. 506 ; IX. 376 ; *the only two of mankind* : P. L. III. 66 ; IX. 415.

Man-like, *adj.* resembling a man in form : P. L. VIII. 471.

Manly, (1) *adj.* (a) characteristic of a man ; *manly prime or youthful bloom* : C. 289 ; *manly grace* : P. L. IV. 490.

(b) suited to a man ; *comp.*, *with manlier objects we must try his constancy* : P. R. II. 225.

(c) strong, brave, courageous, *sup.* : P. R. II. 167.

(2) *adv.* as befits a man : P. L. IV. 302.

Manna, *sb.* the food by which the children of Israel were sustained in the wilderness : P. R. I. 351 ; II. 312 ; or, possibly, the sweet syrup exuded from certain plants ; *fig., his tongue dropt manna* : P. L. II. 113.

Manner, *sb.* (a) form of executing, way, mode : P. R. I. 50.

(b) *pl.* behaviour, bearing : P. R. IV. 83.

Manoa (Mánoa, *disyl.* : S. A. 1441, 1548, 1565 ; possibly Mánoá, *trisyl.* : S. A. 328), *sb.* the father of Samson : S. A. 328, 1441, 1548, 1565.

Mansion, *sb.* dwelling-place, abode ; used of heaven : Ps. CXXXVI. 93 ; *empyreal mansion* : P. L. III. 699 ; *before the starry threshold of Jove's court my mansion is* : C. 2 ; of hell ; *unhappy, ill mansion* : P. L. I. 268 ; II. 462 ; VI. 738 ; *dolorous mansions* : N. O. 140 ; of Paradise ; *thy mansion wants thee, Adam* : P. L. VIII. 296 ; *fig.,* of the human body : Il P. 92.

Manslaughter, *sb.* the killing of men by men : P. L. XI. 693.

Mantle, (1) *sb.* loose outer garment : P. L. III. 10 : *his mantle hairy* : L. 104 ; *his mantle blue* : L. 192 ; *fig., the moon ... o'er the dark her silver mantle threw* : P. L. IV. 609 ; *night ... over the pole thy thickest mantle throw* : P. 30.

(2) *vb. intr.* (a) to serve as a mantle or covering ; *wings ... came mantling o'er his breast* : P. L. v. 279.

(b) to spread out ; *her white wings mantling proudly* : P. L. VII. 439.

part. adj. **mantling,** spreading ; *mantling vine* : P. L. IV. 258 ; C. 294.

Manure, *vb. tr.* to cultivate : P. L. XI. 28.

vbl. sb. **manuring,** cultivation : P. L. IV. 628.

Many, (1) *adj.* (a) great in number, numerous : P. L. I. 128, 700 ; III. 473 ; v. 101 ; x. 1084 ; XI. 256 ; P. R. II. 188 ; III. 315, 342 ; IV. 321 ; S. A. 915 ; C. 526, 537, 946 ; *many feet, hands* : S. A. 111, 1260 ; *many days, years, ages* : P. L. XI. 254, 534. 767 ; XII. 602 ; P. R. II. 11, 80 ; *many more causes* : P. L. IX. 730 ; *many ways to die* : P. L. x. 1005 ; *many shapes of death* : P. L. XI. 467 ; *so many* : P. L. III. 611 ; IV. 429 ; VI. 24 ; VIII. 28 ; XII. 282, 283 ; P. R. II. 441 ; III. 137 ; IV. 124, 482 ; S. A. 65 ; *how many are thy foes* : Ps. III. 1, 2 ; *many are the sayings of the wise* : S. A. 652 ;

many are the trees of God : P. L.
IX. 618; *knowing their advantages
too many* : S. A. 1401; following
the *sb.* : P. L. VI. 336; with a
number; *many millions* : Ps. III.
15.

(*b*) being one of many, not
few; with *sing. sb.*, and followed
by *indef. art.* : P. L. I. 709, 727;
II. 548, 618, 620, 651; III. 465,
642, 741; IV. 229; V. 346; VI.
387, 658; IX. 183, 434, 517; X.
311; XI. 351; P. R. IV. 411,
569; S. A. 542, 918; V. Ex. 74;
L'A. 95, 101, 139; *many a rood*
P. L. I. 196; *many a league* : P.
L. II. 929; IV. 164; X. 274, 438;
P. R. III. 269; *many a region,
realm, province*, etc. : P. L. II.
619; IV. 234; VI. 76, 77; P. R.
I. 118; *many a structure, edifice,
tower* : P. L. I. 733; P. R. IV.
55; C. 935; *many a hard assay* :
P. R. I. 261; IV. 478; *many an
age* : P. R. I. 16; *many a slain* :
S. A. 439; *many a friend* : C. 949.

(*c*) being of a certain number :
S. A. 194; *how many ages as the
ages of men* : P. R. I. 48; *how
many battles fought, how many
kings destroyed* : P. L. XII. 261,
262; *so many* : P. L. XI. 323;
*ten thousand fathoms … as many
miles* : P. L. II. 938.

(2) *absol.* or *sb.* many persons :
P. L. VI. 624; VII. 144; XII. 530;
P. R. II. 89, 155; *many there be* :
Ps. IV. 25; *as many as are re-
stored* : P. L. III. 289; *as many as
offered life neglect not* : P. L. XII.
425; *the ruin of so many* : P. L.
V. 567; *where so many died* : S.
A. 287; *how many* : P. R. II. 193.

Maple, *adj.* made of the wood of the
maple-tree : C. 391.

Mar, *vb. tr.* (*a*) to injure, ruin : P.
L. IX. 136.

(*b*) to disfigure : P. L. IV. 116.

Marasmus, *sb.* a wasting away of
the flesh : P. L. XI. 487.

Marble, (1) *sb.* the hard limestone;
(*a*) used in buildings : P. R. IV.
60; *fig.*, as a symbol of insensibility to physical impressions;
forget thyself to marble : Il P. 42;
*make us marble with too much con-
ceiving* : W. S. 14.

(*b*) statue or image : N. O. 195.

(*c*) tomb : M. W. 1.

(2) *adj.* (*a*) made of marble : C.
916.

(*b*) clear, bright, shining; *pure
marble air* : P. L. III. 564.

March, (1) *sb.* (*a*) the regular advance
of a body of angels; P. L. V. 778;
X. 747; P. R. I. 115; *flying
march* : P. L. II. 574; V. 688;
high above the ground their march :
P. L. VI. 72; *roving on in confused march* : P. L. II. 615.

(*b*) journey : P. L. I. 413.

(3) *vb. intr.* (*a*) to go; *when he
(Israel) passed from Egypt marching* : P. L. II. 488.

(*b*) to advance by measured and
regular steps : P. R. III. 303; *a
bannered host … marching* : P. L.
II. 886; used of angels, who
march through the air : P. L. VI.
77.

(*c*) to journey : P. L. XII. 40.

Marchioness, *sb.* the wife of a Marquis : M. W. 74.

Margaret, *sb.* Lady Margaret Ley :
S. X. 14. *See* **Earl.**

Margent, *sb.* margin, border; *slow
Meander's margent green* : C. 232.

Margiana, *sb.* a province of the
Parthian Empire lying between
Hyrcania on the west and Bactria
on the east : P. R. III. 317. *See*
Bactrian, Hyrcanian.

Mariner, *sb.* seaman, sailor : P. L.
IV. 558; *Tuscan mariners* : C. 48.

Marish, *sb.* marsh : P. L. XII. 630.

Maritime, *adj.* bordering on the
sea : P. L. XI. 398.

Mark, (1) *sb.* (*a*) significant sign by
which a thing is known; *the mark
of fool set on his front* : S. A. 496.

(*b*) token; *marks of honour* : S.
A. 992.

(*c*) object of endeavour : S. XII.
13.

(2) *vb. tr.* (*a*) to observe particularly, take note of, regard : P.
L. IV. 129, 401, 568; IX. 528; A.
14; *the way he came not having
marked* : P. R. I. 297; *to mark
what of their state* : P. L. IV. 400;
*to mark how spring our tended
plants* : P. L. V. 21; said of God;
God … to mark their doings : P. L.
XII. 50; *God … marks the just
man* : P. R. III. 61; *absol.* : Ps.
VI. 15.

(*b*) to pay attention to, give
heed to; *mark what I areed thee* :
P. L. IV. 962; *hear and mark to
what end I have brought thee hither* :
P. R. III. 349; *absol.* : P. L. IX.
72.

Marle, *sb.* soil : P. L. I. 296.

Marocco, *sb.* Morocco, the most western of the Barbery States of northern Africa : P. L. I. 584 ; XI. 404.

Marriage, *sb.* the union of a man and woman in wedlock : P. L. v. 223 ; XI. 684 ; S. A. 224 ; *to seek in marriage* : S. A. 320.

   attrib. pertaining to wedlock ; *marriage rites* : P. L. VIII. 487 ; XI. 591.

Marriageable (márriageáble), *adj.* fitted for marriage ; *fig., the vine... about him twines her marriageable arms* : P. L. v. 217.

Marriage-choice, *sb.* selection of a wife : S. A. 420.

Marriage-faith, *sb.* vows made at marriage : S. A. 1115.

Marriage-feast, *sb.* feast made at the celebration of a marriage : M. W. 18.

Marry, *vb. tr. fig.,* to unite closely to ; *soft Lydian airs, married to immortal verse* : L'A. 137.

   vbl. sb. **marrying,** the act of entering into wedlock : P. L. XI. 716.

Mars, *sb.* the Roman god of war : P. R. III. 84.

Marshalled, *part. adj. marshalled feast,* a feast at which the guests are arranged or disposed by a marshal : P. L. IX. 37.

Martial, *adj.* pertaining to war ; *martial equipage* : P. R. III. 304 ; *sound* : P. L. I. 540.

Martyrdom, *sb.* submission to death or extreme suffering for the sake of principle : P. L. IX. 32.

Martyred, *part. adj.* having suffered death for the sake of religious belief : S. XVIII. 10.

Marvel, *vb. intr.* to be filled with astonishment, wonder : P. L. IX. 551.

Mary, *sb.* (*a*) the mother of Jesus : P. R. II. 105 ; *his mother Mary* : P. R. II. 60 ; *Mary, second Eve* : P. L. v. 387 ; x. 183.

   (*b*) the sister of Martha (Luke x. 42) : S. IX. 5.

Masculine, *adj.* male ; *spirits masculine* : P. L. x. 890.

Mask, *sb.* a play or dramatic spectacle in which the performers, at least originally, wore masks ; *mask and antique pageantry* : L'A. 128 ; *mixed dance and wanton mask* : P. L. IV. 768 ; *fig.* : P. 19 ;

the world's vain mask : S. XXII. 13.

Mass, *sb.* (*a*) body of coherent matter ; *formless mass* : P. L. III. 708 ; *fluid* : P. L. VII. 237 ; *conflagrant* : P. L. XII. 548 ; *fig., mass of sinful flesh* : P. R. I. 162.

   (*b*) collection *of things* : Ariosto I. 3.

Massacre, *sb.* slaughter : P. L. XI. 679.

Massy, *adj.* (*a*) consisting of a mass ; *the massy ore* : P. L. I. 703.

   (*b*) having much weight or bulk ; *massy bar, pillar* : S. A. 147, 1633, 1648 ; *shield, spear* : P. L. I. 285 ; VI. 195 ; *iron, gold* : P. L. II. 878 ; v. 634 ; *two massy clods of iron* : P. L. XI. 565 ; *massy keys* : L. 110.

Massy-proof (not compound in original text), *adj.* massive and able to bear up the incumbent weight(?) : Il P. 158.

Mast, *sb.* the beam by which the sails and rigging of a vessel are supported : P. L. I. 297.

Master, *sb.* (*a*) one who has authority, ruler : S. A. 1215, 1404 ; applied to Christ : N. O. 34.

   (*b*) one who has another under his control, employer : C. 501 ; *we should serve him* (God) *as a grudging master* : C. 725.

   See **Task-master, Work-master.**

Mastering, *gerund,* conquering ; *by mastering heaven's Supreme* : P. L. IX. 125.

Master-work, *sb.* chief or most important work : P. L. VII. 505.

Mastery, *sb.* (*a*) rule, dominion : P. L. II. 899.

   (*b*) skill : P. L. IX. 29.

Match, (1) *sb.* one fitted to cope with another : S. A. 1164 ; *now unequal match to save himself against a coward armed* : S. A. 346.

   (2) *vb. tr.* (*a*) to bring together into harmonious relation ; *ill matching words and deeds* : P. L. v. 113.

   (*b*) to join as equals in combat : P. L. II. 720.

   (*c*) to equal ; *Eternal Might to match with their inventions they presumed so easy* : P. L. VI. 631.

   (*d*) to unite in wedlock : P. L. XI. 685.

   See **Over-match.**

Matchless, *adj.* having no equal : P. L. II. 487 ; VI. 341 ; *O Powers*

matchless, but with the Almighty:
P. L. I. 623; *matchless Gideon*:
S. A. 280; *matchless in might*: S.
A. 178; *in cunning*: P. R. IV.
10; said of God; *heaven's matchless King*: P. L. IV. 41; *thy
matchless Sire*: P. R. I. 233.

(b) used of qualities or actions;
matchless strength, deeds, etc.: P.
L. VI. 457; X. 404; P. R. I. 233;
S. A. 1740; S. XIV. 3.

Mate, *sb*. (*a*) companion, associate:
P. L. I. 192, 238; VI. 608; D. F. I.
24; *among the beasts no mate for
thee was found*: P. L. VIII. 594;
*whether the Muse or Love call thee
his mate*: S. I. 13; *fig., strength,
while virtue was her mate*: S. A.
173; used of fish; *part, single or
with mate, graze the sea-weed*: P.
L. VII. 403.

(b) wife: P. L. VIII. 576; X.
899.

(c) match; *no mate for you*:
P. L. IV. 828.

See **Ill-mated, Steers-mate.**

Material, (1) *adj.* consisting of
matter; *this world's material
mould*: P. L. III. 709.

(2) *sb.* component matter or
substance: P. L. III. 709; VI. 478.

Matin, *sb.* morning salutation; *the
first cock his matin rings*: L'A.
114.

attrib. pertaining to or heard in
the morning; *matin song*: P. L.
V. 7; *trumpet*: P. L. VI. 526;
evening harps and matin: P. L.
VII. 450.

Matrimonial, *adj.* pertaining to the
state of marriage; *matrimonial
love*: P. L. IX. 319; *treason*: S.
A. 959.

Matron, *sb.* (*a*) a married woman:
P. L. I. 505; M. W. 23; *first
matron, Eve*: P. L. XI. 136;
Philistian matron: S. A. 722.

(b) a woman of age and dignity;
*fig., that crowned matron, sage
white-robed Truth*: D. F. I. 54.

attrib. belonging to a wife: P.
L. IV. 501.

Matter, *sb.* (1) that out of which
anything is made; *one first matter
all endued with various forms*: P.
L. V. 472; *matter unformed and
void*: P. L. VII. 233; object-
matter, as acted upon by a cause:
P. L. X. 807.

(b) material stuff: P. L. X.
1071.

(2) material or subject of thought
or expression; *solicit not thy
thoughts with matters hid*: P. L.
VIII. 167; *the copious matter of
my song*: P. L. III. 413; *high
matter thou enjoinest me*: P. L. V.
563.

(b) the contents of a writing;
both matter, form, and style: S.
XI. 2.

(3) subject for action, affair: S.
A. 1348; or, possibly, in sense
(2); *some great matter*: P. L. IX.
669; S. A. 1638.

(4) a thing worthy of consideration: P. L. III. 613; P. R. IV.
329.

(5) an inducing cause or occa-
sion; *matter to me of glory*: P. L.
V. 738; *matter of glorious trial*:
P. L. IX. 1177; *matter of scorn*:
P. L. IX. 951.

(6) importance, consequence;
what matter where: P. L. I. 256.

Mature, (1) *adj.* (*a*) having attained
full development in age or powers,
ripe: P. L. X. 882; *birth mature
of this our native heaven*: P. L.
V. 862; *mature in knowledge*: P.
L. IX. 803; *judgement mature*: P.
R. III. 37; *for death mature*:
P. L. XI. 537.

(b) completely elaborated; *his
godlike office now mature*: P. R.
I. 188; *sup., maturest counsels*:
P. L. II. 115.

(2) *vb. tr.* (*a*) to bring to a state
of full development, ripen; *till
time mature thee to a kingdom's
weight*: P. R. IV. 282; *all kinds
...for destruction to mature*: P.
L. X. 612.

(b) to elaborate; *these thoughts
full counsel must mature*: P. L. I.
660.

Maugre, *prep.* in spite of, notwithstanding: P. L. III. 255; IX. 56;
P. R. III. 368.

Maw, *sb.* stomach; used with reference to death: P. L. II. 847; X.
601, 991; *fig., hireling wolves whose
gospel is their maw*: S. XVI. 14.

Maxim, *sb.* summary statement of
an accepted principle: P. R. III.
400; S. A. 865.

May, *sb.* the fifth month of the
year; *flowery, bounteous, propitious May*: M. M. 3, 5; S. I. 4.

attrib. blooming during the
month of May: P. L. IV. 501.

See **a-Maying.**

*May, *vb.* (*pres. 2d sing.* may'st: P.
L. v. 76; vi. 894, 903; vii. 94,
etc.; *negative*, mayn't : U. C. ii.
18; *pret.* might; *2d sing.*
might'st: P. R. iv. 100; S. A.
422, etc.) used with the simple
infinitive ; (**1**) in the principal
clause ; (*a*) denoting subjective
ability : P. L. xi. 141; C. 382,
423 ; *well we may afford our givers
their own gifts*: P. L. v. 316; *how
may I adore thee, Author of this
universe*: P. L. viii. 359; *ere long
I might perceive strange alteration
in me*: P. L. ix. 598.

(*b*) denoting objective possibility : P. L. x. 1079 ; *nor that
sweet grove ... might with this
Paradise ... strive*: P. L. iv. 274 ;
his eye might there command: P.
L. xi. 385 ; *with easy eye, thou
may'st behold*: P. R. iii. 293.

(*c*) denoting possibility with
contingency : P. L. i. 650; ii.
25, 274 ; viii. 93; ix. 826 ; *my
dwelling, haply, may not please ...
your sense*: P. L. iv. 378 ; *chance
may lead where I may meet some ...
Spirit of Heaven*: P. L. iv. 530 ;
our number may affright: C. 148 ;
used in asking a question ; *where
may she wander now?*: C. 351 ;
to avoid bluntness in asking a
question ; *might she the wise
Latona be?*: A. 20.

(*d*) denoting opportunity, liberty, or permission: P. L. i. 261 ;
vii. 544; ix. 660; C. 747 ; *we
may no longer stay*: P. L. xii.
594 ; *who can advise may speak*:
P. L. ii. 42 ; *happier thou may'st
be*: P. L. v. 76 ; *of this tree we
may not taste*: P. L. ix. 651.

(*e*) denoting a wish: P. L. ix.
1084 ; x. 834; xi. 535 ; P. R. ii.
125 ; Il P. 167 ; C. 601, 924 ; L. 19.

(**2**) in dependent clauses, as
auxiliary, but often retaining
something of the idea of power or
possibility ; (*a*) in sb., adj., or
adv. clause : P. L. ii. 525 ; iii.
189 ; v. 234; vi. 148, 299 ; vii.
115, 128 ; xi. 858.

(*b*) in purpose clause : P. L.
iii. 54, 180 ; vi. 559 ; *that ... I
may assert eternal Providence*:
P. L. i. 25 ; *that we may so suffice
his vengeful ire*: P. L. i. 148;
*that .. he might heap on himself
damnation*: P. L. i. 214; *loud
that all may hear*: P. L. vi. 567.

(*c*) in result clause ; *that whom
they hit none on their feet might
stand*: P. L. vi. 592; *that Orpheus'
self may heave his head*: L'A. 145.

(*d*) in concessive clause ; *darkness enters ... though darkness there
might well seem twilight here*: P.
L. vi. 11.

(*e*) in causal clause ; *possible to
swerve since reason ... may meet
some specious object*: P. L. ix. 360.

(*f*) in conditional clause; in
the protasis, the apodosis containing the subj.: P. L. v. 493; viii.
121 ; ix. 46, 1025 ; containing
can: P. L. ii. 210; containing
should: P. L. ii. 83; vi. 503 ;
the apodosis ellipt.: P. L. vi.
595.

in the apodosis, the protasis
containing the indic.: S. A. 649,
736, 1477 ; the protasis ellipt.:
P. L. v. 785.

(*g*) in indirect question : P. L.
ii. 573, 677 ; iii. 272 ; S. A. 743.

Maze, *sb.* (*a*) an intricate and con-
fusing network of paths ; *this
woody maze*: P. R. ii. 246 ; *the
blind mazes of this tangled wood*:
C. 181 ; *the yellow-skirted fays ...
leaving their moon-loved maze*: N.
O. 236.

fig. the complex coils of a serpent's body : P. L. ix. 490; the
involutions of the dance: P. L.
v. 622 ; intricate passages of
music : L'A. 142.

(*b*) entanglement of thought :
P. L. ii. 561 ; x. 830.

Mazy, *adj.* resembling a maze ; *the
serpent ... in whose mazy folds*: P.
L. ix. 161 ; *the crisped brooks rolling ... with mazy error*: P. L. iv.
239.

Me. See I.

Mead, *sb.* meadow: V. Ex. 94; L'A.
90.

Meadow, *sb.* low level land covered
with grass : L'A. 75 ; *green
meadow, meadows green*: P. L.
vii. 460 ; P. R. ii. 185 ; *twilight
meadows*: C. 844.

Meadow-ground, *sb.* ground used as
a meadow : P. L. xi. 648.

Meagre, *adj.* lean, thin ; *the meagre
shadow* (death): P. L. x. 264 ;
blue meagre hag: C. 434.

Mean, *adj.* (*a*) low, humble : P. L.
iv. 62; *mean suitors*: P. L. xi.
9 ; *office, estate, lot*: P. L. ix.
39 ; xii. 351 ; S. ii. 10 ; *mean*

pretence : P. L. VI. 421 ; *comp.*, *meaner thoughts* : P. L. VI. 367 ; *sup.* : P. L. XI. 231.

(b) common, trivial, insignificant : P. L. VIII. 473 ; *mean recompense* : P. L. II. 981 ; *applause* : S. XXI. 2.

(c) contemptible; *sup.*, *perverts best things to worst abuse, or to their meanest use* : P. L. IV. 204.

Mean, (1) *adj. absol.* an average measure : S. A. 207.

(2) *sb. pl.* that which is used to effect a purpose or attain an end, agency, instrumentality : P. L. III. 228 ; XII. 279 ; P. R. III. 89, 355, 356, 394; IV. 152, 475; S. A. 315 ; *to find means of evil* : P. L. I. 165 ; *the means of thy deliverance* : S. A. 603 ; *great acts require great means of enterprise* : P. R. II. 412 ; *by means of thee* : S. A. 444 ; *by what means* : P. L. X. 1062; XII. 234 ; *what offered means* : S. A. 516 ; *by which means* : S. A. 562 ; *by this means* : C. 644 ; *by all means* : S. A. 795 ; *some other means I have* : C. 821.

Mean, *vb.* (*pres. 2d sing.* mean'st : P. R. IV. 230 ; *pret.* and *past part.* meant) (1) *tr.* (a) to intend, purpose, design : P. L. X. 545 ; P. R. II. 99 ; with *acc.* and *dat.* : P. L. IX. 1152; Ps. VII. 10 ; with *acc.* and *to* : C. 765 ; in *passive* : A. 35 ; with *acc.* and *inf.*, the *inf.* omitted : P. L. IX. 690; C. 591 ; with *prep. inf.* : P. L. II. 684; IV. 632; V. 723; VI. 120, 290, 854; IX. 860; P. R. I. 155; III. 404; IV. 161; S. A. 1644; L'A. 152; the *inf.* omitted : P. R. IV. 230.

(b) to have in mind, think of in speaking : P. L. VIII. 527 ; P. R. II. 6 ; C. 417, 418; *ye were the two she meant* : C. 578; *unless be meant whom I conjecture* : P. L. X. 1033; *License they mean when they cry Liberty* : S. XII. 11.

(c) to signify, denote, import : P. L. III. 272 ; IX. 553; P. R. I. 83 ; II P. 120; *what meant that caution joined* : P. L. V. 513; *what mean those coloured streaks in heaven* : P. L. XI. 879; *spiritual power and civil, what each means* : S. XVII. 10 ; *immediate dissolution, which we thought was meant by death* : P. L. X. 1050; *by that seed is meant thy great Deliverer* : P. L.

XII. 149 ; to be intended to have meaning ; *each stair mysteriously was meant* : P. L. III. 516.

(2) *intr.* to be minded or disposed ; *love hath oft, well meaning, wrought much woe* : S. A. 813. *vbl. sb.* **meaning** ; (a) intention, design : C. 754.

(b) sense, signification : P. L. VII. 5 ; IX. 1019 ; P. R. IV. 516. See Ill-meaning.

Meander, *sb.* a river of Asia Minor rising in Phrygia and emptying into the Ægean Sea : C. 232.

Meanly, *adv.* poorly, unworthily ; *all meanly wrapt in the rude manger* : N. O. 31.

Meanwhile (meánwhile : P. L. II. 767 ; IV. 260; C. 102 ; meanwhile : P. L. III. 333 ; VI. 186 ; XI. 133 ; elsewhere beginning a line or following the cæsura, where either accent is possible) (1) *adv.* in the meantime, during the interval : P. L. I. 752; II. 629, 767 ; III. 333, 418; IV. 260, 539, 633; V. 350, 443, 503, 711 ; VI. 186, 293, 354, 493; VII. 162, 192, 417 ; IX. 739; X. 1, 229, 585; XI. 133, 738; XII. 315; P. R. I. 183; II. 1 ; S. A. 256, 604; C. 102; L. 32.

(2) (meánwhile), *sb.* meantime ; *in the meanwhile* : S. A. 479.

Measure, I. *sb.* (1) standard of judgement or award : P. L. VI. 265.

(2) a limited or ascertained extent or quantity : S. A. 1439; *love without end, without measure grace* : P. L. III. 142 ; *full to the utmost measure of what bliss human desire can seek* : P. L. V. 517 ; *secure of surfeit where full measure only bounds excess* : P. L. V. 639 ; *to know in measure what the mind may well contain* : P. L. VII. 128 ; *it must be still in strictest measure even to that same lot* : S. II. 10.

(b) capacity ; *not surpassing human measure* : P. L. VII. 640.

(c) treatment : P. L. I. 513.

(3) regulated motion ; *faltering measure*, irregular beating of the heart : P. L. IX. 846.

(4) a grave and solemn dance : P. R. I. 170.

II. *vb. tr.* (1) to determine the extent of in space ; *a vessel measured by cubit* : P. L. XI. 730; in time ; *time ... measures all things durable by present, past, and future* :

P. L. v. 581 ; *nine times the space that measures day and night* : P. L. I. 50.

(2) to estimate, judge of, determine the relative value or greatness of : P. L. VI. 821 ; VII. 603 ; *to measure life learn thou betimes* : S. XXI. 9 ; *measuring things in heaven by things on earth* : P. L. VI. 893.

(3) to pass over : P. L. IV. 776.

(*b*) to cover or include ; *how soon hath thy prediction ... measured this transient world* : P.L. XII. 554.

(*c*) to pass over with the eye, view : L'A. 70.

(*d*) to reach, attain ; *my age had measured twice six years* : P. R. I. 210.

part. adj. **measured**, characterized by regularity of movement, rhythmical : A. 71.

See **Various-measured, Well-measured.**

Meat, *sb.* food : Ps. LXXXI. 68 ; *pl.* : P. R. II. 328, 341 ; solid food ; *meats and drinks* : P. L. V. 451 ; XI. 473 ; P. R. II. 265.

Meath, *sb.* a sweet beverage : P. L. v. 345.

Meddling, *part. adj.* meddlesome, officious : C. 846.

Mede, *sb. pl.* the inhabitants of Media : P. R. III. 376.

Media, *sb.* the country in Asia lying south and west of the Caspian Sea : P. L. IV. 171 ; as forming part of the Parthian Empire : P. R. III. 320.

Mediation, *sb.* intercession in favour of another : P. L. III. 226.

Mediator, *sb.* one who interposes to restore harmony between two persons ; applied to Christ as mediating between God and man : P. L. X. 60 ; XII. 240.

Medicinal (méd'cinal : C. 636 ; médcinal : S. A. 627), *adj.* having the power of healing, remedial : S. A. 627 ; C. 636.

Meditate, *vb. tr.* to exercise oneself in or apply oneself to ; *meditate my rural minstrelsy* : C. 547 ; *meditate the thankless muse* : L. 66.

part. adj. **meditated**, planned, designed : P. L. IX. 55.

Meditation, *sb.* deep and continued thought, contemplation : P. L. XII. 605 ; Ps. V. 2 ; *holy, holiest contemplations* : P. R. I. 195 ; II. 110 ; *personified* : C. 386.

Medusa, *sb.* one of the Gorgons : P. L. II. 611. *See* **Gorgon.**

Medway, *sb.* a river in Kent emptying into the Thames : V. Ex. 100.

Meed, *sb.* reward, recompense : L. 14, 84.

Meek, *adj.* (*a*) of gentle disposition or temper : P. L. VIII. 217 ; XI. 437, 451 ; S. A. 1036 ; *our Saviour meek* : P. R. IV. 401, 636 ; *subverting ... worldly-wise by simply meek* : P. L. XII. 569.

(*b*) full of or characterized by gentleness ; *meek aspect, regard* : P. L. III. 266 ; P. R. III. 217.

(*c*) peaceful ; *blest kingdoms meek of joy and love* : L. 177.

(*d*) submissive, humble ; *meek demeanour* : P. L. XI. 162 ; *surrender, submission* : P. L. IV. 494 ; XII. 597 ; *humiliation* : P. L. X. 1092, 1104 ; *reverence* : P. L. V. 359.

Meek-eyed, *adj.* having gentle eyes ; *the meek-eyed Peace* : N. O. 46.

Meekly, *adv.* submissively, humbly : P. R. II. 108 : P. 21 ; S. XIV. 3.

Meet, *adj.* fit, suitable, proper : P. L. III. 234 ; IX. 711 ; P. R. III. 442 ; IV. 232 ; M. W. 16 ; *though to Nature seeming meet* : P. L. XI. 604 ; *as is meet* : P. L. III. 675 ; *as meet is* : P. L. IX. 1028.

absol. what is proper : P. L. VIII. 448.

Meet, *vb.* (*pres. 2d sing.* meet'st : P. L. V. 175 ; *pret.* and *past part.* met) I. *tr.* (1) to come into the same place with or into the presence of : P. L. II. 955 ; Il P. 28 ; *Raphael ... with reverence I must meet* : P. L. XI. 237 ; *as man ... to meet man* : P. L. XI. 240 ; *Alpheus ... stole under seas to meet his Arethuse* : A. 31.

(2) to come face to face with by approaching from an opposite direction : P. L. V. 350 ; VI. 532, 882 ; IX. 847, 849 ; X. 349 ; *when the angels met Jacob in Mahanaim* : P. L. XI. 213 ; *where art thou, Adam, wont with joy to meet my coming* : P. L. X. 103 ; *if Earth ... with her part averse from the Sun's beam meet Night* : P. L. VIII. 139 ; *fig.*, to experience ; *run to meet what he would most avoid* : C. 363.

(*b*) to go or move in a direction toward ; *Moon, that now meet'st the orient Sun* : P. L. V. 175.

(c) to come in contact with; *to meet the rudeness ... of such late wassailers*: C. 178.

(d) perhaps with a blending of the meaning: to match, equal: P. L. x. 390.

(3) to come into physical contact with: P. L. II. 931; VI. 323; *half her swelling breast met his*: P. L. IV. 496; to be united or contiguous to; *the rapid current ... met the nether flood*: P. L. IV. 231; *where heaven with earth and ocean meets*: P. L. IV. 540; used with reference to that which is perceived by one of the five senses; *blaze on blaze first met his view*: P. L. VI. 18; *more is meant than meets the ear*: Il P. 120; *her eye hath met the virtue of this magic dust*: C. 165; *purer air meets his approach*: P. L. IV. 154.

(4) to come across, light upon, fall in with, find: P. L. II. 742; IV. 530; x. 905; L'A. 20; C. 572; S. XIII. 14; *faery damsels met in forest side*: P. R. II. 359; *who seek in these true wisdom ... her false resemblance only meets*: P. R. IV. 320; *matter new to gaze the Devil met*: P. L. III. 613; *Reason ... may meet some specious object*: P. L. IX. 360; *to meet no danger*: P. L. IX. 1176; *what they met*: P. L. x. 285; *each thing met*: P. L. IX. 449; to experience, suffer: P. L. IX 271; x. 775.

(5) to come to, befall; *Satan, whom repulse upon repulse met*: P. R. IV. 22.

(6) to encounter as an enemy: P. L. II. 722; VI. 128, 131, 247; IX. 325; S. A. 1123; *to meet the noise of his almighty engine, he shall hear infernal thunder*: P. L. II. 64; *till the ... wrath meet thy flight sevenfold*: P. L. IV. 913.

II. *intr.* (a) to come together; *where shall we ... meet*: S. xx. 3; *the loveliest pair that ever since in love's embraces met*: P. L. IV. 322; *when meet now such pairs*: P. L. VIII. 57; *Corydon and Thyrsis met*: L'A. 83.

(b) to come face to face from opposite directions: P. L. IV. 863.

(c) to assemble, congregate: P. L. I. 574; VI. 93; XI. 722; *all beasts that in the field or forest meet*: P. L. VIII. 20; with the purpose expressed by the *prep. inf.*: P. L.

VI. 156; S. A. 1588, 1656; C. 948; Ps. LXXXVI. 50.

(d) to join; *our circuit meets full west*: P. L. IV. 784; to be united or contiguous: P. R. III. 258; IV. 385; *the confines met of ... Heaven and of this World*: P. L. x. 321.

(e) to come together in battle: P. L. VI. 439; P. R. III. 337; *when two such foes met armed*: P. L. VI. 688; *angel ... with angel ... in fierce hosting meet*: P. L. VI. 93.

(*f*) meet with, come upon, fall in with: P. L. VIII. 609; x. 599, 879.

part. adj. meeting, that goes out to meet (the music): L'A. 138.

vbl. sb. meeting, a coming together: P. L. x. 350; assembly: P. L. V. 778.

Megæra, *sb.* one of the Furies: P. L. x. 560. *See* Fury.

Melancholy, (1) *sb.* (a) melancholia: P. L. XI. 485.

(b) grave and serious reflection, meditation: C. 546; *personified*; *loathed, divinest Melancholy*: L'A. 1; Il P. 12; vocative: Il P. 175.

(2) *adj.* (a) caused or affected by the 'humour' called black bile or melancholy: P. L. XI. 544; *a melancholy blood*: C. 810. *See* Humour.

(b) sad, mournful: Il P. 62.

Melesigenes, *sb.* a name of Homer, given him because he was believed to have been born near the river Meles, which empties into the Gulf of Smyrna: P. R. IV. 259.

Melibœan, *adj.* that made at Melibœa, a maritime town of Thessaly: P. L. XI. 242.

Melibœus, *sb.* the name of a shepherd common in pastoral poetry; here probably referring to Spenser; cf. F. Q. II. x. 14-19: C. 822.

Melind (Melínd), *sb.* the northernmost of the provinces of Zanzibar. "Melinde is the name of a little kingdom, on the South of the Realm of Adea, in the Higher Æthiopia, from which parted by the River Raptus." Heylyn, *Cos.* 1657, p. 990: P. L. XI. 399.

Mellifluous, *adj.* flowing with sweetness, honey-sweet; *mellifluous dews*: P. L. V. 429; *fig., from whose mouth issued forth mellifluous streams*: P. R. IV. 277.

Mellowing, *part. adj.* bringing to maturity : L. 5.

Melodious, *adj.* containing or producing melody, musical ; *melodious harmony* : V. Ex. 51 ; *hymns* : P. L. v. 656 ; *murmurs, chime, noise* : P. L. v. 196 ; xi. 559 ; S. M. 18 ; *part* : P. L. iii. 371 ; *time* : N. O. 129 ; used of poetry ; *melodious tear* : L. 14.

Melody, *sb.* music ; *melody of birds* : P. L. viii. 528.

Melt, *vb.* (1) *intr.* (*a*) to disappear, vanish : N. O. 138.

(*b*) to be softened to pity or tenderness : P. L. iv. 389 ; L. 163.

(2) *tr.* to reduce from a solid to a fluid state by means of heat : P. L. xi. 566.

part. adj. **melting**, moving, affecting ; *the melting voice through mazes running* : L'A. 142.

Member, *sb.* a functional organ of an animal body ; used of death ; *shape had none distinguishable in member, joint, or limb* : P. L. ii. 668.

Membrane, *sb.* the tissue covering the separate members of the body : P. L. viii. 625.

Memnon, *sb.* the son of Tithonus and Eos. He was king of the Ethiopians, and was famous for his beauty : Il P. 18.

Memnonian, *adj. Memnonian palace,* the acropolis of Susa erected to the honour of Memnon : P. L. x. 308.

Memorable (memoráble), *adj.* worthy to be remembered : P. R. iii. 96 ; S. A. 956.

Memorial, *sb.* something to preserve remembrance, record, monument : P. L. i. 362 ; vi. 355 ; P. R. ii. 445 ; inscription ; *in their glittering tissues bear emblazoned holy memorials* : P. L. v. 593.

Memory, *sb.* (*a*) the power or faculty of producing states of consciousness representative of the past : P. L. xi. 154 ; C. 206.

(*b*) the fact of such production, remembrance : Ps. LXXXIII. 16 ; *wakes the bitter memory* : P. L. iv. 24 ; *be honoured ever with grateful memory* : P. L. viii. 650 ; with the genitive ; *from his memory inflame their breasts* : S. A. 1739.

(*c*) the length of time covered by the faculty of remembrance ; *before his* or *thy memory* : P. L. vii. 66, 637.

(*d*) the state of being remembered : P. L. xii. 46 ; *Shakespeare … dear son of memory, great heir of fame* : W. S. 5.

(*e*) that which calls to remembrance, memorial : P. L. xi. 325 ; *cancelled from heaven and sacred memory* : P. L. vi. 379.

Memphian, *adj.* of Memphis, the capital of Egypt. " They call it now Cairum, or Alcair." Mercator *Atlas*, 1635, p. 818 : P. L. i. 307, 694 ; N. O. 214. See **Alcairo.**

Menace, (1) *sb.* threat ; *sign of battle make and menace high* : C. 654.

(2) *vb. tr.* to threaten : P. L. ix. 977.

Mend, *vb. tr.* to improve upon ; *Justice divine mends not her slowest pace for prayers* : P. L. x. 859.

Mental, *adj.* pertaining to the mind, intellectual : P. L. xi. 418.

Mention, (1) *sb.* a brief statement about a person or thing : P. L. viii. 200 ; S. A. 331.

(2) *vb. tr.* to speak of briefly, refer to, name : P. L. ii. 820 ; P. R. i. 45 ; ii. 327 ; iii. 92 ; S. A. 978 ; Ps. LXXXVII. 11, 13 ; *and offered fight will not dare mention* : S. A. 1254 ; *no more be mentioned then of violence against ourselves* : P. L. x. 1041.

Merchant, *sb.* one who buys and sells goods : P. L. ii. 639.

Merciful, *adj.* exercising forbearance or pity, compassionate : P. L. xii. 565 ; Ps. LXXXVI. 56.

Mercury, *sb.* the Roman god who was identified with the Greek Hermes ; here as a patron of the dance : C. 963.

Mercy, *sb.* compassionate leniency toward wrong-doers ; used of God towards men : P. L. xii. 346 ; S. A. 512 ; *pl.* : Ps. v. 17, 18 ; CXXXVI. 395 ; *esp.* of God in judging man or in providing salvation for him : P. L. iii. 202 ; *grace and mercy* : P. L. i. 218 ; *favour, grace, and mercy* : P. L. x. 1096 ; *Father of mercy and grace* : P. L. iii. 401 ; *mercy and justice* : P. L. iii. 132, 134 ; iii. 407 ; *I shall temper so justice with mercy* : P. L. x. 78 ; *I intend mercy colleague with justice* : P. L. x. 59.

personified : N. O. 144 ; Ps. LXXXV. 41 ; (not in the original text) : D. F. I. 53.

as an exclamation of surprise or fear ; *mercy guard me !* : C. 695 ; *mercy of heaven !* : S. A. 1509.

Mercy-seat, *sb.* the place of expiation in heaven : P. L. XI. 2 ; the golden lid of the ark of the covenant, which was sprinkled with the blood of the expiatory victim on the day of atonement : P. L. XII. 253.

Mere, *adj.* simple, only, nothing but : P. L. IV. 316 ; IX. 413 ; *privation mere of light* : P. R. IV. 400 ; *to the utmost of mere man* : P. R. IV. 535 ; *this is mere moral babble* : C. 807 ; nobody but : F. of C. 8.

Merely, *adv.* only, solely : P. L. V. 774 ; VIII. 22 ; T. 6 ; U. C. II. 15.

Meriba, *sb.* the place where the Children of Israel murmured against Moses because of a lack of water : Ps. LXXXI. 32.

Meridian, *adj.* of or pertaining to midday : P. L. IV. 30 ; *the full-blazing sun, which now sat high in his meridian tower* : P. L. IV. 30 ; *meridian hour* : P. L. IV. 581.

Merit, I. *sb.* (*a*) that which is deserved, due honour or reward : P. L. III. 319.

(*b*) that for which a person deserves honour or reward : P. L. V. 80 ; P. R. II. 464 ; S. A. 1011 ; *sense of injured merit* : P. L. I. 98 ; *a race of men ... by degrees of merit raised* : P. L. VII. 157 ; *by merit raised to that bad eminence* : P. L. II. 5 ; used with reference to Christ ; *by merit more than birthright son of God* : P. L. III. 309 ; *who by right of merit reigns* : P. L. VI. 43 ; *by merit called my Son* : P. R. I. 166 ; the righteousness of Christ which is imputed to man : P. L. III. 290 ; *my merit those shall perfect* : P. L. XI. 35 ; *pl., his merits to save them* : P. L. XII. 409.

(*c*) worthiness, excellence : P. L. II. 21 ; X. 259.

II. *vb.* (1) *tr.* to be entitled to, be worthy to have, deserve : P. L. I. 575 ; IV. 418 ; IX. 995 ; S. A. 734 ; *merit praise* : P. L. III. 697 ; P. R. II. 456 ; *nought merits but dispraise* : P. L. VI. 382 ; *what most merits fame* : P. L. XI. 699 ; *ere I merit my exaltation* : P. R. III. 196.

(2) *intr.* to earn honour or reward ; *amply have merited of me* : P. L. X. 388.

part. adj. **merited,** deserved : P. L. VI. 153.

Meritorious, *adj.* worthy of praise or honour : S. A. 859.

Meroë, *sb.* the Isle of Meroë, a large tract of country in Ethiopia between the Nile and its tributary the Atbara River : P. R. IV. 71.

Merriment, *sb.* noisy sport, frolic : C. 172.

Merry, *adj.* full of mirth ; *merry wakes and pastimes* : C. 121 ; used of bells which ring gaily ; *when the merry bells ring round* : L'A. 93.

Mess, *sb.* dish : L'A. 85.

Message, *sb.* a communication sent by a messenger : P. L. IV. 833 ; XI. 299 ; XII. 174 ; S. A. 1307, 1343, 1345, 1352, 1391, 1443 ; *high, solemn, heavenly message* : P. L. V. 289, 290 ; P. R. I. 133 ; the messenger bringing the communication : S. A. 635.

Messenger, *sb.* one who bears a communication or goes on an errand : S. A. 1384 ; *ethereal messenger* : P. L. VIII. 646 ; *winged* : P. L. III. 229 ; VII. 572 ; *a messenger from God foretold thy birth* : P. R. I. 238 ; *after him, the surer messenger, a dove sent forth* : P. L. XI. 856.

Messiah, *sb.* the Anointed One, Christ, as participating in the Divine Government in heaven : P. L. V. 664, 691, 765, 883 ; VI. 43, 68, 718, 775, 796, 881 ; as the Saviour of the world : P. L. XII. 244, 359 ; P. R. I. 272 ; II. 32, 43 ; Ps. II. 5 ; *called Jesus Messiah, son of God* : P. R. II. 4 ; preceded by the *def. art.* : P. R. I. 245, 261 ; IV. 502.

Metal, *sb.* the hard, heavy, and lustrous element : P. L. III. 592, 595 ; L. 110 ; *metals of drossiest ore* : P. L. V. 442 ; *graven in metal* : P. L. XI. 573 ; *fig.* a trumpet composed of metal : P. L. I. 540.

See **Sphere-metal.**

Metallic, *adj.* consisting of metal : P. L. I. 673.

Meteor, *sb.* the transient luminous body seen in the atmosphere : P. L. I. 537.

Meteorous (metéorous), *adj.* like a meteor : P. L. XII. 629.

Methink (*pret.* methought), *vb. impers.* it seems to me, it appears to me : P. L. IV. 478 ; with clause : P. L. V. 35 ; VIII. 462 ; X. 243 ; XI. 151 ; S. A. 368, 1515 ; C. 171 ; S. X. 11 ; XXIII. 1 ; the clause represented by *so*: C. 482 ; parenthetically : P. L. V. 50, 85, 91, 114 ; VIII. 295, 355 ; X. 1029.

Method, *sb.* plan of action : P. R. IV. 540.

Metropolis, *sb.* chief city : P. L. III. 549 ; Pandemonium, the seat of government in hell : P. L. X. 439.

Mexico, *sb.* the country of North America : P. L. XI. 407.

Michael, *sb.* the archangel, leader of the celestial armies : P. L. II. 294 ; VI. 44, 202, 250, 321, 411, 686, 777 ; sent by God to expel man from Paradise : P. L. XI. 99, 295, 334, 412, 453, 466, 515, 530, 552, 603, 683, 787 ; XII. 79, 285, 386, 466.

Mickle, *adj.* great; *a noble Peer of mickle trust and power* : C. 31.

Microscope, *sb.* the optical instrument ; *fig., my aery microscope*: P. R. IV. 57.

Mid (in the original texts *mid* is joined to its noun with a hyphen in : *mid-hours* : P. L. V. 376; *mid-noon*: P. L. V. 311 ; *mid-day*: P. L. VIII. 112; C. 384 ; *mid-course*: P. L. XI. 204. See the following compound words), *adj.* middle ; *in mid sky* : P. L. VI. 314 ; *tower the mid aereal sky* : P. L. VII. 442 ; *night sits monarch yet in the mid sky* : C. 957.

Mid-air (mid-áir), *sb.* the midst of the air : P. L. VI. 536 ; probably the *media regio* of the mediæval physicists, the region of clouds and cold ; *two black clouds ... join their dark encounter in mid-air* : P. L. II. 718 ; *in mid air summons all his mighty peers, within thick clouds and dark*: P. R. I. 39 ; *my afflicted powers to settle here on earth or in mid air* : P. L. IV. 940.

Midas, *sb.* the Phrygian king who wished to award the prize of musical composition to Pan instead of to Apollo ; for this Apollo gave him ass's ears : S. XIII. 4.

Mid-course (mid-coúrse), *sb.* the middle of the course ; *ere day's mid-course* : P. L. XI. 204.

Mid-day (mid-dáy : P. L. VIII. 112), *sb.* the middle of the day, noon : P. L. VIII. 112.
attrib. noonday ; *the mid-day sun* : C. 384.

Middle, (1) *sb.* (*a*) the middle part of the human body, the waist : P. L. II. 653.
(*b*) the air ; *considered all things visible in heaven, or earth, or middle*: P. L. IX. 605.
(2) *adj.* equally distant from the extremes or limits : P. L. I. 14 ; IV. 195 ; V. 280, 339 ; IX. 1097 ; *of middle age one rising* : P. L. XI. 665 ; *middle spirits ... betwixt the angelical and human kind*: P. L. III. 461; *middle air,* etc., probably the *media regio* (*see* Mid-air) ; *thence on the snowy top of cold Olympus ruled the middle air* : P. L. I. 516 ; *Satan ... was gone up to the middle region of thick air* : P. R. II. 117 ; *through middle empire of the freezing air* : D. F. I. 16 ; *the dreadful Judge in middle air shall spread his throne* : N. O. 164.

Mid-heaven (mid-héaven), *sb.* the middle of the heavens ; *through, in mid-heaven*: P. L. III. 729; XII. 263 ; the midst of heaven ; *he ... rode through mid heaven* : P. L. VI. 889; *though in mid heaven*: P. L. IX. 468.

Mid-hour (mid-hóur), *sb.* (*a*) *pl.* the hours between noon and evening : P. L. V. 376.
(*b*) *mid-hour of night*, midnight: S. IX. 13.

Midian, *sb.* the nation dwelling principally in the country north of Arabia and east of the Gulf of Akabah : Ps. LXXXIII. 33.

Midnight (midníght : P. L. V. 667 ; IX. 58), *sb.* the middle of the night : P. L. V. 667 ; *at midnight* : P. L. IX. 58 ; *personified* : L'A. 2.
attrib. pertaining to or occurring in the middle of the night ; *midnight hour* : Il P. 85 ; *midnight air, vapour* : P. L. IV. 682 ; IX. 159 ; *torches* : C. 130 ; *march* : P. L. V. 778 ; *search* : P. L. IX. 181 ; *plaint* : N. O. 191 ; *revels, ball, shout and revelry* : P. L. I. 782 ; IV. 768 ; C. 103.

Midnight-stroke, *sb.* a blow given at the middle of the night P. L. : XII. 189.

Mid-noon (mid-nóon), *sb.* noon : P. L. v. 311.

Midriff, *sb.* diaphragm ; *smote him into the midriff* : P. L. xi. 445.

Mid-sea (mid-séa), *sb.* the open sea : P. L. vii. 403.

Midst, (1) *sb.* the middle or central part or person ; *but still greatest he the midst* : P. L. x. 528 ; *to sit the midst of Trinal Unity* : N. O. 11 ; *his head the midst* : P. L. ix. 184 ; *he through the midst ... passed* : P. L. x. 441 ; *through midst of heaven* : P. L. iii. 358 ; v. 251 ; *in the midst* : P. L. i. 224 ; vi. 99, 417 ; xi. 432 ; P. R. ii. 294 ; iv. 31 ; with the implication of being surrounded or hard pressed ; *i' the midst of all mine enemies* : Ps. vi. 15 ; *in my midst of sorrow* : S. A. 1339.

(2) *adv.* in the middle : P. L. ii. 508 ; v. 165.

(3) *prep.* amidst ; *a voice from midst a golden cloud* : P. L. vi. 28.

Mid-volley (mid-vólley), *sb.* the middle of a volley ; *checked his thunder in mid-volley* : P. L. vi. 854.

Midway, *sb.* the middle of the way or journey : P. L. xi. 631 ; *their thoughts proved fond and vain in the mid-way* : P. L. vi. 91.

Might, *sb.* (1) power, strength, efficiency ; (*a*) used of God or Christ : P. L. i. 110, 643 ; vii. 615 ; Ps. lxxx. 12 ; lxxxii. 25 ; cxxxvi. 25 ; *Eternal Might* = God : P. L. vi. 630 ; *the dear might of him that walked the waves* : L. 173 ; *esp.* the power of God as resting upon or operating through Christ : P. L. iii. 398 ; v. 720 ; vi. 710 ; vii. 223 ; *armed with thy might* : P. L. vi. 737 ; *Son who art alone my word, my wisdom, and effectual might* : P. L. iii. 170 ; *my overshadowing spirit and might with thee I send along* : P. L. vii. 165 ; used of angels : P. L. ii. 192 ; vi. 116, 229, 377 ; *fearless to be o'ermatched by living might* : P. L. ii. 855 ; *Satan ... collecting all his might* : P. L. iv. 986 ; *nor odds appeared in might* : P. L. vi. 320 ; used of sin and death ; *my substitutes ... of matchless might issuing from me* : P. L. x. 404.

concr. the might of Gabriel fought* : P. L. vi. 355.

(*b*) used of animals ; *the ... elephant ... used all his might* : P. L. iv. 346 ; of things ; *by might of waves* : P. L. xi. 830 ; *the might of hellish charms* : C. 613.

(*c*) physical strength : P. L. xi. 689 ; S. A. 178, 588, 1083, 1271, 1293.

(*d*) mental power ; *they consult with all their might* : Ps. lxxxiii. 17.

(2) power, dominion, influence ; used of men : Ps. lxxxii. 7 ; H. B. 13 ; of gods : P. L. i. 506.

Mighty, *adj.* (1) powerful ; *a mighty hunter* : P. L. xii. 33.

(*b*) used of God or Christ : Ps. cxxxvi. 90 ; *mighty king* : P. L. vii. 608 ; *mighty Father* : P. L. v. 735, 836 ; vi. 890 ; *mighty Pan* : N. O. 89 ; used of angels, esp. of Satan : P. L. i. 136 ; ii. 456, 719, 991 ; *mighty cherubim, seraphim, etc.* : P. L. i. 665 ; vi. 638, 841 ; x. 650 ; P. R. i. 40 ; *their mighty chief* : P. L. i. 566 ; x. 455 ; *their mighty Paramount* : P. L. ii. 508 ; *comp.* : P. L. vi. 32 ; used of the gods, *comp.* : P. L. i. 512.

(*c*) used of things ; *mighty spell, art* : V. Ex. 89 ; C. 63.

(*d*) great in physical strength : S. A. 556, 706.

(2) having wide rule or authority ; *mighty king* : P. R. iii. 167 ; *sup.* : P. R. iii. 262 ; *mighty nation, monarchy, etc.* : P. L. v. 748 ; xii. 124 ; *sup.* : P. L. ii. 307 ; xi. 387.

(3) serving as a sign of power and authority ; *mighty standard* : P. L. i. 533.

(4) very large, vast ; *mighty sphere, frame* : P. L. vii. 355 ; viii. 81 ; *mass* : Ariosto ii. 3 ; *quadrate* : P. L. vi. 62 ; perhaps with blending of sense (1) ; *mighty stature, bone, strength* : P. L. i. 222 ; xi. 642 ; S. A. 1602 ; *mighty wings* : P. L. i. 20.

(5) momentous, important ; *mighty works, deeds, etc.* : P. R. i. 186 ; ii. 448 ; *comp.* : P. L. i. 149 ; *sup.* : S. A. 638.

absol. (*a*) those high in rank and power : S. A. 1272.

(*b*) *sup.* those possessing the greatest power ; used of God or angels, *the* or *their mightiest* : P. L. i. 99 ; vi. 112, 200, 386 ; *thou mightiest* : P. L. VI. 710; *the hands of mightiest* : P. L. VI. 459.

Mild, (1) *adj.* (*a*) moderate in action or disposition, gentle, tender, kind : P. L. IV. 479 ; P. R. IV. 134; used of God or angels : P. L. II. 546; X. 96; XI. 151, 234 ; *mild Heaven* : S. XXI. 11 ; *comp.* : P. L. II. 816; used of beasts : P. R. I. 810.

(*b*) characterized by gentleness or kindness; *mild answer* : P. L. IX. 226 ; *temper* : P. L. X. 1046 ; *comp.*, *milder thought* : P. L. VI. 98.

(*c*) temperate, genial, pleasant; *mild zone, regions* : P. L. II. 397; C. 4 ; *mild evening, night* : P. L. IV. 647, 654 ; X. 847 ; *comp.*, *the milder shades of Purgatory* : S. XIII. 14.

(*d*) peaceful, undisturbed : P. R. II. 125.

(*e*) calm ; *mild ocean* : N. O. 66.

(*f*) soft, low ; *mild voice, echoes, whispers* : P. L. V. 16 ; P. 53; L. 136.

(*g*) moderate in degree, not hard to bear ; *his mild yoke* : S. XIX. 11 ; *this horror will grow mild* : P. L. II. 220.

(**2**) *sb.* mildness, gentleness : P. R. II. 159.

(**3**) *adv.* gently, kindly : P. L. V. 371 ; VI. 28 ; VII. 110 ; X. 67 ; • XI. 286.

Mildew, *sb. attrib.* producing a state of decay : C. 640.

Mildly, *adv.* gently, kindly : P. L. VIII. 317.

Mildness, *sb.* gentleness, kindness, clemency : P. L. VI. 735 ; *thy looks, the heaven of mildness* : P. L. IX. 534.

Mile, *sb.* the measure of length : P. L. II. 938.

Mile-End, *sb.* *Mile-End Green*, a common in the Hamlet of Milend Old Towne, in the Parish of St. Dunstan's, Stepney, London. Stow, *Surrey of London*, revised by Srype, 1720, map at page 46 : S. XI. 7.

Militant, *adj.* (*a*) engaged in warfare : P. L. VI. 61.

(*b*) equipped for warfare : P. L. X. 442.

Military, *adj.* (*a*) of or pertaining to war : P. L. VI. 45.

(*b*) of or befitting a soldier ; *military vest of purple* : P. L. XI.

241 ; *military obedience, pride* : P. L. IV. 955 ; P. R. III. 312.

Milk, *sb.* the fluid with which female animals feed their young : P. L. IX. 582.

Milkmaid, *sb.* a woman who milks cows : L'A. 65.

Milky, *adj.* resembling milk ; (*a*) pure or sweet as milk (?) : P. L. V. 306 ; S. A. 550.

(*b*) *milky way*, the luminous band of stars encircling the heavens ; *the Galaxy, that milky way* : P. L. VII. 579.

Mill, *sb.* the machine for grinding grain : S. A. 41, 1093 ; *the* or *their public. mill* : S. A. 1327, 1393.

Million, *sb.* a very great but indefinite number ; always *pl.* : P. L. II. 55 ; P. R. I. 359 ; *by millions* : P. L. II. 997 ; VI. 48 ; with *of* ; *millions of spirits*, etc. ; P. L. I. 609 ; IV. 677 ; VI. 220 : *millions of flaming swords* : P. L. I. 664 ; *millions of spinning worms* : C. 715.

Mimic, (1) *adj.* imitative : P. L. V. 110.

(**2**) *sb.* one who imitates, actor, player : S. A. 1325.

Mincing, *part. adj.* taking short dainty steps : C. 964.

Mincius, *sb.* the Mincio, a river in Lombardy, Italy, which empties into the Po near Mantua : L. 86.

Mind, I. *sb.* (1) that which feels, wills, and thinks : the soul : P. L. V. 34 ; VIII. 525 ; IX. 1125 ; XII. 444 ; S. A. 611, 745, 1336 ; *the mind and inward faculties* : P. L. VIII. 541 ; *union of mind, or in us both one soul* : P. L. VIII. 604 ; *the mind through all her powers irradiate* : P. L. III. 52 ; *the mind and will depraved* : P. L. X. 825 ; *evil into the mind of God or man may come* : P. L. V. 117 ; *hindered not Satan to attempt the mind of man* : P. L. X. 8 ; *fame ... that last infirmity of noble mind* : L. 71 ; *greatness of, amplitude of, magnitude of* : P. L. VIII. 557 ; P. R. II. 139 ; S. A. 1279 ; *ease of, anguish of, calm of* : P. L. IX. 1120 ; S. A. 600, 1758 ; *immortal, exalted, virtuous, generous*, etc. : P. L. I. 559 ; IV. 55 ; P. R. II. 206, 479 ; V. Ex. 33 ; Il P. 4, 91 ; C. 211 ; *untroubled, troubled* : P. R. IV. 401 ; S. A. 185 ; *servile* :

S. A. 412, 1213; used of angels:
P. L. II. 521; v. 786; *one who
brings a mind not to be changed by
place or time. The mind in its
own place*: P. L. I. 253, 254; *the
mind and spirit remains invincible*:
P. L. I. 139; *heavenly minds*: P.
L. IV. 118; *ambitious mind*: P.
L. II. 34.

(*b*) in contrast with the body:
P. L. IV. 618; IX. 238; S. A. 18,
52, 1298; C. 663; *feed at once
both body and mind*: P. L. IX.
779; *prodigious births of body or
mind*: P. L. XI. 687; *allure mine
eye, much less my mind*: P. R. IV.
113; *the outward shape, the unpolluted temple of the mind*: C.
461; *vested all in white, pure as
her mind*: S. XXIII. 9.

(2) the faculty of perceiving
divine things, of knowing good
and hating evil; *their minds how
darkened*: P. L. IX. 1053.

(3) the intellective faculty, the
understanding, the power of con-
sidering and judging: P. L. VIII.
188; IX. 213; X. 1011, 1015,; P.
R. II. 221; S. A. 1638; *I will
excite their minds with more desire
to know*: P. L. IV. 522; *to know
in measure what the mind may well
contain*: P. L. VII. 128; *all my
mind was set serious to learn*: P.
R. I. 202; *extend thy mind o'er
all the world in knowledge*: P. R.
IV. 223; *if there be aught of presage
in the mind*: S. A. 1387; *a spirit
of phrensy sent, who hurt their
minds*: S. A. 1676; used of God:
P. L. II. 189; XI. 144; used of
the serpent; *with capacious mind
considered all things*: P. L. IX.
603; used of angels: P. L. III.
705; VI. 444; *what power of
mind, foreseeing*: P. L. I. 626.

(4) thought, feeling, desire, intention, purpose: Ps. LXXXIII.
18; *I know your friendly minds*:
S. A. 1508; *sudden mind arose in
Adam*: P. L. V. 452; used of
angels: P. L. VI. 613; *change his
constant mind*: P. L. V. 902;
change...that fixed mind: P. L.
I. 97; *new minds may raise in us*:
P. L. V. 680.

(5) memory, remembrance: P.
L. XII. 15; P. R. II. 105; *brought
to my mind*: C. 619; *calling* or
call to mind: P. L. X. 1030; XI.
898.

II. *vb.* (1) *tr.* (*a*) to think upon,
consider: P. R. II. 258; *as not to
mind from whence they grow*: P.
L. VI. 477.

(*b*) to call to mind, remember:
P. L. XI. 156.

(*c*) to make to think, remind;
with *acc.* and *of*: P. L. IV. 612.

(*d*) to take notice of: P. L. II.
212.

(*e*) to watch over: P. L. IX.
358.

(2) *intr.* (*a*) to be inclined, intend, purpose; with *prep. inf.*:
S. A. 1603; *so minded*, having
this intention: P. L. IV. 583;
disposed to think in this way: P.
L. VIII. 444.

(*b*) to give heed, take note: P.
L. IX. 519.

Mindless, *adj.* unmindful, not re-
gardful; *of* omitted: P. L. IX.
431.

Mine, *sb.* (*a*) underground excavation for the purpose of digging
out metals: P. L. V. 443; *swart
faery of the mine*: C. 436.

(*b*) subterranean passage dug
under the wall of a fortification:
P. L. XI. 656.

*Mine, *poss. pron.* (1) of or belonging to me; with *sb.*; *mine eye* or
ear: P. L. II. 808; III. 193; IV.
358; v. 36; VIII. 310, 335; XI.
598; XII. 274; P. R. III. 390;
IV. 112; S. A. 459; P. 43; L'A.
69; *mine enemies*: Ps. VI. 15,
21; *mine own*: P. L. II. 863; S.
A. 45; used for *my* when separated from the *sb.*; *mine and love*'s
prisoner: S. A. 808.

(2) *absol.* that or those belonging to me; (*a*) referring to a
preceding *sb.*: P. L. II. 807; III.
735; IV. 489, 637; IX. 916; S. A.
1155; with *of*; *no decree of mine*:
P. L. X. 43; *is this the recompense
of mine to thee*: P. L. IX. 1164.

(*b*) not referring to a *sb.*; *my*
nation or people: S. A. 291; *my*
nature or being: P. L. IX. 957; *my*
part or duty: P. L. X. 69; *my*
afflictions or evils: P. L. X.
738.

Mineral, (1) *sb.* the solid inorganic
substance, dug from veins be-
neath the surface of heaven: P.
L. VI. 517.

(2) *adj.* of minerals; *sublimed
with mineral fury*: P. L. I.
235.

Minerva, *sb.* the Latin name for Athene, the virgin daughter of Zeus and the goddess of wisdom: C. 448.

Mingle, *vb.* (1) *tr.* (*a*) to mix : P. L. VI. 513.

(*b*) to join, bring into association; *earth with hell to mingle* : P. L. II. 384.

(*c*) to stir up ; *there mingle broils* : P. L. VI. 277.

(**2**) *intr.* to become joined, be mixed ; *as earth and sky would mingle* : P. R. IV. 453 ; *humours black that mingle with my fancy* : S. A. 601.

part. adj. **mingled,** varied or blended : C. 994.

Minim, *sb.* very diminutive being; *minims of nature* : P. L. VII. 482.

Minister, I. *sb.* (*a*) one who executes the commands of another : S. A. 706 ; *spirits of air ... thy gentle ministers* : P. R. II. 375 ; the angels, servants and messengers of God or attendants upon man ; *empyreal, flaming, bright* : P. L. V. 460 ; IX. 156 ; XI. 73.

(*b*) one who acts as a dispenser ; *the minister of Law* : P. L. XII. 308; *Death's ministers, not men* : P. L. XI. 676 ; used of angels ; *his ministers of vengeance* : P. L. I. 170.

II. *vb.* (**1**) *tr.* to furnish, supply : P. L. IV. 664.

(**2**) *intr.* to act as a minister or attendant ; *to minister about his altar* : P. R. I. 488 ; *to serve at table* : P. L. V. 444.

part. adj. **ministering,** acting as attendants : P. L. VI. 167.

vbl. sb. **ministering,** ministry : P. L. VI. 182.

Ministrant, *adj.* ministering ; *Dominations, Angels ministrant* : P. L. X. 87 ; P. R. II. 385.

Ministry, *sb.* (*a*) the office or duty of a minister ; *their ministry performed, and race well run* : P. L. XII. 505.

(*b*) ministration, service : P. L. VII. 149.

Minstrelsy, *sb.* (*a*) music and lyric song : C. 547.

(*b*) a body of singers and players; *the minstrelsy of heaven* : P. L. VI. 168.

Mintage, *sb.* that which is formed as if by coining ; *reason's mintage, charactered in the face* : C. 529.

Minute, *sb.* the sixtieth part of an hour : P. L. X. 91.

Minute-drops, *sb.* drops that fall at intervals of a minute : Il P. 130.

Miracle, *sb.* (*a*) that which excites astonishment, wonder : P. L. IX. 562 : *the miracle of men* : S. A. 364.

(*b*) an occurrence transcending the common course of nature and brought about by divine power : P. L. XII. 501 ; Ps. CXXXVI. 13 ; *by miracle* : P. R. I. 337 ; S. A. 1528.

Miraculous, *sb.* supernatural : S. A. 587.

Mire, *sb.* deep mud ; *to trample thee as mire* : P. L. IV. 1010 ; *pl.* morass, fen : P. L. IX. 641.

attrib. abounding with mire ; *the fields are dank and ways are mire* : S. XX. 2.

Mirror, *sb.* (*a*) an object having a nearly perfect reflecting surface; used *fig.* of the moon : P. L. VII. 377 ; of water : P. L. IV. 263.

(*b*) exemplar ; *O mirror of our fickle state* : S. A. 164.

Mirth, *sb.* (*a*) gaiety, jollity, merriment : P. L. I. 786 ; S. A. 1613 ; C. 955 ; S. XXI. 6 ; *they swim in mirth* : P. L. IX. 1009 ; *the tumult of loud mirth* : C. 202 ; *mirth, and youth, and warm desire* : M. M. 6 ; *to make them mirth* : P. L. IV. 346 ; *concr.* those indulging in mirth ; *far from all resort of mirth* : Il P. 81.

(*b*) joy : P. 1.

(*c*) Euphrosyne, one of the Graces : L'A. 13, 38, 152.

Miry, *adj.* muddy ; *miry soil* : Ps. LXXXI. 23.

Misbecoming, *adj.* unbecoming, unseemly : C. 372.

Miscellaneous, *adj.* mixed, promiscuous : P. R. III. 50.

Mischance, *sb.* misfortune, mishap ; *by mischance* : D. F. I. 44 ; M. W. 27.

Mischief, *sb.* (*a*) misfortune, calamity: P. L. X. 895 ; XI. 450.

(*b*) harm, hurt, injury : P. L. II. 141 ; *after all his injury done* : P. R. IV. 440 ; *his mischief ... turns on his head* : Ps. VII. 57.

(*c*) the doing of injury ; *intent on mischief* : P. L. VI. 503 ; *he ... to mischief swift* : P. L. IX. 633 ; *thoughts of mischief* : P. L. IX. 472 ; *implements, instrument of mischief* : P. L. VI. 488 ; X. 167.

Mischievous, *adj.* bent on injury : P. L. II. 1054.

Miscreated, *part. adj.* deformed ; *thy miscreated front* : P. L. II. 683.

Misdeed, *sb.* evil deed : P. L. X. 1080 ; S. A. 747.

Misdeem, *vb. intr.* to misjudge : P. L. IX. 301 ; with *of* : P. R. I. 424.

Misdo, *vb.* (*pret.* misdone) (1) *tr.* to do amiss, perform wrongly : S. A. 911.

(2) *intr.* to act amiss, err in conduct : P. R. I. 225.

Miser, *sb.* niggard : C. 399.

Miserable (miseráble), *adj.* (*a*) unhappy, wretched : P. L. IX. 126, 1139 ; X. 839, 930 ; P. R. I. 411, 471 ; S. A. 703 ; *O miserable mankind !* : P. L. XI. 500 ; *me miserable !* : P. L. IV. 73 ; *O miserable of happy !* : P. L. X. 720 ; *O yet more miserable !* : S. A. 101 ; *happier far than miserable* : P. L. II. 98 ; *to be weak is miserable* : P. L. I. 157 ; *miserable it is to be to others cause of misery* : P. L. X. 981.

(*b*) causing or attended by unhappiness or wretchedness ; *miserable pain, change, plight, troubles* : P. L. II. 752 ; S. A. 340, 480 ; Ps. v. 27 ; *days* : S. A. 762.

Misery, *adj.* extreme unhappiness, wretchedness, suffering : P. L. I. 90 ; II. 459 ; IV. 92 ; X. 726, 928, 982, 997 ; XI. 476 ; P. R. I. 341, 398, 470 ; S. A. 1469 ; C. 73 ; Ps. CXXXVI. 78 ; *endless, eternal misery* : P. L. I. 142 ; VI. 904 ; X. 810 ; *of happiness and final misery* : P. L. II. 563 ; *death as utmost end of misery* : P. L. X. 1021 ; *pain is perfect misery* : P. L. VI. 462 ; *into nature brought misery* : P. L. VI. 268 ; *personified* : P. L. IX. 12.

Misfortune, *sb.* (*a*) adverse fortune, bad luck : P. L. X. 900.

(*b*) evil accident, calamity : C. 286.

Misgive, *vb.* (*pret.* misgave) *tr.* to give doubt to, make apprehensive ; with pron. object ; *his heart ... misgave him* : P. L. IX. 846.

Misguide, *vb. tr.* to lead astray in action : S. A. 912.

Mishap, *sb.* ill chance, misfortune : P. L. X. 239 ; L. 92.

Misinform, *vb. tr.* to give wrong instruction to ; *reason ... misinform the will* : P. L. IX. 355.

Misjoin, *vb. tr.* to join unfitly ; *mimic fancy ... misjoining shapes* : P. L. V. 111.

Mislead, *vb.* (*pret.* and *past part.* misled) *tr.* (*a*) to guide wrongly, lead astray : P. L. IX. 640.

(*b*) to lead astray in conduct or thought : P. R. I. 226 ; *absol.* : P. R. IV. 309.

part. adj. misled, wrongly directed : C. 200.

Mislike, *vb. tr.* to dislike, be averse to ; *Israel ... misliked me* : Ps. LXXXI. 48.

Misrepresent, *vb. intr.* to convey a false impression : S. A. 124.

Misrule, *sb.* (*a*) absence of control, disorder ; *the loud misrule of chaos* : P. L. VII. 271.

(*b*) bad rule, misgovernment : P. L. X. 628.

Miss, *vb. tr.* (*a*) to fail in aiming at, not to hit ; *fig., missing what I aimed* : P. R. IV. 208.

(*b*) to fail to gain or obtain ; *to gain a sceptre, oftest better missed* : P. R. II. 486 ; *their full tribute never miss* : C. 925.

(*c*) to fail to find ; *miss the way* : P. L. III. 735 ; X. 262 ; XI. 15.

(*d*) to fail, come short of ; with *prep. inf.* : P. L. VI. 499.

(*e*) to perceive and feel the want of, deplore the absence of : P. L. IX. 857 ; X. 104 ; P. R. II. 9 ; S. A. 927 ; Il P. 65.

(*f*) *pres. part.* absent ; *Moses was in the mount and missing long* : P. R. II. 15 ; *past part.* apart ; *Mercy and Truth, that long were missed, now joyfully are met* : Ps. LXXXV. 41.

(*g*) *absol.* or *intr.* to fail : P. R. II. 77.

Mission, *sb.* that for which a person is destined : P. R. II. 114.

Missive, *adj.* missile ; transferred epithet ; *balls of missive ruin* : P. L. VI. 519.

Mist, *sb.* (*a*) the thin vapour suspended in the atmosphere at or near the earth's surface : P. L. X. 694 ; *evening mist* : P. L. XII. 629 ; *dewy mist* : P. L. VII. 333 ; *like a black mist low-creeping* : P. L. IX. 180 ; *fig.* : L. 126 ; as intercepting vision ; *involved in rising mist* : P. L. IX. 75 ; *wrapt in mist of midnight vapour* : P. L. IX. 158 ; *black usurping mists* : C. 337 ; *in mist,* not clearly and distinctly

seen : P. L. v. 435 ; *personified* :
P. L. v. 185.

  (*b*) *fig.* that which intercepts
intellectual or spiritual vision : P.
L. III. 53.

Mistake, I. *sb.* error, blunder : P.
L. x. 900.

  II. *vb.* (*pret.* mistook ; *past part.*
mistaken) (**1**) *tr.* to misunderstand,
misapprehend : A. 4.

  (**2**) *intr.* to do wrong, err : C.
815.

  part. adj. **mistaken,** wrong, in
error ; *I was ... quite mistaken* : S.
A. 907.

Misthink, *vb.* (*pret.* misthought),
intr. to think erroneously ; with
of : P. L. IX. 289.

Mistress, *sb.* (*a*) a woman having
power or authority : A. 36 ; applied to Eve ; *sovran mistress* : P.
L. IX. 532.

  (*b*) a woman beloved and
courted : A. 106.

Mistrust, *sb.* the want of confidence,
doubt : P. L. IX. 357, 1124.

Mistrustful, *adj.* wanting confidence,
doubtful ; with *in* : P. L. II. 126.

Misty, *adj.* containing or filled with
mist or clouds ; *misty air* : P. L.
I. 595 ; *the misty regions of wide
air* ; V. Ex. 41.

Misused (*trisyl.*), *part. adj.* applied
to an improper purpose : C. 47.

Mitigate, *vb. tr.* to make milder or
less severe ; *mitigate ... troubled
thoughts* : P. L. I. 558 ; *their* or
his doom : P. L. x. 76 ; XI. 41.

Mitred, *part. adj.* covered with a
sacerdotal head-dress ; *his mitred
locks* : L. 112.

Mix, *vb.* (**1**) *tr.* (*a*) to mingle, blend,
unite : P. L. II. 913 ; *do they mix
irradiance* : P. L. VIII. 616 ; *fairest
colours mixed* : P. L. IX. 577 ; *gay
enamelled colours mixed* : P. L. IV.
149 ; *not to mix tastes* : P. L. v.
334 ; one thing *with* another ;
*thunder mixed with hail, hail mixed
with fire* : P. L. XII. 181, 182 ;
rain with lightning mixed : P. R.
IV. 412 ; *and with the centre mix the
pole* : P. L. VII. 215 ; *the ... sun ...
with terrestrial humour mixed* : P.
L. III. 610 ; *destruction with creation might have mixed* : P. L. VIII.
236 ; *I ... mixed with bestial slime* :
P. L. IX. 165 ; *sighs and prayers ...
mixed with incense* : P. L. XI. 24 ;
affliction mixed with ... pride : P.
L. I. 58 ; *sadness ... mixed with*

pity : P. L. x. 24 ; *decencies ...
mixed with love* : P. L. VIII. 602.

  (*b*) to intermingle ; *mixing intercession sweet* : P. L. x. 228 ;
mixing somewhat true : P. R. I.
433 ; *too much of self-love mixed* :
S. A. 1031.

  (*c*) to join, combine, associate ;
*grey-headed men with warriors
mixed* : P. L. XI. 662 ; *the heroic
race ... mixed with auxiliar gods* :
P. L. I. 579.

  (*d*) to intermarry : P. L. XI. 686.

  (*e*) to produce by mingling ingredients : C. 526, 674.

  (*f*) to create or form ; *works of
nature's hand ... unkindly mixed* :
P. L. III. 456.

  (*g*) to throw into confusion,
confound ; *his throne itself mixed
with Tartarean sulphur* : P. L. II.
69.

  (**2**) *intr.* (*a*) to be or become
mingled or blended : P. L. v. 182 ;
if spirits embrace, total they mix :
P. L. VIII. 627 ; with *with* : P. L.
XI. 529 ; *flesh to mix with flesh* :
P. L. VIII. 629 ; *evil ... mix no
more with goodness* : C. 594 ; *evil
... impossible to mix with blessedness* : P. L. VII. 58.

  (*b*) to be joined or associated ;
*he mixed among those friendly
powers* : P. L. VI. 21 ; *to mix with
thy discernments* : S. A. 969.

  part. adj. **mixed** ; (*a*) indiscriminate ; *mixed dance*, the dancing
of men and women together :
P. L. IV. 768.

  (*b*) united : S. M. 3.

Mixture, *sb.* (*a*) union : Il P. 26.

  (*b*) admixture, somewhat mingled or added : P. L. XI. 51.

  (*c*) that which results from
mixing ; *fig., any mortal mixture
of earth's mould* : C. 244.

Moab, *sb.* the nation descended from
Moab, the son of Lot's eldest
daughter : Ps. LXXXIII. 23 ; *Moab's
sons* : P. L. I. 406.

Moan, (**1**) *sb.* (*a*) lamentation : S.
XVIII. 8.

  (*b*) grief, sorrow : M. W. 55.

  (**2**) *vb. intr.* to lament : N. O.
191.

Mock, *vb. tr.* (*a*) to make sport of by
mimicry, deride : P. L. XII. 59.

  (*b*) to disappoint with false expectation ; *mock us with his blest
sight* : P. R. II. 56 ; *why am I
mocked with death* : P. L. x. 774.

(c) to set at nought, defy: P. L. IV. 628.

Mode, sb. (a) manner, way: P. R. II. 340.

(b) pattern, design: P. L. I. 474.

Model, (1) sb. a representation in miniature: P. L. III. 509.

(2) vb. tr. to execute a representation of, imitate in form: P. L. VIII. 79.

Moderate, (1) adj. (a) avoiding extremes, acting temperately: S. A. 1464.

(b) not excessive, medium: C. 769.

(2) adv. in a moderate manner; live moderate: P. L. XII. 351.

Moderation, sb. freedom from excess, due restraint: P. L. XI. 363.

Modern, adj. pertaining to the present time, late, recent: P. L. XI. 386; S. A. 653; C. 45.

Modest, adj. (a) not bold, unobtrusive: P. L. IV. 310.

(b) full of bashful reserve indicating a chaste mind: S. A. 1036.

Modesty, sb. (a) reserve proceeding from absence of self-esteem, unobtrusiveness: P. R. III. 241.

(b) reserve proceeding from a chaste character, delicacy of feeling: P. L. VIII. 501.

Modin, sb. a city or village of Judea, the ancestral house of the Maccabæan family. Its exact locality is uncertain: P. R. III. 170.

Mogul, sb. Great Mogul, the sovereign of the Mogul empire: P. L. XI. 391.

Moist, (1) adj. (a) moderately wet, damp: C. 918; the winds blow moist: P. L. X. 1066; exhalation dusk and moist: P. L. XI. 741; fish ... attend moist nutriment: P. L. VII. 408; a nymph ... with moist curb sways the smooth Severn: C. 825; referring to the clouds or vapour on the surface of the moon; her moist continent: P. L. V. 422.

(b) accompanied with tears; our moist vows: L. 159.

(c) absol. the sea: P. L. III. 652.

(2) sb. (a) moisture: P. L. V. 325.

(b) one of the supposed qualities which in combination with another determined the nature or 'complexion' of a body, personified: P. L. II. 898.

Moisture, sb. wetness, humidity: P. L. VII. 282; VIII. 256.

Mole, sb. the animal Talpa: P. L. VII. 467.

Mole, sb. a massive structure, a causeway: P. L. X. 300.

Mole, sb. a river of Surrey, England: V. Ex. 95.

Molest, vb. tr. to trouble, disturb, harass: P. L. VIII. 186; P. R. IV. 498; S. A. 1525.

Moloch, sb. Molech, the god of the Ammonites: N. O. 205; as identified with one of the fallen angels: P. L. I. 392, 417; II. 43; VI. 357.

Molten, adj. liquid: C. 931. See **Crystal.**

Moly, sb. an herb of magic power: C. 636.

Mombaza, sb. one of the provinces of Zanzibar. "Mombaza is the name of another of these petit kingdoms ... so called from Mombaza, the Chief City of it, situate from Melinde about 70 miles, in a little Island." Heylyn, Cos. 1657, p. 990: P. L. XI. 399.

Moment, sb. (a) force sufficient to turn the scale, fig.: P. L. VI. 239; X. 45.

(b) an instant: P. L. II. 907; in a moment: P. L. I. 544; IV. 51; VI. 509; VII. 154; P. R. IV. 162; S. A. 1559; Ps. VI. 24; in one moment: P. L. II. 609.

(c) importance, consequence; of public moment: P. L. II. 448.

Mona, sb. the isle of Anglesey: L. 54.

Monarch, sb. supreme ruler: P. L. I. 599; V. 832; P. R. III. 237, 262; Europe ... and all her jealous monarchs: S. XV. 3; applied to God: P. L. I. 638; Heaven's awful monarch: P. L. IV. 960; applied to Satan: P. L. II. 467; X. 375; fig., Night sits monarch yet in the mid sky: C. 957.

Monarchal, adj. befitting a monarch: P. L. II. 428.

Monarchy, sb. (a) supreme power, absolute authority: P. L. V. 795; X. 379; the throne and monarchy of God: P. L. I. 42.

(b) kingdom, empire: P. L. II. 307; P. R. IV. 150; that first golden monarchy: P. R. III. 277; the monarchies of the earth: P. R. III. 246; the monarchy of Heaven: P. R. I. 87.

Money, *sb.* wealth, riches : P. R. II. 422.

'Mongst, *prep.* (*a*) amongst, surrounded by : L'A. 4.

(*b*) by (the members of a group) generally : D. F. I. 14.

Monster, *sb.* (*a*) the sphinx : P. R. IV. 572. ‛

(*b*) an unnatural and deformed creature : P. L. II. 795 ; *complicated monsters, head and tail* : P. L. x. 523 ; *oughly-headed monsters* : C. 695 ; applied to death : P. L. II. 675 ; x. 596, 986.

(*c*) a person morally deformed : P. R. IV. 100, 128 ; *Dalila, that specious monster* : S. A. 230.

See **Sea-monster.**

Monstrous, *adj.* (*a*) out of the ordinary course of nature, unnatural : P. L. II. 625 ; III. 456 ; *monstrous shapes* : P. L. I. 479.

(*b*) huge, enormous : P. L. I. 197 ; x. 514.

(*c*) shocking, horrible ; *monstrous sight* : P. L. VI. 862 ; or extraordinary in number, kind, and degree ; *diseases ... a monstrous crew* : P. L. XI. 474.

(*d*) of monsters ; used instead of a sb. as first part of a compound ; *monstrous forms* : C. 605 ; *monstrous rout* : C. 533 ; *the monstrous world* ; the world teeming with monsters : L. 158.

Montalban, *sb.* a name famous in medieval romances, the castle of the knight Renaud, in Guienne, France. The geographies give it as a town in the province of Quercu, a division of Guienne. Heylyn, *Cos.* 1666, p. 209 ; also Moll, *Geography* 1701, p. 107 : P. L. I. 583.

Montezume, *sb.* Montezuma, the Aztec chief of Mexico who was conquered by Cortez : P. L. XI. 407.

Month, *sb.* the interval from one new moon to the next : P. L. III. 581 ; VIII. 69 ; N. O. 1 ; C. 114.

Monthly, *adv.* performed in a month : P. L. III. 728.

Monument, *sb.* (*a*) that by which the memory of a thing is preserved ; *these redundant locks ... vain monument of strength* : S. A. 570.

(*b*) something built in memory of actions or persons : P. L. I.

695 ; XI. 326 ; used of the causeway from hell *to* earth : P. L. x. 258 ; a structure erected at a grave in memory of the dead : S. A. 1734 ; *fig.* : W. S. 8.

Monumental, *adj.* memorial ; *monumental oak* : Il P. 135.

Mood, *sb.* (*a*) state of mind as regards passion or feeling, disposition, humour ; *calm, constant mood* : P. L. IX. 920 ; C. 371 ; *gamesome, careless, senseless* : P. L. VI. 620 ; P. R. IV. 450 ; S. XII. 9.

(*b*) mode, a system of dividing the intervals of an octave by placing the steps and half steps in certain arbitrary positions ; *Dorian mood* : P. L. I. 550 ; *fig., that strain was of a higher mood* : L. 87 ; *of dissonant mood from his complaint* : S. A. 662.

Moon, *sb.* (*a*) the satellite that revolves round the earth : P. L. I. 440, 596 ; II. 1053 ; IV. 723 ; VII. 356 ; U. C. II. 29 ; C. 116, 374 ; S. XII. 7 ; XXII. 5 ; Ps. VIII. 10 ; *the new moon* : Ps. LXXXI. 9 ; *now reigns full-orbed the moon* : P. L. VI. 42 ; *the labouring moon eclipses at their charms* : P. L. II. 665 ; *dazzling the moon* : P. L. IV. 798 ; *the moon haste to thy audience* : P. L. VII. 104 ; *imagined lands and regions in the moon* : P. L. v. 263 ; *to the corners of the moon* : C. 1017 ; as inhabited : P. L. III. 459 ; virtually the first part of a compound, *moon-light* : P. L. IV. 655.

vocative : P. L. v. 175 ; XII. 266 ; *thou, fair moon, ... stoop thy pale visage* : C. 331.

denoted by a feminine pronoun : P. L. I. 287 ; VII. 375 ; VIII. 142 ; x. 656 ; Il P. 67 ; Ps. CXXXVI. 33 ; *whence in her visage round those spots* : P. L. v. 418 ; *nor doth the moon no nourishment exhale from her moist continent to higher orbs* : P. L. v. 421 ; *silent as the moon ... hid in her vacant interlunar cave* : S. A. 87 ; more definitely personified with the characteristics of the goddess Diana ; *overhead the moon sits arbitress* : P. L. I. 784 ; *in her pale dominion checks the night* : P. L. III. 726 ; *rising in clouded majesty, at length apparent queen* : P. L. IV. 606 ; *the gems of heaven, her starry train* : P. L. IV. 648.

(b) the satellite of any planet;
*other suns ... with their attendant
moons*: P. L. VIII. 149.
   See **Half-moon.**
Mooned (*disyl.*), *adj.* (a) crescent-
shaped : P. L. IV. 978.
   (b) *mooned Ashtaroth*, Ashtoreth,
goddess of the moon: N. O. 200.
   See **Horn** (1) (a) and (2) (b).
Moon-loved (lovèd, *disyl.*), *adj.* loved
by the moon: N. O. 236.
Moon-struck, *adj.* caused by the in-
fluence of the moon ; *moon-struck
madness*: P. L. XI. 486.
Moor, *vb. intr.* to anchor a boat : P.
L. I. 207.
Moorish, *adj.* marshy, boggy ; *moor-
ish fen* : C. 433.
Moory, *adj.* marshy ; *moory dale* :
P. L. II. 944.
Moping, *part. adj.* yielding to gloom
and despondency : P. L. XI. 485.
Moral, *adj.* pertaining to rightness
and oughtness in conduct : P. L.
XII. 298 ; *moral prudence, virtue* :
P. R. IV. 263, 351 ; *verdict* : S. A.
324 ; *mere moral babble* : C. 807.
*More (*comp. of* much *or* many), (1)
adj. (a) greater ; *more wrath, woe,
desire, warmth*, etc. : P. L. I. 54 ;
III. 553 ; IV. 327, 523 ; V. 302 ;
VIII. 94 ; S. A. 388 ; C. 789 ; *in
number more* : S. A. 1667.
   (b) in addition, additional ;
more worlds, angels, hands : P. L.
II. 916 ; IX. 146, 207 ; *causes* : P.
L. IX. 730.
   absol. (a) a greater or superior
thing ; *what can heaven show
more ?* : P. L. II. 273.
   (b) something or some persons
additional ; *all these and more came
flocking* : P. L. I. 522 ; *he ... and
many more* : P. L. III. 473 ; *took
more than enough* : P. L. VIII.
537 ; *of pain .. will covet more* : P.
L. II. 35 ; *more in this place to utter
is not safe* : P. L. V. 682 ; *to know
no more* : P. L. IV. 637.
   (2) *adv.* (a) to a greater extent
or degree : P. L. I. 11, 681 ; II.
22, 698, 908 ; III. 200 ; VI. 421 ;
VIII. 571 ; *more than half* : S. A.
79 ; *more strongly* : C. 806 ; *is
more a king* : P. R. II. 467 ; *no
more than*, as little as : P. L. VI.
349 ; *the more ... the more* : P. L.
VIII. 573 ; P. R. III. 40 ; *the more
... so much more* : P. L. IX. 119.
   used before adjectives or adverbs
to form the comparative degree :

P. L. I. 120 ; II. 52, 192 ; III.
460 ; IV. 215, 330 ; before monosyllables ; *more apt* : P. R. II.
454 ; *bold* : P. L. IX. 664 ; *cool* :
P. L. V. 370 ; X. 95 ; *deaf* : S. A.
960 ; *dread* : P. L. II. 16 ; *fell* :
P. L. II. 539 ; *fierce* : P. L. II.
599 ; *fresh* : P. R. IV. 435 ; *glad* :
P. L. IV. 150 ; *green* : P. R. IV.
435 ; *gross* : P. L. I. 491 ; *just* :
Cir. 15 ; *lewd* : P. L. I. 490 ; *loth* :
P. L. X. 109 ; *mild* : P. L. II. 546 ;
meek : P. L. XI. 437 ; *pure* : P. L.
V. 475 ; P. R. I. 77 ; *safe* : P. L.
VII. 24 ; XI. 814 ; *soft* : P. L. IX.
458 ; *sweet* : P. L. II. 555 ; V. 68 ;
XII. 221 ; *swift* : P. L. VII. 176 ;
true : P. R. I. 431 ; *wise* : P. L.
VII. 425 ; *near* : P. L. V. 830 ; A.
40 ; *oft* : S. A. 268.
   (b) farther ; *more to west* : P.
R. IV. 71.
   (c) in addition, besides, again :
P. L. IX. 1090 ; XII. 418 ; S. A.
1129 ; *once more* : P. L. I. 268 ;
II. 393, 721 ; III. 175 ; IV. 941 ;
XI. 75, 125 ; XII. 211 ; S. A. 742 ;
no more : P. L. III. 264, 340 ; IV.
838 ; V. 659 ; VII. 144 ; IX. 827 ;
X. 958 ; XI. 745 ; *never more* : P.
L. IX. 859 ; P. R. I. 405 ; IV. 610 ;
to be no or *never more*, to be dead
or no longer in existence : P. L.
II. 146 ; XI. 200 ; C. 559.
Moreh, *sb. plain of Moreh*, a place
in central Palestine near Shechem
(R.V. *oak of Moreh*, Gen. XII. 6) ;
P. L. XII. 137.
Morn, *sb.* morning : P. L. I. 208 ;
IV. 773 ; V. 30, 310, 428 ; VI. 748 ;
IX. 191, 848, 1136 ; P. R. IV. 438,
439 ; N. O. 1 ; L'A. 107 ; Ps.
LXXXVIII. 56 ; *from morn to noon
he fell* : P. L. I. 742 ; *a summer's
morn* : P. L. IX. 447 ; *the stars of
morn* : P. L. XII. 422 ; *fair Morn
orient in heaven* : P. L. VI. 524 ;
Morn purples the east : P. L. VII.
29 ; *blushing like the Morn* : P. L.
VIII. 511 ; *short blush of morn* : P.
L. XI. 184 ; *tresses like the morn* :
C. 753 ; *odorous breath of morn* :
A. 56 ; feminine gender : P. R. II.
281 ; *breath of Morn* : P. L. IV. 641,
650 ; joined to *even* or *evening* : P. L.
III. 42 ; V. 202, 628 ; VII. 252, 260,
338, 386, 448, 550 ; P. R. II. 268.
   fig. as a symbol of purity and
brilliance ; *Sons of Morn* : P. L.
V. 716 ; *morn of light* : S. M. 28.
   See **Light** and **Son.**

personified, often with the characteristics of the goddess Aurora: P. L. v. 168; M. W. 45; L'A. 54; Il P. 122; C. 139; *Morn ... with rosy hand unbarred the gates of light*: P. L. vi. 2; *went forth the Morn ... arrayed in gold empyreal*: P. L. vi. 12; *the Morn began her rosy progress*: P. L. xi. 173; *the opening eyelids of the Morn*: L. 26; *still morn went out with sandals grey*: L. 187; *Morn, her rosy steps ... advancing*: P. L. v. 1.

Morning, *sb.* the first part of the day: P. L. v. 145, 211; ix. 800; P. R. iv. 221, 451; Ps. v. 6, 7; *the morning shines* or *shine*: P. L. v. 20; vii. 108; *ere fresh morning streak the east*: P. L. iv. 623; *fig.* as a symbol of purity and brilliance; *Sons of Morning*: N. O. 119. *See* Son.

personified: P. L. v. 124; *Morning fair ... in amice grey*: P. R. iv. 426.

attrib. of or pertaining to the first part of the day; *morning hour*: C. 920; *morning sun, planet, ray, sky*: P. L. iv. 244; vii. 366; C. 622; L. 171; *light*: N. O. 73; *dew-drops*: P. L. v. 746; *even and morning chorus*: P. L. vii. 275; *morning incense*: P. L. ix. 194; *trumpets*: S. A. 1598; *fig.*, *our Morning Star*, Christ: P. R. i. 294.

Morning-hour, *sb.* the first hour of the morning: P. L. viii. 111.

Morning-light, *sb.* the light of morning: P. L. xi. 204.

Morning-star, *sb.* Lucifer; *personified, his countenance, as the morning-star that guides the starry flock*: P. L. v. 708; *morning-star ... leads with her the flowery May*: M. M. 1.

Morning-watch, *sb.* the watch of the night which lasted from 2 A.M. to sunrise; here, apparently, the break of day: P. L. xii. 207.

Morpheus, *sb.* the god of dreams: Il P. 10.

Morrice, *sb.* morris-dance, *fig.*: C. 116.

Morrow, *sb.* the next day after the present, to-morrow: P. L. v. 33; C. 317.

attrib. of to-morrow; *by morrow dawning*: P. L. iv. 588; *by morrow evening*: P. L. iv. 662.

See **Good-morrow, To-morrow.**

Morsel, *sb.* mouthful, bite; used of that which death devours: P. L. ii. 808; x. 605.

Mortal, (1) *adj.* (*a*) subject to death, destined to die: P. L. iii. 214; viii. 331; x. 796; P. R. i. 86; C. 802; *mortal men*: P. L. i. 51; iii. 268; xii. 248; P. R. i. 234; S. A. 168, 1682; *mortal creatures, seed, wight*: P. R. ii. 157; S. A. 1439; D. F. I. 41; *mortal clay*: N. O. 14; *mortal mixture of earth's mould*: C. 244; *mortal frailty*: C. 686.

(*b*) of or pertaining to man as subject to death, human; *mortal minds, sight, voice, ear*, etc.: P. L. i. 559; iii. 55; vii. 24; xii. 9, 236; S. A. 639; N. O. 95; A. 62; *food*: P. L. xi. 54; *things*: P. L. i. 693; P. R. iv. 318; *prowess, strength*: P. L. i. 588; S. A. 349.

(*c*) of this world as contrasted with heaven; *mortal dross*: T. 6; *soil*: L. 78.

(*d*) occurring at the time of death; *mortal change*, death: P. L. x. 273; C. 10; *mortal passage*, passage from mortality: P. L. xi. 366.

(*e*) destructive to life, either temporal or eternal, or both; deadly; *mortal sting, dart, dint, snare*: P. L. ii. 653, 729, 813; iii. 253; iv. 8; *wound, injury, pain*: P. L. vi. 348, 434; xii. 384; *taste*: P. L. i. 2; *crime, sin*: P. L. iii. 215; ix. 1003; *mortal sentence*, the sentence dooming man to death: P. L. x. 48; *day that must be mortal to us*, the day on which death is to come: P. L. xi. 273.

(*f*) to the death; *mortal combat, duel, fight*: P. L. i. 766; S. A. 1102, 1175.

(*g*) deadly, implacable: P. L. iii. 179.

(2) *sb. pl.* man, human beings in general: P. L. ii. 1032; P. R. iv. 454; S. A. 523, 817; V. Ex. 66; Il P. 153; *vocative*: C. 997, 1018.

Mortality, *sb.* (*a*) the condition of being subject to death: D. F. I. 35.

(*b*) death: P. L. x. 776.

Mortification, *sb.* the death of one part of an animal body while the rest is alive; used *fig.* of grief: S. A. 622.

Mosaic, *sb.* inlaid work, *fig.*: P. L. IV. 700.

Mosco, *sb.* Moscow, the capital of Moscovia or Russia: P. L. XI. 395.

Moses, *sb.* the leader of the Israelites from the Land of Egypt, and the lawgiver and organizer of the Israelitish nation: P. L. XII. 170, 198, 211, 237, 241, 307; P. R. I. 352; II. 15; *questions fitting Moses' chair*: P. R. IV. 219; *Moses' law*: P. R. IV. 225.

Mossy, *adj.* overgrown with or abounding in moss: P. L. V. 392; IX. 589; P. R. II. 184; Il P. 169; C. 276.

*Most, I. *adj.* (*comp. of* much *or* many) **(1)** greatest in degree or extent; *most reason, repose,* etc. : P. L. VI. 126; P. R. III. 232; S. A. 406; C. 591, 592; *the Most High,* God: P. L. I. 40; V. 699, etc. *See* **High.**

absol. (*a*) the greatest degree; *of all reproach the most*: S. A. 446.

(*b*) the greatest number: P. L. VI. 166, 500; C. 67, 747; *the most*: S. A. 190; *these most*: P. L. II. 906.

(*c*) the greatest part: P. L. III. 596.

(2) greatest in number; *most men*: P. R. I. 482; *things, deeds*: S. A. 942, 972.

II. *adv.* in a very high or the highest degree, chiefly, principally: P. L. I. 187; II. 122; VI. 791; VIII. 196; X. 78; P. R. I. 440; S. A. 67; C. 363; before all others: P. L. XII. 354.

used before adjectives or adverbs to form the superlative degree: P. L. II. 258, 763; V. 624; VIII. 85; IX. 1093; P. R. III. 27; IV. 205; S. A. 1001; Il P. 76; *most likely, surely, truly*: P. L. IX. 365; D. F. I. 36; U. C. II. 1; before monosyllables; *most fit*: A. 76; *just*: P. L. III. 294; VI. 726; *mild*: Ps. LXXXVI. 53; *true*: C. 386; *right*: Ps. LXXXVI. 37.

Mote, *sb.* small particle of dust visible in a ray of sunlight: Il P. 8.

Mother, *sb.* (*a*) female parent: P. L. VIII. 498; D. F. I. 71; M. W. 33; S. XVIII. 8; *Cybele, mother of a hundred gods*: A. 22; *Ashtaroth, heaven's queen and mother*: N. O.

201; applied to Mary, the mother of Christ: P. L. XII. 368; P. R. I. 86, 227; II. 60, 136; III. 154; IV. 216, 639; *virgin mother*: N. O. 3; vocative: P. L. XII. 379; applied to Circe : C. 57, 63, 153, 253, 523.

applied to Eve as the mother of mankind: P. L. IV. 492; IX. 644; XII. 624 : *mother of mankind* : P. L. I. 36; VI. 159; vocative: P. L. V. 388; *mother of human race*: P. L. IV. 475; *mother of all things living*: P. L. XI. 160.

applied to sin: P. L. II. 792, 849; X. 602.

(*b*) *fig.* an appellation of the earth; *Earth, all-bearing mother*: P. L. V. 338; *the great mother*: P. L. VII. 281; *my, thy mother's lap*: P. L. X. 778; XI. 536.

(*c*) *fig.* that which has produced or given birth to something; *wisdom-giving Plant, mother of science*: P. L. IX. 680; *Greece, mother of arts*: P. R. IV. 240.

attrib. fig. mother *tree*: P. L. IX. 1106; or appositive; *mother earth*: P. L. I. 687; P. R. IV. 566.

Motherly, *adj.* pertaining to a mother: P. R. II. 64.

Motion, I. *sb.* **(1)** the passing from one place to another, change of position; *in our proper motion we ascend*: P. L. II. 75; *instinctive motion*: P. L. VIII. 259; *prodigious motion felt and rueful throes*: P. L. II. 780; *motion of swift thought*: P. L. VI. 192; the advance of an armed body: P. L. VI. 532; XII. 592.

(*b*) the continuous motion of heavenly bodies in their spheres: P. L. III. 582; VIII. 35, 115; *their planetary motions*: P. L. X. 658; *Heaven ... rolled her motions*: P. L. VII. 500; *the planet Earth ... three different motions move*: P. L. VIII. 130; *in their motions harmony divine*; P. L. V. 625; *the low world in measured motion draw after the heavenly tune*: A. 71; *whose love their motion swayed*: S. M. 22.

(*c*) used abstractly; *time ... applied to motion*: P. L. V. 581; *more swift than time or motion*: P. L. VII. 177; with a play upon the word; *time numbers motion yet ... motion numbered out his time*: U. C. II. 7, 8.

(*d*) any movement of the body expressive of character: P. L. VI. 302; VIII. 223; IX. 674; P. R. IV. 601.

(2) the power of moving: P. L. II. 151.

(3) impulse, incitement: P. R. I. 290; S. A. 1382; *he sorrows now, repents, ... my motions in him*: P. L. XI. 91.

(4) proposal, scheme: P. L. II. 191.

II. *vb.* (1) *tr.* to propose: S. A. 222.

(2) *intr.* to make a proposal, offer plans: P. L. IX. 229.

Motionless, *adj.* incapable of motion: C. 819.

Mould, (1) *sb.* the form into which a fused metal is run to obtain a cast: P. L. XI. 571; *a various mould*: P. L. I. 706; *fig.*: P. L. VII. 470; Ps. VII. 53.

(2) *vb. tr.* to shape, fashion; with two *acc.*, *to mould me man*: P. L. X. 744.

Mould, *sb.* (*a*) the ground, soil; *the bright surface of this ethereous mould*: P. L. VI. 473; as the substance of the human body; *Adam, Earth's hallowed mould*: P. L. V. 321; *mortal mixture of earth's mould*: C. 244.

(*b*) the earth; *this sin-worn mould*: C. 17.

(*c*) the constituent material of anything, substance: P. L. IV. 360; *etherial mould*: P. L. II. 139; VII. 356; *ethereous*: P. L. VI. 473; *terrestrial, earthly, human*: P. L. IX. 485; N. O. 138; A. 73; *this world's material mould*: P. L. III. 709; *stony*: P. L. VI. 576; or, possibly, shape, form: P. L. II. 355.

See **Garden-mould.**

Mound, *sb.* a wall of earth: P. L. IV. 134.

Mount, (1) *sb.* mountain: P. L. XI. 320; A. 55; *flaming mount*: P. L. V. 598; XI. 216; *as a mount raised on a mount*: P. L. V. 757; *this specular mount*: P. R. IV. 236; *the guarded mount*, St. Michael's mount in Cornwall: L. 161; *Mount Amara*: P. L. IV. 281; *Carmel*: P. L. XII. 144; *Casius*: P. L. II. 593; *Ephraim*: S. A. 988; *Hermon*: P. L. XII. 142; *Ida*: P. L. V. 382; *Palatine*: P. R. IV. 50; *Sion*: P. L.

III. 530; *Aonian Mount*: P. L. I. 15; *Atlas Mount*: P. L. XI. 402; Niphates: P. L. IV. 569; *Assyrian Mount*: P. L. IV. 126; *Indian mount*, probably the Imaus Mountains: P. L. I. 781; *the Mount of Sinai, Mount Sinai, the Mount*: P. L. XII. 227; P. R. I. 351; II. 15; N. O. 158; *this Mount of Paradise*: P. L. XI. 829; used as a symbol of magnitude; *a mount of alabaster*: P. R. IV. 547.

(2) *vb. intr.* (*a*) to ascend, rise aloft: L. 172; with *up*: D. F. I. 15.

(*b*) to get on horseback; *death ... not mounted yet on his pale horse*: P. L. X. 589.

part. adj. **mounted**; (*a*) that has ascended; *his mounted scale*: P. L. IV. 1014; *the mounted sun*: P. L. V. 300.

(*b*) placed in position and with the parts adjusted ready for use: P. L. VI. 572.

Mountain, *sb.* an elevation of land rising high above the surrounding country: P. L. VI. 575; XI. 567, 728; P. R. III. 253; IV. 39; L'A. 73; Ps. LXXXIII. 56; CXIV. 13; *immediately the mountains huge appear*: P. L. VII. 285; *mountains in her* (the moon's) *spotty globe*: P. L. I. 291; *high mountain*: P. L. XI. 851; P. R. III. 252; IV. 26; *huge-bellied*: Ps. CXIV. 11; *lonely, wild*: N. O. 181; P. 51; *holy*: Ps. LXXXVII. 1; *Alpine mountains*: St. XVIII. 2; the mountain of Paradise: P. L. IV. 226; VIII. 303; X. 1065; the mountains in heaven: P. L. VI. 649, 652, 697, 842; *two brazen mountains*: P. L. VII. 201.

the Mountain of the Congregation: P. L. V. 766. *See* **Congregation.**

the offensive mountain, the Mount of Offence, the southern summit of the Mount of Olives, so called because of the 'high places' that Solomon built there for the gods of his foreign wives: P. L. I. 443.

as immovable or mighty in strength: P. L. VI. 197; S. A. 1648.

as a symbol of great magnitude; *surging waves as mountains*: P. L. VII. 214; *mountains of ice*: P. L. X. 291.

attrib. (*a*) growing on a mountain : P. L. I. 613.

(*b*) pertaining to a mountain ; *mountain watch* : C. 89.

Mountaineer, *sb.* the inhabitant of a mountain regarded as a barbarous person : C. 426.

Mountain-nymph, *sb.* a nymph whose home is in the mountains ; *the mountain-nymph, sweet Liberty* : L'A. 36.

Mountain-pard, *sb.* mountain leopard : C. 444.

Mountain-top, *sb.* the top of a mountain : P. L. II. 488 ; P. R. III. 265.

Mourn, *vb.* (*pres. 3d sing.* mourneth : C. 235) (1) *tr.* (*a*) to grieve for, lament : P. L. XI. 760 ; N. O. 204 ; *whose success Israel in long captivity still mourns* : P. R. III. 279.

(*b*) to express or utter mournfully : C. 235.

(2) *intr.* to grieve, express sorrow : P. L. I. 458 ; S. A. 1752 ; N. O. 188 ; Ps. LXXXVIII. 28 ; *ye flaming Powers ... now mourn* : Cir. 6 ; *the woods and desert caves ... mourn* : L. 41.

vbl. sb. **mourning,** grief, sorrow : S. A. 1712.

Mourner, *sb.* one who grieves or laments : P. 56.

Mournful, *adj.* (*a*) expressing sorrow : P. 28.

(*b*) doleful, dreary : P. L. I. 244.

Mouth, *sb.* (1) the orifice adapted for the reception of food and the utterance of speech : P. L. II. 517 ; V. 83 ; IX. 187 ; S. XI. 10 ; *oped the mouths of idolists* : S. A. 452 ; *from whose mouth issued forth mellifluous streams* : P. R. IV. 276 ; *the mouth of God* : P. R. I. 350 ; *barked with wide Cerberean mouths* : P. L. II. 655 ; perhaps nearer : voice, speech : P. L. IV. 513 ; X. 547 ; P. R. I. 428 ; *to hear her dictates from thy mouth* : P. R. I. 482 ; *kings and nations from thy mouth consult* : P. R. III. 12 ; *celebrated in the mouths of wisest men* : S. A. 866 ; *Discord with a thousand various mouths* : P. L. II. 967 ; *filling each mouth with envy or with praise* : S. XV. 2.

fig. danger's mouth : S. A. 1522 ; put for the whole person ; *blind mouths* : L. 119.

(2) something resembling a mouth : (*a*) the entrance to a cave, etc. ; *cave's mouth* : P. L. XI. 569 ; *the mouth of Hell* : P. L. X. 288, 636 ; XII. 42.

(*b*) the opening of a piece of ordnance by which the charge issues : P. L. VI. 576.

(*c*) that part of a stream where its waters are discharged : P. L. XII. 158 ; *river's mouth* : P. L. IX. 514.

See **Double-mouthed, Furnacemouth.**

Move, *vb.* I. *tr.* (1) to cause to change place, set in motion, propel : P. L. II. 876 ; VI. 405 ; *then shall this Mount ... be moved out of his place* : P. L. XI. 830 ; *who moved their stops and chords* : P. L. XI. 560 ; *an engine moved with wheel and weight* : U. C. II. 9 ; *spheres moved contrary with thwart obliquities* : P. L. VIII. 132.

(*b*) to dance ; *fig., move their starry dance* : P. L. III. 579.

(2) to stir up ; (*a*) to incite *a person* to action : P. R. II. 407 ; *Adam thus 'gan Eve to dalliance move* : P. L. IX. 1016 ; *if kingdom move thee not, let move thee zeal* : P. R. III. 171 ; *zeal moved thee* : S. A. 895 ; with *acc.* and *prep. inf.* : P. L. I. 29 ; VI. 790 ; VII. 91 ; VIII. 116, 293 ; P. R. I. 424 ; V. Ex. 2 ; C. 247.

absol., or the vb. is *intr.* to exert influence : P. L. XI. 91.

(*b*) to incite, arouse, awaken : P. L. V. 554 ; *passion in him move* : P. L. VIII. 585 ; *heaven ... move new broils* : P. L. II. 837 ; *to move his laughter* : P. L. VIII. 77 ; *to inspire* ; *voluntary move harmonious numbers* : P. L. III. 37.

(*c*) to be the cause or occasion of : S. A. 1452 ; *what moves thy inquisition* : P. R. III. 200.

(3) to begin, commence : P. L. IV. 409.

(4) to stir to deep feeling, excite the emotions of : P. L. IV. 902 ; IX. 1143 ; XI. 453 ; *dumb things would be moved to sympathize* : C. 796 ; *as to passion moved* : P. L. IX. 667.

(5) to propose ; *reconcilement move* : S. A. 752.

II. *intr.* (1) to change place or position : P. L. IX. 677 ; *likest gods they seemed, stood they or*

moved : P. L. VI. 302 ; *the rest his
look bound with Gorgonian rigour
not to move* : P. L. X. 297 ; *gates
... on golden hinges moving* : P. L.
VII. 207.

(*b*) used of the revolution or
rotation of heavenly bodies : P. L.
III. 719 ; VIII. 33, 70 ; X. 652 ;
three different motions move : P. L.
VIII. 130 ; *that move in mystic
dance* : P. L. V. 177 ; *move in
melodious time* : N. O. 129.

(**2**) to go, walk, advance : P. L.
I. 284 ; II. 675 ; V. 310 ; U. C. II.
2 ; *why move thy feet so slow* : P.
R. III. 224 ; *yet on she moves* : S.
A. 726 ; *with ... labour hard moved
on* : P. L. II. 1022.

(*b*) to march : P. L. I. 549 ;
under spread ensigns moving : P.
L. VI. 533 ; *the great hierarchal
standard was to move* : P. L. V.
701 ; *with on* : P. L. I. 561 ; VI.
63, 68 ; *onward move embattled* :
P. L. VI. 550.

(*c*) to move in the dance ; *in
celestial measures moved, circling
the throne* : P. R. I. 170; probably
also, *singing in their glory move* :
L. 180 ; *fig., the sounds and seas ...
in wavering morrice move* : C. 116.

(**3**) to have the power of motion :
P. L. VII. 534 ; VIII. 264, 276, 281.

(**4**) to succeed ; *how war may
best ... move* : S. XVII. 8.

(**5**) to be emotionally affected ;
my heart still moves with thine : P.
L. X. 359.

part. adj. (*a*) **moving**, being in
motion : P. L. VII. 415 ; used of
heavenly bodies ; *moving fires* : P.
L. VII. 87 ; being alive and having
the power of motion ; *myself my
sepulchre, a moving grave* : S. A.
102.

(*b*) **moved** ; *that first moved*, the
Primum Mobile : P. L. III. 483.
See **First-moving**.

Mover, *sb.* one who imparts motion;
the great First Mover's hand : P.
L. VII. 500.

Mow, *vb. tr.* to cut down ; *fig.,
whatever thing the scythe of Time
mows down* : P. L. X. 606.

Mower, *sb.* one who cuts down
grain : L'A. 66.

Mozambic (Mozámbic), *sb.* the province on the east coast of Africa :
P. L. IV. 161.

***Much**, (**1**) great in quantity or
extent ; *much converse, pleasure,*

blood, etc. : P. L. IX. 247, 1022 ;
XI. 791 ; P. R. I. 107, 341 ; III.
391 ; S. A. 658 ; L. 84 ; *pre-
eminent by so much odds* : P. L.
IV. 447 ; *much instrument of war* :
P. R. III. 388 ; *how much* : Dante
1 ; *so much* : P. L. X. 622 ; P. R.
III. 133 ; *thus much* : P. L. IV.
899 ; *too much* : P. L. V. 783.

absol. (*a*) a great deal, a large
quantity ; *yet much remains to
conquer* : S. XVI. 9 ; *too much of
ornament* : P. L. VIII. 538 ; *the
rule of not too much* : P. L. XI.
531 ; *so much of death ... as dyed
her cheeks with pale* : P. L. X.
1008 ; *much of the soul they talk* :
P. R. IV. 313 ; *many things* : P. L.
IV. 31 ; *he had much to see* : P. L.
XI. 415 ; *much I have heard of thy
prodigious might* : S. A. 1082.

(*b*) a great or strange thing;
*thought not much to clothe his
enemies* : P. L. X. 219.

(*c*) a great advantage ; *won so
much on Eve* : P. R. IV. 5.

(**2**) *adv.* (*a*) to a great degree,
to a great extent ; modifying a
vb. : P. L. I. 119 ; II. 210 ; IV.
451 ; IX. 202; X. 20 ; XI. 235 ; S.
A. 1526 ; *how much* : P. L. II.
480 ; *so much* : P. L. II. 293 ; VIII.
600 ; *too much* : S. A. 970 ; *much
more* or *less* : P. L. III. 220, 402 ;
VI. 495 ; modifying an adj. adv.
or phrase ; *much deject* : Ps. VI.
3 ; *much more wonder* : P. R. II.
303 ; *much fairer, heavier, better,*
etc. : P. L. V. 53 ; X. 836 ; XI.
599 ; S. A. 1442 ; S. II. 7 ; *much
more sweet*, etc. : P. L. V. 68 ; X.
221, 501 ; *much nearer*, etc. : P.
R. IV. 237 ; S. A. 828 ; *so much
the stronger, nearer, rather, more* :
P. L. I. 92 ; II. 1008 ; III. 51 ; V.
8 ; *like to end as much in vain* : P.
L. IV. 833 ; *men ... think me much
a foe* : P. R. I. 387.

(*b*) very ; *in much uneven scale* :
P. R. II. 173.

(*c*) nearly, almost ; *much like* :
M. W. 62, 67 ; C. 57.

Much-humbled, *adj.* greatly humili-
ated : P. L. XI. 181.

Mud, *sb.* mire : C. 931.

Mulciber, *sb.* a surname of Vulcan,
the god of fire : P. L. I. 740.

Mule, *sb.* the animal *Mulus* : P. R.
III. 335.

Multiform, *adj.* having many forms :
P. L. V. 182.

Multiply, *vb.* (1) *tr.* to make greater in number, quantity, or degree: P. L. VII. 398; *where nature multiplies her fertile growth*: P. L. V. 318; *optic skill of vision, multiplied through air*: P. R. IV. 41; *what can I multiply ... but curses on my head*: P. L. X. 732; *thy sorrow I will greatly multiply*: P. L. X. 193; *multiplies my fear*: P. R. I. 69; *multiply ten thousandfold the sin*: P. L. XI. 677; perhaps rather, to make great in number: *multiply a race of worshippers*: P. L. VII. 630; *his image multiplied*: P. L. VIII. 424.

(2) *intr.* to increase in number, produce offspring, be prolific: P. L. VII. 396, 531; X. 730; XII. 17.

Multitude, *sb.* (*a*) numerousness; *number to this day's work is not ordained, nor multitude*: P. L. VI. 810.

(*b*) a great number: P. L. X. 554; *multitude of eyes*: P. L. VI. 847; *multitude of thoughts*: P. R. I. 196.

used of men or angels: P. L. VII. 138; *to him shalt bear multitudes like thyself*: P. L. IV. 474; *heaven, surcharged with potent multitude*: P. L. II. 836; *grown in multitude*: P. L. XII. 352; as assembled or gathered together, a throng: P. L. I. 351, 702; *as the sound of seas, through multitude that sung*: P. L. X. 643; *the multitude of my redeemed*: P. L. III. 260; *the multitude of angels*: P. L. III. 345; *of labouring pioneers a multitude*: P. R. III. 331; *pl.*: P. L. V. 716; VI. 31; P. R. II. 470; *in multitudes*: P. L. X. 26; perhaps with blending of sense (*c*); *the hasty multitude admiring entered*: P. L. I. 730; *his captive multitude*: P. L. II. 323.

(*c*) the common people, the populace, the rabble: P. R. II. 420; S. A. 696.

See **Over-multitude.**

Mummer, *sb.* a masked buffoon: S. A. 1325.

Mural, *adj.* pertaining to a wall: P. L. VI. 879.

Murder, *sb.* the unlawful killing of human beings: S. A. 1186.

Murderer. *See* **Murtherer.**

Murderous, *adj.* guilty of murder: P. R. II. 76.

Murky, *adj.* dark, obscure; *the murky air*: P. L. X. 280.

Murmur, I. *sb.* (*a*) a low and indistinct sound; *bees industrious murmur*: P. R. IV. 248; *the ... stream, whose liquid murmur*: P. L. VII. 68; *fountains ... as ye flow, melodious murmurs*: P. L. V. 196; *as the sound of waters deep, hoarse murmur*: P. L. V. 873; *such murmur ... as when hollow rocks retain the sound of ... winds*: P. L. II. 284.

(*b*) muttered charms; *murmurs made to bless*: A. 60; *with many murmurs mixed*: C. 526.

(*c*) the utterance of grievance, complaint: S. XIX. 9.

II. *vb.* (1) *intr.* (*a*) to utter words indistinctly, mutter: P. L. IV. 1015.

(*b*) to express discontent or disapproval: P. R. III. 108.

(2) *tr.* to utter indistinctly; *Charybdis murmured soft applause*: C. 259.

part. adj. **murmuring**; (*a*) making a low continuous sound; *murmuring waters, streams*: P. L. IV. 260; VIII. 263.

(*b*) consisting of a low continuous noise; *murmuring sound of waters*: P. L. IV. 453.

vbl. sb. **murmuring**, a low continuous sound; *the waters murmuring*: Il P. 144.

Murrain, *sb.* the infectious disease among cattle: P. L. XII. 179.

Murtherer, *sb.* one who commits murder: S. A. 832, 1180.

Musæus, *sb.* the mythical poet of Greece: Il P. 104.

Muse, I. *sb.* wonder, surprise: P. L. VII. 52.

II. *vb.* (1) *intr.* to give oneself up to thought, ponder, meditate: P. L. IX. 744; S. A. 1017.

(2) *tr.* to meditate on; *what he meant I mused*: P. R. II. 99; *musing and much revolving ... how best the mighty work he might begin*: P. R. I. 185; *the nations muse a vain thing*: Ps. II. 2.

part. adj. **musing**, occupied with contemplation; *musing meditation*: C. 386; indicating absorption in contemplation; *musing gait*: Il P. 38.

vbl. sb. **musing**, meditation: P. R. IV. 249.

Muse, *sb.* (*a*) one of the nine goddesses, the daughters of Zeus and

Mnemosyne, who presided over the liberal arts : P. L. VII. 6; where the Muses haunt : P. L. III. 27 ; the Muses' bower : S. VIII. 9 ; hears the Muses in a ring aye round about Jove's altar sing : Il P. 47 ; Calliope : P. L. VII. 37 ; L. 58, 59 ; probably also : S. I. 13.

(b) the inspiring power of poetry personified; my wandering Muse: V. Ex. 53 ; my muse with Angels did divide to sing : P. 4 ; the Heavenly Muse, called also Urania (see Urania) : P. L. I. 6, 376 ; III. 19 ; N. O. 15 ; what the sage poets, taught by the heavenly Muse, storied of old in high immortal verse: C. 515 ; Sicilian Muse, the inspirer of the poetry of Theocritus : L. 133.

(c) poetry itself : L. 66.

(d) poet, bard : L. 19.

Music, sb. (a) the science and art of the rhythmic and harmonic combination of tones : S. XIII. 2.

(b) vocal or instrumental melody or harmony : P. L. XI. 592; P. R. IV. 332 ; such sweet compulsion doth in music lie : A. 68; the fair music that all creatures made to their great Lord: S. M. 21; made by fairies; jocund music : P. L. I. 787; made by angels: N. O. 117; P. 1; Cir. 2; aerial music : P. L. V. 548; music sweet : N. O. 93 ; sweet music breathe ... sent by some spirit to mortals good : Il P. 151 ; the music of the spheres : A. 74.

Musical, adj. melodious, harmonious ; musical as is Apollo's lute : C. 478 ; sweet bird ... most musical : Il P. 62.

Musk rose, sb. the flower Rosa moschata : C. 496 ; L. 146.

Musky, adj. laden with the perfume of musk ; west winds with musky wing : C. 989.

Must, sb. the unfermented juice of the grape ; the wine-press where sweet must is poured : P. R. IV. 16.

*****Must,** vb. used as an auxiliary with the simple infinitive ; (1) to be obliged ; (a) by a physical necessity ; by the Tree of Knowledge he must pass : P. L. IX. 849; his room where he must lodge : U. C. I. 15.

(b) by a moral necessity ; I must not quarrel with the will of highest dispensation : S. A. 60; I must

not omit a father's timely care : S. A. 602 ; with first approach of light, we must be risen : P. L. IV. 624.

(c) by a logical necessity : P. L. II. 206, 278 ; of worse deeds worse sufferings must ensue : P. L. IV. 26 ; needs must the Power that made us ... be infinitely good : P. L. IV. 412; which else to several spheres thou must ascribe : P. L. VIII. 131; subtle he needs must be who could seduce angels: P. L. IX. 307.

(d) by fate, the command of God, or the power of circumstances : P. L. I. 244 ; II. 89, 246, 914 ; I else must change their nature : P. L. III. 124; him thy care must be to find : P. L. IV. 575; if I must contend : P. L. IV. 851 ; who will but what they must by destiny : P. L. V. 533 ; man, whom death must end : P. L. X. 797; with labour I must earn my bread : P. L. X. 1054; weakly to a woman must reveal it : S. A. 50.

(e) little more than an emphatic use ; I ... must confess to find ... delight : P. L. VIII. 523.

(f) almost = will ; these thoughts full counsel must mature : P. L. I. 660.

(g) with the infinitive omitted : Ps. I. 16 ; I must after thee : P. L. X. 363; thou ... must with me along : P. L. X. 250 ; who aspires must down as low as high he soared : P. L. IX. 169.

(2) to be destined to : P. L. XI. 770 ; thou art gone and never must return : L. 38; this must not yet be so : N. O. 151.

Muster, I. sb. the assemblage of troops for battle : P. R. III. 308.

II. vb. (1) tr. to collect, assemble ; mustering all his waves : V. Ex. 44 ; mustering all her wiles : S. A. 402 ; mustering their rage : P. L. II. 268.

(2) intr. to assemble as troops : P. L. XI. 645.

Mutable, adj. inconstant, unstable : P. L. V. 237 ; so mutable are all the ways of men : S. A. 1407 ; I saw thee mutable of fancy : S. A. 793.

Mute, adj. (a) silent, not speaking : P. L. I. 618 ; II. 420 ; III. 217 ; VIII. 222 ; X. 18 ; XI. 31 ; P. R. I. 12, 459 ; voice, unchanged to hoarse or mute : P. L. VII. 25.

(*b*) not uttered or expressed ; *the rural ditties were not mute* : L. 36 ; or, perhaps nearer to sense (*d*), not having sufficient power for expression ; *eloquence flourished, since mute* : P. L. IX. 672.

(*c*) not accompanied by words ; *heaven by these mute signs in nature shows* : P. L. XI. 194.

(*d*) not having the power of speech, dumb : P. L. IX. 557, 563, 748 ; S. A. 672 ; *long they sat as stricken mute* : P. L. IX. 1064 ; *Satan stood a while as mute* : P. R. III. 2 ; *the deeds themselves, though mute, spoke* : S. A. 248 ; *and the mute Silence hist along* : Il P. 55.

Mutely, *adj.* silently : V. Ex. 6.

Mutiny, *sb.* rebellion ; *fig., these elements in mutiny had from her axle torn the steadfast earth* : P. L. II. 926.

Mutter, (1) *sb.* a murmured charm : C. 817.

(2) *vb. tr.* to emit a low rumbling sound of ; *muttering thunder* : P. L. IX. 1002.

Mutual, *adj.* (*a*) reciprocally given and received, interchanged ; *mutual amity, help, love,* etc. : P. L. IV. 376, 727 ; VIII. 58, 385 ; C. 741 ; *accusation* : P. L. IX. 1187 ; *slaughter* : P. L. VI. 506.

(*b*) equally affecting two or more, shared alike ; *mutual guilt* : P. L. IX. 1043 ; *league* : P. L. I. 87 ; taking part one after another or in succession ; *with mutual wing easing their flight* : P. L. VII. 429.

(*c*) alternating ; *the mutual flowing of the seas* : U. C. II. 31.

*****My,** *poss. pron.* of or belonging to me : P. L. II. 683, 738 ; III. 133 ; IV. 38 ; *obj. gen.* : S. A. 738 ; before a vowel : P. L. I. 13 ; II. 197, 783, 785 ; III. 195, 248 ; IV. 488, 939 ; V. 18 ; VI. 47 ; VIII. 211, 441 ; X. 781 ; P. R. II. 146 ; Il P. 150 ; C. 506 ; L. 88 ; followed by *own* : P. L. IX. 956 ; X. 727, 831 ; P. R. IV. 191 ; S. A. 78 ; used emphatically : P. L. I. 261 ; II. 51, 197 ; X. 952, 955 ; transposed ; *in my midst of sorrow,* in the midst of my sorrow : S. A. 1339.

Myriad, *sb.* a vast but indefinite number : P. L. I. 87 ; V. 684 ; VI. 24 ; VII. 201 ; *myriads of immortal spirits* : P. L. I. 622.

Myrrh, *sb.* (*a*) the tree *Balsamodendron myrrha* : P. L. V. 23, 292 ; IX. 629 ; C. 937.

(*b*) the resinous exudation from this tree used as a perfume ; *incense, myrrh, and gold* : P. L. XII. 363 ; P. R. I. 251.

Myrrhine, *adj.* of murra, a precious material of which costly vases and cups were made ; by the best authorities conjectured to be the agate : P. R. IV. 119.

Myrtle, *sb.* the tree or shrub *Myrtus communis* : P. L. IV. 262, 694 ; IX. 219, 627 ; L. 2.

attrib. of or from this tree ; *myrtle wand* : N. O. 51 ; *myrtle band* : P. L. IX. 431.

Myself, *pron.* (1) *emphatic* ; (*a*) in apposition with a *pron.* : P. L. VII. 170 ; X. 820 ; P. R. I. 198 ; S. A. 234, 375.

(*b*) as subject of a *vb.* ; *myself and all the angelic host ... our happy state hold* : P. L. V. 535 ; *myself am hell* : P. L. IV. 75 ; *myself was distant* : P. R. IV. 453 ; with an *inf.* ; *either to undergo myself the total crime* : P. L. X. 127 ; the *vb.* omitted ; *myself my sepulchre* : S. A. 102.

(2) *refl.* : P. L. II. 828 ; IV. 450 ; VIII. 267 ; IX. 959 ; X. 117 ; S. A. 965 ; *myself I thought born to that end* : P. R. I. 204 ; *nor hope to be myself less miserable* : P. L. IX. 126 ; with a *prep.* : P. L. III. 244 ; V. 95, 607 ; VIII. 278 ; S. A. 401, 809, 824 ; *prep.* omitted ; *unworthy ... myself* : S. A. 1425 ; following *but* ; *whom have I to complain of but myself* : S. A. 46 ; as an exclamation : S. A. 1334.

Mysterious, *adj.* (*a*) worshipped by secret rites : C. 130.

(*b*) involved in mystery, obscure, unintelligible, unexplained : P. L. IV. 312 ; *the rites mysterious of connubial love* : P. L. IV. 743 ; *wedded love, mysterious law* : P. L. IV. 750 ; *in mysterious terms* : P. L. X. 173 ; *some strange mysterious dream* : Il P. 147 ; full of the sense of mystery or full of awe ; *mysterious reverence* : P. L. VIII. 599.

Mysteriously, *adv.* symbolically : P. L. III. 516.

Mystery, *sb.* (*a*) a hidden purpose or counsel ; *who have profaned the mystery of God* : S. A. 378 ; or, perhaps, secret office or duty ; *of thyself so apt, in regal arts and regal mysteries* : P. R. III. 249.

(*b*) a secret truth or doctrine ; *the sublime notion and high mystery ... of chastity* : C. 785; apparently a blending of (*a*) and (*b*) ; *the sacred mysteries of heaven* : P. L. XII. 509.

Mystic, *adj.* (*a*) incomprehensible in form and movement ; *fires* (stars) *that move in mystic dance* : P. L. V. 178.

(*b*) mythical : P. L. IX. 442.

Mystical, *adj.* mystic ; *days they spent in ... mystical dance* : P. L. V. 620.

N

Naiad, *sb.* (*pl.* Naiades), one of the nymphs of springs and rivers : P. R. II. 355 ; C. 254.

Nail, *vb. tr.* to fasten with nails ; *Sisera ... through the temples nailed* : S. A. 990; *to the cross* : P. L. XII. 413, 415.

Naked, *adj.* having no clothes on, nude : P. L. IV. 319; V. 382, 444; IX. 1074, 1117, 1139 ; X. 117, 121, 212; *her swelling breast naked* : P. L. IV. 496; *their naked limbs* : P. L. IV. 772; applied to a condition of or due to nakedness ; *in naked majesty* : P. L. IV. 290; *in naked beauty* : P. L. IV. 713; *naked glory* : P. L. IX. 1115 ; *her naked shame* : N. O. 40.

fig., innocence ... was gone ... from about them, naked left to guilty shame : P. L. IX. 1057; unclothed in language ; *I have some naked thoughts* : V. Ex. 23.

Nakedness, *sb.* (*a*) *concr.* naked body; *he clad their nakedness with skins of beasts* : P. L. X. 217; *fig., inward nakedness ... with his robe of righteousness arraying* : P. L. X. 221.

(*b*) absolute divestment; *emptied his glory even to nakedness* : Cir. 20.

Namancos, *sb.* a citadel a short distance east of Cape Finisterre. Mercator, *Atlas* 1636, vol. 2. map at page 347 : L. 162.

Name, I. *sb.* (1) a personal or particular appellation : P. L. I. 361, 365, 374, 376; IV. 36; V. 658, 776; VII. 5; VIII. 357; X. 649, 867; XI. 171; XII. 36, 140, 515;

S. A. 677, 974 ; C. 208; S. XI. 10; *Dagon his name* : P. L. I. 462; *Peor his other name* : P. L. I. 412; *Urania by that name* : P. L. VII. 1 ; *Satan, for I glory in the name* : P. L. X. 386 ; *Jesus ... his name* : P. L. XII. 311; *Manoa ... that name* : S. A. 331 ; *Sabrina is her name* : C. 826 ; *Humber ... the Scythian's name* : V. Ex. 99; *whose name Jehovah is* : Ps. LXXXIII. 65 ; *names of old renown, Osiris, Isis, Orus* : P. L. I. 477; *no place is yet distinct by name* : P. L. VII. 536 ; *all the stars thou knew'st by name* : P. L. XII. 577.

(*b*) used in periphrastic phrase for the person ; *the dreaded name of Demogorgon* : P. L. II. 964.

(*c*) a person as represented by his name : P. L. V. 707 ; P. R. II. 189, 447 ; *exalted high above all names in heaven* : P. L. XII. 458; *the brand of infamy upon my name denounced* : S. A. 968 ; *my name ... may stand defamed* : S. A. 975; *Israel's name ... may be lost in memory* : Ps. LXXXIII. 15.

(2) a common, generic, or collective appellation : P. L. VII. 493; XI. 277; C. 749; Ps. LXXXVIII. 16 ; *general names of Baalim and Ashtaroth* : P. L. I. 421 ; *by numbers that have name* : P. L. VIII. 114; *simples of a thousand names* : C. 627 ; *birds ... to receive their names* : P. L. VI. 76; VIII. 344; *woman is her name* : P. L. VIII. 496; *names, Fortune and Fate* : P. R. IV. 316; *love, by name to come called Charity* : P. L. XII. 584; *the name of servitude* : P. L. VI. 174; *heroic name*, the appellation of hero or heroic : P. L. IX. 40; *that name* : P. L. IX. 44.

(3) the name used for everything which the name covers ; (*a*) that which is aroused in the mind by hearing or remembering the name; *Death ... the hideous name* : P. L. II. 788 ; *O sacred name of faithfulness* : P. L. IV. 950; *that same vaunted name Virginity* : C. 738; *our country is a name so dear* : S. A. 894.

(*b*) the divine majesty and perfection of God, those qualities by which God reveals himself to men : S. A. 1429 ; Ps. V. 36 ; VII. 63 ; VIII. 2; LXXX. 76 ; LXXXVI.

32, 39, 44; cxxxvi. 5; *his great name assert*: S. A. 467; *vindicate the glory of his name*: S. A. 475; *glorious is thy name*: Ps. viii. 24; used similarly of a god: P. L. i. 738.

(c) glory, honour, renown: P. L. vi. 373; W. S. 6; S. viii. 7; xv. 1; *thy name shall be the copious matter of my song*: P. L. iii. 412; *shall make thy name to live*: D. F. I. 77; *get themselves a name*: P. L. xii. 45.

(d) reputation; *thou bear'st the highest name for valiant deeds*: S. A. 1101.

(e) memory: M. W. 60.

(f) *in the name of*, by the command and authority of: C. 868.

(4) race; *half the Angelic Name*: P. L. ix. 142; kind; *all fish ... exquisitest name*: P. R. ii. 346.

II. *vb. tr.* (1) to give an appellation to: P. L. viii. 352, 439; C. 325; with two *acc.*: P. L. vii. 252; C. 58; *Heaven he named the Firmament*: P. L. vii. 274; *naming thee the Tree of Knowledge*: P. L. ix. 751; *so I name this king*: P. L. xii. 326; *worth naming Son of God by voice from Heaven*: P. R. iv. 539; in passive: P. L. i. 80; v. 839; xii. 62; *him named Almighty*: P. L. vi. 294; *be named ... heretics*: F. of C. 11; with phrase; *Cocytus named of lamentation*: P. L. ii. 579.

(b) to address as or style; *among the Thrones, or named of them the highest*: P. L. xi. 296.

(2) to mention by name, speak of: P. L. i. 574; P. R. iii. 95; S. A. 982; *whom the fables name*: P. L. i. 197; *though in Holy Writ not named*: P. R. ii. 8; *nor do I name of men the common rout*: S. A. 674.

(3) to speak the name of: P. L. viii. 272.

vbl. sb. **naming**, ability to give a name to: P. L. viii. 359.

Nameless, *adj.* without a name: P. L. vi. 380.

Naphtha, *sb.* a fluid variety of asphalt: P. L. i. 729.

Narcissus, *sb.* the beautiful youth beloved by the nymph Echo: C. 237.

Nard, *sb.* the aromatic plant: P. L. v. 293; C. 991.

Narrow, (1) *adj.* (a) measuring relatively little from side to side, not broad; *narrow frith, space, vent*: P. L. ii. 919; vi. 104, 583.

(b) limited in extent, small, circumscribed; *narrow room, limits, circuit*, etc.: P. L. i. 779; iv. 207, 384; ix. 323; xi. 341; S. A. 1117; *comp.*: P. L. vii. 21.

(c) scrutinizing, careful; *narrow search, scrutiny*: P. L. iv. 528; ix. 83; *comp.*: P. R. iv. 515.

(2) *adv. comp.* to a more limited space: P. L. vii. 22.

Nathless, *adv.* nevertheless, notwithstanding: P. L. i. 299.

Nation, *sb.* a people, either as a race or as a political unit: P. L. i. 385, 598; xi. 792; xii. 97, 126, 147, 329, 440, 450, 499, 503; P. R. i. 79, 98, 432, 442; ii. 473; iii. 12, 76; iv. 47, 122, 135, 202, 362; S. A. 268, 1494; Ps. ii. 1; vii. 25; lxxx. 35; lxxxii. 28; lxxxvi. 29; lxxxvii. 23; H. B. 14; *to nations yet unborn*: P. L. iv. 663; *subdue nations*: P. L. xi. 692; *all nations now to Rome obedience pay*: P. R. iv. 80; *law of nations*: S. A. 890; *in whom all nations shall be blest*: P. L. xii. 277; *all nations they shall teach*: P. L. xii. 446; *all nations, Jew, or Greek, or Barbarous*: P. R. iii. 118; the Philistine nation: S. A. 857, 877; the Israelitish nation: P. L. xii. 113, 164, 414; S. A. 218, 565, 1182, 1205, 1425; Ps. lxxxiii. 14; *one peculiar nation*: P. L. xii. 111; *from him will raise a mighty nation*: P. L. xii. 124; Wales: C. 33.

National, *adj.* (a) due to one's country; *national obstriction*: S. A. 312.

(b) common to the whole people of a country; *sins national*: P. L. xii. 317.

Native, (1) *adj.* (a) conferred or derived by birth or origin, inborn, natural rather than acquired; *native form*: P. L. iii. 605; *vigour*: P. L. vi. 436; *subtlety*: P. L. ix. 93; *honour, innocence, righteousness*: P. L. iv. 289; ix. 373, 1056; *brightness*: P. R. i. 378; *wood-notes*: L'A. 134.

(b) of or pertaining to one by birth, or to the place of birth or origin; *native seat*: P. L. i. 634;

II. 76, 1050; VI. 226; *land*: P.
R. III. 437; *home*: C. 76; *dust*...
our native home: P. L. X. 1085;
I must return to native dust: P. L.
XI. 463; *soil*: P. L. XI. 270, 292;
XII. 129; *Heaven*: P. L. V. 863;
X. 467; *Light ... from her native
East to journey*: P. L. VII. 245;
native element: P. L. VII. 16;
language: P. L. XII. 54; P. R.
IV. 333; V. Ex. 1; *fig.* being the
source of a river: P. L. I. 450.

(c) indigenous; *native perfumes*: P. L. IV. 158.

(d) being the place of birth;
Greece ... native to famous wits: P.
R. IV. 241.

(2) *sb.* one deriving birth or
origin from a certain place; *Native
of Heaven*: P. L. V. 361; *Natives
and Sons of Heaven*: P. L. V. 790;
Native of Thebes: P. R. II. 313.

Nativity, *sb.* (a) birth: P. R. I. 242;
S. A. 1141.

(b) native place or state: P. L.
VI. 482.

Natural, *adj.* (a) according to the
laws of its nature: P. L. X. 740.

(b) implanted at birth, innate:
V. Ex. 87; *natural necessity,
pravity*: P. L. X. 765; XII. 288.

(c) genuine, not artificial; *natural tears*: P. L. XII. 645.

Nature, *sb.* (a difficult word; often
impossible to discriminate with
any certainty between meanings)
(a) the forces and processes of the
world, conceived as producing all
things and preserving the order
of things according to fixed laws:
P. L. III. 49; IV. 314; VIII. 534;
Nature's whole wealth: P. L. IV.
207; *minims of nature*: P. L.
VII. 482; *the prime end of Nature*:
P. L. VIII. 541; *all Nature's works
or works of God*: P. L. XII. 578;
Nature's law, law of Nature: P.
L. X. 805; XI. 49; XII. 29; *the
stars that Nature hung in heaven*:
C. 198; *Nature and Fate had had
no strife*: M. W. 13; *those dainty
limbs, which Nature lent*: C. 680;
sleep ... called by Nature: P. L.
VIII. 459; opposed to *art*: P. L.
IV. 242; *Nature taught Art*: P.
R. II. 295.

more or less clearly personified:
C. 739, 745; *Nature breeds*: P. L.
II. 624; *ye Elements, the eldest birth
of Nature's womb*: P. L. V. 181;
the ... works of Nature's hand: P.

L. III. 455; *Nature's desire*: P.
L. V. 45; *Nature, wise and frugal*:
P. L. VIII. 26; feminine gender:
P. L. VIII. 561; IX. 624; P. R.
II. 332; C. 710, 772; *beldam
Nature in her cradle was*: V.
Ex. 46; *Nature ... played at will
her virgin fancies*: P. L. V. 294;
*like Nature's bastards not her
sons*: C. 727; *Nature ... she good
cateress*: C. 762; *Nature ... her
reign*; N. O. 101; *how Nature
paints her colours*: P. L. V. 24;
*how Nature multiplies her fertile
growth*: P. L. V. 318; *Nature
seems fulfilled in all her ends*:
P. L. XI. 602; *keep unsteady
Nature to her law*: A. 70; *Nature
... sighing through all her works*:
P. L. IX. 782.

(b) the created universe: P. L.
VIII. 153; X. 892; XI. 182, 194;
P. R. I. 13; D. F. I. 45; *the
originals of Nature*: P. L. VI.
511; *the rising birth of Nature*:
P. L. VII. 103; *extinguish life in
Nature*: P. L. IV. 667; *the scale
of Nature*: P. L. V. 509; *Nature's
concord broke*: P. L. VI. 311;
nature's chime: S. M. 20; *into
Nature brought misery*: P. L. VI.
267; perhaps personified; *Night
and Chaos, ancestors of Nature*:
P. L. II. 895; feminine gender:
P. L. II. 1037; *the womb of
Nature and perhaps her grave*:
P. L. II. 911.

as influenced by the acts of
man: P. L. IX. 1001; feminine
gender; *Nature had doffed her
gaudy trim*: N. O. 32; all created
things; *whom universal nature
did lament*: L. 60.

(c) the sum of innate properties
and powers by which one person
or being differs from another,
inherent character and disposition: P. L. III. 126; IX. 27; C.
411; *what between us made the
odds, in nature none*: P. L. VI.
442; *a superior nature*: P. L. V.
360; *their nature also to thy nature
join*: P. L. III. 282; *to assume
man's nature*: P. L. III. 304;
human nature: P. R. III. 231;
Spiritual Natures: P. L. V. 402;
all angelic nature: P. L. V. 834;
applied to animals: P. L. VII.
493; VIII. 353; X. 169.

(d) essential character; *to the
place conformed ... in nature*: P.

L. II. 218 ; *thy will by nature free* :
P. L. v. 527 ; *Silence ... deny her
nature* : C. 559 ; *a rib crooked by
nature* : P. L. x. 885.

(*e*) the physical constitution or
being of man : P. L. IV. 633 ; v.
452 ; P. R. II. 230, 249, 253, 265;
when Nature rests : P. L. v. 109 ;
pure Nature's healthful rules : P.
L. XI. 523 ; *Nature within me
seems in all her functions weary of
herself* : S. A. 599 ; possibly with
blending of sense (*a*) ; *I feel the
link of nature draw me* : P. L. IX.
914; *the bond of Nature* : P. L. IX.
956; *instinct of nature* : S. A. 1545.

(*f*) the moral constitution of
man ; *law of nature* : S. A. 890 ;
perhaps both the physical and
moral constitution, or in sense (**1**) ;
the bent of Nature : P. L. XI. 597;
though to Nature seeming meet : P.
L. XI. 604.

(*g*) the instinctive sense of what
is truth or right : P. L. VIII. 506;
God and Nature bid the same : P.
L. VI. 176 ; *Nature's light, light of
Nature* (*see* Light) : P. R. IV. 228,
352.

Naught or **Nought,** (**1**) *sb.* or *pron.*
not anything : P. L. III. 207, 453;
VI. 382; P. R. IV. 161 ; S. A.
779 ; N. O. 218 ; C. 204 ; *naught
else regarded* : P. L. IX. 786 ; *to
me worth naught* : P. R. III. 393 ;
*his might continues in thee .. not
for naught* : S. A. 588 ; *to their
masters gave me up for nought* : S.
A. 1215 ; *bring to naught* : P. L.
III. 158 ; *come to nought* : P. R.
I. 181 ; *set at nought* : C. 444.

(**2**) *adv.* not at all : P. L. II.
679 ; P. R. IV. 208.

Navel, *sb.* central point ; *the navel of
this hideous wood* : C. 520.

Nay, *adv.* (*a*) no ; *to say us nay* : S.
A. 1729.

(*b*) not only so, but : P. L IV.
71 ; IX. 1159; P. R. IV. 6 ; S. A.
350 ; C. 271, 659 ; U. C. II. 17.

Nazareth, *sb.* the town in Galilee :
P. R. I. 23 ; II. 79.

Nazarite, *sb.* one bound by a peculiar
vow to be set apart from others
for the service of God : S. A. 318,
1359 ; *my vow of Nazarite* : S. A.
1386.

Neæra, *sb.* the name of a maiden
common in pastoral poetry : L. 69.

Near, I. *adj.* (*a*) being close by,
adjacent ; *sup.* : P. L. I. 192 ; II.

958 ; *comp.*, seen from a comparatively short distance ; *nearer
view* : P. L. VI. 81 ; P. R. IV.
514 ; S. A. 723.

(*b*) short, direct ; *sup.*, *the
nearest way* : S. XXI. 10.

II. *adv.* (**1**) at or to a point not
far distant, close ; (*a*) used of
place : C. 486 ; Ps. VII. 48 ; *more
near* : A. 40 ; *too near* : C. 491 ;
so near : P. L. IX. 221 ; C. 616 ;
Ps. LXXXIV. 4 ; with a *prep.*,
near about : P. L. IV. 133 ; *near at hand* :
L'A. 33 ; *near to* : P. L. IV. 425 ;
near upon : N. O. 44.

comp. : P. L. IV. 133, 399 ; IX.
434, 578 ; P. R. III. 364 ; S. A.
1229, 1631 ; *much nearer* : P. R.
IV. 237 ; *so much the nearer danger* :
P. L. II. 1008 ; with *to* : P. L. I.
785 ; v. 476 ; *sup.*, *nearest to his
throne* : P. L. III. 649.

followed by a *sb.* without *to* ;
by some authorities classed as
prep. (see also *Next* and *Nigh*) :
P. L. II. 609 ; IV. 787 ; VII. 55 ;
IX. 220 ; x. 347, 389, 562 ; S. A.
725 ; Il P. 68 ; C. 567 ; *comp.*,
nearer his presence : P. L. v. 358;
nearer our ancient seat : P. L. II.
394 ; *sup.*, *nearest my heart* : P.
L. IV. 484.

(*b*) used of time : *that I to manhood am arrived so near* : S. II. 6.

(**2**) closely, intimately ; *it touched
his deity full near* : D. F. I. 10 ;
so near related : S. A. 786 ; *more
near united* : P. L. v. 830; deeply ;
pierce more near his heart : Cir.
28.

comp. : P. L. VII. 62 ; *with woe
nearer acquainted* : P. R. I. 400;
sup. : P. L. v. 622.

(**3**) so as to approximate ; *nearest to the present aid* : C. 90.

Nearly, *adv.* intimately : P. L. v.
721.

Near-ushering, *adj.* preceding at a
short distance : C. 279.

Neat, *adj.* nice, delicate ; *neat repast* : S. XX. 9.

Neat-handed, *adj.* deft, dexterous :
L'A. 86.

Neatness, *sb.* elegance, grace and
beauty : Hor. O. 5.

Nebaioth, *sb.* the eldest son of
Ishmael, here used for Ishmael :
P. R. II. 309.

Nebo, *sb.* the mountain in the land
of Moab, the highest summit of
the range of Abarim : P. L. I. 407.

Necessary, *adj.* indispensable, essential : S. A. 90.

Necessitate, *vb. tr.* to make necessary, render unavoidable : P. L. x. 44.

    part. adj. **necessitated,** given because of an inevitable determination of the will ; *our necessitated (service)* : P. L. v. 530.

Necessity, *sb.* (*a*) imperative exigency ; *necessity, the tyrant's plea* : P. L. iv. 393 ; *necessity subdues me* : P. L. x. 131.

    (*b*) the law of being ; *natural necessity* : P. L. x. 765.

    (*c*) that which must be, fate ; *personified, the daughters of Necessity* : A. 69 ; *tangled in the fold of dire Necessity* : S. A. 1666 ; *Necessity and Chance approach not me* : P. L. vii. 172.

    (*d*) the inevitable determination of the will by a cause : P. L. iii. 110 ; v. 528 ; vii. 172.

Neck, *sb.* the part of the body of an animal connecting the head and the trunk ; *the swan with arched neck* : P. L. vii. 438 ; *burnished neck of verdant gold* : P. L. ix. 501 ; *sleek enamelled neck* : P. L. ix. 525 ; as bearing the yoke, *fig.* : P. L. v. 787 ; *God ... his just yoke laid on our necks* : P. L. x. 1046 ; put for the whole body : P. L. iii. 395.

    fig., sturdiest oaks, bowed their stiff necks : P. R. iv. 418 ; *the neck of crowned Fortune* : S. xxi. 5.

Necromancer, *sb.* sorcerer : C. 649.

Nectar, *sb.* (*a*) the drink of the god ; *nectar, drink of gods* : P. L. ix. 838 ; *immortal nectar* : V. Ex. 39 ; the drink of angels ; *rubied nectar* : P. L. v. 633 ; used by way of ablution to confer immortality : L. 175.

    (*b*) a delicious and salubrious drink ; *brooks ... ran nectar* : P. L. iv. 240 ; *vines yield nectar* : P. L. v. 428.

Nectared, *adj.* (*a*) mingled with nectar ; used of a bath which confers immortality : C. 838 ; hence, divine, immortal ; *thy nectared head* : D. F. I. 40.

    (*b*) delicious as nectar : C. 479.

Nectarine, *adj.* delicious as nectar : P. L. iv. 332.

Nectarous, *adj.* (*a*) nectarine : P. L. v. 306.

    (*b*) resembling nectar : P. L. vi. 332.

Need, (1) *sb.* (*a*) a lack of something necessary, want, necessity : P. L. iv. 419 ; v. 629 ; Ps. cxxxvi. 86 ; P. R. ii. 254, 397 ; *if need be* : S. A. 1483 ; *if need were* : C. 219 ; *in time of need* : Ps. lxxx. 2 ; *they all had need* : P. R. ii. 318 ; followed by a sb. without *of ; he had need all circumspection* : P. L. ii. 413 ; *thou hast need much washing* : S. A. 1107 ; *had need the guard* : C. 394 ; followed by a sb. with *of* : P. L. ix. 731 ; P. R. ii. 253 ; *if need were of ... strength* : P. L. ix. 311 ; *stand in need of nothing* : V. Ex. 81 ; with a clause ; *no need that thou should'st propagate* : P. L. viii. 419 ; with simple *inf.* : P. L. vi. 625.

    (*b*) indigence, distress, extremity : C. 287 ; *in hard-besetting need* : C. 857 ; *almost pine with need* : Ps. lxxxvi. 4 ; *at need,* in the time of extremity : P. L. ix. 260 ; S. A. 1437.

    II. *vb.* (*pres. 2d sing.* need'st : P. L. viii. 564 ; S. A. 1379 ; V. Ex. 11 ; W. S. 6 ; *3d sing.* need : P. R. ii. 249 ; C. 362, 752 ; elsewhere needs ; *pret.* needed) (1) *tr.* to have necessity for, want, lack, require : P. L. iii. 340 ; iv. 617 ; v. 214, 384 ; vii. 126 ; viii. 564, 628 ; x. 80 ; P. R. iii. 399 ; S. A. 1345 ; N. O. 82 ; W. S. 1, 6 ; S. 122 ; S. xix. 9 ; *more tuneable than needed lute or harp* : P. L. v. 151 ; *other light she needed none* : P. L. vii. 378 ; *which needs not thy belief* : P. L. viii. 136 ; *when we need refreshment* : P. L. ix. 236 ; *he ... no other doctrine needs* : P. R. iv. 290 ; *no preface needs* : P. L. xi. 251 ; S. A. 1554.

    with *prep. inf.* : P. L. ii. 341 ; v. 414 ; *need ... to fear* : S. A. 1526 ; with simple *inf.* : V. Ex. 11 ; *need doubt* : S. A. 1379 ; *need fear* : P. L. x. 409, 1082 ; P. R. iii. 385 ; *know* : P. R. i. 292 ; *seek* : P. R. iv. 325 ; *walk* : P. L. ix. 246 ; *not need repeat* : P. L. vi. 318 ; *what need a man forestall his date of grief* : C. 362 ; absol. : P. L. ii. 53 ; v. 302 ; *if nature need not, or God support nature without repast, though needing* : P. R. ii. 249, 251 ; *where most needs* : P. L. ix. 215.

(2) *intr.* to be wanted or necessary ; *impers., whereof here need no account* : P. L. IV. 235 ; *what need a vermeil-tinctured lip for that* : C. 752.

Needless, (1) *adj.* not requisite, unnecessary : P. L. IX. 1140 ; C. 942 ; *riches are needless* : P. R. IV. 484.

(2) *adv.* without cause : P. L. VII. 494.

Needs, *adv.* of necessity, unavoidably ; used with the vb. *must* : P. L. II. 277 ; III. 105 ; IV. 412 ; V. 556 ; VI. 456, 693 ; IX. 307, 942 ; XII. 10, 383 ; S. A. 840, 1044, 1519.

Ne'er. *See* **Never.**

Neglect, (1) *sb.* (*a*) the not doing a thing that should be done : C. 510.

(*b*) the omission of due attention, slight : V. Ex. 16.

II. *vb. tr.* (*a*) not to heed or accept, be indifferent to : S. A. 291 ; *my day of grace, they who neglect* : P. L. III. 199 ; *offered life neglect* : P. L. XII. 426.

(*b*) not to treat with due care or respect, slight : S. A. 481, 944.

(*c*) to omit to perform, leave undone : P. L. III. 738.

part. adj. **neglected,** uncared for : C. 743.

Negus, *sb.* the hereditary title of the kings of Abyssinia : P. L. XI. 397.

Neighbour, (1) *sb.* one who lives near another : S. A. 180.

attrib. dwelling near, adjacent; *neighbour woodman, villager, foe* : C. 484, 576 ; Ps. LXXX. 27.

(2) *vb. intr.* to lie near, be adjacent ; *his nether empire neighbouring round* : P. L. IV. 145.

part. adj. **neighbouring,** situated or dwelling near by ; *neighbouring moon* : P. L. III. 459, 726 ; *hills* : P. L. V. 547 ; VI. 663 ; XI. 575 ; *plain, plains* : P. L. XII. 136 ; P. R. III. 319 ; *arms* : P. L. II. 395 ; *nations* : P. R. III. 76 ; *eyes* : L'A. 80.

Neighbourhood, *sb.* (*a*) the state of dwelling near, proximity : P. L. I. 400.

(*b*) adjoining district, vicinity ; *my ... ancient neighbourhood* : C. 314 ; *gentle neighbourhood of grove and spring* : P. 52.

(*c*) neighbours collectively : Hor. Epist. 5.

***Neither,** (1) *absol.* or *pron.* not one or the other : P. L. IV. 1007 ; IX. 1188 ; X. 791.

(2) *conj.* (*a*) not either ; correlative with *nor* : P. L. II. 939 ; III. 682 ; IV. 509, 650 ; V. 146 ; VI. 322 ; VIII. 596 ; IX. 124 ; L. 52 ; *neither Sea, nor Shore, nor Air, nor Fire* : P. L. II. 912 ; *neither had I trangressed, nor thou with me* : P. L. IX. 1161 ; *neither wealth nor honour, arms nor arts* : P. R. IV. 368 ; correlative with *or* : P. R. I. 268 ; correlative with *and* : P. L. XI. 773 ; the correlative clause omitted : P. L. II. 482.

(*b*) and not, nor yet : P. L. II. 811.

Nepenthes, *sb.* a magic potion which banished pain and sorrow : C. 675.

Neptune, *sb.* Poseidon, the god of springs, rivers, and seas, and also of the islands of the seas : P. L. IX. 18 ; P. R. II. 190 ; C. 18 ; L. 90 ; *green-eyed Neptune* : V. Ex. 43 ; *earth-shaking* : C. 869.

Nereus, *sb.* the sea-god who was called ' the Ancient One of the Sea.' He was the father of the Nereids, the goddesses of the sea ; *aged, hoary Nereus* : C. 835, 871.

Nerve, *sb.* (*a*) sinew, tendon ; *fig., the brute Earth would lend her nerves, and shake* : C. 797 ; *how war ... may best move by her two main nerves, iron and gold* : S. VII. 8 ; rather, the bodily power of sensation and motion : C. 660.

(*b*) one of the structures by which sensations and impulses are transmitted to and from organs : P. L. XI. 415.

(*c*) bodily strength, muscular power : S. A. 1646 ; *the nerve of mortal arm* : S. A. 639.

Nest, *sb.* the bed formed by a bird for the incubation and rearing of its young : P. L. IV. 601 ; S. A. 1694 ; *brooding nest* : Ps. LXXXIV. 12 ; *fowls in their clay nests* : P. R. I. 501.

See **Ground-nest.**

Net, *sb.* snare ; *amorous net, nets* : P. L. XI. 586 ; P. R. II. 162.

Nether, *adj.* (*a*) lying below in position, lower : P. L. II. 784 ; *nether flood, ocean* : P. L. IV. 231 ; VII. 624 ; *nether empire, world* : P. L. IV. 145 ; XI. 328 ; opposed to *upper* : P. L. I. 346.

(b) pertaining to hell; *nether empire*: P. L. II. 296.

(c) having the rule of Hades; *nether Jove*: C. 20. *See* Jove.

Nethermost, *adj.* lowest: P. L. II. 956, 969.

*****Never**, *adv.* (a) not ever, at no time: P. L. I. 66, 352; II. 721; III. 4, 590; contracted to *ne'er*: U. C. II. 18; C. 127, 131, 177; Ps. LXXXVII. 22.

(b) in no degree, not at all: P. L. I. 108, 657; IV. 98; *ne'er so*, to whatever degree: S. A. 212.

Never-ceasing, *adj.* at no time stopping: P. L. II. 654.

Never-ending, *adj.* continued forever: P. L. II. 221.

Nevertheless, *adv.* none the less, notwithstanding: P. L. X. 970.

New, I. *adj.* (1) recently come into existence, lately made; *new wine*: P. L. IX. 1008; *creation*: P. L. III. 661; *world* or *worlds*: P. L. I. 650; II. 403, 867; IV. 34, 113, 391; VII. 209; X. 257, 377, 721; *new ... pontifice*: P. L. X. 348; *race*: P. L. II. 348; III. 679; recently constituted or established; *new Presbyter*: F. of C. 20; *schools of Academics, old and new*: P. R. IV. 278.

(2) lately introduced to one's knowledge, not before known, recently discovered; *new lands*: P. L. I. 290; *fresh woods and pastures new*: L. 193; *object*: P. L. IX. 222; *creatures new to sight*: P. L. IV. 287; *new and strange*: P. L. VI. 571; *strange point and new*: P. L. V. 855; *what happens new*: P. R. I. 334; *new matter*: P. L. III. 613; *subject*: S. XI. 3; *device*: P. R. IV. 443; C. 941; *joys*: N. O. 66; *acquist of ... experience*: S. A. 1755.

(b) recently obtained; *new kingdom*: P. L. X. 406.

(c) recently come; *new possessor*: P. L. I. 252; *this newcomer, Shame*: P. L. IX. 1097.

(3) other than the former, different; recently produced by change, fresh (some of the following may belong to (4)): P. L. IV. 205; VII. 68; IX. 175, 667; X. 972; P. R. II. 38; III. 266; *new names*: P. L. I. 365; *flesh*: P. L. XI. 4; *abode*: N. O. 18; *new*

Heaven and Earth: P. L. III. 335; X. 647; *new Heavens, new Earth*: P. L. XII. 549; *haunt*: P. L. IV. 184; *Lords*: P. L. VI. 451; *laws*: P. L. V. 679, 680; XI. 228; *broils, troubles, quarrels*: P. L. II. 837; IV. 575; XI. 103; P. R. II. 126; S. A. 1329; *rebellions*: S. XV. 6; *foes*: S. XVI. 11; *counsels, commands*: P. L. V. 681, 691; *covenant*: P. L. XI. 867; *honours*: P. L. V. 780; *minds*: P. L. V. 680; *life*: P. L. III. 294; *courage, hope, joy*, etc.: P. L. I. 279; III. 137; IV. 106; V. 431; IX. 843, 985; XI. 138; P. R. II. 58; L'A. 69; C. 967; *praise*: P. L. V. 184; *strength*: P. L. X. 243; *speech*: P. L. XII. 5.

(4) additional, repeated; *new Babels*: P. L. III. 468; *new war, subjection*: P. L. I. 645; II. 239; *league*: P. L. II. 319; *utterance*: P. L. IV. 410; *strength*: P. R. IV. 566.

(5) renewed; *new moon*: Ps. LXXXI. 9.

II. *adv.* (a) lately, recently, freshly: P. L. I. 774; IX. 852; P. R. I. 328; S. A. 1447; M. W. 40.

(b) anew, afresh: P. L. VIII. 311.

(c) so as to restore to a former state of purity; *till fire purge all things new*: P. L. XI. 900.

See Ever-new.

New-arrived, *absol.* the new arrived, those who have but just come to a place: P. L. X. 26.

New-baptized, *absol.* the new-baptized, those who have recently received baptism: P. R. II. 1.

New-born, *adj.* very lately born: N. O. 116.

New-created, *adj.* recently created; *new-created world*: P. L. III. 89; IV. 937; VII. 554; X. 481.

New-declared, *absol.* this new-declared, this man who has been recently made known: P. R. I. 121.

New-enlightened, *adj.* recently filled with light: N. O. 82.

New-enlivened, *adj.* reanimated, again revived: C. 228.

New-fangled, *adj.* new-fashioned, novel: V. Ex. 19.

New-felt, *adj.* newly experienced: P. L. X. 263.

New-graven, *adj.* recently sculptured; *fig.*, *affirming it thy star, new-graven in heaven*: P. R. I. 253.

New-intrusted, *adj.* recently given in trust: C. 36.

Newly, *adv.* recently, just: U. C. I. 18.

New-made, *adj.* (*a*) recently created; *new-made world*: P. L. VII. 617; Ps. CXXXVI. 26.
(*b*) recently dug: C. 472.

New-reaped, *adj.* recently cut: P. L. XI. 431.

New-risen, *adj.* just above the horizon: P. L. I. 594.

News, *sb.* fresh information, tidings: P. L. VI. 20; XI. 263; S. A. 1569; *glad, joyous news*: S. A. 1444; P. 3; *unwelcome, ill, evil*: P. L. X. 21; P. R. I. 64; S. A. 1538.

New-spangled, *adj.* freshly or brilliantly gleaming: L. 170.

New-waked, *past part.* just awakened: P. L. VIII. 4, 253.

New-welcome, *adj.* recently welcomed: M. W. 71.

Next, I. *adj.* (**1**) nearest in position: C. 185.
(**2**) immediately following: M. W. 67; *next holiday*: C. 959; *command*: P. L. IV. 864; *design*: P. L. V. 33.
(**3**) nearest in rank or relation; *next subordinate*: P. L. V. 671; *mate*: P. L. I. 238; *next in worth*: P. L. I. 378; *next in military prowess*: P. L. VI. 45; with *to*; *this glory next to thee*: P. L. III. 239; *with next to almighty arm*: P. L. VI. 316; followed by a sb. without *to*; *one next himself in power*: P. L. I. 79.
(*b*) direct in line of succession; *his next son*: P. L. XII. 332.
(*c*) closely connected by being of the same tribe: S. A. 1507.
(*d*) dearest: C. 501.
absol. (*a*) the person nearest; *Gabriel to his next in power*: P. L. IV. 781.
(*b*) the person succeeding another: P. R. IV. 295; S. A. 227; V. Ex. 58.
II. *adv.* (**1**) in the nearest position; *next under*: V. Ex. 41; *stood ... next to*: P. L. IV. 220; followed by sb. without *to*: P. L. I. 383; M. W. 62; or in sense (**2**); *next him ... stood up*: P. L. II. 43.

(**2**) immediately after, in the place or turn immediately succeeding: P. L. I. 406, 457; II. 439, 965; VI. 446, 653; VIII. 449; IX. 174; X. 645; XI. 169, 436; P. R. III. 417; IV. 253, 272; C. 916; L. 103; *next behind*: P. L. I. 446; *when next we meet*: P. L. VI. 439; *Socrates (who next more memorable?)*: P. R. III. 96; with *to*: P. L. IX. 807.
(*b*) secondly; *first ... next*: P. L. II. 19; III. 383, 466; IV. 948; VII. 489; IX. 950; X. 604.
(**3**) so as to approach nearest in rank or position; *Fancy next, her office holds*: P. L. V. 102; followed by a sb. without *to*; *next him ... Chance governs*: P. L. II. 909.

Nibbling, *part. adj.* biting off and eating small bits: L'A. 72.

Nice, *adj.* (*a*) difficult to please, exacting, fastidious; *to taste think not I shall be nice*: P. L. V. 453; over-fastidious, squeamish; *the nice Morn on the Indian steep*: C. 139.
(*b*) dainty, fine, choice; *a nice and subtle happiness*: P. L. VIII. 399.
(*c*) accurate, exact; *not nice Art ... but Nature boon*: P. L. IV. 241; *sup.,* applied *with nicest touch*: P. L. VI. 584.
absol. a fastidious person: P. R. IV. 157.

Nicely, *adv.* fastidiously, critically: P. R. IV. 377.

Niger, *sb.* the river in western Africa; *Niger flood*: P. L. XI. 402.

Niggard, *sb.* miser: C. 726.

Nigh, *adv.* (**1**) close at hand, near; (*a*) used of distance: P. L. VI. 533; VIII. 564; IX. 482, 595; X. 864; XII. 625; P. R. I. 332; II. 262; IV. 489, 582; S. I. 10; Ps. VII. 6; *draw* or *drew nigh*: P. L. III. 645, 646; V. 82; XI. 238; S. A. 178; Ps. LXXXVIII. 12; *so far ... so nigh*: P. L. IX. 433; *far and nigh*: P. L. VI. 295; P. R. IV. 122; *nigh in her sight*: P. L. XI. 184; *nigh on the plain*: P. L. I. 700; *nigh at hand*: P. L. IV. 552; IX. 256; *nigh to*: P. R. II. 20; followed by a sb. without *to*: P. L. IV. 861; IX. 514; *sup.,* *nighest is far*: P. R. I. 332.
(*b*) used of time: P. L. IV. 366; *some further change awaits us nigh*:

P. L. XI. 193; *nigh at hand*: P.
R. I. 20; S. A. 593; followed by
a *sb.* without *to*; *which nigh the
birth now rolling*: P. L. IV. 15.
(2) nearly, almost: P. L. II.
940; X. 159, 632; P. R. I. 36;
converts it nigh to joy: S. A. 1564;
well nigh half: P. L. IX. 141.
Nigh-hand, *adv.* near at hand, close
by: P. L. III. 566.
Night, *sb.* (*a*) the time of darkness
between sunset and sunrise: P. L.
I. 343, 500; IV. 550, 557, 688,
724; V. 31, 128, 166, 206; VII.
351, 380, 584; VIII. 139; IX. 211,
635; XII. 264; P. R. II. 279;
S. A. 88; L'A. 107; C. 123, 222,
285; *that, this, her night*: P. L.
I. 503; V. 30, 35, 93, 96, 227;
U. C. I. 15; A. 39; C. 948; *in
one night*: P. L. I. 487; IX. 140;
day and night: P. L. I. 50; II.
505; IV. 613, 680; VI. 8; VIII.
24; IX. 51; XI. 826, 898; S. A.
807; *days and nights*: P. L. X.
680; *six nights and days*: P. L.
IX. 137; *seven continued nights*:
P. L. IX. 63; *the wheel of Day and
Night*: P. L. VIII. 136; *not day
nor night*: S. A. 404; *to divide the
Day from Night*: P. L. VII. 341;
Darkness, Night he named: P. L.
VII. 251; *the hour of night*: P. L.
IV. 611; P. R. II. 260; *the mid-
hour of night*: S. IX. 13; *all night*
or *all night long*: P. L. II. 286;
III. 545; IV. 603, 657; V. 657;
VII. 436; XII. 206; *by night*: P.
L. III. 514; IV. 665; V. 261, 547;
IX. 58; X. 342; XII. 365; P. R.
I. 244; C. 432; *by day ... by night*:
P. L. VII. 348; VIII. 143; XII.
203, 257; *night by night*: C. 532;
night's hemisphere: P. L. IX. 52;
*the circling canopy of Night's ex-
tended shade*: P. L. III. 557;
while night invests the sea: P. L.
I. 207; *her* (the moon's) *pale
dominion checks the night*: P. L.
III. 732; *the stars of night*: P. L.
V. 745; *bird of night*: P. L. VIII.
518; *peaceful was the night*: N.
O. 61; *fresh dews of night*: L.
29; *night bids us rest*: P. L. IV.
633; *what hath night to do with
sleep*: C. 122; *sleepless night* or
nights: P. L. IX. 63; XI. 173;
night or loneliness: C. 404; *still
as night*: P. L. II. 308; *the still
night*: P. L. X. 846; *in deep of
night*: P. L. IV. 674; A. 61; *cold

the night: P. L. X. 1070; *black ...
as night*: P. L. II. 670; *dark ...
night*: P. 7; *the shades of Night*:
P. L. IV. 1015; *O night and shades*:
C. 580; *gloomy as Night*: P. L.
VI. 832; *dismal, ominous*: P. R.
IV. 452, 481; *empty-vaulted*: C.
250; *the night so foul*: P. R. IV.
426; *a night of storm*: P. R. IV.
436; *dews and damps of night*: P.
R. IV. 406; *each ... night to defend
him from the dew*: P. R. I. 304.
feminine gender; *silent Night,
with this her solemn bird*: P. L.
IV. 647, 654; *Night ... with her
shadowy cone*: P. L. IV. 776;
more definitely *personified*, sometimes with the characteristics of
the mythological goddess; *shamefaced, listening night*: N. O. 111;
Cir. 5; *rugged brow of Night*:
Il P. 58; *Night with her will
bring Silence*: P. L. VII. 105;
Night with her sullen wing: P. R.
I. 500; *crossed the car of Night*:
P. L. IX. 65; vocative: P. 29;
Il P. 121; *O thievish Night*: C.
195; masculine gender; *startle
the dull night from his watch-
tower in the skies*: L'A. 42; *Night
sits monarch yet in the mid sky*:
C. 957; as the child of Darkness: P. R. IV. 398.
in heaven: P. L. V. 645, 699;
day without night: P. L. V. 162;
all night: P. L. VI. 1; *by night*:
P. L. VI. 416; *dim Night*: P. L.
V. 700; *ambrosial*: P. L. V. 642;
feminine gender: P. L. VI. 406;
dim Night her shadowy cloud: P.
L. V. 685; personified: P. L. VI.
14; *conscious Night*: P. L. VI. 521.
(*b*) the absence of light, darkness: P. L. III. 726; *thy soul ... to
incorporate with gloomy night*: S.
A. 161; *Chaos, that reigns here
in double night of darkness and of
shades*: C. 335.
personified as the consort of and
co-ruler with Chaos: P. L. I. 543;
II. 133, 970, 1036; III. 18; *sable-
vested*: P. L. II. 962; *the womb
of ... Night*: P. L. II. 150; X.
477; *the frown of Night*: P. L.
III. 424; *the sceptre of old Night*:
P. L. II. 1002; *the standard ... of
ancient Night*: P. L. II. 986;
*eldest Night and Chaos, ancestors
of Nature*: P. L. II. 894; rather,
the realm of Night: P. L. II. 439;
III. 71.

(c) obscurity ; *things ... the invisible king ... hath suppressed in night* : P. L. VII. 123.

(d) a time of loneliness and sorrow : S. XXIII. 14.

See **Birth-night.**

Night-foundered, *adj.* lost in the darkness of night : P. L. I. 204 ; C. 483.

Night hag, *sb.* a witch who flies abroad in the night : P. L. II. 662.

Nightingale, *sb.* the bird *Daulias luscinia* : P. L. IV. 771 ; S. I. 1 ; as feminine gender (but *see* P. L. V. 41) ; *wakeful* : P. L. IV. 602 ; *solemn, love-lorn* : P. L. VII. 435 ; C. 234 ; *fig., your dear sister ... poor hapless nightingale* : C. 566.

Nightly, (1) *adj.* happening or appearing in the night : P. L. IX. 22 ; *nightly trance* : N. O. 179 ; *ill, harm* : A. 48 ; Il P. 84.

(2) *adv.* by night, every night : P. L. I. 440 ; II. 642 ; III. 32 ; IV. 685 ; V. 714 ; VII. 29, 580 ; IX. 47 ; C. 113, 225, 883.

Night-raven, *sb.* the night-heron (?) : L'A. 7.

Night-steed, *sb.* one of the horses harnessed to the chariot of Night : N. O. 236.

Night-wanderer, *sb.* one travelling by night : P. L. IX. 640.

Night-warbling, *adj.* singing in the night : P. L. V. 40.

Night-watch, *sb.* a division of the night ; *village cock count the night-watches to his feathery dames* : C. 347 ; during which a soldier is on guard : P. L. IV. 780.

Nile, *sb.* the river of Egypt : P. L. I. 343 ; *river Nile* : P. L. XII. 157 ; *fig.* the river put for the country : P. L. I. 413 ; N. O. 211.

Nilotic, *adj.* of or bordering on the river Nile ; *Meroë, Nilotic isle* : P. R. IV. 71.

Nilus, *sb.* the Nile : P. L. IV. 283.

Nimble, *adj.* light and quick in motion, swift ; *nimble feet, tread, glance* : P. L. IV. 866 ; VI. 73 ; XI. 442.

Nine, *adj.* eight and one : A. 64 ; *nine days* : P. L. VI. 871 ; *the Muses nine* : P. L. VII. 6 ; *nine times the space* : P. L. I. 50.

Ninefold, (1) *adj.* composed of nine tones or notes ; *ninefold harmony* : N. O. 131.

(2) *adv.* nine times : P. L. II. 436.

Nineveh, *sb.* the capital of the Assyrian empire : P. R. III. 275.

Ninus, *sb.* according to the Greek tradition, the founder of Nineveh : P. R. III. 276.

Nip, (1) *sb.* sharp frost-bite ; *winter's nip* : M. W. 36.

(2) *vb. tr.* to blast ; *bloom of spring nipt with the lagging rear of winter's frost* : S. A. 1577.

Niphates, *sb.* a mountain range on the southern border of Armenia, west of Lake Van : P. L. III. 742.

Nisibis, *sb.* the most important city of Mesopotamia, the capital under the Parthian empire : P. R. III. 291.

Nisroch, *sb.* one of the fallen angels : P. L. VI. 447.

Nitre, *sb.* saltpetre ; *some tumultuous cloud, instinct with fire and nitre* : P. L. II. 937.

Nitrous, *adj.* containing nitre ; *nitrous powder, foam* : P. L. IV. 815 ; VI. 512.

*No, (1) *adj.* not any or an, none : P. L. I. 63, 282, 362, 492 ; C. 774 ; *no other* : P. L. IV. 420 ; V. 534 ; in a clause introduced by *nor* : P. L. V. 421.

(2) *adv.* not in any degree, in no respect ; with comparatives ; *no better* : P. L. IV. 915 ; P. R. I. 248 ; *greater* : P. R. II. 27 ; *higher* : P. L. XII. 576 ; *less* : P. L. I. 144, 647 ; II. 414 ; *longer* : P. L. X. 365 ; XII. 594 ; *more* : P. L. IV. 22 ; VI. 349 ; *profaner* : Il P. 140 ; *sooner* : P. L. III. 344 ; X. 357.

No, *adv.* (a) nay, not so ; the particle of denial or negation : P. L. II. 60 ; V. 242 ; P. R. II. 86 ; III. 431 ; S. A. 1481 ; D. F. I. 34 ; N. O. 149 ; in iteration or amplification of a previous negative : P. L. IX. 124, 913 ; S. A. 928, 1113.

(b) not ; *the last of me or no* : S. A. 1426 ; *whether they serve willing or no* : P. L. V. 533.

Nobility, *sb.* persons of high rank collectively : S. A. 1654.

Noble, I. *adj.* (1) distinguished by birth or rank : S. A. 218, 1166 ; *noble birth* : M. W. 5 ; *house, stem* : M. W. 54 ; A. 82 ; *Peer* : C. 31 ; *Lord and Lady* : C. 966.

(2) high in excellence or worth ; (a) lofty, magnanimous ; *noble minds* : L. 71.

(b) excellent, superior, great:
noble stroke : P. L. VI. 189 ; *task* :
S. XXII. 11.

comp. : P. L. XI. 411 ; *nobler
task* : S. XV. 9 ; *herb, plant, and
nobler birth* : P. L. IX. 111 ;
creatures ... two of far nobler shape :
P. L. IV. 288 ; *the inner man, the
nobler part* : P. R. II. 477.

sup. noblest architects : P. R. IV.
52 ; *trees of noblest kind* : P. L.
IV. 217 ; *meats of noblest sort* : P.
R. II. 341.

(c) great, magnificent, splendid ;
used of the stars : P. L. VIII. 34 ;
comp. : P. L. VIII. 28.

(3) proceeding from or indicative of greatness of mind ; *noble
deeds* : P. R. IV. 99 ; *a death so
noble* : S. A. 1724 ; *noble grace,
virtues* : C. 451 ; S. X. 12 ; *comp.* :
P. L. II. 116 ; XI. 655 ; *sup.* :
P. L. I. 552.

absol. persons of lofty character :
P. L. XII. 221.

II. *adv.* nobly, magnanimously ;
comp., nobler done : P. R. II. 482.

Nobleness, *sb.* magnanimity, lofti-
ness of character : P. L. VIII. 557.

Nobly, *adv.* splendidly, magnificently : P. R. IV. 239.

Nocent, *adj.* hurtful, injurious : P.
L. IX. 186.

Nocturnal, *adj.* of or belonging to
the night ; *nocturnal note* : P. L.
III. 40 ; *sport* : C. 128 ; *nocturnal
... rhomb* : P. L. VIII. 134. *See*
Rhomb.

Nod, *sb.* a quick short downward
motion of the head ; *duck or nod* :
C. 960 ; *nods and becks* : L'A. 28.

Nodding, *part. adj.* bending, overhanging ; transferred epithet, *this
drear wood, the nodding horror of
whose shady brows* : C. 38.

Noise, (1) *sb.* (a) sound, usually of a
loud and disagreeable character ;
sometimes a mixture of confused
sounds : P. L. II. 957 ; VIII. 243 ;
S. A. 1472, 1508, 1513 ; C. 170,
369 ; *loud, thundering, outrageous,
infernal, insufferable, barbarous* :
P. L. II. 921 ; VI. 487, 587, 667,
867 ; S. XII. 3 ; *spattering* : P. L.
X. 567 ; *jangling noise of words* :
P. L. XII. 55 ; *the noise of riot* :
P. L. I. 498 ; *of endless war* : P.
L. II. 896 ; *of conflict* : P. L. VI.
211 ; *of drums* : P. L. I. 394 ; *of
his almighty engine* : P. L. II. 64 ;
of ruin ... the noise : S. A. 1515 ;

noise ... or universal groan : S. A.
1511 ; *the noise of folly* : Il P. 61 ;
*such noise as I can make to be heard
farthest* : C. 227 ; the barking of
dogs : P. L. II. 657 ; the sound of
the winds : P. L. X. 705.

(b) outcry, clamour : S. A. 16.

(c) report, rumour : S. A. 1088.

(d) music ; *the stringed noise* :
N. O. 97 ; *that melodious noise* :
S. M. 18.

(2) *vb. intr.* to sound : P. R.
IV. 488.

Noisome, *adj.* (a) hurtful, noxious :
A. 49.

(b) loathsome : P. L. XI. 478.

None, I. *adj.* not any, no ; always
following the sb. : P. L. III. 219,
669, 738 ; V. 538 ; VIII. 624 ; XI.
673 ; P. R. II. 288 ; IV. 184, 487 ;
terms of peace yet none : P. L. II.
331 ; *that shape had none* : P. L.
II. 667 ; *living or lifeless, to be
found was none* : P. L. III. 443 ;
further way found none : P. L. IV.
174 ; *though men were none* : P. L.
IV. 675 ; *insect or worm durst enter
none* : P. L. IV. 704 ; *other rites
observing none* : P. L. IV. 737 ;
other light she needed none : P. L.
VII. 378 ; *man to till the ground
none was* : P. L. VII. 333 ; *conviction to the serpent none* : P. L.
X. 84 ; *they his gifts acknowledged
none* : P. L. XI. 612 ; *tidings of
him none* : P. R. II. 62 ; *other
place none can than Heaven* : P.
L. V. 362 ; *when answer none
returned* : P. L. VIII. 285 ; *that
rest or intermission none I find* : P.
L. II. 802.

II. *pron.* (1) no one, nobody ;
(a) *sing.* : P. L. I. 273, 690 ; II.
32, 33, 255, 300, 423, 466, 776,
814 ; III. 289 ; IV. 45 ; V. 59, 62,
850 ; VI. 159 ; VII. 124 ; VIII. 233,
406 ; IX. 92, 1140 ; P. R. I. 323 ;
II. 146, 315 ; III. 289, 358 ; S. A.
344, 531, 1628 ; A. 72 ; Ps. LXXXV.
8 ; LXXXVI. 25 ; *to none but me* :
P. L. III. 182 ; *if none regard* : P.
L. V. 44 ; *Abdiel than whom none* :
P. L. V. 805 ; *none arguing stood* :
P. L. VI. 508 ; *since none but thou
can end it* : P. L. VI. 702 ; *by his
gait none of the meanest* : P. L. XI.
231.

(b) *pl.* : P. L. V. 791 ; *none but
such* : P. L. III. 202 ; *none but such
as are good men* : C. 702 ; *in at
this gate none pass ... but such* : P.

L. IV. 579 ; *whom they hit, none on their feet might stand* : P. L. VI. 592 ; *none are* : P. L. X. 80 ; P. R. II. 177 ; *laws which none shall find left them* : P. L. XII. 522.

(2) not any, not one : P. L. III. 132, 235 ; IV. 80, 81 ; V. 99, 860 ; VI. 442 ; X. 820 ; XI. 837 ; P. R. II. 318 ; C. 137 ; *no thought of flight, none of retreat* : P. L. VI. 237 ; *I in none of these find place* : P. L. IX. 118 ; *torment less than none of what we dread* : P. L. X. 998 ; *all glory arrogate, to God give none* : P. R. IV. 315 ; *ease to the body some, none to the mind* : S. A. 18.

Nook, *sb.* (*a*) a secluded place or recess : P. L. IV. 789 ; *in a shady nook* : P. L. IX. 277 ; *this dark sequestered nook* : C. 500.

(*b*) *fig.* body ; *this fleshly nook* : Il P. 92.

(*c*) receptacle; *filled each hollow nook* : P. L. I. 707.

Noon, *sb.* (*a*) the time when the sun is in the meridian, midday : P. L. IX. 219 ; X. 93 ; *high noon* : P. L. V. 174 ; *the hour of noon* : P. L. IX. 739 ; *morn to noon* : P. L. I. 734 ; *feast and noon* : S. A. 1612 ; *the heat of noon* : P. L. V. 231 ; *the blaze of noon* : S. A. 80 ; *by noon* : P. L. IX. 401 ; *at noon* : P. L. III. 616 ; IV. 627 ; XII. 1 ; P. R. II. 292 ; *at highth of noon* : P. L. IV. 564.

(*b*) time of greatest power and influence ; *their highth of noon* : S. A. 683.

(*c*) time of greatest brilliancy ; *the ... moon, riding near her highest noon* : Il P. 68.

attrib. of the time of noon ; *the noon sky* : P. R. II. 156.

See **Mid-noon.**

Noontide, *adj.* midday ; *noontide bowers* : P. L. IV. 246 ; *repast* : P. L. IX. 403 ; *air* : P. L. II. 309.

*****Nor,** *conj.* (*a*) and not ; correlative with *neither* : P. L. II. 940 ; III. 682 ; IV. 509 ; V. 147 ; VI. 323 ; IX. 1161 ; P. R. III. 45 ; L. 54 ; S. XX. 8 ; *neither* omitted : P. L. IV. 1009 ; VI. 810 ; *as fearing God nor man* : P. R. IV. 304 ; *attendance none shall need, nor train* : P. L. X. 80 ; correlative with *nor* : P. L. II. 341 ; III. 83 ; IV. 741 ; VII. 6 ; XI. 307 ; *nor God nor man* : P. L. V. 60 ; *nor skilled nor*

studious : P. L. IX. 42 ; *thou hast nor ear, nor soul* : C. 784 ; *nor gentle purpose, nor endearing smiles ... nor youthful dalliance* : P. L. IV. 338 ; *nor ... hill, nor ... vale, nor wood, nor stream* : P. L. VI. 70 ; *Pan or Sylvan never slept, nor Nymph nor Faunus haunted* : P. L. IV. 707.

with various other negatives used in the first member of the sentence or clause ; *created thing naught valued he nor shunned* : P. L. II. 679 ; *who never wanted means, nor ... just cause* : S. A. 316 ; *never touched ... nor conspired* : P. L. XI. 426 ; *no bars of hell, nor all the chains* : P. L. III. 82 ; *no obstacle ... nor shade* : P. L. III. 615 ; *no sight, nor motion* : P. L. VI. 192 ; *no change, nor ... desire* : P. L. VIII. 526 ; *no more contend, nor blame each other* : P. L. X. 958 ; *not tied ... nor founded* : P. L. I. 427 ; *thou ... didst not spare, nor stop* : P. L. III. 394 ; *not love, nor hope* : P. L. IX. 475 ; *not God, ... nor Fate* : P. L. IX. 927.

(*b*) and ... not ; without a correlative : P. L. I. 715 ; III. 32 ; VI. 359 ; VII. 494 ; VIII. 486 ; IX. 382 ; S. A. 930 ; *nor only Paradise ... but the starry cope of Heaven* : P. L. IV. 991 ; introducing a sentence : P. L. I. 364 ; *Nor can I miss the way* : P. L. X. 262 ; *Nor can this be* : P. L. XII. 395 ; *Nor did Israel scape the infection* : P. L. I. 482 ; with another negative in the clause ; *Nor doth the moon no nourishment exhale* : P. L. V. 421 ; *Nor did they not perceive the evil plight* : P. L. I. 335 ; *nor could his eye not ken* : P. L. XI. 396. See also **Neither.**

North, (1) *adv.* to or in the north : P. R. IV. 78 ; *the mount that lies from Eden north* : P. L. IV. 569.

(2) *sb.* (*a*) that one of the cardinal points of the compass which is on the right hand when one faces in the direction of the setting sun ; *from the north* : P. L. X. 654 ; *to the north* : P. L. VI. 79.

(*b*) a district or country lying toward the north ; *these other wheel the north* : P. L. IV. 783 ; *the populous North*, the land of the Goths, Huns, and Vandals :

P. L. I. 351; *the false North,*
Scotland; S. XV. 7; a part of
heaven; *the quarters of the North*:
P. L. V. 689; *the limits of the
North*: P. L. V. 755; *the spacious
North*: P. L. V. 726.

(c) the northern part; with *of*:
P. L. X. 695.

(d) the northern side; *on the
north*: P. R. IV. 28, 448.

North-east, *adj.* coming from between the north and east; *north-
east winds*: P. L. IV. 161.

Northern, *adj.* dwelling in or coming
from the north; *all his northern
powers*: P. R. III. 338.

Northward, *adv.* toward the north:
P. L. XII. 139.

North-wind, *sb.* the wind blowing
from the north: P. L. II. 489;
XI. 842.

Norumbega, *sb.* a region on the
Atlantic coast of North America;
it "hath on the North-east,
Nova Scotia; on the South-west,
Virginia." Heylyn, *Cos.* 1666, p.
1024; also Mercator, *Atlas*, 1636,
vol. 2, map at p. 435: P. L. X.
696.

Norway, *sb. attrib.* adjacent to Norway; *Norway foam*: P. L. I. 203.

Norwegian, *adj.* of Norway: P. L.
I. 293.

Nostril, *sb.* the nasal orifice: P. L.
VII. 525; IX. 196; the *sing.* for
the *pl., upturned his nostril wide*:
P. L. X. 280.

***Not,** the particle of negation,
denial, refusal, or prohibition:
P. L. I. 106, 109, 241; II. 122;
C. 414; *I ... could not but taste*:
P. L. V. 86; *whether to hold them
wise or not*: P. L. IV. 908;
*whether he durst accept the offer
or not*: S. A. 1255; *I had not
thought to have unlocked my lips*:
C. 756. *See also* **Nor.**

with a vb. without the auxiliary
do ; if I fail not: P. L. I. 167; *I
give not Heaven for lost*: P. L. II.
13; *I boast not*: P. L. II. 52; *long
I sat not*: P. L. II. 778; *he staid
not to inquire*: P. L. III. 571;
come not too near: C. 491; *further
know I not*: C. 580; *I state not
that*: S. A. 424; *know ye not me?*
P. L. IV. 828; *he drew not nigh
unheard*: P. L. III. 645; *yet not
true life thereby regained*: P. L.
IV. 196; *which not nice Art ...
poured forth*: P. L. IV. 241; *not

the more cease I to wander: P. L.
III. 26; *yet not rejoicing in his
speed*: P. L. IV. 13; *they ... not
once perceive*: C. 74; *am I not
sung?*: S. A. 203.

Note, *sb.* (a) importance, distinction,
renown: P. R. II. 306.

(b) a musical character representing a tone: S. XIII. 3.

(c) a musical sound, melody,
music; *pl.*: L'A. 139; Il P. 106;
artful voice warble immortal notes:
S. XX. 12; used of the music of
angels; *sing., celestial voices ...
responsive each to other's note*: P.
L. IV. 683; *pl.*: N. O. 116; *with
notes angelical*: P. L. II. 548; of
the music of birds; *sing., the
wakeful bird ... tunes her nocturnal
note*: P. L. III. 40; *pl.*: P. L.
II. 494; V. 199; *the Attic bird
trills her thick-warbled notes*: P.
R. IV. 246; *O Nightingale, ... thy
liquid notes*: S. I. 5; *cleared up
their choicest notes*: P. R. IV. 437.

used *fig.* of poetry; *with other
notes than to the Orphean lyre*: P.
L. III. 17; *I must change these
notes to tragic*: P. L. IX. 6; *set
my harp to notes of saddest woe*:
P. 9.

See **Wood-notes.**

Nothing, (1) *sb.* (a) no thing, not
any thing: P. L. I. 27; IV. 418;
VIII. 571; IX. 232, 345, 722; XII.
186; P. R. II. 169; III. 79, 129,
135; IV. 157, 158; S. A. 474, 801,
881, 966, 1033, 1233, 1385, 1408,
1424, 1528, 1721, 1723; *think
nothing hard*: P. L. VI. 495; *I
shall want nothing*: S. A. 1484;
in need of nothing: V. Ex. 81;
good for nothing else: S. A. 1163;
nothing said: L. 129; *that he
nothing knew*: P. R. IV. 294;
apprehended nothing high: P. L.
IX. 574; *fancies built on nothing*:
P. R. IV. 292; *nothing wear but
frieze*: C. 722; *nothing wants but
that thy shape*: P. L. X. 869; *of
wisdom nothing more than mean*:
S. A. 207; *nothing of all these evils*:
S. A. 374.

(b) non-existence; *on this side
nothing*: P. L. II. 101; *reduce to
nothing this essential*: P. L. II.
97; *to nothing brought*: P. R. III.
389.

(2) *adv.* not at all; *nothing
loth*: P. L. IX. 1039; *swayed*:
P. L. X. 1010.

Notice, *sb.* (*a*) attention, regard : S. A. 250.

(*b*) information, intelligence : S. A. 1536.

Notion, *sb.* (*a*) conception, idea : C. 785.

(*b*) fancy, conception founded on imagination ; *notions vain* : P. L. VIII. 187.

(*c*) mind, understanding ; *as earthly notion can receive* : P. L. VII. 179.

Notorious, *adj.* known to everybody ; *notorious murder* : S. A. 1186.

Notus, *sb.* the south wind : P. L. X. 702.

Nought. *See* **Naught.**

Nourish, *vb.* (1) *tr.* (*a*) to supply with nutriment ; *which these soft fires* (the stars) ... *nourish* : P. L. IV. 670 ; *Air, and ye Elements, ... nourish all things* : P. L. V. 183.

(*b*) to encourage, cherish ; *thy thoughts ... nourish them* : P. R. I. 230.

(2) *intr.* to be nutritious, afford nourishment : P. L. V. 325.

Nourisher, *sb.* one who nourishes ; applied to God : P. L. V. 398.

Nourishment, *sb.* food, nutriment : P. L. XI. 533 ; *flowers and their fruit, man's nourishment* : P. L. V. 483 ; *wisdom to folly, as nourishment to wind* : P. L. VII. 130 ; *nor doth the Moon no nourishment exhale* : P. L. V. 421.

Novelty, *sb.* a new and strange thing : P. L. X. 891.

Novice, *adj.* befitting a beginner or one inexperienced ; *novice modesty* : P. R. III. 24ʰ.

*****Now**, (1) *adv.* (*a*) at the present time, at this juncture ; used chiefly in vivid narration : P. L. III. 484 ; IV. 160, 205, 611, 735 ; V. 38 ; C. 351 ; *I can now no more* : P. L. VIII. 630 ; *now to my charms* : C. 150 ; *and now a stripling Cherub he appears* : P. L. III. 636 ; *of pure now purer air meets his approach* : P. L. IV. 153 ; *now one, now other* : P. L. IV. 397 ; *now high, now low* : P. L. VIII. 126 ; *now meet'st the orient Sun, now fliest* : P. L. V. 175 ; *now hid, now seen* : P. L. IX. 436 ; *and now ... and now* : L. 190 ; *first ... now* : P. L. II. 1004 ; IX. 950 ; *late ... now* : S. A. 179 ; *long after ... now* : P. L. III. 497 ; *now ... erst* : P. L.

II. 469 ; *once ... now* : P. L. I. 90, 316 ; S. A. 22 ; *then ... now* : P. L. II. 820 ; *now ere* : P. L. V. 699 ; beginning a sentence : P. L. III. 56, 362 ; IV. 172, 604 ; V. 642 ; IX. 192.

iteratively ; *Now, now* : P. R. II. 35.

ere now, before this time : P. L. II. 831 ; Ps. III. 20 ; *till now*, until this time : P. L. II. 744 ; IV. 466 ; VI. 208, 429, 432 ; IX. 858, 1023 ; X. 369 ; C. 264.

(*b*) in these present times : P. L. IX. 70 ; X. 690 ; *when meet now such pairs, in love.. joined* : P. L. VIII. 57.

(*c*) a short time ago ; *but now* : P. L. I. 777.

(*d*) things being so, under these circumstances : P. L. VI. 165 ; *this now fenceless world* : P. L. X. 303 ; *thine now is all this world* : P. L. X. 372 ; *and now ... all mankind must have been lost* : P. L. III. 222 ; *thou know'st me now* : S. A. 1081.

(2) *conj.* it being the case that, since ; *the heavy change, now thou art gone* : L. 37, 38.

now that, seeing that, since : S. XX. 2.

Nowhere, *adv.* in no place : P. L. III. 411, 620 ; IV. 448 ; P. R. IV. 472.

Noxious, *adj.* hurtful, harmful ; *noxious vapour* : P. L. II. 216 ; *worm* : P. R. I. 312 ; *the serpent ... though to thee not noxious* : P. L. VII. 498 ; *to the other five* (stars) *... of noxious efficacy* : P. L. X. 660 ; applied to a storm : P. R. IV. 460.

Null, *vb. tr.* to destroy : S. A. 935.

Number, (1) *sb.* (*a*) the computed quantity, as many or as few as are counted or admitted : P. L. III. 706 ; X. 888 ; S. A. 1667 ; *their number last he sums* : P. L. I. 571 ; *I their number heard* : P. L. VI. 769 ; *Hell, her numbers full* : P. L. III. 332 ; *the number of her days* : M. W. 11 ; *our number may affright* : C. 148 ; *equal in number to that godless crew* : P. L. VI. 49 ; as many as are requisite (to make the harmony perfect) : P. L. IV. 687.

(*b*) a collection of units or individuals, an indefinite aggregation : P. L. VII. 147 ; XI. 480 ;

XII. 503 ; *the number of thy wor-shippers* : P. L. VII. 613 ; *such numbers of our nation* : S. A. 857 ; *to repair his numbers* : P. L. IX. 144.

a multitude ; *numbers without number* : P. L. III. 346 ; *numbers numberless* : P. R. III. 310 ; *numbers thither flock* : S. A. 1450 ; the fact of there being a multitude (of opponents) : P. L. V. 901.

(*c*) body, company ; *he, the head, one of our number becomes* : P. L. V. 843.

(*d*) a numeral figure ; *distance inexpressible by numbers that have name* : P. L. VIII. 114 ; the sing. collectively ; *to describe whose swiftness number fails* : P. L. VIII. 38.

(*e*) plurality ; *Man by number is to manifest his single imperfection* : P. L. VIII. 422.

(*f*) the quality of being numerous ; *number to this day's work is not ordained* : P. L. VI. 809.

(*g*) the capacity of being counted ; *without number* : P. L. I. 791 ; III. 346.

(*h*) musical measure ; *in tones and numbers hit by voice* : P. R. IV. 255 ; *move their starry dance in numbers* : P. L. III. 580.

(*i*) poetic measure, verse, poetry ; *harmonious numbers* : P. L. III. 38 ; *thy easy numbers flow* : W. S. 10.

(*j*) a part of a whole, detail ; but, by a play upon the word, with blending of sense (*a*) ; *through all numbers absolute, though One* : P. L. VIII. 421.

(**2**) *vb. tr.* (*a*) to count, enumerate, reckon : P. R. III. 410 ; A. 59 ; *his ransom ... shall willingly be paid and numbered down* : S. A. 1478.

(*b*) to serve to compute ; *time numbers motion* : U. C. II. 7 ; to serve to measure ; *motion numbered out his time* : U. C. II. 8.

(*c*) to make to comprise or include a number ; *though numbered such as each divided legion might have seemed a numerous host* : P. L. V. 229.

(*d*) to limit to a small number ; *his days are numbered* : P. L. XI. 40.

(*e*) to include in a list or class *with* : S. A. 1295 ; in the list of

readers ; *numbering good intellects* : S. XI. 4.

part. adj. **numbered** ; (*a*) fixed as to number ; *certain numbered days* : P. L. X. 576.

(*b*) enumerated : P. L. VIII. 19.

Numberless, *adj.* innumerable : P. L. I. 344, 780 ; VII. 492 ; P. R. III. 310 ; Il P. 7 ; *Angels numberless* : P. L. IX. 548 ; *numberless ... Spirits* : P. L. VII. 197 ; *army numberless* : P. L. VI. 224 ; *pavilions* : P. L. V. 653 ; *stars* : P. L. III. 719 ; that cannot be computed in numbers ; *swiftness ... numberless* : P. L. VIII. 108.

Numbing, *part. adj.* depriving of the power of motion : C. 853.

Numbness, *sb.* torpor : S. A. 571.

Numerous, (**1**) *adj.* (*a*) consisting of a great many individuals ; *numerous offspring* : P. L. IV. 385 ; *hatch* : P. L. VII. 418 ; *brigad, host, chivalry* : P. L. I. 675 ; II. 993 ; VI. 231, 830 ; P. R. III. 344.

(*b*) great in number, not a few : P. L. XII. 167 ; *mankind, so numerous* : P. L. XI. 752 ; *numerous orbs* : P. L. X. 397 ; *stars* : P. L. VII. 621 ; *eyes* : P. L. XI. 130 ; *servitude* : P. L. XII. 132 ; *mercies* : Ps. V. 18.

(*c*) rhythmical, melodious ; *numerous verse* : P. L. V. 150.

(**2**) *adv.* with a great number : P. L. V. 389.

Nun, *sb.* a female recluse ; applied to Melancholy : Il P. 31.

Nuptial, (**1**) *adj.* pertaining to marriage or to the marriage ceremony ; *nuptial feast* : S. A. 1194 ; *torch* : P. L. XI. 590 ; *bower* : P. L. VIII. 510 ; XI. 280 ; *bed* : P. L. IV. 710 ; *league* : P. L. IV. 339 ; *choice* : S. A. 1734 ; *love* : S. A. 385 ; *sanctity* : P. L. VIII. 487 ; *embraces* : P. L. X. 994 ; *nuptial song*, the song at 'the marriage supper of the Lamb' (Rev. XIX. 6-9) : L. 176.

(**2**) *sb. pl.* marriage : S. A. 1023.

Nurse, (**1**) *sb.* (*a*) a woman who suckles or tends an infant : V. Ex. 61.

(*b*) one who cares for and cherishes another ; *fig.*, *Wisdom's ... best nurse, Contemplation* : C. 377.

(**2**) *vb. tr.* (*a*) to bring up, rear : L. 23 ; to train, educate ; *nursed in princely lore* : C. 34.

(b) to tend in sickness or infirmity, care for : S. A. 1487, 1488.

(c) to promote growth in, foster ; *to nurse the saplings* : A. 46.

part. adj. **nursing**, exercised in caring for one who is infirm : S. A. 924.

Nursery, *sb.* that which is the object of a nurse's care ; *bud and bloom, her nursery* : P. L. VIII. 46.

Nursling, *sb.* one who is highly favoured and tenderly cared for : S. A. 633.

Nurture, *sb.* upbringing, rearing : S. A. 362.

Nut-brown, *adj.* brown as a ripe and dried nut : L'A. 100.

Nutriment, *sb.* that which nourishes, food ; *corporal nutriment* : P. L. V. 496 ; (fish) *attend moist nutriment* : P. L. VII. 408.

Nymph, *sb.* an inferior goddess ; *spec.* Circe : C. 54 ; Euphrosyne : L'A. 25 ; a nymph of the waters, a Naiad or Nereid : C. 883 ; L. 50 ; Sabrina : C. 824 ; a nymph of the mountains or woods, an Oread or a Dryad : P. L. IV. 707 ; N. O. 188 ; Il P. 137 ; *a quivered nymph* : C. 422 ; *nymphs of Diana's train* : P. R. II. 355 ; Echo : C. 230 ; the characters in the Arcades : A. 1, 33, 96.

See **Mountain-nymph, Sea-nymph, Water-nymph, Wood-nymph.**

Nymph-like, *adj.* characteristic of a nymph, light and graceful : P. L. IX. 452.

Nyseian, *adj. Nyseian isle*, the birthplace of Bacchus : P. L. IV. 275. *See* **Triton.**

O

O, *interj.* an exclamation prefixed to an expression of ; (a) earnest address : P. L. I. 128, 622 ; II. 119, 430 ; with the added idea of joy : P. L. III. 274, 275 ; of reproach or indignation : P. L. V. 877 ; C. 815.

(b) solemn invocation : P. L. I. 17.

(c) surprise, pain, or sorrow : P. L. II. 496 ; IV. 358 ; V. 542 ; IX. 404 ; X. 741.

(d) surprise, joy, or gladness : P. L. III. 410 ; IV. 521 ; V. 92.

Oak, *sb.* (a) the tree *Quercus* : P. L.

I. 613 ; Il P. 60, 135 ; L. 186 ; *ancient, aged* : P. R. I. 305 ; L'A. 82 ; *sturdiest* : P. R. IV. 417.

(b) the wood of this tree : P. L. VI. 574.

Oaken, *adj.* of the wood or the branches of the oak-tree ; *oaken bower* : A. 45 ; *staff* : S. A. 1123.

Oar, *sb.* the pole with a broad end used to row boats : P. L. II. 942.

Oary, *adj.* serving the purpose of an oar ; *oary feet* : P. L. VII. 440.

Oat, *sb.* the shepherd's pipe ; *fig.* pastoral song : L. 88.

Oaten, *adj.* made of the stem of the oat ; *oaten stops* : C. 345 ; *flute* : L. 33.

Oath, *sb.* a solemn asseveration or promise made by God : P. L. II. 352.

Ob, *sb. river Ob*, the river Obi in western Siberia : P. L. IX. 78.

Obdurate (obdúrate), *adj.* hardhearted, inexorable, unyielding : P. L. XII. 205 ; *obdurate pride* : P. L. I. 58.

absol. those who are unyielding ; *the obdurate* : P. L. VI. 790.

Obdure (obdurèd, *trisyl.* : P. L. II. 568), *vb. tr.* to make stubborn or obstinate : P. L. VI. 785.

part. adj. **obdured**, obdurate ; *the obdured breast* : P. L. II. 568.

Obedience, *sb.* (a) dutiful compliance with a known law, submission to authority ; *all nations now to Rome obedience pay* : P. R. IV. 80 ; submission to the authority of God : P. L. III. 190, 191 ; V. 514, 522 ; IX. 368 ; *sign of, proof of, pledge of* : P. L. III. 95 ; IV. 428, 520 ; VIII. 325 ; *while our obedience holds* : P. L. V. 537 ; *under long obedience tried* : P. L. VII. 159 ; *he may seduce thee also from obedience* : P. L. VI. 902 ; *obedience to the law of God* : P. L. XII. 397 ; *whilst they stood in first obedience* : S. M. 24 ; the submission of Christ to God : P. L. XII. 403, 408 ; P. R. I. 4 ; Cir. 25 ; *filial obedience* : P. L. III. 269 ; of angels : P. L. III. 107 ; VIII. 240 ; P. R. I. 422 ; *just obedience* : P. L. VI. 740 ; *military obedience* : P. L. IV. 955.

(b) moving as if influenced by ; *obedient to the moon he spent his date in course reciprocal* : U. C. II. 29.

Obedient, *adj.* complying with a command, submissive to authority or control : P. L. v. 501, 514 ; *such delight hath God in men obedient* : P. L. XII. 246 ; *the serpent ... not noxious, but obedient* : P. L. VII. 498.

Obey, *vb.* (*pres. 2d sing.* obey'st : P. R. I. 452) **(1)** *tr.* to submit to the rule or authority of : P. L. II. 865 ; IX. 570 ; X. 145 ; S. A. 895 ; *Judæa ... obeys Tiberius* : P. R. III. 159 ; the person obeyed being God : P. L. v. 551 ; VI. 741 ; IX. 701 ; *Him whom to love is to obey* : P. L. VIII. 634 ; the gods : S. A. 900.

(*b*) to comply with, perform : S. A. 1372 ; *that sole command, so easily obeyed* : P. L. VII. 48 ; *the high injunction ... which they not obeying* : P. L. x. 14 ; *divine commands obeyed* : P. L. v. 806 ; *his divine behests obey* : P. L. VI. 185 ; *thy bidding they obey* : P. L. XI. 112 ; *what thou bidd'st unargued I obey* : P. L. IV. 636.

(*c*) to act in accordance with ; *what obeys Reason is free* : P. L. IX. 351 ; *Reason in man obscured, or not obeyed* : P. L. XII. 86.

(*d*) to act in answer to ; *all obeyed the wonted signal* : P. L. v. 704.

(*e*) to act as compelled by ; *the sea his rod obeys* : P. L. XII. 212.

(*f*) *absol.* to do what is commanded ; to be obedient : P. L. XII. 126 ; P. R. III. 194 ; S. A. 1641 ; *I learn that to obey is best* : P. L. XII. 561 ; *thou ... like a fawning parasite, obey'st* : P. R. I. 452 ; *best reign who first well hath obeyed* : P. R. III. 196 ; *the Serpent ... not obeying* : P. L. IX. 868.

fig., *the earth obeyed* : P. L. VII. 453 ; *my tongue obeyed* : P. L. VIII. 272.

(2) *intr.* to be obedient *to* ; *to their General's voice they soon obeyed* : P. L. I. 337.

Object, I. *sb.* **(1)** something presented to the sight or other senses : P. L. III. 621 ; VIII. 609 ; *this double object in our sight* : P. L. XI. 201 ; *objects new casual discourse draw on* : P. L. IX. 222 ; *an object that excels the sense* : P. L. VIII. 456 ; *objects divine ... impair and weary human sense* : P. L. XII. 9.

(2) something presented to the mind ; *Reason ... may meet some specious object* : P. L. IX. 361.

(3) something which on being seen excites a particular emotion ; *before the present object languishing with like desire* : P. L. x. 996 ; *such object hath the power to soften ... severest temper* : P. R. II. 163 ; *manlier objects* : P. R. II. 225 ; *objects of delight* : S. A. 71 ; *object more enticing* : S. A. 559.

(*b*) sight ; *not proof enough such object to sustain* : P. L. VIII. 535.

(*c*) spectacle ; *a gaze or pitied object* : S. A. 568.

(4) that to which action is directed ; *just object of his ire* : P. L. x. 936.

II. *vb. tr.* to bring forward as an adverse reason ; *thou wilt object his will* : P. L. IV. 896.

Oblige, *vb. tr.* to render liable to punishment : P. L. IX. 980.

Oblique (óblique : P. L. III. 564), **(1)** *adj.* diverging from a straight line or course ; *oblique way, tract* : P. L. III. 564 ; IX. 510.

(2) *adv.* in a slanting direction ; *they ... pushed oblique the centric Globe* : P. L. x. 671.

Obliquity, *sb.* the position of being neither parallel nor at right angles, but inclined to each other ; *several spheres ... moved contrary with thwart obliquities* : P. L. VIII. 132.

Oblivion, *sb.* (*a*) the cessation of remembering, forgetfulness ; *Lethe, the river of oblivion* : P. L. II. 583 ; *the gloomy land of dark oblivion* : Ps. LXXXVIII. 52.

(*b*) the state of being forgotten or of being lost to memory ; *in dark oblivion let them dwell* : P. L. VI. 380.

Oblivious, *adj.* causing forgetfulness ; *the oblivious pool* : P. L. I. 266.

Obloquy, *sb.* calumny, abuse, slander : P. L. v. 813 ; P. R. III. 131 ; S. A. 452.

Obnoxious, *adj.* liable, subject, exposed ; *obnoxious ... to all the miseries of life* : S. A. 106 ; *to shame obnoxious* : P. L. IX. 1094 ; *obnoxious ... to basest things* : P. L. IX. 170.

Obscene (óbscene), *adj.* impure, lewd : P. L. I. 406.

Obscure (óbscure : P. L. II. 132), (1)
adj. (*a*) devoid of or deficient in
light, dark, dim, gloomy : P. L.
I. 429 ; XI. 283 ; applied to hell
or chaos ; *that obscure sojourn* :
P. L. III. 15 ; *place of doom obscure* : P. L. IV. 840 ; *the vast
profundity obscure* : P. L. VII.
229 ; *unvoyageable gulf obscure* :
P. L. X. 366 ; *voyage ... obscure* :
P. L. VIII. 230.

(*b*) enveloped in darkness, and
so eluding sight,; *with obscure
wing* : P. L. II. 132 ; *in mist of
midnight vapour glide obscure* : P.
L. IX. 159.

(*c*) hidden or remote from public view or knowledge ; *live
obscure* : P. R. I. 287 ; *life ... obscure in savage wilderness* : P. R.
III. 22 ; *they walk obscure* : S. A.
296.

(*d*) unknown to fame : P. R. I.
24 ; *old age obscure* : S. A. 572.

(*e*) imperfectly understood ; *to
know at large of things ... obscure
and subtle* : P. L. VIII. 192 ; not
clearly known ; *a land and times
obscure* : P. R. III. 94.

(2) *sb.* obscurity, darkness ; *the
palpable obscure*, chaos : P. L. II.
406.

(3) *adv.* dimly, indistinctly : P.
L. I. 524.

(4) *vb.* (obscurèd, *trisyl.* : C.
536) *tr.* (*a*) to make dark, darken ;
*obscured with smoke, all Heaven
appeared* : P. L. VI. 585 ; to
deprive of brightness, dim ; *with
passions foul obscured* : P. L. IV.
571.

(*b*) to lessen the glory of : P.
L. V. 841.

(*c*) to cover or hide from view,
conceal : P. L. IX. 1086 ; *the
excess of glory obscured* : P. L. I.
594.

(*d*) to cover with obscurity,
keep unknown : P. L. IX. 797 ;
to conceal from knowledge the
purpose of ; *his absence ... he obscures* : P. R. II. 101.

(*e*) to deprive of power or influence ; *Reason in Man obscured* :
P. L. XII. 86.

part. adj. **obscured** ; (*a*) hidden,
concealed : C. 536.

(*b*) humble, lowly ; *life obscured* : S. A. 688.

Obscurely, *adv.* (*a*) not plainly or
clearly : P. L. XII. 543.

(*b*) not conspicuously ; *aloof obscurely stood* : S. A. 1611.

Obsequious, *adj.* promptly obedient,
compliant, dutiful ; *obsequious
majesty* : P. L. VIII. 509 ; *obsequious Darkness* : P. L. VI. 10 ;
*the uprooted hills ... went obse-
quious* : P. L. VI. 783.

Obsequy, *sb.* funeral ceremonies :
S. A. 1732.

Observe, *vb. tr.* (1) to attend to in
practice, follow, obey ; *to observe
... his will* : P. L. VII. 78 ; *laws to
be observed* : P. L. XI. 228 ; *absol.* :
P. L. X. 430 ; Ps. LXXXI. 14.

(*b*) to adhere to, follow : P. R.
IV. 477 ; *observe the rule* : P. L.
XI. 530.

(*c*) to wait for and follow the
direction of ; *ever to observe his
providence* : P. L. XII. 563.

(2) to celebrate in the prescribed way ; *other rites observing none* :
P. L. IV. 737.

(3) to regard, honour ; *of God
observed* : P. L. XI. 817 ; to hold
in honour, reverence ; *yet observed
their dread Commander* : P. L. I.
588.

(4) to take notice of, perceive,
mark : P. L. IX. 94 ; *to observe
the sequel* : P. L. X. 334 ; *what
thence couldst thou observe* : P. R.
III. 235 ; *to find here observed his
lustre visibly impaired* : P. L. IV.
849 ; *absol.* : P. L. XI. 191 ; Ps.
V. 23.

(5) to subject to systematic
inspection for scientific purposes ;
*observes imagined lands ... in the
Moon* : P. L. V. 262.

Obstacle, *sb.* hindrance, obstruction :
P. L. III. 615 ; VIII. 624.

Obstinacy, *sb.* stubbornness : P. L.
X. 114.

Obstriction, *sb.* obligation : S. A. 312.

Obstruct, *vb. tr.* (*a*) to block, render
impassable : P. L. X. 636 ; *ere the
tower obstruct Heaven-towers* : P.
L. II. 52.

(*b*) to come in the way of ;
obstruct his sight : P. L. V. 257.

Obtain, *vb. tr.* (1) to procure, gain,
get : P. R. II. 73 ; *obtained ... the
crown* : P. R. III. 168 ; *thy kingdom ... thou never shalt obtain* : P.
R. III. 354 ; *thy request ... obtain* :
P. L. VII. 112 ; XI. 47 ; *leave,
honour, peace, pardon, forgiveness* : P. L. II. 250 ; III. 660 ; X.
938 ; S. A. 814, 909.

(b) to acquire, achieve; *if answerable style I can obtain*: P. L. IX. 20.

(c) to be permitted to return to; *could obtain ... my former state*: P. L. IV. 93.

(2) to reach, arrive at; *obtains the brow of some ... hill*: P. L. III. 546.

(b) to attain, reach; *obtain his end*: P. L. III. 156.

(3) to possess, occupy; *he who obtains the monarchy of Heaven*: P. R. I. 87.

Obtrude, *vb. (pres. 2d sing.* obtrud'st: P. R. IV. 493) *tr.* to thrust forward unduly, force upon anyone: P. R. II. 387; IV. 493; C. 759; with *on*: P. L. XI. 504.

Obtrusive, *adj.* given to thrusting oneself upon others, forward: P. L. VIII. 504.

Obtuse, *adj.* not keenly sensitive; *thy senses then obtuse*: P. L. XI. 541.

Obvious, *adj.* (a) being in the way: P. L. VI. 69.

(b) advancing to meet one: P. L. VIII. 504.

(c) exposed; *to the evil turn my obvious breast*: P. L. XI. 374; *the eye ... so obvious and so easy to be quenched*: S. A. 95.

(d) open; *is obvious to dispute*: P. L. VIII. 158.

(e) perfectly evident; *obvious duty*: P. L. X. 106.

Occasion, (1) *sb.* (a) opportunity, favourable time: S. A. 224, 237, 425; *let us not slip the occasion*: P. L. I. 178; *not to let the occasion pass*: P. L. V. 453; *not let pass occasion*: P. L. IX. 480; *find some occasion*: S. A. 423; *do they not seek occasion*: S. A. 1329; *nor will occasion want*: P. L. II. 341; *to lay hold on this occasion*: S. A. 1716.

personified, on Occasion's forelock watchful wait: P. R. III. 173.

(b) motive, reason for action: P. R. III. 174.

(c) exigency: C. 91.

(d) *pl.* business, affairs: S. A. 1596.

(e) event, occurrence: L. 6.

(f) *by occasion*, indirectly: P. L. IX. 974.

(2) *vb. tr.* to cause, bring about: P. L. XII. 475.

Occasionally, *adv.* incidentally: P. L. VIII. 556.

Ocean, *sb.* (a) the great sea, the main: P. L. VII. 412; XI. 827; C. 976; S. XIX. 13; *over all the face of Earth main ocean flowed*: P. L. VII. 279; *Earth, with her nether ocean*: P. L. VII. 624; *where Heaven with Earth and Ocean meets*: P. L. IV. 540; *the Sun .. at even sups with the Ocean*: P. L. V. 426; *old Ocean smiles*: P. L. IV. 165; *whispering new joys to the mild ocean*: N. O. 66; *spec.* the Atlantic: H. B. 7; the Pacific: P. L. IX. 80; the Red Sea: Ps. CXIV. 13.

(b) chaos; *dark illimitable ocean*: P. L. II. 892; the waters of chaos; *in ocean or in air*: P. L. III. 76.

(c) *crystalline ocean*, the Crystalline sphere: P. L. VII. 271. *See* **Sphere.**

(d) the lake of hell; *yon boiling ocean*: P. L. II. 183.

attrib. of the great sea; *ocean wave*: P. L. III. 539; *bed*: L. 168; *isles*: P. L. IV. 354.

Ocean-brim, *sb.* the margin of the ocean forming the horizon: P. L. V. 140.

Ocean-stream, *sb.* the waters of the ocean; *that swim the ocean-stream*: P. L. I. 202.

Oceanus, *sb.* a Titan and the god of the river Oceanus which was supposed to encircle the whole earth: C. 868.

October, *sb.* the tenth month of the year; *wet October's torrent flood*: C. 930.

Odd, *sb. pl.* (a) inequality, difference: P. L. IV. 447; *nor odds appeared in might*: P. L. VI. 319; *what between us made the odds*: P. L. VI. 441.

(b) advantage, superiority: P. L. IX. 820; X. 374; *Juno dares not give her odds*: A. 23.

Ode, *sb.* a poem intended or adapted to be sung: N. O. 24; *Dorian lyric odes*: P. L. IV. 257; *they in Heaven their odes and vigils tuned*: P. R. I. 182.

Odious, *adj.* hateful: P. L. II. 781; IX. 880; Ps. LXXXVIII. 34, 35; *odious din of war*: P. L. VI. 408; *offerings*: P. L. I. 475; *truth*: P. L. XI. 704.

Odiously, *adv.* (a) hatefully: S. A. 873.

(b) disgustingly: Ariosto II. 2.

Odoriferous, *adj.* laden with perfume : P. L. IV. 157.

Odorous (odórous : P. L. V. 482), *adj.* ·fragrant : P. L. IV. 166 ; *each odorous bushy shrub* : P. L. IV. 696 ; *flower, spirits odorous breathes* : P. L. V. 482 ; *the odorous banks, that blow flowers* : C. 993 ; *trees wept odorous gums* : P. L. IV. 248 ; *odorous oil* : P. 16 ; *perfume* : S. A. 720 ; *the odorous breath of morn* : A. 56 ; *thy odorous lamp* : S. IX. 10.

Odour, *sb.* (*a*) sweet scent, fragrance : P. L. IX. 579 ; *the buxom air, embalmed with odours* : P. L. II. 843 ; *fresh gales ... flung odours from the spicy shrub* : P. L. VIII. 517 ; *gentlest gale Arabian odours fanned* : P. R. II. 364 ; *north-east winds blow Sabæan odours* : P. L. IV. 162 ; *then strews the ground with ... odours from the shrub* : P. L. V. 349 ; *flowering odours* : P. L. V. 293 ; *covering the earth with odours, fruits, and flocks* : C. 712 ; in heaven ; *his altar breathes ambrosial odours* : P. L. II. 245.

(*b*) a substance that emits a sweet scent, spices : S. A. 987 ; frankincense and myrrh : N. O. 23 ; perfumed water or ointment : C. 106 ; Hor. O. 1.

Œchalia, *sb.* the name of several cities in Greece, here probably of that in the western part of Thessaly : P. L. II. 542.

O'er. *See* Over.

O'erblown, *part.* having ceased : P. L. I. 172.

O'ercome, *vb. tr.* to conquer, overpower : P. R. I. 161 ; S. A. 51.

O'erflow, *vb. intr.* to be more than full : P. L. VIII. 266.

O'erfraught, *part.* loaded too heavily ; *the sea o'erfraught* : C. 732.

O'ergrown, *part.* grown beyond the natural size : L. 40.

O'erlaid, *part.* covered ; *o'erlaid with black,* covered or veiled with a superficial darkness : Il P. 16.

O'erleap, *vb. tr.* to clear by leaping : P. L. IV. 583.

O'ermatch, *vb. tr.* to surpass, excel : P. L. II. 855.

O'erpower, *vb. tr.* to subdue, defeat : P. L. I. 145.

O'ershade, *vb. absol.* to cast a shade over ; *where thy bower o'ershades* : P. L. V. 376.

O'ershadow, *vb. tr.* to shelter, protect : P. R. I. 140.

O'erspread, *vb. tr.* to spread over ; *the dusky clouds ... o'erspread heaven's cheerful face* : P. L. II. 489.

O'erthrow *vb.* (*pret.* o'erthrew) *tr.* to lay prostrate, vanquish : P. L. I. 306.

O'erwatch, *vb. tr.* to weary with too much watching : P. L. II. 288.

O'er-weary, *vb. tr.* to overcome with weariness : P. L. VI. 392.

O'erwhelm, *vb. tr.* to overthrow, overpower : P. L. I. 76 ; VI. 489 ; to bring to ruin, crush : S. A. 370.

O'er-worn, *part.* worn out : S. A. 123.

Œta, *sb.* a mountain in the extreme southern part of Thessaly : P. L. II. 545.

*Of, *prep.* (1) of position or direction ; from, away from : P. L. X. 695 ; *out of* : P. L. I. 386 ; II. 433. *See* also **Out.**

(2) of separation or privation : P. L. I. 610 ; III. 251 ; IX. 392 ; S. A. 1188 ; *disburden of* : P. L. IX. 624 ; *rob of* : C. 390 ; *cleared of* : P. L. VIII. 179 ; *the cure of all* : P. L. IX. 776 ; *loss of* : P. L. I. 4 ; *empty of* : P. L. XI. 616 ; *devoid of* : P. L. II. 151 ; *waxing well of* : C. 1000 ; *quit of* : P. L. XI. 549 ; *secure of* : P. L. IV. 791 ; V. 639.

(3) of origin or source ; (*a*) racial or local origin ; *sprung of old Anchises' line* : C. 923 ; *of Satan sprung* : P. L. X. 591 ; *of famous Arcady ye are* : A. 28 ; *of evil sprung* : P. L. V. 98 ; *sin ... of thee begot* : P. L. XII. 286 ; *sleep, bred of unkindly fumes* : P. L. IX. 1050 ; *of man extracted* : P. L. VIII. 496 ; *sons of Eve* : P. L. I. 364 ; *stock of David* : P. L. XII. 326.

of the origin of a name ; *named of lamentation loud* : P. L. II. 579.

(*b*) from ; *won of Earth* : P. R. I. 63 ; *out of the ground wast taken* : P. L. X. 207 ; *intend advantage of my labours* : S. A. 1259 ; *sought of thee* : S. A. 889 ; *of whom ... expect* : P. R. III. 126 ; *of him to ask* : P. L. VIII. 53.

(4) of the source of action or emotion ; (*a*) out of, from ; *of my own accord* : S. A. 1643 ; *of ... favour* : S. A. 273 ; *of his grace* :

P. L. X. 767; *of herself, them-selves*: P. L. VIII. 137; XI. 685.

(*b*) of the cause or motive of an action or feeling; *rings of*: S. XXII. 12; *of grace beseeching him*: P. L. X. 1082; *of choice to incur*: P. L. IX. 992; *God made thee of choice his own*: P. L. X. 766.

following sbs. or adjs.; from, because of: P. L. I. 98; *experience of this great event*: P. L. I. 118; *amazement of their change*: P. L. I. 313; *joy of*: P. L. VI. 617; *pride of*: P. R. III. 410; *swoonings of despair*: S. A. 631 *afraid of*: P. L. X. 117; *fearless of*: P. L. XI. 811; *weary of*: S. A. 596.

(5) of the agent: P. L. V. 406; VI. 804; *favoured of Heaven*: P. L. I. 30; *of whom to be dispraised*: P. R. III. 56; *beloved of God*: P. R. I. 379; *forsaken of*: P. L. V. 878; *of Javan's issue held Gods*: P. L. I. 508.

(*b*) following sbs.; *works of God*: P. L. III. 695; *prey of whirlwinds*: P. L. II. 182; *sent by*; *visions of God*: P. L. XI. 377; *made by*; *law of God*: P. L. XII. 397.

(6) of means, material, or substance; (*a*) *great things of small ... we can create*: P. L. II. 258; *out of our evil to bring forth good*: P. L. I. 163; *composed of*: P. R. I. 407; *produce of*: P. L. XII. 470.

(*b*) of transformation from a former state; *of pure now purer air*: P. L. IV. 153; *of incorrupt corrupted*: P. L. XI. 56; *miserable of happy*: P. L. X. 720; *of guests ... slaves*: P. L. XII. 167.

(*c*) following sbs. or adjs.: P. L. I. 280, 690; II. 176; III. 440; L'A. 21; *steps of gold*: P. L. III. 541; *a pomp of winning graces*: P. L. VIII. 61; *army of fiends*: P. L. IV. 953; *space of seventy years*: P. L. XII. 345; *land of, stream of, valley of*: P. L. I. 343, 399, 404; *name of*: P. L. IV. 951; V. 776; *fact of arms*: P. L. II. 124; *full of*: P. L. VI. 622.

(7) of the subject-matter of thought, feeling, or action; with regard to; in reference to; about: P. L. I. 1, 580; II. 51; *hear of*: P. L. VII. 53; *judge of*: P. L. VIII. 448; *dreamed of*: P. L. V. 32; *complain of*: S. A. 46; *despair of*: S. A. 1171; *admonish*

of: P. L. XI. 812; *advise of*: P. L. V. 234; *repent of*: P. L. XII. 474; *of love they treat*: P. L. XI. 588.

(*b*) following sbs. or adjs.: P. L. I. 55, 107; *contemplation of*: P. L. V. 511; *sure of*: P. L. I. 158; *ignorant of*: P. R. IV. 310; *incapable of*: P. L. II. 140.

(8) expressing the relation of objective genitive; *the glimmering of*: P. L. I. 182; *the tossing of*: P. L. I. 184; *the bearing well of*: S. A. 655; *desire of wandering*: P. L. IX. 1136; *search of this new world*: P. L. II. 403; *toil of battle*: P. L. I. 319; *the trial of men*: P. L. I. 366; *taste of that ... fruit*: P. L. XI. 85; *the esteem of wise*: P. L. IV. 886; *ministers of vengeance*: P. L. I. 170.

(9) in respect of; *exact of taste*: P. L. IX. 1017; *fallible of future*: P. L. VI. 429; *ripe ... of his full-grown age*: C. 59; *higher of the genial bed*: P. L. VIII. 598; *short of knowing*: P. R. IV. 288.

(10) of quality or distinguishing mark: P. L. I. 65, 85, 181; II. 186; X. 978; *whom ... of monstrous size*: P. L. I. 197; *throne of royal state*: P. L. II. 1; *den of shame*: P. L. II. 58; *tree of danger*: P. L. IX. 864; *fruit ... of virtue to make wise*: P. L. IX. 778; *fellowships of joy*: P. L. XI. 80; *enterprise of small enforce*: S. A. 1223; *in time of truce*: P. L. XI. 244; *years of mourning*: S. A. 1712.

(11) in partitive use: P. L. I. 238, 368, 765; II. 34; III. 668; C. 805; *cloud of locusts*: P. L. I. 341; *what ... of merit*: P. L. II. 21; *share of pain*: P. L. II. 30; *precious of all trees*: P. L. IX. 795; *fairest of her daughters*: P. L. IV. 324; *of all his works ... hugest*: P. L. I. 201; *Holiest of Holies*: P. R. IV. 349.

(*b*) followed by a poss. pron.: L. 102; *no decree of mine*: P. L. X. 43.

(*c*) some of: P. L. VIII. 320; *taste of pleasure*: P. L. IX. 477; *reach also of the Tree of Life*: P. L. XI. 94.

(12) belonging or pertaining to; (*a*) *sojourners of Goschen*: P. L. I. 309; *seat of man*: P. L. III. 632; *top of, gates of*, etc.: P. L. I. 7,

171, 174, 233, 300; II. 129; III.
739; *wealth of*: P. L. II. 2; *the
race of time*: P. L. XII. 554;
works of day past: P. L. V. 33.

(*b*) belonging to a place as lord
or master: P. L. I. 32, 204, 272;
queen of heaven: P. L. I. 438;
King of Israel: P. R. I. 254.

(*c*) belonging to a person or
thing as something possessed or
as a quality: P. L. I. 42, 401;
VIII. 585; P. R. III. 314; S. VIII.
11; *leaves of thy ... book*: W. S.
11; *strength of Gods*: P. L. I.
116; *force of ... winds*: P. L. I.
231; *glory of Him*: P. L. I. 370;
dedicated to; *grove of Daphne*:
P. L. IV. 273; *oracle, temple of
God*: P. L. I. 12, 402.

(**13**) during, in: P. L. III. 328;
W. S. 2; Il P. 101; *of this age*:
P. R. II. 209; *of old, late, yore*:
P. L. II. 38, 77; Il P. 23; *of
yesterday*: P. L. V. 67.

See **Unthought-of.**

***Off**, (1) *adv.* (*a*) to a distance,
away; *fly, bear, draw, drive off*:
P. L. III. 494, 559; IV. 782; VII.
32; C. 456; *removed his tents far
off*: P. L. XI. 727; *all approach
far off to fright*: P. L. XI. 121.

(*b*) at a distance, distant; *off
at sea*: P. L. IV. 161; *far off*:
P. L. II. 582, 636, 643, 1047; III.
88, 422; IV. 14; VI. 768; C.
229; *dwell far off all anxious cares*:
P. L. VIII. 185; distant in time:
P. R. III. 397.

(*c*) away from a certain attach-
ment, position, or relation; *beat
off*: P. R. IV. 17; *brush*: A. 50;
pull: U. C. I. 16; *purge*: P. L.
II. 141, 400; *put*: P. L. III. 240;
IX. 713; C. 82; *shake*: S. A.
409; *throw*: P. L. III. 362; *wash*:
S. A. 1727. *See* also the verbs:
Break, Cast, Come, Cut, Fall, Fly,
Set, Throw.

(**2**) *prep.* **from off**, away from:
P. L. I. 184; C. 896; *it stood
retired from off the files*: P. L.
VI. 339; *blows from off*: L. 94;
down from: Il P. 130; *from off
the boughs ... we brush ... dews*: P.
L. V. 428; up from; *he rears
from off the pool*: P. L. I. 221;
ascended from off the altar: S. A.
26.

See **Far-off, Putting-off.**

Offal, *sb.* putrid flesh, carrion: P.
L. X. 633.

Offence, *sb.* transgression, sin, fault:
S. A. 1218; *beauty ... hath strange
power, after offence returning*: S.
A. 1004; the sin of man in eating
the forbidden fruit: P. L. V. 34,
355, 410; IX. 726; X. 171, 854.

See **Self-Offence.**

Offend, *vb.* (1) *tr.* (*a*) to attack,
assail; *we may offend our yet
unwounded enemies*: P. L. VI. 465.

(*b*) to harm, injure; *how we
may ... most offend our enemy*: P.
L. I. 187.

(*c*) to wound the feelings of,
displease, annoy, anger: S. A.
1333, 1414; Il P. 21; *a world
offended*: P. L. XI. 811; *let not
my words offend thee, Heavenly
Power*: P. L. VIII. 379; *whom,
not to offend, with reverence I must
meet*: P. L. XI. 236; *He* (God)
thereat offended: P. L. X. 488;
God is every-day offended: Ps.
VII. 44; *be not so sore offended,
Son of God*: P. R. IV. 196.

absol. not mind us, not offending:
P. L. II. 212.

(*d*) to sin against: S. A. 515.

(**2**) *intr.* to commit a fault, sin:
P. L. V. 135; X. 110, 916.

*part.adj.***offended**; (*a*) displeased,
disgusted; *the offended taste*: P.
L. X. 566.

(*b*) angered; *the offended Deity*:
P. L. XI. 149.

Offensive, *adj.* of offence or sin;
the offensive mountain: P. L. I.
443. *See* **Mountain.**

Offer, (1) *sb.* (*a*) a tender or proposal
to be accepted or rejected: P. R.
III. 380; IV. 155, 171; S. A. 1255.

(*b*) a thing presented for acceptance; *I would not taste thy
treasonous offer*: C. 702.

(**2**) *vb. tr.* (*a*) to present to God
or Christ as an act of worship or
devotion, sacrifice; *as a sacrifice
glad to be offered*: P. L. III. 270;
thereon offer sweet-smelling gums:
P. L. XI. 327; *to offer incense,
myrrh, and gold*: P. L. XII. 363;
fig., *offer the offerings just of
righteousness*: Ps. IV. 23; to
present to an idol; *offered first
to idols*: P. R. II. 328.

(*b*) to present for acceptance or
rejection: P. L. II. 469; IX. 802;
P. R. II. 399; IV. 156, 160, 190,
468; S. A. 390; C. 64; *contemn
riches, though offered*: P. R. II.
449; *life for life I offer*: P. L.

III. 237 ; *life offered* : P. L. XI.
506 ; *none offering fight* : S. A.
344 ; with *prep. inf.* : *offered himself to die* : P. L. III. 409 ; *offering to combat thee* : S. A. 1152.
part. adj. **offered** ; (*a*) presented
for acceptance or rejection ; *offered
fight* : S. A. 1253 ; *aid, means* : P.
R. IV. 377, 493 ; S. A. 516 ; *grace,
good, peace, life* : P. L. III, 187 ;
V. 63 ; VI. 617 ; XII. 425.
(*b*) attempted ; *the offered wrong* :
P. L. IX. 300.
vbl. sb. **offering**, something presented to God in worship or
devotion, a sacrifice : P. L. XI.
441, 456 ; S. A. 519 ; *from off the
altar where an offering burned* :
S. A. 26 ; *atonement for himself,
or offering meet* : P. L. III. 234 ;
*ambrosial flowers, our servile offer-
ings* : P. L. II. 246 ; *fig.* : Ps. IV.
23 ; presented to an idol ; *Ahaz
...his odious offerings* : P. L. I.
475.
See **Honest-offered, Wine-offering**.

Office, *sb.* (*a*) service, attention : S.
A. 924 ; D. F. I. 70 ; *strive in
offices of love* : P. L. X. 960.
(*b*) a duty attaching to one's position, a service falling or assigned
to one : P. R. I. 374 ; *therein
stands the office of a king* : P. R.
II. 463 ; *'tis my office best to help
ensnared chastity* : C. 908 ; *his
heavenly office* : P. R. I. 28 ; *publish his godlike office* : P. R. I.
188 ; *this office of his mountain
watch* : C. 89 ; *to sit in hateful
office here confined* : P. L. II. 859 ;
office mean : P. L. IX. 39.
(*c*) that which is performed by
a particular thing, function : P.
L. VII. 344 ; *the Star of Hesperus
whose office is* : P. L. IX. 49 ; *to
the blanc Moon her office they prescribed* : P. L. X. 657 ; *Death ...
his office* : P. L. X. 1002.
(*d*) a position to which certain
duties are attached : P. L. XII.
240, 311 ; *kind office of a chamberlin* : U. C. I. 14 ; *fig., Fancy
next her office holds* : P. L. V. 103.

Officer, *sb.* (*a*) one who performs a
service for another ; *officers of
vengeance* : C. 218.
(*b*) a public functionary : S. A.
1306.

Officiate, *vb. tr.* to supply ; *to officiate light* : P. L. VIII. 22.

Officious, *adj.* eager or ready to
serve : P. R. II. 302 ; *their* (the
stars) *bright officious lamps* : P. L.
IX. 104 ; ministering ; *not to Earth
are those bright luminaries officious* : P. L. VIII. 99.

Offspring, *sb.* issue of the body,
child or children, descendants ;
sing., an offspring : D. F. I. 76 ;
collect., a beauteous offspring :
P. L. XI. 613 ; *pl.* : P. L. VIII.
86 ; X. 781 ; XI. 358, 755 ; C.
34 ; *your numerous offspring* : P.
L. IV. 385 ; *human offspring* : P.
L. IV. 751 ; *the shepherd lad whose
offspring on the throne of Judah
sat* : P. R. II. 440 ; *those Ten Tribes
whose offspring* : P. R. III. 375.
(*b*) applied to Sin or Death as
sprung from Satan : P. L. II.
781 ; X. 238, 349.
(*c*) *fig. Offspring of Heaven and
Earth*, applied to Adam as created
by God out of earth, and thus
partaking of both the heavenly
and earthly natures : P. L. IX.
273 ; *Offspring of Heaven*, applied
to the fallen angels as created in
or by heaven, or by God (cf. P.
L. IV. 43 ; V. 859-863 ; IX. 146) :
P. L. II. 310 ; *Evil ... thy offspring*,
possibly with allusion to Sin : P.
L. VI. 276 ; *holy Light, offspring
of Heaven* : P. L. III. 1 ; *Darkness ... louring Night, her shadowy
offspring* : P. R. IV. 399.

*Oft, (1) *adv.* (*a*) many times, frequently : P. L. III. 185, 661 ; IV.
405 ; V. 112, 374 ; *as oft* : P. L.
IX. 400, 515 ; X. 568, 852 ; *full
oft* : P. L. II. 763 ; S. A. 759 ; A.
42 ; *how oft* : P. L. II. 263 ; *more
oft* : P. L. I. 493 ; S. A. 268,
1287 ; *so oft* : P. L. I. 275 ; VI.
94 ; IX. 1082 ; P. R. IV. 4 ; *sup.* :
P. L. V. 489 ; P. R. II. 228, 486 ;
S. A. 1030.
(*b*) in many instances : P. R. IV.
464 ; S. A. 692, 704, 1008, 1062.
(2) *adj.* frequent ; *oft experience* :
S. A. 382 ; *converse* : C. 459.

Often, *adv.* frequently : P. L. I.
387 ; P. R. I. 199 ; S. A. 351 ;
N. O. 74 ; L'A. 74 ; C. 569 ; *how
often* : P. L. IV. 680 ; *so often* :
A. 29 ; S. XXI. 4.

Oft-invocated, *part. adj.* frequently
invoked : S. A. 575.

Oft-times, *adv.* on many occasions,
in many cases : P. L. I. 166 ;
VIII. 571 ; P. R. I. 472 ; IV. 460.

Og, *sb.* the Amorite king of Bashan, one of the giants ' of the remnant of the Rephaim ': S. A. 1080; Ps. cxxxvi. 69.

Oh, *interj.* an exclamation expressive of; (*a*) earnest address: D. F. I. 41.

(*b*) solemn invocation: Ps. vi. 8; lxxxiii. 49; lxxxvi. 10, 57.

(*c*) surprise, regret, pain, or sorrow: P. L. i. 75, 84; iv. 58; ix. 1084; x. 819, 888; xii. 115; Hor. O. 5.

(*d*) earnest denial: D. F. I. 34.

Oil, *sb.* the unctuous liquid; as a product of the soil; *corn, wine, and oil*: P. L. xii. 19; *fertile of corn the glebe, of oil, and wine*: P. R. iii. 259; used for feeding lamps, *fig.*: C. 199; used for anointing purposes: P. 16; *and through the porch and inlet of each sense dropt in ambrosial oils*: C. 840.

Old, I. *adj.* (*sup.* eldest, q.v.) (**1**) advanced in years: P. R. iv. 90, 91; C. 852; S. x. 8; *prophets, seers old*: P. L. iii. 36; P. R. iii. 15; *a sibyl old*: V. Ex. 69; qualifying proper names; *Old Anchises*: C. 923; *Damœtas*: L. 36; *Glaucus*: C. 874; *Hobson*: U. C. i. 1; *Hyrcanus*: P. R. iii. 367; *Laertes*: P. L. ix. 441; *Manoah*: S. A. 328, 1441; *Melibœus old*: C. 822; *Old Proteus*: P. L. iii. 604; *Simeon*: P. R. ii. 87.

comp., made older than thy age: S. A. 1489.

absol. persons advanced in years; *old and young*: P. L. xi. 668; *young and old*: L'A. 97.

(**2**) *old age*, the latter period of life: P. L. xi. 538; S. A. 572, 700, 925, 1487, 1488.

(**3**) having existed long, or long occupied or in use: P. L. ix. 101.

(*b*) weak, feeble: Ps. vi. 4.

(**4**) practised, experienced, skilled; *in sage counsel old*: S. xvii. 1; *warriors*: P. L. i. 565; S. A. 139.

(**5**) dating far back into the past; (*a*) that has been from the beginning, primeval; *old Night*: P. L. i. 543; ii. 1002; *the Anarch old*: P. L. ii. 988; *darkness old*: P. L. iii. 421; *Saturn old*: P. L. i. 519; *old Ocean*: P. L. iv. 165; *Cham*: P. L. iv. 276; *old truth*: U. C. ii. 8; applied to Satan;

the old Serpent, Dragon: P. R. ii. 147; N. O. 168.

(*b*) of ancient origin; *an old ... nation*: C. 33.

(*c*) made long ago; *old conquest*: P. R. i. 46.

(*d*) of long standing or continuance; *old renown, repute, respect, experience*: P. L. i. 477, 639; S. A. 333; Il P. 173.

(**6**) belonging to an age now past; (*a*) of or pertaining to the distant past, belonging to a bygone age; *giants old*: S. A. 148; *heroes old*: P. L. i. 552; xi. 243; V. Ex. 47; *prophets*: P. R. iii. 178; *fables*: P. L. xi. 11; *old bards*: L. 53; *schools of Greece*: C. 439; *Law*: S. xxiii. 6; *Academics old and new*: P. R. iv. 278; *old or modern bard*: C. 45.

(*b*) associated with ancient times, long renowned; *Bellerus old*: L. 160; *Mount Casius old*: P. L. ii. 593; *the Emims old*: S. A. 1080; *old Euphrates*: P. L. i. 420; *Kishon old*: Ps. lxxxiii. 37; *Ninus old*: P. R. iii. 276; *old Lycœus*: A. 98; *Olympus*: P. L. vii. 7; *Salem old*: P. R. ii. 21.

(*c*) relating to past times; *city of old or modern fame*: P. L. xi. 386.

(*d*) former: P. L. iv. 666.

(**7**) belonging to an earlier period; *new Presbyter is but old Priest writ large*: F. of C. 6.

II. *sb.* **of old**, from or in the beginning; from, of, or in early times; long ago: P. L. ii. 38; iii. 568; vii. 200; ix. 145, 670; x. 226; P. R. ii. 174, 358; iii. 378; S. A. 1533; N. O. 119; C. 516; S. xviii. 3; Ps. vii. 52; lxxxi. 13; H. B. 9; *long of old*: P. R. iv. 604.

Olive, *sb.* the leaves of the olive-tree as a symbol of peace: N. O. 47.

Olive-grove, *sb.* a grove of olive-trees; *the olive-grove of Academe*: P. R. iv. 244.

Olive-leaf, *sb.* a leaf of the olive-tree: P. L. xi. 860.

Olympian, *adj.* (*a*) held at Olympia in Greece; *the Olympian games*: P. L. ii. 530.

(*b*) *Olympian hill*, Mount Olympus: P. L. vii. 3.

Olympias, *sb.* the wife of Philip II. of Macedon, here as the mother of Alexander the Great by Jupiter Ammon : P. L. IX. 509.

Olympus, *sb.* the mountain on the borders of Macedonia and Thessaly, the abode of the gods : D. F. I. 44 ; *top of old Olympus* : P. L. VII. 7 ; *snowy top of cold Olympus* : P. L. I. 516 ; *high Olympus* : P. L. X. 583.

Omen, *sb.* prognostication : S. A. 967.

Ominous, *adj.* (a) foreboding or predicting evil : P. L. II. 123.

(b) full of portents and signs of evil ; *ominous night, wood* : P. R. IV. 481 ; C. 61.

Omission, *sb.* the failure to do something which ought to be done : S. A. 691.

Omit, *vb. tr.* to fail to use, neglect : S. A. 602.

Omnific, *adj.* all-creating : P. L. VII. 217.

Omnipotence, *sb.* infinite power ; an attribute of God or Christ : P. L. V. 722 ; VI. 159 ; VIII. 108 ; *girt with omnipotence* : P. L. VII. 194 ; *Second Omnipotence,* Christ : P. L. VI. 684.

Omnipotent, *adj.* infinite in power ; applied to God : P. L. III. 372 ; IV. 725 ; VI. 227 ; IX. 927 ; to the acts of God ; *omnipotent decree* : P. L. II. 198.

absol. the Omnipotent, God : P. L. I. 49, 273 ; IV. 86 ; V. 616 ; VI. 136 ; VII. 136, 516.

Omnipresence, *sb.* the quality of being omnipresent ; *his omnipresence fills land, sea, and air* : P. L. XI. 336 ; God himself : P. L. VII. 590.

Omniscient, *adj.* all-knowing ; used of God : P. L. VI. 430 ; VII. 123 ; X. 7.

*On, I. *prep.* (1) above and in contact with or supported by, upon ; *lit.* and *fig.* : P. L. I. 6, 195, 427 ; II. 181 ; III. 179 ; IV. 194, 350 ; S. A. 146 ; *the bee sits on the bloom* : P. L. V. 25 ; *bore him on their shields* : P. L. VI. 337 ; *others on ground walked* : P. L. VII. 442 ; *on his throne* : P. L. II. 138 ; VI. 88 ; *incumbent on the dusky air* : P. L. I. 226 ; *grounds his courage on despair* : P. L. II. 126 ; *on thee his ... spirit rests* : P. L. III. 389.

(b) used of the earth, sea, etc. : P. L. II. 589 ; III. 440 ; *on dry land he lights* : P. L. I. 227 ; *lets them pass, as on dry land* : P. L. XII. 197 ; but usually with the meaning : within the superficial limits or bounds of : P. L. I. 104 ; IX. 67 ; C. 209 ; *on earth* : P. L. II. 484 ; III. 64, 283 ; IV. 5 ; V. 224 ; VII. 581 ; *on sea* : P. L. X. 693 ; *on the plain* : P. L. III. 466.

(c) of the part of the body which supports one : P. L. VI. 194, 592 ; IX. 497 ; *lights on his feet* : P. L. IV. 183.

(d) of the means of conveyance : P. L. IV. 974 ; VI. 573 ; VII. 441 ; *on foot* : P. L. III. 941 ; *on wing* : P. L. I. 345 ; VI. 74 ; *on the ... wave* : P. L. II. 1042 ; *on the winds* : P. L. V. 269 ; *on the trading flood* : P. L. II. 640 ; *on a sunbeam* : P. L. IV. 556.

(e) of an axis or pivot : P. L. V. 255 ; VII. 207, 381 ; VIII. 165 ; *on hinges* : P. L. II. 881 ; *Earth ... on her centre hung* : P. L. VII. 242.

(2) in contact with : P. L. I. 287 ; III. 627 ; V. 323 ; *his flowing hair in curls on either cheek* : P. L. III. 641 ; *every herb ... grew on the green stem* : P. L. VII. 337 ; *border on* : P. L. II. 959 ; III. 537.

(3) close to, near : P. L. XII. 143 ; P. R. IV. 93.

(4) of position with reference to a place or thing ; *lit.* and *fig.*, *on the north* : P. R. IV. 28, 448 ; *on ... hand, side, part,* etc. : P. L. I. 222, 276, 578 ; II. 108 ; III. 218 ; IV. 179 ; VI. 362 ; IX. 7 ; *on the larboard* : P. L. II. 1019 ; *on high* : P. L. VI. 60.

(b) of background ; against ; *displayed on the open firmament of heaven* : P. L. VII. 390.

(5) in ; *I was never present on the place* : S. A. 1085.

(6) of the time of an occurrence : P. L. V. 582 ; VII. 593 ; IX. 67, 556 ; S. A. 1741 ; *on a summer's morn* : P. L. IX. 447 ; *on a day* : P. L. V. 579.

(b) at : P. L. V. 311.

(7) of occasion ; *on their march* : P. L. I. 413.

(8) of manner, state, or condition : *on winged speed* : P. L. V. 744 ; *on a sudden* : P. L. II. 752, 879 ; V. 51 ; *on a heap* : P. L. VI. 389 ; *on duty* : P. L. I. 333.

(9) of the basis or reason of action or feeling : S. A. 258 ; *on*

promise made: P. L. II. 238 ; *on other surety*: P. L. V. 538; *on my experience*: P. L. IX. 988; *on purpose*: P. L. IV. 584.

(10) of motion or direction to or towards ; *lit.* and *fig.*: P. L. II. 4; IV. 671 ; V. 343; *a spark lights on ... powder*: P. L. IV. 815; *heap on himself damnation*: P. L. I. 215; *on me let thine anger fall*: P. L. III. 237 ; *all power on him transferred*: P. L. VI. 678 ; *entering on studious thoughts*: P. L. VIII. 40 ; *lay hands on that ... key*: C. 13.

(*b*) of the incidence of a stroke, etc.: P. L. I. 668 ; VI. 188, 209 ; *fig.*, *the torrid clime smote on him*: P. L. I. 298.

(*c*) of the instrument; *all sounds on fret*: P. L. VII. 597 ; *grate on their scrannel pipes*: L. 124.

(*d*) of cumulative addition: P. L. II. 995; IV. 508 ; *blaze on blaze*: P. L. VI. 18.

(11) in an aspect or direction towards or with relation to: P. L. III. 722 ; V. 124, 907 ; VI. 590; IX. 1013 ; C. 222 ; *Zephyrus on Flora breathes*: P. L. V. 16 ; *Jupiter on Juno smiles*: P. L. IV. 500; *look on me*: P. L. IV. 462; IX. 687 ; *gaped on us*: P. L. VI. 577.

(*b*) above ; *the Sun ... rise on the Earth*: P. L. VIII. 161.

(12) into ; *thy bold entrance on this place*: P. L. IV. 882.

(13) through ; *on the washy ooze deep channels wore*: P. L. VII. 303.

(14) over so as to shut in ; *Hell ... on them closed*: P. L. VI. 875.

(15) of the person or thing to which action or feeling is directed: P. L. II. 123 ; IV. 620 ; VI. 265 ; VII. 295 ; VIII. 95 ; *mercy, shewn on man*: P. L. I. 219 ; *influence on their fault*: P. L. III. 118 ; *introduce law and edict on us*: P. L. V. 798 ; *on their Orbs impose ... revolution*: P. L. VIII. 30 ; *on him found deadly*: P. L. IX. 932.

(*b*) of the business of action or the object of desire : P. L. III. 533; V. 290; VII. 573 ; IX. 414; C. 502 ; *on some great charge employed*: P. L. III. 629; *on his great expedition*: P. L. VII. 193 ; *bound on a voyage*: P. L. VIII. 230 ; *intent on, bent on*: P. L. I. 786 ; III. 85 ; IV. 568 ; V. 332.

(16) towards or against with hostile intent: P. L. I. 354 ; VI. 831 ; S. A. 262 ; *back on thy foes to return*: P. L. VI. 39 ; *warred on*: P. L. I. 576.

(17) in regard to : S. A. 1228 ; L. 83 ; S. XIV. 9 ; *consulting on the sum of things* : P. L. VI. 673.

of the object of mental activity ; about, over ; *thought on*: P. L. IV. 198 ; *pored on*: S. XI. 4.

(18) from ; *trophies won on me* : S. A. 470 ; *this revenge on you* : P. L. IV. 387 ; *to be revenged on men* : P. L. IV. 4.

II. *adv.* (*a*) in the position of being in contact with, or supported by, the upper surface of something : L'A. 132.

(*b*) in the position of covering or being in contact with the body: P. L. III. 479; VI. 714; S. A. 717 ; *a kingly crown had on*: P. L. II. 673; *fig.*, *putting off human, to put on Gods*: P. L. IX. 714.

(*c*) so as to possess or control : P. L. II. 1001.

(*d*) forward in space or time: P. L. I. 561, 678 ; II. 614, 715 ; IV. 268 ; V. 50; VI. 63 ; VIII. 484 ; S. XX. 6 ; with the vb. omitted ; *let's on*: C. 599; forward in action: P. L. VII. 61 ; S. A. 638, 1677.

(*e*) with onward action, continuously : P. L. IX. 180; XI. 633; *sleep, say on*: P. L. IV. 773; VIII. 228 ; *pay on*: S. A. 489.

(*f*) into being or action: P. L. V. 233 ; S. A. 375 ; *casual discourse draw on*: P. L. IX. 223 ; *puts on swift wing*: P. L. II. 631 ; *new part puts on*: P. L. IX. 667.

See also the words: Bring, Come, Rely, Wait.

*Once, I. *adv.* (1) one time only ; *once a year* : P. R. IV. 234 ; *once before*: D. F. I. 50; *once ... no more*: L. 131 ; *again ... once*: S. A. 932 ; *once and again*: P. L. XI. 857; *once again*: P. L. VI. 618; P. R. II. 17; S. A. 1174; *once more*: P. L. I. 268; II. 721 ; IV. 941; XI. 75, 125; XII. 211 ; S. A. 742; *for once*: P. L. III. 689; V. Ex. 68.

(*b*) *all at once*, all at the same time, together : P. L. II. 476 ; VI. 582; on a sudden : P. L. II. 61.

(*c*) *at once*, at one and the same time : P. L. III. 59, 543 ; IV. 56,

148, 853; without delay, immediately: P. L. I. 59; II. 155, 475; V. 228.

(*d*) on one occasion: M. W. 23.

(2) at any time, ever, at all: S. A. 197, 368; *not once*: C. 74; *when once her eye hath met*: C. 164; *if once they hear that voice*: P. L. I. 274; only, merely; *thee once to gain companion of his woe*: P. L. VI. 907.

(3) at one time in the past, formerly: P. L. I. 607; II. 613; III. 353; IV. 39, 828; IX. 1125; X. 296; P. R. III. 162; S. A. 22, 633; S. X. 1; *now ... once*: P. L. I. 316; II. 748; VI. 270; X. 587; P. R. IV. 132; S. A. 1417; P. 40.

II. *conj. adv.* when or if once, as soon as; *once dead*: P. L. III. 233; *found*: P. L. VI. 500; *known*: P. L. II. 839; *joined*: S. A. 1037; *passed*: P. L. II. 1023; *warned*: P. L. IV. 125.

One, I. *adj.* (1) being of the smallest cardinal number; the sb. omitted or understood; *twenty to one*: U. C. I. 3; *summers three times eight save one*: M. W. 7.

(2) one and no more, a single: P. L. I. 32; II. 383; IV. 545, 546; V. 830; VI. 140, 520; IX. 628; X. 633; XI. 256, 753; P. R. I. 307; S. A. 649, 1518; C. 582; *one night*: P. L. I. 487; IX. 140; L'A. 107; *one night or two*: P. L. IX. 211; *one day*: P. L. VI. 423; *one day or seven*: S. A. 1016; *one day ... six nights and days*: P. L. IX. 136; *one short hour*: P. L. X. 923; *all in one moment*: P. L. II. 609; *one man*: P. L. IX. 545; XI. 219, 876; *one just man*: P. L. XI. 890; *one faithful man*: P. L. XII. 113; *out of one man a race of men innumerable*: P. L. VII. 155; *one man's fault*: P. L. X. 823; *one peculiar nation*: P. L. XII. 111; *one whole world*: P. L. XI. 874; *one stroke*: P. L. I. 488; II. 702; VI. 317; X. 809, 855; *at one gate ... at another*: S. A. 560; *one foot ... the other*: P. L. VII. 228.

(*b*) the sb. omitted but understood from the context: P. L. V. 783, 784, 834; VIII. 421; predicatively; *and what is one*: P. L. IX. 546.

(3) one made up of several components, a united; *they shall*

be *one flesh, one heart, one soul*: P. L. VIII. 499; *our union ... one heart, one soul in both*: P. L. IX. 967; *Heaven to Earth, one kingdom*: P. L. VII. 161; *one realm Hell and this World*: P. L. X. 391.

(4) uniformly the same: C. 133.

(5) one in substance, the same, identical; *as one continued brake*: P. L. IV. 175; *one Celestial Father gives to all*: P. L. V. 403; *one great sire*: P. L. VI. 95; *one first matter*: P. L. V. 472; *one individual soul*: P. L. V. 610; *one spirit in them ruled*: P. L. VI. 848; predicatively; *I with thee am one*: P. L. XI. 44.

(6) one in kind; *one guilt, one crime*: P. L. IX. 971; predicatively; *had been all one*: P. L. VI. 165.

(7) united in thought or feeling; predicatively; *we were one*: P. L. V. 678.

(8) a particular, a certain: P. L. III. 50; XI. 646; *that one beast*: P. L. IX. 769; *that one talent*: S. XIX. 3; *this one, this easy charge*: P. L. IV. 421.

(*b*) *one day*, on a certain day: P. R. I. 189; at some future time: P. L. II. 178, 734; S. A. 794.

(*c*) *one while*, at one time: P. R. I. 216.

(*d*) *absol.*, with *of*: P. L. III. 648; IV. 573; VI. 24; P. R. III. 362; *like one of us man is become*: P. L. XI. 84; *one of the Heavenly host*: P. L. XI. 230; *one of our number*: P. L. V. 843.

II. *absol.* or *pron.* (*a*) a certain one, some one, an individual: P. L. VII. 66; VIII. 295; X. 945; XI. 564; XII. 24; P. R. IV. 317; *one next himself in power*: P. L. I. 79; *one who brings a mind not to be changed*: P. L. I. 252; *as one who chose his ground*: P. L. IV. 406; *close at mine ear one called me*: P. L. V. 36; *to introduce one greater*: P. L. XII. 242; *as one who prayed*: S. A. 1637; *one Almighty is*: P. L. V. 469.

one ... the other: P. R. III. 84; S. A. 974; *the one ... the other*: P. L. II. 650; VIII. 387; P. R. III. 256; *now one ... now other*: P. L. IV. 397; *as one leads the other*: P. R. III. 53; *in one another's arms*: P. L. IV. 506.

one by one, singly : P. L. v.
697 ; S. A. 1457.

(b) any one whatever; *while
one might walk to Mile-End Green* :
S. xi. 7.

(c) a thing of the kind already
mentioned ; *God's altar ... one of
Syrian mode* : P. L. i. 474.

(d) person ; *every one* : V. Ex.
76 ; *some one* : P. L. vi. 503 ; C.
483 ; *the Holy One*, God : P. L.
vi. 359 ; xii. 248 ; S. A. 1427 ;
the or *that Evil One*, Satan : P. L.
ix. 463 ; P. R. iv. 194 ; *a woman;
who finds one virtuous* : S. A.
1047 ; *some fair one* : D. F. I. 11.

Only, I. *adj.* (a) one (or two), of
which there exists no more of the
kind : P. L. iv. 428 ; ix. 28 ; xi.
304 ; V. Ex. 55 ; *my, his*, or *thy
only Son* : P. L. ii. 728 ; iii. 64,
79, 403 ; v. 604, 718, 815 ; *the
only son of light* : P. L. xi. 808 ;
the only two of mankind : P. L.
iii. 65 ; ix. 415 ; *the only God* :
P. L. xii. 562 ; *the only righteous* :
P. L. xi. 701 ; *the only evil* : P.
L. iii. 683 ; *the, my*, or *this only
peace, strength*, etc. : P. L. iii.
274 ; x. 921 ; S. A. 460, 630 ;
that only Tree of Knowledge : P.
L. iv. 423.

(b) acting alone, sole : P. L. v. 5.

II. *adv.* (1) no one than, nothing
more or else than, nothing but,
alone, solely, merely ; (a) preceding what it modifies : P. L.
iii. 105 ; v. 206, 779, 897 ; viii.
14 ; ix. 129, 923 ; x. 1043 ; xii.
67, 581 ; P. R. ii. 13, 220, 404 ;
iv. 177 ; S. A. 557, 863 ; C. 126,
765 ; S. xix. 14 ; *only to discover* :
P. L. i. 64 ; *only to shine* : P. L.
viii. 155 ; *judgest only right* :
P. L. iii. 155 ; *know'st only good* :
P. L. iv. 895 ; *only this I know* :
P. L. v. 402 ; *his only dreaded
bolt* : P. L. vi. 491 ; *think only
what concerns thee* : P. L. viii.
174 ; *left only in these written
records* : P. L. xii. 513 ; *only in
his arm the moment lay* : P. L. vi.
239 ; *the invisible king, only omniscient* : P. L. vii. 123.

(b) following what it modifies :
P. L. iii. 281, 398, 701 ; v. 366,
639 ; viii. 447, 532, 616 ; ix. 380 ;
x. 832, 841, 931, 936, 1051 ; xi.
336, 689, 765 ; P. R. i. 226 ; ii.
478 ; iv. 320, 364 ; S. A. 264,
1123, 1190, 1659 ; *men only dis-*

agree : P. L. ii. 497 ; *for evil only
good* : P. L. ii. 623 ; *if true here
only* : P. L. iv. 251 ; *he for God
only* : P. L. iv. 299 ; *stand only* :
P. L. vi. 810 ; *to know this only* :
P. R. iv. 294 ; *gold though offered
only* : S. A. 390 ; *so only can high
justice rest appaid* : P. L. xii.
401 ; *man lives not by bread only* :
P. R. i. 349.

(c) separated from what it
modifies : P. L. iii. 268 ; ix. 327 ;
xi. 618 ; P. R. ii. 229, 289, 336 ;
S. A. 912, 1742 ; V. Ex. 25 ; U.
C. ii. 34 ; N. O. 37 ; M. W. 39 ;
only supreme in misery : P. L. iv.
91 ; *one gate there only was* : P.
L. iv. 178 ; *but only used for
prospect* : P. L. iv. 199 ; *do they
only stand by ignorance* : P. L.
iv. 518 ; *as only fit for gods* : P.
L. v. 69 ; *they only set on sport* :
S. A. 1679 ; the modified word
omitted : P. R. iv. 420.

(d) *not only ... but* : P. L. iv.
668 ; viii. 338 ; ix. 681 ; xii.
447 ; S. A. 617, 1654 ; *not of war
only, but* : S. xvi. 2 ; *not of Earth
only, but* : P. L. viii. 178 ; *not to
do only, but* : P. L. x. 826 ; the
but clause omitted : P. L. x. 461 ;
S. A. 579 ; *nor only ... but* : P. L.
iv. 991 ; ix. 1121 ; S. A. 687 ;
*nor he their outward only ... but
inward* : P. L. x. 220.

(2) without any one else, alone :
P. R. iv. 466.

Only-begotten, *adj.* singly begotten :
P. L. iii. 80.

Onset, *sb.* attack, assault : P. L. ii.
364 ; vi. 98.

Onward, *adv.* forward ; (a) in position : P. L. ii. 675 ; v. 298 ; vi.
550, 768, 831 ; *a little onward
lend thy guiding hand* : S. A. 1.

(b) in time ; *from this day onward* : P. L. x. 811.

(c) in progress ; *steer right onward* : S. xxii. 9.

Ooze, *sb.* soft mud : P. L. vii. 303.

Oozy, *adj.* (a) consisting of ooze ;
*the weltering waves their oozy
channel keep* : N. O. 124.

(b) wet with the slime of the
sea ; *his oozy locks* : L. 175.

Opacous, *adj.* not transparent ; *the
firm, opacous globe* : P. L. iii.
418 ; *this opacous Earth* : P. L.
viii. 23.

Opal, *sb. attrib.* of the opal : P. L.
ii. 1049.

Opaque, *adj.* not transparent ; *body opaque* : P. L. III. 619.

Ope, *vb. tr.* (*a*) to open, undo, unclose ; *ope his leathern scrip* : C. 626 ; *ope thine eyes* : P. L. XI. 423 ; *oped the mouths* : S. A. 452.

(*b*) to unlock : C. 14 ; *absol.* : L. 111.

Open, I. *adj.* (*a*) not shut : P. L. X. 419 ; *open fly ... the infernal doors* : P. L. II. 879 ; *the gates wide open stood* : P. L. II. 884 ; *the gates ... stood open wide* : P. L. X. 232 ; *the cataracts of Heaven set open* : P. L. XI. 825 ; *open left the cell of fancy* : P. L. VIII. 460 ; *will his ear be open* : P. L. X. 1061 ; *whose ear is ever open* : S. A. 1172.

(*b*) having the door or lid removed ; *an open grave their throat* : Ps. v. 28.

(*c*) not surrounded by barriers ; *open field* : P. L. X. 533.

(*d*) unconfined, free, clear ; *open sky* : P. L. III. 514 ; IV. 721 ; *firmament of heaven* : P. L. VII. 390.

(*e*) unobstructed ; *open sight* : P. L. V. 138.

(*f*) not covered over : P. L. IV. 245 ; S. A. 1609.

(*g*) exposed to general view ; *in open show* : P. L. X. 187 ; carried on without concealment, not secret ; *open war* : P. L. I. 662 ; II. 41, 51, 119, 187 ; *admiration* : P. L. III. 672.

(*h*) unreserved, candid ; used punningly with blending of sense (*a*) ; *open breast, front and breast* : P. L. VI. 560, 611.

(*i*) accessible, available ; *shall that be shut to Man which to the Beast is open?* : P. L. IX. 692.

II. *vb.* (*pres. 2d sing.* open'st : P. L. IX. 809) (1) *tr.* (*a*) to set open or unclose ; used of the doors or gates of heaven : P. L. VII. 205, 575 ; P. R. I. 281 ; N. O. 148 ; of the doors of hell : P. L. I. 724 ; of other things ; *open when, and when to close the ridges of grim war* : P. L. VI. 235 ; used *lit.* and *fig.* of the eyes (*see* Eye) : P. L. IX. 708, 866, 985, 1053, 1071 ; XI. 429.

absol. of the gates of hell ; *Sin opening* : P. L. X. 234 ; *she opened* : P. L. II. 883.

(*b*) to make open, provide free access to or egress from ; *Tar-*

tarus, which ready opens wide his fiery chaos : P. L. VI. 54 ; *the Earth ... opening her fertile womb* : P. L. VII. 454.

(*c*) to make an opening or incision in : P. L. VIII. 465.

(*d*) to make ; *opened into the hill a ... wound* : P. L. I. 689.

(*e*) to make free for passage, *fig.* : P. L. VII. 158 ; *thou open'st Wisdom's way* : P. L. IX. 809 ; *to evil ... opening the way* : P. L. IX. 865.

(*f*) to disclose, display ; *what if all her stores were opened* : P. L. II. 175 ; *opened ... a woody scene* : P. R. II. 294 ; *flowers that open now their ... smells* : P. L. V. 127 ; *herbs ... opening their various colours* : P. L. VII. 318.

(2) *intr.* (*a*) to become open or unclosed : P. L. VII. 565, 569 ; *opened from beneath ... a passage down to the Earth* : P. L. III. 526 ; *fig.*, *a lower deep still threatening to devour me opens wide* : P. L. IV. 77.

(*b*) to come asunder, disclose a gap : P. L. II. 755 ; VI. 860 ; *Heaven opened* : P. R. I. 30.

(*c*) to expand : P. L. VI. 481.

part. adj. **opening** ; (*a*) *the opening gulf*, the gulf stretching out from the river, or used for a sb., the entrance of the gulf : P. L. XI. 833.

(*b*) unclosing, expanding ; *opening eyelids* : L. 26 ; *bud* : P. L. XI. 277.

gerund or *vbl. sb.* **opening**, (*a*) unclosing ; *my opening* : P. L. II. 777 ; *mine eyes true opening* : P. L. XII. 274.

(*b*) passage : P. L. III. 538.

See **Self-opened**.

Opener, *sb.* that which opens the eyes ; *opener mine eyes* : P. L. IX. 875 ; *true opener of mine eyes* : P. L. XI. 598.

Openly, *adv.* (*a*) publicly : P. R. I. 288.

(*b*) unreservedly, without disguise : S. A. 398.

Operation, *sb.* action, agency, effect : P. L. VIII. 323 ; IX. 706, 1012.

Ophion, *sb.* one of the Titans and the first ruler of Olympus : P. L. X. 581.

Ophir, *sb.* the region from which Solomon obtained gold : P. L. XI. 400. *See* **Sofala.**

Ophiuchus, *sb.* the constellation: P. L. II. 709.

Ophiusa, *sb.* *isle Ophiusa,* the isle of serpents, an island in the Mediterranean east of Spain and south of the Pityusæ Isles: P. L. X. 528.

Opiate, *adj.* inducing sleep: P. L. XI. 133.

Opinion, *sb.* (a) judgement formed on evidence that does not produce knowledge: P. L. VIII. 78; *call our knowledge or opinion*: P. L. v. 108.

(b) a legal judgement: Hor. Epist. 4.

(c) reputation, public opinion: P. L. II. 471.

Opium, *sb.* the juice of the poppy as a narcotic; *fig., death's benumbing opium*: S. A. 630.

Opportune, (1) *adj.* (a) seasonable; *opportune excursion*: P. L. II. 396.

(b) conveniently exposed, open; *the woman opportune to all attempts*: P. L. IX. 481.

(2) quasi-*adv.*. advantageously, conveniently; *which of all most opportune might serve his wiles*: P. L. IX. 85.

Opportunely, *adv.* seasonably: P. R. II. 396.

Opportunity, *sb.* convenient time, favorable circumstances: P. R. IV. 531; *Danger will wink on Opportunity*: C. 401.

Oppose, *vb.* (1) *tr.* (a) to speak against, endeavour to frustrate with adverse argument: P. L. II. 419; *that tongue ... durst oppose a third part of the Gods*: P. L. VI. 155; *Abdiel ... the current of his fury thus opposed*: P. L. v. 808.

(b) to interpose as an obstacle: P. L. VI. 254.

(c) to withstand, resist, combat: P. R. I. 96; *power with adverse power opposed*: P. L. I. 103; *to oppose the attempt*: P. L. II. 610; to endeavour to hinder or thwart; *fiercely opposed my journey*: P. L. x. 478; *to oppose his high decree*: P. L. v. 717; *thy providence to oppose*: Ps. VIII. 8.

(2) *intr.* (a) to offer resistance: P. L. I. 41; with *against*; *arms against such hellish mischief fit to oppose*: P. L. VI. 636.

(b) to bring forward in opposition; *what had I to oppose against such ... arguments*: S. A. 862.

part. adj. **opposing,** resisting, hindering: C. 600.

Opposite, (1) *adj.* (a) placed over against, contrary in position; *that opposite fair star*: P. L. III. 727.

(b) hostile, antagonistic: P. L. II. 298; P. R. III. 358.

(2) *sb.* opposite aspect, opposition; *their planetary...aspects, in sextile, square, and trine, and opposite*: P. L. x. 659.

(3) quasi-*adv.* in or to an opposite position; *forth-stepping opposite*: P. L. VI. 128; *less bright the Moon, but opposite in levelled west*: P. L. VII. 376; *just opposite a shape ... appeared*: P. L. IV. 460; *two broad suns their shields blazed opposite*: P. L. VI. 306.

Opposition, *sb.* (a) opposite position; *in opposition sits grim Death*: P. L. II. 803.

(b) the relative position of two heavenly bodies when their longitudes differ by 180°: P. L. VI. 314.

(c) antagonism, hostility: P. L. XI. 664; P. R. III. 250; IV. 386; S. A. 1050.

Oppress, *vb. tr.* (a) to press down, crush; *main promontories flung ... oppressed whole legions*: P. L. VI. 655.

(b) to overpower; *fig., sleep oppressed them*: P. L. IX. 1045.

(c) to weigh down, burden; *absol., knowledge ... oppresses else with surfeit*: P. L. VII. 129.

(d) to subdue, overwhelm: P. L. II. 13.

(e) to trouble, harass, afflict: S. A. 1269; *with want oppressed*: P. R. II. 331; used of an enemy: P. R. II. 44; S. A. 232.

Oppression, *sb.* (a) pressure; *sleep... with soft oppression seized my drowsed sense*: P. L. VIII. 288.

(b) the tyrannical exercise of power, tyranny: P. L. XI. 672.

Oppressor, *sb.* one who tramples on the rights of another, a tyrant: S. A. 233, 1272.

Opprobrious, *adj.* dishonourable, disgraceful, shameful: P. L. x. 222; associated with disgrace, held in dishonour; *opprobrious hill, den*: P. L. I. 403; II. 58.

Ops, *sb.* the Roman goddess of plenty, identified with Rhea, the wife of Cronus: P. L. x. 584.

Optic, *sb.* pertaining to or assisting the sight ; *optic skill of vision* : P. R. IV. 40 ; *optic glass, tube,* the telescope : P. L. I. 288 ; III. 590.

*Or, *conj.* the co-ordinating particle introducing an alternative : P. L. I. 96, 121, 270 ; II. 207 ; IX. 44 ; *to submit or yield* : P. L. I. 108 ; *to explore or to disturb* : P. L. II. 971 ; *I repent or change* : P. L. I. 96 ; *inclination or sad choice leads* : P. L. II. 524 ; *his seasons, hours, or days, or months, or years* : P. L. VIII. 69 ; *sharp, smooth, swift, or slow* : P. L. II. 902 ; *head, hands, wings, or feet* : P. L. II. 949 ; *beast, bird, insect, or worm* : P. L. IV. 704 ; *swims, or sinks, or wades, or creeps, or flies* : P. L. II. 950.

(*b*) correlative with *either* : P. L. I. 424 ; II. 230, 365 ; IX. 1176.

(*c*) the first member of the alternative introduced by other words ; by *nor* : P. L. I. 211, 738 ; *Nor did they not perceive the evil plight ... or the fierce pains not feel* : P. L. I. 336 ; by *whether* : P. L. III. 524 ; v. 190 ; *whether of open war or covert guile* : P. L. II. 41 ; *whether true, or fancied so* : P. L. IX. 789.

(*d*) *or ... or* in the sense of *either ... or ; or east or west* : P. L. X. 685 ; *or in behalf of man, or to invade* : P. L. XI. 102.

(*e*) *or ... or* in the sense of *whether ... or ; or peace or not* : S. A. 1074.

(*f*) *or else* : P. L. II. 397 ; S. A. 694, 770 ; N. O. 91 ; U. C. I. 3 ; C. 484 *See* **Else.**

(*g*) otherwise, else ; *awake, arise, or be forever fallen* : P. L. I. 330 ; *some ... peasant sees, or dreams he sees* : P. L. I. 784.

(*h*) introducing a sentence and expressing an alternative with the preceding sentence, or little more than continuing the narration : P. L. I. 318, 322 ; II. 134 ; III. 7 ; X. 107 ; XI. 881.

Oracle, *sb.* (1) the medium by which a god was supposed to make known his will to men : P. R. IV. 275 ; *the Oracles are dumb* : N. O. 173 ; such a medium presenting the will of Satan : P. R. I. 395, 430, 456.

(2) the medium of divine communication ; (*a*) Christ ; *his living*

Oracle : P. R. I. 460 ; the Holy Spirit ; *an inward oracle* : P. R. I. 463.

(*b*) the Most Holy Place in the Jewish temple where God appeared in the cloud upón the mercy-seat : P. L. I. 12.

(*c*) the breast-place worn by Aaron ; *the oracle Urim and Thummim* : P. R. III. 13.

(3) divine message : P. L. X. 182.

Oracling, *vbl. sb.* the uttering of oracles : P. R. I. 455.

Oraculous, *adj.* possessing the power of revealing the will of God : P. R. III. 14.

Orator, *sb.* an eloquent public speaker : P. L. IX. 670 ; P. R. IV. 267, 353.

Oratory, *sb.* eloquence : P. L. XI. 8 ; *the oratory of Greece and Rome* : P. R. III. 360.

Orb, I. *sb.* (1) something of circular form ; (*a*) *the rocky orb ... his ample shield* : P. L. VI. 254.

(*b*) a wheel ; *the orbs of his fierce chariot* : P. L. VI. 828.

(*c*) circle, ring ; *in orbs of circuit inexpressible they stood, orb within orb* : P. L. v. 594, 596.

(2) one of the celestial spheres (*see* Sphere) : P. L. VIII. 30 ; *the luminous inferior orbs* : P. L. III. 420 ; *the fixed Stars, fixed in their orb that flies* : P. L. v. 176 ; *Cycle and Epicycle, Orb in Orb* : P. L. VIII. 84 ; *the utmost Orb,* the Primum Mobile : P. L. II. 1029.

(3) one of the celestial bodies ; sometimes the globe or disk of this body : P. L. v. 422 ; VIII. 152, 156 ; IX. 109 ; X. 397 ; *these shining orbs* : P. L. III. 668, 670 ; *in their glimmering orbs did glow* : N. O. 75 ; used of the sun ; *the Sun's orb* : P. L. VII. 361 ; *the Sun's lucent orb* : P. L. III. 589 ; *the Prime Orb* : P. L. IV. 592 ; used of the moon ; *whose orb ... the Tuscan artist views* : P. L. I. 287.

(*b*) the earth ; *the orb he roamed* : P. L. IX. 82.

(*c*) used of the universe ; *the hollow universal orb* : P. L. VII. 257.

(4) the eye or eyeball ; *these dark orbs no more shall treat with light* : S. A. 591 ; *hath quenched their orbs* : P. L. III. 25 ; *these*

eyes ... *their seeing have forgot*;
*nor to their idle orbs doth sight
appear*: S. XXII. 4.

(5) a complete period or sphere
of action ; *when fatal course had
circled his full orb* : P. L. v. 862.

II. *vb. tr.* to encircle; *orbed in
a rainbow*: N. O. 143.

part. adj. **orbed,** circular ; *his
orbed shield* : P. L. VI. 543.

See **Full-orbed.**

Orbicular, (1) *adj.* spherical : P. L.
X. 381.

(2) quasi - *adv.* with circular
motion ; *that rolled orbicular* : P.
L. III. 718.

Orc, *sb.* a sea-monster : P. L. XI.
835.

Orcus, *sb.* the Latin name for the
god of the lower world, here an
attendant upon the throne of
Chaos : P. L. II. 964.

Ordain, *vb. tr.* (1) to institute, establish : Ps. LXXXI. 17.

(2) to set in order, prepare : P.
L. IV. 215.

(3) to appoint, decree, destine,
order; *their great Senate ... to rule
by laws ordained* : P. L. XII. 226;
they themselves ordained their fall :
P. L. III. 127.

(*b*) used of God: P. L. III. 126;
VI. 175, 809 ; VII. 343 ; VIII. 106;
IX. 470 ; XI. 164 ; S. XXI. 11 ; *all
things as the will of God ordained
them* : P. L. IX. 344; *the work
ordained* : P. L. VII. 590 ; *for
whom all these his works ... he ordained* : P. L. III. 665 ; *for thee
I have ordained it* : P. L. VI. 700;
his punishment ordained : P. L. X.
1039 ; *here their prison ordained* :
P. L. I. 71 ; *with two acc.* ; *ordained me some inferior angel* : P.
L. IV. 58 ; *thy will by nature free* :
P. L. V. 526 ; *thy nurture holy* :
S. A. 362 ; *them ordain his dark
materials to create more worlds* :
P. L. II. 915 ; in passive : P. L.
IV. 729 ; V. 615 ; VIII. 297 ; *thee,
ordained his drudge* : P. L. II.
732 ; *thou shalt be what thou art
ordained* : P. R. IV. 473 ; *with
prep. inf.* : P. R. III. 152 ; *our
being ordained to govern* : P. L. V.
802 ; *with acc. and dat.* ; *ordain
them laws* : P. L. XII. 230.

(*c*) *absol.* or *intr.* the law that so
ordains : P. L. II. 201 ; *so God
ordains* : P. L. IV. 636.

(4) to determine ; *whose wisdom*

had ordained good out of evil to
create : P. L. VII. 187.

See **Pre-ordain.**

Order, I. *sb.* (1) rank, position : P.
L. I. 506 ; *orders and degrees jar
not with liberty* : P. L. V. 792.

(2) each of the nine ranks or
grades into which the angels are
divided in the system of the
Pseudo-Dionysius the Areopagite:
P. L. v. 591 ; X. 443 ; *under their
hierarchs in orders bright* : P. L.
v. 587 ; *thou rulest the angelic
orders* : S. A. 672 ; *to rule ... the
Orders bright* : P. L. I. 737 ; *each
order bright sung triumph* : P. L.
VI. 885 ; *to those bright Orders
uttered thus his voice* : P. L. X.
615.

(3) formal disposition, sequence
or succession of things in time or
space : P. L. V. 334 ; XI. 736.

(*b*) the condition in which everything is in its right place, and
performs its proper function ;
order from disorder sprung : P. L.
III. 713.

(4) conformity to law or established authority, public order: P.
L. II. 280.

(5) state, condition ; *all things
in best order* : P. L. IX. 402.

(6) a military position in which
the shield was hung on the left
arm, and the spear held erect by
the right side : P. L. I. 569 ; or
the meaning is, military array :
P. L. VI. 548.

(7) authoritative direction, command ; *by order of* : S. A. 1447.

(8) **in order** ; (*a*) in proper
sequence according to rank : P. L.
II. 507 ; according to position in
space ; *from land to land in order* :
P. L. IV. 663.

(*b*) having the separate elements
properly disposed with reference
to each other ; *nests in order
ranged of ... fowl* : S. A. 1694 ;
*their engines and their balls ... in
order set* : P. L. VI. 522, or
merely, position ; *bright-harnessed
Angels sit in order serviceable* : N.
O. 244 ; or, the proper position ;
*at a stately sideboard ... in order
stood tall stripling youths* : P. R.
II. 351.

(9) **in order to,** for the purpose
of : S. A. 1608.

(10) **out of order,** not in orderly
arrangement ; *earth's foundations*

all ... are out of order gone : Ps.
LXXXII. 20.

II. vb. tr. (a) to ordain, regulate;
used of God : P. R. III. 112 ; S.
A. 30.

(b) absol. to command ; seemed
so ordering : P. L. VIII. 377.

part. adj. **ordered**; (a) arranged
methodically and harmoniously :
P. 49.

(b) held in the proper military
position; ordered spear and shield :
P. L. I. 565.

Orderly, adj. characterized by regular arrangement : P. L. VI. 74.

Ore, sb. (a) the mineral; metallic
ore : P. L. I. 673 ; massy : P. L.
I. 703 ; metals of drossiest ore : P.
L. V. 442.

(b) a metal; spec. iron and
brass ; the liquid ore he drained
into fit moulds : P. L. XI. 570 ;
gold ; the all-worshipped ore : C.
719 ; the golden : C. 933 ; fig.
splendid radiance; the day-star ...
with new-spangled ore flames in
the ... sky : L. 170.

Oread, sb. a mountain-nymph: P. L.
IX. 387.

Oreb, sb. a prince of Midian : Ps.
LXXXIII. 41.

Oreb, sb. Mount Horeb, by some
scholars held to be a lower peak
of Mount Sinai, by others a
general name for the whole mountain of which Sinai is a particular
peak. In Ortelius Theatri Orbis
Terrarum, 1624, the map Palæs-
tina at page 2, Sinai and Horeb
are given as two distinct peaks,
Sinai lying north of Horeb : P. L.
I. 484 ; XI. 74 ; on the secret top
of Oreb, or of Sinai, didst inspire
that shepherd : P. L. I. 7.

Organ, sb. (a) the seat of a specific
faculty ; the organs of her fancy :
P. L. IV. 802.

(b) the musical instrument : P.
L. I. 708; XI. 560; pealing : Il P.
161 ; all organs of sweet stop : P.
L. VII. 596 ; fig., of the spheres ;
let the bass of heaven's deep organ
blow : N. O. 130.

Organic, adj. acting as an organ ;
serpent tongue organic : P. L. IX.
530.

Orgy, sb. a rite connected with the
worship of Chemos : P. L. I. 415.

Orient, sb. (a) eastern, or possibly
in sense (b) ; orient wave : N. O.
231.

(b) brilliant, shining; the orient
Sun : P. L. V. 175 ; beams : P. L.
VI. 15 ; light : P. L. VII. 254 ;
morning-light : P. L. XI. 205 ;
gems : P. L. II. 507 ; pearl : P. L.
IV. 238 ; V. 2 ; colours : P. L. I.
546 ; liquor : C. 65.

(c) rising ; fair Morn orient in
Heaven : P. L. VI. 524 ; the Sun,
when first ... he spreads his orient
beams : P. L. IV. 644 ; at the
brightening orient beam : P. L. II.
399.

Orifice, sb. opening, aperture : P. L.
VI. 577.

Original, (1) adj. (a) that belonged
at the beginning to the person or
thing in question ; original brightness : P. L. I. 592 ; darkness : P.
L. II. 984.

(b) initial, first ; the mortal Sin
original : P. L. IX. 1004 ; crime :
P. L. XI. 424 ; lapse : P. L. XII.
83.

(2) sb. (a) source : P. L. IX.
150 ; shall curse their frail original,
Adam as the author of sin : P. L.
II. 375.

(b) pl. original elements ; the
originals of Nature : P. L. VI. 511.

Orion, sb. the constellation : P. L. I.
305.

Orison, sb. prayer : P. L. V. 145 ;
XI. 137.

Ormus, sb. a city on an island at the
entrance of the Persian Gulf : P.
L. II. 2.

Ornament, sb. (a) something employed to adorn, embellishment ;
on her bestowed too much of ornament : P. L. VIII. 538 ; outward :
S. A. 1025 ; arms ... their ornament : S. A. 1132 ; fig., of faith,
of purity, our wonted ornaments :
P. L. IX. 1076.

(b) the action of adorning ;
mantling o'er his breast with regal
ornament : P. L. V. 280.

Ornate, adj. adorned, decorated: S.
A. 712.

Orontes, sb. a river of northern Syria
emptying into the Mediterranean :
P. L. IV. 273 ; IX. 80.

Orphean, adj. of Orpheus : P. L.
III. 17.

Orpheus, sb. the son of Calliope and
the mythical poet and musician of
ancient Greece : L'A. 145 ; Il P.
105 ; L. 58.

Orus, sb. Horus, the sun-god of
Egypt, the son of Isis and Osiris,

generally represented with the head of a hawk : N. O. 212 ; as identified with one of the fallen angels : P. L. I. 478.

Osier, *sb.* a species of willow: P. R. II. 26 ; C. 891.

Osiris, *sb.* the chief male deity of the Egyptians, incarnated in or represented by Apis, the Sacred Bull : N. O. 213 ; as identified with one of the fallen angels : P. L. I. 478.

Ostentation, *sb.* display, parade : P. R. III. 387.

*Other, (1) *adj.* (a) the remaining of two ; preceded by the def. art. or a pron. : P. L. I. 412 ; II. 666 ; III. 725 ; IV. 488 ; VI. 485 ; VIII. 139 ; X. 128, 414 ; *his other half* : P. L. V. 560 ; *the other side* : P. L. II. 108 ; P. R. IV. 159 ; S. A. 768, 1609 ; *the other part* : P. L. VI. 413 ; XI. 431 ; *the other goal* : C. 100 ; *the other door* : P. L. VI. 9 ; *thy other self* : P. L. VIII. 450 ; *the other life* : P. L. III. 450 ; *the other sort* : P. L. VI. 376.

(b) the remaining, the rest of the ; with plural sb. ; *his other parts* : P. L. I. 194 ; *five other wandering fires* : P. L. V. 177 ; *the other five their planetary motions* : P. L. X. 657 ; *all other parts* : C. 72.

(c) existing besides, or distinct from, that already mentioned ; not this ; additional : P. L. II. 806 ; VI. 442, 807 ; IX. 251 ; *other joy, care* : P. L. IX. 478, 813 ; preceded by a modifying word ; *the other service* : P. R. I. 427 ; *no other service, guide, doctrine* : P. L. IV. 420 ; P. R. I. 336 ; IV. 290 ; *other place, surety, harm none* : P. L. V. 361, 538 ; P. R. IV. 486 ; *each other creature* : P. R. II. 406 ; *some other place, power* : P. L. II. 977 ; IV. 61 ; X. 787 ; *such other trial* : S. A. 1643 ; *those other two* : P. L. III. 33.

with plural sb. : P. L. IV. 63, 84, 736 ; V. 259, 618, 884 ; VI. 354 ; VIII. 480 ; IX. 103 ; S. A. 105, 916, 1526 ; C. 961 ; L. 174 ; *other worlds* : P. L. III. 566 ; VIII. 175 ; X. 237 ; *other stars, suns* : P. L. VII. 364 ; VIII. 123, 148 ; *other creatures* : P. L. VII. 507 ; VIII. 169, 411, 546 ; *two other drops* : P. L. V. 132.

(d) different : P. L. IV. 360, 582 ; X. 538, 861 ; S. A. 1096,

1236 ; C. 684 ; *no other way* : P. L. XI. 527 ; *what other way I see not* : P. R. I. 338 ; *some other way* : P. L. X. 894 ; P. R. II. 254 ; *other notes than* : P. L. III. 17 ; *noise other than* : P. L. VIII. 243 ; *of other care ... than* : L. 116 ; *I discern thee other than thou seem'st* : P. R. I. 348 ; *far other* : P. L. IX. 1012 ; X. 862 ; XI. 171 ; P. R. II. 132 ; S. A. 875 ; C. 612.

(2) *absol.* or *pron.* (a) the remaining of two ; *the other* : P. L. III. 131, 132 ; VII. 444 ; XI. 443, 458 ; S. A. 208 ; *this other* : P. L. XI. 60 ; S. A. 387 ; *that* : P. R. II. 478 ; *these other* : P. L. IV. 783 ; *the one ... the other* : P. L. VIII. 387 ; P. R. III. 256 ; *one ... the other* : P. L. VII. 228 ; P. R. III. 84 ; S. A. 974 ; *each cast at the other* : P. L. II. 714 ; *each in other's countenance read* : P. L. II. 422 ; *each other, each to other, each the other, each from other* ; *see* **Each.**

(b) another person or thing of the kind mentioned : P. L. VIII. 581 ; *no other* : P. L. V. 534 ; P. R. I. 100 ; *now one ... now other* : P. L. IV. 398 ; *any other of* : D. F. I. 55 ; *some way or other* : S. A. 1252.

(c) another person ; *some other* : P. L. III. 211 ; S. A. 1302 ; *no other* : S. A. 723.

pl. other persons ; *others* : P. L. I. 216 ; II. 469, 546 ; IV. 880 ; V. 241 ; VI. 528 ; IX. 127, 805 ; XI. 655 ; XII. 37 ; P. R. II. 61 ; IV. 297 ; *all others* : P. R. I. 273 ; II. 174 ; S. A. 815 ; *others of some note* : P. R. II. 306 ; *in power of others* : S. A. 78 ; *as others use* : L. 67.

pl. other trees, animals, tents, etc. : P. L. IV. 249, 350 ; VII. 437, 442 ; XI. 558.

(3) *adv.* otherwise : P. L. I. 607.

Otherwhere, *adv.* in another place : P. 25.

Otherwise, *adv.* in a different way or manner : P. R. IV. 212 ; *far otherwise* : P. L. VI. 398 ; VIII. 529 ; IX. 984 ; *all otherwise* : S. A. 590 ; in elliptical phrase ; *if otherwise,* if the matter turn out differently from that mentioned : C. 318.

Oughly-headed, *adj.* having hideous heads : C. 695.

Ought, *vb.* (*pres. 2d sing.* ought'st : S. A. 329) to be bound in duty ; with simple *inf.*; *who ought rather admire* : P. L. VIII. 74 ; with *prep. inf.* ; *how thou ought'st to receive him* : S. A. 329 ; *ought to have still remembered* : P. L. X. 12 ; the infinitive omitted : P. R. IV. 288 ; S. A. 874.

Ounce, *sb.* the common lynx : P. L. IV. 344 ; VII. 466 ; C. 71.

*****Our**, *poss. pron.* of or belonging to us ; with *sb.* : P. L. I. 141, 163 ; II. 434 ; V. 628 ; *our like mouths* : S. XI. 10 ; *obj. gen.* : P. L. II. 137, 210, 825 ; VIII. 242 ; X. 368 ; without *sb.*, *our own* : P. L. II. 366.

(*b*) referring to the human race : P. L. I. 3, 29 ; II. 872 ; III. 65 ; IV. 6 ; Cir. 12 ; or to the body of Christians : P. R. I. 406 ; II. 283 ; IV. 25.

(*c*) referring to the poet ; *our tedious song should here have ending* : N. O. 239 ; *we salute thee with our early song* : M. M. 9.

Ours, *pers. pron.* that or those belonging to us ; referring to a preceding *sb.* : P. L. IV. 629 ; V. 629, 726 ; X. 1040 ; *absol.* our power : P. L. V. 489 ; *our army* : P. L. VI. 200.

Ourselves, *pron. pl.* (*a*) emphatic ; in apposition with *we* : P. L. VIII. 186.

(*b*) *refl.* : P. L. VI. 467 ; X. 999 ; with a *prep.* : P. L. II. 225, 253, 254 ; IX. 654 ; X. 1002, 1037, 1042.

Ouse, *sb.* a river of Yorkshire, England : V. Ex. 92.

*****Out**, I. *prep.* (*a*) of motion or direction ; from within, away from ; *from out* : P. L. II. 823 ; X. 282 ; XI. 855.

(*b*) **of** source or origin ; *from out* ; S. A. 1703 ; N. O. 28 ; *from out the purple grape crushed the ... wine* : C. 46.

II. *adv.* (**1**) of motion or direction from within a space : P. L. I. 621 ; II. 997 ; VII. 416 ; XII. 42 ; *driven out from bliss* : P. L. II. 86 ; *set out from Heaven* : P. L. VIII. 111.

(**2**) forth from the presence of a person ; *out from* : P. L. V. 613 ; VI. 52 ; *driven out the ungodly from his sight* : P. L. VII. 185 ; from one's home or company ; *turned me out* : S. A. 539.

(**3**) from among others : S. A. 1326 ; C. 630.

(**4**) of extension in space or time ; *stretched out* : P. L. I. 209 ; VIII. 102 ; *spread out* : P. L. VI. 827 ; *draw out* : P. L. X. 801 ; *why am I ... lengthened out to deathless pain* : P. L. X. 774.

(**5**) to extinction : P. L. XII. 188 ; *beat out life* : P. L. XII. ; *groaned out his soul* : P. L. XI. 447 ; *eyes put out* : S. A. 33 ; *blot out mankind* : P. L. XI. 891 ; *names ... blotted out* : P. L. I. 362 ; *rase quite out their native language* : P. L. XII. 54.

(**6**) to an end, to a conclusion : U. C. II. 8 ; *run out thy race* : T. 1 ; to exhaustion ; *wearied out* : S. A. 405.

(**7**) to a solution ; *riddle ... found out* : P. R. IV. 574.

(**8**) into a state of activity ; *burst out into sudden blaze* : L. 74.

(**9**) so as to be heard, aloud ; *cried out* : P. L. II. 787 ; *ring out* : N. O. 125.

(**10**) in the way of disclosure ; *speak them out* : S. A. 1569.

(**11**) with ellipsis of the *vb.* *go* : S. A. 748.

(**12**) **out of** ; (*a*) from within : P. L. II. 758 ; VII. 456 ; X. 464 ; *rise out of his grave* : P. L. XII. 423 ; *the way ... that out of Hell leads* : P. L. II. 433 ; *wind out of such prison* : P. L. VI. 660 ; *root them out of Heaven* : P. L. VI. 855 ; *out of Heaven shalt look* : P. L. III. 257 ; *out of Heaven the ... voice I heard* : P. R. I. 84 ; *thundering out of Sion* : P. L. I. 386 ; *from out of* : P. L. X. 317.

(*b*) from (a source, origin, or material) : P. L. I. 164 ; IV. 216 ; VI. 137 ; VII. 155 ; *the heavens and earth rose out of Chaos* : P. L. I. 10 ; *out of Darkness called up Light* : P. L. V. 179 ; *out of these hard stones be made thee bread* : P. R. I. 343 ; *spun out of Iris' woof* : C. 83 ; *the tusked boar out of the wood* : Ps. LXXX. 53 ; *out of the mouths of babes ... thou hast founded strength* : Ps. VIII. 5 ; *work ease out of pain* : P. L. II. 261 ; *out of evil seek to bring forth good* : P. L. I. 163.

because of, on account of : S. A. 880.

(c) from (a condition); *out of order* : Ps. LXXXII. 20.

(d) of separation or deprivation; from ; *sense of pleasure we may well spare out of life* : P. L. VI. 460 ; *delivered ... out of thine* (hands) : S. A. 439 ; *flattered out of all* : P. L. x. 42 ; *put him out of breath* : U. C. II. 12.

(e) from within the range of : P. L. x. 867.

(f) having lost ; *out of hope* : P. L. VIII. 481.

See also the words : Draw, Fall, Find, Keep, Lay, Season, Shut, Spin, Toil, Wear.

See **Unmeasured-out.**

Outbrake, *vb. intr.* to burst forth : N. O. 159.

Outbreathe, *vb. tr.* to express, utter : P. R. II. 29.

Outcast, *vb. tr.* to expel, exile ; *outcast from God* : P. L. II. 694 ; *us, outcast, exiled* : P. L. IV. 106.

part. adj. **outcast,** rejected, forsaken : P. R. II. 309.

Outcry, *sb.* (a) a loud cry : P. L. II. 726, 737 ; a confused noise, uproar : S. A. 1517.

(b) a loud noise ; *with an oaken staff ... raise such outcries on thy clattered iron* : S. A. 1124.

Outdo (óutdo : P. L. III. 298) *vb.* (*part.* outdone) *tr.* (a) to excel, surpass : P. L. I. 696.

(b) to defeat ; *Heavenly love shall outdo Hellish hate* : P. L. III. 298.

Outfly, *vb.* (*pret.* outflew) *intr.* to come suddenly into view : P. L. I. 663.

Outgo, *vb. tr.* to outdo, surpass : V. Ex. 79.

Outgrow, *vb.* (*pret.* outgrew) *tr.* to pass beyond the limits of : P. L. IX. 202.

Outlandish, *adj.* foreign and extravagant ; *outlandish flatteries* : P. R. IV. 125.

Outlast, *vb. tr.* to outlive : D. F. I. 3.

Outlaw, *sb.* robber : C. 399.

Outlive, *vb. tr.* to live longer than, survive : P. L. XI. 538.

part. adj. **outliving,** being longer than the day ; *long outliving night* : P. 7.

Outmost, *adj.* farthest outward : P. L. II. 1039.

Out-pour, *vb. tr.* (a) to cause to flow out : S. A. 544.

(b) to send forth ; *numbers num-*berless the city gates outpoured* : P. R. III. 311.

Outrage, *sb.* the violent infraction of law and order, violence : P. L. I. 500 ; x. 707.

Outrageous, *adj.* unrestrained, violent, furious ; *the Abyss ... outrageous as a sea* : P. L. VII. 212 ; *the gates .. belching outrageous flames* : P. L. x. 232 ; *this huge convex of fire, outrageous to devour* : P. L. II. 435 ; *noise* : P. L. v. 587.

Outrageously, *adv.* audaciously, atrociously : Ps. LXXXIII. 6.

Outshine, *vb.* (*pret.* outshone) *tr.* to shine brighter than : P. L. I. 86.

(b) to surpass in magnificence or splendour : P. L. II. 2.

Outside, *sb.* the outer surface ; *the bare outside of this World* : P. L. III. 74 ; *the outside bare of this round World* : P. L. x. 317 ; the exterior of a building ; *many a fair edifice ... outside and inside* : P. R. IV. 58 ; the external person as distinguished from the mind : P. L. VIII. 568, 596.

Outspread, *vb. tr.* to expand, extend ; *all this globous Earth in plain outspread* : P. L. v. 649 ; used of wings : P. L. I. 20 ; VII. 235 ; Ps. LXXX. 6 ; *fig., my glory ... there outspread* : Ps. VII. 17.

Outstretch, *vb. tr.* (a) to extend or place at full length : U. C. II. 17 ; *on the ground outstretched he lay* : P. L. x. 851.

(b) to extend in area : P. R. III. 254 ; *beheld the Earth outstretched* : P. L. v. 88.

Outward, (1) *adj.* (a) of or from the outside ; *outward view* : S. XXII. 2.

(b) of or pertaining to the body as distinguished from the mind or soul ; *outward acts* : S. A. 1368 ; *shape* : C. 460 ; *lustre* : P. L. I. 97 ; *ornament* : S. A. 1025 ; *show* : P. L. VIII. 538 ; *calm, strength* : P. L. IV. 120 ; IX. 312 ; *freedom, liberty* : P. L. XII. 95, 100 ; *light* : S. A. 160 ; *inward faculties ... outward also* : P. L. VIII. 543 ; *nor he their outward only ... but inward nakedness* : P. L. x. 220.

(c) of or pertaining to outer form as distinguished from inner substance ; *rites* : P. L. XII. 534.

(d) external to one's person ; *outward aid* : P. L. VIII. 642 ; *force* : P. L. IX. 348 ; S. A. 1369.

(2) *adv.* on or in the body as distinguished from the mind : P. L. VIII. 221 ; P. R. IV. 145.

Outwatch, *vb. tr.* to watch longer than : Il P. 87.

Outwear, *vb.* (*pret.* outworn) *tr.* (*a*) to wear out : Ps. LXXXVII. 22.

(*b*) to exhaust in strength; *with age outworn* : S. A. 580.

*Over or **O'er,** (1) *prep.* (*a*) higher up than, above : P. L. III. 521, 527 ; VI. 757 ; XI. 864 ; XII. 252 ; P. R. IV. 543 ; *over whose heads they roar* : P. R. IV. 463 ; *over them ... Death his dart shook* : P. L. XI. 491 ; *another world hung o'er my realm* : P. L. II. 1005 ; *the Sun ... hovering o'er the ocean-brim* : P. L. V. 140; *o'er his sceptre bowing low* : P. L. VI. 746 ; *upborne with ... wings over the vast Abrupt* : P. L. I. 409 ; *clouds rattling on over the Caspian* : P. L. II. 716.

fig. till many years over thy head return : P. L. XI. 534.

(*b*) in or to a position on the surface of, or so as to cover : P. L. IV. 258 ; V. 279 ; XI. 206, 240 ; Il P. 36 ; *over Heaven inducing darkness* : P. L. VI. 406 ; *Night ... over the pole thy thickest mantle throw* : P. 30; *the Moon ... o'er the dark her silver mantle threw* : P. L. IV. 609 ; *casts a gleam over this tufted grove* : C. 225 ; *the louring element scowls o'er the darkened landskip snow or shower* : P. L. II. 491.

(*c*) on all parts of the surface of, everywhere on ; *over all the face of Earth main ocean flowed* : P. L. VII. 278 ; *light was over all* : S. A. 84.

(*d*) from place to place on the surface of, throughout; *wandering o'er the earth* : P. L. I. 365 ; *wide over all the plain ... their camp extend* : P. L. V. 648.

(*e*) throughout every part of ; *birds ... summoned over Eden* : P. L. VI. 76 ; *to subdue and quell, o'er all the earth* : P. R. I. 218 ; *extend thy mind o'er all the world* : P. R. IV. 223 ; *eloquence ... fulmined over Greece* : P. R. IV. 270.

(*f*) above in authority or power; *God over all supreme* : P. R. IV. 186 ; *lord over* : P. L. XII. 69 ; *dominion, monarchy, victory, etc., over* : P. L. IV. 431 ; V. 795 ; XII. 420 ; S. A. 1290 ; *reign, rule,*

triumph, etc., over : P. L. V. 820; IX. 941, 1130; X. 196 ; XII. 453 ; S. A. 267 ; *temperance over appetite* : P. L. VII. 127.

(*g*) beyond in degree or quantity ; *over wrath grace shall abound* : P. L. XII. 478.

(*h*) of motion that passes above and to the other side : P. L. IV. 191 ; *thrown ... o'er the crystal battlements* : P. L. I. 742; *fly o'er* : P. L. III. 494; *leaps o'er the fence* : P. L. IV. 187.

(*i*) from side to side of, to the other side of, across : P. L. I. 296, 520 ; II. 620 ; III. 359 ; IV. 538 ; VI. 75, 840 ; VIII. 301 ; X. 432 ; S. A. 1530; *ferry over this Lethean sound* : P. L. II. 604 ; *while o'er the necks thou drov'st* : P. L. III. 395 ; *rode tilling o'er the waves* : P. L. XI. 746; *a river o'er the marish glides* : P. L. XII. 630 ; *a way or passage over* : P. L. II. 102 ; III. 530 ; X. 257, 309, 472 ; *the mole ... over the foaming Deep* : P. L. X. 301.

(*j*) on the other side of, across ; *I hear the ... curfew sound over some ... shore* : Il P. 75.

(2) *adv.* (*a*) above ; *waved over by that flaming brand* : P. L. XII. 643.

(*b*) above so as to cover the surface : S. XIV. 10 ; *scribbled o'er* : P. L. VIII. 83; *fig., ambition varnished o'er with zeal* : P. L. II. 485.

(*c*) out of possession or power : P. R. IV. 23; S. A. 121, 629. See **Give.**

Over-arch, *vb. tr.* to form into an arch above ; *shades* or *shade high over-arched* : P. L. I. 304 ; IX. 1107.

Overawe, *vb. tr.* to restrain or control by awe : P. L. IX. 460.

Overbuild, *vb.* (*past part.* overbuilt) *tr.* to span with a structure : P. L. X. 416.

Over-cloy, *vb. tr.* to fill to overflowing : Ps. IV. 34.

Overcome, *vb.* (*pret.* and *past part.* overcame) (1) *tr.* (*a*) to overpower, conquer, subdue : P. L. IX. 313; S. A. 365 ; *who overcomes by force hath overcome but half his foe* : P. L. I. 649; *not so is overcome Satan* : P. L. XII. 390 ; *what is else not to be overcome* : P. L. I. 109 ; *with non-material object* ;

will overcome their noxious vapour:
P. L. II. 215; *overcome this dire
calamity*: P. L. I. 189.

(*b*) to overwhelm, render helpless or ineffectual; *overcome with
rage*: P. L. IV. 857; *with female
charm*: P. L. IX. 999; *perseverance overcame whate'er his
cruel malice could invent*: P. R.
I. 148.

(2) *absol.* or *intr.* (*a*) to be vic-
torious: P. L. I. 648; *in battle*:
P. L. XI. 691; *till Israel overcome*:
P. L. XII. 267; *reason overcome*:
P. L. VI. 126.

(*b*) to obtain the mastery; *to
overcome by suffering*: P. L. XI.
374.

Over-exquisite, *adj.* excessively exact, too careful or discriminating:
C. 359.

Over-fond, *adj.* fond to excess,
doting: P. L. XI. 289.

Overgrow, *vb.* (*pret.* not used; *past
part.* overgrown) (1) *tr.* to cover
with growth; *with thicket* or
branches overgrown: P. L. IV.
136, 627.

(2) *intr.* to grow beyond the
fit size: P. L. IX. 210.

Overgrowth, *sb.* excessive growth:
P. L. XII. 166.

Overhang, *vb.* (*pret.* overhung) *intr.*
to jut over: P. L. IV. 547.

Over-hardy, *adj.* overbold, very
daring: Ps. CXXXVI. 70.

Overhead, *adv.* over one's head,
aloft, on high: P. L. I. 784; IV.
137; VI. 212; IX. 1038.

Overhear, *vb.* (*pret.* overheard) *tr.*
to hear what is not addressed to
the hearer: P. L. IX. 276.

Overjoy, *vb. tr.* to transport with
gladness: P. L. V. 67; VIII.
490.

Over-just, *adj.* just to excess: S. A.
514.

Over-labour, *vb. tr.* to fatigue with
excessive labour: S. A. 1327.

Overlay, *vb.* (*pret.* not used; *past
part.* overlaid) *tr.* (*a*) to surmount; *pillars overlaid with
golden architrave*: P. L. I. 714.

(*b*) to span: P. L. X. 370; *overlay with bridges rivers proud*: P.
R. III. 333.

(*c*) to cover the surface of;
cedar overlaid with gold: P. L.
XII. 250.

Overleap, *vb. tr.* to leap to the other
side of: P. L. IV. 181.

Overlive, *vb. intr.* to continue in life
beyond a stated time: P. L. X.
773.

Overlove, *vb. tr.* to love to excess, be
too fond of: P. L. X. 1019.

Over-match, (1) *sb.* one who is too
skilful to be overcome: P. R. IV.
7.

(2) *vb. tr.* to defeat by superior
skill: P. R. II. 146.

Overmuch, (1) *adj. absol.* too much
importance or power: P. L. VIII.
565.

(2) *adv.* in too great a degree:
P. L. IX. 1178; S. A. 213.

Over-multitude, *vb. tr.* to exceed in
number: C. 731.

Overpass, *vb. tr.* to pass by without
regard or consideration: P. R.
II. 198.

Overply, *vb. tr.* to use to excess,
exhaust by too much use: S. XXII.
10.

Over-potent, *adj.* too powerful: S.
A. 427.

Overpower, *vb. tr.* (*a*) to overcome
with superior force, conquer: P.
L. II. 237; VI. 419.

(*b*) to overwhelm, master; *my
earthly, by his heavenly over-
powered*: P. L. VIII. 453; *over-
powered by thy request, who could
deny thee nothing*: S. A. 880.

Overpraising, *sb.* excessive praise:
P. L. IX. 615.

Overreach, *vb. tr.* to get the better
of through cunning or sagacity:
P. L. IX. 313; X. 879; P. R. IV.
11.

Over-ripe, *adj.* more than the necessary number; *thy years are over-
ripe*: P. R. III. 31.

Overrule, *vb. tr.* to control, sway;
overruled their will: P. L. III.
114; *thy will ... not over-ruled*: P.
L. V. 527; *overruled ... their
might*: P. L. VI. 228.

Overrun, *vb. tr.* to harass by hostile
incursions: P. R. III. 72.

Overshadow, *vb. tr.* to cover with a
shadow, shade: P. L. XII. 187;
P. R. IV. 148.

part. adj. **overshadowing**, *fig.*
covering or filling with creative
power: P. L. VII. 165.

Overspread, *vb. tr.* to cover com-
pletely; *with her green shade ...
the hills were overspread*: Ps.
LXXX. 42; to extend over; *all
Heaven ... with ruin overspread*:
P. L. VI. 670.

Over-strong, *adj.* strong to excess :
S. A. 1590.

Over-sure, *adj.* sure to excess, too
confident : P. R. II. 142.

Overtake, *vb.* (*pret.* overtook) *tr.* (*a*)
to come up to in pursuit, catch :
P. L. II. 792 ; Ps. VII. 14.

(*b*) to come upon unexpectedly,
surprise and overcome ; *Joy shall
overtake us as a flood* : T. 13.

Overtask, *vb. tr.* to impose too heavy
a task upon : C. 309.

Overthrow, (**1**) *sb.* fall, defeat ; *sad,
indecent* : P. L. I. 135 ; VI. 601 ; *in
Adam's overthrow* : P. R. I. 115.

(**2**) *vb.* (*pret.* overthrew ; *past
part.* overthrown) *tr.* (*a*) to throw
down, prostrate : U. C. I. 4.

(*b*) to defeat, vanquish : P. L.
II. 992 ; VI. 372 ; S. A. 1698 ;
*Dagon hath presumed, me over-
thrown* : S. A. 463 ; *Satan ... whom
folly overthrew* : P. L. IV. 905.

part. absol. those who are prostrate ; *the overthrown he raised* :
P. L. VI. 856.

Over-tire, *vb. tr.* to weary to excess,
fatigue to exhaustion : S. A. 1632.

Overtrust, *vb. intr.* to have too much
confidence ; *to worth in women
overtrusting* : P. L. IX. 1183.

Overture, *sb.* proposal, offer ; used
punningly : P. L. VI. 562.

Overturn, *vb. tr.* (*a*) to upset, overthrow : P. L. VI. 390.

(*b*) to subvert, destroy ; *pain ...
overturns all patience* : P. L. VI.
463.

(*c*) to overpower, conquer, vanquish ; *desire of wine ... many a
famous warrior overturns* : S. A.
542.

Over-watch, *vb. tr.* to fatigue by long
watching : S. A. 405.

Overween, *vb. intr.* to think arrogantly : S. IX. 6 ; to be too self-
confident ; *him overweening to
overreach* : P. L. X. 878.

vbl. sb. **overweening,** arrogance,
presumption : P. R. I. 147.

Overwhelm, *vb. tr.* (*a*) to flow over
so as to submerge : P. L. XI. 748 ;
*the waves return, and overwhelm
their war* : P. L. XII. 214.

(*b*) to crush with sudden ruin ;
*all her sons ... overwhelmed and
fallen* : S. A. 1559.

(*c*) to overpower ; *with shame
nigh overwhelmed* : P. L. X. 159.

Over-woody, *adj.* producing branches
rather than fruit : P. L. V. 213.

Owe, *vb. tr.* (*a*) to be indebted in, under
obligation to render : P. L. IX.
1141 ; with the *dat.* ; *owe them
absolute subjection* : S. A. 1405 ;
with *to* : S. XVII. 12 ; *to me owe
... deliverance* : P. L. III. 181 ; *to
him ... praises* : P. L. IV. 444 ; *to
the infinitely Good ... thanks* : P.
L. VII. 76 ; *to thee duty and service* : P. R. II. 325 ; *to me ... no
less than for deliverance what we
owe* : P. L. VI. 468 ; with clause
and *to* : P. L. V. 521 ; *that thou
art happy owe to God* : P. L. V.
520.

absol. to be under obligation :
P. L. IV. 53, 56.

(*b*) to be indebted to ; *experience, next to thee I owe* : P. L. IX.
807.

vbl. sb. **owing,** indebtedness : P.
L. IV. 56.

Owl, *sb.* the bird *Strix* : S. XII. 4.

*Own, I. *adj.* (**1**) belonging to oneself or itself, proper, individual ;
(*a*) used after a poss. pron. : P. L.
I. 188 ; II. 70, 360 ; III. 86, 129 ;
IV. 819 ; V. 236 ; VII. 526 ; VIII.
641 ; IX. 464 ; X. 344 ; XII. 110 ;
offspring ... thine own begotten : P.
L. II. 782 ; *our own right hand
shall teach us* : P. L. V. 864 ;
himself is his own dungeon : C.
385 ; *our own loss how repair* : P.
L. I. 188 ; *to regain our own right* :
P. L. II. 231 ; *seek our own good* :
P. L. II. 253 ; *bear my own deserv-
ings* : P. L. X. 727 ; *draw their
own ruin* : S. A. 1267 ; *in his own
temple* : P. L. I. 460 ; *with his
own folly* : P. L. III. 153 ; *upon
his own head* : P. L. III. 220 ;
under her own weight : P. L. XII.
539 ; *of my own accord* : S. A.
1643 ; *within his own clear breast* :
C. 381 ; *thy discernments ... my
own* : S. A. 970 ; *the strength he was
to cope with, or his own* : P. R. IV.
9 ; *his glory, not their own* : P. R.
III. 143.

(*b*) used after a *sb.* in the possessive ; *God's own ear listens* :
P. L. V. 626 ; *nature's own work
it seemed* : P. R. II. 295.

(**2**) *absol.* possession, peculiar
nature, etc. : P. L. II. 366 ; VIII.
549 ; X. 738 ; *the bond of Nature
draw me to my own, my own in thee* :
P. L. IX. 956, 957 ; *God made thee
of choice his own* : P. L. X. 766 ;
he to his own a comforter will send :

P. L. XII. 486 ; *offer ... to me my own* : P. R. IV. 191 ; *one of these ...make sure thy own* : P. R. III. 363.

of your own, belonging to you : C. 969 ; *what of my own*, what belongs to me : P. R. II. 381 ; *of his own*, of or in himself : P. R. III. 134.

II. *vb. tr.* (*a*) to possess : M. W. 6 ; II P. 113.

(*b*) to acknowledge as one's own ; *Son owned from Heaven by his Father's voice* : P. R. II. 85.

(*c*) to acknowledge as approved or accepted ; *thee he regards not, owns not* : S. A. 1157 ; *the Lord will own, and have me in his keeping* : Ps. VI. 20.

Owner, *sb.* master : S. A. 1261.

Ox, *sb.* (*pl.* oxen : P. L. XI. 647), adult male of the domestic *Bos taurus* : P. L. VIII. 396 ; *fair oxen* : P. L. XI. 647 ; *the grazed or laboured ox* : P. L. I. 486 ; C. 291.

Oxus, *sb.* a river forming part of the boundary between Tartary and Persia, and emptying into the Aral Sea : P. L. XI. 389.

P

Pace, (1) *sb.* (*a*) step : S. A. 110 ; *ten paces* : P. L. VI. 193 ; *following pace for pace* : P. L. X. 589.

(*b*) the manner or rate of walking : C. 145 ; *heavy* : P. L. VI. 551 ; *majestic* : C. 870 ; *fig.*, *the Earth ... with inoffensive pace* : P. L. VIII. 164 ; *the heavy plummet's pace* : T. 3 ; *Justice ... mends not her slowest pace* : P. L. X. 859.

(2) *vb. intr.* to step ; *fig.*, *the Earth ... paces even* : P. L. VIII. 165 ; *the sun ... pacing* : C. 100.

See **Slow-paced.**

Pacific, *adj.* indicative of peace : P. L. XI. 860.

Pack, *vb. tr.* to put together, stow, *fig.* : V. Ex. 12.

Packing, *vbl. sb.* collusion, trickery : P. of C. 14.

Pact, *sb.* compact, agreement : P. R. IV. 191.

Padan-Aram, *sb.* apparently a name given to the northern part of Mesopotamia : P. L. III. 513.

See **Title-page.**

Pageantry, *sb.* theatrical spectacles : L'A. 128.

Pain, (1) *sb.* (*a*) penalty, punishment : P. L. X. 964, 1025.

(*b*) suffering or distress of body or mind : P. L. I. 558 ; II. 34, 88, 147, 207, 219, 461, 544, 567 ; IV. 888, 892, 910, 915, 918, 921, 925, 948 ; VI. 280, 394, 397, 431, 454 ; IX. 283, 487 ; X. 470 ; XI. 601 ; P. R. IV. 305 ; C. 687 ; *implacable* : P. L. VI. 657 ; *lasting, endless, deathless* : P. L. I. 55 ; II. 30 ; X. 775 ; *miserable, grievous* : P. L. II. 752 ; X. 501 ; *uncouth* : P. L. VI. 362 ; *mortal* : P. L. XII. 384 ; *in pain* : P. L. I. 125 ; *fellowship in pain* : P. R. I. 401 ; *vows made in pain* : P. L. IV. 97 ; *to have their lot in pain* : P. L. I. 608 ; *work ease out of pain* : P. L. II. 261 ; *remove the sensible of pain* : P. L. II. 278 ; *then Satan first knew pain* : P. L. VI. 327 ; *quelled with pain, which all subdues* : P. L. VI. 457 ; *pain is perfect misery* : P. L. VI. 462 ; *pain of longing, of death, of absence* : P. L. IV. 511 ; IX. 694, 861 ; *pain and woe, woe and pain* : P. L. II. 608, 695 ; *fear and pain* : P. L. II. 783 ; *agony and pain* : P. L. II. 861 ; *pleasure and pain* : P. L. II. 586 ; *house of pain*, hell : P. L. II. 823 ; VI. 877.

pl. : S. A. 105, 615 ; *fierce, inhuman, horrid* : P. L. I. 336 ; XI. 511 ; S. A. 501 ; *support our pains* : P. L. I. 147 ; *end of all my pains* : S. A. 576 ; *pains and slaveries* : S. A. 485.

pl. the throes of child-birth : P. L. X. 1051.

(*c*) trouble, difficulty : P. L. IV. 271 ; *pl.* : P. R. IV. 479.

(*d*) labour, exertion, effort ; *pl.* : P. R. II. 401.

(2) *vb. tr.* to cause bodily suffering to : P. L. VI. 404 ; S. A. 617.

Painful, *adj.* attended with or causing suffering of body or mind ; *painful steps, passages, diseases* : P. L. I. 562 ; XI. 528 ; S. A. 699 ; *superstition* : P. L. III. 452.

Paint, *vb. tr.* (*a*) to adorn with colours ; *Mists and Exhalations ... the sun paint your fleecy skirts* : P. L. V. 187.

(*b*) to variegate, diversify, or to display ; *Nature paints her colours* : P. L. V. 24.

part. adj. **painted** ; (*a*) adorned with frescoes : P. R. IV. 253.

(b) adorned with colours; *painted wings* : P. L. VII. 434 ; *heavens* : Ps. CXXXVI. 18.

Pair, I. *sb.* (1) two things of a kind used together; of wings : P. L. v. 278, 280.

(2) two of opposite sexes; (a) a man and woman united by love or marriage : P. L. VIII. 58 ; XI. 10 ; used of Adam and Eve ; *human pair* : P. L. v. 227 ; IX. 197 ; *wedded* : P. L. VIII. 605 ; *loveliest, gentle, happy, blest* : P. L. IV. 321, 336, 534, 774 ; *hapless, sinful* : P. L. x. 342 ; XI. 105.

(b) a mated couple of animals : P. L. VII. 459; VIII. 394; XI. 735.

(3) two persons of the same kind taken together : C. 236 ; *the Hellish pair ... Sin ... Death* : P. L. x. 585 ; *blest pair of Sirens ... Voice and Verse* : S. M. 1.

II. *vb. intr.* to be equal or a match *with* : S. A. 208.

Palace, *sb.* (a) a royal residence : P. L. I. 497 ; XII. 177 ; P. R. II. 300 ; *Mount Palatine, the imperial palace* : P. R. IV. 51 ; *Susa, his Memnonian palace* : P. L. x. 308; *the palace of great Lucifer* : P. L. v. 760 ; *fig., the palace of eternity*, heaven : C. 14 ; *the Sun's orb ... great palace now of Light* : P. L. VII. 363.

(b) any magnificent residence : P. L. XI. 750 ; P. R. IV. 35.

(c) hall or court : Ps. LXXXIII. 48.

Palace-gate, *sb.* the gate of a royal residence : P. L. III. 505.

Palace-hall, *sb.* the hall of a royal residence; *fig., Heaven ... her high palace-hall* : N. O. 148.

Palate, *sb.* the sense of taste : P. L. IX. 1020.

Palatine, *sb. Mount Palatine*, one of the seven hills of Rome : P. R. IV. 50.

Pale, *sb.* enclosure : Il P. 156.

Pale, (1) *adj.* (a) of a whitish or ashen appearance, lacking colour, wan : P. L. IX. 894 ; S. XXIII. 4 ; *deadly pale* : P. L. XI. 446 ; *with shuddering horror pale* : P. L. II. 616 ; used of death, spirits; *Death ... his pale horse* : P. L. x. 590 ; *the flocking shadows pale* : N. O. 232 ; of the moon; *thy pale visage* : C. 333.

a transferred epithet; *the Moon ... her pale course* : P. L. I. 786 ;

her pale dominion : P. L. III. 732; *Night ... thy pale career* : Il P. 121.

(b) inducing pallor ; *pale fear* : P. L. VI. 393.

(c) lacking intensity or depth of colour ; *pale primrose, jessamine* : M. M. 4 ; L. 143 ; *poplar pale* : N. O. 185 ; used of light : P. L. I. 183.

(2) *sb.* paleness, pallor : P. L. IV. 115 ; x. 1009.

Pale-eyed, *adj.* having dim eyes : N. O. 180.

Pales, *sb.* the Roman goddess of pastures : P. L. IX. 393.

Palestine, *sb.* the country of the Philistines, Philistia : P. L. I. 80, 465 ; S. A. 144, 1099 ; N. O. 199.

Pall, *sb.* cloak, mantle : Il P. 98.

Pallet, *sb.* bed ; *fig., the low-roosted lark from her thatched pallet* : C. 318.

Palm, *sb.* the inner part of the hand : C. 918.

Palm, *sb.* (a) the tree *Palma; branching palm* : P. L. IV. 139; VI. 885; S. A. 1735 ; *cedar, pine, or palm* : P. L. IX. 435 ; *Jericho, city of palms* : P. R. II. 21.

(b) a branch of this tree worn as a sign of victory : S. M. 14.

Palmer, *sb.* a pilgrim who had visited the holy places in Jerusalem, in sign of which he carried a palm-branch or palm-leaf : C. 189.

Palm-tree, *sb.* the tree *Palma* : P. L. VIII. 212.

Palmy, *sb.* abounding in palm-trees : P. L. IV. 254.

Palpable, *adj.* that may be felt, perceptible to the touch; *the palpable obscure* : P. L. II. 406 ; *palpable darkness* : P. L. XII. 188.

Pampered, *part. adj.* indulged unduly ; *fig., fruit trees ... reached too far their pampered boughs* : P. L. v. 214.

See **Lewdly-pampered.**

Pan, *sb.* the 'goat-footed, two-horned god of shepherds' ; *universal, mighty, bounteous* : P. L. IV. 266; N. O. 89 ; C. 176 ; *Pan or Sylvanus, Sylvan* : P. L. IV. 707 ; C. 268 ; as the lover of Syrinx : P. R. II. 190 ; A. 106.

Pandemonium, *sb.* the capital of Satan : P. L. I. 756 ; x. 424.

Pandora, *sb.* the first woman ; she was created by Hephæstus at the command of Zeus, in revenge or the fire stolen from heaven by Prometheus. The gods endowed her with all gifts, and Hermes brought her to Epimetheus that she might bring ruin on mankind : P. L. IV. 714.

Paneas, *sb.* an old name of Cæsarea Philippi, a city situated in a valley at the foot of Mount Hermon. On neighbouring mountain was a grotto or cave sacred to Pan, called the Paneion, whence the city and district took the name *Paneas* : P. L. III. 535.

Pang, *sb. pl.* sudden and keen spasms of pain : P. L. II. 703 ; Cir. 27 ; M. W. 68 ; *colic pangs* : P. L. XI. 484 ; *Earth trembled ... as again in pangs* : P. L. IX. 1001 ; or probably, sudden and sharp mental anguish : S. A. 660.

Panim, *sb.* pagan : P. L. I. 765.

Panope, *sb.* one of the Nereids : L. 99.

Panoply, *sb.* a complete suit of armour ; *golden, celestial* : P. L. VI. 527, 760.

Pansy, *sb.* the flower *Viola tricolor* : P. L. IX. 1040 ; C. 851 ; *the pansy freaked with jet* : L. 144.

Paquin (Páquin), *sb.* Peking, the capital of China : P. L. XI. 390.

Parable, *sb.* a fable or apologue ; *a sin that Gentiles in their parables condemn* : S. A. 500.

Parade, *sb.* an assembling of soldiers for inspection or display ; *the Cherubim ... stood armed ... in warlike parade* : P. L. IV. 780.

Paradise, *sb.* (1) the abode of Adam and Eve in the garden of Eden : P. L. III. 354, 733 ; IV. 241, 282, 422, 752, 991 ; V. 226, 446 ; VII. 45 ; VIII. 171, 319 ; IX. 406, 476, 619, 796 ; X. 2, 17, 326, 398, 585, 598 ; XI. 29, 48, 104, 123, 210, 259 ; XII. 586, 642 ; P. R. I. 52 ; II. 141, 604, 611 ; *delicious, blissful, fair* : P. L. IV. 132, 208, 379 ; *the blissful seat of Paradise* : P. L. III. 527 ; *the happy seat of Man* : P. L. III. 632 ; *this Paradise of Eden* : P. L. IV. 274 ; *of Paradise and Eden's happy plains* : P. L. V. 143 ; *of Paradise or Eden* : P. L. XI. 342 ; *wall of, gate of, cliff of, hill of, Mount of* : P. L. IV. 143, 542 ; V. 275 ; XI. 378, 830 ; *Tigris, at the foot of Paradise* : P. L. IX. 71 ; *fair fruit, like that which grew in Paradise* : P. L. X.

551 ; *joys of Paradise, dear bought* : P. L. X. 742 ; *must I leave thee, Paradise* : P. L. XI. 269.

(2) the abode of God and the angels and the final abode of the blessed : P. L. III. 478 ; *eternal Paradise of rest* : P. L. XII. 314.

(*b*) the final abode after death ; *the Paradise of Fools* : P. L. III. 496.

(3) the earth after the second coming of Christ ; *Earth shall be all Paradise* : P. L. XII. 464.

(4) a state of bliss due to reconciliation with God brought about by Christ ; *sing recovered Paradise to all mankind* : P. R. I. 3 ; *regained lost Paradise* : P. R. IV. 608 ; *a fairer Paradise is founded now* : P. R. IV. 613.

(5) a place compared to Paradise, a place of supreme bliss ; *in heavenly paradises dwell* : P. L. V. 500 ; *Man placed in a paradise* : P. L. X. 484 ; a state of supreme bliss ; *shalt possess `a Paradise within thee* : P. L. XII. 587.

Paradox, *sb.* a proposition involving an apparent contradiction or absurdity : P. R. IV. 234.

Paragon, *vb. tr.* to compare, parallel : P. L. X. 426.

Parallax, *sb.* the apparent displacement of an object observed, caused by the actual change of position of the observer : P. R. IV. 40.

Parallel, *adj.* lying in the same plane but never meeting : P. L. V. 141.

Paramount, *sb.* one highest in rank and power : P. L. II. 508.

Paramour, *sb.* lover ; *fig., Nature ... to wanton with the Sun, her lusty paramour* : N. O. 36.

Paranymph, *sb.* the particular friend of the bridegroom who went with him to bring home his bride : S. A. 1020.

Parasite, *sb.* a sycophant ; *a fawning parasite* : P. R. I. 452.

Parch, *vb. tr.* to dry up, scorch ; *the ... sword of God ... began to parch that temperate clime* : P. L. XII. 636 ; *parched with scalding thirst* : P. L. X. 556.

part. adj. **parching,** shrivelling or withering with çold ; *parching air* : P. L. II. 594 ; *wind* : L. 13.

Pard, *sb.* leopard : P. L. IV. 344.

See **Mountain-pard.**

Pardon, I. *sb.* (1) the overlooking of an offence and the treatment of the offender as if it had not been committed : S. A. 771, 814 ; *such pardon ... as I give my folly* : S. A. 825 ; *my pardon no way assured* : S. A. 738.

(*b*) the forgiveness of sin granted by God : P. L. IV. 80 ; V. 848 ; S. A. 521, 1171 ; *pardon beg* or *begged* : P. L. X. 1089, 1101 ; *infinite in pardon was my Judge* : P. L. XI. 167.

(2) the remission of sin granted by the Roman Catholic Church : P. L. III. 492.

(3) courteous indulgence, allowance : V. Ex. 7.

II. *vb. absol.* to grant forgiveness : Ps. LXXXVI. 14.

Parent, *sb.* (1) a father or mother; *pl.* : P. L. I. 393 ; X. 904 ; S. A. 25, 220, 886, 1487 ; *the Ionian gods ... Heaven and Earth, their boasted parents* : P. L. I. 510 ; *sing.,* used of Sin as the mother of Death : P. L. II. 805 ; of Satan as the father of Sin and Death : P. L. X. 331, 354.

(*b*) a progenitor; used of Adam and Eve : P. L. XII. 638 ; *our first parents* : P. L. IV. 6 ; *our two first parents* : P. L. III. 65 ; *our grand Parents* : P. L. I. 29.

(2) author, source; *Parent of good* : P. L. V. 153.

Parentage, *sb.* extraction, birth ; *low of parentage* : P. R. I. 235.

Parle, *sb.* discussion : P. L. VI. 296; a conference to settle disputed points : P. R. IV. 529 ; *let weakness, then, with weakness come to parle* (*see* come) : S. A. 785.

Parley, *sb.* speech ; *blandished parleys* : S. A. 403 ; conversation ; *Echo ... sweet Queen of Parley* : C. 241.

Parliament, *sb.* the supreme legislative body of Great Britain : S. X. 5 ; F. of C. 15.

Parricide, *sb.* a murderer of a father : S. A. 832.

Parsimonious, *adj.* thrifty, frugal ; *the parsimonious emmet* : P. L. VII. 485.

Part, I. *sb.* (1) division of a whole ; a piece, portion, division, quantity or number taken from the whole or considered by itself : P. L. VIII. 138 ; *the third part of Heaven's sons* or *host* : P. L. II.

692 ; V. 710 ; *a third part of the Gods* : P. L. VI. 156 ; *the greatest part of mankind* : P. L. I. 367 ; *far the greater part* : P. L. VII. 145 ; *the other part* : P. L. XI. 431 ; *her other part* : P. L. VIII. 139 ; *that part* : S. A. 1463 ; *each ... part* : P. L. III. 584 ; *the moral part* : P. L. XII. 298.

(*b*) without the article : P. L. II. 528, 531 ; III. 595 ; VI. 516, 519 ; VII. 293, 403, 410, 425 ; IX. 72 ; XI. 430, 643 ; XII. 230, 231, 336 ; *another part* : P. L. II. 570 ; *his ... wrath whose thou feel'st as yet least part* : P. L. X. 951 ; *most part* : P. R. III. 232 ; *far greater part* : P. L. XII. 533 ; *not all parts like* : P. L. III. 593 ; with *of* : *of his kingdom lose no part* : P. L. II. 325 ; *of that same fruit held part* : P. L. V. 83 ; *of sapience no small part* : P. L. IX. 1018 ; *part of our sentence* : P. L. X. 1031 ; *part of what I suffer* : P. R. II. 248 ; *part of my soul* : P. L. IV. 487.

(2) a portion of the body of man or angel : P. L. I. 194 ; IX. 1093 ; X. 886 ; S. A. 624 ; *some, each part* : P. L. VIII. 534 ; IX. 673 ; *every part* : P. L. VI. 345 ; S. A. 93 ; *in what part* : S. A. 48, 394, 395 ; *all parts* : S. A. 96 ; C. 72 ; *those middle parts* : P. L. IX. 1097 ; *those mysterious parts* : P. L. IV. 312 ; *the inward parts* : C. 466 ; *the inner man, the nobler part* : P. R. II. 477 ; of the body of an animal ; *his hinder parts* : P. L. VII. 465.

(3) a portion, a share : P. L. XI. 765 ; *as thou hast part* : P. L. IX. 879 ; *to give ye part with me* : S. A. 1453 ; *sole part of all these joys* : P. L. IV. 411.

(*b*) lot in life ; *the better part with Mary and with Ruth* : S. IX. 5.

(4) a person's share in some action, function, duty : P. L. I. 267 ; VI. 565 ; *our better part remains to work* : P. L. I. 645 ; *Nature! she hath done her part* : P. L. VIII. 561 ; *Nature ... her part was done* : N. O. 105 ; *God ... hath done his part* : P. L. IX. 375 ; *to do my part* : S. A. 1217.

(*b*) *on the part of,* as regards the share in the action of : P. L. IX. 7, 8 ; *on my part,* as far as I am concerned : P. L. X. 817.

(5) an assumed character : P. L. IX. 667; rôle as in the drama : P. L. X. 155. P. R. II. 240.

(6) the melody assigned to one of the voices in a concerted piece of music : P. L. III. 371.

(7) a portion of a territory, region, quarter : P. L. VI. 354 ; *in other part* : P. L. XI. 564, 660 ; *met from all parts* : S. A. 1656.

(8) side in a contract or contest : P. L. IV. 63 ; VI. 413 ; *to our part loss* : P. L. II. 770 ; *on my part* : P. R. III. 399.

(9) **in part**, partly, to some extent, to some degree : P. L. II. 380 ; IV. 670 ; V. 405 ; IX. 1119 ; X. 716 ; XI. 513 ; S. A. 72, 681 ; *in some part* : S. A. 746.

II. *vb.* (1) *tr.* (*a*) to separate, sunder ; *him ... parted ... from thy orbicular World* : P. L. X. 380 ; *from thy state mine never shall be parted* : P. L. IX. 916 ; *from life ... parted* : Ps. LXXXVIII. 17.

(*b*) to form a boundary between : P. L. II. 660 ; *the brook that parts Egypt from Syrian ground* : P. L. I. 420.

(2) *intr.* (*a*) to depart, go away ; *part hence* or *thence* : P. L. IV. 872 ; S. A. 1229, 1447, 1481 ; C. 56.

(*b*) to go away from each other : P. L. IV. 784 ; V. 252 ; VIII. 652 ; IX. 848 ; in elliptical phrase ; *since to part*, since we are to part, or since you are about to depart : P. L. VIII. 645.

part from, to separate or go away from, leave : P. L. XI. 282 ; *was I never to have parted from thy side* : P. L. IX. 1153 ; *with God not parted from him* : S. A. 1719 ; *Faith and Love, which parted from thee never* : S. XIV. 1 ; to give up, surrender : P. R. III. 155 ; *from that right to part* : S. A. 1056 ; *to part from truth* : P. R. I. 472.

part with, to give up, surrender : P. R. IV. 161.

part. adj. (*a*) **parting**, going away, departing : P. L. IX. 276 ; N. O. 186 ; setting ; *the parting sun* : P. L. VIII. 630.

(*b*) **parted**, arranged with a line of division between the parts ; *his parted forelock* : P. L. IV. 302.

vbl. sb. **parting**; (*a*) the mutual separation of two persons : P. L. IV. 1003.

(*b*) departure; *our parting hence* : P. L. XII. 590.

Partake, *sb.* (*pret.* partook ; *past part.* partaken) (1) *tr.* to have a part or share in : S. A. 1455 ; *this enterprise none shall partake with me* : P. L. II. 466 ; *partake his punishment* ; P. L. VI. 903 ; *partake full happiness with me* : P. L. IX. 818.

(*b*) to eat or drink of : P. R. II. 277 ; *with him partook rural repast* : P. L. IX. 3.

(*c*) to be informed of ; *let her partake with thee what thou hast heard* : P. L. XII. 598.

(*d*) to participate in, enjoy ; *partake the season* : P. L. IX. 199.

(2) *intr.* to have a portion or lot in common with others ; *to partake with us* : P. L. II. 374 ; *with me I see not who partakes* : P. L. VIII. 364.

(*b*) to take and eat food : P. L. V. 75.

part. adj. **partaken**, shared : C. 741.

Partaker, *sb.* one who takes a part of : P. L. IV. 731.

Parthenope, *sb.* one of the Sirens : C. 879.

Parthian, *adj.* of or pertaining to Parthia or the Parthian Empire : P. R. III. 290, 299, 362 ; IV. 73.

absol. the Parthian, the Parthian king or the Parthian Empire : P. R. III. 294, 363, 369 : IV. 85.

Partial, *adj.* biased in favour of oneself : P. L. II. 552.

Participate, *vb.* (1) *tr.* to have a share in ; *participate all rational delight* : P. L. VIII. 390.

(*b*) to partake of ; *participating god-like food* : P. L. IX. 717.

(2) *intr.* to have a share in common with others ; with *in* : S. A. 1507.

(*b*) to share food *with* : P. L. V. 494.

Particular, *adj.* circumstantial, detailed : S. A. 1595.

Partition, *sb.* (*a*) that by which different parts are separated : P. L. VII. 267.

(*b*) compartment ; *man ... lodged in a small partition* : P. L. VIII. 105.

Partly, *adv.* in some measure, not wholly : P. R. I. 262.

Partner, *sb.* sharer : P. L. IV. 411 ; *the partner of my life* : P. L. X.

128 ; *partners in my love*: S. A.
810.

See **Co-partner.**

Party, *sb.* side in a contest : P. L.
II. 368.

Pass, *vb.* (*pret.* passed ; *past part.*
passed and past ; *perfect* formed
with the auxiliary *have* : P. L. v.
554, 675, 754 ; IX. 1144 ; X. 227 ;
P. R. II. 106, 245 ; S. A. 811 ;
with *be* : P. L. IV. 160 ; VI. 699,
895 ; L. 132) I. *intr.* (1) to go on,
proceed : P. L. III. 498 ; with *on* :
P. L. IV. 319, 689 ; VII. 432 ; C.
430 ; *to and fro* : P. L. II. 1031 ;
III. 534 ; *hand in hand* : P. L. IV.
321, 689.

(2) to proceed *to* (a place or
destination) : P. R. III. 439 ; Ps.
CXIV. 3 ; Ariosto II. 1 ; *them that
pass down to the dismal pit* ; Ps.
LXXXVIII. 13 ; *passes to bliss* ; S.
IX. 13.

(3) to travel : P. R. I. 322.

(4) to undergo change ; *I was
then passing to my former state* :
P. L. VIII. 290.

(5) to go away or depart *from* :
P. L. I. 487 ; *from amidst them
forth he passed* : P. L. v. 903.

(6) to go by : P. L. IX. 452 ; X.
714 ; C. 302 ; L. 21 ; *let a ...
maiden pass* : C. 402 ; *I named
them as they passed* : P. L. VIII.
352.

(7) to elapse, come to an end :
P. L. VII. 253 ; XI. 600 ; *two
days are ... passed* : P. L. VI. 699 ;
thus passed the night : P. R. IV.
426.

(*b*) of things in time ; to slip
by ; *passed unnoticed* : P. L. IX.
231 ; to cease ; *the dread voice is
past* : L. 132.

(8) to go through, obtain passage : P. L. II. 438, 1023 ; XII.
196 ; Ps. CXXXVI 50 ; to enter
heaven : P. L. III. 480.

(*b*) to go over ; *this Lethean
sound ... as they pass* : P. L. II.
606.

(9) to be accepted or allowed :
S. A. 811.

(10) to take place, occur, happen : P. L. v. 554 ; VI. 895 ; VIII.
173 ; X. 227 ; P. R. II. 106 ; *bring
to pass* : V. Ex. 72 ; *come* or *came
to pass* : P. L. X. 38 ; S. A. 444 ;
V. Ex. 45.

(11) to be executed : *the mortal
sentence pass* : P. L. X. 48.

II. *tr.* (1) to go by : P. L. III.
481 ; IV. 160 ; v. 291 ; to escape
the notice of in going by ; *in at
this gate none pass the vigilance
here placed* : P. L. IV. 579.

(2) to go through or over : P.
L. I. 352 ; II. 438 ; v. 754 ; *regions
they passed* : P. L. v. 748 ; *all
path ... that passes that way* : P. L.
IV. 177 ; *these gates ... which none
can pass* : P. L. II. 776 ; *passing
now the ford* : P. L. XII. 130.

(3) to be spoken by : P. L. IX.
1144 ; *what decree ... hath passed
the lips of Heaven's Almighty* : P.
L. v. 675.

(4) to live through, spend : P.
L. v. 31 ; P. R. I. 303 ; II. 245 ;
to pass commodiously this life : P.
L. X. 1083.

(5) to pledge ; *thy word is
passed* : P. L. III. 227.

In combination with other
words ; (*a*) **pass away,** to cease
to be : N. O. 139.

(*b*) **pass by** ; to go over : C.
539 ; to go past : P. L. IX. 849.

(*c*) **let pass,** to allow to slip by
without taking any advantage or
notice of ; *not to let the occasion
pass* ; P. L. v. 453 ; *not let pass
occasion* : P. L. IX. 479 ; *let pass
no advantage* : P. R. II. 233 ; *glory
... let it pass* : P. R. III. 151 ; *let
pass ... the kingdoms of this world* :
P. R. IV. 209.

(*d*) **pass through,** to go from
side to side or end to end of,
traverse : P. L. IV. 225 ; VI. 330 ;
X. 443 ; Ps. LXXXI. 19 ; *through
gates, doors,* etc. : P. L. II. 684,
886, 1017 ; X. 233, 419 ; XI. 16 ;
through the high streets : S. A.
1458 ; *I passed through ways* : P.
L. v. 50 ; *through glade, vale* :
P. L. II. 619 ; C. 79 ; Ps. LXXXIV.
21 ; *through the spheres of watchful fire* : V. Ex. 40 ; *through fire* :
P. L. I. 395 ; *through all the Hierarchies intends to pass* : P. L. v.
693.

part. adj. **past** ; (*a*) gone by,
done with, over ; predicatively
after *be* ; *the bitterness of death is
past* : P. L. XI. 158 ; *that care
now is past* : P. L. XI. 776 ; *my
riddling days are past* : S. A.
1064 ; *that past* : P. L. X. 341.

(*b*) belonging to a former time,
that is gone, passed away ; *past
ages* : P. L. III. 328 ; *past ex-*

ample : P. L. x. 840 ; following the sb.: P. L. iv. 762 ; 932 ; xii. 14, 604 ; P. R. i. 300 ; S. A. 685 ; *day, ages, times past* : P. L. v. 33 ; P. R. iii. 294 ; S. A. 22 ; *deeds long past* : P. L. v. 113 ; *knowledge past* : P. L. i. 628.

vbl. sb. **passing**, the going over or across : P. R. iii. 436 ; *the difficulty of passing back* : P. L. x. 252.

Passage, *sb.* (*a*) the action of going from one place to another: P. L. x. 260.

(*b*) transition from this life to the next ; *thy mortal passage* : P. L. xi. 366.

(*c*) opportunity or right to pass : P. L. xi. 122 ; *to have their passage out*, to be allowed to pass out ; V. Ex. 24.

(*d*) a way leading from one place to another, road, path, route : P. L. iii. 528 ; iv. 232 ; x. 304 ; *I toiled out my uncouth passage* : P. L. x. 475 ; *secret passage find to the inmost mind* : S. A. 610 ; a way to death ; *these painful passages* : P. L. xi. 528.

Passenger, *sb.* wayfarer, traveller : C. 39.

Passing, *adv.* very, exceedingly : P. L. xi. 717 : P. R. ii. 155.

Passion, *sb.* (**1**) powerful feeling, intense emotion: P. L. ii. 564 ; ix. 667 ; *inward* : S. A. 1006 ; *holy* : Il P. 41 ; *all passion spent* : S. A. 1758 ; *each passion ... ire, envy, and despair* : P. L. iv. 114 ; pity or sorrow: P. L. i. 605.

(*b*) *pl.*: P. R. ii. 467 ; iv. 266 ; *foul, upstart, lawless* : P. L. iv. 571 ; xii. 88 ; P. R. ii. 472 ; *high passions—anger, hate*, etc.: P. L. ix. 1123.

(*c*) an outburst of passion ; *his bursting passion into plaints thus poured* : P. L. ix. 98 ; *some fit of passion* : P. L. x. 627 ; *in a troubled sea of passion tost* : P. L. x. 718 ; *his fierce passion* : P. L. x. 865.

(**2**) sexual desire : P. L. viii. 530, 585, 588 ; *wanton passions* : P. L. i. 454, rather in a weaker sense, amorous feeling, love: P. L. viii. 635.

Passive, *adj.* unresisting, submissive : P. L. iii. 110 ; *fig.*, *the passive air upbore their nimble tread* : P. L. vi. 72.

Past, (**1**) *sb.* time preceding the present ; without the art. : P. L. ix. 926 ; *past, present, and future*: P. L. v. 582 ; what happened in the past : P. L. iii. 78.

(**2**) *prep.* (*a*) further on than: P. L. ix. 628.

(*b*) beyond the reach and compass of : P. L. iii. 62 ; *past shame, hope, cure* : P. R. iv. 342 ; S. A. 120, 912 ; *past thy preventing* : P. R. iv. 492.

Pastime, *sb.* amusement, diversion : P. L. viii. 375 ; *pl.* sports, games: C. 121.

Pastoral, *adj.* of or pertaining to shepherds : *pastoral reed* : P. L. xi. 132 ; C. 345.

Pastry, *sb.* the crust of a pie : P. R. ii. 343.

Pasture, (**1**) *sb.* (*a*) ground on which cattle or other beasts graze : P. R. iii. 260 ; L. 193.

(*b*) food taken by grazing : P. L. iv. 351 : *fig.*, *graze the seaweed, their pasture* : P. L. vii. 404.

(**2**) *vb. intr.* to graze : P. L. vii. 462 ; xi. 653.

part. adj. **pasturing**, grazing : P. L. ix. 1109.

Paternal, *adj.* of or by a father ; *paternal rule* : P. L. xii. 24 ; characteristic of a father : P. L. xi. 353.

(*b*) of his own father ; *the omnific Word ... on the wings of Cherubim uplifted, in paternal glory rode* : P. L. vii. 219.

(*c*) that is a father ; *Paternal Deity* : P. L. vi. 750.

Path, *sb.* (*a*) track, footway : P. L. ii. 976 ; ix. 244 ; xi. 371 ; P. R. i. 322 ; C. 37, 569 ; *all path of man or beast* : P. L. iv. 177 ; *to found a path over this main*: P. L. x. 256.

(*b*) a course of action or conduct: P. L. xi. 631 ; *the path of truth* : P. L. vi. 173 ; *paths of righteousness* : P. L. xi. 814 : *the path to Heaven* : C. 303.

See **Sea-path**.

Pathless, *adj.* having no footway, untrodden: P. R. i. 296 ; *heaven's wide pathless way* : Il P. 70.

Patience, *sb.* (*a*) a calm and composed temper in grief or suffering : P. L. ii. 569 ; vi. 464 : S. A. 1287 ; D. F. I. 75 ; *thy wrongs with saintly patience borne* : P. R.

III. 93; *the better fortitude of patience* : P. L. IX. 32; *extolling patience as the truest fortitude* : S. A. 654; *those whom patience finally must crown* :. S. A. 1296; *personified* : S. XIX. 8.

(*b*) forbearance with others: P. L. XI. 361; S. A. 755.

(*c*) calmness in waiting for something : P. R. II. 102.

(*d*) steadfastness or constancy in the midst of trial or suffering : P. L. XII. 583; P. R. I. 426; III. 92; C. 971.

Patient, *adj.* bearing evils or suffering with calmness and fortitude : S. A. 1623; *O patient Son of God* : P. R. IV. 420; *patient Job* : P. R. III. 95.

Patiently, *adj.* calmly, submissively, meekly : P. L. XI. 112, 287, 551; P. R. II. 432.

Patriarch, *sb.* the progenitor of a tribe or race : P. L. IV. 762; *spec.* Adam : P. L. V. 506; IX. 376; Noah : P. L. XII. 117; Abraham : P. L. XII. 151.

Patrimony, *sb.* heritage : P. L. X. 818 : P. R. III. 428 : S. A. 1482.

Patron, *sb.* (*a*) a protector; *patrons of mankind* : P. L. XI. 696.

(*b*) an advocate; *on Man's behalf patron ... none appeared* : P. L. III. 219.

(*c*) a defender; *patron of liberty* : P. L. IV. 958.

Patroness, *sb.* a female tutelary deity; *fig., Night, best patroness of grief* : P. 29; the muse Urania; *my celestial Patroness* : P. L. IX. 21.

Pattern, *sb.* a model deserving imitation : P. L. VII. 487.

Paul, *sb.* the apostle to the Gentiles : F. of C. 10.

Pause, (1) *sb.* a temporary stop in action : P. L. III. 561; VI. 162; in speaking : P. L. V. 562.

(2) *vb. intr.* (*a*) to intermit action for a short time : P. L. V. 64; IX. 744; to intermit speech : P. L. XII. 2, 466.

(*b*) to wait, rest : S. XXI. 7.

Pave, *vb. tr.* to cover with a pavement : P. L. II. 1026; X. 473.

See **Coral-paven, Star-paved.**

Pavement, *sb.* the hard solid surface-covering of a floor or road : P. L. I. 726; III. 363; *the riches of Heaven's pavement, trodden gold* : P. L. I. 682; *through Heaven ... a*

broad and ample road, whose dust is gold, and pavement stars : P. L. VII. 578.

Pavilion, (1) *sb.* tent : P. L. V. 653; *fig., the throne of Chaos, and his dark pavilion spread wide on the wasteful Deep* : P. L. II. 960.

(2) *vb. tr.* to fill with tents : P. L. XI. 215.

Paw, (1) *sb.* the foot of a beast having nails or claws; of a lion, tiger, wolf : P. L. IV. 343, 408; L. 128; S. XVI. 13.

(2) *vb. intr.* to strike with the paw : P. L. VII. 464.

Pay, *vb.* (*pret.* and *past part.* paid) *tr.* (*a*) to hand over the amount of, give money in discharge of : S. A. 1477; *fig.*: P. L. III. 246; *thy ransom paid* : P. L. XII. 424; *that rigid score* : S. A. 432; *pay the rigid satisfaction* : P. L. III. 211; *Death ... hath paid his ransom* : S. A. 1573.

(*b*) to reward, requite : P. L. XI. 452 : *pay my underminers in their coin* : S. A. 1204.

(*c*) to give, render : *pay thee fealty* or *homage* : P. L. VIII. 344; P. R. II. 375; *pay him thanks* : P. L. IV. 47; *his praise due paid* : C. 776; *obedience* : P. L. III. 107; *to Rome obedience pay* : P. R. IV. 80.

absol. to render gratitude : P. L. IV. 53, 56.

(*d*) to discharge, perform; *paid their vows* : P. L. I. 441; *their orisons, each morning duly paid* : P. L. V. 145; *spent in worship, paid to whom we hate* : P. L. II. 248.

(*e*) to suffer, undergo : P. L. X. 1026; *pay on my punishment* : S. A. 489.

(*f*) *pay for,* to atone for; *some blood more precious must be paid for Man* : P. L. XII. 293.

Paynim, *sb.* a pagan : P. R. III. 343.

Peace, I. *sb.* (1) a state of national tranquillity, freedom from war, cessation of hostilities : P. L. I. 660; II. 228, 292, 329, 332; XI. 781; P. R. III. 91; S. XVI. 10; *terms of peace* : P. L. II. 331; *weeds of peace* : L'A. 120; *peace to corrupt no less than war* : P. L. XI. 784; *she strikes a universal peace through sea and land* : N. O. 52.

(*b*) a time of peace ; *works of peace* : P. R. III. 80 ; *in peace* : P. L. XI. 796.

(2) public order and security ; *dwell long time in peace* : P. L. XII. 23 ; *public peace* : P. L. XII. 317 ; *who first broke peace in Heaven* : P. L. II. 690 ; *thou disturbed Heaven's blessed peace* : P. L. VI. 267 ; or in sense (1) : S. XVII. 5.

(3) friendly relations between individuals, harmony, concord : P. L. XII. 355 ; S. A. 1073, 1074 ; Ps. VII. 10 ; *comes he in peace* : S. A. 1070 ; *between us two let there be peace* : P. L. X. 924 ; *household peace* : P. L. X. 908 ; *in their dwellings peace* : P. L. VII. 183 ; *suing for peace* : S. A. 966 ; between God and man : P. L. III. 263 ; N. O. 7 ; between God and Satan : P. L. IV. 104.

(*b*) nearer in meaning to : pardon, mercy : P. L. X. 938 ; *besought his peace* : P. L. X. 913 ; *the smell of peace toward Mankind* : P. L. XI. 38 ; *betokening peace from God* : P. L. XI. 867.

(*c*) the author of peace ; *O thou ... the only peace found out for mankind* : P. L. III. 274.

(4) an undisturbed state, usually of the mind, quiet, tranquillity, calmness : P. L. IX. 1126 ; XI. 815 ; S. A. 1049 ; *where peace and rest can never dwell* : P. L. I. 65 ; definitely of the mind : P. L. IX. 981 ; S. A. 1757 ; *find peace within* : P. L. IX. 333 ; *be at peace within* : Ps. IV. 22 ; *to their thoughts firm peace recovered* : P. L. V. 210 ; *peace returned home to my breast* : P. L. XI. 153 ; *peace of thought* : P. L. XII. 558 ; *of conscience* : P. L. XII. 296 ; *my conscience and internal peace* : S. A. 1334 ; *in peace* : P. L. XI. 117, 507 ; S. XVII. 14 ; Ps. IV. 37 ; *in calm and sinless peace* : P. R. IV. 425 ; *the sweet peace that goodness bosoms ever* : C. 368.

(*b*) *personified* : Il P. 45.

(*c*) secure tranquillity; used in expressions of well-wishing or salutation : S. A. 1445 ; M. W. 48 ; *bid fair peace be to my sable shroud* : L. 22.

(5) used with a blending of two or more of the above senses : P. L. XI. 667 ; N. O. 63 ; S. XVI. 4 ;

God proclaiming peace, yet live in hatred ... and levy cruel wars : P. L. II. 499 ; *war so near the peace of God in bliss* : P. L. VII. 55 ; *preserve freedom and peace to men* : P. L. XI. 580 ; *New Earth ... founded in ... peace* : P. L. XII. 550 ; used quibblingly : P. L. VI. 560, 617.

personified : S. 16 ; *the meek-eyed Peace* : N. O. 46 ; *peace shall lull him in her flowery lap* : V. Ex. 84.

(6) *hold my, his, thy peace* : P. L. X. 135; Ps. LXXXIII. 2; Eurip. 4. *See* **Hold.**

II. *vb. intr.* to be silent or calm ; *imper.* : P. L. VII. 216 ; S. A. 60 ; C. 359.

Peaceable, *adj.* disposed to peace : P. R. III. 76.

Peaceful, *adj.* (*a*) making for peace, friendly : P. L. X. 946.

(*b*) full of peace, free from strife, calm, tranquil ; *peaceful counsels* : P. L. II. 279 ; *sloth* : P. L. II. 227 ; *days, night* : P. L. XI. 600 ; N. O. 61 ; *end* : S. A. 709 ; *hermitage* : Il P. 168.

Peal, (1) *sb.* a loud outburst of sound ; used of the sound of a trumpet : P. L. III. 329 ; of the barking of dogs ; *rung a hideous peal* : P. L. II. 656 ; of a volley of words : S. A. 906 ; *a peal of words* : S. A. 235.

(2) *vb. tr.* to din or assail ; *nor was his ear less pealed with noises loud* : P. L. II. 920.

part. adj. **pealing,** giving out loud sounds ; *the pealing organ* : Il P. 161.

Pearl, *sb.* (*a*) the white and shining body secreted within the shell of various bivalve mollusks ; *sing. collect.* : P. L. II. 4 ; *orient pearl* : P. L. IV. 238 ; *studs of pearl* : P. R. IV. 120 ; *a bright sea flowed ... of liquid pearl* : P. L. III. 519.

(*b*) a drinking vessel made of pearl ; *rubied nectar flows in pearl* : P. L. V. 634.

(*c*) *fig.* drops of dew ; *orient pearl* : P. L. V. 2 ; *pearls of dew* : M. W. 43.

(*d*) something very precious ; *this is got by casting pearl to hogs* : S. XII. 8.

Pearled (*disyl.*), *part. adj.* adorned with pearls : C. 834.

See **Icy-pearled.**

Pearly, *adj.* (*a*) resembling pearls in size or shape : P. L. v. 430.

(*b*) abounding in mother-of-pearl : P. L. VII. 407.

Peasant, *sb.* a rustic, a countryman : P. L. I. 783.

Pebble, *sb.* a small rounded stone : P. R. IV. 330.

Peccant, *adj.* sinning ; *peccant Angels* : P. L. XI. 70.

Peculiar, (1) *adj.* (*a*) that characterizes one as distinct from others, one's own : P. L. v. 15 ; *each man's peculiar load* : P. R. I. 402.

(*b*) independent, individual; *each peculiar power forgoes his wonted seat* : N. O. 196.

(*c*) particular, special ; *chosen of peculiar grace* : P. L. III. 183.

(*d*) *one peculiar nation*, a nation chosen of God for his own people : P. L. XII. 111.

(2) *sb.* that which belongs to one to the exclusion of others, exclusive possession : P. L. VII. 368.

Peel, *vb. tr.* to plunder, spoil ; *peeling their provinces* : P. R. IV. 136.

Peep, *vb. intr.* to look pryingly through a small aperture ; *fig.*, *the nice Morn ...from her cabined loop-hole peep* : C. 140.

Peer, *sb.* (1) an equal in rank : P. L. I. 39 ; v. 812 ; an equal in attainments ; *young Lycidas, and hath not left his peer* : L. 9.

(2) companion, associate : P. L. VI. 127.

(3) a nobleman ; (*a*) of England, an earl : C. 31.

(*b*) one of the twelve peers of France ; *the peers of Charlemain* : P. R. III. 343.

(*c*) one of high rank and power among the followers of Satan : P. L. I. 618 ; P. R. I. 40 ; *Satan and his peers* : P. L. I. 757 ; *the grand Infernal Peers* : P. L. II. 507 ; *the great consulting Peers* : P. L. x. 456 ; in direct address ; *O Peers* : P. L. II. 119, 445.

Peerage, *sb.* the body of peers ; *Charlemain with all his peerage feel* : P. L. I. 586.

Peering, *part. adj.* appearing, coming into view : N. O. 140.

Peerless, *adj.* unequalled : P. L. IV. 608 ; A. 75.

Pegasean, *adj.* of Pegasus, the winged horse of the Muses : P. L. VII. 4.

Pellean (Pelléan), *adj.* from Pella in Macedonia, the birthplace of Alexander the Great : P. R. II. 196.

Pelleas, *sb.* the knight of Arthur's Round Table : P. R. II. 361.

Pellenore, *sb.* the knight of Arthur's Round Table : P. R. II. 361.

Pelops, *sb.* the father of Atreus and the grandfather of Agamemnon : Il P. 99.

Pelorus (Pelórus), *sb.* Cape Faro, the northeastern cape of Sicily : P. L. I. 232.

Pen, *sb.* feather : P. L. VII. 421.

Pen, *vb.* (*pret.* not used ; *past part.* penned : C. 344 ; elsewhere pent) *tr.* (*a*) to confine, shut in ; *with the force of winds and waters pent* : S. A. 1647 ; *one who long in populous city pent* : P. L. IX. 445.

(*b*) to shut up in a fold : C. 344 ; *shepherds pen their flocks* : P. L. IV. 185.

part. adj. **pent** ; (*a*) encased in armour : P. L. VI. 657.

(*b*) shut up in a fold : C. 499.

Penal, *adj.* (*a*) inflicted as punishment : P. L. I. 48.

(*b*) payable as a penalty ; *the penal forfeit* : S. A. 508.

Penalty, *sb.* punishment : P. L. IX. 775 ; x. 15, 753, 1022 ; XI. 197 ; *death is the penalty imposed* : P. L. VII. 545 ; *death, the penalty of thy transgression* : P. L. XII. 399.

on penalty of death, with the liability of incurring death : P. L. XII. 398.

Penance, *sb.* (*a*) penitence : S. A. 738.

(*b*) punishment : P. L. II. 92 ; x. 550.

Pencil, *sb.* an artist's paint-brush ; *by shading pencil drawn* : P. L. III. 509.

Pendent, *adj.* (*a*) hanging, suspended : P. L. I. 727 ; *this pendent World* : P. L. II. 1052.

(*b*) overhanging ; *pendent shade, rock* : P. L. IV. 239 ; x. 313.

Pendulous, *adj.* hanging, suspended ; *the pendulous round Earth* : P. L. IV. 1000.

Penetration, *sb.* the act of penetrating or piercing : P. L. III. 585.

Penitent, (1) *adj.* repentant, contrite : P. L. x. 1097 ; XII. 319 ; P. R. III. 421 ; S. A. 502, 754.

(2) *sb. the penitent*, one who is repentant : S. A. 761.

Pennon, *sb.* a wing ; *rising on stiff pennons* : P. L. VII. 441 ; *fluttering his pennons vain* : P. L. II. 933.

Pensioner, *sb.* a gentleman in the personal service of a king ; *fig.*, *dreams, the fickle pensioners of Morpheus' train* : Il P. 10.

Pensive, *adj.* (*a*) engaged in, or addicted to, earnest and somewhat sorrowful musing : P. L. IV. 173 ; *pensive here I sat alone* : P. L. II. 777 ; *pensive I sat me down* : P. L. VIII. 287 ; *come, pensive Nun* : Il P. 31 ; full of serious or sad thoughts ; *fig.*, *cowslips wan that hang the pensive head* : L. 147.

(*b*) conducive to thoughtfulness; *pensive secrecy of desert cell* : C. 387 ; *pensive trance*, a trance in which the soul is engaged in the contemplation of sorrowful things: P. 42.

Pentateuch, *sb.* the first five books of the Old Testament : P. R. IV. 226.

Penuel, *sb.* a city on or near the river Jabbok. The exact location is uncertain : S. A. 278.

Penurious, *adj.* parsimonious to a fault : C. 726.

People (peoplé : S. A. 1533), I. *sb.* (1) the whole body of persons composing a community or nation : P. L. XII. 181 ; H. B. 10 ; used of the Israelitish nation ; *his, thy, my, that people* : P. L. XII. 171, 309, 483 ; P. R. II. 48 ; IV. 132 ; S. A. 317, 681, 1158, 1533 ; Ps. III. 24 ; LXXX. 20 ; LXXXI. 33, 45, 53, 63 ; LXXXIII. 9 ; LXXXV. 6, 23, 31 ; CXXXVI. 57.

(*b*) the inhabitants collectively; *in multitude the Ethereal people ran* : P. L. X. 27 ; *this day a solemn feast the people hold to Dagon* : S. A. 12.

(*c*) the whole company of persons gathered in one place : S. A. 1473, 1601, 1620.

(2) the commonalty, the populace ; *the people* : P. R. III. 48 ; S. A. 1421 ; *what the people but a herd confused* : P. R. III. 49.

II. *vb. tr.* (*a*) to inhabit ; *fig.*, *the gay motes that people the sunbeams* : Il P. 8.

(*b*) to stock with inhabitants : P. L. X. 889.

See **Victor-people.**

Peor, *sb.* Baal-Peor, the form of Baal worshipped at Mount Peor, a mountain of Moab : P. L. I. 412 ; N. O. 197.

Peræa, *sb.* a region of undefined limits east of the Jordan : P. R. II. 24.

Perceive *vb.* (*pres. 2d sing.* perceiv'st : P. L. VIII. 566) *tr.* to become aware of, gain a knowledge of, discover with the eye or the mind : P. L. I. 335 ; II. 299 ; VI. 19 ; VIII. 41 ; IX. 598 ; P. R. I. 227 ; C. 74 ; with two *acc.*; *perceive thee purposed not to doom frail man* : P. L. III. 404 ; *perceived all set on enmity* : S. A. 1201 : with *acc.* and *prep. inf.*; *I perceive thy mortal sight to fail* : P. L. XII. 8 ; with clause : P. L. VI. 623 ; *I did perceive it was the voice* : C. 563 ; *perceiving how openly ... she purposed to betray me* : S. A. 397 ; *absol.*, *as thou thyself perceiv'st* : P. L. VIII. 566.

Perched, *part. adj.* used as a perch or resting place for birds : S. A. 1693.

Perdition, *sb.* (*a*) utter destruction, ruin : D. F. I. 67.

(*b*) hell : P. L. I. 47 ; the place of the dead, the Hebrew *Abaddon*: Ps. LXXXVIII. 47.

Perfect, I. *adj.* (1) without blemish or defect, lacking in nothing ; *perfect sight* : P. L. IV. 577 ; *beauty* : P. L. IV. 634 ; *good* : P. L. V. 399 ; *diapason* : S. M. 23 ; *Hero* : P. 13 ; *this woman ... thy perfect gift* : P. L. X. 138 ; *what seemed in thee so perfect* : P. L. IX. 1179 ; *thy heart contains of good, wise, just, the perfect shape* : P. R. III. 11 ; *the Stoic ... perfect in himself* : P. R. IV. 302 ; or, possibly, absolutely just ; *perfect witness of all-judging Jove* : L. 82.

(*b*) pure, without alloy ; *perfect gold* : P. L. V. 442.

(*c*) without moral blemish, sinless : P. L. VIII. 642 ; XI. 876 ; *this perfect man* : P. R. I. 166 ; *God made thee perfect* : P. L. V. 524 ; *spirits ... perfect while they stood* : P. L. V. 568.

(2) full, complete, entire ; *perfect forms* : P. L. VII. 455 ; *our bliss full and perfect is* : N. O. 166 ; used of God ; *thou in thyself art perfect* : P. L. VIII. 415.

(*b*) absolute; *perfect thraldom*: S. A. 946.

(*c*) exact; *thy perfect image*: P. L. II. 764.

(*d*) entire, utter; *pain is perfect misery*: P. L. VI. 462; *so perfect is their misery*: C. 73.

(*e*) *life more perfect*, life of higher type: P. L. IX. 689.

(*f*) fit; *the perfect season*: P. R. IV. 468.

(*g*) very plain or distinct; *the tumult ... was ... perfect in my listening ear*: C. 203.

(3) right as regards number or form; *perfect phalanx, ranks*: P. L. I. 550; VI. 71.

(4) sincere, genuine; *tears of perfect moan*: M. W. 55.

(5) real, genuine; *a perfect dove*: P. R. I. 83.

II. *vb. tr.* to make faultless: P. L. XI. 36.

Perfection, *sb.* (1) the highest attainable degree of development or excellence: P. L. V. 472; *Earth ... to receive perfection from the Sun's ... ray*: P. L. IV. 673; *the new-created World ... of absolute perfection*: P. L. X. 483.

(*b*) a high degree of attainment or knowledge: P. R. I. 209.

(2) freedom from blemish or weakness, supreme excellence, completeness; used of persons: P. L. IX. 964; X. 150; *in thee ... what of perfection can in man be found*: P. R. III. 230.

(3) that which brings completeness; said of Eve in relation to Adam: P. L. V. 29.

(4) a quality or endowment of supreme excellence; *pl.*, *complete, absolute*: P. L. V. 353; P. R. II. 138; *thee, adorned with all perfections*: P. L. IX. 1031.

Perfectly, *adv.* absolutely, completely: P. L. IX. 707; T. 15.

Perfidious, *adj.* faithless, treacherous; *perfidious hatred, fraud*: P. L. I. 308; V. 880; used *fig.* of a thing; *that ... perfidious bark*: L. 100.

Perform, *vb. tr.* (*a*) to do, accomplish, achieve, execute: P. L. I. 699; IV. 418; VII. 164; S. A. 1626, 1641; *war wearied hath performed what war can do*: P. L. VI. 695; *thy prodigious might and feats performed*: S. A. 1083; *the exploit performed successfully*: P. R. I. 102.

(*b*) to carry into effect, execute: S. A. 1218; *to perform thy terms*: P. L. X. 750; *nor man the moral part perform*: P. L. XII. 298; *absol.*: P. L. XII. 299.

(*c*) to fulfil, discharge: *perform that office*: D. F. I. 70; *their ministry performed*: P. L. XII. 505; *absol.* to fulfil expectation: P. R. II. 49.

(*d*) to celebrate; *due rites performed*: P. L. XI. 440.

(*e*) to cause, produce; *cold performs the effect of fire*: P. L. II. 595.

vbl. sb. **performing**, the act of putting into execution: P. L. XI. 300.

Performance, *sb.* deed, achievement: P. L. X. 502.

Perfume (perfúme) *sb.* sweet odour, fragrance: P. L. IV. 158; *odorous*: S. A. 720; *rich distilled*: C. 556.

*****Perhaps**, *adv.* possibly, perchance: P. L. I. 166, 655; II. 70, 362, 835; III. 588; IV. 791; VI. 616; VII. 85; VIII. 77, 205; IX. 139, 610, 928; P. R. II. 452; III. 430; S. A. 112.

Peril, *sb.* danger, hazard; *peril great*: P. L. IX. 922; X. 469; *with peril*: P. L. I. 276; *suffer peril*: C. 40.

Perilous, *adj.* (*a*) full of danger; *perilous wilds, flood*: C. 424; L. 185.

(*b*) attended with or involving danger; *perilous attempt, enterprises*: P. L. II. 420; S. A. 804; *edge of battle*: P. L. I. 276.

Period, *sb.* (*a*) an epoch or age: P. L. II. 603; *the World's great period*: P. L. XII. 467.

(*b*) a complete sentence: C. 585.

Peripatetic, *sb. pl.* the followers of Aristotle collectively as a school of philosophy: P. R. IV. 279.

Perish, *vb. tr.* (*a*) to be destroyed; *as far as Gods ... can perish*: P. L. I. 139; *the Spirit of Man ... cannot together perish with this corporeal clod*: P. L. X. 785; to come to naught; *those thoughts ... to perish*: P. L. II. 149.

(*b*) to cease to live, die: S. A. 676, 1512; Ps. II. 26; LXXX. 67; to die both a physical and moral death; *in him* (Adam) *perish all men*: P. L. III. 287.

Permission, *sb.* liberty granted, allowance, leave: P. L. I. 212;

IX. 378 ; *do as thou find'st permission from above* : P. R. I. 496 :
thou hast permission on me : P. R.
IV. 175.

Permissive, *adj.* (*a*) that allows permission, unhindering : P. L. III.
685.

(*b*) permitted, allowed ; *permissive freedom, glory* : P. L. VIII.
435 ; X. 451.

Permit, *vb.* (1) *tr.* (*a*) to intrust,
commit : P. L. XI. 554.

(*b*) to suffer or allow to be or
to come to pass : P. L. VI. 674 :
with *acc.* and *dat.* ; *permitting
him ... venial discourse* : P. L. IX.
4 ; with *dat.* and *prep. inf.* :
P. L. XII. 90 ; P. R. I. 483 ;
S. A. 1159, 1495 ; in passive ; *their
lost shape, permitted, they resume* :
P. L. X. 574 ; *the kingdoms of the
world to thee were given! permitted
rather* : P. R. IV. 183 : with *prep.
inf.* ; *thy Lord longer in this Paradise to dwell permits not* : P. L.
XI. 260.

(2) *absol.* or *intr.* to give leave
or permission : P. L. IV. 1009 ;
IX. 885 ; 1159 ; to be favourable,
give opportunity ; *if the air will
not permit* : Il P. 77.

Pernicious, *adj.* destructive, harmful : S. A. 1400 ; *fire* : P. L. VI.
849 ; *fallen such a pernicious
highth* : P. L. I. 282 ; *a fact pernicious to thy peace* : P. L. IX.
981 : full of or fraught with destruction : P. L. VI. 520.

Perpetual (1) *adj.* (*a*) continuing or
continued without intermission :
P. L. IV. 760 ; *perpetual inroads,
fight* : P. L. II. 103 ; VI. 693 ;
storms : P. L. II. 588 ; *feast* : C.
479 ; *agony* : P. L. II. 861 ; *circle,
round* : P. L. V. 182 ; VI. 6 ; or
the meaning may be : that holds
everywhere, universal ; *Heaven's
perpetual king* : P. L. I. 131.

(*b*) to continue forever, everlasting : P. L. XI. 108 ; N. O. 7.

(2) *adv.* continually, always :
P. L. VII. 306 ; X. 679.

Perpetuity, *sb.* eternity : P. L. X.
813.

Perplex, (pérplexed : C. 37) *vb. tr.*
(*a*) to make tangled or involved ;
*the undergrowth ... had perplexed
all path of man* : P. L. IV. 176.

(*b*) to render confused or obscure ; *to perplex ... counsels* : P.
L. II. 114.

(*c*) to trouble with suspense,
anxiety, or uncertainty ; distract :
P. L. I. 599 ; II. 525 ; IX. 19 ; XII.
274 ; P. R. IV. 1.

part. adj. (*a*) **perplexing,** dis-
tracting : P. L. VIII. 183.

(*b*) **perplexed,** tangled, involved : C. 37.

Perplexity, *sb.* bewilderment, dis-
traction of mind : P. R. II. 38 ;
pl. : S. A. 304.

Persecute, *vb. intr.* to harass or
afflict others : Ps. VII. 50.

Persecution, *sb.* the infliction of pain
or death as a punishment for adhering to a religious creed : P. L.
XII. 531.

Persecutor, *sb.* one who afflicts
others on account of religious
principles : P. L. XII. 497.

Persepolis, *sb.* the capital of Persia
Proper and the chief capital of
the Persian Empire under Cyrus :
P. R. III. 284.

Perseverance, *sb.* persistency, constancy : P. R. I. 148.

Persevere, *vb. intr.* (*a*) to persist in
what is begun, be steadfast : P.
L. V. 525 ; XII. 532.

(*b*) to remain steadfastly ; *and
persevere upright* : P. L. VII. 632.

vbl. sb. **persevering,** constancy :
P. L. VIII. 639.

Persian, *adj.* of Persia ; *the Persian
bay*, the Persian Gulf : P. R. III.
273.

absol. the Persian, the king of
Persia : P. L. XI. 393.

Persist, *vb. tr.* (*a*) to continue
steadily in one course of action :
P. L. III. 197 ; IX. 377.

(*b*) to continue to be, remain ;
persisted happy : P. L. X. 874 ;
deaf : S. A. 249.

Person, *sb.* (1) a character as in the
drama : P. L. X. 156 ; P. R. II. 240.

(2) a human being, an individual : P. L. IX. 41, 444 ; S. A.
1211 ; *a person separate to God* :
S. A. 31 ; *a private person* : S. A.
1208.

(3) bodily form, external appearance : S. XXIII. 11 ; *a fairer
person* : P. L. II. 110.

(*b*) *in person*, with bodily presence, not by representative : S.
A. 851.

(*c*) body ; *lest some ill-greeting
touch attempt the person of our
unowned sister* : C. 406.

Personate, *vb. tr.* to represent or to

celebrate; *in fable, hymn, or song, so personating their gods* : P. R. IV. 341.

Persuade, *vb.* (1) *tr.* (*a*) to urge the acceptance of, advise ; *persuade immediate war* : P. L. II. 121.

(*b*) to prevail upon by argument or entreaty : P. L. IX. 979 ; with *acc.* and *prep. inf.*: P. R. III. 44.

(**2**) *refl.* to convince oneself ; *I persuade me,* I am convinced : S. A. 586 ; with clause : S. A. 1495 ; D. F. I. 29.

Persuader, *sb.* that which influences one to action : P. L. IX. 587.

Persuasion, *sb.* (*a*) the act of influencing the mind of another by argument, or by an appeal to the feelings: P. R. I. 223 ; *ruling them by persuasion* : P. R. 230.

(*b*) a reason or argument that influences the mind : S. A. 658.

(*c*) settled opinion, conviction, belief ; *persuasion in me grew* : P. L. XI. 152 ; *deceive you to persuasion ... of like succeeding here* : P. R. II. 142.

Persuasive, *adj.* having the power of winning the mind of another ; *persuasive accent, words, tongues, rhetoric* : P. L. II. 118 ; IX. 737 ; P. R. II. 159 ; IV. 4.

Persuasively, *adv.* convincingly : P. L. IX. 873.

Pert, *adj.* lively, alert : C. 118.

Perturbation, *sb.* disquiet of mind or body : P. L. IV. 120 ; X. 113.

Peru, *sb.* the country in South America : P. L. XI. 408.

Peruse, *vb. tr.* to survey, scrutinize : P. L. VIII. 267 ; P. R. I. 320.

Perverse, *adj.* (1) turned away from what is right, wilfully wrong or evil ; *a world perverse* : P. L. XI. 701 ; *the Spirits perverse* : P. L. II. 1030 ; turned aside from the true end or purpose ; *Nature breeds, perverse, all monstrous ... things* : P. L. II. 625.

(*b*) existing because of wilful wrong-doing ; *this perverse commotion* : P. L. VI. 706.

(**2**) stubborn, untractable, self-willed : P. L. VI. 37, 562.

(**3**) untoward or unfortunate *event* : P. L. IX. 405 ; S. A. 737.

Perverseness, *sb.* wickedness, stubbornness : P. L. X. 902 ; *in Heavenly Spirits could such perverseness dwell?* : P. L. VI. 788.

Pervert, *vb. tr.* (*a*) to turn another way, avert ; *our labour must be to pervert that end* : P. L. I. 164.

(*b*) to distort from the true end, purpose, or meaning : Ps. LXXXII. 5 ; *perverts best things to worst abuse*: P. L. IV. 203 ; *they pervert pure Nature's healthful rules to loathsome sickness* : P. L. XI. 523.

(*c*) to turn from right conduct, corrupt : P. L. III. 92 ; X. 3.

part. adj. **perverted,** corrupted : P. L. XII. 547.

Pest, *sb.* a destructive being, a bane ; applied to death : P. L. II. 735.

Pester, *vb. tr.* to annoy, trouble, harass : C. 7.

Pestilence, *sb.* an epidemic malignant disease : P. R. III. 412 ; *wide-wasting, slaughtering* : P. L. XI. 487 ; D. F. I. 68 ; *a comet .. from his horrid hair shakes pestilence* : P. L. II. 711.

Pestilent, *sb.* tending to produce a plague, pestilential: P. L. X. 695.

Pet, *sb.* fit : C. 721.

Peter, *sb. Saint Peter,* the apostle to whom the keys of heaven were given : P. L. III. 484.

Petition, *sb.* a prayer addressed to God : P. L. XI. 10 ; S. A. 650.

Petrific, *adj.* having the power to turn things to stone : P. L. X. 294.

Petsora, *sb.* or Pechora, a river of northern Russia emptying into a bay of the same name : P. L. X. 292.

Petty, *adj.* (*a*) small ; *petty rills* : C. 926.

(*b*) inconsiderable, trifling: *petty trespass, enterprise*: P. L. IX. 693 ; S. A. 1223.

(*c*) inferior ; *petty kings, god* : P. R. IV. 87 ; S. A. 529.

Phalanx, *sb.* line or order of battle : P. L. I. 550 ; IV. 979 ; *in cubic phalanx* : P. L. VI. 399.

Phantasm, *sb.* (*a*) apparition, spectre; applied to death : P. L. II. 743.

(*b*) that which is produced by the imagination, vision: P. L. IV. 803.

Phantasy. *See* **Fantasy.**

Pharaoh, *sb.* the title of the ancient kings of Egypt ; *spec.,* the king who made Joseph governor of Egypt : P. L. XII. 163 ; the king who was ruling at the time of the Exodus : P. L. I. 342 ; Ps. CXXXVI. 41.

Pharian, *adj.* probably derived from Pharos, an island opposite ancient Alexandria in Egypt; *Pharian fields,* Egypt: Ps. CXIV. 3.

Pharphar, *sb.* a river of Damascus: P. L. I. 469.

Philip, *sb.* the King of Macedon and the father of Alexander the Great: P. R. III. 32.

Philistean (Philistéan), *adj.* Philistian: P. L. IX. 1061.

Philistia, *sb.* the strip of land lying along the Mediterranean coast from Ekron to the border of Egypt: Ps. LXXXVII. 14.

Philistian, *adj.* of or pertaining to Philistia or its inhabitants: S. A. 39, 42, 216, 482, 722, 831, 1371, 1655, 1714.

Philistine (Philistine: S. A. 577; elsewhere, Philistíne), *sb.* one of the warlike people who inhabited Philistia and contested the possession and sovereignty of it with the Israelites: S. A. 1099; the people as a whole; *sing. collect.*: S. A. 238; *pl.*: S. A. 251, 434, 577, 808, 1189, 1192, 1363, 1523; Ps. LXXXIII. 27.

Phillis, *sb.* the name of a shepherdess common in pastoral poetry: L'A. 86.

Philomel, *sb.* the nightingale; Philomela, the daughter of Pandion, king of Athens, when fleeing from Tereus, her sister's husband, who had violated her, was changed into the nightingale: Il P. 56.

Philosopher, *sb.* alchemist; *that stone ... philosophers in vain so long have sought*: P. L. III. 601.

Philosophic, *adj.* characteristic of or befitting a philosopher: P. R. IV. 300.

Philosophy, *sb.* the science of things divine and human; *false philosophy*: P. L. II. 565; *sage, divine*: P. R. IV. 272; C. 476.

Phineus, *sb.* the King of Salmydessus in Thrace; he was blind and a soothsayer: P. L. III. 36.

Phlegeton, *sb.* the river of hell: P. L. II. 580.

Phlegra, *sb.* the old name for the peninsula of Pallene, the westernmost of the three peninsulas of Chalcidice projecting into the Ægean Sea: P. L. I. 577.

Phœbus, *sb.* (*a*) a surname of Apollo, the god of the sun; *the drouth of Phœbus*: C. 66; *the hindmost wheels of Phœbus' wain*: C. 190; the god of music and poetry: P. R. IV. 260; L. 77; S. XIII. 10. (*b*) muse; *to this horizon is my Phœbus bound*: P. 23.

Phœnician, *sb. pl.* the inhabitants of Phœnicia: P. L. I. 438.

Phœnix, *sb.* the fabulous Arabian bird of great beauty that existed single and rose again from its own ashes: P. L. V. 272.

Phrenzy, *sb.* madness: P. L. XI. 485; S. A. 1675.

Phylactery, *sb.* an amulet consisting of strips of parchment inscribed with certain texts from the Old Testament; it was worn on the forehead or on the left arm, *fig.*: F. of C. 17.

Pick, *vb. tr.* to choose; *they must pick me out*: S. A. 1326.

Pickaxe, *sb.* a pick with a sharp point on one side and a broad blade on the other: P. L. I. 676.

Picture, *sb.* a votive tablet on which a shipwreck was painted: Hor. O. 14.

Piece, *sb.* fragment; *dash to pieces*: P. L. VI. 489; P. R. IV. 149.

Pied, *adj.* party-coloured, variegated: L'A. 75.

Piemontese, *sb.* the inhabitants of Piedmont: S. XVIII. 7.

Pierce, *vb.* (1) *tr.* (*a*) to thrust through with a sharp instrument; used *fig.* of the wound made; *pierced with wound*: P. L. VI. 435.

(*b*) to force a way into or through; *the might of Gabriel ... pierced the deep array of Moloch*: P. L. VI. 356.

(*c*) to penetrate or permeate; *Voice and Verse ... dead things with inbreathed sense able to pierce*: S. M. 4; *soft Lydian airs ... such as the meeting soul may pierce*: L'A. 138.

(*d*) to affect keenly with pain: Cir. 28.

(2) *intr.* to penetrate, enter; *through my very soul a sword shall pierce*: P. R. II. 91; *so deep the power of those ingredients pierced*: P. L. XI. 417; *where wounds of deadly hate have pierced so deep*: P. L. IV. 99; to penetrate the ear: S. A. 1568.

part. adj. **piercing,** penetrating; *piercing fires, ray*: P. L. II. 275; III. 24.

Piety, *sb.* (*a*) zealous devotion to one's country: S. A. 993.

(*b*) devout obedience to God, godliness: P. L. VI. 144; XI. 452, 799; XII. 321.

Pilaster, *sb.* a square engaged pillar: P. L. I. 713.

Pile, *sb.* a massive building: P. L. I. 722; II. 591; *fig.* of the body; *his pile high-built and proud*: S. A. 1069; the mass of the building; *the glorious Temple reared her pile*: P. L. IV. 547.

Pile, *vb.* (*part.* pilèd, *disyl.*: V. Ex. 42; W. S. 2) *tr.* to heap up: P. L. v. 394; *tables ... piled with Angels' food*: P. L. v. 632; *a table ... with dishes piled*: P. R. II. 341; with *up*: P. L. IV. 544; *pile up every stone*: P. L. XI. 324.

part. adj. **piled,** heaped up; *the labour of an age in piled stones*: W. S. 2; *lofts of piled thunder*: V. Ex. 42.

Pilfering, *part. adj.* filching: C. 504.

Pilgrim, *sb.* one who travels to a place esteemed sacred: P. L. III. 476.

attrib. characteristic of a pilgrim: P. R. IV. 427.

Pillar, *sb.* (*a*) a column or columnar mass: P. L. VI. 572, 573; P. R. IV. 58; S. A. 1606, 1630; *two massy pillars*: S. A. 1633, 1648; *pillars massy-proof*: Il P. 158.

fig. a column of fire; *pillar of fire*: P. L. XII. 202, 203; *fiery*: P. L. XII. 208.

(*b*) a supporter; *he ... seemed a pillar of state*: P. L. II. 302.

Pillared, *adj.* supported by or as by pillars; *the pillared frame of Heaven*: P. R. IV. 455; *the pillared firmament*: C. 598; *a pillared shade*: P. L. IX. 1106.

Pillow, *vb. tr.* to rest on for support; *fig., the sun ... pillows his chin upon an orient wave*: N. O. 231.

Pilot, *sb.* the steersman of a ship: P. L. I. 204; V. 264; S. A. 198, 1044; Saint Peter; *the Pilot of the Galilean Lake*: L. 109.

See **Land-pilot.**

Pin. *sb.* a peg used to hold something in place; *pins of adamant*: P. L. X. 318.

Pinch, *vb. tr.* to squeeze with the fingers: L'A. 103.

part. adj. **pinching,** nipping *cold*: P. L. X. 691.

Pindarus, *sb.* Pindar, the Greek lyric poet: S. VIII. 11.

Pine, *sb.* the tree *Pinus*: P. L. IV. 139; VI. 198; IX. 435; X. 1076; XI. 321; Il P. 135; C. 184: *tallest*: P. L. I. 292; P. R. IV. 416; *mountain*: P. L. I. 613; *Thessalian*: P. L. II. 544; in direct address; *ye Pines*: P. L. v. 193; IX. 1088.

Pine, *vb.* (1) *tr.* (*a*) to starve; *the clouds will pine his entrails*: P. L. II. 77; *pined with hunger*: P. R. I. 325.

(*b*) to grieve for: P. L. IV. 848.

(2) *intr.* (*a*) to be afflicted or tortured, or to starve: P. L. II. 601; *with eternal famine pine*: P. L. X. 597; *pines with want*: C. 768; or to waste away; *I am poor, and almost pine with need*: Ps. LXXXVI. 3.

(*b*) to be consumed; *pined with vain desire*: P. L. IV. 466; *with pain of longing pines*: P. L. IV. 511.

part. adj. **pining,** wasting away the body: P. L. XI. 486.

Pinfold, *sb.* the place in which beasts are confined; *fig.* of the world: C. 7.

Pink, *sb.* the flower *Dianthus*: C. 851; *the white pink*: L. 144.

Pinnace, *sb.* a small light sailing-vessel: P.L. II. 289.

Pinnacle, *sb.* a small ornamental structure rising above the roof or coping of a building: P. L. III. 550: P. R. IV. 549.

Pioneer, *sb.* one of a company of foot-soldiers who march before an army and prepare for its coming: P. L. I. 676; P. R. III. 330.

Pious, *adj.* (*a*) godly, devout: P. R. I. 463.

(*b*) proceeding from reverential affection; *pious awe*: P. L. v. 135; from reverence for God or a god; *pious sorrow*: P. L. XI. 362; used ironically: S. A. 955.

Pipe, (1) *sb.* (*a*) a tubular wind instrument: P. R. II. 363; S. A. 1616; used in the marching of an army: P. L. I. 561; in religious celebration; *the solemn pipe*: P. L. VII. 595; by shepherds or rustics: C. 86; *Arcadian, sylvan*: P. L. XI. 132; P. R. I. 480; *gamesome*: C. 173; *scrannel*: L. 124.

(*b*) an organ-pipe: P. L. I. 709.

(2) *vb. intr.* (*a*) to play on a pipe : C. 823.

(*b*) to sound shrilly ; *winds are piping loud* : Il P. 126.

Pit, *sb.* (1) a hole or ditch : Ps. VII. 55, 56.

(2) a gulf or abyss; (*a*) applied to hell : P. L. I. 91 ; *this* or *the infernal pit* : P. L. I. 657 ; II. 850 ; IV. 965 ; X. 464 ; *the pit of Hell* : P. L. I. 381 ; *the bottomless pit* : P. L. VI. 866 ; *fig.* an abyss of affliction : Ps. LXXXVIII. 25.

(*b*) the grave : Ps. LXXXVIII. 14.

Pitch, (1) *sb.* (*a*) point of elevation, height ; P. L. II. 772 ; *fig.* : P. L. VIII. 198.

(*b*) degree ; *highest pitch of human glory* : P. L. XI. 693 ; *lowest pitch of abject fortune* : S. A. 169.

(2) *vb. tr.* to set up, place : P. L. XII. 136 ; *they pitch against me their pavilions* : Ps. III. 18.

Pitch, *sb.* asphalt : P. L. XI. 731.

Pitchy, *adj.* very dark, black : P. L. I. 340.

Piteous, *adj.* (*a*) compassionate ; *a piteous eye* : Ps. CXXXVI. 77 ; *piteous of her woes* : C. 836.

(*b*) miserable, pitiful, sad : P. L. X. 1032.

Pity, (1) *sb.* (*a*) compassion : S. A. 814 ; S. IX. 8 ; the compassion of God or angels : P. L. III. 402, 405 ; v. 220 ; X. 25 ; D. F. I. 33 ; *his heart to pity incline* : P. L. X. 1061.

(*b*) a matter of regret : P. L. XI. 629.

(2) *vb. tr.* to feel pity or compassion for : P. L. IV. 374 ; used of God : Ps. IV. 6 ; *pity me, Lord* : Ps. VI. 3 ; LXXXVI. 9 ; *pitying how they stood before him naked to the air* : P. L. X. 211 ; *absol.* : P. L. X. 1059.

part adj. **pitied,** compassionated : S. A. 568.

Placable, *adj.* willing to forgive : P. L. XI. 151.

Place, I. *sb.* (1) a portion of space occupied or to be ·occupied by a person or thing, spot, site, locality, region : P. L. II. 260 ; III. 442, 591 ; IV. 891 ; V. 361 ; VII. 535 ; IX. 69 ; X. 315, 787 ; XI. 305, 836 ; XII. 142, 464, 618 ; P. R. I. 321, 412, 416 ; II. 396 ; IV. 600 ; S. A. 254 ; C. 156, 201,

305, 326, 570; *holiest place* : P. L. IV. 759 ; *cursed* : C. 939 ; *unfrequented, uncouth, removed* : S. A. 17, 333 ; Il P. 78 ; *be gathered now, ye waters ... into one place* : P. L. VII. 284 ; *a mind not to be changed by place or time. The mind is its own place* : P. L. I. 253, 254 ; *nor from Hell...can fly by change of place* : P. L. IV. 23 ; *Heaven...this world...Hell... these three places* : P. L. X. 324 ; used of heaven or a spot therein : P. L. I. 75 ; v. 682 ; *pl.* : P. L. v. 364.

(*b*) set apart or used for a particular purpose : P. L. X. 953, 1086, 1098 ; XI. 477 ; S. A. 1624 ; *place of judgment* : P. L. X. 932 ; *the place of her retire* : P. L. XI. 267 ; *the place of those encounters* : S. A. 1085 ; *where to choose their place of rest* : P. L. XII. 647 ; *assigned some narrow place* : S. A. 1117 ; for purposes of worship : S. A. 1359 ; *high place* : P. L. v. 732 ; used of the Earth as the seat of man : P. L. II. 345, 360, 840, 977 ; *that place is Earth* : P. L. III. 724 ; *a place foretold should be* : P. L. II. 830 ; *a place so heavenly* : P. L. X. 624 ; of Paradise or a spot therein : P. L. IV. 246, 562, 729, 843, 882, 894 ; IX. 444 ; XI. 303 ; *such place hast here to dwell* : P. L. v. 373 ; *place by place* : P. L. XI. 318 ; used of hell : P. L. I. 70, 318, 625 ; II. 217, 317 ; IV. 385 ; X. 241 ; P. R. I. 362 : *place of doom, of punishment* : P. L. IV. 840 ; VI. 53.

(*c*) allotted or belonging to a particular person or thing : P. L. VI. 405 ; VII. 240 ; P. R. I. 39 ; D. F. I. 46 ; Ps. LXXX. 37 ; *each had his place appointed* : P. L. III. 720: *the uprooted hills retired each to his place* : P. L. VI. 782 ; *this Mount of Paradise .. moved out of his place* : P. L. XI. 831 ; *to serve the Lady of this place* : A. 105 ; or in sense (**10**) ; *so may we hold our place* : P. R. II. 125 ; with blending of sense (**3**) : P. L. v. 614 ; VII. 135.

(*d*) characterized by a particular thing ; *the place of horror* : S. A. 1550 ; *a place of bliss* : P. L. II. 832 ; *the place of Evil* : P. L. VI. 276.

(*e*) the spot where a thing

belongs according to the law of its being ; *heavy, though in their place* : P. L. x. 741.

(*f*) the site of birth : P. L. xii. 363 ; P. R. i. 252 ; *place of birth* : P. L. xii. 364.

(*g*) a fitting or suitable spot : P. L. iv. 745.

(2) town, city : P. R. ii. 19.

(3) a dwelling-place, an abode : P. L. iv. 690 ; P. R. iv. 373 ; *I in none of these find place* : P. L. ix. 119 ; *fig.*: V. Ex. 25 ; used of heaven : P. L. ii. 235 : *into fraud drew many whom their place knows here no more* : P. L. vii. 144.

(4) space in general ; *where ... time, and place, are lost* : P .L. ii. 894.

(5) position, relation ; *restored by thee ... to place of new acceptance* : P. L. x. 971.

(6) room, stead : P. R. iv. 101.

(7) opportunity, chance : P. L. iv. 79 ; S. A. 910.

(8) right to be or exist ; *force upon free will hath here no place* : P. L. ix. 1174.

(9) *in place*, present : S. A. 1751.

(10) social or official status : P. L. i. 759 ; position, rank, office : P. L. xi. 635 ; xii. 516 ; *the highest place* : P. L. ii. 27 ; *in place thyself so high above thy peers* : P. L. v. 812 ; *the place wherein God set thee above her* : P. L. x. 148.

II. *vb. tr.* (*a*) to put, set : P. L. i. 387 ; v. 476 ; vii. 360 ; x. 447 ; P. R. iv. 553 ; *placed Heaven from Earth so far* : P. L. viii. 120 ; *power ... God hath in his mighty angels placed* : P. L. vi. 638 ; *I will place within them ... my umpire Conscience* : P. L. iii. 194 ; to fix, settle, or locate (a person *in* a place) : P. L. ii. 833 ; iii. 66, 90 ; iv. 416 ; v. 516 ; viii. 170 ; x. 745 ; *Man placed in a paradise* : P. L. x. 484 ; *they, in their earthly Canaan placed* : P. L. xii. 315.

(*b*) to station *a watch* or *guard* : P. L. vi. 412 ; viii. 559 ; xi. 118 ; *none pass the vigilance here placed* : P. L. iv. 580.

(*c*) to establish ; *his son Herod placed on Judah's throne* : P. R. ii. 424.

(*d*) to assign a station or posi-

tion to ; *thou art placed above me* : P. R. i. 475.

(*e*) to base, found, repose : Petr. 3 ; *sanctitude ... in true filial freedom placed* : P. L. iv. 294 ; *others in virtue placed felicity* : P. R. iv. 297 ; *the weal or woe in thee is placed* : P. L. viii. 638.

See **Biding-place, Dwelling-place, Well-placed.**

Placid, *adj.* gentle, calm, peaceful : P. R. iii. 217.

Plague, (1) *sb.* (*a*) one who brings suffering and distress ; *destroyers ... and plagues of men* : P. L. xi. 697.

(*b*) panic, terror ; *in their souls infixed plagues* : P. L. vi. 838.

(2) *vb. tr.* to afflict, harass : P. L. ii. 174 ; vi. 505 ; x. 572.

Plain, (1) *sb.* an expanse of level ground : P. L. iv. 243 ; vii. 299 ; ix. 116 ; xi. 349, 576, 580, 649, 673 ; xii. 41 ; P. R. iii. 333 ; iv. 27, 543 ; *a spacious plain* : P. L. xi. 556 ; P. R. iii. 254 ; *the subjected* : P. L. xii. 640 ; *sunny* : P. L. viii. 262 ; *on plains* : C. 823 ; *mountain, whose high top was plain* : P. L. viii. 303 ; *lay hills plain* (*see* Lay) : P. R. iii. 332 ; *Sechem and the neighboring plain* : P. L. xii. 136 ; *plains of Sericana* : P. L. iii. 437 ; *Astracan, over the snowy plains* : P. L. x. 432 ; *Atropatia, and the neighboring plains* : P. R. iii. 319 ; *Rabba and her watery plain* : P. L. i. 397 ; *the plain of Senaar* : P. L. iii. 466 ; *Eden's happy plains* : P. L. v. 143 ; in heaven : P. L. v. 648, 649 ; vi. 15 ; *the plains of Heaven* : P. L. i. 104 ; in hell : P. L. i. 350, 700 ; ii. 528 ; *yon dreary plain* : P. L. i. 180 ; used *fig.* of water ; *a liquid plain* : P. L. iv. 455.

(2) *adj.* (*a*) easily understood, clear : P. R. iv. 296.

(*b*) unsophisticated, simple ; *plain fishermen* : P. R. ii. 27.

(*c*) unassisted, unaided : S. A. 1279.

(*d*) unadorned, simple : Hor. O. 5.

(*e*) *absol. in plain*, in plain terms, frankly : P. L. ix. 758.

(3) *adv.* so as to leave no doubt, clearly : P. L. ix. 285 ; P. R. ii. 87 ; iv. 193 ; S. A. 1256 ; *sup.* : P. R. iv. 361.

Plain, *vb. intr.* to lament : P. L. IV. 504.

part. adj. **plaining,** expressing sorrow : P. 47.

Plainly, *adv.* clearly, *sup.* : P. L. XII. 151.

Plaint, *sb.* an audible expression of sorrow, lamentation : P. L. X. 343 ; XI. 499, 762 ; N. O. 191 ; *proceeded in her plaint* : P. L. X. 913 ; *pl.* : P. L. IX. 98 ; P. R. II. 29, 58 ; D. F. I. 37.

Planet, *sb.* a star revolving in its orbit : P. L. III. 481 ; V. 621 ; *planets ... real eclipse then suffered* : P. L. X. 413 ; *the planets in their stations listening stood* : P. L. VII. 563 ; *the morning planet* : P. L. VII. 366 ; *the planet Earth* : P. L. VIII. 129 ; as influencing life upon the earth : P. L. VI. 313 ; II P. 96 ; *the cross dire-looking planet* : A. 52.

Planetary, *adj.* pertaining to a planet : P. L. X. 658.

Planet-strook, *adj.* blasted : P. L. X. 413.

Plank, *sb.* board : P. L. I. 772.

Plant, (1) *sb.* a vegetable, esp. one bearing flowers or edible fruit : P. L. IV. 240, 438 ; V. 193, 327 ; P. R. IV. 461 ; S. A. 362 ; A. 48 ; L. 78 ; *our tended plants* : P. L. V. 22 ; *every virtuous plant* : C. 621 ; *the flocks ... rose as plants* : P. L. VII. 473 ; in combination or contrast with *herb, fruit, flower,* etc. : P. L. VI. 475 ; VII. 335 ; IX. 111, 206 ; P. R. IV. 434 ; *spec.* the tree of life : P. L. IV. 199 ; the tree of knowledge : P. L. V. 58 ; IX. 837 ; *wisdom-giving* : P. L. IX. 679.

(2) *vb. tr.* (*a*) to put in the ground for growth : P. L. IV. 424 ; Ps. I. 7 ; LXXX. 36, 62.

(*b*) to furnish with plants : P. L. VII. 538 ; VIII. 305 ; *plant it round with shade of laurel* : S. A. 1734.

(*c*) to place, locate ; *Paradise ... in the east of Eden planted* : P. L. IV. 210 ; *whose dwelling God hath planted here* : P. L. IV. 884.

(*d*) to put ; *there plant eyes* : P. L. III. 53.

(*e*) to establish ; *therein plant a generation* : P. L. I. 652.

Plantation, *sb.* the act of planting seeds or vegetables : P. L. IX. 419.

Planter, *sb.* one who plants a garden ; applied to God : P. L. IV. 691.

Plat, *sb.* a small piece of ground, a plot ; *a plat of rising ground* : II P. 73 ; *this flowery plat* : P. L. IX. 456.

Platane, *sb.* the plane-tree : P. L. IV. 478.

Plate, *sb.* armour composed of sheets of metal : P. L. VI. 368.

part. adj. **plated,** covered with plate-armour : S. A. 140.

See **Breast-plate.**

Plato, *sb.* the Greek philosopher : P. L. III. 472 ; P. R. IV. 245 ; II P. 89.

Plausible, *adj.* worthy of approval, commendable : P. R. III. 393.

Play, I. *sb.* (*a*) movement ; *hold them play,* keep them moving or in action : S. A. 719.

(*b*) exercise or occupation intended for pleasure, amusement, diversion, sport : P. L. IX. 528 ; *childish play* : P. R. I. 201 ; *sport and play* : S. A. 1679 ; *lamb or kid, that tend their play* : P. L. IX. 583 ; *two gentle fawns at play* : P. L. IV. 404 ; *shepherds, back! enough your play* : C. 958 ; sexual intercourse ; *amorous play* : P. L. IX. 1045.

II. *vb.* (1) *intr.* (*a*) to move irregularly ; *curls on either cheek played* : P. L. III. 641 ; to hover ; *vapour ... about their spirits had played* : P. L. IX. 1048.

(*b*) to engage in exercise or occupation for pleasure, sport, gambol, frolic : L'A. 97 ; C. 301 ; L. 52, 99 ; *bended dolphins play* : P. L. VII. 410 ; *frisking played all beasts* : P. L. IV. 340 ; *the water-nymphs that in the bottom played* : C. 833 ; *Zephyr with Aurora playing* : L'A. 19 ; *fig., winds with reeds ... play* : P. L. II. 26.

(*c*) to engage in active exercise for the amusement of others : S. A. 1340, 1448 ; *creatures ... to come and play before thee* : P. L. VIII. 372.

(*d*) to make music : P. L. VII. 10.

(2) *tr.* (*a*) to have sexual intercourse : P. L. IX. 1027.

(*b*) to put in operation, execute : P. L. V. 295.

See **Sword-player.**

Plea, *sb.* (*a*) defence : L. 90.

(*b*) that which is alleged in support or justification, reason, excuse : P. R. III. 149 ; S. A. 834 ; *righteous plea* : P. L. x. 30 ; *weakness for no plea* : S. A. 843 ; *necessity, the tyrant's plea* : P. L. IV. 394.

Plead, *vb.* (**1**) *intr.* to urge reasons, use arguments ; with *prep. inf.* : P. L. XI. 41.

(**2**) *tr.* (*a*) to speak for, defend : P. L. II. 379.

(*b*) to allege in extenuation or justification : S. A. 421, 833.

part. adj. **pleaded,** urged in support of an action : P. L. VIII. 510.

Pleasant, *adj.* (*a*) affording pleasure, delightful ; *pleasant valley, garden, walk,* etc. : P. L. I. 404 ; IV. 28, 215 ; VII. 625 ; VIII. 306 ; IX. 418, 448 ; XI. 179, 607 ; P. R. I. 118 ; II. 289 ; III. 255 ; Hor. O. 2 ; Ps. LXXXIV. 3 ; *soil* : P. L. IV. 214 ; *pleasant the sun* : P. L. IV. 642 ; *labour, task* : P. L. IV. 625 ; IX. 207 ; *his works, pleasant to know* : P. L. III. 703 ; *time* : P. L. V. 38 ; *smell, fruit,* etc. : P. L. V. 84, 445 ; VII. 540 ; VIII. 215 ; *sup.* : P. L. VIII. 212 ; *green* : P. L. VII. 316 ; *the ... harp with pleasant string* : Ps. LXXXI. 8.

(*b*) witty, facetious : P. L. VI. 628.

Please, *vb.* (**1**) *tr.* (*a*) to be agreeable to ; impers., *as him pleases best* : P. L. VIII. 169 ; *so it pleases him* : S. A. 311 ; in passive ; *yet, so pleased* : P. L. VIII. 429.

(*b*) to give delight or satisfaction to, gratify : P. L. II. 387 ; VIII. 57, 449 ; IX. 26, 949 ; P. R. IV. 157, 369 ; S. A. 219 ; L'A. 117 ; S. VIII. 3 ; *to please thy gods* : S. A. 896 ; *he pleased the ear* : P. L. II. 117 ; *pleased so well our victor's ear* : P. R. IV. 337 ; *please ... sense* : P. L. IV. 378 ; IX. 580 ; *please ... appetite, taste* : P. L. V. 304 ; VII. 49 ; C. 714 ; in passive ; *Silence was pleased* : P. L. IV. 604 ; *pleased,* delighted, gratified : P. L. II. 845 ; III. 257 ; IV. 463, 464 ; VIII. 248 ; X. 105 ; S. A. 511 ; *less therefore to be pleased* : S. A. 900 ; *this is my Son beloved,—in him am pleased* : P. R. I. 85 ; *the Almighty*

Father, pleased with thy ... song : P. L. VII. 11 ; *thus far to try thee ... I was pleased* : P. L. VIII. 437 ; *well pleased* : P. L. III. 241 ; IV. 164 ; V. 617 ; VI. 728 ; XI. 71 ; XII. 625 ; P. R. I. 286 ; *better pleased* : P. L. IV. 167.

(**2**) *intr.* (*a*) to like, choose : the pron. as subject : P. L. I. 423 ; II. 270 ; P. R. II. 395 ; IV. 164 ; *such as he pleased* : P. L. V. 825 ; *as they please* : P. L. VI. 351. used in polite request ; *please to taste* : P. L. V. 397.

(*b*) to give delight or satisfaction : P. L. II. 291, 762 ; IV. 640 ; IX. 453.

part. adj. **pleasing,** giving pleasure, delightful : P. L. IX. 453, 503 ; P. R. I. 479 ; *pleasing light* : P. L. V. 42 ; *savour* : P. L. XI. 26 ; *poison* : C. 526 ; *play* : P. R. I. 202 ; *slumber* : C. 260 ; *sorcery* : P. L. II. 566 ; *concord* : S. A. 1008 ; *fit of melancholy* : C. 546.

See **Well-pleasing.**

Pleasingly, *adv.* pleasantly, happily : P. L. IX. 794.

Pleasure, *sb.* (**1**) delight, gratification, enjoyment : P. L. II. 586 ; III. 107 ; IX. 477 ; XI. 604 ; P. R. IV. 305 ; *sense of* : P. L. VI. 459 ; *to taste of* : P. L. IX. 477 ; *taste no pleasure, though in pleasure, solitary* : P. L. VIII. 402 ; *pleasure to do ill* : P. R. I. 423 ; *took or takes pleasure* : P. L. IX. 455 ; Il P. 50 ; *pl.* : P. L. IV. 535 ; L'A. 40 ; Il P. 175.

(*b*) definitely, delight of the senses : P. L. IX. 596, 1022, 1024 ; X. 1013, 1019 ; XI. 794 ; *carnal, corporal* : P. L. VIII. 593 ; P. R. IV. 299 ; *pleasure and voluptuous life* : S. A. 534 ; *all taste of* : P. L. XI. 541 ; *the air such pleasure loth to lose* : N. O. 99 ; *pl.* : C. 668 ; *mine eye hath caught new pleasures* : L'A. 69.

(*c*) *with pleasure,* gladly, willingly : C. 77.

(**2**) that which affords delight or gratification : P. L. VI. 641 ; VIII. 50, 402 ; IX. 470 ; *pl.* : P. L. VIII. 480 ; IX. 120 ; P. R. III. 28.

(**3**) kindness, favour ; *do me once a pleasure* : V. Ex. 17.

Plebeian, *adj.* belonging to the lower ranks : P. L. X. 442.

Pledge, *sb.* that which is given or
considered as a warrant or security, gage, pawn ; *pledge of hope,
obedience, immortality, strength* :
P. L. I. 274 ; III. 95 ; IV. 200 ;
VIII. 325 ; S. A. 535 ; *the pledge
of my ... vow* : S. A. 1144 ; *under
pledge of vow* : S. A. 378 ; *Dawn,
sure pledge of day* : P. L. V.
168.

    fig. offspring, child : L. 107 ;
pledge of dalliance : P. L. II. 818 ;
pledges of Heaven's joy : S. M. 1.

Pleiad, *sb. pl.* the group of small
stars in the constellation Taurus :
P. L. VII. 374.

Plenipotent, *adj.* possessing full
power : P. L. X. 404.

Plenteous, *adj.* (*a*) abundant, copious : P. L. X. 600 ; *plenteous
crop* : P. L. XII. 18 ; *acts of
hateful strife* : P. L. VI. 263.

    (*b*) yielding abundance, pro-
ductive : Ps. IV. 35.

Plenteously, *adv.* copiously : P. L.
VII. 392.

Plenty, *sb.* abundance, fullness : P.
L. VIII. 94 ; C. 718 ; *in plenty* :
Ps. LXXXV. 51 ; an abundance of
fruit : P. L. IX. 594.

Plight, *sb.* state, condition : S. A.
1729 ; *evil, bad, saddest*, etc. :
P. L. I. 335 ; IX. 1091 ; S. A. 480 ;
P. 13 ; C. 372 ; *lowly, lowliest* :
P. L. X. 937 ; XI. 1 ; *possibly,
mood or strain* : Il P. 57.

    (*b*) a distressed .condition : P.
L. VI. 607.

Plighted, *part. adj.* folded : C. 301.

Plot, (1) *sb.* scheme, intrigue : P. L.
II. 193 ; F. of C. 14 ; Ps. LXXXIII.
10.

    (2) *vb. tr.* to scheme, contrive :
P. L. V. 240 ; *plotting how he may
seduce* : P. L. VI. 901 ; *plotting
how the Conqueror least may reap* :
P. L. II. 338.

    See **Garden-plot**.

Plough, *vb. tr.* to make *a way* as
with a plough : S. XVI. 4.

Ploughman, *sb.* one who ploughs :
P. L. VII. 983 ; L'A. 63.

Pluck, *vb. tr.* (*a*) to pull off, gather,
or pick *fruit, berries*, etc. : P. L.
V. 84, 327 ; X. 560 ; C. 296 ; L.
3 ; *fig., thou ... not harshly plucked,
for death mature* : P. L. XI. 537.

    absol. to pick fruit : P. L. V.
65 ; VIII. 309 ; IX. 595, 781.

    (*b*) to **strip** by picking the fruit
or leaves : Ps. LXXX. 51.

    (*c*) to pull, tear ; *from their
foundations they plucked the seated
hills* : P. L. VI. 644 ; *the pride of
her carnation train, plucked up* :
M. W. 38.

Plumb-down, *adv.* straight down :
P. L. II. 933.

Plume, I. *sb.* (1) feather ; (*a*) as
part of the plumage of angels :
P. L. III. 642 ; V. 286.

    (*b*) worn as an ornament ;
*cease to admire, and all her
plumes fall flat* : P. R. II. 222.

    (*c*) *pl. fig.* the wings of birds :
P. L. VII. 432 ; or birds on the
wing : C. 730.

    (2) plumage ; *two birds of gayest
plume* : P. L. XI. 186.

    (3) a token of honour or vic-
tory ; *to win from me some plume* :
P. L. VI. 161.

    II. *vb. tr.* to dress as a bird its
plumage ; *fig., Wisdom ... plumes
her feathers* : C. 378.

    part. adj. **plumed**, adorned with
plumes (?) : P. L. IV. 989.

Plummet, *sb.* a plumb-line : T. 3.

Plumy, *adj.* feathered : P. R. IV.
583.

Plunge, *vb. tr.* to cast or throw suddenly ; *plunge us in the flames* :
P. L. II. 172 ; *in that abortive
gulf* : P. L. II. 441 ; *in the womb
of ... Night* : P. L. X. 476 ; *fig.* : P.
L. X. 844.

Plurality, *sb.* the holding of two or
more benefices by the same person
at the same time ; *the widowed
whore Plurality* : F. of C. 3.

Pluto, *sb.* the bestower of wealth, a
name given euphemistically to
Hades, the god of the lower
world : L'A. 149 ; Il P. 107.

Plutonian, *adj.* resembling that of
Pluto, infernal : P. L. X. 444.

Ply, *vb.* (1) *tr.* to apply oneself to,
work at ; *ply their ... work* : P. L.
IX. 201 ; *ply the sampler* : C. 750.

    (2) *intr.* to proceed with dili-
gence or haste : P. L. II. 642,
954.

Poem, *sb.* a composition in verse :
P. L. IX. 41 ; P. R. IV. 260, 332.

Poet, *sb.* a writer of poetry ; *sage* : C.
515 ; *youthful* : L'A. 129 ; *sad
Electra's poet* (*see* Electra) : S.
VIII. 13.

Point, I. *sb.* (*a*) sharp end ; used of
a sunbeam : P. L. IV. 590.

    (*b*) an exactly defined part of
space ; *the western point* : P. L.

IV. 862; place, spot; *this shrubby
point* : C. 306 ; a quarter of the
heavens ; *eastern point of Libya* :
P. L. III. 557.

(c) a definite part of time ; *the
point of dawn* : N. O. 86.

(d) the precise proposition or
question in dispute : P. L. V.
855; *shalt thou dispute with Him
the points of liberty* : P. L. V.
823 ; *points and questions fitting
Moses' chair* : P. R. IV. 219.

(e) one of the degrees into
which the mariner's compass is
divided : P. L. IV. 559.

(f) degree ; *destruction at the
utmost point* : S. A. 1514.

II. *vb.* (1) *tr.* to indicate the
place of by pointing : P. L. XII.
143.

(2) *intr.* to indicate direction
or position or call attention with
or as with the finger : P. L. III.
733 ; *pointed at* : P. R. II. 51 ;
Faith pointed with her golden rod:
S. XIV. 7 ; *seem to point,* seem to
be directed towards them : P. R.
IV. 463.

part. adj. **pointing,** ending in a
point : P. L. I. 223.

Poise, (1) *sb.* weight ; *fig., an equal
poise of hope and fear* : C. 410.

(2) *vb. tr.* (a) to give weight to :
P. L. II. 905.

(b) to balance ; *Earth ... upon
her centre poised* : P. L. V. 579.

Poison, *sb.* a substance that, introduced into the body, tends to
change the body or to impair
health : C. 526 ; *the secret poison
of misused wine* : C. 47.

Poisonous, *adj.* venomous: S. A. 763.

Polar, *adj.* pertaining to, or issuing
from, the region near the poles of
the earth ; *polar circles* : P. L. X.
681 ; *winds* : P. L. V. 266; X.
289.

Pole, *sb.* (a) one of the two extremities of the axis of the earth ; *the
poles of Earth* : P. L. X. 669 ;
from pole to pole : P. L. IX. 66 ;
and with the centre mix the pole :
P. L. VII. 215; the south pole :
P. L. II. 642 ; of the axis of the
globe or universe : P. L. I. 74 ;
from pole to pole : P. L. III. 560 ;
not rapt above the pole : P. L. VII.
23 ; *pl.* the universe ; *the wheeling poles* : V. Ex. 34.

(b) the firmament or sky : P. L.
IV. 724 ; P. 30 ; C. 99.

Policy, *sb.* prudent wisdom in the
management of affairs : P. L. II.
297 ; P. R. III. 391.

Polish, *vb. tr.* to make elegant,
refine : P. L. XI. 610.

part. adj. **polished,** burnished :
N. O. 241.

Politic, *adj.* pertaining to government ; *politic maxims* : P. R. III.
400.

Politician, *adj.* intriguing; *politician
lords* : S. A. 1195.

Pollute, *vb. tr.* to defile or corrupt
morally : P. L. X. 167.

part. adj. (a) **polluting,** causing
moral defilement : P. L. X. 631.

(b) **polluted,** corrupt, morally :
P. L. XII. 110 ; **pollute** : N. O. 41.

Pollution, *sb.* moral defilement, im-
purity : P. L. XII. 355.

Pomona, *sb.* the goddess of fruits
and fruit-trees : P. L. V. 378 ;
IX. 393, 394.

Pomp, *sb.* (a) a solemn or magnificent procession : S. A. 436, 1312;
used of angels ; *the bright pomp
ascended* : P. L. VII. 564 ; probably also the following, but the
meaning may be (c) : P. L. II.
510; P. R. I. 457 ; L'A. 127 ;
nearer in meaning to : religious
festivity, celebration : S. A. 449.

(b) train, retinue : P. L. V.
354 ; *fig., on her ... a pomp of
winning Graces waited* : P. L.
VIII. 61.

(c) splendour, magnificence : P.
L. I. 372; II. 257; XI. 748; P. R.
III. 246; S. A. 357; W. S. 15.

Pompey, *sb.* Cneius Pompey, The
Great : P. R. III. 35.

Pompous, *adj.* splendid, showy :
P. R. II. 390.

Pond, *sb.* a small body of standing
water : P. L. IX. 641.

Ponder, *vb.* (1) *tr.* (a) to weigh :
P. L. IV. 1001.

(b) to weigh in the mind, reflect
upon : P. L. XII. 147; *pondering
the danger* : P. L. II. 421; *his
voyage* : P. L. II. 919.

(2) *intr.* to think, reflect ; *so,
thus pondering* : P. L. VI. 127;
P. R. II. 105.

Ponderous, *adj.* very heavy : P. L.
I. 284.

Ponent, *adj.* west : P. L. X. 704.

Pontic, *adj.* of Pontus : P. R. III.
36. *See* **Pontus.**

Pontifical, *adj.* pertaining to bridge-
building : P. L. X. 313.

Pontifice, *sb.* bridge : P. L. x. 348.

Pontus, *sb.* (*a*) Pontus Euxinus, the Black Sea : P. L. IX. 77; P. R. II. 347.

(*b*) the country in Asia Minor south of the Black Sea : P. L. V. 340.

Pool, *sb.* (*a*) a small pond : P. L. IX. 641.

(*b*) sea or lake ; *the Asphaltic Pool* : P. L. I. 411 ; *the Pool Mæotis* : P. L. IX. 77; *the Tauric pool* : P. R. IV. 79 (*see* the proper names) ; the burning lake of hell: P. L. I. 221 ; *the oblivious pool* : P. L. I. 266 ; *the Stygian Pool* : P. L. III. 14.

Poor, *adj.* (*a*) destitute of wealth or of property, indigent, needy : P. L. XII. 133; P. R. II. 447; Ps. LXXXII. 10 ; *I am poor* : Ps. LXXXVI. 3 ; *poor Socrates* : P. R. III. 96.

(*b*) mean, low : P. 17.

(*c*) to be pitied, unfortunate, wretched: S. A. 366; C. 566; *poor miserable captive thrall* : P. R. I. 411.

absol. those in need ; *the poor* : Ps. LXXXII. 13 ; *sup.*, *the poorest in my tribe* : S. A. 1479.

Pope, *sb.* Pope Silvester I. : Dante 3.

Poplar *sb.* the tree *Populous* : N. O. 185.

Popular, *adj.* of or pertaining to the people at large ; *popular vote* : P. L. II. 313 ; *noise, feast* : S. A. 16, 434; *praise* : P. R. II. 227; *faults heaped to the popular sum* : P. L. XII. 338; used *fig.* of ants ; *her popular tribes of commonalty* : P. L. VII. 488.

Populous, *adj.* (*a*) composed of many units, numerous ; *populous rout* : Ps. III. 16 ; *bees ... pour forth their populous youth* : P. L. I. 770 ; or possibly *adv.* ; *swarm populous* : P. L. II. 903.

(*b*) well-peopled : P. L. IX. 445 ; *the populous North* : P. L. I. 351 ; *Heaven, yet populous* : P. L. VII. 146.

Porch, *sb.* a vestibule or entrance to a building : P. L. I. 762 ; a portico or colonnade : P. R. IV. 36 ; *the sacred porch* : P. L. I. 454 ; *fig.*, *the porch and inlet of each sense* : C. 839.

Porcupine, *sb.* the animal *Hystrix cristata* : S. A. 1138.

Pore, *sb.* a minute perforation in a membrane of the body : S. A. 97.

Pore, *vb. intr.* to examine or read carefully ; with *on* : S. XI. 4.

Porous, *adj.* having pores, pervious, permeable; *through veins of porous earth* : P. L. IV. 228 ; *the Sun's orb made porous* : P. L. VII. 361.

Port, *sb.* (*a*) gate ; *their ivory port* : P. L. IV. 778.

(*b*) harbour for ships, haven : P. L. II. 1044; *the empire of Negus to his utmost port Ercoco* : P. L. XI. 397 ; *fig.*, *worst is my port* : P. R. III. 209.

Port, *sb.* carriage, bearing, demeanour : P. L. XI. 8 ; *of regal port* : P. L. IV. 868 ; *their port was more than human* : C. 297.

Portal, *sb.* door, gate : P. L. III. 508 ; *Heaven ... opened wide her blazing portals* : P. L. VII. 575.

attrib. of a gate ; used *fig.* of the mouth ; *driving dumb Silence from the portal door* : V. Ex. 5.

Portcullis, *sb.* a strong sliding door made to protect a gate : P. L. II. 874.

Ported, *part. adj.* *ported spears*, spears held with both hands diagonally across the breast so that the upper part crosses opposite the middle of the left shoulder : P. L. IV. 980.

Portend, *vb. tr.* to betoken, signify, foreshow ; *portending hollow truce*: P. L. VI. 578 ; *strange events* : P. R. II. 104 ; *hope of peaceful days* : P. L. XI. 600 ; *good, success* : P. L. XII. 596; S. I. 7 ; with *acc.* and *dat.*; *a kingdom they portend thee*: P. R. IV. 389 ; with clause : S. A. 590.

Portent (portént), *sb.* an omen of ill : P. R. I. 395 ; IV. 491.

Portentous, *adj.* (*a*) wonderful ; *this portentous bridge* : P. L. X. 371.

(*b*) foreshadowing evil ; *a sign portentous* : P. L. II. 761.

Portion, *sb.* (*a*) part assigned, share : P. L. II. 33.

(*b*) lot, fate, destiny : P. L. I. 72.

Portraiture, *sb.* pictures or images collectively : Il P. 149.

Portray, *vb. tr.* to adorn with pictures ; *shields ... with boastful argument portrayed* : P. L. VI. 84.

Portress, *sb.* a female keeper of a gate ; *the Portress of Hell-gate* : P. L. II. 746.

Possess, *vb. tr.* (*a*) to have, hold, enjoy : P. R. IV. 302 ; *love once possessed* : S. A. 1005 ; *life* : P. L. III. 243 ; *virtues* : S. X. 14 ; *shalt possess a Paradise within thee* : P. L. XII. 586.

(*b*) to make oneself master of, take possession of : P. L. II. 365, 979 ; X. 623 ; *they had by this possessed the towers of Gath* : S. A. 266 ; to come into the possession or control of ; *thou shalt by right the nations all possess* : Ps. LXXXI. 28.

(*c*) to give possession or control; *say thou wert possessed of David's throne* : P. R. III. 357 ; *possessed of happiness* : P. L. VIII. 404.

(*d*) to occupy in person and, generally, to rule over : P. L. V. 366, 790 ; X. 466 ; XI. 339 ; *the ·Earth ... as lords possess it* : P. L. VIII. 340 ; *this Universe we have possessed* : P. R. I. 49 ; *we possess the quarters of the North* : P. L. V. 688 ; *creatures that possess Earth, Air, and Sea* : P. L. IV. 431 ; to provide inhabitants for, or the meaning may be : to hold the control or rule of ; *Heaven ... retains number sufficient to possess her realm, though wide* : P. L. VII. 147.

(*e*) to have power over, dominate, rule : P. L. IX. 1137 ; *what fury ... possesses thee* : P. L. II. 729 ; *doubt possesses me* : P. L. IX. 251 ; *the Devil ... his brutal sense ... possessing* : P. L. IX. 189; probably also ; *fancies fond with gaudy shapes possess* : II P. 6.

Possession, *sb.* (*a*) the having or holding of something, ownership, occupancy : P. L. IV. 941 ; *to seize possession of* : P. L. XI. 222.

(*b*) things owned or controlled ; *as thy possession I on thee bestow the Heathen* : Ps. II. 17 ; used of lands or realms : P. L. XI. 103 ; P. R. III. 156 ; *fig., lest ... Darkness ... regain her old possession* : P. L. IV. 666 ; *in possession*, in what you may occupy and control : P. L. X. 461.

(*c*) control ; *that grounded maxim ... took full possession of me* : S. A. 869.

(*d*) the state of being under the control of devils : P. R. IV. 628.

Possessor, *sb.* one who occupies and rules over a place : P. L. I. 252.

Possible, *adj.* (*a*) that may be or may happen ; *if possible* : S. A. 490, 771 ; with *prep. inf.* ; *holds it possible to turn* : P. L. V. 441.

(*b*) having the power ; with *prep. inf.* : P. L. IX. 359.

Possibly, *adv.* in any way, by any power : P. L. V. 515.

Post, *sb.* a piece of timber set upright and intended as a support : S. A. 147.

Post, (1) *vb. intr.* to go or come with speed, hasten : D. F. I. 59 ; S. XIX. 13.

(2) *adv.* with speed, hastily ; *sent ... post to Egypt* : P. L. IV. 171 ; *evil news rides post* : S. A. 1538.

Posterity, *sb.* (*a*) descendants collectively : P. L. III. 209.

(*b*) succeeding generations collectively : P. L. VII. 638 ; X. 818 ; S. A. 977.

Posture, *sb.* position, attitude : P. L. IV. 876 ; *abject* : P. L. I. 322; *in posture to displode their second tire* : P. L. VI. 605.

Pot, *sb.* the carrying of pots ; *I set his shoulder free ; his hands from pots* : Ps. LXXXI. 23.

Potable, *adj.* drinkable ; *rivers run potable gold* : P. L. III. 608.

Potent, *adj.* (*a*) powerful ; used of persons : P. L. II. 836 ; *the potent Victor* : P. L. I. 95 ; *arm, tongue, voice* : P. L. II. 318 ; VI. 135 ; VII. 100 ; used of things ; *potent rod* : P. L. I. 338 ; XII. 211 ; *the Sun's more potent ray* : P. L. IV. 673 ; having magic power ; *potent herbs* : C. 255.

(*b*) having great authority ; *two potent Thrones* : P. L. VI. 366.

See **Over-potent.**

Potentate, *sb.* a person of high rank and power, prince, ruler ; used of Satan or his angels : P. L. V. 706 ; P. R. I. 117 ; *his potentates to council called* : P. L. VI. 416 ; *his Potentates in council sat* : P. R. II. 118 ; in direct address : P. L. I. 315 ; apparently used as one of the nine orders of angels ; *Seraphim and Potentates and Thrones* : P. L. V. 749 ; a member of this order : P. L. XI. 231 ; *Cherub and Seraph, Potentates and Thrones* : P. L. VII. 198.

Potion, *sb.* drink, draught : C. 68.

Potter, *sb.* one who makes earthen vessels : Ps. II. 21.

Pour, *vb. tr.* (1) to cause to flow in a stream: P. L. XII. 21; P. R. IV. 16.

(2) to rain; *pour* or *poured rain*: P. L. XI. 825; P. R. IV. 411; *this day will pour down ... no ... shower, but rattling storm of arrows*: P. L. VI. 544.

(3) to cause to flow as in a stream; in various *fig.* uses; (*a*) to send forth as in a stream; *a multitude ... the populous North poured ... from her frozen loins*: P. L. I. 352; *Heaven-gates poured out ... her ... bands*: P. L. II. 997; *bees ... pour forth their populous youth*: P. L. I. 770.

(*b*) to assemble in multitudes; *about his chariot were poured numberless Cherub and Seraph*: P. L. VII. 197.

(*c*) to yield or produce in abundance: P. L. V. 296; *flowers ... Nature boon poured forth*: P. L. IV. 243; *Nature pour her bounties forth*: C. 710.

(*d*) to confer or bestow abundantly: P. L. VIII. 220; XII. 498; *on whom ... these graces poured*: P. L. III. 674; *such grace ... on their shape hath poured*: P. L. IV. 365.

(*e*) to offer or present in large measure; *pour abundance*: P. L. V. 314.

(*f*) to cause to overwhelm; *on himself ... vengeance poured*: P. L. I. 220; *God's indignation on these godless poured*: P. L. VI. 811.

(*g*) to utter; *his ... passion into plaints thus poured*: P. L. IX. 98.

See **Out-poured**.

Poverty, *sb.* want of wealth; *founded in ... humble poverty*: Petr. 1; indigence, penury; *in poverty*: P. R. II. 415, 451; S. A. 697; *in lowest poverty*: P. R. II. 438.

Powder, (1) *sb.* gunpowder: P. L. IV. 815.

(2) *vb. tr.* to sprinkle, stud: P. L. VII. 581.

Power, *sb.* (1) the strength or ability residing in a thing, or exerted or put forth by a thing (sometimes with blending of sense (3)); *creatures ... tender all their power*: P. R. II. 327; (*a*) residing in or exerted by persons, esp. by man: P. L. II. 356; x. 1004; XII. 200; P. R. II. 163; *Man ... less in power*: P. L. II. 350; *free will*

and power to stand: P. L. IV. 66; *his power left free to will*: P. L. V. 235; *to persevere he left it in thy power*: P. L. V. 526; *the danger lies within his power*: P. L. IX. 349; *godlike power*: P. L. VI. 301; *to change thee Winter had no power*: D. F. I. 28; *sad Virgin! that thy power might raise Musæus from his bower*: Il P. 103; *no goblin or ... faery ... hath hurtful power*: C. 437; the power of God, Christ, or angels: P. L. I. 637; v. 159, 458; VI. 637; VIII. 279; x. 801; P. R. IV. 494, 528; *equal God in power*: P. L. VI. 343; *all power on him transferred*: P. L. VI. 678; *thy power above compare*: P. L. VI. 705; *sceptre and power, thy giving*: P. L. VI. 730; *Jehovah! infinite thy power*: P. L. VII. 603; *fomented by his virtual power*: P. L. XI. 338; *my power that right to use*: P. R. II. 380; the power of Satan or his angels: P. L. x. 531; P. R. II. 394; IV. 103; *diabolic power*: P. L. IX. 95; *to our power*: P. L. II. 336; *power to give*: P. R. II. 393; *such power was given him then*: P. R. III. 251; *by our own quickening power*: P. L. V. 861; *Satan ... prodigious power had shown*: P. L. VI. 247; *demons ... whose power*: Il P. 95; the power of sin or death: P. L. II. 884; x. 255, 284; *if your joint power prevail*: P. L. x. 408; *Sin, there in power before*: P. L. x. 586.

(*b*) residing in or exerted by things: P. L. VI. 319; IX. 680; N. O. 127; C. 801; S. I. 8; VIII. 13; (music) *nor wanting power to mitigate*: P. L. I. 556; *beauty hath strange power*: S. A. 1003; *Voice and Verse ... your ... mixed power employ*: S. M. 3; *apt words have power to suage*: S. A. 184; *masters' commands come with a power*: S. A. 1404; *spells ... of power to cheat the eye*: C. 155; *such power to stir up joy*: C. 677; *mutters of dissevering power*: C. 817; *power of mind, of harmony, of chastity, of verse*: P. L. I. 626; P. R. IV. 254; C. 782, 858; *power of these ingredients*: P. L. XI. 417.

(*c*) without relation to the thing in which it resides; *what power*: V. Ex. 89; *no power*: P. L. x. 251.

(2) strength or ability acting as an agent; that issuing from God: P. L. x. 515; S. A. 1150; *his power creation could repeat*: P. L. IX. 945; *Power Divine his way prepared*: P. L. VI. 780; *his sire the Power of the Most High*: P. L. XII. 369; *the power of the Highest o'ershadow her*: P. R. I. 139.

(3) authority, dominion, command, control (often with blending of sense (1)): P. L. IV. 429; P. R. II. 45; IV. 65, 82; S. A. 1054; C. 31; *both spiritual power and civil*: S. XVII. 10; *secular, carnal power*: P. L. XII. 517, 521; *have me in their civil power*: S. A. 1367; *in power of others*: S. A. 78; *get into my power the key*: S. A. 798; *in my* or *thy power*: P. L. IX. 820; x. 986; S. A. 430, 745; the authority of God, Christ, or angels: P. L. I. 112, 241; IV. 781, 881; v. 739, 796, 821; *all power I give thee*: P. L. III. 317; *to himself engrossed all power*: P. L. V. 776; *kingdom and power and glory*: P. L. VI. 815; *with glory and power to judge both quick and dead*: P. L. XII. 460; the authority of Satan or his angels: P. L. I. 79, 736, 753; v. 660; P. R. I. 61; *he knew his power not yet expired*: P. R. IV. 394; *this imperial sovranty ... armed with power*: P. L. II. 447; the dominion of death: P. L. III. 242; *Death over him no power shall long usurp*: P. L. XII. 420.

(b) *concr.* one who rules; *tyrannic power*: P. R. I. 219; S. A. 1275.

(c) a position of authority, *pl.*: P. R. III. 30.

(d) influence, control; *charms no more on me have power*: S. A. 935.

(4) a being exercising power; applied to God; *the Power that made us*: P. L. IV. 412; *Heavenly Power*: P. L. VIII. 379; to a god or tutelary spirit: N. O. 196; *as to the Power that dwelt therein* (the tree): P. L. IX. 835; *I am the Power of this fair wood*: A. 44; *that power which erring men call Chance*: C. 587; to a sea-nymph; *their powers*=them: Il P. 21.

(5) potentate, ruler, sovereign:

P. L. II. 955; *ye Powers of this nethermost Abyss*: P. L. II. 968; applied to God or Christ; *the acknowledged Power Supreme*: P. L. IV. 956; *the Filial Power*: P. L. VII. 587; *the Almighty Power*: P. L. I. 44.

fig., *unworthy powers to reign over free reason*: P. L. XII. 91.

(6) applied to an angel; (a) as a prince in heaven or hell: P. L. IV. 61, 63; *the godlike*: P. L. VIII. 249; *the Angelic*: P. L. XI. 126; *the regent Powers*: P. L. v. 697; *essential Powers*: P. L. v. 841; *Powers that erst in Heaven sat on thrones*: P. L. I. 360.

(b) as one of the host of heaven or hell; *pl.* sometimes perhaps equivalent to (8) (b): P. L. III. 390, 397; IV. 939; VI. 22; x. 395; *the Powers of Heaven*: P. L. v. 824; *ethereal Powers*: P. L. III. 100; XII. 577; P. R. I. 163; *Stygian, Infernal Powers*: P. L. II. 875; IX. 136; *powers of Darkness*: P. L. III. 256; *Powers of Air*, etc.: P. R. I. 44; II. 124; in direct address: P. L. II. 456; III. 213; VII. 162; x. 34; Cir. 1.

(7) the sixth of the nine orders of angels: P. L. II. 11, 310; III. 320; v. 601, 772, 840; x. 86, 460; used of the fallen angels as ruling the air: P. L. x. 186.

(8) ability or strength resting upon armies, armed force: P. R. III. 299; Ps. CXXXVI. 54; used of angels: P. L. I. 103; II. 102; v. 728; VI. 134, 223.

(b) *pl.* band, army, host: P. R. III. 338; S. A. 251, 1110, 1190; used of angels: P. L. I. 186, 622; II. 522; VI. 786, 898; XI. 221; *Satan with his Powers*: P. L. v. 743; *the banded Powers of Satan*: P. L. VI. 85; *the Powers Militant that stood for Heaven*: P. L. VI. 61; *Michael and his Powers*: P. L. VI. 686.

(9) a faculty of the mind: P. L. III. 52, 176; IX. 600, 1048.

Powerful, *adj.* (a) having great ability or strength, mighty, efficient: P. L. x. 247; *powerful key*: P. L. II. 774; *hand*: C. 903; *art*: P. L. III. 602; *his powerful Word and Spirit*: P. L. VII. 208; *sup.*, *what Heaven's Lord had powerfullest to send against us*: P. L. VI. 425.

(b) having great authority or ability to rule : P. R. III. 155.

(c) having great influence or control : P. L. IX. 587; *arguments* : S. A. 862; *beauty's powerful glance* : P. L. VIII. 533 ; *the jealousy of love* : S. A. 791 ; *all-controlling* ; *powerful destiny* : P. L. IV. 58.

See **All-powerful.**

Practice, *sb.* customary performance, custom : S. A. 114.

Practise, *vb. tr.* (a) to make use of habitually ; *practised falsehood* : P. L. II. 122; *absol.* : P. L. II. 124.

(b) to exercise oneself in, study; *practise how to live secure* : P. L. XI. 802.

part. adj. **practised,** learned from practice : P. L. IV. 945.

See **Well-practised.**

Prætor, *sb.* the Roman magistrate : P. R. IV. 63.

Praise, I. *sb.* (1) commendation bestowed, high approbation, laudation, honour : P. L. III. 106 ; IV. 638 ; IX. 800 ; XI. 617 ; P. R. II. 464 ; III. 51, 56 ; M. W. 12 ; A. 11 ; C. 271 ; L. 76 ; S. XIII. 6. XV. 2 ; Eurip. 3 ; *the praise of men* : P. L. III. 453 ; VI. 376 ; *the people's praise* : P. R. III. 48 ; *popular praise* : P. R. II. 227 ; *her beauty's praise* : Il P. 20 ; *to speak thy praise* : P. L. IX. 749 ; *a crown of deathless praise* : C. 973 ; *immortal praise* : A. 75 ; *merit praise* : P. L. III. 697 ; P. R. II. 456 ; *I the praise yield thee* : P. L. IX. 1020 ; *pl.* : P. R. III. 64 ; S. A. 175 ; S. XVI. 8.

(b) something said in commendation : Ps. LXXXVI. 17.

(2) the glorification of God ; sometimes nearer in meaning to : devotion with thanksgiving, worship : P. L. III. 414, 415 ; IV. 46, 676 ; VII. 187 ; C. 776 ; Ps. VI. 10 ; VII. 61 ; VIII. 3 ; CXIV. 6 ; *spiritual creatures ... with ceaseless praise his works behold* : P. L. IV. 679 ; *whose praise be ever sung* : P. L. V. 405 ; *hymns of high praise* : P. L. VI. 745 ; *pl.* : P. L. III. 147 ; IV. 444 ; Ps. CXXXVI. 9 ; as rendered by the sun, the stars, air, etc.: P. L. V. 172, 179, 184, 191, 192, 196, 199, 204 ; IX. 195.

(b) the glorification of Dagon : S. A. 1621 ; *pl.* : S. A. 436, 450.

(3) ground of approbation : P. R. II. 251.

II. *vb. tr.* (1) to commend, applaud, extol : P. R. III. 52; S. A. 420 ; *praise the work* : P. L. I. 731 ; *virtue, resolution, abstinence* : P. L. IX. 693 ; S. A. 1410 ; C. 709 ; S. X. 12 ; with clause : P. L. II. 480.

(2) to glorify or worship (God) : P. L. III. 676 ; IV. 436 ; VII. 258 ; Ps. LXXXIV. 18 ; LXXXVI. 41 ; LXXXVIII. 43 ; CXXXVI. 2 ; *to praise their Maker* : P. L. V. 147; *Sion's songs ... where God is praised aright* : P. R. IV. 348 ; used of a star : P. L. V. 169.

(b) to glorify or thank (a god); *praising the bounteous Pan* : C. 176.

Prance, *vb. intr.* to move proudly with high steps ; *horses ... prancing* : P. R. III. 314.

Prank, *vb. tr.* to deck, adorn ; *fig., rules pranked in reason's garb* : C. 759.

Pravity, *sb.* moral perverseness, wickedness : P. L. XII. 288.

Pray, *vb.* (1) *intr.* to address God devoutly in adoration or petition : P. L. III. 190 ; V. 209 ; XI. 2 ; P. R. I. 490 ; S. A. 1637 ; Ps. IV. 28 ; *unto thee I pray* : Ps. V. 4 ; *he will instruct us praying* : P. L. X. 1081 ; *unskilful with what words to pray* : P. L. XI. 32 ; *repents, and prays contrite* : P. L. XI. 90 ; with *for* : S. A. 351 ; *I prayed for children* : S. A. 352 ; *for* omitted ; *answer what I prayed* : Ps. LXXXVI. 24.

(2) *tr.* (a) to ask earnestly, beg : V. Ex. 15.

(b) to make devout petition to (God) ; *if we pray him* : P. L. X. 1060 ; *O hear me, I thee pray* : Ps. LXXXVI. 2.

Prayer, *sb.* (a) entreaty, petition : S. A. 961 ; *flattering prayers* : S. A. 392.

(b) devout supplication to God : P. L. III. 191 ; X. 859 ; XI. 146, 149, 307, 311 ; S. A. 359, 649 ; Ps. IV. 6 ; V. 8 ; VI. 18 ; LXXXIV. 29 ; LXXXVI. 19 ; LXXXVIII. 5 ; *thy people's prayer* : Ps. LXXX. 20 ; *at thy prayer* : S. A. 581 ; *prayers and vows* : S. A. 520 ; *thy prayers are heard* : P. L. XI. 252 ; *if prayers could alter high decrees* ; P. L. X. 952 ; *to Heaven their prayers flew up*: P. L. XI. 14; *up to thee my prayer doth hie*: Ps. LXXXVIII. 55 ; *sighs and prayers, ... in this golden censer, mixed with incense*: P. L. XI. 24 ; *the Spirit of prayer*, the Holy Spirit as inciting the heart of man to prayer: P. L. XI. 6.

Preach, *vb. tr.* to inculcate by or as by a sermon ; *preached conversion and repentance*: P. L. XI. 723 ; *salvation shall be preached*: P. L. XII. 448 ; with clause ; *preaching how meritorious ... it would be*: S. A. 859.

Preamble (preámble), *sb.* prelude : P. L. III. 367.

Precede, *vb.* (1) *tr.* to go before in time, exist before : P. L. IX. 327.
(2) *intr.* to have power, prevail : P. L. X. 640.

Precedence, *sb.* a prior place or superior position : P. L. II. 33.

Precept, *sb.* (*a*) instruction or direction as a rule of action ; *the Sun had first his precept so to move*: P. L. X. 652.
(*b*) a rule of conduct, maxim, *sententious*: P. R. IV. 264 ; *fetch their precepts from the Cynic tub*: C. 708.

Precinct (precínct), *sb.* a bounded space; *the precincts of light*: P. L. III. 88.

Precious, *adj.* of great worth, highly prized or esteemed : P. L. III. 611 ; v. 132 ; S. A. 538 ; *precious gems*: C. 719 ; *riches...the precious bane*: P. L. I. 692 ; *vialed liquors*: C. 847 ; *some blood more precious*: P. L. XII. 293 ; *precious beams*: P. L. IX. 106 ; *the stars ... their precious influence*: N. O. 71 ; *of precious cure*; C. 913 ; equivalent to the superlative ; *precious of all trees*: P. L. IX. 795.

Precipice, *sb.* headlong declivity ; *the precipice of Heaven*: P. L. I. 173.

Precipitance, *sb.* headlong hurry : P. L. VII. 291.

Precipitant, *adj.* falling or descending headlong : P. L. III. 563.

Precipitate, *vb. tr.* to hurl headlong: P. L. VI. 280.

Precise, *adj.* definitely appointed ; *the hour precise*: P. L. XII. 589.

Predestination, *sb.* a decree of God by which from eternity all things have been immutably determined : P. L. III. 114.

Predicament, *sb.* used punningly with the double meaning of: part assigned and category : V. Ex. 56.

Predict, *vb. tr.* to foretell, prophesy: P. R. III. 356.

Prediction, *sb.* prophecy : P. L. XII. 553 ; P. R. III. 354, 394 ; *worthy of his ... high prediction*: P. R. I. 142 ; *call in doubt divine prediction*: S. A. 44.

Predominant, *adj.* ruling ; *the Sun ... predominant in heaven*: P. L. VIII. 160.

Pre-eminence, *sb.* superiority in rank and power : P. L. V. 661 ; XI. 347.

Pre-eminent, *adj.* superior, supreme: P. L. IV. 447 ; *in goodness and in power pre-eminent*: P. L. VIII. 279.

Preface, *sb.* preliminary remarks : P. L. IX. 676 ; XI. 251 ; P. R. II. 115 ; S. A. 1554.

Prefer, *vb. tr.* (*a*) to promote, advance : S. A. 464, 1672.
(*b*) to like better than, choose : P. L. IX. 99 ; P. R. IV. 303 ; S. A. 1019 ; *and, me preferring*: P. L. I. 102 ; *man prefer, set God behind*: S. A. 1374 ; *there be who faith prefer*: P. L. VI. 144 ; with *before*: P. L. I. 17 ; II. 255; VIII. 52 ; P. R. IV. 84.

Prefix (prefixèd, *trisyl.*: D. F. I. 59), *vb. tr.* to appoint beforehand; *time, date prefixed*: P. R. I. 269; IV. 392.
part. adj. **prefixed**, occupied before : D. F. I. 59.

Pregnant, *adj.* (*a*) being with child: P. L. II. 779.
fig., *my sorrows loud had got a race of mourners on some pregnant cloud*: P. 56 ; productive ; *dove-like sat brooding on the vast abyss, and mad'st it pregnant*: P. L. I. 22 ; *neither Sea, nor Shore ... but all these in their pregnant causes mixed*: P. L. II. 913.
(*b*) impregnated, filled ; *pregnant with infernal flame*: P. L. VI. 483.

Prelate, *sb. attrib.* who is a high dignitary of the church ; *your Prelate Lord*: F. of C. 1.

Pre-ordain, *vb. tr.* to decree beforehand : P. R. I. 127.

Prepare, *vb.* (1) *tr.* (*a*) to make fit or ready : P. L. I. 700 ; XI. 571 ; *his way prepared*: P. L. VI. 780 ; P.

R. I. 272; *prepared for dinner savoury fruits*: P. L. v. 303; *his supper on the coals prepared*: P. R. II. 273.

(*b*) to bring into a certain state of mind, fit for some action: P. L. IX. 381; XI. 365; *in mind prepared ... for death*: P. L. XII. 444; *prepare thee for another sight or scene*: P. L. XI. 555, 637.

(*c*) to provide; *ministering light prepared*: P. L. IV. 664; *to prepare fit entertainment*: P. L. v. 689; or in sense (*a*): P. L. I. 70; VIII. 299.

(*d*) to make, construct; *compasses, prepared in God's ... store*: P. L. VII. 225.

(2) *intr.* to make one's self ready: P. L. XI. 126; with *prep. inf.*: P. L. I. 615.

part. adj. **prepared**, provided or made ready: P. L. VI. 738.

vbl. sb. **preparing**, preparation: P. R. III. 389.

Presage, (1) *sb.* (*a*) prognostic, omen: P. L. VI. 201; P. R. I. 394.

(*b*) prescience, foreknowledge; *if there be aught of presage in the mind*: S. A. 1387.

(2) *vb. tr.* (*a*) to foreshow, foretoken: P. L. XII. 613.

(*b*) to foretell, predict: V. Ex. 70; *absol.*: P. L. I. 627.

part. adj. **presaging**, foretokening: M. W. 44.

Presbyter, *sb.* an elder in the Presbyterian Church: F. of C. 20.

Prescribe, *vb. tr.* to set down authoritatively, ordain, appoint: P. L. x. 657; *bounds prescribed*: P. L. III. 82; IV. 878, 909; *my breeding ... prescribed*: S. A. 30.

Prescript (prescrípt), *sb.* command: P. L. XII. 249; decree, edict: S. A. 308.

Presence, *sb.* (*a*) the state of being in a certain place or company: P. L. IX. 836; S. A. 1321; C. 950; used of God: P. L. XI. 341, 351; *withdraw his presence from among them*: P. L. XII. 108; self-manifestation; *he voutsafed Presence Divine*: P. L. XI. 319.

(*b*) close proximity, immediate company; *knowledge in her presence falls degraded*: P. L. VIII. 551; situation face to face with God: P. L. x. 100; Ps. CXIV. 15; *in his* or *thy presence*: P. L. II. 240; III. 265; XII. 563; *unto thy*

presence: Ps. LXXXVIII. 5; *in God's presence*: P. L. III. 649; *in presence of the Almighty Father*: P. L. VII. 11; with an angel: P. L. v. 358.

(*c*) person; used of God; *charioting his godlike presence*: S. A. 28; *Presence Divine*: P. L. VIII. 314; *Sovran Presence*: P. L. x. 144.

(*d*) companionship, society: P. L. IX. 858.

Present, (1) *adj.* (*a*) being in a certain place, not absent: P. L. I. 20; IX. 316; S. A. 1378; *the present object*: P. L. x. 996; *I was never present on the place*: S. A. 1085; used of God: P. L. XI. 351; *where is not He present?*: P. L. VII. 518; *though present in his angel*: P. L. XII. 201.

(*b*) being at this time, not past or future: P. L. IV. 762; x. 651; XI. 871; *present lot, state*: P. L. II. 223; P. R. I. 200; C. 789; *aid, need*: C. 90, 287; *pain, evils, misery*: P. L. II. 34, 281, 459; *journey*: P. L. II. 985; *knowledge past or present*: P. L. I. 628.

(2) *sb.* the time now passing; *for the present*: P. L. IX. 1092; *at present*: S. A. 1446; in combination with *past, future*: P. L. v. 582; or what is now happening: P. L. III. 78; the time and that which it involves: P. L. x. 340.

(3) *sb.* gift: D. F. I. 74; N. O. 16.

(4) *adv.* near in space, close by: P. R. I. 258.

(5) *vb. tr.* (*a*) to bring into the presence of: P. L. VI. 26.

(*b*) to bring before the vision: P. R. IV. 38.

(*c*) to bring before the mind, reveal: S. M. 5; to suggest: P. L. IX. 213; to cause one to remember: S. A. 21.

(*d*) to offer for acceptance; *me ... presented with a universal blank of Nature's works*: P. L. III. 48.

(*e*) to lay before one who judges, submit: P. L. XI. 21; S. XIX. 5.

(*f*) to confront in hostility; *front to front presented stood*: P. L. VI. 106.

(*g*) to offer the opportunity for: P. L. IX. 974.

(*h*) to represent, act: Il P. 99.

Presentment, *sb.* representation, picture: C. 156.

See **Self-preservation**.

Preserve, *vb. tr.* (*a*) to defend from injury or destruction: Ps. LXXXV. 24; *life preserves*: P. R. II. 372; *preserve my soul*: Ps. LXXXVI. 5.

(*b*) to keep in the same state; *preserve unhurt our minds*: P. L. VI. 443; *preserved these locks unshorn*: S. A. 1143.

(*c*) to secure permanence to, make lasting: P. L. XI. 579, 873.

President, (**1**) *adj.* presiding; *his Angels president in every province*: P. R. I. 447.

(**2**) *sb.* the presiding officer of an assembly: S. X. 1.

Press, *vb.* (**1**) *tr.* (*a*) to exert weight against: P. L. IV. 501.

(*b*) to crush, squeeze; *from sweet kernels pressed*: P. L. V. 346; *as he were pressed to death*: U. C. II. 26.

(*c*) to enjoin, urge; *pressed how just it was*: S. A. 854.

(**2**) *intr.* to weigh, oppress, afflict: Ps. LXXXVIII. 30.

See **Wine-press.**

Presume, *vb.* (**1**) *tr.* (*a*) to undertake, venture, dare: P. L. IX. 921; S. A. 1209; with *prep. inf.*: S. A. 462; *absol.*: P. L. XII. 530.

(*b*) to suppose, imagine; with two *acc.*: P. L. X. 50; *Eternal Might to match with their inventions they presumed so easy*: P. L. VI. 631.

(**2**) *intr. or absol.* (*a*) to speak overboldly: P. L. VIII. 356; P. R. III. 345.

(*b*) to proceed presumptuously, make one's way overconfidently: P. L. VII. 13; *earthly sight, if it presume*: P. L. VIII. 121; to rely *on* as a ground for boldness; *presume not on thy God*: S. A. 1156.

part. adj. **presumed,** taken for granted or intended beforehand: P. L. IX. 405.

Presumption, *sb.* arrogance, insolence: C. 431.

Presumptuous, *adj.* arrogant, overbold, insolent: P. L. IV. 912; VIII. 367; *hope*: P. L. II. 522; *a joy presumptuous to be thought*: S. A. 1531.

Presumptuously, *adv.* arrogantly, insolently: S. A. 498.

Pretence, *sb.* (*a*) pretext: P. L. XII. 520; *under pretence of*: S. A. 1196; C. 160.

(*b*) a claim or right asserted: P. L. VI. 421; *our just pretences*: P. L. II. 825.

Pretend, *vb.* (*pres. 2d sing.* pretend'st: P. R. I. 430) (**1**) *tr.* (*a*) to spread before as a screen; *that too heavenly form, pretended to hellish falsehood*: P. L. X. 872.

(*b*) to put forward as an excuse: P. L. V. 244; *pretending so commanding to consult*: P. L. V. 768; *pretending first wise to fly pain*: P. L. IV. 947.

(*c*) to feign; *thy love ... pretended*: S. A. 873.

(*d*) to allege or declare falsely; with *prep. inf.*: P. R. I. 73.

(*e*) to intend, mean (?): S. A. 212.

(**2**) *intr.* to lay claim *to*: P. R. I. 430.

Pretext (pretéxt), *sb.* a motive assigned: S. A. 901.

Prevail, *vb. intr.* (**1**) to be superior in power or influence, triumph: P. L. IX. 873; X. 40, 258; *affection prevailing over fear*: S. A. 740; used of sin or death: U. C. I. 9; *if your joint power prevail*: P. L. X. 408.

(*b*) to conquer an enemy, be victorious; with *against*: P. L. VI. 795; with *o'er*: P. R. III. 167.

(**2**) to succeed in persuading or convincing a person: S. A. 661, 869.

part. adj. **prevailing,** victorious: P. L. IV. 973.

Prevalent, *adj.* (*a*) victorious: P. L. VI. 411.

(*b*) powerful, efficacious: P. L. XI. 144.

Prevenient, *adj.* going before; *prevenient grace*, grace which acts upon the sinner before repentance: P. L. XI. 3.

Prevent, *vb. tr.* (**1**) to go or come before, forestall: N. O. 24; Ps. LXXXVIII. 56.

(**2**) to hinder (a person) from some action, restrain: P. L. II. 739; S. A. 1103; C. 285.

(**3**) to keep from occurring, render impossible, ward off: V. Ex. 73; *to prevent such horrid fray*: P. L. IV. 996; *the harass of their land*: S. A. 256; *evil*: P. L. XI. 773.

(*b*) to hinder, obstruct; *reply*: P. L. II. 467; *tidings*: P. L. X. 37; *murmur*: S. XIX. 8.

(4) to keep from existing ; *to prevent the race unblest* : P. L. X. 987.

(5) *absol.* to interpose a hindrance : C. 573.

vbl. sb. **preventing,** power to hinder : P. R. IV. 492.

Prevention, *sb.* (*a*) the act of forestalling an enemy : P. L. VI. 320.

(*b*) obstacle, hindrance : P. L. VI. 129.

Preventive, *adj.* hindering : F. of C. 16.

Prey, (1) *sb.* (*a*) spoil, booty : P. L. XI. 793 ; *sacred things ... a prey to that proud city* : P. L. XII. 341.

(*b*) that which is seized to be devoured ; *a region scarce of prey* : P. L. III. 433 ; *new haunt for prey* : P. L. IV. 184 ; *to dogs and fowls a prey* : S. A. 694 ; used *fig.* of that which is the prey of sin or death : P. L. II. 806 ; X. 268, 609 ; *all things shall be your prey* : P. L. II. 844 ; *Man and all his World to Sin and Death a prey* : P. L. X. 490 ; *all my trees their prey* : P. L. XI. 124 ; *thou wilt not leave me in the ... grave his prey* : P. L. III. 248 ; of the prey of Satan or his angels ; *nearer to view his prey* : P. L. IV. 399 ; *the whole included race, his purposed prey* : P. L. XI. 124 ; *roaming to seek their prey on Earth* : P. L. I. 382.

(*c*) one who is given into the power of another, a victim : C. 574 ; Ps. LXXX. 5 ; *me to the Uncircumcised a welcome prey* : S. A. 260 ; *each ... the sport and prey of racking whirlwinds* : P. L. II. 181.

(*d*) the act of seizing in order to devour ; *tigers at their prey* : C. 534 ; used *fig.* of Satan ; *the Fiend ... bent on his prey* : P. L. III. 441.

(2) *vb. intr.* to bring injury *on* : S. A. 613.

Prick, *vb. intr.* to spur on, ride rapidly ; with *forth* : P. L. II. 536.

Prickle, *sb.* the thorn of a leaf : C. 631.

Pride, *sb.* **(1)** inordinate self-esteem : P. L. X. 874, 1044 ; XI. 795 ; C. 761 ; Ps. LXXXIII. 45 ; *high conceits engendering pride* : P. L. IV. 809 ; *her female pride* : P. R. II. 219 ; *swell or swollen with pride* :

P. R. III. 81 ; S. A. 532 ; *be it not done in pride* : C. 431 ; *philosophic* : P. R. IV. 300 ; used of Satan or his angels : P. L. I. 36, 572 ; IV. 40 ; V. 665 ; P. R. IV. 570 ; *obdurate, wonted, considerate, monarchal* : P. L. I. 58, 527, 603 ; II. 428 ; *quell their pride* : P. L. V. 740 ; *dash their pride* : P. L. X. 577 ; *his pride humbled* : P. L. VI. 341.

(*b*) national arrogance : S. A. 286 ; *the Carthaginian pride* : P. R. III. 35.

(2) an act indicating pride ; *the pride of numbering Israel* : P. R. III. 409.

(3) self-respect : P. L. IV. 310.

(4) that which causes pride or exultation : M. W. 37 ; *young Hyacinth, the pride of Spartan land* : D. F. I. 26.

(5) glorious beauty ; *summer's pride* : P. L. VII. 478 ; splendour ; *military pride* : P. R. III. 312.

Priest, *sb.* one who officiates in a sacred office ; (*a*) at the altar of God : P. L. I. 494 ; XII. 353 ; P. R. I. 257 ; III. 169 ; *the hypocrite or atheous priest* : P. R. I. 487 ; applied to Christ : P. L. XI. 25 ; P. 15.

(*b*) at the altar of a deity : S. A. 857, 1653 ; N. O. 180 ; *the well-feasted priest* : S. A. 1419 ; *Egypt and her priests* : P. L. I. 480 ; *Dagon and his priests* : S. A. 1463 ; *Cotytto ... befriend us thy vowed priests* : C. 136 ; of men regarded as gods : P. R. III. 83 ; used *fig.* of a person ; *to honour thee, the priest of Phœbus' choir* : S. XIII. 10.

(*c*) in the Anglican or Roman Catholic Church (as a contraction of the Gr. πρεσβύτερος) : F. of C. 20.

Prime, (1) *adj.* (*a*) first in rank or importance, chief ; *us, his prime creatures* : P. L. IX. 940 ; *architect, Angel* : P. L. X. 356 ; XI. 598 ; *the Sun ... the Prime Orb* : P. L. IV. 592 ; *prime wisdom, work, decree* : P. L. VIII. 194 ; S. A. 70, 85 ; *end, cause* : P. L. VIII. 540 ; P. R. III. 123 ; S. A. 234.

(*b*) best : P. L. IX. 200.

(*c*) early : P. R. II. 200.

(*d*) being in the best or most vigorous time of life : P. L. XI. 245.

(2) *sb.* or *absol.* (*a*) beginning; *in her prime of love*: S. A. 388.

(*b*) the first hour or period of the day : P. L. v. 21 ; *that sweet hour of prime*: P. L. v. 170.

(*c*) youth : P. L. IX. 395; *Nature here wantoned as in her prime*: P. L. v. 295; the earliest period of youth : P. L. III. 637.

(*d*) the most vigorous time of life ; *manly prime or youthful bloom*: C. 289 ; *dead ere his prime*: L. 8.

(*e*) full health and vigour : S. IX. 1.

(*f*) one first in rank or importance : P. L. I. 506; VI. 447; *the choice and prime of those ... champions*: P. L. II. 423 ; *the prime in splendour*: P. R. I. 413; or, possibly, the first one in time ; *O prime of Men*: P. L. v. 563.

Primitive, *adj.* first : P. L. v. 350.

Primrose (primróse : M. M. 4), *sb.* the flower *Primula ; silken, pale, rathe*: D. F. I. 2 ; M. M. 4 ; L. 142.

attrib. of primroses : C. 671.

Prince, *sb.* (*a*) sovereign, ruler, lord : P. L. v. 355 ; C. 325 ; Ps. II. 3 ; LXXXII. 24 ; LXXXIII. 42, 44 ; *Prince Memnon's*: II P. 18 ; *the princes of my country*: S. A. 851 ; applied to angels : P. L. I. 735 ; XI. 298 ; to Christ ; *Prince of Light* : N. O. 62; applied to Satan or his angels ; *Prince* or *Princes of Hell*: P. L. II. 313; IV. 871 ; X. 621 ; *Prince of the Air, of Air* : P. L. X. 185; XII. 454 ; *of Darkness*: P. L. X. 383; P. R. IV. 441 ; in direct address : P. L. I. 128, 315 ; P. R. II. 121.

(*b*) a leader in war ; *Michael, of celestial armies prince*: P. L. VI. 44 ; *Prince of Angels* : P. L. VI. 281.

Princedom, *sb.* principality, the seventh of the nine orders of angels : P. L. III. 320 ; X. 87 ; *Thrones, Dominations, Princedoms, Virtues, Powers*: P. L. v. 601, 772, 840 ; X. 460.

Princely, *adj.* (*a*) having the rank of a prince : P. L. I. 359; XI. 220.

(*b*) pertaining to a ruler ; *yon princely shrine*: A. 36.

(*c*) becoming a prince; *princely counsel, lore*: P. L. II. 304; C. 34.

Principality, *sb.* the seventh of the nine orders of angels : P. L. VI. 447 ; used of the fallen angels as ruling the air : P. L. X. 186.

Principle, (1) *sb.* that by which anything is moved or regulated : U. C. II. 10.

(2) *vb. tr.* to establish in certain principles : S. A. 760.

Print, (1) *sb.* a mark made by pressure ; *print of step* : A. 85 ; *fig.*, *no print of the approaching light*: N. O. 20.

(2) *vb. tr.* to characterize in print as : F. of C. 11.

Printless, *adj.* leaving no mark : C. 897.

Prison, *sb.* (*a*) a place of confinement : P. L. VI. 660 ; applied to hell : P. L. I. 71; II. 59, 434; IV. 824, 906 ; P. R. I. 364.

(*b*) a public building for the confinement of criminals : P. L. XI. 725; *the common prison*: S. A. 6, 1161 ; *calamitous* : S. A. 1480 ; *fig.*, *thy bondage or lost sight, prison within prison*: S. A. 153.

Prisoned, *part. adj.* restrained from liberty : C. 256.

Prisoner, *sb.* one confined in a prison : S. A. 7, 1308, 1460 ; *fig.*, *love's prisoner*: S. A. 808.

Prison-house, *sb.* prison : S. A. 922.

Prithee, a corruption of *pray thee* ; without subject expressed : C. 512, 615.

Private, *adj.* (*a*) personal, respecting particular individuals, opposed to *public* ; *private respects, reward* : S. A. 868, 1465.

(*b*) removed from public view, not open, secret : P. L. v. 109 ; *in private*, secretly : P. R. IV. 94.

(*c*) not invested with public function, unofficial ; *private life* : P. R. II. 81; III. 22, 232; *person* : S. A. 1208, 1211 ; *in private*, not publicly : P. R. IV. 509.

(*d*) affording privacy and quiet : P. R. IV. 331.

(*e*) alone, not accompanied : P. R. IV. 639.

Privation, *sb.* deprivation, loss : P. R. IV. 400.

Privilege, *sb.* a particular right, immunity, or advantage : P. L. VII. 589 ; *by privilege of death and burial* : S. A. 104.

Privy, *adj.* acting secretly or by stealth ; *the grim wolf with privy paw* : L. 128.

Prize, *sb.* something gained as a reward of exertion or contest: L'A. 122.

Prize, *vb. tr.* to value highly, esteem: Ps. IV. 11.

Proboscis, *sb.* the trunk of an elephant: P. L. IV. 347.

Proceed, *vb.* (*pres. 2d sing.* proceed'st: P. R. IV. 125) *intr.* (*a*) to go on, continue: P. L. XI. 672; L. 88; *proceeded in her plaint*: P. L. X. 913.

(*b*) to go, come, or issue *from*: P. L. X. 824; XII. 381; *one Almighty is, from whom all things proceed*: P. L. V. 470; *the gods are first ... all from them proceeds*: P. L. IX. 719; *man as from a second stock proceed*: P. L. XII. 7; *each word proceeding from the mouth of God*: P. R. I. 350.

(*c*) to arise from or be caused by; with *from*: P. L. IX. 94; *suggestions, which proceed from anguish of the mind*: S. A. 599; with *of;* *of good still good proceeds*: P. L. IX. 973.

(*d*) to set to work, take measures, act; *how with Mankind I proceed*: P. L. XI. 69; *to judgment he proceeded*: P. L. X. 164; with *prep. inf.*: P. L. VII. 69; P. R. IV. 125.

Process (procéss), *sb.* (*a*) the continuous proceeding: P. L. VII. 178.

(*b*) course; *process of time*: P. L. II. 297.

Procession, *sb.* a succession of angels moving with ceremonious solemnity: P. L. VII. 222.

Procinct, *sb. in procinct*, ready, at hand: P. L. VI. 19.

Proclaim, *vb. tr.* to declare or announce openly: P. L. V. 784; P. R. I. 70; IV. 474; *God proclaiming peace*: P. L. II. 499; *life to all*: P. L. XII. 407; with two *acc.; proclaimed me him*: P. R. I. 275; *proclaims him come*: P. L. XII. 361; in passive: P. L. V. 663.

(*b*) to publish or promúlgate by heralds or the sound of trumpets *council, tribunal*, etc.: P. L. I. 754; III. 325; S. A. 435, 1598; *Fame ... proclaims most deeds*: S. A. 972.

Proclaimer, *sb.* one who makes something known by public announcement; applied to John the Baptist: P. R. I. 18.

Proconsul, *sb.* the Roman officer who was charged with the government of a province: P. R. IV. 63.

Procreation, *sb.* the act of begetting, the generation of young: P. L. VIII. 597.

Procure, *vb. tr.* to bring about, cause: P. L. II. 225.

Prodigious, *adj.* (*a*) unnatural, monstrous: P. L. II. 625; *births of body or mind*: P. L. XI. 687.

(*b*) very great in extent; *prodigious motion*: P. L. II. 780; *length*: P. L. X. 302.

(*c*) very great in degree; *prodigious power, might*: P. L. VI. 247; S. A. 1083.

Prodigy, *sb.* portent: P. R. IV. 482.

Produce, *vb. tr.* (1) to bring forward, offer to view or consideration: P. R. I. 150; IV. 184.

(2) to bring into existence; (*a*) to generate: P. L. IX. 721; XI. 29; *the ... Sun ... produces ... many precious things*: P. L. III. 610; *rain produce fruits*: P. L. VIII. 146.

(*b*) to create; *space may produce new Worlds*: P. L. I. 650; *his Word all things produced*: P. R. III. 122.

(*c*) to beget (offspring): P. L. XI. 687.

(*d*) to bring forth; *all this good of evil shall produce*: P. L. XII. 470.

(3) to bring about, cause: P. L. X. 692; S. A. 1346.

(4) to bring into form, make; *Fancy .. wild work produces*: P. L. V. 112.

Product, *sb.* that which is begotten, offspring: P. L. XI. 683.

Productive, *adj.* having the power of producing: P. L. IX. 111.

Proem, *sb.* preface, introduction: P. L. IX. 549.

Profane, (1) *adj.* (*a*) done with irreverence: S. A. 1362; speaking irreverently: C. 781.

(*b*) *comp.* less initiated: Il P. 140.

absol. those who are irreverent toward God: S. A. 693.

(2) *vb. tr.* to treat with irreverence, pollute, desecrate: P. L. IV. 951; IX. 930; S. A. 377; *with cursed things his holy rites ... profaned*: P. L. I. 390.

Profess, *vb. tr.* (*a*) to acknowledge publicly or openly, avow ; with *prep. inf.* :* P. R. IV. 293.

refl. with the pron. omitted ; *professing next the spy*: P. L. IV. 948 ; in passive ; *thy country's foe professed* : S. A. 884.

(*b*) to make protestations of ; *nuptial love professed* : S. A. 385.

Proffer, *vb. tr.* to propose for acceptance : P. L. II. 425 ; to hold out or present for acceptance : P. R. II. 330.

Profit, I. *sb.* (*a*) that which is useful or helpful : P. R. IV. 345.

(*b*) pecuniary gain : S. A. 1261.

II. *vb.* (**1**) *tr.* to be of use to, benefit, advantage: P. L. VI. 909; *what profits then our inward freedom?*: P. L. IX. 761.

(**2**) *intr.* to be of use, bring good : P. L. VIII. 571.

Profluent, *adj.* flowing : P. L. XII. 442.

Profound, (**1**) *adj.* (*a*) deep, abysmal ; *void, gulf*, etc. : P. L. II. 438, 592, 858 ; Ps. LXXXVIII. 25 ; *sup.*, *profoundest Hell* : P. L. I. 251 ; N. O. 218.

(*b*) concerned with things intellectually deep ; *profound dispute* : P. R. IV. 214.

(*c*) intense ; *darkness profound* : P. L. VII. 233.

(**2**) *sb.* the abyss of chaos ; *I travel this profound*: P. L. II. 980.

Profundity, *sb.* the abyss of chaos ; *the vast profundity obscure* : P. L. VII. 229.

Profuse, (**1**) *adj.* liberal to excess, lavish, prodigal : P. L. VIII. 286 ; A. 9.

(**2**) *adv.* lavishly, prodigally : P. L. IV. 243.

Progenitor, *sb.* parent ; used of Adam : P. L. V. 544 ; XI. 346.

Progeny, *sb.* (*a*) offspring, children : P. L. III. 96 ; XI. 107 ; XII. 138 ; S. XII. 6 ; used of Adam and Eve as coming into being through the volition of God : P. L. V. 503.

fig., *Progeny of Heaven* : P. L. II. 430 ; *Progeny of Light* : P. L. V. 600. *See* **Heaven, Light.**

(*b*) descent, lineage : P. R. IV. 554.

Progress, *sb.* (*a*) a going forward ; *the Morn ... begins her rosy progress* : P. L. XI. 175.

(*b*) a journey of state : P. L. IV. 976.

Progressive, *adj.* going forward, advancing : P. L. VIII. 127.

Prohibit, *vb. tr.* to hinder, prevent : P. L. II. 437.

Prohibition, *sb.* interdiction : P. L. IV. 433 ; IX. 760 ; *the Tree of Prohibition*, the prohibited tree : P. L. IX. 645.

Project, (**1**) *sb.* scheme, plan : P. R. III. 391.

(**2**) *vb. tr.* to scheme, plan : P. L. II. 329.

Prolific, *adj.* having the quality of generating; *warm prolific humour* : P. L. VII. 280.

Prologue, *sb.* preface, introduction : P. L. IX. 854.

Prolong, *vb. tr.* (*a*) to lengthen in time : N. O. 100 ; *prolonged or prolong life* : P. L. XI. 331, 547 ; *prolong our expectation* : P. R. II. 41.

(*b*) to put off, postpone : P. R. IV. 469.

Promiscuous, (**1**) *adj.* mingled indiscriminately, miscellaneous, confused : P. L. I. 380.

(**2**) *adv.* indiscriminately : P. R. III. 118.

Promise, (**1**) *sb.* (*a*) a declaration by which one person binds himself to another to do something ; *on promise made* : P. L. II. 238 ; IV. 84 ; made by God: P. L. XII. 322 ; *by promise* : P. L. XII. 137.

(*b*) that which is promised by God : P. L. XII. 155 ; S. A. 38 ; one who is promised ; *a Comforter ... the promise of the Father* : P. L. XII. 487.

(**2**) *vb. tr.* to make a promise of, engage to do or give : P. L. XI. 413 ; S. A. 635 ; *thou hast promised from us two a race* : P. L. IV. 732 ; *promise wonders in her change* : S. A. 753 ; with *acc.* and *to* ; *great joy he promised to his thoughts* : P. L. IX. 843 ; in passive with *to*: P. L. XII. 260, 519, 542 ; *absol.*, *so promised he* : P. L. IV. 589.

part. adj. **promised** : P. L. IX. 1070 ; *race, seed, kingdom* : P. L. XI. 331 ; XII. 623 ; P. R. I. 265 ; *the Promised Land* : P. L. III. 531 ; P. R. III. 157, 439 ; *their promised land* : P. L. XII. 172.

Promontory, *sb.* (*a*) mountain-ridge : P. L. VI. 654.

(*b*) headland : P. L. VII. 414 ; *each beaked promontory* : L. 94.

Promote, *vb. tr.* (*a*) to contribute to the growth or establishment of, forward ; *promote all truth* : P. R. I. 205 ; *good works in her husband* : P. L. IX. 234.

(*b*) to raise up ; *did I solicit thee from darkness to promote me* : P. L. X. 745.

Promotion, *sb.* advancement : P. R. III. 202.

Prompt, (1) *adj.* (*a*) ready and unstudied ; *prompt eloquence* : P. L. V. 149.

(*b*) ready and willing ; *prompt obedience* : P. L. VIII. 240.

(2) *vb. tr.* (*a*) to move to action, incite : C. 229 ; *rage prompted them* : P. L. VI. 635 ; with *acc.* and *prep. inf.* : P. R. II. 456 ; S. A. 318 ; S. XII. 1.

(*b*) to suggest to the mind ; *divine impulsion prompting how thou might'st find some occasion to infest our foes* : S. A. 422.

(*c*) to aid, assist (?) : P. L. IX. 854.

part. adj. **prompted,** inspired ; *my prompted song* : P. R. I. 12.

Prone, *adj.* (*a*) being or moving with the head forward as a brute ; *a creature … not prone* : P. L. VII. 506 ; *these erect from prone* : P. L. VIII. 433 ; used of the serpent ; *on his belly prone* : P. L. X. 514 ; *prone on the ground* : P. L. IX. 497.

(*b*) lying flat ; *his other parts … prone on the flood* : P. L. I. 195.

(*c*) moving downward ; *the sun … with prone career* : P. L. IV. 353 ; descending abruptly ; *thither prone in flight he speeds* : P. L. V. 266.

(*d*) accompanied by a bowing or bending down in token of reverence or humility ; *they bend with awful reverence prone* : P. L. II. 478 ; *with supplication prone* : S. A. 1459.

(*e*) inclined or disposed ; *prone to pardon* : Ps. LXXXVI. 13.

Pronounce, *vb. tr.* (*a*) to declare or announce solemnly or officially : P. L. IV. 761 ; *from us, his foes pronounced* : P. R. III. 120 ; *absol.*, *so Fate pronounced* : P. L. II. 809 ; to declare or proclaim publicly and formally ; *our laws* : S. XXI. 3 ; with two *acc.* : P. R. IV. 275 ; used of God : P. L. V. 814 ; VIII. 333 ; *judgment, curse, penalty*

pronounced : P. L. X. 197, 640, 1022 ; *his will* : P. L. II. 352 ; XI. 83 ; with two *acc.* : P. R. IV. 513 ; *him Lord pronounced* : P. L. IX. 154 ; *him* or *me his beloved Son* : P. R. I. 32, 284 ; *it Death to taste* : P. L. IV. 427.

(*b*) to speak : P. L. IX. 553 ; *fit strains pronounced, or sung* : P. L. V. 148.

(*c*) to enunciate correctly ; *want of well pronouncing Shibboleth* : S. A. 289.

Proof, (1) *sb.* (*a*) trial, experiment, test : P. L. IX. 1142 ; *put to proof* : P. L. I. 132 ; *by proof* : P. L. II. 101, 686 ; V. 865 ; P. R. I. 11, 130, 400.

(*b*) evidence, testimony, confirmation : P. L. IX. 967 ; *high proof ye now have given to be the race of Satan* : P. L. X. 385 ; *proof … of true allegiance* : P. L. III. 103 ; *of his fatal guile* : P. L. IV. 350 ; *of their obedience* : P. L. IV. 520 ; *for proof* : P. L. IV. 1010 ; P. R. IV. 621 ; S. A. 1145.

demonstration, exhibition : S. A. 526, 1314 ; *proof of strength* : S. A. 1475, 1602.

(*c*) impenetrability : S. A. 134.

(2) *adj.* able to resist morally : P. L. VIII. 535 ; *proof against temptation* : P. L. IX. 298 ; P. R. IV. 533 ; *against all assaults* : P. L. X. 882.

See **Massy-proof, Star-proof, Virtue-proof.**

Prop, (1) *sb.* support, stay : P. L. IX. 433.

(2) *vb. tr.* to support by placing something under : P. L. IX. 210.

Propagate, *vb.* (1) *tr.* to multiply by natural generation : P. L. VIII. 580.

(2) *intr.* to be multiplied by generation : P. L. VIII. 420.

part. adj. **propagated,** begotten ; *fig., all that I … shall beget, is propagated curse* : P. L. X. 729.

Propense, *adj.* inclined, disposed : S. A. 455.

Proper, *adj.* (one's) own, peculiar ; *our proper motion* : P. L. II. 75 ; *his proper shape* : P. L. III. 634 ; V. 276 ; *red, Love's proper hue* : P. L. VIII. 619 ; my own ; *convert . to proper substance* : P. L. V. 493.

Properly, *adv.* in a strict sense : P. L. X. 791.

Property, *sb.* essential attribute, peculiar quality : V. Ex. 87 ; C. 469.

Prophecy, *sb.* a prediction under divine inspiration : S. A. 473 ; concerning the coming of Christ : P. L. XII. 325 ; P. R. IV. 381.

Prophesy, *vb. tr.* to predict by divine inspiration : P. R. IV. 108.

Prophet, *sb.* (1) soothsayer, seer : P. L. III. 36.

(2) one who by divine inspiration declares to men the will of God : P. R. IV. 226, 356 ; *Balaam ... a prophet yet inspired* : P. R. I. 491 ; *those young prophets ... sought lost Eliah* : P. R. II. 18 ; Elijah : P. R. II. 270, 312 ; Ezekiel : P. 37 ; one who so speaks concerning the coming of Christ : P. L. XII. 243 ; P. R. III. 178, 352 ; IV. 503 ; applied to John the Baptist as the herald of the Messiah : P. R. I. 70, 80, 328 ; II. 51.

(*b*) one who claims to speak by divine inspiration : P. R. I. 375.

(*c*) the books written by the prophets : P. R. I. 260.

(3) proclaimer, foreteller ; *O prophet of glad tidings* : P. L. XII. 375.

Prophetic, *adj.* (*a*) containing prophecy : P. R. III. 184 ; having the character of prophecy : Il P. 174.

(*b*) pertaining to prophecy, oracular ; *the prophetic cell* : N. O. 180.

(*c*) foretelling future events ; *prophetic Anna* : P. R. I. 255 ; concerned with future events : P. L. II. 346.

Propitiation, *sb.* that which appeases ; used of Christ as furnishing by his life and death a ground for the forgiveness of sins : P. L. XI. 34.

Propitious, *adj.* (*a*) favourably disposed, gracious : P. L. V. 507 ; *the jolly hours lead on propitious May* : S. I. 4 ; used of God : P. L. XII. 612 ; *my Maker, be propitious while I speak* : P. L. VIII. 380.

(*b*) indicative of a readiness to be gracious ; *propitious fire from heaven* : P. L. XI. 441.

Proportion, (1) *sb.* comparative relation in amount or degree : P. L. VIII. 385 ; IX. 711 ; C. 773.

(2) *vb. tr.* to adjust in suitable relations : P. L. V. 479 ; S. A. 209.

part. adj. **proportioned,** granted in suitable measure : C. 330.

Proportional, *adj.* having a due comparative relation, corresponding : P. L. IX. 936.

Proposal, *sb.* a plan offered for acceptance : S. A. 487 ; *pl.* terms of peace proposed ; used quibblingly : P. L. VI. 618.

Propose, *vb.* (*pres. 2d sing.* proposest : P. L. VIII. 400 ; X. 1038) *tr.* (*a*) to offer for consideration or acceptance : P. R. IV. 370 ; *counsel, terms, ransom* : P. L. II. 380 ; X. 757 ; S. A. 1471 ; *I ... have proposed what both from men and angels I receive* : P. R. IV. 199 ; *absol., as thou proposest* : P. L. X. 1038.

(*b*) to offer or present for solution : S. A. 1200 ; *that Theban monster that proposed her riddle* : P. R. IV. 572 ; for discussion : *to propose what might improve my knowledge or their own* : P. R. I. 212.

(*c*) to place before as something to be done, point out as a goal to be reached : P. L. II. 447 ; VIII. 400 ; with *prep. inf.* : P. R. I. 371.

(*d*) to speak, utter : P. L. VIII. 64.

part. adj. **proposed,** offered for acceptance ; *God's proposed deliverance* : S. A. 292.

Propound, *vb. tr.* to offer for consideration or acceptance ; used punningly : P. L. VI. 567, 612 ; to propose ; *dar'st thou to the Son of God propound to worship thee* : P. R. IV. 178.

Propriety, *sb.* that which is held as an exclusive possession : P. L. IV. 751.

Prose, *sb.* language not conformed to poetical measure ; *in prose or numerous verse* : P. L. V. 150 ; *in prose or rhyme* : P. L. I. 16.

Prosecute, *vb. tr.* (*a*) to make efforts to obtain ; *prosecute the means of thy deliverance* : S. A. 603.

(*b*) to pursue for redress or punishment ; *gods unable to ... prosecute their foes* : S. A. 897.

Proserpin (Prosérpin) *sb.* Proserpina : P. L. IV. 269.

Proserpina (Prosérpina) *sb.* the daughter of Ceres, the wife of Pluto, and the queen of the infernal regions : P. L. IX. 396.

Prospect, *sb.* (*a*) the view of things within the reach of the eye, sight, survey : P. L. IV. 144; *the amplest reach of prospect* : P. L. XI. 380; *in prospect* : P. L. VII. 556; X. 89; XII. 143; *the ground, under a cloud in prospect*, to anyone looking at or viewing it: P. L. VII. 423.

(*b*) that which is presented to the eye, scene, view : P. L. III. 548; *the Earth... a prospect wide and various* : P. L. V. 88; *to ken the prospect round* : P. R. II. 286; *on that prospect strange their... eyes they fixed*: P. L. X. 552; *so large the prospect* : P. R. III. 263.

(*c*) a place affording an extensive view : P. L. III. 77; or in sense (*a*) : P. L. IV. 200.

Prospective-glass, *sb.* a glass in which may be seen future events ; *Time's long and dark prospective glass*: V. Ex. 71.

Prosper, *vb. intr.* to thrive; (*a*) to succeed, be fortunate; used of persons : P. L. II. 39; X. 360; XII. 316; *by force or fraud weening to prosper* : P. L. VI. 795.

(*b*) to grow, flourish ; *her fruits and flowers, to visit how they prospered* : P. L. VIII. 45.

(*c*) to turn out fortunately ; *what he takes in hand shall prosper*: Ps. I. 10.

Prosperity, *sb.* success, good fortune: P. L. II. 39.

Prosperous, *adj.* (*a*) favourable, advantageous ; *things* : P. L. II. 259; *either state to bear, prosperous or adverse* : P. L. XI. 364; *the way found prosperous* : P. R. I. 104.

(*b*) fortunate, successful ; *in prosperous days* : S. A. 191; *with prosperous wing* : P. R. I. 14.

(*c*) thriving, flourishing : C. 270.

Prostituting, (1) *gerund*, the act of surrendering to base uses ; *by prostituting holy things to idols* : S. A. 1358.

(2) *vbl. sb.* the act of offering the body to indiscriminate sexual intercourse for hire : P. L. XI. 716.

Prostrate (prostráte : P. L. VI. 841) *adj.* (*a*) lying at one's length : P. L. I. 280.

(*b*) lying or bowed low in the posture of extreme humility or supplication : P. L. X. 1087, 1099; Ps. LXXXVIII. 4; with blending of the ideas : overcome and lying on the ground : P. L. VI. 841.

Prostration, *sb.* the act of bowing down in humility and adoration : P. L. V. 782.

Protect, *vb. tr.* to guard, defend, shield : S. VIII. 4; *the faithful side ... still shades thee and protects* : P. L. IX. 266.

Protection, *sb.* shelter, defense, *Lord ... under thy protection* : Ps. VII. 3; *nor was I under their protection* : S. A. 887.

Protest, *vb. tr.* to call upon as a witness, appeal to : P. L. X. 480.

Proteus, *sb.* the sea-god who tended the flocks (the beasts of the sea) of Poseidon, and who had the power of assuming every possible shape in order to escape the necessity of prophesying : P. L. III. 604. *See* **Carpathian**.

Proud, *adj.* (*a*) full of inordinate self-esteem, arrogant, haughty : P. L. IX. 383; XII. 25; P. R. I. 219; S. A. 1462; Ps. LXXXIII. 7; *the Tempter proud*: P. R. IV. 569, 595; *Cherub*: P. L. IV. 971; *Aspirer*: P. L. VI. 89; *victors*: P. L. VI. 609; *crowned Fortune proud* : S. XVI. 5; *sup.*: P. L. XII. 497; P. R. III. 99; imperious; lordly; *nation, cities, kings* : P. L. II. 533; XII. 342; C. 33; Ps. LXXX. 35; LXXXVII. 11; *proud king Ahab*: P. R. I. 372; proudly disregardful, disdainful : P. L. IV. 770; elated with success : P. L. III. 159.

(*b*) indicative of pride ; *proud step, pile* : P. L. IV. 536; S. A. 1069; *the proud crest of Satan* : P. L. VI. 191.

(*c*) proceeding from pride, daring, bold, presumptuous ; *battle*, etc.: P. L. I. 43; II. 691; VII. 609; XII. 72; *imaginations, argument, excuse*: P. L. II. 10; V. 809; X. 764.

(*d*) being a ground of pride ; *proud honour* : P. L. I. 533; lofty, magnificent : P. L. X. 424; *proud towers* : P. L. V. 907; grand; *armies ranked in proud array* : S. A. 345; strong; *proud arms* : S. A. 137; great, large; *rivers proud* : P. R. III. 334.

(*e*) full of mettle: P. L. IV. 858. *absol.* one who is arrogant; *the proud*: P. L. VI. 789; Ps. LXXXVI. 49; in direct address ; *Proud, art thou met ?* : P. L. VI. 131.

Proudly, *adv.* (*a*) arrogantly, haughtily, boldly : P. R. IV. 580 ; S. A. 55 ; Ps. LXXXI. 58.

(*b*) in a lofty or stately manner : P. L. VII. 439.

(*c*) as indicating pride or arrogance ; *he, above the rest ... proudly eminent* : P. L. I. 590.

(*d*) to a great height ; *towers and temples proudly elevate* : P. R. IV. 34.

Prove, *vb.* (1) *tr.* (*a*) to make trial of, test : P. L. IX. 616 ; *gave into my hands Uzzean Job, to prove him* : P. R. I. 370.

(*b*) to render certain, demonstrate, show : P. L. VI. 170 ; with two *acc.*; *how dost thou prove me these?* : S. A. 1181 ; with clause : U. C. II. 1.

(*c*) to experience, feel ; *which we had proved ... to burn* : Ps. LXXXV. 11 ; to enjoy : C. 123 ; U. C. II. 1.

(2) *intr.* to be found or shown to be by experience or trial ; followed by an *inf.*; *those pearls ... prove to be presaging tears* : M. W. 44 ; followed by a *sb.* : P. L. IV. 985 ; X. 963 ; C. 592 ; *God may prove their foe* : P. L. II. 369 ; *I shall prove a bitter morsel* : P. L. II. 808 ; *the contrary she proves* : S. A. 1037 ; followed by an *adj.* or *adv.* : P. L. VI. 117 ; VIII. 388 ; X. 761 ; S. A. 1400, 1575 ; *so much the stronger proved he* : P. L. I. 92 ; *which the stronger proves* : P. L. VI. 819 ; *his good proved ill* : P. L. IV. 48 ; *thoughts proved fond* : P. L. VI. 90 ; *false* : P. L. VI. 271 ; IX. 333 : S. A. 227 ; *proves not so* : P. L. VI. 428.

(*b*) nearer in meaning to : to be, become : P. L. III. 119 ; X. 664 ; XI. 123 ; S. A. 64, 351, 1262.

Proverb, *vb. tr.* to speak of proverbially ; *am I not ... proverbed for a fool?* : S. A. 203.

Provide, *vb. tr.* (*a*) to furnish, supply : P. L. VI. 520 ; C. 187 ; *absol.* : P. L. X. 1058.

(*b*) to procure beforehand, make ready, prepare : P. L. VIII. 363 ; X. 237 ; *till I provided Death* : P. L. XI. 61.

part. adj. **providing**, furnishing food and comfort : P. R. II. 310.

Providence, *sb.* (*a*) the care and guardianship of God : P. L. II. 559 ; *assert Eternal Providence* :
P. L. I. 25 ; *his providence* P. L. I. 162 ; XII. 564 ; P. R. I. 445 ; III. 440 ; *all our fears lay on his providence* : P. R. II. 54 ; *thy providence* : S. A. 670 ; Ps. VIII. 8.

(*b*) God as exercising care and guardianship : S. A. 1545 ; *Providence their guide* : P. L. XII. 647 ; *eye me, blest Providence* : C. 329.

Provident, *adj.* careful, cautious in preparing for future exigencies ; with *of* : P. L. V. 828 ; *the ... emmet, provident of future* : P. L. VII. 485.

Province, *sb.* (*a*) a country under Roman dominion : P. R. III. 158 ; IV. 63, 136 ; under Parthian dominion : P. R. III. 315.

(*b*) an administrative division of a country ; *his Angels president in every province* : P. R. I. 448 ; as ruled over by Satan or his angels : P. R. I. 118 ; in heaven ; *many a tract of Heaven ... many a province* : P. L. VI. 77.

Provision, *sb.* that which is provided for future use ; *she* (Nature), *good cateress, means her provision only to the good* : C. 765 ; a store of food provided ; *till men grow up to their provision* : P. L. IX. 623 ; victuals, food : P. R. II. 402 ; *pl.* : P. L. XI. 732.

Provoke, *vb. tr.* (*a*) to incite or arouse to action ; *this right hand provoked* : P. L. VI. 154 ; with *acc.* and *prep. inf.* : P. L. X. 1027 ; XII. 318.

(*b*) to instigate, stir up ; *war* : P. L. I. 644, 645 ; *anger, envy* : P. L. IV. 916 ; IX. 175 ; to be the cause of ; *peril great provoked* : P. L. IX. 922.

(*c*) to arouse to anger : S. A. 237, 643 ; to incense (God) : P. L. II. 82 ; S. A. 446.

Prow, *sb.* the forepart of a ship : P. L. XI. 746.

Prow, *adj.* valiant, *sup.* : P. R. III. 342.

Prowess, *sb.* bravery, valour : P. L. XI. 789 ; P. R. III. 19 ; S. A. 286 ; Ps. CXXXVI. 62 ; *the glory of prowess* : S. A. 1098 ; *mortal, military* : P. L. I. 588 ; VI. 45.

Prowling, *part. adj.* roaming about stealthily in search of prey : P. L. IV. 183.

Prudence, *sb.* wisdom, sagacity, discretion : P. R. IV. 263.

Prudent, *adj.* (*a*) politic, provident: P. L. II. 468.

(*b*) wise, sagacious; *so steers the prudent crane her annual voyage*: P. L. VII. 430.

Prune, *vb. tr.* to cut off superfluous twigs or branches: P. L. IV. 438; IX. 210.

Pry, *vb. intr.* to look searchingly with scrutinizing curiosity : P. L. I. 665 ; IX. 159.

Psalm, *sb.* a sacred poem or song: S. M. 15 ; *pl.* those contained in the Book of Psalms : P. R. IV. 335.

Psaltery, *sb.* the stringed musical instrument : Ps. LXXXI. 7.

Psyche, *sb.* a beautiful maiden who became the wife of Cupid. Against his wish, she revealed his name to her sisters, whereupon he left her. She then wandered alone over the earth compelled by the jealousy of Venus to perform many labours. At the prayer of Cupid, she was restored to her husband and granted immortality : C. 1005.

Public, (1) *adj.* (*a*) pertaining to the whole people of a state ; *public peace, good* : P. L. XII. 317 ; P. R. I. 204 ; S. A. 867 ; *faith, fraud* : S. XV. 12, 13 ; *cares* : P. R. IV. 96 ; *officer, servant* : S. A. 1306, 1615 ; pertaining to all the inhabitants of hell ; *public care, moment, reason* : P. L. II. 303, 448 ; IV. 389.

(*b*) open to all the people ; *public mill* : S. A. 1327, 1393; shared in by all; *public scorn* : P. L. X. 509.

(*c*) given before all, open to the knowledge of all: S. A. 992, 1314; *in public*, before the people at large, in open view : P. R. II. 52, 84.

(2) *sb.* the general body of people constituting a nation ; *the public* : P. R. II. 465 ; Eurip. 2.

Publish, *vb. tr.* (*a*) to make generally and openly known ; *publish his godlike office* : P. R. I. 188 ; *publish grace to all* : P. L. II. 238.

(*b*) to reveal : S. A. 777 ; *have published his holy secret* : S. A. 498.

Puissance, *sb.* strength, power, might : P. L. V. 864 ; VI. 119.

Puissant, *adj.* (*a*) strong, mighty; *puissant legions* : P. L. I. 632; *thy puissant thigh* : P. L. VI. 714 ;

powerful ; *puissant words and murmurs made to bless* : A. 60.

(*b*) having great power or influence ; *puissant friends* : P. R. II. 425.

(*c*) accomplished with might or power ; *puissant deeds* : P. L. XII. 322.

Pull, *vb. tr.* to draw, haul, tug: L'A. 103 ; *the edifice ... upon their heads and on his own he pulled* : S. A. 1589 ; *pulled up ... the gates* : S. A. 146 ; *pulled off his boots* : U. C. I. 16 ; *absol.* : S. A. 1626 ; *fig.*, *pulled down the same destruction on himself* : S. A. 1658.

Pulp, *sb.* the soft succulent part of fruit: P. L. IV. 335.

Pulse, *sb.* the esculent seeds of leguminous plants : P. R. II. 278 ; C. 721.

Punctual, *adj.* resembling a point in size ; *Earth, this punctual spot* : P. L. VIII. 23.

Punic, *adj.* of the Carthaginians : P. L. V. 340 ; P. R. III. 102.

Punish, *vb. tr.* (*a*) to inflict suffering or restraint on as a punishment for sin : P. L. II. 159 ; *punished in the shape he sinned* : P. L. X. 516 ; *to ... punish mortals* : P. L. II. 1032.

(*b*) to requite by visiting penalty upon the offender ; *my crime ... will be punished* : P. R. III. 214.

(*c*) to inflict as a punishment ; *satisfied with what is punished* : P. L. II. 213.

part. adj. **punished,** suffering the penalty of sin : P. L. X. 803.

Punisher, *sb.* one who inflicts a penalty ; applied to God : P. L. IV. 103.

Punishment, *sb.* (*a*) the infliction of a penalty : P. L. VI. 807.

(*b*) penalty inflicted for sin or crime : P. L. XI. 520, 710 ; S. A. 504 ; *pay on my punishment* : S. A. 489 ; *servile* : S. A. 413 ; *capital* : S. A. 1225; *the punishment of dissolute days* : S. A. 702 ; that inflicted upon Satan or his angels: P. L. II. 699 ; IV. 911 ; V. 881 ; X. 242, 544, 1039 ; *their place of punishment, the gulf of Tartarus* : P. L. VI. 53; *his punishment, eternal misery* : P. L. VI. 904 ; *eternal, arbitrary* : P. L. I. 155 ; II. 334 ; that inflicted upon Adam or Eve: P. L. X. 133, 768, 949 ; XII. 404.

Puny, *adj.* feeble, weak, insignificant : P. L. II. 367.

Purchase, (1) *sb.* (*a*) acquisition : P. L. x. 579.

(*b*) prey, booty : C. 607.

(2) *vb. tr.* to acquire, gain, obtain : P. L. IV. 101 ; *a world who would not purchase with a bruise* : P. L. x. 500.

Pure, *adj.* (1) absolute, perfect, unmixed : P. L. I. 425 ; *more spirituous and pure* : P. L. v. 475 ; *pure intelligential substances* : P. L. v. 407 ; *intelligence* : P. L. VIII. 180 ; *breath of life* : P. L. x. 784.

comp. our purer essence : P. L. II. 215 ; *of Elements the grosser feeds the purer* : P. L. v. 416 ; *purer fire* : C. 111.

sup. purest Spirits or spirits : P. L. v. 406 ; S. A. 613 ; *Spirits of purest light, purest at first* : P. L. VI. 660, 661.

(2) free from anything extraneous that impairs or pollutes, clear, clean, unspotted, unsullied : P. L. III. 7 ; VI. 758 ; x. 632 ; XI. 50 ; P. R. III. 27 ; *the pure Empyrean* : P. L. III. 57 ; *the pure firmament* : Ps. VIII. 11 ; *air* : P. L. III. 564 ; IV. 153 ; VII. 264 ; XI. 285 ; P. R. IV. 239 ; *the breath of heaven* : S. A. 10 ; *Light ... quintessence pure* : P. L. VII. 244 ; *Heaven and Earth, renewed, shall be made pure* : P. L. x. 638 ; *elixir, waters, rivers,* etc. : P. L. III. 607 ; IV. 456, 806 ; S. A. 548, 1727 ; C. 912 ; L. 175 ; S. XIV. 14 ; *blood* : P. L. IV. 805 ; *vessels, viands* : P. L. v. 348 ; P. R. II. 370 ; *weeds* : C. 16 ; *vested all in white, pure as her mind* : S. XXIII. 9.

comp. purer air : P. L. IV. 153.

sup. Heaven's purest light : P. L. II. 137.

(3) free from moral defilement, guiltless, innocent, chaste ; used of persons : P. L. IV. 316 ; v. 100 ; VIII. 623 ; P. R. II. 63 ; Il P. 31 ; S. IX. 14 ; *created, as thou art .. holy and pure* : P. L. XI. 606 ; *thou ... upright and pure* : P. L. IV. 837 ; *pure of sinful thought* : P. L. VIII. 506 ; *the Virgin pure* : P. R. I. 134 ; *a virgin pure* : C. 826 ; *upright heart and pure* : P. L. I. 18 ; *pure Nature's healthful rules* : P. L. XI. 523 ; used of God or Christ : P. R. I. 74, 77, 486.

(4) not arising from or involving any evil ; used of actions : P. L. IV. 747, 755 ; *kisses pure* : P. L. IV. 502 ; *life pure* : P. L. XII. 444 ; *whatever pure thou in the body enjoy'st* : P. L. VIII. 622 ; perhaps the meaning is nearer to holy ; *this pure cause* : C. 794.

(5) free from that which vitiates; (*a*) genuine, sincere, true ; *pure sanctitude, adoration,* etc. : P. L. IV. 293, 737 ; IX. 452 ; F. of C. 9.

(*b*) free from that which is untrue or false ; *records pure* : P. L. XII. 513 ; *kept thy truth so pure of old* : S. XVIII. 3.

(*c*) perfect ; *song of pure concent* : S. M. 6.

(6) not impaired in any manner, sound ; *pure digestion* : P. L. v. 4.

(7) clear-sighted, discerning : L. 81.

absol. that which is absolute spirit : P. L. VIII. 627.

Pure-eyed, *adj.* clear-sighted : C. 213.

Purfled, *part. adj.* ornamented with a border ; used *fig.* of the rainbow : C. 995.

Purgatory, *sb.* the place described by Dante in which the souls of those dying penitent are purified from venial sins : S. XIII. 14.

Purge, *vb. tr.* (*a*) to make clean or whole ; *purged ... the visual nerve* : P. L. XI. 414.

(*b*) to purify by removing that which defiles : P. L. XII. 548 ; *till fire purge all things new* : P. L. XI. 900.

(*c*) to clear away, remove, expel : P. L. III. 54 ; *downward purged the ... dregs* : P. L. VII. 237 ; with *off* : P. L. II. 141 ; *purge him off* : P. L. XI. 52 ; *purge off this gloom* : P. L. II. 400.

Purification, *sb.* the process of cleansing ceremonially : S. XXIII. 6.

Purify, *vb. tr.* to make pure, free from sin : P. R. I. 74.

Purity, *sb.* (*a*) moral cleanness, freedom from sin, innocence : P. L. IV. 745 ; IX. 1075 ; S. A. 319.

(*b*) chastity : C. 427.

Purlieu (purliéu), *sb.* (*a*) the open ground on the border of a forest : P. L. IV. 404.

(*b*) *pl.* the environs of a place, outskirts ; *in the purlieus of Heaven* : P. L. II. 833.

Purling, *part. adj.* rippling, murmuring: P. R. II. 345.

Purloin, *vb. tr.* to steal: P. L. II. 946.

Purple, (1) *adj.* of the colour of purple: P. L. I. 451; IX. 429; *purple grape*: P. L. IV. 259; C. 46; *flower*: D. F. I. 27; *wings*: P. L. IV. 764; *beams*: S. XIV. 10.

(2) *sb.* (*a*) the colour formed by the mixture of blue and red: P. L. IV. 596; VII. 479.

(*b*) cloth of this colour; *a military vest of purple*: P. L. XI. 241.

(3) *vb. tr.* to give a brilliant colour to; *Morn purples the East*: P. L. VII. 30; *purple all the ground with vernal flowers*: L. ,141.

Purpose, (1) *sb.* (*a*) that which a person proposes or intends to do, design, plan, intention, aim: P. L. VII. 614; P. R. II. 101; *my eternal purpose*: P. L. III. 172; *execute their aery purposes*: P. L. I. 430; *forerunners of his purpose*: P. L. XI. 195; *the Father in his purpose hath decreed*: P. R. III. 186; *change his purpose*: S. A. 1406; with *prep. inf.* indicating the design or intention: P. L. II. 971; III. 90; VI. 675; VII. 78; XII. 301; P. R. I. 444; IV. 93; S. A. 1498; *on purpose*, with design, intentionally: P. L. IV. 584.

(*b*) advantage, use; *to no purpose*: S. A. 569.

(*c*) discourse, conversation: P. L. IV. 337; VIII. 337.

(2) *vb. tr.* (*a*) to propose, intend, design: C. 284; with *prep. inf.*: S. A. 399.

(*b*) to resolve, determine; with *prep. inf.*: P. L. III. 404.

part. adj. **purposed;** (*a*) intended, designed; *thy purposed business*: V. Ex. 57; *no purposed foe*: P. L. IV. 373; *his purposed prey*: P. L. IX. 416.

(*b*) determined: P. R. I. 127.

Purposely, *adj.* designedly, intentionally: Ps. VII. 49.

Purse, *vb. tr.* to put in a purse or bag; with *up*: C. 642.

Pursue, *vb. tr.* (1) to follow; *his volant touch ... fled and pursued ... the resonant fugue*: P. L. XI. 563.

(2) to follow with the view of overtaking and seizing or harassing: P. L. I. 308; II. 79, 165, 945; VI. 52, 715; IX. 15; Ps. VII.

13; LXXXIII. 57; LXXXVIII. 68; *pursuing whom he late dismissed*: P. L. XII. 195; *I pursue thy lingering*: P. L. II. 701; *pursued with terrors and with furies*: P. L. VI. 858; to chase (bird or beast): P. L. XI. 188, 202.

(*b*) *absol.* or *intr.*: P. L. II. 790, 998; XII. 205, 206.

(3) to go in search of, seek to find: C. 503.

(4) to strive to gain; (*a*) to try or seek to regain: P. L. II. 249.

(*b*) to seek to accomplish: P. L. I. 15.

(5) to keep in view; used of the eye: P. L. IV. 125, 572; IX. 397; XI. 192.

(6) to dwell upon; *whom my thoughts pursue with wonder*: P. L. IV. 362.

(7) to be present with; *one doubt pursues me still*: P. L. X. 783; *dire imagination still pursues me*: S. A. 1544.

(8) to seek to injure, persecute: S. A. 1275.

(9) to continue; (*a*) to carry on, continue; *pursue vain war*: P. L. II. 8.

(*b*) to carry on, prosecute; *God's ... work pursued*: S. XVI. 6.

(*c*) to proceed with; *meditations, temptation, importunity*: P. R. I. 195; II. 405; IV. 24.

(*d*) to continue in the use or practice of; *pursue thy way of gaining David's throne*: P. R. IV. 470.

(*e*) to proceed along; *his way*: P. L. II. 524, 949.

Pursuer, *sb.* one who follows another in hostility: P. L. I. 326; P. R. III. 325.

Pursuit, *sb.* the act of following with a view of overtaking and seizing or harassing: P. L. I. 170; III. 397; VI. 538; P. R. III. 306; S. A. 280; C. 829.

Purvey, *vb.* (1) *tr.* to provide; *Nature ... hath purveyed ... her choicest store*: P. R. II. 333.

(2) *intr.* to provide food: P. L. IX. 1021.

Push, (1) *sb.* a setting in motion; *the push of fate*, the last moment before, or the moment when, fate begins to act: P. R. IV. 470.

(2) *vb. tr.* (*a*) to impel by pressure; *they ... pushed oblique the centric Globe*: P. L. X. 670; *waters*

...*pushed a mountain from his seat*: P. L. vi. 197; *this Mount ...pushed by the horned flood*: P. L. xi. 831; *the clouds ... pushed with winds*: P. L. x. 1074.

Put, *vb.* (*pret.* and *past part.* put) *tr.* (*a*) to oblige, constrain, compel: S. A. 37; *who puts me, loath, to this revenge*: P. L. iv. 386; *for possession put to try*: P. L. iv. 941.

(*b*) to place, set, lay: P. L. ii. 517; iv. 1002.

fig.: P. L. x. 497; *between thee and the Woman I will put enmity*: P. L. x. 179; *into the hands of their deliverer puts invincible might*: S. A. 1271; *into my heart more joy... thou hast put*: Ps. iv. 32.

(*c*) to bring into some specified state or condition: P. R. ii. 218; *put to proof*: P. L. i. 132; *to second rout*: P. L. iv. 3; *in doubt*: P. L. iv. 888; *to suspicious flight*: C. 158; *into misbecoming plight*: C. 372; *under his feet*: Ps. viii. 18.

In combination with other words; (*a*) **put down**, to put out of employment: U. C. ii. 20.

(*b*) **put forth**, to stretch out: P. L. vi. 583; to yield; *let the Earth put forth...grass*: P. L. vii. 310; to emit; *inward light ...puts forth no visual beam*: S. A. 163; to make manifest; *his regal state put forth*: P. L. i. 641; to exert; *strength, goodness*: P. L. vi. 853; vii. 171.

(*c*) **put off**, to lay aside; *put off these ... robes*: C. 82; *this glory ... put off*: P. L. iii. 240.

(*d*) **put on**, to clothe oneself with: P. L. iii. 479; *put on ... arms*: S. A. 1119; *fig.*, *to put on Gods*: P. L. ix. 714; to assume; *new part puts on*: P. L. ix. 667; *terrors, mildness*: P. L. vi. 734, 735; to bring into action; *puts on swift wings*: P. L. ii. 631.

(*e*) **put out**, to destroy the sight of: S. A. 33, 1103, 1160; to deprive *of*; *put him out of breath*: U. C. ii. 12.

vbl. sb. or *gerund*, **putting-off**, the act of laying aside; *the putting-off these ... disguises*: P. L. iv. 739; *by putting-off Human*: P. L. ix. 713.

Pygmean, *adj.* of the Pygmies, the mythical race of dwarfs dwelling in India; P. L. i. 780.

Pyramid, *sb.* that which is pyramidal in form; *a pyramid of fire*: P. L. ii. 1013.

(*b*) a pinnacle: P. L. v. 758.

(*c*) a sepulchral monument: W. S. 4.

Pyrrha, *sb.* (*a*) the wife of Deucalion; P. L. xi. 12. *See* **Deucalion.**

(*b*) the name of a girl: Hor. O. 3.

Pythian, *adj.* of Pytho, an old name for that part of Phocis in which Delphi was situated: P. L. x. 530; for Delphi itself: P. L. ii. 530.

Python, *sb.* the serpent which the earth, warmed by the sun, brought forth after the flood sent by Zeus: P. L. x. 531.

Q

Quadrate, *sb.* square; *the Powers Militant ... in mighty quadrate joined*: P. L. vi. 62.

Quadrature, *sb.* a territory square in shape; *the empyreal bounds, his quadrature*: P. L. x. 381.

Quaff, *vb.* (1) *tr.* to drink freely and copiously; *fig.*, *quaff immortality and joy*: P. L. v. 638.

(2) *intr.* to drink: P. R. iv. 118.

Quaint, *adj.* (*a*) clever, ingenious: P. L. viii. 78.

(*b*) skilfully or cunningly made or designed; *impresses quaint*: P. L. ix. 35; *a sceptre or quaint staff*: S. A. 1303; beautiful, pretty; L. 139; possibly with blending of sense (*c*); *curl the grove with ringlets quaint*: A. 47.

(*c*) strange, unfamiliar, curious: N. O. 194; *my quaint habits*: C. 157.

Qualm, *sb.* a fit of sickness: P. L. xi. 481

Quarrel, (1) *sb.* a ground or cause of complaint: S. A. 1329.

(2) *vb. intr.* to find fault; *I must not quarrel with the will of highest dispensation*: S. A. 60.

See **Love-quarrel.**

Quarry, *sb.* (*a*) a place where precious stones are taken from the rocks: P. L. v. 759.

(*b*) a mass of stone: P. 46.

Quarry, *sb.* an intended prey; *the grim Feature* (death) *... sagacious of his quarry*: P. L. x. 281.

Quarter, (1) *sb.* (*a*) one of the four parts into which the horizon is divided ; *ye Winds, that from four quarters blow* : P. L. v. 192.

(*b*) a particular region of country, district, locality : P. L. vi. 530 ; *the quarters of the North* : P. L. v. 689.

(*c*) assigned position : P. L. iii. 714.

(2) *vb. tr.* to divide ; possibly, to divide into four parts : C. 29.

part. adj. **quartered,** belonging to the four quarters of the horizon ; *the quartered winds* : P. R. iv. 202.

Quaternion, *sb.* a fourfold combination : P. L. v. 181.

Queen, *sb.* **(1)** a female sovereign, the consort of a king : V. Ex. 47 ; Cassiopeia, the wife of Cepheus, king of Ethiopia : Il P. 19.

(2) a woman whose position is in some way comparable to that of a queen ; (*a*) applied to Eve ; P. L. viii. 60 ; *Queen of this Universe* : P. L. ix. 684.

(*b*) goddess: A. 94, 109 ; Diana: C. 442, 446 ; Aphrodite : C. 1002; *Astarte, queen of heaven* : P. L. i. 439 ; *Ashtaroth, Heaven's queen* : N. O. 201 ; *fig., the Moon ... apparent queen* : P. L. iv. 608.

(*c*) a saint in heaven : M. W. 74.

(*d*) mistress ; *she shall be my queen* : C. 265.

(*e*) a woman of pre-eminence ; *queen ... on Beauty's throne* : P. R. ii. 212 ; *fig., Echo ... sweet Queen of Parley* : C. 241.

(3) something having a pre-eminence comparable to that of a queen ; *Rome, Queen of the Earth* : P. R. iv. 45.

See **Harvest-queen.**

Quell, *vb. tr.* (*a*) to put an end to, destroy, suppress; *quell the might of hellish charms* : C. 613 ; *strength ... quelled with pain* : P. L. vi. 457 ; *their pride* : P. L. v. 740 : S. A. 286.

(*b*) to overcome, subdue, vanquish : P. L. vi. 386 ; P. R. i. 218 ; iii. 35 ; S. A. 563, 1272 ; Ps. cxxxvi. 10 ; *who shall quell the adversary serpent* : P. L. xii. 311; *let them fall by their own counsels quelled* : Ps. v. 30 ; *compassion quelled his best of man* : P. L. xi. 496 ; *awe from above had quelled his heart* : P. L. iv. 860.

Queller, *sb.* one who deprives another of power ; used of Christ : P. R. iv. 634.

Quench, *vb. tr.* (*a*) to extinguish the fire of ; *fig., resist Satan's assaults, and quench his fiery darts* : P. L. xii. 492.

(*b*) to destroy the sight of : P. L. iii. 25 ; S. A. 95.

(*c*) to slake (thirst) ; *quench the drouth of Phœbus* : C. 66 ; *fig., quench not the thirst of glory* : P. R. iii. 38.

(*d*) a blending of the ideas : to put an end to and to extinguish : P. L. ii. 939.

Quest, *sb.* search, pursuit : D. F. I. 18 ; A. 34 ; C. 321 ; *on his quest* : P. L. ix. 414; *following ... the quest of* : P. R. i. 315 ; *with wandering quest* : P. L. ii. 830.

Question, (1) *sb.* (*a*) that which is asked, query : P. L. iv. 887 ; S. A. 1254.

(*b*) a subject for discussion : P. R. iv. 219.

(2) *vb. tr.* (*a*) to ask a question of, interrogate : L. 93.

(*b*) to doubt, hold as uncertain : P. L. iii. 166 ; ix. 720.

(*c*) to call in question, oppose : P. L. iv. 882.

Quick, (1) *adj.* (*a*) mentally vigorous or alert, *sup.* : P. R. iii. 238.

(*b*) rapid, swift : P. L. v. 269 ; vi. 597 ; vii. 405 ; viii. 259.

(*c*) that takes place rapidly or is soon over, not delayed : P. L. vi. 619 ; P. R. ii. 172; *quick ... change* : C. 841 ; *return* : P. L. ix. 399 ; C. 284 ; *destruction* : S. A. 764; *command* : C. 41.

(2) *sb.* or *absol.* living persons ; *to judge both quick and dead* : P. L. xii. 460.

(3) *adv.* without delay : P. L. iv. 1004; P. R. iii. 323; *then quick about thy purposed business* : V. Ex. 57.

Quicken, *vb. tr.* (*a*) to restore life to : U. C. ii. 16 ; *fig.* to make alive spiritually : Ps. lxxx. 75.

(*b*) to stimulate, rouse ; *quickened appetite* : P. L. v 85 ; *hunger and thirst* : P. L ix. 587.

part. adj. **quickening,** giving life : P. L. v. 8o1.

Quickly, *adv.* without delay, very soon : P. R. ii. 400; D. F. I. 42; M. W. 16 ; C. 1014.

Quiet, (1) *sb.* (*a*) the absence of disturbance ; *personified* : Il P. 45.
in quiet, in freedom from political disturbance : P. R. III. 360.
(*b*) rest, repose : Ps. LXXXIII. 50 ; *may thy grave peace and quiet ever have* ; M. W. 48.
(2) *adj.* (*a*) free from social disturbance ; *the quiet state of men* : P. L. XII. 80.
(*b*) not distressed, at peace : P. L. XI. 272.
(3) *vb. tr.* to calm, tranquillize ; *what may quiet us in a death so noble* : S. A. 1724.

Quietly, *adv.* calmly, tranquilly : P. R. III. 192.

Quill, *sb.* a musical pipe ; *fig.* probably with the meaning : mood, strain : L. 188.

Quiloa (Quilóa), *sb.* one of the provinces of Zanzibar. "Quiloa lieth on the south of Mombaza. It took this name from Quiloa the chief town thereof, situate in a little island." Heylyn, *Cos.* 1657, p. 991 : P. L. X. 399.

Quintessence (qúintessénce : P. L. III. 716), *sb.* the 'fifth essence,' as distinguished from the four elements, earth, water, air, and fire ; *this ethereal quintessence of Heaven*: P. L. III. 716 ; *Light ... quintessence pure* : P. L. VII. 244.

Quintilian, *sb.* the Roman rhetorician : S. XI. 11.

Quintius, *sb.* Lucius Quintius Cincinnatus who was taken from the plough to the dictatorship of Rome : P. R. II. 446.

Quip, *sb.* a smart or witty saying : L'A. 27.

Quire, *sb.* **(1)** a band of singers who perform the music in church service : Il P. 162 ; in the worship of a god : H. B. 6.
(2) a company of singers in general ; (*a*) at a wedding : M. W. 17.
(*b*) used of angels : P. L. XII. 366 ; P. R. I. 242 ; N. O. 115 ; S. M. 12 ; *the Angel Quire* : N. O. 27 ; *heavenly, celestial, Angelic* : P. L. IV. 711 ; VII. 254 ; P. R. IV. 593.
(*c*) *fig.* the *quire of creatures wanting voice* : P. L. IX. 198 ; *the starry quire* : C. 112 ; or the meaning may be : the music made by a company of singers ; *the birds their quire apply* : P. L. IV. 264.

(*d*) *Phœbus' quire*, the Muses : S. XIII. 10.
(3) each of the nine orders of angels in the heavenly hierarchy : P. L. V. 251 ; *the quires of Cherubim* : P. L. III. 666 ; sing. collect. *all the Heavenly Quire stood mute* : P. L. III. 217.

Quit, *vb. tr.* **(1)** to set free, deliver ; with *of* : P. L. XI. 548.
(*b*) *refl.* to free or rid oneself *of* ; in passive ; *quit of all impediment* : P. L. VI. 548.
(2) to acquit, absolve ; *quits her of unclean* : S. A. 324.
(*b*) to discharge from liabilities ; *fig.*, *I ... glad to scape so quit* : P. R. I. 447.
(3) *refl.* to bear oneself, behave ; *Samson hath quit himself like Samson* : S. A. 1709.
(4) to remit ; *God will relent, and quit thee all his debt* : S. A. 509.
(5) to cease to have, use, or be occupied with : P. R. III. 241 ; *I did but prompt the age to quit their clogs* : S. XII. 1.
(*b*) to be free from ; *how to quit the yoke of God's Messiah* : P. L. V. 882.
(*c*) to resign, give up : P. L. III. 307 ; X. 627 ; S. A. 1484.
(6) to go away from, leave (a place) : P. L. VII. 440 ; (a person) : P. L. IV. 770 ; to part from ; *this earthy grossness quit* : T. 20.
(7) to pay ; *quit the debt ... of ... gratitude* : P. L. IV. 51.

Quite, *adv.* completely, wholly ; (*a*) used with a vb. : P. L. II. 93, 96 ; III. 50, 173 ; XI. 712 ; XII. 28 ; P. R. II. 224 ; IV. 352 ; S. A. 469, 907 ; C. 336, 468, 527, 728 ; N. O. 67 ; L'A. 149 ; Ps. VI. 24 ; LXXXIII. 39 ; following the vb. ; *dismissing quite* : P. L. II. 282 ; *redeem thee quite* : P. L. XI. 258 ; *vanished quite* : P. R. II. 402 ; *extinguished quite* : S. A. 1688 ; *cut off quite* : S. A. 1158.
(*b*) with an adj. adv. or phrase ; *regardless quite of* : P. L. IV. 317 ; *to rase quite out* : P. L. XII. 54 ; *quite at a loss* : P. R. IV. 366.

Quiver, *sb.* the case for holding arrows : P. L. III. 367 ; VI. 764 ; IX. 390.

Quivered, *part. adj.* furnished with a quiver : C. 422.

Quoth, *vb.* (only in *pret.* quoth) *tr.*
to say, declare : U. C. II. 17 ; L.
107.

R

Rabba, *sb.* the capital city of the
Ammonites situated on the river
Jabbok : P. L. I. 397.

Rabbi, *sb.* an expounder of the
Jewish law : P. R. IV. 218.

Rabble, *sb.* a disorderly crowd, mob :
P. R. III. 50.

Race, *sb.* (*a*) the course of life : P.
L. XII. 505 ; *my race of glory run* :
S. A. 597.

(*b*) the daily course of the sun
through the heavens : P. L. VII.
99.

(*c*) the course of time ; *this
transient World, the race of Time* :
P. L. XII. 554 ; *till thou run out
thy race* : T. 1.

(*d*) a contest of speed : P. L.
II. 529 ; IX. 33.

Race, *sb.* (1) offspring, posterity,
descendants ; *the race of Satan* :
P. L. X. 385 ; *fig.* : P. L. VII. 33.

(*b*) the production of offspring :
P. L. VII. 530.

(2) tribe, nation, people : P. L.
I. 577 ; P. R. III. 423 ; *Pygmean
race* : P. L. I. 780 ; *the unforeskinned race* : S. A. 1100 ; *the
race elect* : P. L. XII. 214 ; as
descended from a specified ancestor : P. L. XII. 104, 163 ; *the race
of Israel* : P. L. I. 432 ; P. R. II.
310 ; *Abraham's race* : S. A. 29 ;
his race who slew his brother : P. L.
XI. 608.

(3) a great division of living
beings ; (*a*) applied to mankind,
as including Adam and Eve : P.
L. II. 834 ; *human race* : P. L. VI.
896 ; *race of mankind* : P. L. II.
382 ; III. 161 ; *some new race,
called Man* : P. L. II. 348 ; *this
new happy race of Men* : P. L. III.
679 ; *the whole race lost* : P. L. III.
280 ; *instead of Spirits malign, a
better race* : P. L. VII. 189 ; as
descended from Adam and Eve :
P. L. VI. 501 ; VII. 45 ; VIII. 339 ;
X. 607, 988 ; XI. 331 ; *race of
mankind* : P. L. XI. 13 ; *the race
of Man* : P. L. XI. 782, 786 ;
human race : P. L. IV. 475 ; *from
us two a race* : P. L. IV. 732 ; *out
of one man a race of men* : P. L.
VII. 155 ; *to bring into the World*

a woeful race : P. L. X. 984 ; *in
them the whole included race* : P.
L. IX. 416.

(*b*) applied to angels ; *the race
of Heaven thus trampled* : P. L.
II. 194.

(4) a group or class of persons ;
that sober race of men : P. L. XI.
621 ; with blending of sense (1) ;
multiply a race of worshippers : P.
L. VII. 630 ; *a race of mourners* :
P. 56.

Rack, *vb. tr.* to torture mentally :
P. L. I. 126 ; P. R. III. 203.

part. adj. **racking,** causing great
physical pain : P. L. XI. 481 ;
racking whirlwinds : P. L. II. 182.
See **Joint-racking.**

Radiance, *sb.* brightness shooting in
rays or beams : P. L. VII. 194.

Radiant, *adj.* (*a*) emitting rays of
light, shining brightly ; *the radiant sun* : P. L. II. 492 ; *Morn ...
with radiant finger* : P. R. IV.
428 ; *Virtue ... with radiant feet* : N.
O. 146 ; *a radiant white* : P. L.
XI. 206 ; used of a precious stone :
P. L. VI. 761 ; used of that which
is in heaven, of Christ, angels,
etc. : P. L. III. 63 ; *radiant visage,
files, forms* : P. L. III. 646 ; IV.
797 ; V. 457 ; *shrine, seat* : P. L.
III. 379 ; X. 85 ; *cloud* : P. L. VII.
247.

(*b*) appearing in the form of
rays ; *radiant light* : P. L. III.
594 ; C. 374 ; *sheen* : M. W. 73 ;
bright, probably owing to the
emission of rays of light from
shining objects ; *radiant state* : A.
14.

(*c*) full of splendour and magnificence ; *radiant courts* : P. R.
III. 237.

Rafter, *sb.* one of the beams giving
the slope to a roof and supporting
the roof covering : C. 324.

Rag, *sb.* a torn and formless fragment of cloth ; *fluttered into rags* :
P. L. III. 491 ; *pl.* worn and mean
garments : S. A. 415.

Rage, I. *sb.* (1) violent anger, furious
passion : P. L. IX. 16 ; Ps. VII.
20 ; *all in rage* : P. L. XII. 58 ; *in
his rage* : P. L. XII. 194 ; *bends his
rage* : Ps. VIII. 8 ; *wake my sudden
rage* : S. A. 953 ; attributed to
God or angels : P. L. I. 95 ; II.
144 ; VI. 635 ; *to disordered rage
let loose the reins* : P. L. VI. 696 ; to
Satan or his angels : P. L. III.

80; v. 845; vi. 199, 813; viii. 244; P. R. i. 38; *vast Typhœan rage*: P. L. ii. 539; *inflamed, overcome, swoln with rage*: P. L. iv. 9, 857; P. R. iv. 499; *waxing more in rage*: P. L. iv. 969; *vent his rage*: P. R. iv. 445; to death: P. L. ii. 791; *on me let Death wreak all his rage*: P. L. iii. 241.

(*b*) the fury of battle; *Punic rage*: P. R. iii. 102; in heaven: P. L. vi. 217.

(2) violence; used of fire, thunder: P. L. ii. 67, 171, 581; *thunders ... mustering their rage*: P. L. ii. 268; *thunder ... winged with ... rage*: P. L. i. 175.

(3) passionate desire; with *prep. inf.*: S. A. 836.

(4) vehement martial ardour; *instead of rage deliberate valour breathed*: P. L. i. 553.

II. *vb. intr.* (1) to be furious with anger: P. L. xi. 444; to rave in fury; *they raged against the Highest*: P. L. i. 666.

(2) to move furiously: P. L. vi. 211.

(*b*) to have a high degree of intensity; *thy anger ... rages*: S. A. 963.

(*c*) to be at the height; *battle when it raged*: P. L. i. 277; to break out violently; *the wrath ... raging into sudden flame*: P. L. v. 891.

(*d*) to be violent: S. A. 619.

(3) to be furiously eager; *raging to pursue the righteous*: S. A. 1275.

part. adj. **raging**, moving or acting with violence; *raging fires, fire, sea*: P. L. ii. 213, 600; x. 286.

Ragged, *adj.* rough, shaggy: L'A. 9.

Rail, *vb. intr.* to use opprobrious language; with *at*: S. xii. 6.

Rain, I. *sb.* water falling in drops through the atmosphere: P. L. viii. 146; x. 1063; xi. 743, 826, 894; P. R. iv. 412; S. A. 1062.

II. *vb.* (1) *intr.* (*a*) to send or pour down rain; *God hath not yet rained upon the Earth*: P. L. vii. 331; *clouds may rain*: P. L. viii. 146.

(*b*) to fall like rain; *tears rained at their eyes*: P. L. ix. 1122.

(2) *tr.* to cause to pour down like rain; *God rained from heaven manna*: P. R. ii. 312; *fig.* to spread abroad, shed; *bright eyes rain influence*: L'A. 122.

Rainbow, *sb.* the arch formed by the reflection and refraction of rays of light from rain; *the colours of the rainbow*: C. 300; *the florid hue of rainbows*: P. L. vii. 446; *orbed in a rainbow*: N. O. 143.

Raise, *vb.* I. *tr.* (1) to lift and place in a standing posture: P. L. vi. 856; viii. 300; xi. 422; *raised by quick instinctive motion*: P. L. viii. 258; *on his side leaning half raised*: P. L. v. 12.

(2) to restore to life: P. L. iii. 258, 296; to cause to rise *from* and appear in life; *raise Musœus from his bower*: Il P. 104.

(3) to incite; with *acc.* and *prep. inf.*: P. L. i. 99; L. 70.

(4) to rouse up, stimulate; *utmost vigour raise*: P. L. ix. 314; *appetite, raised by the smell*: P. L. ix. 740; *to better hopes his ... mind .. had raised*: P. L. x. 1012.

(*b*) to encourage, inspire: P. L. ii. 468, 521.

(*c*) to reanimate, revive; *raised their fainting courage*: P. L. i. 529.

(5) to build or pile up, construct; *as a mount raised on a mount*: P. L. v. 758; *that mountain ... high raised upon the rapid current*: P. L. iv. 226; *where plain was raise hill*: P. R. iii. 333; *raised of grassy turf their table was*: P. L. v. 391; to create, produce; *to raise magnificence*: P. L. ii. 272; *Eden raised in the ... Wilderness*: P. R. i. 7.

(*b*) to found, establish: Petr. 2.

(6) to bring into existence, produce; *God ... from him will raise a mighty nation*: P. L. xii. 123; *God voutsafes to raise another world from him*: P. L. xi. 877; *raise ... new Heavens*: P. L. xii. 547; to create, and with blending of sense (11): P. L. ix. 177; *that raised us from the dust*: P. L. iv. 416.

(7) to cause to come into existence or to appear: P. R. i. 124; *provoking God to raise them enemies*: P. L. xii. 318.

(8) to produce (a sound); *raise such outcries on thy clattered iron*: S. A. 1124.

(*b*) to sing : Ps. VII. 62.

(9) to give rise to, cause, originate *war*, *troubles*, etc.: P. L. I. 43 ; IV. 574 ; V. 226 ; VI. 224 ; XI. 103, 796 ; *ambition*, *hopes*, etc.: P. L. IV. 60, 806 ; V. 680 ; P. R. II. 64 ; III. 59 ; S. A. 839 ; *inflammation* : S. A. 625.

(*b*) to create; *to raise that name*: P. L. IX. 43.

(10) to move to a higher position, lift : P. L. IV. 590 ; *though new rebellions raise their Hydra heads* : S. xv. 6.

(11) to advance to a higher rank or position, exalt in power : P. L. II. 5, 427 ; III. 162 ; S. A. 172 ; *what raised Antipater* : P. R. II. 423 ; *I was no private*, *but a person raised ... to free my country* : S. A. 1211 ; *whom God hath ... raised as their deliverer* : S. A. 273.

(*b*) to bring out of (a condition of distress) : Ps. LXXXII. 11.

(*c*) to extol, laud : A. 8.

(12) to elevate to a higher mental or spiritual position : P. L. VII. 157 ; VIII. 430 ; IX. 667 ; *raised to highth of noblest temper heroes old* : P. L. I. 551 ; to a sufficiently high mental position ; *capacity not raised to apprehend ... what is best* : S. A. 1028.

(*b*) to make higher or nobler (the mind, thoughts) : P. L. I. 23 ; P. R. I. 232.

(13) to cause to appear; *grisly spectres*, *which the Fiend had raised* : P. R. IV. 430.

(14) to bring together ; *raised incessant armies* : P. L. VI. 138.

II. *intr.* to rise *from* : P. L. X. 457.

See **High-raised, Self-raised.**

Rally, *vb. tr.* to reassemble ; *to ... fight rallied their Powers* : P. L. VI. 786.

part. adj. **rallied,** reassembled : P. L. I. 269.

Ram, *sb.* a male sheep : C. 497 ; Ps. CXIV. 11.

Ramath-lechi, *sb.* Ramath-lehi, the scene of Samson's slaughter of the thousand Philistines with the jaw-bone of an ass ; its location is uncertain (spelled Ramath-lechi in Vulg.) : S. A. 145.

Ramiel, *sb.* one of the rebel angels : P. L. VI. 372.

See **Thick-rammed.**

Ramoth, *sb.* Ramoth Gilead, a city east of the Jordan : P. R. I. 373.

Ramp, (1) *sb.* leap, spring : S. A. 139.

(2) *vb. intr.* to rear on the hind legs as in the act of springing : P. L. IV. 343.

Rampant, *adj.* rearing on the hind legs : P. L. VII. 466.

Rampart, *sb.* a mound of earth raised for the defence of a place : P. L. I. 678.

Rancour, *sb.* malignant hatred or spitefulness : P. L. X. 1044 ; *hellish rancour* : P. L. IX. 409.

Random, *sb.* at *random*, heedlessly, carelessly ; *lies at random* : S. A. 118 ; *at random yielded up* : P. L. X. 628 ; without thought or consideration ; *thy words at random* : P. L. IV. 930.

Range, (rangèd, *disyl.*: P. L. II. 522) *vb.* (1) *tr.* (*a*) to draw up in ranks : P. L. XI. 644 ; P. R. III. 322 ; *millions ranged for fight* : P. L. VI. 48.

(*b*) to arrange, dispose ; (birds) *ranged in figure* : P. L. VII. 426 ; *nests in order ranged* : S. A. 1694 ; *bristles ranged like those that ridge the back of ... boars* : S. A. 1137.

(2) *intr.* to rove at large, roam : P. L. IV. 621 ; *his World ... to range in* : P. L. X. 492 ; *range in the air* : P. R. I. 366 ; to go or pass here and there : P. L. VI. 248.

fig. lust ... *among the bestial herds to range* : P. L. IV. 754 ; *that destruction wide may range* : P. L. IX. 134.

part. adj. **ranged,** drawn up in ranks : P. L. II. 522.

Rank, (1) *sb.* (*a*) a line of persons ; *trip no more in twilight ranks* : A. 99.

(*b*) a number of soldiers ranged abreast ; *pl.* : P. L. I. 616 ; VI. 71 ; *sworded seraphim are seen in glittering ranks* : N. O. 114 ; army, forces ; *embattled ranks* : P. L. XII. 213 ; *fig.* : A. 59.

(*c*) one of several rows of trees placed at different levels : P. L. IV. 140.

(2) *vb. tr.* (*a*) to draw up in ranks : P. L. II. 887 ; *stood ranked of Seraphim another row* : P. L. VI. 604 ; *their armies ranked* : S. A. 345.

(b) *fig.* to set in order ; *O flowers ... who now shall ... rank your tribes* : P. L. XI. 278.

Rank, *adj.* foul ; *rank vapours, mist* : C. 17 ; L. 126.

Rankle, *vb. intr.* to fester, ulcerate ; used *fig.* of grief : S. A. 621.

Ransack, *vb. tr.* to pillage, plunder : P. L. I. 686.

Ransom, (1) *sb.* (*a*) the paying of money for the release of a prisoner : S. A. 604.

(b) the price paid or demanded for such release : S. A. 483, 1460, 1471 ; *his ransom ... shall willingly be paid* : S. A. 1476 ; *fig., Death ... hath paid his ransom* : S. A. 1573.

the price paid or set for the redemption of man : P. L. III. 221 ; XII. 424 ; used *fig.* of Christ ; *both ransom and Redeemer voluntary* : P. L. X. 61.

(2) *vb. tr.* to redeem ; *ransomed with his* (Christ's) *own dear life* : P. L. III. 297.

Rap. *See* **Rapt.**

Rapacious, *adj.* characterized by voracity ; *Death's rapacious claim* : P. L. XI. 258.

Rape, *sb.* (*a*) the act of carrying away a woman by force : D. F. I. 9.

(b) the violation of a woman : P. L. XI. 717 ; the violation of Sin by Death : P. L. II. 794 ; *transf.* sodomy : P. L. I. 505.

Raphael, *sb.* the archangel : P. L. VI. 363 ; sent by God to warn Adam and Eve : P. L. V. 224, 561 ; VIII. 64, 217 ; *the sociable Spirit* : P. L. V. 221 ; *the affable Archangel* : P. L. VII. 40 ; *not sociably mild, as Raphael* : P. L. XI. 235.

Rapid, *adj.* moving swiftly : P. L. II. 532 ; IV. 227 ; VI. 711 ; XI. 853.

Rapine, *sb.* pillage, robbery, plunder : P. R. IV. 137 ; S. XV. 14 ; *fig., rapine sweet* : P. L. IX. 461.

Rapt, *past part.* (*a*) seized and carried off ; *what accident hath rapt him from us* : P. R. II. 40.

(b) taken and carried up, transported ; *not rapt above the pole* : P. L. VII. 23 ; carried up into heaven ; *rapt in a chariot* : P. L. III. 522 ; *in a balmy cloud* : P. L. XI. 706.

part. adj. **rapt,** transported with emotion : Il P. 40 ; C. 794.

Rapture, *sb.* (*a*) force of movement ; *with torrent rapture* : P. L. VII. 299.

(b) transport of mind, ecstasy : P. L. IX. 1082 ; *holy rapture* : P. L. V. 147 ; *their souls in blissful rapture took* : N. O. 98 ; *woods and rocks had ears to rapture* : P. L. VII. 36.

(c) the expression of ecstatic feeling : C. 247 ; *they ... waken raptures high* : P. L. III. 369.

Rare, *adj.* (*a*) of slight consistence, not dense ; *they limb themselves, and colour, shape, or size assume ... condense or rare* : P. L. VI. 353 ; *absol.* matter that is rare : P. L. II. 948.

(b) being or keeping far apart ; *they walked ... those rare and solitary, these in flocks* : P. L. VII. 461.

(c) of a kind seldom found, exceptional ; *comp., the rarer thy example stands* : S. A. 166 ; seldom achieved : P. L. III. 21 ; few in number : Il P. 101.

(d) remarkable for excellence ; *inventors rare* : P. L. XI. 610 ; *to waylay some beauty rare* : P. R. II. 186 ; *of colour glorious and effect so rare* : P. L. III. 612.

Rarely, *adv.* seldom, not often : P. L. XII. 537 ; S. A. 1047.

Rase, *vb. tr.* (*a*) to remove by scraping ; *fig.* : P. L. III. 49 ; *their names ... blotted out and rased ... from the Books of Life* : P. L. I. 362 ; *to rase quite out their native language* : P. L. XII. 53.

(b) to level with the ground, demolish : P. L. II. 923.

Rash, *adj.* (*a*) acting without due consideration, hasty, impetuous : P. L. XI. 860 ; XII. 76 ; P. R. IV. 8 ; *I was a fool, too rash* : S. A. 907 ; *her rash hand* : P. L. IX. 780 ; *the rash hand of bold Incontinence* : C. 397.

(b) characterized by or proceeding from rashness ; *rash revolt* : P. R. I. 359 ; *misdeed* : S. A. 747 ; *zeal* : P. L. V. 851.

Rashly, *adv.* inconsiderately, presumptuously : S. A. 43.

Rashness, *sb.* presumptious haste or boldness : P. L. XII. 222.

Rate, *sb.* degree ; *thy strength they know surpassing human rate* : S. A. 1313.

Rathe, *adj.* blooming early in the year ; *the rathe primrose* : L. 142.

Rather, *adv.* (1) *the rather,* the more readily (for this reason): P. L. III. 51 ; P. R. I. 326.

(2) more properly speaking, more truly or correctly ; (*a*) with *than* : P. R. III. 402 ; *that stone ...imagined rather oft than elsewhere seen* : P. L. III. 599 ; *all was but a show, rather than solid virtue* : P. L. X. 884.

(*b*) without *than* ; expressing opposition or contrast to the preceding statement : P. L. III. 697 ; IV. 236 ; V. 829 ; IX. 332, 694, 902 ; X. 1026 ; XI. 503, 548 ; P. R. I. 390 ; II. 144 ; III. 162, 174 ; IV. 183, 207, 316, 338, 444 ; S. A. 421 ; *what fear I then ? Rather what know to fear* : P. L. IX. 773 ; *they have slain thy son. Thy son is rather slaying them* : S. A. 1517 ; *the fellows of his crime, the followers rather* : P. L. I. 606 ; *no light ; but rather darkness* : P. L. I. 63 ; *this happy place imparts to thee no happiness...rather inflames thy torment* : P. R. I. 418.

(*c*) *or rather,* introducing a more correct statement : P. L. X. 494 ; P. R. I. 74 ; S. A. 661, 1118, 1154.

(3) in a certain degree ; *rather opportunely* : P. R. II. 396.

(4) more properly or justly : P. L. VIII. 75 ; *to me reproach rather belongs* : P. L. XI. 166.

(5) more readily or willingly, with or in preference ; (*a*) with *than* : S. A. 216 ; *I incline to hope rather than fear* : C. 412 ; *brutish forms rather than human* : P. L. I. 482 ; expressing choice between two courses of action : P. L. IX. 969, 979 ; P. R. III. 218 ; *rather than be less cared not to be at all* : P. L. II. 47 ; *much rather ... than* : S. A. 1478.

(*b*) without *than* ; expressing contrast to the preceding statement : P. L. II. 60, 149, 252 ; III. 7 ; IX. 819 ; *of him to ask chose rather* : P. L. VIII. 54 ; *willingly chose rather death with thee* : P. L. IX. 1167 ; *choosing rather inglorious life* : P. L. XII. 219 ; *here rather let me drudge* : S. A. 573 ; *much rather* : S. A. 828.

(*c*) *had rather,* to choose, prefer ; with simple *inf.* : P. L. VI. 166 ; V. Ex. 29.

Rational, *adj.* (*a*) endowed with reason : P. L. II. 498 ; V. 409.

(*b*) characterized by or springing from reason : P. L. VIII. 587 ; *rational liberty* : P. L. XII. 82 ; *delight* : P. L. VIII. 391.

Rattle, *vb. intr.* to move rapidly and with a rattling sound ; *clouds ... come rattling on* : P. L. II. 715.

part. adj. **rattling,** making a clattering noise ; *rattling storm of arrows* : P. L. VI. 546.

Rave, *vb. intr.* to act boisterously, rage ; *the mild Ocean ...forgot to rave* : N. O. 67 ; *how green-eyed Neptune raves* : V. Ex. 43.

Ravel, *vb. intr.* to become confused : S. A. 305.

Raven, *sb.* the bird *Corvus corax* : P. R. II. 267 ; *from out the ark a raven flies* : P. L. XI. 855.

attrib. black as a raven ; *the raven down of darkness* : C. 251.

See **Night-raven.**

Ravenous, *adj.* voracious : P. L. X. 274 ; P. R. II. 269 ; used of death ; *his ravenous maw* : P. L. X. 991 ; used of hell ; *his ravenous jaws* : P. L. X. 637.

Ravin, *sb.* plunder, prey : P. L. X. 599.

Ravishment, *sb.* transport, ecstasy, rapture : P. L. II. 554 ; V. 46 ; IX. 541 ; C. 245.

Ray, *sb.* (1) a beam of light ; (*a*) from the sun : P. L. V. 301 ; VIII. 372 ; *the setting Sun ... levelled his evening rays* : P. L. IV. 543 ; *the Sun ... shot parallel to the Earth his dewy ray* : P. L. V. 141 ; *the eastern ray* : S. A. 548 ; *thy piercing ray* : P. L. III. 24.

(*b*) from a shining object : P. L. III. 625.

(*c*) from a resplendent being ; *on his Son with rays direct shone full* : P. L. VI. 719 ; *rays of Bethlehem* (see Bethlehem) : N. O. 223.

fig. the sacred rays of Chastity : C. 425 ; *thy beauty's heavenly ray* : P. L. IX. 607.

(*d*) *Heaven's rays,* the light of heaven as analogous to the light of the sun on earth : P. L. VI. 480.

(2) light, radiance : P. L. VIII. 140 ; *the Sun's more potent ray* : P. L. IV. 673 ; *the morning ray* : C. 622.

(3) *visual ray,* the power of vision : P. L. III. 620.

Razor, *sb.* the instrument used for shaving : S. A. 1167.

Reach, I. *sb.* (*a*) the extent to which a person may stretch out the hand : P. L. IX. 591.

(*b*) power of apprehension, range of thought : S. A. 62, 1380; *the reach of human sense*: P. L. v. 571; *human reach no further knows*: P. L. x. 793.

(*c*) range of the eye : P. L. XI. 380 ; Ps. CXXXVI. 94.

(*d*) continuous stretch or extent : P. L. x. 323.

II. *vb.* (1) *tr.* (*a*) to stretch forth, extend : P. L. v. 213.

(*b*) to lay hold of with the hand ; *absol.* with *of* : P. L. XI. 94.

(*c*) to succeed in influencing; *to reach the organs of her fancy* : P. L. IV. 801.

(*d*) to extend to : P. L. II. 1029 ; *his stature reached the sky* : P. L. IV. 988.

(*e*) to arrive at, get to : P. L. II. 606.

to come to ; *reach my ear* : S. A. 177.

to carry to ; *Eternity, whose end no eye can reach* : P. L. XII. 556.

(*f*) to arrive at, attain : P. L. VI. 131 ; *thy desire … leads to no excess that reaches blame* : P. L. III. 697.

(*g*) to succeed in comprehending : P. L. VII. 75.

(2) *intr.* (*a*) to stretch out the hand : P. L. IX. 732, 779.

(*b*) to make a stretch of a certain length ; *with solitary hand, reaching beyond all limit* : P. L. VI. 140 ; *without modifying phrase ; all other beasts … envying stood, but could not reach* : P. L. IX. 593.

(*c*) to extend : P. L. II. 644 ; *a city and tower, whose top may reach to Heaven* : P. L. XII. 44.

See **Forth-reaching.**

Read, *vb.* (*pret.* and *past part.* read) (1) *tr.* (*a*) to peruse ; *the Law of God I read* : P. R. I. 207.

(*b*) to learn by perusal ; *absol.* : P. R. IV. 116.

fig. to discover, understand : P. L. IV. 1011 ; VIII. 68 ; *if I read aught in heaven, or heaven write aught of fate* : P. R. IV. 382.; *each in other's countenance read his own dismay* : P. L. II. 422.

(*c*) to utter aloud : F. of C. 19 ; *the summons read* : P. L. I. 798.

(2) *intr.* to peruse a book : P. R. IV. 322.

vbl. sb. **reading,** the act of perusing books : P. R. IV. 323.

See **Stall-reader.**

Readily, *adv.* with facility, easily, promptly : P. L. VIII. 272.

Readiness, *sb.* the state of being in due preparation for what is to be done : P. R. II. 144.

Re-admit, *vb. tr.* to admit again : S. A. 1173.

Ready, *adj.* (*a*) in a state of preparation for action or use : P. L. III. 650 ; v. 132 ; *Tartarus, which ready opens wide his fiery chaos* : P. L. VI. 54 ; *innumerable hands were ready* : P. L. VI. 509 ; *with prep. inf.* : P. L. III. 72 ; *stands ready to* : P. L. II. 854 ; VI. 561 ; L. 131.

(*b*) willing ; *with prep. inf.* : S. A. 1483 ; *sup.* : Ps. LXXXVI. 54 ; *attrib., his ready harbinger* : N. O. 49.

(*c*) immediately liable ; *ready to expire* : Ps. LXXXVIII. 62.

(*d*) immediately available ; *sup., the … readiest recompense* : P. R. III. 128.

(*e*) lying directly before one, direct, near ; *the way is ready* : P. L. IX. 626 ; *sup., readiest path, way* : P. L. II. 976 ; XII. 216 ; C. 305.

Real, *adj.* (*a*) actually existing as a thing : P. L. VIII. 310 ; *if what is evil be real* : P. L. IX. 969 ; *what kingdom, real or allegoric* : P. R. IV. 390.

(*b*) genuine ; *real eclipse* : P. L. x. 413 ; *hunger* : P. L. v. 437 ; *darkness* : S. A. 159 ; *dignity* : P. L. x. 151.

Reality, *sb.* that which has real existence : P. L. VIII. 575.

Realm, *sb.* a kingdom : P. L. IV. 234, 1002 ; VI. 186 ; P. R. II. 422, 458 ; *and made one realm, Hell and this World* : P. L. x. 391, 392 ; *the realm of Aladule* : P. L. x. 435 ; *realm of Bocchus* : P. R. IV. 72 ; *of Congo* : P. L. XI. 400 ; *of Gaul* : H. B. 8 ; *of Pharaoh* : P. L. I. 342 ; XII. 162 ; *Seon's realm* : P. L. I. 409 ; *as ruled over by Satan or his angels* : P. R. I. 118.

(*b*) in heaven ; *Heaven … retains number sufficient to possess her realms* : P. L. VII. 147 ; *the happy realms of light* : P. L. I. 85.

(c) chaos as the kingdom of Night : P. L. II. 133, 972, 1005.
(d) the air as the kingdom of Satan : P. L. X. 189 ; XII. 455.
(e) the earth as Adam's kingdom : P. L. VIII. 375.

Realty, *sb.* sincerity : P. L. VI. 115.
Reap, *vb. tr.* (a) to cut down and gather : P. L. XII. 18.
fig., *reaping immortal fruits of joy and love* : P. L. III. 67 ; *plotting how the Conqueror least may reap his conquest* : P. L. II. 339.
(b) to get or bring in return ; *I ... suing for peace, reap nothing but repulse and hate* : S. A. 966 ; *fill thy ... lamp with ... hope that reaps not shame* : S. IX. 11.
See **New-reaped.**

Reaper, *sb.* one who cuts and gathers grain : P. L. IX. 842 ; XI. 434.
Rear, *sb.* (a) the hindmost part of an army : P. L. II. 78 ; *van and rear* : P. L. V. 589.
fig., *the lagging rear of winter's frost* : S. A. 1577 ; *the rear of darkness* : L'A. 50.
(b) the back part ; *serpent ... not with indented wave ... but on his rear* : P. L. IX. 497.
Rear, *vb. tr.* (a) to lift to a standing posture : P. L. VIII. 316 ; XI. 758 ; to an erect position ; *he rears from off the pool his mighty stature* : P. L. I. 221 ; *reared her lank head* : C. 836.
(b) to construct by building up : P. L. I. 464 ; V. 653 ; C. 798 ; *altars I would rear* : P. L. XI. 323.
fig., *hast reared God's trophies* : S. XVI. 6.
(c) to bring up, nourish : S. A. 555.
(d) to train to an upright position ; *who now will rear ye* (plants) *to the Sun* : P. L. XI. 278.
(e) to have or hold in an upright position : P. L. IV. 699 ; in an elevated position ; *the glorious Temple reared her pile* : P. R. IV. 546.
(f) to direct ; *up to a hill anon his steps he reared* : P. R. II. 285.
Re-ascend, *vb. intr.* to ascend again : P. L. I. 633 ; with *up* : P. L. III. 20 ; *our Deliverer up to Heaven must reascend* : P. L. XII. 480.
Reason, I. *sb.* (1) reasoning ; *whose reason I have tried unsound and false* : P. L. VI. 120.

(2) cause of action, ground, motive : P. R. II. 485 ; S. A. 811, 864 ; C. 162 ; *good reason* : P. L. VIII. 443 ; P. R. IV. 526 ; *main* : P. L. II. 121 ; *no reason* : P. L. IV. 895 ; S. I. 12 ; *my pleaded reason* : P. L. VIII. 510 ; *public reason* : P. L. IV. 389 ; *make the worse appear the better reason* : P. L. II. 114.
(3) the intellectual faculty in man and brute : P. L. IX. 113, 600 ; in man as distinguished from the intelligence of brutes : P. L. IX. 243 ; C. 529 ; *not prone and brute as other creatures, but endued with sanctity of reason* : P. L. VII. 508 ; *smiles from reason flow to brute denied* : P. L. IX. 239 ; the power of judging rightly, of knowing truth from falsehood or right from wrong : P. L. VI. 125, 126 ; IX. 1130 ; XII. 86, 92 ; S. A. 322, 323 ; *true liberty ... with right reason dwells* : P. L. XII. 84 ; *Will and Reason* (*Reason also is Choice*) : P. L. III. 108 ; *the soul Reason receives, and Reason in her being, Discursive, or Intuitive* : P. L. V. 487 ; *Love ... hath his seat in Reason* : P. L. VIII. 591 ; *our Reason is our Law* : P. L. IX. 654 ; *instinct of nature seems, or reason ... to have guided me aright* : S. A. 1546 ; *who reason for their law refuse—right reason for their law* : P. L. VI. 41, 42 ; *nations will decline so low from virtue, which is reason* : P. L. XII. 98.
more or less clearly *personified* : P. L. V. 102 ; VIII. 554 ; XII. 89 ; feminine gender : P. L. V. 106 ; IX. 352, 360.
(b) inherent power (?) : P. L. I. 248.
(c) evidence of intelligence ; *in their* (beasts') *looks much reason* : P. L. IX. 559.
(4) the conformity of something to the dictates of reason ; *in reason* : P. L. V. 794 ; *with reason* : P. L. II. 431.
(5) that which is agreeable to reason, that which recommends itself to the enlightened intelligence : P. L. IV. 755 ; *words clothed in reason's garb* : P. L. II. 226 ; *rules pranked in reason's garb* : C. 759 ; *his .. words, impregned with reason* : P. L. IX. 738 ; *as reason was* : S. A. 1641 ;

our ... Saviour replied ... "And reason, etc.": P. R. II. 122.

II. vb. intr. (a) to exercise the faculty of reason: P. L. VIII. 25, 374 ; IX. 765, 872.

(b) to engage in discussion, argue : P. L. II. 558 ; P. R. IV. 233.

part. adj. **reasoning**, expressing an argument or proof for an opinion ; reasoning words: P. L. IX. 379.

vbl. sb. **reasoning**, discriminating thought or discussion, argument : P. L. VIII. 85 ; pl. : P. L. X. 830 ; S. A. 322, 875.

Reasonless, adj. not grounded upon reason : P. L. IV. 516 ; S. A. 812.

Re-assemble, vb. tr. to bring together again : P. L. I. 186.

Reassume, vb. tr. to receive again ; into his blissful bosom reassumed in glory as of old : P. L. X. 225.

Reave (past part. reft), vb. tr. to take away by force : L. 107.

Rebeck, sb. a musical instrument, an early form of the violin: L'A. 94.

Rebel, (1) adj. (a) refusing obedience to lawful authority : P. L. I. 484; used of the fallen angels : P. L. III. 677; rebel host: P. L. VI. 647 ; Angels, Spirits, Thrones : P. L. I. 38 ; IV. 823 ; VI. 199.

(b) refractory ; rebel to all law : P. L. X. 83.

(2) sb. one who refuses obedience to lawful authority; whether I be dextrous to subdue thy rebels : P. L. V. 742.

(3) vb. intr. to rise in opposition against the lawful authority of God : Ps. II. 12; against thee they have rebelled : Ps. V. 32 ; of the fallen angels : P. L. VI. 899; who hath rebelled against his worthier : P. L. VI. 179.

part. adj. absol. rid Heaven of these rebelled : P. L. VI. 737.

Rebellion, sb. armed resistance to the ruler of a country, insurrection : P. L. XII. 36, 37; I ... presumed single rebellion: S. A. 1210; new rebellions raise their Hydra heads : S. XV. 6; resistance to the authority of God : Ps. V. 31; the insurrection led by Satan : P. L. I. 363 ; V. 715 ; VI. 269.

Rebellious, adj. (a) defying lawful authority; used of the fallen angels: P. L. VII. 140; rebellious rout, crew; P. L. I. 747; IV. 952; VI. 50.

transf. in proud rebellious arms : P. L. II. 691 ; his own rebellious head: P. L. III. 86.

absol. those, or his rebellious : P. L. I. 71 ; VI. 414.

(b) characteristic of rebels ; rebellious fight : P. L. VI. 786.

Rebound, vb. intr. to bound, leap ; with joy and fear his heart rebounds : P. L. I. 788.

part. adj. **rebounding**, bounding back : P. L. X. 417.

Rebuff, sb. a repelling blow or blast; the strong rebuff of some tumultuous cloud : P. L. II. 936.

Rebuild, vb. tr. to build a second time : P. R. III. 281.

Rebuke, sb. reproof, reprimand ; sharply thou hast insisted on rebuke: P. R. I. 468; such rebuke : P. L. VI. 342 ; grave, just : P. L. IV. 844 ; IX. 10.

Recall, I. sb. the possibility of being revoked ; other decrees against thee are gone forth without recall : P. L. V. 885.

II. vb. tr. (1) to call back (a person) : P. L. I. 169; P. R. II. 55 ; to a state ; recalled to life prolonged and promised race : P. L. XI. 330.

(b) to bring back; past who can recall : P. L. IX. 926.

(c) to summon back ; his attention thus recalled : P. L. XII. 422.

(2) to call back to the mind; to mind recalling : P. R. II. 106.

(3) to revive ; how soon would highth recall high thoughts : P. L. IV. 95.

Recant, vb. tr. to retract : P. L. IV. 96.

Receive, vb. (pres. 2d sing. receiv'st: P. L. IX. 109) I. tr. (1) to accept (something offered) : P. L. III. 106 ; IV. 309 ; XI. 37.

(2) to lift or take up; on their plumy vans received Him : P. R. IV. 583.

(3) to take in, allow to enter : P. L. VI. 55 ; VII. 361 ; the void profound of ... Night receives him: P. L. II. 439 ; Hell ... received them whole: P. L. VI. 875 ; Earth; there first received, his (the sun's) beams : P. L. VIII. 96 ; fig. : P. L. VI. 721.

(b) to give accommodation to, admit ; the fiery surge ... received us falling : P. L. I. 174 ; Hell, receive thy new possessor : P. L. I. 252.

(c) to afford proper space to : P. L. IV. 384.

(d) to attain unto ; *what of perfection ... human nature can receive* : P. R. III. 231.

(e) to have the sensation of, feel ; *receive familiar the fierce heat* : P. L. II. 218.

(4) to apprehend mentally : P. L. VII. 179 ; used punningly with blending of sense (3) : P. L. VI. 624.

(5) to welcome, greet : P. L. V. 781 ; P. R. I. 74 ; *fit entertainment to receive our king* : P. L. V. 690 ; used punningly with blending of the meaning : to meet with resistance : P. L. VI. 561.

(b) to salute upon approach, greet in a certain manner : P. L. VI. 22 ; XII. 609 ; S. A. 329.

(c) to entertain as a guest : P. L. V. 315.

(6) to admit : P. L. XI. 707 ; *into glory him received* : P. L. VI. 891 ; *receive them into bliss* : P. L. XII. 462.

(7) to accept in a certain capacity : S. A. 1214 ; *receive me for thy husband* : S. A. 883.

(8) to accept or regard in a specified manner : P. L. VII. 78 ; VIII. 386 ; *receive with joy the tidings* : P. L. XII. 503 ; *with delight received* : P. R. IV. 263.

(b) to regard as ; *these words I as a prophecy receive* : S. A. 473.

(9) to get or gain from another or others : P. L. V. 423 ; VIII. 35 ; P. R. IV. 200 ; *to receive ... knee-tribute* : P. L. V. 781 ; *glory he receives ... from all nations* : P. R. III. 117 ; *receiving from his mother Earth new strength* : P. R. IV. 566.

(b) to attain by the aid of another ; *receive perfection from the Sun's ... ray* : P. L. IV. 672.

(c) to get, gain ; *she alone receives the benefit* : P. L. VIII. 89.

(d) to experience, feel ; *from his sight received beatitude* : P. L. III. 61.

(10) to have conferred or bestowed upon one : P. L. IV. 54 ; VI. 152 ; VIII. 343 ; IX. 309 ; XI. 505, 636 ; P. R. II. 381 ; III. 137 ; C. 684 ; Dante 3 ; *from thee receive new life* : P. L. III. 294 ;

whence the soul Reason receives : P. L. V. 487 ; *to receive their names of thee* : P. L. VI. 75 ; *render back all I received* : P. L. X. 750 ; *he receives gift* : P. L. XII. 137 ; *to receive the testimony of Heaven* : P. R. I. 77 ; *he who receives light from above* : P. R. IV. 288 ; to have given to one ; *a promise shall receive* : P. L. XII. 322.

(11) to have inflicted upon one : P. L. VI. 349 ; IX. 284 ; X. 639 ; P. R. IV. 623 ; Ps. CXIX. 10 ; *Death his death's wound shall then receive* : P. L. III. 252 ; *this greeting on thy impious crest receive* : P. L. VI. 188 ; *against his will he can receive no harm* : P. L. IX. 350 ; *receive such a discomfit* : S. A. 468.

(12) to have imposed on one : P. L. VII. 119 ; *receive strict laws* : P. L. II. 240 ; *his charge received* : P. L. V. 248.

II. *absol.* or *intr.* to be a recipient ; *as ye have received, so have ye done* : P. L. VI. 805 ; *thou* (the earth) *centring receiv'st from all* : P. L. IX. 109.

Receptacle (réceptácle : P. L. XI. 123), *sb.* a place which receives and keeps something ; *the great receptacle of ... waters he called Seas* : P. L. VII. 307 ; *lest Paradise a receptacle prove to Spirits foul* : P. L. XI. 123.

Reception, *sb.* (a) admission ; *all hope is lost of my reception into grace* : P. R. III. 205.

(b) an occasion of ceremonious greeting : P. L. V. 769.

(c) the capacity for receiving : P. L. X. 807.

Recess, *sb.* a place of retirement, a remote or secret spot ; *grots and caves of cool recess* : P. L. IV. 258 ; *this flowery plat, the sweet recess of Eve* : P. L. IX. 456 ; *Athens ... in her sweet recess, city or suburban* : P. R. IV. 242 ; applied to the bower of Adam and Eve : P. L. IV. 708 ; to Paradise : P. L. XI. 304 ; to hell : P. L. II. 254 ; a secret or private room : P. L. I. 795.

Reciprocal, *adj.* (a) having an alternate backward and forward motion : U. C. II. 30.

(b) contributing each to the other in return : P. L. VIII. 144.

Reck, *vb. tr.* (*a*) to have a care *of* so as to be troubled thereby; *of God ... he recked not* : P. L. II. 50.

(*b*) to care, mind ; *I reck not* : P. L. IX. 173.

(*c*) *impers.*, to concern, trouble ; *what recks it them?* : L. 122 ; *of night or loneliness it recks me not* : C. 404.

Reckon, *vb.* (1) *tr.* (*a*) to include in the number of : Ps. LXXXVIII. 13.

(*b*) to regard, consider ; *him I reckon not in high estate* : S. A. 170 ; *reckon'st thou thyself with Spirits of Heaven* : P. L. II. 696 ; *Religion ... reckons thee her eldest son* : S. XVII. 14.

(2) *intr.* to judge ; *if thou reckon right* : P. L. VIII. 71.

vbl. sb. **reckoning**, account ; *I pursed it up, but little reckoning made* : C. 642 ; *of other care they little reckoning make* : L. 116.

Reclaim, *vb. absol.* to recall from wrong-doing : P. L. VI. 791.

Recline, *adj.* recumbent, reclining : P. L. IV. 333.

Recoil, (1) *sb.* the act of springing back : P. L. II. 880.

(2) *vb. intr.* (*a*) to rebound or spring back to the starting point; *fig.*, *his dire attempt ... like a devilish engine back recoils upon himself* : P. L. IV. 17 ; *revenge on itself recoils* : P. L. IX. 172 ; *evil on itself shall back recoil* : C. 593.

(*b*) to draw back or retreat from an enemy : P. L. VI. 391 ; *fig.* : Ps. CXIV. 9 ; to stagger back from the effects of a blow : P. L. VI. 194.

(*c*) to start back in fear or horror : P. L. II. 759.

Recollect, *vb. tr.* to summon up, rally : P. L. I. 528 ; *fierce hate he recollects* : P. L. IX. 471.

Recomfort, *vb. tr.* to inspire with fresh hope or courage : P. L. IX. 918.

Recommend, *vb. intr.* to make acceptable : P. L. IV. 329 ; P. R. I. 301.

Recompense, (1) *sb.* (*a*) reparation made to a person for wrong done him : S. A. 910 ; *in thy large recompense* : L. 184,

(*b*) compensation for loss sustained : P. L. II. 981.

(*c*) return for something given or received : P. L. IV. 47 ; VIII.

5 ; IX. 995 ; P. R. III. 128 ; *in recompense* : P. L. IX. 994 ; *the Sun, that light imparts to all, receives from all his alimental recompense* : P. L. V. 425.

(2) *vb. tr.* (*a*) to give compensation to : P. L. XII. 495.

(*b*) to make up for : P. L. X. 1052 ; *recompense dole with delight* : P. L. IV. 893 ; *the low Sun, to recompense his distance, ... had rounded still the horizon* : P. L. X. 683.

(*c*) to make compensation for ; *to recompense my rash ... misdeed* : S. A. 746.

Reconcile, *vb. tr.* (*a*) to restore to friendship after estrangement : *fig.*, *water with fire in ruin reconciled* ; P. R. IV. 413 ; *winds to seas are reconciled* : S. A. 962.

(*b*) to win again to friendship ; *let him live before thee reconciled* : P. L. XI. 39.

Record, (1) *sb.* (*a*) an account of something preserved in writing ; *pl.* : P. L. XII. 513 ; *of their names in Heavenly records now be no memorial* : P. L. I. 361.

(*b*) that which keeps a thing in memory, memorial ; *pl.* : P. L. XII. 252.

(2) *vb. tr.* (*a*) to set down in writing, put on record : S. A. 984 ; *in thy book record their groans* : S. XVIII. 5 ; in emblazonry : P. L. V. 594.

(*b*) to mark : *even and morn recorded the third Day* : P. L. VII. 338.

Recorder, *sb.* the musical instrument of the flagiolet class : P. L. I. 551.

Recount, *vb. tr.* to tell in detail or in order : P. L. X. 228 ; *recount his praises* : P. R. III. 64 ; *recount almighty works* : P. L. VII. 112.

Recover, *vb.* (1) *tr.* (*a*) to get again, regain ; *recover speech, words, breath* : P. L. IV. 357 ; XI. 499 ; S. A. 1555 ; *heart* : P. L. X. 966 ; *glory* : S. A. 1098 ; *peace* : P. L. V. 210.

(*b*) to make up for, retrieve : P. L. II. 22.

(2) *intr.* to regain soundness of body ; *Adam ... from the cold sudden damp recovering* : P. L. XI. 294.

part. adj. **recovered**, regained : P. L. I. 240 ; P. R. I. 3.

Recreant, *adj.* unfaithful to duty ; *who ... turned recreant to God* : P. R. III. 138.

Recure, *vb. tr.* to cure, heal : P. L. XII. 393.

Red, (1) *adj.* (*a*) of a colour resembling that of blood ; *red fire* : N. O. 159 ; *lightning* : P. L. I. 175.

(*b*) flushed ; *mine enemies ... grown red with shame* : Ps. VI. 22.

(*c*) characterized by violence suggestive of fire ; *arm again his red right hand to plague us* : P. L. II. 174.

(2) *sb.* the colour of red ; *fiery red* : P. L. IV. 978 ; *cloudy red* : N. O. 230.

See **Rosy-red**.

Redeem, *vb. tr.* (*a*) to save, deliver ; *redeem thee quite from Death's rapacious claim* : P. L. XI. 258 ; *thy ransom paid, which Man from Death redeems* : P. L. XII. 424.

(*b*) to deliver from sin and its consequence : P. L. III. 281, 299 ; XII. 434.

(*c*) to make atonement for : *to redeem Man's mortal crime* : P. L. III. 214.

(*d*) to make good ; *redeem our loss* : N. O. 153.

past part. absol. those delivered from sin and its consequences ; *my redeemed* : P. L. III. 260 ; XI. 43.

Redeemer, *sb.* the Saviour of man, Christ : P. L. X. 61 ; XII. 445, 573.

Redemption, *sb.* (*a*) deliverance from sin and its consequences by the atonement of Christ : P. L. XII. 408 ; N. O. 4 ; *work redemption for mankind* : P. R. I. 266.

(*b*) a ransom ; *for his redemption all my patrimony* : S. A. 1482 ; *without redemption all mankind must have been lost* : P. L. III. 222.

(*c*) the possibility of deliverance ; *his place ordained without redemption* : P. L. V. 615.

Redouble, *vb. tr.* (*a*) to repeat : P. L. IV. 562.

(*b*) to re-echo : S. XVIII. 9.

part. adj. **redoubled**, (*a*) made twice as great ; *my redoubled love and care* : S. A. 923.

(*b*) repeated : P. L. VI. 370.

Redound, *vb. tr.* (*a*) to be in excess : P. L. V. 438.

(*b*) to rebound ; *fig.* : P. L. VII. 57 ; X. 737 ; *revenge, that shall redound upon his own rebellious head* : P. L. III. 85.

(*c*) to result ; *though thereby worse to me redound* : P. L. IX. 128.

part. adj. **redounding**, abounding, abundant : P. L. II. 889.

Redress, (1) *sb.* remedy, relief : S. A. 619.

(2) *vb. tr.* (*a*) to set right again, mend : P. L. IX. 219.

(*b*) to reform, amend ; *this wicked earth redress* : Ps. LXXXII. 26.

Red-Sea, *sb.* the sea between Arabia and Africa ; *the Red Sea and Jordan once he cleft* : P. R. III. 438.

attrib., *the Red-Sea coast* : P. L. I. 306.

Reduce, *vb. tr.* (*a*) to bring or lead back : P. L. X. 438.

(*b*) to bring back *to* a certain condition : P. L. II. 983 ; *reduce me to my dust* : P. L. X. 748.

(*c*) to bring *to* a certain condition : P. L. VI. 514 ; *reduce to nothing this essential* : P. L. II. 96.

(*d*) to bring *under* the control or authority of : P. L. III. 320 ; VI. 777 ; *reduced a province under Roman yoke* : P. R. III. 158.

(*e*) to bring down ; *to servitude reduce man* : P. L. XII. 89 ; *reduce their foe to misery* : S. A. 1468 ; to bring down to a lower rank or position : P. L. V. 843.

(*f*) to diminish ; *to smallest forms reduced their shapes* : P. L. I. 790.

Redundant, *adj.* (*a*) with a wave-like motion : P. L. IX. 503.

(*b*) abounding to excess ; *these redundant locks* : S. A. 568.

Reed, *sb.* (1) one of the tall straight stems of grass growing on the banks of streams or in other wet places : P. R. II. 26 ; *smooth-sliding Mincius crowned with vocal reeds* : L. 86.

(*b*) used for carrying fire : P. L. VI. 519, 582 ; *a reed ... tipt with fire* : P. L. VI. 579.

(*c*) *transf.* used of other plants ; *the balmy reed* : P. L. V. 23 ; *the corny reed* : P. L. VII. 321.

(2) a reed made into a musical pipe ; *pastoral reed* : P. L. XI. 132 ; C. 345.

Re-edify, *vb. tr.* to rebuild: P. L. XII. 350.

Reeking, *part. adj.* that rises as vapour: P. L. VIII. 256.

Reel, *vb. intr.* to turn round and round, whirl: Ps. LXXXIII. 51.

Re-embattle, *vb. tr.* to form again in line of battle: P. L. VI. 794.

Re-enter, *vb. tr.* to enter again: P. L. II. 397.

Refer, *vb. tr.* to assign, ascribe: S. A. 1015.

Refine, *vb. tr.* (a) to free from impurities: P. L. XII. 548; to make pure or of the nature of spirit: P. L. V. 475.

(b) to raise to a higher spiritual level: P. L. XI. 63.

(c) to free from what is coarse or gross; *love refines the thoughts*: P. L. VIII. 589.

Reflect, *vb. tr.* to throw back (light): P. L. VI. 18; *light ... though but reflected*: P. L. III. 723; *his gathered beams reflected*: P. L. X. 1071.

part. adj. **reflected**, thrown back; *reflected purple*: P. L. IV. 596.

Reflection, *sb.* (a) the action of throwing back light: P. L. VII. 367.

(b) reflected light: P. L. III. 428.

Reflourish, *vb. intr.* to thrive anew: S. A. 1704.

Reflux, *sb.* a flowing back: P. L. X. 739.

Reform, *vb. tr.* to change for the better by alteration or reconstruction; *reform yon flowery arbours*: P. L. IV. 625; *O Earth ... built with second thought, reforming what was old*: P. L. IX. 101.

Refrain, *vb.* (1) *tr.* to restrain; *nor from the Holy One ... refrained his tongue blasphemous*: P. L. VI. 360.

(2) *intr.* to forbear, abstain: S. XXI. 14; with *prep. inf.*: S. A. 1565.

Refresh, *vb.* (1) *tr.* to impart fresh vigour to: P. L. IX. 1027; *ambrosial drink, that soon refreshed him*: P. R. IV. 591; *from heavenly feast refreshed*: P. R. IV. 637.

(2) *intr.* or *absol.* to reinvigorate oneself: S. A. 551.

vbl. sb. **refreshing**, refreshment; *from above, secret refreshings that*

repair his strength and fainting spirits: S. A. 665.

Refreshment, *sb.* (a) the fact or state of being refreshed: C. 687.

(b) that which gives new vigour; *meats and drinks, nature's refreshment*: P. R. II. 265; *we need refreshment, whether food, or talk between*: P. L. IX. 237.

Reft. *See* **Reave.**

Refuge, *sb.* (a) shelter or protection from danger or distress: P. L. IX. 119; X. 839; XI. 673.

(b) a place of safety: P. L. II. 168.

Refulgent, *adj.* resplendent, gleaming; *in arms they stood of golden panoply, refulgent host*: P. L. VI. 527.

Refusal, *sb.* the denial of something offered or demanded: P. R. II. 323; S. A. 1330.

Refuse, *vb. tr.* (a) to decline to accept: P. L. V. 492; P. R. II. 329; to reject the offer of: P. L. II. 470, 471.

(b) to decline to submit to; *who reason for their law refuse*: P. L. VI. 41; *refused those terms*: P. L. X. 756; *refuse subjection to his empire*: P. L. XII. 31; to decline to take part in: P. L. IV. 743.

(c) to decline to admit to a specified position; *would'st be thought my God*; *and storm'st, refused*: P. R. IV. 496.

(d) to decline; with *prep. inf.*: P. L. II. 451, 452; P. R. I. 278.

Refute, *vb. tr.* to overthrow by argument or other means, prove to be false: P. R. IV. 233; S. A. 1220; *self-destruction ... sought refutes that excellence thought in thee*: P. L. X. 1016.

Regain, *vb. tr.* (a) to recover possession of: P. L. I. 270; II. 230; P. R. II. 441; *to regain thy right*: P. R. III. 163; *lest total Darkness should by night regain her old possession*: P. L. IV. 665; *regained lost Paradise*: P. L. IV. 608; *the blissful seat*: P. L. I. 5; *love*: P. L. X. 972; S. A. 1004; *life*: P. L. IV. 197.

(b) to rejoin; *to regain my severed company*: C. 274.

(c) to gain, accomplish: P. R. III. 371.

See **Half-regained.**

Regal, *adj.* (*a*) of or belonging to a king: P. L. XII. 323; P. R. II. 183, 461; used of that which belongs to God or Christ; *regal state*: P. L. I. 640; *power*: P. L. v. 739; *sceptre*: P. L. III. 339, 340; v. 816; *stooping his regal head*: P. 15; *regal arts and regal mysteries*: P. R. II. 248.

(*b*) befitting a king or resembling that of a king; *regal virtues*: P. R. IV. 98; *a table richly spread in regal mode*: P. R. II. 340; used of that which pertains to angels; *regal port*: P. L. IV. 869; *ornament*: P. L. v. 280; to Satan; *his high throne ... was placed in regal lustre*: P. L. X. 447.

fig., *trumpets regal sound*: P. L. II. 515.

Regard, I. *sb.* (1) aspect, look; *with stern regard*: P. L. IV. 877; X. 866; *with regard benign*: P. L. XI. 334; *meek regard*: P. R. III. 217; look, watch; *passed ... his eye with choice regard from Paneas to Beërsaba*: P. L. III. 534.

(2) importance; *a certain shepherd lad, of small regard to see to*: C. 620.

(3) attention, consideration, interest; *the regard of Heaven on all his ways*: P. L. IV. 620; *with some regard to what is just and right*: P. L. XII. 16.

(*b*) have *regard of*; to take care of, provide for; *of thee these forty days none hath regard*: P. R. II. 315.

(*c*) *with regard of*, taking into consideration: P. L. II. 281; *with no regard of*: S. A. 684.

(4) esteem, affection: P. L. I. 653.

II. *vb. tr.* (1) to take notice of, show an interest in: S. A. 1157; Ps. LXXXII. 9; LXXXVIII. 22.

(*b*) to take thought or care for; *regard thyself*: S. A. 1333.

(2) to take into account or consideration: P. L. XII. 357; *Eve, intent now only on her taste, naught else regarded*: P. L. IX. 787.

(*b*) to pay attention or heed to; *who denies to know their God, or message to regard*: P. L. XII. 174.

(*c*) to show consideration for; *should I of these the liberty regard*: P. R. III. 427.

absol. or *intr.* to give heed: P. L. v. 44.

Regardless, *adj.* careless, indifferent; *regardless whether*: P. L. XII. 47; *regardless of*: P. L. III. 408; P. R. IV. 317; S. A. 303.

Regency, *sb.* a district under the control of a regent; *regencies of Seraphim and Potentates*: P. L. v. 748.

Regenerate, *part. adj.* made anew spiritually; *made new flesh regenerate grow*: P. L. XI. 5.

Regent, (1) *sb.* (*a*) that which rules; *the glorious lamp ... regent of day*: P. L. VII. 371.

(*b*) one who rules; applied to angels; *Uriel, Regent of the Sun*: P. L. III. 690; IX. 60; to Satan or his angels: P. R. I. 117.

(2) *adj.* acting as regent: P. L. v. 697, 698.

Regiment, *sb.* a body of soldiers: P. L. I. 758.

Region, *sb.* (1) a tract of land or portion of space of considerable but indefinite extent, district, country, clime: P. R. II. 155; *embassies from regions far remote*: P. R. IV. 67; *if thence he scape, into whatever world or unknown region*: P. L. II. 443; *dwell ... in these regions of the World*: P. R. I. 392; *what worlds or what vast regions hold the immortal mind*: Il P. 90.

(*b*) a district or portion of space in heaven: P. L. v. 748, 750; XI. 77; *the eternal regions*: P. L. III. 349; *the least of whom could ... arm him with the force of all their regions*: P. L. VI. 223; applied to hell: P. L. I. 242; the portion of chaos taken in the creation of the universe: P. L. II. 982.

(*c*) a district in the sun: P. L. III. 606; in the moon: P. L. v. 263.

(*d*) a place or country having a certain character; *a region scarce of prey*: P. L. III. 433; in heaven; *from skirt to skirt a fiery region*: P. L. VI. 80; *before the threshold of Jove's court ... in regions mild*: C. 4; in hell; *regions of sorrow*: P. L. I. 65; *many a dolorous region*: P. L. II. 619.

(2) one of the successive portions into which the air is divided; *the World's first region*: P. L. III. 562; *the middle region of thick*

air: P. R. II. 117; *misty regions of wide air*: V. Ex. 41; *the Airy region, the region,* the upper air: P. L. VII. 425; N. O. 103.

Register, *vb. tr.* to record, enroll: P. L. XII. 335.

Regorge, *vb. tr.* to devour to repletion: S. A. 1671.

Regret, *sb.* sorrow caused by the loss of something: P. L. X. 1018.

Regular, *adj.* following in form and arrangement an established rule: P. L. V. 623.

Regulus, *sb.* the celebrated Roman general who, at the sacrifice of his own life, dissuaded his countrymen from making peace with Carthage: P. R. II. 446.

Reign, I. *sb.* (1) royal power, sovereignty; *Saturn's reign*; the Golden Age: Il P. 25; used of Chaos; *sable-vested Night, the consort of his reign*: P. L. II. 963.

(*b*) the sovereignty of God: P. L. I. 102; the sovereignty of Christ in heaven: P. L. V. 841; *his great vicegerent reign*: P. L. V. 609; a blending of the two ideas: the rule of Christ upon earth, and the sovereignty of Christ in the kingdom of God to be established after the destruction of the world: P. L. XII. 330, 370; P. R. III. 178, 179, 184, 216.

(*c*) the power of Satan upon earth: P. R. I. 125.

(*d*) *fig.,* Nature...to think...her *reign had here its last fulfilling*: N. O. 106.

(2) sway; *the Prince of Light his reign of peace...began*: N. O. 63.

(3) kingdom, realm; *the reign of Chaos and old Night*: P. L. I. 543; *from the element each of his reign allotted*: P. R. II. 123; applied to the earth as the realm of Diana: H. B. 4; *fig.* the realm of the moon: P. L. VII. 381.

II. *vb.* (1) *intr.* (*a*) to hold or exercise sovereign authority: P. L. II. 454; P. R. II. 442; III. 195; V. 832; *equal over equals to let reign*: P. L. V. 820; *Alcinous reigned*: P. L. V. 341; *so Jove usurping reigned*: P. L. I. 514; of Chaos: P. L. II. 909; V. 578; C. 334.

used of God: P. L. I. 124, 637; II. 59, 324, 814; V. 680; X. 549;

Ps. LXXXIV. 45; of Christ in heaven: P. L. III. 315, 318; VI. 43, 888; upon earth, perhaps with blending as in the *sb.* (*b*) (see the *sb.*): P. R. III. 180, 215, 385; IV. 492; *to reign David's true heir*: P. R. III. 404.

used of Satan or his angels: P. L. II. 451; IV. 961; VI. 183, 293; *here we may reign*: P. L. I. 261; *to reign is worth ambition*: P. L. I. 262; *better to reign in Hell than serve in Heaven*: P. L. I. 263; *here thou shalt monarch reign*: P. L. X. 375; of sin or death: P. L. II. 698, 868; X. 399.

used *fig.* of things; *the beast that reigns in woods*: P. L. XI. 187; *now reigns full-orbed the moon*: P. L. V. 41; *Love reigns, reigned*: P. L. IV. 765; V. 449; *Accident...shall reign as king*: V. Ex. 75; of the rule of reason over the body or the body over reason: P. L. XII. 91; P. R. II. 466, 478, 480.

(*b*) to hold sway; *Belial ... in courts and palaces ... reigns*: P. L. I. 497.

used of things: P. L. XI. 543; *luxury late reigned*: P. L. XI. 751; *surfeit*: C. 480; *sin*: P. L. XII. 286.

(2) *tr.* to rule, govern: P. L. IV. 112.

Rein, (1) *sb.* bridle; *fig., some say the sun was bid turn reins*: P. L. X. 672; *let their eyes rove without rein*: P. L. XI. 586; *to ... rage let loose the rein*: P. L. V. 696; *give the reins to thought* or *grief*: S. A. 302, 1578.

(2) *vb. tr.* to restrain by a bridle: P. L. IV. 858.

Reinforcement, *sb.* augmentation of strength: P. L. I. 190.

Reins, *sb. pl.* (*a*) kidneys: P. L. VI. 346; S. A. 609.

(*b*) the seat of the affections and emotions: Ps. VII. 39.

Reinspire, *vb. tr.* to breathe fresh life into; *till Favonius reinspire the frozen earth*: S. XX. 6.

Reinstall, *vb. tr.* (*a*) to seat anew; *reinstall thee in David's royal seat*: P. R. III. 372.

(*b*) to replace, restore: D. F. I. 46; (man to Paradise): P. R. IV. 615.

Reiterated, *part. adj.* repeated again and again: P. L. I. 214.

Reject, *vb.* (*pres. 2d sing.*: P. R. IV. 156) *tr.* (*a*) to throw or cast forth; *bitter ashes, which the offended taste with spattering noise rejected*: P. L. X. 567.

(*b*) to refuse to receive or obey *commands, forewarning*: P. L. IV. 523 ; XI. 876.

(*c*) to refuse to accept or take advantage of *sceptre, riches, aid,* etc.: P. L. V. 886 ; P. R. II. 457 ; IV. 156, 376, 467 ; S. A. 516.

(*d*) to refuse to treat with kindness ; *reject the penitent*: S. A. 760.

Rejoice, *vb.* (1) *intr.* to feel or express joy : P. L. VIII. 314 ; X. 120 ; P. R. II. 37 ; Ps. LXXXV. 23 ; *inly rejoiced* : P. R. I. 228 ; *make rejoice thy servant's soul* : Ps. LXXXVI. 10 ; with *at* : P. L. XI. 869 ; with *in* : P. L. II. 487 ; IV. 13 ; V. 641 ; *rejoice in doing* : P. L. II. 339 ; *I in thy persevering shall rejoice* : P. L. VIII. 639 ; with *for* : P. L. XI. 875 ; with clause: P. L. XII. 475 ; used of angels : P. L. V. 163; of Satan : P. L. X. 396 ; with *at* : P. L. V. 851.

(*b*) used of beasts : P. L. VIII. 392.

(*c*) used *fig.* of things ; *Heaven rejoiced, and soon repaired her mural breach* : P. L. VI. 878.

(2) *tr.* to make joyful, gladden: S. A. 1455.

vbl. sb. **rejoicing,** the feeling and expression of joy : P. L. VII. 180.

Relapse, *sb.* a falling back into a former state of sin : P. L. IV. 100; of hopelessness : P. R. II. 30.

Relate, *vb. tr.* (*a*) to tell, narrate : P. L. VIII. 9, 203, 204 ; VII. 84 ; *what is to come I will relate* : P. L. XII. 11 ; with the event told as obj.: P. L. XI. 319.

(*b*) to tell of, describe : P. L. V. 564 ; *brief related whom they brought* : P. L. IV. 875 ; *Eve her night related* : P. L. V. 94; *you to relate them* (virtues) *true* : S. X. 13 ; *relate thee* : to tell of thy power and works ; P. L. VII. 604.

(*c*) *absol.* or *intr.* : P. L. VI. 298 ; VIII. 208 ; *thus they relate* : P. L. I. 746 ; *Adam relating* : P. L VIII. 51 ; *relate by whom* : S. A. 1563 ; *I might relate of thousands* : P. L. VI. 373.

part. adj. **related,** being similar in nature : S. A. 786.

Relater, *sb.* one who tells a story, narrator : P. L. VIII. 52.

Relation, *sb.* (*a*) the act of telling, recital ; *but thy relation now* : P. L. VIII. 247 ; *have we not ... by relation heard* : P. R. II. 182 ; *make this relation,* relate this : C. 617.

(*b*) that which is told, account: P. L. V. 556 ; *give us ... relation more particular* : S. A. 1595.

(*c*) connection by blood, kinship : P. L. IV. 756 ; P. R. IV. 519.

Relax, *vb. tr.* (*a*) to make less compact in form ; *relax their serried files* : P. L. VI. 599.

(*b*) to make less tense ; *his joints relaxed* : P. L. IX. 89.

Release, (1) *sb.* liberation from bondage ; *release from Hell* : P. R. I. 409.

(2) *vb. tr.* (*a*) to set free ; *from death released* : P. L. XI. 197.

(*b*) to remit : N. O. 6.

Relent, *vb. tr.* to become less obdurate or severe, yield: P. L. IV. 79 ; *what ... wonders move the obdurate to relent* : P. L. VI. 790 ; to feel compassion ; *soon his heart relented* : P. L. X. 940; used of God : P. L. II. 237 ; X. 1093 ; S. A. 509.

Relentless, *adj.* not knowing pity ; *relentless thoughts* : P. L. IX. 130.

Relic. *See* **Relique.**

Relief, *sb.* (*a*) the alleviation of pain or distress : P. L. X. 976 ; S. I. 12.

(*b*) that which removes suffering and want : P. R. II. 309.

Relieve, *vb.* (*a*) to free from suffering and want ; *us relieve with food* : P. R. I. 344.

(*b*) to free from mental suffering : S. A. 472; *this only hope relieves me* : S. A. 460.

(*c*) to release : S. A. 5.

Religion, *sb.* (*a*) the belief in, and allegiance in manner of life to, God : P. L. XI. 667 ; XII. 535 ; S. A. 412; to a god : S. A. 854, 872, 1420.

(*b*) the Christian Church ; *on thy firm hand Religion leans in peace* : S. XVII. 13.

(*c*) the rites and ceremonies pertaining to religion : P. L. I. 372.

Religious, *adj.* (*a*) pious, godly : P. L. xi. 622.

(*b*) of or pertaining to religion, prompting to religion ; *religious rites* : P. L. xii. 231 ; S. A. 1320 ; *a dim religious light* : Il P. 160.

Relique (spelled relic: P. L. v. 273) *sb.* (*a*) the body of a deceased person: W. S. 3 ; the body of the phœnix : P. L. v. 273.

(*b*) something held sacred by the Roman Catholic Church because connected with a saint : P. L. iii. 491.

Relish, *sb.* pleasing taste or flavour: P. L. ix. 1024.

Reluctance, *sb.* resistance : P. L. ii. 337 ; *reluctance against God and his just yoke* : P. L. x. 1045.

Reluctant, *adj.* (*a*) striving against opposing force, resisting : P. L. x. 515 ; *smoke to roll in wreaths reluctant flames*, flames forcing a way through the smoke : P. L. vi. 58.

(*b*) caused by unwillingness of mind : P. L. iv. 311.

Rely, *vb. intr.* (*a*) to repose confidence, trust, depend ; with *on* : P. L. vi. 238 ; ix. 373 ; Ps. lxxxiv. 47.

(*b*) to rest *on*; *on whom we send the weight of all, and our last hope, relies* : P. L. ii. 416.

Remain, *vb. intr.* (1) to continue in a place; used of persons : P. R. ii. 1, 243 ; S. A. 1549 ; of things; *thy face, wherein no cloud of anger shall remain* : P. L. iii. 263 ; *strength ... remaining in those locks* : S. A. 587.

(2) to continue in a specified state or condition : P. L. ii. 320 ; v. 773 ; ix. 464 ; x. 989 ; xii. 14 ; P. R. i. 17 ; iv. 326 ; S. A. 912 ; C. 72 ; *free they must remain* : P. L. iii. 124 ; *I had remained in ignorance* : P. L. ix. 808 ; *we had then remained still happy* : P. L. ix. 1138 ; *the mind remains invincible* : P. L. i. 139.

(3) to stay or be left behind after others have gone ; *only the ... Tempter still remained* : P. R. ii. 404 ; used of things : P. L. vi. 115 ; U. C. ii. 34 ; *and* (a part) *of the sixth Day yet remained* : P. L. vii. 504 ; *while her faith to me remains* : P. L. x. 129 ; *something yet of doubt remains* : P. L. viii. 13.

(*b*) to be left at the close ; *war ... wherein remained ... to our Almighty Foe clear victory* : P. L. ii. 768.

(*c*) to continue to be or exist ; *though hunger still remain* : P. R. ii. 255 ; with *dat.*, *while breath remains thee* : S. A. 1126.

(*d*) to continue forever ; *they, his people, should remain* : Ps. lxxxi. 63.

(4) to be left to be dealt with, done, suffered, or offered : P. L. x. 502 ; *half yet remains unsung* : P. L. vii. 21 ; *a worse thing yet remains* : S. A. 433 ; *this one prayer remains* : S. A. 649 ; with *prep. inf.* : P. L. i. 645 ; *much remains to conquer* : S. xvi. 9 ; with *dat.* ; *the easier conquest now remains thee* : P. L. vi. 38 ; *what remains him less than unknown dangers* : P. L. ii. 443 ; *me ... higher argument remains* : P. L. ix. 43.

Remark, *vb. tr.* to point out; *his manacles remark him* : S. A. 1309.

Remarkable, *adj.* worthy of note : S. A. 1388.

Remarkably, *adv.* in a manner worthy of note, extraordinarily : P. L. ix. 982 ; P. R. ii. 106.

Remediless (remédiless), *adj.* irreparable : P. L. ix. 919 ; *all my evils, all remediless* : S. A. 648 ; *that may not be turned aside* ; *rightful doom remediless* : Cir. 17.

Remedy, *sb.* that which corrects or counteracts an evil : P. L. x. 1079 ; *of evil, then, so small as easy think the remedy* : P. L. vi. 438 ; *Death becomes his final remedy* : P. L. xi. 62.

Remember, *vb.* (*pres. 2d sing.* rememberest : P. L. v. 674; remember'st : P. L. v. 857; vii. 561) *tr.* (*a*) to recall to mind, recollect : P. L. iv. 449 ; v. 674 ; P. R. i. 46 ; ii. 196, 445 ; C. 416 ; *remember'st thou thy making* : P. L. v. 857 ; *remember with what mild ... temper he both heard and judged* : P. L. x. 1046 ; *absol.* in parenthetic clause : P. L. vii. 561 ; P. R. iii. 66.

(*b*) to have in memory, preserve unforgotten ; *heads without name, no more remembered* : S. A. 677.

(*c*) to bear in mind : P. L. x. 12; *imper.* : P. L. viii. 327 ; *remember what I foretell thee* : P. R. iv. 374

remember, and fear to transgress:
P. L. VI. 912; used of God: Ps.
VIII. 12; LXXXVIII. 21; *remembering Abraham*: P. R. III. 434; *remembering mercy*: P. L. XII. 346.

Remembrance, *sb*. (*a*) the faculty or
power of remembering: P. L.
VIII. 204.

(*b*) the act of remembering; *lest
fierce remembrance wake my sudden
rage*: S. A. 952.

(*c*) the state of being remembered; *in death no remembrance
is of thee*: Ps. VI. 10.

(*d*) **have in remembrance**, to
remember, keep in mind: P. L.
III. 704.

(*e*) **bring to remembrance**, to
cause one to recall to mind: S.
A. 277.

Remiss, *adj*. (*a*) not tense, slack;
fig. lacking in perception and
understanding: P. L. VIII. 387.

(*b*) slow in action because wanting strength, languid; *pain...
makes remiss the hands of mightiest*:
P. L. VI. 458.

(*c*) negligent, dilatory: S.A. 239.

Remission, *sb*. forgiveness, pardon:
S. A. 835.

Remit, *vb. tr*. (*a*) to send back: S.
A. 687.

(*b*) to diminish in intensity,
abate; *willingly doth God remit
his ire*: P. L. XI. 885; *his anger*:
P. L. II. 210.

(*c*) to refrain from exacting,
give up: S. A. 1470.

Remorse, *sb*. (*a*) intense and painful
sorrow and regret due to a consciousness of guilt: P. L. IV. 109;
X. 1098; *feigned remorse*: S. A.
752; *sweet remorse*: P. L. V. 134.

(*b*) sympathetic sorrow, pity,
compassion: P. L. I. 605; *without
remorse*: P. L. V. 566; XI. 105; *sting
of amorous remorse*: S. A. 1007.

Remorseless, *adj*. pitiless; *remorseless cruelty*: M. W. 29; *fig*., *the
remorseless deep*: L. 50.

Remote, (1) *adj*. (*a*) distant in space,
not near: P. L. III. 609; P. R.
IV. 598; *far remote*: P. L. VII.
369; P. R. IV. 67; *wide remote*:
P. L. IV. 284; *many a league
remote*: P. L. X. 274; *Heaven is
... remote to see*: P. L. IX. 812;
situated or living at a distance;
nations, neighbouring or remote:
P. R. III. 76; *sup*., *remotest kings*:
S. XV. 4.

fig. gone astray; *from the paths
of truth remote*: P. L. VI. 173.

(*b*) distant in relation, separated; *to know... of things remote
from use*: P. L. VIII. 191.

(2) *adv*. from a distance, afar
off; *thunder heard remote*: P. L.
II. 477.

Remove, I. *sb*. (*a*) the change of
place; *by quick contraction or
remove*: P. L. VI. 597.

(*b*) the departure or withdrawal
from a place; *in signal of remove*:
P. L. XII. 593.

II. *vb*. (removèd, *trisyl.*: Il P.
78) (1) *tr*. (*a*) to bring or cause to be
brought away from a place; *to
remove him, thee*: P. L. XI. 96,
260; *to Heaven removed*: P. L.
III. 356; *removed his tents far off*:
P. L. XI. 727.

fig., *the sentence, from thy head
removed*: P. L. X. 934; *removed
the stony from their hearts*: P. L.
XI. 3.

(*b*) to place or put at a distance;
*to remove his ways from human
sense*: P. L. VIII. 119.

removed, placèd at a distance:
remote; *chaos far removed*: P.L.
VII. 272; *thus far removed*: P.L.
II. 211, 321; *more removed*: P.L.
II. 835; *too far removed*: P. R.
IV. 87; *as far removed from God
as*: P. L. I. 73.

(*c*) to place at another time;
*the instant stroke of death... re-
moved far off*: P. L. X. 211.

(*d*) to take away by causing to
cease; *from Adam's eyes the film
removed*: P. L. XI. 412; *remove
the sensible of pain*: P. L. II. 277;
fear of death: P. L. IX. 702;
sin, temptation: P. L. XII. 290;
S. A. 1051; to take away from
connection with something; *remove their swelling epithets*: P. R.
IV. 343.

(*e*) to take away by death,
destroy: P. L. XI. 889.

(2) *intr*. to move from one place
to another; *remove behind them*:
P. L. XII. 204.

part. adj. **removed**, secluded:
Il P. 78.

Rend, *vb*. (used only in *pres.*) *tr*. (*a*)
to tear asunder, split; *rend the
woods*: P. L. X. 700; *sky*: P. L.
XII. 182.

(*b*) to remove with violence,
tear; with *up*; P. L. II. 540.

Render, *vb. tr.* (*a*) to give in return: P. R. III. 130; with *acc.* and *dat.*: P. L. VIII. 6; with *acc.* and *to*: Ps. VII. 11; to deal in return; *can my ears unused hear these dishonours, and not render death*: S. A. 1232.

(*b*) to give back, return to the giver; *render back all I received*: P. L. X. 749; with *acc.* and *dat.*: D. F. I. 75.

(*c*) to make to be, cause to become; with two *acc.*: P. L. II. 130, 459; VI. 602; VIII. 196; IX. 823; *render thee a king*: P. R. IV. 283; *renders them useless*: S. A. 1282; with *acc.* and *prep.* phrase; *render thee the Parthian at dispose*: P. R. III. 369.

vbl. sb. **rendering,** the act of surrendering life or of giving an account of life; *my appointed day of rendering up*: P. L. XI. 551.

Renew, *vb. tr.* (*a*) to give new life and force to, revive: P. L. II. 1012; *life in us renew*: Ps. LXXXV. 28; *his lapsed powers*: P. L. III. 175.

(*b*) to recreate in purity and perfection equal to that of the former state; *Heaven and Earth renewed*: P. L. X. 638; XI. 66.

(*c*) to take again, reassume; *Heaven his wonted face renewed*: P. L. VI. 783.

(*d*) to give or make again; *my covenant ... renewed*: P. L. XI. 116; *prayers and vows renewed*: S. A. 520; to grant again, bestow anew: S. A. 1357.

(*e*) to repeat, reiterate; *the birds their notes renew*: P. L. II. 494.

(*f*) to begin or make again, recommence *speech, reply, words,* etc.: P. L. II. 389: III. 226; VIII. 337; IX. 321, 1183; X. 543; XI. 140, 499; P. R. II. 367; III. 6, 346; *that song*: S. M. 25; *the assault, fresh assaults*: P. L. IV. 19, 570: S. A. 331; *her monthly round still ending, still renewing*: P. L. III. 729.

Renounce, *vb. tr.* (*a*) to disclaim: P. L. III. 291; *with stiff vows renounced his Liturgy*: F. of C. 2.

(*b*) to give up, lay aside; *these titles must we renounce*: P. L. II. 312; *I ... renounce deity for thee*: P. L. IX. 884.

(*c*) to abandon; *thou wilt renounce thy seeking*: S. A. 828.

Renovation, *sb.* a making anew, resurrection; *waked in the renovation of the just*: P. L. XI. 65.

Renown, *sb.* fame, glory: P. L. III. 34; VI. 378; XII. 154; *who, under names of old renown*: P. L. I. 477; *high*: P. L. XI. 688; *long*: P. R. IV. 84; *great in renown*: P. R. I. 136; *fame shall be achieved, renown on earth*: P. L. XI. 698; *glory and renown*: P. L. VI. 422; P. R. III. 60.

Renowned, (*trisyl.*: A. 29) *part. adj.* famous, illustrious; used of persons: P. L. IX. 670; XII. 321; S. A. 988, 1079; *renowned Alcinous*: P. L. IX. 440: *Samson*: S. A. 125, 341; *far renowned the Ionian gods*: P. L. I. 507; *that renowned flood ... divine Alpheus*: A. 29; used of things or acts: P. L. III. 549; IX. 1101; *Rome ... so far renowned*: P. R. IV. 46; *exploit, victories*: P. L. III. 465; S. XVI. 11.

Repair, (1) *sb.* restoration; *sought repair of sleep*: P. L. VIII. 457.

(2) *vb. tr.* (*a*) to restore or make whole again after loss or injury; *Heaven ... repaired her mural breach*: P. L. VI. 878; *repaired what hunger ... had impaired*: P. R. IV. 591; *refreshings that repair his strength*: S. A. 665; to fill up anew; *to repair his numbers*: P. L. IX. 144.

fig. to revive or lift up again; *the day-star ... anon repairs his drooping head*: L. 169.

(*b*) to make amends for *loss, detriment*: P. L. I. 188; III. 678; VII. 152; to make good the loss of; *showered roses, which the morn repaired*: P. L. IV. 773.

Repair, *vb. intr.* to go to a specified place, resort; with *to*: P. L. X. 1087, 1099; *thence to the famous Orators repair*: P. R. IV. 267; *fig.,* to their fountain, other stars repairing*: P. L. VII. 365.

Repast, *sb.* (*a*) a meal; *sweet repast*: P. L. VIII. 214; *neat*: S. XX. 9; *rural*: P. L. IX. 4; joined to *repose*: P. L.. V. 232; *noontide repast, or afternoon's repose*: P. L. IX. 403; *sweet repast or sound repose*: P. L. IX. 407; *in heaven; sweet*: P. L. V. 630.

(b) food : P. R. II. 250; C. 688 ; *gnaw my bowels, their repast* : P. L. II. 800.

Repay, *vb.* (only in *pret.* and *past part.* repaid) *tr.* (a) to requite ; *spite then with spite is best repaid* : P. L. IX. 178.

(b) to make return to : P. R. IV. 188 ; *she him as wantonly repaid* : P. L. IX. 1015 ; *the snake with youthful coat repaid* : P. L. X. 218.

Repeal, *vb. tr.* to recall, put an end to ; *Adam soon repealed the doubts that in his heart arose* : P. L. VII. 59.

Repeat, (1) *sb.* repetition : P. L. VI. 318.

(2) *vb. tr.* (a) to do or make again ; *though his power Creation could repeat* : P. L. IX. 946 ; *repulse repeated* : P. L. VI. 601 ; *revolution* : P. L. VIII. 32 ; *reserved alive to be repeated the subject of their cruelty* : S. A. 645.

(b) to say again, iterate : P. L. IX. 400.

(c) to say over, recite, rehearse : P. L. VII. 494.

part. adj. **repeated**, recited : S. VIII. 12.

Repel, *vb. tr.* (1) to drive or thrust away : P. L. X. 866.

(b) to check the advance of; *gowns, not arms, repelled the fierce Epirot* : S. XVII. 3.

(c) to resist *temptation* : P. L. VIII. 643.

(2) to frustrate, defeat : P. R. IV. 446.

(3) to render ineffectual *attempt, violence* : P. L. VII. 611 : IX. 284.

Repent, *vb.* (1) *intr.* (a) to change one's mind : P. L. X. 75.

(b) to feel sorrow or regret for something done : P. L. I. 96.

(c) to feel sorrow on account of sin and to turn to God seeking his pardon : P. L. III. 190; XI. 90, 255 ; used of Satan : P. L. IV. 93.

(2) *tr.* (a) to feel repentance for; *repent the sin* : S. A. 504.

(b) *refl.* to give oneself sorrow or regret on account of ; *God ... repenting him of Man depraved* : P. L. XI. 886 ; *whether I should repent me now of sin by me done* : P. L. XII. 474.

part. adj. **repenting**, full of regret ; *fig., God may ... with repenting hand abolish his own works* : P. L. II. 369.

vbl. sb. **repenting**, regret: S. XXI. 6.

Repentance, *sb.* (a) the recognition of and sorrow for sin, with a desire to abandon it : S. A. 821 ; with a desire to be saved by God from it : P. L. III. 191 ; used with reference to Satan : P. L. IV. 80.

(b) the hearty amendment of life with sorrow for past sins ; *the great Proclaimer ... cried Repentance* : P. R. I. 20 ; *to them preached repentance* : P. L. XI. 724.

Repentant, *adj.* experiencing repentance, sorrowful for sin : P. L. XI. 1 ; P. R. III. 435 : S. A. 751.

Repine, *vb. intr.* to murmur in discontent, be unhappy and indulge in complaint : P. L. VI. 460 ; P. R. II. 94 ; with *at* : S. A. 995.

Replenish, *vb. tr.* to fill or stock abundantly : P. L. VIII. 371 ; *the waters thus with fish replenished* : P. L. VII. 447.

Replete, *adj.* filled ; *his words replete with guile* : P. L. IX. 733 ; *our Sire, replete with joy and wonder* : P. L. XII. 468.

Reply, I. *sb.* answer, response : P. L. II. 467 ; VIII. 209 ; IX. 321.

II. *vb.* (1) *tr.* to return for an answer ; *confounded ... what to reply* : P. R. III. 3 ; *nor had what to reply* : P. R. IV. 2.

with the answer as object sentence : P. L. IV. 969 ; IX. 377 ; XI. 552 ; P. R. I. 337, 346 ; II. 319 ; L. 77 ; S. XIX. 9 ; *whereto ... the Arch-Fiend replied* : P. L. I. 156; *whereto Satan replied* : P. L. VI. 469 ; *to whom ... replied* : P. L. II. 688 ; IV. 659, 946 ; V. 468, 506 ; IX. 290, 655, 1162 ; X. 118 ; P. R. III. 121, 203 ; IV. 109, 154, 195, 499.

(2) *intr.* to make answer : P. L. II. 1010 ; IV. 857 ; Ps. III. 11 ; *thus replied* : P. L. III. 273 ; IV. 903 ; V. 852 ; VIII. 4, 65, 368, 378 ; IX. 614 ; X. 161 ; XII. 468, 552 ; *to whom thus* : P. L. IV. 440; VI. 171 ; VIII. 179, 595 ; IX. 272, 342, 567 ; X. 124, 144, 602, 966 ; XI. 370, 453 ; XII. 574 ; P. R. I. 406 ; II. 378, 432 ; III. 43, 108 ;

IV. 285 ; *thus Eve to him replied* :
P. L. IX. 960 ; *Adam ... thus to
Eve replied* : P. L. X. 1012 ; *Satan
... thus to our Saviour replied* : P.
R. IV. 367 ; *to whom thus the
Portress of Hell-gate replied* : P.
L. II. 746 ; *to whom the great
Creator thus replied* : P. L. III. 167.

Report, (1) *sb.* (*a*) an account brought
or taken back : P. L. III. 704 ; v.
869 ; S. X. 8.

(*b*) that which people say or
tell, rumour ; *to see ... if thy appearance answer loud report* : S.
A. 1090 ; or in sense (*a*); *O change
beyond report* : S. A. 117.

(2) *vb. tr.* (*a*) to bring back an
account of ; *they beseech that Moses
might report to them his will* : P.
L. XII. 237.

(*b*) to tell, relate : P. L. VI. 21;
*who knows how he may report thy
words* : S. A. 1350.

(*c*) to reveal, make known; *sin,
which these dun shades will ne'er
report* : C. 127.

Repose, I. *sb.* (*a*) rest : P. L. v.
233 ; P. R. II. 275 ; S. A. 406 ;
afternoon's repose : P. L. IX. 403 ;
sound : P. L. IX. 407 ; rest in
sleep : P. L. IV. 612.

(*b*) a place of rest ; *worst is my
port ... and my ultimate repose* :
P. R. III. 210.

II. *vb.* (1) *tr.* to refresh by rest:
P. L. I. 319.

(2) *intr.* (*a*) to lie at rest, sleep:
P. L. IV. 450 ; *where young Adonis
oft reposes ... in slumber soft* : C.
999.

(*b*) to recline ; *on flowers re-
posed* : P. L. v. 636.

(*c*) to rest in confidence : P. L.
v. 28.

Re-possess, *vb. tr.* to regain possession of : P. L. I. 634.

Reprehend, *vb. tr.* to reprove, rebuke : Ps. VI. 1.

Represent, *vb. tr.* (*a*) to bring before
one ; *O thou, who future things
canst represent as present* : P. L.
XI. 870.

(*b*) to bring to the mind ; *things
which the five watchful senses represent* : P. L. v. 104; *various
objects, from the sense variously
representing* : P. L. VIII. 610; *to
be the medium through which (a
thing) is brought to the mind ;
damps and dreadful gloom ; which
to his evil conscience represented*

all things with double terror : P. L.
x. 849.

(*c*) to typify : P. L. XII. 255 ;
to suggest by being like ; *this
happy place ... representing lost
bliss* : P. R. I. 418.

Repress, *vb. tr.* to check, restrain :
S. A. 543.

Reprieve, *sb.* suspension of the execution of a death sentence : S.
A. 288.

Reproach, (1) *sb.* (*a*) severe censure or
blame : P. L. XI. 165, 811 ; *I led
the way ... bitter reproach* : S. A.
823 ; *for the testimony of truth
hast borne universal reproach* : P.
L. VI. 34 ; *pl.* : P. R. IV. 387 ;
amorous reproaches : S. A. 393.

(*b*) a state of disgrace, shame ;
to thy reproach : P. R. III. 66.

(*c*) the occasion or cause of
disgrace or shame : S. A. 446 ;
D. F. I. 14 ; *thought barrenness
in wedlock a reproach* : S. A. 353.

(2) *vb. tr.* to censure with
severity, upbraid : P. L. IX. 1098.

Reproachful, *adj.* full of or receiving reproach ; *a reproachful life* :
P. L. XII. 406.

Reprobate, *adj.* morally abandoned,
depraved : P. L. I. 697 ; P. R. I.
491 ; *to sense reprobate* : S. A. 1685.

Reproof, *sb.* censure for a fault,
rebuke : P. R. I. 477.

Reprove, *vb. tr.* to reprehend,
blame : P. L. x. 761.

Reptile, *sb.* a creeping animal; used
collectively for fishes of all kinds;
*let the waters generate reptile with
spawn abundant* : P. L. VII. 388.

Repulse, (1) *sb.* (*a*) the condition of
being driven back ; used of an
army : P. L. I. 630 ; *if on they
rushed, repulse repeated* : P. L.
VI. 600.

(*b*) the fact or condition of
being checked or foiled in an
attempt : P. L. IX. 384 ; P. R.
IV. 623 ; *reap nothing but repulse
and hate* : S. A. 966 ; *Satan whom
repulse upon repulse met ever* : P.
R. IV. 21.

(2) *vb. tr.* (*a*) to drive back (an
enemy) : P. L. II. 142 ; Ps.
LXXXIII. 38 ; to drive or thrust
away (a person) : P. L. x. 910.

(*b*) to check, frustrate, foil :
P. R. I. 6 ; *beauty ... hath strange
power ... nor can easily be repulsed* : S. A. 1006; *repulsed whatever wiles of foe* : P. L. x. 10.

Repute, *sb.* reputation : P. L. I. 639 ; II. 472.

Request, (1) *sb.* petition, entreaty : P. L. VII. 111, 635 ; S. A. 356 ; *all thy request for Man, accepted Son, obtain* ; *all they request* : P. L. XI. 46, 47 ; *thus Adam made request* : P. L. v. 561 ; *at* or *by thy request* : P. L. VI. 894 ; S. A. 881 ; C. 900 ; *for her request* : M. W. 17.

(2) *vb. tr.* to ask, entreat; with *acc.* and *prep. inf.*: S. A. 1630 ; *did I request thee, Maker, ... to mould me man* : P. L. X. 743.

Require, *vb. tr.* (*a*) to have necessity for, want, need : P. L. III. 735 ; VIII. 425 ; P. R. III. 17; *yon flowery arbours ... require more hands than ours* : P. L. IV. 628 ; *food ... those pure intelligential substances require* : P. L. v. 408 ; *no outward aid require* : P. L. VIII. 642 ; *the branches would require thy utmost reach* : P. L. IX. 590 ; *great acts require great means of enterprise* : P. R. II. 412.

(*b*) to claim as of right or by authority, demand, exact : P. L. IV. 308 ; S. A. 1314 ; used of God : P. L. IV. 419 ; *our voluntary service he requires* : P. L. v. 529 ; *requires glory from men ... glory he requires* : P. R. III. 113, 117.

Requisite, *adj.* necessary, indispensable : P. R. I. 464.

Requital, *sb. in requital,* as a reward : C. 626.

Requite, *vb. tr.* (*a*) to return an equivalent for ; *so requite favour renewed* : S. A. 1356.

(*b*) to recompense, reward ; *he can requite thee* : S. VIII. 5.

Resalute, *vb. tr.* to greet anew : P. L. XI. 134.

Rescue, (1) *sb.* means of deliverance from an enemy : Ps. VII. 6.

(2) *vb. tr.* (*a*) to save or deliver from violence, danger, etc. : P. L. XI. 682 ; *rescued from Death by force* : S. XXIII. 4 ; *rescue from the hands of wicked men ... him that help demands* : Ps. LXXXII. 14.

(*b*) to deliver by force of arms : P. R. I. 217.

part. absol. his rescued, those delivered by him : P. L. XII. 199.

Resemblance, *sb.* (*a*) similarity, likeness : P. L. IV. 364 ; VI. 114.

(*b*) something similar, similitude, image ; *fairest resemblance of thy Maker fair* : P. L. IX. 538 ; *human count'nance, the express resemblance of the gods* : C. 69 ; *true wisdom ... her false resemblance* : P. R. IV. 320 ; *some such resemblances ... I find of our last evening's talk in this thy dream* : P. L. v. 114.

Resemble, *vb.* (*pres. 2d sing.* resemblest : P. L. IV. 839) *tr.* to be like to : P. L. v. 622 ; *Heaven resembles Hell* : P. L. II. 268 ; *the emptier waste, resembling air* : P. L. II. 1045 ; used of persons ; *therein least resembling thy great Father* : P. R. III. 110 ; *I understand ... her resembling less his image* : P. L. VIII. 543 ; *thou resemblest now thy sin* : P. L. IV. 839.

Resent, *vb. tr.* to take ill, be indignant at : P. L. IX. 300.

Reserve, (1) *sb.* something excepted : P. L. v. 61 ; P. R. IV. 165.

(2) *vb. tr.* (*a*) to keep back, keep in store for the future ; *such pleasure she reserved* : P. L. VIII. 50.

(*b*) to keep or preserve for another purpose ; *smells, reserved from night* : P. L. v. 128 ; *this intellectual food for beasts reserved* : P. L. IX. 768 ; used with reference to persons : P. L. XI. 501 ; *his doom reserved him to more wrath* : P. L. I. 54 ; *we are ... reserved ... to eternal woe* : P. L. II. 161 ; without *prep.* ; *reserved his captive multitude* : P. L. II. 322 ; to keep in a certain condition ; with two *acc.* ; *reserved alive to be ... the subject of their cruelty* : S. A. 645.

(*c*) to hold in possession, retain : P. L. XII. 71.

Reside, *vb. intr.* to dwell : P. L. XII. 114 ; Ps. LXXXIV. 17 ; *whatever Power or Spirit of the nethermost Abyss might in that noise reside* : P. L. II. 957 ; *till I* (Sin), *in Man residing through the race* : P. L. x. 607 ; used of God : P. L. II. 265 ; XII. 284 ; *Heaven where God resides* : P. L. VIII. 112.

Residence, *sb.* (*a*) the act of dwelling in a place ; *where ... Angels held their residence* : P. L. I. 734 ; *I* (Chaos) *upon my frontiers here keep residence* : P. L. II. 999 ;

fig., *something holy ... to testify his hidden residence* : C. 248.

(*b*) a place of abode, dwelling-place : C. 974; *transf.*, *fish within their watery residence* : P. L. VIII. 346.

Resign, *vb. tr.* to give up from possession, surrender : P. L. XI. 287; *desirous to resign ... all I received* : P. L. X. 749; *resign this earthly load of death, called life* : S. XIV. 3; *sceptre and power* : P. L. VI. 731.

(*b*) to give up or hand over *to* a person or thing : V. Ex. 58; *resigned to him his heavenly office* : P. R. I. 27; *to her thou didst resign thy manhood* : P. L. X. 148; *Wisdom to Simplicity resigns her charge* : P. L. III. 688; *Death ... to second life ... resigns him up with Heaven and Earth renewed* : P. L. XI. 66.

(*c*) to bring or lead *up to; Law appears imperfect, and but given with purpose to resign them ... up to a better covenant* : P. L. XII. 30.

Resist, *vb. tr.* (*a*) to withstand, oppose : P. L. II. 192; S. A. 1753; *His high will whom we resist* : P. L. I. 162; *that mortal dint ... none can resist* : P. L. II. 814; *a man ... far abler to resist all his solicitations* : P. R. I. 151; *absol.* : P. L. IV. 1013.

used of things : P. L. VI. 323; *spiritual armour, able to resist Satan's assaults* : P. L. XII. 491.

(*b*) to put aside or refuse to accept; *weakness to resist Philistian gold* : S. A. 830.

Resistance, *sb.* the power of exerting force in opposition : P. L. VI. 838.

Resistless, *adj.* that may not be withstood; *power resistless* : S. A. 1404; *resistless eloquence* : P. R. IV. 268; that may not be obstructed or barred; *to force resistless way* : P. L. II. 62.

Resolute, *adj.* constant in pursuing a purpose, determined, firm; *sup.* : P. R. II. 167.

Resolution, *sb.* (*a*) something determined upon, a settled purpose : S. A. 1344, 1410; *with thee certain my resolution is to die* : P. L. IX. 907; *let us seek some safer resolution* : P. L. X. 1029.

(*b*) resoluteness, firmness, undaunted courage : P. L. I. 191;

II. 468; *in his face I see sad resolution* : P. L. VI. 541; *with doubtful feet and wavering resolution* : S. A. 732.

Resolve, *vb. tr.* (*a*) to dispel or banish *doubt* : P. L. VIII. 14.

(*b*) to free from perplexity or doubt : S. A. 305.

(*c*) to free from uncertainty, inform; *resolve me, then, O soul most surely blest* : D. F. I. 36.

(*d*) to fix in purpose, determine; *with a grain of manhood well resolved* : S. A. 408; *with prep. inf.* : P. L. I. 120; V. 668; IX. 585, 968; XII. 109; P. R. IV. 444; C. 183; S. XXI. 5; *with clause; I resolve Adam shall share with me* : P. L. IX. 830.

(*e*) to determine on, decide : P. L. IX. 97; S. A. 1390; *war ... must be resolved* : P. L. I. 662; *this was at first resolved* : P. L. II. 201; *great things resolved* : P. L. II. 392; *childless days resolved* : P. L. X. 1038.

absol. or *intr.* : P. L. IX. 97; *in time thou hast resolved* : S. A. 1390.

See **Best-resolved.**

Resonant, *adj.* repeating the same notes, re-echoing; *resonant fugue* : P. L. XI. 563.

Resort, (1) *sb.* (*a*) the act of going to a place; *he excluded my resort* : P. R. I. 367.

(*b*) a place frequented; *far from all resort of mirth* : Il P. 81; or the assembling of people; *in the various bustle of resort* : C. 379.

(2) *vb. intr.* (*a*) to betake one's self, go : C. 952; to go in answer *to; the Sons of Light hasted, resorting to the summons* : P. L. XI. 80.

(*b*) to go frequently or habitually : S. A. 1738.

Resound, *vb.* (1) *intr.* (*a*) to sound or ring again; *the rigid interdiction, which resounds yet dreadful in mine ear* : P. L. VIII. 334.

(*b*) to sound back, echo, reverberate : P. L. I. 315; XI. 592; P. R. II. 290; *all Heaven resounded* : P. L. VI. 218; *the Earth, the air resounded* : P. L. VII. 561.

(*c*) to be celebrated; *what resounds in fable or romance of Uther's son* : P. L. I. 579.

(2) *tr.* (*a*) to give back the sound of : P. L. X. 862; *caves ... back resounded Death* : P. L. II.

789 ; *thy throne encompassed shall
resound thee ever blest* : P. L. III.
149.

(*b*) to spread the fame of, celebrate : P. L. V. 178 ; S. XVI. 8.

part. adj. **resounding**, echoing ;
the resounding shore : N. O. 182 ;
*give resounding grace to all Heaven's
harmonies* : C. 243.

Respect, *sb.* (*a*) esteem, regard : S.
A. 333.

(*b*) consideration, motive : S.
A. 868.

(*c*) point, particular : P. R. IV.
521.

(*d*) *in respect of*, in regard to,
as to : S. A. 316.

Respiration, *sb.* refreshing ; *till the
day appear of respiration to the
just* : P. L. XII. 540.

Respire, *vb. intr.* to breathe : S. A.
11.

Respite, (1) *sb.* (*a*) an interval of rest ;
gave respite to the ... steeds : C.
553.

(*b*) time granted before the
execution of a sentence ; *to spend
... the respite of that day that must
be mortal to us both* : P. L. XI. 272.

(2) *vb. tr.* to relieve by a pause ;
respite ... pain : P. L. II. 461 ;
day-labour : P. L. V. 232.

Resplendence, *sb.* exceeding brilliance, splendour : P. L. V. 720.

Resplendent, *adj.* splendid, brilliant ;
Moon's resplendent globe : P. L.
IV. 723 ; used of Christ or angels :
P. L. X. 66 ; *resplendent locks* : P.
L. III. 361 ; very beautiful ; *re-
splendent Eve* : P. L. IX. 568.

Responsive, *adj.* answering : P. L.
IV. 683.

Rest, I. *sb.* (*a*) the absence or cessation of motion or labour, repose :
P. L. I. 185 ; II. 802 ; S. A. 14,
406 ; U. C. II. 11 ; C. 689 ; *the
Creator, in his holy rest through all
eternity* : P. L. VII. 91 ; *eternal
Paradise of rest* : P. L. XII. 314 ;
void of rest : P. L. VI. 415 ; *post
o'er land and ocean without rest* :
S. XIX. 9 ; *earn rest from labour
won* : P. L. XI. 375 ; *seat of rest* :
H. B. 4 ; *day of rest* : S. A. 1297.

(*b*) sleep as a condition of repose : P. L. IV. 611, 613, 617 ;
unquiet rest : P. L. V. 11 ; *betook
him to his rest* : P. R. IV. 403 ; in
heaven ; *disposed all but the unsleeping eyes of God to rest* : P. L.
V. 647.

(*c*) freedom or relief from that
which disturbs, peace, quiet, ease :
P. L. II. 618 ; IX. 1120 ; *think not
here to trouble holy rest* : P. L. VI.
272 ; *sweet rest seize thee evermore* :
M. W. 50 ; *where peace and rest
can never dwell* : P. L. I. 66 ; *at
rest* : N. O. 216.

(*d*) abode ; *where to choose their
place of rest* : P. L. XII. 647 ;
permanent abode ; *dust, our final
rest and native home* : P. L. X. 1085.

II. *vb. intr.* (1) to be without
motion ; *where Earth now rests
upon her centre poised* : P. L. V.
578.

(2) to cease from action or
labour, take rest, find repose : P.
L. I. 185 ; P. R. I. 39 ; S. XIV.
13 ; *in yonder shady bower to rest* :
P. L. V. 368 ; *determined there to
rest at noon* : P. R. II. 292 ; *this
day from battle rest* : P. L. VI.
802 ; *the anguish of my soul that
suffers not ... thoughts to rest* : S.
A. 459 ; used of God : P. L. VII.
592 ; *resting on that day from all
his work* : P. L. VII. 593.

fig., the harp ... rested not : P.
L. VII. 595.

(3) to be free from whatever
disturbs, be quiet or at peace : P.
L. X. 778.

(4) to rest in sleep ; *Night bids
us rest* : P. L. IV. 633 ; *when
Nature rests* : P. L. V. 109 ; *laid
her Babe to rest* : N. O. 238.

(5) to be dead ; *I shall shortly
be with them that rest* : S. A. 598.

(6) to stand or lie in a certain
position ; *over the tent a cloud shall
rest by day* : P. L. XII. 257 ; *on
thee his ample spirit rests* : P. L.
III. 389.

(*b*) to lie in repose ; *fig., on
whose barren breast the labouring
clouds do often rest* : L'A. 74.

(7) to trust or rely *in* : Ps.
LXXXIV. 48.

(8) to be or remain ; *while they
rest unknown* : C. 361 ; *that thou in
me...may'st ever rest well pleased* :
P. L. V. 71 ; *so only can high justice
rest appaid* : P. L. XII. 401 ; *the
credit of whose virtue rest with thee* :
P. L. IX. 649.

(*b*) to remain unused ; *let Euclid
rest* : S. XXI. 7.

(*c*) to remain to be done ; *but
fallen he is ; and now what rests* :
P. L. X. 48.

vbl. sb. **resting,** resting-place :
P. L. I. 237.

Rest, *sb.* (*a*) that which is left over,
the remainder ; *the rest* : P. L. I.
671 ; III. 721 ; IV. 547 ; VII. 240 ;
VIII. 71, 105 ; X. 296, 1008 ; P. R.
IV. 344 ; S. A. 1470 ; *the rest were
long to tell* : P. L. I. 507 ; XII.
260 ; *envy bid conceal the rest* : A.
13 ; *the rest is true* : P. L. IV. 900 ;
the rest commit to me : P. R. II.
233.

(*b*) the others ; *the rest* : P. L.
II. 54 ; III. 185 ; VI. 162, 662 ;
VII. 510 ; XII. 112, 533 ; *o'er the
rest* : P. 26 ; *among, amongst the
rest* : P. R. IV. 511 ; C. 629 ;
above the rest : P. L. I. 589 ; II.
455 ; III. 184 ; IX. 564 ; X. 532 ;
P. R. IV. 48 ; *Charity, the soul of
all the rest* : P. L. XII. 585 ; *what
reward awaits the good, the rest
what punishment* : P. L. XI. 710 ;
the rest were all retired : P. L. X.
422; *the rest are barbarous* : P. R.
IV. 86 ; *all the rest are held* : V.
Ex. 50 ; *the rest are numberless* :
P. L. VII. 492 ; in elliptical
phrase : as regards the others :
P. L. IX. 653.

Restless, *adj.* (*a*) always moving,
never quiet ; *restless let them reel* :
Ps. LXXXIII. 51 ; characterized
by constant motion ; *restless revolution, change* : P. L. VIII. 31 ;
C. 596.

(*b*) unquiet ; *restless thoughts* :
P. L. II. 526 ; S. A. 19.

Restorative, *adj.* capable of renewing strength ; *sweet restorative
delight* : P. R. II. 373.

Restore, *vb. tr.* (*a*) to bring back (a
person) to a former place or
position : P. L. I. 5 ; *these if from
servitude thou shalt restore* : P. R.
III. 381 ; *restored ... to place of
new acceptance* : P. L. X. 971.

(*b*) to bring back to a former
state of acceptance with God : P.
L. III. 288, 289 ; Ps. VI. 7 ;
LXXXV. 14 ; *man fallen shall be restored* : P. R. I. 405.

(*c*) to heal, cure : C. 690.

(*d*) to renew after destruction ;
*the world destroyed and world re-
stored* : P. L. XII. 3 ; *to restore
the race of mankind drowned* : P.
L. XI. 12.

(*e*) to re-establish after interruption ; *equity restored* : P. R. I.
220.

(*f*) to give or bring back, return ; *the kingdom shall to Israel
be restored* : P. R. II. 36 ; *the
Promised Seed shall all restore* :
P. L. XII. 623 ; *his eye-sight ... by
miracle restored* : S. A. 1528 ; *restore the truth ... that thou hast
banished from thy tongue* : C. 691 ;
with *acc.* and *dat.* ; *God will restore him eye-sight* : S. A. 1503.

Restorer, *sb.* one who restores another to a former state ; used of
Christ ; *destined, restorer of Mankind* ; P. L. X. 646.

Restrain, *vb. tr.* to hinder from
action, check : P. L. IX. 868 ; XI.
498.

part. adj. **restrained,** restricted :
P. L. VIII. 628.

Restraint, *sb.* (1) the act of restrain-
ing or hindering from action : P.
L. IX. 1170 ; *not enough severe in
thy restraint* : P. L. IX. 1184.

(2) that which limits or hinders
from action, restriction, prohibition ; *transgress his will for one
restraint* : P. L. I. 32.

(*b*) that which checks or directs
growth : P. L. IX. 209.

(*c*) that which confines or shuts
in ; *through all restraint broke loose* :
P. L. III. 87.

(3) reserve ; *greedily she ingorged without restraint* : P. L. IX.
209 ; *full sight of her without
restraint* : S. XXIII. 8.

Result, *sb.* (*a*) conclusion, issue :
P. L. VI. 619.

(*b*) the final decision of a council :
P. L. II. 515.

Resume, *vb. tr.* (*a*) to take again ;
*resume his seat at God's right
hand* : P. L. XII. 465 ; *their lost
shape* : P. L. X. 574.

(*b*) to recover ; *resume new
courage* : P. L. I. 278 ; *new hope* :
P. R. II. 58.

(*c*) to continue after interruption ; *speech resumes* : P. L. XII.
5.

Resurrection, *sb.* the rising again
of Christ from the dead : P. L.
XII. 436.

Retain, *vb. tr.* (*a*) to hold back ;
*I might perceive strange alteration
in me ... though to this shape re-
tained* : P. L. IX. 601.

(*b*) to hold or keep in possession ; *Heaven ... retains number
sufficient to possess her realm* : P.
L. VII. 146.

(c) to continue to have or possess; *Man, retaining still divine similitude*: P. L. XI. 512; *his love*: P. L. v. 501; *his power*: P. L. x. 532; *her maiden gentleness*: C. 842.

(d) to keep within itself; *the Sun's orb ... firm to retain her (light's) gathered beams*: P. L. VII. 362.

Retinue, (retínue) *sb.* the suite of a prince: P. L. v. 355; P. R. II. 419.

Retire, I. *sb.* retirement; *the place of her retire*: P. L. XI. 267.

(2) *vb.* (perfect formed with the auxilliary *be*: P. L. x. 423; S. A. 253; retirèd, *trisyl.*: ll P. 49; C. 376) *intr.* (b) to draw or fall back: P. L. x. 423; *back to his chariot where it stood retired*: P. L. VI. 338; *women ... skilled to retire, and in retiring draw hearts after them*: P. R. II. 161; used of an army: P. L. VI. 307; *the front ... to either flank retired*: P. L. VI. 570; *both retired, victor and vanquished*: P. L. VI. 409.

(a) to return; *the uprooted hills retired each to his place*: P. L. VI. 781.

(c) to fall back or retreat from a foe or from battle: P. L. x. 433: C. 656; *retire, or taste thy folly*: P. L. II. 686; *here Nature first begins her farthest verge, and Chaos to retire ... a broken foe*: P. L. II. 1038.

(d) to go away, withdraw: P. L. VII. 170; P. R. II. 40; *him (God) ... from this new World retiring*: P. L. x. 378; *Truth shall retire bestuck with slanderous darts*: P. L. XII. 535.

(e) to go away or part from action, from company, or from a public to a more private place: P. L. XI. 237; P. R. III. 164; *had we best retire?*: S. A. 1061; *where she sat retired in sight*: P. L. VIII. 41; *others apart sat on a hill retired*: P. L. II. 557; *some wandering Spirit ... in thick shade retired*: P. L. IV. 532; *Wisdom ... though secret she retire*: P. L. IX. 810; with *to, into, unto*, or *from*: S. A. 253; *Reason retires into her private cell*: P. L. v. 108; *he indeed retired unto the Desert*: P. R. III. 166; *from Rome retired to Capreæ*: P. R. IV. 91; *from the popular*

noise: S. A. 16; *from the heat of noon*: P. L. v. 231.

part. in seclusion, alone: P. L. IX. 537.

(f) to go to bed; *all things now retired to rest*: P. L. IV. 611.

part. adj. **retired**, (a) apart from public view or public action; *retired solitude*: C. 376; *Leisure*: ll P. 49.

(b) not intruding upon the notice, unassuming: P. L. VIII. 504,

vbl. sb. **retiring**, the act of drawing back: P. R. II. 161.

Retirement, *sb.* (a) the act of retiring from the company of a person: P. L. IX. 250.

(b) the place of withdrawal from public life; *the olive-grove of Academe, Plato's retirement*: P. R. IV. 245.

Retort, *vb. tr.* to reply resentfully; with the answer as obj. sentence: P. L. x. 751.

part. adj. **retorted**, flung back; *with retorted scorn*: P. L. v. 906.

Retreat, (1) *sb.* (a) the retirement of an army before an enemy: P. L. x. 435; *flight or foul retreat*: P. L. I. 555; *flight or faint retreat*: P. L. VI. 799; *no thought of flight, none of retreat*: P. L. VI. 237.

(b) a place of retirement and security; used of hell: P. L. II. 317.

(2) *vb. intr.* to withdraw to a retreat or quiet place: P. L. II. 547.

part. adj. **retreating**, withdrawing; *the retreating sea*: P. L. XI. 854.

Retrench, *vb. tr.* to diminish: P. R. I. 454.

Retribution, *sb.* the allotment of reward and punishment after death: P. L. III. 454.

Retrograde, *adj.* moving backward: P. L. VIII. 127.

Return, I. *sb.* (a) the act of coming or going back: P. L. IX. 405, 839; x. 253; P. R. I. 297; *short retirement urges sweet return*: P. L. IX. 250; *his charge of quick return*: P. L. IX. 399; *purposed quick return*: C. 284; *on return*: P. R. IV. 64; *at return of Him so lately promised*: P. L. XII. 541; *new solace in her return*: P. L. IX.

844; *greater now in thy return*: P. L. VII. 604.

used of that which returns periodically; *their* (the stars) *swift return diurnal*: P. L. VIII. 21; *the sweet return of morn*: P. R. IV. 438.

(*b*) recompense, requital: P. L. IV. 42; *unsuitable return for so much good*: P. R. III. 132.

II. *vb.* (*pres. 2d sing.* return'st: P. L. VI. 151; XII. 610; perfect formed with the auxiliary *have*: P. L. x. 240; with *be*: P. R. II. 140) (**1**) *tr.* (*a*) to send or cast back; *which returns light back to them*: P. L. VIII. 157.

(*b*) to bring or lead back (a person to a place): P. L. VII. 16; P. R. IV. 374; S. A. 517.

(*c*) *refl.* to bring oneself back; *Satan ... now returns him*: P. L. IV. 906.

(*d*) to cause to go back; *lest ... fear return them back to Egypt*: P. L. XII. 219.

(*e*) to restore to a former state of reconciliation with God: Ps. LXXX. 29, 77.

(*f*) to surrender; *force him to return his purchase back*: C. 607.

(*g*) to give in requital: P. R. III. 129, 130; *what peace can we return*: P. L. II. 335.

(*h*) to give back in response: P. L. II. 736; *answer*: P. L. III. 693; VIII. 285; IX. 226: P. R. I. 467; II. 172; III. 181; *hiss for hiss returned*: P. L. x. 518; with *acc.* and *dat.*; *returned them loud acclaim*: P. L. II. 520.

(**2**) *intr.* (*a*) to come or go back: P. L. II. 527; IV. 534; x. 455: P. R. I. 324; II. 115; S. A. 1390; C. 194; *imper.*: S. A. 1332; L. 132, 133; Ps. VII. 28; LXXX. 57; *Return, fair Eve*: P. L. IV. 481; with an adv., adj., or phrase indicating time, place, purpose, manner, or condition: P. L. II. 839; III. 159, 261; VI. 151, 187; IX. 57, 278; x. 34, 240, 341, 346; XI. 348; XII. 610, 632: P. R. II. 24, 61, 140, 302; IV. 639; S. A. 1750; L. 38; S. XIX. 6; Ps. VI. 23; *at midnight*: P. L. IX. 58; *on the eighth*: P. L. IX. 67; *by noon*: P. L. IX. 401; *at eve*: P. R. I. 318; *I ... to the place of judgment will return*: P. L. x.

932; *from Egypt home returned*: P. R. II. 79; *the great Creator from his work returned*: P. L. VII. 567; *scarce from the tree returning*: P. L. IX. 850; *we now return to claim our just inheritance*: P. L. II. 37; *pleased I soon returned*: P. L. IV. 463; *Uriel to his charge returned*: P. L. IV. 590; *yet one returned not lost*: P. L. VI. 25; *the great Son returned victorious*: P. L. VII. 135; *successful*: P. L. x. 462; *he shall return of them derided*: P. L. XI. 816; *the wiser*: P. R. I. 439; with *back*: P. L. VI. 39, 606; XII. 171; Ps. LXXXV. 4; with *up*: P. L. VII. 552; VIII. 245; x. 224.

used of things, abstractions, or personifications: P. L. II. 799; VI. 879; XI. 859; XII. 213; P. R. IV. 17; N. O. 142; *from whom all things proceed, and up to him return*: P. L. v. 470; *soon his clear aspect returned*: P. L. VIII. 337; *vigour soon returns*: P. L. I. 140; *peace returned home to my breast*: P. L. XI. 153; *Justice shall not return ... scorned*: P. L. x. 54; *soon we shall see our hope, our joy, return*: P. R, II. 57; *beauty ... after offence returning*: S. A. 1004; *this ... gift of strength again returning*: S. A. 1355; *his scattered spirits returned*: P. L. XI. 294; *all honour done to him returns our own*: P. L. v. 845.

(*b*) to come or go back to a former state or condition: P. L. v. 276; x. 770; XI. 200, 463; *falsehood ... returns of force to its own likeness*: P. L. IV. 812; *till thou return unto the ground*: P.L. x. 206; *thou ... shalt to dust return*: P. L. x. 208; *return to folly*: Ps. LXXXV. 35; *Lord ... calmly did'st return from thy fierce wrath*: Ps. LXXXV. 10.

(*c*) to repeat a visit: P. L. VIII. 651.

(*d*) to appear or begin again after a periodical revolution; *seasons, morn, years*: P. L. III. 41; v. 30; XI. 534; *ere the third dawning light return*: P. L. XII. 422; *fig.*, *when the fresh blood ... returns brisk as the April buds in primrose season*: C. 670.

(*e*) to answer: P. L. IV. 576.

Reveal, *vb.* (*past part. trisyl.*: P. L.
VII. 122) *tr.* (*a*) to make known,
divulge : S. A. 50, 383, 491; *some
great act ... revealed to Abraham's
race*: S. A. 29; *whether on hill ... or
harboured in one cave, is not revealed*: P. R. I. 307; *absol.*: S. A.
782, 800; to disclose (to man
superhuman knowledge): P. L.
VI. 895; VII. 71, 122; XII. 151,
272; *thus far hath been revealed
not of Earth only, but of highest
Heaven*: P. L. VIII. 177; *reveal
to Adam what shall come in future
days*: P. L. III. 113; *secrets of
another world .. not lawful to reveal*: P. L. V. 570; *what concerns
my knowledge God reveals*: P. R.
I. 293.

(*b*) to expose to sight : P. R. II.
50: *last in the clouds from Heaven
to be revealed* : P. L. XII. 545.

Revel, (1) *sb.* merrymaking, frolic:
P. L. I. 782.

(2) *vb. intr.* (*a*) to dance, frolic ;
fig., *revels the spruce and jocund
Spring*: C. 985.

(*b*) to take great pleasure : P.
L. IV. 765,

Reveller, *sb.* one who leads a dissolute life ; *Bacchus and his re-
vellers*: P. L. VII. 33.

Revelry, *sb.* merry-making: C. 103;
or, possibly, the Revels, a kind of
dance forming a part of a masque
or pageant : L'A. 127.

Revenge, (1) *sb.* (*a*) the return of an
injury, the execution of venge-
ance : P. L. X. 1036; S. A. 1591,
1660; *set on revenge*: S. A. 1462;
used with reference to God or
angels : P. L. X. 242; to Satan
or his angels : P. L. II. 105,
129, 987; III. 160; IV. 390; VI.
905; IX. 171; *study of revenge*:
P. L. I. 107; *pride waiting
revenge*: P. L. I. 604; *desperate*:
P. L. II. 107; III. 85; *dire*:
P. L. II. 128; *common*: P. L. II.
371; *in wished hour of my revenge*: P. L. VI. 151; *who puts
me loth to this revenge*: P. L. IV.
386.

(*b*) the desire for vengeance,
vindictiveness : S. A. 484; used
with reference to Satan : P. L. I.
35; II. 337, 1054; IV. 123; IX.
168, 466.

(2) *vb. absol.*, or *passive* to take
vengeance : S. A. 1468; *Samson
... on his enemies fully revenged*:

S. A. 1712; *the Dragon ... to be
revenged on men*: P. L. IV. 4.

Reverence, (1) *sb.* (*a*) a feeling of
profound respect : P. L. VIII. 599;
mingled with awe and affection :
P. L. X. 915.

(*b*) the outward manifestation
of reverend feeling : P. L. V. 359;
XI. 237 ; *in Heaven ... reverence
none neglect*: P. L. III. 738 ; *towards him they bend with awful
reverence prone*: P. L. II. 478.
the bowing down as evidence of
reverence ; *whom with low reverence I adore*: A. 37; *first low
reverence done*: P. L. IX. 835; *I
saw the Prophet do him reverence* :
P. R. I. 80.

(2) *vb. tr.* (*a*) to regard with
reverence, venerate: P. L. XI. 525.

(*b*) to show respect to, honour :
P. L. XI. 346.

(*c*) to worship, bow down to :
S. A. 1463.

Reverend, *adj.* worthy to be revered,
entitled to veneration or respect ;
a or *thy reverend sire*: P. L. XI.
719; S. A. 326; *Camus, reverend
sire*: L. 103; in direct address ;
reverend Sire: S. A. 1456; *Manoa*:
S. A. 1548.

Reverent, *adj.* (*a*) feeling or showing
reverence : P. L. III. 349; *fall
before him reverent*: P. L. X.
1088, 1100.

(*b*) full of or characteristic of
reverence ; *reverent awe*: P. R.
II. 220.

Reverse, (1) *adj.* opposite in direction : P. L. VI. 326.

(2) *vb. tr.* (*a*) to turn in an
opposite direction : C. 816.

(*b*) to set aside ; *his doom ...
not to reverse*: P. L. XI. 41.

Revile, *sb.* reproach : P. L. X. 118.

Reviling, *vbl. sb.* upbraiding, reproach : P. L. X. 1048.

Revisit, *vb.* (*pres. 2d. sing.* revisit'st :
P. L. III. 23) *tr.* to seek again,
return to ; *holy Light ... thee I
revisit now ... Thee I revisit safe*;
P. L. III. 13, 21; *thou revisit'st
not these.eyes* : P. L. III. 23.

Revive, *vb.* (1) *intr.* (*a*) to return to
life after death : P. L. XII. 420 ;
S. A. 1740; C. 840.

(*b*) to recover strength and
courage: P. L. I. 279; VI. 493;
XI. 871; *how reviving to the spirits
of just men long oppressed*: S. A.
1268.

(c) to regain freshness and beauty ; *the fields revive* : P. L. II. 493.

(2) *tr.* (*a*) to rouse from depression or despair : S. A. 187.

(*b*) to renew spiritual life and power ; *absol.*: Ps. LXXXV. 22.

(*c*) to arouse *hope* : P. L. VI. 497.

part. adj. **revived**, returned to life, reanimated : P. L. IX. 440.

Revoke, *vb. tr.* (*a*) to recall (a promise) : P. R. III. 356.

(*b*) to annul by recalling, repeal ; *revoke the high decree* : P. L. III. 126.

Revolt, (1) *sb.* rebellion against God ; *on the part of man revolt and disobedience* : P. L. IX. 7 ; the revolt of Satan or his angels : P. L. I. 611 ; II. 326 ; III. 117 ; VI. 262 ; *foul revolt* : P. L. I. 33 ; *leagued with millions more in rash revolt* : P. R. I. 359.

(2) *vb. tr.* to rebel ; *still revolt when Truth would set them free* : S. XII. 10 ; to rebel against God : P. L. VI. 740.

part. adj. **revolted**, having rebelled against God ; *revolted Spirit, multitudes, rout* : P. L. IV. 835 ; VI. 31 ; X. 534.

Revolter, *sb.* a rebel : S. A. 1180.

Revolution, *sb.* (*a*) the act of moving completely around a circular course : P. L. VIII. 31 ; *fig.*: U. C. II. 6.

(*b*) a recurrent period of time : P. L. II. 597.

(*c*) a return to a point previously occupied : P. L. X. 814.

Revolve, *vb. tr.* (*a*) to cause to turn about as upon an axis ; *she* (the moon) *shines, revolved on heaven's great axle* : P. L. VII. 381.

(*b*) to unroll ; *I again revolved the Law and Prophets* : P. R. I. 259.

(*c*) to meditate on : P. R. IV. 281 ; *some great matter in his mind revolved* : S. A. 1638 ; *much revolving* : P. L. IV. 31 ; *irresolute of thoughts revolved* : P. L. IX. 88 ; *much revolving ... how best the mighty work he might begin* : P. R. I. 185.

Reward, (1) *sb.* that which is given in requital of good or evil, return, recompense ; (*a*) of good : P. L. XI. 459 ; P. R. III. 104 ; *thy reward was of his grace* : P. L. X.

767 ; *what reward awaits the good* : P. L. XI. 709 ; *public marks ... of reward* : S. A. 992 ; *glory, the reward that sole excites...most erected spirits* : P. R. III. 25 ; *in reward*, as a recompense : P. L. VII. 628.

(*b*) of evil : P. L. VI. 153, 910 ; *all who have their reward on earth* : P. L. III. 451 ; *shameful death their due reward* : P. R. III. 87 ; remuneration ; *their aim private reward* : S. A. 1465.

(2) *vb. tr.* to recompense for good ; *to reward his faithful* : P. L. XII. 461 ; for evil ; *servile mind rewarded well with servile punishment* : S. A. 413.

Rhea, *sb.* the wife of Saturn and the mother of Jove : P. L. I. 513 ; the wife of Ammon : P. L. IV. 279. *See* **Ammon.**

Rhene, *sb.* the river Rhine : P. L. I. 353.

Rhetoric, *sb.* eloquent language, oratory : P. R. IV. 4 ; *enjoy your dear wit and gay rhetoric* : C. 790.

Rheum, *sb. pl.* rheumatism : P. L. XI. 488.

Rhodope, *sb.* a mountain in the western part of Thrace : P. L. VII. 35.

Rhomb, *sb.* (*a*) that which has the shape and motion of a wheel ; *nocturnal and diurnal rhomb*, the Primum Mobile whose revolution produced the phenomena of day and of night : P. L. VIII. 134. *See* **Sphere.**

(*b*) a line of battle in the shape of a rhomb or diamond : P. R. III. 309.

Rhyme, *sb.* verse, poetry ; *things unattempted yet in prose or rhyme* : P. L. I. 16 ; *build the lofty rhyme* : L. 11.

Rib, *sb.* (*a*) one of the curved bones springing from the vertebral column ; *strains that might create a soul under the ribs of Death* : C. 562 ; the rib used in the creation of Eve : P. L. VIII. 466, 469 ; IX. 1154 ; X. 884 ; *should God create another Eve, and I another rib afford* : P. L. IX. 912.

(*b*) the side of the body over the ribs ; *his arms clung to his ribs* : P. L. X. 512.

(*c*) that which resembles a rib in size or shape ; *ribs of gold* : P. L. I. 690.

Rich, I. *adj.* (1) having large possessions, wealthy: S. A. 722; *rich burgher*: P. L. IV. 189; or lavish; *sup., the gorgeous East with richest hand*: P. L. II. 3.

(2) abounding in wealth; *rich Mexico*: P. L. XI. 407; *Cathaian coast*: P. L. X. 292; *comp.*: P. L. XI. 408.

(3) of great value and beauty, magnificent, splendid: P. L. III. 504; *rich gems*: C. 22; *marble*: M. W. 1; *achieved ... high titles, and rich prey*: P. L. XI. 793; *sup., richest texture*: P. L. X. 446; *robes*: V. Ex. 21.

fig., Earth, in her rich attire: P. L. VII. 501.

(*b*) precious; *sup.*: P. 44.

(*c*) splendidly attired; *rich retinue*: P. L. V. 355; splendidly built, furnished, or adorned; *rich abode*: Ps. LXXXIV. 39.

(*d*) brilliant in colour; *with rich inlay broidered the ground*: P. L. IV. 701.

(4) luxuriant, fruitful; *rich trees*: P. L. IV. 248.

(5) full and satisfying to the sense of smell; *rich perfumes*: C. 566.

sup. absol. the one having greatest wealth: S. A. 1479.

II. *adv.* richly, splendidly; *rich emblazed*: P. L. I. 538.

Rich-clad, *adj.* clad in costly and splendid garments: P. R. II. 352.

Riches, *sb.* abundant possessions, wealth: P. R. II. 427, 449, 453, 458; IV. 298, 536; *all the riches of this world*: P. L. XII. 580; *the All-giver would be unthanked ... not half his riches known*: C. 724; *pl., riches are mine*: P. R. II. 429; *are needless*: P. R. II. 484; gold regarded as wealth; *admiring more the riches of Heaven's pavement*: P. L. I. 682; *riches grow in Hell*: P. L. I. 691.

Richly, *adv.* in a costly and splendid manner; *a table richly spread*: P. R. II. 340; *women richly gay in gems*: P. L. XI. 582; with great beauty or brilliance of colour; *windows richly dight*: Il P. 159.

Rid, *vb.* (used only in the *pres.*) *tr.* (*a*) to put out of the way; *by death to rid me hence*: S. A. 1263.

(*b*) to free, clear, deliver; *rid*

Heaven of these rebelled: P. L. VI. 737.

See **Bed-rid.**

Riddance, *sb.* the act of clearing away; *these blossoms ... ask riddance*: P. L. IV. 632.

Riddle, *sb.* enigma: S. A. 1016, 1200; *that Theban monster that proposed her riddle*: P. R. IV. 573.

Riddling, *part. adj.* in which one speaks in riddles; *my riddling days*: S. A. 1064.

Ride, *vb.* (*pres. 2d sing.* ridest: C. 135; *pret.* and *past part.* rode) I. *intr.* (1) to go or come on horseback: P. L. I. 764; *the wondrous horse of brass on which the Tartar king did ride*: Il P. 115; *fig., evil news rides post*: S. A. 1538.

(2) to be borne along in a chariot; *young Pompey ... in triumph had rode*: P. R. III. 36; *the great Thisbite, who on fiery wheels rode up to Heaven*: P. R. II. 17; *as in a cloudy chair ascending rides*: P. L. II. 930; *thy cloudy ebon chair, wherein thou ridest with Hecat'*: C. 135; used of Christ: P. L. VI. 840; VII. 219; *he on the wings of Cherub rode sublime*: P. L. VI. 771; *though Heaven's King ride on thy wings*: P. L. IV. 974; *he ... rode, triumphant through mid Heaven*: P. L. VI. 888; *up he rode*: P. L. VII. 557; *ride forth*: P. L. VII. 166.

(*b*) to be borne along in a similar manner; *who from thy father's field rode up in flames*: S. A. 1433.

(3) to be borne along on water; *the floating vessel ... rode tilting o'er the waves*: P. L. XI. 747.

(4) to move along; *when the Sun with Taurus rides*: P. L. I. 769; *Hesperus ... rode brightest*: P. L. IV. 606; *the ... moon, riding near her highest noon*: Il P. 68; *seven ... nights he rode with darkness*: P. L. IX. 63; *the night hag ... riding through the air*: P. L. II. 663.

II. *tr.* (*a*) to pass or travel through; *others ... ride the air*: P. L. II. 540; *forced to ride the ... Abyss*: P. L. X. 475.

(*b*) to tyrannize over: F. of C. 7.

Rider, *sb.* one who rides on horseback: P. R. III. 314; S. A. 1324.

Ridge, (1) *sb.* (*a*) a long and narrow elevation ; *a ridge of pendent rock* : P. L. x. 313 ; *waters ... rise in ... ridge direct* : P. L. vii. 293.

(*b*) an extended line of hills or mountains ; *a ridge of hills* : P. R. iv. 29 ; *Senir, that long ridge of hills* : P. L. xii. 146 ; *Imaus ... snowy ridge* : P. L. iii. 432.

(*c*) the strip of ground thrown up by a plough (?) ; *fig.* ranks of soldiers drawn up in line of battle : P. L. vi. 236.

(2) *vb. tr.* to cover with ridges : S. A. 1137.

Ridiculous, *adj.* worthy of laughter or contempt : S. A. 1361, 1501 ; *turned me out ridiculous, despoiled, shaven* : S. A. 539 ; *their gods ridiculous* : P. R. iv. 342 ; *weaponless himself, made arms ridiculous* : S. A. 131 ; *the building left ridiculous* : P. L. xii. 62.

Rife, *adj.* (*a*) prevalent, current : P. L. i. 650 ; S. A. 866.

(*b*) clear, plain ; *the tumult of loud mirth was rife, ... in my listening ear* : C. 203.

Rifle, *vb. tr.* to plunder ; *rifled the bowels of their mother Earth* : P. L. i. 687.

Rift, (1) *sb.* fissure : P. R. iv. 411.

(2) *vb. tr.* to cleave ; *the people with a shout rifted the air* : S. A. 1621.

part. adj. **rifted**, cleft ; *rifted rocks* : C. 518.

Rig, *vb. tr.* to fit with the necessary tackle : L. 101 ; *fig.* : S. A. 200.

Right, I. *adj.* (1) straight, direct ; *the setting sun ... with right aspect against the eastern gate of Paradise levelled his evening rays* : P. L. iv. 541.

(2) conforming to the principles of justice and the moral law ; in the predicate : P. L. i. 247 ; ix. 570 ; *it were but right to reduce me to my dust* : P. L. x. 747 ; *with some regard to what is just and right* : P. L. xii. 16 ; *what thou hast said is just and right* : P. L. iv. 443 ; used of the ways of God ; *whose ways are just and right* : Ps. lxxxiv. 44 ; *thy way most right* : Ps. lxxxvi. 37.

(*b*) recognizing and dictating what is right ; *right reason* : P. L. vi. 42 ; xii. 84 ; *Reason he made right* : P. L. ix. 352.

(3) upright, righteous ; *I made him right* : P. L. iii. 98.

(4) being on the side opposite to the left ; *right side* : P. L. vi. 327 ; *right hand coast* : P. L. ii. 633 ; *hand* : L'A. 35 ; used with reference to God or Christ : P. L. ii. 174 ; iii. 279 ; v. 606 ; vi. 762, 835 ; x. 64 ; Ps. lxxx. 61, 69 ; *the right hand of Glory* : P. L. vi. 747 ; *at the right hand of bliss* : P. L. vi. 892 ; *his glory at God's right hand* : P. L. xii. 457 ; with reference to Satan : P. L. ii. 869 ; v. 864 ; vi. 154.

II. *sb.* (1) that which is conformable to justice and the moral law : P. L. ix. 676 ; *they, therefore, as to right belonged so were created* : P. L. iii. 111 ; *spake much of right and wrong* : P. L. xi. 666 ; *till truth and right from violence be freed* : S. xv. 11.

(*b*) justice : Ps. vii. 26 ; *how long will ye pervert the right* : Ps. lxxxii. 5 ; *who can in reason, then, or right, assume monarchy* : P. L. v. 794.

(*c*) rightness ; *self-esteem, grounded on just and right* : P. L. viii. 572.

(2) a just and proper claim or title : P. L. ii. 18 ; iv. 881 ; xii. 68 ; P. R. ii. 325, 379, 380 ; *to try in battle what our power is or our right* : P. L. v. 728 ; *such as live by right his equals* : P. L. v. 795 ; *by right endued with regal sceptre* : P. L. v. 815 ; *who by right of merit reigns* : P. L. vi. 43 ; *by right of war* : P. L. i. 150 ; *hast thou not right to all created things* : P. R. ii. 324 ; with blending of sense (1) ; *of right* : P. L. ix. 611 ; x. 76, 461 ; *that which to God alone of right belongs* : P. R. iii. 141.

(*b*) privilege, prerogative : S. A. 310, 1056 ; *to me the power is given, and by that right I give it thee* : P. R. iv. 104.

(3) that which is due one by just claim or title : P. L. ii. 231 ; P. R. iii. 154, 164 ; *that ... claimed Azazel as his right* : P. L. i. 534 ; *our right as Gods* : P. L. vi. 452 ; *King Messiah might be born barred of his right* : P. L. xii. 360 ; *to be King ... thy deserved right* : P. L. vi. 709.

(4) the side opposite to the left; *to right and left* : P. L. VI. 558, 569; *on his right the radiant image of his glory sat* : P. L. III. 62.

III. *adv.* (*a*) straight, directly : Ps. v. 24 ; *right down* : P. L. III. 562 ; x. 398 ; *right onward* : P. L. VI. 831 ; S. XXII. 9.

(*b*) justly, righteously ; *judgest only right* : P. L. III. 155.

(*c*) not erroneously, truly, correctly ; *if I trust to know ye right* : P. L. v. 789 ; *if thou reckon right* : P. L. VIII. 71 ; *to judge right* : U. C. II. 21 ; *to value right* : P. L. IV. 202.

(*d*) in a suitable manner, properly : P. L. VI. 624 ; C. 854.

(*e*) exactly, just ; *right against* : P. L. I. 402 ; L'A. 59.

Righteous, *adj.* (*a*) upright ; *righteous Job* : P. R. I. 425.

(*b*) holy ; *his righteous altar* : P. L. I. 434.

(*c*) conformable to or in accordance with right, just and good ; *righteous deeds* : P. L. III. 292 ; *cause, plea, decrees* : P. L. VI. 804 ; x. 30, 644 ; *things* : P. R. I. 206 ; *ways* : Ps. LXXXI. 56.

absol. one who is upright ; *to pursue the righteous* : S. A. 1276 ; *the only righteous in a world perverse* : P. L. XI. 701.

Righteousness, *sb.* purity of heart and rectitude of life ; *native righteousness* : P. L. IX. 1056; the state of acceptance and of harmony with God : P. L. XI. 682 ; Ps. IV. 2, 24 ; VII. 32 ; *before them set the paths of righteousness* : P. L. XI. 814 ; *new Heavens, new Earth ... founded in righteousness* : P. L. XII. 550 ; the holiness of God or Christ ; *Lord, lead me in thy righteousness* : Ps. v. 21 ; *such righteousness to them by faith imputed* : P. L. XII. 294 ; *with his robe of righteousness arraying* : P. L. x. 222.

Rightful, *adj.* (*a*) lawful, legitimate : P. L. v. 818.

(*b*) just : Cir. 17.

Rightly, *adv.* (*a*) in the right manner, truly, sincerely : P. L. XII. 418.

(*b*) properly, fitly, suitably : P. L. VII. 2 ; VIII. 439 ; S. M. 18 ; *Eve rightly called, Mother of all Mankind* : P. L. XI. 159 ; *sup.,*

each act is rightliest done : P. R. IV. 475.

(*c*) not erroneously, correctly : II P. 170 ; *comp., destroyers rightlier called* : P. L. XI. 697 ; *rightlier called Powers of Fire* : P. R. II. 123.

Rigid, *adj.* (*a*) held firmly in an upright position ; *rigid spears* : P. L. VI. 83.

(*b*) rigorous, severe : S. A. 433 ; *pay the rigid satisfaction* : P. L. III. 212 ; *the rigid interdiction* : P. L. VIII. 334 ; *rigid threats of death* : P. L. IX. 685 ; austere, cold, stern ; *rigid looks of chaste austerity* : C. 450.

See **Self-rigorous.**

Rigorously, *adv.* without mitigation, inexorably : P. L. XI. 109.

Rigour, *sb.* (*a*) rigidity ; *bound with Gorgonian rigour not to move* : P. L. x. 297.

(*b*) austerity in life ; *personified, Rigour now is gone to bed* : C. 107.

(*c*) the severity or relentlessness of God : P. L. x. 803 ; P. R. I. 363.

Rill, *sb.* a small stream of **water** : P. L. IV. 229 ; L. 24, 186 ; *a thousand petty rills* : C. 926 ; *fuming* : P. L. v. 6 ; *soft* : Ps. CXIV. 18.

Rimmon, *sb.* a god of Syria, identified with one of the fallen angels ; P. L. I. 467.

Rind, *sb.* the thick outer coat or skin ; (*a*) of fruits ; *golden rind* ; P. L. IV. 249 ; *in the rind ... scoop the brimming stream* : P. L. IV. 335.

(*b*) of an animal ; *Leviathan ... his scaly rind* : P. L. I. 206.

(*c*) of man ; *this corporeal rind* : C. 664.

Rined, *adj.* having a rind ; *fruit ... smooth rined* : P. L. v. 342.

Ring, *sb.* (*a*) the circlet of gold worn on the finger : II P. 113.

(*b*) circle : II P. 47.

Ring, I. *sb.* the sound produced by striking metal ; *cymbals' ring* : N. O. 208.

II. *vb.* (*pret.* rang : N. O. 158 ; rung : P. L. II. 655 ; III. 347 ; VI. 204 ; VII. 562, 633 ; IX. 737 ; *past part.* rung) (1) *tr.* (*a*) to produce as by ringing ; *a cry of Hellhounds ... rung a hideous peal* : P. L. II. 655 ; *the first cock his matin rings* : L'A. 114.

(b) to repeat loudly and sonorously : Ps. LXXXI. 4 ; *the faithful armies rung Hosannah* : P. L. VI. 204.

(2) *intr.* (a) to give forth a musical sound ; *ring out, ye crystal spheres* ! : N. O. 125 ; *the merry bells ring round* : L'A. 93.

(b) to resound, reverberate : P. L. III. 347 ; N. O. 158 ; P. 2 ; *the heavens and all the constellations rung* : P. L. VII. 562 ; *the Empyrean rung* : P. L. VII. 633 ; *in her ears the sound yet rings* : P. L. IX. 737 ; *sing.* with compound subject ; *hill and valley rings* : P. L. II. 495.

(c) to be filled with report or talk : S. A. 1449 ; *of which all Europe rings* : S. XXII. 12 ; *whereof all Hell had rung* : P. L. II. 723.

(d) to be celebrated ; *whose name in arms through Europe rings* : S. XV. 1.

Ringlet, *sb.* a curl of hair : P. L. IV. 306 ; *fig.* the foliage of trees : A. 47.

Riot, *sb.* (a) rebellion, insurrection : P. L. X. 521.

(b) boisterous and excessive festivity : P. L. I. 499 ; XI. 715 ; C. 172.

Riotous, *adj.* knowing no restraint, wantonly luxurious : C. 763.

Ripe, *adj.* (a) ready for reaping, gathering, or using : P. L. IV. 323 ; *a field of Ceres ripe for harvest* : P. L. IV. 98 ; *ripe fruit, clusters* : P. L. XI. 535 ; C. 296.

(b) ready for action or for life ; *Comus ... ripe and frolic of his full-grown age* : C. 59.

(c) sufficient in number : P. R. III. 31 ; *ripe years* : P. R. III. 37.

(d) finished ; *when this World's dissolution shall be ripe* : P. L. XII. 459.

See **Over-ripe.**

Ripen, *vb. tr.* to mature ; *had ripened thy just soul* : S. XIV. 2.

Ripeness, *sb.* maturity ; *inward ripeness* : S. II. 7.

Rise, I. *sb.* the act of appearing above the horizon ; *fig.*, *so spake our Morning Star, then in his rise* : P. R. I. 294.

II. *vb.* (*pret.* rose ; *past part.* risen ; perfect tenses formed with the auxiliary *have* : P. L. I. 211 ; II. 726 ; with *be* : P. L. X. 975 ; P. R. II. 127) *intr.* (1) to move

from a lower to a higher position, ascend : P. L. I. 546 ; II. 15 ; V. 188, 191 ; VII. 293 ; (birds) *rising on stiff pennons* : P. L. VII. 441 ; *evening mist risen from a river* : P. L. XII. 630 ; *Ye Mists ... that now rise from hill* : P. L. V. 185 ; *banners rise into the air* : P. L. I. 545 ; *fig.*, *a ... sound rose like a steam of ... perfume* : C. 556.

(2) to get up from a sitting or lying posture, stand up : P. L. I. 211 ; II. 301, 466, 475, 726 ; VIII. 44 ; XI. 665 ; P. R. II. 149 ; IV. 565 ; L. 192 ; *he ... rose from the right hand of Glory* : P. L. VI. 746 ; *from his radiant seat he rose of high collateral glory* : P. L. X. 85 ; *if to fall, but that they rise unvanquished* : P. L. VI. 285 ; *to his message high in honour rise* : P. L. V. 289 ; *as a tiger ... rising, changes oft his couchant watch* : P. L. IV. 405 ; *up rose* : P. L. II. 108 ; *imper.* : P. L. VIII. 296 ; X. 958 ; S. A. 1316.

(b) to get up from bed or sleep : P. L. V. 48 ; P. R. II. 274 ; *we must be risen* : P. L. IV. 624 ; *let us to our fresh employments rise* : P. L. V. 125 ; *so rose ... Samson from the harlot-lap of ... Dalilah* : P. L. IX. 1059 ; with *up* : P. L. IX. 1051 ; P. R. II. 282 ; *up rose the victor Angels* : P. L. VI. 525.

(c) to get up from a repast : S. XX. 10.

(3) to come up or emerge from a place : P. L. IV. 229 ; *till part rose up a fountain ... and with it rose, Satan* : P. L. IX. 73, 74 ; *rise, rise, and heave thy rosy head from thy coral-paven bed* : C. 885.

(b) to come up *out of* : P. R. I. 280 ; *him, rising out of the water* : P. R. I. 80.

(4) to lead away or up ; *what readiest way .. due west it rises from this shrubby point* : C. 306.

(5) to reach a height by increase ; *till inundation rise above the highest hills* : P. L. XI. 828.

(6) to extend upward : P. L. IV. 548.

(7) to appear above the horizon ; used of the sun : P. L. X. 329 ; *whether the Sun ... rise on the Earth, or Earth rise on the Sun* : P. L. VIII. 161 ; of the moon : P. L. IV. 607 ; of the stars : P. L. VII. 385 ; *the star that rose at*

evening : L. 30; *the stars that usher evening rose* : P. L. IV. 355; *the fixed ... rising with the Sun* : P. L. X. 663; *they rise and set* : P. L. IV. 664; *transf.* of morn or dawn: P. L. V. 311; L'A. 44; of evening, even, or darkness : P. L. V. 376; P. R. IV. 397; A. 54; C. 190.

(8) to arise from the grave; used of Christ : P. L. III. 250, 296; X. 185; XII. 422.

(9) to come into existence; (*a*) to come forth, appear; with blending of sense (**1**) or (**2**) : P. L. VII. 459, 468, 472; X. 555; *last rose, as in dance, the stately trees* : P. L. VII. 324; *out of the ground up rose, ... the wild beast* : P. L. VII. 456; *the heavens and earth rose out of Chaos* : P. L. I. 10; *out of the earth a fabric huge rose like an exhalation* : P. L. I. 711; *by whom new Heaven and Earth shall to the ages rise, or down from Heaven descend* : P. L. X. 647; *who did the solid earth ordain to rise above the watery plain* : Ps. CXXXVI. 22.

(*b*) to spring up : P. L. VI. 669; IX. 1123; *I feel new strength within me rise* : P. L. X. 243; *what thoughts ... are risen* : P. L. X. 975; *now storming fury rose* : P. L. VI. 207; *rebellion rising* : P. L. V. 715.

(*c*) to be born : P. L. XII. 326.

(*d*) to be built : H. B. 12.

(*e*) to become audible; *a hideous gabble rises* : P. L. XII. 56. .

(*f*) to be offered or presented; *lest a question rise* : S. A. 1254.

(**10**) to attain (a certain position) by increasing in power; *this nether empire, which might rise ... in emulation opposite to Heaven* : P. L. II. 296.

(**11**) to increase in force; *the South-wind rose* : P. L. XI. 738.

(**12**) to obtain power or authority : P. L. XII. 24.

(**13**) to begin to exert power : Ps. III. 19; *rise Jehovah, in thine ire* : Ps. VII. 19.

(**14**) to become hostile, take up arms in opposition : P. L. V. 725; P. R. II. 127; Ps. III. 3; LXXXI. 58; LXXXVI. 49; *all Hell should rise ... to confound Heaven's purest light* : P. L. II. 135; *against the Omnipotent to rise in arms* : P. L. VI. 136.

part. adj. **rising**; (*a*) ascending mist : P. L. IX. 75.

(*b*) extending upwards : P. L. IX. 498.

(*c*) appearing above the horizon; *rising sun* : P. L. III. 551; IV. 651.

(*d*) higher in level; *a plat of rising ground* : Il P. 73.

(*e*) coming into existence; *the rising World of waters* : P. L. III. 11; *the rising birth of Nature* : P. L. VII. 102.

vbl. sb. **rising**; (*a*) the act of getting up from a sitting position; *his, their rising* : P. L. II. 301, 476.

(*b*) the act of moving from a lower to a higher position spiritually or morally : P. L. IX. 1070; P. R. II. 88.

(*c*) the act of appearing; *Morn, her rising sweet* : P. L. IV. 641.

(*d*) the act of increasing in power; *my rising is thy fall* : P. R. III. 201.

See **New-risen, Sun-rise.**

Rite, *sb.* (*a*) a solemn ceremony connected with the worship of God : P. L. I. 390; IV. 736; XI. 440; XII. 244; *religious rites of sacrifice* : P. L. XII. 231; *outward rites* : P. L. XII. 534; in heaven; *this high temple to frequent with ... solemn rites* : P. L. VII. 149; connected with the worship of a god: C. 125; *religious rites* : S. A. 1320; *idolatrous* : S. A. 1378; *abhorred rites to Hecate* : C. 535; *Peor ... to do him wanton rites* : P. L. I. 414.

(*b*) a usage or ceremony connected with love or marriage; *marriage rites* : P. L. VIII. 487; XI. 591; *love's due rites* : P. L. X. 994; *rites mysterious of connubial love* : P. L. IV. 742.

Rival, *sb.* (*a*) companion : S. A. 387.

(*b*) one who is in pursuit of the same object as another : P. L. II. 472.

Riven, *part. adj.* rent asunder : P. L. VI. 449.

River, *sb.* a considerable stream of water flowing through the land : P. L. IV. 223; VII. 305, 328; IX. 514; XII. 176, 630; P. R. III. 255, 257; Ps. LXXX. 47; *rivers pure* : P. L. IV. 806; *proud* : P. R. III. 334; *wide* : L'A. 76; *silver lakes and rivers* : P. L. VII. 437;.

rivers, woods, and plains: P. L.
VIII. 275; IX. 116; *the river Tri-
ton*: P. L. IV. 276; *the river Ob*:
P. L. IX. 78; *the river Nile*: P. L.
XII. 157; Euphrates, *the great
river*: P. L. XI. 833; Tiber: P.
R. IV. 32; Tigris: P. L. IX. 74;
Severn: C. 842; in heaven; *the
River of Bliss*: P. L. III. 358; in
hell; *four infernal rivers*: P. L.
II. 575; *Lethe, the river of obliv-
ion*: P. L. II. 583; in the sun:
P. L. III. 607; in the moon: P.
L. I. 291.

River-dragon, *sb.* a crocodile; *fig.*
Pharaoh, king of Egypt; *the river-
dragon ... submits to let his sojourners depart*: P. L. XII. 191.

River-horse, *sb.* hippopotamus: P.
L. VII. 474.

Rivers, *sb.* probably a punning use
of the name of one of the sons of
Sir John Rivers: V. Ex. 91.

Rivulet, *sb.* a small stream: P. L.
IX. 420.

Road, *sb.* (*a*) highway: P. R. I.
322; N. O. 22; *the Appian road*:
P. R. IV. 68; in heaven; *the road
of Heaven star-paved*: P. L. IV.
976; *empyreal*: P. L. V. 253;
broad and ample: P. L. VII. 577;
the highway from this world to
hell: P. L. X. 394; *transf.* a path
through the heavens: P. L. VII.
373; *equinoctial road*: P. L. X.
672.

(*b*) journey; *the Sun,...his flaming road begin*: P. L. VIII. 162.

Roam, I. *sb.* the act of wandering;
began ... his roam: P. L. IV. 538.

II. *vb.* (**1**) *intr.* to go from place
to place without any certain direction; *here pilgrims roam*: P. L.
III. 476; *from the pit of Hell
roaming to seek their prey on
Earth*: P. L. I. 382.

(**2**) *tr.* to wander over or through:
P. L. I. 521; *Sons of God, roaming the Earth*: P. R. II. 179; *the
orb he roamed*: P. L. IX. 82; *wild
beasts came forth the woods to
roam*: P. R. I. 502.

Roar, (**1**) *sb.* (*a*) a full, deep, continued
sound; *the roar of thunder*: P.
R. IV. 428; *deep-throated engines
...whose roar*: P. L. VI. 586; *the
far-off curfew ... swinging slow with
sullen roar*: Il P. 76.

(*b*) a loud confused sound, uproar: C. 549; *the hideous roar*:
L. 61.

(**2**) *vb. intr.* (*a*) to utter a full,
deep, continued sound; used of
personifications; *Chaos roared*:
P. L. VI. 871; *the brazen throat of
war had ceased to roar*: P. L. XI.
713; *devouring war shall never
cease to roar*: V. Ex. 86.

(*b*) to make such a sound; *deep
thunders roar*: P. L. II. 267; used
of a storm: P. R. IV. 463; *wild
winds when they roar*: C. 87.

Rob, *vb. tr.* (*a*) to plunder or strip
by violence: P. R. III. 75; *who
would rob a hermit of his weeds*:
C. 390.

(*b*) to deprive *of*: C. 261.

Robber, *sb.* one who steals or plun-
ders: S. A. 1180, 1188; C. 485.

Robe, (**1**) *sb.* (*a*) a loose flowing
garment; *a robe of darkest grain,
flowing with majestic train*: Il P.
33.

(*b*) an official or ceremonial
dress; *in robes of state*: P. R. IV.
64; *Hymen ... in saffron robe*:
L'A. 126.

(*c*) any garment: S. A. 1188;
the envenomed robe: P. L. II. 543;
fig.: V. Ex. 21; *his robe of
righteousness*: P. L. X. 222; *guilty
Shame: he covered, but his robe
uncovered more*: P. L. IX. 1058.

(**2**) *vb. tr.* to clothe; *fig., the
Sun ... robed in flames*: L'A. 61.

See **Sky-robe, White-robed.**

Robustious, *adj.* vigorous, flourishing; *these ... locks robustious*: S.
A. 569.

Rock, *sb.* (**1**) a large mass of stone:
P. L. II. 621; VI. 645; VII. 300,
408; IX. 118; XI. 852; P. R. I.
194; S. XVIII. 8; Ps. LXXXI. 67;
each on his rock transfixed: P. L.
II. 181; *rend up both rocks and
hills*: P. L. II. 540; *woods and
rocks had ears to rapture*: P. L.
VII. 35; *Adonis from his native
rock*: P. L. I. 450; *rifted rocks
whose entrance leads to Hell*: C.
518; *hollow*: P. L. II. 285; *low-
browed, rugged*: L'A. 8; Ps.
CXIV. 17.

(*b*) as forming an eminence or
promontory; *the Tarpeian rock*:
P. R. IV. 49; *the rock of Etham*:
S. A. 253; *when Argo passed
through Bosporus betwixt the justling rocks*: P. L. II. 1018; the
mount of Paradise: P. L. XI. 336.

(*c*) out of which something is
constructed; *threefold the gates*...

three of adamantine rock: P. L.
II. 646; *every bolt and bar of...
solid rock*: P. L. II. 878; *sad
sepulchral rock*: P. 43; probably
also: P. L. IV. 283.

(*d*) as firmly fixed or serving as
a symbol of firmness: P. L. VI.
593; *a solid rock*: P. R. IV. 18;
firmlier fastened than a rock: S.
A. 1398.

(*e*) as a symbol of hardness;
heart of rock: P. L. XI. 494.

(2) a mass of a similar substance; *diamond rocks*: C. 881.

(*b*) out of which something is
constructed: P. L. X. 313; *in a
rock of diamond armed*: P. L. VI.
364; *rocks of gold*: P. L. V. 759;
*the eastern gate of Paradise ... a
rock of alabaster*: P. L. IV. 543.

(*c*) as a symbol of firmness; *as
a rock of adamant ...firm*: P. R.
IV. 533.

(3) a cause of disaster; *rocks
whereon greatest men have oftest
wrecked*: P. R. II. 228.

Rocking, *part. adj.* causing things
to rock; *rocking winds*: Il P.
126.

Rocky, *adj.* (*a*) abounding in rocks:
V. Ex. 97.

(*b*) consisting of or resembling
rock; *rocky pillars*: P. L. IV.
549; *the rocky orb of tenfold
adamant*: P. L. VI. 254; located
in a rock; *a rocky cell*: Ps. IV.
41.

Rod, *sb.* a straight slender piece of
wood or other material; (*a*) an
instrument of punishment; *fig.*,
*an iron rod to bruise and break thy
disobedience*: P. L. V. 887.

(*b*) a symbol of power or authority; *lictors and rods, the
ensigns of their power*: P. R. IV.
65; the rod used by Moses: P.
L. I. 338; XII. 198, 211, 212;
fig., *Faith pointed with her golden
rod*: S. XIV. 7.

(*c*) an enchanter's wand: C.
816; the wand or staff of Hermes;
opiate rod: P. L. XI. 133.

(*d*) *fig.* the sun's ray; *with
touch etherial of Heaven's fiery
rod*: S. A. 549.

Roll, *sb.* list, catalogue: S. A. 290.

Roll, *vb.* I. *tr.* (1) to cause to rotate
or move in a circular course; *roll
the eye*: P. L. XI. 620; with
cognate object; *Heaven ... rolled
her motions*: P. L. VII. 499.

(2) to cause to turn over and
over: Ps. LXXXIII. 39; *them with
all their pomp deep under water
rolled*: P. L. XI. 749; *rolled
mother with infant down the rocks*:
S. XVIII. 7.

(*b*) *fig.* to overthrow or humiliate; *roll in the dust my glory
dead*: Ps. VII. 15.

(3) to move through with a circular motion; *stars, that seem to
roll spaces incomprehensible*: P. L.
VIII. 19.

(4) to impel forward; (*a*) with
the sweeping swelling motion of
water; *Lethe ... rolls her watery
labyrinth*: P. L. II. 583; *the
River of Bliss ... rolls ... her amber
stream*: P. L. III. 359; *Ilissus
rolls his ... stream*: P. R. IV. 249.

(*b*) with the motion of a serpent's body; *rolling her bestial
train*: P. L. II. 873.

(5) to bring with the motion of
waves; *may thy billows roll ashore
the beryl and the golden ore*: C.
932.

II. *intr.* (1) to move onward
while rotating; *the orbs of his
fierce chariot rolled*: P. L. VI.
829; used of heavenly bodies: P.
L. III. 718; IV. 593; V. 578.

(2) to turn round and round;
these eyes, that roll in vain: P. L.
III. 23.

(3) to perform a periodical revolution; *all times and seasons
roll*: P. R. III. 187.

(4) to fall or turn over and
over; *Angel on Archangel rolled*:
P. L. VI. 594; *rolling in dust and
gore*: P. L. XI. 460.

(5) to tumble or be tossed about,
welter: P. L. I. 52; *Cherub and
Seraph rolling in the flood*: P. L.
I. 324.

(*b*) to wallow; *fig.*, *rolling in
brutish vices*: P. R. III. 86; *to
roll with pleasure in a sensual sty*:
C. 77.

(6) to move in general: P. L.
VI. 879; *crystal wall of Heaven ...
rolled inward*: P. L. VI. 861;
fig., *his dire attempt; which, nigh
the birth now rolling*: P. L. IV.
16.

(*b*) to glide as a serpent: P. L.
IX. 631; X. 558.

(*c*) to flow as water: P. L. IV.
238; *wave rolling after wave*: P.
L. VII. 298.

(d) to move as flame or smoke : P. L. VI. 765 ; XII. 183 ; *smoke to roll in dusky wreaths* : P. L. VI. 57 ; *the flames … rolled in billows* : P. L. I. 223.

(7) to emit a deep prolonged sound : P. L. X. 666.

part. adj. **rolling** ; (a) rotating: H. B. 2.

(b) moving as smoke ; *rolling smoke* : P. L. I. 671.

See **Self-rolled.**

Roman, *adj.* of or pertaining to Rome or the Roman Empire : P. R. III. 362 ; *Roman yoke* : P. R. I. 217 ; III. 158.

absol. the *Roman,* the Roman emperor or the Roman Empire : P. R. III. 368.

Romance, *sb.* a tale of chivalry : P. L. I. 580 ; P. R. III. 339.

Rome, *sb.* the city in Italy : P. L. IX. 510 ; P. R. IV. 91 ; S. XVII. 3 ; *free Rome, where eloquence flourished* : P. L. IX. 671 ; *the oratory of Greece and Rome* : P. R. IV. 360 ; the capital of the Roman Empire : P. R. III. 385 ; IV. 81 ; *Rome was to sway the world* : P. L. XI. 405 ; *all nations now to Rome obedience pay* : P. R. IV. 80 ; *Rome, Queen of the Earth* : P. R. IV. 45.

Rood, *sb.* the measure of length : P. L. I. 196.

Roof, *sb.* (1) the exterior upper covering of a house : S. A. 1651 ; *the arched roof* : S. A. 1634 ; *the roof was fretted gold* : P. L. I. 717.

(b) the roof of the bower of Adam and Eve ; *the roof of thickest covert was inwoven shade* : P. L. IV. 692 ; *flowery, arborous* : P. L. IV. 772 ; v. 137 ; *lowly* : P. L. V. 463.

(c) that which resembles a roof ; *the shady roof of branching elm star-proof* : A. 88 ; *the ruined roof of shaked Olympus* : D. F. I. 43 ; *thick overhead with verdant roof embowered* : P. L. IX. 1038.

(2) the inner part of this covering, the ceiling ; *the arched roof* : P. L. I. 726 ; N. O. 175 ; *high embowed* : Il P. 157 ; apparently both the outer and inner part of the house covering : P. R. IV. 58.

(b) the inner covering of hell ; *the horrid roof* : P. L. II. 644.

See **High-roofed, Low-roofed.**

Room, *sb.* (a) space affording opportunity of being or moving : P. L. IV. 383 ; VII. 486 ; *narrow* : P. L. I. 779 ; *in narrow room Nature's whole wealth* : P. L. IV. 207 ; *such vast room in Nature unpossessed* : P. L. VIII. 153.

(b) place or space unoccupied : P. R. I. 248 ; III. 263.

(c) chamber, apartment : V. Ex. 62 ; U. C. I. 15 ; Il P. 79.

(d) place or position considered as occupied or to be occupied by a successor : P. L. IV. 359 ; VII. 190 ; *to advance into our room a creature formed of earth* : P. L. IX. 148 ; *in their room … wolves shall succeed* : P. L. XII. 507 ; *be thou in Adam's room* : P. L. III. 285 ; *to supply perhaps our vacant room* : P. L. II. 835 ; *the shady gloom had given day her room* : N. O. 78.

Roost, *sb.* a place on which birds rest at night : S. A. 1693.

See **Low-roosted.**

Root, I. *sb.* (1) that part of a plant which grows downward into the soil and absorbs nutriment : P. L. V. 479 ; *pl.* : P. L. II. 544 ; Ps. LXXX. 54 ; *we here live on tough roots* : P. R. I. 339 ; as having medicinal properties ; *a small unsightly root, but of divine effect* : C. 629.

(b) *fig.,* of constancy *no root infixed* : S. A. 1032.

(c) **take root,** to put forth roots : P. L. IX. 1105 ; *fig.* to become fixed ; *then shall this Mount of Paradise … there take root* : P. L. XI. 834.

(2) foundation ; *to the roots of Hell* : P. L. X. 299.

(3) source ; *the Tree of Prohibition, root of all our woe* : P. L. IX. 645 ; used of Adam and Eve as the source of mankind : P. L. II. 383 ; of Christ ; *so in thee, as from a second root, shall be restored as many as are restored* : P. L. III. 288.

II. *vb. tr.* (a) to plant and fix in the earth by roots : P. R. IV. 417 ; Ps. LXXX. 38.

(b) to remove completely ; *root them out of Heaven* : P. L. VI. 855.

Root-bound, *adj.* fixed to the earth by roots : C. 662.

Rose, *sb.* (a) the shrub *Rosa* : P. L. IX. 218.

(b) the flower of this shrub : P.
L. IV. 698, 773 ; C. 743 ; L. 45 ;
S. XX. 8 ; *impurpled with celestial
roses* : P. L. III. 364 ; *the roses ...
glowed* : P. L. IX. 426 ; *fresh-
blown* : L'A. 22 ; *faded* : P. L. IX.
893 ; *without thorn the rose* : P. L.
IV. 256 ; *courts thee on roses* : Hor.
O. 2 ; *beds of hyacinth and roses,
where young Adonis oft reposes* :
C. 998 ; *sing. collect.* : P. L. V.
349 ; *summer's rose* : P. L. III. 43.
fig. applied to a person : A. 32.
(c) the fragrance of the rose :
P. L. VIII. 517.
See **Musk-rose.**

Roseate, *adj.* showing the colours of
the rose ; *roseate dews* : P. L. V.
646.

Rosy, *adj.* (a) resembling a rose in
colour ; applied to morn personified ; *her rosy steps* : P. L. V. 1 ;
with rosy hand : P. L. VI. 3 ; *her
rosy progress* : P. L. XI. 175 ; to
a person ; possibly, beautiful as a
rose ; *heave thy rosy head from thy
coral-paven bed* : C. 885.
(b) consisting of roses ; *rosy
twine* : C. 105.

Rosy-bosomed, *adj.* having bosoms
rosy in colour or covered with
rose-coloured garments (?) : C. 986.

Rosy-red, *sb.* the colour of the red
rose : P. L. VIII. 619.

Rot, (1) *sb.* a disease fatal to animals :
P. L. XII. 179.
(2) *vb. intr.* (a) to undergo
natural decomposition : U. C. II.
3.
(b) to become morally rotten :
L. 127.

Rottenness, *sb.* a thing that is unsound or unstable ; *the pillared
firmament is rottenness* : C. 598.

Rough, *adj.* (a) having an uneven
surface, not smooth ; *fruit...rough
or smooth rined* : P. L. V. 342 ;
*fig., hard are the ways of truth, and
rough to walk* : P. R. I. 478 ; presenting an uneven line ; *the rough
edge of battle* : P. L. VI. 108.
(b) shaggy, hairy : L. 34.
(c) boisterous, tempestuous ; *seas
rough with black winds* : Hor. O. 7.
(d) wild ; *Hail, foreign wonder!
whom certain these rough shades
did never breed* : C. 266.
(e) harsh, uncivil ; *comp., a
rougher tongue* : S. A. 1066.
absol. a way or course that is
rugged or broken : P. L. II. 948.

Round, I. *adj.* (a) circular : P. L.
I. 285 ; II. 1048 ; *the Moon ... in
her visage round those spots* : P.
L. V. 419.
(b) cylindrical ; *hollow engines
long and round* : P. L. VI. 484.
(c) spherical ; used of the world :
P. L. II. 832 ; *this round World* :
P. L. III. 419 ; X. 318 ; *the pendulous round Earth* : P. L. IV.
1000.
II. *sb.* (a) a spherical body ;
used of universe ; *to the uttermost
convex of this great round* : P. L.
VII. 267 ; of the moon ; *the hollow
round of Cynthia's seat* : N. O.
102.
(b) the coil of a serpent's body :
P. L. IX. 183.
(c) circuit, revolution ; *the
neighboring Moon ... her monthly
round* : P. L. III. 728 ; *lead in
swift round the months and years* :
C. 114.
(d) a dance in a circle : C. 144 ;
fig. used of the stars in their
motion about the sun : P. L. VIII.
125.
(e) a prescribed circuit of going ;
I fetch my round : A. 54.
(f) recurrent order, rotation ;
*Light and Darkness in perpetual
round lodge and dislodge* : P. L.
VI. 6.
III. adv. (1) on each or every
side, in every direction : P. L.
VII. 371 ; IX. 52 ; S. A. 451 ; L'A.
70 ; enclose, encompass, environ,
etc. *round* : P. L. I. 617 ; II. 266,
435, 511, 862 ; IV. 979 ; V. 876 ;
VII. 27, 90 ; IX. 636 ; XI. 352 ; P.
R. I. 194 ; IV. 422, 481 ; S. A.
194, 257, 846 ; *angels watching
round* : P. L. II. 413 ; *frozen
round* : P. L. II. 602 ; *storms ...
blustering round* : P. L. III. 426 ;
his ... empire neighbouring round :
P. L. IV. 145 ; *darkness hovers
round* : Ps. LXXXVIII. 27 ; *locks
round from his parted forelock
manly hung* : P. L. IV. 302 ; *looked
or looking round* : P. L. VI. 529 ;
XI. 381 ; P. R. I. 295 ; *cast round
thine eyes* : P. R. IV. 61 ; *search
thy coffers round* : V. Ex. 31 ; *bells
ring round* : L'A. 93 ; *no way
round* : P. L. III. 618 ; *far round* :
P. L. I. 666 ; IX. 482 ; *on all sides
round* : P. L. I. 61 ; II. 1015.
(b) **round about,** on every side
of : P. L. II. 653 ; III. 379 ; IV.

21, 401; VIII. 261, 318; IX. 426; X. 448; S. A. 1497; V. Ex. 63; II P. 48; circuitously about: Ps. LXXXVIII. 67; on every side: Ps. III. 17.

(2) with a rotary motion : P. L. VII. 229; A. 66.

(3) *half round*, in the form of a semicircle : S. A. 1606.

(4) with the revolution of time; *our solemn feast comes round* : Ps. LXXXI. 12.

IV. *prep.* (*a*) in such a manner as to encircle : P. L. IV. 661; VIII. 23; IX. 216; circuitously about; *with what delight could I have walked thee round* : P. L. IX. 114.

(*b*) on or to every side of : P. L. IX. 591; X. 439; A. 15.

(*c*) to or from every part of : P. L. IV. 528; Ps. LXXXIV. 15.

(*d*) over; *the potent rod of Amram's son ... waved round the coast* : P. L. I. 340.

V. *vb.* (1) *tr.* to make the circuit of; *the low sun ... had rounded still the horizon* : P. L. X. 684; *to round this globe of Earth* : P. R. I. 365.

(2) *intr.* to make a circuit; *nightly rounding walk* : P. L. IV. 685.

See **Half-rounding.**

Rouse, *vb.* (1) *tr.* (*a*) to cause to start up from sleep; *roused from slumber on that fiery couch* : P. L. I. 377; *fig.*, *rouse the slumbering morn* : L'A. 54.

(*b*) to bring suddenly to an end; *such a peal shall rouse their sleep* : P. L. III. 329.

(*c*) to provoke to activity from inaction : S. A. 1690.

refl. to provoke oneself to activity : Ps. VII. 20.

(*d*) to stir violently, make boisterous; *blustering winds ... had roused the sea* : P. L. II. 287.

(2) *intr.* to start or rise up from sleep : P. L. I. 334; C. 318.

part. adj. **rousing,** stirring to activity : S. A. 1382.

Rout, *sb.* (*a*) band, troop, company; *rebellious, revolted* : P. L. I. 747; X. 534; *vile* : P. L. VII. 34; *monstrous* : C. 533; *the rout that made the hideous roar* : L. 61.

(*b*) the multitude, the rabble; *the idolatrous rout* : S. A. 443; *nor do I name of men the common*

rout : S. A. 674; *the populous rout* : Ps. III. 16.

(*c*) a defeat followed by disordered flight : P. L. II. 770; *deformed, forced* : P. L. VI. 387, 598; *rout on rout* : P. L. II. 995; *so huge a rout* : P. L. VI. 873; *put to rout* : P. L. IV. 3; P. R. II. 218.

Rove, *vb.* I. *intr.* (1) to wander at random, roam, ramble; *thus roving on* : P. L. II. 614; *roving still about the world* : P. R. I. 33; used of animals; *other creatures all day long rove idle* : P. L. IV. 617.

(*b*) to go astray in character or thought; *from that mark how far they rove* : S. XII. 13.

(*c*) used *fig.* of the mind; *apt the mind or fancy is to rove* : P. L. VIII. 188; of thoughts; *some naked thoughts that rove about* : V. Ex. 23.

(2) to march from place to place for war and conquest : P. R. III. 79.

(3) to look here and there; *let their eyes rove without rein* : P. L. XI. 586.

II. *tr.* to wander over, ramble about : P. L. IX. 575; C. 60.

part. adj. **roving,** wandering : P. L. III. 432; C. 485; *fig.*, *these latest scenes confine my roving verse* : P. 22.

vbl. sb. **roving,** the act of wandering; used of the mind : P. L. VIII. 189.

Row, *sb.* line, rank, file; *the shepherds ... in a rustic row* : N. O. 87; *the bright Seraphim in burning row* : S. M. 10; *engines' triple row* : P. L. VI. 650; with *of*; *of Seraphim* : P. L. VI. 604; *of pipes* : P. L. I. 709; *of pillars* : P. L. VI. 572; *of starry lamps* : P. L. I. 727; *of trees, myrtles* : P. L. IV. 146; V. 212; IX. 627.

Row, *vb. tr.* to impel along the surface of the water as if with oars; *the swan ... rows her state with oary feet* : P. L. VII. 439.

Royal, *adj.* of or pertaining to a king : P. L. I. 677; *David's royal seat* : P. R. III. 373; *royal stock of David* : P. L. XII. 325; *the royal towers of great Seleucia* : P. L. IV. 211; *the royal bench of British Themis* : S. XXI. 2; to Satan as king : P. L. V. 756; *a throne of royal state* : P. L. II. 1.

Royal-towered, *adj.* having the royal palaces upon its banks : V. Ex. 100.

Royalty, *sb.* the office and dignity of a king : P. L. II. 451.

Rub, *vb. tr.* to cover over by means of friction : P. L. I. 774.

Rubied, *adj.* being of the colour of the ruby ; *rubied nectar* : P. L. v. 633 ; *lip* : C. 915.

Rubric, *sb.* a calendar of the festival-days prefixed to the Prayer-book and printed in red letter ; *fig.*, *no date prefixed directs me in the starry rubric set* : P. R. IV. 393.

Ruby, *sb.* (*a*) the precious stone of a rich red colour : P. L. III. 597.

(*b*) wine of a ruby colour : S. A. 543.

Ruddy, *adj.* red ; *colours ... ruddy and gold* ; P. L. IX. 578 ; *ruddy flame* : P. L. II. 889 ; used of the waves of the Red Sea : Ps. CXXXVI. 45.

Rude, *adj.* (1) rough ; (*a*) harsh, unpleasing to the sense ; *rude burs* : C. 352.

(*b*) crude, unwrought, unfashioned ; *the rude manger* : N. O. 31.

(2) lacking refinement or elegance, clumsy ; *Art, yet rude* : P. L. IX. 391.

(3) uncivilized, ignorant ; *these beasts ... beholders rude* : P. L. IX. 544.

(4) unkind, uncivil, cruel ; *the rude bird of hate* : S. I. 9 ; *fingers rude* : L. 4 ; *detractions rude* : S. XVI. 2.

(5) violent : *the clouds ... rude in their shock* : P. L. X. 1074 ; *evil tidings, with too rude irruption hitting thy aged ear* : S. A. 1567.

(6) destructive ; *the rude ax* : Il P. 136 ; *sup., with rudest violence* : Ps. LXXX. 52.

Rudeness, *sb.* discourtesy, incivility : C. 178.

Rudiment, *sb.* (*a*) the beginning of action ; *he shall first lay down the rudiments of his great warfare* : P. R. I. 157.

(*b*) a state of inexperience : P. R. III. 245.

Rue, *sb.* the plant *Ruta graveoleus* : P. L. XI. 414.

Rue, *vb. tr.* to grieve for, regret, lament : P. L. I. 134 ; IX. 1180 ; P. R. IV. 181 ; *thy will chose freely what it now so justly rues* : P. L.

IV. 72 ; *Abaddon rues thy bold attempt* : P. R. IV. 624.

Rueful, *adj.* (*a*) lamentable, pitiable: P. L. II. 780.

(*b*) of sorrow or woe ; *Cocytus ... the rueful stream* : P. L. II. 580.

(*c*) expressing sorrow ; *rueful cry* : S. A. 1553.

Ruffled, *part. adj.* angered : S. A. 1138.

See **To-ruffled.**

Rugged, *adj.* (*a*) rough, uneven ; *rugged bark* : C. 354 ; *rocks* : Ps. CXIV. 17 ; *fig.*, *every gust of rugged wings* : L. 93.

(*b*) wrinkled ; *sup.*, *the rugged'st brow* : P. R. II. 164 ; *fig.*, *the rugged brow of Night* : Il P. 58.

(*c*) harsh, grating ; *rugged names* : S. XI. 10.

Ruin, I. *sb.* (1) a falling down, fall ; *Him the Almighty Power hurled headlong ... with hideous ruin* : P. L. I. 46.

(2) fall, overthrow, destruction (material or moral) ; sometimes with blending of sense (*a*) : P. L. II. 1009 ; S. A. 1043, 1267, 1515, 1684 ; Ps. I. 16 ; VII. 60 ; *ruin, destruction at the utmost point* : S. A. 1514 ; *to save the Athenian walls from ruin bare* : S. VIII. 14 ; *so huge a rout encumbered him* (Chaos) *with ruin* : P. L. VI. 874 ; *balls of missive ruin* : P. L. VI. 519 ; the fall or overthrow of the angels : P. L. I. 91 ; v. 567 ; VI. 456 ; P. R. IV. 579 ; *ruin upon ruin* : P. L. II. 995 ; *to fall in universal ruin* : P. L. VI. 797 ; *thou ... a spectacle of ruin* : P. R. I. 415 ; the destruction resulting from their fall ; *now all Heaven had gone to wrack, with ruin overspread* : P. L. VI. 670 ; the fall of man : P. L. IV. 522 ; IX. 275, 493.

(*b*) devastation, desolation : P. R. III. 79.

(3) the state of being overthrown or destroyed ; *his face ... majestic, though in ruin* : P. L. II. 305 ; *water with fire in ruin reconciled* : P. R. IV. 413.

(4) that which brings overthrow : P. L. VI. 193.

(5) the remains of a ruined building ; *and ruin seems of ancient pile* : P. L. II. 590.

II. *vb.* (1) *tr.* to cause the downfall or overthrow of ; *what ruins kingdoms* : P. R. IV. 363 ; *while*

... *I* (Christ) *ruin all my foes* : P.
L. III. 258; *nor appeared less than
Archangel ruined* : P. L. I. 593 ;
to cause the fall of man : P. L. V.
228 ; IX. 906, 950 ; P. R. I. 102.

(2) *intr.* to fall headlong and
with violence : P. L. VI. 868.

part. adj. **ruined,** in a state of
ruin ; *the ruined roof of shaked
Olympus* : D. F. I. 43.

Ruinous, *adj.* destructive, pernicious ; *ruinous assault* : P. L. VI.
216 ; *a storm so ruinous* : P. R.
IV. 436 ; *noises ... ruinous* : P. L.
II. 921.

Rule, I. *sb.* (*a*) the instrument used
for measuring ; *fig.*, *long levelled
rule of streaming light* : C. 340.

(*b*) a formula for the regulation
of conduct, precept, law : P. R.
IV. 283 ; C. 759 ; *rules of civil
government* : P. R. IV. 358 ; *the
known rules of ancient liberty* : S.
XII. 2 ; *Nature's healthful rules* :
P. L. XI. 523 ; *the rule of Not too
much* : P. L. XI. 531.

(*c*) the customary or prescribed
form or quantity ; *Nature ...
played at will her virgin fancies ...
wild above rule or art* : P. L. V.
297.

(*d*) the possession and exercise
of controlling power, dominion,
sway : P. L. IV. 429 ; XII. 581 ;
absolute, imperial : P. L. IV. 301 ;
C. 21 ; *bear rule* : P. L. VIII. 375 ;
X. 155 ; government ; *paternal
rule* : P. L. XII. 24 ; *the rule of
high Olympus* : P. L. X. 582.

fig. of the sun ; *two great Lights
... the greater to have rule by day* :
P. L. VII. 347.

II. *vb.* (*pres. 2d sing.* rul'st : S.
A. 671) (**1**) *tr.* (*a*) to exercise controlling power over, have dominion
over : P. R. II. 469 ; III. 159 ; C.
876 ; Ps. CXXXVI. 66 ; used of
God : P. R. I. 236 ; S. A. 671 ;
with iron sceptre rule us here : P.
L. II. 327 ; of angels : P. L. I.
736; of Satan and his angels; *this
Universe we have ... ruled* : P. R.
I. 49; of man ; *all the Earth he
gave thee to possess and rule* : P. L.
XI. 339; of gods; *ruled the middle
air* : P. L. I. 516.

fig. of the stars ; *the Stars ...
rule the day ... and rule the night* :
P. L. VII. 350.

(*b*) to direct the actions of : P.
L. X. 516.

(*c*) to lead, influence ; *ruling
them by pursuasion* : P. R. IV.
230.

(*d*) to control, restrain ; *wild
Uproar stood ruled* : P. L. III.
711 ; *he who ... rules passions ... is
more a king* : P. R. II. 466.

(2) *intr.* (*a*) to exercise power,
have authority : P. L. II. 907 ;
VI. 177 ; XII. 226 ; S. A. 56 ; used
of God : P. L. II. 351 ; of Satan ;
*thou, Infernal Serpent, shalt not
long rule in the clouds* : P. R. IV.
619 ; of sin and death ; *over man
to rule* : P. L. X. 493 ; of man : P.
L. VII. 520 ; X. 493 ; *to rule over
his works* : P. L. VII. 628 ; *he over
thee shall rule* : P. L. X. 196.

(*b*) to direct, guide, control ;
one spirit in them ruled : P. L. VI.
848 ; *Understanding ruled not* :
P. L. IX. 1127 ; *lets her will rule* :
P. L. IX. 1184.

See **All-ruling.**

Ruminate, *vb. intr.* to chew the
cud : P. L. IV. 352.

Rumour, (**1**) *sb.* popular report : L.
80 ; *personified* as an attendant
upon the throne of Chaos : P. L.
II. 965 ; a report about a particular thing ; *rumours loud that
daunt remotest kings* : S. XV. 4.

(2) *vb. tr.* to tell among the
people, report : S. A. 1600.

part. adj. **rumoured,** reported
as about to be : P. L. IV. 817.

Run, *vb.* (*pres. 3d sing.* runneth :
V. Ex. 95 ; *pret.* run : P. R. I.
441 ; elsewhere ran ; *past part.*
run) I. *intr.* (**1**) to move or go
swiftly on the feet : P. L. XII.
608 ; S. A. 1520, 1541 ; N. O. 24 ;
sometimes ran with supple joints :
P. L. VIII. 268 ; *run to your
shrouds* : C. 147 ; *down the lawns
I ran* : C. 568 ; *they ran, they flew* :
P. L. VI. 642 ; *I can fly, or I can
run* : C. 1013 ; with *prep. inf.* of
purpose : P. L. X. 27 ; M. W. 23 ;
used impersonally without subject
expressed (*L.* cursum est) ; *forthwith ... to his aid was run by Angels
many and strong* : P. L. VI. 335.

(*b*) to attack as an enemy ; *ran
on embattled armies* : S. A. 129 ;
Go ... lest I run upon thee : S. A.
1237.

(2) to move, pass, or go swiftly ;
used of persons : P. R. I. 441 ; S.
A. 1522; of things ; *his eyes that
run through all the Heavens* : P. L.

III. 651 ; *the melting voice through mazes running* : L'A. 142 ; *no voice ... runs through the arched roof* : N. O. 175 ; *the greedy flame runs higher* : Ps. LXXXIII. 55 ; *horror chill ran through his veins* : P. L. IX. 891.

(*b*) **run back,** retrace its course ; *Time will run back* : N. O. 135.

(*c*) **run on,** continue in its course ; *Time will run on smoother* : S. XX. 5.

(3) to hasten, hurry ; *run to meet what he would most avoid* : C. 363.

(4) to flow : V. Ex. 95 ; *the nether flood ... runs diverse* : P. L. IV. 234 ; *Adonis ... ran purple to the sea* : P. L. I. 451.

II. *intr.* (1) to pour forth ; *rivers run potable gold* : P. L. III. 607 ; *the crisped brooks ... ran nectar* : P. L. IV. 240.

(2) to move or pass over or along ; with cognate object ; *ye Elements ... in quaternion run perpetual circle* : P. L. V. 181 ; used of the sun or the heavens : Ps. CXXXVI. 30 ; *the great Light of Day yet wants to run much of his race* : P. L. VII. 98 ; *to run his longitude* : P. L. VII. 372 ; *Heaven such journeys run* : P. L. VIII. 88 ; of time ; *Fly, envious Time, till thou run out thy race* : T. 1.

(*b*) *fig.* to accomplish, perform ; with cognate object ; *my race of glory run* : S. A. 597 ; *their ... race well run* : P. L. XII. 505.

part. adj. **running,** flowing : P. L. VII. 397.

Runner, *sb.* one who runs in a race : S. A. 1324.

Rupture, *sb.* the act of breaking or bursting : P. L. VII. 419.

Rural, *adj.* of or pertaining to the country : P. L. IV. 134, 247 ; *towns, and rural works* : P. L. XI. 639 ; *shrine* : C. 267 ; *queen* : A. 94 ; *weeds* : P. R. I. 314 ; *work, repast, labours* : P. L. V. 211 ; IX. 4, 841 ; *minstrelsy, dance, ditties* : C. 547, 952 ; L. 32 ; *sight ... sound* : P. L. IX. 451.

Rush, *vb. intr.* to move swiftly and impetuously : P. L. II. 726 ; IV. 407 ; *armies rush to battle* : P. L. II. 534 ; *together rushed both battles* : P. L. VI. 215 ; *two planets, rushing from aspect malign* : P. L. VI. 313 ; with *forth* or *abroad* : P. L.

X. 456 ; *forth rushed ... the chariot* : P. L. VI. 749 ; *forth rush ... the winds* : P. L. X. 704 ; *the winds ... rushed abroad* : P. R. IV. 414.

(*b*) **rush on** or **upon,** more swiftly to the attack of an enemy : P. L. VI. 600 ; C. 651 ; *fig., restless thoughts ... rush upon me* : S. A. 21 ; to come upon so as to control ; *that Spirit that first rushed on thee* : S. A. 1435.

(*c*) to pour ; *down rushed the rain* : P. L. XI. 743.

part. adj. **rushing,** moving with great rapidity : P. 36 ; transferred epithet ; *rushing sound of onset* : P. L. VI. 97.

See **Swift-rushing.**

Rush-candle, *sb.* a candle made by dipping a rush in tallow : C. 338.

Rushy-fringed (fringèd, *disyl.*), *adj.* bordered with rushes : C. 890.

Russet, *adj.* of a reddish-brown colour : L'A. 71.

Russian, *adj.* of Russia : P. L. X. 431 ; *the Russian Ksar* : P. L. XI. 394.

Rustic, *adj.* belonging to or characteristic of the country : P. L. XI. 433 ; P. R. II. 299 ; *rustic lays* : C. 849 ; *chatting in a rustic row* : N. O. 87.

Rustling, *part. adj.* giving out a slightly sibilant sound when shaken or moved ; *rustling wings, leaves* : P. L. I. 768 ; IX. 519 ; Il P. 129.

Ruth, *sb.* pity, compassion, tenderness : L. 163 ; S. IX. 8.

Ruth, *sb.* the Moabitish woman who was the wife of Boaz : S. IX. 5.

Rutherford (original text Rotherford), *sb.* Samuel Rutherford, a Scottish divine of the Westminster Assembly : F. of C. 8.

S

Sabbath, *sb.* the seventh day of the week observed as the day on which God rested from his work : P. L. VII. 634.

Sabbath-day, *sb.* the sabbath ; *no journey of a Sabbath-day* : S. A. 149.

Sabbath-evening, *sb.* the evening of the seventh day of the week : P. L. VIII. 246.

Sabean, *adj.* from Saba (Sheba), an old name for the southwestern part of Arabia : P. L. IV. 162.

Sable, *adj.* black ; *sable cloud* : C. 221 ; *my sable shroud* : L. 22 ; *sable stole of cypress lawn* : Il P. 35.

Sable-stoled (stolèd, *disyl.*), *adj.* wearing a black stole or robe : N. O. 220.

Sable-vested, *adj.* robed in black ; *sable-vested Night* : P. L. II. 962.

Sacred, *adj.* (1) set apart for or consecrated to a god : P. L. VII. 331 ; *sisters of the sacred well* : L. 15 ; *wall* : Hor. O. 14 ; *Osiris...within his sacred chest* : N. O. 217 ; set apart for man compared to a god ; *sacred bower* : P. L. IV. 706.

(2) in some way connected with God or holy things ; (*a*) consecrated to holy or religious purposes ; *sacred virtue* : P. R. I. 231 ; *silence* : P. L. V. 557 ; *a plant select and sacred* : S. A. 363.

(*b*) set apart for the use or service of God ; *the sacred hill* : P. L. V. 619 ; VI. 25 ; set apart for or devoted to the worship of God ; *sacred porch, courts, house* : P. L. I. 454 ; P. R. I. 488 ; S. A. 518 ; *feast* : P. L. XII. 21 ; *things* : P. L. XII. 341.

(*c*) concerned with or relating to God or holy things : N. O. 15 ; *sacred song, songs* : P. L. III. 29, 149, 369 ; Ps. LXXXVII. 26 ; concerned with God or his worship ; *the sacred mysteries of Heaven* : P. L. XII. 509.

(*d*) entitled to reverence ; *sacred head* : L. 102 ; *vesture's hem* : A. 83 ; *sacred name of faithfulness* : P. L. IV. 951 ; with blending of sense (*f*) ; *sacred plant, fruit* : P. L. IX. 679, 904, 924.

(*e*) of divine quality or character, holy ; *sacred light* : P. L. IX. 192 ; XI. 134 ; *sacred influence of light* : P. L. II. 1034 ; *precious beams of sacred influence* : P. L. IX. 107 ; *the sacred rays of chastity* : C. 425 ; or the meaning may be : *set apart for Christ* ; *the third sacred morn* : P. L. VI. 748.

(*f*) not to be violated ; *sacred trust* : S. A. 428, 1001.

(*g*) setting apart to a holy office ; *sacred unction* : P. L. VI. 709.

(*h*) of the holy ; *cancelled from ...sacred memory* : P. L. VI. 379.

(3) pure, holy ; *a sacred and home-felt delight* : C. 262 ; *a flame of sacred vehemence* : C. 795.

(4) devoted ; *sacred to abstinence* : P. L. IX. 924.

(5) set apart for evil ; *Man ... to destruction sacred and devote* : P. L. III. 208.

Sacrifice, I. *sb.* (*a*) the act of making an offering to God : P. L. XII. 232 ; P. R. III. 116 ; to a god : P. R. I. 457 ; to Dagon : S. A. 436, 1312, 1612 ; to men treated as gods : P. R. III. 83.

(*b*) that which is offered to God : Seneca 2 ; used with reference to Christ ; *as a sacrifice glad to be offered* : P. L. III. 269 ; that which is offered to a god ; *human sacrifice* : P. L. I. 393.

II. *vb.* (1) *tr.* to make an offering to God of : P. L. XII. 20.

(2) *intr.* to offer up a sacrifice to God : P. L. XI. 438, 451.

Sacrilegious, *adj.* guilty of profaning sacred things, impious : P. R. III. 140 ; S. A. 833.

Sad, *adj.* (1) sober, serious, grave : Il P. 103 ; C. 189 ; or *adv.* seriously, earnestly : P. L. V. 94.

(2) expressing seriousness or gravity ; *with a sad leaden downward cast* : Il P. 43 ; *in his face I see sad resolution* : P. L. VI. 541.

(3) sorrowful, mournful : P. L. IV. 357 ; X. 18 ; XI. 272, 675 ; XII. 603 ; *sad Eve* : P. L. X. 159, 863 ; *the heart of Adam, erst so sad* : P. L. XI. 868 ; *sad Ulysses* : V. Ex. 50 ; *Electra's poet* : S. VIII. 13 ; *yet be not sad* : P. L. V. 116 ; *fig.* of things ; *sad Acheron* : P. L. II. 578 ; *morn* : M. W. 45 ; *rock* : P. 43.

(*b*) or *adv.* sadly ; *his grieved look he fixes sad* : P. L. IV. 28.

(*c*) deep, intense ; *sup., set my harp to notes of saddest woe* : P. 9.

(4) expressing or indicating sorrow ; *some sad drops wept* : P. L. IX. 1002 ; *discourse, complaint, words, song* : P. L. X. 343, 719 ; XII. 609 ; C. 235 ; *demeanour, looks* : P. L. XI. 162 ; P. R. I. 43 ; or in sense (3) ; *sup., a song, in her ... saddest plight* : Il P. 57.

(5) full of or causing sorrow, distressing, grievous, disastrous : P. L. II. 146, 524, 872 ; III. 525 ; S. X. 5 ; *sad decay* : Ps. LXXXVI. 4 ; *sad event, occasion* : P. L. IV. 716 ; S. A. 1551, 1560 ; L. 6 ; *overthrow* : P. L. I. 135 ; *task* : P. L. V. 564 ; IX. 13 ; *tidings* : P. R.

I. 109 ; *experiment*: P. L. x. 967 ; *sentence* : P. L. xi. 109 ; *end* : P. L. x. 977 ; xi. 755 ; *days* : P. L. xi. 40, 272 ; C. 355 ; *dismay, fears* : P. L. ix. 917 ; C. 355 ; *joys* : P. L. ii. 820 ; *sup., to Israelites not saddest the desolation of a hostile city* : S. A. 1560 ; *sad share*, a share of sadness : Cir. 6.

(*b*) full of wretchedness or misery ; *a place .. sad, noisome, dark* : P. L. xi. 478.

(6) quiet or somber in colour : L. 148.

Sadly, *adv.* (*a*) seriously : C. 509.

(*b*) sorrowfully : C. 1002.

Sadness, *sb.* sorrow, grief : P. L. iv. 156 ; x. 23.

Safe, (1) *adj.* (*a*) unharmed, uninjured : P. L. xii. 215, 314.

(*b*) secure from harm or injury : C. 389 ; Ps. iv. 40 ; lxxx. 16, 32, 80 ; *who then safe to the rock of Etham was retired* : S. A. 253 ; *where you may be safe* : C. 320 ; *our great Forbidder, safe with all his spies about him* : P. L. ix. 815 ; *sup.* : P. L. ix. 268 ; *safest he who stood aloof* : S. A. 135 ; not liable to be stolen : C. 400.

(*c*) free from risk or danger : P. L. x. 875 ; *more ... to utter is not safe* : P. L. v. 683 ; *comp., some safer resolution* : P. L. x. 1029.

(*d*) affording safety or security ; *safe abode* : C. 693 ; Ps. lxxxiv. 14 ; *throne* : P. L. ii. 23 ; *shore* : P. L. i. 310 ; *retreat* : P. L. ii. 317 ; *custody, convoy* : S. A. 802 ; C. 81 ; *paths of righteousness* : P. L. xi. 814.

(*e*) trustworthy ; *safe guide* : P. L. xi. 371.

(2) *adv.* (*a*) without injury or harm : P. L. ii. 411 ; iii. 21, 197 ; x. 316.

(*b*) with confidence or surety : P. L. vii. 24 ; *sup., so shalt thou lead safest thy life* : P. L. xi. 365.

Safely, *adv.* without fear, risk, or harm : P. R. iv. 555 ; C. 585.

Safety, *sb.* (1) the state of being unharmed or uninjured ; *in safety* : P. L. ii. 280 ; S. A. 1128 ; Ps. iv. 42.

(*b*) welfare, well-being ; *the general safety* : P. L. ii. 481 ; *some great work, thy glory, and people's safety* : S. A. 681.

(2) freedom or immunity from harm or danger : P. L. vii. 15 ;

P. R. iii. 349 ; S. A. 1002 ; *thy key of strength and safety* : S. A. 799 ; *wherein consisted all thy strength and safety* : S. A. 780.

(3) that which renders free from injury or harm : S. A. 1132.

Saffron, *adj.* orange-yellow in colour ; *in saffron robe* : L'A. 126.

Sagacious, *adj.* keen-scented ; *sagacious of his quarry from so far* : P. L. x. 281.

Sage, I. *adj.* wise, judicious ; *sage Hippotades* : L. 96 ; *Beëlzebub ... sage he stood* : P. L. ii. 305 ; *sage white-robed Truth* : D. F. I. 54 ; *thou Goddess sage and holy !* : Il P. 11.

(*b*) wise and learned ; *the sage poets* : C. 515.

(*c*) containing or embodying wisdom ; *sage Philosophy* : P. R. iv. 272.

(2) sound, well-advised ; *sage counsel* : S. xvii. 1.

(3) grave, serious ; *the sage and serious doctrine of Virginity* : C. 786 ; *great bards beside in sage and solemn tunes have sung* : Il P. 117.

absol. comp. poets who are wiser or more learned ; *whether as some sager sing* : L'A. 17.

II. *sb.* a wise man ; *pl., the schools of ancient sages* : P. R. iv. 251 ; the Magi ; *the eastern sages* : P. L. xii. 362 ; the prophets ; *the holy sages* : N. O. 5.

Sagely, *adv.* wisely, prudently : P. R. iv. 285.

Sail, (1) *sb.* (*a*) the sheet that catches the wind and carries a vessel on : P. L. ix. 515 ; *fig.* : S. A. 718 ; *back with speediest sail Zophiel ... came flying* : P. L. vi. 534 ; *a fiery globe of Angels on full sail of wing* : P. R. iv. 582 ; in a proverbial phrase ; *behoves him now both oar and sail* : P. L. ii. 942.

(*b*) a similar sheet used for carrying on a wagon ; *Chineses drive with sails and wind their cany waggons light* : P. L. iii. 439.

(2) *vb. intr.* (*a*) to be conveyed in a vessel by means of sails : P. L. ii. 638 ; iv. 159 ; *fig.* : S. A. 713.

(*b*) to move through the air by means of wings ; *who after came from Earth sailing wafted by Angels* : P. L. iii. 520 ; *in flight he ... sails between worlds and worlds* : P. L. v. 268.

Sail-broad, *adj.* spreading like a sail: P. L. II. 927.

Saint, *sb.* (1) a holy person: P. L. IV. 762; P. R. IV. 349; S. A. 1288; Ps. LXXXV. 32; *my late espoused saint*: S. XXIII. 1; *thy slaughtered saints*: S. XVIII; 1; *translated Saints*: P. L. III. 461; *to his dear saints he will speak peace*: Ps. LXXXV. 33; applied to Moses; *such wondrous power God to his Saint will lend*: P. L. XII. 200.

(*b*) as a title before a proper name; *Saint Peter*: P. L. III. 484.

(**2**) an angel: P. L. VI. 742, 801, 882; VII. 136; XI. 705; *the winged Saint*: P. L. V. 247; *my armed Saints*: P. L. VI. 47; *the inviolable Saints*: P. L. VI. 398; *attended with ten thousand thousand Saints*: P. L. VI. 767; *from his transcendent seat the Saints among*: P. L. X. 614.

(**3**) one of the blessed dead: M. W. 71; L. 178; *thou bright Saint high sitt'st in glory*: M. W. 61; the holy of both the dead and the living; *then, all thy Saints assembled, thou shalt judge bad men and Angels*: P. L. III. 330.

Sainted, *part. adj.* set apart for the gods: C. 11.

Saintly, *adj.* characteristic of or befitting a saint; *saintly visage*: Il P. 13; *veil of maiden white*: N. O. 42; *show, shout*: P. L. IV. 122; S. M. 9; *patience, chastity*: P. R. III. 93; C. 453.

Sake, *sb.* (always preceded by *for*) (*a*) purpose of obtaining; *for empire's sake*: P. R. III. 45; *for glory's sake*: P. R. III. 46.

(*b*) cause, interest, account; *for his, her, thy sake*: P. L. III. 238; IX. 993; X. 201; *for anger's sake*: P. L. X. 802; *for Truth's, honour's sake*: P. L. XII. 569; P. R. III. 98; S. A. 372; *for dear honour's sake*: C. 864; *for their bellies' sake*: L. 114; *for his Maker's image' sake*: P. L. XI. 514; *for intermission sake*: S. A. 1629.

Sale, *sb.* the act of selling; *God and State they easily would set to sale*: S. A. 1466.

Salem, *sb.* Salim, an apparently well-known place on the west of the Jordan, near which was Ænon where John baptized; its exact location is uncertain: P. R. II. 21.

Salem, *sb.* Jerusalem: P. 39.

Sallow, *adj.* of an unhealthy yellowish colour: C. 709.

Salmanassar, *sb.* Shalmaneser IV., king of Assyria, who beseiged Samaria during the reign of Hoshea (spelled Salmanasar in Vulg.): P. R. III. 278.

Salt, *adj.* inpregnated with salt; *island salt*: P. L. XI. 834; *flood*: C. 19.

Salutation, *sb.* greeting: P. L. V. 386; P. R. II. 107.

Salute, (1) *sb.* salutation, greeting: P. R. II. 67.

(**2**) *vb. tr.* to greet or address with welcome or homage: V. Ex. 7; M. M. 9.

Salvation, *sb.* (*a*) deliverance; *to such as do him fear salvation is at hand*: Ps. LXXXV. 38; heaven as a state in which the soul is delivered from the world or from sin; (Enoch) *to walk with God high in salvation and the climes of bliss*: P. L. XI. 708.

(*b*) deliverance through Christ from the power and penalty of sin: P. L. XII. 441, 448; *this perfect man ... to earn salvation for the sons of men*: P. R. I. 167.

Salve, (1) *sb.* a medicinal substance applied to sores, ointment; *fig.*: S. A. 184.

(**2**) *vb. tr.* to redeem, save; *to salve his credit*: P. R. IV. 12.

Samarchand, *sb.* the capital of Zagathay, a province of Tartary; Mercator *Atlas*, 1636, vol. 2, map at page 413: P. L. XI. 389.

Samaritan, *sb.* an inhabitant of Samaria: P. R. III. 359.

Same, *adj.* (always preceded by the def. art. or the demon. pron.) (**1**) identical, not another: P. L. X. 571; P. R. I. 354; S. A. 232, 1658; *of kind the same*: P. L. V. 490; *the same of kind*: S. A. 786; *fed the same flock*: L. 24; *Jehovah ... thou the same o'er all the earth art one*: Ps. LXXXIII. 67.

(*b*) used for emphasis: P. L. V. 83; *that same watery cloud*: P. L. XI. 882; *this same small neglect*: V. Ex. 16; *that same lot*: S. II. 11.

(*c*) used to express contempt; *that same vaunted name, Virginity*: C. 738.

(2) unchanged, not different;
if I be still the same: P. L. I.
256; *thy shape the same*: P. L.
IV. 835; *the tenor of Man's woe
holds on the·same*: P. L. XI. 633.

(3) of like nature, kind, or
degree: P. L. IV. 66; P. R. III.
413.

absol. the identical person: P.
L. III. 623; not a different thing;
God and Nature bid the same: P.
L. VI. 176; a thing of like kind
or nature: P. L. VIII. 345, 581;
X. 826.

See Self-same.

Samos, *sb.* the small island in the
Ægean Sea: P. L. V. 265.

Sampler, *sb.* a pattern piece of
embroidery: C. 751.

Samson, *sb.* the son of Manoah of
the tribe of Dan, a Nazarite endowed with supernatural strength:
S. A. 1129, 1308, 1563, 1570, 1581,
1601, 1615, 1635, 1657; *Herculean, irresistible, invincible*: P. L.
IX. 1060; S. A. 126, 341; *Samson
hath quit himself like Samson*: S.
A. 1709; in direct address: S. A.
438, 445, 733, 766, 909, 1016,
1076, 1293, 1310, 1348, 1391.

Sanctitude, *sb.* holiness: P. L. IV.
293.

Sanctity, *sb.* (*a*) holiness; *then
Heaven and Earth shall be made
pure to sanctity*: P. L. X. 639;
a holy or sacred faculty or endowment; *a creature ... endued
with sanctity of reason*: P. L.
VII. 508.

(*b*) sacredness; *nuptial sanctity*:
P. L. VIII. 487; *God attributes to
place no sanctity*: P. L. XI. 837.

(*c*) *concr.* a holy being, an
angel; *about him all the Sanctities
of Heaven*: P. L. III. 60.

Sanctuary, *sb.* a holy place where
God dwells or is worshipped;
*our living Dread, who dwells in
Silo, his bright sanctuary*: S. A.
1674; the peculiar abode of God
in heaven: P. L. V. 732; *he sits
shrined in his sanctuary of Heaven*:
P. L. VI. 672; the Jewish tabernacle: P. L. XII. 249; the temple
at Jerusalem: P. L. I. 338; Ps.
LXXXVII. 3.

Sand, *sb.* (1) the water-worn detritus;
(*a*) forming the bed of streams;
*pl., the crisprèd brooks rolling on
orient pearl and sands of gold*: P.
L. IV. 238.

(*b*) *pl.* the mass of sand covering
the shore: C. 117, 209.

(2) *pl.* a tract or region consisting chiefly of sand; *the Libyan
sands*: P. L. I. 355; the grains
of sand composing the soil; *unnumbered as the sands of Barca or
Cyrene's torrid soil*: P. L. II. 903.

Sandy, *adj.* consisting of or abounding in sand; *sandy Ladon's lilied
banks*: A. 97; *sandy perilous
wilds*: C. 424.

Sanguine, *adj.* of blood: P. L. VI.
333; *that sanguine flower*, the
flower that sprang from the blood
of the youth Hyacinth: L. 106.

Sap, *sb.* the vital juice of a plant:
P. L. IX. 837.

Sapience, *sb.* wisdom: P. L. VII.
797; *the Son ... with radiance
crowned of majesty, sapience and
love immense*: P. L. VII. 195;
wisdom in matters determined by
the sense of taste: P. L. IX. 1018.

Sapient, *adj.* wise: P. L. IX. 442.

Sapling, *sb.* a young tree: A. 46.

Sapphire, *sb.* a precious stone;
*Heaven ... with opal towers and
battlements adorned of living sapphire*: P. L. II. 1050; *He ... in
sapphire throned*: P. L. VI. 772.

fig. used of stars; *now glowed
the firmament with living sapphires*:
P. L. IV. 605.

attrib. (*a*) composed of or adorned
with this stone; *a crystal firmament, whereon a sapphire throne*:
P. L. VI. 758; *to wear their
sapphire crowns*: C. 26.

(*b*) of the colour of sapphire;
used of water: P. L. IV. 237.

Sapphire-coloured, *adj.* of the colour
of sapphire: S. M. 7.

Sarmatian, *sb. pl.* the people inhabiting the country of Europe
between the Vistula and Volga
rivers: P. R. IV. 78.

Sarra, *sb.* a name of the city of Tyre
in Phœnicia, celebrated for its
purple dye: P. L. XI. 243.

Satan, *sb.* the prince of the fallen
angels, the adversary of God and
man: P. L. I. 192, 271; II. 5,
300, 380, 427, 630, 674, 707, 736,
968, 988, 1010, 1041; III. 70, 422,
540, 653, 736; IV. 9, 173, 356,
827, 885, 905, 968, 985; V. 225,
743, 756; VI. 85, 109, 191, 246,
324, 414, 469, 557, 607, 900; IX.
53, 75; X. 2, 8, 189, 236, 258,
315, 327, 386, 414, 419, 841, 1034;

XI. 248; XII. 391, 394, 492, 547;
P. R. I. 143, 497; II. 115, 172,
319, 392; III. 1, 146; IV. 21, 194,
365, 562, 581, 634; *the Arch-
Enemy, and thence in Heaven
called Satan*: P. L. I. 82; *Satan
—so call him now; his former name
is heard no more in Heaven*: P. L.
v. 658; *the high capital of Satan
and his peers*: P. L. I. 757; *then
Satan first knew pain*: P. L. VI.
327; *Satan, first in sin*: P. L. X.
172; *saw Satan fall like lightning
down*: P. L. X. 184; *proud seat
of Lucifer ... of that bright star to
Satan paragoned*: P. L. X. 426;
*of Satan sprung, all-conquering
Death*: P. L. X. 591; *this act shall
bruise the head of Satan*: P. L.
XII. 430; in direct address: P. L.
IV. 878, 950, 1006.

Satanic, *adj.* of Satan; *Satanic
strength*: P. R. I. 161; *Satanic
host*: P. L. VI. 392.

Sate, *vb. tr.* to satisfy the appetite
of: P. L. IX. 598; C. 714.

Satiate, *vb. tr.* (*a*) to satisfy fully
the appetite of; *absol.*: P. L.
VIII. 214.

(*b*) to satisfy beyond desire; *if
much converse perhaps thee satiate*:
P. L. IX. 248.

part. or *adj.* **satiate**; (*a*) filled
to satiety: P. L. IX. 792.

(*b*) satisfied; *whether scorn or
satiate fury yield it*: P. L. I. 179.

(*c*) impregnated, saturated; *Earth
... satiate with genial moisture*: P.
L. VII. 282.

Satiety, *sb.* an excess of gratification; *thy words ... bring to their
sweetness no satiety*: P. L. VIII.
216.

Satisfaction, *sb.* (*a*) the sufferings
and death of Christ as satisfying
the requirements of God's justice:
P. L. XII. 419.

(*b*) compensation; *pay the rigid
satisfaction, death for death*: P. L.
III. 212.

Satisfy, *vb.* (1) *tr.* (*a*) to fulfil the
desires or demands of, content,
gratify: P. L. VIII. 180; x. 79;
P. R. II. 229, 254; Ps. LXXXI. 67;
*to satisfy the sharp desire I had of
tasting those fair apples*: P. L. IX.
584; *satisfied ... revenge*: S. A.
484; *to satisfy thy lust*: S. A.
837; *our Supreme Foe ... satisfied
with what is punished*: P. L. II.
212; *to satisfy his* (God's) *rigour*,

never satisfied: P. L. X. 803, 804;
*Death ... to satisfy his ravenous
maw*: P. L. X. 991; *Religion
satisfied*: P. L. XII. 535.

(*b*) to fulfil the conditions of:
Cir. 22.

(2) *intr.* to make reparation;
Man ... shall satisfy for Man: P.
L. III. 295.

See **Self-satisfying**.

Saturn, *sb.* Cronus, the son of
Uranus and Ge, who usurped his
father's throne, and who was himself expelled by his own son
Zeus: P. L. I. 512, 519; Il P.
24; C. 805; or who, according
to the Orphic theogony, usurped
the throne of Ophion and Eurynome: P. L. X. 583.

Satyr, *sb.* a Greek god of the woods,
part man and part goat: P. R.
II. 191; L. 34.

Savage, (1) *adj.* (*a*) wild, uncultivated; *savage hill*: P. L. IV. 172;
wilderness: P. R. III. 23.

(*b*) fierce, cruel; *of savage
hunger, or of savage heat*: C. 358.

(*c*) indicating fierceness, wild,
furious; *savage clamour*: P. L.
VII. 36.

(*d*) *adv.* like an inhabitant of
the wood; *Oh, might I here in
solitude live savage*: P. L. IX.
1085.

(2) *sb.* an uncivilized and fierce
man: C. 426.

Save, I. *vb. tr.* (1) to preserve from
evil, danger, or destruction: P.
L. XI. 820; C. 396; Ps. VII. 2,
42; LXXX. 12; LXXXVI. 60; *whom
his anger saves to punish endless*:
P. L. II. 158; *save me, my God*:
Ps. III. 19; to preserve, guard,
defend, or rescue *from*: P. L. XII.
319; M. W. 36; S. XXIII. 6; *to
save her country from a fierce destroyer*: S. A. 984; *to save the
Athenian walls from ruin*: S. VIII.
14; *to save free conscience from
the paw of hireling wolves*: S. XVI.
13; *my plants I save from nightly
ill*: A. 48.

(*b*) *absol.*: C. 866, 889; *thy
wrath, from which no shelter saves*:
Ps. LXXXVIII. 29.

(*c*) to keep from starvation: P.
R. I. 344.

(*d*) to defend; *to save himself
against a coward armed*: S. A. 347.

(*e*) to keep up, maintain; *to
save appearances*: P. L. VIII. 82.

(2) to rescue from sin and spiritual death : P. L. III. 173, 215; XII. 410; Ps. VI. 8; LXXXVI. 7; LXXXVIII. 1; *to save ... the whole lost race* : P. L. III. 279; *to save a world* : P. L. III. 307; *to save Mankind* : P. R. IV. 635.

(3) to prevent the necessity of, make superfluous; with *acc.* and *dat.*; *Thy fear ... will save us trial* : P. L. IV. 855; *the foe at hand ... will save us long pursuit* : P. L. VI. 538; *save the Sun his labour* : P. L. VIII. 133.

part. adj. **saving**, effecting salvation : P. R. II. 474; *saving health*, salvation : Ps. LXXXV. 13, 27.

II. *conj.* not including, except : P. L. III. 427; V. 380; VIII. 409; XII. 291; *save he who reigns above none can* : P. L. II. 814; *save when they journey* : P. L. XII. 258; *the silent* (time), *save where silence yields to the night-warbling bird* : P. L. V. 39.

III. *prep.* except : P. L. V. 655; II P. 82; *summers three times eight save one* : M. W. 7; *save what* : P. L. I. 182; V. 324; VI. 691; IX. 478.

Saviour, *sb.* Jesus Christ, the Redeemer of mankind : P. L. X. 209; P. R. IV. 506, 615; *Son of God, Saviour of men* : P. L. III. 412; *Saviour to mankind* : P. R. I. 187; *thy Saviour* : P. L. XII. 393, 544; *our Saviour* : P. R. I. 406, 465, 493; II. 283, 338; III. 43, 121, 181, 266, 346, 386; IV. 25, 170, 285, 367, 401, 442, 636.

Savour, (1) *sb.* taste, flavour; *fruits of more pleasing savour* : P. L. XI. 26; *meats of noblest ... savour* : P. R. II. 342; *taste the savour of death from all things there that live* : P. L. X. 269; used with double meaning of physical taste and intellectual discernment and appreciation : P. L. IX. 1019.

(2) *vb. tr.* to indicate the presence of; *savours only rancour and pride* : P. L. X. 1043.

Savoury, *adj.* pleasing to the taste or smell : P. L. IV. 335; V. 304; *the savoury herb* : C. 541; *their savoury dinner* : L'A. 84; *savoury smell, odour* : P. L. V. 84; IX. 579, 741.

Saw, *sb.* maxim, proverb : C. 110.

Say, *vb.* (*pres. 2d sing.* say'st : P. L.

V. 818, 853; VIII. 612; P. R. III. 394; IV. 127; S. A. 822, 1580 *3d sing.* saith : Ps. II. 1; *pret.* said ; *2d sing.* said'st : P. L. VI. 187; IX. 933, 1157; P. R. II. 379; *past part.* said) I. *tr.* (1) to express or declare in words : P. L. IV. 443; VIII. 549; P. R. I. 450; C. 780, 783; Soph. 1; *what best to say canst say* : P. R. III. 8; *praise that shall ... be said of Sion* : Ps. LXXXVII. 18; in absolute construction ; *this said* : P. L. II. 417; IV. 736; V. 64, 818, 833; VII. 524; X. 610.

(b) with clause introduced by *that* : P. L. IX. 656; Ps. LXXXII. 21; *said'st thou not that to all things I had right* : P. R. II. 379.

(c) the thing spoken as object sentence : P. L. I. 243; II. 160; IV. 827, 851, 854; V. 37, 58, 224; VII. 217, 230, 261, 282, 309, 387, 450, 530; VIII. 273, 296, 317; IX. 631, 662, 948; X. 855; XI. 526, 530, 635; XII. 485; P. R. I. 229; II. 323; III. 150; V. Ex. 73; Ps. II. 6, 11, 14; IV. 25; LXXXIII. 13, 45; '*Let there be Light!' said God* : P. L. VII. 243; *and blessed them, saying, 'Be fruitful'* etc. : P. L. VII. 395; *saying, Thou shalt not eat thereof* : P. L. X. 200; *Do they not say, 'How well are come upon him his deserts'?* : S. A. 204; *it shall be said, "Hobson has supped,"* etc. : U. C. I. 17; *then saith my heart, Oh, what is man* : Ps. VIII. 11; to announce; the message as object sentence : S. A. 1392.

(d) parenthetically or following the clause : P. L. VIII. 612; *to say truth, truth to say* : P. L. X. 755; S. A. 215; *means I must use, thou say'st* : P. R. III. 394; *I shall, thou say'st, expel a brutish monster* : P. R. IV. 127; *I gave, thou say'st, the example* : S. A. 822; *all by him fell, thou say'st* : S. A. 1580; *she was pinched and pulled, she said* : L'A. 103.

(e) absol., *say and straight unsay* : P. L. IV. 947; *say and unsay* : P. R. I. 474.

(2) to answer; *confounded what to say* : P. R. III. 2.

(3) to ask; *Thou wilt say, 'Why, then, revealed?'* : S. A. 799.

(4) to tell, make known : P. L. VIII. 505; *say, Muse, their names* :

P. L. I. 376; followed by the clause containing the question (direct or indirect), the request or command; *they found me where they say*: P. L. IV. 900; *imper.*: P. L. I. 27, 28; III. 213; V. 512; IX. 562; XI. 879; N. O. 15; *say where and when their fight*: P. L. XII. 384; *say, Goddess, what ensued*: P. L. VII. 40; *but say, where grows the tree?*: P. L. IX. 617; *but say ... what shall betide the few*: P. L. XII. 479; *say first how died he*: S. A. 1578; *say if he be here*: S. A. 337; *with dat.; say me true if those wert mortal wight*: D. F. I. 41; *absol.*: P. L. IX. 566; S. A. 1456.

(5) to utter in opposition, oppose: L. 129.

(6) to declare; with clause; *time there is for all things, Truth hath said*: P. R. III. 183; *many books, wise men have said, are wearisome*: P. R. IV. 322.

(7) to assert: U. C. II. 25; to affirm; *with hand so various—or might I say contrarious*: S. A. 669.

(8) to judge, decide; *wisest Fate says No*: N. O. 149; with clause; *what it is, hard is it to say*: S. A. 1013.

(9) to suppose, assume; with subjunctive clause; *but say I could repent*: P. L. IV. 93; *but say that death be not one stroke*: P. L. X. 808; *but say thou wert possessed of David's throne*: P. R. III. 357.

II. *intr.* to speak, declare: P. R. III. 8; *thus* or *so say, saying, said,* or *having said*; the thing said immediately preceding or following: P. L. II. 466, 871; III. 736; IV. 536, 797; V. 82, 331, 361, 718; VI. 189, 746; VIII. 300, 644; IX. 179, 385, 780, 834, 917, 990, 1034; X. 85, 157, 272, 410, 504; P. R. II. 244; IV. 394, 450, 541; S. A. 1310; Ps. III, 5; *as thou said'st, as he, they* etc. *said*: P. L. VI. 187; IX. 933, 1157; C. 185, 632, 852; *he said*: P. L. V. 872; VI. 719; P. R. IV. 561; *he or she scarce had said*: P. L. VII. 313; IX. 664; *imper.*: P. L. VII. 640; X. 158.

In combination with other words;

(*a*) **say on,** to continue to speak or relate: P. L. VIII. 228.

(*b*) **say us nay,** to deny or hinder us: S. A. 1729.

(*c*) **some say,** people assert: P. L. X. 575, 668, 671; C. 432.

(*d*) **they say,** it is commonly reported or believed: P. L. IX. 638; P. R. I. 397; *as 'tis said*: N. O. 117.

vbl. sb. **saying,** statement, declaration: P. R. II. 104; S. A. 652.

Scaffold, *sb.* a temporary gallery upon which spectators stand: S. A. 1610.

Scalding, *part. adj.* burning; *scalding thirst*: P. L. X. 556.

Scale, *sb.* one of the thin structures which collectively form the covering of fish: P. L. VII. 401.

Scale, *sb.* (1) the dish of a balance; *the Fiend looked up, and knew his mounted scale aloft*: P. L. IV. 1014.

(*b*) *fig.*, *in the ascending scale of Heaven the stars that usher evening rose*: P. L. IV. 354; *Belial, in much uneven scale thou weigh'st all others by thyself*: P. R. II. 173.

in even scale, neither side having any advantage over the other; *in even scale the battle hung*: P. L. VI. 245; uninfluenced; *his free will, to her own inclining left in even scale*: P. L. X. 47.

(2) the balance itself; *the Eternal ... hung forth in Heaven his golden scales*: P. L. IV. 997.

(3) *pl.* the zodiacal constellation Libra: P. L. X. 676.

Scale, I. *sb.* a ladder or flight of steps; *fig.*, *Love ... is the scale by which to Heavenly Love thou may'st ascend*: P. L. VIII. 591; *flowers ... by gradual scale sublimed to vital spirits aspire*: P. L. V. 483 *the scale of Nature set, from centre to circumference*: P. L. V. 509.

(*b*) a scaling-ladder used in the assault of a fortified place: P. L. XI. 656.

II. *vb.* (1) *tr.* to climb or clamber up: P. L. II. 71.

(2) *intr.* to lead up by steps; *the lower stair, that scaled by steps of gold to Heaven-gate*: P. L. III. 541.

Scaly, *adj.* covered with scales: P. L. I. 206; *scaly crocodile*: P. L. VII. 474; *scaly Triton's winding shell*: C. 873; of a serpent's body; *ended foul in many a scaly* *fold*: P. L. II. 651; transferred epithet; *the Old Dragon...swinges the scaly horror of his folded tail*: N. O. 172.

Scan, *vb. tr. (a) absol.* to read so as to indicate the metrical structure or to divide into feet: S. XIII. 3.

(*b*) to examine critically, scrutinize: P. L. VIII. 74.

Scandal, *sb.* opprobrium, shame, disgrace: S. A. 453; *that hill of scandal (see* Hill): P. L. I. 416.

Scandalous, *adj.* shameful, disgraceful: S. A. 1409.

Scant, *adj.* short in quantity, scarcely sufficient: P. L. IV. 628; *scant allowance of star-light*: C. 308; *judgment scant*: S. A. 1027.

Scape, I. *sb.* escapade, misdemeanour: P. R. II. 189.

II. *vb.* (1) *tr. (a)* to get safely out of or away from; *glorying to have scaped the Stygian flood*: P. L. I. 239.

(*b*) to get free from: Ps. LXXXIII. 64.

(*c*) to succeed in avoiding: S. A. 697; *to scape his punishment*: P. L. IV. 911; *our foe shall scape his punishment*: P. L. X. 1039; to shun, not to be caught in; *and scaped, haply so scaped, his mortal snare*: P. L. IV. 7.

(*d*) to succeed in eluding; *what can scape the eye of God*: P. L. X. 5.

(*e*) to remain uninjured by; *the patriarch...who scaped the Flood*: P. L. XII. 117; to remain untouched by; *nor did Israel scape the infection*: P. L. I. 482.

(2) *intr. (a)* to escape, gain liberty: C. 814; *from his prison scaped*: P. L. IV. 906; *from Hell scaped*: P. L. V. 225.

(*b*) to succeed in avoiding punishment or danger: P. L. I. 749; II. 442; *from thee I can... endure check or reproof, and glad to scape so quit*: P. R. I. 477; to avoid death: S. A. 1659.

Scar, *sb.* hurt, wound; *the scar of these corrosive fires*: P. L. II. 401; *deep scars of thunder*: P. L. I. 601.

Scarce, (1) *adj.* scantily supplied; with *of*; *a region scarce of prey*: P. L. III. 433.

(2) *adv.* hardly, barely; qualifying a *vb.*: P. L. I. 283, 699; II. 284, 541; IV. 874; V. 139, 559; VI. 568; VII. 67, 313, 319; IX.

664; XI. 499; P. R. II. 96; III. 233; S. A. 1525, 1546; *scarce thus at length failed speech recovered*: P. L. IV. 357; *that scarce themselves know how to hold a sheep-hook*: L. 119; *Death discover them scarce men*: P. R. III. 85; *scarce to contribute each Orb a glimpse of light*: P. L. VIII. 155; *scarce a shed could be obtained*: P. L. II. 72; *glory scarce of few is raised*: P. R. III. 59; qualifying an *adj.* or *adv.*: P. L. V. 558; VI. 393; VIII. 306; X. 654, 923; P. R. III. 51; M. W. 20; *distinguishable scarce from Gentiles*: P. R. III. 424; *scarce worth the sight*: P. R. IV. 86; *scarce freely draw the air*: S. A. 7; *scarce half I seem to live*: S. A. 79; qualifying a phrase: P. L. VII. 470; XI. 762; *scarce from the tree returning*: P. L. IX. 850; *scarce with life the shepherds fly*: P. L. XI. 650.

Scarf, *sb.* a strip of fine material forming part of a costume; used *fig.* of the rainbow: C. 995.

Scathe, *vb. tr.* to injure: P. L. I. 613.

Scatter, *vb. tr. (a)* to throw loosely about, strew: S. XVIII. 2.

(*b*) to cover here and there with; *where cattle pastured late, now scattered lies with carcasses*: P. L. XI. 653.

(*c*) to disperse; *scatters the rear of darkness thin*: L'A. 50.

part. adj. **scattered**; (*a*) strewn: P. L. I. 304; separated (from their owners) and lying here and there; *Cherub and Seraph rolling in the flood with scattered arms*: P. L. I. 325.

(*b*) dissipated; *his scattered spirits returned*: P. L. XI. 294.

Scene, *sb. (a)* theatre; *from the daily scene effeminate*: P. R. IV. 142.

(*b*) an action exhibited to spectators; *if cause were to unfold some active scene of various persons*: P. R. II. 239.

(*c*) one of a series of events or situations forming a complete spectacle: P. L. XI. 637; *these latest scenes confine my roving verse*: P. 22.

(*d*) view, landscape; *sylvan, woody scene*: P. L. IV. 140; P. R. II. 294.

Scent, (1) *sb.* smell, odour; *the scent of fruit*: P. L. IX. 587; *of odorous perfume*: S. A. 720; *of carnage*: P. L. X. 267; *of living carcasses*: P. L. X. 277; *fig.*, *gold, though offered only, by the scent conceived... Treason against me*: S. A. 390.

(2) *vb. tr.* to perceive by the smell; *absol.*: P. L. X. 279.

Sceptre, *sb.* (*a*) a staff borne as a symbol of royal power or authority: S. A. 1303; borne by Christ: P. L. VI. 746; by Satan: P. L. IV. 90.

(*b*) the royal power or authority symbolized: P. L. XII. 357; C. 36; *the sceptre from his father Brute*: C. 828; *David's...sceptre*: P. R. III. 405; *Israel's sceptre*: P. R. IV. 480; *to gain a sceptre*: P. R. II. 486; *the sceptre of old Night*: P. L. II. 1002; the power of God or Christ: P. L. VI. 730; *regal sceptre*: P. L. III. 339; v. 816; *iron, golden*: P. L. II. 327; v. 886.

Sceptred, *part. adj.* bearing a sceptre; *Moloch, sceptred king*: P. L. II. 43; *heralds*: P. L. XI. 660; *angels*: P. L. I. 734; or the meaning may be: royal, regal; *Tragedy in sceptred pall*: Il P. 98.

School, *sb.* (*a*) the followers of a particular teacher; *the schools of ancient sages*: P. R. IV. 251; a sect adhering to a certain system of philosophy: S. A. 297; *the old schools of Greece*: C. 439; *the schools of Academics*: P. R. IV. 277.

(*b*) a means of discipline or instruction: P. R. III. 238.

Science, *sb.* knowledge: P. L. IX. 680.

Sciential, *adj.* having power to confer knowledge: P. L. IX. 837.

Scipio, *sb.* Scipio Africanus Major: P. L. IX. 510; P. R. III. 34.

Scoff, *vb.* (1) *intr.* to speak jeeringly, mock: P. L. VI. 568, 629.

(2) *tr.* to mock at; *the Lord shall scoff them*: Ps. II. 9.

Scoop, *vb. tr.* to take up as with a ladle, dip out: P. L. IV. 336.

Scope, *sb.* mark; *fig.*, *the scope of all his aim*: P. L. II. 127; aim, purpose, intention: P. R. I. 494.

Scorch, *vb. tr.* (*a*) to burn superficially without consuming; *with redoubled blow Ariel, and Arioch, ...scorched and blasted*: P. L. VI. 372.

(*b*) to injure by heat; *summer drouth or singed air never scorch thy tresses fair*: C. 929.

part. adj. scorching, burning, parching: P. L. X. 691.

Score, (1) *sb.* amount due, debt; *fig.*: S. A. 433.

(2) *vb. tr.* to record: P. 46.

Scorn, I. *sb.* (*a*) contempt, disdain: P. L. IX. 299; *how deserving contempt and scorn of all*: S. A. 494; *Philistia full of scorn*: Ps. LXXXVII. 14; *in scorn of*: S. A. 137; *had or have in scorn*: S. A. 442; Ps. IV. 8; *added in scorn*: P. R. IV. 550; *thus he in scorn*: P. L. IV. 902; *felt by God or angels*: P. R. I. 415; *whether scorn or satiate fury yield it from our Foe*: P. L. I. 178; *by Satan or his angels*: P. L. I. 619; IV. 827.

(*b*) the expression of contempt or disdain, derision: P. L. XI. 811; *the subject of their cruelty or scorn*: S. A. 646; *pl.*: P. R. III. 191; IV. 387; expressed by angels: P. L. v. 904, 906; *Zephon, answering scorn with scorn*: P. L. IV. 834; *by Satan or his angels*; *the sound of public scorn*: P. L. X. 509; *matter of scorn not to be given the Foe*: P. L. IX. 951; *breath'st ...scorn*: P. L. II. 697.

(*c*) an object of contempt or derision: P. L. XII. 341; *made of all mine enemies the scorn and gaze*: S. A. 34; *of his thunder made a scorn*: P. L. VI. 632.

II. *vb. tr.* (1) to hold in scorn or contempt, disdain: P. L. X. 418; *scorning surprise*: P. L. II. 134; *scorn delights*: L. 72.

(2) to treat with contempt, disregard, despise: P. L. X. 54; S. A. 943; C. 685; *my day of grace, they who neglect and scorn*: P. L. III. 199; *not to scorn the facile gates of Hell*: P. L. IV. 966; *easily scorned all her* (beauty's) *assaults*: P. R. II. 194; *to scorn the sordid world*: D. F. I. 63.

(*b*) to leave with contempt; *wings wherewith to scorn the Earth*: P. L. IX. 1011.

(*c*) to make a mock of, deride: P. L. VI. 40.

Scorner, *sb.* one who holds God or religion in contempt: Ps. I. 4.

Scornful, *adj.* full of contempt, disdainful, insolent: P. L. X. 625; Ps. LXXXIII. 22; *with scornful eye*: P. L. VI. 149; or *adv.* contemptuously, disdainfully: P. L. IV. 536.

Scorpion, *sb.* (*a*) the animal *Scorpio*: P. L. X. 524; *lest with a whip of scorpions I pursue thy lingering*: P. L. II. 701; *fig.*, *his gifts... draw a scorpion's tail behind*: S. A. 360.

(*b*) the zodiacal constellation: P. L. X. 328.

attrib. of the constellation Scorpio; *the Scorpion sign*: P. L. IV. 998.

Scot, *sb.* a native of Scotland: S. XVI. 7.

Scotch, *adj.* of Scotland: F. of C. 12.

Scour, *vb. tr.* to go quickly along in search of something; *he scours the right hand coast*: P. L. II. 633; *scouts each coast... scour*: P. L. VI. 529.

Scourge, (1) *sb.* a lash; used *fig.* as a symbol of punishment: P. L. II. 90.

(2) *vb. tr.* to whip, lash; *Xerxes ... scourged with many a stroke the indignant waves*: P. L. X. 311; to drive as with a lash; *till the wrath... scourge that wisdom back to Hell*: P. L. IV. 914.

Scout, (1) *sb.* one sent out to gain and bring in information: P. L. III. 543; VI. 529; *fig.*, *the blabbing eastern scout, the nice Morn*: C. 138.

(2) *vb. intr.* to go or act as a scout; *with obscure wing scout far and wide into the realm of Night*: P. L. II. 133.

Scowl, *vb. tr.* to drive or send with a scowl; *fig.*, *the louring element scowls o'er the darkened landskip snow or shower*: P. L. II. 491.

Scramble, *vb. intr.* to struggle eagerly and rudely for something; *to scramble at the shearers' feast*: L. 117.

Scrannel, *adj.* making a thin rasping sound (?): *their scrannel pipes of wretched straw*: L. 124.

Screen, *vb. tr.* to shelter, protect: P. R. IV. 30.

Scribble, *vb. tr.* to mark hastily or incorrectly; *the Sphere with Cen-*

tric and Eccentric scribbled o'er: P. L. VIII. 83.

Scribe, *sb.* a man learned in the Mosaic law and in the sacred writings: P. R. I. 261.

Scrip, *sb.* wallet, bag: C. 626.

Scroll, *sb.* schedule, list: P. L. XII. 336; *the Lord shall write it in a scroll*: Ps. LXXXVII. 21.

Scruple, *vb. tr.* to have doubt about, hesitate with regard to: P. R. II. 331; with *prep. inf.*: P. L. IX. 997.

Scrupulous, *adj.* cautious from fear of error; *Advice with scrupulous head*: C. 108.

Scrutiny, *sb.* critical examination: P. R. IV. 515.

Scull, *sb.* a multitude of fish, school, shoal: P. L. VII. 402.

Sculpture, *sb.* a figure cut in a solid substance; *cornice or frieze, with bossy sculptures graven*: P. L. I. 716.

Scum, (1) *sb.* the impurities rising to the surface of boiling liquid: C. 595.

(2) *vb. tr.* to remove the scum, skim: P. L. I. 704.

Scurf, *sb.* scaly or flaky matter; *the rest shone with a glossy scurf*: P. L. I. 672.

Scylla, *sb.* a nymph beloved by Glaucus, who through the jealousy of Circe was changed into a monster surrounded by barking dogs: P. L. II. 660; this monster whose abode was supposed to be a rock on the Italian shore of the Strait of Sicily: C. 257.

Scythe, *sb.* the instrument used in mowing grain: L'A. 66; *fig.*, *whatever thing the scythe of Time mows down*: P. L. X. 606.

Scythian, *sb.* an inhabitant of Scythia, the country comprising that part of Europe north of the Black Sea and south of Sarmatia, and a large undefined tract of country in western and central Asia: P. R. IV. 78; *spec.* Humber, King of the Huns: V. Ex. 99; collectively; *the Parthian king... hath gathered all his host against the Scythian*: P. R. III. 301.

Sdain, *vb. tr.* to disdain, scorn: P. L. IV. 50.

Sea, *sb.* (1) the ocean or a branch of it: P. L. II. 287; III. 472; VII. 212; P. R. III. 258; C. 732; *while night invests the sea*: P. L.

I. 208; *all the earth and all the sea*: P. L. V. 753; *call up…old Proteus from the sea*: P. L. III. 604; *dominion hold over fish of the sea*: P. L. VII. 533; *raging sea*: P. L. X. 286; *the flat sea*: C. 375; *at sea*: P. L. II. 636; IV. 161; masc. gen.; *nor let the sea surpass his bounds*: P. L. XI. 893; *sing.* for *pl.*; *the stern God of Sea*: Hor. O. 16; with proper name; *the Euboic sea*: P. L. II. 546; *the Cronian sea*: P. L. X. 290; *the Blackmoor Sea*: P. R. IV. 72; *pl.* for *sing.*; *Atlantic seas*: P. L. III. 559.

(b) *pl.*: P. L. VII. 396, 399; C. 115, 713; S. A. 961; *the sound of seas*: P. L. X. 642; *seas rough with black winds*: Hor. O. 6; *the mutual flowing of the seas*: U. C. II. 31.

(c) without the art. and in combination or contrast with *land, shore, air, fire*, etc.: P. L. II. 939; X. 666; P. R. II. 344; S. A. 962; *sea and land*: P. L. III. 653; VII. 473; X. 693; XII. 579; N. O. 52; *sea or land*: S. A. 710; *sea and air*: P. L. VII. 521; XI. 337; *sea or air*: P. L. VII. 629; VIII. 341; *Earth, Air, and Sea*: P. L. IV. 432; *now land, now sea*: P. L. IX. 117; *sea he had searched and land from Eden over Pontus*: P. L. IX. 76; *pl.*: P. L. VII. 428; X. 700; *the shores and sounding seas*: L. 154; *o'er lands and seas*: S. VIII. 7; *the great receptacle of waters he called seas*: P. L. VII. 308.

(d) the Mediterranean or a part of it: P. L. II. 660; XII. 142; Ps. LXXX. 46; LXXXIII. 38; *the great western sea*: P. L. XII. 141; *Adonis .. ran purple to the sea*: P. L. I. 451; *see where it* (the Nile) *flows…into the sea*: P. L. XII. 159; the Tyrrhenian Sea: P. R. IV. 28; the Ægean Sea: P. L. X. 309; *pl.*; *Alpheus…stole under seas*: A. 31.

(e) the Red Sea: P. L. XII. 212; Ps. CXIV. 7; *the sea swallows him with his host*: P. L. XII. 195; *the Red Sea*: P. R. III. 438.

(f) the lake of hell; *that inflamed sea*: P. L. I. 300.

(g) applied to the great flood: P. L. XI. 854; *sea covered sea, sea without shore*: P. L. XI. 749, 750;

applied to chaos; *glad that now his sea should find a shore*: P. L. II. 1011; applied to the Crystalline sphere: P. L. III. 518; *the glassy sea*: P. L. VII. 619.

(2) Neptune, the god of the sea: L. 89.

(3) *fig.* something resembling a sea in extent, appearance, etc.; *at his trunk sprouts out a sea*: P. L. VII. 416; *the bright pavement, that like a sea of jasper shone*: P. L. III. 363; *a windy sea of land*: P. L. III. 440; *my couch I make a kind of sea*: Ps. VI. 12; *seas wept from our deep sorrow*: Cir. 9; *a troubled sea of passion*: P. L. X. 718.

(4) as one of the four elements which form the universe: P. L. II. 912; V. 416, 417.

See **Mid-Sea, Red-Sea.**

Sea-beast, *sb.* an enormous sea animal; *that sea-beast, Leviathan*: P. L. I. 200.

Seafaring, *adj.* following the business of seamen: P. L. II. 288.

Sea-girt, *adj.* surrounded by the sea: C. 21; H. B. 9.

Sea-idol, *sb.* the idol that was 'upward man and downward fish'; *Dagon, their sea-idol*: S. A. 13.

Seal, *sb.* the marine animal: P. L. VII. 409; XI. 835.

Seal, (1) *sb.* (a) confirmation, pledge: P. L. IX. 1043.

(b) that which effectually secures; *the seal of silence*: S. A. 49.

(2) *vb. tr.* (a) to attest; *seals obedience first with wounding smart*: Cir. 25.

(b) to shut up, close; *obstruct the mouth of Hell forever, and seal up his…jaws*: P. L. X. 637.

(c) to confine, imprison: P. L. IV. 966.

Seaman, *sb.* mariner: P. L. I. 205.

Sea-mew, *sb.* sea-gull: P. L. XI. 835.

Sea-monster, *sb.* a monstrous marine animal: P. L. XI. 751; a monster in form like those inhabiting the sea; *Dagon his name, sea-monster*: P. L. I. 462.

Sea-nymph, *sb. pl.* the goddesses of the sea, the Nereids: Il P. 21.

Sea-path, *sb.* a course through the sea; *fish that through the wet sea-paths … do slide*: Ps. VIII. 22.

Search, I. *sb.* (*a*) the act of seeking or looking for something : P. L. IX. 181 ; *with narrow search* : P. L. IV. 528 ; IX. 83 ; *our solemn search* : A. 7 ; with *of* : P. L. IV. 799 ; *the search of foreign worlds* : P. L. X. 440 ; *in search of this new World* : P. L. II. 403.

(*b*) investigation, inquiry : P. L. VI. 445.

II. *vb.* (**1**) *tr.* (*a*) to go through and look carefully for something : V. Ex. 31 ; *sea he had searched and land* : P. L. IX. 76.

(*b*) to look for ; *search...a place foretold should be* : P. L. II. 830 ; *searching what was writ concerning the Messiah* : P. R. I. 260.

(*c*) to seek mentally, investigate : P. L. VII. 125 ; XII. 377 ; *absol.* or *intr.* : P. L. VIII. 66.

(**2**) *intr.* to make search : P. L. IV. 789.

See **Shallow-searching.**

Season, (**1**) *sb.* (*a*) a particular period of time : P. R. II. 72 ; *the season, prime for sweetest scents* : P. L. IX. 200 ; *the inclement seasons, rain, ice,* etc. : P. L. X. 1063.

(*b*) one of the four divisions of the year : L'A. 89 ; *the hard season* : S. XX. 5 ; *pl.* : P. L. III. 41 ; VII. 427 ; *all seasons* : P. L. IV. 640 ; V. 323 ; *let them be for signs, for seasons, and for days* : P. L. VII. 342 ; *learn his seasons, hours, or days, or months, or years* : P. L. VIII. 69 ; *change of seasons* : P. L. X. 678.

(*c*) fit, suitable, or allotted time : P. L. III. 187 ; N. O. 35 ; *my, thy, your,* or *his season* : P. R. IV. 146, 380 ; L. 7 ; Ps. I. 8 ; *at season fit* : P. L. XII. 597 ; *the perfect season* : P. R. IV. 468 ; time at which they are to be inhabited : P. L. VII. 623.

out of season, inopportune, inappropriate : P. L. V. 850.

(**2**) *vb. tr.* to fit for the taste ; *fig., till I* (Sin), *in Man residing, ... season him thy last and sweetest prey* : P. L. X. 609.

Seat, I. *sb.* (**1**) that on which one sits, bench, chair, throne : P. L. VIII. 42 ; S. A. 1607 ; C. 916 ; *mossy seats* : P. L. V. 392 ; *the seat of scorners* : Ps. I. 3 ; (Death) *from his seat ... onward came* : P. L. II. 674 ; as occupied by God, Christ, gods, or angels : P. L. X.

614 ; XI. 82 ; *the seat of God* : P. L. XI. 148 ; *from his radiant seat he rose* : P. L. X. 85 ; *his seat at God's right hand* : P. L. XII. 457 ; *the seat of Deity supreme* : P. L. VII. 141 ; *a thousand demi-gods on golden seats* : P. L. I. 796 ; *the enthroned gods on sainted seats* : C. 11 ; *the seat of Jove* : L. 16.

(*b*) *fig., a cloudy chair ... that seat* : P. L. II. 931 ; *Nature from her seat* : P. L. IX. 782.

(*c*) *fig.* the person seated on the throne ; *they led him ... before the seat supreme* : P. L. VI. 27 ; kingly power : P. R. II. 442 ; IV. 469 ; *David's royal seat* : P. R. III. 373.

(**2**) site, situation : P. L. VI. 197 ; *a happy rural seat of various view* : P. L. IV. 247 ; *the blissful seat of Paradise* : P. L. III. 527.

(**3**) place of abode : P. L. XI. 575 ; P. R. IV. 30 ; H. B. 4, 5 ; P. R. II. 125 ; *Hebron, seat of giants old* : S. A. 148.

(*b*) Eden, Paradise, or the world, the abode of man : P. L. I. 5 ; III. 669 ; VII. 329 ; VIII. 299 ; IX. 153 ; X. 237 ; XII. 642 ; *another World, the happy seat of... Man* : P. L. II. 347 ; *Paradise, the happy seat of Man* : P. L. III. 632 ; *Earth, the seat of Man* : P. L. III. 724 ; *this high seat, your Heaven* : P. L. IV. 371 ; *Earth...seat worthier of God* : P. L. IX. 100 ; *the seat of men* : P. L. VII. 623.

(*c*) heaven, the abode of God or angels : P. L. II. 394 ; D. F. I. 59 ; *their, our,* or *his native seat* : P. L. I. 634 ; II. 76, 1050 ; VI. 226 ; *Heaven, thy seat divine* : Ps. LXXX. 58 ; *in thy everlasting seat remainest God alone* : Ps. LXXXVI. 35 ; *Satan to his royal seat* : P. L. V. 756.

(*d*) hell : P. L. I. 243.

(*e*) the moon ; *the hollow round of Cynthia's seat* : N. O. 103.

(*f*) *fig., seat of desolation* : P. L. I. 181 ; *of bliss* : P. L. VI. 273 ; P. R. IV. 612 ; *Love ... hath his seat in Reason* : P. L. VIII. 590 ; *seat of mental sight* : P. L. XI. 418 ; *greatness of mind and nobleness their seat build in her* : P. L. VIII. 557.

(**4**) the place where God or a god is worshipped ; *Rimmon, whose delightful seat was fair Damascus* : P. L. I. 467 ; *each* *peculiar power forgoes his wonted seat*: N. O. 196 ; *durst fix their seats, long after, next the seat of God*: P. L. I. 383.

(5) the capital city or the royal residence, or both : P. L. XI. 386; P. R. III. 262 ; *seat of Cathaian Can*: P. L. XI. 388; *seat of Atabalipa*: P. L. XI. 408; *seat of Montezume*: P. L. XI. 407 ; *of that first golden monarchy the seat*; P. R. III. 277 ; *Pandemonium, city and proud seat of Lucifer*: P. L. X. 424 ; used of Paradise : P. L. XI. 343.

II. *vb. tr.* (*a*) to furnish an abode or residence for : P. L. I. 720.

(*b*) to set firm, establish : P. R. II. 217.

(*c*) to locate : Ps. LXXXVII. 3.'

part. adj. **seated,** firmly rooted : P. L. VI. 644.

See **High-seated, Mercy-seat.**

Sea-weed, *sb.* the plants growing in the sea : P. L. VII. 404.

Sechem, *sb.* Shechem, a city of central Palestine situated between ·Mts. Ebal and Gerezim (spelled Sichem in Vulg.) : P. L. XII. 136.

Second, (1) *adj.* (*a*) next after the first : P. L. VII. 275; IX. 101 ; XI. 859.

(*b*) one more, another : P. L. I. 702; III. 713; VI. 605; IX. 1001; P. R. II. 275 ; S. A. 1391 ; M. W. 25 ; *the Dragon, put to second rout*: P. L. IV. 3 ; *second life*: P. L. XI. 64 ; *fate, stroke*: P. L. II. 17, 713 ; *root, stock, source*: P. L. III. 288 ; XII. 7, 13 ; *Mary, second Eve*: P. L. V. 387 ; X. 183 ; *our second Adam*: P. L. XI. 383; *second Omnipotence*: P. L. VI. 684.

(*c*) subordinate only to God : P. L. XII. 35 ; little inferior in quality or attributes *to* ; *no fair to thine equivalent or second*: P. L. IX. 609 ; *the bliss wherein he sat second to thee*: P. L. III. 409 ; *none I know second to me or like*: P. L. VIII. 407.

absol. (*a*) one next after the first in time : P. L. XII. 321 ; in power : P. L. XII. 162.

(*b*) another existing at the same time : S. A. 1701.

(*c*) a person of the second generation; *second of Satan sprung, all-conquering Death*: P. L. X. 591.

(2) *vb. tr.* (*a*) to do again, repeat : P. L. X. 335.

(*b*) to aid, support : S. A. 1153; *thunder ... seconded thy else not dreaded spear*: P. L. IV. 929.

(*c*) to favour, encourage ; *who appeared to second ... the perilous attempt* : P. L. II. 419.

(*d*) to show approval of ; *his zeal none seconded* : P. L. V. 850.

Secondary, *adj.* inferior, subordinate : P. L. V. 854.

Secrecy, *sb.* (*a*) solitude, seclusion ; *secrecy of desert cell* : C. 387 ; *thou* (God), *in thy secrecy although alone* : P. L. VIII. 427.

(*b*) strict silence regarding matters not to be divulged : S. A. 1002.

Secret, I. *adj.* (1) set apart, remote, solitary ; *the secret top of Oreb* : P. L. I. 6 ; *from out his secret altar* : N. O. 28 ; *high throned in secret bliss* : Cir. 19 ; *in secret shades of woody Ida's inmost grove* : Il P. 28.

(2) hidden, concealed, unrevealed : P. L. II. 838 ; V. Ex. 45.

(*b*) concealed, · hidden, unseen ; *I perhaps am secret* : P. L. IX. 811 ; *secret sluice* : A. 30 ; *the secret flame of midnight torches* : C. 129 ; *secret passage find* : S. A. 610 ; or *adv.* in secret : P. L. VI. 522 ; *though secret she retire,* though she retire into a hidden or concealed place : P. L. IX. 810.

(*c*) hidden and mysterious : P. L. X. 248 ; *the secret power of harmony* : P. R. IV. 254 ; *my heart ... by a secret harmony still moves with thine* : P. L. X. 358 ; *sup., by secretest conveyance* : P. L. X. 249.

(*d*) hidden from others, known only to oneself ; *secret sting of amorous remorse* : S. A. 1007 ; *secret refreshings that repair his strength* : S. A. 665.

(*e*) stealthy : P. L. IV. 7.

(*f*) done without the knowledge of others ; *secret gaze* : P. L. III. 671 ; *in secret*, not publicly or openly : P. L. II. 663, 766 ; V. 672 ; P. R. I. 15.

(*g*) held in privacy ; *secret conclave* : P. L. I. 795.

(3) affording concealment ; *the Most High ... from his secret cloud amidst* : P. L. X. 32.

(4) that should be kept a secret; *the secret gift of God* : S. A. 201.

II. *sb.* (*a*) that which is not or should not be revealed : S. A. 384, 492, 776, 798, 879, 1199 ; *his holy secret* : S. A. 497; *my capital secret* : S. A. 394.

(*b*) a hidden or unrevealed thing or place ; *unfold the secrets of another world* : P. L. v. 569 ; *to explore the secrets ... of his eternal empire* : P. L. vii. 95 ; *the great Architect did ... not divulge his secrets* : P. L. viii. 74 ; *Night and Chaos ... jealous of their secrets* : P. L. x. 478 ; *Chaos and ancient Night ... the secrets of your realm* : P. L. ii. 972 ; *the secrets of the hoary Deep* : P. L. ii. 891 ; *all secrets of the Deep* : P. L. xii. 578.

Sect, *sb.* (*a*) a school of philosophy ; *the sect Epicurean* : P. R. iv. 279.

(*b*) a body of adherents, party : P. L. vi. 147.

Secular, *adj.* (*a*) lasting for ages : S. A. 1707.

(*b*) temporal, worldly, opposed to *spiritual* : P. L. xii. 517 ; S. xvi. 12.

Secure, I. *adj.* **(1)** free from care or fear, dreading no evil, untroubled, unconcerned : P. L. vi. 672 ; *secure delight* : L'A. 91 ; *sleep secure* : P. L. x. 779 ; *dwell or live secure* : P. L. ii. 399 ; xi. 802 ; P. R. iv. 616 ; *here we may reign secure* : P. L. i. 261 ; *till then as one secure sat on his throne* : P. L. i. 638 ; *Heaven's high Arbitrator sit secure in his own strength* : P. L. ii. 359 ; *thou ... secure laugh'st at their vain designs* : P. L. v. 736 ; with *of ; asleep, secure of harm* : P. L. iv. 791.

(*b*) *comp.* less prepared ; *if thou think trial unsought may find us both securer* : P. L. ix. 371.

(*c*) or *adv.* confidently ; *this further consolation yet secure I carry hence* : P. L. xii. 620.

(2) free from apprehension, confident, certain, sure : P. L. v. 238 ; P. R. i. 176 ; *in his face I see sad resolution and secure* : P. L. vi. 541 ; *strength, ... burdensome, proudly secure* : S. A. 55 ; with *of* : P. L. v. 638 ; *secure of our discharge from penalty* : P. L. xi. 196 ; with *prep. inf.* : P. L. ix. 1175.

(3) free from danger, safe, protected : P. L. iv. 186 ; ix. 339 ; xi. 746 ; P. R. iii. 360 ; *in a place ... less secure* : C. 327 ; *if I thought my sister's state secure* : C. 409.

II. *vb. tr.* (*a*) to guard from danger, make safe, protect : P. L. iv. 370 ; Ps. vii. 2 ; *aught that might his happy state secure, secure from outward force* : P. L. ix. 347, 348 ; *how to secure the Lady from surprisal* : C. 618.

(*b*) to make sure of, insure : P. R. iii. 348.

(*c*) to obtain, gain, bring about : P. L. v. 222.

Securely, *adj.* confidently : P. L. vi. 130.

Sedentary, *adj.* (*a*) caused by habitually sitting ; *sedentary numbness* : S. A. 571.

(*b*) fixed, unmoving ; *the sedentary Earth* : P. L. viii. 32.

Sedge, *sb.* the plant *Carex* : P. L. i. 304 ; L. 104.

Sedgy, *adj.* abounding in sedge : V. Ex. 97.

Seditious, *adj.* guilty of sedition ; *seditious Angel* : P. L. vi. 152.

Seduce, *vb. tr.* to draw into evil, lead astray ; *thy equal fear that my firm faith and love can ... be seduced* : P. L. ix. 287 ; used of Satan in relation to man : P. L. iv. 83 ; x. 41, 332 ; *man seduced* : P. L. x. 577 ; *who first seduced them* : P. L. i. 33 ; *Man by him seduced* : P. L. i. 219 ; *him by fraud I have seduced from his Creator* : P. L. x. 485.

Sedulous, *adj.* diligent in application, assiduous : P. L. ix. 27.

See, *vb.* (*pres. 2d sing.* seest : P. L. i. 91, 180 ; ii. 781 ; iii. 80, etc. ; *pret.* saw ; *2d sing.* saw'st : P. L. ii. 796 ; viii. 446 ; xi. 471, 607, etc. ; *past part.* seen) I. *tr.* **(1)** to perceive by the eye, behold ; sometimes with blending of sense **(2)** ; a person : P. L. iii. 623 ; iv. 467, 468 ; v. 56, 157 ; vi. 147, 774 ; viii. 482, 507 ; ix. 436, 508, 546, 1030, 1094 ; x. 104 ; xi. 614 ; xii. 128 ; P. R. i. 246, 384 ; ii. 270 ; iii. 67, 303 ; S. A. 219, 1588 ; A. 95, 109 ; C. 291, 575 ; *this odious offspring whom thou seest* : P. L. ii. 781 ; *Father, to see thy face* : P. L. iii. 262 ; *glad I see thy face* : P. L. v. 29 ; *I see*

bone of my bone...before me: P. L.
VIII. 494; *longing to be seen*: P.
L. X. 877; *have I seen Death*: P.
L. XI. 462; *Death thou hast seen*:
P. L. XI. 466; *see each blissful
deity*: V. Ex. 35; *seraphim are
seen in glittering ranks*: N. O.
114; *Faith...Hope...I see ye
visibly*: C. 216; *those whom last
thou saw'st in triumph...first seen
in acts of prowess*: P. L. XI. 787,
789.

a place: P. L. I. 180; III. 552,
590; VIII. 261, 305, 317; XI. 556;
XII. 51; P. R. II. 288, 289; III.
245; IV. 44, 74, 274; *see there the
olive-grove of Academe*: P. R. IV.
244; *Persepolis...there thou seest*:
P. R. III. 285; *some foreign land
first seen*: P. L. III. 549; *he sees
...Earth*: P. L. V. 258; *in spirit
perhaps he also saw rich Mexico*:
P. L. XI. 406; *the earth no more
was seen*: P. L. XI. 745; *the world
thou hast not seen*: P. R. III. 236.

a thing or action: P. L. I. 455;
II. 191; III. 599; VI. 770, 785;
VIII. 273, 446; IX. 646, 1090; X.
336, 538, 540, 613; XI. 415; XII.
8; S. A. 243; P. 36; Il P. 86;
*Heaven is high...to see from thence
each thing on Earth*: P. L. IX.
812; *saw beneath the originals of
Nature*: P. L. VI. 510; *to see...
his wondrous works*: P. L. III.
662; *to see his glory*: P. L. VI.
792; *he who saw the Apocalypse*:
P. L. IV. 1; *the Fiend saw...all
delight*: P. L. IV. 286; *the more
I see pleasure*: P. L. IX. 119; *the
more he sees of pleasure*: P. L.
IX. 469; *marriages thou saw'st*:
P. L. XI. 684; *to see the hubbub
strange*: P. L. XII. 60; *I see a
storm*: S. A. 1061; *midnight
revels*: P. L. I. 783, 784; esp. a
star or stars: P. L. IV. 997; VII.
369, 370, 579; VIII. 128, 145; *a
star, not seen before*: P. R. I. 249.

(*b*) with two *acc.*: P. L. VIII.
463; XI. 151, 607; *who shouldst be
seen a goddess*: P. L. IX. 546; *the
Son of God was seen most glorious*:
P. L. III. 138; *nor ever saw till now
sight more detestable*: P. L. II.
744; the second *acc.* a *part.*: P. L.
I. 344; II. 66; III. 489, 510; IV.
127, 793; V. 258, 714, 715, 739;
VI. 199, 540, 648, 651; VII. 580;
IX. 369; X. 334, 536, 902; XI.
214, 638; XII. 135, 342; P. R. II.

2, 60, 267; III. 322; N. O. 213;
M. W. 35; C. 294, 471; L. 43;
S. XXIII. 1; Ariosto I. 2; *Hell
saw Heaven ruining*: P, L. VI.
867; *this fair Earth...I see producing*: P. L. IX. 720; *saw the
face of things quite changed*: P. L.
XI. 712; *saw the whole Earth
filled with violence*: P. L. XI. 887;
saw...Dalila floating this way:
S. A. 1071; *to see me girt with
friends*: S. A. 1415; *they saw me
wearied out*: C. 182; *I see one
hither speeding*: S. A. 1539; *see
him forced to things unseemly*:
S. A. 1451.

(*c*) with *acc.* and simple *inf.*:
P. L. I. 544; III. 622; XII. 422;
P. R. IV. 571; N. O. 83; A. 27;
he saw descend the Son of God: P.
L. X. 337; *see him die*: P. L. XI.
459; *thou hast seen one world begin*:
P. L. XII. 6; *I saw the Prophet do
him reverence*: P. R. I. 79; *saw
Satan fall*: P. L. X. 184; *we
shall see our hope...return*: P. R.
II. 57; *an aged man...he saw approach*: P. R. I. 319; *saw the ark
hull on the flood*: P. L. XI. 840.

(*d*) with *prep. inf.*: C. 373; *in
passive*; *be seen to save us by thy
might*: Ps. LXXX. 11.

(*e*) with indirect question introduced by *who*: P. L. VIII. 364;
XI. 561; *thou shalt see whose God
is strongest*: S. A. 1154; *to see of
whom such noise hath walked about*:
S. A. 1088; introduced by *what*:
P. L. XI. 22; P. R. III. 310; IV.
61; *see with what heat these dogs
of Hell advance*: P. L. X. 616;
*seest thou what rage transports our
Adversary*: P. L. III. 80; *see
what life the gods live there*: P. L.
V. 80; introduced by *how*: P. L.
IV. 847; XI. 70; P. R. II. 270;
V. Ex. 35; *that all may see...how
we seek peace*: P. L. VI. 559; *see
how in warlike muster they appear*:
P. R. III. 308; *see how he lies*:
S. A. 118; *have we not seen...how
thou lurk'st*: P. R. II. 182; *see
how from far the star-led wizards
haste*: N. O. 22; introduced by
where: P. L. XII. 158; *saw where
the sword of Michael smote*: P. L.
VI. 250; by *when*: P. L. III. 708;
who saw when this creation was:
P. L. V. 856.

(*f*) parenthetically: P. L. VII.
145; *as thou seest*: P. L. III. 719;

as thou saw'st : P. L. II. 796 ; XI. 471, 707 ; *if ye saw* : P. L. VIII. 277.

(*g*) of personifications ; *Night, oft see me* : Il P. 121 ; *that saw the troubled sea* : Ps. CXIV. 7.

(*h*) of the eye; *mine eye...towers and battlements it sees* : L'A. 77.

(*i*) *absol.* or *intr.* : P. L. II. 993 ; IV. 848; VIII. 43 ; IX. 592; *I saw and heard* : P. R. I. 330 ; *what if God have seen* : P. L. IX. 826.

(2) to perceive mentally, discern, understand : P. L. I. 134 ; IV. 179 ; X. 962 ; XI. 726 ; *now I see his day* : P. L. XII. 276 ; *what other way I see not* : P. R. I. 338 ; *no better way I saw* : S. A. 797.

(*b*) with two *acc.* : S. A. 1440: *when thou art seen least wise* : P. L. VIII. 578 ; *what I see excellent* : P. R. I. 381 ; *I saw thee mutable* : S. A. 793 ; *which when thou seest impartial* : S. A. 826 ; the second *acc.* a *part.* : P. L. V. 679 ; *I see thy fall determined* : P. L. V. 878.

(*c*) with *acc.* and *prep. inf.* ; *I see peace to corrupt* : P. L. XI. 783.

(*d*) with *acc.* and simple *inf.* : N. O. 171 ; *whose excellence he saw transcend his own* : P. L. V. 456 ; *they see Law can discover sin* : P. L. XII. 289.

(*e*) with clause without connective : P. L. VI. 142 ; IX. 1017; XI. 632 ; P. R. I. 94 ; S. A. 960 ; *thou seest it in thy hand* : S. A. 1105 ; *I saw he could not lose himself* : P. R. II. 97 ; *God saw the Light was good* : P. L. VII. 249 ; *I see thou know'st* : P. R. III. 7 ; *thou seest we long to know* : S. A. 1554 ; the clause introduced by *that* : P. L. VII. 309, 395 ; X. 58 ; P. R. II. 393 ; *God saw that it was good* : P. L. VII. 337, 352 ; *I see that most...had rather serve* : P. L. VI. 166.

(*f*) with indirect question ; *see how beauty is excelled* : P. L. IV. 489 ; *thou seest how subtly to detain thee I devise* : P. L. VIII. 206 ; *to see how thou couldst judge* : P. L. VIII. 448 ; *I see all offers... how slight thou valuest* : P. R. IV. 155; *ye see ... how many evils have enclosed me round* : S. A. 193 ; *saw not how ...I served* : S. A. 419 ; *how far they rove we see* : S.

XII. 13 ; *I see what I can do ... is suspect* : P. R. II. 398.

(*g*) parenthetically : P. L. VIII. 227, 399 ; *I, as thou seest, have none* : P. R. II. 318.

(3) to know to be ; *what God for you saw good* : P. L. V. 491 ; *sees good*, permits because good : C. 665 ; to recognize to be ; *with those few art eminently seen that labour up the hill of... Truth* : S. IX. 3.

(4) to go to, seek ; *shalt never see Gath more* : S. A. 1129 ; *my soul doth long ... thy courts to see* : Ps. LXXXIV. 6.

(5) to provide for ; with two *acc.; I will see thee heartened and fresh clad* : S. A. 1317.

(6) to make sure ; *to see that none thence issued forth a spy* : P. L. VIII. 233.

(7) to know by experience, feel, suffer ; *see golden days* : P. L. III. 337 ; *miseries, which Adam saw already* : P. L. X. 715 ; *cause us to see thy goodness* : Ps. LXXXV. 25 ; with indirect question or clause ; *might see how all his malice served but to bring forth infinite goodness* : P. L. I. 216 ; *into what pit fallen thou seest* : P. L. I. 91 ; parenthetically ; *now plenteous as thou seest these acts of hateful strife* : P. L. VI. 263.

(8) to live through; *twelve years he scarce had seen* : P. R. II. 96.

II. *intr.* (*a*) to have the power of sight: P. L. V. 411; VIII. 462; S. A. 75 ; *no wonder if thy perfect sight ... see far and wide* : P. L. IV. 579.

(*b*) to perceive mentally : P. L. III. 54 ; VIII. 578.

(*c*) to look ; *round about him saw* : P. L. X. 448 ; *to see to*, to look at : C. 620.

(*d*) behold ! look ! used to call attention : P. L. I. 169 ; XI. 173; XII. 590; S. A. 326 ; N. O. 237 ; C. 668.

vbl. sb. **seeing**, power of sight ; *their seeing have forgot* : S. XXII. 3.

See **All-seeing**.

Seed, *sb.* (1) that from which plants spring: P. L. VII. 310, 312 ; *fig.* of a human being ; *be thyself Man...made flesh ...of virgin seed* : P. L. III. 284 ; *I can produce a man, of female seed* : P. R. I. 151

(2) offspring, descendant; *sing.* often collectively; *mortal seed*: S. A. 1439; *Joseph's seed*: Ps. LXXX. 4; Christ or mankind as descended from Adam and Eve: P. L. x. 180, 499, 965, 999, 1031; XI. 116, 155, 873; XII. 125, 233, 395, 600; *all nations of the Earth shall in his seed be blest. By that seed is meant thy great Deliverer*: P. L. XII. 148; *our great Expectation shall be called the Seed of Woman*: P. L. XII. 379; *the Woman's Seed*: P. L. XII. 327, 543, 600; P. R. I. 64; *the seed of Eve*: P. R. I. 54; *the Promised Seed*: P. L. XII. 623; race, people; *the chosen seed*: P. L. I. 8.

(*b*) the offspring of the serpent: P. L. x. 180; of all creatures: P. L. XI. 873.

(3) whatever possesses life-giving power: P. L. XI. 26.

Seed-time, *sb.* the proper season for sowing seed: P. L. XI. 899.

Seek, *vb.* (*pres. 2d sing.* seek'st: P. L. VI. 724; VII. 639; VIII. 428; *pret.* sought; *2d sing.* sought'st: P. L. VIII. 316; *past part.* sought) I. *tr.* (1) to go in search of, endeavour to find, look for; a person or animal: P. L. IV. 272, 487, 799; VI. 295; IX. 421; XI. 328; S. A. 193, 252, 1190; C. 302; *whom thou sought'st I am*: P. L. VIII. 316; *to seek their wandering gods disguised in brutish forms*: P. L. I. 480; *to seek in Golgotha him dead*: P. L. III. 476; *sought lost Eliah*: P. R. II. 19; *the prisoner Samson here I seek*: S. A. 1308; *let us seek Death*: P. L. x. 1001; *roaming to seek their prey on Earth*: P. L. I. 382; *seeking asses*: P. R. III. 242; *sought for*: P. L. VI. 151.

a place or thing; *to seek ... some cool friendly spring*: C. 282; *what readiest path*: P. L. II. 975; *new haunt for prey*: P. L. IV. 184; *some better shroud*:. P. L. x. 1067; *that stone ... philosophers in vain so long have sought*: P. L. III. 601; *vain covertures*: P. L. x. 336; an abstract thing; *delight, cares, virtue, wisdom*, etc.: P. L. IV. 894; VIII. 187; P. R. IV. 314, 318, 325; *deliverance, temptation, trial*, etc.: P. L. II. 464; IX. 364, 380, 1140, 1141; *self-*

destruction: P. L. x. 1016; *with indirect question*; *sought where to lie hid*: P. L. IX. 75; *sought ... how to endear, and hold thee to me firmest*: S. A. 795; *absol.* : P. L. IX. 417.

(*b*) to seek as an enemy: P. L. IX. 383.

(*c*) to think out carefully or endeavour to find by thought; *seek some safer resolution*: P. L. x. 1028.

(2) to go or come to; *I seek this unfrequented place*: S. A. 16.

(3) to try to secure or obtain: P. L. VIII. 457; IX. 860, 878; XI. 532; *who sought forbidden knowledge*: P. L. XII. 278; *seeking just occasion*: S. A. 237; *occasion of new quarrels*: S. A. 1329; *when men seek most repose*: S. A. 406; *seek our own good from ourselves*: P. L. II. 252.

(*b*) to endeavour or desire to gain, solicit, ask for: P. L. III. 233; IV. 774; V. 518; IX. 511; x. 752, 762; P. R. I. 336; S. A. 522, 889; Ps. IV. 11; VII. 26; *league with you I seek*: P. L. IV. 375; *terms of peace*: P. L. II. 332; *peace and composure*: P. L. VI. 559; *reconcilement*: P. L. x. 943; *fellowship, social communication*: P. L. VIII. 390, 428; *thy gift of sleep*: P. L. IV. 735; *what love did seek*: Il P. 108; *with prep. inf.*; *let no man seek ... to be foretold what shall befall*: P. L. XI. 770.

(*c*) to win by soliciting; *wert thou sought to deeds*: P. R. III. 16.

(*d*) to ask in marriage: P. R. III. 342; *to seek in marriage*: S A. 320.

(*e*) to desire to know :. P. L. VII. 639.

(4) to aim at, strive after, pursue as an object: P. L. IX. 127; Ps. LXXXVI. 51; *the praise of men*: P. L. III. 453; VI. 376; *fame, riches, wealth, glory*: P. L. VI. 384; P. R. II. 485; III. 44, 105, 106, 110, 134; *our ruin*: P. L. IX. 274; *revenge*: P. L. VI. 151; *sought his life*: P. R. II. 77; *with prep. inf.*; *neither here seek I, no, nor in Heaven to dwell*: P. L. IX. 124.

part. adj. **sought,** carefully collected or chosen; *much persuasion sought*: S. A. 658.

(b) to strive to bring; *while he sought evil to others*: P. L. I. 215.

(5) to try, endeavour; with *prep. inf.*: P. L. I. 163; VI. 724; VII. 613; IX. 255, 1152; X. 719; XI. 148; XII. 165, 515; P. R. III. 347; IV. 143, 526; S. A. 220, 401, 837; C. 699; Ps. CXIV. 8.

II. *intr.* (a) to go or resort *to*: C. 376.

(b) *to seek*, at a loss, under the necessity of searching: P. L. VIII. 197; ignorant what to do: C. 366.

vbl. sb. **seeking**, the act of endeavouring to obtain: P. R. III. 151; by soliciting: S. A. 828.

Seem, *vb.* (*pres. 2d sing.* seem'st: P. L. IX. 371; P. R. I. 327, 348; IV. 212) *intr.* (1) to have the appearance of being, look like, appear to be; (a) the complement a *sb.*: P. L. II. 508, 590, 650, 672; III. 74, 423, 566, 567, 595, 698; IV. 290, 459, 871, 957, 990; V. 310; VI. 12, 230, 232, 244; VII. 415; VIII. 580; XI. 297, 479, 577; P. R. I. 91, 327; II. 295; III. 261; S. A. 661, 772; *Hell then seemed a refuge*: P. L. II. 167; *the Hell I suffer seems a Heaven*: P. L. IV. 78; *a globe far off it seemed*: P. L. III. 423; *he ... seemed a pillar of state*: P. L. II. 301; *substance might be called that shadow seemed, for each seemed either*: P. L. II. 669, 670; *he seems a phœnix*: P. L. V. 271; *war seemed a civil game*: P. L. VI. 667; the complement represented by *so*: P. L. VIII. 117; *so seemed ... the flying Fiend*: P. L. II. 642.

(b) the complement an *adj.* or *part.*: P. L. II. 71, 110, 747, 845; III. 84, 629; IV. 152, 291, 850; V. 617, 624; VI. 91, 615; VIII. 306, 475, 547, 550; IX. 453, 632, 919, 987, 1093, 1179; X. 146, 154, 755, 1095; XI. 10, 599, 602, 604; P. R. I. 348; II. 357; IV. 212, 441; S. A. 332, 376, 595, 703, 1035, 1420, 1443, 1464, 1504; A. 9; *so wide the opening seemed*: P. L. III. 538; *Earth, so steadfast though she seem*: P. L. VIII. 129; *what in me seems wanting*: P. R. II. 450; *their sex not equal seemed*: P. L. IV. 296; *fair it seemed*: P. L. V. 52; *so easy it seemed*: P. L. VI. 499; *seemed entering on stu-*

dious thoughts*: P. L. VIII. 39; seemed so ordering*: P. L. VIII. 376; *seem I ... possessed of happiness*: P. L. VIII. 404; *your eyes, that seem so clear*: P. L. IX. 706; *female of sex it seems*: S. A. 711; *words ... seem into tears dissolved*: S. A. 729; the *part.* omitted: P. L. XI. 614.

with *like*; *likest gods they seemed*: P. L. VI. 301; *like to pillars*: P. L. VI. 573; *like to Heaven*: P. L. VII. 329; *to Pales ... likest she seemed*: P. L. IX. 394.

(c) the complement an *inf.*: P. L. I. 777; II. 122; III. 484; V. 466; VI. 146; VIII. 19; X. 142, 531, 600, 624, 1013; P. R. II. 229; IV. 463, 494; S. A. 1545, 1749; N. O. 195; the *inf.* omitted: P. L. IX. 371; *the ark seems on ground*: P. L. XI. 850.

(d) parenthetically; *as he seemed*: P. L. IV. 565.

(2) to appear to oneself; *I seem in Heaven*: P. L. VIII. 210; *scarce half I seem to live*: S. A. 79.

(3) to appear, be seen, show oneself or itself: P. L. VII. 83; *Goodness thinks no ill where no ill seems*: P. L. III. 689; with *prep. inf.*: S. A. 249.

(4) it **seems**, it appears; used parenthetically: P. L. II. 790; IV. 513, 883; V. 69; VI. 428; IX. 769, 1170; P. R. II. 93; *as seems*: P. L. IX. 105; *as seemed*: P. L. IX. 787; P. R. I. 315; S. A. 1698; *as may seem*: P. R. IV. 355.

part. adj. **seeming**, being such in appearance only, apparent: P. L. X. 11.

vbl. sb. **seeming**, judgement: P. L. IX. 738; *mere shows of seeming pure*: P. L. IV. 316.

Seemingly, *adv.* in appearance only: P. L. V. 434.

Seemly, *adv.* (a) fitly; *sup.*: P. L. IX. 268.

(b) *comp.* with better garments; *seemlier clad*: P. R. II. 299.

Seer, *sb.* one who foresees and foretells future events, prophet: P. R. III. 15; applied to the angel Michael: P. L. XII. 553.

Seize, *vb.* (1) *tr.* (a) to invest with possession; *fig.*, *sweet rest seize thee evermore*: M. W. 50.

(b) to take possession of by force: Ps. LXXXIII. 46; *the seat*

of Deity ... he trusted to have seized:
P. L. VII. 143; *they seize the
sceptre*: P. L. XII. 356; *birthright
seized by younger Saturn*: P. L.
I. 511; *to seize the widowed whore
Plurality*: F. of C. 3; *to get by
force*; *to seize possession of the
Garden*: P. L. XI. 221.

(c) to lay sudden and forcible
hold of, catch, grasp: P. L. IV.
407, 796; XI. 669; C. 653; *thy
gentle hand seized mine*: P. L. IV.
489; *her hand he seized*: P. L.
IX. 1037; *fig.*, *gentle sleep ... with
soft oppression seized my drowsed
sense*: P. L. VIII. 288.

(d) to come upon with sudden
and powerful effect; *amazement
seized*: P. L. II. 758; VI. 198;
*astonishment, horror, admiration,
envy*, etc.: P. L. I. 317; II. 432,
703; III. 271, 552, 553; VI. 647;
to affect, influence; *our sin sore
doth begin his infancy to seize*:
Cir. 14.

(e) to come or happen upon
suddenly; *whose chance on these
defenceless doors may seize*: S.
VIII. 2.

(2) *intr.* (a) to lay hold *on*; *he
shall ... be .. seized on by force*: P.
L. XII. 412.

(b) to come *on*; *woe, which on
our dearest Lord did seize*: P. 10.

Seizure, *sb.* the thing taken possession of: P. L. XI. 254.

Seldom, *adj.* rarely, not often: P.
L. IX. 423; X. 901; P. R. I. 345,
436; IV. 507; S. XI. 4.

Select, (1) *adj.* chosen in preference
to others, choice: P. L. XI. 646;
a plant select and sacred: S. A.
363; *sup.*, *constellations, on that
hour shed their selectest influence*:
P. L. VIII. 513.

(2) *vb. tr.* to make choice of;
*one peculiar nation to select from
all the rest*: P. L. XII. 111.

part. adj. **select,** chosen; *them
of man and beast select for life*:
P. L. XI. 823.

Seleucia, *sb.* a city of Babylonia near
the river Tigris and about forty
miles northeast of Babylon: P. L.
IV. 212; P. R. III. 291.

Self, *sb.* (one's) own being or person; *I now see .. my Self before
me*: P. L. VIII. 495; *thy or my
other self*: P. L. VIII. 450; X.
128; *thy greedy self*: T. 10;
Delia's self: P. L. IX. 388; Or-

pheus' self: L'A. 145; *Wisdom's
self*: C. 375.

Self-balanced, *adj.* balanced by its
own weight, poised by virtue of
its nature; *Earth, self-balanced,
on her centre hung*: P. L. VII.
242.

Self-begot, *adj.* begot by one's own
power: P. L. V. 860.

Self-begotten, *adj.* same as the preceding; *that self-begotten bird*:
S. A. 1699.

Self-condemning, *pres. part.* declaring or admitting oneself guilty:
P. L. IX. 1188.

Self-consumed, *adj.* consumed by
itself; *evil ... self-consumed*: C.
597.

Self-deceived, *adj.* deluded by one's
opinion of one's own power: P. R.
IV. 7.

Self-delusion, *sb.* the deluding of
oneself: C. 365.

Self-depraved, *adj.* corrupted by
oneself: P. L. III. 130.

Self-destruction, *sb.* the destroying
of oneself: P. L. X. 1016.

Self-displeased, *adj.* offended at
oneself: S. A. 514.

Self-esteem, *sb.* a good opinion of
oneself: P. L. VIII. 572.

Self-fed, *adj.* sustained by preying
upon itself; *evil ... self-fed*: C.
597.

Self-killed, *adj.* killed by oneself:
S. A. 1664.

Self-knowing, *adj.* possessing self-
consciousness: P. L. VII. 510.

Self-left, *adj.* left to itself: P. L.
XI. 93.

Self-lost, *past part.* voluntarily
parted with: P. L. VII. 154.

Self-love, *sb.* love of oneself: S. A.
1031.

Self-offence, *sb.* wrong done to oneself: S. A. 515.

Self-open, *vb. intr.* to open of its
own power and without aid: P.
L. V. 254.

Self-preservation, *sb.* preservation
of oneself: S. A. 505.

Self-raised, *past part.* or *adj.* lifted
up by one's own power and with-
out aid from another: P. L. I.
634; created or brought into
being by one's own power: P. L.
V. 860.

Self-rigorous, *adj.* severe or stern
with oneself: S. A. 513.

Self-rolled, *adj.* coiled on itself: P.
L. IX. 183.

Self-same, *adj.* identical, the very same : P. L. VI. 87 ; X. 315 ; XI. 203 ; L. 23.

Self-satisfying, *adj.* giving satisfaction to oneself : S. A. 306.

Self-severe, *adj.* judging oneself severely : S. A. 827.

Self-tempted, *adj.* enticed by oneself to evil : P. L. III. 130.

Self-violence, *sb.* violence inflicted upon oneself : S. A. 1584.

Sell, *vb. tr.* to betray for a price ; *thou alone could ... sell me* : S. A. 940.

Semblance, *sb.* (*a*) countenance, aspect, form : P. L. IX. 607 ; S. II. 5.

(*b*) appearance ; *words, that bore semblance of worth* : P. L. I. 529.

Semele, *sb.* the daughter of Cadmus, king of Thebes, and the mother of Dionysius by Zeus : P. R. II. 187.

Sennaar (Sénnaár), *sb.* Shinar ; *the plain of Sennaar,* the tract of country through which flow the Euphrates and the Tigris, known in later times as Babylonia (spelled Senaar in Vulg.) : P. L. III. 467.

Senate, *sb.* the legislative body of Rome : Hor. Epist. 2 ; the seventy men of the elders of Israel associated with Moses in the government ; *there they shall ...their great Senate choose through the twelve tribes* : P. L. XII. 225.

Senate-house, *sb.* the house in which a senate meets : C. 389.

Senator, *sb.* a member of a senate : S. XVII. 2.

Send, *vb,* (*pret.* and *past part.* sent) I. *tr.* (1) to cause to go from one place to another : P. L. IV. 170 ; P. R. IV. 632 ; S. A. 1160 ; with *advs.* ; *send thee back* : P. L. IX. 410 ; *send thee* or *him from the Garden forth* : P. L. XI. 97, 261 ; *send them forth* : P. L. XI. 117 ; *her branches . down to the sea she sent* : Ps. LXXX. 46.

(*b*) to commission or authorize to go and act : P. L. I. 585 ; II. 402, 415 ; III. 324 ; IV. 842 ; VIII. 647 ; X. 55, 59, 403, 429 ; XI. 356 ; XII. 498 ; P. R. II. 50 ; III. 107 ; IV. 131 ; S. A. 999, 1214 ; C. 219, 972 ; *what Heaven's Lord had powerfullest to send against us* : P. L. VI. 425 ; *us he sends upon*

his high behests for state : P. L. VIII. 238 ; *both Judge and Saviour sent* : P. L. X. 209 ; *he to his own a Comforter will send* : P. L. XII. 486 ; *God hath now sent his living Oracle ... and sends his Spirit of Truth* : P. R. I. 460, 462 ; *Gabriel ...I sent thee to the Virgin pure* : P. R. I. 134 ; *a great Prophet ... is sent harbinger* : P. R. I. 71 ; *Moses and Aaron sent from God* : P. L. XII. 170 ; *among them he a spirit of phrensy sent* : S. A. 1675 ; with *advs. ; my overshadowing Spirit and might with thee I send along* : P. L. VII. 166 ; with *down* : P. L. VII. 72 ; N. O. 46 ; with *forth* : P. R. I. 158 ; *God of Israel, send thy Messiah forth* : P. R. II. 43 ; *Hell shall ... send forth all her kings* : P. L. IV. 383 ; *a dove, sent forth* : P. L. XI. 857 ; with *thither* : P. L. VII. 572 ; with *acc.* and *dat. ; send thee the Angel of thy birth* : S. A. 1431.

(*c*) to cause to go out, compel to leave : N. O. 186.

(2) to cause to be conveyed or transmitted : P. L. VI. 621 ; *what a present thou to God hast sent* : D. F. I. 74 ; with *acc.* and *dat.* : W. W. 59 ; to cause to be borne along ; *his gory visage down the stream was sent* : L. 62.

(3) to cast, hurl ; *he ... was headlong sent* : P. L. I. 750 ; *thunders, which he sent before him* : P. L. VI. 836 ; with *forth* : P. L. VI. 486.

(4) to emit ; (*a*) to give forth or throw out *light, heat* : P. L. VIII. 141 ; X. 1077.

(*b*) to breathe forth ; *sighs ... sent from hearts contrite* : P. L. X. 1091, 1103 ; *all things that breathe ... send up silent praise to the Creator* : P. L. IX. 195.

(*c*) to give forth ; *Cherubic songs ... aërial music send* : P. L. V. 548.

(*d*) to cause to rise ; *the hills ... vapour and exhalation sent up* : P. L. XI. 742.

(5) to cause to come ; (*a*) to inflict : P. L. X. 557 ; P. R. IV. 491 ; Ps. LXXXVIII. 60.

(*b*) to give, grant, bestow : P. L. XII. 612 ; *sweet music ... sent by some Spirit to mortals good* : Il P. 153 ; *when God sends a cheerful hour* : S. XXI. 14.

II. *intr.* **send for**, to request by message to come : S. A. 1730.

part. absol. the person dispatched ; *the sent* : P. L. IV. 852 ; *O sent from Heaven* : P. L. XII. 270.

vbl. sb. **sending**, the act of dispatching a messenger : S. A. 1394.

See **Up·send.**

Sender, *sb.* one who dispatches another : P. L. IV. 852.

Seneschal, *sb.* the officer who had the superintendence of ceremonies and feasts, the house-steward : P. L. IX. 38.

Senir, *sb.* the Amorite name of the whole or a part of the Hermon range of mountains. "Mount Hermon ; a ledge of Hills, which beginning at the East point of the Anti-Libanus, bend directly south : in different places, and by several Nations called by divers names ... by the Amorites, Samir." "Trachonitis is that mountainous and hilly Country, which beginning at the borders of the Ammonites, where the Hills are called the Mountains of Gilead ; extendeth itself Northwards as far as Libanus : the Hills in those parts being by the Jews called Galeed, Syrion, and Hermon." Heylyn, *Cos.* 1657, pp. 706, 716, cf. Ortelius, *Theatrum Orbis Terrarum*, 1624, map at page III. : P. L. XII. 146.

Sense, *sb.* (*a*) one of the five organs by which external objects are perceived : P. L. XI. 265, 540 ; N. O. 127 ; *the five watchful senses* : P. L. V. 104 ; *the porch and inlet of each sense* : C. 839 ; *sight ... other senses* : S. A. 916 ; the sense of touch : P. L. VIII. 579 ; IX. 1031 ; of taste : P. L. IX. 580, 987 ; of sight : P. L. XII. 10 ; Il P. 14 ; *sing. collect.* : P. L. VIII. 289, 456, 609 ; XI. 469 ; A. 62 ; *every lower faculty of sense, whereby they hear, see, smell, touch, taste* : P. L. V. 411 ; *to all delight of human sense exposed ... Nature's whole wealth* : P. L. IV. 206 ; *for Eloquence the Soul, Song charms the Sense* : P. L. II. 556 ; *my dwelling haply may not please ... your sense* : P. L. IV. 379 ; *they in pleasing slumber lulled the sense* : C. 260 ; *to invite the unwary sense* : C. 538.

(*b*) sense-perception or sensation ; *devoid of sense and motion* : P. L. II. 151 ; *give both life and sense* : P. L. V. 485 ; *creatures animate with gradual life of growth, sense, reason* : P. L. IX. 113 ; *say that death be not one stroke ... bereaving sense* : P. L. X. 810 ; *dead things with inbreathed sense able to pierce* : S. M. 4 ; *void of corporal sense* : S. A. 616.

(*c*) perception by the mind, apprehension, feeling : P. L. IX. 315 ; *sense of new joy* : P. L. III. 137 ; *sense of pain* or *of pleasure* : P. L. VI. 394, 459 ; *of endless woes* : P. L. X. 754 ; *of injured merit* : P. L. I. 98 ; *of Heaven's desertion* : S. A. 632.

(*d*) mental power, mind, understanding : P. L. III. 188 ; V. 565 ; VIII. 119 ; P. R. I. 382 ; S. A. 1556 ; *thenceforth endued with human voice and human sense* : P. L. IX. 871 ; *his sense depraved to folly* : S. A. 1042 ; *to sense reprobate* : S. A. 1685 ; *what surmounts the reach of human sense* : P. L. V. 572 ; *all sense*, having the special faculty of thinking and feeling in all parts of the body : P. L. VI. 351.

(*e*) the consciousness of brutes : P. L. IX. 96, 188.

(*f*) thought, meaning, import : P. L. IX. 554 ; P. R. I. 435 ; IV. 296, 517 ; S. A. 176.

Senseless, *adj.* lacking in reason and judgement : S. XII. 9.

Sensible, *sb.* sensibility ; *remove the sensible of pain* : P. L. II. 278.

Sensibly, *adv.* keenly, painfully : S. A. 913.

Sensual, *adj.* (*a*) licentious ; *sup.* : P. R. II. 151.

(*b*) pertaining to or characterized by licentiousness ; *sensual appetite, folly* : P. L. IX. 1129 ; C. 975 ; *to roll with pleasure in a sensual sty* : C. 77.

Sensuality, *sb.* the free indulgence in licentious pleasures : C. 474.

Sentence, (1) *sb.* (*a*) a way of thinking, opinion, decision, judgement : P. L. II. 291 ; IX. 88 ; *my sentence is for open war* : P. L. II. 51.

(*b*) a judicial decision, judgement, verdict, decree : P. L. II. 208 ; pronounced by God or Christ : P. L. III. 145, 332 ; X. 805, 934, 1031 ; XI. 109 ; *to the*

Woman thus his sentence turned : P. L. x. 192 ; *Death, then due by sentence :* P. L. xi. 253 ; *but that the mortal sentence pass on his transgression :* P. L. x. 48 ; *mortality, my sentence :* P. L. x. 776.

(*c*) axiom, maxim : S. A. 1369.

(**2**) *vb. tr.* to pass judgement on, condemn : P. L. x. 97.

Sententious, *adj.* full of meaning, pithy, terse : P. R. iv. 264.

Sentery, *sb.* a sentry, watch, guard : P. L. ii. 412.

Seon, *sb.* Sihon, a king of the Amorites (spelled Sehon in Vulg.) : P. L. i. 409 ; Ps. cxxxvi. 65.

Separate, (**1**) *part.* or *adj.* (*a*) divided from the rest, parted, removed : P. L. vi. 743.

(*b*) by one's self, apart from others : P. L. ix. 422, 424.

(*c*) set apart for a certain purpose, dedicated ; *a person separate to God :* S. A. 31.

(**2**) *vb. tr.* to sever, part, disunite : P. L. ix. 970 ; *Death from sin no power can separate :* P. L. x. 251.

Septentrion, *adj.* northern : P. R. iv. 31.

Sepulchral, *adj.* used as a tomb : P. 43.

Sepulchre (sepúlchre : W. S. 15), (**1**) *sb.* tomb, grave : C. 471 ; *myself my sepulchre, a moving grave :* S. A. 102.

(**2**) *vb. tr.* to entomb, inter : W. S. 15.

Sequel, *sb.* that which follows a course of action, consequence : P. L. iv. 1003 ; x. 334.

Sequent, *adj.* succeeding to the throne ; *a sequent king :* P. L. xii. 165.

Sequestered, *part. adj.* secluded, retired : P. L. iv. 706 ; C. 500.

Seraph, *sb.* (*pl.* seraphim ; *sing.* for *pl.* : P. L. i. 324 ; vii. 198) the highest of the nine orders of angels, or a member of this order : P. L. i. 324 ; vi. 579 ; vii. 113 ; *Cherub and Seraph, Potentates and Thrones :* P. L. vii. 198 ; Uriel : P. L. iii. 667 ; Raphael : P. L. v. 277 ; Abdiel : P. L. v. 875, 896 ; *pl.* : P. L. ii. 750 ; v. 749, 804 ; vi. 604, 841 ; *a globe of fiery Seraphim :* P. L. ii. 512 ; *brightest* or *bright :* P. L. iii. 381 ; S. M. 10 ; *embattled, fighting,*

sworded : P. L. i. 129 ; vi. 249 ; N. O. 113.

Seraphic, *adj.* (*a*) who are seraphim ; *the great Seraphic Lords :* P. L. i. 794.

(*b*) belonging to seraphim : P. L. i. 539.

Serapis, *sb.* the Apis, or Sacred Bull of Egypt, which after death became an Osiris Apis (*Gr.* Serapis), was regarded as united with or almost equal to Osiris, and was worshipped as the god of the lower world. The temples in which the Apis was buried were called Serapeum : P. L. i. 720.

Serbonian, *adj.* that *Serbonian bog,* Lake Serbonis on the northeast coast of Lower Egypt, separated from the sea by only a strip of sand : P. L. ii. 593.

Sere, *adj.* dry, withered : P. L. x. 1071 ; L. 2 ; Ps. ii. 27.

Serenate, *sb.* a song sung by a lover to his lady : P. L. iv. 769.

Serene, (sérene : C. 4), *adj.* (*a*) clear, fair, calm ; *serene air :* C. 4.

(*b*) clear, transparent : P. L. iii. 25. *See* **Drop.**

(*c*) calm, tranquil ; *the Father, without cloud, serene :* P. L. xi. 45 ; *the Son...ineffable, serene :* P. L. v. 734 ; *angel serene :* P. L. viii. 181 ; used of the countenance : P. L. v. 123 ; *with front serene :* P. L. vii. 509 ; of the countenance of God : P. L. x. 1094.

Sericana, *sb.* the geography of *Sericana* is not clear ; possibly the following explains its position. "Serica hath on the East some part of China ; on the South, India Extra Gangem, and some part of the Countrey then inhabited by the Antient Sina : on the North, Altay : on the West, the mountains of Imaus." Heylyn *Cos.* 1657, pp. 854, 855 : P. L. iii. 438.

Serious, (**1**) *adj.* important, momentous, grave : C. 787.

(**2**) *adv.* earnestly, intently : P. R. i. 203.

Serpent, (**1**) *adj.* (*a*) of or composed of serpents ; *serpent kind :* P. L. vii. 482 ; ix. 504.

(*b*) like those of a serpent ; *serpent wings :* S. xv. 8 ; *serpent wiles :* P. R. iii. 5.

(c) moving as a serpent, serpentine, winding :. P. L. VII. 302.

(2) *sb.* (a) a reptile of the order *Ophidia*; *the fiery serpent*: P. R. I. 312 ; those into which the angels of hell were changed : P. L. X. 514, 520, 539 ; the serpent in the Garden of Eden into which Satan entered : P. L. IX. 161, 182, 764, 867, 930, 1150; X. 3, 84, 174, 495, 879, 927, 1034 ; *the serpent sly* : P. L. IV. 347; *subtlest beast of all the field* : P. L. VII. 495 ; IX. 86, 560 ; *the Serpent me beguiled* : P. L. X. 162; *the Fiend, mere serpent in appearance* : P.L. IX. 413 : *the Enemy of Mankind, enclosed in serpent* : P. L. IX. 495; *the accused serpent* : P. L. X. 165; in direct address : P. L. IX. 560, 615, 647 ; the lower part of the body of Sin : P. L. II. 652.

(b) applied to persons as full of treachery ; applied to Satan : P. L. IX. 455, 785 ; XII. 150, 234, 383 ; *infernal Serpent* : P. L. I. 34 ; P. R. IV. 618 ; *the old Serpent* : P. R. II. 147 ; *the adversary Serpent* : P. L. XII. 312 ; *the Serpent, Prince of Air* : P. L. XII. 454 ; *thy seed shall bruise the Serpent's head* : P. L. X. 1032 ; *the Serpent, whom they* (the Heathen) *called Ophion* : P. L. X. 580; applied to Eve : P. L. X. 867 ; to Dalila : S. A. 997.

Serpentine, *adj.* like that of a serpent : P. L. X. 870.

Serpent-tongue, *sb.* the tongue of a serpent : P. L. IX. 529.

Serraliona, *sb.* Sierra Leone, the country on the west coast of Africa : P. L. X. 703.

Serried, *part. adj.* closely compacted or locked together ; *serried shields in thick array* : P. L. I. 548 ; *their serried files* : P. L. VI. 599.

Servant, *sb.* (a) one who is subject to the commands of another : P. L. X. 214; *Samson as a public servant* : S. A. 1615 ; *servant of servants* : P. L. XII. 104.

(b) one who gives himself up wholly to the will of God or Christ : S. A. 1755 ; Ps. LXXXVI. 7, 11, 59; CXXXVI. 73; *as when he washed his servants' feet* : P. L. X. 215 ; *my servant Job* : P. R. III. 67; with blending of (a) and (b) ; *Servant*

of God : P. L. VI. 29 ; one who dedicates himself to Virtue ; *unmindful of the crown that Virtue gives ...to her true servants* : C. 10. *See* **Fellow-servant.**

Serve, *vb.* (*pres. 2d sing.* serv'st : S. A. 1363) I. *tr.* (1) to be in the employment and under the command of : A. 105 ; C. 725.

(2) to be in subjection to the will of, obey the commands of : P. L. VI. 179, 180 ; *fig., in the soul are many lesser faculties that serve Reason as chief* : P. L. v. 101.

(b) to conform to the law and obey the commands of (God or Christ) : P. L. III. 680 ; IV. 943 ; V. 538; VI. 175, 183; VIII. 168 ; X. 767 ; P. R. IV. 177 ; S. A. 585; S. XIX. 5, 11 ; *hearts ... whether they serve willing or no* : P. L. V. 532 ; *who serve idols with God* : P. R. III. 432.

(c) to be in bondage to ; used of nations : P. R. III. 431 ; S. A. 267.

(d) to take as a master or guide, follow ; *the Muse or Love...both them I serve, and of their train am I* : S. I. 14.

(3) to be in subjection to the dictates of or be controlled by *necessity, appetite, passions* : P. L. III. 110; XI. 517, 518 ; P. R. II. 472.

(4) to minister to : P. L. VIII. 87 ; *Earth ... served by more noble than herself* : P. L. VIII. 34.

(5) to wait or attend on for the purpose of serving ; *served by Angels numberless thy daily train*: P. L. IX. 547.

(6) to bring and arrange on the table ; *feast served up in hall* : P. L. IX. 38 ; *fig.* : V. Ex. 14.

(7) to promote the interests of, aid : S. A. 1363 ; *wilt thou then serve the Philistines* : S. A. 577 ; *wherein serve my nation* : S. A. 564 ; *to what may serve his glory best* : S. A. 1429.

(8) to answer the requirements of : P. L. IX. 85 ; *served best his ends* : P. L. IV. 398.

II. *intr.* (1) to be a servant : M. W. 46.

(2) to be in subjection to another : S.A. 419.

(b) to obey the commands or do the will of God or Christ : P. L. v. 681, 802 ; *most ... had rather* serve: P. L. VI. 166; *better to reign in Hell than serve in Heaven*: P. L. I. 263.

(*c*) to be in bondage to another nation: P. R. III. 375, 378, 379; S. A. 240, 1216.

(3) to answer the purpose, avail, suffice: P. L. V. 322; X. 727; *sticks to gather, which might serve against a winter's day*: P. R. I. 316; with *prep. inf.*: P. L. I. 64, 217; II. 385, 999; VI. 440, 599; VII. 115, 614; IX. 1092; XI. 60, 881; S. A. 743; C. 750; with *for*; *for distinction serve of hierarchies, of orders, and degrees*: P. L. V. 590.

Service, *sb.* (*a*) the work of a slave: S. A. 1163.

(*b*) labour performed for another, office or duty done or required: P. L. IV. 420; P. R. I. 427; S. A. 686; *to use him further in some great service*: S. A. 1499; *I had rather ... thy service in some graver subject use*: V. Ex. 30; *do him mightier service as his thralls*: P. L. I. 149; *nor was his service hard*: P. L. IV. 45; *our voluntary service he requires*: P. L. V. 529; *owe not all creatures ... to thee duty and service*: P. R. II. 326; *with all helpful service will comply*: A. 38.

(*c*) the place or position of a servant; *subjected to his service Angel-wings*: P. L. IX. 155.

(*d*) a body of servants, servants collectively; *a swain that to the service of this house belongs*: C. 85.

(*e*) religious worship: Il P. 163; *affright the flamens at their service*: N. O. 244.

Serviceable, *adj.* (*a*) capable of rendering service, useful: P. R. I. 421.

(*b*) ready or prepared for service; *bright harnessed Angels sit in order serviceable*: N. O. 244.

Servile, *adj.* (*a*) proper for a slave; *servile toil*: S. A. 5; *the draff of servile food*: S. A. 574; *punishment*: S. A. 413.

(*b*) characteristic or worthy of a slave; *servile mind* or *minds*: S. A. 412, 1213; *yoke*: P. R. II. 102; *fear*: P. L. XII. 305: *offerings, pomp*: P. L. II. 246, 257.

Servilely, *adv.* slavishly, cringingly: P. L. IV. 959.

Servility, *sb.* the condition of a slave, slavery: P. L. VI. 169.

Servitude, *sb.* (1) the state of subjection to a master, slavery: S. A. 416; *this is servitude—to serve the unwise*: P. L. VI. 178; *corporal servitude*: S. A. 1336; subjection to God: P. L. VI. 175; *in one night freed from servitude inglorious well nigh half the Angelic Name*: P. L. IX. 141.

(*b*) national subjection: P. L. XII. 220; P. R. III. 381; *to free thy country from her heathen servitude*: P. R. III. 176; *nations ... by their vices brought to servitude*: S. A. 269.

(*c*) slavery to the passions: P. L. XII. 89.

(2) servants collectively: P. L. XII. 132.

Session, *sb.* the sitting of a council or court: P. L. II. 514; the last judgement; *at the World's last session*: N. O. 163.

Set, *vb.* (*pret.* and *past part.* set) I. *tr.* (1) to cause to sit or stand *on*: P. L. XI. 382; P. R. IV. 549; *Angels ... set him down on a green bank*: P. R. IV. 586; *are set* = sit: L'A. 84.

(2) to put, place, fix: Ps. LXXXVIII. 26; *I set my printless feet o'er the cowslip's velvet head*: C. 897; *the mark of fool set on his front*: S. A. 496; *in derision sets upon their tongues a various spirit*: P. L. XII. 52.

(*b*) to place *before* (a person); *Heaven is as the book of God before thee set*: P. L. VIII. 67; *if food were now before thee set*: P. R. II. 320; *set before him spread a table of celestial food*: P. R. IV. 587; to place before the eyes; *set women in his eye*: P. R. II. 153; *before mine eyes thou hast set ... much policy*: P. R. III. 390.

(*c*) to place *before* to be done; *what was set before him ... he still performed*: S. A. 1624.

(*d*) to put out for use; *his cream-bowl duly set*: L'A. 106.

(*e*) to place in position (a ladder); *fig., the scale of Nature set from centre to circumference*: P. L. V. 509.

(*f*) to fix in position: P. L. VII. 376; *made the Stars and set them in the firmament*: P. L. VII. 349: *while the Creator great his constellations set*: N. O. 121 ; *the moon and stars, which thou ... hast set in the pure firmament*: Ps. VIII. 10 ; *will therein set his triple-coloured bow*: P. L. XI. 896.

(*g*) to erect, build ; *built like a temple, where pilasters round were set*: P. L. I. 714.

(*h*) to exalt, magnify ; *above the heavens thy praise is set*: Ps. VIII. 3 ; *strove to set her beauty's praise above the Sea-Nymphs*: Il P. 20 ; *Dante shall give Fame leave to set thee higher than his Casella*: S. XIII. 12.

(**3**) to place or establish (a person) in some specified relation to others : P. L. VIII. 382 ; *one step higher would set me highest*: P. L. IV. 51 : *they weened ... on his throne to set the envier of his state*: P. L. VI. 89 ; *which would have set thee on David's throne*: P. R. IV. 378 ; *us ... set over all his creatures*: P. L. IX. 941 ; *the place wherein God set thee above her*: P. L. X. 149.

(*b*) *refl.* to establish oneself : P. L. I. 39.

(**4**) to bring or place before the mind : P. L. XI. 813 ; Ps. V. 24 ; LXXXVI. 52 ; as an opportunity or duty ; *all his great work before him set*: P. R. II. 112; with *prep. inf.*; *this offer sets before thee to deliver*: P. R. III. 380 ; *God hath set before us to return thee home*: S. A. 517.

(**5**) to make or cause to be ; with two *acc.*: P. L. XI. 825 ; *set*, or *sets them, thee, all*, etc. *free*: P. L. II. 822 ; P. R. III. 284 ; S. A. 317, 1412 ; L'A. 149 ; S. XII. 10 ; F. of C. 6 ; Ps. LXXXI. 22; LXXXVI. 47 ; *Death, who sets all free*: S. A. 1572 ; with *acc.* and *adv.* or *phrase*: P. L. V. 357 ; *to set the hearts of men on fire*: D. F. I. 62; *set to work millions of spinning worms*: C. 715 ; *set at large*: Ps. IV. 5 ; *set in order*: P. L. VI. 522.

(**6**) to appoint, determine, ordain : P. L. I. 72; III. 587; *bounds were set to darkness*: P. L. III. 538 ; *to the winds they set their corners*: P. L. X. 664 ; *ransom set*: P. L. III. 221 ; *of time*: P. R. IV. 393 ; *when is not set*: P. L. X. 499 ; *to ordain to be*; *God hath set labour and rest ... to men successive*: P. L. IV. 612.

(**7**) to arrange, make ready ; *tables are set*: P. L. V. 632.

(**8**) to plant: P. L. V. 63 ; Ps. LXXX. 62 ; *the tree ... which I have set ... amid the garden* : P. L. VIII. 324.

(**9**) to adorn as with precious stones : C. 893 ; *their bodies ... were set with eyes*: P. L. VI. 755.

(**10**) to direct or make intent ; *all my mind was set serious to learn*: P. R. I. 202 ; with *on*: P. L. XI. 288 ; P. R. II. 207 ; S. A. 1201 ; *God ... hath set ... on Man his equal love*: P. L. VIII. 227 ; *some ... set on revenge and spite*: S. A. 1462; *they only set on play and sport*: S. A. 1679 ; *thy heart is set on high designs*: P. R. II. 410.

(**11**) to attune ; *set my harp to notes of saddest woe*: P. 9.

II. *intr.* to decline toward and pass below the horizon : P. L. IV. 664 ; VII. 385, 583 ; VIII. 632.

In combination with other words ; (*a*) **set at naught**, to disregard, despise: C. 444.

(*b*) **set behind**, to consider of less importance: S. A. 1375.

(*c*) **set as high esteem on**, to value as highly : P. R. IV. 160.

(*d*) **set foot in**, to enter : P. R. IV. 610.

(*e*) **set forth**, to arrange in order and send out : P. L. VII. 427 ; to represent or make clear to the mind; *to set forth great things by small*: P. L. VI. 310.

(*f*) **set off**, to make more powerful or effective : C. 801 ; to increase the beauty of : P. L. V. 43 ; (?) L. 80.

(*g*) **set on**, to incite to action : P. L. II. 804.

(*h*) **set out**, to begin a journey : P. L. VIII. 111.

(*i*) **set to sale**, to make merchandise of : S. A. 1466.

(*j*) **set upon**, to attack : S. A. 255.

(*k*) **set up**, to establish : P. L. XII. 247.

part. adj. **setting**, passing below the horizon ; *the setting sun* : P. L. I. 744 ; IV. 540.

Setia, *sb.* a city in Latium, Italy, noted for its wine : P. R. IV. 117.

Settle, *vb.* (**1**) *tr.* (*a*) to establish in a permanent abode ; *my afflicted Powers to settle here on Earth* : P. L. IV. 940.

(b) to arrange or conclude *peace*:
S. XVII. 5.

(2) *intr.* (*a*) to be firmly implanted or fixed; *settled in his
face I see sad resolution*: P. L. VI.
540.

(b) to sink to the bottom as
dregs; *evil ... gathered like scum,
and settled to itself*: C. 595.

part. adj. **settled,** tranquil,
quiet: P. L. II. 279.

vbl. sb. pl. **settlings,** sediment,
dregs: C. 810.

Seven, *adj.* six and one: P. L. IX.
93; XII. 158, 255; P. R. IV. 35;
the planets seven: P. L. III. 481;
the seven Atlantic Sisters: P. L.
X. 673; *those seven Spirits that
stand in sight of God's high throne*:
P. L. III. 654; *in one day or
seven*: S. A. 1017.

absol. (*a*) the seven archangels:
P. L. III. 648.

(b) a group of animals seven in
number: P. L. XI. 735.

Sevenfold, *adj.* seven times as great:
P. L. II. 171; IV. 914.

Seventh, *adj.* the ordinal of seven:
P. L. VII. 581, 592.

absol. a thing occupying the
seventh place; *seventh to these,
the planet Earth*: P. L. VIII. 128;
a person of the seventh generation: P. L. XI. 700.

Seven-times-folded, *adj.* made of
seven layers: S. A. 1122.

Seven-times-wedded, *adj.* having
been married seven times: P. L.
V. 223.

Seventy, *adj.* seven times ten: P.
L. XII. 345.

Sever, *vb.* (1) *tr.* (*a*) to separate or
part *from*: S. XIV. 4; Ps.
LXXXVIII. 70.

(b) to divide; *our state cannot
be severed; we are one, one flesh*:
P. L. IX. 958.

(c) to set apart from the rest:
P. L. I. 704.

(d) to determine the limits of,
demarcate; *both spiritual power
and civil ... what severs each*: S.
XVII. 11.

(2) *intr.* to go away or part
from: P. L. IX. 252; *if from me
thou sever not*: P. L. IX. 366.

part. adj. **severed,** from whom
one is parted; *how to regain my
severed company*: C. 274.

Several, *adj.* (*a*) separated, apart:
P. L. V. 697.

(b) separate, individual, particular: P. L. II. 901; v. 477; C.
25; *wandering, each his several
way*: P. L. II. 523; *swift to their
several quarters hasted then the
cumbrous elements*: P. L. III. 714;
the rest to several place disparted:
P. L. VII. 240; *the Creator ... gave
them several charge*: P. L. X. 650;
*each fettered ghost slips to his several
grave*: N. O. 234.

(c) different, distinct; *three
several ways*: P. L. X. 323; *they
both betook them several ways*: P.
L. X. 610.

(d) consisting of an indefinite
number, more than one: P. L.
VIII. 131; P. R. III. 276.

Severe, *adj.* (*a*) serious, grave,
austere; *the Stoic severe*: P. R.
IV. 280; *sanctitude severe and
pure*: P. L. IV. 293, 294; *sup.*,
to soften and tame severest temper:
P. R. II. 164.

(b) harsh, stern, relentless: P.
L. IX. 1169; *Adam severe*: P. L.
IX. 1144; *his grave rebuke, severe
in youthful beauty*: P. L. IV. 845;
in a flame of zeal severe: P. L. V.
807; *custody, doom severe*: P. L.
II. 333; III. 224; used of God:
P. L. X. 1095; Ps. VII. 43; *his
countenance too severe to be beheld*:
P. L. VI. 825; or *adv.*; *then severe
speak to them*: Ps. II. 9.

(c) causing great pain; *these
piercing fires as soft as now severe*:
P. L. II. 276.

See **Self-severe.**

Severely, *adv.* rigorously, sternly:
S. A. 788.

Severity, *sb.* austerity; *personified*:
C. 109.

Severn, *sb.* the river of western
England; *the smooth Severn*: C.
825; *Severn swift*: V. Ex. 96.

Sew, *vb. tr.* to fasten together as by
a thread: P. L. IX. 1112; *leaves,
together sewed*: P. L. IX. 1095.

Sewer, *sb.* the servant who marched
in before the meats, arranged the
dishes on the table, and removed
them after the feast: P. L. IX.
38.

Sewer, *sb.* a drain to carry off water
and waste matter: P. L. IX. 446.

Sex, *sb.* (*a*) the character of being
either male or female; in beasts:
P. L. IX. 574; in man: P. L. IV.
296; VIII. 471; *spirits ... can either
sex assume*: P. L. I. 424; *female*

of sex: S. A. 711; *to add what wants in female sex*: P. L. IX. 822; women in general; *this, her, our, their sex*: P. L. X. 898; P. R. III. 341; S. A. 774, 1026.

fig., *Suns ... Moons ... communicating male and female light, which two great sexes animate the World*: P. L. VIII. 151.

(*b*) nature or character as an accompaniment of sex; *thy frailty and infirmer sex*: P. L. X. 956.

Sextile, *sb.* the aspect of two planets at a distance of sixty degrees from each other: P. L. X. 659.

Shackle, *sb.*, in the *pl.* manacles, fetters: S. A. 1326.

Shade, I. *sb.* (1) the relative obscurity produced by the interception of rays of light; *sing.* and *pl.*: P. L. X. 861; L. 137; *choice of sun or shade*: S. A. 3; *twilight shade of tangled thickets*: N. O. 188; *O night and shades*: C. 580; *in double night of darkness and of shades*: C. 335; *cypress shades*: C. 521; *green*: Ps. LXXX. 41; *unpierced, thick, gloomiest, dark, horrid,* etc.: P. L. IV. 245, 532; VI. 828; X. 716; P. R. I. 194, 296; C. 62, 127, 266, 429; L'A. 8; *chequered*: L'A. 96; *amidst*: A. 42; *among*: P. L. IX. 408; *through*: P. L. IV. 868; *under*: P. L. IV. 572; L'A. 8; P. R. II. 339; *in the shade*: L'A. 96; L. 68; in the sun: P. L. III. 615; in heaven; *Amaranthine shade*: P. L. XI. 78.

(2) darkness; *underground they fought in dismal shade*: P. L. VI. 666; in heaven; *that high mount of God whence light and shade spring both*: P. L. V. 643; the darkness of night; *the shades of Night*: P. L. IV. 1015; *the circling canopy of Night's extended shade*: P. L. III. 557; the twilight of evening: P. L. VIII. 653.

(3) a place where little light enters, a shady or secluded spot: P. L. V. 230; XI. 270; P. R. II. 242, 292; Il P. 28; L. 24; *fountain, or fresh shade*: P. L. V. 203; *horrid shade or dismal den*: P. L. IX. 185; *love to haunt her sacred shades*: P. L. VII. 331; *studious walks and shades*: P. R. IV. 243; *the milder shades of Purgatory*: S. XIII. 14; *along the crisped shades and bowers*: C. 984; *shades of death*: P. L. II. 621;

regions of sorrow, doleful shades: P. L. I. 65.

(*b*) trees forming shade: P. L. III. 734; a wood: H. B. 1.

(4) that which intercepts the light and produces shade; used of trees: P. L. IV. 693; *a pillared shade high overarched*: P. L. IX. 1106; *loop-holes cut through thickest shade*: P. L. IX. 1110; trees or plants: P. L. IV. 451; P. R. IV. 404; *Etrurian shades*: P. L. I. 303; *plant it round with shade of laurel*: S. A. 1734; *loftiest shade, cedar, and pine,* etc.: P. L. IV. 138, 141; *pendent*: P. L. IV. 239; *under a tuft of shade*: P. L. IV. 325.

(5) the shadow of a person; applied to Death in relation to Sin; *thou, my shade inseparable*: P. L. X. 249.

II. *vb.* (*pres. 2d sing.* shad'st: P. L. III. 377) *tr.* (*a*) to cover, screen, hide: P. L. V. 277; VI. 885; *the Tree of Life ... shading the Fount of Life*: P. L. III. 357.

(*b*) to render relatively dim or obscure by means of that which screens; *thou shad'st the full blaze of thy beams*: P. L. III. 377.

(*c*) to protect from harm: P. L. IX. 266.

part. adj. **shading**; (*a*) protecting: P. R. III. 221.

(*b*) used for drawing in gradations of colour; *shading pencil*: P. L. III. 509.

See **Double-shade.**

Shadow, (1) *sb.* (*a*) the faint light and coolness caused by the interception of the sun's rays; *shadows brown*: Il P. 134.

(*b*) darkness: N. O. 206.

(*c*) the dark figure projected by a body when it intercepts the light: P. L. III. 619; *where the shadow both way falls*: P. R. IV. 70; *substance might be called that shadow seemed*: P. L. II. 669.

(*d*) something that follows a person like a shadow; applied to Death: P. L. X. 264; *Sin and her shadow Death*: P. L. IX. 12.

(*e*) an image reflected in the water: P. L. IV. 470.

(*f*) an image or likeness; *though what if Earth be but the shadow of Heaven*: P. L. V. 575.

(*g*) a symbol or prophetic similitude; *religious rites of sacrifice, informing them, by types and shadows, of that destined Seed to bruise the Serpent*: P. L. XII. 233.

(*h*) the slightest trace: P. L. III. 120.

(*i*) an image produced by the imagination: C. 207.

(*j*) a departed spirit; *gloomy shadows damp*: C. 470; *flocking shadows pale*: N. O. 232.

(2) *vb. tr.* (*a*) *absol.* to cast a shadow or cause darkness; *main promontories … in the air came shadowing*: P. L. VI. 655.

(*b*) to cover, screen, protect: P. L. V. 284; *innocence, that as a veil had shadowed them from knowing ill*: P. L. IX. 1055.

(*c*) *absol.* to represent in a shadowy way; *as the dream had lively shadowed*: P. L. VIII. 311.

part. adj. **shadowing,** screening or hiding from view: P. L. VI. 554.

Shadowy, *adj.* (*a*) consisting of or causing shade or darkness; *dim Night, her shadowy cloud withdraws*: P. L. V. 686; *Night … her shadowy cone (see Cone)*: P. L. IV. 776.

(*b*) serving as a type or symbol: P. L. XII. 291, 303.

(*c*) ghostlike, unsubstantial, unreal; *the drudging goblin … his shadowy flail*: L'A. 108; *Darkness … brought in louring Night, her shadowy offspring*: P. R. IV. 399.

(*d*) *adv.* in the manner of a shadow, dimly: P. L. V. 43.

Shady, *adj.* (*a*) full of or affording shade; *shady grove, wood*, etc.: P. L. III. 28; VIII. 262; *the shady roof of branching elm*: A. 88; *shady arborous roof*: P. L. V. 137; *sup.*: P. L. III. 39.

fig. overhanging so as to produce shade; *this drear wood, the nodding horror of whose shady brows*: C. 38.

(*b*) protected from light or heat, shaded; *shady lodge, bower, bank,* etc.: P. L. IV. 720; V. 367; VIII. 286; IX. 277, 420, 1037; P. R. I. 304; *comp.*: P. L. IV. 705.

(*c*) dark, dusky; *shady gloom*: N. O, 77.

Shaft, *sb.* arrow: P. R. III. 305; *fig., here Love his golden shafts employs*: P. L. IV. 763; *the*

thunder … perhaps hath spent his shafts: P. L. I. 176.

See **Silver-shafted.**

Shag, *vb. tr.* to give the appearance of shagginess or roughness; *grots and caverns shagged with horrid shades*: C. 429.

Shaggy, *adj.* covered with a thick rough growth of trees or bushes: P. L. IV. 224; VI. 645; *the shaggy top of Mona*: L. 54.

Shake, *vb.* (*pret.* shook; *past part.* shook: P. L. VI. 219; S. A. 409; shaken: P. L. IX. 287) (1) *tr.* (*a*) to cause to move with quick vibrations, cause to tremble or quiver: P. L. I. 105; II. 882; V. 286; S. A. 1650; *the tawny lion … shakes his brinded mane*: P. L. VII. 466; *an oath that shook Heaven's whole circumference*: P. L. II. 353; *the flaming chariotwheels, that shook Heaven's everlasting frame*: P. L. III. 394; *the rapid wheels that shake Heaven's basis*: P. L. VI. 712; *fig., eloquence … shook the Arsenal*: P. R. IV. 270; to shake the head in sorrow or disapprobation: L. 112.

fig., to disturb; *shook sore their inward state of mind*: P. L. IX. 1124.

(*b*) to brandish: P. L. II. 672; *over them triumphant Death his dart shook*: P. L. XI. 492.

(*c*) to cause to come *from* by a vibratory motion; *fig., a comet … from his horrid hair shakes pestilence and war*: P. L. II. 711.

(*d*) *shake off,* to get free from: S. A. 409.

(*e*) to cause to waver; *my firm faith and love … be shaken*: P. L. IX. 287.

(*f*) to rouse, startle: A. 58.

(2) *intr.* to tremble or quiver; *under his burning wheels the steadfast Empyrean shook*: P. L. VI. 833; used of the Earth: P. L. VI. 219; N. O. 162; C. 797; Ps. CXIV. 15; CXXXVI. 4; to tremble with fear: Ps. LXXXVIII. 59.

part. adj. **shaked,** made to tremble: D. F. I. 44.

See **Earth-shaking.**

Shakespeare, *sb.* the poet: W. S. 1; L'A. 133.

*****Shall,** *vb.* (*pres. 2d sing.* shalt: P. L. III. 257; IV. 472; V. 822, etc.; *pret.* should; *2d sing.* shouldst: P. L. VI. 287; VIII. 420; IX. 279,

etc.) as auxiliary with simple
infinitive; (1) in the principal
clause; (a) denoting necessity,
obligation, duty, or fitness: P. L.
XII. 354; S. A. 208, 783; P. 34;
C. 815; *whose failing I should
conceal*: P. L. X. 130; in direct
question: P. L. XI. 511; *Whom
should I obey but thee?*: P. L. II.
865; *shall that be shut to Man
which to the Beast is open?*: P. L.
IX. 691.

(b) denoting simple futurity;
in 1st person: P. L. I. 259; V.
572; S. A. 598; C. 953; in direct
question: C. 779; *where shall we
find such love?*: P. L. III. 213;
*which way shall I fly infinite
wrath*: P. L. IV. 73; possibly in
2d and 3d person, but in each
instance the meaning shades into
some other sense, as (c) etc.: P.
L. I. 655; IX. 801, 943; X. 80;
S. A. 1347; L. 184; Ps. v. 6.

(c) denoting certainty or inevitability as regards the future;
usually a promise or prophecy for
the future: P. L. I. 657; II. 402,
844; III. 242; IV. 472; V. 389;
VI. 483; VII. 117; X. 54, 181;
XI. 689; XII. 33, 334; *I shall rise
victorious*: P. L. III. 250; *I shall
know*: P. L. IV. 588; *here shalt
thou sit incarnate*: P. L. III. 315;
*children thou shalt bring in sorrow
forth*: P. L. X. 194; *he over thee
shall rule*: P. L. X. 196; *thus it
shall befall him*: P. L. IX. 1182.

(d) denoting possibility or permission; *shalt thou give law to
God?*: P. L. V. 822; =could; *Ye
shall not die. How should ye?*:
P. L. IX. 686.

(e) denoting power or ability;
Whose fountain who shall tell?:
P. L. III. 8.

(f) denoting a command: P.
L. IX. 662; *thou shalt not eat
thereof*: P. L. X. 200; *thou shalt
worship the Lord thy God*: P. R.
IV. 176; periphrastically; *it shall
be said*: U. C. I. 17.

(g) denoting determination: P.
L. V. 62; IX. 859, 916; P. R. I.
150; *I shall let pass no advantage*:
P. R. II. 233; *I shall no more
advise thee*: P. R. IV. 210; *this
enterprise none shall partake with
me*: P. L. II. 466; *that glory never
shall his wrath ... extort from me*:
P. L. I. 110; in parallel con-

struction with *will*: Ps. LXXXIII.
46.

(h) denoting doubt or uncertainty; *But for thee what shall
be done?*: S. A. 478; *What shall
we do*: S. A. 1520; *What should
they do?*: P. L. VI. 600; *that
hallo I should know*: C. 490;
what should it be?: C. 482.

(i) used to soften a statement;
*I should be loth to meet the ...
swilled insolence of such late wassailers*: C. 177.

(2) in dependent clauses; (a)
shall in sb. adj. or adv. clause:
P. L. I. 167; V. 817; IX. 657,
707; *to taste think not I shall be
nice*: P. L. V. 433; *declaring
thee resolved, rather than death ...
shall separate us*: P. L. IX. 970;
*that we never shall forget to love ...
my constant thoughts assured me,
and still assure*: P. L. V. 550;
should in similar clause: P. L.
II. 551, 808; *a place foretold
should be*: P. L. II. 831; *to hear
his famine should be filled*: P. L.
II. 847; *glad that now his sea
should find a shore*: P. L. II.
1011; *easier to transact with me,
that thou shouldst hope*: P. L.
VI. 288; *far be it that I should
write thee sin*: P. L. IV. 758;
*nor is it aught but just that he ...
should win*: P. L. VI. 123; *enjoins
that I should mind thee oft*: P. L.
IX. 358; *I told ye then he should
prevail*: P. L. X. 40; *ill-worthy I
such title should belong to me*: P.
L. XI. 163; *thou art worthy that
thou shouldst not know*: C. 788;
*time is our tedious song should here
have ending*: N. O. 239; *I knew
the time now full, that I no more
should live obscure*: P. R. I. 287.

shall denoting fate or destiny;
whenever that shall be: P. L. II.
809; *while here shall be our home*:
P. L. II. 458; *Prophetic Writ
hath told that it shall never end*:
P. R. III. 185; *all that I ... shall
beget*: P. L. X. 728; *when time
shall be*: P. L. X. 74; P. R. IV.
616.

(b) in a concessive clause: P.
R. IV. 113; *hard is to say ...
though one should musing sit*: S.
A. 1017.

(c) in a final clause introduced
by *lest*: P. L. II. 483; IV. 665;
X. 1057; S. A. 1451.

(d) in conditional clause; *shall* in the protasis, the apodosis containing *shall*: P. R. III. 381; *should* in the protasis, the apodosis containing *could*: P. L. II. 237; containing *may*: P. L. II. 82; containing *might*: P. L. VI. 502; containing *would*: P. L. IX. 911; X. 135; P. R. II. 211; III. 12; containing both *should* and *would*: C. 721; the apodosis omitted or ellipt.: P. L. II. 171; IV. 388; C. 288; *should* in parallel construction with the subj.: P. L. II. 176; VI. 315.

shall in the apodosis, the protasis containing *may*: S. A. 1477; *should* in the apodosis, the protasis containing the indic.: P. L. II. 119; containing the subj.: P. L. VI. 619; S. A. 370; containing *could*: P. L. II. 445; the protasis omitted or ellipt.: P. L. II. 93; X. 778; P. R. I. 382; S. A. 807.

(e) in an exclamation: P. L. VI. 115; S. A. 606; *O pity and shame, that they ... should turn aside*: P. L. XI. 630; *Oh, that men ... should be so stupid grown*: P. L. XII. 116.

(f) in indirect question: P. L. IX. 1152; XII. 378, 474; P. R. II. 485; S. A. 216.

Shallow, *adj.* (*a*) not deep; *shallow brooks*: L'A. 76.

(b) not deep intellectually, superficial: P. R. IV. 327; F. of C. 12; *shallow ignorance*: C. 514; *these beasts ... shallow to discern half what in thee is fair*: P. L. IX. 544; superficial in love, false; *the shallow cuckoo's bill*: S. I. 6.

Shallow-searching, *adj.* searching only the surface: A. 41.

Shame, I. *sb.* (1) a painful feeling of degradation or humiliation: P. L. VI. 340; IX. 312, 313, 1114; X. 113, 159; S. A. 457; Ps. LXXXIII. 64; *past shame*: P. R. IV. 342; *confused with shame*: S. A. 196; *hope that reaps not shame*: S. IX. 11; *grown red with shame*: Ps. VI. 20; *fill with shame their face*: Ps. LXXXIII. 60; *shame, the last of evils*: P. L. IX. 1079; *the Sun ... hid his head for shame*: N. O. 80; *personified*: P. L. IX. 1058.

(2) distress at a breach of decorum or propriety: P. R. IV. 189; esp. at the exposure of one's person: P. L. IX. 1094; X. 336; *guilty shame. Dishonest shame of Nature's works*: P. L. IV. 313; *this new comer, Shame*: P. L. X. 1097.

(3) a person or thing to be ashamed of, a cause of ignominy: P. L. X. 906; XI. 629; S. A. 841; *death to life is crown or shame*: S. A. 1579.

(b) disgrace, dishonour: P. L. II. 564; P. R. III. 136; IV. 14; S. A. 446; *O shame to men!*: P. L. II. 496; *to work ... woe and* or *or shame*: P. L. IX. 255; X. 555; *my ... race of shame*: S. A. 597; *this dark opprobrious den of shame*: P. L. II. 58; *to ways of sin and shame*: Ps. LXXX. 74; *to the shame of*: W. S. 9; a dishonour: P. L. I. 115; *for the shame done to his father*: P. L. XII. 102.

(c) reproach, opprobrium; *my dread of shame among the Spirits*: P. L. IV. 82.

(d) derision, contempt: P. L. X. 546.

(4) the parts of the body which modesty requires to be covered: P. L. IX. 1119; *fig.*: N. O. 40.

II. *vb.* (1) *tr.* (*a*) to make ashamed, cause to feel disgraced: P. L. I. 461; IX. 1139; S. A. 563; Ps. LXXXIII. 62.

(b) to cover with reproach, disgrace: P. L. IX. 384.

(2) *intr.* to be ashamed: P. R. IV. 303.

Shamefaced, *adj.* modest; *the shamefaced Night*: N. O. 111.

Shameful, *adj.* (*a*) filled with a consciousness of shame or humiliation; *shameful silence*: P. R. IV. 22.

(b) disgraceful, dishonourable: S. XV. 12; *shameful garrulity*: S. A. 491; *deeds*: S. A. 1043; *death*: P. L. XII. 413; P. R. III. 87.

Shamefully, *adv.* disgracefully: S. A. 499.

Shameless, *adj.* unabashed: C. 736.

Shape, (1) *sb.* (*a*) outward contour or appearance, form, figure: P. L. I. 428; II. 667; IV. 288, 365, 398, 587; IX. 601; X. 516, 574, 869; XI. 239, 297; P. R. II. 176; IV. 449; *he cast to change his proper shape*: P. L. III. 634; *changing shape*: P. L. X. 333; *to his proper shape returns*: P. L. V.

276 ; *colour, shape, or size assume* :
P. L. VI. 352 ; *think not, revolted
Spirit, thy shape the same* : P. L.
IV. 835 ; *whoever tasted lost his
upright shape* : C. 52 ; *in shape* :
P. L. I. 590 ; II. 704, 756 ; *in his
own shape* : P. L. IV. 819 ; *the
brute Serpent, in whose shape Man
I deceived* : P. L. 495 ; *call up
unbound in various shapes old
Proteus* : P. L. III. 604 ; *comeliness
of* : S. A. 1011 ; *of shape divine* :
P. L. VIII. 295 ; *pleasing was his
shape* : P. L. IX. 503.

often having nearly or quite the
meaning : being or body considered with respect to outward
form : L'A. 4 ; C. 460 ; *godlike
Shapes* : P. L. I. 358 ; *those immortal shapes* : C. 2 ; *to smallest
forms reduced their shapes immense* : P. L. I. 790 ; *monstrous
shapes* : P. L. I. 479 ; *my nether
shape* : P. L. II. 784 ; *his fulgent
head and shape star-bright* : P. L.
X. 450 ; *all their shape spangled
with eyes* : P. L. XI. 129.

(b) definitely : being, creature ;
*just opposite a shape within the
watery gleam appeared* : P. L. IV.
461 ; *what glorious Shape comes
this way moving* : P. L. V. 309 ;
such glorious Shape : P. L. V.
362 ; *saw the Shape still glorious* :
P. L. VIII. 463 ; *those Heavenly
Shapes* : P. L. IX. 1082 ; *four
cherubic Shapes* : P. L. VI. 753 ;
applied to Sin or Death : P. L.
II. 649, 666, 667, 681.

(c) something bodied forth by
the imagination : P. L. V. 111 ;
Il P. 6 ; *aery shapes* : P. L. V.
105 ; *calling shapes* : C. 207.

(d) the way in which a thing
manifests itself ; *saw Virtue in
her shape how lovely* : P. L. IV.
848 ; *if aught...in the shape of
difficulty or danger* : P. L. II.
448 ; mode of acting or operating ; *Death thou hast seen in his
first shape on Man* : P. L. XI. 467.

(e) form, pattern, mould : P.
R. III. 11.

(2) *vb. tr.* to form ; *one shaped
...like one of those from Heaven* :
P. L. V. 55.

Share, (1) *sb.* part, portion : C. 769 ;
*share of endless pain, of woe, of
hazard* : P. L. II. 29, 452 ; X.
961 ; *of wisdom* : S. A. 53 ; *if sad
share with us to bear* : Cir. 6.

(2) *vb. tr.* (a) to apportion ; *the
rest* (thrones) *are barbarous ...
shared among petty kings* : P. R.
IV. 87.

(b) to enjoy or suffer in common *with* others : P. L. I. 267 ;
*Adam shall share with me in bliss
or woe* : P. L. IX. 831 ; to seize
and possess jointly ; *Avarice and
Rapine share the land* : S. XV. 14.

(c) to shear, cut, cleave : P. L.
VI. 326.

Sharp, (1) *adj.* (a) having fine cutting edges or points : P. L. II.
902 ; *sharp sleet of arrowy showers* :
P. R. III. 324.

(b) keen ; *sup., sharpest sight* :
P. L. IX. 91.

(c) eager ; *sharp desire* : P. L.
IX. 584.

(d) violent, fierce ; *sharp contest of battle* : P. L. XI. 800.

(e) painful, distressing, afflict-
ive : P. L. X. 977 ; XI. 63.

(2) *absol.* or *sb.* the condition of
being sharp pointed ; *his visage
drawn he felt to sharp* : P. L. X.
511.

Sharpen, *vb. tr.* (a) to arrange in a
figure with sharp points : P. L.
IV. 978. *See* **Horn.**

(b) to render keen : P. L. III.
620.

Sharpest-sighted, *adj.* having the
quickest discernment : P. L. III.
691.

Sharply, *adv.* severely, rigorously :
P. R. I. 468.

Shatter, *vb. tr.* (a) to scatter : P. L.
X. 1066 ; *shatter your leaves* : L.
6.

(b) to break into pieces ; *all thy
magic structures ... were shattered
into heaps* : C. 799.

part. adj. **shattered**, broken
into pieces ; *the shattered sides of
... Ætna* : P. L. I. 232 ; *arms* :
P. L. VI. 361 ; *to the hazard of thy
brains and shattered sides* : S. A.
1241.

Shave, *vb. tr.* (a) to make bare by
cutting off the hair : S. A. 540.

(b) to skim along on or near the
surface of : P. L. II. 634.

See **Smooth-shaven.**

*She, (1) *pers. pron.* (*dat.* and *acc.*
her) (a) referring to a female
person previously mentioned : P.
L. II. 663 ; IV. 272, 298, 304, 309,
717 ; V. 27, 129, 343, 384 ; VIII. 43 ;
unlocked her all my heart : S. A.

407 ; *nor ... wants her fit vessel* :
P. L. v. 348 ; *that moral verdict
quits her of unclean* : S. A. 324 ;
not previously mentioned but
understood from the context :
L'A. 103.

(*b*) referring to the nightingale :
P. L. IV. 603.

(*c*) referring to various things
with more or less personification ;
to the earth : P. L. VIII. 89, 141 ;
the mind or fancy : P. L. v. 105 ;
VIII. 190 ; light : P. L. VII. 248 ;
the moon : P. L. VII. 378 ; VIII.
143 ; S. A. 88 ; morn : P. L. IV.
650 ; Il P. 123 ; nature : P. L.
VIII. 561 ; N. O. 107 ; night : P.
L. VII. 105 ; peace : N. O. 47 ; a
plant : P. L. v. 216 ; reason : P.
L. v. 111 ; IX. 355 ; silence : C.
558 ; Sin : P. L. II. 727 ; x. 588 ;
Sion : Ps. LXXXVII. 20 ; the soul :
S. A. 97 ; C. 468 ; a star : M. M.
2 ; wisdom : P. L. VIII. 563 ; IX.
810 ; virtue : P. R. II. 456 ; C.
1023.

(*d*) that woman ; *she of Timna* :
S. A. 382 ; as antecedent of *rel.
pron.* : P. L. IX. 509.

(*e*) any woman : P. L. IX. 1186 ;
restraint she will not brook : P.
L. IX. 1184 ; *once joined, the
contrary she proves* : S. A. 1037 ;
as antecedent of *rel. pron.* : C.
421.

(2) *refl. pron. bestirs her* : P. L.
v. 337 ; *betake her* : C. 351 ; *betook her* : P. L. IX. 388.

Sheaf, *sb.* a bundle of stalks of
grain : P. L. XI. 430 ; *to bind the
sheaves* : L'A. 88 ; *the green ear
and the yellow sheaf* : P. L. XI.
435 ; *his hopeful sheaves prove
chaff* : P. L. IV. 984.

Shear, *vb.* (*pret.* shore ; *past part.*
shorn) *tr.* (*a*) to clip with shears ;
*who shore me, like a tame wether,
all my precious fleece* : S. A. 537.

(*b*) to deprive, strip ; *the sun ...
shorn of his beams* : P. L. I. 596 ;
waked shorn of his strength : P. L.
IX. 1062.

(*c*) to reap with a sickle ; *fig.,
shorn the fatal harvest of thy head* :
S. A. 1024.

Shearer, *sb.* one who cuts wool
from sheep ; *fig.* : L. 117.

Shears, *sb.* the two-bladed instrument for cutting ; *fig., the Parliament may with their ... preventive
shears* : F. of C. 16 ; those held

by Atropos, the goddess of fate ;
the abhorred shears : L. 75 ; *the
vital* : A. 65.

Shed, *sb.* a hut or mean dwelling :
C. 323 ; an outhouse : P. R. II.
72.

Shed, *vb.* (*pret.* and *past part.*
shed) *tr.* (*a*) to spread around,
disperse, diffuse ; *the moon ... disastrous twilight sheds* : P. L. I.
597 ; *the Pleiades ... shedding sweet
influence* : P. L. VII. 375 ; *happy
constellations, on that hour shed
their selectest influence* : P. L.
VIII. 513 ; *in part shed down their
stellar virtue* : P. L. IV. 670.

(*b*) to cause to flow out ; *shed
the luscious liquor on the ground* :
C. 652.

(*c*) to let fall ; *all the faded roses
shed* : P. L. IX. 893.

*fig., the draff and filth which
Man's polluting sin ... hath shed on
what was pure* : P. L. x. 631 ; to
cause to grow by shedding
moisture ; *the clouds that shed
May flowers* : P. L. IV. 501 ; to
bring or contribute ; *bid amaranthus all his beauty shed* : L. 149.

Sheen, *sb.* light, brightness, splendour ; *celestial, radiant, azure,
spangled* : N. O. 145 ; M. W. 73 ;
C. 893, 1003.

Sheeny, *adj.* shining ; *the wall of
sheeny Heaven* : D. F. I. 48.

Sheep, *sb.* the animal *Ovis* ; *a flock
of sheep* : Ps. LXXX. 33 ; unchanged
in the *pl.* : N. O. 91 ; *fig.*, those
who depend upon God for guidance and protection : S. XVIII. 6 ;
those who look to the church for
guidance : L. 125.

Sheep-cote, *sb.* a small building or
enclosure for sheltering sheep : P.
R. II. 287, 288.

Sheep-hook, *sb.* a shepherd's crook ;
fig. : L. 120.

Sheep-walk, *sb.* a pasture for sheep :
P. L. XI. 431.

Sheer, *adv.* quite, entirely, clean ;
*thrown ... sheer o'er the crystal
battlements* : P. L. I. 742 ; *sheer
within lights on his feet* : P. L. IV.
182 ; *in half cut sheer* : P. L. VI.
325 ; *oaks ... torn up sheer* : P. R.
IV. 419.

Shelf, *sb.* a reef or shoal in the sea :
C. 117.

Shell, *sb.* (*a*) the hard outer covering
of certain kinds of fruit : P. L.
v. 342.

(*b*) the covering of testaceous animals : P. R. II. 345 ; *their pearly shells* : P. L. VII. 407.

(*c*) the trumpet of Triton which was made of a shell : C. 873.

(*d*) *airy shell* : C. 231. *See* **Aery.**

Shelter, I. *sb.* that which affords safety or protection ; *in thick shelter of black shades imbowered* : C. 62 ; that which protects one from the anger of God : P. R. III. 221 ; *the mountains now might be again thrown on them, as a shelter from his ire* : P. L. VI. 843 ; *thy wrath, from which no shelter saves* : Ps. LXXXVIII. 29.

II. *vb.* (1) *tr.* to cover and protect from exposure or injury : P. R. II. 73 ; IV. 407 ; *besought the Deep to shelter us* : P. L. II. 167 ; *he ... shall in the ark be lodged and sheltered round* : P. L. XI. 824.

(2) *intr.* to take shelter : P. L. XI. 223 ; *the Indian herdsman ... shelters in cool* : P. L. IX. 1109.

part. adj. **sheltered,** protected : P. R. IV. 406.

Shepherd, *sb.* one who tends sheep : P. L. IV. 185 ; XI. 650 ; L'A. 67 ; C. 848 ; L. 49, 165, 182 ; *the homely, slighted, shepherd's trade* : L. 65 ; *the star that bids the shepherd fold* : C. 93 ; *spec.* those to whom the birth of Christ was announced : P. L. XII. 365 ; P. R. I. 244 ; N. O. 85 ; Cir. 3 ; Abel : P. L. XI. 436 ; Lycidas : L. 39 ; Melibœus : C. 823 ; the characters in the Arcades : A. 1, 96 ; in Comus : C. 958 ; Thyrsis : C. 271, 307, 321, 330, 493, 509, 615, 908 ; *fig.*, applied to Moses as the leader of Israel : P. L. I. 8 ; applied to God as the guardian of **Israel** : Ps. LXXX. 1.

attrib. who is a shepherd ; *shepherd lad* : C. 619 ; *the shepherd lad whose offspring on the throne of Judah sat* : P. R. II. 439.

Shepherdess, *sb.* a woman who tends sheep ; *that fair Syrian shepherdess*, Rachel : M. W. 63.

Shibboleth, *sb.* a word given by Jephthah as a test in pronunciation to distinguish his own men from the Ephraimites, who could not pronounce *sh* : S. A. 289.

Shield, I. *sb.* (1) the piece of defensive armour : S. A. 284 ; N. O. 55 ; *emblazoned, brazen* : P. L. IX.

34 ; S. A. 132 ; *seven-times-folded* : S. A. 1122 ; *that snaky-headed Gorgon shield* : C. 447 ; borne by an angel : P. L. VI. 83, 192, 840 ; X. 540 ; *ponderous, orbed* : P. L. I. 284 ; VI. 543 ; *two broad suns their shields* : P. L. VI. 305 ; *the rocky orb of tenfold adamant, his ample shield* : P. L. VI. 255 ; *celestial, golden* : P. L. IV. 553 ; VI. 102 ; *serried, ordered* : P. L. I. 548, 565 ; *clashed on their sounding shields* : P. L. I. 668 ; *bore him on their shields* : P. L. VI. 337 ; *nor wanted in his grasp what seemed both spear and shield* : P. L. IV. 990.

(*b*) the left side or direction : P. L. IV. 785.

(2) that which protects or defends : Ps. v. 39 ; *be now a shield of fire* : S. A. 1434 ; *some good angel bear a shield before us* : C. 658 ; used of God : Ps. III. 7 ; LXXXIV. 31, 41.

II. *vb. tr.* to shelter, protect : P. R. IV. 405.

Shift, (1) *sb.* resource, contrivance ; *extreme shift how to regain my severed company* : C. 273 ; *care and utmost shifts how to secure the lady* : C. 617 ; *pl.* arguments or excuses used as a device to avoid conviction or assent ; *subtle shifts conviction to evade* : P. R. IV. 308 ; *feigned* : S. A. 1116 ; *these shifts refuted* : S. A. 1220.

(2) *vb. tr.* to change the position of ; *a ship ... shifts her sail* : P. L. IX. 515.

Shifter, *sb.* one who practises artifice : U. C. I. 5.

Shine, I. *sb.* light, brightness ; *tapers' holy shine* : N. O. 202.

II. *vb.* (*pret.* shined : S. XXIII. 11 ; elsewhere shone ; *past part.* shone) *intr.* (1) to give or emit light ; (*a*) used of heavenly bodies : P. L. IV. 657, 675 ; VII. 380 ; VIII. 155 ; IX. 104 ; X. 652 ; *the Sun that barren shines* : P. L. VIII. 94 ; *Heaven in all her glory shone* : P. L. VII. 499 ; *the horned moon to shine by night* : Ps. CXXXVI. 33 ; *that globe* (the earth) ... *with light from hence, though but reflected, shines* : P. L. III. 723 ; to appear to be by their shining ; *that shone stars distant, but nighhand seemed other worlds* : P. L. III. 565.

(*b*) used of heavenly beings;
*He ... on his Son with rays direct
shone full* : P. L. VI. 720; to be
seen because of the light emitted;
far off his (Christ's) *coming shone* :
P. L. VI. 768.

(*c*) *fig.* to give light as a sign
of favour or reconciliation : Ps.
LXXX. 7; *cause thou thy face on
us to shine* : Ps. LXXX. 15, 31, 79;
to give light to the mind or soul;
*thou, Celestial Light, shine inward
and the mind through all her powers
irradiate* : P. L. III. 52.

(2) to be bright, gleam : P. L.
I. 672; III. 508; *the glittering
staff... shone like a meteor* : P. L. I.
537; *the bright pavement ... shone* :
P. L. III. 363; *the twelve that
shone in Aaron's breast* : P. L. III.
597; used of Satan; *shone above
them all the Archangel* : P. L. I.
599; of Sin; *shining heavenly
fair* : P. L. II. 757.

(3) to appear; used of light :
P. L. III. 713; of morn or morning : P. L. V. 20; VI. 748; VII.
108; to continue to shine without
interruption; *to them day had
unbenighted shone* : P. L. X. 682.

(4) to be or exist in brightness :
*every thing that is sincerely good ...
shall ever shine about the supreme
throne* : T. 16.

(5) to be visible : P. L. IV. 363;
*in their looks divine the image of
their glorious Maker shone* : P. L.
IV. 292; *in whose look ... mercy
shone* : P. L. X. 1096; *goodness,
in her person shined* : S. XXIII.
11; *princely counsel in his face yet
shone* : P. L. II. 304; with more
or less accompanying brightness
or light : P. R. I. 93; D. F. I.
34; *in him all his Father shone* :
P. L. III. 139; *all his Father in
him shone* : P. L. VII. 196; *in
whose...countenance...the Almighty
Father shines* : P. L. III. 386.

(6) to be eminent, excel, surpass; *mercy ... shall brightest
shine* : P. L. III. 134; *virtue ...
most shines and most is acceptable
above* : S. A. 1052; *above which
only shone filial obedience* : P. L.
III. 268.

part. adj. **shining**, emitting
light; *shining orbs, globes* : P. L.
III. 668, 670; V. 259; bright,
gleaming : P. L. VII. 401; *shining
rock, throne* : P. L. IV. 283; A. 15.

Ship, *sb.* a large sea-going vessel :
P. L. IX. 513; S. A. 714.

Shipwrack, *vb. tr.* to cause to suffer
shipwreck; *fig.* : S. A. 198.

Shiver, (1) *sb. pl.* small fragments;
all to shivers dashed : P. R. IV.
19.

(2) *vb. tr.* to break into small
fragments : Ps. II. 21.

part. adj. **shivered**, broken into
pieces; *shivered armour* : P. L.
VI. 389.

Shiver, *vb. intr.* to shudder, tremble :
P. L. X. 1003; *that saw the
troubled sea, and shivering fled* :
Ps. CXIV. 7.

Shoal, (1) *sb.* a school of fish : P. L.
VII. 400; Ps. VIII. 22.

(2) *vb. tr.* to cause to move in
crowded masses, drive in shoals :
P. L. X. 288.

Shock, *sb.* violent collision : *the
shock of fighting elements* : P. L.
II. 1014; *the clouds ... rude in their
shock* : P. L. X. 1074; the encounter of battle : P. L. V. 207.

Shock, *sb.* a group of sheaves of
grain : Ps. LXXXI. 65.

Shoe, *sb.* (*pl.* shoon) the covering
for the foot : C. 635.

Shoot, I. *sb.* a young branch; *tender
shoots* : C. 296; Ps. LXXX. 56.

II. *vb.* (*pret.* and *past part.*
shot) (1) *intr.* (*a*) to rush or dart
along rapidly; *Tigris ... into a
gulf shot underground* : P. L. IX.
72; *I shoot from heaven* : C. 81.

(*b*) to be thrown out or emitted;
his beams ... shot upward : P. L.
III. 618.

(*c*) to come forth, germinate :
P. L. VI. 480; *the flower new shot
up* : M. W. 40.

(2) *tr.* (*a*) to send forth, throw
out, dart : A. 16; *the Sun ... shot
parallel to the Earth his dewy ray* :
P. L. V. 141; *the mounted Sun shot
down direct his fervid rays* : P. L.
V. 301; *the slope sun his upward
beam shoots against the dusky pole* :
C. 99; (the sun) *shoots invisible
virtue even to the Deep* : P. L. III.
586; *light ... shoots far into the
bosom of dim Night a glimmering
dawn* : P. L. II. 1036.

(*b*) to let fly, discharge, fire :
P. R. III. 323; to send after the
manner of an arrow or a bullet;
*see black fire and horror shot with
equal rage among his Angels* : P.
L. II. 67; *the sulphurous hail,*

shot after us in storm : P. L. I.
172 ; every eye ... shot forth pernicious fire : P. L. VI. 849 ; fig.,
from about her shot darts of desire
into all eyes : P. L. VIII. 62 ;
beauty ... shot forth peculiar graces :
P. L. V. 15.

(c) to strike or hit with a
missile ; fig., Night, shot through
with orient beams : P. L. VI. 15.

part. adj. **shooting,** darting;
shooting star : P. L. IV. 556.

Shop, sb. a place where something
is made ; fig., spinning worms,
that in their green shops weave
the ... silk : C. 716.

Shore, sb. (1) the coast or land
adjacent to or bordering on a
large body of water : P. L. VII.
417 ; P. R. IV. 330 ; S. A. 962 ;
L. 154 ; sea or shore : P. R. II.
344 ; sea without shore : P. L. XI.
750 ; sands and shores : C. 209 ;
shores with forest crowned : P. L.
IX. 117 ; woody : P. L. IX. 1118 ;
wide-watered : Il P. 75 ; resounding : N. O. 182 ; thou art the
Genius of the shore : L. 183 ; Afric
shore : P. L. I. 585 ; the Ægean
shore : P. R. IV. 238 ; the spicy
shore of Araby the blest : P. L. IV.
162 ; the Campanian : P. R. IV.
93 ; the Lesbian : L. 63 ; the
Samoed ; P. L. X. 696 ; the hoarse
Trinacrian : P. L. II. 661 ; the
Tyrrhene : C. 49 ; that adjacent
to the Red Sea : P. L. I. 310 ;
XII. 199, 215 ; to the Mediterranean : P. L. XII. 143 ; middle
shore, those countries bordering
on the Mediterranean : P. L. V.
339 ; fig.: P. L. II. 1011.

(b) land bordering on the lake
of hell : P. L. I. 284 ; the land of
heaven as bordering on chaos :
P. L. VII. 210.

(2) land ; sea, air, and shore :
P. L. X. 666.

(b) boundary or frontier ; Arabian shore : P. L. III. 537.

(c) as one of the four elements
which form the universe : P. L.
II. 912.

Short, (1) adj. (a) not long in space
or extent ; comp.: P. R. IV. 595.

(b) not long in time, of brief
duration ; short hour, time, etc.:
P. L. X. 923 ; XI. 184 ; P. R. IV.
378 ; M. W. 9 ; longest time to
him is short : P. R. I. 56 ; silence,
intermission, absence, etc.: P. L.

I. 797 ; IV. 102 ; V. 562 ; IX. 248,
250 ; P. R. III. 235 ; S. A. 670 ;
D. F. I. 60 ; pleasures, joy : P. L.
IV. 535 ; XI. 628 ; probably with
sb. omitted ; make short : P. L.
X. 1000 ; acting but a short time ;
Hesperus ... short arbiter twixt day
and night : P. L. IX. 50 ; sup.
most quickly effective ; of many
ways to die the shortest choosing :
P. L. X. 1005.

(c) brief, not lengthy ; short
sigh : P. L. XI. 147 ; his message
will be short : S. A. 1307 ; to be
short : Ariosto I. 1.

(d) lacking, deficient ; short of
thy perfection : P. L. IX. 963 ; am
I short of knowing : P. R. IV. 287.

(2) absol. or sb. a short syllable :
S. XIII. 4.

(3) adv. (a) for a time not long
in duration ; live well ; how long
or short permit to Heaven : P. L.
XI. 554.

(b) so as to decrease the distance ; comp., cut shorter many a
league : P. R. III. 269.

(c) so as not to reach a goal ;
come, fall short : P. L. VIII. 414 ;
IX. 174. See the verbs.

Shorten, vb. tr. to abridge, curtail
in time : M. W. 52.

part. adj. **shortened,** made
brief in duration ; in wintry
solstice like the shortened light :
P. 6.

Shortly, adj. in a short time, soon :
S. A. 598.

Shoulder, sb. the parts of the body
about the scapula : P. L. IV. 303 ;
V. 279 ; S. A. 1493 ; thy decent
shoulders : Il P. 36 ; his shoulders
fledge with wings : P. L. III. 627 ;
as bearing or able to bear burdens :
P. L. I. 287 ; on his shoulders
bore, the gates of Azza : S. A. 146 ;
Atlantean shoulders, fit to bear the
weight of mightiest monarchies :
P. L. II. 306.

fig. supporting power or strength :
P. R. II. 462.

Shout, (1) sb. a sudden and loud
outcry of a multitude of people,
expressing exultation or other
emotion : P. L. VI. 200 ; X. 505 ;
S. A. 1472, 1510, 1620 ; a shout
that tore Hell's concave : P. L. I.
542 ; the host of Hell with deafening shout : P. L. II. 520 ; the multitude of Angels, with a shout ...
uttering joy : P. L. III. 345 ; the

shout of battle: P. L. VI. 96 ; with joy and shout : P. L. VII. 256 ; midnight : C. 103 ; saintly : S. M. 9.

(2) vb. intr. to cry aloud in exultation : S. A. 1473.

Shove, vb. tr. to push roughly away: L. 118.

Show or **shew,** I. sb. (a) the act of displaying to view ; show of luxury : P. R. IV. 110.

(b) sight, spectacle ; triumphed in open show : P. L. X. 187.

(c) appearance, semblance : P. L. VIII. 538 ; in show plebeian Angel : P. L. X. 442 ; a crown, golden in show : P. R. II. 459 ; that care, though wise in show: S. XXI. 12 ; such as have more show of worth : P. R. II. 226.

(d) a deceptive appearance, simulation, pretence, pretext: P. L. VIII. 575 ; X. 883 ; mere shows of seeming pure : P. L. IV. 316 ; show of love well feigned : P. L. IX. 492 ; show of zeal and love : P. L. IX. 665 ; practised false-hood under saintly show : P. L. IV. 122.

II. vb. (pres. 2d sing. show'st: P. L. II. 818 ; P. R. IV. 121 ; 3d sing. shew'th : S. II. 4 ; pret. 2d sing. show'dst: S. A. 781 ; past part. shown or shewn) (1) tr. (a) to present to view, exhibit, display : P. L. III. 255 ; VII. 406 ; P. R. II. 13 ; III. 350 ; IV. 121 ; S. A. 1475 ; shown in public : P. R. II. 51 ; in public shown : P. R. II. 84 ; beauty ... must be shown in courts : C. 745 ; every star that Heaven doth shew : Il P. 171 ; with acc. and dat.: P. L. II. 818 ; XI. 384 ; P. R. IV. 88 ; S. A. 1644 ; show me simples : C. 627 ; a land which he will show him : P. L. XII. 123 ; to show them feats : S. A. 1340 ; to show the people proof: S. A. 1601 ; which now the sky ... begins to show us : P. L. X. 1065 ; in passive ; that ... luggage of war there shown me : P. R. III. 401.

(b) to allow to be seen, disclose, discover ; thy shape ... may show thy inward fraud : P. L. X. 870 ; with two acc.; his starry helm ... showed him prime in manhood : P. L. XI. 245.

(c) to make known, reveal, dis-close : P. L. XI. 194 ; it was shown

him so from Heaven : P. R. I. 276 ; to us thy mercy shew : Ps. LXXXV. 26 ; to show forth his goodness : P. R. III. 124 ; mercy, shewn on Man : P. L. I. 218 ; with blending of the idea in (a) : P. L. VI. 247 ; Jehovah's wonders were in Israel shown : Ps. CXIV. 5 ; they show us when our foes walk not upright : P. L. VI. 627 ; to show thee what reward awaits the good : P. L. XI. 709 ; to show thee what shall come : P. L. XI. 357.

(d) to make known beforehand, foreshow : P. L. VI. 161 ; child-hood shows the man, as morning shows the day : P. R. IV. 220, 221 ; to point to ; fears that show no end but death : P. L. X. 1004.

(e) to manifest, demonstrate, prove: P. R. IV. 554 ; S. A. 910, 994 ; as if to show what creatures Heaven doth breed : D. F. I. 61 ; with two acc.: P. L. VIII. 115 ; P. R. I. 141 ; N. O. 227 ; with clause ; that showed thou wast divine : D. F. I. 35 ; to show withal how slight the gift was : S. A. 58 ; in passive : thou art ... shown how light : P. L. IV. 1012.

(f) to point out to, indicate ; with acc. and dat.; thou show'dst me first the way : S. A. 781 ; showed him his room : U. C. I. 15 ; with acc. and prep. phrase : P. L. IV. 558.

(g) to furnish, produce, offer ; what can Heaven show more : P. L. II. 273 ; flowers of more mingled hue than her purfled scarf can shew ; C. 995 ; my late spring no bud or blossom shew'th : S. II. 4 ; to do, accomplish ; whate'er the skill of lesser gods can show ; A. 79.

(h) to impart to, bestow or con-fer upon ; who yet will show us good ?: Ps. IV. 26.

(i) to explain, make clear : C. 512.

(2) intr. (a) to become visible, be seen : P. R. III. 286.

(b) to appear, seem : P. L. VII. 555 ; Wisdom ... like Folly shows : P. L. VIII. 553.

Shower, (1) sb. a short fall of rain : P. L. II. 491 ; IV. 653 ; falling : P. L. V. 190 ; soft : P. L. IV. 646 ; honeyed : L. 140 ; vernal : M. W. 40 ; a shower still : Il P. 127.

fig., *no drizzling shower, but rattling storm of arrows* : P. L. VI. 545 ; *sharp sleet of arrowy showers* : P. R. III. 324.

(2) *vb. tr.* (*a*) to wet with rain ; *when God hath showered the earth* : P. L. IV. 152 ; to flood with water : P. L. XI. 883.

(*b*) to pour down or out abundantly ; *taught the fixed their influence malignant when to shower* ; P. L. X. 662 ; *upon him shower his benediction* : P. L. XII. 124 ; to scatter in abundance ; *the gorgeous East ... showers on her kings barbaric pearl and gold* : P. L. II. 4 ; *the flowery roof showered roses* : P. L. IV. 773 ; *absol.* : P. L. V. 640.

Showery, *adj.* resulting from showers ; *the showery arch*, the rainbow : P. L. VI. 759.

Shrewd, *adj.* sly, cunning : C. 846.

Shriek, (1) *sb.* a sharp and shrill cry : L'A. 4 ; *Apollo ... with hollow shriek the steep of Delphos leaving* : N. O. 178.

(2) *vb. intr.* to utter such a cry : *hellish furies ... shrieked* : P. R. IV. 423.

Shrill, (1) *adj.* sharp or piercing in tone ; *the shrill matin song of birds* : P. L. V. 7.

(2) *adv.* sharply or piercingly ; *echoing shrill* : L'A. 56.

Shrine, (1) *sb.* (*a*) an altar or small chapel sacred to, or hallowed by the presence of, a god : P. L. I. 388 ; *the goddess that in rural shrine dwell'st* : C. 267 ; *before the shrine of Themis* : P. L. XI. 13 ; *through a cloud drawn round about thee like a radiant shrine* : P. L. III. 379 ; *fig.* a throne : A. 36.

(*b*) the place from which oracles were delivered : P. R. I. 438 ; *Apollo from his shrine can no more divine* : N. O. 176.

(*c*) dwelling-place, tabernacle ; *fig.*, *light ... transplanted from her cloudy shrine* : P. L. VII. 360.

(2) *vb. tr.* to enshrine ; *the Almighty Father ... shrined in his sanctuary of Heaven* : P. L. VI. 672.

Shrink, *vb.* (*pret.* shrunk ; *past part.* not used) (1) *intr.* (*a*) to decrease in volume ; *which made their flowing shrink* : P. L. XI. 846.

(*b*) to shrivel ; *all her plumes fall flat, and shrink into a trivial toy* : P. R. II. 223.

(*c*) to draw back from danger or suffering : P. L. II. 205 ; C. 656 ; *shrink from pain* : P. L. IV. 925.

(2) *tr.* (*a*) to cause to decrease in volume ; *the dread voice ... that shrunk thy streams* : L. 133.

(*b*) to draw in ; *Lybic Hammon shrinks his horn* : N. O. 203.

Shroud, I. *sb.* (*a*) a winding-sheet : L. 22.

(*b*) a place of shelter or protection : P. L. X. 1068 ; *run to your shrouds* : C. 147 ; *nought but profoundest Hell can be his shroud* : N. O. 218.

II. *vb.* (1) *tr.* to shelter, protect : P. R. IV. 419.

(2) *intr.* to take shelter ; *if your stray attendance ... shroud within these limits* : C. 316.

Shroud, *sb. pl.* the ropes forming part of a ship's rigging : P. L. II. 1044.

Shrub, *sb.* a woody plant smaller than a tree : P. L. V. 349 ; *odorous, bushy, humble, spicy* : P. L. IV. 696 ; VII. 322 ; VIII. 517 ; *undergrowth of shrubs* : P. L. IV. 176.

Shrubby, *adj.* abounding in shrubs : C. 306.

Shuddering, *part. adj.* (*a*) quaking or trembling because of fear ; transferred epithet ; *a cold shuddering dew dips me all o'er* : C. 802.

(*b*) accompanied by or causing trembling ; *with shuddering horror pale* : P. L. II. 616.

Shun, *vb.* (*pres. 2d sing.* shunn'st : Il P. 61) *tr.* (*a*) to keep clear of, endeavour not to meet, avoid ; *shun the goal with rapid wheels* : P. L. II. 531 ; *on the larboard shunned Charybdis* : P. L. II. 1019 ; *created thing naught valued he nor shunned* : P. L. II. 679 ; *shun his deadly arrow* : P. L. II. 810 ; a person as object : P. R. I. 414 ; *whose higher intellectual more I shun* : P. L. IX. 483 ; *nor shunned the sight of God or Angel* : P. L. IV. 319 ; an abstract thing as object : P. L. VIII. 328 ; IX. 331 : *evil* : P. L. IX. 699 ; *the present* : P. L. X. 339 ; *the noise of folly* : Il P. 61 ; *the broad way* : S. IX. 2 ; with *prep. inf.* ; *shun to taste* : P. L. VIII. 327.

(*b*) to avoid the effects of, provide against ; *to shun the inclement seasons* : P. L. X. 1062.

(c) to seek to escape from, evade; *shunning heat*: P. L. IX. 1108; *danger shunned by me*: P. L. I. 636.

Shut, (1) *sb.* the time of closing; *at shut of evening flowers*: P. L. IX. 278.

(2) *vb.* (*pret.* and *past part.* shut) (a) to make fast by bolts or other fastening; used of the gates of heaven or hell: P. L. VIII. 240; *to keep these gates for ever shut*: P. L. II. 776; *the golden opes, the iron shuts amain*: L. III.; *absol.*: P. L. II. 883.

fig., the heaven his windows shut: P. L. XI. 849.

(b) to close so as to prevent egress or ingress; *though Heaven be shut*: P. L. II. 358; *Hell ... shall be for ever shut*: P. L. III. 333.

(c) to bring together the lids of, close; *when sleep hath shut all eyes*: P. L. IV. 658; *of the eye of God*; *mine eye not shut*: P. L. III. 193; *fig., where day never shuts his eye*: C. 978.

(d) to render inaccessible; *shall that be shut to Man which to the Beast is open*: P. L. IX. 691.

(e) **shut out**, to exclude; *wisdom at one entrance quite shut out*: P. L. III. 50.

(f) **shut up**, to cut off or bar from by confining; *shut up from light*: S. A. 160.

Sibma, *sb.* a place beyond Jordan with extensive vineyards; its exact location is uncertain: P. L. I. 410.

Sibyl, *sb.* a prophetess: V. Ex. 69.

Sicilian, *adj.* of Sicily: L. 133. *See* **Muse.**

Sick, *sb.* or *absol.* diseased persons; *the sick*: P. L. XI. 490.

See **Heart-sick.**

Sicken, *vb. intr.* to fall ill: U. C. II. 15; *speckled Vanity will sicken soon and die*: N. O. 137.

Sickness, *sb.* illness: S. A. 698; *loathsome sickness*: P. L. XI. 524.

Side, *sb.* **(1)** either half of an animal body as divided by the median plane: P. L. I. 207; *right side*: P. L. VI. 327; *he on his side leaning*: P. L. V. 11; *from her side the fatal key ... she took*: P. L. II. 871; *harps ... by their sides like quivers hung*: P. L. III. 366; *by his side ... hung the sword*: P.

L. XI. 246; *side by side*: P. L. IV. 741.

(b) that part between the shoulder and the hip: P. L. VIII. 536; *opened my left side*: P. L. VIII. 465, 536; *being I lent out of my side to thee*: P. L. IV. 484; *from whose dear side I boast me sprung*: P. L. IX. 965; *Laughter holding both his sides*: L'A. 32.

(c) used to denote nearness: P. L. I. 78; IV. 485; XI. 176; *to have never parted from thy side*: P. L. IX. 1153; *to trust thee from my side*: P. L. X. 881; *to stand fast by thy side*: S. A. 1432; *fast by his brethren's side*: P. 21; *on each side went armed guards*: S. A. 1617; *with blending of sense* (1)(b); *leave not the faithful side that gave thee being*: P. L. IX. 265.

(d) either half of the head; *on the left side*: P. L. II. 755.

(e) *fig.* body, person; *left your fair side abandoned*: C. 283; *from her fair ... side twins are to be born*: C. 1009; *pl.*: S. A. 1241.

(2) one of the continuous surfaces of an object limited by terminal lines: P. L. IV. 135, 257, 695; XI. 574; P. R. III. 255; S. A. 1609; L'A. 55; *in the side a door contrived*: P. L. XI. 731; *the shattered side of thundering Ætna*: P. L. I. 232; *to the Western side of that high mountain*: P. R. IV. 25; *the side of yon small hill*: C. 295.

(3) one of the extended marginal parts of a surface; *from side to side*, throughout the whole extent: P. L. V. 393; C. 313; S. XXII. 12.

(4) any part with respect to its direction or situation as contrasted with another part: P. L. III. 427, 722; X. 288; *on the east side of the Garden*: P. L. XI. 118; *all the eastern side ... of Paradise*: P. L. XII. 641; *on the western side*: Ps. LXXX. 41; *that side Heaven*: P. L. II. 1006; *on this side Night*: P. L. III. 71; *on all sides, on either or every side*, in or from all directions: P. L. I. 61; II. 1015; VI. 335, 544, 844; X. 507; P. R. I. 295.

(b) a part of an object opposed to a corresponding part; *before the gates there sat on either side*:

P. L. II. 649; *one gate ... that looked east on the other side* : P. L. IV. 179.

(5) one of two places or positions with reference to an intermediate space : P. L. X. 415; P. R. IV. 33; *on this side Euphrates* : P. L. XII. 114; *on this side ... Genezaret* : P. R. II. 23; *we are at worst on this side nothing* : P. L. II. 101.

(6) one of two parts or positions placed in opposition to each other; (*a*) in the opposition of combat; *on the other side* : P. L. II. 706; IV. 985.

(*b*) in the opposition of thought or opinion; *on the other side* : P. L. II. 108; IX. 888; P. R. IV. 159; S. A. 246, 768.

(7) one of two groups of persons at war, party : P. L. I. 578; *Angels fought on either side* : P. L. VI. 221; or the meaning may be nearly (1) (*e*), person, himself : P. L. VI. 133.

fig., *sands ... levied to side with warring winds* : P. L. II. 905.

(8) line of descent; *by mother's side* : P. R. II. 136; III. 154.

See **Forest-side, Fountain-side, Thicket-side.**

Sideboard, *sb.* side-table : P. R. II. 350.

Sidelong, *adv.* (*a*) obliquely : P. L. VI. 197; IX. 512.

(*b*) on one's side; *sidelong as they sat recline* : P. L. IV. 333.

Sideral, *adj.* produced by the influence of the stars; *sideral blast* : P. L. X. 693.

Sideways, *adv.* toward one side : M. W. 42.

Siding, *adj.* taking one's part, defending : C. 212.

Sidonian, *adj.* of Sidon, the city of Phœnicia : P. L. I. 441.

Siege, *sb.* the act of besetting a fortified place; *lay siege* : P. L. XI. 656; *Heaven, whose high walls fear no ... siege* : P. L. II. 343; *to God his tower intends siege* : P. L. XII. 74.

fig., *the hateful siege of contraries* : P. L. IX. 121; *what sieges girt me round* : S. A. 846.

Sift, *vb. tr.* to examine critically; *sift thee* : P. R. IV. 532.

Sigh, I. *sb.* a deep and long-drawn respiration indicative of sorrow, grief, or anxiety : P. L. IV. 31; XI. 31; S. A. 392; Ps. LXXXVIII.

6; *one short sigh of human breath* : P. L. XI. 147; *words interwove with sighs* : P. L. I. 621; *with our or their sighs the air frequenting* : P. L. X. 1090, 1102; *thoughts, which she in sighs thus clad* : P. R. II. 65; *burn in your sighs* : Cir. 8; *sighs and prayers, which in this golden censer, mixed with incense* : P. L. XI. 23; *their hearts, ... that sighs now breathed* : P. L. XI. 5.

II. *vb.* (1) *intr.* to utter a sigh; *fig.*, *Hell ... sighed from all her caves* : P. L. II. 788; *Nature ... sighing* : P. L. IX. 783.

(2) *tr.* to spend in sighing; *sighing out my days* : Ps. VI. 11.

vbl. sb. **sighing,** the act of expressing sorrow by sighing : N. O. 186.

Sight, *sb.* (1) the power of vision, the faculty of seeing : P. L. VIII. 527; S. A. 157, 1117; *mortal, human, earthly* : P. L. III. 55; VII. 368; VIII. 120; XII. 9; Il P. 14; *sharpest* : P. L. IX. 91; *clearer* : P. L. XI. 413; *my fancied sight* : S. XXIII. 10; *why was the sight to such a tender ball as the eye confined* : S. A. 93; as swift in action : P. L. VI. 191; as lost : S. A. 196, 914; S. XXII. 4; *loss of* : S. A. 67, 152, 645; *blind of* : S. A. 1687; *sight bereaved* : S. A. 1294; used with reference to God or angels; *Uriel ... thy perfect sight* : P. L. IV. 577; *the Eternal Eye, whose sight* : P. L. V. 711.

(*b*) *to sight*, judged by the sight : P. L. VI. 118.

(*c*) *for sight*, to look at : P. L. IV. 217.

(*d*) perhaps the meaning is nearer to the eye as seeing or looking : P. L. IX. 898; *the fruitage fair to sight* : P. L. X. 561; *with what to sight ... was sweet* : P. L. XI. 281; *living creatures, new to sight* : P. L. IV. 287; *surrounds their sight a globe of circular light* : N. O. 109.

(*e*) used *fig.* of the mind; *fancy, my internal sight* : P. L. VIII. 461; *mental sight* : P. L. XI. 418.

(2) the fact of seeing, the perceiving or being perceived by the eye, view : P. L. V. 138; *from his sight received beatitude* : P. L. III.

61 ; *at whose* or *his sight* : P. L.
IV. 34 ; P. R. I. 310 ; *at sight of*
or *whereof* : P. L. III. 554 ; X.
350 ; P. R. III. 345 ; *at sight of
him* : S. A. 1620 ; *the sight of me* :
S. A. 1415 ; *the sight of this ...
spectacle* : S. A. 1542 ; *I trust to
have full sight of her* : S. XXIII.
8 ; *lost sight of* : P. L. IV. 573 ;
not knew by sight : P. R. I. 271 ;
mock us with his blest sight : P. R.
II. 56 ; *in sight* : P. L. VIII. 41, 63 ;
IX. 565 ; X. 324 ; XI. 19 ; *in their,
her, our*, etc. *sight* : P. L. V. 46 ;
X. 683 ; XI. 184, 201 ; Ps. VII.
28 ; LXXX. 10 ; *in sight of* : P. L.
II. 749 ; V. 765 ; IX. 517 ; S. A.
24.

(3) the act of seeing, look,
gaze ; *worth thy* or *the sight* : P.
L. V. 308 ; P. R. IV. 86 ; *nor
shun the sight of God or Angel* : P.
L. IV. 319 ; *covered from his
Father's sight* : P. L. X. 223 ;
sight no obstacle found here : P. L.
III. 615 ; *no cloud, or to obstruct
his sight, star interposed* : P. L. V.
257.

(4) presence : P. L. IX. 294,
310 ; *the pain of absence from thy
sight* : P. L. IX. 861 ; *out of my
sight* : P. L. X. 867 ; the presence
of God : P. L. III. 655 ; VII. 185 ;
T. 18 ; Ps. V. 12 ; *that stand in
sight of God* : P. L. V. 536 ; X.
828 ; God looking on and judging,
in God's judgement or estimation ;
to stand approved in sight of God :
P. L. VI. 36 ; *such grace shall one
just man find in his sight* : P. L.
XI. 890.

(5) something seen or to be
seen, spectacle : P. L. III. 43 ; X.
538 ; XI. 555, 872 ; L'A. 129 ;
sights of woe : P. L. I. 64 ; *O sight
of terror* : P. L. XI. 463 ; *detestable, hateful, monstrous*, etc. : P.
L. II. 745 ; IV. 505 ; VI. 862 ; XI.
493 ; L'A. 4 ; *glorious, nobler,
fair* : P. L. IV. 658 ; XI. 411 ; P.
R. III. 351 ; *rural* : P. L. IX. 451.
at the or *that sight* : P. L. III.
256 ; V. 448, 665 ; VI. 111, 792 ;
XI. 448.

(6) insight, discernment : P. R.
III. 238.

See **Eye-sight, Sharpest-sighted.**

Sign, *sb.* (1) a visible thing announc-
ing the presence of a person,
approaching here in meaning to
banner, standard : P. L. VI. 776.

(2) symbol ; (baptism) *the sign
of washing them from guilt of sin* :
P. L. XII. 442.

(3) mark, token, evidence, proof :
P. L. I. 672 ; II. 831 ; VIII. 342 :
C. 572 ; *an olive-leaf he brings,
pacific sign* : P. L. XI. 860 ; *ill-
luck signs* : C. 845 ; *of his presence
many a sign* : P. L. XI. 351 ; *sign
of remorse, obedience, power, wrath*,
etc. : P. L. I. 605 ; IV. 428, 429 ;
V. 134 ; VI. 58 ; VIII. 514 ; IX.
783, 1077 ; P. R. II. 119 ; *in sign
of sorrow* : P. L. X. 1091, 1103 ;
in sign of worship : P. L. V. 194 ;
token or witness ; *some sign of
good to me afford* : Ps. LXXXVI.
61.

(*b*) a movement of the body
indicating intention ; *sign of
battle* : C. 654.

(*c*) that by which one is
warned ; used of Christ as indicating the will of God and
admonishing men ; *he should be ...
to a sign spoken against* : P. R. II.
89.

(*d*) used of the stars as indicating the quarters of the heavens
and changes in the weather, as
portents of extraordinary events,
and possibly as means of revealing
divine judgements : P. L. VII.
341.

(4) prodigy, portent ; (*a*) any
phenomenon portending future
events, omen, prognostic ; used of
events : P. L. XI. 182 ; *Heaven
by these mute signs in Nature
shows* : P. L. XI. 194 ; *a sure foregoing sign* : P. R. IV. 483 ; *signs
betokening* : P. R. IV. 489 ; *presages
and signs* : P. R. I. 394 ; used of
persons or things ; *called me Sin,
and for a sign portentous held me* :
P. L. II. 760 ; *read thy lot in yon
celestial sign* : P. L. IV. 1011.

(*b*) a manifestation of the power
of God : P. L. VI. 789 ; in mira-
cles : P. L. XII. 175.

(5) a constellation of the Zodiac ;
the Scorpion sign : P. L. IV. 998.

Signal, (1) *adj.* eminent, remarkable : S. A. 338.

(2) *sb.* something that incites
to or directs action : P. L. II. 56 ;
V. 705 ; *a* or *the signal given* : P.
L. I. 347, 776 ; *that voice ... their
surest signal* : P. L. I. 278 ; *the
parting Sun ... my signal to depart* :
P. L. VIII. 632 ; *till winds the*

signal blow: P. L. II. 717; the
Son gave signal high: P. L. XI.
72; in signal of remove: P. L. XII.
593.

See Fore-signify.

Silence, sb. (1) abstinence from
speech or noise: P. L. I. 797; X.
459; sacred: P. L. V. 557;
shameful: P. R. IV. 22; silence
was in Heaven: P. L. III. 218;
with reason hath deep silence ...
seized us: P. L. II. 431; an
unusual stop of sudden silence:
C. 552; broke silence: P. L. IX.
895; X. 353; P. R. IV. 43;
imper., silence, ye troubled waves:
P. L. VII. 216; personified; driving
dumb Silence from the portal door:
V. Ex. 5.

(b) in silence, without words or
noise: P. L. I. 561; II. 994; VI.
64; VII. 594; S. A. 864.

(2) absence of sound or noise,
stillness: P. L. V. 39, 668; Night
... inducing ... silence: P. L. VI.
408; through the soft silence of
the listening night: Cir. 5; breaking the horrid silence: P. L. I.
83; more or less clearly personified: P. L. IV. 600; Night
with her will bring Silence: P. L.
VII. 106; Silence was pleased: P.
L. IV. 604; the mute Silence hist
along: Il P. 55; how sweetly did
they float upon the wings of silence:
C. 250; Silence was took ere she
was ware: C. 557.

(3) absence of mention, oblivion: P. L. XI. 699; eternal
silence be their doom: P. L. VI.
385.

(4) secrecy; the seal of silence:
S. A. 49; the sacred trust of: S.
A. 428; gave up my fort of silence:
S. A. 236.

Silent, adj. (a) not speaking: P. L.
VI. 882; IX. 1063; if I be silent:
P. L. V. 202; be not thou silent ...
O God: Ps. LXXXIII. 1; used fig.
of the countenance; his meek aspect silent yet spake: P. L. III.
267.

(b) making little or no sound;
a slow and silent stream, Lethe:
P. L. II. 582.

(c) fig. not shining; silent as
the moon: S. A. 87.

(d) unmarked or unaccom-
panied by speech or sound; all
things that breathe ... send up silent
praise: P. L. IX. 195; silent cir-

cumspection: P. L. VI. 523; silent
obsequy and funeral train: S. A.
1732.

(e) free from noise, marked
by stillness, quiet; silent Night:
P. L. IV. 647, 654; the silent
(time), hours: P. L. V. 39; VII.
444; the silent air: C. 481; silent
valley, walk: P. L. II. 547; P. R.
II. 261; she (the earth) from west
her silent course advance: P. L.
VIII. 163.

(f) withholding mention: P.
L. IV. 938.

Silently, adj. without noise, quietly:
P. L. II. 842; V. 130.

Silk, sb. the thread produced by the
larvæ of silk-worms; worms ...
weave the smooth-haired silk: C.
716.

Silken, adj. (a) made of silk: P. R.
IV. 76; S. A. 730.

(b) like silk, delicate, tender;
soft silken primrose: D. F. I. 2.

Silly, adj. harmless, innocent: N.
O. 92.

Silo, sb. Shiloh, a town of Ephraim,
the place where the ark was kept
from the days of Joshua to the
time of Samuel (spelled Silo in
Vulg.): S. A. 1674.

Siloa, (Siloa) sb. Siloam, a pool outside the walls of Jerusalem: Siloa's
brook, the pool of Siloam or the
stream flowing from it (spelled
Siloë in Vulg.): P. L. I. 11.

Silver, I. sb. the precious metal:
P. L. III. 595.

II. adj. (1) made of silver: P.
L. III. 644; shooting her beams
like silver threads: A. 16.

(2) resembling silver; (a) applied to the pale lustre of the
moon or the clouds; o'er the dark
her silver mantle threw: P. L. IV.
609; her silver lining: C. 222, 224.

(b) applied to water: bright,
shining; silver lake or lakes: P.
L. VII. 437; C. 865.

(c) applied to sound: soft and
clear; silver chime: N. O. 128.

Silver-buskined, adj. wearing busk-
ins, or half-boots, adorned with
silver, or made of cloth of silver:
A. 33.

Silver-shafted, adj. carrying silver
arrows: C. 442.

Simeon, sb. the devout Jew who
prophesied concerning Christ
(Luke II. 25-35): P. R. I. 255; II.
87.

Similitude, *sb.* (*a*) likeness; *let us make now Man ... in our similitude*: P. L. VII. 520; *Man, retaining still divine similitude*: P. L. XI. 512.

(*b*) one in whom the likeness of another is seen, image; *begotten Son, Divine Similitude*: P. L. III. 384.

Simon, *sb.* Simon Peter, one of the twelve apostles: P. R. II. 7.

Simple, (1) *adj.* (*a*) lowly and unlearned; *simple shepherds*: P. L. XII. 365.

(*b*) plain and insignificant: P. R. II. 348.

(2) *sb. pl.* medicinal herbs: C. 627.

Simplicity, *sb.* artlessness of mind: P. L. III. 687; *personified*; *Suspicion sleeps ... and to Simplicity resigns her charge*: P. L. III. 687.

Simply, *adv.* artlessly, guilelessly; *sat simply chatting*: N. O. 87; *subverting worldly - strong ... by simply meek*: P. L. XII. 569.

Sin, I. *sb.* any want of conformity to or any violation of the law of God: P. L. III. 446; VI. 506; IX. 292, 327; XII. 283, 285, 289; P. R. I. 266; D. F. I. 66; Cir. 12; C. 465; Ps. LXXXIV. 40; LXXXV. 7; *enthralled by sin*: P. L. III. 177; *dead in sins*: P. L. III. 233; *guilt of sin*: P. L. XII. 443; *taint of sin*: S. A. 313; *to ways of sin and shame*: Ps. LXXX. 74; *sins national*: P. L. XII. 316; *the sins of all mankind*: P. L. XII. 416; *Law can discover sin*: P. L. XII. 290; *to wash off sin*: P. R. I. 73; *'tis only daylight that makes sin*: C. 126; *each thing of sin and guilt*: C. 456; *disproportioned sin*: S. M. 19.

(*b*) a particular sinful act specified or understood from the context: P. L. IV. 758; S. A. 499, 504, 1357; F. of C. 4; *that sin in Bethel*: P. L. I. 485; *the sin of him who slew his brother*: P. L. XI. 678; *Can it be sin to know?*: P. L. IV. 517.

(*c*) the sin of Adam and Eve: P. L. IX. 70; X. 16, 133, 791; XI. 427; XII. 429, 474; *the mortal Sin original*: P. L. IX. 1003; *the solace of their sin*: P. L. IX. 1044; *Man's polluting sin*: P. L. X. 631; *dissolution wrought by sin*: P. L. XI. 55; *the sin of Eve*: P. L. XI. 519.

(*d*) the sin of Satan or the other rebel angels; *by sin of disobedience*: P. L. VI. 396: *thou resemblest now thy sin*: P. L. IV. 840; *save what sin hath impaired*: P. L. VI. 691; *Satan, first in sin*: P. L. X. 172; *Satan ... struck with guilt of his own sin*: P. R. III. 147.

(*e*) *personified*: N. O. 138; *esp.* the being that sprang from the head of Satan: P. L. II. 1024; X. 230, 234, 251, 407, 473, 490, 586, 590, 635, 708; XII. 431; *back they recoiled ... and called me Sin*: P. L. II. 760; *Sin, his fair enchanting daughter*: P. L. X. 352; *Sin and her shadow Death*: P. L. IX. 12; *Sin ... and her black attendant Death*: P. L. VII. 546; probably also: P. R. I. 159.

II. *vb.* (1) *intr.* to violate the law of God: P. L. VI. 402; X. 516; 930; Ps. IV. 19; *it was but breath of life that sinned*: P. L. X. 790; *Man ... sins against the high supremacy of Heaven*: P. L. III. 204.

(2) *tr.* to commit; with cognate object; *nor sinned thy sin*: P. L. XI. 427; *impers.*; *ere thus was sinned*: P. L. X. 229.

vbl. sb. **sinning,** the committing of sin; *gross by sinning grown*: P. L. VI. 661.

Sinæan, *adj.* of the Sinæ, an ancient name of the people of China: P. L. XI. 390.

Sinai, *sb.* the mountain of the Sinaitic peninsula whence Moses received the law: P. L. I. 7; *Mount Sinai*: N. O. 158; *the Mount of Sinai*: P. L. XII. 227. See **Oreb.**

Sin-born, *adj.* being the child of Sin: P. L. X. 596.

Sin-bred, *adj.* produced by sin: P. L. IV. 315.

***Since,** (1) *adv.* (*a*) from that time till now: P. L. I. 582; P. R. I. 52; II. 358; *the loveliest pair that ever since in love's embraces met*: P. L. IV. 322; *never since of serpent kind lovelier*: P. L. IX. 504; *where eloquence flourished, since mute*: P. L. IX. 672; *the past time not accurately given by the context*: P. L. IV. 341; IX. 497; XI. 509.

(*b*) subsequently, after and in the meantime: P. L. III. 495; XI. 393; P. R. II. 100; *his trumpet, heard in Oreb since*: P. L. XI.

74 ; *so since into his Church lewd
hirelings climb* : P. L. IV. 192.

(c) before now, ago ; *long since*:
P. R. I. 399 ; IV. 189 ; S. A. 929.

(2) *prep.* ever from the time of,
after : P. L. X. 451 ; XI. 85 ; XII.
83 ; *since created man* : P. L. I.
573 ; *since man on earth* : S. A.
165 ; *since meridian hour, morning hour*, etc.: P. L. IV. 581 ;
VIII. 111 ; IX. 412, 1029; *since
then* : S. A. 884.

(3) *conj.* (a) from the time when,
during the time after : P. L. VI.
686 ; IX. 25, 60 ; X. 233 ; P. R. I.
51 ; II. 107 ; *since Satan fell* : P.
L. IV. 905 ; *since born his sons* :
P. L. IV. 323 ; *not longer than
since I in one night freed* : P. L.
IX. 140 ; *since ... I fell asleep* : P.
L. XII. 613.

(b) inasmuch as, seeing that,
because: P. L. I. 116 ; II. 12,
817 ; IV. 612, 1008 ; V. 363 ; VI.
433 ; VII. 80 ; VIII. 645 ; IX. 710,
1070 ; X. 241, 962 ; XII. 90 ; P.R.
I. 443 ; IV. 368 ; S. A. 843 ; *since
no less than such could* : P. L. I.
144 ; *since God is light* : P. L. III.
3 ; *since now we find* : P. L. VI.
433 ; *since none but thou can end
it* : P. L. VI. 702 ; *since to part,
go* : P. L. VIII. 645 ; *since higher
I fall short* : P. L. IX. 174 ; *since
easier shunned* : P. L. IX. 699 ;
since I as man : P. L. IX. 710.

Sincere, *adj.* (1) not assumed or
feigned, true, genuine ; *sincere
faith, love, delight* : P. L. IX. 320;
X. 915 ; P. R. II. 480 ; S. A. 874.

(b) admissible or convincing ;
proof ... sincere : P. L. III. 103.

(c) assiduous and heedful; *sup.,
your sincerest care* : P. L. X. 37.

(2) characterized or prompted
by moral purity and genuineness;
sincere intent : P. L. III. 192 ; *for
his* (offering) *was not sincere* : P.
L. XI. 443.

(3) morally upright or with unfeigned and upright intentions ;
*Abraham ... may bring them back,
repentant and sincere* : P. R. III. 435.

Sincerely, *adj.* truly, really : T. 14;
C. 454.

Sinew, *sb.* a tendon or a muscle ;
*this strength, diffused ... through all
my sinews* : S. A. 1142 ; *by sinews
weak didst move my ... tongue* : V.
Ex. 1 ; *crumble all thy sinews* : C.
615.

Sinful, *adj.* (a) full of sin, wicked ;
mass of sinful flesh : P. R. I. 162;
the sinful pair : P. L. XI. 105.

(b) morally depraved, evil ; *sinful state* : P. L. III. 186; *thought*:
P. L. VIII. 506; *pollute with sinful
blame* : N. O. 41.

Sinfulness, *sb.* moral corruption,
wickedness: P. L. XI. 360.

Sing, *vb.* (*pres. 2d sing.* sing'st : C.
567 ; *3d sing.* singeth : L'A. 65;
pret. sang : P. L. III. 383 ; VII.
192; L. 186; elsewhere and usually
sung ; *past part.* sung) I. *intr.* (1)
to utter a song : P. L. XI. 619 ; A.
86 ; C. 567, 623 ; S. XIII. 13; Ps.
v. 35 ; LXXXI. 1, 2 ; LXXXVII. 25;
the milkmaid singeth blithe ; L'A.
65 ; *faery ladies ... sweetly singing
round thy bed* : V. Ex. 63 ; used
of angels or saints in heaven : P.
L. X. 643 ; P. R. I. 171; S. M.
28 ; *when Spirits immortal sing* :
P. L. II. 553 ; *a glorious quire of
Angels ... sung to shepherds* : P. R.
I. 243 ; *of old the Sons of Morning
sung* : N. O. 119 ; *the Saints above
... that sing* : L. 180 ; used of the
Muses, etc.: C. 256 ; *the Muses ...
aye round about Jove's altar sing* :
Il P. 48 ; *the celestial Sirens' harmony ... that sing* : A. 65 ; *his
daughters three that sing about the
golden tree* : C. 983 ; with what is
sung preceding and either stated or
described : P. L. VII. 573, 633 ;
thus sang the uncouth swain : L.
186 ; *so sang the Hierarchies* : P.
L. VII. 192.

(b) used of birds or insects : P.
L. V. 198 ; of the lark : L'A. 42 ;
of the nightingale : P. L. III. 39 ;
S. I. 9, 11 ; of the night-raven :
L'A. 7 ; of the bee : Il P. 143.

(2) to blow a signal ; *to arms the
matin trumpet sung* : P. L. VI. 526.

(3) to play on a musical instrument ; *while the hand sung with
the voice* : P. R. I. 172.

(4) to compose poetry : P. L.
III. 18 ; VII. 24 ; V. Ex. 45 ; L.
10, 11 ; said of the muse that in-
spires poetry : *sing, Heavenly
Muse* : P. L. I. 6 ; *my muse with
Angels did divide to sing* : P. 4.

(5) to relate in poetry ; *as some
sager sing* : L'A. 17.

(6) to prophesy ; *the Prophets
... of great Messiah shall sing* : P.
L. XII. 244 ; *so the holy sages once
did sing* : N. O. 5.

II. *tr.* (1) to utter as a song; with cognate object; *amorous ditties*: P. L. XI. 583; *seranate*: P. L. IV. 769; *bid the soul of Orpheus sing such notes*: Il P. 105; *what unshorn Apollo sings*; used of angels or saints; *halleluiahs, psalms*, etc.: P. L. II. 242; VI. 744; X. 642; P. R. IV. 594; S. M. 7, 16; *in fit strains,...sung*: P. L. V. 148; *his carol sung*: P. L. XII. 367; *the heavenly choirs the hymenæan sung*: P. L. IV. 711; '*Open, ye everlasting gates!*' *they sung*: P. L. VII. 565.

(*b*) used of the nightingale; *she ...her amorous descant sung*: P. L. IV. 603.

(2) to celebrate in song, proclaim by song: P. L. VIII. 519; S. A. 983; A. 29; Ps. VII. 63; *am I not sung ...for a fool*: S. A. 203; *they loudest sing the vices of their deities*: P. R. IV. 339; said of angels: P. L. III. 372, 383; VII. 182; Cir. 4; *singing their great Creator*: P. L. IV. 684; *whose praise be ever sung*: P. L. V. 405; *each order bright sung triumph*: P. L. VI. 886; *sing ... their own heroic deeds*: P. L. II. 547; *morning chorus sung the second Day*: P. L. VII. 275; *the Six Days' acts they sung*: P. L. VII. 601; with two *acc.*: P. L. VII. 259; *the angelic song ... that sung thee Saviour*: P. R. IV. 506; *they the Son of God sung victor*: P. R. IV. 637.

(3) to describe or celebrate in poetry: P. R. I. 1, 2; Il P. 117; to compose or write in poetry: P. R. IV. 258.

(4) to prophesy, foretell; *the like shall sing all Prophecy*: P. L. XII. 324; *the Prophets old, who sung thy endless reign*: P. R. III. 178.

Singed (*disyl.*), *part. adj.* burned superficially: P. L. I. 236, 614; *fig.*, inflamed by the sun's rays; *summer drouth or singed air*: C. 928.

Single, I. *adj.* (1) not more than one: P. L. V. 552; *single combatant*: S. A. 344; *in fight withstand me single and unarmed*: S. A. 1111; *his single imperfection*, his imperfection which consists in being only one: P. L. VIII. 423.

(2) having but one on a side; *single fight*: S. A. 1222.

(3) apart from others, by oneself: P. L. X. 817; *the stars voluminous, or single characters*: P. R. IV. 384; *single or in array of battle ranged*: P. L. XI. 644; apart from each other: P. L. IX. 325.

(*b*) alone, unaccompanied: P. L. VII. 403; P. R. I. 323; *a single helpless maiden*: C. 402; *others came single*: P. L. III. 469; *I thus single*: P. L. IX. 536.

(*c*) alone, unaided: P. L. IV. 856; V. 903; *daring single to be just*: P. L. XI. 703; *who single hast maintained ... the cause*: P. L. VI. 30.

(*d*) individual, particular; *yet leader seemed each warrior single*: P. L. VI. 233.

(4) pertaining to one person or thing, individual, opposed to *common* or *general*; *I ... presumed single rebellion*: S. A. 1210; *which bears no single sense*: P. R. IV. 517.

(5) unmixed, complete; *single darkness*: C. 204.

(6) mere, only: C. 369.

absol. one person alone: P. L. IX. 339.

II. *vb. tr.* to select for single combat: S. A. 1092.

Singly, *adv.* (*a*) with no more than one; *those great acts which God hath done singly by me*: S. A. 244.

(*b*) one at a time: P. L. I. 379.

Singular, *adj.* not in accord with the majority, peculiar: P. L. V. 851.

Singularly, *adv.* apart from others, individually; *who dares be singularly good*: P. R. III. 57.

Sinister (sinìster), *adj.* used with the double meaning of left and unlucky: P. L. X. 886.

Sink, *vb.* (*pret.* and *past part.* sunk; perfect tenses formed with *have*: P. L. II. 594; with *be*: P. L. IX. 48; C. 375; L. 167) I. *intr.* (1) to go down, descend, opposed to *rise*: P. L. II. 81.

(*b*) to descend to hell under the sentence of God: P. L. III. 331.

(*c*) to descend below the surface of the earth: *in with the river sunk ... Satan*: P. L. IX. 74; to descend a given depth; *so high as heaved the tumid hills, so low down sunk a hollow bottom*: P. L. VII. 289.

(2) to become submerged in water or something likened to it:

L. 167, 172 ; *swims, or sinks* : P. L.
II. 950 ; *that Serbonian bog...where
armies whole have sunk* : P. L. II.
594 ; *for ever sunk under yon boiling ocean* : P. L. II. 182 ; *though
sun and moon were in the flat sea
sunk* : C. 375.

(3) to fall ; (*a*) to fall *down* to
the ground : P. L. V. 91 ; VIII.
457 ; XI. 420.

(*b*) to be overcome and fall in
battle ; *their heads ... sunk before
the spear* : P. L. I. 436.

(*c*) to be destroyed : P. 40.'

(*d*) to become debased morally;
sunk in carnal pleasure : P. L.
VIII. 593.

(4) to descend and disappear
below the horizon : P. L. IX. 48 ;
so sinks the day-star : L. 168 ; *fig.,
daylight sunk* : P. R. IV. 398.

II. *tr.* to engulf, submerge : L.
102 ; with the double meaning of
to engulf and to overwhelm with
sorrow : P. L. XI. 758.

See **Half-sunk.**

Sinless, *adj.* (*a*) guiltless of sin : P.
L. VII. 61 ; IX. 659 ; X. 690.

(*b*) not arising from or involving
sin ; *sinless peace* : P. R. IV. 425.

Sinner, *sb.* one who commits sin :
Ps. I. 3, 14.

Sinuous, *adj.* winding, tortuous : P.
L. VII. 481.

Sin-worn, *adj.* worn out or decayed
by sin ; *this sin-worn mould* : C. 17.

Sion, *sb.* (*a*) the mount at Jerusalem
on which the temple stood : P. L.
III. 30 ; *Sion hill* : P. L. I. 10 ;
Sion my holy hill : Ps. II. 13 ;
Mount Sion : P. L. III. 530.

(*b*) the temple itself : P. L. I.
386 ; *transf.* heaven, the dwelling-
place of God : Ps. LXXXIV. 28.

(*c*) Jerusalem : P. L. I. 442, 453 ;
Ps. LXXXVII. 5, 18.

(*d*) the Israelites, the people of
God ; *Sion's songs*, the lyrics of
the Old Testament : P. R. IV. 347.

Sip, (**1**) *sb.* a very small draught,
taste : C. 811.

(**2**) *vb. tr.* to take in gradually
as if in drinking ; *every herb that
sips the dew* : Il. P. 172.

Sir, *sb.* (*a*) a respectful title of address : P. R. I. 321 ; S. XI. 8.

(*b*) a title of honour prefixed to
the Christian name of a knight :
S. XI. 12. *See* **Cheek.**

Sire, *sb.* (*a*) sovereign, lord ; *Heaven's
all-ruling Sire* : P. L. II. 264.

(*b*) an old man ; *reverend,
ancient* ; applied to Noah : P. L.
XI. 719, 862 ; to Manoa ; in direct
address : S. A. 1456 ; to Camus :
L. 103.

(*c*) father, progenitor ; applied
to Noah : P. L. XI. 736 ; to Manoa :
S. A. 326 ; to Adam ; *our Sire* :
P. L. IV. 712 ; VIII. 39, 249 ; XI.
460 ; XII. 467 ; *our general sire* :
P. L. IV. 144 ; *our primitive great
Sire* : P. L. V. 350 ; in direct address ; *Sire of men* : P. L. VIII.
218 ; to God as the father of
Christ or angels : P. L. VI. 95 ;
P. R. I. 86, 233 ; *his sire the Power
of the Most High* : P. L. XII. 368 ;
to Satan as the father of Sin : P.
L. II. 817, 849 ; to Zeus : V. Ex.
39.

Siren, *sb. pl.* the nymphs who by
their singing bewitched men : C.
253, 878 ; the singers of the heavens ; *celestial Sirens' harmony, that
sit upon the nine infolded spheres* :
A. 63 ; *fig.*, *blest pair of Sirens,
... sphere-born harmonious sisters,
Voice and Verse* : S. M. 1.

Sirocco, *sb.* the Italian name for the
southeast wind : P. L. X. 706.

Sisera, *sb.* the captain of the army
of Jabin, king of Canaan : S. A.
990 ; Ps. LXXXIII. 35.

Sister, *sb.* (*a*) a female born of the
same parents as another or others ;
applied to the Lady in Comus : C.
350, 366, 407, 408, 414, 486, 564 ;
to the Nereids ; *Panope with all
her sisters* : L. 99 ; to the Muses;
Sisters of the sacred well : L. 15 ;
Himera or Hemera (?) : Il P. 18.

(*b*) *fig.* applied to things closely
allied ; *Urania ... Wisdom, thy
sister* : P. L. VII. 10 ; *sisters,
Voice and Verse* : S. M. 2 ; to
stars : Ps. CXXXVI. 34 ; *the seven
Atlantic sisters* (*see* Atlantic) :
P. L. X. 674.

attrib. who are sisters ; *two
sister Graces* : L'A. 15.

Sit, *vb.* (*pres. 2d sing.* sitt'st : P. L.
III. 376 ; IV. 578 ; V. 156 ; M. W.
61 ; Ps. LXXX. 5 ; *pret.* sat ; *2d sing.*
sat'st : P. L. I. 21 ; IV. 825 ; P. R.
IV. 425 ; *past part.* sat) *intr.*
(**1**) to rest upon the haunches,
occupy a seat ; sometimes with
blending of senses (**7**) or (**8**) : P. L.
II. 648, 724, 777, 778, 803 ; IV.
549 ; VIII. 41, 210 ; IX. 1064 ; X.
230, 864 ; S. A. 4, 1309, 1608,

1652; C. 818, 1002; *who ... in the
seat of scorners hath not sat*: Ps. I. 4;
others apart sat on a hill: P. L.
II. 557; *they sat recline on the
soft downy bank*: P. L. IV. 333;
in the door he sat: P. L. V. 299;
she sits on diamond rocks: C. 881;
in his ... chariot sat: P. L. VI.
100; *sat ... in a rustic row*: N. O.
87; *at his supper sat*: C. 293; *sit
and hear* or *hearken*: P. R. IV.
123; C. 625; *sit and taste*: P. L.
V. 369; *I ... have sat to wonder*:
A. 43; *where God ... with Man ...
used to sit*: P. L. IX. 3; *the hapless pair sat in their sad discourse*:
P. L. X. 343.

(*b*) used of animals; *gazing sat*:
P. L. IV. 351.

(*c*) *fig.* to cling; used of serpents: P. L. X. 559.

(2) to occupy a throne **or** a
similar seat of power, hence often
rather, to exercise power **or**
authority: P. L. II. 456; A. 18,
91; *the god that sits at marriage-
feast*: M. W. 18; *Ashtaroth ...
now sits not girt with tapers' holy
shine*: N. O. 202; with a *sb.* of
position; *as sitting queen adored
on Beauty's throne*: P. R. II. 212;
used of God or Christ: P. L. II.
139, 643, 359; III. 57, 63, 315,
376; V. 597; VI. 747; P. R. II.
440; III. 153; S. M. 8; *as one
secure sat on his throne*: P. L. I.
639; *Him who sits above*: P. L. II.
731; *who sitt'st above*: P. L. V.
156; *where he sits shrined in his
sanctuary*: P. L. VI. 671; *he sits
at the right hand of bliss*: P. L.
VI. 892; *sit on David's throne*: P.
R. I. 240; IV. 146; *to sit the
midst of Trinal Unity*: N. O. 11;
used of angels: P. L. I. 360; II.
5; IV. 829; IX. 164; *Angels ... sat
as Princes*: P. L. I. 735; *Beëlzebub ... none higher sat*: P. L. II.
300; *Uriel ... amid the sun's bright
circle where thou sitt'st*: P. L. IV.
578.

(*b*) used *fig.* of personifications;
with him enthroned sat ... Night:
P. L. II. 962; *the ... sun ... sat high
in his meridian tower*: P. L. IV.
30; *mercy shall sit between, throned*:
N. O. 144; with a *sb.* of position
or office; *chaos umpire sits*: P. L.
II. 907; *Night sits monarch*: C.
957; *the Moon sits arbitress*: P. L.
I. 785.

(3) to set oneself down, take a
seat: P. L. II. 417; VI. 446; P.
R. II. 336; *sit and eat*: P. R. II.
368; *Nay, Lady, sit*: C. 659;
with *down*: P. L. V. 433; X. 448;
P. R. II. 377.

(*b*) *refl.* to seat oneself; *I sat
me down*: P. L. VIII. 287; C. 543;
they sat them down: P. L. IV. 327;
IX. 1121; *sat him down with his
great Father*: P. L. VII. 587.

(4) to crouch down; *why satt'st
thou like an enemy in wait*: P. L.
IV. 825.

(*b*) to rest upon the feet in a
crouching posture; *the bee sits on
the bloom*: P. L. V. 25; used of
Satan in the form of a bird: P. L.
IV. 196, 197.

(*c*) to crouch as a bird on a
nest; *birds of calm sit brooding*:
N. O. 68; used *fig.* of the Spirit
of God; *dove-like sat'st brooding*:
P. L. I. 21.

(5) to remain inactive, not to
engage in the business that should
occupy one; with *pres. part.*: P.
L. X. 235; *to sit ... hatching vain
empires*: P. L. II. 377; *contriving,
lingering, projecting*: P. L. II. 54,
56, 329.

(6) to have a seat or an abiding-
place, be located; *care sat on his
faded cheek*: P. L. I. 602; *deep
on his front ... deliberation sat*:
P. L. II. 303; *that this new comer,
Shame, there sit not*; P. L. IX.
1098; *thy rapt soul sitting in
thine eyes*; Il P. 40; *at his right
hand sat Victory*: P. L. VI. 763;
on his crest sat Horror: P. L. IV.
989.

(7) to be or remain in a specified
position or condition; sometimes
including sense (1): P. L. II. 420,
859; N. O. 244; *the bliss wherein
he sat*: P. L. III. 408; *sit in want*:
P. R. II. 431; *in calm ... peace*:
P. R. IV. 425; *full of cares*: S. A.
805; *though one should musing sit*:
S. A. 1017; *sit* or *sat idle* or *still*:
S. A. 556, 1500; N. O. 59; Ps.
LXXXIII. 3; *Earth sitting still*: P.
L. VIII. 89; *my soul in holy vision
sit*: P. 41; *they sat in fellowships
of joy*: P. L. XI. 79.

(*b*) to be on guard: P. L. X.
421; *sat watch*: P. L. X. 594; *fig.*:
V. Ex. 6.

(8) to be, remain, dwell, or
abide in a place; sometimes with

blending of (1) or (2): P. R. I. 412; S. A. 1491; 11 P. 170; C. 382, 389, 860; A. 64; *where the Persian in Ecbatan sat*: P. L. XI. 393; *thou, bright Saint, high sitt'st in glory*: M. W. 61; *attired with stars we shall forever sit*: T. 21; *thou sitt'st between the cherubs bright*: Ps. LXXX. 5; *gloomy shadows ... sitting by a new-made grave*: C. 472.

(9) to meet in assembly for deliberation: P. L. I. 795; II. 164; P. R. IV. 577; *the Grand in council sat*: P. L. X. 428; *his Potentates in council sat*: P. R. II. 118.

vbl. sb. **sitting**; (*a*) the action of remaining inactive: P. L. III. 164.

(*b*) the occupation or possession of a throne; *no sitting ... on David's throne*: P. R. IV. 107.

Sittim, *sb.* Shittim, the place in the Jordan Valley opposite Jericho where Israel encamped (spelled Settim or Setim in Vulg.): P. L. I. 413.

Situate, *part.* placed, located: P. L. VI. 641.

Situation, *sb.* site, place, spot: P. L. I. 60.

Six, *adj.* five and one: P. L. V. 277; U. C. II. 20; *six days, nights, years*: P. L. VII. 568, 601; IX. 137; P. R. I. 210; *absol.*: P. L. VIII. 128.

Sixth, *adj.* the ordinal of six; *the sixth day*: P. L. VII. 504, 550; *absol.*: P. L. VII. 449.

Size, *sb.* dimension, magnitude: P. L. VI. 352; *monstrous, gigantic*: P. L. I. 197; S. A. 1249.

Skiff, *sb.* a small vessel: P. L. I. 204.

Skilful, *adj.* expert: P. L. IX. 515.

Skill, (1) *sb.* (*a*) knowledge, wisdom: P. L. VIII. 573.

(*b*) readiness and excellence in applying to practical purposes the familiar knowledge of an art or science, practical efficiency: P. L. II. 272; IX. 1112; S. A. 757; C. 273; S. XIII. 5; *the skill of lesser gods*: A. 79; *skill of noblest architects*: P. R. IV. 52; *thy skill of conduct*: P. R. III. 17; *skill of artifice or office mean*: P. L. IX. 39; ability or dexterity in using or controlling the body; *optic skill of vision*: P. R. IV. 40; *to*

stand upright will ask thee skill: P. R. IV. 552.

(2) *vb. intr.* to be versed, be expert; *of these nor skilled nor studious*: P. L. IX. 42; *skilled to retire*: P. R. II. 161; *deep skilled in all his mother's witcheries*: C. 523; *well skilled in every virtuous plant*: C. 620.

Skin, *sb.* (*a*) the natural covering of the human body: Hor. Epist. 6.

(*b*) the hide of an animal: P. L. X. 220; *he clad their nakedness with skins of beasts*: P. L. X. 217.

Skip, *vb. intr.* to take light dancing steps; *fig.* of mountains: Ps. CXIV. 11, 13.

Skirt, I. *sb.* (1) *pl.* garment, probably that below the waist; *dark with excessive bright thy* (God's) *skirts appear*: P. L. III. 380.

(*b*) *fig.*, *Ye Mists ... till the sun paint your fleecy skirts*: P. L. V. 187; *the fluid skirts of that same watery cloud*: P. L. XI. 882.

(*c*) *fig.* the outermost part or limit; *behold though but his utmost skirts of glory*: P. L. XI. 332.

(2) confine, boundary; *from skirt to skirt a fiery region*: P. L. VI. 80.

II. *vb. tr.* to form a garment or covering for: P. L. V. 282.

See **Yellow-skirted.**

Sky, *sb.* (1) the vaulted expanse of heaven, the firmament: P. L. IV. 459; XI. 209; C. 957; *ample sky*: P. L. VIII. 258; *the broad fields of the sky*: C. 979; *fair as the noon sky*: P. R. II. 156; *Sky, Air, Earth, and Heaven*: P. L. IV. 722; *thou ... shalt in the sky appear*: P. L. III. 324; *pl.*: P. 18; L'A. 43; *as apparently reached by something from earth*: P. L. VII. 287; *his stature reached the sky*: P. L. IV. 988; *shout ... it tore the sky*: S. A. 1472; *under sky, under open sky*, with no roof-covering over the head: P. L. III. 514; IV. 721; S. A. 1610.

(*b*) the expanse in which appear the sun and stars: P. L. I. 730; L. 171; *a comet ... in the arctic sky*: P. L. II. 710; *two planets ... in mid sky*: P. L. VI. 314; *through the vast ethereal sky sails between worlds and worlds*: P. L. V. 267.

(*c*) the region where clouds float and storms gather: P. L. II. 534; V. 189; X. 1064; *sky loured*:

P. L. IX. 1002; *the thickened sky*:
P. L. XI. 742; *as earth and sky
would mingle*: P. R. IV. 453; *hail
mixed with fire, must rend the
Egyptian sky*: P. L. XII. 182.

used *fig.* of chaos; *chaos blustering round, inclement sky*: P. L.
III. 426.

(*d*) the region of air above the
earth in which birds fly; *the mid
aerial sky*: P. L. VII. 442.

(2) heaven, the abode of God;
the ethereal sky: P. L. I. 45; *pl.*:
C. 342; *looks commercing with the
skies*: Il P. 39.

(3) firmament, floor: P. L. VI.
772. *See* **Firmament.**

Sky-robe, *sb.* a robe worn in heaven,
or, possibly, like the sky in delicacy, fineness, and colour: C. 83.

Sky-tinctured, *adj.* dyed the colour
of the sky: P. L. V. 285.

Slack, (1) *adj.* (*a*) slow in action,
negligent, remiss: P. R. III. 398;
thou hast not, Lcrd, been slack:
Ps. LXXXV. 2.

(*b*) limp, weak; *from his slack
hand the garland ... dropt*: P. L.
IX. 892.

(2) *vb. tr.* (*a*) to decrease the
speed of, make slower; *they slack
their course*: P. L. IV. 164.

(*b*) to make less intense; *slack
the pain*: P. L. II. 461.

(*c*) *fig.* to relax or smooth; *slack
the avenger's brow*: Ps. VIII. 7.

Slacken, *vb.* (1) *intr.* (*a*) to make less
tense; *fig., to slacken virtue*: P.
R. II. 455.

(*b*) to become less violent; *these
fierce fires will slacken*: P. L. II.
214; to become less severe; *my
penance hath not slackened*: S. A.
738.

Slackness, *sb.* remissness; *Man's
effeminate slackness*: P. L. XI.
634.

Slake, *vb. tr.* to appease, assuage;
to slake his wrath: D. F. I. 66.

Slanderous, *adj.* calumnious; *Truth
... bestuck with slanderous darts*:
P. L. XII. 536.

Slant, *adj.* moving obliquely; *the
slant lightning*: P. L. X. 1075.

Slaughter, *sb.* the act of killing;
slaughter of one foe: S. A. 1518;
wearied with slaughter: S. A.
1583; the carnage of war: P. R.
III. 75; *war and mutual slaughter*:
P. L. VI. 506; *slaughter and
gigantic deeds*: P. L. XI. 659.

Slaughtered, *part. adj.* slain, massa-
cred: S. A. 1667; *thy slaughtered
saints*: S. XVIII. 1; *absol., over
heaps of slaughtered walk his way*:
S. A. 1530.

Slaughtering, *part. adj.* destroying;
slaughtering pestilence: D. F. I. 68.

Slave, *sb.* (*a*) one who is wholly
subject to the will of another:
S. A. 367; *at the mill with slaves*:
S. A. 41; *among the slaves and
asses*: S. A. 1162; used of Samson: S. A. 1224, 1392; of the
Israelites: P. L. XII. 167.

(*b*) one who is in subjection to
vice; *inward slaves*: P. R. IV. 145.
See **Bond-slave.**

Slavery, *sb.* bondage, servitude; *the
slavery of the invading enemy*:
Ps. CXXXVI. 81; *pl., pains and
slaveries*: S. A. 485; applied to
moral bondage: S. A. 418.

Slavish, *adj.* (*a*) of or befitting a
slave; *slavish toil*: Ps. LXXXI.
21; *habit*: S. A. 122.

(*b*) enslaved; *slavish officers of
vengeance*: C. 218.

Slay, *vb.* (*pret.* slew; *2d sing.*
slew'st: S. A. 439; *past. part.*
slain) *tr.* to put to death violently
or kill (beasts): P. L. X. 217;
(men): S. A. 1516, 1517, 1668;
S. XVIII. 7; *who slew his brother*:
P. L. XI. 609, 678; *the unjust the
just hath slain*: P. L. XI. 455;
*nailed to the cross ... slain for
bringing life*: P. L. XII. 414; *who
slew'st them many a slain*: S. A.
439; *Apollo ... did slay ... his
mate*: D. F. I. 24; in war: Ps.
LXXXIII. 38.

past part. absol. those killed:
S. A. 439; *thy slain*: S. A. 1664;
the slain in bloody fight: Ps.
LXXXVIII. 19.

Sleek, (1) *adj.* (*a*) smooth and glossy;
sleek enamelled neck: P. L. IX. 525;
sleek Panope: L. 99; soft (?): *to
live in dimple sleek*: L'A. 30.

(*b*) easy of pronunciation;
*names to our like mouths grow
sleek*: S. XI. 10.

(2) *vb. tr.* (*a*) to make smooth
and glossy; *sleeking her ... locks*;
C. 882.

(*b*) to make insinuating; *that
sleeked his tongue*: P. R. IV. 5.

Sleep, (1) *sb.* (*a*) the state of repose
marked by a general quiescence
of voluntary and conscious func
tions: P. L. IV. 449, 658; XII.

434 ; *in sleep* : P. L. v. 96, 120 ; *God also is in sleep*: P. L. XII. 611 ; *soundest, gentle, dewy* : P. L. VIII. 253, 287 ; IX. 1044 ; *the timely dew of sleep* : P. L. IV. 614 ; *grosser* : P. L. IX. 1049 ; *his sleep was aery light* : P. L. v. 3 ; *thy gift of sleep* : P. L. IV. 735 ; *dreams disturbed his sleep*: P. R. IV. 409 ; *he went to sleep* : P. R. II. 284 ; *sought repair of sleep* : P. L. VIII. 458 ; *mine eye to harbour sleep* : S. A. 459 ; *to violate sleep* : P. L. IV. 883 ; *sleep hath forsook .. me* : S. A. 629 ; *what hath night to do with sleep* : C. 122 ; the sleep of angels : P. L. v. 668, 673 ; *can now thy sleep dissent* : P. L. v. 679 ; of beasts : P. L. IX. 190.

personified : P. L. VII. 106 ; *the litter of close-curtained Sleep* : C. 554 ; *the dewy-feathered Sleep*: Il P. 146.

(*b*) the rest of the grave, death : P. L. III. 329 ; *those ychained in sleep* : N. O. 155.

(2) *vb.* (*pres. 2d sing.* sleep'st : P. L. v. 38, 673 ; L. 160 ; *pret.* slept ; *2d sing.* slept'st : P. L. XI. 369 ; *past part.* not used) *intr.* (*a*) to be in a state of sleep : P. L. I. 333 ; IV. 678, 707, 826 ; v. 38 ; VIII. 463 ; XI. 368, 369 ; XII. 608 ; P. R. I. 311 ; II. 271 ; IV. 407 ; S. A. 1113 ; *embracing slept* : P. L. IV. 771 ; *smote Sisera ... sleeping* : S. A. 990 ; *sleep on, blest pair* : P. L. IV. 773 ; used of angels : P. L. v. 654, 673 ; of beasts : P. L. VII. 414 ; IX. 161, 182, 187.

(*b*) to go to sleep : P. R. II. 263 ; *I lay and slept* : Ps. III. 13 ; *lay me down and sleep* : Ps. IV. 38.

(*c*) *fig.* to remain inactive ; *Suspicion sleeps* : P. L. III. 686 ; *the North-wind sleeps* : P. L. II. 489 ; *nor slept the winds* : P. R. IV. 413.

(*d*) *fig.* to appear still or without motion ; *Earth ... with inoffensive pace that spinning sleeps* : P. L. VIII. 164.

(*e*) to be or lie dead, rest in death : L. 160 ; Ps. LXXXVIII. 18 ; *there I should rest, and sleep secure* : P. L. x. 779.

Sleepless, *adj.* being without sleep, wakeful : P. L. XI. 173 ; P. R. II. 460.

Sleepy, *adj.* causing sleep ; *the sleepy*

drench of that forgetful lake : P. L. II. 73.

Sleet, *sb.* hail mingled with rain ; *fig., shot sharp sleet of arrowy showers* : P. R. III. 324.

Sleight, *sb.* trick, artifice, stratagem : P. L. IX. 92.

Slender, *adj.* slim ; *what slender youth* : Hor. O. 1 ; *slender waist* : P. L. IV. 304.

Slide, *vb.* (only in *pres.*) *intr.* to glide ; *words ... slide through my infant lips* : V. Ex. 4 ; of motion through the air ; *as in air smooth sliding without step* : P. L. VIII. 302 ; *softly sliding down through the turning sphere* : N. O. 47.

part. adj. **sliding**, gliding, *my sliding chariot* : C. 892.

See **Smooth-sliding**.

Slight. (1) *adj.* (*a*) frail, fleeting, perishable : S. A. 59.

(*b*) of little value, trifling, insignificant : V. Ex. 19 ; *secure on no slight grounds* : P. R. III. 349 ; *sup., the slightest recompense* : P. R. III. 128.

(*c*) easily made ; *one slight bound* : P. L. IV. 181.

(2) *adv.* (*a*) disparagingly ; *think not so slight of glory* : P. R. III. 109 ; lightly ; *all offers ... how slight thou valuest* : P. R. IV. 155.

(*b*) inadequately ; *so slight informed* : S. A. 1229.

(3) *vb. tr.* to treat as of little value, disregard intentionally : P. L. VII. 47 ; S. A. 940.

part. adj. **slighted**, treated as of small importance : L. 65.

vbl. sb. **slighting**, the failure to notice one ; *at every sudden slighting* : P. R. II. 224.

Slightly, *adv.* (*a*) with indifference : P. R. II. 198.

(*b*) insecurely ; *gates of Hell too slightly barred* : P. L. IV. 967.

Slime, *sb.* a glutinous substance ; (*a*) soft mud : P. L. x. 530.

(*b*) bitumen ; *asphaltic slime* : P. L. x. 298.

(*c*) that exuded from the body of an animal ; *bestial slime* : P. L. IX. 165.

Slimy, *adj.* of the consistency of slime : P. L. x. 286.

Sling, *sb.* a sudden throw or swing ; *at one sling of thy victorious arm* : P. L. x. 633.

Slinger, *sb.* one who uses the sling as a weapon in war : S. A. 1619.

Slink, *vb.* (*pret.* and *past part.* slunk ; perfect formed with the auxiliary *be* : P. L. IV. 602) *intr.* to creep or steal softly ; *beast and bird ... these to their nest were slunk* : P. L. IV. 602.

(*b*) to move stealthily, sneak ; *he ... slunk into the wood* : P. L. x. 332 ; *back to the thicket slunk the ... Serpent* : P. L. IX. 784.

Slip, I. *sb.* a plant : M. W. 35.

II. *vb.* (1) *intr.* to pass quietly ; *each ... ghost slips to his several grave* : N. O. 234 ; to pass unnoticed, steal away ; *hath any ram slipped from the fold* : C. 498 ; *slipping from his mother's eye* : P. R. IV. 216.

(2) *tr.* to allow to pass unappropriated or unused, lose by oversight ; *let us not slip the occasion* : P. L. I. 178 ; *let slip time* : C. 743.

See **Tinsel-slippered.**

Slit, *vb. tr.* to cut asunder, sever ; *slits the thin-spun life* : L. 76.

Slope, (1) *adj.* (*a*) slanting ; *the slope hills* : P. L. IV. 261.

(*b*) declining, setting ; *the slope sun* : C. 98.

(2) *adv.* obliquely ; *bore him slope downward* : P. L. IV. 591.

(3) *vb. tr.* to direct obliquely, bend ; *the ... flames slope their pointing spires* : P. L. I. 223 ; to direct downward toward the horizon ; *the star ... sloped his westering wheel* : L. 31.

Sloth, *sb.* disinclination to exertion, habitual indolence : P. L. VI. 166 ; *ease and sloth* : P. L. XI. 794 ; *ease and peaceful sloth* : P. L. II. 227.

Slothful, *adj.* averse to exertion ; *his thoughts were ... slothful* : P. L. II. 117.

Slough, *sb.* a place of deep mud : U. C. I. 4.

Slow, (1) *adj.* (*a*) not quick in motion : P. L. II. 902 ; IV. 173 ; VIII. 110 ; Ps. LXXXV. 55 ; *wandering steps and slow* : P. L. XII. 648 ; *slow but firm battalion* : P. L. VI. 533 ; used of a stream : P. L. II. 582 ; *slow Meander* : C. 232 ; *sup. fig., Justice divine mends not her slowest pace* : P. L. X. 859.

(*b*) not occurring or appearing in a short time : P. L. X. 692 ; S. II. 7 ; *revenge, though slow* : P. L. II. 337.

(*c*) not ready to hear ; *mine ear shall not be slow* : P. L. III. 193 ; not prompt to act : *zeal and duty are not slow* : P. R. III. 172.

(*d*) acting with deliberation ; *slow to be angry* : Ps. LXXXVI. 55.

(2) *adv.* (*a*) not quickly ; *slow descends* : P. L. XI. 257 ; *swinging slow* : Il P. 76 ; *footing slow* : L. 103 ; *why move thy feet so slow* : P. R. III. 224.

(*b*) gradually ; *where the bowed welkin slow doth bend* : C. 1015.

Slow-endeavouring, *adj.* accomplishing its object with slowness and difficulty : W. S. 9.

Slowly, *adv.* not quickly : P. L. IV. 541.

Slow-paced, *adj.* moving or coming slowly ; *a slow-paced evil* : P. L. x. 963.

Sluice, (1) *sb.* (*a*) a flood-gate ; *fig., the deep, who now had stopped his sluices* : P. L. XI. 849.

(*b*) a channel for water : A. 30 ; *fig., precious drops* (tears) *that ready stood, each in his crystal sluice* : P. L. v. 133.

(2) *vb. tr.* to draw off by means of a sluice ; *liquid fire sluiced from the lake* : P. L. I. 702.

Slumber, (1) *sb.* sleep ; *in slumber soft* : C. 1001 ; *golden slumber on a bed of heaped Elysian flowers* : L'A. 146 ; *roused from the slumber on that fiery couch* : P. L. I. 377 ; *pl., thou visit'st my slumbers* : P. L. VII. 29 ; *fig., strict Age and sour Sevrity ... in slumber lie* : C. 110 ; a state akin to sleep ; *in pleasing slumber lulled the sense* : C. 260.

(2) *vb. intr.* (*a*) to sleep : P. L. IX. 23 ; used of angels : P. L. I. 321 ; of beasts : P. L. I. 203.

(*b*) *fig.,* to remain inactive ; *despair that slumbered* : P. L. IV. 24.

part. adj. **slumbering,** *fig.* still, quiet ; *the slumbering morn* : L'A. 54 ; not moving ; *the slumbering leaves* : A. 57.

Slumbrous, *adj.* inviting to sleep : P. L. IV. 615.

Sly, *adj.* (*a*) crafty, cunning, artful ; *the serpent sly* : P. L. IV. 347 ; *the spirited sly Snake* : P. L. IX. 613 ; *thou* (Satan) *sly hypocrite* : P. L. IV. 957.

(*b*) showing, or characterized by, craftiness or cunning ; *sly circum-*

spection, *assault, preface, enticement, disguise* : P. L. IV. 537 ; IX.
256 ; P. R. II. 115 ; C. 525, 571.

Small, *adj.* (*a*) little in size, not
large : P. L. I. 204, 575 ; II. 607 ;
V. 258 ; VII. 486 ; IX. 628 ; XI.
734, 753 ; P. R. IV. 35 ; C. 295,
629 ; *the Earth, though, in comparison of Heaven, so small* : P. L.
VIII. 92 ; *Man .. lodged in a small
partition* : P. L. VIII. 105 ; *Capreæ,
an island small* : P. R. IV. 92 ;
comp. : P. L. VII. 433 ; *sup.* : P. L.
I. 779, 789 : II. 1053 ; VII. 477.

(*b*) not large in amount or
degree : P. L. V. 322 ; *some small
reflection gains of glimmering air* :
P. L. III. 428 ; *they augment their
small peculiar* : P. L. VII. 368 ;
*none whose portion is so small of ...
pain* : P. L. II. 33 ; *made small
account of beauty* : P. R. II. 193 ;
no small praise : P. R. III. 56 ;
no small profit : S. A. 1261 ; *small
loss* : V. Ex. 9 ; *small consolation* :
P. R. I. 403 ; *of sapience no small
part* : P. L. IX. 1018.

(*c*) little in moment or importance, insignificant, trivial : P. R.
I. 66 ; C. 620 ; *a petty enterprise of
small enforce* : S. A. 1223 ; *this
same small neglect* : V. Ex. 16 ; *so
small as easy think the remedy* :
P. L. VI. 437 ; *sup.* : P. L. VI. 137 ;
the smallest tittle : P. R. I. 450.

in combination or contrast with
great : P. L. II. 258 ; XII. 566 ; *to
compare small things with greatest* :
P. R. IV. 564 ; perhaps with
blending of sense (*a*) ; *to compare
great things with small* : P. L. II.
922 ; *to set forth great things by
small* : P. L. VI. 311 ; *if great
things to small may be compared* :
P. L. X. 306.

Smart, *sb.* (*a*) sharp keen pain : Cir.
25.

(*b*) distress, suffering : P. L. IV.
102 ; P. R. I. 401 ; the suffering
involved in punishment ; *our
deserved smart* : D. F. I. 69.

Smear, *vb. tr.* to cover or bedaub
with a viscous substance : C. 917 ;
smeared round with pitch : P. L.
XI. 731.

Smell, I. *sb.* (*a*) the sense of smell ;
P. L. VIII. 527 ; *with what to sight
or smell was sweet* : P. L. XI. 281.

(*b*) odour ; *the smell of infant
blood* : P. L. II. 664 ; *the smell of
mortal change on earth* : P. L. X.

272 ; the fragrance of flowers,
fruits, plants, etc. : P. L. IV. 217 ;
V. 127 ; *the smell of field and grove* :
P. L. IV. 265 ; *the smell of grain* :
P. L. IX. 450 ; *of sweetest fennel* :
P. L. IX. 581 ; *cassia's balmy
smells* : C. 991 ; *Flora's earliest
smells* : P. R. II. 365 ; *grateful,
pleasant, fragrant, savoury, ambrosial* : P. L. IV. 165 ; V. 84, 379 ;
IX. 740, 852 ; *his* (God's) *nostrils
fill with grateful smell* : P. L. IX.
197 ; the savour of wine : P. R.
II. 351 ; S. A. 544 ; *fig., the smell
of peace* : P. L. XI. 38.

II. *vb.* (1) *tr.* to perceive by the
nose : P. L. V. 411.

(2) *intr.* to give out an odour :
P. L. VII. 319 ; Ariosto II. 2.

See **Sweet-smelling.**

Smile, (1) *sb.* the contraction of the
features expressive of pleasure,
approbation, or contempt : P. L.
IX. 222 ; XI. 624 ; P. R. II. 193 ;
smiles from reason flow : P. L. IX.
239 ; *endearing* : P. L. IV. 337 ;
bought : P. L. IV. 765 ; *wreathed* :
L'A. 28 ; *the Vision* (God) *bright,
as with a smile more brightened* :
P. L. VIII. 368 ; *the Angel, with
a smile* : P. L. VIII. 618 ; *Death
grinned horrible a ghastly smile* :
P. L. II. 846.

(2) *vb. intr.* (*a*) to contract the
features in giving expression to
pleasure, approbation, or disdain :
P. L. IV. 499 ; S. A. 948, 1057 ;
Jupiter on Juno smiles : P. L. IV.
500 ; used of God or angels : P. L.
III. 257 ; IV. 903 ; V. 718 ; P. R.
I. 129.

fig. of personifications, *old Ocean
smiles* : P. L. IV. 165 ; *the Morn ...
smiling* : P. L. XI. 175 ; *fair Morning first smiles on the world* : P. L.
V. 124.

(*b*) to look gay or joyous : P. L.
VII. 502 ; VIII. 265 ; *in his face
youth smiled* : P. L. III. 638 ; *the
bright pavement ... with celestial
roses smiled* : P. L. III. 364 ; *the
sylvan lodge ... that like Pomona's
arbour smiled* : P. L. V. 378 ;
*with fresh flowerets hill and valley
smiled* : P. L. VI. 784 ; *a bough of
fairest fruit, that downy smiled* :
P. L. IX. 851 ; *else had the spring
perpetual smiled* : P. L. X. 679 ;
to look contented or happy ; *fig.,
smoothing the raven down of darkness till it smiled* : C. 252.

(c) to appear propitious : P. L.
IX. 480.

part. adj. **smiling** ; (a) wearing a smile : N. O. 151 ; *Mercy,
that sweet smiling Youth* : D. F. I.
53.

(b) joyous; *smiling morn* : P. L.
v. 168.

Smite, *vb.* (*pret.* smote ; *past part.*
smit : P. L. III. 29 ; smitten :
P. R. IV. 526 ; smote, Ps. III. 20)
(1) *tr.* (a) to strike : P. L. x. 295 ;
S. A. 990 ; *smote him into the midriff with a stone* : P. L. XI. 445 ;
fig., thou (God) *hast smote ... on the
cheek-bone all my foes* : Ps. III. 20.

(b) to kill, slay : Ps. CXXXVI.
38.

(c) to strike, come in contact
with ; *the morning sun ... smote the
open field* : P. L. IV. 244.

(d) to affect powerfully ; *smit
with the love of sacred song* : P. L.
III. 29 ; *smitten with amazement* :
P. R. IV. 562.

(e) to blast, blight ; *what the
cross dire-looking planet smites* :
A. 52.

(2) *intr.* or *absol.* : (a) to give a
blow or blows : P. L. VI. 324, 591 ;
the sword of Michael smote : P. L.
VI. 250 ; *to smite once, and smite
no more* : L. 131.

(b) to produce the effect as of a
blow, afflict ; *the torrid clime
smote on him sore* : P. L. I. 298.

Smoke, (1) *sb.* the sooty exhalation
from something burning : P. L. I.
237 ; *like the sons of Vulcan, vomit
smoke* : C. 655 ; in heaven : P. L.
VI. 57 ; *obscured with smoke, all
Heaven appeared* : P. L. VI. 585 ;
about him (Christ) *fierce effusion
rolled of smoke* : P. L. VI. 766 ;
in hell ; *rolling, redounding,
surging* : P. L. I. 671 ; II. 889,
928 ; used as a type of all that
renders impure ; *above the smoke
and stir of ... Earth* : C. 5.

(2) *vb. intr.* to emit smoke :
P. L. I. 493 ; *altar smoked* : P. L.
I. 493.

part. adj. **smoking,** *fig.* fierce,
hot : Ps. LXXX. 19.

Smoky, *adj.* stained with smoke :
C. 324.

Smooth, (1) *adj.* (a) having an even
surface : P. L. I. 725 ; II. 902 ;
v. 342 ; *smooth leaves* : P. L. IX.
1095 ; *the smooth enamelled green* :
A. 84.

(b) level and free from obstructions ; *a passage broad, smooth* :
P. L. x. 305 ; *fig., his way to
peace is smooth* : S. A. 1049.

(c) free from hair : C. 290.

(d) not ruffled, gently flowing ;
used of water : P. L. IV. 459 ;
smooth Adonis : P. L. I. 450 ;
smooth Severn : C. 825 ; *Medway
smooth* : V. Ex. 100 ; of an image
seen in the water ; *that smooth
watery image* : P. L. IV. 480 ;
the *sb.* omitted or the *adj.* used
as *sb.* =smooth seas : P. L. VII.
409.

(e) gently moving ; *bears thee
soft with the smooth air along* :
P. L. VIII. 166.

(f) gentle and insinuating ;
this answer smooth returned : P. R.
I. 467.

(g) agreeable or pleasant to the
ear : P. R. I. 479 ; harmonious :
S. XIII. 8.

(h) easy and elegant, free from
anything disagreeable or unpleasant : P. L. XI. 615.

(i) deceptive, fallacious : P. R.
IV. 295 ; S. A. 872.

(2) *adv.* (a) evenly, without jar ;
in air smooth sliding : P. L. VIII.
302 ; *fig.* agreeably ; *comp., time
will run on smoother* : S. XX. 6.

(b) gently, soothingly : P. L. II.
816.

(3) *vb.* (smoothèd, *disyl.* : P. L.
I. 772) *tr.* (a) to make smooth,
take the wrinkles from ; *smooth the
rugged'st brow* : P. R. II. 164 ;
*fig., smoothing the rugged brow of
Night* : Il P. 58.

(b) to stroke, rub gently and so
render smooth ; *fig., smoothing the
raven down of darkness* : C. 251.

(c) to put down or repress ;
each perturbation smoothed : P. L.
IV. 120.

(d) to make agreeable to the
ear, render harmonious ; *harmony
divine so smooths her charming
tones* : P. L. v. 626.

(e) to make flattering : Ps.
v. 28.

part. adj. **smoothed,** rendered
even in surface : P. L. I. 772.

Smooth-dittied, *adj.* sweetly sung or
played : C. 86.

Smooth-haired, *adj.* woven of
smooth threads or having an even
surface : *the smooth-haired silk* :
C. 716.

Smoothly, *adv.* (*a*) gently or quietly ; *smoothly the waters kissed* : N. O. 65.

(*b*) agreeably or successfully : C. 1012.

Smooth-shaven, *adj.* having the grass smoothly and closely cut : Il P. 66.

Smooth-sliding, *adj.* flowing gently and evenly : L. 86.

Smouldering, *part. adj.* burning with inward fire while throwing out smoke ; *the red fire and smouldering clouds outbreak* : N. O. 159.

Smutty, *adj.* of the colour of soot, black : P. L. IV. 817.

Snake, *sb.* a serpent : P. L. X. 2l8 ; the serpent into which Satan entered, or Satan in the serpent ; *the wily snake* : P. L. IX. 91 ; *the spirited sly Snake* : P. L. IX. 613 ; *with the Snake conspired* : P. L. XI. 426 ; *so glistered the dire Snake* : P. L. IX. 643.

Snaky, *adj.* (*a*) pertaining to snakes : P. L. VII. 484.

(*b*) composed of or entwined with snakes ; *snaky locks* : P. L. X. 559.

(*c*) having wholly or partly the form of a snake ; *the snaky sorceress* : P. L. II. 724 ; *Typhon huge ending in snaky twine* : N. O. 226.

(*d*) treacherous, deceitful ; *snaky wiles* : P. R. I. 120.

Snaky-headed, *adj.* having snakes for hair : C. 447.

Snare, (**1**) *sb.* a gin ; *fig.*, a device, trick, or allurement by which one is entangled, entrapped, or led into evil : P. R. III. 191 ; IV. 611 ; S. A. 409, 845 ; P. 11 ; *mortal, fatal, deadly* : P. L. IV. 8 ; P. R. I. 441 ; C. 567 ; *war and hostile snare* : P. L. XII. 31 ; *well-woven* : P. R. I. 97 ; *female* : P. L. X. 897 ; *riches ... the wise man's ... snare* : P. R. II. 454 ; *to bring my feet again into the snare* : S. A. 931 ; *into the snare I fell of fair fallacious looks* : S. A. 532 ; *hug him into snares* : C. 164 ; a person who entraps another or leads him into evil : S. A. 230 ; *I ... became thy snare* : P. L. XI. 165.

(**2**) *vb. tr.* to take by guile, entrap : P. L. X. 873.

Snatch, *vb. tr.* (*a*) to seize suddenly : C. 815 ; to obtain by force and

before the due time ; *death so snatched* : P. L. X. 1025.

(*b*) to seize and transport ; *snatch him hence* : P. R. II. 56 ; *a cloud ... snatched him hence* : P. L. XI. 670.

Sneeze, *sb.* a sudden and violent ejection of air through the nose and mouth with an audible sound : P. R. IV. 458.

Snow, *sb.* the vapour of the atmosphere precipitated in soft white flakes : P. L. II. 491, 591 ; X. 1063 ; *armed with ... snow* : P. L. X. 698 ; *which had forbid the snow from cold Estotiland* : P. L. X. 685 ; as found in the air or clouds ; *hills of snow* : V. Ex. 42 ; as a symbol of purity ; *innocent snow* : N. O. 39.

Snow-soft, *adj.* soft with snow ; *he* (Winter) *descended from his snow-soft chair* : D. F. I. 19.

Snowy, *adj.* covered with snow ; *snowy plains, hills* : P. L. X. 432 ; C. 927 ; *the snowy top of cold Olympus* : P. L. I. 515 ; *Imaus ... snowy ridge* : P. L. III. 432 ; *snowy Alp* : S. A. 628.

Snuff, *vb. tr.* to draw in through the nose, inhale : P. L. X. 272.

***So,** I. *adv.* (**1**) in or to this or that degree or extent ; (*a*) preceded or followed by a clause indicating the degree or extent ; *the more I see pleasures about me, so much more I feel torment within me* : P. L. IX. 120 ; the clause introduced by *as* : P. L. X. 1008 ; S. A. 415 ; *so much to him due of hazard more as he above the rest high honoured sits* : P. L. II. 454 ; *so clear as in no face* : S. XXIII. 12.

(*b*) the degree or extent indicated by a previous statement ; *so much the stronger proved he* : P. L. I. 92 ; *so thick bestrown ... lay these* : P. L. I. 311 ; *so numberless were those* : P. L. I. 344 ; *so thick the aery crowd swarmed* : P. L. I. 775 ; *so much hath Hell debased me, to what I was in Heaven* : P. L. IX. 487 ; *so much the nearer danger* : P. L. II. 1008 ; *so well he feigned* : P. L. III. 639 ; by a following statement : P. L. XI. 417 ; C. 73 ; *so far the happier lot, enjoying thee* : P. L. IV. 446.

(*c*) the degree or extent not indicated, but to be inferred from the context ; sometimes hardly more than an intensive : P. L. IV.

53, 72, 423 ; *what transports thee
so ?* : P. L. VIII. 567 ; *whereof so
rife there went a fame* : P. L. I.
650 ; *philosophers in vain so long
have sought* : P. L. III. 601 ; *so
oft* : P. L. I. 275 ; VI. 94 ; *so late* :
P. L. I. 114 ; *so near* : P. L. II.
609 ; *so highly* : P. L. I. 30 ; *so
wide* : P. L. IX. 203 ; *so wise* : P.
L. II. 155.

(*d*) followed by a clause or infinitive phrase of result ; the
clause introduced by *that* : P. L. IV.
376 ; XI. 876 ; XII. 97 ; P. R. III.
262 ; *he called so loud that all the
hollow deep ... resounded* : P. L. I.
314 ; *hath so prevailed that I have
also tasted* : P. L. IX. 873 ; *so oft
prevailed that* : P. R. III. 167 ; *so
swift ... that* : P. L. VI. 190 ; introduced by *but that* : P. R. I.
362 ; the phrase introduced by
as : P. L. II. 425 ; IX. 235 ; *so
prevalent as to concern the mind of
God* : P. L. XI. 144 ; *so stupid ...
as to forsake* : P. L. XII. 116 ; *so
incense God, as to leave them* : P.
L. XII. 338 ; *so void of fear ... as
offer them to me* : P. R. IV. 189 ;
*so fond are mortal men ... as their
own ruin on themselves to invite* :
S. A. 1682.

(2) in this or that manner ; (*a*)
preceded or followed by a clause
introduced by *as* indicating the
manner : P. L. V. 572 ; *so told as
earthly notion can receive* : P. L.
V. 179 ; *as armies ... so the watery
throng* : P. L. VII. 297 ; *for as
Earth, so he the World built* : P.
L. VII. 269.

(*b*) in a manner previously
stated : P. L. I. 209 ; II. 248 ; *so
spake* : P. L. I. 125 ; II. 704 ; III.
681 ; IV. 393 ; VII. 174 ; *so sung* :
P. L. VII. 573, 633 ; *not so waked
Satan* : P. L. V. 657 ; *that little
which is left so to defend* : P. L.
II. 1000.

(*c*) in such a manner ; followed
by a clause of result ; the clause
introduced by *that* : P. L. VI. 322 ;
introduced by *as that ; accepted
so as that more willingly thou* : P.
L. V. 465 ; introduced by *as* : P.
L. IV. 966 ; V. 334 ; X. 652 ; *supported so as shall amaze* : P. L.
XII. 496 ; *so found as well I saw* :
P. R. II. 97 ; *so as we need not
fear to pass commodiously this
life* : P. L. X. 1082 ; *may succeed*

so as perhaps shall grieve him : P.
L. I. 166.

(*d*) introducing a wish ; *so were
I equalled with them in renown* :
P. L. III. 34 ; *so may some gentle
Muse ... favour my destined urn* :
L. 19.

(3) in a like or corresponding
manner or degree ; preceded by a
clause introduced by *as* indicating
the manner or degree : P. L. X.
215 ; *as in him perish all men, so
in thee ... shall be restored* : P. L.
III. 287 ; *as ye have received, so
have ye done* : P. L. VI. 805 ; *as
God in Heaven is centre ... so thou* :
P. L. IX. 108 ; introduced by *so ;
so high ... so low* : P. L. VII. 288.

(4) by this or that means : P.
L. I. 148 ; *so to add what wants
in female sex* : P. L. IX. 821 ; *so
both himself and us to glorify* : N.
O. 154.

(5) as said or implied ; taking
the place of or implying a preceding word or statement, sometimes almost equivalent to *such,
this, that* : P. R. III. 97 ; IV. 362 ;
S. A. 149, 818 ; *so is my will* : P.
L. III. 184 ; *be it so* : P. L. I. 245 ;
for so the popular vote inclines :
P. L. II. 313 ; *so Fate pronounced* :
P. L. II. 809 ; *proves not so* : P.
L. VI. 428 ; *so I name this king* : P.
L. XII. 326 ; *this must not yet be
so* : N. O. 150 ; *God so commanded* : P. L. IX. 652 ; *true, or
fancied so* : P. L. IX. 789 ; *so he
departing gave command* : P. L.
X. 429 ; *wrongs, and worse than
so* : P. 11 ; *and it was so* : P. L.
VII. 545 ; taking the place of a
following statement ; *if so befall* :
P. L. XII. 444.

(6) such being the case, accordingly : P. L. III. 120 ; V. 542 ; X.
490 ; *so may'st thou be translated
to the skies* : C. 242 ; *so farewell
hope* : P. L. IV. 108 ; *yet so most
reason is that reason overcome* : P.
L. VI. 125 ; *so should I purchase
dear short intermission* : P. L. IV.
101 ; *yet so perhaps thou shalt not
die* : P. L. IX. 927 ; *so Death becomes his final remedy* : P. L. XI.
61 ; in that case ; *I should so have
lost all sense* : P. R. I. 382.

II. *conj.* on condition that, provided that : P. R. II. 255 ; *I reck
not, so it light well aimed* . P. L.
IX. 173.

Soak, *vb. intr.* to lie in and become saturated with a fluid; *the body .. soaked in his enemies' blood*: S. A. 1726.

Soar, I. *sb.* the height attained in flying; *within soar of towering eagles*: P. L. v. 270.
II. *vb.* (1) *intr.* (*a*) to mount on wings, fly aloft: P. L. II. 634; *soaring on main wing*: P. L. VI. 243; *him that yon soars on golden wing*: II P. 52; *can soar as soon to the corners of the moon*: C. 1016.
(*b*) to rise in thought or imagination: P. L. VII. 3; *thy thoughts ... let them soar*: P. R. I. 230; *the deep transported mind may soar*: V. Ex. 33; *my ... song ... intends to soar*: P. L. I. 14.
(*c*) to aspire or rise in social position: P. L. IV. 829; IX. 170.
(2) *tr.* to mount in; *soaring the air sublime*: P. L. VII. 421.

Sober, *adj.* (*a*) not arising from intemperance, dispassionate, rational; *sober certainty of waking bliss*: C. 263.
(*b*) grave, serious: Il P. 32; *that sober race of men*: P. L. XI. 621; earnest, serious; *Nature .. her sober laws*: C. 766.
(*c*) subdued in colour, somber: P. L. IV. 599.

Sociable (sóciáble), *adj.* disposed to be friendly, companionable; *Raphael, the sociable Spirit*: P. L. v. 221.

Sociably (sóciábly), *adv.* affably; *not sociably mild, as Raphael*: P. L. XI. 234.

Social, *adj.* of society; *social communication*: P. L. VIII. 429.

Society, *sb.* (*a*) companionship, fellowship, company: P. L. VIII. 586; IX. 1007; *among unequals what society can sort*: P. L. VIII. 383; *solitude sometimes is best society*: P. L. IX. 249; *recommend such solitude before choicest society*: P. R. I. 302.
(*b*) a body of persons connected by a common bond; *the Saints above, in ... sweet societies*: L. 179.

Sock, *sb.* the light shoe worn by comic actors in the ancient drama; used *fig.* for comedy; *if Jonson's learned sock be on*: L'A. 132.

Socrates, *sb.* the philosopher of Greece; *the low-roofed house of Socrates*: P. R. IV. 274; *poor Socrates*: P. R. III. 96.

Sodom, *sb.* the city of Syria situated near the Dead Sea: P. L. I. 503; x. 562.

Soe'er, *adv.* separated from the word with which it is usually compounded; *in what place soe'er*: P. L. II. 260. *See* **Whatsoever.**

Soever, *adv.* same as preceding; *which way soever men refer it*: S. A. 1015. *See* **Whichsoever.**

Sofala, *sb.* the southernmost of the provinces of Zanzibar. "Sofala lieth on the South of Mozambique ... so called from Sofala the chief city, situate in a little Island." Heylyn, *Cos.* 1657, p. 991: P. L. XI. 400.

Soft, I. *adj.* (1) yielding easily to pressure, not hard; *soft downy bank*: P. L. IV. 334; *sup., Earth's freshest, softest lap*: P. L. IX. 1041.
(*b*) readily changing form (cf. P. L. VI. 348); *Spirits ... can either sex assume, or both; so soft ... is their essence pure*: P. L. I. 424.
(2) affecting the senses in an agreeable manner; (*a*) low, gentle, or melodious to the ear; not loud or harsh; *soft applause, sound*: C. 259, 555; *soft lays, lay, ditties, airs*: P. L. VII. 436; XI. 584; L'A. 136; L. 44; S. I. 8; *comp.*: P. 27; *soft tunings*: P. L. VII. 598; making little sound; *soft foot*: P. L. XI. 848; making gentle music; *soft recorders, pipes, pipe*: P. L. I. 551, 561; C. 86.
(*b*) pleasing to the touch, light and *gentle; sleep ... with soft oppression*: P. L. VIII. 288; *dew of sleep ... with soft slumberous weight*: P. L. IV. 615; smooth and fine; *soft ... locks*: C. 882; mild and agreeable; *soft fires, air*: P. L. II. 276, 400; IV. 667; *fig., soft silence of the listening night*: Cir. 5.
(*c*) refreshing; *slumber soft*: C. 1001.
(3) gentle, tender, loving: P. L. IV. 479; S. A. 1036.
(*b*) characterized by gentleness or love; *soft embraces, words, delicacy*: P. L. IV. 471; x. 865; C. 681.
(4) tender, delicate: P. L. IX. 458; D. F. I. 2; *to starve in ice their soft ethereal warmth*: P. L. II. 601.

(5) mild or gentle in action or motion ; *Earth … that spinning sleeps on her soft axle* : P. L. VIII. 165 ; *soft wings* : P. R. II. 365.

(b) gently blowing : P. L. X. 98.

(c) gently falling or flowing : P. L. IV. 646 ; Ps. LXXXVII. 27.

II. *adv.* gently ; (a) with little noise ; *whispering soft* : P. L. IV. 326 ; *breathe soft* : P. L. V. 193.

(b) without jar or discomfort : P. L. VIII. 254 ; P. R. IV. 583 ; *Earth … bears thee soft with the smooth air along* : P. L. VIII. 166.

(c) with little force : P. L. IX. 386 ; *her hand soft touching* : P. L. V. 17.

See **Snow-soft.**

Soft-ebbing, *adj.* flowing gently : P. L. VII. 300.

Soften, *vb. tr.* (a) to render less hard in substance : P. L. VII. 280.

(b) to make less intractable ; *I behold them softened* : P. L. XI. 110 ; *soften stony hearts* : P. L. III. 189.

(c) to make gentle or effeminate : S. A. 534 ; *to soften and tame severest temper* : P. R. II. 163.

part. adj. **softened,** rendered less hard : P. 46 ; *her softened soil* : P. L. VIII. 147.

Softly, *adv.* gently, quietly : Il P. 150 ; *softly sliding down* : N. O. 47 ; *imper.* approach quietly and slowly : S. A. 115.

Softness, *sb.* gentleness, tenderness, love : P. L. IV. 298.

Sogdiana, *sb.* the northeastern province of the Parthian Empire, lying between the rivers Oxus and Jaxartes : P. R. III. 302.

Soil, *sb.* (a) the ground as fertile or as having a particular character : P. L. XI. 98, 262 ; C. 633 ; *labouring the soil* : P. L. XII. 18 ; *a better soil* : A. 101 ; *Cyrene's torrid soil* : P. L. II. 904 ; *light the soil* : P. R. IV. 239 ; *miry* : Ps. LXXXI. 23 ; *mortal* : L. 78 ; as producing serpents ; *the soil bedropt with blood of Gorgon* : P. L. X. 526 ; in the moon : P. L. VIII. 147 ; in heaven : P. L. VI. 510 ; in hell : P. L. I. 691 ; *this desert soil* : P. L. II. 270 ; *the burnt soil* : P. L. I. 562 ; used of the solid substance of chaos ; *the aggregated soil* : P. L. X. 293.

(b) country, land ; *native soil* :

P. L. XI. 270, 292 ; XII. 129 ; *in this pleasant soil his … garden God ordained* : P. L. IV. 214 ; used of hell : P. L. I. 242.

Soil, *vb. tr.* (a) to make dirty, befoul : P. L. IX. 1076 ; S. A. 123 ; *soiled their crested helmets* : S. A. 141 ; *soil these pure ambrosial weeds* : C. 16.

(b) to defile, violate : *soil her virgin purity* : C. 427.

Sojourn, (1) *sb.* (a) temporary residence or stay : P. R. III. 235.

(b) a place of temporary stay : P. L. III. 15.

(2) *vb. intr.* to dwell for a time, stay temporarily : P. L. XII. 159 ; *she* (light) *in a cloudy tabernacle sojourned* : P. L. VII. 249.

Sojourner, *sb.* a temporary resident : P. L. XII. 192 ; *the sojourners of Goshen* : P. L. I. 309.

Solace, (1) *sb.* (a) comfort, consolation, alleviation : P. L. VI. 905 ; C. 348.

(b) pleasure and delight : P. L. IX. 844 ; P. R. IV. 334 ; *love's disport … the solace of their sin* : P. L. IX. 1044.

(c) that which brings comfort and joy ; *thee … an individual solace* : P. L. IV. 486 ; *life yet hath many solaces* : S. A. 915.

(2) *vb. tr.* (a) to cheer ; *the smaller birds with song solaced the woods* : P. L. VII. 434.

(b) to make amends for by gaining comfort and joy ; *Man … with his like to help or solace his defects* : P. L. VIII. 419.

Soldan, *sb.* the sultan of Turkey : P. L. I. 764.

Soldiery, *sb.* soldiers collectively : S. A. 1498.

Sole, *sb.* the bottom of the foot : P. L. I. 237.

Sole, *adj.* (a) alone in its kind, being without another : P. L. I. 160 ; III. 276 ; IV. 411, 751 ; VIII. 51 ; IX. 533, 653 ; X. 935, 941, 973 ; S. A. 376 ; *sole king* : P. L. II. 325 ; *victor* : P. L. VI. 880 ; *Eve* : P. L. IX. 227 ; *Man, sole lord of all* : P. L. X. 401 ; *bird* : P. L. V. 272 ; *command, dominion* : P. L. III. 94 ; IV. 33 ; VII. 47 ; VIII. 329 ; *reigning* : P. L. I. 124 ; following the word it modifies ; *the glory sole* : P. L. IX. 135 ; perhaps· rather : chief, principal : P. L. IV. 411.

(b) acting alone, only; *sole fugitive*: P. L. IV. 923; following the word it modifies; *whose he sole appoints*: P. L. VI. 808; *on him sole depend*: P. L. XII. 564; *glory, the reward that sole excites ... erected spirits*: P. R. III. 26.

(c) unaccompanied, alone: P. R. II. 110; *I go this uncouth errand sole*: P. L. II. 827; *sole, or responsive each to other's note*: P. L. IV. 683; *I ... sole undertook the dismal expedition*: P. R. I. 100.

absol. one who is alone; *O sole in whom my thoughts find all repose*; P. L. V. 28.

Solemn, *adj.* (1) marked by or attended with religious rites and ceremonies, sacred; *solemn days, day*: P. L. V. 618; VII. 202; *feast, rites, festivals*: P. L. I. 390; VII. 149; S. A. 12, 983, 1311; Ps. LXXXI. 12.

(2) devout, reverential; *solemn adoration, devotion*: P. L. III. 351; *sup.*: S. A. 1147.

(b) arising from or marked by reverence or devotion; perhaps with blending of sense (3) (c); *our solemn search*: A. 7.

(3) fitted to excite or express serious or devout thoughts, impressive, awe-inspiring: P. L. I. 557; *solemn vision*: C. 457; *given with solemn hand*: S. A. 359; *songs, strain, choir*, etc.: V. Ex. 49; N. O. 17, 115; S. M. 9; Il. P. 117; producing solemn music; *the solemn pipe*: P. L. VII. 595.

(b) imposing, impressive; *more solemn than the tedious pomp that waits on princes*: P. L. V. 354.

(c) marshalled, stately, and devout; *solemn troops and sweet societies*: L. 179.

(d) awe-inspiring and of great consequence; *that solemn message*: P. R. I. 133.

(4) earnest, serious; *solemn purpose*: P. L. VII. 78.

(5) serious in demeanour, grave: P. R. II. 354; used of the nightingale from the gravity or melancholy of its song: P. L. IV. 648, 655; VII. 435.

(b) august, majestic, awful; *one of the Heavenly Host ... solemn and sublime*: P. L. XI. 236; *a solemn Angel*: P. L. XII. 364.

(6) formal in character; *a solemn council*; P. L. I. 755.

Solemn-breathing, *adj.* used *fig.* of a sound; arousing in the hearer a feeling of awe and reverence: C. 555.

Solemnity, *sb.* a religious rite: C. 142; nearer in meaning to a ceremonial or festal occasion: A. 39; C. 746.

Solemnize, *vb. tr.* to celebrate; *to solemnize this feast*: S. A. 1656; *evening and morn solemnized the fifth Day*: P. L. VII. 448.

Solemnly, *adv.* (a) reverently, devoutly: S. A. 1731.

(b) formally: S. A. 678.

Solicit, *vb. tr.* (a) to trouble, distress; *solicit not thy thoughts with matters hid*: P. L. VIII. 167.

(b) to tempt, entice; *that fruit ... solicited her longing eye*: P. L. IX. 743.

(c) to exhort, admonish, urge; *absol.*: S. A. 852.

(d) to petition, pray; with *acc.* and *prep. inf.*: P. L. X. 744.

Solicitation, *sb.* (a) temptation, enticement: P. R. I. 152.

(b) earnest request, suit: S. A. 488.

Solicitous, *adj.* anxious, uneasy, greatly concerned: P. R. II. 120; III. 200; *solicitous what chance might intercept their Emperor*: P. L. X. 428.

Solid, *adj.* (a) compact, firm, and unyielding: P. L. X. 286; *solid earth*: Ps. CXXXVI. 22; *rock*: P. L. II. 878; P. R. IV. 18; *land that ever burned with solid, as the lake with liquid fire*: P. L. I. 229.

(b) genuine, true, real; *solid good, virtue*: P. L. VIII. 93; X. 884; S. XXI. 10; sound and worthy of confidence; *the solid rules of civil government*: P. R. IV. 358.

absol. a solid substance: P. L. VI. 323.

Solitary, *adj.* (a) without companions; *those rare and solitary, these in flocks*: P. L. VII. 461; living or reigning alone; *solitary Saturn*: Il. P. 24.

(b) by oneself, unattended, companionless; *solitary flight*: P. L. II. 632; *though in pleasure, solitary*: P. L. VIII. 402.

(c) lonely; *solitary way*: P. L. XII. 649.

(d) single, only one ; *with solitary hand* : P. L. VI. 139.

Solitude, *sb.* (a) the state of being alone : P. L. VIII. 369 ; *in solitude what happiness* : P. L. VIII. 364 ; *blissful solitude* : P. L. III. 69 ; *might I here in solitude live savage* : P. L. IX. 1085 ; *thus entertained with solitude* : P. L. X. 105 ; *the better to converse with solitude* : P. R. I. 191 ; *solitude sometimes is best society* : P. L. IX. 249 ; *recommend such solitude before choicest society* : P. R. I. 302 ; the absence or want of companionship ; *with dangers compassed round, and solitude* : P. L. VII. 28.

(b) a deserted or lonely place : P. R. II. 304 ; *sweet retired solitude* ; C. 376.

Solomon, *sb.* the king of Israel : P. R. II. 201, 206 ; *the wisest heart of Solomon* : P. L. I. 401 ; *the heart of wisest Solomon* : P. R. II. 170.

Solstice, *sb.* the time at which the sun is at its greatest declination : P. 6.

Solstitial, *adj.* at the time of the solstice : P. L. X. 656.

Solution, *sb.* (a) explanation : P. L. VIII. 14 ; S. A. 306.

(b) the means of deciding or ending (a battle) : P. L. VI. 694.

Solve, *vb. tr.* (a) to find an answer to (a riddle) : P. R. IV. 573, 574 ; S. A. 1200.

(b) to decide, determine ; *solve high dispute with conjugal caresses* : P. L. VIII. 55.

*****Some,** *adj.* (a) denoting a person or thing conceived or thought of, but not definitely known or specified ; often nearly or quite equivalent to the indefinite article : P. L. IV. 404, 816 ; VI. 161 ; *some message* : P. L. V. 290 ; *part* : P. L. VIII. 534 ; *unkindness* : P. L. IX. 271 ; *orator* : P. L. IX. 670 ; *glade, tree, cave* : P. L. IX. 1085, 1095 ; XI. 569 ; *misfortune* : P. L. X. 900 ; *spirit* : Il. P. 153 ; *beauty, goddess, virgin* : P. R. II. 186 ; D. F. I. 48 ; L'A. 79 ; C. 148 ; *some one* : P. L. VI. 503 ; C. 483 ; *some other* : P. L. III. 211 ; S. A. 1302 ; *some way or other* : S. A. 1252 ; usually followed by another *adj.* : P. L. I. 204, 294, 783 ; XII. 99 ; P. R. I. 290 ; S. A. 680 ; C. 70 ; Il. P. 5 ; *some capital city* : P. L. II. 924 ; *foreign land* : P. L.

III. 548 ; *mild zone* : P. L. II. 397 ; *new race* : P. L. II. 348 ; *worse way* : P. L. II. 83 ; *dire revenge* : P. L. II. 128 ; *great charge* : P. L. III. 628 ; *dreadful thing* : P. L. IV. 426 ; *cursed fraud* : P. L. IX. 904 ; *such resemblances* : P. L. V. 114.

(b) denoting an indefinite number ; *some days* : P. L. XI. 198 ; P. R. I. 183 ; *some ages past* : P. R. III. 294 ; *some flowers* : M. W. 57 ; *some naked thoughts* : V. Ex. 23 ; *some gay creatures* : C. 299 ; *some few* : C. 771.

(c) denoting an indefinite quantity or amount ; *some glimpse of joy* : P. L. I. 524 ; *some small reflection* : P. L. III. 428 ; *some little cheering* : C. 348 ; *ease to the body some* : S. A. 18 ; *some disadvantage* : P. L. VI. 431 ; *regard* : P. L. XII. 16 ; *note* : P. R. II. 306.

absol. or *sb.* (a) certain persons not definitely specified : P. L. III. 459 ; IV. 281 ; S. XI. 6 ; *some say* : P. L. X. 575, 668, 671 ; C. 432.

(b) an indefinite part or number of persons or things as distinguished from the rest : P. L. XI. 425, 471, 557 ; P. R. IV. 69 ; S. A. 1461 ; *the work some praise* : P. L. I. 731 ; *some I have chosen* : P. L. III. 183 ; *what God commands ... to some* : P. L. IV. 747 ; *some of serpent kind* : P. L. VII. 482 ; *some of Saturn's crew* : C. 805.

Something, *sb.* (a) a certain thing indefinitely conceived or stated : P. L. VIII. 201 ; X. 1014 ; P. R. I. 96 ; S. A. 1383 ; V. Ex. 67 ; *his heart, divine of something ill* : P. L. IX. 845 ; *with something Heavenly fraught* : P. L. XI. 207 ; *something holy lodges in that breast* : C. 246 ; *fain would I something say* : C. 783 ; *something in thy face did shine* : D. F. I. 34 ; *to something like prophetic strain* : Il. P. 174.

(b) an indefinite part ; *something yet of doubt remains* : P. L. VIII. 13.

Sometime (sometime : P. L. IX. 824 ; Il. P. 97), *adv.* (a) at an indefinite future time : P. L. IX. 824.

(b) at times, now and then : L'A. 57 ; Il. P. 97.

Sometimes (sómetimes : P. L. v.
79 ; vi. 242 ; viii. 268 ; xii. 97 ;
L'A. 91 ; S. xx. 3 ; elsewhere
sometímes), *adv.* (*a*) at times,
occasionally, now and then : P. L.
iii. 517 ; vi. 148 ; vii. 495 ; ix.
249, 675 ; xii. 97 ; P. R. i. 330,
367 ; ii. 13, 277 ; L'A. 91 ; C.
380 ; S. xx. 3 ; *sometimes ... sometimes* : P. L. ii. 632, 633 ; iv. 27,
29 ; v. 79 ; viii. 268 ; *sometimes
... then* : P. L. vi. 242 ; *sometimes, anon* : P. R. i. 304.

(*b*) at any time, ever ; *nor sometimes forget* : P. L. iii. 32.

Somewhat (probably somewhăt :
P. L. vi. 615 ; S. A. 1244), (1)
sb. something ; *mixing somewhat
true to vent more lies* : P. R. i.
433.

(2) *adv.* in some degree or
measure : P. L. ii. 521 ; vi. 615 ;
S. A. 1244 ; L. 17.

Somewhere, *adv.* in some place : P.
L. ix. 256.

Son, *sb.* (1) a male child : P. L. iii.
463 ; iv. 757 ; x. 760 ; xi. 319,
736 ; xii. 101, 153, 155, 160, 161,
332 ; P. R. iii. 84 ; iv. 90 ; S. A.
1248, 1485, 1487 ; M. W. 24 ; C.
56 ; S. xxi ; Ps. lxxxvi. 60 ;
Terah's faithful son : Ps. cxiv. 1 ;
Israel ... son of Isaac : P. L. xii.
268 ; *her son, outcast Nebaioth* :
P. R. ii. 308 ; *his son Herod* : P.
R. ii. 424 ; *Amram's son* : P. L.
i. 339 ; *Eli's sons* : P. L. i. 495 ;
ten sons of Jacob : P. R. iii. 377 ;
the son of Macedonian Philip : P.
R. iii. 31 ; *Tobit's son* : P. L. iv.
170 ; *the unwiser son of Japhet* : P.
L. iv. 716 ; *Cytherea's son* ; P. L.
ix. 19 ; *Laertes' son* : P. L. ix.
441 ; *her florid son, young Bacchus* :
P. L. iv. 278 ; *Cupid, her famed
son* : C. 1004 ; *Lencothea's ... son* :
C. 876 ; *the sons of Vulcan* : C.
655 ; *Jove's great son,* Heracles :
S. xxiii. 3 ; Orpheus : P. L. vii.
38 ; L. 59 ; *Uther's son* : P. L. i.
580 ; *Rhea's son* : P. L. i. 513 ;
Earth's son, Antæus : P. R. iv.
563 ; *Earth's sons,* the Giants or
the Titans : P. L. i. 778 ; D. F. I.
47 ; *Maia's son* : P. L. v. 285 ;
Samson : S. A. 335, 353, 354,
1443, 1446, 1460, 1486, 1488,
1516, 1517 ; in direct address : S.
A. 420, 503.

(*b*) applied to Christ in his
earthly life ; *thou art no son of*
mortal man : P. R. i. 234 ; as the
son of Joseph : P. R. i. 23 ; as
the son of Mary : P. L. x. 183 ;
P. R. ii. 61, 109 ; *high are thy
thoughts, O Son !* : P. R. i. 230 ;
as begotten by the Holy Ghost
and hence the son of God : P. R.
i. 88, 135, 166, 176 ; ii. 85, 260 ;
N. O. 2 ; *his beloved Son* : P. R. i.
32, 285 ; *my Son beloved* : P. R.
i. 85 ; *not therefore joins the Son
Manhood to Godhead* : P. L. xii.
388 ; *Son of God or the Son of
God* : P. L. xii. 381 ; P. R. i.
11, 122, 136, 173, 183, 329, 335,
342, 346, 385 ; ii. 4, 242, 303,
368 ; iii. 1, 145, 252 ; iv. 109,
178, 190, 365, 396, 420, 431, 484,
501, 513, 517, 539, 550, 555, 580,
602, 626, 636 ; in direct address :
P. R. ii. 377 ; iv. 196, 451 ; *Hail,
Son of the Most High* : P. R. iv. 633.

(*c*) applied to Christ in heaven
as the only begotten of God : P.
L. v. 835, 847 ; vi. 676, 887 ; vii.
135 ; xi. 20 ; *Son both of God and
Man* : P. L. iii. 316 ; *my, his,* or
thy Son or *only Son* : P. L. ii.
678 ; iii. 64, 79, 403 ; v. 604, 718,
815 ; vi. 678, 719, 725 ; vii. 138,
518 ; x. 70 ; Ps. ii. 15 ; *the Son* ;
P. L. iii. 343 ; v. 597, 733, 743 ;
vi. 824 ; vii. 192 ; x. 64, 645 ;
xi. 72 ; Ps. ii. 25 ; *Son of God or
the Son of God* : P. L. iii. 138,
224, 309, 412 ; v. 662 ; vi. 799 ;
x. 338 ; in direct address : P. L.
iii. 80, 168, 169, 384, 398, 412 ;
v. 719 ; vi. 680 ; vii. 163 ; x. 56,
634 ; xi. 46.

(*d*) applied to Death as the son
of Satan and Sin : P. L. ii. 728,
743, 804, 818 ; x. 363 ; *O Son,
why sit we here* : P. L. x. 235 ;
thou, son and grandchild both : P.
L. x. 384.

(*e*) *fig., Religion ... reckons thee
her eldest son* : S. xvii. 14 ; applied to men as the sons of nature :
C. 717, 727 ; to a river : V. Ex. 91
to substance : V. Ex. 73 ; *good
luck befriend thee, Son* : V. Ex. 59.

(2) a male descendant however
distant : P. L. iv. 324 ; *sons of
gods* : P. L. xi. 696 ; *David's
sons* : P. L. xii. 357 ; applied to
Christ : P. L. xii. 327 ; *Adam's
son* : P. L. iii. 286 ; *then hear, O
Son of David* : P. R. iv. 500.

(*b*) *pl.* descendants in general :
P. L. i. 364 ; iii. 290 ; v. 389 ;

VII. 626; VIII. 637; X. 819; XI.
348, 758; XII. 145; P. R. IV.
614; H. B. 12; *Israel's sons*: P.
R. III. 406; S. A. 1177; *Moab's
sons*: P. L. I. 406; *Geryon's sons*:
P. L. XI. 410; *the sons of Abraham's loins*: P. L. XII. 447; *the
sons of Anak, of Caphtor, of
Lot*: S. A. 528, 1713; Ps. LXXXIII.
32; *the sons of Eden*: P. L. IV.
213.

(3) an adult male, a man : P. L.
XII. 64, 80.

(4) people ; *one whole world of
wicked sons*; P. L. XI. 875.

(5) one who is connected with
or belongs to a person or thing by
some kind of close relationship,
one whose character partakes
largely of some quality ; usually
with the genitive of the person,
thing, or quality ; (*a*) *Son of Man*,
used of Christ as partaking of the
nature of man : Ps. LXXX. 71 ; or
in sense (1) (*b*) ; *Son both of God
and Man*: P. L. III. 316; used
periphrastically for *man* with the
suggestion of weakness in contrast with angels or gods ; *sons of
men*: P. L. VI. 505; P. R. I. 167,
237; II. 192; S. A. 1294.

(*b*) applied variously to angels
as created by God or as partaking
of the heavenly nature : P. L. III.
658; VI. 46, 95; *Sons of God* :
P. L. V. 447; P. R. I. 368;
IV. 197; *O Sons, like one of us
Man is become*: P. L. XI. 84;
Ethereal Sons: P. L. V. 863;
Heaven's ancient Sons: P. R. II.
121; *Heaven's Sons*: P. L. II.
692; *Sons of Heaven*: P. L. I.
654; V. 790; *Sons of Light*: P.
L. V. 160; XI. 80; *Son of Morn*
or *Morning*: P. L. V. 716; N. O.
119; to Satan : P. R. IV. 518; to
the fallen angels : P. R. II. 179.

(*c*) applied to man as created
by God : P. L. II. 373; *Sons of
God*: P. R. IV. 197, 520; Ps.
LXXXII. 22; *thy youngest son*: P.
L. III. 151; *Son of Heaven and
Earth*, Adam as created by God
out of earth, and hence partaking
of both the heavenly and earthly
natures : P. L. V. 519.

(*d*) with reference to the
country, nation, tribe, or city in
which a man is born or to which
he belongs : P. L. I. 353; IV. 213;
S. A. 240, 1558.

(*e*) one who is a follower of
another, one who is prompted to
action by and obeys the will of
another ; *the sons of Belial* : P. L.
I. 501; *Sons of God*: P. L. XI.
622; one who follows the example
of another in belief ; *sons of
Abraham's faith* : P. L. XII. 448.

(*f*) *son of light*, man as perceiving and following the truth
of God : P. L. XI. 808.

(*g*) *Sons of Darkness*, the rebel
angels: P. L. VI. 715.

(*h*) *son of despite*, one created
because of malice or hatred : P.
L. IX. 176.

(*i*) *son of memory* : W. S. 5.

Song, *sb.* (1) an utterance in musical
modulation, a singing : P. L. V.
204; VIII. 243; IX. 800; *Song
charms the Sense* : P. L. II. 556;
sylvan pipe or song : P. R. I. 480;
by angels ; *triumphant song* : Cir.
2; in heaven : P. L. V. 619;
trained up in feast and song : P.
L. VI. 167.

(*b*) the singing of birds : P. L.
VII. 433.

(*c*) the music of the spheres :
P. L. V. 178; combined with the
singing of angels ; *such holy song*;
N. O. 133.

(2) that which is sung or is to
be sung, lay, strain : P. L. I. 441;
X. 862; XI. 594; P. R. IV. 341;
S. M. 25; L. 36; Ps. LXXXI. 5;
*tale or song, from old or modern
bard* : C. 44; *our Hebrew songs*:
P. R. IV. 336; *Sion's songs*: P.
R. IV. 347; *lyric, smooth-dittied,
warbled, well-measured* : S. A.
1737; C. 86, 854; S. XIII. 1;
sacred, solemn : P. L. III. 148;
V. Ex. 49; Ps. LXXXVII. 26;
flashy : L. 123; *the songs of
Sirens sweet* : C. 878; *Urania ...
thy celestial song* : P. L. VII. 12;
the goddess ... by blest song : C.
268; sung by angels : P. L. IV.
687; X. 648; *the angelic song in
Bethlehem field* ; P. R. IV. 505;
in heaven : P. L. III. 413; S. M.
6; *with songs to hymn his throne* :
P. L. IV. 944; *with songs ... circle
his throne* : P. L. V. 161; *Heaven
and Earth shall high extol thy
praise, with ... sacred songs* : P. L.
III. 148; *sacred song* : P. L. III.
369; *cherubic songs* : P. L. V. 547;
nuptial song ; L. 176; in hell : P.
L. II. 552.

(b) sung by birds ; *shrill matin song of birds*: P. L. v. 7 ; by the lark : P. R. ii. 281 ; by the nightingale : Il. P. 56 ; *sad* : C. 235 ; *love-laboured* : P. L. v. 41.

(3) a poem or poetry : P. L. vii. 30 ; P. R. i. 12 ; *smit with the love of sacred song* : P. L. iii. 29 ; *heroic song* : P. L. ix. 25 ; *my adventurous song* : P. L. i. 13 ; a lyric poem, an ode : N. O. 239 ; P. 8 ; M. M. 9 ; recital in verse : P. L. vii. 107.

See **Even-song.**

Sonorous, *adj.* giving out sound, resonant : P. L. i. 540.

*****Soon, (1)** *adv.* (*a*) in a short time, before long, presently, shortly, quickly : P. L. i. 78, 127, 140, 278 ; ii. 140, 816, 866, 931 ; iii. 273, 621 ; iv. 822, 946 ; vi. 878 ; vii. 56, 418 ; viii. 336 ; ix. 182 ; *odious soon* : P. L. ix. 880 ; *there soon they chose the fig-tree* : P. L. ix. 1100 ; *answered soon* : P. L. x. 596 ; *beholding soon* : P. L. xii. 50 ; *our foes found soon occasion* : S. A. 425 ; *as soon* : P. L. i. 705 ; iv. 464 ; vi. 432 ; C. 1016 ; *soon as* : P. L. v. 138, 667 ; ix. 888, 1046 ; C. 68 ; *as soon as* : P. R. ii. 383 ; *full soon* : P. L. ii. 805 ; vi. 384 : Ps. iii. 11 ; *how soon* : P. L. iv. 94, 95 ; Cir. 12 ; *so soon* : P. L. ii. 376 ; S. A. 1019, 1585 ; *so soon as* : P. R. iv. 332 ; *too soon* : P. L. x. 586 , P. R. i. 57 ; S. A. 1566.

comp. : P. R. i. 441 ; *no sooner ... but* : P. L. iii. 344 ; x. 357 ; xi. 822 ; S. A. 20 ; D. F. I. 1 ; without *conj.; no sooner... he* : P. L. iii. 403 ; *the sooner*, without correlative word : S. A. 426, 1537 ; correlative with *the happier* : P. R. iii. 179 ; *the sooner for*, the more quickly because of : P. L. vi. 595.

sup. : P. L. iv. 893 ; ix. 181 ; S. A. 1419.

(*b*) at an early time ; *comp., sooner or later* : P. L. x. 613.

(*c*) easily, likely : P. R. ii. 451 ; *comp.* : C. 323.

(2) *adj.* appearing in a short time ; *be it less or more, or soon or slow* : S. ii. 9.

Soot, *sb.* the black substance disengaged from fuel in the process of combustion : P. L. x. 570.

Sooth, (1) *adj.* true, trustworthy ;

no word is ... sooth : Ps. v. 26 ; *sup., the soothest shepherd* : C. 823.

(2) *sb.* truth ; *tell me sooth* : D. F. I. 51.

Soothe, *vb. tr.* to restore to tranquillity, calm, quiet : P. L. ix. 1006.

part. adj. **soothing,** calming, gentle : P. R. iii. 6.

Soothsaying, *part. adj.* able to foretell future events : C. 874.

Sooty, *adj.* (*a*) producing soot : P. L. v. 440.

(*b*) black ; *the sooty flag of Acheron* : C. 604.

Sophi, *sb.* a title of the ruler of Persia under the Sufawi Dynasty : P. L. x. 433.

Sorcerer, *sb.* magician : N. O. 220 ; applied to Comus : C. 521, 940.

Sorceress, *sb.* a female sorcerer ; applied to Sin ; *the snaky Sorceress* : P. L. ii. 724 ; to Dalila : S. A. 937.

Sorcery, *sb.* magic art, enchantment : P. L. i. 479 ; C. 587 ; used *fig.* of charming or enticing speech ; *a pleasing sorcery, could charm pain for a while* : P. L. ii. 566 ; *to fence my ear against thy sorceries* : S. A. 937.

Sord, *sb.* sward, turf : P. L. xi. 433.

Sordid, *adj.* morally foul, base ; *the sordid world* : D. F. I. 63.

Sore, (1) *adj.* (*a*) causing bodily pain : M. W. 49.

(*b*) violent, fierce ; *sore battle* : S. A. 287 ; *sore hath been their fight* : P. L. vi. 687.

(2) *sb.* a diseased and painful spot on the body : S. A. 607 ; *fig.* grief, sorrow : S. A. 184.

(3) *adv.* so as to cause mental or physical suffering, painfully, grievously, violently, greatly : P. R. i. 89 ; Cir. 13 ; *the torrid clime smote on him sore* : P. L. i. 298 ; *so sore the griding sword ... passed through him* : P. L. vi. 328 ; *thy wrath...full sore doth press on me* : Ps. lxxxviii. 30 ; *trouble did thee sore assail* : Ps. lxxxi. 25 ; *shook sore their inward state of mind* : P. L. ix. 1124 ; *sore toiled, beset, offended, hurried, troubled* : P. L. vi. 449 ; x. 124 ; P. R. iv. 196, 402 ; Ps. vi. 6.

Sorec, *sb. vale of Sorec*, the home of Dalilah. Its locality is not certainly known : S. A. 229.

Sorrow, (1) *sb.* (*a*) pain or distress of mind, grief, sadness, misery, affliction : P. L. II. 605 ; x. 717 ; XII. 613 ; P. R. II. 69 ; S. A. 1564 ; Ps. LXXXVIII. 37 ; *regions of sorrow* : P. L. I. 65 ; *sad Acheron of sorrow, black and deep* : P. L. II. 578 ; *a world of woe and sorrow* : P. L. VIII. 333 ; *hourly born with sorrow* : P. L. II. 797 ; *thy sorrow I will greatly multiply* : P. L. x. 193 ; *children thou shalt bring in sorrow forth* : P. L. x. 195 ; *thou in sorrow shalt eat thereof* : P. L. x. 201 : *of sorrow thy full load* : S. A. 214 ; *chilling grip of sorrow* : P. L. XI. 264 : *sorrow and pain* : P. L. I. 558 ; *sorrow and dejection and despair* ; P. L. XI. 301 ; *tears and sorrow* : P. L. x. 757 ; *shame and sorrow* : S. A. 457 ; *sorrows and labours* : P. R. IV. 386 ; *to thy sorrow* : S. A. 1154 ; *in my midst of sorrow* : S. A. 1339 ; *in spite of sorrow* : L'A. 45 ; *pious, deep, dark* : P. L. XI. 362 ; Cir. 9 ; P. 33 ; *from these gates sorrow flies far* : C. 668 ; repentance : P. L. x. 1092, 1104

(*b*) the expression of grief, lamentation : D. F. I. 73 ; P. 8, 55.

(*c*) a cause of grief, one for whom a person grieves : L. 166.

(2) *vb. intr.* to feel sorrow, grieve, be sad : P. L. XI. 117 ; S. A. 1347 ; *I sorrowed at thy captive state* : S. A. 1603 ; *he sorrows now, repents, and prays* : P. L. XI. 90.

vbl. sb. **sorrowing,** the expression of grief, lamenting, mourning : M. W. 53.

Sorry, *adj.* (*a*) grieved ; as an expression of regret ; *I am sorry what this stoutness will produce* : S. A. 1346.

(*b*) poor, mean ; *cheeks of sorry grain* : C. 750.

Sort, (1) *sb.* (*a*) rank or position in society ; *all the lords, and each degree of sort* : S. A. 1608.

(*b*) kind, species ; *all sorts are here that all the earth yields* : P. L. VII. 541 ; *meats of noblest sort* : P. R. II. 341 ; *every sort of gymnic artist* : S. A. 1323 ; a class of men or angels ; *Spirit of happy sort* : P. L. IV. 128 ; *Spirit of other sort* : P. L. IV. 582 ; *the first, the other, a different, the third* : P.

L. III. 129 ; VI. 376 ; XI. 574 ; P. R. IV. 296.

(*c*) way, manner ; *to Adam in what sort shall I appear?* : P. L. IX. 816 ; or degree : P. R. IV. 198.

(2) *vb. intr.* (*a*) to issue, result ; *among unequals what society can sort, what harmony* : P. L. VIII. 384.

(*b*) to agree with, fit, suit : P. L. x. 651 ; P. R. I. 200.

Sottish, *adj.* foolish : P. L. I. 472.

Soul, *sb.* (1) the incorporeal part of man ; that which feels, thinks, and wills : P. R. IV. 313.

(*b*) as in or distinguished from the body : P. R. II. 476 ; S. A. 156 ; D. F. I. 21 ; *strains that might create a soul under the ribs of Death* : C. 561 ; *if it be true that light is in the soul, she all in every part* : S. A. 92 ; apparently in contrast with *spirit* as free from body ; *flesh to mix with flesh, or soul with soul* : P. L. VIII. 629.

(*c*) as the seat of the feelings, desires, affections ; as affected by joy, delight, longing, sorrow, etc. : Ps. LXXXIV. 5 ; LXXXVI. 11, 12 ; LXXXVIII. 10, 57 ; *the anguish of my soul* : S. A. 458 ; *through my very soul a sword shall pierce* : P. R. II. 90 ; *for Eloquence the Soul, Song charms the Sense* : P. L. II. 556 ; as affected by music : V. Ex. 50 ; N. O. 98 ; L'A. 138 ; C. 256 ; used of God or angels ; *united as one individual soul, for ever happy* : P. L. v. 610 ; *O Son, in whom my soul hath chief delight* : P. L. III. 168 ; *such as in their souls infixed plagues* : P. L. VI. 837.

one soul, the union of man and wife in oneness of living, feeling, thinking : P. L. VIII. 499 ; IX. 967 ; *union of mind, or in us both one soul* : P. L. VIII. 604.

(*d*) as the seat of the moral life, as liable to sin but as designed for everlasting life : P. L. XI. 724 ; S XIX. 4 ; Ps. VI. 8 ; LXXXVI. 5, 46 ; *teach the erring soul* : P. R. I. 224 ; *he that hides a dark soul* : C. 383 ; *ripened thy just soul to dwell with God* : S. XIV. 2 ; *to bind our souls with secular chains* : S. XVI. 12 ; fem. gender : C. 454, 467 ; in contrast with the body : C. 462 ; used of Christ ; *my unspotted soul* : P. L. III. 248.

(e) as the seat of the mind ; *in the soul are many lesser faculties, that serve Reason as chief* : P. L. v. 100 ; *whence the Soul Reason receives, and Reason is her Being* : P. L. v. 486 ; with blending of (1) (c); *worthy to subdue the soul of Man, or passion in him move* : P. L. VIII. 585 ; *thou hast nor ear, nor soul, to apprehend* : C. 784 ; *thy rapt soul sitting in thine eyes* : Il P. 40 ; *there doth my soul in holy vision sit* : P. 41.

(2) the animating or essential part ; *thou Sun ... of this great World both eye and soul* : P. L. v. 171 ; *Charity, the soul of all the rest* : P. L. XII. 584 ; *soul of harmony* : L'A. 144.

(3) the spirit after its departure from the body : D. F. I. 36 ; T. 19 ; M. W. 72 ; *the soul of Orpheus* : Il P. 105 ; *O soul of Sir John Cheek* : S. XI. 12.

(4) life : Ps. VII. 5, 13 ; *part of my soul I seek thee* : P. L. IV. 487 ; *groaned out his soul* : P. L. XI. 447.

(5) that in which there is life, being, creature : P. R. III. 125 ; applied to angels : P. L. VI. 165 ; *every soul in Heaven shall bend the knee* : P. L. v. 816.

living soul, soul living : P. L. VIII. 154 ; applied to man ; *thou becam'st a living soul* : P. L. VII. 528 ; to the beasts, birds, etc. : P. L. v. 197 ; VII. 388, 392, 451.

Sound, *adj.* (a) whole, uninjured : P. L. VI. 444.

(b) unbroken and deep, undisturbed ; *sound repose, sleep* : P. L. IX. 407 ; *sup.* : P. L. VIII. 253.

Sound, *sb.* a narrow passage of water ; *the sounds and seas* : P. L. VII. 399 ; C. 115 ; *this Lethean sound* : P. L. II. 604.

Sound, I. *sb.* that which is perceived by the ear : C. 942 ; the character or the source of the sound specified : P. R. II. 403 ; *jarring, stunning, whirlwind, battle's sound* : P. L. II. 880, 952 ; VI. 749 ; N. O. 53 ; *harmonious, rural, humming* : P. L. VII. 206 ; IX. 451 ; P. R. IV. 17 ; *of blustering winds, of thunder, of waters, of torrent floods, of leaves, of rustling leaves, of seas* : P. L. II. 286, 476 ; IV. 453 ; v. 5, 872 ; VI. 829 ; IX. 518 ; x. 642 ; *of bees* : P. R. IV.

247 ; *of dance* : P. L. VIII. 243 ; *of onset, of riot* : P. L. VI. 97 ; C. 171 ; *of public scorn* : P. L. x. 508.

(b) a sound made by the voice : N. O. 193 ; in speech : S. A. 660 ; *articulate sound* : P. L. IX. 557 ; *of words* : S. A. 176 ; *of his persuasive words* : P. L. IX. 736.

(c) a musical sound, whether of the voice or of a musical instrument : P. L. I. 711 ; IV. 686 ; VI. 64 ; N. O. 101 ; *harmonious, divine, inimitable, solemn-breathing, glad* : P. L. VIII. 606 ; S. M. 3 ; A. 78 ; C. 555 ; L. 35 ; *of hymns, of song* : P. L. III. 147 ; VIII. 243 ; *of pastoral reed* : C. 345 ; *of harps, of harp and organ* : P. L. VII. 558 ; XI. 558 ; *all sounds on fret by string* : P. L. VII. 597 ; the sound of the trumpet : P. L. I. 531, 540, 754 ; II. 515 ; XII. 229 ; P. R. I. 19 ; Ps. LXXXI. 10.

(d) words ; *thou clothe my fancy in fit sound* : V. Ex. 32.

II. *vb.* (1) *intr.* to give out a sound ; *rebecks sound* : L'A. 94 ; *the far-off curfew sound* : Il P. 74 ; used of a trumpet : P. L. VI. 204 ; XI. 76 ; P. 26.

(2) *tr.* (a) to make sound, blow ; or possibly (1) *intr.*; *Michael bid sound the ... trumpet* : P. L. VI. 202.

(b) to announce by a sound ; *the crested cock ... sounds the silent hours* : P. L. VII. 443.

(c) to celebrate, proclaim; *sound his praise* : P. L. v. 172.

part. adj. **sounding,** giving forth sounds : P. L. I. 668 ; II. 517 ; L. 154.

Sound, *vb. tr.* to test the depth of ; *fig.*, to sound or taint integrity : P. L. v. 703.

Sound-board, *sb.* a thin piece of wood so placed in an organ as to enhance the power and quality of the tones : P. L. I. 709.

Sour, *adj.* austere, morose ; *sour Severity* : C. 109.

Source, *sb.* one who or that which gives rise to something : S. A. 64, 664 ; *wedded Love ... true source of offspring* : P. L. IV. 750 ; used of man ; *I ... am graced the source of life* : P. L. XI. 169 ; *this second source of men* : P. L. XII. 13 ; *on me ... as the source and spring of all corruption* : P. L. x. 832.

South, (1) *adv.* to or toward the south : P. L. x. 686 ; xi. 401 ; xii. 139.

(2) *sb.* (*a*) that one of the cardinal points of the compass which is on the left hand when one faces in the direction of the setting sun ; *from the south* : P. L. x. 655, 701 ; *to south the Persian bay* : P. R. iii. 273.

(*b*) a district or country lying toward the south : P. R. iv. 69 ; *the South* : P. L. i. 750 ; *the south of Susiana* : P. R. iii. 320; *these ... coast the south* : P. L. iv. 782.

Southern, *adj.* situated in the south : P. R. iv. 28.

Southmost, *adj.* situated farthest toward the south : P. L. i. 408.

Southward, *adv.* toward the south : P. L. iv. 223.

South-west, *sb.* that point of the compass equally distant between south and west : P. R. iv. 237.

South-wind, *sb.* the wind blowing from the south : P. L. xi. 738.

Sovran, (1) *adj.* (*a*) supreme : P. L. viii. 647.

(*b*) supreme in power ; *sovran Jove* : C. 41 ; *wonder not, sovran mistress* : P. L. ix. 532; *sovran Reason* : P. L. ix. 1130; used of God or Christ : P. L. i. 246; *sovran King, Presence, Lord, Priest* : P. L. viii. 239 ; x. 144 ; N. O. 60 ; P. 15 ; *Planter, Architect* : P. L. iv. 691 ; v. 256 ; of that which pertains to or issues from God ; *sovran voice* : P. L. vi. 56 ; P. R. i. 84 ; *power, will* : P. L. i. 753 ; vii. 79 ; xi. 83 ; *throne* : P. L. v. 656 ; *gift* : P. L. v. 366 ; *sentence* : P. L. iii. 145.

(*c*) supremely efficacious, potent : P. L. iii. 22 ; C. 639 ; *O sovran, virtuous, precious of all trees* : P. L. ix. 795.

(2) *sb.* an absolute monarch ; applied to God : P. L. ii. 244; or *absol.* one who is supreme in power ; *thee* (Eve) *of right declared sovran of creatures* : P. L. ix. 612.

Sovranty, *sb.* supreme rule, absolute authority : P. L. ii. 446 ; xii. 35.

Sow, *vb.* (*pret.* sowed ; *past part.* sown) (1) *tr.* (*a*) to scatter over, besprinkle ; *fig., sowed the earth with orient pearl* : P. L. v. 2 ; *sowed with stars the heaven* : P. L. vii. 358.

(*b*) *fig.* to spread abroad ; *to sow a jangling noise of words* : P. L. xii. 55.

(2) *intr.* to scatter seed for the purpose of growth ; *the lily and rose, that neither sowed nor spun* : S. xx. 8 ; *fig., thy seed sown ... in his heart* : P. L. xi. 27 ; *their martyred blood and ashes sow* : S. xviii. 10.

See **Thin-sown.**

Space, *sb.* (1) unlimited extension ; (*a*) as an agent ; *space may produce new worlds* : P. L. i. 650.

(*b*) as occupied ; *nor vacuous the space* : P. L. vii. 169 ; *that which yields or fills all space* : P. L. vii. 89.

(2) extent of surface, distance ; *stars, that seem to roll spaces incomprehensible* : P. L. viii. 20; *ample, narrow, little* : P. L. i. 725 ; vi. 104 ; x. 320 ; P. R. ii. 339.

(3) an interval of time, period : P. L. ix. 463; *nine times the space that measures day and night* : P. L. i. 50 ; *the space of seven continued nights* : P. L. ix. 63 ; *of seventy years* : P. L. xii. 341.

(*b*) a short time, a space : P. L. ii. 717 ; xi. 498 ; P. R. i. 169.

Spacious, *adj.* (1) of great extent, extensive, vast : P. L. ii. 974 ; iii. 430 ; *the spacious North* : P. L. v. 726 ; *this continent of spacious Heaven* : P. L. vi. 474 ; *a spacious World* : P. L. x. 467 ; *plain* : P. L. xi. 556 ; P. R. iii. 254.

(*b*) wide, large; *spacious wound, gap* : P. L. i. 689 ; vi. 861.

(*c*) *adv. who built so spacious* : P. L. viii. 102.

(2) affording large or ample room ; *spacious hall, theatre* : P. L. i. 762 ; S. A. 1605 ; *who ... possess this spacious ground* : P. L. v. 367.

Spade, *sb.* the implement for digging : P. L. i. 676 ; P. R. iii. 331.

Span, *vb. tr. fig.* to pronounce in reading verse : S. xiii. 2.

Spangle, *vb. tr.* to sprinkle with spangles or small bright objects ; *all their shape spangled with eyes* : P. L. xi. 130 ; *thousand thousand stars ... spangling the hemisphere* : P. L. vii. 384.

part. adj. **spangled** ; (*a*) set with stars ; *in spangled sheen* : C. 1003.

(b) bright as if covered with spangles ; *all the spangled host* : N. O. 21.

See **New-spangled.**

Spare, I. *adj.* parsimonious, frugal ; *spare Fast, Temperance*: II P. 46 ; C. 767.

II. *sb.* or *absol.* the condition of being thin or lean ; *his visage drawn he felt to ... spare*: P. L. x. 511.

III. *vb.* (1) *tr.* (a) to refrain from employing freely : P. L. III. 393.

(b) to withhold the use or the doing of, omit, forbear : S. A. 487 ; *we might have spared our coming*: P. L. IX. 647 ; with *prep. inf.*: P. L. II. 739 ; IX. 596 ; S. XX. 13.

(c) to do without, give up : L. 113 ; *sense of pleasure we may well spare out of life*: P. L. VI. 460 ; *I spare thee from my bosom* : P. L. III. 278.

(d) to refrain from injury to, leave undisturbed : S. VIII. 10 ; *dim sadness did not spare that time celestial visages*: P. L. x. 23.

(2) *intr.* to be parsimonious or frugal : P. L. v. 320.

Sparely, *adv.* rarely, seldom : L. 138.

Spark, *sb.* a particle of fire emitted from a burning body : P. L. IV. 814.

Sparkle, (1) *sb.* (a) a spark : P. L. VI. 766.

(b) scintillation ; *swift as the sparkle of a glancing star* : C. 80.

(2) *vb. intr.* to shine, gleam : S. A. 544 ; used of eyes or of that which shines through the eyes : P. L. I. 194 ; *joy sparkled in all their eyes* : P. L. II. 388 ; *I see bright honour sparkle through your eyes* : A. 27.

part. adj. **sparkling,** gleaming, glittering : P. L. III. 507.

Spartan, *adj.* of Sparta ; *Spartan land* : D. F. I. 26 ; *the Spartan Twins* (*see* Twin) : P. L. x. 674.

Spasm, *sb.* a violent and involuntary contraction of the muscles : P. L. XI. 481.

Spattering, *part. adj.* made in sputtering ; *a spattering noise* : P. L. x. 567.

Spawn, *sb.* the offspring of fish : P. L. VII. 388 ; C. 713.

Speak, *vb.* (*pres. 2d sing.* speak'st : P. R. IV. 487 ; *pret.* spoke : S. A. 248 ; elsewhere spake ; *2d sing.* spak'st : P. L. VIII. 444 ; *past part.* spoken : P. L. III. 171 ; P. R. II. 90 ; spoke : P. L. x. 517 ; S. A. 727 ; Ps. LXXXVII. 10) I. *tr.* (1) to express in words, utter, declare : P. L. II. 50 ; III. 171 ; P. R. I. 256 ; II. 337 ; *most glorious things of thee abroad are spoke* : Ps. LXXXVII. 10 ; *spake much of right and wrong* : P. L. XI. 666 ; *to speak thy praise* : P. L. IX. 749 ; *speak the truth* : S. XIV. 12 ; *a lie* : Ps. v. 15 ; *he speaks or will speak peace* : Ps. LXXXV. 31, 33 ; the thing spoken as object sentence : P. L. VII. 339.

(2) to declare, make known ; *the deeds ... spoke loud the doer* : S. A. 248 ; *the Heaven's wide circuit, let it speak the Maker's high magnificence*: P. L. VIII. 100.

(3) to use in oral utterance ; *to speak all tongues* : P. L. XII. 501.

(4) to inflict or impose by a command : C. 804.

II. *intr.* (1) to employ the vocal organs in speech, utter words : P. L. VIII. 222 ; *to speak I tried, and forthwith spake* : P. L. VIII. 271 ; *he ... knows, and speaks, and reasons*: P. L. IX. 765 ; *didst move my ... tongue to speak* : V. Ex. 2 ; with blending of (2) ; *he would have spoke, but hiss for hiss returned* : P. L. x. 517.

(2) to give verbal expression to thought ; sometimes to discourse formally and publicly : P. L. II. 42 ; VIII. 3, 380, 444 ; IX. 1150 ; Eurip. 2 ; *he or she speaks or spake* : P. L. I. 663 ; II. 735 ; S. A. 178 ; *he now prepared to speak* : P. L. I. 616 ; *she makes address to speak* : S. A. 731 ; *I'll speak to her* : C. 264 ; *the Lord shall ... speak to them* : Ps. II. 10 ; *so or thus speaking* or *spake* ; the thing spoken immediately preceding or following : P. L. I. 125, 271 ; II. 228, 309, 429, 704, 705 ; III. 135, 681 ; IV. 114, 393, 492, 844, 977 ; v. 27, 246, 599, 616, 694, 743, 849, 896 ; VI. 56, 281, 450, 722, 824 ; VII. 174 ; VIII. 39, 249, 349, 376, 434 ; IX. 318, 376, 494, 552 ; x. 63, 1097 ; XI. 181 ; XII. 466, 624 ; P. R. I. 168, 294, 320, 465 ; II.

147; III. 1, 145, 441; IV. 365;
thus spake to: P. L. III. 79, 143;
IV. 781, 877; V. 672; VI. 800;
VII. 138, 518; IX. 646; XI. 192,
225; P. R. I. 129; the *perf. inf.*
used for the *pres.; about to have
spoke*: S. A. 727; *imper.*: C. 490,
492; Ps. IV. 20; *speak ... ye Sons
of Light*: P. L. V. 160; to be expressed in words; *so spake this
oracle*: P. L. X. 182.

(*b*) **speak against**, to refuse
assent to or acceptance of: P. R.
II. 90.

(*c*) **speak out**, to tell quickly or
fully: S. A. 1569.

(*d*) *fig.* to reveal one's thoughts
and desires; *his meek aspect silent
yet spake*: P. L. III. 267.

(3) to command; *speak thou,
and be it done*: P. L. VII. 164.

(4) to talk, converse: C. 357;
with *of*: P. L. VIII. 199; IX. 966;
of fellowship I speak: P. L. VIII.
389; *those terrors which thou
speak'st of*: P. R. IV. 487.

(5) to tell or make known in
recorded speech; *the Law and
Prophets ... of whom they spake I
am*: P. R. I. 262.

(6) to give forth sound; *the
trumpet spake not to the armed
throng*: N. O. 58.

Speakable, *adj.* having the power of
speech: P. L. IX. 563.

Spear, *sb.* (*a*) the weapon of warfare:
S. VIII. 9; *the idle spear*: N. O.
55; *thy spear a weaver's beam*:
S. A. 1121; *at one spear's length*:
S. A. 348; *shield and spear*: S. A.
132, 284; *sing. collect.*: P. L. I.
436; borne by an angel: P. L. I.
292, 347; IV. 810, 929; XI. 248;
with ordered spear and shield: P.
L. I. 565; *what seemed both spear
and shield*: P. L. IV. 990; *down
fell both spear and shield*: P. L.
X. 542; *shields, helms, and spears*:
P. L. IV. 553; *a forest huge of
spears*: P. L. I. 547; *couch their
spears*: P. L. II. 536; *ported,
rigid, massy*: P. L. IV. 980; VI.
83, 195; *at the spear*, in the use
of, or when using, the spear: P.
L. II. 204.

(*b*) a man armed with a spear:
S. A. 1619.

(*c*) the right side or direction:
P. L. IV. 785.

Special, *adj.* express, particular: P.
L. II. 1033; S. A. 273; *under his*

special eye, directly and closely
watched by him: S. A. 636.

Specious, *adj.* superficially, but not
really, fair, just, or right: P. L.
IX. 361; *deeds, gifts*: P. L. II.
484; P. R. II. 391; *outward
rights and specious forms*: P. L.
XII. 534; *that specious monster,
my accomplished snare*: S. A.
236.

Speck, *vb. tr.* to mark in spots: P.
L. IX. 429.

Speckled, *adj.* plague - spotted,
tainted, polluted; *speckled vanity*:
N. O. 138.

Spectacle, *sb.* (*a*) a show, sight; *this
so horrid spectacle*: S. A. 1542;
an exhibition; *a spectacle of ruin*:
P. R. I. 415.

(*b*) a great public show or exhibition: S. A. 1604.

Speech, *sb.* (*a*) the power of speaking: P. L. IX. 600; *failed speech*:
P. L. IV. 357.

(*b*) the action of speaking, the
expression of thought in words:
P. L. IV. 409; IX. 1133; XII. 5;
*cannot without process of speech be
told*: P. L. VII. 178; *thy tongue
not made for speech*: P. L. IX.
749; *leave of*: P. L. VIII. 377;
faltering: P. L. II. 989.

(*c*) that which is spoken: P. L.
V. 459; a formal and public
speech: P. L. II. 389.

(*d*) manner of speaking: P. R.
II. 301.

Speechless, *adj.* not speaking from
present inability, silent: P. L.
IX. 894.

Speed, I. *sb.* (1) good fortune, prosperity, success: P. L. IV. 13.

(2) rapidity of movement, swiftness, celerity: P. L. III. 643;
VIII. 38; C. 573; *bent all on
speed*: P. L. IV. 568; *winged with
speed*: P. L. I. 674; *with or on
winged speed*: P. L. IV. 788; V.
744; *to thy speed add wings*: P.
L. II. 700; *incorporeal*: P. L.
VIII. 37; *speed almost spiritual*:
P. L. VIII. 110; *the speed of Gods*:
P. L. X. 90; *the Sun himself withheld his wonted speed*: N. O. 79;
the Hours ... whose speed: T. 3;
the ... thunder made all speed: P.
L. IV. 928; *with speed, with what
spēed, with all speed*: P. L. V.
313, 730; VI. 307; X. 410; P. R.
II. 116; S. A. 1316, 1343, 1345,
1728; D. F. I. 60.

(b) a rapid going or progress:
P. L. v. 252; a speedy journey;
bent on speed: P. L. xii. 2.

(3) haste, hurry; *speed in his
looks*: S. A. 1304.

II. *vb.* (*pret.* sped; *past part.*
sped: P. L. iii. 740; L. 122;
speeded: P. R. iii. 267) (1) *intr.*
(a) to be fortunate, prosper, succeed: P. L. x. 40; Ps. lxxxiii.
41, 42; *imper.*: P. L. ii. 1008.

(b) to move rapidly, go or pass
swiftly: P. L. v. 267; x. 954; S.
xix. 12; *I see one hither speeding*:
S. A. 1539; and hence, to reach a
place in a comparatively short
time; *well have we speeded*: P. R.
iii. 267.

(2) *tr.* (a) to cause to move
rapidly; *sped with hoped success*:
P. L. iii. 740.

(b) to provide quickly for: L.
122.

Speedily, *adv.* in a short time: P. L.
v. 692.

Speedy, (1) *adj.* (a) moving swiftly:
P. L. ii. 516; *sup.*, *the speediest
of thy winged messengers*: P. L.
iii. 229.

(b) characterized by swiftness;
comp., *speedier flight*: P. L. xi. 7;
sup., *speediest sail*: P. L. vi. 534.

(c) not delayed or delaying,
prompt, ready: P. L. i. 156;
each to other speedy aid: P. L. ix.
260; *speedy death*: S. A. 650;
sup., *my speediest friend*: S. A.
1263.

(2) *adv.* without delay, quickly:
S. A. 1681.

Spell, I. *sb.* a form of words
supposed to have occult power;
breathed spell: N. O. 179; any
means of enchantment: S. A.
1132, 1139; C. 919; *the very
lime-twigs of his spells*: C. 646;
old soothsaying Glaucus' spell: C.
874; *magic, mighty, dazzling,
guileful, numbing*: S. A. 1149; V.
Ex. 89; C. 154, 537, 853.

II. *vb.* (*pret.* not used; *past
part.* spelled) (1) *tr.* to make out
point by point, discover by careful
study; *by what the stars ... give
me to spell*: P. R. iv. 385; *the
drift of hollow states hard to be
spelled*: S. xvii. 6.

(2) *intr.* (a) to read by telling
the letters singly: S. xi. 7.

(b) to engage in careful observation and study *of*: Il P. 170.

Spend, *vb.* (*pret.* and *past part.*
spent) *tr.* (a) to expend, employ,
let loose; *to spend all his rage*:
P. L. ii. 144.

(b) to consume, exhaust, use
up: P. L. ix. 145; P. R. iv.
443; *the thunder ... perhaps hath
spent his shafts*: P. L. i. 176; *all
his darts were spent*: P. R. iv.
366; *all passion spent*: S. A.
1758; *my light is spent*: S. xix. l.

(c) to pass or employ *hours,
days*: P. L. iii. 417; v. 618; ix.
1187; xii. 22; *thy life*: P. R. iii.
232; *his date*: U. C. ii. 29; *eternity*: P. L. ii. 248; *to spend the
respite of that day*: P. L. xi. 271.

(d) to exhaust or overweary:
P. L. viii. 457.

adj. or *part.* **spent**, gone, passed;
the day is not yet spent: P. L.
viii. 206; *ere yet my life be spent*:
Ps. lxxxviii. 54.

Spet, *vb. tr.* to spit, throw out from
the mouth; *fig.*, *darkness spets
her thickest gloom*: C. 132.

Sphere, I. *sb.* (1) a globe; *the Sun a
mighty sphere he framed*: P. L.
vii. 355; the sun as ruled over by
Uriel; *this day ... came to my
sphere a Spirit*: P. L. iv. 564;
the moon: H. B. 2.

(b) *sphere of fortune*, the globe
upon which the goddess Fortuna
was represented as standing: S.
A. 172.

(2) the orb or globe of the universe: P. L. viii. 82; N. O. 48.

(b) *Diurnal Sphere*, the astro-
nomical universe which appears to
revolve around the earth in
twenty-four hours: P. L. vii. 22.

(3) one of the orbs or hollow
globes which were supposed to
revolve about the earth as a
common centre, and in which the
heavenly bodies were set: P. L.
viii. 131; *O Sun ... above thy
sphere*: P. L. iv. 39; *passing
through the spheres of watchful
fire*: V. Ex. 40; *the starry quire,
who, in their nightly watchful
spheres*: C. 113; *two planets ...
their jarring spheres confound*: P.
L. vi. 315.

(b) as producing music; *fairest
of Stars ... praise him in thy sphere*:
P. L. v. 169; *ring out, ye crystal
spheres*: N. O. 125; *the celestial
Sirens' harmony, that sit upon the
nine infolded spheres*: A. 64.

(c) *that crystalline sphere*, the ninth orb, supposed by some to be 'the waters which were above the firmament' (Gen. I. 7): P. L. III. 482.

(d) *that high first-moving sphere*, the Primum Mobile, the tenth and last orb, which was supposed to be of a hard and opaque substance. This first received motion, and then communicated it to all the other orbs: D. F. I. 39.

(4) the orbs collectively with their heavenly bodies, the stellar universe; *yonder starry sphere of planets and of fixed*: P. L. V. 620; *thus they in Heaven, above the Starry Sphere*: P. L. III. 416.

(5) field of existence, circuit of influence or activity: P. L. V. 477.

(6) inherent potentiality or power: P. L. X. 808.

(7) atmosphere, air: C. 241.

II. *vb. tr.* to ensphere, encircle; *Light... sphered in a radiant cloud*: P. L. VII. 247.

Sphere-born, *adj.* arising from the harmony produced by the movements of the spheres, each of the notes of the gamut being represented by a planetary sphere (?): S. M. 2.

Sphere-metal, *sb.* a material as durable as that of which the spheres are composed: U. C. II. 5.

Sphery, *adj.* of the spheres; *sphery chime*: C. 1021.

Spicy, *adj.* (a) aromatic, fragrant; *spicy shrub*: P. L. VIII. 517; *drugs*: P. L. II. 640; flavoured with spices; *spicy nut-brown ale*: L'A. 100.

(b) abounding in aromatic plants; *spicy shore, forest*: P. L. IV. 162; V. 298.

Spill, *vb.* (*past part.* spilt) *tr.* to shed *blood*: P. L. XI. 791.

Spin, *vb.* (*pret.* and *past part.* spun) (1) *tr.* (a) to weave; *these my sky robes, spun out of Iris' woof*: C. 83.

(b) to draw out and twist into threads; *fig.*, *and between spun out the Air*: P. L. VII. 241.

(2) *intr.* (a) to draw out and twist fibre into threads; *the lily and rose, that neither sowed nor spun*: S. XX. 9.

(b) to revolve rapidly; *Earth... spinning sleeps on her soft axle*: P. L. VIII. 164.

part. adj. **spinning**, forming threads as silkworms: C. 715.
See **Thin-spun.**

Spindle, *sb.* the small pendent bar for twisting and winding the fibres drawn from the distaff; *the adamantine spindle ... on which the fate of gods and men is wound*: A. 66.

Spire, *sb.* (a) that which shoots taperingly to a point; *flames ... slope their ... spires*: P. L. I. 223.

(b) the tapering part of a steeple; *glistering, glittering, golden*: P. L. III. 550; IV. 54, 548.

Spire, *sb.* the coil of a serpent's body: P. L. IX. 502.

Spirit, I. *sb.* (1) the vital principle which bestows and governs the phenomena of life; *taint the animal spirits, that from pure blood arise*: P. L. IV. 805; *flowers and their fruit ... to vital spirits aspire, to animal*: P. L. V. 484; *a rib, with cordial spirits warm*: P. L. VIII. 466; *his scattered spirits returned*: P. L. XI. 294; *all his spirits became entranced*: P. L. XI. 420; probably also; *to the inmost mind ... and on her purest spirits prey*: S. A. 613.

(2) that which feels, thinks, and wills; the soul: P. R. I. 215; IV. 324; S. A. 1238; *my spirit some transporting cherub feels*: P. 38; *pl.*: P. L. IX. 1048; *kindle my rapt spirits*: C. 794; or in sense (3); *all her spirits composed to meek submission*: P. L. XII. 596; *how reviving to the spirits of just men*: S. A. 1269; *bathe the drooping spirits in delight*: C. 812.

(b) as conferred upon or breathed into man by God; *expressing well the spirit within thee, my image*: P. L. VIII. 440; *the Spirit of Man, which God inspired*: P. L. X. 784.

(c) of angels; *the mind and spirit remains*: P. L. I. 139; *have left us this our spirit and strength entire*: P. L. I. 146.

(d) as contrasted with outward forms; *in the worship persevere of Spirit and Truth*: P. L. XII. 533; *disciplined ... from flesh to spirit*: P. L. XII. 303.

(e) *in spirit*, with the eyes of the soul, in a vision: P. L. XI. 406.

(3) temper of mind, cheerfulness, courage: P. L. XI. 545; *I*

feel my genial spirits droop: S.
A. 594; *fainting*: S. A. 666; *new-
enlivened*: C. 228.

(4) the disposition or influence
which fills and governs the soul
or the being: P. L. VI. 848; XII.
53; *the spirit of love*: P. L. VIII.
477; *a spirit of phrensy*: S. A.
1675.

(5) a simple essence devoid of
matter and possessed of the power
of knowing, willing, acting; *till
body up to spirit work*: P. L. V.
478; *your bodies may at last turn
all to spirit*: P. L. V. 497; as in
the chariots of God; *instinct with
spirit*: P. L. VI. 752; *within them
Spirit lived*: P. L. VII. 204.

(*b*) God's power and agency,
often the Holy Spirit: P. L. III.
389; VII. 209; XI. 611; XII. 488,
514, 519, 523; P. R. I. 8, 189;
S. A. 1435; *my overshadowing
Spirit*: P. L. VII. 165; *his brooding wings the Spirit of God outspread*: P. L. VII. 235; *the Spirit,
poured first on his Apostles*: P. L.
XII. 497; *in likeness of a dove the
Spirit descended*: P. R. I. 31;
*the Spirit descended on me like a
dove*: P. R. I. 282; *Thou, O
Spirit*: P. L. I. 17; *the Spirit of
Grace*: P. L. XII. 525; *his Spirit
of Truth*: P. R. I. 462; *the Spirit
of prayer*: P. L. XI. 6.

(*c*) an angel; applied to both
the faithful and the fallen angels:
P. L. I. 423, 490, 609; III. 737;
IV. 83, 128, 582; V. 406, 439; VI.
167, 344, 596, 660; VII. 199; VIII.
626; P. R. II. 237; Il P. 153;
*Spirits of Heaven, the Heavenly
host of Spirits*, etc.: P. L. II. 687,
696, 825; IV. 361, 531; V. 374,
837; VI. 788; VIII. 615; *eternal,
ethereal, immortal, celestial, blessed*,
etc.: P. L. I. 318, 622, 658, 789;
II. 553; III. 101, 136, 360; VI.
333; *reprobate, damned, perverse*,
etc.: P. L. I. 697; II. 482, 1030;
IV. 823; VII. 189, 610; XI. 124;
P. R. II. 122; *armed, warring*:
P. L. I. 101; V. 566; *masculine*:
P. L. X. 890; *those seven Spirits
that stand in sight of God's high
throne*: P. L. III. 654; applied to
Satan: P. L. III. 553, 630; IV.
565, 793; P. R. I. 358; *think not,
revolted Spirit*: P. L. IV. 835; *O
Spirit accused*: P. L. V. 877;
thee, ambitious Spirit: P. R. IV.

495; to Mammon: P. L. I. 679;
to Moloch: P. L. II. 44; to Uriel:
P. L. III. 691; to Raphael: P. L.
V. 221; *O favourable Spirit*: P.
L. V. 507; to Belial: P. R. II.
150; to Ithuriel and Zephon: P.
L. IV. 786.

(*d*) any supernatural being;
*middle Spirits...betwixt the angeli-
cal and human kind*: P. L. III.
461; *Spirit* or *Spirits of the* or *this
nethermost Abyss*: P. L. II. 956,
969; *Spirits of air*: P. R. II. 374;
a demon; *a flame which...some
evil spirit attends*: P. L. IX. 638;
the gods; *bright aereal spirits*:
C. 3.

(6) a disembodied soul: S. M.
14; *the spirit of Plato*: Il P. 89;
tell me, bright Spirit: D. F. I. 38.

(7) a human being considered
with respect to his peculiar characteristics; *most erected, deepest,
timely-happy*: P. R. III. 27; V.
Ex. 22; S. II. 8; *fame is the spur
that the clear spirit doth raise*: L.
70.

(8) perfume: P. L. V. 482.

(9) *spirits of balm*, a liquid composed of balm and alcohol: C. 674.

II. *vb. tr.* to animate, bring into
individual existence and action:
P. L. III. 717.

Spirited, *adj.* possessed by a spirit;
the spirited sly Snake: P. L. IX.
613.

Spiritless, *adj.* wanting courage: P.
L. VI. 852.

Spiritous, *adj.* having the quality of
spirit: P. L. V. 475; VI. 479.

Spiritual, *adj.* (*a*) consisting of spirit:
P. L. V. 573; *spiritual substance,
creatures, Natures*: P. L. IV. 585,
677; V. 402; *Man, in part
spiritual*: P. L. V. 406; like that
of spirits; *speed almost spiritual*:
P. L. VIII. 110.

(*b*) of or pertaining to the spirit:
P. R. I. 10; *spiritual armour,
power, laws*: P. L. XII. 491, 518,
521.

(*c*) pertaining to the church,
ecclesiastical: S. XVII. 10.

Spit, *sb.* a slender pointed prong
used in roasting meat: P. R. II.
343.

Spite, (1) *sb.* (*a*) a disposition to
thwart and disappoint the wishes
of others, or an act springing
from such a disposition: P. L. II.
385; IX. 178; S. A. 1462.

(b) chagrin, mortification; *for* ... *spite*: P. R. IV. 12, 574.

(c) *in spite of*, in defiance of, in opposition to, notwithstanding: P. L. I. 619; II. 393; L'A. 45.

(2) *vb. tr.* to thwart malignantly, vex, annoy: P. L. II. 384; IX. 147, 177.

Spleen, *sb.* ill-will, secret malice; *fret their spleen*: S. IX. 7.

Splendid, *adj.* magnificent: P. L. II. 252.

Splendour, *sb.* (a) great brightness; *the golden Sun, in splendour likest Heaven*: P. L. III. 572; *a third* (angel), *of ... faded splendour wan*: P. L. IV. 870.

(b) magnificence, pomp, glory: P. L. II. 447; P. R. I. 413; II. 366; *from eternal splendours flung*: P. L. I. 610; *eminence and glory*: P. L. V. 796; *magnificent and shining garments*; *clad in splendour*: A. 92.

Spoil, I. *sb.* (1) the plunder taken in war; *bring home spoils*: P. L. XI. 692; *Rome ... with the spoils enriched of nations*: P. R. IV. 46.

(b) anything taken by force or unjustly from another: P. L. XII. 172; *a creature formed of earth, and him endow ... with heavenly spoils, our spoils*: P. L. IX. 151; *gales ... stole those balmy spoils*: P. L. IV. 159; taken by death: P. L. III. 251; garments taken as spoil: S. A. 1203.

(2) the act of plundering, pillage: P. L. II. 1009.

(3) injury, damage, destruction: S. A. 1191.

II. *vb.* (*pret.* and *past part.* spoiled) *tr.* (a) to strip of possessions by violence, plunder: P. R. III. 75; *rising from his grave, spoiled Principalities and Powers*: P. L. X. 186; *Death ... spoiled of his vaunted spoil*: P. L. III. 251.

(b) to injure, ruin, destroy: P. L. XI. 832; M. W. 30.

Sponge, *sb. worth a sponge*, deserving to be obliterated: P. R. IV. 329.

Spongy, *adj.* seeming to imbibe like a sponge; *the spongy air*: C. 154.

Spontaneous, *adj.* without the intervention of external agency, voluntarily: P. L. VII. 204.

Sport, (1) *sb.* (a) amusement, diversion, entertainment; *to make them sport*: S. A. 1328; *set on sport*: S. A. 1679; *personified*: L'A. 31.

(b) a mode of amusement, pastime, game: S. A. 1614; *at their sport*: C. 953; *by their sports to blood inured of fighting beasts*: P. R. IV. 139; the licentious rites of Cotytto: C. 128.

(c) a plaything; *the sport of winds*: P. L. III. 493; *of whirlwinds*: P. L. II. 181.

(d) a laughing-stock; *turned to sport her importunity*: S. A. 396.

(2) *vb. intr.* to amuse oneself, play, frolic: L. 68; *sporting the lion ramped*: P. L. IV. 343; *fish ... sporting with quick glance*: P. L. VII. 405.

Sportful, *adj.* playful, frolicsome: P. L. IV. 396.

Spot, *sb.* (1) a stain, blot: S. XXII. 2.

(2) a stain upon moral purity: P. L. V. 119; upon both moral and physical purity: S. XXIII. 5.

(3) a bit of surface differing from the rest in colour: P. L. VII. 479.

(b) a dark place on the disk of the moon: P. L. V. 419; VIII. 145.

(4) a particular locality, a place: P. L. III. 588; V. 266; IX. 439; *that spot ... is Paradise*: P. L. III. 733; *this dim spot which men call Earth*: C. 5.

(5) something very minute, a particle; *Earth, this punctual spot*: P. L. VIII. 23; *this Earth, a spot, a grain*: P. L. VIII. 17.

Spotless, *adj.* free from moral blemish, pure: P. L. IV. 318.

Spotted, *part. adj.* marked with spots: C. 444.

Spotty, *adj.* spotted; *her* (the moon's) *spotty globe*: P. L. I. 291.

Spousal, (1) *adj.* pertaining to marriage: S. A. 389.

(2) *sb.* nuptials, marriage; *the amorous bird of night sung spousal*: P. L. VIII. 519.

Spouse, (1) *sb.* a wife; *the spouse of Tobit's son*: P. L. IV. 169; *the sapient king ... with his fair Egyptian spouse*: P. L. IX. 443; applied to Eve: P. L. IV. 742; V. 129.

(2) *vb. tr.* to take for a wife: *fig.* of the vine: P. L. V. 216.

Spout, *vb. tr.* to throw out with force as through a narrow orifice: P. L. VII. 416; *Hell should spout her cataracts of fire*: P. L. II. 176.

Spray, *sb.* twig, branch: P. R. IV. 437; S. I. 1.

Spread, *vb.* (*pret.* and *past part.* spread) I. *tr.* (1) to distribute over a surface : P. L. iv. 255 ; *spread out* : C. 398.

(*b*) to shed upon a surface ; *the Sun ... spreads his orient beams, on herb*, etc. : P. L. iv. 643.

(2) to extend to the full size, expand ; said of wings : P. L. ii. 928 ; vii. 434 ; L'A. 6 ; *spread out* : P. L. vi. 827.

(*b*) to stretch out and fix in position ; *under state of richest texture spread* : P. L. x. 446 ; *his dark pavilion spread* : P. L. ii. 960 ; to erect, set up ; *in middle air shall spread his throne* : N. O. 164.

(3) to lay out, display something to be viewed : P. L. xi. 638.

(4) to reach out, extend : V. Ex. 93 ; used of trees, plants, etc. : P. L. ix. 1087, 1103 ; *spread their branches* : P. L. vii. 324 ; *spreads her verdant leaf* : C. 622.

(*b*) to stretch out *to ; my hands to thee I spread* : Ps. lxxxviii. 40.

(*c*) to stretch out in area ; *spread his aery flight ... over the vast Abrupt* : P. L. ii. 407 ; *wide was spread that war* : P. L. vi. 241.

(*d*) to cause to flow over an area ; *where Deva spreads her wizard stream* : L. 55.

(5) to send out in all directions ; *what radiant state she spreads* : A. 14 ; to disseminate, diffuse : P. L. x. 412 ; *foul contagion spread* : L. 127.

(6) to cause to be known, publish : S. A. 1429 ; *he can spread thy name* : S. viii. 7.

(7) to arrange or lay in order : P. R. iv. 587 ; *a table richly spread* : P. R. ii. 340.

(8) to set forth, recount in full ; *spread before him how highly it concerns his glory* : S. A. 1147.

II. *intr.* (*a*) to become dispersed or distributed : P. L. i. 354 ; xi. 343.

(*b*) to be propagated or disseminated : P. L. v. 715 ; *contagion spread both of thy crime and punishment* : P. L. v. 880.

(*c*) to become extended ; *waters ... spread into a liquid plain* : P. L. iv. 454.

(*d*) to expand, grow ; used of trees : P. R. iv. 148 ; L. 81.

part. adj. (1) **spreading**, extending over a comparatively wide area ; *these fair spreading trees* : P. L. x. 1067 ; either a transferred epithet with this meaning, or used by inversion for the *sb.* spread ; *under the spreading favour of these pines* : C. 184.

(2) **spread** ; (*a*) extended *wings* : P. L. ii. 1046.

(*b*) displayed *ensigns* : P. L. ii. 886 ; vi. 533.

Spring, I. *sb.* (1) the vernal season : S. A. 1576 ; *the frolic wind that breathes the spring* : L'A. 18 ; *else had the spring perpetual smiled* : P. L. x. 678 ; personified : P. L. v. 394 ; *the Hours ... led on the eternal Spring* : P. L. iv. 268 ; *revels the ... jocund Spring* : C. 985.

(*b*) *fig.* the early part of life : S. ii. 4.

(2) a thicket ; *yonder spring of roses* : P. L. ix. 218.

(3) an issue of water from the earth, fountain ; *woods and springs* : P. R. ii. 374 ; *grove and spring* : P. 52 ; *fountain or spring* : P. L. xi. 78 ; *springs and showers* : Ps. lxxxiv. 24 ; *clear, haunted, cool, friendly* : P. L. iii. 28 ; N. O. 184 ; C. 282 ; *Castalian spring* (*see* Castalian) : P. L. iv. 274.

(*b*) the source of a river ; *the springs of Ganges or Hydaspes* : P. L. iii. 435.

(4) that from which something originates ; *me ... the source and spring of all corruption* : P. L. x. 832.

II. *vb.* (*pret.* and *past part.* sprung ; *perfect* formed with the auxiliary *be* : P. L. vi. 312) *intr.* (*a*) to leap, bound : P. L. vii. 465 ; *out of thy head I sprung* : P. L. ii. 758 ; *I sprung into swift flight* : C. 578 ; with *up* or *upward* : P. L. viii. 259 ; *up they sprung upon the wing* : P. L. i. 331 ; *springs upward, like a pyramid of fire* : P. L. ii. 1013 ; to leap into fuller growth : P. L. viii. 46.

(*b*) to rise *from* a source : L. 16 ; *a fountain ... from the dry ground to spring* : S. A. 582.

(*c*) to rise as from a source, issue, proceed, originate ; with *from* or *of* : P. L. ii. 381 ; v. 98 ; vii. 58 ; xi. 22 ; xii. 476 ; *order from disorder sprung* : P. L. iii.

713; *new hope to spring out of despair*: P. L. XI. 138; *Light ... sprung from the Deep*: P. L. VII. 245; *from her ashes spring new Heaven and Earth*: P. L. III. 334; *that high mount of God whence light and shade spring*: P. L. V. 644.

(*d*) to take one's birth or origin, be derived; with *from* or *of*: P. L. IX. 965; XI. 425; XII. 113; A. 28; *second of Satan sprung, all-conquering Death*: P. L. X. 591; *sprung of old Anchises' line*: C. 923.

(*e*) to come into being, begin to act: P. L. XII. 353; *among the constellations war were sprung*: P. L. VI. 312; with blending of sense (*c*) or (*f*); *a grove ... sprung up with this their change*: P. L. X. 548; *cause light again within thy eyes to spring*: S. A. 584.

(*f*) to rise out of the ground and grow by vegetative power: P. L. V. 21, 480.

See **Day-spring**.

Spring-time, *sb.* spring: P. L. I. 669.

Sprinkle, *vb. tr.* (*a*) to scatter *drops*: C. 911.

(*b*) to besprinkle, overspread with particles of: P. L. III. 642.

Sprout, *sb.* a shoot of a plant: A. 59.

Spruce, *adj.* dainty, fine; *revels the spruce and jocund Spring*: C. 985.

Spume, *sb.* froth, scum: P. L. VI. 479.

Spur, *sb.* that which impels to action, incitement: L. 70.

Spurious, *adj.* illegitimate, bastard; *conceived, her spurious first-born, Treason against me*: S. A. 391.

Spurn, *vb. tr.* (*a*) to thrust away with the foot: P. L. II. 929.

(*b*) to strike with the foot: S. A. 138.

Spy, (1) *sb.* one secretly watching or so sent to watch the movements of others: P. L. II. 970; IV. 948; VIII. 233; IX. 815; S. A. 386, 1197.

(2) *vb. tr.* (*a*) to gain sight of, see, perceive: P. L. IV. 403, 1005; IX. 424; V. Ex. 61; *thee he spied from far*: D. F. I. 17.

(*b*) to discover by search; *a dove ... to spy green tree*: P. L. XI. 857; to discover and ex-

plore; *spy this new-created World*: P. L. IV. 936.

See **Half-spied**.

Squadron, *sb.* a body of soldiers drawn up in a square; sometimes perhaps merely: a part of an army, a troop: P. L. VI. 251; XI. 652; of angels: P. L. I. 356; *angelic, embattled, shadowing*: P. L. IV. 977; VI. 16, 554; *in squadrons*: P. L. II. 570; N. O. 21; *stood in squadron joined*: P. L. IV. 863.

Squadroned, *part. adj.* drawn up in a squadron: P. L. XII. 367.

Square, (1) *sb.* (*a*) a quadrilateral surface: P. L. V. 393.

(*b*) the position of two planets at a distance of ninety degrees from each other: P. L. X. 659.

(2) *adj.* rectangular and equilateral: P. L. II. 1048.

(3) *vb.* (squarèd *disyl.*: P. L. I. 758) *tr.* (*a*) to draw up into a square; *squared in full legion*: P. L. VIII. 232.

(*b*) to adapt, suit; *square my trial to my ... strength*: C. 329.

part. adj. **squared**, drawn up in the form of a square: P. L. I. 758.

Squat, *vb. intr.* to sit close to the ground, crouch: P. L. IV. 800.

Squint, *adj.* looking askance; *squint suspicion*: C. 413.

Stable, (1) *sb.* a building for horses or cattle; that in which Christ was born: P. R. II. 74; N. O. 243.

(2) *vb. intr.* to dwell, *sea-monsters whelped and stabled*: P. L. XI. 752.

part. adj. **stabled**, in their dens: C. 534.

Stablish, *vb. tr.* to establish, fix unalterably: P. L. XII. 347.

Stack, *sb.* a large pile of grain in the sheaf: L'A. 51.

Staff, *sb.* (*a*) a stick carried for support or used as a weapon; *oaken staff*: S. A. 1123; *a sceptre or quaint staff*: S. A. 1303.

(*b*) the pole of a flag: P. L. I. 535.

Stag, *sb.* male deer: P. L. VII. 469.

Stage, *sb.* the floor on which theatrical performances are exhibited; *fig.* the drama as acted: L'A. 131; Il P. 102; *fig.* a place where something is publicly exhibited; *wherewith the stage of Earth and Air did ring*: P. 2.

Staid, *adj.* sedate, sober, grave : Il P. 16.

Stain, (1) *sb.* (*a*) taint, tarnish, blemish ; a blending of the ideas of physical and moral taint ; *the ethereal mould, incapable of stain* : P. L. II. 140 ; *Heaven and Earth, renewed, shall be made pure to sanctity that shall receive no stain* : P. L. X. 639.

(*b*) moral taint or pollution : S. A. 325.

(*c*) a cause of moral pollution : Il P. 26.

(2) *vb. tr.* (*a*) to discolour, spot : P. L. VI. 334.

(*b*) to soil with guilt, bring reproach on, pollute : P. L. IX. 1076 ; *stain his honour* : S. A. 1166 ; *stain my vow of Nazarite* : S. A. 1386.

Stair, *sb.* (*a*) one of a series of steps to mount by : P. L. III. 516, 540.

(*b*) *pl.* a flight or series of such steps : P. L. III. 510, 523.

Stake, *sb.* a stick sharpened at one end for driving into the ground ; used *fig.* for a sword : C. 491.

Stalk, *sb.* the stem of a plant ; *hangs or withers on the stalk* : P. L. V. 323 ; C. 744 ; *tender, green* : P. L. v. 337, 480 ; IX. 428.

Stalk, *vb. intr.* to walk with a stately step : S. A. 1245 ; *a lion now he stalks* : P. L. IV. 402.

Stall-reader, *sb.* one who reads books at the stall where they are sold : S. XI. 5.

Stand, A. *sb.* the place where a person stands, station : P. L. IV. 395 ; *the princely Hierarch in their bright stand there left his powers* : P. L. XI. 221.

B. *vb.* (*pret.* stood ; *2d sing.* stood'st : P. L. IV. 837 ; XI. 759 ; P. R. III. 409 ; IV. 420 ; *past part.* stood) I. *intr.* (1) to be in an upright position on the feet, take or maintain an upright and stationary position : P. L. I. 357, 379 ; II. 305 ; III. 622 ; VI. 579 ; VII. 210 ; VIII. 464 ; IX. 277, 425 ; X. 211 ; P. R. II. 298 ; S. A. 1610 ; M. W. 21 ; C. 297 ; *Eve ... stood to entertain her guest* : P. L. V. 383 ; *on the beach ... he stood* : P. L. I. 300 ; *the wary Fiend stood on the brink of Hell* : P. L. II. 918 ; *the bright surface ... whereon we stand* : P. L. VI. 473 ; *by them stood Orcus* : P. L. II. 963 ; *about him stood all the Scantities of Heaven* : P. L. III. 61 ; *where he stood so high above* : P. L. III. 555 ; *near him stood* : P. L. IV. 787 ; *beside it stood* : P. L. V. 54 ; *he ... before her stood* : P. L. IX. 523 ; *he by the brook of Cherith stood* : P. R. II. 266 ; *stood at my head a dream* : P. L. VIII. 292 ; *where he stood among the mightiest* : P. L. VI. 111 ; an *adj. part.* or *phrase* indicating position or condition ; some of the following may belong under (10) : P. L. IV. 846, 986 ; VI. 448, 581, 604 ; XI. 564 ; *black it stood as night* : P. L. II. 670 ; *like Maia's son he stood* : P. L. V. 285 ; *in orbs, in circles, in station* : P. L. V. 595, 631 ; X. 535.

(*b*) opposed to the action of moving, rising, falling : P. L. IV. 720, 863 ; VI. 391 ; IX. 677 ; P. R. IV. 554 ; *none on their feet might stand* : P. L. VI. 592 ; *on thy feet thou stood'st* : P. L. XI. 759 ; *stood armed to their night-watches* : P. L. IV. 779 ; *fell whence he stood* : P. R. IV. 571 ; *standing else as rocks* : P. L. VI. 593.

(*c*) to be in an upright position and also to rise ; *he, above the rest ... stood like a tower* : P. L. I. 591.

(2) to remain erect ; said of a tree : P. L. I. 615.

(3) to continue morally upright : P. L. III. 99, 101 ; IV. 66 ; V. 522 ; VI. 911 ; *do they only stand by ignorance* : P. L. IV. 518 ; *in this we stand or fall* : P. L. V. 540 ; *freely they stood who stood, and fell who fell* : P. L. III. 102 ; *glorious once and perfect while they stood* : P. L. V. 568 ; *stand fast* : P. L. VIII. 640.

(4) to stop moving or acting, be or become motionless : P. L. X. 504 ; XI. 264 ; XII. 263 ; P. R. IV. 561 ; S. XIX. 14 ; *stood they or moved* : P. L. VI. 302 ; *on she moves ; now stands* : S. A. 726 ; *now tripped, now solemn stood* : P. R. II. 354 ; *Sun, in Gibeon stand* : P. L. XII. 265 ; *waters ... stood unmoved* : P. L. IV. 455 ; *the sea ... awed by the rod of Moses so to stand* : P. L. XII. 198.

(*b*) to remain inactive ; *the hooked chariot stood* : N. O. 56.

(*c*) to stop advancing or fighting, halt ; used of an army or of combatants: P. L. I. 563; II. 716, 720; VI. 633, 634; *front to front presented stood* : P. L. VI. 106; *when to advance or stand* : P. L. VI. 234; *imper.* : P. L. VI. 810; *stand still in bright array ye saints; here stand* : P. L. VI. 801.

(5) to have a position, be placed or situated : P. L. IV. 326; VII. 200; X. 547; XI. 385; P. R. IV. 238; P. 39; *where stood her temple* : P. L. I. 442; *the ascending pile stood fixed* : P. L. I. 723; *an imperial city stood* : P. R. IV. 33; *an altar as the landmark stood:* P. L. XI. 432; *his chariot where it stood* : P. L. VI. 338; *there stood a hill* : P. L. I. 670; *amid them stood the Tree of Life* : P. L. IV. 218.

(6) to take or maintain a position; *he shall stand on even ground against his mortal foe* : P. L. III. 178; *stand upon our guard* : C. 487; to ward off condemnation or destruction; *the wicked shall not stand in judgment* : Ps. I. 12.

(b) to maintain one's ground in battle : P. L. I. 630; *stand firm* : P. L. IV. 873.

(c) *stand against*, to withstand, oppose oneself to : P. L. II. 28.

(d) *stand between* or *'twixt* (one and something feared), to protect one from : P. R. III. 219; D. F. I. 69.

(e) *stood for*, fought on the side of : P. L. VI. 62.

(7) to exist, be ; *to him no temple stood* : P. L. I. 492; *one fatal tree there stands* : P. L. IV. 514; *the rarer thy example stands* : S. A. 166.

(8) to continue in being, endure, last : P. L. V. 602; XII. 527; *if I was, I am; relation stands* : P. R. IV. 519; *Gaza yet stands* : S. A. 1558.

(9) to continue in power, maintain authority: P. L. II. 897.

(10) to be or remain in a certain position, condition, or state; often including or with a blending of sense (1) ; (a) with an *adv.* : P. L. II. 888; III. 516; X. 712; *stand, stands*, or *stood ready* : P. L. II. 854; III. 650; V. 132; VI. 561; L. 131; *stand fast by* : S. A. 1431; *standing still* : P. L. VIII. 127.

(b) with a *prep. phrase* : P. L. II. 240; IV. 356; V. 535; VI.

526 ; VII. 23 ; P. R. II. 351 ; S. A. 1637 ; *stand in arms* : P. L. II. 55 ; *stand in sight of God's high throne* : P. L. III. 654; *whilst they stood in first obedience* : S. M. 23; *Expectation stood in horror* : P. L. VI. 306 ; *he shall stand in need of clothing*: V. Ex. 81; *in evil strait this day I stand before my Judge* : P. L. X. 125 ; *at interview both stood* : P. L. VI. 555 ; *stood at gaze the adverse legions*: P. L. VI. 205.

(c) with an accompanying *sb. adj.* or *part.* ; sometimes almost or quite equivalent to the auxiliary *be* ; with a *sb.* ; *though the cross doctors all stood bearers* : U. C. II. 19.

with an *adj.* : P. L. XI. 321 ; XII. 473 ; P. R. I. 258 ; *faithful, unterrified, happy,* etc. : P. L. I. 611 ; II. 707 ; IV. 59, 837 ; XI. 1, 14 ; *unmindful* : P. L. VI. 369 ; *adverse* : P. L. VI. 489 ; *mute, silent, speechless* : P. L. III. 217 ; VI. 882 ; IX. 894 ; *open* : P. L. II. 884 ; X. 232 ; *the thickened sky like a dark ceiling stood*: P. L. XI. 743.

with the *pres. part.* : P. L. VI. 580 ; XI. 645 ; *arguing, scoffing, listening, spelling* : P. L. VI. 508, 629 ; VII. 563 ; S. XI. 7 ; *doubting, longing, admiring* : P. L. IV. 983 ; IX. 593 ; X. 352 ; P. R. I. 169 ; *shivering* : P. L. X. 1003 ; with the *past part.* : P. L. V. 249 ; VI. 36, 785 ; *re-embattled, fixed* : P. L. VI. 794 ; VIII. 3 ; XII. 555 ; P. R. III. 146 ; N. O. 70 ; *ruled, appointed* : P. L. III. 711 ; VI. 565 ; *unshaken, unwearied, collected* : P. L. IV. 64 ; VI. 403 ; IX. 673 ; P. R. IV. 420 ; *acquitted, confirmed* : P. L. X. 827 ; XI. 71 ; *cursed, defamed* : P. L. X. 818 ; S. A. 977 ; *abstracted, astonied, perplexed, amazed* : P. L. IX. 463, 890 ; P. R. III. 1 ; IV. 2 ; C. 565.

(11) to come, go, rise, retire ; with an adverb noting motion or rest after motion; *stood aloof* : P. L. I. 380 ; S. A. 135, 1611; *nearer* : S. A. 1631 ; *nigh* : P. L. XII. 626 ; *up* : P. L. II. 44 ; V. 807 ; P. R. III. 409 ; *up stood the corny reed* : P. L. VII. 321 ; *stand upright* : P. R. IV. 551 ; *upright stood on his feet* : P. L. VIII. 261 ; *stood without* : S. A. 1659.

(12) to lie or consist *in ; therein stands the office of a king* : P. R. II. 463.

II. *tr.* to bear up against, endure : P. L. IV. 926.

In combination with other words; (*a*) **in opinion stand,** to be generally considered as: P. L. II. 471.

(*b*) **stand in the admiration of,** to be admired by: P. R. II. 220.

(*c*) **stand one in stead,** to be serviceable or advantageous to one : P. R. I. 473.

(*d*) **stand under,** to endure : P. L. VIII. 454.

part. adj. **standing** ; (*a*) *waged on foot* : P. L. VI. 243; P. R. III. 328.

(*b*) *without ebb or flow; standing lake* : P. L. XI. 847.

Standard, *sb.* an ensign of war, banner : P. L. V. 589; VII. 297; (Satan) *upreared his mighty standard* : P. L. I. 533; *the great hierarchal standard* : P. L. V. 701; *the standard ... of ancient Night* : P. L. II. 986.

Star, *sb.* (1) one of the luminous celestial bodies : P. L. III. 61; V. 258; VI. 754; VII. 348, 357, 383, 577, 620, 621; VIII. 80, 123, 135, 142; XII. 576; D. F. I. 43; Il P. 171; C. 197; S. XXII. 5; Ps. VIII. 10; *this ethereal quintessence of Heaven .. turned to stars* : P. L. III. 718; *sowed with stars the heaven* : P. L. VII. 358; *that milky way ... powdered with stars* : P. L. VII. 581; *this pendent World, in bigness as a star* : P. L. II. 1052; *the stars hide their diminished heads* : P. L. IV. 34; *other stars repairing in their golden urns draw light* : P. L. VII. 364; *the stars that usher evening* : P. L. IV. 355; *the stars of morn* : P. L. XII. 422; *the stars grow high* : C. 956; *falling, shooting, glancing* : P. L. I. 745; IV. 556; C. 80; *fixed* : P. L. V. 176; *blasted, faint* : P. L. X. 412; C. 331; *autumnal* : P. R. IV. 619; *innumerable, numbered* : P. L. III. 565; VIII. 19; *innumerable as the stars of night, or stars of morning* : P. L. V. 745, 746; as virtually part of a compound ; *to star or sunlight* : P. L. IX. 1087.

(*b*) *spec.* that which indicated the birth-place of Christ : P. L. XII. 360; P. R. I. 249; *thy star, new-graven in heaven* : P. R. I. 253; *Heaven's youngest-teemed star* : N. O. 240; Sirius; *the swart star* : L. 138; Aries; *the fleecy star* : P. L. III. 558; *star of Arcady,* Callisto, the daughter of Lycaon, king of Arcadia, who was changed into the constellation of the Greater Bear, by which the Greek mariners directed their course (*see* Calisto) : C. 341; Venus, called Hesperus when the evening star, Lucifer when the morning star: *fairest of stars* : P. L. V. 166; Hesperus: P. L. VII. 104; *the Star of Hesperus* : P. L. IX. 48; possibly also; *the star that bids the shepherd fold* : C. 93; *the star that rose at evening bright* : L. 30; Lucifer: P. L. VII. 133; X. 426; the moon: P. L. III. 727; the sun: P. L. X. 1069.

(*c*) as indicating or influencing human destiny : P. R. IV. 383; perhaps *personified* : N. O. 69.

(*d*) *fig.* Christ; *our Morning Star* : P. R. I. 294.

(2) that which resembles the stars of heaven in shape or brilliance; as forming the pavement of heaven : P. L. VII. 578; as worn by the blessed in heaven; *attired with stars* : T. 21; used of the appearance of the diamond; *the unsought diamonds would .. so bestud with stars* : C. 734.

See **Day-star, Evening-star, Morning-star.**

Star-bright, *adj.* resembling a star in brilliance : P. L. X. 450.

Stare, *vb. intr.* to gaze steadily with the eyes wide open : S. XI. 11; with *at* : S. A. 112.

Star-led, *adj.* guided by a star; *star-led wizards* : N. O. 23.

Starless, *adj.* without stars : P. L. III. 425.

Star-light (stár-light: P. L. IV. 656; star-líght: C. 308), *sb.* the light proceeding from the stars : C. 308; *glittering* : P. L. IV. 656.

Star-paved, *adj.* paved with stars P. L. IV. 976.

Star-proof, *adj.* impervious to the light of stars : A. 89.

Starred, *part. adj.* placed in the heaven as a star : Il P. 19.

Starry, *adj.* (*a*) of stars; *their starry dance* : P. L. III. 580.

(b) abounding with stars; *starry sphere, pole, zone*: P. L. III. 416; IV. 724; V. 281, 620; *cope of Heaven*: P. L. IV. 992.

(c) composed of stars; *starry host, train, flock*: P. L. IV. 606, 649; V. 709; *choir*: C. 112; *rubric*: P. R. IV. 393; *threshold of Jove's court*: C. 1.

(d) resembling stars; *starry eyes*: P. L. VII. 446; shining like stars; *starry lamps, helm, front*: P. L. I. 728; XI. 245; P. 18.

(e) covered or set with that which resembles stars in shape or brilliance; *starry wings*: P. L. VI. 827.

Start, *vb. intr.* to move suddenly, rise or go abruptly; *I started back, it started back*: P. L. IV. 462, 463; *started* or *starts up*: P. L. IV. 813, 819; *out of the woods he starts*: P. R. IV. 449.

Startle, *vb. tr.* to excite by sudden apprehension or fear, alarm, arouse: C. 210; *singing, startle the dull night*: L'A. 42.

part. adj. **startled**, showing alarm: P. L. V. 26.

Starve, *vb. tr.* to cause to perish with cold, benumb: P. L. II. 600.

part. adj. **starved**, suffering for lack of the loved one; *the starved lover*: P. L. IV. 769.

See **Half-starved.**

Star-ypointing, *adj.* pointing toward the stars: W. S. 4.

State, I. *sb.* (1) mode of existence; condition of life; position, situation, circumstances of nature or fortune: P. L. IV. 38, 400; VIII. 176, 403; IX. 123, 958; X. 19, 619; XI. 363; P. R. II. 203; IV. 601; C. 408; *settled state of order*: P. L. II. 279; *the quiet state of men*: P. L. XII. 80; *thus have I told thee all my state*: P. L. VIII. 521; *from thy state mine never shall be parted*: P. L. IX. 915; *our state of splendid vassalage*: P. L. II. 251; *their state of good*: S. M. 24; *state of bliss*: P. L. V. 241, 543; *inward state of mind*: P. L. IX. 1125; *fickle*: P. L. IX. 948; S. A. 164; *happy, happier*: P. L. I. 29, 141; II. 24; IV. 519, 775; V. 234, 504, 536, 830; VIII. 331; IX. 337, 347; *sinful, fallen, wretched*, etc.: P. L. III. 186; XI. 180, 501; P. R. III. 189, 218; S. A. 338, 708, 1603; C. 475; *his or*

my former state: P. L. II. 585; IV. 94; VIII. 290; *my present state*: P. R. I. 200; *fraternal*: P. L. XII. 26; rather condition of faith or loyalty: P. L. XI. 71.

(2) political or social status, station, rank: P. L. V. 288.

(3) dignity, pomp, splendour, magnificence: P. R. III. 246; Ps. VIII. 16; *high on a throne of royal state*: P. L. II. 1; *mark what radiant state she spreads*: A. 14; *the painted heavens so full of state*: Ps. CXXXVI. 18; *in himself was all his state*: P. L. V. 353.

(b) dignity, stateliness, majesty: Il P. 37; *he, kingly, from his state inclined not*: P. L. XI. 249.

(c) *in state*, with dignity and pomp: C. 948.

(d) *rows her state*, moves with the dignity of a barge of state: P. L. VII. 440.

(e) progress accompanied with splendour and magnificence; *where the great sun begins his state*: L'A. 60.

(f) *concr.* a throne: A. 81.

(4) the power, greatness, majesty, or glory attendant upon high place; *God-like imitated state*: P. L. II. 511; attendant upon God; *the envier of his state*: P. L. VI. 89; *he who envies now thy state*: P. L. VI. 900; *his state is kingly*: S. XIX. 11; *his regal state put forth at full*: P. L. I. 640; *us he sends upon his high behests for state*: P. L. VIII. 239; or the meaning may be the installation into a chair of state: C. 35.

(5) the canopy over a throne: P. L. X. 445.

(6) the people united under one government as well as the government itself, the body politic: S. A. 892; Ps. LXXXII. 2; *God and state*: S. A. 1465; *a pillar of state*: P. L. II. 302; *the drift of hollow states*: S. XVII. 6; *what can be juster in a state*: Eurip. 5.

(b) *robes of state*, robes indicating official position in the state: P. R. IV. 64.

(7) the persons representing a body politic; *those Infernal States*: P. L. II. 387.

II. *adj.* of or pertaining to the whole community or body politic, public; *state livery*: S. A. 1616.

III. *vb. tr.* to express the particulars of, enter into a discussion of : S. A. 424.

State-affairs, *sb.* matters of public concern ; used *fig.* with reference to bees : P. L. I. 775.

Stately, (1) *adj.* grand, lofty, dignified, imposing ; used of a building, etc. : P. L. I. 723 ; *the Capitol ... lifting his stately head :* P. R. IV. 48 ; *a stately ship :* S. A. 714 ; *a stately side-board :* P. R. II. 350 ; of trees : P. L. VII. 324 ; *forest oaks ... their stately growth :* P. L. I. 614 ; *sup.* : P. L. IX. 435 ; *a woody theatre of stateliest view :* P. L. IV. 142.

(2) *adv.* in a majestic manner : P. L. V. 201.

Station, *sb.* (1) the place where a person stands : P. R. IV. 584.

(2) a place or position appointed or assigned to a person : P. L. VII. 146 ; *I ... kept not my happy station :* P. R. I. 360 ; *their fixed station :* P. L. XII. 627 ; to the sun or the planets ; *so wondrously was set his station :* P. L. III. 587 ; *planets in their station listening stood :* P. L. VII. 563.

(*b*) *in station,* on guard ; *all yet left of that revolted rout ... in station stood :* P. L. X. 535.

(3) one appointed to watch, guard, sentinel : P. L. II. 412.

Statist, *sb.* statesman : P. R. IV. 354.

Statue, *sb.* a sculptured figure : P. R. IV. 37 ; *if I but wave this wand ... you* (are) *a statue :* C. 661.

Stature, *sb.* (*a*) height, size ; *stature as of gods :* P. L. I. 570 ; *likest gods ... in stature :* P. L. VI. 302 ; *his stature reached the sky :* P. L. IV. 988.

(*b*) body as it possesses height : P. L. VII. 509 ; *he rears from off the pool his mighty stature :* P. L. I. 222.

Statute, *sb.* edict, law : Ps. LXXXI. 13 ; Hor. Epist. 2.

Stay, I. *sb.* (*a*) support : P. L. X. 921 ; *happy all those who have in him their stay :* Ps. II. 28.

(*b*) standstill ; *was at stay,* had ceased : U. C. II. 6.

(*c*) continuance in a place, sojourn ; *if he intends our stay in that dark durance :* P. L. IV. 898 ; forbearance of departure : P. L. IX. 372 ; *desiring more her stay :* P. L.

IX. 398 ; *wish her stay :* P. L. VIII. 43.

(*d*) delay, tarrying ; *a little stay will bring some notice :* S. A. 1536 ; *wondered, Adam, at my stay :* P. L. IX. 856.

II. *vb.* (*pret.* and *past part.* stayed or staid) (1) *tr.* (*a*) to cause to come to a standstill, stop ; *then stayed the fervid wheels :* P. L. VII. 224 ; *stay thy ... chair :* C. 134 ; *stayed her flight :* C. 832 ; *stays not on,* does not make to cease with : P. L. XII. 73.

(*b*) to cause to cease ; *that fury stayed :* P. L. II. 938.

(*c*) to delay, hinder : P. L. X. 253.

(*d*) to wait for : P. L. IV. 470.

(2) *intr.* (*a*) to cease going, moving, or acting : P. L. III. 742 ; VI. 325 ; VII. 218 ; *the Son of God went on and stayed not :* P. R. IV. 485 ; *imper.* : A. 26.

(*b*) to come to an end, cease ; *nor yet staid the terror there :* P. R. IV. 421.

(*c*) to delay, linger, tarry, wait : P. R. II. 326 ; V. Ex. 25 ; *Satan staid not to reply :* P. L. II. 1010 ; *he staid not to inquire :* P. L. III. 571.

(*d*) to wait before coming to a definite conclusion ; *imper.* : S. A. 43 ; C. 820.

(*e*) to continue in a place, remain : P. L. IX. 1134 ; XII. 594 ; S. A. 1520 ; D. F. I. 64 ; S. XIV. 6 ; *longer I durst not stay :* C. 577 ; *stay longer on Earth :* P. L. XII. 436 ; *with thee to go is to stay here :* P. L. XII. 616 ; *the wife ... seemliest by her husband stays :* P. L. IX. 268 ; *by the rushy-fringed bank ... my sliding chariot stays :* C. 892 ; *he* (God) *also went invisible, yet stayed :* P. L. VII. 589.

Stead, *sb.* (*a*) place which another had ; *in my stead :* A. 355.

(*b*) assistance, service ; *stand him more in stead :* P. R. I. 473 ; *do thee little stead :* C. 611.

Steadfast, *adj.* (*a*) firmly fixed in position, established, stable ; *the steadfast Earth :* P. L. II. 927 ; *the planet Earth, so steadfast :* P. L. VIII. 129 ; *the steadfast Empyrean :* P. L. VI. 833.

(*b*) firm in mind or purpose, constant : Il P. 32 ; unwavering, unchanging ; *steadfast hate :* P. L. I. 58.

(*c*) steadily directed towards an object; *steadfast gaze*: N. O. 70.

Steady, *adj.* (*a*) having a regular even motion; *steady wing*: P. L. v. 268.

(*b*) persistent; *sup.*, *my steadiest thoughts*: P. L. xii. 377.

Stealth, *sb.* (*a*) a clandestine or underhand proceeding; *by stealth*, clandestinely: P. L. ii. 945; ix. 68.

(*b*) a thing stolen: C. 503.

Steam, *sb.* rising vapour, exhalation; *a steam of rich distilled perfumes*: C. 556; the smoke and vapour rising from sacrifice and exhaling a pleasant odour: P. L. xi. 442.

Steaming, *part. adj.* emitting vapour: P. L. v. 186.

See **Grisamber-steamed.**

Steal, *vb.* (*pret.* stole; *past part.* stolen; P. L. x. 20; xi. 125; S. ii. 2; stole: P. L. iv. 719; C. 195) (1) *tr.* (*a*) to take clandestinely and without right: *him who had stole Jove's ...fire*: P. L. iv. 719; to take away stealthily; *darkness ... had stole them from me*: C. 195; *Time ... stolen on his wing my three-and-twentieth year*: S. ii. 2; *gales ... whisper whence they stole those balmy spoils*; P. L. iv. 158.

(*b*) to procure or effect clandestinely; *the ... Fiend had stolen entrance*: P. L. x. 20.

(2) *intr.* to move stealthily, move or creep softly; *a soft ... sound ... stole upon the air*: C. 557; used of water: P. L. xi. 847; A. 31.

part. adj. **stolen,** taken unlawfully: P. L. xi. 125.

Steed, *sb.* a horse used for occasions of state or for war: P. L. ix. 35; *proud*: P. L. iv. 858; *fiery*: P. L. ii. 531; vi. 17; *foaming*: P. L. xi. 643; *fiery foaming*: P. L. vi. 391; *the ... steeds that draw the litter of ... Sleep*: C. 553; as passing through the air; *rapt in a chariot drawn by fiery steeds*: P. L. iii. 522; *rapt in a balmy cloud, with winged steeds*: P. L. xi. 706; *fig.* the poet's Muse considered as a Pegasus; *lest from this winged steed unreined ... dismounted*: P. L. vii. 17.

See **Night-steed.**

Steel, *sb.* (*a*) a compound or alloy of iron; *inflexible as steel*: S. A.

816; *Chalybean-tempered steel*: S. A. 133.

(*b*) armour, coat of mail; *arm the obdured breast ... as with triple steel*: P. L. ii. 569; *clad in complete steel*: C. 421; *cuirassiers all in steel*: P. R. iii. 328.

Steep, I. *adj.* (1) precipitous, sheer; *steep hill, glade*: P. L. iv. 172, 231; *wilderness*: P. L. iv. 135; used of a way leading up or down a precipitous place: P. L. ii. 71; vii. 299; used of the appearance of the ocean at the horizon; *his glowing axle doth allay in the steep Atlantic stream*: C. 97.

(2) moving through a precipitous course; *throws his steep flight*: P. L. iii. 741; used of the sun as it passes from the zenith to the horizon; *the great Light of Day yet wants to run much of his race, though steep*: P. L. vii. 99.

(*b*) falling precipitously; *the waters steep of Meriba*: Ps. lxxxi. 31.

(3) intense, very great; *steep force, ruin steep*: P. L. vi. 324; Ps. vii. 20.

II. *sb.* (*a*) a precipitous place: P. L. ii. 948; *from the steep of echoing hill*: P. L. iv. 680.

(*b*) a mountain or mountains; *the Indian steep*: C. 139; *the Ismenian steep* (*see* Ismenian): P. R. iv. 575; *the steep of Delphos* (*see* Delphos): N. O. 178; possibly Kerig-y-Druidion in South Denbighshire; *the steep where your old bards, the famous Druids, lie*: L. 52.

Steer, *vb.* (1) *tr.* to pursue in a certain direction, direct; *steers his flight*: P. L. i. 225; *so steers the prudent crane her annual voyage*: P. L. vii. 430; *steering his zenith*; directing his course to or towards the zenith: P. L. x. 328.

(2) *intr.* (*a*) to guide a vessel by means of a rudder: P. L. ii. 1020; ix. 515.

(*b*) to direct one's course; *the tread of many feet steering this way*: S. A. 111; *with radiant feet the tissued clouds down steering*: N. O. 146.

(*c*) to conduct oneself, direct one's conduct: S. xxii. 8.

Steersman, *sb.* one who steers a vessel, pilot: P. L. ix. 513.

Steers-mate, *sb.* the assistant of the pilot : S. A. 1045.

Stellar, *adj.* of or pertaining to the stars ; *stellar virtue* : P. L. IV. 671.

Stem (1) *sb.* (*a*) the branch of a plant, stalk : P. L. VII. 337.

(*b*) the stock of a family, race, ancestry : A. 82.

(2) *vb. intr.* to make headway as a ship : P. L. II. 642.

Stench, *sb.* a disgusting smell : P. L. I. 237.

Step, I. *sb.* (1) *a* single separate movement made by the leg in walking ; *smooth sliding without step* : P. L. VIII. 302 ; *not like those steps on Heaven's azure* : P. L. I. 296 ; *of his steps the track divine* : P. L. XI. 354; with an *adj.* indicating condition or manner ; *proud step* : P. L. IV. 536 ; *pl.*, *dark* : S. A. 2 ; *uneasy, easy* : P. L. I. 295 ; P. R. I. 120 ; *painful, lonely* : P. L. I. 562 ; II. 828 ; *I hear the tread of hateful steps* : C. 92 ; *they had engaged their wandering steps too far* : C. 193.

(*b*) put for the person : *far off his steps adore* : P. L. XI. 333.

(*c*) *step by step*, by gradual and regular progress : P. R. I. 192.

(2) walk, course ; *from the tree her step she turned* : P. L. IX. 834 ; *up to a hill anon his steps he reared* : P. R. II. 285.

(*b*) passage, course ; *now Morn, her rosy steps ... advancing* : P. L. v. 1.

(*c*) course of conduct ; *set thy ways right before where my step goes* : Ps. v. 24.

(3) one of the treads in a ladder or stairs : P. L. III. 541.

(4) the space passed over by one movement of the foot ; *one step* : P. L. IV. 22.

(5) degree in progress or advance ; *thought one step higher would set me highest* : P. L. IV. 50 ; *by steps we may ascend to God* : P. L. v. 512.

(6) foot ; *by human steps untrod* : P. R. I. 298 ; *where no print of step hath been* : A. 85 ; or in sense (2) ; *turned thitherward in haste his travelled steps* : P. L. III. 501.

(7) manner of walking ; *grace was in all her steps* ; P. L. VIII. 488 ; *decent, nymph-like* : P. L. III. 644 ; IX. 452 ; *pilgrim, care-*

ful : P. R. IV. 427 ; S. A. 327 ; *youthful* : S. A. 1442 ; *even* : Il P. 38 ; *wandering steps and slow* : P. L. XII. 648.

(8) one of a series of proceedings, measure, means : C. 12.

II. *vb. intr.* (*a*) to advance or recede by a movement of the foot ; *step aside* : C. 168 ; *back stepped* : P. L. IV. 820.

(*b*) to go or walk a short distance : C. 185.

See **Forth - stepping, Leaden-stepping, Stepdame.**

Stepdame, *sb.* stepmother : P. L. IV. 279 ; C. 830.

Stern, (1) *adj.* (*a*) austere, harsh, rigorous ; *stern Achilles* : P. L. IX. 15 ; *God of Sea* : Hor. O. 16.

(*b*) proceeding from or indicating austerity ; *stern brow* : P. R. IV. 367 ; *frown* : C. 446 ; *regard* : P. L. IV. 877 ; x. 866.

(2) *adv.* sternly, severely, rigorously : P. L. VI. 171 ; L. 112 ; *frowning stern* : P. L. IV. 924.

Sternly, *adv.* with severity, rigorously : P. L. VIII. 333 ; P. R. I. 406.

Stick, *sb.* a branch of a tree or shrub cut or broken off : P. R. I. 316.

Stick, *vb.* (*pret.* not used ; *past part.* stuck) (1) *tr.* to fasten ; *his foul esteem sticks no dishonour on our front* : P. L. IX. 330.

(2) *intr.* to be stopped or checked in progress ; *he's here stuck in a slough* : U. C. I. 4.

Stiff, *adj.* (*a*) rigid, not pliant ; *oaks bowed their stiff necks* : P. R. IV. 418.

(*b*) firm, strict, inexorable ; *stiff vows* : F. of C. 2.

(*c*) strong ; *stiff pennons* : P. L. VII. 441.

Stifle, *vb. tr.* to suffocate, smother : P. L. XI. 313.

*****Still,** (1) *adj.* (*a*) remaining in place, motionless ; *stand* or *standing still* : P. L. VI. 801 ; VIII. 127 ; XII. 263 ; *kings sat still* : N. O. 59 ; *Earth sitting still* : P. L. VIII. 89.

(*b*) remaining inactive ; *regain thy right by sitting still* : P. R. III. 164 ; *sit thou not still, O God* : Ps. LXXXIII. 3.

(*c*) free from sound or noise, quiet, noiseless ; *the woods are still* : S. I. 2 ; *a shower still* : Il P. 127 ; silent ; *attention still as night* : P. L. II. 308.

(d) calm, peaceful ; with more or less blending of quiet, noiseless ; *still Evening, night, morn* : P. L. IV. 598 ; X. 846 ; L. 187 ; *some still removed place* : Il P. 78.

(e) soft and low in tone ; *lute, or viol still* : P. 28.

(2) *adv.* (a) constantly, ever, always : P. L. I. 68, 165 ; III. 618 ; V. 184 ; VIII. 61 ; X. 120 ; XII. 106 ; *her monthly round still ending, still renewing* : P. L. III. 729 ; *a grateful mind by owing owes not, but still pays* : P. L. IV. 56 ; *still as they thirsted* : P.L. IV. 336 ; *be bounteous still to give us only good* : P. L. V. 205 ; *the one intense, the other still remiss* : P.L. VIII. 387 ; *be good and friendly still* : P. L. VIII. 651 ; *with good still overcoming evil* : P. L. XII. 566.

(b) in future no less than formerly : P. L. X. 376 ; XI. 352 ; S. II. 10.

(c) now as in the past, to this time. yet : P. L. I. 256, 791 ; II. 74, 658, 1001 ; III. 467 ; *Satan, still in gaze as first* : P. L. IV. 356 ; *still thy words at random, as before* : P. L. IV. 930 ; *still to gaze* : P. L. V. 47 ; *still thou err'st* : P. L. VI. 172 ; *thought him still speaking* : P. L. VIII. 3 ; *saw the shape still glorious* : P. L. VIII. 464 ; *though hunger still remain* : P. R. II. 255.

(d) again, once more ; *I mention still him* : P. L. III. 92.

(e) in increasing degree, even yet ; *that still lessens the sorrow* : S. A. 1563 ; used with comparatives ; *greedier still* : P. R. IV. 141 ; *still less resolved* : S. A. 305 ; *still longer* : P. L. VIII. 252.

(f) for all that, nevertheless : C. 842.

(3) *vb. tr.* (a) to make still, render calm, restrain ; *to still the wild winds* : C. 87.

(b) to make to cease ; *Morning ... stilled the roar of thunder* : P. R. IV. 428.

Sting, (1) *sb.* (a) the sharp organ with which certain animals inflict a wound ; *fig.*, (Sin) *a serpent armed with mortal sting* : P. L. II. 653 ; *Death ... of his mortal sting disarmed* : P. L. III. 253 ; *Sin and Death ... fix far deeper in his head their stings* : P. L. XII. 432 ;

thoughts ... armed with deadly stings : S. A. 623.

(b) the act or manner of stinging or the pain resulting ; *she's gone—a manifest serpent by her sting* : S. A. 997.

(c) that which gives acute pain or the pain given ; *the sting of famine* : P. R. II. 257 ; *sting of amorous remorse* : S. A. 1007.

(2) *vb.* (*past part.* stung) *tr.* to pain acutely ; *the subtle Fiend, though inly stung with anger* : P. R. I. 466.

Stink, *vb.* (in *pres.*) *intr.* to emit an unpleasant odour : Ariosto II. 2.

Stint, *vb. tr.* to make to cease, check ; *to stint the enemy* : Ps. VIII. 7.

Stir, I. *sb.* commotion, tumult, disturbance ; *what stir on Earth* : P. L. V. 224 ; *the smoke and stir of this dim spot which men call Earth* : C. 5.

II. *vb. tr.* (1) to agitate, disturb ; *from the bottom stir the hell within him* : P. L. IV. 19 ; *stir the constant mood of her calm thoughts* : C. 371.

(2) to rouse to action, make active ; *these raging fires will slacken, if his breath stir not their flames* : P. L. II. 214 ; to rouse, awaken ; *stirred in me sudden appetite* : P. L. VIII. 308.

(3) **stir up** ; (a) to instigate, incite : P. L. I. 35 ; *stir them up ... to afflict thee* : S. A. 1251 ; *stirring up Sin against Law to fight* : P. L. XII. 288.

(b) to bring about, cause, excite : C. 174 ; *stir up joy* : C. 677.

Stoa, *sb.* a roofed colonnade ; *the painted Stoa*, the Poecile at Athens, which was adorned by Polygnotus, and in which Zeno taught his philosophy : P. R. IV. 253.

Stock, (1) *sb.* (a) a wooden block ; *stocks and stones*, the images or other material objects of worship in the Catholic Church : S. XVIII. 4.

(b) the original progenitor of a race : P. L. XII. 7.

(c) race, family, lineage ; *the royal stock of David* : P. L. XII. 325 ; *of stock renowned as Og* : S. A. 1079 ; *thou ancient stock of Israel* : Ps. LXXXI. 35.

(2) *vb. tr.* to provide with animals : C. 152.

Stoic, (1) *adj.* (*a*) of or pertaining to the Stoics : C. 707.

(*b*) composed of the disciples of Zeno : P. R. IV. 280.

(2) *sb.* a disciple, or the disciples collectively, of the philosopher Zeno : P. R. IV. 300.

Stole, *sb.* scarf (?), veil (?) ; *sable stole of cypress lawn over thy decent shoulders drawn* : Il P. 35.

See **Sable-stoled.**

Stone, *sb.* (1) a piece of rock of small or moderate size : P. L. XI. 324, 445, 658 ; *out of these hard stones be made thee bread* : P. R. I. 343; *to dash thy foot against a stone* : P. R. IV. 559 ; *a stone that shall dash to pieces all monarchies* : P. R. IV. 149 ; *the labour of an age in piled stones* : W. S. 2.

(2) the hard material of which rock consists ; *she freezed her foes to congealed stone* : C. 449; *to worship their own work in wood and stone for gods* : P. L. XII. 119.

(*b*) *Atlantic stone,* probably marble from near Mt. Atlas : P. R. IV. 115.

(*c*) as a substance dug from veins beneath the surface of heaven ; *part hidden veins digged up ... of mineral and stone* : P. L. VI. 517.

(3) a piece of rock used for a special purpose (*see* Stock) : S. XVIII. 4.

(4) a precious stone : P. L. III. 592, 596 ; *stone of costliest emblem* : P. L. IV. 702 ; the philosopher's stone, supposed to have the property of turning baser metals into gold : P. L. III. 598, 600.

(5) the disease arising from a calculus ; *intestine stone and ulcer* : P. L. XI. 484.

See **Flint-stone.**

Stony, *adj.* (*a*) made of stone : P. L. VI. 576 ; *in stony fetters* : C. 819; *the winds within their stony caves* : P. R. IV. 414.

(*b*) abounding with stones ; *the stony Mœnalus* : A. 102.

(*c*) hardened, obdurate ; *stony hearts* : P. L. III. 189.

absol. hard flesh ; used *fig.* for wickedness, evil ; *removed the stony from their hearts* : P. L. XI. 4.

Stoop, *vb.* (1) *intr.* (*a*) to bend or reach forward or down : P. L. VIII. 465 ; IX. 427 ; *Heaven itself would stoop to her* : C. 1023 ; *the wandering moon, as if her head she bowed, stooping through a fleecy cloud* : Il P. 72.

(*b*) to swoop upon prey ; *the bird of Jove, stooped from his aery flight* : P. L. XI. 185.

(*c*) to alight or fly low from flight : P. L. III. 73 : *each bird stooped on his wing* : P. L. VIII. 351.

(*d*) *fig.* to bow down, yield, submit ; *Dagon must stoop* : S. A. 468 ; *Death ... stoop inglorious* : P. L. III. 352.

(2) *tr.* to bow or bend down ; *he ... stooped his regal head* : P. 15 ; *fair moon ... stoop thy pale visage* : C. 333.

Stop, (1) *sb.* (*a*) pause, intermission ; *an unusual stop of sudden silence* : C. 552.

(*b*) that by which the sounds of wind instruments are regulated ; *harp and organ, and who moved their stops and chords* : P. L. XI. 561 ; *pastoral reed with oaten stop* : C. 345 ; with an *adj.* indicating the character of the music; *organs of sweet stop* : P. L. VII. 596 ; *tender stops of various quills* : L. 188.

(2) *vb.* (*past part.* stopt) *tr.* (*a*) to close up by obstructing ; *mountains of ice, that stop the ... way* : P. L. X. 291.

(*b*) to shut, make fast ; *the deep, who now had stopt his sluices* : P. L. XI. 848.

(*c*) to hinder from proceeding, stay : P. L. III. 394 ; XII. 166.

Store, I. *sb.* (1) a stock accumulated, supply, hoard : P. L. II. 175 ; V. 314, 322 ; *some ... valley spread her store* : P. L. IV. 255 ; *a greater store of fruit* : P. L. IX. 621 ; *Nature ... hath purveyed ... her choicest store* ; P. R. II. 334 ; *she* (Nature) *no whit encumbered with her store* : C. 774.

(*b*) *in store,* laid up, hoarded : P. L. V. 128.

(*c*) treasure ; *the casket of Heaven's richest store* : P. 44.

(2) a large number or quantity, plenty, abundance : P. L. III. 444; Ps. LXXXVII. 7 ; *store of ladies* : L'A. 121 ; *evil store* : P. L. IX. 1078 ; *trouble store* : Ps. LXXXVIII. 9.

(3) a place where supplies are kept for future use, storehouse :

P. L. VI. 515; Ps. IV. 34; *the golden compasses, prepared in God's eternal store*: P. L. VII. 226.

II. *vb. tr.* (*a*) to provide, furnish: C. 720; *his bow, and quiver, with three-bolted thunder stored*: P. L. VI. 764; *his head ... well stored with subtle wiles*: P. L. IX. 184.

(*b*) to stock, supply; *powder... some magazine to store*: P. L. IV. 816; *her waxen cells with honey stored*: P. L. VII. 492.

(*c*) to lay up in reserve; *light ... stored in each Orb*: P. L. VIII. 152; *in what part my strength lay stored*: S. A. 395.

vbl. sb. **storing**, the act of putting away for future use; *by frugal storing*: P. L. V. 324.

Storehouse, *sb.* a repository; *my heart hath been a storehouse long of things and sayings*: P. R. II. 103.

Stork, *sb.* the bird *Ciconia*: P. L. VII. 423.

Storm, I. *sb.* (**1**) a tempest: Hor. O. 7; *a night of storm*: P. R. IV. 436; *the sulphurous hail, shot after us in storm*: P. L. I. 172; *a frozen continent ... beat with perpetual storms*: P. L. II. 588; *the ever-threatening storms of Chaos*: P. L. III. 425.

(*b*) *fig.* a furious flight of missiles; *rattling storm of arrows*: P. L. VI. 546; an outburst of anger or defiance: S. A. 1061.

(**2**) calamity, distress: P. L. IX. 433.

II. *vb.* (*pres. 2d sing.* storm'st: P. R. IV. 496) (**1**) *tr.* to attack, assault; *to storm me*: S. A. 405.

(**2**) *intr.* to be in a passion, rage: P. L. XII. 59; P. R. IV. 496; *thy furious foes ... storm outrageously*: Ps. LXXXIII. 6; to rage in war; *Bellona storms*: P. L. II. 922.

part. adj. **storming**, of or pertaining to war; *storming fury*: P. L. VI. 207.

Stormy, *adj.* (*a*) tempestuous, boisterous, full of wind and rain; *stormy gust, blasts*: P. L. X. 698; P. R. IV. 418.

(*b*) abounding in storms; *stormy Hebrides*: L. 156.

Story, (**1**) *sb.* (*a*) a connected account of memorable events, history; *others of some note, as story tells,*

have trod this wilderness: P. R. II. 307; the history of the Old Testament; *all our Law and Story strewed with hymns*: P. R. IV. 334; of the New Testament: P. L. XII. 506.

(*b*) account, recital: P. L. VII. 51; the recital to God of one's affliction or desires; hence, prayer: Ps. III. 8.

(*c*) a tale, whether true or fictitious: L'A. 101; S. XIII. 11; *the story of Cambuscan bold*: Il P. 110.

(*d*) the experience or career of an individual; *my, her, his story*: P. L. VIII. 205, 522; IX. 886; L. 95; *much like to thee in story*: M. W. 62.

(**2**) *vb. tr.* to relate in narrative: C. 516.

part. adj. **storied**, adorned with stained glass representing scenes from scriptural or church history; *storied windows*: Il P. 159.

Stoutly, *adv.* proudly, boldly: L'A. 52.

Stoutness, *sb.* resoluteness, persistency, stubbornness: S. A. 1346.

Straggling, *part. adj.* wandering away and becoming separated from the main body: C. 499.

Straight (strait: P. L. II. 948), (**1**) *adj.* without bend, not crooked; *the one winding, the other straight*: P. R. III. 256; *made intricate seem straight*: P. L. IX. 632.

absol. a way or course that is level: P. L. II. 948.

(**2**) *adv.* (*a*) without deviating from a direct course, directly: P. L. X. 90.

(*b*) immediately, without delay, at once: P. L. I. 531, 723; II. 959; III. 647; IV. 405, 476; V. 287; VI. 613; VII. 453; VIII. 257; X. 361; P. R. I. 259, 275; IV. 581; S. A. 385; L'A. 69; C. 835; S. XII. 3; Ps. LXXXV. 30; *straight side by side were laid*: P. L. IV. 741; *to say and straight unsay*: P. L. IV. 947; *he straight obeys*: P. L. XII. 126; *haste thee straight*: V. Ex. 17; *he ended straight*: U. C. II. 10; *this will cure all straight*: C. 811.

Strain, (**1**) *sb.* (*a*) tune, melody: L'A. 148; *solemn strain*: N. O. 17; *artful*: C. 494; *took in strains that might create a soul under the ribs of Death*: C. 561; used of what is spoken rather than sung ; *that strain I heard was of a higher mood* : L. 87 ; *nor holy rapture wanted they ... in fit strains pronounced, or sung unmeditated* : P. L. v. 148.

(*b*) manner of speaking ; *to something like prophetic strain* : Il P. 174.

(**2**) *vb. tr.* (*a*) to stretch to the utmost tension ; *straining all his nerves* : S. A. 1646 ; *fig., matters now are strained up to the highth* : S. A. 1348.

(*b*) to exert to the utmost ; *my earthly ... strained to the highth in that celestial colloquy* : P. L. viii. 454.

Strait, (**1**) *adj.* (*a*) narrow, confined ; *comp., in straiter limits bound* : N. O. 169.

(*b*) near, intimate ; *league with you I seek ... so strait* : P. L. iv. 376 ; *strait conjunction with this sex* : P. L. x. 898.

(**2**) *sb.* difficulty, distress ; *in evil strait* : P. L. x. 125 ; *in poverty and straits* : P. R. ii. 415 ; *in straits and in distress* : Ps. iv. 3.

Straiten, *vb. tr.* (*a*) to confine, hem in : P. L. ix. 323.

(*b*) to hamper, inconvenience for room : P. L. i. 776.

part. adj. **straitening**, impeding progress ; *nor obvious hill, nor straitening vale* : P. L. vi. 70.

Strand, *sb.* the shore of the sea : C. 876 ; of the lake of hell : P. L. i. 379 ; of a river ; *born on Eurotas' strand* : D. F. I. 25.

Strange, *adj.* (*a*) foreign, alien, belonging to another country : P. L. ii. 69.

(*b*) not before known, unfamiliar, new ; *strange horror seize thee* : P. L. ii. 703 ; *creatures new to sight and strange* : P. L. iv. 287 ; *strange point and new* : P. L. v. 855 ; *new and strange* : P. L. vi. 571 ; *the tongue I heard was strange* : Ps. lxxxi. 20.

(*c*) unusual, surprising, remarkable, wonderful ; sometimes with blending of (*b*) : P. L. i. 707 ; ii. 737, 1024 ; v. 116, 556 ; vi. 91 ; ix. 1135 ; x. 552, 799 ; P. R. iv. 40 ; C. 628 ; *into strange vagaries fell* : P. L. vi. 614 ; *things so high and strange* : P. L. vii. 53 ; *passion first I felt, commotion strange* : P. L. viii. 531 ; *I might perceive*

strange alteration in me : P. L. ix. 599 ; *strange hath been the cause* : P. L. ix. 861 ; *my journey strange* : P. L. x. 479 ; *a wonder strange* : P. L. xi. 733 ; *the hubbub strange* : P. L. xii. 60 ; *strange events* : P. R. ii. 104 ; *beauty ... hath strange power* : S. A. 1003 ; *strange to think* : U. C. ii. 32 ; *some strange mysterious dream* : Il P. 147.

Strangely, *adv.* unusually, remarkably : Ariosto i. 3.

Stranger, *sb.* (*a*) one of another country or place : P. L. xii. 358 ; in direct address ; *I know thee, stranger* : P. L. ii. 990.

(*b*) one not belonging to the house, a guest ; *to honour and receive our heavenly stranger* : P. L. v. 316 ; in direct address ; *Heavenly Stranger, please to taste* : P. L. v. 397.

Strangle, *vb. tr.* to choke, suffocate ; *Nature's bastards, not her sons, who would be ... strangled with her waste fertility* : C. 729.

Stratagem, *sb.* artifice, plot, scheme ; *ye stratagems of Hell* : P. R. i. 180.

Straw, *sb.* a stalk or stem of grain : L. 124.

Straw-built, *adj.* constructed of straw ; *their* (bees') *straw-built citadel* : P. L. i. 773.

Stray, I. *adj.* having wandered away : C. 315 ; *some stray ewe* : P. R. i. 315.

II. *vb. intr.* (**1**) to wander from a direct course or out of the proper limits : P. L. iii. 476 ; *I never from thy side henceforth to stray* : P. L. xi. 176 ; *my wandering Muse, how thou dost stray* : V. Ex. 53 ; *not a blast was from his dungeon strayed* : L. 97.

(*b*) to spread ; *fire which on a sudden strays* : Ps. lxxxiii. 54.

(**2**) to wander idly about : P. L. viii. 283 ; *where the nibbling flocks do stray* : L'A. 72 ; *part, single or with mate ... through groves of coral stray* : P. L. vii. 405.

(*b*) to gleam here and there in or on (?) ; *the azure sheen ... that in the channel strays* : C. 895.

part. adj. **strayed**, that has wandered away ; *a strayed ewe* : C. 503.

Streak, (**1**) *sb.* a line of colour different from the ground ; *those coloured streaks in Heaven* : P. L. xi. 879.

(2) *vb. tr.* to mark or variegate with lines of colour different from the ground ; *ere fresh morning streak the east* : P. L. IV. 623 ; *these ... streaking the ground with sinuous trace* : P. L. VII. 481.

Stream, I. *sb.* (1) a current of water ; (*a*) the ocean ; *the steep Atlantic stream* : C. 97.

(*b*) a river or rivulet, or the steady current in either : P. L. IV. 233 ; S. A. 1726 ; L. 174 ; *washed by streams from underground* : P. L. XI. 569 ; *liquid lapse of murmuring streams* : P. L. VIII. 263 ; *current, running, ebbing* : P. L. VII. 67, 397 ; C. 19 ; *watery* : Ps. I. 8 ; *soft* : Ps. LXXXVII. 27 ; *haunted* : L'A. 130 ; *the stream of utmost Arnon* : P. L. I. 398 ; *Abbana and Pharphar, lucid streams* : P. L. I. 469 ; *Ganges or Hydaspes, Indian streams* : P. L. III. 436 ; *the double-founted stream, Jordan* : P. L. XII. 144 ; *Jordan's clear streams* : Ps. CXIV. 9 ; *Choaspes, amber stream* : P. R. III. 288 ; *Deva spreads her wizard stream* : L. 55 ; *the stream ... the swift Hebrus* : L. 62 ; *Darwen stream* : S. XVI. 7 ; *the Severn* : C. 850 ; *smooth Severn stream* : C. 825 ; *pl.* : C. 884 ; in heaven : P. L. VI. 70 ; *living streams* : P. L. V. 652 ; in hell ; *Cocytus ... the rueful stream* : P. L. II. 580 ; *a slow and silent stream, Lethe* : P. L. II. 582.

as a place of baptism ; *baptizing in the profluent stream* : P. L. XII. 442 ; *consecrated* : P. R. I. 72 ; *laving* : P. R. I. 280.

(*c*) the volume of water in either ; *unite their streams* : P. L. IV. 263 ; *Ilissus rolls his whispering stream* : P. R. IV. 250 ; *Alpheus ... shrunk thy streams* : L. 133 ; in heaven ; *the River of Bliss ... rolls ... her amber stream* : P. L. III. 359 ; in hell ; *four infernal rivers ... disgorge ... their baleful streams* : P. L. II. 576.

(2) the water of a river or fountain : P. L. IV. 336 ; *drink the clear stream* : C. 722 ; *allure thee from the cool crystalline stream* : S. A. 546 ; in heaven ; *drink thy fill of pure immortal streams* : S. XIV. 14 ; in hell ; *to reach the tempting stream* : P. L. II. 607.

(3) a current of any other fluid ;

milky stream : P. L. V. 306 ; *a stream of nectarous humour* : P. L. VI. 332.

(4) something issuing as a stream ; of light or air as issuing from a source or flowing continuously : P. L. III. 7 ; *some strange mysterious dream wave at his wings, in airy stream* : Il P. 148 ; of wisdom : P. R. IV. 277.

II. *vb. intr.* (*a*) to move in a continuous current, flow continuously ; *rivers ... stream* : P. L. VII. 306 ; *life-blood streaming* : P. L. VIII. 467.

(*b*) to stretch out in a line, float at full length : P. L. I. 537 ; v. 590.

part. adj. **streaming**, radiating in a stream ; *streaming light* : C. 340.

See **Ocean-stream**.

Streamer, *sb.* flag, pennon ; *fig.* : S. A. 718.

Street, *sb.* a public way in a city or town : P. L. I. 501 ; S. A. 204, 343, 1402 ; *high street* : S. A. 1458, 1599 ; *the streets of Sodom* : P. L. I. 503 ; *the streets of Bethlehem* : P. R. II. 78.

Strength, *sb.* (1) physical force or power ; (*a*) of a person : P. L. IX. 312, 1062 ; XI. 539 ; P. R. II. 276 ; S. A. 47, 53, 58, 63, 127, 173, 394, 536, 570, 665, 780, 799, 938, 1011, 1136, 1141, 1212, 1228, 1360, 1363, 1439, 1475, 1496, 1502, 1503, 1644 ; Ps. II. 6 ; *receiving from his mother Earth new strength* : P. R. IV. 566 ; *a strength equivalent to angels* : S. A. 342 ; *in strength all mortals I excelled* : S. A. 522 ; *thou in strength all mortals dost exceed* : S. A. 817 ; *thy strength ... surpassing human* : S. A. 1313 ; *this consecrated gift of strength* : S. A. 1355 ; *heaven-gifted, glorious, immeasurable*, etc. : S. A. 36, 206, 586, 1602 ; *mortal* : S. A. 349.

(*b*) of a thing ; solidity, hardness, toughness ; *the brittle strength of bones* : P. L. I. 427.

(2) inherent ability or power residing in or put forth by a person ; sometimes with blending of sense (1) : P. L. I. 696 ; VI. 381 ; IX. 484 ; P. R. III. 402 ; C. 415, 418 ; the strength of God, Christ, or angels : P. L. II. 360 ; P. R. II. 234 ; IV. 9 ; Ps. VIII. 6 ; LXXX. 11 ; LXXXVI. 59 ; *the*

strength of Gods: P. L. I. 116; the strength of Heaven: C. 416; O God of strength: Ps. LXXXIII. 3; upheld by strength, or chance, or fate: P. L. I. 133; the image of thy strength: S. A. 706; his strength concealed: P. L. I. 641; half his strength he put not forth: P. L. VI. 853; with more strength to foil thy enemy: P. L. XII. 389; the strength of Satan or his angels: P. L. I. 146, 240; II. 410; VI. 820; we feel strength undiminished: P. L. I. 154; withered all their strength: P. L. VI. 850; crush his strength: P. L. XII. 430; with the Eternal to be deemed equal in strength: P. L. II. 47; to suffer, as to do, our strength is equal: P. L. II. 200; Satan, I know thy strength: P. L. IV. 1006; Satanic strength: P. R. I. 161; strength and might: P. L. VI. 116; valour or strength: P. L. VI. 457; the strength of Sin: P. L. X. 243.

(b) guiding power; led by the strength of the Almighty's hand: Ps. CXIV. 4.

(c) power of endurance: C. 330.

(3) power of mind, intellectual force: P. L. X. 9.

(4) moral power: Ps. VIII. 6; journey on from strength to strength: Ps. LXXXIV. 25; happy whose strength in thee doth bide: Ps. LXXXIV. 19; exercised in resisting temptation: S. A. 789.

(b) fortitude, courage: P. L. XI. 138.

(5) power resting upon armies: P. L. I. 572; in strength each armed hand a legion: P. L. VI. 231; those locks that of a nation armed the strength contained: S. A. 1494; to strength and counsel joined think nothing hard: P. L. VI. 494.

(6) one who is regarded as an embodiment of strength, that in which reliance is placed: P. L. X. 921; applied to God: Ps. LXXXI. 1; Living Strength: P. L. I. 433.

(7) the body as having great physical power; basks at the fire his hairy strength: L'A. 112.

(8) a place unapproachable because of its strength: P. L. VII. 141.

Strenuous, adj. accompanied by exertion and labour: S. A. 271.

Stretch, vb. (1) tr. to cause to reach, draw out, extend: P. L. VI. 80; all the earth, and all the sea, from one entire globose stretched into longitude: P. L. V. 754; with out: P. L. XI. 380; his line stretched out so far: P. L. VIII. 102; the sun had stretched out all the hills, caused the shadows of the hills to lengthen: L. 190; to extend between specified points: P. L. IV. 210.

(2) intr. (a) to be continuous over a distance, reach: P. L. II. 1003.

(b) to lie at full length; leviathan ... on the deep stretched like a promontory: P. L. VII. 414; stretched out: P. L. I. 209; L'A. 111.

Strew, vb. (pres. strew: P. L. V. 348; V. Ex. 64; M. W. 58; L. 151; strow: P. L. I. 302; past part. strewed: P. L. XI. 439; P. R. IV. 334; C. 838; strown: P. L. VI. 389) tr. (a) to scatter, spread loosely; fig., strew all their blessings on thy sleeping head: V. Ex. 64.

(b) to intersperse; our Law and Story strewed with hymns: P. R. IV. 334.

(c) to cover with things scattered, by sprinkling or casting loosely about: P. L. V. 348; XI. 439; M. W. 58; all the ground with ... armour strown: P. L. VI. 389; leaves that strow the brooks: P. L. I. 302; nectared lavers strewed with asphodil: C. 838; to strew the laureate hearse: L. 151.

Strict, adj. (a) severe, rigorous, exacting; strict laws, etc.: P. L. II. 241; IX. 903; XII. 304; necessity, fate: P. L. V. 528; VI. 869; X. 131; age: C. 109; sup., strictest bondage: P. L. II. 321.

(b) exact, accurate, careful; strict watch: P. L. IV. 562; sup.: P. L. IV. 783; IX. 363; senteries: P. L. II. 412; sup., strictest purity: S. A. 319; measure: S. II. 10.

Strictly, adv. (a) rigorously, severely: P. L. III. 402, 405; IX. 235; D. F. I. 33.

(b) closely, carefully, with nice accuracy: L. 66.

Stride, (1) sb. a long step indicative of pride and haughtiness: S. A. 1067; Satan, with vast and haughty strides: P. L. VI. 109;

stalking with less unconscionable strides: S. A. 1245; *came ... with horrid strides*: P. L. II. 676.

(2) *vb.* (*pret.* strode) *intr.* to walk with long steps; *Hell trembled as he strode*: P. L. II. 676.

Strife, *sb.* (*a*) angry contention, discord, conflict, battle: P. L. I. 623; II. 31; VI. 289; S. A. 460; *live in hatred, enmity, and strife*: P. L. II. 500; *yet shall he live in strife*: V. Ex. 85; *their strife pollution brings upon the temple*: P. L. XII. 355; *Chaos judge the strife*: P. L. II. 233; *the strife of glory*: P. L. VI. 290; *hateful*: P. L. VI. 264.

(*b*) a contest for superiority: P. L. VI. 823; *Nature and Fate had had no strife*: M. W. 13; *the strife of mercy and justice*: P. L. III. 406.

(*c*) a cause of contention or conflict: Ps. LXXX. 25.

Strike, *vb.* (*pret.* strook: P. L. VI. 863; *past part.* struck: P. R. III. 146; S. A. 1686; strook: P. L. II. 165; P. R. IV. 576; N. O. 95; strucken: P. L. IX. 1064) (1) *intr.* to inflict a blow; *Death ... delayed to strike*: P. L. XI. 492.

(2) *tr.* (*a*) to assail or overcome; *strook with Heaven's ... thunder*: P. L. II. 165.

(*b*) to bring suddenly and completely into some state; *strucken mute*: P. L. IX. 1064.

(*c*) to effect or impress suddenly and forcibly; *strook them with horror*: P. L. VI. 863; *struck with guilt*: P. R. III. 146; *with dread and anguish*: P. R. IV. 576; *with amaze*: S. A. 1645; *with blindness internal*: S. A. 1686.

(*d*) to produce by strokes of the fingers; *such music ... never was by mortal finger strook*: N. O. 95.

(*e*) to produce with sudden force; *she* (Peace) *strikes a universal peace*: N. O. 52.

See **Awe-strook, Heart-strook, Moon-struck, Planet-strook.**

String, *sb.* a tightly stretched cord or wire of a musical instrument, by the vibration of which tones are produced; *sing. collect.*: P. L. VII. 597; *such notes as warbled to the string*: Il P. 106; *touch the warbled string*: A. 87; *loudly*

sweep the string: L. 17; *harp with pleasant string*: Ps. LXXXI. 8; *pl.* stringed instruments; *chiming*: P. R. II. 363; *softer*: P. 27.

Stringed (*disyl.*), *adj.* produced by stringed instruments: N. O. 97.

Strip, *vb.* (*pret. 2d sing.* stripp'dst) *tr.* to deprive of utterly, rob, plunder: S. A. 1188.

Stripe, *sb.* a blow struck in whipping, lash: P. L. II. 334; P. R. IV. 388.

Stripling, *sb. attrib.* in the state of adolescence, youthful, young; *a stripling Cherub*: P. L. III. 636; *youths*: P. R. II. 352.

Strive, *vb.* (*pres. 2d sing.* striv'st: S. A. 841; *pret.* strove; *past part.* not used) *tr.* (*a*) to endeavour earnestly; *with prep. inf.*: S. A. 841; V. Ex. 78; Il P. 19; C. 8; Ps. LXXXIII. 11; *with clause*; *strive in offices of love how we may lighten each other's burden*: P. L. X. 959.

(*b*) to contend, struggle, battle, fight: P. L. IV. 859; *no good for which to strive*: P. L. II. 31; *strive here for mastery*: P. L. II. 899; *Antæus strove with Jove's Alcides*: P. R. IV. 564.

(*c*) to contend for superiority; vie; *three that in Mount Ida naked strove*: P. L. V. 382; *Egypt with Assyria strove in wealth*: P. L. I. 721; *with this Paradise of Eden strive*: P. L. IV. 275.

Stroke, *sb.* (*a*) a cut or blow with a weapon: P. L. II. 713; VI. 317; *the rude ax with heaved stroke*: Il P. 136; *one stroke of this dart*: P. L. II. 702; *a noble stroke he lifted high*: P. L. VI. 189; *some ... by violent stroke shall die*: P. L. XI. 471; *what stroke shall bruise the Victor's heel*: P. L. XII. 385; *the lash of a scourge*; *scourged with many a stroke the ... waves*: P. L. X. 311.

(*b*) any sudden and special effect produced as if by a blow: P. L. XI. 268; *the stroke of that long-threatened wound*: P. R. I. 59; used of the sudden infliction of death: P. L. I. 488; X. 52; *the stroke of death*: P. 20; *the instant stroke of death*: P. L. X. 210; *not one stroke, as I supposed*: P. L. X. 809; *one thrice-acceptable stroke*: P. L. X. 855.

See **Midnight-stroke.**

Strong, I. *adj.* (1) capable of exerting great bodily force, powerful; used of persons : S. A. 52, 816 ; *the Danite strong* : P. L. IX. 1059; *charmed thee strong* : S. A. 1134 ; *his mighty champion strong* : S. A. 556 ; *comp.* : P. L. IX. 311 ; *sup.*, *strongest of mortal men* : S. A. 168 ; of animals : P. R. III. 313.

(2) powerful in resources or inherent ability, having means for exercising or resisting force, mighty ; (*a*) used of persons : Ps. LXXXII. 8 ; *hand* : P. R. III. 168 ; *strong siding champion, Conscience* : C. 212 ; of God, Christ, or angels : Ps. LXXX. 72 ; *Spirits, Angels* : P. L. IV. 786 ; VI. 336 ; *hand* : Ps. LXXXVI. 34 ; *comp.*, *the stronger proved he* : P. L. I. 92 ; *which the stronger proves* : P. L. VI. 819 ; *sup.* : P. L. II. 44 ; *whose God is strongest* : S. A. 1155 ; of sin and death : P. L. X. 409.

(*b*) used of things ; *strong hold* : P. L. VI. 228 ; *prison, city, island strong* : P. L. II. 434 ; XI. 655 ; P. R. IV. 92.

(3) resisting decay or destruction, having vital energy : Ps. LXXX. 64.

(4) possessing moral and mental force, firm in character : P. L. VIII. 633.

(5) acting with power, forcible, effective ; *strong rebuff* : P. L. II. 936 ; *inducement* : P. L. IX. 934 ; *motion* : P. R. I. 290 ; able to endure, unyielding, firm ; *strong sufferance* : P. R. I. 160.

(6) containing much alcohol ; *sup.*, *strongest wines, drinks* : S. A. 553, 554.

(7) intense in degree ; *strong inclination* : P. L. X. 265 ; *pangs* : Cir. 27 ; *comp.*, *stronger hate* : P. L. IX. 491, 492.

comp. absol. one more powerful; *provoke our stronger* : P. L. II. 83.

II. *adv.* so as to resist attack : P. L. VIII. 241.

See **Over-strong, Worldly-strong**.

Strongly, *adv.* powerfully, forcibly, effectively : P. L. X. 262 ; *try her yet more strongly* ; C. 806 ; *comp.* : Hor. Sat. II. 2 ; resolutely ; *strongly to suffer* : P. L. I. 147.

Structure, *sb.* that which is built, a building, an edifice ; *in Heaven by many a towered structure high* : P. L. I. 733 ; *the palace of great Lucifer (so call that structure ...)* : P. L. V. 761 ; *all thy magic structures* : C. 798 ; applied to stairs or a ladder : P. L. III. 503; probably rather, the mode or form of building ; *compass huge, and high the structure* : P. R. IV. 52 ; *Ecbatana her structure vast there shows* : P. R. III. 286.

(*b*) *fig.* the human body : S. A. 1239.

Struggle, *vb. tr.* to put forth violent effort, strive earnestly against opposing force : P. L. VI. 659 ; with *prep. inf.* : P. L. II. 606.

Strut, *vb. intr.* to walk with a pompous gait ; *the cock ... stoutly struts* : L'A. 52.

Stub, *sb.* the end of a shrub or plant remaining after the main part has been cut away : P. R. I. 339.

Stubble, *sb.* the lower ends of grain-stalks left in the ground by the reaper : Ps. LXXXIII. 52; as without strength or firmness ; *earth's base built on stubble* : C. 599.

Stubborn, *adj.* (*a*) characterized by persistence, obstinately maintained ; *stubborn patience* : P. L. II. 569.

(*b*) not to be moved by reason, persistently obdurate ; *stubborn heart* : P. L. XII. 193 ; not to be exorcised ; *stubborn unlaid ghost* : C. 434.

absol. those who are obdurate ; *the stubborn* : P. R. I. 226.

Stud, *sb.* an object forming a small protuberant ornament ; *studs of pearl* : P. R. IV. 120.

Studious, *adj.* (*a*) inquiring for truth, seeking knowledge, contemplative ; *studious thoughts, musing* : P. L. VIII. 40; P. R. IV. 249.

(*b*) eager to attain something, zealous, desirous ; *studious ... of arts* : P. L. XI. 609 ; *of these ... studious* : P. L. IX. 42.

(*c*) devoted to the purposes of study or contemplation ; *studious walks and shades* : P. R. IV. 243 ; *cloister's pale* : Il P. 156.

Study, I. *sb.* zealous endeavour, thoughtful care : P. L. XI. 577 ; *study of revenge* : P. L. I. 107.

II. *vb.* (1) *tr.* to apply the mind to ; *to study household good* : P. L. IX. 233.

(2) *intr.* to meditate, reflect; *in his law he studies day and night*: Ps. I. 6.

part. adj. **studied**, carefully thought out : S. A. 658.

Stuff, (1) *sb.* raw material, substance : P. L. XII. 43.

(2) *vb. tr.* to fill to distention, cram : P. L. X. 601.

Stumble, *vb.* (1) *intr.* to walk unsteadily in a moral sense; *that they may stumble on*: P. L. III. 201.

(2) *tr.* to cause to fall, trip up : P. L. VI. 624.

Stunning, *part. adj.* deafening : P. L. II. 952.

Stupendious, *adj.* of wonderful magnitude or degree, astounding; *that stupendious bridge*: P. L. X. 351 ; *force* : S. A. 1627.

Stupid, *adj.* wanting in understanding, foolish, senseless : P. L. XII. 116.

Stupidly, *adv.* as in a condition of stupor; *he remained stupidly good*: P. L. IX. 465.

Sturdy, *adj.* hardy, enduring, strong ; *sup.*: P. R. IV. 417.

Sty, *sb.* a place of bestial debauchery; *his throne now made a sty*: P. R. IV. 101 ; *to roll with pleasure in a sensual sty*: C. 77.

Stygian, *adj.* (*a*) of or pertaining to the river Styx, and hence to hell : *Stygian flood, Pool*: P. L. I. 239; III. 14 ; *council, Powers, throng*: P. L. II. 506, 875 ; X. 453.

(*b*) resembling that of hell; *Stygian cave, darkness*: L'A. 3 ; C. 132.

Style, (1) *sb.* (*a*) mode of expressing thought in speaking or writing; *our Prophets ... their majestic, unaffected style*: P. R. IV. 359; in speaking : P. L. IX. 1132; *their orisons ... paid in various style*: P. L. V. 146; in writing : P. L. IX. 20 ; S. XI. 2.

(*b*) title, appellation : P. L. II. 312.

(2) *vb. tr.* to give the designation to, entitle ; with two *acc.*: P. L. VI. 289; in passive : P. L. XII. 33; *he, Almighty styled*: P. L. IX. 137; *to be styled great conquerors*: P. L. XI. 695 ; *thou, Lord ... art styled most merciful*: Ps. LXXXVI. 55.

Styx, *sb.* the river of hell : P. L. II. 577.

Subduct, *vb. tr.* to take away: P. L. VIII. 536.

Subdue, *vb. tr.* (1) to conquer and bring into permanent subjection ; *the Earth ; subdue it*: P. L. VII. 532; *to subdue the world*: P. R. IV. 252 ; *whose strength ... might have subdued the Earth*: S. A. 174; *nations*: P. L. XI. 691, 792; *absol.*: P. R. III. 71.

(2) to vanquish or overcome by force of arms : P. L. V. 741 ; VI. 259 ; P. R. I. 218, 226 ; IV. 126 ; Ps. CXXXVI. 69 ; *boasting I could subdue the Omnipotent*: P. L. IV. 85 ; *to subdue by force who reason for their law refuse*: P. L. VI. 40.

(*b*) to crush or put down ; *subdue rational liberty*: P. L. XII. 81.

(3) to conquer by other means; *subdue my vanquisher* (death) : P. L. III. 250 ; *fate inevitable subdues us*: P. L. II. 198 ; *necessity subdues me*: P. L. X. 132 ; *by the barber's razor best subdued*: S. A. 1167.

(4) to prevail over by any mild influence, gain complete sway over : P. L. VIII. 584.

(5) to render subservient ; *to subdue us to his will*: P. L. VI. 427.

(6) to reduce to weakness, deprive of power ; *pain, which all subdues*: P. L. VI. 458.

Subject, (1) *adj.* being under the power or dominion of another; with *to*: S. A. 1182; V. Ex. 74.

(2) *sb.* (*a*) one who owes allegiance to a government : S. A. 886.

(*b*) one who is the cause or occasion of something ; *the subject of their cruelty or scorn*: S. A. 646.

(*c*) something about which thought or the artistic constructive faculty is employed, theme ; V. Ex. 30 ; S. XI. 3 ; *this subject for heroic song*: P. L. IX. 25.

(3) *vb. tr.* (*a*) to make subservient ; *subjected to his service Angel-wings*: P. L. IX. 155.

(*b*) to make liable, expose ; *subject him to so foul indignities*: S. A. 371 ; *subject him to anarchy within*: P. R. II. 471.

(*c*) to bring under dominion, subdue ; with *to*: P. L. XII. 93; *my nation was subjected to your lords*: S. A. 1205.

(*d*) to subdue by bringing under the sway of some influence; *absol.*: P. L. VIII. 607.

part. adj. **subjected**, lying under or at the foot of : P. L. XII. 640.

Subjection, *sb.* (*a*) the state of being under the power or sway of another, or the act of so submitting oneself ; the sway that of a ruler or master : P. L. XII. 32 ; S. A. 1405 ; *I sdained subjection* : P. L. IV. 50 ; *on promise made of new subjection* : P. L. II. 239 ; of a husband or wife : P. L. IV. 308 ; *thy love, not thy subjection* : P. L. VIII. 570 ; X. 153.

(*b*) the state of being subject to an influence ; *both in subjection now to sensual appetite* : P. L. IX. 1128.

(*c*) the bowing down in token of submission : P. L. VIII. 345.

Sublime (súblime : C. 785) (1) *adj.* (*a*) borne aloft, uplifted ; *on the wings of Cherub rode sublime* : P. L. VI. 771 ; high, lofty, or almost *adv.* on high, aloft ; *the air sublime* : P. L. II. 528 ; III. 72 ; VII. 421 ; P. R. IV. 542.

(*b*) elevated with hope or happiness, elated ; *sublime with expectation* : P. L. X. 536 ; *their hearts were jocund and sublime* : S. A. 1669.

(*c*) exalted in excellence, great, noble : P. L. X. 1014.

(*d*) dealing with lofty ideas, awaking feelings of awe, solemn ; *that celestial colloquy sublime* : P. L. VIII. 455 ; *the sublime notion ... of Virginity* : C. 785.

(*e*) of lofty mien, noble, commanding : P. L. IV. 300 ; XI. 236.

(2) *vb. tr.* (*a*) to refine, purify : P. L. V. 483.

(*b*) to sublimate : P. L. I. 235.

Sublunar, *adj.* situated beneath the moon : P. L. IV. 777.

Submiss, *adj.* humble, submissive : P. L. IX. 377 ; P. R. I. 476 ; *at his feet I fell submiss* : P. L. VIII. 316 ; *with submiss approach* : P. L. V. 359.

Submission, *sb.* the yielding of oneself to the power or authority of another : P. L. IV. 81 ; *feigned submission* : P. L. IV. 96 ; *who can think submission* : P. L. I. 661 ; to the wishes, commands, or laws of another ; *coy, meek, filial* : P. L. IV. 310 ; XII. 597 ; S. A. 511.

Submissive, *adj.* (*a*) willing to submit, obedient, humble : P. L. X. 942.

(*b*) expressing submission, showing humility : P. L. IV. 498.

Submit, *vb.* (1) *tr.* to surrender to the power of another, yield ; *will ye submit your necks* : P. L. V. 787 ; *absol.*, *submits to let his sojourners depart* : P. L. XII. 191.

(2) *intr.* to yield oneself to the power of another : P. L. I. 108 ; IV. 85 ; to the commands, laws, or wishes of another : P. L. X. 769 ; XI. 526 ; *to the hand of Heaven I submit* : P. L. XI. 372 ; *to his great bidding I submit* : P. L. XI. 314 ; *to thy husband's will thine shall submit* : P. L. X. 196 ; *repentant, to submit* : S. A. 751 ; *again transgresses, and again submits* : S. A. 758.

Subordinate, *sb.* one inferior in power and rank : P. L. V. 671.

Suborn, *vb. tr.* to incite secretly to an evil act : P. L. IX. 361.

Subscribe, *vb. intr.* to give consent, assent as if by writing one's name ; *Fate subscribed not* : P. L. XI. 182 ; *hope would fain subscribe* : S. A. 1535.

Subsequent, *adj.* following in time, happening at a later time : S. A. 325.

Subserve, *vb. intr.* to serve in an inferior capacity, be subordinate : S. A. 57.

Subsist, *vb. intr.* (*a*) to retain the existing state, continue, remain ; *subsist in battle* : P. R. III. 19 ; *firm we subsist* : P. L. IX. 359.

(*b*) to have continued existence, live : P. L. X. 922 ; C. 686.

Substance, *sb.* (*a*) the material of which anything is made : *various degrees of substance* : P. L. V. 474 ; *her* (the moon's) *substance* : P. L. V. 420 ; of which a person is constituted : P. L. V. 493 ; *their armour ... into their substance pent* : P. L. VI. 657 ; *creatures ... of what mould or substance* : P. L. II. 356 ; *if our substance be indeed divine* : P. L. II. 99 ; *empyreal, spiritual, ethereal* : P. L. I. 117 ; IV. 585 ; VI. 330.

(*b*) that which exists by itself, a being ; *or substance might be called that shadow seemed* : P. L. II. 669 ; *intelligential* : P. L. V. 408 ; *corporeal* : P. L. VIII. 109.

(c) real or essential part, that which constitutes the thing itself : P. L. I. 529 ; XI. 775.

Substantial, *adj.* (*a*) actually existing, real, true : P. L. IV. 485.

(*b*) strong, stout, solid : P. L. IV. 189.

Substantially, *adv.* with reality of existence, really ; *in him all his Father shone substantially expressed* : P. L. III. 140.

Substitute, *sb.* one acting with delegated power in the place of another : P. L. VIII. 381 ; X. 403.

Subterranean, *adj.* situated below the surface of the earth ; *subterranean wind* : P. L. I. 231.

Subtle, *adj.* (*a*) delicate, refined ; *a nice and subtle happiness* : P. L. VIII. 399.

(*b*) sly, cunning, artful, crafty ; *Time, the subtle thief of youth* : S. II. 1 : used of Satan : P. L. IX. 307, 324 ; *the subtle Fiend* : P. L. II. 815 ; X. 20 ; P. R. I. 465 ; II. 323 ; *sup., subtlest beast of all the field* : P. L. VII. 495 ; IX. 86, 560.

(*c*) sagacious, discerning, shrewd : P. L. IV. 786.

(*d*) artfully contrived, cunningly or skilfully devised ; *subtle magic, art* : P. L. I. 727 ; VI. 513 ; *wiles, shifts* : P. L. IX. 184 ; P. R. IV. 308.

(*e*) profound, difficult of understanding : P. L. VIII. 192.

Subtlety, *sb.* (*a*) artifice, cunning : P. L. II. 358 ; IX. 93 ; P. R. I. 144.

(*b*) a device or stratagem ; *liable to fall by weakest subtleties* : S. A. 56.

Subtly, *adv.* artfully or cunningly in a good sense : P. L. VIII. 207.

Suburb, *sb.* a region or place adjacent to a city or village ; *pl. Modin and her suburbs* : P. R. III. 170 ; *fig., the smoothed plank, the suburb of their* (bees') *straw-built citadel* : P. L. I. 773.

Suburban, *adj.* situated in the suburbs : P. R. IV. 243.

Subvert, *vb. tr.* (*a*) to overcome ; *by things deemed weak subverting worldly-strong* : P. R. I. 124.

(*b*) to overthrow or ruin morally : P. L. XII. 568.

Succeed, *vb. intr.* (*a*) to follow, come after, be subsequent ; *of all ages to succeed* : P. L. X. 733 ; *woes are to succeed* : P. L. IV. 535.

(*b*) to take the place which another has left ; *wolves shall succeed for teachers* : P. L. XII. 508.

(*c*) to have a successful termination : P. L. I. 166 ; S. A. 908.

vbl. sb. **succeeding,** success, prosperous termination : P. R. II. 143.

Success, *sb.* (*a*) the termination of an enterprise, issue, result, fortune : P. L. II. 9, 123 ; *that thy success may show destruction to the rest* : P. L. VI. 161 ; *ill, bad* : P. L. IV. 932 ; P. R. IV. 1.

(*b*) the favourable termination of an enterprise, prosperous issue, good fortune : P. L. X. 239 ; P. R. III. 278 ; *so main to our success* : P. L. VI. 471 ; *my success with Eve* : P. R. II. 141 ; *success in love* : S. I. 7 ; *them to acquaint with these successes* : P. L. X. 396 ; *hoped* : P. L. III. 740 ; P. R. IV. 578 ; *hope of* : P. R. I. 105 ; *desperate of* : P. R. IV. 23 ; *good* : S. A. 1454.

Successful, *adj.* (*a*) having attained what one wishes : P. L. X. 463.

(*b*) *successful hope*, hope of success or of a prosperous issue of an undertaking : P. L. I. 120.

Successfully, *adv.* with a favourable termination, fortunately : P. R. I. 103.

Succession, *sb.* order or series of descendants : P. L. XII. 331.

Successive, *adj.* following in order one after the other ; *day and night, to men successive* : P. L. IV. 614.

Successor, *sb.* one who takes the place which another has left : P. R. III. 373 ; *successor in thy bed* : S. A. 1021.

Succinct, *adj.* girded up : P. L. III. 643.

Succoth, *sb.* a city of Israel east of Shechem and near the Jordan. Its exact location is uncertain : S. A. 278.

Succour, (1) *sb.* aid, help, assistance : P. L. IX. 642.

(2) *vb. tr.* to relieve, lighten, remove ; *succour our just fears* : F. of C. 18.

*****Such,** *adj.* (1) of that or the like kind or degree ; (*a*) that with which comparison is made given in the context ; immediately followed by a *sb.* : P. L. II. 290 ; III.

107 ; IV. 42, 163 ; V. 31 ; VI. 342 ; VII. 294 ; IX. 145 ; X. 1026 ; P. R. I. 492 ; S. A. 290 ; N. O. 117 ; II P. 26 ; *if he had seen such two* : C. 575 ; *when meet now such pairs, in love* : P. L. VIII. 58 ; *such joy, pleasure* : P. L. IV. 92 ; VIII. 50 ; IX. 455 ; N. O. 99 ; *such fire to use* : P. L. X. 1078 ; *some such resemblances* : P. L. V. 114 ; as subject or predicate of *be* ; *such are the courts of God* : P. L. V. 650 ; *such are those ... shadows* : C. 470 ; followed by the *indef. art.* : S. A. 1045 ; *such a tomb* : W. S. 16 ; *such a rural Queen* : A. 94 ; *such a scant allowance* : C. 308.

(*b*) that with which comparison is made stated and introduced by *as* : P. L. II. 284 ; V. 582 ; C. 677 ; S. VIII. 6 ; *no such company as* : P. L. VIII. 446 ; *such pardon ... as* : S. A. 825 ; *such discourse ... as may advise him* : P. L. V. 233 ; *such place ... as may not oft invite* : P. L. V. 373 ; *such abundance ... as leaves a greater store* : P. L. IX. 620 ; *such notes as ... drew iron tears* : II P. 106 ; *a virgin, such as was herself* : C. 856 ; *bounds ... such as bound* : P. L. III. 539 ; *laws ... such as appertain to civil justice* : P. L. XII. 230 ; *such a frown ... as* : P. L. II. 713 ; *such a horrid clang as* : N. O. 157 ; *such a foe as* : P. L. IV. 372.

introduced by *that* : P. L. II. 765 ; VI. 703 ; XI. 890 ; P. R. III. 18 ; U. C. I. 3 ; *such delight hath God ... that* : P. L. XII. 245 ; *such perfection that* : P. R. I. 209 ; *in such pomp dost lie that kings* : W. S. 15 ; *that* omitted : P. L. XII. 622.

introduced by *who* ; *such a foe is rising, who intends* : P. L. V. 724 ; *such an enemy we have, who seeks our ruin* : P. L. IX. 274 ; *such an enemy is risen to invade us, who no less threatens* : P. R. II. 126.

introduced by *where* or *when* ; *clothe my fancy in fit sound : such where the ... mind may soar* : V. Ex. 33 ; *in such a season born, when scarce a shed could be obtained* : P. R. II. 72 ; *such wherein appeared obscure some glimpse of joy* : P. L. I. 523.

(*c*) explained by an infinitive phrase which follows ; *such commission from above I have received, to answer thy desire* : P. L. VII. 118 ; *such ambush ... waited ... to intercept thy way* : P. L. IX. 408.

(*d*) followed by an *adj.* : P. L. V. 149, 362 ; VI. 401, 636 ; S. A. 862 ; W. S. 6 ; C. 245 ; *such restless resolution* : P. L. VIII. 31 ; *such vast room* : P. L. VIII. 153 ; *such fatal consequence* : P. L. X. 364 ; *such wondrous power* : P. L. XII. 200 ; *such cooling drink as the ... woods provide* : C. 186 : *such impetuous fury ... that* : P. L. VI. 591.

(2) the same as previously mentioned or specified, not other ; without the *art.* : P. L. I. 70, 237 ; III. 371 ; IV. 379 ; V. 26, 521 ; VI. 253 ; *such thou art* : P. L. IX. 292 ; *such was their song* : P. L. X. 648 ; *such were those Giants* : P. L. XI. 688 ; *such was the splendour* : P. R. II. 366 ; *expel a Devil who made him such* : P. R. IV. 129 ; *such ye seem* : S. A. 332 ; *aspiring to be such* : P. L. IV. 526 ; *such audacious neighborhood* : P. L. I. 399 ; *such bold words* : P. L. V. 66.

(3) by omission of the correlative, used emphatically ; so great, extreme, intense, etc.: P. L. VI. 114, 688 ; VIII. 88 ; IX. 1024 ; XII. 81 ; S. A. 357 ; followed by the *indef. art.* : P. L. VIII. 36 ; X. 267 ; C. 711 ; *fallen such a pernicious highth* : P. L. I. 282 ; *such a numerous host* : P. L. II. 993 ; *such a peal shall rouse their sleep* : P. L. III. 329 ; *such a petty trespass* : P. L. IX. 693 ; *such a viper* : S. A. 1001 ; *such a sacred and home-felt delight* : C. 262.

absol. as *sb.* or *pron.* (*a*) such a person or persons : P. L. I. 145 ; *how such as stood like these* : P. L. I. 629 ; *let such bethink them* : P. L. II. 73 ; *none but such from mercy I exclude* : P. L. III. 202 ; *how can God with such reside ?* : P. L. XII. 284 ; *what delight to be by such extolled* : P. R. III. 54 ; *such are from God inspired* : P. R. IV. 350 ; *from such as nearer stood* : S. A. 1631 ; *enow of such as ... creep, and intrude* : L. 114 ; *such of shape*, one of such shape : P. L. XI. 297.

(b) a person previously mentioned or described ; *such ... seize fast* : P. L. IV. 796 ; a thing : C. 519 ; *that detriment, if such it be* : P. L. VII. 153 ; *the Elysian fields (if such there were)* : D. F. I. 40.

Suck, *vb. tr.* (*a*) to draw in with the mouth ; *there I suck the liquid air* : C. 980.

(b) to absorb or drink in ; *your (flowers) ... eyes, that on the green turf suck the honeyed showers* : L. 140.

Suckling, *sb.* an unweaned child : Ps. VIII. 5.

Sudden, (1) *adj.* (*a*) happening, coming, or acting quickly and without warning : P. L. X. 963 ; XI. 293 ; P. R. II. 224 ; *sudden onset* : P. L. II. 364 ; *vengeance, rage* : P. L. VI. 279 ; S. A. 953 ; *adoration* : C. 452 ; *appetite* : P. L. VIII. 308 ; *silence* : C. 552 ; *coming* : C. 954 ; *blaze, flame* : P. L. I. 665 ; IV. 818 ; V. 891 ; X. 453 ; S. A. 1691 ; A. 2 ; L. 74 ; *view* : P. L. II. 890 ; III. 542 ; *mind* : P. L. V. 452 ; *hand* : P. L. II. 738 ; acting at once and without previous training or knowledge ; *my sudden apprehension* : P. L. VIII. 354.

(b) hastily devised or prepared : P. R. I. 96.

(2) *adv.* suddenly ; *so sudden to behold the grisly King* : P. L. IV. 821 ; *pavilions ... sudden reared* : P. L. V. 653 ; *every leaf, that sudden flowered* : P. L. VII. 317 ; *for sudden all at once* : P. L. VI. 582.

(3) *sb. on a sudden*, all at once and without notice : P. L. II. 752, 879 ; V. 51, 632 ; IX. 900 ; Ps. LXXXIII. 54.

Suddenly, *adv.* (*a*) all at once, unexpectedly : P. L. V. 90 ; VIII. 468 ; *air suddenly eclipsed* : P. L. XI. 183 ; *suddenly at head appeared Satan* : P. L. VI. 556 ; *suddenly stood at my head a dream* : P. L. VIII. 292 ; *suddenly a man before him stood* : P. R. II. 298.

(b) presently, immediately : P. L. X. 341 ; without preparation : S. A. 1565.

Sue, *vb. intr.* to beg, entreat ; *him who ... sues for life* : S. A. 512 ; *suing for peace* : S. A. 965 : *sue for grace* : P. L. I. 111.

Suffer, *vb.* (*pres. 2d sing.* suffer'st : S. A. 744) (**1**) *tr.* (*a*) to support bravely, bear, endure : P. L. I. 147 ; P. R. III. 194.

(b) to be affected by, undergo, experience ; *their tender age might suffer peril* : C. 40 ; *the air, that now must suffer change* : P. L. X. 213 ; *planets ... real eclipse then suffered* : P. L. X. 414.

(c) to bear or undergo with pain, either physical or mental or both : P. L. II. 162, 163 ; X. 470 ; P. R. II. 249 ; III. 97, 101, 192 ; S. A. 233, 744 ; *the Hell I suffer seems a Heaven* : P. L. IV. 78 ; *to suffer here chains* : P. L. II. 195 ; *suffering death* : P. L. XII. 398 ; P. R. III. 98 ; *suffering the punishment of dissolute days* : S. A. 701.

(d) to allow, permit : C. 809 ; with *acc.* and *prep. inf.* : P. L. III. 248 ; S. A. 458 ; *I suffer them to enter* : P. L. X. 623 ; *suffer the hypocrite ... to tread his sacred courts* : P. R. I. 487 ; *absol.* : P. L. VI. 701.

(**2**) *intr.* (*a*) to feel or undergo pain of body or mind : P. L. I. 158.

(b) to be in pain of body or mind without sinking, endure evils with patience : P. L. II. 199 ; *who best can suffer best can do* : P. R. III. 195.

vbl. sb. **suffering,** the bearing of pain or distress ; *in* or *by suffering* : P. L. II. 340 ; XI. 375 ; *suffering for Truth's sake is fortitude* : P. L. XII. 569 ; or the pain borne ; *pl.* : P. L. IV. 26 ; P. 25 ; *to such unsightly sufferings be debased* : P. L. XI. 510 ; *of all thy sufferings think the heaviest* : S. A. 445.

Sufferance, *sb.* (*a*) patience or endurance under suffering : P. R. I. 160.

(b) allowance, permission, leave, P. L. VIII. 202 ; *this my long sufferance* : P. L. III. 198 ; *God's high sufferance* : P. L. I. 336 ; *the sufferance of supernal power* : P. L. I. 241.

Sufferer, *sb.* one who sustains an evil : S. A. 1525.

Suffice, *vb.* (**1**) *tr.* to be equal to the demands of, satisfy, content : P. L. V. 451 ; *let it suffice thee* : P. L. VIII. 620 ; *happier had it sufficed him to have known good* : P. L. XI.

88 ; *the strength whereof sufficed him forty days* : P. R. II. 276 ; *suffice his vengeful ire* : P. L. I. 148.

(2) *intr.* to be enough or adequate : P. L. II. 411 ; *I will clear their senses dark what may suffice* : P. L. III. 189 ; *suffices that to me strength is my bane* : S. A. 63 ; with *prep. inf.* : P. L. IV. 328 ; VII. 113, 114.

Sufficient, *adj.* (*a*) equal to the end proposed, enough, adequate ; *sufficient thanks* : P. L. VIII. 5 ; *penalty* : P. L. X. 753 ; *introduction* : P. R. III. 247 ; with *prep. inf.* : P. L. II. 102 ; VI. 427 ; S. A. 1212 ; *number sufficient to possess her realms* : P. L. VII. 147 ; *absol.* ; *sufficient that thy prayers are heard* : P. L. XI. 252.

(*b*) of competent power, fit, capable, able : P. L. II. 404 ; with *prep. inf.* : P. L. III. 99 ; IX. 43.

Sufficiently, *adv.* to a degree that answers the purpose, adequately : P. L. VIII. 404.

Suffrage, *sb.* a vote given in the choice of a person for a position : P. L. II. 415.

Suffusion, *sb.* that which is spread over : P. L. III. 26.

Suggest, *vb. tr.* to hint, intimate, insinuate : P. R. I. 355.

part. adj. **suggested**, indicated, intimated, or implied ; *tells the suggested cause* : P. L. V. 702.

Suggestion, *sb.* (*a*) hint, intimation ; P. L. I. 685 ; S. A. 599.

(*b*) prompting to do evil, temptation : P. L. III. 129 ; IX. 90.

Suit, (1) *sb.* the litigation of a right in a court of justice : Hor. Epist. 3.

(2) *vb. tr.* to agree, accord ; *the one intense, the other still remiss, cannot well suit with either* : P. L. VIII. 388.

See **Civil-suited**.

Suitable, *adj.* fitting, appropriate : P. L. III. 639.

Suitor, *sb.* one who begs for something, petitioner ; P. L. XI. 9.

Sullen, *adj.* (*a*) gloomy, dismal, dark ; *a sullen day* : S. XX. 4 ; *Night with her sullen wing* : P. R. I. 500 ; with blending of the meaning morose ; *sullen Moloch* : N. O. 205.

(*b*) slow-moving, sluggish ; V. Ex. 95.

(*c*) dull, heavy ; *curfew ... swinging slow with sullen roar* : Il P. 76.

Sulphur, *sb.* the mineral substance : P. L. I. 69 ; *ever-burning* : P. L. I. 674 ; *Tartarean* : P. L. II. 69.

Sulphurous, *adj.* composed of or mixed with sulphur ; *sulphurous and nitrous foam* : P. L. VI. 512 ; *sulphurous fire*, gunpowder : P. L. XI. 658 ; *sulphurous hail*, hail accompanied with lightning : P. L. I. 171.

Sultan, *sb.* (*a*) monarch, ruler ; applied to Satan : P. L. I. 348.

(*b*) the ruler of Turkey : P. L. XI. 395.

Sultry, *adj.* (*a*) exceedingly hot or passionate ; *a sultry chafe* : S. A. 1246.

(*b*) heard at the time of oppressive heat : L. 28.

Sum, (1) *sb.* (*a*) the highest point, the crowning feature, that which completes ; *last, the sum of all, my Father's voice* : P. R. I. 283 ; *thou hast attained the sum of wisdom* : P. L. XII. 575 ; *brought my story to the sum of earthly bliss* : P. L. VIII. 522.

(*b*) the aggregate amount, whole : P. L. XII. 338 ; *the sum of things*, all things together : P. L. VI. 673.

(*c*) the outcome of many circumstances, result : S. A. 1557.

(2) *vb. tr.* (*a*) to combine into a total, add together, compute : P. L. I. 571.

(*b*) to bring together, collect ; *in her look sums all delight* : P. L. IX. 454 ; *my strength ... in what part summed* : S. A. 395 ; with *up* : P. L. VIII. 473 ; *their known virtue ... all summed up in Man* : P. L. IX. 113.

(*c*) to have reached the full growth of the feathers ; *with prosperous wing full summed* : P. R. I. 14.

(*d*) to complete the growth of the feathers, or possibly the meaning may be to preen ; *they summed their pens* : P. L. VII. 421.

Sumless, *adj.* that cannot be computed : P. L. VIII. 36.

Summer, *sb.* the warmest season of the year ; *the summer long* : P. R. IV. 246 ; in the genitive ; *summer's day* : P. L. I. 449 ; as the

longest day of the year : P. L. I.
744 ; *summer's morn* : P. L. IX.
447 ; *noontide air* : P. L. II. 309 ;
heat : P. L. X. 656 ; *cloud* : P. R.
III. 222 ; *rose* : P. L. III. 43 ;
pride, honour : P. L. VII. 478 :
D. F. I. 3.

(*b*) as a season of joy and delight ; *there eternal summer dwells*:
C. 988.

(*c*) *pl.* used for the whole year ;
summers three times eight : M. W.
7.

attrib. of or pertaining to summer ; *summer eves* : L'A. 130 ;
drouth : C. 928 ; *fly* : S. A. 676.

Summon, *vb. tr.* (*a*) to give notice
to appear at a specified place,
cite ; *to council summons all his ...
peers* : P. R. I. 40 ; *the total kind
of birds ... summoned over Eden* :
P. L. VI. 75 ; *fish ... not hither
summoned* : P. L. VIII. 347.

(*b*) to call on ; *I summon all ...
to be in readiness* : P. R. II. 143.

(*c*) to call into action, arouse :
P. L. IX. 374.

part. adj. **summoning,** acting
as a summoner : P. L. III. 325.

Summons, *sb.* (*a*) an authoritative
call to appear at a place named,
citation : P. L. I. 757, 798 ; *the
summons high* : P. L. XI. 81 ; *imperial* : P. L. V. 584.

(*b*) a request or entreaty to
appear at a place named : C. 888.

Sumptuous, *adj.* (*a*) costly, luxurious, splendid : P. R. IV. 114.

(*b*) richly and splendidly attired : S. A. 1072.

Sun, *sb.* (1) the celestial body that
is the main source of heat and
light in the solar system : P. L.
III. 8 ; IV. 792 ; V. 370, 746 ; VII.
406 ; IX. 721 ; X. 529, 663, 1078 ;
XI. 278 ; XII. 263 ; P. R. IV. 432;
S. A. 86 ; C. 374, 736 ; S. XXII.
5 ; *for yet the Sun was not* : P. L.
VII. 247 ; *the Sun a mighty sphere
he framed* : P. L. VII. 354 ; *when
the Sun with Taurus rides* : P. L.
I. 769 ; *while the Sun in Aries
rose* : P. L. X. 329 ; *the Sun, now
fallen beneath the Azores* : P. L.
IV. 591 ; *the sun's bright circle* : S.
VIII. 8 ; *the Sun's orb* : P. L. VII.
361 ; *the Sun's lucent orb* : P. L.
III. 589 ; *the Sun's axle* : P. L. X.
670 ; *the golden Sun, in splendour
likest Heaven* : P. L. III. 572 ;
the sun paint your fleecy skirts

with gold : P. L. V. 187 ; *the
Sun's more potent ray* : P. L. IV.
673 ; *a glorious angel ... whom
John saw also in the Sun* : P. L.
III. 623 ; *Uriel, regent of the Sun*:
P. L. III. 690 ; IX. 60 ; *Uriel ...
amid the Sun's bright circle where
thou sitt'st* : P. L. IV. 578 ; *the sun
was set* : P. L. VII. 582 ; *the Sun
in western cadence low* : P. L. X.
92 ; *the sun had stretched out all
the hills* : L. 190 ; *morning, rising,
orient* : P. L. IV. 244, 651 ; V.
175 ; *mid-day* : C. 384 ; *setting,
declined, parting, falling* : P. L.
I. 744 ; IV. 352 ; VIII. 630 ; C. 30;
arch-chemic : P. L. III. 609 ; in
direct address : P. L. IV. 37 ;
Thou Sun : P. L. V. 171 ; VIII.
273 ; *Sun, in Gibeon stand* : P. L.
XII. 265.

(*b*) neuter gender : P. L. VIII.
94.

(*c*) masculine gender : P. L. V.
558 ; VIII. 133, 139, 255 ; IX. 48 ;
X. 651 ; II P. 131 ; *what if the
Sun be centre to the World* : P. L.
VIII. 122 ; *whether the Sun ... rise
on the Earth, or Earth rise on the
Sun* : P. L. VIII. 160, 161 ; *new-
risen, rising* : P. L. I. 594 ; III.
551 ; *mounted* : P. L. V. 300 ;
setting, low : P. L. IV. 540 ; X.
682 ; *radiant, full-blazing,* etc.;
P. L. II. 492 ; IV. 29, 150, 642 ;
XI. 844 ; more definitely personified : P. L. X. 688 ; N. O. 229 ;
C. 98 ; L'A. 60 ; *the Sun ... at
even sups with the Ocean* : P. L.
V. 423 ; with the characteristics
of the sun-god Apollo : N. O. 36,
79 ; S. XII. 7 ; *by the Sun's team
untrod* : N. O. 19 ; *the tell-tale
Sun* : C. 141 ; *some say the Sun
was bid turn reins* : P. L. X. 671 ;
*the Sun ... with wheels yet hovering
o'er the ocean-brim* : P. L. V.
139 ; of Helios ; *Circe, the daughter of the Sun* : C. 51.

(2) any heavenly body which is
the centre of a system : P. L.
VIII. 148.

(3) that which resembles the
sun in brightness : P. L. VI. 305.

(4) sunshine : S. A. 3.

(5) the source of moral light
and glory, God : N. O. 83 ; Christ :
Ps. LXXXIV. 41.

(6) the sun-god of Egypt, Ra,
worshipped especially at Helio-
polis ; *a phœnix ... to enshrine his*

relics in the Sun's bright temple:
P. L. V. 273.

Sun-beam (sun-béam), *sb.* a ray of
the sun : P. L. IV. 556 ; Il P. 8.

Sun-bright, *adj.* like the sun in
brightness : P. L. VI. 100.

Sun-clad, *adj.* clothed in radiance ;
the sun-clad power of chastity : C.
782.

Sunlight, *sb.* the light of the sun :
P. L. IX. 1087.

Sunny, *adj.* (*a*) bright like those of
the sun : P. L. III. 625.

(*b*) exposed to the rays of the
sun ; *sunny hill, plains* : P. L. III.
28 ; VIII. 262 ; P. R. IV. 447.

Sun-rise (sun-rise), *sb.* the first
appearance of the sun above the
horizon : S. A. 1597.

Sunshine (sunshine), *sb.* the light of
the sun : P. L. III. 616.

attrib. sunshiny, bright with the
light of the sun : C. 959 ; L'A. 98.

Sup, *vb. intr.* to eat the evening
meal : U. C. I. 18 ; *fig., the Sun...
at even sups with the Ocean* : P. L.
V. 426.

Superficially, *adv.* shallowly, slightly :
P. L. VI. 476.

Superfluous, (1) *adj.* (*a*) more than
is needed, unnecessary, excessive,
useless : P. L. V. 325 ; IX. 308 ;
S. XXI. 13.

(*b*) creating more than is needed ;
with superfluous hand : P. L. VIII.
27.

(**2**) *adv.* in a useless or unnecessary manner : P. L. IV. 832.

Superior, *adj.* (*a*) higher in rank,
position, or office : P. L. X. 147 ;
superior Fiend, Spirits, lord : P.
L. I. 283 ; III. 737 ; P. R. IV.
167 ; *superior voice of their great
potentate* : P. L. V. 705.

(*b*) surpassing in quality or
degree, more excellent or eminent :
P. L. XI. 636 ; *superior love, judgment* : P. L. IV. 499 ; P. R. IV. 324.

(*c*) greater or surpassing in
power ; *her words set off by some
superior power* : C. 801 ; *sway* :
P. L. IX. 1131 ; in eminence,
power, or goodness ; used of persons : P. L. V. 360 ; VI. 443 ; IX.
825.

(*d*) too great to be affected by
the cause implied : P. L. V. 905 ;
VIII. 532.

Supernal, *adj.* heavenly ; *supernal
grace, power* : P. L. I. 241 ; VII.
573 ; XI. 359.

Supernumerary, *adj.* exceeding the
necessary number : P. L. X. 887.

Superscription, *sb.* (*a*) words inscribed on a coin ; *fig., how
counterfeit a coin they are who
'friends' bear in their superscription* : S. A. 190.

(*b*) the address on a letter, inscription : U. C. II. 34.

Superstition, *sb.* (*a*) the belief in
and reverence for things which
are not proper objects of worship :
P. L. III. 452 ; the worship of a
false god : S. A. 15.

(*b*) pagan religious doctrines or
practices : P. L. XII. 512.

Superstitious, *adj.* influenced by a
belief in the gods : P. R. II. 296.

Supper, *sb.* the evening meal ; *the
hour of supper* : P. L. IX. 225 ; *at
his supper sat* : C. 293 ; *found his
supper on the coals* : P. R. II. 273 ;
*the chewing flocks had ta'en their
supper* : C. 541.

Supper-fruit, *sb.* fruit to be eaten at
the evening meal : P. L. IV. 331.

Supplant, *vb. tr.* to trip up, take off
one's feet : P. L. X. 513.

part. adj. **supplanted,** overthrown morally : P. R. IV. 607.

Supple, *adj.* pliant, flexible, easily
bent ; *supple knee, joints* : P. L.
V. 788 ; VIII. 269.

Suppliant, (1) *adj.* expressive of
humble entreaty ; *with suppliant
knee* : P. L. I. 112.

(**2**) *sb.* a humble petitioner : P.
L. X. 917 ; S. A. 1173.

Supplication, *sb.* (*a*) a humble and
earnest prayer to God : P. L. V.
867 ; XI. 31 ; Ps. VI. 19 ; LXXXVI. 17.

(*b*) a humble and earnest request, petition : S. A. 1459.

Supply, (1) *sb.* a quantity of something furnished, stock, store : P.
L. XI. 740.

(**2**) *vb. tr.* (*a*) to furnish with
what is wanted, provide : P. L.
X. 1001 ; S. A. 926 ; to make provision for, satisfy ; *with full hand
supplies their need* : Ps. CXXXVI.
86.

(*b*) to fill a place, occupy instead
of some one else : P. L. II. 834 ;
to take the place of ; *a comfortable heat...which might supply the
Sun* : P. L. X. 1078.

Support, (1) *sb.* (*a*) a means of
holding up ; *two massy pillars,
that to the arched roof gave main
support* : S. A. 1634.

(b) a means of maintaining or keeping up; *to think strongest drinks our chief support of health*: S. A. 554.

(2) *vb. tr.* (a) to keep from falling or sinking; *to support each flower*: P. L. IX. 427; *to support uneasy steps*: P. L. I. 295.

(b) to maintain in physical vigour; *God support nature without repast*: P. R. II. 250.

(c) to sustain or uphold by spiritual aid; *what is low raise and support*: P. L. I. 23; to sustain mentally and spiritually: P. L. XII. 496; *What supports me, dost thou ask?*: S. XXII. 9.

(d) to endure or bear without being overcome: P. L. I. 147; X. 834.

(e) to keep up, maintain; *industrious to support tyrannic power*: S. A. 1274.

Suppose, *vb. (pres. 2d sing.* supposest: P. L. VIII. 86) (1) *tr.* (a) to think or believe to be true, with the implication that the belief is false: P. L. I. 451; *Mount Amara...by some supposed true Paradise*: P. L. IV. 281; with *prep. inf.; supposing here to find his son*: S. A. 1443; *to find out that...I suppose*: C. 307; with two *acc.; supposing him some neighbor villager*: C. 576; with clause; *supposests that bodies bright*: P. L. VIII. 86; *I suppose ...we should*: P. L. VI. 617.

(b) to assume as true for the sake of argument or experiment; with two *acc.; supposed not incorruptible*: P. L. IX. 297; with clause; *suppose he should relent*: P. L. II. 237.

(c) to assume as existing because of the consequences; *that swift nocturnal and diurnal rhomb supposed*: P. L. VIII. 134.

(d) to imply, take for granted: P. R. III. 355.

(2) *intr.* to be of opinion, think, presume; *as I or he suppose or supposed*: P. L. IV. 130; X. 809; S. A. 334; *as dull fools suppose*: C. 477.

Suppress, *vb. tr.* to withhold from disclosure, conceal: P. L. VII. 123.

Supremacy, *sb.* the highest power or authority; *the high supremacy of Heaven*: P. L. III. 205; *his high supremacy*: P. L. I. 132.

Supreme (súpreme: P. L. I. 735; II. 217; T. 17; C. 217) *adj.* (1) highest in power; *Fate supreme*: P. L. X. 480; used of God or Christ: P. L. I. 248; VI. 814; *God, King, Lord,* etc.: P. L. I. 735; II. 236; VII. 142, 515; *our Supreme Foe*: P. L. II. 210; *Power Supreme*: P. L. IV. 956; *Head Supreme*: P. L. III. 319; *the Supreme Good*: C. 217; *God over all supreme*: P. R. IV. 186; of that which belongs or pertains to God; *throne* or *seat supreme*: P. L. V. 670; VI. 27; X. 28; XI. 82; *the supreme throne*: T. 17; *supreme decree*: P. L. III. 659; *thy will supreme*: P. L. X. 70.

(b) holding the highest place; *I ...only supreme in misery*: P. L. IV. 91.

(2) highest in degree, greatest possible; *pomp supreme*: P. L. II. 510.

absol. one who is highest in power or authority, or who has power over all: P. R. I. 99; God; *Heaven's Supreme*: P. L. IX. 125; *Supreme of Things*: P. L. VIII. 414; *O Supreme of Heavenly Thrones*: P. L. VI. 723.

Surcease, *vb. tr.* to cease, stop, leave off: P. L. VI. 258; with *prep. inf.*: S. A. 404; Ps. LXXXV. 35.

Surcharge, *vb. tr.* to overload, overburden: C. 728; Ps. LXXXVIII. 10; *Heaven, surcharged with ... multitude*: P. L. II. 836; *plant ...with fruit surcharged*: P. L. V. 58; *flower surcharged with dew*: S. A. 728; *Adam with such joy surcharged*: P. L. XII. 373; *with aggravations not surcharged*: S. A. 769.

Sure, (1) *adj.* (a) certainly knowing, free from doubt, assured; *of* omitted; *this I am sure*: S. A. 424.

(b) fully persuaded, confident; *be sure*: P. L. II. 323; IV. 841; VI. 647; XII. 485; S. A. 465, 1385, 1408; *he may be sure*: P. L. XI. 772; *of this be sure*: P. L. I. 158.

(c) certain of obtaining; *to be sure of Paradise*: P. L. III. 478; *of the first be sure*: P. L. IX. 1080; *be sure to find what I foretold*: P. R. IV. 477; *be sure thou ...hast gained*: S. IX. 11; *comp., surer to prosper*: P. L. II. 39; certain of retaining; *to be sure of our omnipotence*: P. L. V. 721.

(*d*) to be relied on, trustworthy: P. R. IV. 483; *sure guess*: C. 310; *pledge of day*: P. L. V. 168; *comp., the surer messenger*: P. L. XI. 856; *sup., their surest signal*: P. L. I. 278.

(*e*) certain to be, infallible, unfailing: P. L. II. 154; Ps. CXXXVI. 4, 96; *for sure*, surely, certainly: P. R. II. 35.

(*f*) stable, steady: P. L. VII. 267, 586.

(2) *adv.* (*a*) assuredly, certainly: P. L. II. 32; P. 48; C. 246, 493; *that sure was worse*: P. L. II. 169; *good unknown sure is not had*: P. L. IX. 756; *eternal sure*: P. R. IV. 391; *sure I'll ne'er be fetched*: U. C. II. 18; *some virgin sure*: C. 148.

(*b*) firmly, securely, safely; *make sure*: P. L. X. 402; P. R. III. 363; *comp., let him surer bar his iron gates*: P. L. IV. 897; *sup., he might surest seize them*: P. L. IV. 407.

See Over-sure.

Surely, *adv.* assuredly, certainly, undoubtedly: P. L. IV. 923; N. O. 60; U. C. I. 9; Ps. LXXXV. 37; *O Soul most surely blest*: D. F. I. 36.

Surety, *sb.* that which makes certain, a ground of security: P. L. V. 538.

Surface (surfáce: P. L. VI. 472), *sb.* the exterior part, outside; *the aged Earth...shall from the surface to the centre shake*: N. O. 162; *bright surface of this ethereous mould*: P. L. VI. 472.

Surfeit, *sb.* the indulgence in anything to satiety; in physical pleasure: P. L. XI. 795; in intellectual or emotional pleasure: P. L. VII. 129; C. 480; *quaff immortality and joy, secure of surfeit*: P. L. V. 639; *there may in grief be surfeit*: S. A. 1562.

Surge, *sb.* large swelling waves collectively, billows: P. L. X. 417; *the fiery surge*: P. L. I. 173.

Surging, *part. adj.* rising and rolling onward as waves; *surging waves*: P. L. VII. 214; P. R. IV. 18; *fig., in the surging smoke*: P. L. II. 928; *enclosed in serpent...fold above fold, a surging maze*: P. L. IX. 499.

Surmise, (1) *sb.* (*a*) a conjecture made on slight evidence, supposition: P. L. IX. 333.

(*b*) thought, fancy; *let our frail thoughts dally with false surmise*: L. 153.

(2) *vb. tr.* to infer on slight evidence; with two *acc.*: P. L. XI. 340.

Surmount, *vb. tr.* to surpass, exceed; *surmounts my reach*: S. A. 1380; *surmounts the reach of human sense*: P. L. V. 571.

Surname, *vb. tr.* to have an appellation added to the original name; *he surnamed of Africa*: P. R. II. 199; *those surnamed Peripatetics*: P. R. IV. 279.

Surpass, *vb.* (*pres. 2d sing.* surpassest: P. L. VIII. 359) *tr.* (*a*) to go beyond in size; *in bigness to surpass Earth's giant sons*: P. L. I. 778.

(*b*) to exceed in degree or amount: P. L. VII. 640; *thy strength...surpassing human rate*: S. A. 1313; *surpass common revenge*: P. L. II. 370; in excellence or power; *Delia's self in gait surpassed*: P. L. IX. 389; *Thou... surpassest far my naming*: P. L. VIII. 359.

(*c*) to overrun; *the sea surpass his bounds*: P. L. II. 894.

part. adj. **surpassing**, transcendent: P. L. IV. 32.

Surprisal, *sb.* the act of taking unawares or the state of being so taken; *to secure the lady from surprisal*: C. 618; *lest he pretend surprisal*: P. L. V. 245.

Surprise, (1) *sb.* a coming upon unawares, a taking suddenly and without preparation: P. L. II. 134; *by flight or by surprise*: P. L. VI. 87.

(2) *vb. tr.* (*a*) to come upon suddenly and unexpectedly, take or assail off one's guard: P. L. IV. 814; S. A. 381, 1285; *lest Sin surprise thee*: P. L. VII. 547; *by some fair appearing good surprised*: P. L. IX. 354; *pain surprised thee*: P. L. II. 753; *them... joy surprised*: P. L. VI. 774.

(*b*) to seize or take prisoner suddenly: P. L. XI. 218; XII. 453; *Virtue may be...surprised by unjust force*: C. 590.

(*c*) to overpower, confound; *with fear surprised*: P. L. VI.

393, 394; *with deep dismay*: P. R.
I. 108; *by fallacy*: P. R. I. 155.
Surrender, *sb.* the yielding of one's
self to another: P. L. IV. 494.
Surround, *vb. tr.* to encompass, encircle, enclose: P. L. II. 796; Ps.
VII. 26; *as with a shield thou wilt
surround him*: Ps. V. 39; *ever-
during dark surrounds me*: P. L.
III. 46; to occupy completely; *at
last surrounds their sight*: N. O. 109.
part. adj. **surrounding**, encompassing *fires, waste*: P. L. I. 346;
C. 403.
Survey, (1) *sb.* a comprehensive
view: P. L. VIII. 24.
(2) *vb. tr.* (*a*) to view anything
in its entirety, take a comprehensive view of: P. L. III. 69;
his eye surveyed the dark idolatries:
P. L. I. 456; *God saw, surveying
his great work*: P. L. VII. 353;
absol.: P. L. III. 555.
(*b*) to view scrutinizingly, inspect, examine: P. L. VIII. 268;
P. R. I. 37; S. A. 1089, 1227;
*fig., take good heed my hand survey
not thee*: S. A. 1230.
(*c*) to look on, see, view: P. L.
VI. 476.
Survive, *vb. tr.* to live after the
death of, outlive: S. A. 1706.
Sus, *sb.* a province of Morocco;
Mercator *Atlas*, 1636, p. 429: P.
L. XI. 403.
Susa, *sb.* the capital of Susiana and
the winter residence of the Persian kings: P. L. X. 308; P. R.
III. 288.
Susiana, *sb.* a province of the Parthian Empire lying north of the
Persian Gulf and east of the
Tigris River: P. R. III. 321.
Suspect, (1) *sb.* suspicion: V. Ex. 27.
(2) *vb.* (*past part.* suspect: P.
R. II. 399; suspected: P. L. XII.
165) *tr.* (*a*) to imagine to exist,
surmise: P. L. X. 140; with two
*acc.; whom he suspected raised
to end his reign*: P. R. I. 124.
(*b*) to regard with mistrust, distrust: S. A. 272; *a nation...
grown suspected to a sequent king*:
P. L. XII. 165; *what I can do or
offer is suspect*: P. R. II. 399.
(*c*) to hold to be uncertain,
doubt: P. L. IX. 337.
Suspend, *vb. tr.* to hinder temporarily from action or operation,
interrupt, delay; *I suspend their
doom*: P. L. VI. 692; to hold in

rapt attention; *the harmony ...
suspended Hell*: P. L. II. 554.
Suspense, (1) *sb.* a state of uncertainty: S. A. 1569.
(2) *past part.* undecided where
to turn or what to expect, in
suspense; *Expectation held his
look suspense*: P. L. II. 418; *we,
suspense*: P. L. VI. 580; *the great
Light of Day ... suspense in heaven*:
P. L. VII. 99.
Suspicion, *sb.* the unreasonable imagination and apprehension of
something ill: P. L. IX. 1124;
squint suspicion: C. 413; *personified; Suspicion sleeps at Wisdom's
gate*: P. L. III. 686.
Suspicious, *adj.* (*a*) given to suspicion, inclined to mistrust, distrustful: P. L. IX. 92; *of him
suspicious*: P. R. IV. 96.
(*b*) exciting suspicion, questionable; *his life ... little suspicious to
any king*: P. R. II. 82; *knowledge
... suspicious*: P. L. IV. 516.
(*c*) caused by suspicion; *suspicious flight*: C. 158.
Sustain, (1) *sb.* one who upholds
another; *my sustain was the Lord*:
Ps. III. 14.
(2) *vb. tr.* (*a*) to uphold, support: P. L. IX. 336.
(*b*) to keep alive, support,
nourish: P. L. XII. 75; *whatever
was created needs to be sustained*:
P. L. V. 415; *we ... sustained by
him with many comforts*: P. L. X.
1083; to provide with the means
of subsistence; *my labour will
sustain me*: P. L. X. 1056.
(*c*) to endure without falling or
yielding, bear up against: P. L.
VIII. 535; *sustained one day in
doubtful fight*: P. L. VI. 423; *all
the world could not sustain thy
prowess*: P. R. III. 19; *our doom*:
P. L. II. 209; *hostile scorn*: P. L.
V. 904; *sorrow, affliction*, etc.: P.
L. XI. 302; S. A. 1258.
(*d*) to suffer, undergo: P. L.
IX. 978; *ill able to sustain his full
wrath*: P. L. X. 950.
Sustenance, *sb.* that which supports
life; *lying is thy sustenance*: P. R.
I. 429.
Swaddling, *part. adj.* used in swath-
ing a child: N. O. 228.
Swage, *vb. tr.* to assuage, quiet,
soothe: P. L. I. 556; *swage the
tumours of a troubled mind*: S. A.
184.

Swain, *sb.* a rustic, usually a shepherd : C. 84, 951 ; *dull* : C. 634 ; *some unheedy* : M. W. 38 ; *spec.* the singer of Lycidas : L. 186 ; Lycidas : L. 92, 113 ; the Spirit as Thyrsis : C. 497, 900 ; Meliboeus : C. 852 ; Satan in disguise : P. R. I. 337 ; the characters in the Arcades : A. 26.

Swallow, *sb.* the bird *Hirundo* : Ps. LXXXIV. 11.

Swallow, *vb. tr.* to cause to disappear, engulf, devour ; *the sea swallows him* : P. L. XII. 196 ; with *up* : P. L. IX. 642 ; *our... happy state here swallowed up in endless misery* : P. L. I\ 142 ; *the shortened light soon swallowed up in dark...night* : P. 7 ; *thoughts... swallowed up and lost in the wide womb of uncreated Night* : P. L. II. 149.

Swan, *sb.* the bird *Cygnus* : P. L. VII. 438.

Swarm, (1) *sb.* a large number or body of insects ; *a swarm of flies* : P. R. IV. 15 ; *a deadly swarm of hornets* : S. A. 19.

(2) *vb. intr.* (*a*) to come forth in great numbers ; *swarming next appeared the female bee* : P. L. VIII. 489 ; to light in great numbers ; *a darksome cloud of locusts swarming down* : P. L. XII. 185.

(*b*) to throng in multitudes : P. L. I. 776 ; II. 903 ; *in prosperous days they* (friends) *swarm* : S. A. 192 ; *a multitude of thoughts at once awakened in me swarm* : P. R. I. 197.

(*c*) to be filled with multitudes ; *the spacious hall...thick swarmed* : P. L. I. 767 ; *each creek and bay, with fry innumerable swarm* : P. L. VII. 400.

(*d*) to breed multitudes ; *not so thick swarmed once the soil* : P. L. X. 526.

See **Thick-swarming.**

Swart, *adj.* (*a*) swarthy, very dark : C. 436.

(*b*) causing swarthiness ; *the swart star,* Sirius, the dog-star, so called because supposed to be connected with the oppressive heat of summer which blackens vegetation : L. 138.

Sway, I. *sb.* (*a*) inclination, preponderance ; *turn the sway of battle* : P. L. VI. 234.

(*b*) swing, sweep : P. L. VI. 251.

(*c*) rule, dominion : P. L. II. 984 ; *temperate* : P. R. III. 160 ; *Neptune, besides the sway of every salt flood* : C. 18 ; *the Old Dragon ...his usurped sway* : N. O. 170 ; control, mastery : P. L. IV. 308 ; *Appetite ... usurping over Reason, claimed superior sway* : P. L. IX. 1131 ; *the jealousy of love, powerful of sway* : S. A. 791.

II. *vb.* (1) *intr.* to bear rule, have dominion : S. XVIII. 11 ; *there let him* (God) *still victor sway* : P. L. X. 376.

(2) *tr.* (*a*) to cause to move, or to direct the movements of ; *whose love their motion swayed* : S. M. 22.

(*b*) to cause to bend or move aside : P. L. IV. 983.

(*c*) to rule, govern : Ps. II. 18 ; *where Rome was to sway the world* : P. L. XI. 405 ; *his full sceptre sway,* rule with his power : P. R. III. 405 ; to manage, control ; *a gentle Nymph ... with moist curb sways the smooth Severn stream* : C. 825.

(*d*) to influence or direct in conduct : P. L. X. 1010 ; *not swayed by female usurpation* : S. A. 1059 ; *lest passion sway thy judgment to do aught* : P. L. VIII. 635.

Swear, *vb.* (*pret.* swore ; *past part.* sworn) (1) *intr.* to utter a solemn declaration ; *so Jove hath sworn* : C. 1011.

(2) *tr.* (*a*) to utter or affirm in a solemn manner ; *his covenant sworn to David* : P. L. XII. 346 ; *by myself have sworn to him shall bow all knees in Heaven* : P. L. V. 607 ; *the just decree of God, pronounced and sworn, that to his only Son ... every soul in Heaven shall bend the knee* : P. L. V. 814.

(*b*) to promise in a solemn manner, vow : P. L. IV. 96 ; *have ye sworn to adore the Conqueror* : P. L. I. 322.

(*c*) to declare upon oath ; *the ...nurse hath sworn she did them spy* : V. Ex. 61.

Sweat, (1) *sb.* the moisture exuded from the skin ; *balmy sweat* : P. L. VIII. 255 ; *in the sweat of thy face thou shalt eat bread* : P. L. X. 205 ; *labour...with sweat imposed* : P. L. XI. 172.

(2) *vb. intr.* (*a*) to exude moisture ; *the chill marble seems to sweat* : N. O. 195.

(*b*) to perspire from hard labour, toil, drudge : L'A. 105.

Sweaty, *adj*. moist with sweat : P. L. XI. 434.

Swede, *sb*. the Swedish people, and esp. the Swedish army : S. XXI. 8.

Sweep, *vb.* (only in *pres.*) (**1**) *intr.* to pass with swift but stately motion ; *Tragedy in sceptred pall come sweeping by* : Il P. 98.

(**2**) *tr.* to pass the hand over with a long quick stroke ; *sweep the string* : L. 17.

Sweet, I. *adj.* (**1**) pleasing to the sense of taste : P. R. II. 265 ; *sweet kernels* : P. L. V. 346 ; *must* : P. R. IV. 16 ; *repast* : P. L. V. 630 ; VIII. 214 ; IX. 407 ; *O fruit divine, sweet of thyself, but much more sweet thus cropt* : P. L. V. 68 ; *the sweet poison of misused wine* : C. 47 ; *sup.*, *season him* (man) *thy last and sweetest prey* : P. L. X. 609.

(**2**) pleasing to any of the other senses ; (*a*) to the sense of smell : P. L. XI. 281 ; *odours sweet* : N. O. 23 ; *flowers* : P. L. IX. 408 ; *dews and flowers* : P. L. V. 212 ; *smelling* or *smelt sweet* : P. L. VII. 319 ; Ariosto II. 2 ; *sup.*, *sweetest scents* : P. L. IX. 200 ; *fennel* : P. L. IX. 581.

(*b*) to the ear : P. L. III. 346 ; *voices sweet* : P. L. I. 712 ; *accent* : P. L. IX. 321 ; *preamble*, *song*, *music* : P. L. III. 367 ; S. A. 1737 ; N. O. 93 ; Il P. 151 ; C. 878 ; *all organs of sweet stop* : P. L. VII. 596 ; or in sense (3), *sup.* : Il P. 56.

(*c*) to the sight : P. L. XI. 281 ; *sweet garland wreaths* : C. 850.

(*d*) to the touch ; *the breath of heaven fresh blowing, pure and sweet* : S. A. 10.

(**3**) pleasing to the mind or emotional nature, charming, delightful, attractive, agreeable, grateful : P. L. II. 608 ; VIII. 602 ; IX. 272, 473, 899 ; X. 359 ; A. 68 ; L. 179 ; *so sweet a child* : D. F. I. 71 ; *the Law of God I read, and found it sweet* : P. R. I. 207 ; *grace* or *graces* : P. L. IV. 298 ; M. W. 15 ; *joys, remorse, delight*, etc. : P. L. II. 820 ; V. 134 ; IX. 171 ; P. R. II. 373 ; C. 261, 368 ; *life, captivity, rest, solitude* : P. L. XII. 221 ; V. Ex. 52 ; M. W. 50 ; C. 376 ; used of a place : P. L. IX. 115 ; *sweet recess* :

P. L. IX. 456 ; XI. 303 ; P. R. IV. 242 ; *grove of Daphne* : P. L. IV. 272 ; of a time of day : P. L. III. 42 ; V. 170 ; P. R. IV. 438 ; *the breath of Morn, her rising sweet* : P. L. IV. 641 ; *sweet the coming-on of Evening* : P. L. IV. 646 ; of an action : P. L. IV. 328 ; *nor walk by moon ... without thee is sweet* : P. L. IV. 656 ; *our delightful task ... with thee were sweet* : P. L. IV. 439 ; *sweet ... delay, return* : P. L. IV. 311 ; IX. 250 ; *embraces* : P. L. X. 994 ; *rapine* : P. L. IX. 461 ; *discourse, communion, intercession*, etc. : P. L. II. 555 ; V. 637 ; IX. 238, 909 ; X. 228 ; XII. 5 ; *comp.* : P. L. VIII. 211.

(*b*) used as a term of endearment or admiration : Ps. LXXXV. 43 ; *the mountain-nymph, sweet Liberty* : L'A. 33 ; *sweet bird* : Il P. 61 ; *sweet Echo* : C. 230 ; *sweet Queen of Parley* : C. 241 ; *sup.*, *sweetest nymph* : C. 230 ; *sweetest Shakespeare* : L'A. 133.

(*c*) gracious, kind, gentle ; *shedding sweet influence* : P. L. VII. 375 ; *the radiant sun, with farewell sweet* : P. L. II. 492.

II. *sb.* (**1**) that which is pleasing to the sense of taste : P. L. IX. 986 ; *taste thy sweet* : P. L. V. 59 ; *fig.*, *divine Philosophy ... a perpetual feast of nectared sweets* : C. 479.

(**2**) that which is pleasing to the sense of smell : P. L. V. 296 ; *those odorous sweets* : P. L. IV. 166 ; *cassia, nard, and balm, a wilderness of sweets* : P. L. IV. 294 ; *the bee ... extracting liquid sweet* : P. L. V. 25.

(**3**) that which delights the mind ; (*a*) pleasure ; *the sweet of life* : P. L. VIII. 184 ; *domestic sweets* : P. L. IV. 760 ; *night hath better sweets to prove* : C. 123.

(*b*) graciousness, charm : P. R. II. 160.

III. *adv.* (*a*) in a manner pleasing to the ear ; *how sweet thou sing'st* : C. 567 ; *sup.*, *tunes sweetest his ... song* : P. L. V. 41.

(*b*) happily, blissfully : C. 1005.

(*c*) kindly, graciously ; *sweet smiling youth* : D. F. I. 53.

Sweet-briar, *sb.* the flower *Rosa rubiginosa* : L'A. 47.

Sweeten, *vb. tr.* to make sweeter to the sense of smell : C. 496.

Sweetly, *adv.* in a manner agreeable to the sense of hearing: V. Ex. 63 ; Cir. 4 ; C. 249.

Sweetness, *sb.* (*a*) the quality of being pleasing to the ear ; *thy words... bring to their sweetness no satiety* : P. L. VIII. 216 ; used of music : Il P. 164 ; *lute or harp to add more sweetness* : P. L. V. 152 ; *linked sweetness* : L'A. 140.

(*b*) loveliness of disposition, gentleness, kindness : S. XXIII. 11.

(*c*) joy, delight : P. L. VIII. 475.

Sweet-smelling, *adj.* fragrant ; *herbs, gums* : P. L. IV. 709 ; XI. 327.

Swell, *vb.* (*pret.* not used ; *past part.* swoln) *intr.* (*a*) to grow bigger, increase in size ; *the sea... would swell* : C. 732 ; *the hungry sheep... swoln with wind* : L. 126.

(*b*) to be puffed up or filled *with pride* : P. R. III. 81 ; S. A. 532 ; *with rage* : P. R. IV. 499.

(*c*) to act arrogantly ; *thy furious foes now swell* : Ps. LXXXIII. 5.

part. adj. **swelling** ; (*a*) rounded ; *her swelling breast* : P. L. IV. 495.

(*b*) bombastic ; *swelling epithets* : P. R. IV. 343.

Swerve, *vb. intr.* (*a*) to turn aside from the right or intended course : P. L. VI. 386.

(*b*) to go astray from right or duty : P. L. V. 238 ; IX. 359 ; with *from* : Ps. LXXXI. 16 ; *to swerve from truth* : P. L. V. 902.

Swift, I. *adj.* (1) moving with great speed, rapid, quick, fleet : P. L. I. 326 ; II. 902 ; VIII. 133 ; *he... to mischief swift* : P. L. IX. 633 ; *swift flights of angels* : P. R. II. 385 ; *puts on swift wing* : P. L. II. 631 ; *the swift stag* : P. L. VII. 469 ; *floods* : P. L. VII. 295 ; *thought* : P. L. VI. 192 ; *comp.* : P. L. II. 791 ; *sup.* : P. L. VI. 535.

(*b*) flowing rapidly ; *Severn swift* : V. Ex. 96 ; *swift Hebrus* : L. 63.

(*c*) passing rapidly ; *sup.*, *swiftest minutes* : P. L. X. 91.

(2) made with or requiring great speed ; *swift race* : P. L. II. 529 ; *prevention* : P. L. VI. 320 ; *wheel* : P. L. VI. 326 ; *ascent* : P. L. X. 224 ; *flight* : C. 579 ; *winged expedition swift as the lightning glance* : S. A. 1284 ; *lead in swift round the months and years* : C. 114 ; *bear his swift errands* : P.

L. III. 652 ; carried out or performed with great speed ; *immediate are the acts of God, more swift than time or motion* : P. L. VII. 176.

(3) quick, prompt : P. L. VIII. 21 ; *will be swift to aid* : C. 855.

(*b*) coming quickly and unexpectedly ; *swift destruction* : P. L. V. 907.

(4) instant, immediate ; *swift descent* : P. L. XI. 127.

II. *adv.* with speed, rapidly : P. L. III. 582, 714 ; VI. 190, 596 ; *swift as a shooting star* : P. L. IV. 556 ; *swift as the sparkle of a glancing star* : C. 80 ; *incredible how swift* : P. L. IV. 593.

Swiftly, *adv.* rapidly, quickly, speedily : P. L. IX. 631 ; V. Ex. 28.

Swiftness, *sb.* rapid motion : P. L. VIII. 107 ; *speed, to describe whose swiftness number fails* : P. L. VIII. 38.

Swift-rushing, *adj.* moving or approaching with great rapidity : D. F. I. 67.

Swilled, *part. adj.* drunken : C. 178.

Swim, *vb.* (*pret.* and *past part.* swum) (1) *intr.* (*a*) to move in or through water by natural means of propulsion : P. L. II. 950 ; XI. 626 ; *there leviathan... sleeps or swims* : P. L. VII. 414.

(*b*) to overflow, abound ; *they swim in mirth* : P. L. IX. 1009 ; *now swim in joy* : P. L. XI. 625.

(*c*) to be supported on water, float : P. L. XI. 753 ; *the floating vessel swum* : P. L. XI. 745.

(2) *tr.* to move in or through by such means ; *leviathan.. hugest that swim the ocean stream* : P. L. I. 202 ; *Water... by .. fish ... was swum* : P. L. VII. 503.

Swim, *vb.* (*pret.* swum) *intr.* to have a giddy sensation : P. L. II. 753.

Swine, *sb.* the animal *Sus* : C. 53 ; *pl.*, *a herd of swine* : P. R. IV. 630.

Swing, *vb.* (only in *pres.*) (1) *intr.* to wave to and fro while suspended, oscillate : Il P. 76.

(2) *tr.* to support and move to and fro ; *swing thee in the air* : S. A. 1240.

Swinge, *vb. tr.* to dash about violently, lash ; *the Old Dragon... swinges the scaly horror of his folded tail* : N. O. 172.

Swinish, *adj.* beastly : C. 776.

Swinked, *part. adj.* wearied with labour : C. 293.

Swooning, (1) *vbl. sb.* the act of fainting ; *these swoonings of despair* : S. A. 1631.

(2) *part. adj. swooning bed,* a bed where one has swooned : U. C. II. 17.

Sword, *sb.* (1) the weapon consisting of a long blade fixed in a hilt : S. A. 1165 ; C. 601, 611 ; *hostile* : S. A. 692 ; worn or used by Christ or angels : P. L. VI. 714 ; XI. 247 ; *the brandished sword of God* : P. L. XII. 633 ; *the sword of Michael* : P. L. II. 294 ; VI. 250, 320 ; *the sword of Satan* : P. L. VI. 324 ; *flaming, fiery* : P. L. I. 664 ; VI. 304 ; XII. 592 ; *of a sword the flame* : P. L. XI. 120 ; *avenging* : P. L. VI. 278 ; *griding* : P. L. VI. 329.

(*b*) *fig.* a means of punishment : Ps. VII. 46.

(*c*) *fig.* war or power ; *adjure the civil sword* : F. of C. 5 ; *to know both spiritual power and civil ... the bounds of either sword to thee we owe* : S. XVII. 12.

(*d*) *fig.* extreme anguish : P. R. II. 91.

(2) that which is used as a sword ; *the jaw of a dead ass, his sword of bone* : S. A. 143.

Sworded, *part. adj.* armed with a sword ; *sworded seraphim* : N. O. 113.

Sword-law, *sb.* government by force : P. L. XI. 672.

Sword-player, *sb.* fencer : S. A. 1323.

Syene, *sb.* a city of Upper Egypt on the confines of Ethiopia, marking the southernmost boundary of the Roman Empire : P. R. IV. 70.

Syllable, *vb. tr.* to pronounce clearly, utter : C. 208.

Sylvan, *adj.* (*a*) of or pertaining to a wood ; *sylvan lodge* : P. L. V. 377 ; rustic ; *sylvan pipe* : P. R. I. 480.

(*b*) abounding with woods ; *a sylvan scene* : P. L. IV. 140.

Sylvan, *sb.* Sylvanus : Il P. 134 ; *Satyr, or Faun, or Silvan* : P. R. II. 191 ; *Pan or Sylvan* : C. 268.

Sylvanus, *sb.* the god of the woods ; *Pan or Sylvanus* : P. L. IV. 707.

Sylvestro, *sb.* Pope Silvester I. : Ariosto 4.

Sympathize, *vb. intr.* to have or exhibit sympathy ; *that dumb things would be moved to sympathize* : C. 796 ; *Nature ... with her great Master so to sympathize* : N. O. 34.

Sympathy, *sb.* (*a*) a feeling similar to or identical with that which another feels ; *looks of sympathy and love* : P. L. IV. 465 ; a similarity of suffering ; *horror on them fell, and horrid sympathy* : P. L. X. 540.

(*b*) physical attraction at a distance : P. L. X. 246.

Symphonious, *adj.* harmonious : P. L. VII. 559.

Symphony, *sb.* harmony of sounds, either vocal or instrumental, or both ; *choral symphony* : P. L. V. 162 ; *angelic* : N. O. 132 ; *charming* : P. L. III. 368 ; XI. 595 ; *dulcet* : P. L. I. 712.

Synod, *sb.* (*a*) a deliberative assembly ; *well have ye judged ... Synod of Gods* : P. L. II. 391 ; *a third part of the Gods, in synod met* : P. L. VI. 156 : *let us call to synod all the Blest through Heaven's wide bound* : P. L. XI. 67.

(*b*) the conjunction of two or more planets : P. L. X. 661.

Syrian, *adj.* of or pertaining to Syria, the country in Asia : P. L. I. 421, 448, 474 ; XI. 218 ; M. W. 63.

Syrinx, *sb.* an Arcadian nymph who, pursued by Pan, fled into the river Ladon, and was changed into a reed : P. R. II. 188 ; A. 106, 107.

Syrtis, *sb.* Syrtis Major and Syrtis Minor, the ancient names of two gulfs off the northern coast of Africa, the modern gulfs of Cabes and Sidra. They were well known for their quicksands ; hence here used for a quicksand : P. L. II. 939.

Syrup, *sb.* a flavoured solution of sugar in water : C. 674.

T

Tabernacle, *sb.* (1) a temporary shelter, tent, booth ; *celestial tabernacles* : P. L. V. 654.

(*b*) *fig.* the human body of Christ ; *fleshly tabernacle* : P. R. IV. 599 ; P. 17 ; the clouds as the abode of light ; *she in a cloudy tabernacle sojourned* : P. L. VII. 248.

Table] 535 [Take

(2) the portable tent-like structure that served the Israelites as a sanctuary during their wandering in the wilderness : P. L. XII. 247.

(3) *pl.* the temple at Jerusalem : Ps. LXXXIV. 3.

Table, *sb.* the article of furniture on which food is served : P. R. II. 340, 384, 402 ; *before him spread a table of celestial food* : P. R. IV. 588 ; *citron tables* : P. R. IV. 115 ; as made of turf : P. L. V. 391, 392 ; *at table Eve ministered* : P. L. V. 443 ; in heaven ; *tables are set, and on a sudden piled with Angels' food* : P. L. V. 632.

See **Council-Table.**

Tacit, *adj.* secret : S. A. 430.

Tackle, *sb.* the ropes of a ship, cordage : P. L. II. 1044 ; *fig.* : S. A. 717.

Tail, *sb.* the hindmost part of a serpent or dragon : P. L. X. 523 ; *a scorpion's tail* : S. A. 360 ; *the Old Dragon … swinges the scaly horror of his folded tail* : N. O. 172.

Taint, (1) *sb.* a moral stain or blemish, corruption : P. L. X. 631 ; *without taint of sin* : S. A. 312 ; both physical and moral ; *washed from spot of child-bed taint* : S. XXIII. 5.

(2) *vb. tr.* (*a*) to render impure, contaminate, infect ; *to sound or taint integrity* : P. L. V. 704 ; *taint the animal spirits* : P. L. IV. 804.

(*b*) to corrupt morally ; *eject him, tainted now* : P. L. XI. 52.

(*c*) to stain, sully ; *the truth with superstitions … taint* : P. L. XII. 512.

Take, *vb.* (*pret.* took ; *2d sing.* took'st : P. L. II. 765 ; S. A. 838, 1591 ; *past part.* taken : P. L. X. 207 ; XI. 98, 262 ; P. R. II. 177 ; ta'en : C. 541 ; U. C. I. 13 ; took : C. 558 ; N. O. 20 ; W. S. 12) *tr.* (1) to lay hold of with the hand, grasp, seize : P. L. III. 365 ; *by the hand he took me* : P. L. VIII. 300 ; *in his hand he took the golden compasses* : P. L. VII. 225.

(2) to bring into one's possession ; (*a*) to seize, capture : S. A. 1183, 1203.

(*b*) to obtain in marriage ; *the next I took to wife* : S. A. 227.

(3) to appropriate, make one's own : P. R. III. 140.

(4) to invest oneself with, assume ; *take the weeds and likeness of a swain* : C. 84 ; *took his image whom they served* : P. L. XI. 517.

(5) to receive : S. A. 826 ; W. S. 12 ; *heaven … hath took no print of the approaching light* : N. O. 20.

(*b*) to receive as news ; *then take the worst in brief* : S. A. 1570.

(*c*) to receive as true or honest ; *I take thy word* : C. 321.

(6) to have the sense of, feel : Ps. V. 9 ; *such joy thou took'st* : P. L. II. 765 ; *took envy* : P. L. VI. 793 ; *pleasure took* : P. L. IX. 455 ; *takes his pleasure* : 11 P. 50.

(7) to infect or affect with some emotion : V. Ex. 20 ; used of music ; *took with ravishment the … audience* : P. L. II. 554 ; *the stringed noise, as all their souls in blissful rapture took* : N. O. 98.

(8) to charm, captivate : P. R. II. 177 ; used of music ; *the Sirens … would take the prisoned soul* : C. 256 ; *Silence was took ere she was ware* : C. 558.

(9) to lay hold of and bear away or remove : P. L. VIII. 536 ; *from her side the fatal key … she took* : P. L. II. 872 ; *of light by far the greater part he took* : P. L. VII. 359 ; *took from thence a rib* : P. L. VIII. 465.

(*b*) to lift and bear away : P. R. IV. 394 ; with *up* : P. R. III. 251 ; D. F. I. 46.

(*c*) to bear, convey : S. A. 1345.

(10) to remove from others and lead away ; *to him takes a chosen band of Spirits* : P. R. II. 236.

(11) to make or create ; *thou out of the ground wast taken* : P. L. X. 207 ; *the ground whence he was taken* or *thou wast taken* : P. L. XI. 98, 262.

(12) to judge, deem ; *I took it for a faery vision* : C. 298.

(13) joined to a sb., with which it forms an expression approximately equivalent in sense to the corresponding vb. ; *take account* : P. L. IV. 622 ; *care of* : S. A. 928 ; *choice* : P. L. XI. 100 ; *their fill* : P. L. IX. 1043 ; *fire* : Ps. II. 27 ; LXXXIII. 53 ; *heed* : P. L. VIII. 635 ; S. A. 1230 ; *full possession* : S. A. 869 ; *root* : P. L. IX. 1105 ; XI. 834 ; *seat* : P. L. XI. 82 ; *supper* : C. 541 ; *thought* : P. L. IX. 1004 ; *take alarm*, to obey a

summons to arms : P. L. VI. 549;
take flight, to fly : P. R. II. 241 ;
to depart : D. F. I. 42 ; to proceed
on their way : N. O. 72 ; *take leave*,
to bid farewell : P. L. III. 739.

In combination with other words;
(*a*) take away, to remove : U. C.
I. 16.

(*b*) take in, to admit, receive :
C. 834 ; to obtain : C. 20 ; to
receive into the mind through the
ear : C. 561.

(*c*) take in hand, to undertake :
Ps. I. 10.

(*d*) take on, to assume the burden of : S. A. 241.

(*e*) take up, to set up, begin :
P. 51 ; to enter into and sojourn ;
had ta'en up his latest inn : U. C.
I. 13.

(*f*) take ... way, to go over a
certain path : P. L. IX. 847 ; XI.
223 ; XII. 649 ; to use means : S.
A. 838, 1591.

Tale, *sb.* (*a*) number : L'A. 67.

(*b*) something told, story, narrative : L'A. 115 ; C. 44 ; *the tale
of Troy divine* : Il P. 100.

See Love-tale, Tell-tale.

Talent, *sb.* mental power considered
as a trust, faculty, gift : S. XIX. 3.

Talk, I. *sb.* (*a*) discourse, speech,
conversation : P. R. IV. 171 ; *our
last evening's talk* : P. L. V. 115 ;
*no more of talk where God or Angel
Guest ... familiar used to sit* : P. L.
IX. 1 ; *talk ... food of the mind* :
P. L. IX. 237 ; *tedious, foul* : P.
R. IV. 307 ; C. 464.

(*b*) report, rumour : S. A. 188.

(*c*) a subject of talk ; *to ... be
their talk* : P. R. III. 55.

II. *vb.* (1) *intr.* (*a*) to communicate or exchange ideas by speech :
P. R. I. 485 ; *talking like this
world's brood* : Ps. IV. 27 ; *so
talked* : P. L. IX. 613 ; P. R. IV.
484 ; *thus talking* : P. L. IV. 689 ;
as they talked : P. L. XI. 444 ;
with him talked : P. L. XI. 322 ;
P. R. II. 6 ; *Satan, talking to his
nearest mate* : P. L. I. 192 ; with
of : P. L. IV. 970 ; P. R. IV. 125.

(*b*) to discuss, argue ; *much of
the soul they talk* : P. R. IV. 313.

(2) *tr.* (*a*) to express in words ;
*whatever hypocrites austerely talk
of purity* : P. L. IV. 744.

(*b*) to discuss or reason about ;
the trepidation talked : P. L. III.
483.

Tall, *adj.* having more than average
height : P. L. IV. 288, 477 ; *a
Cherub tall* : P. L. I. 534 ; *tall
stripling youths* : P. R. II. 352;
timber, saplings, wood : P. L. XI.
728 ; A. 46 ; C. 270 ; *cedars* : Ps.
LXXX. 43 ; *sup., tallest pine, pines* :
P. L. I. 292 ; P. R. IV. 416.

Talon, *sb.* the claw of a bird of
prey ; *harpies' ... talons* : P. R. II.
403.

Tame, (1) *adj.* having lost its native
wildness, domesticated : S. A.
538, 1695.

(2) *vb. tr.* (*a*) to reduce from a
wild to a domestic state, make
gentle ; *she tamed the brinded
lioness* : C. 443.

(*b*) to bring into subjection,
conquer, subdue : P. L. XII. 191 ;
*I thought gyves and the mill had
tamed thee* : S. A. 1093 ; *hunger,
that each other creature tames* : P.
R. II. 406 ; *to soften and tame
severest temper* : P. R. II. 163 ; to
conquer or subdue in war : P. L.
VI. 686.

Tamely, *adv.* submissively, without
opposition : P. L. II. 1028.

Tangle, (1) *sb.* (*a*) interlaced locks ;
the tangles of Neæra's hair : L. 69.

(*b*) a fold or coil of a serpent's
body ; *he ... swiftly rolled in tangles* :
P. L. IX. 632.

(2) *vb. tr.* to entangle, ensnare ;
hearts ... tangled in amorous nets :
P. R. II. 162 ; *tangled in the fold
of dire Necessity* : S. A. 1665.

part. adj. (1) tangling, growing
thickly and confusedly together :
P. L. IV. 176.

(2) tangled, dense and pathless ;
tangled wood, thickets : N. O. 188;
C. 181.

Tanned, *part. adj.* browned by
exposure to the sun ; *the tanned
haycock* : L'A. 90.

Tantalus, *sb.* the king who was
punished in the lower world by
being placed up to his chin in
water and under a loaded fruit
tree ; the water and fruit retreated
whenever he sought to satisfy his
thirst or hunger : P. L. II. 614.

Taper, *sb.* a candle ; *taper clear* :
L'A. 126 ; *gentle* : C. 337 ; *tapers'
holy shine* : N. O. 202.

Tapestry, *sb.* *attrib.* hung with
tapestry ; *tapestry halls* : C. 324.

Taprobane, *sb.* the ancient name of
Ceylon : P. R. IV. 75.

Tardy, *adj.* not performed at the appointed time : P. L. X. 853.

Targe, *sb.* shield : P. L. IX. 1111.

Tarpeian, *adj. Tarpeian rock,* the southern peak of the Capitoline Hill at Rome ; apparently here applied to the whole hill, including the northern peak, the Arx : P. R. IV. 49.

Tarsus, *sb.* the capital of Cilicia ; *ancient* : P. L. I. 200 ; *like a stately ship of Tarsus* : S. A. 715.

Tartar, (1) *sb.* a native of Tartary, the country of Central Asia. " It is situate in the North, on the East it hath the most potent kingdome of China; on the South India, the Rivers Ganges and Oxus, on the West the Caspian Sea and Poland, from thence it confineth on Moscovie, and on the North the freezing Sea." Mercator *Atlas,* 1635, p. 860 ; see also Heylyn *Cos.,* 1657, p. 840 : P. L. III. 432 ; the Tartar army : P. L. X. 431.

(2) *adj.* of Tartary : Il P. 115.

Tartarean, *adj.* of hell : P. L. II. 69.

Tartareous, *adj.* resembling that of hell : P. L. VII. 238.

Tartarus, *sb.* hell ; *the gulf of* : P. L. VI. 54 ; *this gloom of* : P. L. II. 858.

Task, *sb.* (*a*) labour imposed, work to be done : P. L. IX. 221 ; C. 18, 1012 ; *our pleasant task enjoined* : P. L. IX. 207 ; *our delightful task, to prune these growing plants* : P. L. IV. 437 ; *my task of servile toil* : S. A. 5 ; *to grind in brazen fetters under task* : S. A. 35 ; *the work ... by task transferred from Father to the Son* : P. L. V. 854 ; *this must be our task in Heaven* : P. L. II. 246 ; *my noble task* : S. XXII. 11 ; *sad* : P. L. V. 564.

(*b*) work voluntarily undertaken : P. R. I. 427 ; III. 368 ; *to do ought good never will be our task* : P. L. I. 159 ; *sad* : P. L. IX. 13 ; or in sense (*a*) : V. Ex. 8 ; *yet a nobler task awaits thy hand* : S. XV. 9.

Task-master, *sb.* one who imposes a task upon another ; applied to God : S. II. 14.

Tasseled, *part. adj.* decorated with tassels ; *tasseled horn* : A. 57.

Taste, I. *sb.* (*a*) the act of tasting, gustation : P. L. IX. 786, 931 ; *whose mortal taste brought death into the World* : P. L. I. 2 ; *the*

water flies all taste : P. L. II. 613 ; *his taste of that defended fruit* : P. L. XI. 85 ; *whose taste* : P. L. IX. 747 ; *their taste* : P. R. II. 371.

(*b*) experience ; *your taste is now of joy* : P. L. IV. 369 ; *thy senses ... all taste of pleasure must forgo* : P. L. XI. 541.

(*c*) the particular sensation excited in the organs of taste, flavour, relish : P. L. VII. 49 ; *of Attic taste* : S. XX. 10 ; *not to mix tastes ... but bring taste after taste upheld with kindly change* : P. L. V. 335, 336 ; the flavour of fruit : P. L. IV. 217 ; *of taste to please true appetite* : P. L. V. 304 ; *taste so divine* : P. L. IX. 986 ; *delicious* : P. L. IV. 251 ; of wine : S. A. 545.

(*d*) the sense of taste by which the relish of things is perceived : P. L. VIII. 527 ; X. 563, 566 ; *this fruit ... inviting to the taste* : P. L. IX. 777 ; *to please and sate the curious taste* : C. 714 ; used with the double meaning of (*d*) and (*e*) ; *I see thou art exact of taste and elegant* : P. L. IX. 1017.

(*e*) intellectual appreciation ; *bred only and completed to the taste of lustful appetence* : P. L. XI. 618.

II. *vb.* (1) *tr.* (*a*) to try, prove ; *have tasted him* : P. R. II. 131 ; with two *acc.*; *hath been tasted such* : P. L. IX. 867 ; *absol.* : S. A. 1091.

(*b*) to perceive by the sense of taste ; *taste the savour of death* : P. L. X. 268.

(*c*) to eat or drink of : P. L. V. 369, 397 ; VII. 539 ; C. 66, 702 ; *these earthly fruits to taste* : P. L. V. 464 ; *human food* : P. R. I. 308 ; II. 247 ; *whose charmed cup whoever tasted* : C. 52 ; the thing eaten being the forbidden fruit : P. L. IV. 423, 515 ; V. 77 ; VII. 543 ; IX. 925 ; X. 13 ; *to taste that tree* : P. L. IV. 427 ; *taste thy sweet* : P. L. V. 59 ; *tasting those fair apples* : P. L. IX. 585 ; *this fair fruit* : P. L. IX. 972 ; *the fatal fruit* : P. L. X. 4 ; *a tree of danger tasted* : P. L. IX. 864.

absol. or *intr.* : P. L. V. 432 ; C. 813 ; to eat the forbidden fruit : P. L. IV. 527 ; V. 61, 65, 86 ; IX. 688, 732, 742, 753, 770, 866, 874, 881, 883, 935, 988, 1024.

(d) to know by experience; *such delight till then ... in fruit she never tasted* : P. L. IX. 788 ; *my day of grace ... shall never taste* : P. L. III. 199 ; *wilt taste no pleasure* : P. L. VIII. 401 ; to undergo the results of ; *taste thy folly* : P. L. II. 686.

(2) *intr.* (*a*) to try the flavour of food : P. L. V. 411.

(*b*) to eat : P. L. V. 412 ; *of the tree ... shun to taste* : P. L. VIII. 327 ; *of this tree we may not taste* : P. L. IX. 651 ; *whereof we wretched seldom taste* : P. R. I. 345.

(*c*) to have experience ; *to taste of pleasure* : P. L. IX. 476.

part. adj. **tasted,** *at that tasted fruit,* at the eating of that fruit : P. L. X. 687.

Tauric, *adj.* pertaining to the Chersonesus Taurica, the modern Crimea ; *the Tauric pool,* the Sea of Azof : P. R. IV. 79.

Tauris, *sb.* Tabreez or Tabriz, the capital of the province of Azerbaijan in northwestern Persia : P. L. X. 436.

Taurus, *sb.* the zodiacal constellation : P. L. I. 769 ; X. 673.

Tawny, *adj.* of a brownish yellow colour ; *the tawny lion* : P. L. VI. 464 ; *tawny sands* : C. 117.

Tax, *vb. tr.* to censure, blame : S. A. 210.

Teach, *vb.* (*pret.* taught ; *2d sing.* taught'st : S. XI. 14 ; *past part.* taught) *tr.* (1) to point out, show ; *well hast thou taught the way* : P. L. V. 508.

(2) to impart knowledge to, instruct : P. L. XII. 446 ; Ps. II. 23 ; *his Spirit taught them* : P. L. XI. 612 ; *teach the erring soul* : P. R. I. 224 ; *as men divinely taught* : P. R. IV. 357 ; *poets taught by the heavenly Muse* : C. 515 ; *by experience taught* : P. L. V. 826 ; VIII. 190 ; *by temperance taught* : P. L. XI. 531.

(3) to impart the knowledge of, instruct in understanding or using : P. R. IV. 261, 309, 357, 361 ; *to teach his final will* : P. R. I. 461 ; *Socrates ... what he taught* : P. R. III. 97 ; *taught, our laws* : S. XXI. 3 ; *to teach the truth* : Hor. Sat. I. 1.

(4) to impart knowledge to concerning, instruct in ; with *dat.* and *acc.* : P. L. XII. 440 ; S. A.

874 ; *teach me ... thy way* : Ps. LXXXVI. 37 ; *thou taught'st Cambridge and King Edward Greek* : S. XI. 14 ; in passive : P. L. V. 698 ; XII. 572 ; F. of C. 8 ; *Nature taught Art* : P. R. II. 295 ; *hill or valley ... taught his praise* : P. L. V. 204 ; *rhetoric, that hath been so well taught her dazzling fence* : C. 791 ; with *dat.* and *clause* : P. L. I. 8 ; IV. 915 ; *to teach thee that God attributes to place no sanctity* : P. L. XI. 836.

(*b*) to assign, appoint, prescribe; *taught the fixed their influence malign* : P. L. X. 661 ; or to direct, instruct ; *came sevens and pairs ... as taught their order* : P. L. XI. 735.

(*c*) to instruct or train in knowledge of how to do something : P. L. I. 685 ; with *dat.* and *acc.* *our own right hand shall teach us highest deeds* : P. L. V. 865 ; with *acc.* and *prep. inf.* of the thing done : P. L. V. 786 ; X. 1062 ; C. 1020 ; *teach light to counterfeit a gloom* : Il P. 80 ; *taught the tongue to speak thy praise* : P. L. IX. 748 ; *I taught your shades to answer* : P. L. X. 861 ; *taught our English music how to span* : S. XIII. 2 ; in passive : P. L. III. 19 ; VIII. 182 ; IX. 1068 ; *the ravens taught to abstain* : P. R. II. 269.

(5) *absol.* or *intr.* to impart knowledge, instruct : P. R. IV. 220, 227.

Teacher, *sb.* one who teaches : P. L. XII. 508; *the teachers of our Law* : P. R. I. 212 ; *the lofty grave Tragedians ... teachers best* : P. R. IV. 262 ; applied to Michael : P. L. XI. 450 ; a preceptor, instructor : Hor. Sat. I. 2.

Team, *sb.* two or more horses harnessed together for drawing a chariot ; *fig., the heaven, by the Sun's team untrod* : N. O. 19.

Tear, *sb.* a drop of the liquid secreted by the lacrimal gland ; S. A. 200 ; *a gentle tear* : P. L. V. 130 ; *your fiery essence can distil no tear* : Cir. 7 ; *pl.* : P. L. IX. 1121 ; X. 910 ; S. A. 729 ; P. 35, 48 ; Ps. LXXX. 21, 22, 23 ; *with tears watering the ground* : P. L. IX. 1089, 1101 ; *a world of tears* : P. L. XI. 627 ; *another flood, of tears and sorrow a flood* : P. L. XI. 757 ; *my bed I water with* *my tears* : Ps. VI. 13 ; *dewed in tears* : P. L. XII. 373 ; *wipe the tears ... from his eyes* : L. 181 ; *natural, iron* : P. L. XII. 645 ; Il P. 107 ; *parents'* : P. L. I. 393 ; *tears, such as angels weep* : P. L. I. 620 ; rather the act of shedding tears, weeping : P. L. XI. 110 ; S. A. 51, 735 ; *gave him up to tears* : P. L. XI. 497 ; *nothing is here for tears* : S. A. 1721 ; *father's* : S. A. 1459 ; *in tears* : P. L. XI. 674.

(*b*) *fig.* of the water or dew on or in flowers : M. W. 44 : *fill their cups with tears* : L. 150.

(*c*) *fig.* a poem : M. W. 55 ; *some melodious tear* : L. 14.

Tear, *vb.* (*pret.* tore ; *past part.* torn) I. *tr.* (1) to pull apart or in pieces, rend : P. L. II. 1044 ; N. O. 187 ; *who tore the lion as the lion tears the kid* : S. A. 128 ; *to tear thee joint by joint* : S. A. 953 ; *that wild rout that tore the Thracian bard* : P. L. VII. 34 ; *fig., lest he tear my soul asunder* : Ps. VII. 5 ; *absol.* : Ps. VII. 6.

(*b*) *fig.* of the effect of sounds ; *it tore the sky* : S. A. 1472; *a shout that tore Hell's concave* : P. L. I. 542 ; *the air, and all her entrails tore* : P. L. VI. 588 ; of the effect of a combat; *the Elements ... disturbed and torn* : P. L. IV. 994.

(2) to remove violently, drag away, wrench ; *a hill torn from Pelorus* : P. L. I. 232 ; *from her axle torn the steadfast Earth* : P. L. II. 926 ; to uproot violently; *up by the roots tore ... pines* : P. L. II. 543 ; *oaks ... torn up sheer* : P. R. IV. 419.

II. *intr.* to move or rush with violence : P. L. II. 783.

Tease, *vb. tr.* to comb or card (wool): C. 751.

Teat, *sb.* the dug of a beast : P. L. IX. 581.

Tedded, *part. adj.* stirred up and spread loosely about for drying : P. L. IX. 450.

Tedious, *adj.* wearisome, tiresome, too long : P. L. VIII. 389 ; IX. 30 ; *tedious pomp* : P. L. V. 354 ; *bliss* : P. L. IX. 880 ; *talk, song* : P. R. IV. 307 ; N. O. 239 ; *waste of time* : P. R. IV. 123.

Teem, *vb. tr.* to bring forth, produce ; *the Earth ... teemed at a*

birth innumerous living creatures : P. L. VII. 454 ; *that self-begotten bird ... from out her ashy womb now teemed* : S. A. 1703.

part. adj. **teeming,** prolific ; *teeming flocks* : C. 175.

See **Youngest-teemed.**

Telassar, *sb.* a city in western Mesopotamia : P. L. IV. 214.

Telescope, *sb.* the optical instrument for enlarging the image of a distant object on the retina of the eye : P. R. IV. 42.

Tell, *vb.* (*pres.* tell'st : P. L. IV. 588 ; v. 553 ; *pret.* told, *2d sing.* told'st : P. R. I. 137 ; C. 694 ; *past part.* told) I. *tr.* (1) to count, enumerate : L'A. 67.

(*b*) *fig.* to live through ; *summers three times eight she had told* : M. W. 8.

(2) to narrate, recount, relate : P. L. v. 553 ; VII. 101 ; P. R. IV. 113 ; *Eve ... her story told* : P. L. IX. 886 ; *with stories told* : L'A. 101 ; *the rest were long to tell* : P. L. I. 507 ; XII. 261 ; *long were to tell what I have done* : P. L. X. 469 ; with *dat.* and *acc.* : C. 43 ; *I told thee all my state* : P. L. VIII. 521 ; *tell us the sum* : S. A. 1557 ; with clause : L'A. 105 ; *for Man to tell how human life began* : P. L. VIII. 250 ; *tell ... how green-eyed Neptune raves* : V. Ex. 43 ; *if Art could tell how* : P. L. IV. 236 ; *as is told thou didst* : Ps. LXXXIII. 35.

(*b*) to narrate stories of ; *heroes old, such as the wise Demodocus once told* : V. Ex. 48.

(3) to make known, reveal, declare : P. L. III. 8 ; XI. 298 ; P. R. IV. 472 ; S. A. 1433 ; Ps. CXXXVI. 9 ; LXXXVIII. 45 ; H. B. 3 ; *telling their ... faculties* : C. 628 ; *tells the suggested cause* : P. L. V. 702 ; *cannot without process of speech be told* : P. L. VII. 178 ; with *dat.* and *acc.* : P. L. II. 739 ; v. 238 ; with *dat.* and *clause* : P. L. IV. 37 ; VIII. 280 ; P. R. I. 137 ; II. 320 ; III. 396 ; S. A. 202, 1319 ; U. C. II. 23 ; C. 400 ; *tell them that ... I am to haste* : P. L. V. 685 ; *to tell thee all what thou command'st* : P. L. IX. 569 ; *I told ye then he should prevail* : P. L. X. 40 ; *told them the Messiah now was born* : P. R. I. 245 ; *That thou art naked who hath told thee?* :

P. L. X. 122 ; in passive ; *as we
are told* : P. L. IX. 863 ; the
clause omitted : P. R. IV. 467 ;
D. F. I. 38, 51 ; with *acc.* and
to : P. L. XII. 364 ; S. A. 1199 ;
with *clause* : P. L. III. 667 ; v.
698 ; P. R. IV. 153 ; *Prophetic
Writ hath told that it shall never
end* : P. R. III. 184 ; *tell, tell ...
how came I thus* : P. L. VIII. 276,
277 ; the *clause* abbreviated : P. L.
III. 575.

II. *intr.* (*a*) to give an account
or description ; with *of* : P. L.
III. 54 ; *tells of some infernal
Spirit* : P. L. IV. 793 ; *of whom
thou tell'st* : P. L. IV. 588 ; *those
who .. tell of Babel* : P. L. I. 693 ;
tell of deeds : P. R. I. 14 ; with
dat. : C. 240 ; *I'll tell ye* : C. 513 ;
to tell thee : C. 509 ; with *dat.* and
of : C. 236, 458 ; *the safe abode
thou told'st me of* : C. 694.

(*b*) to declare, say ; used parenthetically ; *as seamen tell* : P. L.
I. 205 ; *ye who best can tell* : P. L.
V. 160 ; *so fables tell* : P. R. II.
215 ; *as story tells* : P. R. II.
307 ; *as romances tell* : P. R. III.
339.

vbl. sb. **telling**, the act of making known ; *which might else in
telling wound* : P. L. XI. 299.

See **Half-told.**

Tell-tale, *adj.* that reveals secrets ;
the tell-tale Sun : C. 141.

Temir, *sb.* Tamerlane, the great
Tartar conqueror : P. L. XI. 389.

Temper, I. *sb.* (*a*) temperament,
constitution ; *to the place conformed in temper and in nature* :
P. L. II. 218 ; *our temper changed
into their temper* : P. L. II. 276.

(*b*) disposition or frame of mind,
humour ; *noblest temper* : P. L. I.
552 ; *mild and gracious* : P. L. X.
1047 ; *severest* : P. R. II. 164.

(*c*) the condition of metal as
regards its hardness and brittle-
ness ; *his ponderous shield, ethereal
temper* : P. L. I. 285 ; *celestial
temper* ; *concr.* that which has
been tempered in heaven : P. L.
IV. 812.

II. *vb.* (*pres. 2d sing.* temper'st) :
S. A. 670) *tr.* (**1**) to prepare by
mixing : P. L. V. 347.

(**2**) to mix in the proper proportions ; *fig., most erected spirits,
most tempered pure ethereal* ; P.
R. III. 27.

(*b*) to bring to a proper state or
consistency : P. L. IV. 670 ; VI. 480.

(*c*) to adjust, dispose, or distribute ; *thou ... temper'st thy providence* : S. A. 670.

(**3**) to modify by blending ;
temper joy with fear : P. L. XI.
361 ; *I shall temper so justice with
mercy* : P. L. X. 77.

(**4**) to attune : P. L. VII. 598 ;
*the rural ditties ... tempered to the
oaten flute* : L. 33.

(**5**) to bring to a certain degree
of hardness ; *those bright arms,
though heavenly tempered* : P. L.
II. 813 ; *the sword ... tempered so
that neither keen nor solid might
resist that edge* : P. L. VI. 322.

part. adj. **tempered**, restrained,
moderate : C. 32.

vbl. sb. **tempering**, the action of
bringing to a proper state ; *I have
... drawn empyreal air, thy tempering* : P. L. VII. 15.

See **Chalybean-tempered.**

Temperance, *sb.* moderation in the
indulgence of any natural appetite, especially in that of eating
and drinking : P. L. XI. 805, 807 ;
XII. 583 ; P. R. II. 408 ; III. 92 ;
S. A. 558 ; *temperance ... in what
thou eat'st and drink'st* : P. L. XI.
531 ; *if all the world should, in a
pet of temperance, feed on pulse* :
C. 721 ; *Knowledge ... needs no less
her temperance over appetite* : P.
L. VII. 127 ; *personified* ; *the holy
dictate of spare Temperance* : C.
767.

Temperate, *adj.* (*a*) observing self-
restraint in the indulgence of the
natural appetites : P. L. IV. 134.

(*b*) arising from eating and
drinking not in excess ; *temperate
vapours* : P. L. V. 5.

(*c*) unmarked by passion or
violence, just ; *temperate sway* :
P. R. III. 160.

(*d*) moderate as regards temperature, mild : P. L. XII. 636.

Temperately, *adv.* calmly ; P. R. II.
378.

Tempest, (**1**) *sb.* (*a*) a violent storm :
P. L. II. 290 ; P. R. IV. 465 ; Ps.
LXXXIII. 58 ; in hell ; *a fiery tem-
pest* : P. L. II. 180 ; in chaos : P.
L. III. 429.

(*b*) *fig.* a violent fit of anger or
other passion : S. A. 1063 ; *thy
anger ... still rages, eternal tempest* : S. A. 964.

(c) a tumult or loud noise : P.
L. VI. 190.

(2) *vb. tr.* to create a violent
disturbance in : P. L. VII. 412.

Tempestuous, (1) *adj.* (a) moving in
the manner of a tempest ; *whirlwinds of tempestuous fire* : P. L.
I. 77.

(b) productive of storms : P. L.
X. 664.

(2) *adv.* as a tempest, with
great violence ; *tempestuous fell
his arrows* : P. L. VI. 844.

Temple, *sb.* (1) an edifice consecrated to one or more deities and
forming a seat of their worship :
P. L. I. 713 ; P. R. I. 449 ; III.
268 ; IV. 34 ; S. A. 1378 : *sing.
collect.* : S. VIII. 11 ; consecrated
to Astoreth : P. L. I. 443 ; to
Belial ; *to him no temple stood* :
P. L. I. 492 ; to Dagon : P. L. I.
460, 463 ; S. A. 1146. 1370 ; to
Moloch : P. L. I. 402 ; to Peor
and Baalim : N. O. 198 ; to Diana :
H. B. 6 ; to the sun-god Ra (*see*
Sun) : P. L. V. 274.

(2) an edifice consecrated to the
worship of God : P. L. I. 18,
494.

(b) the seat of the Jewish worship at Jerusalem : P. L. XII.
340 : Ps. LXXXIV. 37 ; LXXXVII.
4 ; *the clouded ark of God ... shall
in a glorious temple enshrine* : P.
L. XII. 334 ; *I ... will towards thy
holy temple worship low* : Ps. V.
20 ; *the Temple of God* : P. L. I.
402 ; *the Temple* : P. L. XII. 356 ;
P. R. I. 211, 256 ; III. 161 ; IV.
217 ; *the glorious Temple* : P. R.
IV. 546.

(c) *fig.* the peculiar dwelling-
place of God in heaven : P. L. VI.
890 ; *this high temple* : P. L. VII.
148.

(3) used *fig.* of Christians as
the dwelling-place of the Spirit
of God ; *his living temples* : P. L.
XII. 527.

(4) used *fig.* of the body ; *the
unpolluted temple of the mind* : C.
461.

Temple, *sb.* the region on each side
of the head in front of the ear
and above the zygoma : S. A.
990.

Temporal, *adj.* pertaining to this
world or to time, not spiritual,
not eternal ; *temporal death* : P.
L. XII. 433.

Tempt, *vb. tr.* (a) to put to trial,
try, test : P. L. IX. 281.

(b) to invite, induce : S. A.
358 ; *tempted our attempt* : P. L.
I. 642 ; *hope ... tempts belief* : S.A.
1535 ; to incite, persuade, prevail upon ; *those who tempted me* :
S. A. 801.

(c) to incite or entice to evil,
seduce : P. L. II. 1032 ; V. 846 ;
P. R. IV. 13 ; *tempt the Son of
God* : P. R. IV. 431, 580 ; *tempt
not the Lord thy God* : P. R. IV.
561 ; *absol.* : P. L. IX. 296, 328 ;
X. 14 ; P. R. I. 143, 178 ; IV.
611 ; *on the fruit she gazed, which
to behold might tempt* : P. L. IX.
736.

(d) to attempt, venture on, try
to reach : P. L. II. 404.

part. adj. **tempting,** inviting,
alluring : P. L. II. 607 ; VIII. 308 ;
IX. 595.

past part. absol. one who is
enticed to evil ; P. L. IX. 297.

See **Self-tempted.**

Temptation (témptation : P. R. II.
405) *sb.* an enticement to evil : P.
L. IV. 65 ; S. A. 427, 1051 ; P.
24 ; esp. Satan's enticement of
Adam or Eve or of Christ :
P. R. I. 123 ; IV. 617 ; *listen not
to his temptations* : P. L. VI. 908 ;
*his fraudulent temptation thus
began* : P. L. IX. 531 ; *his temptation pursued* : P. R. II. 405 ; *all
temptation to transgress repel* : P.
L. VIII. 643 ; *not proof against,
proof against* : P. L. IX. 299 : P.
R. IV. 533 ; *seek not temptation* :
P. L. IX. 364 ; *victory over* : P. R.
IV. 595 ; *by vanquishing* : P. R.
IV. 608 ; *fierce* : P. 24.

Tempter, *sb.* one who incites to evil ;
applied to Satan : P. L. X. 39 ;
P. R. IV. 617 ; *the Tempter* : P.
L. IX. 549, 655, 665, 678 ; X. 552 ;
XI. 382 ; P. R. I. 5 ; II. 366 ; III.
108, 203, 265 ; IV. 2, 43, 154,
408, 569, 595 ; *the tempter .. of
mankind* : P. L. IV. 10 ; *thou
stood'st up his tempter* : P. R. II.
409 ; *guileful, importune* : P. L.
IX. 567 ; P. R. II. 404.

Ten, *adj.* nine and one : P. L. II.
671 ; VI. 193 ; XII. 190 ; P. R.
III. 377 ; L'A. 109 ; *for one tree
had been forbidden ten* : P. L. IX.
1026 ; *those ten tribes* : P. R. III.
374, 403 ; *ten years* : U. C. I. 7 ;
four times ten days : P. R. II.

245 ; *twice ten degrees* : P. L. X.
669 ; *ten thousand* : P. L. I. 545 ;
II. 934 ; III. 488 ; V. 588 ; VI.
767, 836 ; VII. 559 ; P. R. III. 411 ;
ten thousandfold : P. L. XI. 678.

Tend, *vb. intr.* (1) to move in a
specified direction, hold a certain
course ; *thither let us tend* : P. L.
I. 183 ; *to Paradise first tending* :
P. L. X. 326 ; *this way some other
tending* : S. A. 1302.

(*b*) *fig.* of development from
lower to higher forms : P. L. V.
476 ; of growth ; *tending to wild* :
P. L. IX. 212.

(*c*) to move in a certain direction morally ; *this latter, as the
former world, shall tend from bad
to worse* : P. L. XII. 106.

(2) to take a specified course of
action ; *the way which to her ruin
now I tend* : P. L. IX. 493.

(3) to exert an influence in a
certain direction, have a bent,
aim, incline : P. L. III. 372 ;
with *prep. inf.* : P. L. III. 694 ;
with *to* ; *tending to some relief of
our extremes* : P. L. X. 976.

Tend, *vb.* (1) *tr.* (*a*) to attend, wait
on, serve ; *to tend his eyes* : S. A.
1490 ; *fig., Despair tended the
sick* : P. L. XI. 490 ; with *on* ;
tended on by glory and fame : P.
R. IV. 371 ; to watch over, guard ;
*flaming ministers to watch and
tend their earthly charge* : P. L.
IX. 156.

(*b*) to take care of : P. L. IX.
801 ; *to tend plant, herb, and
flower* : P. L. IX. 206 ; *these
flowers* : P. L. IV. 438 ; *tend my
flocks* : C. 531 ; *tends his pasturing
herds* : P. L. IX. 1109.

(*c*) to be attentive to ; *lamb or
kid, that tend their play* : P. L.
IX. 583 ; to follow as an occupation ; *to tend the ... shepherd's
trade* : L. 65.

(2) *intr.* to wait on as a servant ; *may ever tend about thee to
old age* : S. A. 925.

part. adj. **tended**, cared for :
P. L. V. 22.

Tendance, *sb.* the work of caring for
(plants) P. L. VIII. 47 ; or it may
be *concr.* that which is cared for ;
*garden-plot ... their tendance or
plantation for delight* : P. L. IX.
419.

Tender, *adj.* (*a*) gentle, fond ; *tender
love* : P. L. IX. 357.

(*b*) expressive of sensitive feeling, gentle ; *O flowers ... which I
bred up with tender hand* : P. L.
XI. 276.

(*c*) sensitive to the touch of the
fingers ; *he touched the tender
stops* : L. 188.

(*d*) easily broken or injured ;
such a tender ball as the eye : S. A.
94 ; *sup., mangle my ... tenderest
parts* : S. A. 624 ; used of growing things ; young and green or
delicate ; *to support each flower of
tender stalk* : P. L. IX. 428 ; *he on
the tender grass would sit* : C. 624 ;
grazing the tender herb : P. L. IV.
253 ; *stalk, grass*, etc.: P. L. V.
337 ; VII. 315 ; C. 296 ; M. W.
35 ; Ps. LXXX. 56.

(*e*) youthful ; *tender age* : C.
40 ; young and feeble ; *the tender
mouths of latest bearth* : Ps. VIII.
4.

Tender, *vb. tr.* to offer, present ; P.
R. II. 327.

Tenderly, *adv.* fondly : P. L. IX.
991.

Tendril, *sb.* the plant organ that
coils spirally around another body
for the purpose of support : P. L.
IV. 307.

Tenement, *sb.* dwelling, abode : P.
R. IV. 274.

Teneriffe, *sb.* the mountain on Teneriffe, one of the Canary Islands :
P. L. IV. 987.

Tenfold, (1) *adj.* ten times as much
or as many, ten times repeated :
P. L. VI. 78, 255, 872.

(2) *adv.* in a ten times greater
degree, so as to be ten times repeated : P. L. II. 705 ; P. R. I.
41.

Tenor, *sb.* prevailing course : P. L.
XI. 632.

Tent, *sb.* (*a*) a portable lodge : P.
L. XI. 557, 581, 592, 727 ; *those
tents thou saw'st so pleasant were
the tents of wickedness* : P. L. XI.
607 ; *I see his tents pitched about
Sechem* : P. L. XII. 135 ; used by
angels encamped ; *I fly these
wicked tents devoted* : P. L. V.
890 ; *their glittering tents* : P. L.
V. 291.

(*b*) the Jewish tabernacle (*see*
Tabernacle) : P. L. XII. 256 ; *the
clouded ark of God, till then in
tents wandering* : P. L. XII. 333.

Tenth, *adj.* the ordinal of ten : P.
L. VI. 194.

Tepid, *adj.* moderately warm : P. L.
VII. 417.

Terah, *sb.* the father of Abraham :
Ps. CXIV. 1.

Teredon, *sb.* a city of Babylonia
situated on the Persian Gulf : P.
R. III. 292.

Term, (1) *sb.* (*a*) the termination or
end of life : U. C. II. 14.

(*b*) expression, word : P. L. X.
173 ; with a definite meaning in
the science of music ; *our Psalms
with artful terms inscribed* : P. R.
IV. 335.

(*c*) *pl.* conditions, stipulations,
propositions : P. L. VI. 621 ; X.
757 ; P. R. IV. 173 ; C. 684 ;
terms of peace : P. L. II. 331 ;
terms of composition : P. L. VI.
612 ; *thy terms too hard, by which
I was to hold the good I sought
not* : P. L. X. 751.

(**2**) *vb. tr.* to call ; *which ... may
be termed her own* : C. 419.

Ternate (Térnate), *sb.* one of the
Molucca Islands : P. L. II. 639.

Terrace, *sb.* an open balcony : P. R.
IV. 54 ; or more likely, a raised
level space supported by masonry
or a bank of turf : C. 935.

Terrene, *sb.* the earth : P. L. VI.
78.

Terrestrial, *adj.* of or pertaining to
the earth ; *terrestrial moon,
heaven* : P. L. VIII. 142 ; IX. 103 ;
humour : P. L. III. 610 ; *mould* :
P. L. IX. 485.

Terrible, *adj.* exciting fear, awe, or
dread ; used of persons : P. L. IX.
490 ; XI. 233 ; P. R. II. 160.

(*b*) horrible ; of persons or
things ; *grim and terrible* : P. L.
II. 682 ; *fierce as ten Furies, terrible
as Hell* : P. L. II. 671 ; *the ways
that lead to his* (Death's) *grim
cave ... to sense more terrible at
the entrance than within* : P. L.
XI. 470.

(*c*) fearful, formidable ; of
things ; *in terrible array* : P. L.
VI. 106 ; *example* : P. L. VI. 910.

Terrific, *adj.* exciting fear, dreadful ; *hairy mane terrific* ; P. L.
VII. 497.

Terrify, *vb. tr.* to fill with extreme
fear, strike with terror : P. L. X.
338 ; *war terrify them* : P. L. XII.
218 ; *absol.*: P. R. I. 179.

(*b*) to subdue by means of fear ;
thinking to terrify me to thy will :
P. R. IV. 496.

Territory, *sb.* (*a*) the extent of land
under the dominion of a sover-
eign : P. L. III. 375 ; IV. 82.

(*b*) an extensive tract of land,
region : P. L. XI. 638.

Terror, *sb.* (*a*) extreme fear, awe, or
dread felt or communicated : P. L.
X. 850 ; Ps. LXXXVIII. 60 ; *terror,
seized the rebel host* : P. L. VI.
647 ; *the thunder when to roll with
terror* : P. L. X. 667 ; *with terror
of that blast* : N. O. 161 ; *the terror of this arm* : P. L. I. 113 ; *the
terror of thy power* : P. L. VI.
134 ; *O sight of terror* : P. L. XI.
464 ; *the terror of his voice* : P. R.
IV. 627 ; *though terror be in love* :
P. L. IX. 490.

(*b*) one who, or that which,
causes extreme fear, awe, or
dread : P. R. IV. 421, 431, 482,
487 ; *mighty Powers, terror of
Heaven* : P. L. II. 457 ; *pursued
with terrors* : P. L. VI. 859 ; applied to Death ; *the grisly Terror* :
P. L. II. 704 ; some of the following may belong in (*a*) : P. L. XII.
238 ; *with conscious terrors* : P.
L. II. 801 ; *with terrors ... compassed round of mine own brood* :
P. L. II. 862 ; *the Son ... into
terror changed his countenance* :
P. L. VI. 824 ; *I ... can put on
thy terrors* : P. L. VI. 735 ; *all
terror hide* : P. L. XI. 111 ; *I thy
terrors undergo* : Ps. LXXXVIII.
63 ; *Medusa with Gorgonian terror
guards the ford* : P. L. II. 611.

Test, *sb.* trial, proof : S. A. 1151.

Testify, *vb.* (**1**) *intr.* to bear witness,
make declaration ; *a reverend sire
... testified against their ways* : P.
L. XI. 721 ; *I testify to thee* : Ps.
LXXXI. 34.

(**2**) *tr.* (*a*) to bear witness to,
declare as true : C. 440 ; *absol.*,
as this place testifies : P. L. I.
625.

(*b*) to make known, declare,
reveal : C. 248.

Testimony, *sb.* (*a*) the proof of a
fact, witness, evidence : Ps.
LXXXI. 17 ; *to receive the testimony
of Heaven* : P. R. I. 78.

(*b*) the act of bearing witness ;
for the testimony of truth : P. L.
VI. 33.

(*c*) the law of God written on
the tables of stone : P. L. XII. 251.

Tethys, *sb.* the wife of Oceanus :
C. 870. *See* **Oceanus.**

Tetrachordon, *sb.* a Greek word meaning four-stringed ; here the title of a pamphlet on the subject ' Expositions upon the Four chief Places in Scripture which treat of Marriage, or Nullities in Marriage ' : S. XI. 1.

Tetrarch, *sb.* a subordinate ruler ; applied to the fallen angels ; *tetrarchs of Fire, Air, Flood* : P. R. IV. 201.

Texture, *sb.* (*a*) woven fabric : P. L. X. 446.
(*b*) structure ; *nor in their liquid texture mortal wound receive* : P. L. VI. 348.

Thame, *sb.* the river Thames in England : V. Ex. 100.

Thammuz, *sb.* the god of the Syrians, the Greek Adonis : P. L. I. 452 ; N. O. 204 ; as identified with one of the fallen angels : P. L. I. 446. *See* **Adonis.**

Thamyris, *sb.* a Thracian bard who boasted he could conquer the Muses in singing, but whose temerity was punished with blindness : P. L. III. 35.

* **Than,** (**1**) *adv.* then : N. O. 88.
(**2**) *conj.* when, as, or if compared with ; the particle used after comparatives or comparative expressions to introduce the second member of the comparison : P. L. I. 482, 593 ; II. 193 ; IV. 629 ; V. 362 ; IX. 1033 ; *better to reign ... than serve* : P. L. I. 263 ; *what can be worse than to dwell here* : P. L. II. 86 ; *more warmth than Adam needs* : P. L. V. 302; *worse than fables yet have feigned* : P. L. II. 627 ; *less than if this frame of heaven were falling* : P. L. II. 924 ; *more dread than from no fall* : P. L. II. 16 ; *other notes than to the Orphean lyre* : P. L. III. 17 ; *fairer than by day* : P. L. V. 53 : *worse than so* : P. ll ; *thou than they less hardy* : P. L. IV. 919 ; *less than he* : P. L. I. 257 ; *mightier than they* : P. L. VI. 32 ; *served by more noble than herself* : P. L. VIII. 34 ; *me than thyself more miserable* : P. L. X. 929 ; *than which* : P. L. IX. 263 ; followed by the *acc.* ; *sight more detestable than him and thee* : P. L. II. 745 ; *than whom* : P. L. I. 490 ; II. 299 ; V. 805 ; X. 529 ; S. XVII. 2.

Thank, (**1**) *sb.* *pl.* gratitude ex-

pressed ; P. L. VIII. 5 ; used ironically : P. L. X. 736 ; expressed to God : P. R. III. 127 ; *pay him thanks* : P. L. IV. 47 ; *we to him ... owe ... daily thanks* : P. L. IV. 445 ; *to the infinitely Good we owe immortal thanks* : P. L. VII. 77.
(*b*) *fig.* a return for labour expended ; *a better soil shall give ye thanks* : A. 101.
(**2**) *vb. tr.* to express gratitude to ; *thank the gods* : C. 177 ; *the Giver* (God) *would be better thanked* : C. 775 ; used ironically ; *for this we may thank Adam* : P. L. X. 736 ; *thank him* (God) *who puts me, loath, to this revenge* : P. L. IV. 386.

Thankless, *adj.* ungrateful, profitless : L. 66.

***That** (*pl.* those) I. *demon. pron.*
(**1**) referring to a person or thing mentioned, implied, or understood : P. L. I. 381, 432 ; *let those contrive who need* : P. L. II. 52 ; *wider than that of after-times ... though that were large* : P. L. III. 529, 530 ; *those few* : P. L. XI. 777 ; S. IX. 3.
(*b*) opposed to *this* : P. L. VII. 476 ; *those male, these feminine* : P. L. I. 422 ; *those rare ... these in flocks* : P. L. VII. 461 : *that fondly lost, this other served* : P. L. XI. 59 ; opposed to *us* ; *rule us here, as ... those in Heaven* : P. L. II. 328.
(**2**) referring to a sentence or a part of a sentence : P. L. I. 114 ; II. 145 ; *that done* : P. L. IX. 199 ; *that be far from thee* : P. L. III. 153 ; *that implies not violence* : P. L. IV. 901 ; *nor less for that* : P. L. V. 874 ; *through them I mean to pass, that be assured* : P. L. II. 685 ; *Why should that cause thy refusal ?* : P. R. II. 322 ; *let that come* : P. R. III. 204 ; *I state not that* : S. A. 424 ; *that were a joy* : S. A. 1531 ; *with that ... he took the Son of God* : P. R. III. 251 ; *with that thy gentle hand seized mine* : P. L. IV. 488.
II. *demon. adj.* the (one) specially designated : P. L. I. 444 ; *that ... Angel* : P. L. II. 991 ; *that shepherd* : P. L. I. 8 ; *those other two* : P. L. III. 33 ; *that sea-beast* : P. L. I. 200 ; *that sea* : P. L. I. 300 ; *that couch* : P. L. I.

377 ; *stone*: P. L. III. 600 ; *tree*: P. L. V. 57 ; *time* : P. L. IV. 489; *day* : P. L. VI. 246 ; *hour* : P. L. VIII. 512 ; *night* : P. L. I. 503.

(*b*) opposed to *this ; those happy places ... these* : P. L. V. 364 ; *this ...that other* : P. R. II. 478.

(*c*) used emphatically in pointing to a person ; *that phantasm call'st my son* : P. L. II. 743 ; in dislike ; *that hill of scandal* : P. L. I. 416 ; *that tongue* : P. L. VI. 154.

(*d*) followed by a *poss. pron. ; those his children dear* : P. L. X. 330 ; *those their conquerors* : P. R. III. 78 ; *those thy boisterous locks* : S. A. 1164.

III. *rel. pron.* (1) introducing a subordinate clause restricting the antecedent : P. L. I. 50 ; *he that has light* : C. 381 ; *him that drinks* : C. 527 ; *leaves that strow the brooks* : P. L. I. 302 ; *the brook that parts Egypt from Syrian ground* : P. L. I. 420 ; *the heroic race ... that fought at Thebes* : P. L. I. 578 ; *the law ... that so ordains* : P. L. II. 201 ; *the twelve that shone in Aaron's breastplate* : P. L. III. 597 ; *all path of man that passed that way* : P. L. IV. 177 ; *the stars that usher evening* : P. L. IV. 355.

(2) introducing a subordinate clause in apposition to or descriptive of the antecedent = who, which : P. L. X. 389 ; *you ... that have been tired*: C. 688 ; *O foolishness of men ! that lend their ears* : C. 706 ; *blind mouths ! that scarce themselves know* : L. 119 ; *the Herald of the Sea, that came in Neptune's plea* : L. 90 ; *Lady, that in the prime* : S. IX. 1 ; *me, that am already bruised* : Ps. LXXXVIII. 59 ; *his baleful eyes, that witnessed* : P. L. I. 57 ; *the ... bird, that now awake tunes* : P. L. V. 40 ; *winds, that from four quarters blow* : P. L. V. 192 ; *fire ... that withered all their strength* : P. L. VI. 850 ; *words, that bore semblance of worth* : P. L. I. 528 ; *conscience wakes despair that slumbered* : P. L. IV. 24 ; *hope never comes that comes to all* : P. L. I. 67 ; = he who : P. L. III. 220.

IV. *conj.* (1) introducing a clause ; (*a*) that is the subject or object of the principal verb : P.

L. I. 531 ; *who can yet believe ... that* : P. L. I. 632 ; *let none admire that riches grow in Hell* : P. L. I. 691; *know that in the soul are* : P. L. V. 100 ; *far be it that I should write thee* : P. L. IV. 758 ; *that he never will is sure* : P. L. II. 153 ; *most reason is that reason overcome* : P. L. VI. 126 ; *think not but that I know these things* : P. R. IV. 286 ; *doubt not but that sin will reign*: P. L. XII. 285 ; *but that thou shouldst ... I expected not to hear* : P. L. IX. 279 ; *it cannot be but that success attends him* : P. L. X. 239 ; omitted ; *God saw the Light was good*: P. L. VII. 249.

(*b*) that is is a necessary complement of some part of the principal sentence : P. L. IV. 562 ; *a fame in Heaven that He erelong intended to create* : P. L. I. 651 ; *glad that now his sea should find a shore*: P. L. II. 1011 ; *that word ... that Man should find grace* : P. L. III. 145 ; *the just decree of God ... that to his only Son* : P. L. V. 815 ; *which gives me hope ... that thou never wilt consent to do* : P. L. V. 120.

(2) the principal sentence elliptical or omitted ; (*a*) introducing a clause or sentence expressive of surprise or sorrow ; *that such resemblance of the Highest should yet remain* : P. L. VI. 114 ; *that I ... am now constrained into a beast* : P. L. IX. 163 ; *that men ... should be so stupid grown* : P. L. XII. 115.

(*b*) introducing a wish : Ps. LXXXI. 53 ; *O that I never had ! :* S. A. 228.

(*c*) *not that*, not because ; *not that I less endure* : P. L. IV. 925 ; *not that they durst* : P. L. VIII. 237.

(3) redundant after *whilst ; whilst ... thy easy numbers flow, and that each heart hath* : W. S. 10.

(4) introducing a purpose ; in order that : P. L. I. 24, 148, 214, 647 ; III. 201 ; X. 70 ; XI. 475 ; P. R. IV. 493 ; *all mist from thence purge ... that I may see* : P. L. III. 54 ; *ambitious to win ... that thy success may show* : P. L. VI. 161 ; *to right and left the front unfold, that all may see* : P. L. VI. 559 ; *seduce them to our party, that*

their God may prove their foe: P. L. II. 368.

(5) introducing a consequence or result : P. L. II. 783, 882, 1041; III. 381; VI. 490; IX. 1007; S. A. 759 ; *the birds their notes renew...that hill and valley rings*: P. L. II. 495; *shook his plumes, that heavenly fragrance filled the circuit*: P. L. V. 286 ; *the hills were crowned ... that Earth now seemed like Heaven* : P. L. VII. 328 ; *hast thou turned the least of these ... to fall, but that they rise*: P. L. VI. 285.

(*b*) correlative with *so*: P. L. I. 314; II. 34; VI. 191, 666; VIII. 472; IX. 986; X. 140; XI. 877; *so quickened appetite that I...could not but taste*: P. L. V. 85; *so charming left his voice that he ... stood fixed to hear* : P. L. VIII. 2 ; *so dear I love him that with him all deaths I could endure*: P. L. IX. 832; *not so confined ... but that*: P. R. I. 363; *so ... as that*: C. 369.

(*c*) correlative with *such*: P. L. VI. 592; XI. 891; XII. 246; P. R. I. 209 ; *thy skill of conduct would be such that all the world could not sustain thy prowess*: P. R. III. 18.

(6) introducing a cause or reason; in that, because : P. L. VI. 23 ; *wept that he had lived so long inglorious*: P. R. III. 41 ; *for envy that his brother's offering found ... acceptance*: P. L. XI. 456; preceded by *for* ; *for that to me thou seem'st the man*: P. R. I. 327; by *now*; *now that the fields are dank*: S. XX. 2 ; for this or that reason ; *was she thy God, that her thou didst obey before his voice*: P. L. X. 145.

(7) following *but* in a conditional clause ; *nor ever thence had risen ... but that the will ... of all-ruling Heaven left him at large*: P. L. I. 211 ; *would full soon devour ... but that he knows*: P. L. II. 806 ; *what rests, but that the mortal sentence pass*: P. L. X. 48.

Thatched, *part. adj.* covered with thatch : C. 318.

Thaw, I. *sb.* the melting of ice : P. L. XII. 194.

II. *vb.* (1) *intr.* to pass from a frozen to a liquid state, dissolve : P. L. II. 590.

(2) *tr.* to undo ; *thaw the numbing spell*: C. 853.

*The, (1) *def. art.* used to specify or limit substantives or words used as substantives : P. L. I. 1, 3, 74, 266, 288 ; *the beach*: P. L. I. 299 ; *the torrid clime*: P. L. I. 297 ; *the Heathen World*: P. L. I. 375.

(*b*) before adjectives used absolutely ; *the Mightiest*: P. L. I. 99 ; *the twelve that shone*: P. L. III. 597 ; *one of the seven*: P. L. III. 648 ; *the good*: P. L. XI. 710 ; *the best*: P. L. IV. 852 ; *the living*: P. L. III. 327 ; *the greater ... the less*: P. L. VII. 347, 348.

(*c*) before a verbal substantive or gerund ; *the glimmering of*: P. L. I. 182 ; *the tossing of*: P. L. I. 184 ; *the coming of*: P. L. IV. 7 ; *the putting-off these troublesome disguises*: P. L. IV. 739.

(*d*) before an adverb ; *the when and how*: P. R. IV. 472.

(*e*) used before a single thing as representing the whole, any or all ; *the egg*: P. L. VII. 418 ; *the eagle and the stork ... their eyries build*: P. L. VII. 423 ; before proper names ; *the Swede ... the French*: S. XXI. 8 ; *the Scythian*; P. R. III. 301.

(*f*) used instead of a possessive pronoun ; *roused from the slumber*: P. L. I. 377 ; *the Father knows the Son*: P. R. I. 176.

(*g*) used with a title ; *the Lady of this place*: A. 105 ; *the Sultan*: P. L. XI. 395.

(*h*) denoting what is well known; *speak the truth ... before the Judge*: S. XIV. 13 ; *the African bold*: S. XVII. 4.

(*i*) omitted ; *removed from God and light of Heaven*: P. L. I. 73 ; *to pass Rhene or the Danaw*: P. L. I. 353 ; *at foot of Heaven's ascent*: P. L. III. 485 ; *when first evening was*: P. L. VII. 260.

(2) *adv.* used to modify words in the comparative degree ; (*a*) correlatively ; *by how much ... by so much* ; *the more thou know'st, the more she will acknowledge thee*: P. L. VIII. 573, 574 ; *the happier ... the sooner*: P. R. III. 179 ; the second *the* omitted ; *more woe, the more your taste is now of joy*: P. L. IV. 369 ; *good, the more communicated, more abundant grows*: P. L. V. 71 ; *rather merits praise the more it seems excess*: P. L. III. 698 ; cor-

related with *by how much*; *the rarer thy example stands, by how much*: S. A. 166.

(*b*) without correlation; in some degree; *the better to converse with solitude*: P. R. I. 190; *down they fell...the sooner for their arms*: P. L. VI. 595; *so much the rather*: P. L. III. 51; *I ask the rather, and the more admire*: P. R. I. 326; *the willinger I go*: P. L. IX. 382.

Theatre, *sb.* (*a*) a building adapted to the representation of spectacles: P. R. IV. 36; S. A. 1605.

(*b*) a place rising by steps like the seats of a theatre: P. L. IV. 141.

Theban, *adj.* of Thebes in Greece; *that Theban monster*: P. R. IV. 572.

Thebes, *sb.* the city of ancient Egypt situated on the Nile: P. L. V. 274.

Thebes, *sb.* the chief city of Bœotia, Greece; *the heroic race ... that fought at Thebes and Ilium*: P. L. I. 572; *Tragedy ... presenting Thebes, or Pelops' line*: Il P. 99.

Thebez, *sb.* used instead of Tishbeh, a place in Gilead, the birth-place of Elijah: P. R. II. 313.

Thee. *See* **Thou.**

Them. *See* **They.**

***Their**, *poss. pron.* of or belonging to them: P. L. I. 31, 71, 278; III. 59; *disturb his inmost counsels from their destined aim*: P. L. I. 168; *the flames...slope their pointing spires*: P. L. I. 223; *thunders ...mustering their rage*: P. L. II. 268; *their own*: P. L. I. 240; II. 549; III. 117; *obj. gen.*; *imports their loss*: C. 287; *their making*: P. L. III. 113.

(*b*) the *sb.* understood from the context; *his attractive virtue and their own*: P. L. VIII. 124; *not God's likeness, but their own*: P. L. XI. 521.

(*c*) the antecedent a collective or singular *sb.* or *pron.*: P. L. XI. 846; *the Angelic throng .. their camp extend*: P. L. V. 651; *I did but prompt the age to quit their clogs*: S. XII. 1; *Heaven ... rolled her motions, as the great First Mover's hand first wheeled their course*: P. L. VII. 501; *all flesh corrupting each their way*: P. L. XI. 889; *each with their kind*: P. L. VIII. 393; *each in their kind*: P. L. VII. 453.

(*d*) modifying a singular *sb.*; *an open grave their throat, their tongue they smooth*: Ps. V. 28; *cedars...advanced their lofty head*: Ps. LXXX. 44.

Theirs, *poss. pron.* referring to a preceding *sb.* or *pron.*: P. L. IX. 806; S. A. 888; *all is not theirs*: P. L. IV. 513; *his obedience ... becomes theirs*: P. L. XII. 409; and antecedent of a *rel. pron.*: P. L. XII. 400, 434.

Theme, *sb.* a subject on which one speaks: S. XIV. 12.

Themis, *sb.* the goddess of justice: P. L. XI. 14; used *fig.* for a court of justice; *the royal bench of British Themis*: S. XXI. 2.

***Themselves**, *pron.* (1) *emphat.*: P. L. I. 793; *so warned he them, aware themselves*: P. L. VI. 547; *themselves disdaining to approach thy temples*: P. L. I. 448.

(*b*) in apposition with a *sb.* or *pron.*; *the deeds themselves*: S. A. 248; *they themselves*: P. L. III. 116, 128; P. R. III. 174.

(*c*) as subject of the verb *be;* *themselves were they who wrought*: P. R. III. 414.

(2) *refl.*: P. L. I. 525; II. 17; III. 125; VI. 352; X. 100; XI. 516; XII. 45, 515; P. R. III. 421; S. A. 897; C. 75; with a *prep.*: P. L. III. 122; VII. 158; IX. 110; X. 547; XI. 522, 685; P. R. III. 424; *among themselves*, with each other: P. L. II. 501; VI. 628.

***Then**, (1) *adv.* (*a*) at that time: P. L. I. 374; II. 167; IV. 129; VII. 383; *had Earth been then*: P. L. VI. 218; *then was not guilty shame*: P. L. IV. 313; *the stairs were then let down*: P. L. III. 523; *if ever, then, then had the Sons of God*: P. L. V. 446, 447; *just then*: P. L. IX. 278; *then soon*: P. L. IX. 470; *then, when I am thy captive*: P. L. IV. 970; *then when the Dragon ... came*: P. L. IV. 3; *then ... when*: P. L. II. 258; VI. 144; X. 756; XI. 253; *when night darkens the streets, then wander forth*: P. L. I. 501; *then retires ... when Nature rests*: P. L. V. 108; *regular then most when most irregular they seem*: P. L. V. 624; *then verified when Jesus ... saw*: P. L. X. 182. *ere then*, before that time: P. L. IV. 971; *since then*: S. A. 884; *till then*, until that time: P. L. I.

93, 638 ; ii. 690 ; vii. 313 ; viii. 206 ; ix. 766, 787 ; x. 640 ; xi. 198 ; xii. 90, 333.

(b) next in order, next or immediately afterward : P. L. i. 225 ; ii. 716 ; iii. 260 ; iv. 31, 395 ; v. 15 ; vii. 224 ; ix. 201 ; *myself I then perused* : P. L. viii. 267 ; *I directed then my walk* : P. L. v. 49 ; *then from pole to pole he views* : P. L. iii. 560 ; *first...then* : P. L. iii. 69 ; vii. 356 ; *by Judges first, then under Kings* : P. L. xii. 320 ; *then ... then* : P. L. vii. 239 ; *then ... now* : P. L. ii. 820.

(c) at another time ; *now .. then* : P. L. ii. 634 ; v. 269 ; *now high, now low, then hid* : P. L. viii. 126 ; *a lion now he stalks ... then as a tiger* : P. L. iv. 403 ; *sometimes ... then* : P. L. iii. 37 ; vi. 243 ; *sometimes ... now ... then* : P. L. ii. 634.

(2) *conj.* if it be so, in that case, therefore : P. L. i. 153, 162, 264 ; ii. 329, 747 ; v. 122 ; vi. 428 ; viii. 397 ; ix. 285, 357 ; *then I shall be no more* : P. L. ix. 827 ; *war, then, war ... must be resolved* : P. L. i. 661 ; *the ascent is easy, then* : P. L. ii. 81 ; *what fear we then?* : P. L. ii. 94 ; *what burden then?* : P. L. iv. 57 ; *O, then, at last relent!* : P. L. iv. 79 ; *since ... then* : P. L. iii. 5 ; *then ... when* : P. L. iii. 606.

(b) used in offering a substitute ; *behold me, then* : P. L. iii. 236 ; *not of myself ; by some great Maker then* : P. L. viii. 278.

*Thence, *adv.* (a) from that place : P. L. i. 210, 415 ; ii. 442, 929 ; iv. 194, 582 ; vii. 536, 554 ; viii. 233 ; ix. 62, 81 ; x. 399, 675 ; xi. 390, 405 ; xii. 458 ; P. R. i. 10, 82 ; ii. 76 ; iii. 271 ; N. O. 74 ; C. 56, 946 ; *from thence* : P. L. iii. 53 ; iv. 453 ; viii. 466 ; ix. 812 ; xi. 107 ; P. R. iii. 340 ; C. 1016.

(b) after that : P. L. i. 515 ; xi. 718 ; P. R. i. 203.

(c) from that source : P. L. i. 234 ; iv. 806 ; vii. 190 ; viii. 608 ; x. 344 ; *from thence* : P. L. vii. 616 ; xi. 532.

(d) for that cause or reason : P. L. i. 82, 404 ; ii. 521 ; iv. 474 ; v. 666 ; ix. 1185 ; x. 969 ; xii. 33, 343 ; P. R. i. 77 ; *from thence* : P. L. vii. 510.

Thenceforth (thénceforth : S. xiv. 13) *adv.* from that time forward : P. L. iii. 265, 333 ; ix. 602, 870 ; x. 214 ; xi. 802 ; P. R. i. 79 ; iv. 514 ; S. xiv. 13 ; *from thenceforth* : P. L. xii. 109.

Theologian, *sb.* one versed in theology : P. L. v. 436.

*There, *adv.* (a) in or at that place : P. L. i. 47, 76 ; ii. 184, 355, 601, 986 ; iii. 90, 249, 570 ; iv. 195, 465 ; v. 81, 689 ; vi. 277 ; vii. 20 ; viii. 173 ; *there ... here* : P. L. vi. 11 ; **vii.** 156 ; ix. 1148 ; *there where* : C. 428 ; *there ... where* : P. L. iv. 829 ; vi. 117 ; ix. 541 ; x. 599 ; *where he abides, think there thy native soil* : P. L. xi. 292 ; in pointing to a place : P. R. iii. 280, 285, 288.

here and there, in this place and that : P. R. iii. 263 ; C. 936.

(b) to that place ; *our sudden coming there* : C. 954.

(c) at that point of action ; *nor staid the terror there* : P. R. iv. 421.

(d) used as an indefinite grammatical subject, the real subject following the *vb.* : P. L. i. 651 ; *there stood a hill* : P. L. i. 670 ; *nor did there want cornice* : P. L. i. 715 ; *where there is, then, no good* : P. L. ii. 30 ; *if there be in Hell fear* : P. L. ii. 84 ; *let there be Light* : P. L. vii. 243 ; the real subject preceding ; *one gate there only was* : P. L. iv. 178 ; *one fatal tree there stands* : P. L. iv. 514 ; the subject omitted : S. A. 295 ; U. C. ii. 25 ; *lives there who loves his pain?* : P. L. iv. 888 ; *there be who faith prefer* : P. L. vi. 143 ; the subject understood ; *there is* : P. L. xi. 530.

Thereafter, *adv.* (a) after that manner, as governed by that : P. L. ii. 50.

(b) according ; *thereafter as I like the giver* : P. R. ii. 321.

Thereat, *adv.* at that, on that account : P. L. x. 487.

Thereby (théreby : P. L. ix. 128 ; P. R. iii. 107 ; S. A. 425) *adv.* by that, by that means, in consequence of that : P. L. iii. 695 ; iv. 197 ; ix. 128 ; xi. 360, 792 ; xii. 96 ; P. R. iii. 107 ; S. A. 425, 941 ; D. F. I. 12, 62.

*Therefore, *adv.* for this or that reason, on that account, conse-

quently, accordingly : P.L. II. 187 ;
III. 111 ; IV. 935 ; V. 229 ; VI.
464, 699, 817 ; VII. 516 ; VIII.
198, 608 ; IX. 212 ; X. 393 ; XI.
30, 314 ; XII. 90, 588 ; P. R. I.
176, 206 ; II. 18, 426 ; III. 362 ;
S. A. 834, 1053 ; C. 77 ; *God,
therefore, cannot hurt ye* : P. L.
IX. 700 ; *go, therefore, mighty
Powers* : P. L. II. 456 ; *Man,
therefore, shall find grace* : P. L.
III. 131 ; *I therefore came* : P. L.
V. 372 ; *say therefore on* : P. L.
VIII. 228 ; *therefore so abject is
their punishment* : P. L. XI. 520 ;
because ... therefore : P. L. III.
313 ; *therefore ... therefore* : P. L.
XI. 702 ; *and therefore* : P. L. XII.
287, 307.

Therein, (thérein : P. L. I. 652 ; II.
833 ; V. 522 ; VIII. 340 ; X. 483 ;
XI. 838, 896 ; P. R. II. 463 ; III.
109 ; S. A. 299) *adv.* (*a*) in that
place, in it or them : P. L. I. 652 ;
II. 833 ; III. 390 ; V. 575 ; VIII. 340 ;
X. 483 ; XI. 838, 895, 896 ; XII.
250 ; S. A. 299 ; Ps. CXXXVI. 74.

(*b*) in that thing or respect ;
thy obedience ; therein stand : P.
L. V. 522 ; *the sense of touch ... if
aught therein enjoyed* : P. L. VIII.
584 ; referring to a clause : P. R.
II. 463 ; *think not so slight of
glory, therein least resembling thy
great Father* : P. R. III. 109.

Thereof, *adv.* (*a*) of it or that ;
some public proof thereof : S. A.
1314 ; *eat'st, eat,* or *eats thereof* :
P. L. VIII. 329 ; IX. 663, 706,
724 ; X. 200, 202.

(*b*) from it or that : C. 740 ;
more good thereof shall spring :
P. L. XII. 476.

Thereon, *adv.* (*a*) on it or that : P.
L. XI. 326 ; S. M. 8.

(*b*) in consequence of that, from
that ; *thy joy thereon conceived* :
S. A. 1505.

Therewith, *adv.* with it or that : S.
XIX. 5.

These. *See* **This.**

Thessalian, *adj.* of Thessaly : P. L.
II. 544.

Thestylis, *sb.* the name of a peasant,
common in pastoral poetry : L'A.
88.

Thetis, *sb.* one of the Nereids : C.
877. *See* **Nereus.**

** **They,** I. *pers. pron.* (*dat.* and *acc.*
them) (1) referring to persons or
things mentioned or understood :

P. L. I. 33, 75, 370 ; *all may
pluck her, as they go* : Ps. LXXX.
51 ; *they all him followed* : P. L.
X. 532 ; *how their love express
they* : P. L. VIII. 616 ; *alone as
they* : P. L. IV. 340 ; *which cost
them woe* : P. L. I. 414 ; *returned
them loud acclaim* : P. L. II. 520 ;
got them names : P. L. I. 365 ; *he
makes them slaves* : P. L. XII.
167 ; *as likes them best* : P. L. VI.
353 ; *who slew'st them many a
slain* : S. A. 439 ; *listened them a
while* : C. 551.

(*b*) opposed to *these* ; *they to
their grassy couch* ; *these to their
nests* : P. L. IV. 601.

(*c*) the antecedent a collective
sb. ; *the wild beast ... among the
trees in pairs they rose* : P. L. VII.
459 ; *let us make now Man ... and
let them rule* : P. L. VII. 520.

(*d*) used emphatically for *who*
in the beginning of a clause or
sentence : P. L. II. 640 ; III. 331 ;
used for *these* or *those* : P. L. III.
579 ; P. R. I. 182 ; *thus they in
Heaven* : P. L. III. 416 ; in the
middle of the sentence ; *with them
of men and beast select for life* : P.
L. XI. 822.

(2) these or those persons or
things ; *they below would grow inured
to light* : C. 734 ; as antecedent of a
rel. pron. : P. L. I. 419 ; III. 478 ;
VIII. 74 ; XII. 418 ; *them who shall
believe* : P. L. XII. 441 ; *absolve
them who renounce* : P. L. III.
291 ; *them who stood and them
who failed* : P. L. III. 101 ; *say
they who counsel war* : P. L. II.
160 ; *end them in his anger whom
his anger saves* : P. L. II. 158 ;
them that bide : P. L. III. 321 ;
they whom I favour : P. R. II. 430 ;
they that overween : S. IX. 6 ; the
descendants ; *them of Hagar's
blood* : Ps. LXXXIII. 23 ; the inhabitants ; *they of Tyre* : Ps.
LXXXIII. 27.

(3) persons indefinitely ; *they
say* : P. L. IX. 638 ; *do they not
say* : S. A. 204.

II. *refl. band them* : S. A. 1753 ;
bethink : P. L. II. 73 ; *betook* : P.
L. VI. 663 ; X. 610 ; *sat them down* :
P. L. IV. 327 ; IX. 1121.

Thick, I. *adj.* (1) having numerous
separate individuals set or lying
close together, crowded together,
arranged compactly : P. L. IV.

980 ; ll P. 7 ; *Angel Forms ...
thick as autumnal leaves* : P. L. I.
302 ; *the Sanctities of Heaven stood
thick as stars* : P. L. III. 61 ;
shields in thick array : P. L. I.
548 ; *the ... constellations thick* : P.
L. III. 577 ; *houses, wood* : P. L.
IX. 446 ; P. R. IV. 448 ; *with*
blending of (3) ; *so thick a cloud he
comes* : P. L. VI. 539 ; *sup.* : P. L.
X. 411 ; *thickest legions* : P. L. II.
537 ; *wood, trees,* etc.: P. L. IV.
693 ; IX. 1100 ; X. 101.

(*b*) carried on by great numbers
crowded together ; *sup., thickest
fight* : P. L. VI. 308.

(*c*) situated at short distances
from each other ; *the strict sentries
and stations thick* : P. L. II. 412.

(*d*) following each other in
quick succession ; *flashing thick
flames* : P. L. VI. 751.

(2) covered or set closely *with* :
P. L. III. 507.

(3) not transparent or clear,
dense, dark ; *the middle region of
thick air* : P. R. II. 117 ; *thick
clouds, shade,* etc. : P. L. II. 264 ;
IV. 532 ; VIII. 653 ; P. R. I. 41 ;
thick shelter of black shades : C.
62 ; *thick and gloomy shadows* :
C. 470 ; *sup.* : P. L. IX. 1110 ; C.
132 ; Ps. LXXXVIII. 27 ; *Night ...
thy thickest mantle* : P. 30.

(*b*) used of a liquid ; turbid ;
so thick a drop : P. L. III. 25.

II. *adv.* (*a*) in large numbers
and close together, compactly,
densely : P. L. I. 311 ; VI. 16 ;
VII. 320 ; IX. 426, 1038 ; *loose
garlands thick thrown off* : P. L.
III. 362 ; *swarmed* : P. L. I. 767,
775 ; X. 526 ; *entwined, interwoven,* etc.: P. L. IV. 174 ; P. R.
II. 263 ; IV. 405 ; *set* : C. 893 ;
sowed : P. L. VII. 358 ; *comp.* : P.
L. X. 559.

(*b*) in rapid succession ; *thick
and fast* : P. L. II. 754.

Thickened, *part. adj.* obscured with
clouds : P. L. XI. 742.

Thicket, *sb.* a thick growth of small
trees or shrubs : P. L. IV. 681 ;
VII. 458 ; IX. 179, 628, 784 ; *with
thicket overgrown* : P. L. IV. 136 :
the high thicket : A. 58 ; *tangled* :
N. O. 188.

Thicket-side, *sb.* the border of a
thicket : C. 185.

Thick-laid, *adj.* used in profusion :
P. R. IV. 343.

Thick-rammed, *adj.* driven down in
numbers and close together : P.L.
VI. 485.

Thick-swarming, *adj.* being crowded
or densely filled ; *thick-swarming
now with ... monsters* : P. L. X.
522.

Thick-warbled, *adj.* sung with many
rapid trills and runs : P. R. IV.
246.

Thick-woven, *adj.* growing close
together and intertwining their
branches : P. L. IX. 437.

Thief, *sb.* one who steals : P. L. IV.
188 ; applied to Satan ; *this first
grand Thief* : P. L. IV. 192 ; *the
... thief of Paradise* : P. R. IV.
604 ; *fig., Time, the subtle thief of
youth* : S. II. 1.

Thievish, *adj.* practising theft ; *fig.,
O thievish Night* : C. 195.

Thigh, *sb.* the part of the leg
between the hip and the knee ; as
covered with wings : P. L. V. 282 ;
as the place where the sword is
borne ; *swords, drawn from the
thighs of mighty Cherubim* : P. L.
I. 664 ; *my almighty arms, gird
on, and sword upon thy puissant
thigh* : P. L. VI. 714 ; the corresponding part in insects ; *the bee
with honied thigh* : ll P. 142.

Thin, *adj.* (*a*) having the component
parts diffused, not dense, rare ;
thin air : P. L. XII. 76 ; P. R. I.
499 ; *comp.* : P. L. VIII. 348.

(*b*) limited in number, scanty ;
comp. : P. L. IX. 142 ; *fig.,* few
and straggling ; *scatters the rear
of darkness thin* : L'A. 50.

* **Thine,** *poss. pron.* (1) of or belonging to thee ; with *sb.* ; *thine eye,
ear,* etc.: P. L. III. 700 ; XI. 30,
423, 711 ; P. R. III. 245 ; IV. 61 ;
S. A. 1160 ; *anger* : P. L. III. 237 ;
ire : Ps. VII. 19 ; *thine own* : P.
L. II. 782 ; VII. 121 ; VIII. 641 ;
S. A. 217 ; used for *thy* when
separated from the *sb.* ; *between
thine and her seed* : P. L. X. 180 ;
obj. gen. ; *thine and of all thy sons
the weal* : P. L. VIII. 637.

(*b*) the *sb.* understood from the
context ; *Man's nature, lessen or
degrade thine own* : P. L. III.
304 ; *thy trophies! which thou
view'st as not thine own* : P. L. X.
355.

(2) *absol.* that or those belonging to thee ; (*a*) referring to a
preceding *sb.* : P. L. III. 157 ; IV.

1008 ; v. 37 ; vi. 699 ; viii. 319 ; xii. 453 ; *whose god is God, thine, or whom I with Israel's sons adore* : S. A. 1177 ; *to a following sb.* ; *thine this universal frame* : P. L. v. 154 ; *thine now is all this World* : P. L. x. 372 ; *with of* ; *that sacred head of thine* : L. 102. (*b*) not referring to a *sb.* ; *thy* followers : P. L. vi. 180 ; *thy* husband : P. L. iv. 473 ; *thy part or duty* : P. L. x. 68 ; *thy people* : S. A. 1169.

Thing, *sb.* (*a*) a separable or distinguishable object of thought, whatever exists or is conceived to exist as a separate entity, any object or substance ; often including sense (*b*), sometimes sense (*c*): P. L. v. 511, 575 ; vi. 137, 298, 477 ; vii. 240 ; viii. 565 ; ix. 449, 1025 ; x. 248 ; P. R. ii. 400; iii. 122 ; Ariosto i. 4 ; *a mighty mass of things* : Ariosto i. 3 ; *the sum of things* : P. L. vi. 673 ; *face of things* : P. L. vii. 636 ; *each thing on Earth* : P. L. ix. 813 ; *whatever thing Death be* : P. L. ix. 695 ; *whatever thing the scythe of Time mows down* : P. L. x. 605 ; *Light ethereal, first of things* : P. L. vii. 244 ; *Night, eldest of things* : P. L. ii. 962 ; *the moon ... sets off the face of things* : P. L. v. 43 ; *things that live* : P. L. v. 474 ; *to discern things in their causes* : P. L. ix. 682 ; *what thing good prayed for* : S. A. 350 ; *every thing that is sincerely good* : T. 14 ; *whatever thing is good* : Ps. LXXXV. 50 ; *each thing bad* : T. 9 ; *things false and vain* : Ps. iv. 12 ; *each thing of sin and guilt* : C. 456 ; *lifeless, dead, dumb* : P. L. x. 707 ; S. M. 4 ; C. 796 ; *precious, best, sacred, holy,* etc. : P. L. iii. 611 ; iv. 203 ; xii. 341 ; P. R. i. 489 ; S.A. 1358 ; C. 703 ; *cursed, dreadful, basest* : P. L. i. 389 ; iv. 426 ; ix. 171 ; *all things* : P. L. iii. 155, 446, 448, 675 ; iv. 434 ; 559, 611, 692, 752, 999 ; v. 46, 183, 470, 581 ; vi. 708 ; vii. 227, 591 ; viii. 340, 363, 476, 493, 524 ; ix. 402, 722 ; x. 269, 380, 850 ; xi. 56, 161, 900 ; P. R. ii. 305, 324, 379 ; iii. 111 ; iv. 224, 296, 435 ; S. A. 926 ; C. 217 ; *whose eye views all things* : P. L. ii. 190 ; *all things shall be your*

(Death's) *prey* : P. L. ii. 844 ; *all things under Heaven* : P. L. xii. 618 ; *all things visible in Heaven* : P. L. ix. 604 ; *nature and all things* : P. L. iv. 667 ; *all eternal things* : P. L. v. 103 ; *the mighty Father made all things* : P. L. v. 837 ; *all things that breathe* : P. L. ix. 194 ; *all things smiled* : P. L. viii. 265 ; *the Gods who all things know* : P. L. ix. 804 ; *all things fair and good* : P. L. ix. 605 ; *Supreme of Things,* God : P. L. viii. 414 ; *that which is made or constructed* ; *mortal things* : P. L. i. 693 ; *a place* ; *things by their names I call* : P. L. xii. 140.

(*b*) being, creature : P. L. ii. 625, 679 ; iv. 563 ; *what thing thou art* : P. L. ii. 741 ; *what thing of sea or land* : S. A. 710 ; *no evil thing that walks* : C. 432 ; *creeping, living* : P. L. vii. 452, 523, 534 ; *all things living* : P. L. ix. 539 ; xi. 160.

(*c*) affair, event, occurrence, action, deed, circumstance, matter, respect, particular ; sometimes including (*a*) or (*b*): P. L. vi. 311 ; vii. 53, 70 ; viii. 159, 196, 199 ; ix. 824 ; x. 306 ; xi. 579 ; xii. 567 ; P. R. i. 137, 258 ; ii. 103 ; iii. 70 ; iv. 286, 564 ; S. A. 250, 942 ; C. 458 ; S. xxi. 11 ; *the face of things* : P. L. xi. 712 ; *great things of small* : P. L. ii. 258 ; *to compare great things with small* : P. L. ii. 922 ; *things yet are in confusion* : S. A. 1592 ; *things past and to come* : P. R. i. 300 ; *secret things that come to pass* : V. Ex. 45 ; *gracious things thou hast revealed* : P. L. xii. 271 ; *things invisible to mortal sight* : P. L. iii. 55 ; *to know of things above his world* : P. L. v. 455 ; *things above Earthly thought* : P. L. vii. 82 ; *things not revealed* : P. L. vii. 122 ; *measuring things in Heaven by things on Earth* : P. L. vi. 893 ; *things remote from use* : P. L. viii. 191 ; *God hath wrought things as incredible* : S. A. 1532 ; *the nations muse a vain thing* : Ps. ii. 2 ; *great, glorious,* etc. : P. L. ii. 392 ; P. R. i. 69, 206 ; ii. 195, 208, 426, 448 ; Ps. LXXXVII. 9 ; Hor. Sat. ii. 1 ; *vulgar, adverse, unseemly,* etc. : P. R. iii. 51, 189 ; S. A. 433,

1451 ; *mournful* : P. 28 ; *un-attempted, too high*, etc. : P. L. I. 16 ; VIII. 10, 121 ; *present, future* : P. L. X. 651 ; XI. 870 ; *mortal* : P. R. IV. 318 ; IX. 343 ; X. 7 ; P. R. III. 182, 239, 355 ; *all things invite to peaceful counsels* : P. L. II. 278 ; *him who all things can* : P. L. XI. 308 ; *time there is for all things* : P. R. III. 183 ; *image of thee in all things* : P. L. VI. 736.

Think, *vb.* (*pres. 2d sing.* think'st : P. L. VIII. 110, 403 ; X. 592 ; P. R. I. 347 ; II. 177 ; III. 163 ; *pret.* and *past part.* thought) I. *tr.* (**1**) to form as a conception, say to oneself mentally : Ps. VII. 7 ; with clause or sentence ; *full little thought they than that the mighty Pan was ... come* : N. O. 88 ; '*O poor hapless nightingale,' thought I* : C. 566.

(**2**) to form a mental idea of, imagine ; *a joy presumptuous to be thought* : S. A. 1531 ; *absol.* : P. L. IX. 830 ; *sight of terror ... horrid to think* : P. L. XI. 465.

(**3**) to grasp intellectually, conceive ; *who can think submission* : P. L. I. 661.

(**4**) to contemplate mentally, meditate on, consider : C. 755 ; *think only what concerns thee* : P. L. VIII. 174 ; *think what a present thou to God hast sent* : D. F. I. 74 ; *not to think how vain ... to rise in arms* : P. L. VI. 135.

(**5**) to hold as an opinion, believe, suppose, conclude ; (*a*) with *clause* : P. L. IV. 50 ; IX. 555, 1179 ; X. 1049 ; P. R. II. 13, 177 ; S. A. 908, 1092 ; D. F. I. 10 ; N. O. 105 ; P. 55 ; U. C. I. 12 ; *who had thought this clime had held* : A. 24 ; *think not I shall be nice* : P. L. V. 433 ; *I thought I then was passing* : P. L. VIII. 289 ; *were it I thought death ... would ensue* : P. L. IX. 977 : *I ... doubt to think he will* : S. A. 1534 ; *if thou think trial unsought may find us* : P. L. IX. 370 ; the clause introduced by *that* : P. L. IV. 675 ; VI. 164 ; IX. 938 ; *think not but that I know these things* : P. R. IV. 286.

(*b*) the clause or phrase elliptical ; the construction probably *acc.* and *inf.*, or *inf.* alone : P. L. X. 219 ; S. A. 445 ; *to give a king-dom hath been thought ... nobler done* : P. R. II. 481 ; *think there thy native soil* : P. L. XI. 292 ; *think'st thou such force in bread* : P. R. I. 347 ; *there be who think not God at all* : S. A., 295 ; *that excellence thought in thee* : P. L. X. 1017 ; with *acc.* and *inf.* phrase ; *I do not think my sister so to seek* : C. 366.

(*c*) with two *acc.* : P. L. IV. 432 ; V. 665 ; VI. 437, 500 ; VII. 139, 635 ; VIII. 3, 110, 581 ; IX. 308, 319, 857 ; P. R. I. 204, 387 ; II. 146 ; IV. 514, 520 ; S. A. 231, 352, 553, 930, 1335 ; C. 408 ; *think thee unbefitting* : P. L. IV. 759 ; *think not ... thy shape the same* : P. L. IV. 835 ; *I thought it thine* : P. L. V. 37 ; *think nothing hard* : P. L. VI. 495 ; *whom fled we thought* : P. L. VI. 538 ; in passive : P. L. V. 576 ; *Sofala* (*thought Ophir*) : P. L. XI. 400 ; *wouldst be thought my God* : P. R. IV. 495 ; *thought extinguished* : S. A. 1688 ; *omniscient thought* : P. L. VI. 430.

(*d*) parenthetically ; *as I thought* : P. L. IX. 1119 ; S. A. 870.

(**6**) to conceive of as a thing possible, have a suspicion of, imagine ; *Goodness thinks no ill* : P. L. III. 688 ; *they thought no ill* : P. L. IV. 320 ; with *clause ; ye little think how nigh your change approaches* : P. L. IV. 366 ; *I thought where all thy ... wiles would end* : S. A. 871 ; *absol.* : P. R. IV. 11 ; *who could have thought ?* : P. L. IV. 794.

(**7**) to mean, intend, purpose ; with *prep. inf.* : P. L. VII. 611 ; X. 564, 1021 ; P. R. IV. 496 ; D. F. I. 6 ; M. W. 39 ; C. 756 ; *would think to charm my judgment* : C. 758 ; *what he for news had thought to have reported* : P. L. VI. 20 ; rather, to hope, expect : P. L. III. 480 ; *think not here to trouble holy rest* : P. L. VI. 271 ; *nor think thou ... to awe* : P. L. VI. 282 ; *think'st thou to regain thy sight* : P. R. III. 163 ; *think not to find me slack* : P. R. III. 398 ; *we ... think to burst out into sudden blaze* : L. 74.

II. *intr.* (**1**) to dwell in mind or meditate *on* or *upon* : P. L. IV. 198 ; Ps. VIII. 13.

(**2**) to believe, suppose, imagine ; *strange to think* : U. C. II. 32 ;

him thought he by the brook of
Cherith stood : P. R. II. 266.

(3) to entertain a particular
sentiment or opinion ; with of :
P. L. X. 592 ; what think'st thou
...of me : P. L. VIII. 403 ; think
not so slight of glory : P. R. III.
109 ; less think than, consider as :
P. L. VIII. 224.

See **Low-thoughted.**

Thin-sown, adj. thinly interspersed :
P. R. IV. 345.

Thin-spun, adj. drawn out and
twisted into a slender thread ;
fig., the thin-spun life : L. 76.

Third, adj. (a) next after the
second : P. R. IV. 296 ; morn,
Day, light : P. L. VI. 748 ; VII.
338 ; XII. 421.

(b) being one of three equal
parts ; thy third reign, the Earth :
H. B. 3 ; the third part of Heaven's
sons : P. L. II. 692 ; the third part
of Heaven's host : P. L. V. 710 ; a
third part of the Gods : P. L. VI. 156.

absol. (a) the one next after the
second : P. L. I. 705 ; IV. 869 ; V.
283 ; VI. 699 ; X. 82 ; S. A. 1466.

(b) one in the third generation ;
the third from Abraham : P. L.
XII. 267.

(c) one existing at the same
time as two others : S. A. 1701.

Thirst, I. sb. suffering or uneasiness from want of drink : P. L.
V. 305 ; P. R. I. 339 ; S. A. 551,
582 ; C. 67, 678 ; the current
stream ... heard new thirst excites :
P. L. VII. 68 ; wholesome : P. L.
IV. 330 ; joined to hunger : P. L.
VIII. 213 ; IX. 586 ; X. 568 ; P.
R. IV. 593 ; scalding thirst and
hunger fierce : P. L. X. 556 ; used
fig. with reference to the sun or
the earth : P. L. XI. 846 ; the
rapid current, which, through veins
of porous earth with kindly thirst
up-drawn : P. L. IV. 228.

(b) an eager desire ; thirst of
glory : P. R. III. 38 ; of knowledge : P. L. VIII. 8.

(II.) vb. (1) intr. to feel or suffer
thirst : P. L. IV. 336 ; who thirst
and hunger still : P. R. IV. 120.

(2) tr. to desire eagerly ; we
thirst to hear : S. A. 1456.

Thirsty, adj. (a) suffering for want
of drink : C. 524.

(b) dry, parched, arid : P. L.
V. 190 ; Baca's thirsty vale : Ps.
LXXXIV. 21.

Thirty, adj. three times ten : S. A.
1186, 1197 ; V. Ex. 94.

* **This** (pl. these), I. demon. pron.
(1) referring to a person or thing
mentioned, referred to, or present
in place or thought : P. L. I. 317,
437 ; IV. 771 ; V. 77 ; VI. 284 ;
this is old age : P. L. XI. 538 ;
this, this is he : S. A. 115 ; either of
these : S. A. 1292 ; this which fills
all space : P. L. VII. 88 ; which
these he breathed : P. L. XII. 374.

(b) opposed to that : P. L. X.
563 ; I state not that ; this I am
sure : S. A. 424 ; this ... that other :
P. R. II. 476 ; opposed to they ;
they to their grassy couch, these to
their nests : P. L. IV. 601 ; to he ;
he with Olympias, this with her :
P. L. IX. 509 ; to worse ; or this,
or worse : P. L. IX. 265.

(c) the antecedent a collective
sb. ; these, the late Heaven-banished
host : P. L. X. 436.

(d) the time, day, year, etc.
referred to ; by this : P. L. X. 19 ;
XI. 208, 293 ; S. A. 266, 485 ; ere
this : P. L. X. 240 ; ere these : P.
R. III. 32.

(2) referring to a sentence or a
part of a sentence : P. L. II. 152,
186, 247 ; III. 272 ; this knows
my Punisher : P. L. IV. 103 ; this
said : P. L. IV. 736 ; this let him
know : P. L. V. 243 ; this saw his
hapless foes : P. L. VI. 785 ; is
this, then, worst—thus sitting : P.
L. II. 163 ; this only to consult,
how etc. : P. L. V. 779 ; only this
I know, that one Celestial Father
gives to all : P. L. V. 402 ; this is
servitude—to serve the unwise : P.
L. VI. 178.

II. demon. adj. the (one) specially designated as present in
place or thought : P. L. I. 24,
182 ; II. 14 ; III. 71 ; IV. 367 ; V.
98 ; IX. 25 ; this gulf : P. L. I.
329 ; advantage : P. L. II. 35 ;
this side nothing : P. L. II. 101 ;
this Hell : P. L. II. 167 ; this far
his over-match : P. R. IV. 7 ; this
time, hour : P. L. II. 348, 934 ;
IV. 963 ; morn : P. L. IX. 1136 ;
evening : P. L. IV. 792 ; night :
P. L. V. 227 ; this day, to-day :
P. L. IV. 564 ; V. 229, 313, 603 ;
VI. 170, 539, 802 ; the present
time ; at this day : P. L. IX. 1102.

(b) opposed to that : P. L. I.
244 ; that grove ... this Paradise :

P. L. IV. 274 ; *that .. this other*:
P. L. XI. 60; opposed to *other ;
this or the other life*: P. L. III.
450.

(c) used emphatically; *this right
hand*: P. L. VI. 154 ; *this Heaven
itself*: P. L. VI. 291 ; *this one
tree*: P. L. IX. 1026 ; *these forty
days*: P. R. II. 315.

(d) followed by a *poss. pron.* :
P. L. I. 146 ; *these our motions*:
P. L. II. 191 ; *this my long sufferance*: P. L. III. 198; *these his
wondrous works*: P. L. III. 663 ;
this thy dream: P. L. V. 115.

Thisbite, *sb.* a native of Thisbe ; *the
great Thisbite*, Elijah the Tish-
bite (in Vulg. Elias Thesbites) :
P. R. II. 16.

Thistle, *sb.* the common prickly
weed : P. L. X. 203 ; C. 352.

*****Thither,** *adv. (a)* to that place : P.
L. I. 183, 357, 674 ; II. 596, 954,
1054 ; III. 573 ; IV. 593, 963 ; V.
266, 770 ; VII. 290, 572 ; IX. 630 ;
X. 629 ; XI. 200, 433, 837 ; XII.
75 ; P. R. I. 250 ; II. 291 ; S. A.
1450, 1521, 1738 ; C. 987 ; *thither
to arrive I travel* : P. L. II. 979 ;
whence thither brought : P. L. IV.
452 ; *though thither doomed* : P.
L. IV. 890 ; *thither let us bend all
our thoughts* : P. L. II. 354 ;
*thither with heart ... directed in
devotion* : P. L. VII. 513.

(b) in that place or part; *I
have thither packed the worst* : V.
Ex. 12.

Thitherward, *adv.* toward that place,
in that direction : P. L. III. 500 ;
*up I sprung, as thitherward en-
deavouring* : P. L. VIII. 260.

Thone, *sb.* according to Strabo XVII.
800, a king of the city of Thon in
Egypt : C. 675.

Thorn, *sb. (a)* a sharp prickle growing from the stem of a plant,
spine ; *without thorn the rose* : P.
L. IV. 256.

(b) *fig.* that which wounds or
causes suffering ; *the contrary she
proves—a thorn intestine* : S. A.
1037 ; *a crown ... is but a wreath
of thorns* : P. R. II. 459.

(c) a thorn-bearing shrub or
tree : P. L. X. 203.

See **White-thorn.**

Thoroughfare, *sb.* passage, travel ;
*Hell and this World...one continent
of easy thoroughfare* : P. L. X.
393.

Those.   *See* **That.**

*****Thou** (*dat.* and *acc.* thee), **(1)** *pers.
pron.* always used for the second
person in P. L., P. R., and S. A.
except in P. L. II. 1007 ; S. A.
1511 where *you* is used. In
Comus there is possibly a remnant
of the Elizabethan use of : **(1)**
superiority to servants; the
Brothers use *thou* to the Shepherd : C. 497, 509 ; but the Shepherd once uses *thou* to the
Brother : C. 611. **(2)** contempt
to strangers or inferiors ; the
Lady always uses *thou* to Comus :
C. 692, 697, etc.; Comus always
you to the Lady : C. 277, 279,
etc. On the other hand, where
we should expect *thou* as indicating affection between the
Brothers, they use *you* : C. 398,
415, 416, 417, 584.

(a) referring to the person addressed : P. L. I. 180 ; II. 689 ; *if
thou beest he* : P. L. I. 84 ; *both
thou and they* : P. L. II. 693 ;
thee, Author of all being : P. L.
III. 374 ; *thou of those seven Spirits
...the first* : P. L. III. 654 ; *none
but thou can end it* : P. L. VI. 702 ;
*the easier conquest now remains
thee* : P. L. VI. 38 ; *thorns ... it
shall bring thee forth* : P. L. X.
203 ; *this ominous night that closed
thee round* : P. R. IV. 481 ; *thou
being by* : P. L. IX. 1147 ; *thou
leading* : P. L. X. 267 ; used for
*thine ; this glory next to thee freely
put off* : P. L. III. 239 ; as antecedent of a *rel. pron.*; *chiefly Thou,
O Spirit, that dost prefer* : P. L. I.
17 ; *thou, who highly thus to entitle* :
P. L. XI. 169.

used emphatically : P. R. III.
198, 199, 407.

with imperatives ; *reign thou* :
P. L. VI. 183 ; *joy thou* : P. L.
VIII. 170.

(b) referring to various things
with more or less personification ;
to chaos : P. L. VII. 216; chastity :
C. 215 ; a city : Ps. LXXXVII. 10,
27 ; conscience : P. L. X. 843 ;
Death : P. L. X. 267 ; the earth :
P. L. VIII. 274 ; IX. 114; echo :
C. 236 ; evil : P. L. IV. 110;
experience : P. L. IX. 809; heaven :
P. L. VI. 564 ; hell : P. L. I. 251 ;
hope : C. 214; language : V. Ex.
7, 10 ; light : P. L. III. 7 ; loss of
sight : S. A. 67 ; love : P. L. IV.

753 ; May : M. M. 9 ; melancholy : II P. 23 ; mirth : L'A. 25 ; the moon : P. L. XII. 266 ; the Muse : P. L I. 11 ; V. Ex. 53 ; night : C. 196 ; the nightingale : S. I. 13 ; Paradise : P. L. XI. 269 ; a river : L. 85 ; Sin : P. L. X. 266 ; a star : P. L. V. 167 ; the sun : P. L. IV. 32 ; VIII. 273 ; time : T. 9 ; a tree : P. L. IX. 751.

(2) *refl. pron.* haste thee : P. L. XI. 104 ; prepare thee : P. L. XI. 555.

*Though, *conj.* (1) notwithstanding that, in spite of the fact that, albeit ; introducing an indicative clause expressing a fact : P. L. I. 279, 624 ; III. 245 ; VII. 170 ; VIII. 289 ; P. R. I. 92 ; N. O. 77 ; *happy though thou art* : P. L. V. 75 ; *though all by me is lost*: P. L. XII. 621 ; *though 1 have lost much lustre* : P. R. I. 377 ; *though...yet* : P. L. II. 18 ; V. 426 ; XI. 330 ; P. 45 ; *though ... but* : P. L. VII. 331.

(*b*) the clause elliptical : P. L. I. 791 ; II. 13, 104, 498 ; III. 14, 305 ; IV. 169, 706 ; V. 580 ; VI. 265, 457 ; VII. 26, 148 ; VIII. 215 ; IX. 171, 377, 390 ; X. 830 ; XI. 117, 177 ; XII. 140, 410 ; P. R. I. 466 ; IV. 454 ; S. A. 844, 1687 ; *our present lot appears for happy though but ill* : P. L. II. 224 ; *majestic, though in ruin* : P. L. II. 305 ; *nor man the least, though last created* : P. L. III. 278 ; *light from hence, though but reflected* : P. L. III. 723 ; *his will though free yet mutable* : P. L. V. 236 ; *see, though from far* : P. R. III. 303.

(2) however true it may be, granting that, even if ; introducing an indicative clause expressing a possibility or supposition ; *hope no higher, though all the stars thou knew'st by name* : P. L. XII. 576 ; introducing a similar subjunctive clause : P. L. I. 361, 576 ; VIII. 117 ; IX. 490, 648, 810 ; X. 794 ; XII. 37 ; P. R. III. 229 ; S. A. 323, 1398, 1706 ; L. 167 ; *what though the field be lost* : P. L. I. 105 ; *though Heaven be shut* : P. L. II. 358 ; *though that were large* : P. L. III. 530 ; *though men were none* : P. L. IV. 675 ; *though Heaven's King ride on thy wings* : P. L. IV. 973 ; *the planet Earth, so steadfast though she seem* : P.

L. VIII. 129 ; *though his power creation could repeat* : P. L. IX. 945 ; *though hunger still remain* : P. R. II. 255 ; *though that seat of earthly bliss be failed* : P. L. IV. 612 ; *though one should musing sit* : S. A. 1017 ; *though here thou see him die* : P. L. XI. 459.

(*b*) the clause elliptical : P. L. I. 262 ; II. 251 ; VI. 297 ; IX. 296 ; X. 878 ; XI. 332 ; P. R. II. 449.

(3) if ; *though but endeavoured with sincere intent* : P. L. III. 192.

(4) and yet, however, still ; introducing a modifying clause added as an after-thought : P. L. I. 507 ; II. 790 ; IV. 167, 295 ; V. 394 ; VII. 112 ; VIII. 598 ; X. 135 ; P. R. III. 215 ; *though darkness there might well seem twilight here* : P. L. VI. 11.

Thought, *sb.* (1) the action or power of thinking ; *thy goodness beyond thought* : P. L. V. 159 ; *change beyond ... thought* : S. A. 117 ; *nor motion of swift thought* : P. L. VI. 192.

(*b*) thinking, cogitation, meditation, reflection ; *give the reins to wandering thought* : S. A. 302 ; *pl.* : P. R. I. 190 ; *entering on studious thoughts* : P. L. VIII. 40 ; *thou linger'st in deep thoughts detained of the enterprise* : P. R. III. 227 ; *perplexed with thoughts what would become of me* : P. L. XII. 275 ; *others apart sat ... in thoughts more elevate* : P. L. II. 558.

(*c*) serious consideration, sober reflection ; *Adam took no thought* : P. L. IX. 1004 ; *pondering the danger with deep thoughts* : P. L. II. 421.

(2) the product of thinking, a notion, reflection, idea, conception, opinion, design : P. L. I. 88, 659 ; III. 171 ; V. 96, 332, 552, 676, 712 ; VI. 90 ; IX. 288, 473, 918 ; X. 608, 788, 975 ; C. 210 ; S. XXII. 13 ; *feed on thoughts* : P. L. III. 37 ; *how far from thought to make us less* : P. L. V. 828 ; *irresolute of thoughts revolved* : P. L. IX. 88 ; *with thought that they must be* : P. L. XI. 770 ; *thought following thought* : P. R. I. 192 ; *a multitude of thoughts* : P. R. I. 196 ; *thoughts, my tormentors* : S. A. 623 ; *second, first* : P. L. IX. 101, 213 ; *youthful* : C. 669 ; *growing* : P. R. I. 227 ; *naked* : V. Ex.

23 ; *high, firmer, steadiest*, etc. :
P. L. IV. 95; VI. 98; XI. 498 ;
XII. 377 ; P. R. I. 229 ; II. 258 ;
S. XXI. 5; *troubled, abject, restless,*
etc. : P. L. I. 557 ; II. 526 ; IV.
19, 807 ; V. 384 ; VI. 367 ; VIII.
183, 187 ; IX. 130, 572 ; P. R. II.
65 ; S. A. 19 ; *sinful, foul* : P. L.
VIII. 506 ; C. 383 ; with *of* : P.
L. II. 630 ; P. R. I. 299 ; S. A.
524 ; *the thought ... of lost happiness* : P. L. I. 54 ; *no thought of
flight* : P. L. VI. 236 ; *all thoughts
of war* : P. L. II. 384 ; *thoughts of
mischief* : P. L. IX. 471.

(3) *pl.* the meaning is nearly or
quite : the mind as thinking ; but
perhaps some of the following
belong in (2) or (4) : P. L. I. 680 ;
II. 354 ; VI. 629 ; IX. 603 ; X.
1008 ; P. R. II. 107 ; S. A. 459,
590, 1383 ; N. O. 92 ; C. 192, 371 ;
L. 153 ; *those thoughts that wander
through eternity* : P. L. II. 148 ;
*whom my thoughts pursue with
wonder* : P. L. IV. 362 ; *lift our
thoughts to Heaven* : P. L. IV.
688 ; *my thoughts find all repose* :
P. L. V. 28 ; *to their thoughts
firm peace recovered* : P. L. V.
209 ; *within our thoughts amused* :
P. L. VI. 581 ; *solicit not thy
thoughts with matters hid* : P. L.
VIII. 167 ; *to attain ... all human
thoughts come short* : P. L. VIII.
414 ; *Love refines the thoughts* : P.
L. VIII. 590 ; *well thy thoughts
employed* : P. L. IX. 229 ; *great
joy he promised to his thoughts* : P.
L. IX. 843 ; or manner of thinking,
disposition of mind ; *his thoughts
were low* : P. L. II. 115.

(4) understanding, intellect,
mind, heart, soul : L. 189 ; *nor
was Godhead from her thought* : P.
L. IX. 790 ; *hath in his thought to
try in battle* : P. L. V. 727 ;
*things to their thought so unimagin-
able as hate* : P. L. VII. 53 ;
things above Earthly thought : P.
L. VII. 82 ; *what thought can
measure thee* : P. L. VII. 603 ;
whatever can to ...thought be formed :
P. L. IX. 898 ; *greatly in peace of
thought* : P. L. XII. 558 ; *fixed* :
P. L. I. 560 ; *unexperienced* : P.
L. IV. 457.

(5) care ; *anxious thought* : S.
A. 659.

(6) trifle ; *worth a thought* : C.
505.

Thousand, (1) *adj.* composed of ten
hundred ; usually of an indefinitely
large number : P. L. I. 796 ; V.
249 ; VII. 382 ; VIII. 601 ; S. A.
144 ; L'A. 62 ; C. 205, 455, 627,
926 ; Ps. LXXXIV. 36 ; *flowerets of
a thousand hues* : L. 135 ; *Discord
with a thousand various mouths* :
P. L. II. 967 ; *thousand echoes* :
N. O. 100 ; *the Cherubic host in
thousand choirs* : S. M. 12 ;
thousand thousand stars : P. L.
VII. 383 ; *twenty thousand ...
chariots of God* : P. L. VI. 769 ;
ten thousand : P. L. I. 545 ; VI.
836 ; VII. 559 ; P. R. III. 411 ;
ten thousand fathom : P. L. II.
934 ; *leagues* : P. L. III. 488 ; *ten
thousand thousand* : P. L. V. 588 ;
VI. 767.

(2) *sb.* ten hundred ; used for
any great number ; always *pl.* :
P. L. I. 760 ; VI. 373 ; P. R. III.
304 ; S. XIX. 12 ; *when thousands
err* : P. L. VI. 148 ; *thou instilled
thy malice into thousands* : P. L.
VI. 270 ; *by thousands* : P. L. VI.
48, 594.

Thousandfold, *adv.* thousand times ;
multiply ten thousandfold : P. L.
XI. 678.

Thracian, *adj.* of Thrace : P. L. VII.
34. *See* **Bard.**

Thraldom, *sb.* bondage, slavery : S.
A. 946.

Thrall, *sb.* (*a*) a person in bondage,
slave : P. L. X. 402 ; S. A. 370,
1622 ; *a poor miserable captive
thrall* : P. R. I. 411 ; *his thralls by
right of war* : P. L. I. 149.

(*b*) bondage, slavery ; *led thee
out of thrall* : Ps. LXXXI. 28.

Thrascias, *sb.* the north-north west
wind : P. L. X. 700.

Thread, *sb.* a slender cord composed
of two or more filaments twisted
together : S. A. 261 ; *shooting her
beams like silver threads* : A. 16.

Threat, (1) *sb.* a menace : P. L. IV.
968 ; V. 889 ; VI. 287 ; *the threats
of Gabriel* : P. L. IX. 53 ; *wind of
airy threats* : P. L. VI. 283 ; *those
rigid threats of death* : P. L. IX.
685 ; *the threats of malice* : C. 586.

(2) *vb. tr.* to menace : C. 39.

Threaten, *vb.* (1) *tr.* (*a*) to declare or
show an intention of bringing
evil on, menace ; *the void profound
of unessential Night ... with utter
loss of being threatens him* : P.
L. II. 441 ; the evil as object ;

faces threatening war: P. L. XI. 641.

(*b*) to hold out to as a penalty ; *the Serpent ... is become not dead, as we are threatened*: P. L. IX. 870 ; the penalty as object ; to hold out as a penalty or punishment ; *death ... threatened*: P. L. IX. 715 ; *threatening cruel death*: S. A. 1198 ; *no less threatens than our expulsion down to Hell*: P. R. II. 128 ; with *prep. inf.*: P. L. IV. 77 ; VI. 359 ; S. XVI. 12.

(*c*) to give ominous indication of ; *cataracts of fire ... threatening hideous fall*: P. L. II. 177 ; to portend ; (storms) *threaten ill*: P. R. IV. 464.

(2) *intr.* (*a*) to utter menaces : P. L. II. 705 ; IV. 968 ; IX. 939 ; S. A. 852.

(*b*) to give indication of danger ; used of storms : P. R. IV. 489.

vbl. sb. **threatening**, threat, menace : Ps. LXXXVIII. 66.

See Ever - threatening, Long-threatened.

Threatener, *sb.* one who threatens another with a penalty ; applied to God : P. L. IX. 687.

Three, *adj.* two and one : P. L. II. 645 ; VIII. 130 ; XI. 736, 866 ; C. 969 ; *from the well of life three drops*: P. L. XI. 416 ; *three ways, places*: P. L. X. 323, 324 ; *days*: P. L. XII. 188 ; P. R. III. 412 ; *three years' day*: S. XXII. 1 ; *summers three times eight*: M. W. 7 ; *the Sirens three*: C. 253 ; *his daughters three*: C. 982.

absol. three persons or things : P. L. X. 364 ; *three that in Mount Ida ... strove*: P. L. V. 382 ; *virtue, valour, wisdom ... these three*: P. R. II. 433.

Three-and-twentieth, *adj.* twenty third : S. II. 2.

Three-bolted, *adj.* formed of three shafts ; *three-bolted thunder*: P. L. VI. 764.

Threefold, *adj.* multiplied by three : P. L. II. 645.

Threescore, *adj.* sixty : P. R. III. 411.

Thresh, *vb. tr.* to beat out from the husk : L'A. 108.

Threshing-floor, *sb.* the floor on which grain is beaten out from the husk : P. L. IV. 984.

Threshold, *sb.* entrance, door, gate *Hell's dark threshold*: P. L. X.

594 ; *the starry threshold of Jove's court*: C. 1.

Thrice, *adv.* (*a*) three times : P. L. I. 619 ; IV. 115 ; IX. 64 ; S. A. 392, 396 ; C. 914, 915 ; *from the centre thrice to the utmost pole*: P. L. I. 74 ; *thrice threefold the gates*: P. L. II. 645 ; *defies thee thrice to single fight*: S. A. 1222 ; *thrice fugitive about Troy wall*: P. L. IX. 16.

(*b*) in a threefold degree, fully, perfectly ; *thrice happy*: P. L. III. 570 ; VII. 625, 631 ; in three respects (?) ; *thrice great Hermes*: Il P. 88.

Thrice-acceptable (ácceptáble), *adj.* perfectly acceptable, much desired : P. L. X. 855.

Thrift, *sb.* frugality, economy : C. 167.

Thrill, *vb. tr.* to penetrate and cause a keen and exquisite emotion in : N. O. 103.

Thrive, *vb.* (only in *pres.*) *intr.* (*a*) to prosper, flourish, be successful : P. L. II. 261 ; X. 236 ; P. R. I. 114.

(*b*) to grow rich ; *thrive in wealth*: P. R. II. 430.

(*c*) to grow vigorously, increase in size and strength : S. A. 637.

Throat, *sb.* the voice ; *fig.*, the *brazen throat of war had ceased to roar*: P. L. XI. 713.

See Deep-throated.

Throe, *sb. pl.* the pains of childbirth : P. L. II. 780 ; M. W. 26.

Throne, I. *sb.* (1) a royal seat ; sometimes including also the sovereign power : A. 15 ; *Artaxerxes' throne*: P. R. IV. 271 ; the throne of God or Christ ; *in middle air shall spread his throne*: N. O. 164 ; *the chariot of Paternal Deity ... whereon a sapphire throne*: P. L. VI. 758 ; the throne of Satan : P. L. II. 1 ; X. 445 ; *adore me on the throne of Hell*: P. L. IV. 89 ; *I should ill become this throne*: P. L. II. 445 ; of Chaos : P. L. II. 959 ; of Jove ; *the thunderous throne*: V. Ex. 36.

(*b*) the peculiar seat or abode of God or Christ in heaven : P. L. I. 639 ; II. 68, 138, 267 ; III. 148, 314, 649 ; V. 585 ; VI. 5, 88, 133, 426, 834 ; VII. 137, 556 ; XI. 20 ; *the holy mount of Heaven's high-seated top, the imperial throne of Godhead*: P. L. VII. 585 ;

shook his throne: P. L. I. 105 ;
*lowly reverent towards either throne
they bow*: P. L. III. 350 ; *with
songs ... circle his throne*: P. L. V.
163 ; *circling the throne and singing*: P. R. I. 171 ; *high, sovran,
Almighty, supreme*: P. L. III.
655 ; V. 656, 868 ; X. 28 ; XI. 82 ;
T. 17 : *sapphire-coloured* : S. M.
7 ; *fatal*: P. L. II. 104 ; *hereditary*: P. L. XII. 370.

(*c*) *fig., sitting ... on Beauty's
throne*: P. R. II. 212.

(*d*) used of a throne-chariot :
P. L. VI. 103 ; *the fiery-wheeled
throne*: Il P. 53 ; *fig., cloudy
throne*: D. F. I. 56 ; the chariot
of the Sun : P. L. IV. 597 ; N. O.
84.

(2) a royal abode ; *Samarchand
... Temir's throne* : P. L. XI. 389.

(3) royal estate or sovereign
power ; sometimes including sense
(1) : P. L. XII. 323 ; P. R. III.
395 ; IV. 100 ; *on Judah's throne,
on the throne of Judah* : P. R. II.
424, 440 ; *David's throne, on
David's throne, on the throne of
David* : P. R. I. 240 ; III. 153,
169, 357, 383, 408 ; IV. 108, 147,
379, 471 ; *the throne of Cyrus* : P.
R. III. 33 ; *the sovereign power
of God* : P. L. X. 382 ; P. R. IV.
603 ; *the throne and monarchy of
God* : P. L. I. 42 ; *banded against
his throne* : P. L. II. 320 ; *the
assessor of his throne* : P. L. VI.
679 ; *to celebrate or hymn his
throne* : P. L. II. 241 ; IV. 944 ;
the power of angels ; *Powers that
erst in Heaven sat on thrones* : P.
L. I. 360 ; of Satan : P. L. V.
725 ; *established in a safe unenvied
throne* : P. L. II. 23.

(4) *pl.* kingdoms, monarchies :
P. R. IV. 85.

(5) God as occupying a throne ;
*leave ... unobeyed, the Throne
supreme* : P.L. V. 670.

(6) the third of the nine orders
of angels or a member of this
order : P. L. II. 310 ; III. 320 ; V.
749 ; VII. 198 ; X. 86 ; *Thrones,
Dominations, Princedoms, Virtues,
Powers* : P. L. V. 601, 772, 840 ;
X. 460 ; apparently applied to
any angels high in authority, but
in each case the meaning may be
the order : P. L. II. 430 ; V. 363 ;
VI. 841 ; P. R. II. 121 ; *the rebel
Thrones* : P. L. VI. 199 ; *two

potent Thrones* : P. L. VI. 366 ;
of the Thrones above : P. L. XI.
232 ; *among the Thrones* : P. L.
XI. 296 ; *Supreme of Heavenly
Thrones, God* : P. L. VI. 723.

II. *vb.* (thronèd *disyl.*: P. L. I.
28) *tr.* to place on or as on a
throne ; *Mercy ... throned in celestial sheen* : N. O. 145 ; used of
God or Christ : P. L. VI. 890 ;
high throned above all highth : P.
L. III. 58 ; *throned inaccessible* :
P. L. III. 377 ; *in sapphire* : P. L.
VI. 772 ; *Jehovah...throned between
the Cherubim* : P. L. I. 386 ;
*throned in highest bliss, in the
bosom of bliss* : P. L. III. 305 ;
P. R. IV. 596.

part. adj. **throned**, that sit on
thrones or hold authority : P. L.
I. 128.

See **High-throned.**

Throng, I. *sb.* (1) a great number of
persons crowded closely together :
P. L. XI. 671.

(2) a great number of persons,
multitude, host ; *throngs of
knights* : L'A. 119 ; *the armed
throng* : N. O. 58 ; of angels :
P. L. IV. 831 ; IX. 112 ; *the throng
of his apostasy* : P. R. I. 145 ; *the
Angelic throng* : P. L. V. 650 ; VI.
308 ; *the Stygian throng* : P. L. X.
453.

(*b*) *the throng*, the mass of people,
the multitude : S. XIII. 5 ; with
blending of sense (1) : S. A. 1609.

(*c*) *fig.* of water ; *the watery
throng, wave rolling after wave* :
P. L. VII. 297.

II. *vb.* (1) *tr.* (*a*) to fill with a
crowd ; *all access was thronged* :
P. L. I. 761 ; *the gate with dreadful faces thronged* : P. L. XII. 644;
to store with a multitude ;
*Nature ... thronging the seas with
spawn* : C. 713.

(*b*) to bring together in a
crowd, or *intr.* to come together
in a crowd ; *helmets thronged* :
P. L. VI. 83 ; *of goats or timorous
flock together thronged* : P. L. VI.
857.

(2) *intr.* (*a*) to crowd or press
together : P. L. I. 780 ; of inanimate things ; *restless thoughts
... rush upon me thronging* : S. A.
21 ; *a thousand fantasies begin to
throng into my memory* : C. 206.

(*b*) to be full, teem ; *with herds
the pastures thronged* : P.R. III. 260.

Throttle, *vb. tr.* to choke, strangle : P. R. IV. 568.

*Through, I. *prep.* (1) from end to end or side to side of, into at one side and out at another : P. L. II. 684, 886 ; *my way lies through your spacious empire* : P. L. II. 974 ; *Argo passed through Bosporus* : P. L. II. 1018 ; *through utter and through middle Darkness borne* : P. L. III. 16 ; *the River of Bliss through midst of Heaven rolls* : P. L. III. 358 ; *through the shaggy hill* : P. L. IV. 224 ; *he passed ... through groves* : P. L. V. 292 ; *the griding sword ... passed through him* : P. L. VI. 330.

(2) over the whole surface or extent of, in all directions in, throughout : P. L. I. 177 ; V. 253 ; *known ... through the Heathen World* : P. L. I. 375 ; *through the coast of Palestine* : P. L. I. 464 ; *through the void immense to search* : P. L. II. 829 ; *the mind through all her powers irradiate* : P. L. III. 52 ; *through the infinite host* : P. L. V. 874 ; *Satan ... ranging through the dire attack* : P. L. VI. 248 ; *through all her numbers absolute* : P. L. VIII. 421.

(3) of passage in and out of, along, or within some medium : P. L. I. 395 ; *through the gloom were seen* : P. L. I. 544 ; *looks through ... the air* : P. L. I. 595 ; *riding through the air* : P. L. II. 663 ; *through a cloud* : P. L. III. 378 ; *drained through a limbec* : P. L. III. 605 ; *through veins of porous earth ... up-drawn* : P. L. IV. 227 ; *through plate and mail* : P. L. VI. 368 ; *through mine ear* : II P. 164 ; *through your eyes* : A. 27 ; *through the soft silence* : Cir. 5.

(*b*) of hindrance ; *through restraint, opposition* : P. L. III. 87 ; S. A. 1050.

(4) of passage in the midst of or among ; *bear him safe through the strict sentries* : P. L. II. 412 ; *through the shock of fighting elements ... wins his way* : P. L. II. 1014 ; *through the spicy forest onward come* : P. L. V. 298 ; *through groves of coral stray* : P. L. VII. 404 ; *their course through thickest constellations held* : P. L. X. 411 ; *advance through the wild Desert* : P. L. XII. 216.

(5) from the beginning to the end of, during the course of : P. L. VII. 92 ; *through eternity* : P. L. II. 148 ; *through the ... night* : P. L. X. 846 ; *through many an age* : P. R. I. 16.

(*b*) of continuance ; *I, in Man residing through the race* : P. L. X. 607 ; *through his short course* : S. A. 670.

(6) of experience ; *through hard assays* : C. 972.

(*b*) over all the steps of ; *lead me through the world's vain mask* : S. XXII. 13.

(*c*) by way of ; *through pangs fled to felicity* : M. W. 68.

(7) by means of : P. L. II. 262 ; *the high repute which he through hazard huge must earn* : P. L. II. 473 ; *him, through their malice fallen* : P. L. III. 400 ; *kindled through agitation to a flame* : P. L. IX. 637 ; *through Sin to Death exposed* : P. L. X. 407 ; *working through love* : P. L. XII. 489.

(8) by reason of, in consequence of, on account of : P. L. I. 366 ; II. 156 ; *through pain* : P. L. II. 544 ; *through dire change befallen us* : P. L. II. 820 ; *through unquiet rest* : P. L. V. 11 ; *through pride* : P. L. V. 665 ; *sloth* : P. L. VI. 166 ; *expectation* : P. L. IX. 789 ; *frailty* : S. A. 369 ; *thirst* : C. 67.

II. *adv.* from one side to the other ; *shot through* : P. L. VI. 15 ; *cut through* : Ps. LXXXVIII. 66.

Throughout, (1) *adv.* in every part : P. L. VI. 833 ; *throughout dominion hold* : P. L. VII. 532 ; *Spirits that live throughout* : P. L. VI. 344.

(2) *prep.* (*a*) in every part of : P. L. I. 754 ; Ps. LXXXI. 37 ; *throughout the world* : P. R. II. 443 ; IV. 150 ; *the spacious North* : P. L. V. 726 ; *the fluid mass* : P. L. VII. 237.

(*b*) during the course of ; *throughout the year* : S. XXII. 5.

Throw, *vb.* (*pres. 2d sing.* throw'st : S. A. 689 ; *pret.* threw : *past part.* thrown) *tr.* (1) to fling, hurl, cast ; *from Heaven ... thrown* : P. L. I. 741 ; *Lichas from the top of Œta threw* : P. L. II. 545 ; *mountains ... thrown on them* : P. L. VI. 843 ; *throw ... wreaths into her stream* : C. 850 ; *the crumbled earth above them threw* : P. L. VII. 468 ; *their*

arms away they threw : P. L. VI.
639 ; *themselves they threw down* :
P. L. VI. 864 ; almost=to bring :
L. 139.
    fig., flouts at us they throw : Ps.
LXXX. 28 ; *the flowery May, who
from her green lap throws the
yellow cowslip* : M. M. 3.
    (2) to cause to fall, cast down ;
(*a*) to bring down from an exalted
position ; *throw'st them lower* : S.
A. 689 ; *ambition threw me down* :
P. L. IV. 40 ; *fig., thrown from
his hope* : P. R. IV. 3.
    (*b*) to conquer ; *by thee threw
down the aspiring Dominations* :
P. L. III. 391.
    (*c*) to slay and leave uncared for,
abandon ; *or left thy carcass where
the ass lay thrown* : S. A. 1097.
    (3) to cause to rise ; *God had
thrown that mountain* : P. L. IV.
225.
    (4) to lay, spread ; *fig.* : P. 30 ;
*on her naked shame ... the saintly
veil ... to throw* : N. O. 42 ; *the
Moon ... o'er the dark her silver
mantle threw* : P. L. IV. 609.
    (5) to direct, turn ; *round he
throws his .. eyes* ; P. L. I. 56.
    In combination with other
words ; (*a*) **throw forth** ; to send
out, emit ; P. L. II. 755 ; to cause
to grow, produce : Ps. LXXXV. 51.
    (*b*) **throw off**, to cast aside : P.
L. III. 362 ; to discard, give up ;
*because you have thrown off your
Prelate Lord* : F. of C. 1.
    (*c*) **throw out**, to reject : P. L.
X. 887.
    (*d*) **throw ... flight**, fly swiftly :
P. L. III. 562, 741.
Thrust, *vb.* (only in *past part.*) *tr.*
to drive with force, push : P. L.
II. 857 ; *I to Hell am thrust* : P.
L. IV. 508 ; *into a dungeon thrust* :
S. A. 367.
Thummim, P. R. III. 14. *See* **Urim.**
Thunder (1) *sb.* (*a*) the loud noise fol-
lowing a flash of lightning : P. L.
II. 477 ; IX. 1002 ; X. 666 ; Ps.
LXXXI. 29 ; *the roar of thunder* :
P. R. IV. 429 ; *thunder mixed with
hail* : P. L. XII. 181 ; *he ... in
hunder, lightning, and loud trum-
pet's sound ordain them laws* :
P. L. XII. 229.
    (*b*) a noise resembling that of
thunder : S. A. 1651 ; in heaven
or hell ; *he shall hear infernal
thunder* : P. L. II. 66 ; *his throne,*

from whence deep thunders roar :
P. L. II. 267 ; *the infernal doors
... grate harsh thunder* : P. L. II.
882 ; *in thunder uttered thus his
voice* : P. L. X. 33.
    (*c*) a shaft of lightning accom-
panied by thunder and hurled, or
to be hurled, at the object struck ;
the wrath of Jove speaks thunder :
C. 804 ; used by God for the
expulsion of the rebel angels from
heaven : P. L. I. 93, 258, 601 ; II.
166, 294 ; III. 393 ; VI. 632, 713,
854 ; VII. 606 ; P. R. I. 90 ; *in
his right hand grasping ten thousand thunders* : P. L. VI. 836 ;
three-bolted : P. L. VI. 764 ; *the
thunder, winged with red lightning* :
P. L. I. 174 ; *his thunder .. devouring fire* : P. L. V. 893 ; *the blasting
volleyed thunder* : P. L. IV. 928.
    fig. of the shot of a cannon : P.
L. VI. 606 ; of the action of Samson ; *his cloudless thunder bolted
on their heads* : S. A. 1696.
    (*d*) lightning ; *thunder blue* : A.
51.
    (2) *vb. intr.* (*a*) to give forth
peals of thunder, resound with
thunder : P. R. IV. 410.
    (*b*) to make a loud noise, re-
sound ; *the ... trump of doom must
thunder through the deep* : N. O.
156 ; *fig., that fear comes thundering back* : P. L. X. 814.
    (*c*) to utter denunciations,
threats, or commands ; *Jehovah
thundering out of Zion* : P. L. I.
386 ; to contain threats or commands : S. A. 1353 ; to resound
with denunciations ; *his dreadful
voice no more would thunder in my
ears* : P. L. X. 780.
    part. adj. **thundering** ; (*a*)
sending forth a sound like thunder : P. L. I. 233.
    (*b*) like that of thunder : P. L.
VI. 487.
Thunderbolt, *sb.* a shaft of lightning;
linked : P. L. I. 328 ; applied *fig.*
to the shot from a cannon :
chained : P. L. VI. 589.
Thunder-clasping, *adj.* grasping
thunderbolts : Ps. CXXXVI. 37.
Thunderer, *sb.* one who thunders ;
the Thunderer, God : P. L. II. 28 ;
VI. 491.
Thunderous, *adj.* full of or emitting
thunder ; *the thundrous clouds* :
P. L. X. 702 ; or the meaning may
be, awe-inspiring because of the

thunder ; *the thunderous throne* :
V. Ex. 36.

Thunderstruck, *past part.* struck
dumb, amazed : P. L. VI. 858 ;
P. R. I. 36.

* **Thus,** *adv.* (**1**) in this or that manner
or way ; (*a*) referring to some-
thing present and in view : P. L.
I. 137, 266, 328 ; II. 741, 784,
914 ; IV. 505 ; V. 68 ; VIII. 277 ;
*thus sitting, thus consulting, thus
in arms* : P. L. II. 164 ; *thus
trampled, thus expelled* : P. L. II.
194 ; *thus alone* : P. L. III. 699.

(*b*) referring to what precedes
or has been said : P. L. I. 192,
559, 789 ; II. 226, 378, 486 ; III.
416 ; *thus saying* : P. L. II. 466,
870 ; *thus they relate* : P. L. I.
746 ; *thus was this place* : P. L.
IV. 246 ; *thus was the first Day* ;
P. L. VII. 252 ; *thus was Sabbath
kept* : P. L. VII. 634 ; *ere thus was
sinned* : P. L. X. 229.

(*c*) referring to what follows
or is about to be said : P. L. II.
10, 309 ; IV. 787 ; *thus began* : P.
L. I. 83 ; II. 118, 680 ; *thus
answered, replied* : P. L. I. 127,
272 ; II. 746 : *his speech he thus
renews* ; P. L. II. 389 ; *to whom
Satan, turning boldly, thus* : P. L.
II. 968.

(**2**) to this or that degree, distance, or extent ; *thus high* : P.L.
II. 7, 8 ; *low* : P. L. II. 81 ;
wondrous fair : P. L. V. 155 ; *thus
early* : P. L. IX. 457 ; *long* : P. R.
II. 105 ; III. 378 ; *forlorn* : P. L.
IV. 374 ; *largely* : P. L. VIII. 7 ;
distempered : P. L. IX. 1131 ; *over-
fond* : P. L. XI. 289 ; *thus far* :
P. L. I. 587 ; II. 22 ; VI. 700 ; X.
370 ; *thus far removed* : P. L. II.
211 ; *thus far extend* : P. L. VII.
230 ; *thus much, as much as this* :
P. L. IV. 899.

(**3**) consequently, so : P. L. X.
837.

Thwart, (**1**) *adj.* lying or moving
crosswise or transverse ; *several
spheres ... moved contrary with
thwart obliquities* : P.L. VIII. 132;
*Notus and Afer ... thwart of these
... Eurus and Zephyr* : P. L. X.
703 ; moving across the sky ; *the
slant lightning, whose thwart flame* :
P. L. X. 1073.

(**2**) *vb. tr.* to pass over or
across ; *a shooting star in autumn
thwarts the night* : P. L. IV. 557.

part. adj. **thwarting,** injurious,
hurtful : A. 51.

* **Thy,** *poss. pron.* of or belonging to
thee ; (*a*) referring to a person ;
with a *sb.* : P. L. I. 130 ; II. 699 ;
III. 145 ; IV. 471 ; VI. 142 ; *thy
few in arms* : P. R. III. 20 ; *thy so
true ... love* : P. L. IX. 982 ; *I
pursue thy lingering* : P. L. II.
701 ; *obj. gen.* : P. L. VI. 740 ;
before a vowel ; *thy empyreal mansion* : P. L. III. 699 ; *thy inward
fraud* : P. L. X. 871 ; *offspring* :
P. L. XI. 358 ; *eyes* : S. A. 584 ;
abundance : P. L. IV. 730 ; *unvalued book* : W. S. 11 ; *thy other
self* : P. L. VIII. 450 ; *thy else
not dreaded spear* : P. L. IV. 929 ;
thy own : P. L. IX. 379 ; S. A.
218, 844 ; M. W. 52 ; used emphatically : P. R. II. 425 ; III.
200 ; without a *sb.* ; *one of these
thou must make sure thy own* :
P. R. III. 363.

(*b*) referring to various things
with more or less personification ;
to death : P. L. II. 683 ; echo :
C. 231 ; hell : P. L. I. 252 ; language : V. Ex. 7 ; light : P. L. III.
22 ; May : M. M. 7 ; melancholy :
L'A. 9 ; mirth : L'A. 35 ; the
moon : C. 333 ; the Muse : P. L.
I. 13 ; night : C. 197 ; the nightingale : S. I. 5 ; the serpent : P. L.
X. 181 ; Sion : P. L. III. 31 ; a
star : P. L. V. 169 ; the sun : P.
L. IV. 33 ; time : T. 1 ; a tree :
P. L. V. 59 ; the world : P. L.
VII. 230.

Thyestean, *adj. Thyestean banquet* ;
Atreus, in revenge for a crime,
slew the children of his brother
Thyestes and served them to him
at a banquet. Because of this
transgression, the sun turned his
course for one day from west to
east : P. L. X. 688.

Thyme, *sb.* the plant *Thymus* : L.
40.

Thyrsis, *sb.* the name of a shepherd
common in pastoral poetry : L'A.
83 ; as the name of the Attendant
Spirit who personates the shepherd in Comus : C. 494, 512, 657.

* **Thyself,** *pron.* (**1**) *emphat.* : P. L.
IV. 961 ; *among the gods thyself a
goddess* : P. L. V. 78 ; *in place
thyself so high* : P. L. V. 812 ; *thyself half-starved* : P. L. X. 595 ;
thyself as false : P. L. X. 868 ; *me
than thyself more miserable* : P. L.

x. 929 ; *thyself not free* : P. L. VI. 181.

(*b*) in apposition with a *pron.*; *thou thyself* : P. L. III. 162 ; VIII. 566 ; IX. 299 ; P. R. II. 175 ; C. 616.

(*c*) as subject of a *vb.*; *be thyself Man* : P. L. III. 283 ; *thyself expect to feel* : P. L. IV. 972.

(2) *refl.* : P. L. II. 696 ; v. 833 ; x. 156 ; P. R. I. 344 ; IV. 555 ; S. A. 213, 914 ; with a *prep.* : P. L. IV. 448 ; v. 68 ; VI. 265 ; VIII. 400, 428 ; x. 949 ; P. R. IV. 284 ; S. A. 789, 1590.

Tiar, *sb.* a tiara, coronet ; *of beaming sunny rays a golden tiar circled his head* : P. L. III. 625.

Tiberius, *sb.* the Roman Emperor : P. R. III. 159.

Tide, *sb.* stream, flood, torrent : P.L. XI. 854 ; L. 157.

Tiding, *sb. pl.* news, intelligence : P. L. v. 870 ; x. 36, 346 ; XI. 302 ; XII. 504 ; *tidings of him* : P. R. II. 62 ; *great, glad* : P. L. XI. 226 ; XII. 375 ; *sad, evil* : P. R. I. 109 ; S. A. 1567.

Tidore, *sb.* one of the Molucca Islands : P. L. II. 639.

Tie, *vb. tr.* to bind, confine, restrict ; *their essence ... not tied or manacled with joint or limb* : P. L. I. 426 ; *the chains that tie the hidden soul of harmony* : L'A. 143 ; *tie him to his own prescript* : S. A. 308.

Tiger, *sb.* the animal *Felis tigris* : P. L. IV. 403 ; *the ounce, the libbard and the tiger* : P. L. VII. 467 ; *wolves or tigers* : C. 534 ; *bears, tigers, ounces* : P. L. IV. 344 ; *ounce or tiger* : C. 71 ; *the lion and fierce tiger* : P. R. I. 313.

Tigris, *sb.* the river : P. L. IX. 71.

Tile, *sb.* a plate of baked clay used in covering roofs : P. L. IV. 191.

*Till, (1) *prep.* to the time of : P. L. III. 458 ; v. 31, 35 ; VI. 10, 262, 396 ; VII. 380, 435 ; IX. 219, 596 ; XI. 550 ; XII. 207 ; *till now* : P. L. II. 744 ; *till then* : P. L. I. 93. *See* Now and Then.

(2) *conj.* to the time that or when ; followed by the indicative ; *till on dry land he lights* : P.L. I. 227 ; *till ... to all the fowls he seems a phœnix* : P. L. v. 270 ; *till ... thou stood'st* : P. L. XI. 758 ; *till ... the sea swallows him* : P. L. XII. 194 ; followed by the sub-

junctive : P. L. v. 187 ; VII. 107 ; XI. 828 ; *till one greater Man restore us* : P. L. I. 4 ; *till his great Chief return* : P. L. II. 527 ; *till this meridian heat be over* : P. L. v. 369 ; *till body up to spirit work* : P. L. v. 478 ; *till ... she learn* : P. L. VIII. 190 ; *till thou return* : P. L. x. 206 ; *till day droop* : P. L. XI. 178 ; *till truth were freed* : P. R. I. 220 ; *till truth ... be freed* : S. XV. 11.

Tillage, *sb.* the cultivation of the soil, husbandry : P. L. XI. 434.

Tilt, *vb. tr.* to move unsteadily, toss : P. L. XI. 747.

   part. adj. **tilting,** used in the tourney : P. L. IX. 34.

Tilth, *sb.* tillage-land, cultivated soil : P. L. XI. 430.

Timber, *sb.* trees yielding wood suitable for building : P. L. XI. 728.

Timbrel, *sb.* a musical instrument resembling the tambourine : P. L. I. 394 ; S. A. 1617 ; Ps. LXXXI. 6.

Timbreled, *part. adj.* sung to the sound of the timbrel : N. O. 219.

Time, *sb.* (1) the general idea or fact of successive existence, 'measure of duration : P. L. IX. 70 ; S. II. 12 ; *Time ... measures all things* : P. L. v. 580 ; *time numbers motion* : U. C. II. 7 ; *the speed of Gods time counts not* : P. L. x. 91 ; *more swift than time or motion* : P. L. VII. 177 ; *where ... time, and place, are lost* : P. L. II. 894 ; *in length of time* : P. L. II. 274 ; *long process of time* : P. L. II. 297 ; *periods of time* : P. L. II. 603 ; *tract of time* : P. L. v. 498 ; *Time will run on smoother* : S. XX. 5 ; *Time will run back* : N. O. 135 ; *till time mature thee* : P. R. IV. 282 ; *I forget all time* : P. L. IV. 639 ; *personified* : V. Ex. 71 ; T. 1, 22 ; *the scythe of Time* : P. L. x. 606 ; as masc. gender : S. II. 1.

(2) a particular part of duration, either a point or a period ; esp. as characterized by the occurrence of some event or series of events : P. L. XII. 23, 316 ; P. R. I. 56 ; *any time this ten years* : U. C. I. 7 ; *at curfew time* : C. 435 ; *now is the pleasant time* : P. L. v. 38 ; *we know no time when we were not as now* : P. L. v. 859 ; *long time in even scale the battle hung* : P. L. VI. 245 ; *in*

time of truce, of dearth, of need: P. L. XI. 244; XII. 161; Ps. LXXX. 20; *this* or *that time*: P. L. II. 348; IV. 489; VIII. 474; P. R. IV. 507; *what time*: P. L. I. 36; C. 291; L. 28; Ps. IV. 18; *for the* or *a time*: P. L. IX. 464; P. R. II. 14; *at which time, at any time*: P. L. II. 774; P. R. IV. 558; *in short time, in a little time*: P. R. IV. 378; S. A. 1126.

(*b*) *pl.* age, epoch: P. R. III. 94; *the times of great Messiah*: P. L. XII. 243.

(3) a point in or a portion of duration available, suitable, or allotted for some special purpose: P. L. IV. 6; P. R. I. 58; III. 396, 433; IV. 174, 475; N. O. 239; *time there is for all things*: P. R. III. 183; *when time shall be*: P. L. III. 284; X. 74; P. R. IV. 616; *the time is come*: P. R. II. 43; *sent before their time*: P. R. IV. 632; *for other things mild Heaven a time ordains*: S. XXI. 11; *time may come when men with angels may participate*: P. L. V. 493; *at times when men seek most repose*: S. A. 406; *no time for lamentation*: S. A. 1708; *no time ...for long indulgence*: P. R. I. 109; *not instant, but of future time*: P. L. X. 345; *he in whose hand all times and seasons roll*: P. R. III. 187; *due, appointed, prefixed*: P. L. XII. 152; P. R. I. 269; III. 182, 440; Ps. LXXXI. 11; *full*: P. L. XII. 301; *fulness of time*: P. R. IV. 380; *I knew the time now full*: P. R. I. 286.

(*b*) the portion of duration allotted to the present order of things; contrasted with *eternity*: *the race of Time, till Time stand fixed*: P. L. XII. 554, 555.

(*c*) the portion of duration allotted to a human life; *numbered out his time*: U. C. II. 8; *short time of breath*: M. W. 9.

(*d*) life, existence, power, or dominion; *his people ...their time should have no end*: Ps. LXXXI. 64.

(*e*) the hour of death: U. C. II. 23.

(*f*) leisure; *waste of time*: P. L. IV. 123; free or unoccupied time; *to drive the time away*: U. C. II. 15.

(*g*) opportunity; *if you let time slip*: C. 743.

(4) the state of things at a particular time, circumstances: P.L. I. 253; *under change of times*: S. A. 695; *present times past*: S. A. 22.

(5) a recurrent instance or occasion: P. L. X. 24; *certain times to appear to his disciples*: P. L. XII. 437; *each*: S. A. 397; *the fourth*: S. A. 402.

(*b*) the renewal of action; *the second time returning*: P. L. XI. 859; *eat the second time*: P. R. II. 275.

(*c*) the addition of a number to itself; *three times*: M. W. 7; *four*: P. L. IX. 65; P. R. II. 245; *nine*: P. L. I. 50.

(6) musical measure; *move in melodious time*: N. O. 129.

(7) **at** times, now and then: P. R. I. 228.

(8) **in** time; (*a*) in the course of events, eventually: P. L. II. 210.

(*b*) before it is too late: P. L. V. 848.

(*c*) at the right moment: P. R. III. 298; S. A. 1390.

See After-times, Oft-times, Seed-time, Seven-times-folded, Seven-times-wedded, Spring-time, Vintage-time.

Timelessly, *adv.* unseasonably: D. F. I. 2.

Timely, (1) *adj.* seasonable, opportune; *the timely dew of sleep*: P. L. IV. 614; *care, rest*: P. L. X. 1057; S. A. 602; C. 689.

(2) *adv.* at the right moment, opportunely: P. L. III. 728; S. I. 9; *to forewarn us timely*: P.L. VII. 74; or early; *Heaven hath timely tried their youth*: C. 970.

Timely-happy, *adj.* fortunate or successful in early life: S. II. 8.

Timna, *sb.* Timnath, a town of the Philistines situated on the northern boundary of Judah: S. A. 219, 383, 795.

Timnian, *adj.* of Timna: S. A. 1018.

Timorous, *adj.* (*a*) fearful of danger, lacking courage, timid: P. R. III. 241; *to nobler deeds timorous*: P. L. II. 117; *a ...timorous flock*: P. L. VI. 857.

(*b*) indicating or arising from fear; *timorous doubt*: S. A. 740.

Tincture, *sb.* absorption: P. L. VII. 367.

See **Sky-tinctured, Vermeil-tinctured.**

Tine, *vb. tr.* to light, kindle ; *tine the slant lightning* : P. L. X. 1075.

Tinsel, *adj.* made of a fabric interwoven with gold or silver threads : P. L. IX. 36.

Tinsel-slippered, *adj.* wearing bright or shining slippers ; *Thetis' tinsel-slippered feet* : C. 877.

Tip, (1) *sb.* point, end : C. 914.

(2) *vb.* (*past part.* tipt) *tr.* to furnish or cover on the end ; *a reed ... tipt with fire* : P. L. VI. 580.

Tipsy, *adj.* indicating or proceeding from inebriation : C. 104.

Tire. *sb.* a row of guns, battery ; *to displode their second tire of thunder* : P. L. VI. 605.

Tire, *vb. tr.* to fatigue, weary : S.A. 1326 ; C. 688.

See **Over-tire.**

Tiresias, *sb.* the blind sooth-sayer of Thebes : P. L. III. 36.

Tissue, *sb.* cloth interwoven with gold or silver : P. L. V. 592.

Tissued, *part. adj.* brilliant in colour ; *the tissued clouds* : N. O. 146.

Titan, *sb.* Oceanus, the eldest son of Uranus and Ge, and the father of the Titans ; identified with one of the fallen angels : P. L. I. 510.

Title, (1) *sb.* an appellation significant of position, dignity, or rank : P. L. II. 311 ; XII. 516 ; P. R. IV. 199 ; *magnific, imperial, high* : P. L. V. 773, 801 ; XI. 793 ; *Mother of Mankind ... ill-worthy I such title* : P. L. XI. 163 ; *man over men he made not lord—such title to himself reserving* : P. L. XII. 70.

(2) *vb. tr.* (*a*) to designate by the title of, name, call ; *false titled Sons of God* : P. R. II. 179 ; *must be titled Gods* : P. R. III. 81.

(*b*) to give a right to be entitled ; with two *acc.* ; *whose lives religious titled them the Sons of God* : P. L. XI. 622.

Title-page, *sb.* the page which contains the title of a book : S. XI. 6.

Tittle, *sb.* minute part, iota : P.R. I. 450.

Titular, *adj.* existing in the title only, nominal : P. L. V. 774.

*To, I. *prep.* (usually not repeated before the second substantive : P. L. VIII. 582 ; IX. 280 ; but sometimes ; *to person or to poem* : P. L. IX. 41 ; *either to God or to each other* : P. L. X. 111, 112 ; also usually omitted before the second infinitive : P. L. I. 147, 473, 556, 644 ; II. 384, 1032 ; III. 662 ; IV. 859, 947 ; V. 369 ; but occasionally ; *either to undergo ... or to accuse* : P. L, X. 126, 127 ; both uses ; *to sing, to dance, to dress, and troll the tongue* : P. L. XI. 619, 620.)

(1) in the direction of ; *to the north* : P. L. VI. 79 ; *wheeling to the shield* : P. L. IV. 785 ; *to right and left the front unfold* : P. L. VI. 558 ; in the same direction as ; *a meteor streaming to the wind* : P. L. I. 537.

(2) toward and ending at ; (*a*) of a place : P. L. I. 47 ; C. 376 ; *Josiah drove them thence to Hell* : P. L. I. 418 ; *ran purple to the sea* : P. L. I. 451 ; *we ascend up to our native seat* : P. L. II. 76 ; *bore him slope downward to the Sun* : P. L. IV. 591 ; *hurried back to fire* : P. L. II. 603 ; *from the centre thrice to the utmost pole* : P. L. I. 74 ; *the way ... out of Hell leads up to Light* : P. L. II. 433.

(*b*) of a condition ; *transform oft to the image of a brute* : P. L. I. 371 ; *exalted to such power* : P. L. I. 736 ; *condemned ... to utter woe* : P. L. II. 87 ; *unchanged to hoarse or mute* : P. L. VII. 25.

(*c*) of an action or a thing to be accomplished : P. L. I. 129 ; *let us to our fresh employments rise* : P. L. V. 125 ; *from dance to sweet repast they turn* : P. L. V. 630 ; *lead forth to battle* : P. L. VI. 46 ; *to arms the matin trumpet sung* : P. L. VI. 525.

(*d*) of an end, purpose, design, destination, etc.; with many shades of meaning in noting the relations between words : P. L. IX. 242 ; *he should be ... to a sign spoken against* : P. R. II. 89 ; *she ... means her provision only to the good* : C. 765 ; *to nobler sights Michael from Adam's eyes the film removed* : P. L. XI. 411 ; *to his Godhead sing* : P. L. II. 242 ; *live to ourselves* : P. L. II. 254 ; *sharpened his visual ray to objects*

distant *far* : P. L. III. 621 ; *to
their glory named Thrones* : P. L.
v. 839 ; *put to proof* : P. L. I.
132 ; *left him at large to his own
dark designs* : P. L. I. 213 ;
armed to their night watches : P.
L. IV. 780 ; *worship paid to whom
we hate* : P. L. II. 249 ; *invoke thy
aid to my ... song* : P. L. I. 13 ;
my will concurred not to my being :
P. L. X. 747 ; *naked to the air* :
P. L. X. 213 ; *fair to the eye* : P.
L. IX. 777.

(*e*) of time ; *destined to that
good hour* : P. L. II. 848 ; *Heaven
and Earth shall to the ages rise* :
P. L. X. 647.

(**3**) as far as ; (*a*) of a point in
space ; *from head to foot* : P. L.
VI. 625 ; *from wing to wing* :
P. L. I. 617 ; *the one seemed
woman to the waist* : P. L. II.
650 ; *piled up to the clouds* : P. L.
IV. 544 ; *all Earth had to her
centre shook* : P. L. VI. 219.

(*b*) of degree ; *to the highth of
this great argument* : P. L. I. 24 ;
to the highth enraged : P. L. II.
95 ; *created all such to perfection* :
P. L. V. 472 ; *made pure to
sanctity* : P. L. X. 639 ; *to black
mortification* : S. A. 622 ; *fruit
be here to excess* : P. L. IX. 648.

(*c*) of a point in time ; *to this
hour* : P. L. II. 934 ; *to the end
persisting* : P. L. III. 197 ; *to this
day* : S. A. 145.

(**4**) close to or against : P. L.
v. 83 ; *put to their mouths the
sounding Alchymy* : P. L. II. 517.

(**5**) of addition ; *to thy speed
add wings* : P. L. II. 700 ; *the hills
to their supply vapour ... sent up* :
P. L. XI. 740.

(*b*) in addition to ; *it gives you
life to knowledge* : P. L. IX. 687.

(**6**) of junction or union ; *Earth
...linked ... to that side Heaven* :
P. L. II. 1006 ; *fit body to fit head* :
P. L. IV. 953 ; *to his wife adhere* :
P. L. VIII. 498 ; *their nature to thy
nature join* : P. L. III. 282 ; *join
him to thy aid* : P. L. VI. 294.

(**7**) of result ; *dash to pieces* :
P. L. VI. 489 ; P. R. IV. 149 ; *to
havoc hewn* : P. L. VI. 449 ; *gone
to wrack* : P. L. VI. 670.

(**8**) of comparison ; compared
with : S. A. 950 ; *to which the
Hell I suffer seems a Heaven* : P.
L. IV. 78 ; *to Heavenly Spirits*

bright *little inferior* : P. L. IV.
361 ; *what this garden is to all the
earth* : P. L. V. 752 ; equal or
like *to* : P. L. I. 654 ; II. 349, 391 ;
to what I was in Heaven : P. L.
IX. 487 ; *all taste of pleasure must
forgo to what thou hast* : P. L. XI.
542 ; *a lower world, to this obscure* :
P. L. XI. 283.

(*b*) with ; *that bright star to
Satan paragoned* : P. L. X. 426.

(**9**) of harmony or agreement ;
the contrary to his high will : P.
L. I. 161 ; *irreconcilable to our
grand Foe* : P. L. I. 122.

(*b*) in answer to ; *resorting to
the summons* : P. L. XI. 81.

(**10**) of opposition or antithesis ;
front to front : P. L. II. 716 ; *with
forked tongue to forked tongue* :
P. L. X. 519.

(*b*) against ; *to all temptations
armed* : P. L. IV. 65.

(**11**) in correspondence or accompaniment with : P. L. I. 561 ;
*to many a row of pipes the sound-
board breathes* : P. L. I. 709 ;
*moved on ... to the sound of instru-
mental harmony* : P. L. VI. 64 ;
*with other notes than to the
Orphean lyre I sung* : P. L. III.
17 ; *responsive each to other's note* :
P. L. IV. 683 ; *hoarse murmur
echoed to his words applause* : P.
L. V. 873.

(**12**) according to, in accordance
with ; *to our power* : P. L. II.
336 ; *as to right belonged* : P. L.
III. 111 ; *to his wish* : P. L. IX.
423 ; *to thy heart's desire* : P. L.
VIII. 451.

(**13**) out of respect for ; *to his
state and to his message high in
honour rise* : P. L. V. 288, 289.

(*b*) before and out of reverence
for ; *bowing lowly down to bestial
gods* : P. L. I. 435.

(**14**) in relation to, with respect
to, as regards, as to : P. L. I. 51 ;
*to his own edicts found contradict-
ing* : S. A. 301 ; *the ways of God
to men* : P. L. I. 26 ; *to me
deserves no less than for deliverance what we owe* : P. L. VI. 467 ;
to their foes a laughter : P. L. VI.
603.

(*b*) in the relation of, as ; *the
next I took to wife* : S. A. 227.

(**15**) in the estimation of ; *a
monument of merit high to all the
infernal host* : P. L. X. 259.

(16) before; *to his speed gave way* : P. L. v. 252.

(*b*) in front of, before; *to the fringed bank ... her crystal mirror holds* : P. L. IV. 262.

(17) by; *suspected to a sequent king* : P. L. XII. 165.

(18) of; *what if the Sun be centre to the World* : P. L. VIII. 123.

(19) over; *to every limb suitable grace diffused* : P. L. III. 638.

(20) supplying the place of the dative case; with a *sb.* or *adj.*; *free leave ... to all things else* : P. L. IV. 434; *foe to God and Man* : P. L. IV. 749; *to me ... alike is Hell* : P. L. x. 597; *new to sight* : P. L. IV. 287; *fairer to my fancy* : P. L. v: 53; *liable to fear* : P. L. VI. 397; the indirect object : P. L. II. 333; *to whom ... thus began* : P. L. I. 81; *then were they known to men* : P. L. I. 374.

(21) used with the infinitive; *intends to soar* : P. L. I. 14; *vainly hope to be invulnerable* : P. L. II. 812; *to be weak is miserable* : P. L. I. 157; *what is else not to be overcome* : P. L. I. 109; the *inf.* modifying a *sb.* or *adj.*; *desire to hear* : P. L. v. 555; *confidence to equal God* : P. L. VI. 343; *impossible to climb* : P. L. IV. 548; an *acc.* as subject of the *inf.*; *found ... new hope to spring* : P. L. XI. 138; *forbids us then to taste* : P. L. IX. 753; the perfect *inf.* used for the present : S. A. 848; *he trusted to have equalled* : P. L. I. 40; *thou couldst not seem ... to have fed* : P. L. v. 467; *thy hope was to have reached* : P. L. VI. 131; *had thought to have reported* : P. L. VI. 22; *he trusted to have seized* : P. L. VII. 143; *armed complete to have discovered* : P. L. x. 10; the *inf.* used instead of a *vbl. sb.* or *gerund* : P. L. IX. 779; x. 8; *which cost Ceres all that pain to seek her* : P. L. IV. 272; *to taste think not I shall be nice* : P. L. v. 433; *to graze the herb all leaving* : P. L. x. 711; *such pleasure took the Serpent to behold* : P. L. IX. 455; used instead of a *part.*; *still to owe* : P. L. IV. 53; used instead of a clause; *a race to fill the earth* : P. L. IV. 733.

(22) used with the *vbl. sb.*; *to the bearing well of all calamities* : S. A. 655.

(23) used with a *vb.* that at present takes no *prep.*; *to their General's voice they soon obeyed* : P. L. I. 337; *befell or befallen to* : P. L. VII. 45; XI. 451.

II. *adv.* forward; *to and fro* : P. L. I. 772; II. 605, 1031; III. 533; VI. 328, 643, 665; S. A. 1649.

Toad, *sb.* the animal *Bufo* : P. L. IV. 800; S. XI. 13.

Tobias, *sb.* the son of Tobit : P. L. v. 222.

Tobit, *sb.* the hero of the Apocryphal Book of Tobit : P. L. IV. 170.

To-day, *adv.* on the present day : S. XXI. 5.

Toe, *sb.* one of the digits of the foot; used for the whole foot or the fore part of the foot; *trip it ... on the light fantastic toe* : L'A. 34; *other trippings to be trod of lighter toes* : C. 962.

Together, *adv.* (*a*) with each other; *both together went into the thickest wood* : P. L. IX. 1099; *together both ... we drove a-field* : L. 25; *both together heard* : L. 27; *best keep together* : S. A. 1521; *lay deep their plots together* : Ps. II. 4.

(*b*) at the same time : P. L. VI. 316; *that pure breath of life ... cannot together perish with this corporeal clod* : P. L. x. 785.

(*c*) in a company, in or into a body; *he together calls ... the Regent powers* : P. L. v. 696; *together thronged* : P. L. VI. 857; *together crowded drove* : P. L. x. 287; *together drive mountains of ice* : P. L. x. 290; *the clouds together drove* : P. L. XI. 739; *fishermen ... together got* : P. R. II. 28.

(*d*) so as to be closely joined; *together sewed* : P. L. IX. 1095, 1112.

(*e*) the one against the other; *together rushed both battles* : P. L. VI. 216.

Toil, I. *sb.* labour, exertion, effort : P. L. II. 1041; C. 687; *servile toil* : S. A. 5; *incessant, irksome* : P. L. I. 698; IX. 242; *toil of their sweet gardening labour* : P. L. IV. 327; *the toil of battle* : P.

L. I. 319 ; *warlike toil*: P. L. VI. 257.

II. *vb.* (*pres. 2d sing.*, toil'st : P. R. IV. 498) (1) *tr.* (*a*) to exhaust by toil ; *as one ... escaped from cruel fight sore toiled*: P. L. VI. 449.

(*b*) to accomplish by great effort ; *I toiled out my uncouth passage*: P. L. X. 475.

(2) *intr.* to put forth effort, labour : P. R. IV. 498.

Toil, *sb.* net, snare ; *riches ... the toil of fools*: P. R. II. 453 ; *thy gins and toils*: S. A. 933.

Toilsome, *adj.* laborious, fatiguing : P. L. IV. 439 ; XI. 179.

Tolerable (tóleráble), *adj.* possible to be endured, supportable: P. L. X. 977 ; *cold and heat scarce tolerable*: P. L. X. 654 ; *render Hell more tolerable*: P. L. II. 460.

Tomb, *sb.* a place where a dead body is deposited ; (*a*) a grave ; *a low-delved tomb*: D. F. I. 32 ; *by dead Parthenope's dear tomb*: C. 879 ; *the ... mother's womb was not long a living tomb*: M. W. 34.

(*b*) a monument erected to enclose, and preserve the memory of, the dead : S. A. 1792 : probably also : S. A. 986 ; *fig.* of poetry : W. S. 16.

To-morrow, *adv.* on the day after the present : P. L. IV. 623 ; L. 193.

Tone, *sb.* a musical sound in relation to its volume, quality, duration, and pitch ; *learn the secret power of harmony, in tones or numbers hit by voice or hand*: P. R. IV. 255 ; *harmony divine so smooths her charming tones*: P. L. V. 626.

Tongue, *sb.* (1) the organ within the mouth as an organ of speech ; in man : P. L. VIII. 272 ; IX. 674 ; *to dress, and troll the tongue*: P. L. XI. 620 ; *move my first endeavoring tongue to speak*: V. Ex. 2 ; *smooth on the tongue discoursed*: P. R. I. 479 ; *arm his profane tongue with contemptuous words*: C. 781 ; *the tongues ... glibbed with lies*: P. R. I. 374 ; *God ... sets upon their tongues a various spirit*: P. L. XII. 53 ; *to live upon their tongues, and be their talk*: P. R. III. 55 ; in angels or other supernatural beings ; *though his tongue dropped manna*: P. L. II. 112 ;

that tongue, inspired with contradiction: P. L. VI. 154 ; *airy tongues that syllable men's names*: C. 208 ; in the serpent : P. L. IX. 554 ; *the tongue not made for speech to speak thy praise*: P. L. IX. 749 ; as that by which the hissing of a serpent is made : P. L. X. 507, 518.

(*b*) a person as speaking ; *a rougher tongue draws hitherward*: S. A. 1066 ; *though fallen on ... evil tongues*: P. L. VII. 26.

(2) speech, language : P. L. VI. 360 ; *rhetoric that sleeked his tongue*: P. R. IV. 5 ; *their tongue they smoothed*: Ps. V. 28 ; *nor tongue ineloquent*: P. L. VIII. 219 ; *enchanting tongues persuasive*: P. R. II. 158 ; *my tongue but little grace can do thee*: V. Ex. 10 ; *tongue of Seers old infallible*: P. R. III. 15 ; *who, though with the tongue of angels, can relate*: P. L. VI. 297 ; *what words or tongue of Seraph can suffice*: P. L. VII. 113 ; *what thought can measure thee, or tongue relate thee*: P. L. VII. 603 ; *potent tongue*: P. L. VI. 135 ; *truth and honesty ... banished from thy tongue*: C. 692 ; *Virtue has no tongue to check her pride*: C. 761.

(*b*) a national language : S. XIII. 8 ; *to speak all tongues*: P. L. XII. 501 ; *the tongue I heard was strange*: Ps. LXXXI. 20.

(*c*) a nation as distinguished by its language ; *Babylon, the wonder of all tongues*: P. R. III. 280.

See **Serpent-tongue.**

Tongue-battery, *sb.* a volley of words: S. A. 404.

Tongue-doughty, *adj.* valiant in speech, bragging : S. A. 1181.

***Too,** *adv.* (*a*) in excessive degree, more than enough ; *too large*: P. L. IV. 730 ; VIII. 104 ; *little*: P. L. X. 600 ; *secure*: P. L. V. 238 ; XI. 196 ; *desirous*: P. L. X. 947 ; *divine*: A. 44 ; *rash, rude*: S. A. 907, 1567 ; *far*: P. R. IV. 87 ; C. 193 ; *near*: C. 491 ; *high*: P. L. VI. 899 ; VIII. 121 ; *late*: P. L. VI. 147 ; IX. 44 ; *soon*: S. A. 1568 ; *much*: P. L. VIII. 538 ; XI. 531 ; S. A. 970 ; *well*: C. 563 ; S. A. 878.

(*b*) in addition, also ; *I mean that too*: C. 418 ; *methought so too*: C. 482.

Tool, *sb.* (*a*) an implement used in executing any piece of manual work : ¡P. L. XI. 572 ; *gardening tools* : P. L. IX. 391.

(*b*) a weapon ; *warlike tools* : S. A. 137 ; *the tools of death* : Ps. VII. 48.

Tooth, *sb.* one of the bony structures in the jaw ; *of men abhorred hast broke the teeth* : Ps. III. 23.

Top, *sb.* the highest part of anything, summit : P. L. III. 504 ; XII. 44 ; *the holy mount of Heaven's high-seated top* : P. L. VII. 585.

(*b*) the summit of a hill or mountain : P. L. XI. 851, 852 ; *a flaming mount, whose top brightness had made invisible* : P. L. V. 598 ; *their tops ascend the sky* : P. L. VII. 287 ; *a hill ...from whose top the hemisphere of Earth in clearest ken stretched out* : P. L. XI. 378 ; *high* : P. 'L. VIII. 303 ; P. R. II. 286 ; *grisly, shaggy* : P. L. I. 670 ; VI. 645 ; *the secret top of Oreb* : P. L. I. 6 ; *the top of Fesolé* : P. L. I. 289 ; *the snowy top of cold Olympus* : P. L. I. 515 ; *the top of old Olympus* : P. L. VII. 6 ; *the top of Œta* : P. L. II. 545 ; *the shaggy top of Mona* : L. 54 ; *Niphates' top* : P. L. III. 742 ; *Sinai, whose grey top* : P. L. XII. 227 ; *the top of Virtue's hill* : P. R. II. 217 ; used both *lit.* and *fig.*; *top of speculation* : P. L. XII. 588.

(*c*) the summit of a tree : P. L. IV. 142 ; *wave your tops, ye Pines* : P. L. V. 193 ; *the forest oaks or mountain pines, with singed top* : P. L. I. 614.

(*d*) the zenith ; *the star ... the top of Heaven doth hold* : C. 94.

(*e*) the highest point or degree ; *the top of eloquence* : P. R. IV. 354 ; *the top of wondrous glory* : S. A. 167.

II. *vb. tr.* to cap, crown ; *topt with golden spires* : P. R. IV. 548.

See **Cedar-top, Hill-top, Mountain-top.**

Topaz, *sb.* the precious stone : P. L. III. 597.

Tophet, *sb.* a grove or garden (?) in the Valley of Hinnom ; probably it was once the royal music-garden or grove, but because of its defilement by idol-worship, it became an abomination : P. L. I. 404. *See* **Gehenna.**

Torch, *sb.* a blazing brand, flambeau ; *midnight torches* : C. 130 ; *the nuptial torch* : P. L. XI. 590.

Torment, (1) *sb.* (*a*) that which causes extreme pain of body or anguish of mind : P. L. II. 196 ; IV. 510 ; *sulphur and strange fire, his own invented torments* : P. L. II. 70 ; *our torments also may ... become our elements* : P. L. II. 274 ; =hell : P. R. IV. 632.

(*b*) intense bodily or mental pain : P. L. IV. 893 ; VIII. 244 ; X. 998 ; P. R. IV. 305 ; S. A. 606 ; *I feel torment within me* : P. L. IX. 121 ; *the happy place inflames thy torment* : P. R. I. 418 ; *under what torments inwardly I groan* : P. L. IV. 88.

(2) *vb. tr.* (*a*) to bring intense mental suffering upon : P. L. XI. 769 ; *the thought ...torments him* : P. L. I. 56 ; *the expectation ... torments me* : P. R. III. 208 ; *no fear of worse ... would torment me* : P. L. X. 781.

(*b*) to throw into a state of commotion or disorder ; *soaring on main wing, tormented all the air* : P. L. VI. 244.

part. adj. **tormenting,** causing mental pain : P. L. IV. 505.

Tormentor, *sb.* that which gives mental pain ; *his tormentor, Conscience* : P. R. IV. 130 ; *thoughts, my tormentors* : S. A. 623.

Torrent, *adj.* (*a*) rushing in a stream, pouring forth with violence ; *waves of torrent fire* : P. L. II. 581 ; *the sound of torrent floods* : P. L. VI. 830 ; *October's torrent flood* : C. 930.

(*b*) like that of a torrent ; *wave rolling after wave .. with torrent rapture* : P. L. VII. 299.

Torrid, *adj.* (*a*) parched and dry with the heat of the sun ; *Cyrene's torrid soil* : P. L. II. 904 ; intensely hot ; used of hell ; *the torrid clime* : P. L. I. 297.

(*b*) having power to parch, scorching, burning : P. L. XII. 634.

Tortuous, *adj.* full of twists or turns, sinuous : P. L. IX. 516.

Torture, (1) *sb.* (*a*) extreme anguish of body or mind ; *racking torture* : P. L. XI. 481 ; *suspense in news is torture* : S. A. 1569 ; *torture without end still urges* : P. L. I. 67.

(*b*) that which causes such anguish ; *turning our tortures into horrid arms against the Torturer* : P. L. II. 63.

(2) *vb. tr.* to cause to suffer anguish of mind : P. L. IX. 469.

part. adj. **torturing**, in which punishment is inflicted ; *the torturing hour* : P. L. II. 91.

Torturer, *sb.* one who tortures ; used of God : P. L. II. 64.

To-ruffled (not compound in original text), *past part.* completely disarranged : C. 380.

Toss, *vb.* (*past part.* tossed and tost) *tr.* (*a*) to fling or throw about ; *tost and fluttered into rags* : P. L. III. 490 : as by the motion of waves ; *as in a raging sea tossed up and down* : P. L. x. 287 ; *fig.*, *in a troubled sea of passion tost* : P. L. x. 718.

(*b*) to agitate, disturb ; *their inward state of mind ... now tost and turbulent* : P. L. IX. 1126.

vbl. sb. **tossing** ; (*a*) the heaving to and fro : *the tossing of these fiery waves* : P. L. I. 184.

(*b*) the turning of the body on this side and on that ; *dire was the tossing* : P. L. XI. 489.

Total, (1) *adj.* (*a*) whole, entire ; *the total kind of birds* : P. L. VI. 73 ; *the total crime* : P. L. x. 127.

(*b*) absolute in degree, utter ; *total eclipse* : S. A. 81 ; *darkness* : P. L. IV. 665.

(2) *adv.* throughout the whole being ; *if Spirits embrace, total they mix* : P. L. VIII. 627.

Touch, I. *sb.* (*a*) the sense of touch : P. L. x. 563 ; *if the sense of touch whereby mankind is propagated* : P. L. VIII. 579.

(*b*) the physical contact of one body with, or the impact of one body upon, another : P. L. VI. 485, 520 ; *their reeds ... applied with nicest touch* : P. L. VI. 584 ; *no falsehood can endure touch of celestial temper* : P. L. IV. 812 ; *fig.* of the rays of the sun ; *with one virtuous touch, the arch-chemic Sun* : P. L. III. 608 ; *with touch ethereal of Heaven's fiery rod* : S. A. 549 ; used for the person ; *lest some ill-greeting touch attempt the person of our unowned sister* : C. 406 ; or *vb.* (*a*) : P. L. VIII. 617.

(*c*) the action of the hand on a

musical instrument ; *heavenly touch of instrumental sounds* : P. L. IV. 686 ; *to what unshorn Apollo sings to the touch of golden wires* : V. Ex. 38 ; or the peculiar manner in which a player uses his instrument ; *his volant touch* : P. L. XI. 561.

(*d*) a suggestion ; *with touch of blame* : P. L. IX. 1143.

(*e*) a musical note or strain ; *swage with solemn touches troubled thoughts* : P. L. I. 557.

II. *vb.* (1) *tr.* (*a*) to be or come in physical contact with ; esp. with the hand : S. A. 951, 1107 ; C. 918 ; L. 77 ; *her hand soft touching* : P. L. v. 17 ; *Ithuriel with his spear touched lightly* : P. L. IV. 811 ; the thing touched being the forbidden tree : P. L. VII. 46 ; IX. 651, 663, 688 ; XI. 425 ; *fig.*, of the rays of the sun ; *touched with Heaven's rays* : P. L. VI. 479.

absol. or *intr.* : P. L. IX. 742, 925.

(*b*) a blending of senses (*a*) and (*h*) ; *her fruits and flowers ... touched by her fair tendance* : P. L. VIII. 47 ; *from out his altar touched with hallowed fire* : N. O. 28 ; *touched with the flame* : S. A. 262.

(*c*) with the double meaning : to come in contact with and to treat briefly in speech : P. L. VI. 566.

(*d*) to impair, injure ; *fog to touch the prosperous growth of this tall wood* : C. 270 ; *thou canst not touch the freedom of my mind* : C. 663.

(*e*) to allude to in speaking : P. L. IX. 380.

(*f*) to play upon : A. 87 ; *to hear the lute well touched* : S. xx. 11 ; *touched their golden harps* : P. L. VII. 258 ; *touch their immortal harps* : S. M. 13 ; *he touched the tender stops* : L. 188.

(*g*) to act upon, affect ; *if ye have power to touch our senses* : N. O. 127 ; *what of sweet before hath touched my sense* : P. L. IX. 987.

(*h*) to influence, impel strongly ; *touch ... his free will* : P. L. x. 45.

(*i*) to concern, relate to : D. F. I. 10.

(2) *intr.* (*a*) to be in contact :
P. L. VIII. 530.

(*b*) to perceive by means of
physical contact : P. L. V. 411.

vbl. sb. **touching,** the act of
coming in contact : P. R. II. 370.

Tough, *adj.* not easily broken or
masticated ; *we here live on tough
roots* : P. R. I. 339.

Tour *sb.* (probably for *tower*), high
or lofty flight : P. L. XI. 185.

Tournament, *sb.* (*a*) a mock combat
of two opposing parties of mounted
men clothed in armour and provided with blunted weapons : P.
L. IX. 37.

(*b*) an encounter, shock of
battle ; *with cruel tournament the
squadrons join* : P. L. XI. 652.

Tourney. *See* **Turney.**

Toward, *prep.* (*a*) in the direction
of, in a course leading to : P. L.
I. 284, 669 ; II. 631 ; VIII. 231 ;
IX· 495 ; X. 64 ; A. 81 ; C. 100 ;
L. 31 ; Ps. LXXXIV. 16 ; CXIV.
14 ; *toward the springs of Ganges* :
P. L. III. 435 ; *toward Namancos* : L. 162 ; *toward the four
winds* : P. L. II. 516 : *toward the
pole* : P. L. II. 642 ; *toward the
coast of Earth* : P. L. III. 739 ;
toward Heaven : P. L. VIII. 257 ;
toward solid good what leads : S.
XXI. 10 ; *to that same lot ... toward
which Time leads* : S. II. 12.

(*b*) with respect to, in relation
to, as regards : S. A. 682 ; Ps.
LXXXV. 16 ; *the smell of peace
toward Mankind* : P. L. XI. 38 ;
great thy mercy is toward me : Ps.
LXXXVI. 45.

Towards, *prep.* (*a*) in the direction
of, in a course leading to : P. L.
II. 477, 873 ; III. 89 ; IV. 27, 29 ;
VI. 648 ; X. 28, 288 ; XI. 848,
854 ; Ps. V. 20 ; *towards the west* :
P. L. XII. 40 ; *towards Canaan* :
P. L. XII. 215 ; *lowly reverent
towards either throne they bow* :
P. L. III. 350 ; (stars) *towards
his all-cheering lamp turn swift
their various motions* : P. L. III.
581.

(*b*) with respect to, in relation
to, as regards : S. A. 334, 668,
772, 792, 911 ; *his heart relented
towards her* : P. L. X. 941 ; *God
towards thee hath done his part* :
P. L. IX. 375 ; *justification towards
God* : P. L. XII. 296.

Tower, I. *sb.* a structure very tall

in proportion to its depth and
width, whether isolated or forming part of another building : P.
R. III. 268 ; IV. 34 ; L'A. 77 ; C.
935 ; *loftiest, lofty* : P. L. I. 499 ;
XI. 640 ; *some high lonely* : Il P.
86 ; *the royal towers of great
Seleucia* : P. L. IV. 211 ; *fair Jerusalem ... lifted high her towers* :
P. R. IV. 545 ; *the towers of Salem
... once glorious towers* : P. 39, 40 ;
sing. collect. : S. VIII. 11 ; in
heaven : P. L. I. 749 ; V. 907 ;
*with ... towers from diamond quar-
ries* : P. L. V. 758 ; as a symbol
of strength ; *he stood like a tower* :
P. L. I. 591 ; *fig.* of the zenith :
*the full-blazing Sun ... high in his
meridian tower* : P. L. IV. 30.

(*b*) as used for purposes of
defense ; *the towers of Gath* : S.
A. 266 ; *the tower of Babel* : P. L.
XII. 44, 51 ; *to God his tower intends siege* : P. L. XII. 73 ; apparently on the walls of heaven ;
*o'er Heaven's high towers to force
resistless way* : P. L. II. 62 ; *the
towers of Heaven are filled with
armed watch* : P. L. II. 129 ; *opal
towers and battlements* : P. L. II.
1049 ; as borne on the back of an
elephant : P. R. III. 329.

II. *vb.* (1) *intr.* (*a*) to rise aloft
like a tower : P. L. II. 635 ; IX.
498 ; *Satan ... came towering* : P.
L. VI. 110.

(*b*) to fly high, soar : P. R. II.
280.

(2) *tr.* to soar into ; *they ...
tower the mid aerial sky* : P. L.
VII. 441.

part. adj. (1) **towering,** soaring
aloft : P. L. V. 271.

(2) **towered** ; (*a*) furnished with
towers ; *towered structure, cities* :
P. L. I. 733 ; L'A. 117.

(*b*) wearing a crown adorned
with turrets ; *towered Cybele* : A.
21.

See **Heaven-tower, High-towered, Royal-towered, Watch-tower.**

Town, *sb.* a considerable collection
of dwelling-houses : P. L. XI.
639 ; *the Galilean towns* : P. R.
III. 233 ; *town or village* : P. R. I.
332 ; *town or city* : P. R. II. 22 ;
the town, London : S. XI. 3.

Toy, *sb.* (*a*) a gewgaw, bauble ;
applied *fig.* to women : P. R. II.
177 ; *to language* : V. Ex. 19 ; *to
joys* : Il P. 4.

(*b*) that which is of no value or importance ; *collecting toys and trifles for choice matters* : P. R. IV. 328 ; *a trivial toy* : P. R. II. 223 ; C. 502.

(*c*) wanton play, caress, fondling ; *toy of amorous intent* : P.L. IX. 1034.

Trace, (1) *sb.* track, trail : P. L. VII. 481.

(**2**) *vb. tr.* (*a*) to follow the track of ; *his ... footstep trace* : P. L. XI. 329.

(*b*) to discover to be by following ; *a liar traced* : P. L. IV. 949.

(*c*) to follow step by step ; *to trace the ways of highest agents* : P. L. IX. 682.

(*d*) to make one's way through; *tracing the wild desert* : P. R. II. 109 ; *trace huge forests* : C. 423.

Trace, *sb. pl.* the harness for draught-oxen : C. 292.

Track, *sb.* (*a*) footprint ; *of his steps the track divine* : P. L. XI. 354 ; trace, vestige ; *far from track of men* : P. R. I. 191.

(*b*) course, path : P. L. II. 1025 ; x. 314, 367.

Tract, *sb.* (*a*) continued duration ; *tract of time* : P. L. V. 498.

(*b*) track, course : P. L. IX. 510.

(*c*) a region of indefinite extent : C. 30 ; *many a tract of Heaven* : P. L. VI. 76 ; *the deep tract of Hell* : P. L. I. 38.

Trade, *sb.* (*a*) practice, usage ; *trade of violence,* habitual violence in dealing with others : Ps. VII. 58.

(*b*) occupation ; *shepherd's trade*: L. 65.

Trading, *part. adj.* moving in a steady course or current ; *the trading flood* : P. L. II. 640.

Tradition, *sb.* a belief, or a body of beliefs and usages, handed down from age to age by oral communication : P. L. X. 578 ; *how refute their ... traditions* : P. R. IV. 234 ; *the truth with ... traditions taint* : P. L. XII. 512.

Traduce, *vb. tr.* to misrepresent, defame, caluminate : S. A. 979.

Tragedian, *sb.* an actor of tragedy : P. R. IV. 261.

Tragedy, *sb.* the dramatic representation of a serious, lofty, and complete action : Il P. 97.

Tragic, *adj.* expressive of tragedy, mournful, sorrowful ; *I now must change these notes to tragic* : P. L. IX. 6.

Trail, *vb. tr.* to draw along, drag : S. A. 1402.

Train, I. *sb.* (1) that which is drawn along behind or which forms the hinder part ; applied to hair ; *the loose train of thy ... hair* : C. 863.

(*b*) the extension of a dress skirt ; *a robe ... flowing with majestic train* : Il P. 34.

(*c*) the tail of a bird ; *the crested cock ... whose gay train adorns him* : P. L. VII. 444.

(*d*) the hinder part of the body of a serpent : P. L. IV. 349 ; of Satan in the serpent ; *his tortuous train* : P. L. IX. 516 ; the lower part of the body of Sin ; *rolling her bestial train* : P. L. II. 873 ; *fig.,* rivers ... *draw their humid train* : P. L. VII. 306.

(**2**) a body of followers or attendants, retinue, following : P. L. V. 351 ; X. 80 ; *a damsel train*: S. A. 721 ; *Angels numberless, thy daily train* : P. L. IX. 548 ; *from his ark the ancient sire descends, with all his train* : P. L. XI. 862 ; *a cumbrous train of herds and flocks, and numerous servitude* : P. L. XII. 131 ; *Osiris, Iris, Orus, and their train* : P. L. I. 478 ; *Delia's train* : P. L. IX. 387 ; *Diana's train* : P. R. II. 355 ; *Morpheus' train* : Il P. 10 ; *the Muse or Love ... of their train am I* : S. I. 14 ; the retinue of God or Christ : P. L. VII. 574 ; *him all his train followed in bright procession* : P. L. VII. 221 ; the retinue of Satan : P. L. V. 767 ; VI. 143.

(*b*) *fig.* of the stars ; *Fairest of Stars, last in the train of Night* : P. L. V. 166 ; *this fair Moon, and these the gems of Heaven, her starry train* : P. L. IV. 649 ; of flowers : M. W. 37.

(**3**) a succession of connected things ; *train of words* : P. R. III. 266.

(**4**) a procession ; *funeral train*: S. A. 1732.

(**5**) something used to allure, wile, artifice : P. L. XI. 624 ; S. A. 932 ; *my wily trains* : C. 151 ; *fair fallacious looks, venereal trains* : S. A. 533.

II. *vb. tr.* (*a*) to draw along, drag : P. L. VI. 553.

(b) to educate, teach ; *minister-ing Spirits, trained up in feast and song* : P. L. VI. 167.

Traitor, *sb.* one who betrays a trust: S. A. 832 ; C. 690 ; *she sought to make me traitor to my-self* : S. A. 401.

Traitor-angel, *sb.* an angel who proves false to allegiance ; applied to Satan : P. L. II. 689.

Traitress, *sb.* a woman who betrays a trust : S. A. 725.

Trample, *vb. tr.* (a) to tread under foot ; *trampling the ... grass* : N. O. 215.

(b) *fig.* to crush, overcome ; *to trample thee as mire* : P. L. IV. 1010 ; *the race of Heaven thus trampled* : P. L. II. 195.

Trance, *sb.* a state in which the soul seems to have passed out of the body into another state of being, rapture, ecstasy : P. L. VIII. 462 ; *nightly trance or breathed spell* : N. O. 179 ; *pensive trance ... and ecstatic fit* : P. 42.

Transact, *vb. intr.* to deal, treat : P. L. VI. 286.

Transcend, *vb. tr.* to surpass, exceed : P. L. V. 457.

Transcendent, *adj.* (a) situated high above others, or surpassing others in splendour ; *from his transcend-ent seat the Saints among* : P. L. X. 614.

(b) very high and remarkable in degree, surpassing ; *trans-cendent brightness, glory* : P. L. I. 86 ; II. 427.

Transfer, *vb. tr.* to convey from one person to another, transmit ; *by task transferred from Father to his Son* : P. L. V. 854 ; *to thee I have transferred all judgment* : P. L. X. 56 ; *all power on him transferred* : P. L. VI. 678 ; *to transfer the guilt on him* : P. L. X. 165 ; *that fault ... transfer on Israel's governors* : S. A. 241 ; *whose sins ... must be transferred upon my head* : P. L. I. 267.

Transfix, *vb. tr.* to fasten by some-thing sharp thrust through ; *with linked thunderbolts transfix us* : P. L. I. 329 ; *caught in a fiery tempest ... each on his rock trans-fixed* : P. L. II. 181.

Transform, *vb. tr.* to alter in shape or appearance, change from one shape to another : P. L. IV. 824 ; C. 527 ; *all my nether shape thus*

grew transformed : P. L. II. 785 ; *the Tuscan mariners transformed* : C. 48 ; with *to* : P. L. I. 370 ; *all transformed alike, to serpents all* : P. L. X. 519 ; *of serpent kind ...to which transformed Ammonian Jove* : P. L. IX. 507 ; *those hinds that were transformed to frogs* : S. XII. 5 ; *transformed him to a purple flower* : D. F. I. 27.

Transfuse, *vb. tr.* to transfer by pouring ; *fig., transfused on thee his ample Spirit rests* : P. L. III. 389 ; *into thee such virtue and grace immense I have transfused* : P. L. VI. 704.

Transgress, *vb.* (1) *tr.* to violate (the command of God regarding the Tree of Knowledge) : P. L. IX. 902 ; Cir. 21 ; *transgress the sole command* : P. L. III. 94 ; *my sole command transgressed* : P. L. VIII. 330.

(2) *intr.* (a) to violate the law of God, sin : P. L. IV. 880 ; Ps. v. 23 ; to break the command of God regarding the Tree of Know-ledge : P. L. VII. 47 ; IX. 1161 ; XI. 253 ; *fear to transgress* : P. L. VI. 912 ; *all temptation to trans-gress repel* : P. L. VIII. 643 ; *wil-fully transgressing* : P. L. V. 244.

(b) to disregard the authority of a person, disobey : S. A. 758.

vbl. sb. **transgressing**, the viola-tion of God's command : P. L. IX. 1169.

Transgression, *sb.* (a) the act of breaking God's command or law : S. A. 1356 ; the sin of Adam and Eve : P. L. X. 49 ; *death, the penalty to thy transgression due* : P. L. XII. 399 ; of Satan : P. L. IV. 879.

(b) a breach of duty, offence ; *how cunningly the sorceress dis-plays her own transgressions* : S. A. 820.

Transgressor, *sb.* one who trans-gresses : P. L. X. 72 ; XI. 164.

Transient, *adj.* of short duration ; *this transient World* : P. L. XII. 554.

Transition, *sb.* a passing from one subject to another ; *with transi-tion sweet, new speech resumes* : P. L. XII. 5.

Transitory. *adj.* existing for a short time only, short-lived : P. L. III. 446 ; *they are transitory, the king-doms of this world* : P. R. IV. 209.

Translate, *vb. tr.* to convey from one place to another, remove ; *so may'st thou* (echo) *be translated to the skies* : C. 242.

part. adj. **translated,** conveyed to heaven without natural death ; *translated saints* : P. L. III. 461.

Translucent, *adj.* transparent, clear ; *fountain or fresh current ... translucent* : S. A. 548 ; *wave* : C. 861.

Transmigration, *sb.* the passing from one place to another : P. L. X. 261.

Transparent, *adj.* admitting the passage of light without irregular diffusion ; *God made the firmament ... transparent, elemental air* : P. L. VII. 265.

Transpicuous, *adj.* transparent ; *the wide transpicuous air* : P. L. VIII. 141.

Transpire, *vb. intr.* to pass off as an exhalation ; *what redounds transpires through Spirits with ease* : P. L. V. 438.

Transplant, *vb. tr.* to remove from one place and establish in another; *light ... transplanted from her cloudy shrine* : P. L. VII. 360 ; *fig.,* *them who ... live in thee transplanted* : P. L. III. 293.

Transport, *vb. tr.* (*a*) to convey from one place to another : P. L. I. 231.

(*b*) to carry away by strong emotion, enrapture : P. L. VIII. 529, 530, 567 ; *with what sweet compulsion thus transported to forget* : P. L. IX. 474 ; to render beside oneself with passion ; *what rage transports our Adversary* : P. L. III. 81 ; *transported with some fit of passion* : P. L. X. 626.

part. adj. (*a*) **transporting,** that bears one away ; *some transporting cherub* : P. 38.

(*b*) **transported,** exalted ; *the deep transported mind* : V. Ex. 33.

Transubstantiate, *vb. absol.* to change from one substance to another : P. L. V. 438.

Transverse, *adv.* (*a*) crosswise, athwart ; *blows them transverse* : P. L. III. 488 ; *away from the right direction morally* ; *drove me transverse* : S. A. 209.

(*b*) across (the keys of the piano) ; *his volant touch ... pursued transverse the resonant fugue* : P. L. XI. 563.

Trap, *vb. tr.* to take by stratagem, ensnare : C. 699.

Trapping, *sb.* ornamental harness for a horse ; *tinsel trappings* : P. L. IX. 36.

Travail, *sb.* (*a*) labour, toil ; *our empire ... earned with travail difficult* : P. L. X. 593.

(*b*) labour in childbed, parturition : M. W. 49 ; *fig.,* *he travails big with vanity* : Ps. VII. 51.

Travel, *vb.* (1) *intr.* (*a*) to make a journey ; *to travel with Tobias* : P. L. V. 222.

(*b*) to move ; *if Earth ... fetch day, travelling east* : P. L. VIII. 138.

(2) *tr.* to journey through ; *I travel this profound* : P. L. II. 980.

part. adj. **travelled,** weary with travel ; *his travelled steps* : P. L. III. 501.

Traveller, *sb.* one who makes a journey ; *the traveller's benison* : C. 332 ; *weary, lonely* : C. '64, 200.

Traverse (travérse : P. L. I. 568), (1) *adv.* across ; *soon traverse the whole battalion views* : P. L. I. 568.

(2) *vb. tr.* to cross in travelling, pass over or through; *many a walk traversed* : P. L. IX. 434 ; *thrice the equinoctial line he circled ... traversing each colure* : P. L. IX. 66.

Treacherously, *adv.* perfidiously : S. A. 1023.

See **Wedlock-treachery.**

Tread, I. *sb.* a stepping or walking: S. A. 111 ; *the tread of hateful steps* : C. 91 ; *the tread of nimble feet* : P. L. IV. 866 ; *the passive air upbore their* (angels') *nimble tread* : P. L. VI. 73.

II. *vb.* (*pret.* trod ; *past part.* trod : P. R. II. 307 ; IV. 620 ; C. 569, 961 ; S. XIV. 6 ; Ps. LXXXVI. 5 ; as *adj.* trodden : P. L. I. 682 ; IX. 572) (1) *intr.* to place the foot down, step, walk : P. L. IV. 632; *the cowslip's velvet head, that bends not as I tread* : C. 899 ; *ye that ... stately tread, or lowly creep* : P.L. V. 201.

(2) *tr.* (*a*) to step or walk on, in, or through ; *paths ... often trod by day* : C. 569 ; *trod this wilderness* : P. R. II. 307 ; *to tread his sacred courts* : P. R. I. 488 ; *to*

tread the unfounded Deep : P. L.
II. 828 ; *treading the crude consistence* : P. L. II. 941 ; with *on* : C.
635 ; *the ground whereon she trod* :
P. L. IX. 526.

fig. to keep (a certain course)
morally ; *I have trod thy ways* :
Ps. LXXXVI. 5 ; *to tread paths
indirect* : P. L. XI. 630.

(*b*) to crush under the foot ;
fig., *thy works ... stayed not behind,
nor in the grave were trod* : S.
XIV. 6 ; to conquer, subdue ;
*whom he shall tread at last under
our feet* : P. L. X. 190 ; with
down : P. L. I. 327 ; *trod down
under his feet* : P. R. IV. 620.

(*c*) to dance ; *other trippings to
be trod* : C. 961.

part. adj. **trodden**, pressed with
the foot ; *the trodden herb* : P. L.
IX. 572 ; *Heaven's pavement,
trodden gold* : P. L. I. 682.

See **Well-trod.**

Treason, *sb.* (*a*) a breach of allegiance
to God as a sovereign : P. L. III.
207.

(*b*) a breach of faith ; *matrimonial treason* : S. A. 959 ; *personified ; her spurious first-born,
Treason against me* : S. A. 391.

Treasonous, *adj.* leading or enticing
to an act of treason (against
virtue) : C. 702.

Treasure, *sb.* (*a*) riches ; *get wealth
and treasure* : P. R. II. 427 ; *all
treasures and all gain esteem as
dross* : P. R. III. 29.

(*b*) the precious metals : P. L.
I. 688 ; or as money, coin ; *the
unsunned heaps of miser's treasure* :
C. 399.

(*c*) that which is regarded as
very precious : V. Ex. 18.

Treasury, *sb.* the department of
government which has control of
the public revenue ; *England's ...
Treasury* : S. x. 2.

Treat, *vb.* (1) *tr.* to behave to,
conduct oneself toward : P. R. II.
335.

(2) *intr.* (*a*) to handle in speaking or writing ; *of love they treat* :
P. L. XI. 588 ; *Tragedians ...
treat of fate, and chance* : P. R.
IV. 264.

(*b*) to negotiate ; *to treat about
thy ransom* : S. A. 482.

(*c*) to have dealings ; *these dark
orbs no more shall treat with light* :
S. A. 591.

Trebisond, *sb.* a city of Asia Minor
situated on the shore of the Black
Sea : P. L. I. 584.

Treble, *adj.* threefold ; *treble confusion* : P. L. I. 220.

Tree, *sb.* the perennial woody plant
having a single self-supporting
stem or trunk : P. L. IV. 644 ; v.
309 ; VII. 459 ; VIII. 306, 313,
321 ; IX. 660, 1095, 1118 ; XI.
124, 320, 832 ; P. R. II. 354 ; C.
147 ; Ps. I. 7 ; *the trees of God* :
P. L. V. 390 ; VII. 538 ; IX. 618 ;
the trees in or of Paradise : P.L. IV.
421 ; XI. 28 ; *precious of all trees
in Paradise* : P. L. IX. 795 ; *like
a tree spreading and overshadowing all the earth* : P. R. IV. 147 ;
*daughters grow about the mother
tree* : P. L. IX. 1106 ; *a dove, sent
forth ... to spy green tree* : P. L.
XI. 858 ; *all trees of noblest kind* :
P. L. IV. 217 ; *goodliest* : P. L.
IV. 147 ; VIII. 304 ; *rich* : P. L.
IV. 248 ; *dropping* : P. R. IV.
434 ; *stately* : P. L. VII. 324 ;
thickest, thick interwoven, tufted :
P. L. X. 101 ; P. R. II. 263 ; L'A.
78 ; *fair spreading* : P. L. X.
1067 ; *the fair Hesperian tree* : C.
393 ; *the golden* : C. 983 ; in hell :
P. L. X. 558.

(*b*) the Tree of Life, in paradise ; *the Tree of Life* : P. L. III.
354 ; IV. 194, 218, 424 ; VIII. 326;
IX. 73 ; XI. 94, 122 ; *that high
tree* : P. L. IV. 395 ; *the middle
tree and highest* : P. L. IV. 195 ;
in heaven ; *ambrosial fruitage
fetched from the Tree of Life* :
P. R. IV. 589 ; used not of one
particular tree, *pl.*; *in Heaven the
trees of life ambrosial fruitage
bear* : P. L. V. 426 ; *by living
streams among the trees of life* :
P. L. V. 652.

(*c*) the Tree of Knowledge :
P. L. IV. 427 ; V. 57 ; IX. 591,
594, 617, 651, 723, 727, 834, 850,
863, 1026 ; X. 122, 143, 199 : *the
Tree of Knowledge* : P. L. IV.
221 ; IX. 751, 848 ; *the tree of
interdicted Knowledge* : P. L. V.
51 ; *the tree which tasted works
Knowledge of good and evil* : P.L.
VII. 542 ; *the tree whose operation
brings Knowledge of good and evil* :
P. L. VIII. 323 ; *that only Tree of
Knowledge* : P. L. IV. 423 ; *that
or one forbidden tree* : P. L. I. 2 ;
X. 554 ; *the interdicted Tree* : P.

L. VII. 46 ; *the excepted tree* : P.
L. XI. 426 ; *the Tree of Prohibition* : P. L. IX. 644 ; *one fatal
tree* : P. L. IV. 514 ; *a tree of
danger* : P. L. IX. 863 ; *goodly,
fair, virtuous* : P. L. IX. 576, 661,
1033.

(d) *fig.* a mother : M. W. 30.

See **Fig-tree, Fruit-tree, Garden-
tree, Palm-tree.**

Tremble, *vb. intr.* to shake, quake ;
when mountains tremble : S. A.
1648 ; used of inanimate things
as affected by emotion, by fear or
terror ; *Hell trembled as he strode* :
P. L. II. 676 ; *Hell trembled at
the hideous name* : P. L. II. 788 ;
Earth trembled from her entrails :
P. L. IX. 1000 ; *the Mount of
Sinai, whose grey top shall tremble* :
P. L. XII. 228.

part. adj. **trembling**; (a)shaking
involuntarily ; *my trembling ears* :
L. 77.

(b) quivering ; *the trembling
leaves* : P. L. IV. 266.

(c) causing trembling or quaking; *trembling fear* : P. R. I. 451.

Tremesen, *sb.* one of the Barbary
states of northern Africa. " The
kingdome of Teleusium which
they call Tremesen. ... The Metropolis is Telusina. ... In the same
Country there is also Algiers, a
great Citty and well fortified."
Mercator *Atlas,* 1635, p. 816.
" Called also the Kingdom of
Algiers, from the City so named,
sometimes the Seat Royal of their
Kings." Heylyn *Cos.* 1657, p.
949 : P. L. XI. 404.

Trench, *vb. tr.* to dig a ditch around
for defence : P. L. I. 677.

Trent, *sb.* the Council of Trent : F.
of C. 14.

Trent, *sb.* the river rising in Stafford-
shire, England : V. Ex. 93.

Trepidation, *sb.* libration, the real
or apparent oscillating motion of
a body on each side of its mean
position : P. L. III. 483.

Trespass, (1) *sb.* the violation of a
law of God, transgression, sin :
S. A. 691 ; the sin of Adam or
Eve : P. L. IX. 693 ; *the fatal
trespass done by Eve* : P. L. IX.
889 ; *nor Eve to iterate her former
trespass* : P. L. IX. 1006.

(2) *vb. intr.* to violate a law of
God, transgress, sin : P. L. III.
122 ; Ps. LXXXV. 36.

Tress, *sb.* a lock or ringlet of hair ;
a garland to adorn her tresses : P.
L. IX. 841 ; *with flower-inwoven
tresses torn the Nymphs* : N. O.
187 ; *golden* : P. L. IV. 305 ; *the
flowing gold of her loose tresses* :
P. L. IV. 497 ; *tresses like the morn* :
C. 753 ; *discomposed, disordered* :
P. L. V. 10 ; X. 911 ; *fig.* the
shrubbery along the banks of a
river : C. 929.

See **Golden-tressed.**

Trial, *sb.* (a) the act of proving or
testing by exercise, use, examination, etc. : C. 592 ; *trial ... of my
strength* : S. A. 1643 ; *the trial of
their fortitude* : S. A. 1288 ; *trial
of exceeding love* : P. L. IX. 961 ;
this happy trial of thy love : P. L.
IX. 975 ; the testing of a person's
judgement ; *for trial only brought* :
P. L. VIII. 447 ; of a person's
moral uprightness or obedience to
God : P. R. III. 196 ; IV. 206 ;
the trial of man : P. L. I. 366 ;
thy trial choose with me : P. L. IX.
316 ; *trial will come unsought* : P.
L. IX. 366 ; *if thou think trial
unsought* : P. L. IX. 370 ; *our
trial, when least sought* : P. L. IX.
380 ; *matter of glorious trial* : P.
L. IX. 1177.

(b) a combat decisive of the
merits of a case ; *the trial of mortal
fight* : S. A. 1175.

(c) a determining attempt ; *save
us trial what the least can do* : P.
L. IV. 855.

(d) that which tries, hardship,
affliction : C. 329.

(e) an examination at the bar of
God : Ps. I. 13.

Tribe, *sb.* (a) one of the hereditary
or political divisions of a united
people ; *by families and tribes* : P.
L. XII. 23 ; *the daughters of my
tribe* : S. A. 876 ; esp. a political
division consisting of all the
descendants of one of the twelve
sons of Jacob : S. A. 242, 265 ; *the
twelve tribes* : P. L. XII. 226 ; *those
Ten Tribes* : P. R. III. 374, 403 ;
those captive tribes : P. R. III. 414 ;
those happy tribes : P. L. III. 532 ;
*Dan, Judah, and the bordering
tribes* : S. A. 976 ; the tribe of
Dan : S. A. 217, 1479, 1540 ; applied *fig.* to one of the divisions
in the organization of a community of ants ; *her popular tribes
of commonalty* : P. L. VII. 488.

(b) a group of plants of indefinite rank : P. L. XI. 279.

Tribulation, *sb.* suffering, affliction ; *life tried in sharp tribulation* : P. L. XI. 63 ; *pl.*: P. L. III. 336 ; P. R. III. 190.

Tribunal, *sb.* a court of justice : S. A. 695 ; the court of God for the trial of moral beings on the day of judgement ; P. L. III. 326.

Tributary, *adj.* subordinate ; *his tributary gods* : C. 24.

Tribute, *sb.* something given or rendered as by a subordinate to a superior ; *fig.*: P. L. V. 343 ; *Earth ... receives as tribute ... her warmth and light* : P. L. VIII. 36 ; *may thy ... waves ... their full tribute never miss from a thousand petty rills* : C. 925 ; perhaps the meaning is nearer, contribution, something added to a common stock ; *rivers ... joined their tribute to the sea* : P. R. III. 258.

See **Knee-tribute.**

Trick, (1) *sb.* a scheme involving deceit, artifice, stratagem : F. of C. 13.

(2) *vb. tr.* to deck, ornament ; *the day-star ... tricks his beams* : L. 170 ; *till civil-suited Morn appear, not tricked* : Il P. 123.

Trident, *sb.* a three-forked sceptre : P. L. X. 295 ; C. 27.

Trifle, *sb.* something of slight value, an insignificant fact or object : P. R. IV. 329 ; *the kingdoms of the world, to thee I give ... no trifle* : P. R. IV. 165.

Triform, *adj.* having three forms or phases ; probably also with allusion to the moon as Luna, Diana, and Proserpina ; *the ... Moon ... her countenance triform* : P. L. III. 730.

Trill, *vb. tr.* to sing quaveringly ; *the Attic bird trills her ... notes* : P. R. IV. 246.

Trim, (1) *adj.* (a) in good order, well-adjusted ; *tackle trim* : S. A. 717 ; well-ordered, tidy, nice ; *gardens* : Il P. 50 ; *meadows* : L'A. 75.

(b) pretty, fine ; *wood-nymphs, decked with daisies trim* : C. 120.

(2) *sb.* ornamental dress ; *fig., Nature ... had doffed her gaudy trim* : N. O. 33.

Trimming, *vbl. sb.* that which is added for ornament : V. Ex. 19.

Trinacrian, *adj.* of Trinacria, an old name of Sicily ; *the hoarse Trinacrian shore* : P. L. II. 661.

Trinal, *adj.* threefold ; *Trinal Unity* : N. O. 11.

Trine, *sb.* the aspect of two planets at a distance of a hundred and twenty degrees from each other : P. L. X. 659.

Trip, (1) *sb.* error, mistake, blunder : V. Ex. 3.

(2) *vb. intr.* (a) to move quickly with light and nimble steps ; *the faery ladies ... tripping to the room* : V. Ex. 62 ; *under the trees now tripped ... nymphs of Diana's train* : P. R. II. 354.

(b) to dance ; *trip the pert fairies* : C. 118 ; *Nymphs and Shepherds ... trip no more* : A. 99 ; *come, and trip it* : L'A. 33.

part. adj. **tripping,** moving quickly and lightly ; used of water ; *tripping ebb* ; P. L. XI. 847.

vbl. sb. **tripping,** a dance ; *other trippings to be trod* : C. 961.

Triple (triplé : P. L. V. 750), *adj.* (a) threefold ; *triple steel* : P. L. II. 569 ; *the triple tyrant,* the Pope who wears the tiara as symbolic of his threefold sovereignty, temporal, spiritual, and purgatorial : S. XVIII. 12.

(b) consisting of three parts or divisions ; *in triple knot* : C. 581 ; *a triple mounted row of pillars* : P. L. VI. 572 ; *those cursed engines' triple row* : P. L. VI. 650.

(c) disposed or ranked in groups of threes ; *Seraphim and Potentates and Thrones in their triple degrees* : P. L. V. 750.

Triple-coloured, *adj.* consisting of three colours : P. L. XI. 897.

Triton, *sb.* a river of Africa that rises in Libya Interior, flows north, and empties into the Syrtis Minor. In its course it flows through a lake, Tritonis Palus, in the centre of which is the island of Nysa. This is according to Ortelius, *Theatrum Orbis Terrarum,* 1624, map at page XXXVI. : P. L. IV. 276.

Triton, *sb.* the sea-god who had the body of a god and the tail of a fish. He was the herald of Poseidon, whose orders he blew through a shell : C. 873.

Triumph (triúmph : P. L. I. 123 ; III. 338 ; X. 186, 572 ; XII. 452 ;

P. R. III. 36 ; T. 22), I. *sb.* (*a*)
the solemn procession marking
the entry of a victorious leader
into Rome : P. R. IV. 138; *young
Pompey ... in triumph had rode* :
P. R. III. 36; applied to the
entry of Christ into heaven ; *I
through the ample air in triumph
high shall lead Hell captive* : P. L.
III. 254 ; applied to the entry of
Satan into hell ; *thou ... hold'st in
Hell no triumph* : P. R. IV. 624 ;
in a more general sense, the
honour received for great achievement : P. L. XI. 695.

(*b*) a public festivity or exhibition ; *triumphs or festivals* : P. L.
XI. 723 ; *triumph, pomp, and
games* : S. A. 1312 ; probably a
tournament ; *where throngs of
knights...high triumphs hold* : L'A.
120.

(*c*) victory in war : P. L. XI.
788 ; applied to the contest of
Christ with Satan ; *victory and
triumph to the Son of God, now
entering his great duel* : P. R. I. 173.

(*d*) exultation over victory, rejoicing : P. L. X. 546 ; *each order
bright sung triumph* : P. L. VI.
886 ; *great triumph and rejoicing
was in Heaven* : P. L. VII. 180 ;
or in sense (*a*) ; *to see in triumph
issuing forth their glorious Chief* :
P. L. X. 537.

(*e*) a cause of rejoicing : S. A.
426.

II. *vb.* (**1**) *intr.* (*a*) to celebrate
a victory by a triumphal pro-
cession ; of Christ ; *rising from
his grave ... triumphed in open
show* : P. L. X. 186 ; *triumphing
through the air over his foes* : P.
L. XII. 452.

(*b*) to gain a victory over an
enemy ; *lest the Adversary* (Satan)
triumph : P. L. IX. 948; *triumphing over ... thee, O Time* : T. 22.

(*c*) to rejoice over victory : P.
L. I. 123 ; *to triumph in victorious
dance* : C. 974 ; *the just ... with
Joy and Love triumphing* : P. L.
III. 338.

(**2**) *tr.* to exult over ; *Man whom
they triumphed once lapsed* : P. L.
X. 572.

Triumphal, (**1**) *adj.* (*a*) used in
commemorating or celebrating a
victory : P. R. IV. 37 ; used of
the chariot of Christ ; *his triumphal
chariot* : P. L. VI. 881.

(*b*) bringing or giving victory ;
*triumphal with triumphal act have
met* : P. L. X. 390.

(**2**) *sb.* a token of victory ;
*brought joyless triumphals of his
hoped success* : P. R. IV. 578.

Triumphant, *adj.* (*a*) used in celebrating a triumph or stately procession ; *draw'st his* (God's)
*triumphal wheels in progress
through the road of Heaven* : P. L.
IV. 975.

(*b*) rejoicing, exulting ; *triumphant song* : Cir. 2.

(*c*) victorious ; *lead ye forth
triumphant out of this infernal
pit* : P. L. X. 464 ; *Death* : P. L.
XI. 491 ; used of Christ : P. L. V.
693 ; *he celebrated rode, triumphant
through mid Heaven* : P. L. VI.
889.

Trivial, *adj.* of little worth or
significance ; *trivial weapon* : S.
A. 142, 263 ; *toy* : P. R. II. 223 ;
C. 502.

Troll, *vb. tr.* to roll ; here probably
with the meaning, to move so as
to speak fluently or glibly ; *troll
the tongue* : P. L. XI. 620.

Troop, (**1**) *sb.* (*a*) a number of people
assembled together, company,
band ; *that fair female troop* : P.
L. XI. 614 ; *with these in troop
came Astoreth* : P. L. I. 437 ; *the
Saints above, in solemn troops* : L.
179 ; *who pass in troop or caravan* :
P. R. I. 323.

(*b*) a body of soldiers : P. R.
III. 311 ; *spurned them to death by
troops* : S. A. 138.

(**2**) *vb. intr.* to march in a body
or company : P. L. I. 760 ; *as
armies...troop to the standard* : P.
L. VII. 297 ; *the grisly legions that
troop under the sooty flag of
Acheron* : C. 603 ; *the flocking
shadows pale troop to the infernal
jail* : N. O. 233.

Trophy, *sb.* something taken from
the enemy and set or hung up as
a token of victory ; *statues and
trophies* : P. R. IV. 37 ; *trophies
hung* : S. A. 1736 ; Il P. 118.

(*b*) hence, any memorial of
victory ; *seraphic arms and
trophies* : P. L. I. 539 ; *thy magnific deeds, thy trophies* : P. L.
X. 355 ; *these boasted trophies won
on me* : S. A. 470 ; *Cromwell ...
hast reared God's trophies* : S. XVI.
6.

Tropic, (1) *adj.* lying in the Tropic of Cancer; *the Tropic Crab*: P. L. x. 675.

(2) *sb.* either *tropic*, each of the two regions, the arctic and antarctic; used here for the north and the south: P. R. iv. 409.

Trot, *sb.* a gait faster than a walk and slower than a run: U. C. ii. 4.

Trouble, (1) *sb.* (a) disturbance, affliction, distress, difficulty, suffering, perplexity: P. L. v. 34, 96; P. R. ii. 87, 126; *lest the Fiend ... some new trouble raise*: P. L. xi. 103; *on the quiet state of men such trouble brought*: P. L. xii. 81; *when trouble did thee sore assail*: Ps. lxxxi. 25; *trouble he hath conceived of old*: Ps. vii. 52; *more trouble is behind*: S. A. 1300; *they stood a while in trouble*: P. L. vi. 634; *trouble store*, store of trouble: Ps. lxxxviii. 9; *pl., to raise new troubles*: P. L. iv. 575; *dangers, troubles, cares*: P. R. ii. 460; *their inside, troubles miserable*: Ps. v. 27.

(b) labour, pains: S. A. 487.

(2) *vb. tr.* to disturb, afflict, distress, perplex: P. L. iv. 315; Ps. ii. 11; lxxxiii. 61, 62; *think not here to trouble holy rest*: P. L. vi. 272; *no more be troubled how to quit the yoke of God's Messiah*: P. L. v. 882; *God ... will trouble all his host*: P. L. xii. 209; *be not ... troubled at these tidings*: P. L. x. 36; *troubled at his bad success*: P. R. iv. 1; *Nature ... troubled*: P. R. ii. 333; *all my bones ... are troubled*: Ps. vi. 6.

part. adj. **troubled**; (a) put in commotion, agitated; *troubled sky, waves, sea*: P. L. ii. 534; vii. 216; Ps. cxiv. 7; *sea of passion*: P. L. x. 718.

(b) perplexed, distressed; *troubled thoughts*: P. L. i. 557; iv. 19; P. R. ii. 65; *mind*: S. A. 185.

Troublesome, *adj.* causing annoyance, vexatious: P. L. iv. 740.

Troy, *sb.* the famous city of the Trojans, destroyed by the Greeks after ten years' siege; *the tale of Troy divine*: Il P. 100; *to thy sons another Troy shall rise*: H. B. 12.

attrib. of Troy; *thrice fugitive about Troy wall*: P. L. ix. 16.

Truce, *sb.* (a) a temporary cessation of hostilities: P. R. iv. 529;

heroes old in time of truce: P. L. xi. 244; *Night ... grateful truce imposed*: P. L. vi. 407; *hollow truce*: P. L. vi. 578.

(b) respite; *truce to his restless thoughts*: P. L. ii. 526.

True, I. *adj.* (1) conformable to fact or reality: P. L. ix. 788, 1069; P. R. i. 433; S. A. 823; S. xix. 6; *O thought horrid, if true*: P. L. x. 789; *Hesperian fables true, if true, here only*: P. L. iv. 250, 251; *the rest is true*: P. L. iv. 900; *my fears are true*: C. 511; *I find it true*: C. 644; *'tis most true that*: C. 385; *if it be true that*: S. A. 91; *true is*: P. L. vi. 430; x. 494; *'tis true*: P. R. i. 358; *true; and thou*: S. A. 430.

(b) real, authentic; *by some supposed true Paradise*: P. L. iv. 282; *Jordan, true limit eastward*: P. L. xii. 145.

(c) conformable to reality and to reason or law; *other doctrine ... though granted true*: P. R. iv. 290.

(2) exact, accurate; *true Image of the Father*: P. R. iv. 596.

(3) perfect, complete: Il P. 95.

(4) legitimate, rightful; *true successor, heir, king*: P. R. iii. 373, 405, 441; *the true anointed King Messiah*: P. L. xii. 358.

(b) not unlawfully assumed but rightful; *whence true authority in men*: P. L. iv. 295.

(5) faithful, loyal, steadfast; *God ... most true*: Ps. lxxxvi. 56; *Virtue ... her true servants*: C. 10; constant, firm; *true allegiance, love, patience*: P. L. iii. 104; ix. 982; xi. 361.

(6) not counterfeited, false, or pretended; genuine; real; actual: P. L. xi. 598; xii. 274; D. F. I. 45; *our Babe, to show his Godhead true*: N. O. 227; *of taste to please true appetite*: P. L. v. 305; *nor known till now true relish*: P. L. ix. 1024; *new acquist of true experience*: S. A. 1756; *reconcilement, freedom, liberty, slavery*: P. L. iv. 98, 294; xii. 83; S. A. 418; Eurip. 1; *life*: P. L. iv. 196; *delight, Love, glory, applause*: P. L. viii. 384, 589; P. R. iii. 60, 63; *virtue, worth, good, wisdom*: P. L. xi. 790; P. R. i. 231; iii. 139: iv. 319; *sup., truest fortitude*: S. A. 654; or

pure, free from evil; *wedded Love
...true source of human offspring*:
P. L. IV. 750 ; *true virginity* : C.
437 ; *virgin* : C. 905.

(7) sure, unerring, trustworthy;
if mine ear be true : C. 170; *all
oracles by thee are given, and what
confessed more true* : P. R. I. 431.

(*b*) fine or discriminating because trained or educated ; *to all
true tastes excelling*: P. R. IV. 347.

(*c*) in harmony and hence able
to comprehend and appreciate ;
list, mortals, if your ears be true :
C. 997.

II. *adv.* with truth, rightly ;
Oh, say me true : D. F. I. 41 ;
both judge you to relate them true :
S. x. 13.

Truly, *adv.* (*a*) not only in appearance but actually : P. L. IV. 491;
*that which alone can truly rein-
stall thee in David's royal seat* : P.
R. III. 372 ; *not truly penitent* :
S. A. 754.

(*b*) certainly, surely : U. C. II.
1 ; Ps. LXXXIV. 46.

Trump, *sb.* trumpet ; *the wakeful
trump of doom* : N. O. 156 ; *fig.,*
Cremona's trump, the Latin poem
The Christiad, written by Marco
Girolamo Vida of Cremona : P. 26.

Trumpery, *sb.* something of no real
value used for purposes of deceit ;
*eremites and friars...with all their
trumpery* : P. L. III. 475.

Trumpet, *sb.* the musical wind-
instrument, used for military
purposes or for blowing a signal :
P. L. VII. 296 ; P. R. I. 19 ; N.
O. 58 ; *trumpets' lofty sound* : Ps.
LXXXI. 10 ; *the morning trumpets
festival proclaimed* : S. A. 1598 ;
*God...will himself, in thunder,
lightning, and loud trumpet's sound
ordain them laws* : P. L. XII. 229;
in heaven or hell : P. L. I. 754 ;
XI. 74 ; *the warlike sound of
trumpets loud* : P. L. I. 532 ;
trumpet's regal sound : P. L. II.
515 ; *to arms the matin trumpet
sung* : P. L. VI. 526 ; *the loud
ethereal trumpet from on high gan
blow* : P. L. VI. 60 ; *Michael bid
sound the Archangel trumpet* : P.
L. VI. 203.

See **Angel-trumpet**.

Trunk, *sb.* (*a*) the main body or
stock of a tree : P. L. IX. 589.

(*b*) the proboscis of the leviathan:
P. L. VII. 416.

Trust, I. *sb.* (*a*) reliance, confidence;
my trust is in the living God : S. A.
1140 ; *O ever-failing trust in mortal strength* : S. A. 348.

(*b*) confident expectation, hope :
P. L. II. 46.

(*c*) that which is committed to
one for use or safe-keeping : C.
682 ; a public duty or office for
which account is to be rendered ;
*a noble Peer of mickle trust and
power* : C. 31.

(*d*) that which is confided to
one to be kept inviolate ; *his most
sacred trust of secrecy*: S. A. 1001;
to violate the sacred trust of silence:
S. A. 428.

II. *vb.* (1) *tr.* (*a*) to repose confidence in, rely upon : P. L. x.
877 ; *I ... trust thy honest-offered
courtesy* : C. 322.

(*b*) to confide the care or disposal of ; *nor should'st thou have
trusted that to a woman's frailty* :
S. A. 783 ; *my vessel trusted to me
from above* : S. A. 199 ; *trusting
all his wealth with God* : P. L. XII.
133.

(*c*) to permit to be ; *to trust thee
from my side* : P. L. x. 881.

(*d*) to hope or expect confidently ; with *acc.* and *prep. inf.;
trust themselves to fear no second
fate*: P. L. II. 17; with *prep. inf.;
I trust to have full sight of her* : S.
XXIII. 7 ; *he trusted to have
equalled* : P. L. I. 40 ; *he trusted
to have seized* : P. L. VII. 143 ;
with clause ; *in trusting he will
accept thee* : S. A. 1178 ; *I trust
she is not* : C. 370.

(*e*) to feel sure, be confident ;
if I trust to know ye right : P. L.
v. 788.

(2) *intr.* to place confidence or
rely (*in* God or Christ) : P. L. VI.
119 ; XII. 328 ; Ps. IV. 24 ; v. 33;
LXXXVI. 8 ; *who rightly trust in
this his satisfaction* : P. L. XII.
418.

Truth, *sb.* (1) conformity to fact or
reality : P. R. III. 443 ; *his persuasive words, impregned ... with
truth* : P. L. IX. 738 ; *revolt when
Truth would set them free* : S.
XII. 10 ; *without a crime 'gainst
old truth* : U. C. II. 8 ; *counterfeited* : P. L. v. 771.

(2) that which is true, a statement or belief that represents or
conforms to fact or reality : P. L.

X. 755; S. A. 215; S. XIV. 12;
Hor. Sat. I. 1; Ariosto II. 3; *if
truth were known*: U. C. I. 5; *to
part from truth*: P. R. I. 472;
*my semblance might deceive the
truth*: S. II. 5; *utter odious truth*:
P. L. XI. 704.

(*b*) esp. that which is true
respecting God, or the execution
of his purposes through Christ,
or respecting the duties of man:
P. L. XII. 482; P. R. I. 446, 453;
II. 34; *hast maintained...the cause
of truth*: P. L. VI. 32; *for the
testimony of truth*: P. L. VI. 33;
in debate of truth: P. L. VI. 122;
the truth with superstitions...taint:
P. L. XII. 511; *to guide them in all
truth*: P. L. XII. 490; *an inward
oracle to all truth requisite*: P. R.
I. 464; *disciplined from shadowy
types to truth*: P. L. XII. 303; *in
the worship persevere of Spirit and
Truth*: P. L. XII. 533; *them who
kept thy truth so pure of old*: S.
XVIII. 3; *suffering for Truth's
sake*: P. L. XII. 569; possibly
*personified; Truth shall retire
bestuck with slanderous darts*: P.
L. XII. 535.

(*c*) the essence of truth as found
in God; *his Spirit of Truth*, the
Holy Spirit: P. R. I. 462.

(*d*) the Scriptures as setting
forth the truth: P. R. III. 183.

(*e*) a true or right system of
government: S. XVI. 4.

(3) veracity: C. 691; *thou pretend'st to truth*: P. R. I. 430.

(4) virtue, integrity, uprightness, righteousness: P. L. IV.
293; VI. 381; XI. 807; P. R. I.
220; S. A. 1276; C. 971; Ps.
LXXXVI. 38; *spake ... of religion,
truth, and peace*: P. L. XI. 667;
*born to promote all truth, all
righteous things*: P. R. I. 205;
truth, duty, so enjoining: S. A.
870; *hard are the ways of truth*:
P. R. I. 478; *to guide nations in
the way of truth*: P. R. II. 473;
*till truth and right from violence be
freed*: S. XV. 11; *the hill of
heavenly Truth*: S. IX. 4; *truth...
like to a flower shall bud and
blossom*: Ps. LXXXV. 45.

(*b*) *personified*: Ps. LXXXV. 41;
*Truth and Justice then will down
return to men*: N. O. 141; *shall
Truth fail to keep her word*: P. L.
X. 856; *that crowned Matron,*

sage white-robed Truth: D. F. I.
54; possibly also: P. L. III. 338;
T. 16.

(5) a blending of the ideas of (1)
and (4); *from the path of truth
remote*: P. L. VI. 173; *to swerve
from truth*: P. L. V. 902; *Socrates
...for truth's sake suffering death
unjust*: P. R. III. 98.

Try, *vb.* (1) *tr.* (*a*) to put to the test,
prove: P. L. VI. 418; P. R. IV.
532; C. 970; Ps. VII. 38; LXXXI.
31; *thus far to try thee, Adam*:
P. L. VIII. 437; *I shall first be
tried in humble state*: P. R. III.
189; *they ... under long obedience
tried*: P. L. VII. 159; *to try her
husband*: S. A. 754; *most perfect
Hero, tried in heaviest plight*: P.
13; *can hearts not free be tried*: P.
L. V. 532; *life tried in sharp
tribulation*: P. L. XI. 63; *thy
virtue tried*: P. L. IX. 317; *try
his constancy*: P. R. II. 225;
temperance, obedience ... tried: P.
L. XI. 805; P. R. I. 4.

(*b*) to prove to be by testing;
*whose reason I have tried unsound
and false*: P. L. VI. 120.

(*c*) to make experiment of, to
know or seek to know by experiment or experience: P. L. IX.
860; *to try thee now more dangerous to his throne*: P. L. X. 382;
*where we might have tried each
other's force*: S. A. 1086; *to try
their art*: S. A. 1399; *his puissance ... I mean to try*: P. L. VI.
120; *evil hast not tried*: P. L.
IV. 896; with clause: P. L. I.
269; IV. 941; V. 727; P. R. IV.
198; *by proof to try who is our
equal*: P. L. V. 865; *to try ...
which the stronger proves*: P. L.
VI. 818.

(*d*) to make experimental use
of; *if they list to try conjecture*:
P. L. VIII. 75; *all guile on him to
try*: P. R. I. 123; *this will I try*:
C. 858.

(*e*) to undertake, attempt; with
prep. inf.: P. L. VIII. 271; X. 254.

(*f*) to tempt: C. 806.

(2) *intr.* to make an effort, endeavour: C. 793; *at least to try,
and teach the erring soul*: P. R. I.
224.

Tub, *sb.* the open wooden vessel;
here that in which Diogenes is
said to have lived; *Cynic tub*: C.
708. See **Cynic.**

Tube, *sb.* a hollow cylinder ; *optic tube*, a telescope : P. L. III. 590.

Tuft, *sb.* (*a*) a cluster, clump; *a tuft of shade* : P. L. IV. 325 ; *tuft of grove* : P. L. IX. 417.

(*b*) a clump of trees, a grove ; *with high woods the hills were crowned, with tufts the valley* : P. L. VII. 327.

Tufted, *part. adj.* adorned with or growing in tufts ; *tufted grove, trees* : C. 225 ; L'A. 78 ; *the tufted crow-toe* : L. 143.

Tug, *vb. intr.* to pull with great effort: S. A. 1650.

Tumble, *vb. intr.* to move in a headlong manner, flow rapidly : C. 927.

Tumid, *adj.* rising above the general level ; *the tumid hills* : P. L. VII. 288.

Tumour, *sb.* a morbid swelling; *fig.*, *the tumours of a troubled mind* : S. A. 185.

Tumult, (**1**) *sb.* commotion, disturbance, uproar : P. L. II. 1040; VI. 674 ; *the tumult of loud mirth* : C. 202; *pl.* : P. L. V. 737; *personified* as an attendant upon the throne of Chaos : P. L. II. 966.

(**2**) *vb. intr.* to make a tumult, be in a great commotion ; *why do the Gentiles tumult* : Ps. II. 1.

Tumultuous, *adj.* (*a*) full of commotion ; *some tumultuous cloud* : P. L. II. 936.

(*b*) agitated or disturbed by passion ; *boils in his tumultuous breast* : P. L. IV. 16.

Tun, *sb.* a large cask : P. L. IV. 816.

Tuneable, *adj.* tuneful, musical, harmonious ; *more tuneable than needed lute or harp to add more sweetness* : P. L. V. 151 ; *tunable as sylvan pipe or song* : P. R. I. 480.

Tune, (**1**) *sb.* (*a*) an air, a melody ; *the heavenly tune* : A. 72 ; *fig.* : S. A. 661 ; *pl.* poems or poetry; *sage and solemn tunes* : Il P. 117.

(*b*) the state of being in the proper pitch or key ; *keep in tune with Heaven* : S. M. 26.

(**2**) *vb.* (*pres. 2d sing.* tunest : S. XIII. 11) *tr.* (*a*) to put in tune; *harps ever tuned* : P. L. III. 366.

(*b*) to give utterance to in musical sounds ; *harps, that tuned Angelic harmonies* : P. L. VII. 559 ; *they in Heaven their odes and vigils tuned* : P. R. I. 182 ; *the*

wakeful bird ... tunes her nocturnal note : P. L. III. 40 ; *the night-warbling bird ... tunes sweetest his love-laboured song* : P. L. V. 41 ; *the solemn nightingale ... tuned her soft lays* : P. L. VII. 436 ; or to set to music : S. XIII. 11.

(*c*) to celebrate in music ; *tune his praise* : P. L. V. 196.

(*d*) to give utterance to ; *his proem tuned* : P. L. IX. 549.

(*e*) to bring into correspondence with something, attune, adapt ; *to sorrow must I tune my song* : P. 8.

vbl. sb. **tuning**, harmony, music : P. L. VII. 598.

Tuneful, *adj.* (*a*) melodious; *tuneful song* : S. XIII. 1.

(*b*) producing melody ; *tuneful birds* : P. R. II. 290.

Turbant, *sb.* a turban, oriental headdress : P. R. IV. 76.

Turbulency, *sb.* a disturbance, commotion ; *pl.* : P. R. IV. 462.

Turbulent, *adj.* (*a*) disturbed, agitated : P. L. IX. 1126.

(*b*) causing disturbance or confusion, making trouble : P. R. IV. 461 ; S. A. 552, 1040.

Turchestan-born (Turchéstan), *adj.* having come from Turchestan : P. L. XI. 396.

Turf, *sb.* earth covered with grass ; *grassy turf* : P. L. V. 391 ; XI. 324 ; C. 280 ; *green* : L. 140.

Turkis, *adj.* of the colour of the turquoise : C. 894.

Turkish, *adj.* of Turkey : P. L. X. 434. · *See* **Horn.**

Turm, *sb.* a turma, among the Romans a company of cavalry consisting of thirty, or later thirty-two, men : P. R. IV. 66.

Turn, I. *sb.* (**1**) time or opportunity coming successively to each of a number of persons ; *then in the east her turn she shines* : P. L. VII. 380.

(*b*) *by turns*, alternately; *Light and Darkness ... lodge and dislodge by turns* : P. L. VI. 7 ; *at intervals* : P. L. II. 598.

(**2**) a kind action ; *this turn hath made amends* : P. L. VIII. 491.

II. *vb.* (**1**) *tr.* (*a*) to cause to rotate : P. L. VII. 228 ; *turn the adamantine spindle round* : A. 66 ; or to move in a circular course ; *towards his all-cheering*

lamp (stars) *turn swift their ...
motions* : P. L. III. 582 ; or to unfasten (?), or *intr.* to go round with
the key (?) ; *in the key-hole turns
the intricate wards* : P. L. II. 876.

(*b*) to change the position,
course, or direction of : P. L. III.
624, 646 ; IV. 536 ; VI. 881 ; *turn
the sway of battle* : P. L. VI. 234 ;
*some say the Sun was bid turn
reins* : P. L. X. 672 ; *the Sun ...
turned his course* : P. L. X. 688 ;
*he bid his Angels turn askance the
poles of Earth* : P. L. X. 668 ;
turn to me thy face : Ps. LXXXVI.
57 ; *to the evil turn my obvious
breast* : P. L. XI. 373 ; *turned
thitherward ... his travelled steps* :
P. L. III. 500 ; *his back he turned
on those proud towers* : P. L. V.
906 ; *from the tree her step she
turned* : P. L. IX. 834 ; *toward
Heaven my wondering eyes I
turned* : P. L. VIII. 257.

refl. to change one's own position ; *Adam ... turned him* : P. L.
IV. 410.

(*c*) to twist about, writhe : S.
A. 139.

(*d*) to cause to change (from
one object or purpose to another),
direct, bend, influence ; *hast thou
turned the least of these to flight* :
P. L. VI. 284 ; *turned ... the eye of
Eve to mark his play* : P. L. IX.
527 ; *his words to Eve he turned* :
P. L. IX. 920 ; *to the Woman thus
his sentence turned* : P. L. X. 192 ;
turn my hand against all those :
Ps. LXXXI. 59 ; *to speculations ... I
turned my thoughts* : P. L. IX. 603.

(*e*) to cause to return to God ;
turn us : Ps. LXXX. 13 ; LXXXV. 14.

(*f*) to change (one thing *to* or
into another) ; alter in nature,
form, or aspect : P. L. V. 420 ;
X. 546 ; P. R. II. 37, 220 ; C.
462 ; *to blood ... the rivers must be
turned* : P. L. XII. 176 ; *to turn,
metals ... to perfect gold* : P. L. V.
441 ; *turn this Heaven itself into
the Hell thou fablest* : P. L. VI.
291 ; *turning our tortures into
horrid arms* : P. L. II. 63 ; *corporeal to incorporeal turn* : P. L.
V. 413 ; *turns wisdom to folly* : P.
L. VII. 129 ; *evil turn to good* : P.
L. XII. 471 ; *turned to sport her
importunity* : S. A. 396 ; *all now
was turned to jollity* : P. L. XI.
714.

(*g*) to put, use, apply : P. L.
XII. 510 ; to use in bringing
about ; *turn his labours ... to peaceful end* : S. A. 708.

(**2**) *intr.* (*a*) to move round, revolve ; *the gate ... on golden hinges
turning* : P. L. V. 255.

(*b*) to move so as to face in a
different direction : P. L. II. 968 ;
III. 736 ; IV. 721 ; V. 332 ; VIII.
507 ; P. R. III. 293 ; L. 21 ; *aside
the Devil turned* : P. L. IV. 502 ;
back I turned : P. L. IV. 480 ;
from her turned : P. L. X. 909 ; *to
his guide turned* : P. L. XI. 675 ;
used of God : Ps. LXXXV. 21 ;
Turn, Lord : Ps. VI. 7 ; used of a
river ; *why turned Jordan toward
his crystal fountains* : Ps. CXIV. 14.

(*c*) to change the position of the
body in bed : P. L. IV. 741.

(*d*) to face in a different direction morally ; *turn aside to tred
paths indirect* : P. L. XI. 630.

(*e*) to direct thought, effort,
or attention ; *to sweet repast they
turn* : P. L. V. 630 ; *to their
sports they turned* : S. A. 1614 ;
he will ... turn from his displeasure :
P. L. X. 1093.

(*f*) to be changed ; *this ethereal
quintessence ... turned to stars* : P.
L. III. 718 ; *your bodies may at
last turn all to spirit* : P. L. V.
497.

followed by a predicate = to
become ; *the priest turns atheist* :
P. L. I. 495 ; *the ... squadron ...
turned fiery red* : P. L. IV. 978 ;
all shall turn degenerate : P. L. XI.
806 ; *who ... turned recreant to
God* : P. R. III. 138.

(*g*) to come back, return : P. L.
IX. 330 ; *his mischief ... turns on
his own head* : Ps. VII. 58.

In combination with other words ;
(*a*) **turn back**, to flee before an
enemy : P. L. VI. 562.

(*b*) **turn forth**, to bring to view :
C. 222, 224.

(*c*) **turn out** or **hence**, to drive
out, expel : S. A. 539 ; to avert,
ward off : D. F. I. 67.

(*d*) **turn up** or **upward**, to bring
the under side or part on top ; *up
they turned wide the celestial soil* :
P. L. VI. 509 ; *a sea ... up from
the bottom turned by furious winds* :
P. L. VII. 213 ; to invert ; *the
bottom of the mountains upward
turned* : P. L. VI. 649.

part. adj. **turning**, rotating : N. O. 48.

vbl. sb. **turning**, a winding path : C. 569.

Turney, *sb.* tournament : Il P. 118.

Turnus, *sb.* the king of the Rutulians in Italy, whose betrothed, Lavinia, was given by her father to Æneas : P. L. IX. 17.

Turret, *sb.* a small tower rising above a larger structure : P. R. IV. 54.

attrib. resembling a turret in form : P. L. IX. 525.

Turtle, *sb. attrib.* of a turtle-dove ; *the meek-eyed Peace ... with turtle wing the amorous clouds dividing* : N. O. 50.

Tuscan, *adj.* of or pertaining to Tuscany ; *the Tuscan artist* : P. L. I. 288 ; *air* : S. XX. 12 ; *mariners* : C. 48.

Tusked (*disyl.*), *adj.* provided with tusks or long pointed teeth : Ps. LXXX. 53.

Twain, *adj.* two ; *two massy keys he bore of metals twain* : L. 110 ; predicatively ; *they were but twain* : C. 284 ; *in twain*, asunder : Ps. CXXXVI. 45.

absol. two separate persons ; *thou and I long since are twain* : S. A. 929.

Tweed, *sb.* the river forming part of the boundary between England and Scotland : V. Ex. 92.

Twelve, *adj.* eleven and one; *twelve sons, tribes, years* : P. L. XII. 155, 226 ; P. R. II. 96 ; the *sb.* understood from the context ; *to the twelve that shone in Aaron's breast-plate* : P. L. III. 597.

See **Three-and-twentieth**.

Twenty, *adj.* nineteen and one; *twenty thousand* : P. L. VI. 769 ; the *sb.* omitted ; *twenty to one* : U. C. I. 3.

Twice, *adv.* two times : P. L. IX. 859 ; P. R. II. 314 ; III. 281 ; S. A. 24, 361, 635 ; *twice ten degrees* : P. L. X. 669 ; *twice six years* : P. R. I. 210.

Twice-battered, *adj.* bruised and broken two times : N. O. 199.

Twig, *sb.* a branch or shoot of a tree : P. L. IX. 1105.

See **Lime-twig**.

Twilight, *sb.* (*a*) the faint light perceived after the setting of the sun : P. L. VI. 12 ; *twilight from the east came on* : P. L. VII. 583 ;

twilight ... short arbiter 'twixt day and night : P. L. IX. 50 ; in heaven ; *grateful twilight* : P. L. v. 645 ; *personified ; Twilight gray had in her sober livery all things clad* : P. L. IV. 598.

(*b*) the faint light during an eclipse of the sun ; *disastrous twilight* : P. L. I. 597.

attrib. (*a*) formed at the time of twilight ; *trip no more in twilight ranks* : A. 99.

(*b*) faintly lighted, shady, dim, obscure ; *twilight shade, groves* : N. O. 188 ; Il P. 133 ; *at eve visits the herds along the twilight meadows* : C. 844.

Twin, (1) *sb.* one of two children born at a birth : C. 1010 ; *the Spartan Twins*, Castor and Polydeuces, the twin sons of Leda, wife of Tyndareus, King of Sparta. By command of Zeus they were changed into the constellation Gemini, as the reward of their mutual affection and fidelity : P. L. X. 674.

(2) *vb. tr.* to unite closely, link together ; *true liberty ... which always with right reason dwells twinned* : P. L. XII. 85.

Twin-born, *adj.* born at the same birth ; *Latona's twin-born progeny* : S. XII. 6.

Twine, (1) *sb.* a convolution, twist, coil ; *the serpent sly ... wove with Gordian twine his braided train* : P. L. IV. 348; *Typhon huge ending in snaky twine* : N. O. 226 : *rosy twine*, entwined roses : C. 105.

(2) *vb. tr.* to wind around, coil : P. L. v. 216.

Twisted, *part. adj.* (*a*) formed by winding one thread around another : Ps. II. 8.

(*b*) intertwined ; *in twisted braids of lilies knitting the loose train of thy ... hair* : C. 862.

(*c*) interlaced ; *the twisted eglantine* : L'A. 48.

Twitch, *vb. tr.* to pull quickly, pluck with a jerky movement : L. 192.

'Twixt, *prep.* (1) between ; (*a*) of local position ; *'twixt van and rear* : P. L. v. 589 ; *'twixt host and host* : P. L. VI. 104 ; *'twixt high and nether Jove* : C. 20 ; *'twixt Africa and Ind* : C. 606.

(*b*) of relation or intercourse ; *'twixt God and Dagon* : S. A. 462 ; *fig., twilight ... arbiter 'twixt day*

and night : P. L. IX. 51 ; *'twixt us and our deserved smart* : D. F. I. 69,
(2) in reference to more than two things = among ; *'twixt upper, nether, and surrounding fires* : P. L. I. 346.
Two, (1) *adj.* one and one : P. L. IV. 1002 ; VI. 313 ; X. 1072 ; XI. 186 ; XII. 169 ; P. R. III. 255 ; IV. 85 ; S. A. 261 ; C. 291 ; followed by another adjective : P. L. IV. 404, 786, 820 ; V. 132 ; VI. 305, 688 ; VII. 201 ; X. 289 ; XI. 57 ; XII. 197, 254, 431 ; P. R. III. 361 ; L'A. 15, 82 ; C. 1010 ; L. 110 ; S. XVII. 8 ; *our two first parents* : P. L. III. 65 ; *those two fair creatures* : P. L. IV. 790 ; *two potent Thrones* : P. L. VI. 366 ; *two great Lights* : P. L. VII. 346 ; *two great sexes* : P. L. VIII. 151 ; *two massy clods* : P. L. XI. 565 ; *two grand foes* : P. R. I. 159 ; *two main* or *massy pillars* : S. A. 1606, 1633, 1648 ; *two days* : P. L. VI. 684, 685, 699 ; *years* : V. Ex. 6.
(*b*) the sb. omitted but understood from the context ; *one night or two* : P. L. IX. 211 ; *two sons of Jacob, two of Joseph* : P. R. III. 377.
absol. two things, creatures, or persons : P. L. III. 33 ; V. 366 ; *two of far nobler shape* : P. L. IV. 288 ; *the hands' dispatch of two gardening* : P. L. IX. 203 ; *the only two of mankind* : P. L. IX. 415 ; *ye were the two* : C. 578 ; *these* or *those two* : P. L. IV. 505, 874 ; X. 82 ; XI. 454 ; S. A. 209 ; *you two* : P. L. IV. 382 ; X. 397 ; *us two* : P. L. IV. 732 ; X. 924, 990 ; *such two* : C. 575.
(2) *adv.* two *and* two, by twos, in pairs : P. L. VIII. 350.
Two-handed, *adj.* requiring two hands to wield ; *huge two-handed sway* : P. L. VI. 251 ; *that two-handed engine* : L. 130.
Tyne, *sb.* a river of Northumberland, England : V. Ex. 98.
Type, *sb.* (*a*) that by which something is prefigured, a prophetic similitude ; *religious rites of sacrifice, informing them, by types* : P. L. XII. 232 ; *disciplined from shadowy types to truth* : P. L. XII. 303.
(*b*) an image, representation ; *Gehenna ... the type of Hell* : P. L. I. 405.

Typhoëan, *adj.* like that of Typhoëus : P. L. II. 539.
Typhon, *sb.* (*a*) Typhoëus, the son of Ge, who made war on the Olympian gods. The upper part of his body was that of a man, the lower part that of a serpent ; he had invincible arms, and from his shoulders grew a hundred serpent heads : P. L. I. 199 ; N. O. 226.
(*b*) Typho, the Egyptian god of evil ; here identified, at least in form, with the above : N. O. 226.
Tyrannic, *adj.* despotic, unjustly severe ; *tyrannic power* : P. R. I. 219 ; S. A. 1275.
Tyrannize, *vb. intr.* to rule despotically, play the tyrant : P. L. XII. 39.
Tyrannous, *adj.* despotic ; *his empire tyrannous* : P. L. XII. 32.
Tyranny, *sb.* absolute power arbitrarily or unjustly administered, despotic government : P. L. XII. 95 ; S. A. 1291 ; *our grand Foe ... holds the tyranny of Heaven* : P. L. I. 124 ; *this dark opprobrious den ... the prison of His tyranny* : P. L. II. 59.
Tyrant, *sb.* one who exercises power arbitrarily or unjustly, a despot : P. L. XII. 96 ; Ps. CXXXVI. 10 ; *necessity, the tyrant's plea* : P. L. IV. 394 ; applied to Pharaoh ; *the lawless tyrant* : P. L. XII. 173 ; to the Pope ; *the triple tyrant* : S. XVIII. 12 ; to God ; *this infernal pit ... the ... dungeon of our tyrant* : P. L. X. 466.
Tyre, *sb.* the city of Phœnicia : Ps. LXXXIII. 27 ; LXXXVII. 15.
Tyrian, *adj.* of or pertaining to Tyre or to Phœnicia : N. O. 204 ; serving as a guide to Phœnician mariners : C. 342. *See* **Cynosure.**
Tyrrhene, *adj.* *the Tyrrhene shore,* the shore of Italy bordering on the Tyrrhenian Sea : C. 49.

U

Ugly, *adj.* (*a*) repulsive or hideous in appearance ; *a crowd of ugly serpents* : P. L. X. 539 ; *O sight of terror, foul and ugly to behold!* : P. L. XI. 464 ; *comp.* : P. L. II. 662.
(*b*) suggesting evil, or full of that which is disagreeable ; *ugly dreams* : P. R. IV. 408.

Ulcer, *sb.* an open sore ; *intestine ... ulcer*: P. L. XI. 484.

Ultimate, *adj.* last, final : P. R. III. 210.

Ulysses, *sb.* Odysseus, the king of Ithaca, whose adventures as he returned from Ilium are told in the Odyssey: P. L. II. 1019; *wise*: C. 637 ; *sad* : V. Ex. 50.

Umbrage, *sb.* that which affords a shade, foliage : P. L. IX. 1087.

Umbrageous, *adj.* shady : P. L. IV. 257.

Umpire, *sb.* one to whose arbitration a question is referred ; *Chaos umpire sits* : P. L. II. 907 ; *I will place within them as a guide my umpire Conscience*: P. L. III. 195.

Unable, *adj.* not able, lacking the necessary power or resources ; *with prep. inf.* : P. L. X. 165, 750 ; *gods unable to acquit themselves* : S. A. 896.

Unacceptable (unacceptáble), *adj.* not acceptable, not welcome : P. L. II. 251.

Unaccomplished, *adj.* not perfected, incomplete ; *the unaccomplished works of Nature's hand* : P. L. III. 455.

Unacquainted, *adj.* lacking acquaintance, not familiar ; *my unacquainted feet* : C. 180.

Unactive, *adj.* inactive, not doing anything : S. A. 1705.

(*b*) not working ; *other animals unactive range* : P. L. IV. 621.

(*c*) not engaged in public activity; *his life private, unactive*: P. R. II. 81.

(*d*) inoperative, producing no effect ; *the Sun ... his beams, unactive else* : P. L. VIII. 97.

Unadmonished, *adj.* not cautioned : P. L. V. 245.

Unadored, *adj.* not worshipped ; *his name ... unadored* : P. L. I. 738.

Unadorned (*tetrasyl.* unadornèd : P. L. IV. 305 ; C. 23), *adj.* simple, plain, not ornamented ; *the bare Earth ... unadorned* : P. L. VII. 314 ; *the unadorned bosom of the deep* : C. 23 ; *her unadorned golden tresses* : P. L. IV. 305.

Unadventurous, *adj.* not seeking risk, not bold or resolute : P. R. III. 243.

Unaffected, *adj.* plain, natural, not artificial : P. R. IV. 359.

Unagreeable, *adj.* not conformable, unsuitable ; *adventurous work, yet*

to thy power and mine not unagreeable : P. L. X. 256.

Unaided, *adj.* not assisted : P. L. VI. 141.

Unalterably, *adv.* unchangeably, immutably : P. L. V. 502.

Unaltered, *adj.* unchanged ; *with unaltered brow* : P. R. I. 493.

Unamazed, *adj.* not amazed, unastonished : P. L. IX. 552.

Unanimous, *adj.* being of one mind, consentient; *in festivals of joy and love unanimous* : P. L. VI. 95 ; *unanimous they all commit the care ...to him* : P. R. I. 111; *both in one faith unanimous* : P. L. XII. 603 ; or *adv.* together ; *this said unanimous* : P. L. IV. 736.

Unanswered, *adj.* not answered, not replied to : P. L. VI. 163.

Unappalled, *adj.* undismayed, undaunted : P. R. IV. 425.

Unapparent, *adj.* that cannot be seen, not visible ; *to hear thee tell ... the rising birth of Nature from the unapparent Deep* : P. L. VII. 103.

Unappeasable, *adj.* not to be appeased, implacable : S. A. 963.

Unapproached (*tetrasyl.* unapproachèd), *adj.* not to be approached ; *God ... in unapproached light dwelt* : P. L. III. 4.

Unapproved, *adj.* not regarded or treated with approval : P. L. V. 118.

Unargued, *adj.* without debate ; *what thou bidd'st unargued I obey*: P. L. IV. 636.

Unarmed (*trisyl.* unarmèd : C. 582), *adj.* not provided with arms or weapons, defenceless : S. A. 126 ; *withstand me single and unarmed* : S. A. 1111 ; *on their whole host I flew unarmed* : S. A. 263 ; used of angels : P. L. VI. 595 ; *the unarmed youth of Heaven* : P. L. IV. 552; of Christ; *he, all unarmed, shall chase thee ... from thy demoniac holds* : P. R. IV. 626 ; not provided with any defence ; *the unarmed weakness of one virgin, alone and helpless* : C. 582.

Unassailed, *adj.* not attacked, free from harm : C. 220.

Unassayed, *adj.* not subjected to trial, untested ; *what is faith, love, virtue, unassayed* : P. L. IX. 335.

Unattempted, *adj.* not essayed, not undertaken ; *things unattempted*

yet in prose or rhyme : P. L.
I. 16.

Unattended, *adj.* having no retinue :
P. L. VIII. 60.

Unattending, *adj.* not attentive, not
listening : C. 272.

Unaware, (1) *adj.* giving no heed,
unmindful of the consequences :
P. L. II. 156.

(2) *adv.* without warning, unexpectedly, suddenly : P. L. III.
547 ; *fall into deception unaware* :
P. L. IX. 362.

Unawares, *adv.* unexpectedly, by
surprise : P. L. II. 932 ; V. 731 ;
S. A. 1522.

Unbar, *vb. tr.* to unlock, open ; *the
circling Hours, with rosy hand
unbarred the gates of Light* : P. L.
VI. 4.

Unbecoming, *adj.* unseemly, unsuitable ; *no unbecoming deed* : P.
L. VI. 237.

Unbefitting, *adj.* unsuitable to, not
proper for ; *think thee unbefitting
holiest place* : P. L. IV. 759.

Unbegot, *adj.* not yet begotten ; *it
lies, yet ere conception, to prevent
the race unblest, to being yet unbegot* : P. L. X. 988.

Unbeheld, *adj.* not looked upon, unseen : P. L. IV. 674.

Unbelief, *sb. concr.* one who refuses to
believe ; *such there be, but unbelief
is blind* : C. 519.

Unbenighted, *adj.* never visited by
darkness ; *to them day had unbenighted shone* : P. L. X. 682.

Unbenign, *adj.* malignant : P. L. X.
661.

Unbesought, *past part.* not sought
by entreaty, not implored : P. L.
X. 1058.

Unbid, *past part.* unbidden, un-
desired ; *thorns also and thistles it
shall bring thee forth unbid* : P. L.
X. 204.

Unblamed, *adj.* free from censure,
without blame ; *discourse, joy unblamed* : P. L. IX. 5 ; XII. 22 ;
may I express thee unblamed? : P.
L. III. 3.

Unblemished, *adj.* pure, spotless ;
thou unblemished form of Chastity! :
C. 215.

Unblenched, *adj.* undaunted, uncon-
founded ; *with unblenched majesty* :
C. 430.

Unblest, *adj.* cursed, unhallowed,
wretched : Ps. v. 14 ; *the race
unblest* : P. L. X. 988 ; *unblessed*

enchanter vile : C. 907 ; *the sole of
unblest feet* : P. L. I. 238.

Unborn, *adj.* (*a*) not born ; *to nations
yet unborn* : P. L. IV. 663 ; *O
miserable Mankind ... better end
here unborn* : P. L. XI. 502.

(*b*) not yet existing, not created ;
Chaos and the World unborn : P.
L. VII. 220.

Unbosom, *vb. tr.* to reveal, disclose,
unfold : S. A. 879 ; *grove and
spring would soon unbosom all
their echoes* : P. 53.

Unbottomed, *adj.* bottomless ; *the
dark, unbottomed, infinite Abyss* :
P. L. II. 405.

Unbound, *adj.* unconfined, unrestrained ; *call up unbound ... old
Proteus* : P. L. III. 603.

Unbounded, *adj.* having no bounds,
unlimited ; *the ... unbounded Deep* :
P. L. X. 471 ; *hope* : P. L. IV. 60.

Unbroken, *adj.* undisturbed, uninterrupted : P. L. II. 691.

Unbuckle, *vb. tr.* to loose from
buckles, unfasten ; *his starry helm
unbuckled* : P. L. XI. 245.

Unbuild, *vb. tr.* to pull down, demolish ; *fig., unbuild his living
temples, built by faith* : P. L. XII.
526 ; *absol. ; how they will wield
the mighty frame* (of Heaven) ;
how build, unbuild : P. L. VIII. 81.

Uncalled, *past part.* unsummoned,
uninvited : P. L. IX. 523.

Uncelebrated, *past part.* not com-
memorated, unhonoured : P. L.
VII. 253.

Uncertain, *adj.* (*a*) not surely or
exactly known : P. L. III. 76 ; C.
300.

(*b*) not knowing what to think
or do : P. R. IV. 326.

Uncessant, *adj.* incessant, unremitting, ceaseless ; *with uncessant
care* : L. 64.

Unchangeable, *adj.* that cannot be
changed, immutable ; *the high decree unchangeable* : P. L. III. 127.

Unchanged, *adj.* not changed, unaltered ; *with mortal voice unchanged to hoarse or mute* : P. L.
VII. 24.

Unchaste, *adj.* not continent, lewd :
S. A. 321, 325 ; *by unchaste looks* :
C. 464.

Unchecked, *adj.* not restrained,
unhindered : P. L. VIII. 189.

Uncheerful, *adj.* gloomy, dark,
joyless ; *at death's uncheerful
door* : Ps. LXXXVIII. 11.

Uncircumcised, *adj.* not circumcised : S. A. 1364.

absol. those not circumcised, the Philistines ; *the Uncircumcised* : S. A. 260, 640.

Uncircumscribed, *adj.* unlimited, unrestricted ; *though I, uncircumscribed, myself retire, and put not forth my goodness* : P. L. VII. 170.

Unclean, *adj.* (1) impure according to the Mosaic law : S. A. 321, 324, 1364 ; perhaps including also sense (2) : S. A. 1362.

(*b*) causing ceremonial defilement ; *meats by the law unclean* : P. R. II. 328.

(2) morally impure ; *reproach us as unclean* : P. L. IX. 1098.

Unclouded, *adj.* not obscured by a cloud ; *blazed forth unclouded deity* : P. L. X. 65.

Uncoloured, *adj.* being of one single colour, not diversified by clouds ; *the uncoloured sky* : P. L. V. 189.

Uncompassionate, *adj.* pitiless : S. A. 818.

Uncompounded, *adj.* not mixed, simple ; *for Spirits ... so soft and uncompounded is their essence pure* : P. L. I. 425.

Unconcerned, *adj.* not anxious, not affected ; *the Morn, all unconcerned with our unrest* : P. L. XI. 174.

Unconfirmed, *adj.* not strengthened by additional testimony : P. R. I. 29.

Unconform, *adj.* dissimilar, unlike ; *he sees, not unconform to other shining globes, Earth* : P. L. V. 259.

Unconjugal, *adj.* unfitting the marriage relation : S. A. 979.

Unconniving, *adj.* not giving aid or encouraging a wrong by silence or forbearance ; *by rigour unconniving* : P. R. I. 363.

Unconquerable (uncónqueráble), *adj.* (*a*) incapable of being vanquished, not to be overcome ; *strength ... to sight unconquerable* : P. L. VI. 118.

(*b*) incapable of being subdued and brought under control ; *the unconquerable will* : P. L. I. 106.

Unconquered, *adj.* not vanquished, unsubdued ; *Minerva ... unconquered virgin* : C. 448.

Unconscionable (uncónscionáble), *adj.* enormous, vast ; *unconscionable strides* : S. A. 1245.

Unconsumed, *adj.* not destroyed by fire : P. L. I. 69 ; *impaled with circling fire, yet unconsumed* : P. L. II. 648.

Uncontrollable, *adj.* that cannot be controlled or restrained : S. A. 1754.

Uncontrolled (*tetrasyl.* uncontrollèd), *adj.* irresistible (?) ; *the uncontrolled worth of this pure cause* : C. 793.

Uncoupled, *adj.* having no wife ; *uncoupled bed* : D. F. I. 13.

Uncouth (úncouth), *adj.* (*a*) not known, strange, unfamiliar ; with the implication of unpleasant, uncanny, or fearsome ; *uncouth way, passage, place, cell* : P. L. II. 407 ; X. 475 ; S. A. 333 ; L'A. 5 ; *voyage uncouth* : P. L. VIII. 230 ; *uncouth errand* : P. L. II. 827 ; *dream, pain* : P. L. V. 98 ; VI. 362.

(*b*) rustic, awkward ; *the uncouth swain* : L. 186.

Uncover, *vb.* (*pres. 2d sing.* uncover'st : S. A. 842) *tr.* to lay bare, disclose : S. A. 842 ; *absol.* to lay open to view ; *guilty shame he covered, but his robe uncovered more* : P. L. IX. 1059.

Uncreate, *vb. tr.* to deprive of existence : P. L. V. 895 ; *absol.* ; *so God shall uncreate* : P. L. IX. 943.

part. adj. **uncreated** ; (*a*) not brought into existence ; *misery, uncreated till the crime of thy rebellion* : P. L. VI. 268.

(*b*) existing without being created ; *in the wide womb of uncreated Night* : P. L. II. 150.

Uncropt, *adj.* not plucked : P. L. IV. 731.

Unction, *sb.* the act of anointing with oil in consecration to office : P. L. VI. 709.

Unctuous, *adj.* impregnated with an oily or fatty substance ; *a wandering fire, compact of unctuous vapour* : P. L. IX. 635.

Unculled, *adj.* not separated, not selected : P. L. XI. 436.

Undaunted, *adj.* fearless, intrepid ; *he patient, but undaunted* : S. A. 1623 ; *Abdiel .. his own undaunted heart explores* : P. L. VI. 113 ; used of Satan : P. L. II. 677, 955 ; IV. 851.

Undazzled, *adj.* unblinded by brilliance : P. L. III. 614.

Undecked, *adj.* unadorned : P. L.
v. 380.
Undefiled, *adj.* unpolluted, pure :
P. L. IV. 761.
Undelayed, *adj.* unhindered : Ps.
VII. 59.
Undelighted, *adj.* not filled with
delight, displeased : P. L. IV. 286.
*Under, I. *prep.* (1) below, beneath,
so as to be lower than or covered
by : P. L. III. 322; IV. 239, 451;
VI. 142, 215; VII. 402; X. 190;
XI. 740; S. A. 140; A. 31; C.
294; *under the cope of Hell* : P.
L. I. 345; *the Abyss long under
darkness cover* : P. L. I. 659; *sunk
under yon boiling ocean* : P. L. II.
183; *under the mid-day sun* :
C. 384; *under the open sky* :
P. L. III. 514; *under foot the
violet* : P. L. IV. 700; *from under
...roof* : P. L. V. 137; *under
ground* : P. L. VI. 196; IX. 72;
under heaven : P. L. VII. 283;
under virgin veil : S. A. 1035;
under the ribs of Death : C. 562;
*Mount Amara...under the Ethiop
line* : P. L. IV. 282; *ere the high
lawns appeared under the opening
eyelids of the Morn* : L. 26.
(*b*) concealed by ; *under shade* :
P. L. IV. 572.
(*c*) beneath and fashioned by ;
*under his forming hands a creature
grew* : P. L. VIII. 470.
(**2**) of supporting, sustaining,
undergoing, etc.; *under wrath* :
P. L. III. 275; *the World...under
her own weight groaning* : P. L.
XII. 539; = to ; *under the frown
of Night starless exposed* : P. L.
III. 424.
(**3**) subject to ; (*a*) of submission or subjection ; *under his
great vicegerent reign abide* : P. L.
v. 609; *under Roman yoke* : P. R.
III. 158; *the nations under yoke* :
P. R. IV. 135; *under the inevitable
curb* : P. L. II. 322; *his gloomy
power* : P. L. III. 242; *long
obedience* : P. L. VII. 159.
(*b*) of power, government, leadership, or guidance : P. L. V. 687;
VI. 67; *under Thee, as Head
Supreme* : P. L. III. 319; *under
their hierarchs* : P. L. V. 587;
under thy conduct : P. L. I. 130;
under kings : P. L. XII. 320;
under paternal rule : P. L. XII. 24.
(*c*) of influence or operation :
P. L. IX. 208; *under amazement,*

hope, torments, etc. : P. L. I. 313;
II. 498; IV. 88; IX. 774; X. 1003;
XI. 511; *under change of times* :
S. A. 695; *under judgments imminent* : P. L. XI. 725; compelled
by ; *under task* : S. A. 35.
(**4**) bound by; *under ban* : P.
L. IX. 925; *seal of silence* : S. A.
49; *pledge of vow* : S. A. 378.
(**5**) beneath the concealment or
guise of ; *under saintly show* : P.
L. IV. 122; *show of love* : P. L.
IX. 492; *pretence* : S. A. 1196;
C. 160; with the designation of ;
under the name of King Anointed :
P. L. V. 776; *under usual names* :
P. R. IV. 316.
(**6**) of shelter or protection ;
under the lee : P. L. I. 207; *his
special eye* : S. A. 636; *protection* :
S. A. 887; Ps. VII. 2.
(**7**) having the duty of, in the
position of ; *the bands of Angels
under watch* : P. L. V. 288.
(**8**) during the time of ; *under
conscious Night* : P. L. VI. 521.
II. *adv.* (*a*) in a lower position :
V. Ex. 41.
(*b*) in subjection : V. Ex. 78.
Undergo, *vb.* (*pret.* underwent; *past
part.* undergone) *tr.* (1) to pass or
go through as an experience,
suffer, bear : P. 12; *undergo eternal punishment* : P. L. I. 155;
undergo like doom : P. L. IX. 953;
one guilt, one crime : P. L. IX.
971; *this annual humbling* : P. L.
X. 575; *underwent a quick immortal change* : C. 841; *I thy
terrors undergo* : Ps. LXXXVIII. 63.
(**2**) to undertake, perform ;
other labour to be undergone : P.
R. II. 132.
(*b*) to take the blame of ; *to
undergo myself the total crime* :
P. L. X. 126.
Underground, *adv.* beneath the surface of the earth : P. L. VII. 301,
469; XI. 570; in heaven : P. L.
VI. 666; wrongly printed for
under ground, for meaning of
ground see **Earth** (**5**) : Il P. 94.
Undergrowth, *sb.* a growth of smaller
plants among larger ones : P. L.
IV. 175.
Underling, *sb.* one who is under
another's authority, subordinate :
V. Ex. 76.
Undermine, *vb.* *absol.* to injure
secretly or in an underhand way :
P. R. I. 179.

Underminer, *sb.* one who secretly injures another, a secret enemy : S. A. 1204.

Underneath, (1) *adv.* below, beneath : P. L. I. 701 ; III. 518 ; IV. 225 ; v. 87 ; VI. 659 ; P. R. IV. 456 ; V. Ex. 95 ; *to the Earth's dark basis underneath* : P. R. IV. 456 ; *the waters underneath from those above dividing* : P. L. VII. 268 ; *above, about, or underneath* : Il P. 152.

(2) *prep.* under, below : P. R. IV. 544.

Understand, *vb.* (*pret.* and *past part.* understood) *tr.* (*a*) to receive the idea or the meaning of ; *each to other calls, not understood* : P. L. XII. 58 ; *of the most I would be understood* : S. A. 191.

(*b*) to perceive the meaning or nature of, comprehend : P. L. VIII. 352 ; XII. 376 ; P. R. I. 436, 437; *nor was jealousy understood* : P. L. v. 450 ; *toy of amorous intent, well understood of Eve* : P.L. IX. 1035 ; *not but by the Spirit understood* : P. L. XII. 514 ; *I ... seek to understand my adversary* : P. R. IV. 527 ; with clause : P. L. IV. 55 ; *understood not all was but a show* : P. L. X. 883 ; with two *acc.* ; *well I understand ... her the inferior* : P. L. VIII. 540 ; *absol.*: P. R. II. 100 ; Ps. LXXXII. 17 ; used quibblingly in both a physical and intellectual sense : P. L. VI. 625, 626.

(*c*) to take to be or to mean ; *his own doom ; which understood not instant* : P. L. X. 344.

(*d*) to take for granted, assume: P. L. VIII. 345 ; *war, open or understood* : P. L. I. 662.

vbl. sb. **understanding**, the intellectual faculty, mind, reason : P. L.v. 486; VI. 444 ; *Understanding ruled not, and the Will heard not her lore* : P. L. IX. 1127.

Undertake, *vb.* (*pret.* undertook ; *past part.* not used) (1) *tr.* to take upon oneself, promise to perform ; *undertake the perilous attempt*: P. L. II. 419 ; *undertook the dismal expedition* : P. R. I. 100 ; *that office* : P. R. I. 374 ; with *prep. inf.*: P. L. IV. 934.

(2) *intr.* or *absol.* to pledge oneself, promise ; *so I undertook before thee* : P. L. X. 74 ; *I, as I undertook* : P. R. II. 129.

Undeserved, *adj.* not merited, not rightfully possessed : P. L. XII. 27.

Undeservedly, *adv.* not rightfully : P. L. XII. 94.

Undesirable, *adj.* not to be wished : P. L. IX. 824.

Undetermined, *adj.* not settled, undecided ; *Heaven ... undetermined square or round* : P. L. II. 1048.

Undiminished, *adj.* unimpaired, unabated ; *strength undiminished* : P. L. I. 154 ; *undiminished brightness* : P. L. IV. 836.

Undiscording, *adj.* not discordant in sound, harmonious : S. M. 17.

Undisguised, *adj.* not concealed although covered by a false appearance ; *the Arch-Fiend, now undisguised* : P. R. I. 357.

Undismayed, *adj.* undaunted, fearless : P. L. II. 432 ; VI. 417.

Undissembled, *adj.* undisguised, open ; *undissembled hate* : S. A. 400.

Undisturbed (*tetrasyl.* undisturbèd), *adj.* calm, peaceful, serene : S. M. 6.

Undo, *vb.* (*pret.* not used ; *past part.* undone) *tr.* (*a*) to reverse what has been done, annul : *past who can recall, or done undo?* : P. L. IX. 926 ; *so God shall ... do, undo* : P. L. IX. 944.

(*b*) to unfasten, unloose : C. 904.

(*c*) to ruin morally : P. L. III. 235.

Undoubted, *adj.* indisputable, unquestioned ; *the undoubted Son of God* : P. R. I. 11 ; sure, unfailing; *undoubted sign* : P. L. I. 672.

Undoubtedly, *adv.* without doubt, indubitably : P. L. X. 1093.

Undrawn, *adj.* not pulled or dragged; *the chariot of Paternal Deity ... undrawn, itself instinct with spirit*: P. L. VI. 751.

Undreaded, *adj.* not feared : P. L. X. 595.

Undying, *adj.* not subject to death : P. L. VI. 739.

Unearned, *adj.* not merited by labour : P. L. IX. 225.

Uneasy, *adj.* causing pain or discomfort ; *uneasy steps, station* : P. L. I. 295 ; P. R. IV. 584.

Unemployed, *adj.* having no employment, unoccupied, idle ; S. A. 580 ; *other creatures all day long rove idle, unemployed* : P. L. IV. 617.

Unenchanted, *adj.* that cannot be enchanted ; *dragon-watch with unenchanted eye* : C. 395.

Unendeared, *adj.* not accompanied with endearment ; *the bought smile of harlots ... unendeared* : P. L. IV. 766.

Unenvied, *adj.* exempt from the envy of others, uncoveted : P. L. II. 23.

Unequal, (1) *adj.* ill-matched, not having an equal power or advantage, disproportioned ; *too unequal work we find* : P. L. VI. 453 ; *against unequal arms to fight* : P. L. VI. 454 ; *now unequal match to save himself against a coward armed* : S. A. 346.

(2) *sb.* one not equal to another in station or power ; *among unequals what society can sort* : P.L. VIII. 383.

Unequalled, *adj.* unparalleled, unrivalled : P. L. IX. 983.

Unespied, *adj.* not seen, undiscovered : P. L. IV. 399 ; VI. 523.

Unessential, *adj.* not having real essence or substance ; *the void profound of unessential Night* : P. L. II. 439.

Uneven, *adj.* not perfectly horizontal or level, not balanced ; *fig., in much uneven scale thou weigh'st all others by thyself* : P. R. II. 173.

Unexampled, *adj.* without a parallel, unmatched : P. L. III. 410.

Unexempt, *adj.* from which there is no immunity ; *the unexempt condition by which all mortal frailty must subsist* : C. 685.

Unexpected, *adj.* not looked for, unforeseen : P. L. VI. 774 ; XI. 268 ; P. R. II. 29.

Unexpectedly, *adv.* at an unlooked for time, suddenly : S. A. 1750.

Unexperienced, *adj.* not having knowledge or power gained from experience ; *I thither went with unexperienced thought* : P. L. IV. 457 ; *the wisest, unexperienced, will be ever timorous* : P. R. III. 240.

Unexpert, *adj.* inexpert, unskilled : P. L. II. 52.

Unexpressive, *adj.* inexpressible, unutterable ; *harping in loud and solemn quire, with unexpressive notes* : N. O. 116 ; *the unexpressive nuptial song* : L. 176.

Unextinguishable (únextínguisháble), *adj.* inextinguishable, unquenchable : P. L. II. 88.

Unfaithful, *adj.* not having faith in God or Christ, unbelieving or disloyal ; *to judge the unfaithful dead* : P. L. XII. 461 ; *his faithful, left among the unfaithful herd* : P. L. XII. 481.

Unfasten, *vb. tr.* to loose, undo : P. L. II. 879.

Unfeared, *adj.* not feared or dreaded : P. L. IX. 187.

Unfeigned (*trisyl.* unfeignèd : P. L. 744), *adj.* not pretended, sincere, true, genuine ; *of sorrow unfeigned and humiliation meek* : P. L. X. 1092, 1104 ; *unfeigned union of mind* : P. L. VIII. 603 ; sung with sincere purpose or feeling ; *unfeigned halleluiahs* : P. L. VI. 744.

Unfelt, *adj.* (*a*) not perceived ; *pangs unfelt before* : P. L. II. 703.

(*b*) not experienced ; *sweetness into my heart unfelt before* : P. L. VIII. 475.

Unfinished, *adj.* not finished, incomplete : S. A. 1027.

Unfit, *adj.* not fit, unqualified ; *I am a man but ...for that name unfit* : Ps. LXXXVIII. 16.

Unfold, *vb. tr.* (*a*) to open the parts or leaves of ; *Hell shall unfold ... her widest gates* : P. L. IV. 381 ; *Heaven ... unfold her crystal doors* : P. R. I. 82 ; *to right and left the front unfold* : P. L. VI. 558.

(*b*) to display, exhibit, show ; *unfolding bright toward the right hand his glory* : P. L. X. 63 ; *if cause were to unfold some active scene of various persons* : P. R. II. 239.

(*c*) to make known, disclose, reveal : Il P. 89 ; *unfold ... the secrets of his eternal empire* : P.L. VII. 94 ; *the secrets of another world* : P. L. V. 568 ; *to unfold the drift of hollow states* : S. XVII. 5 ; *thy faithfulness unfold* : Ps. LXXXVIII. 48 ; *the sage and serious doctrine of Virginity* : C. 786 ; with indirect question ; *unfold ... whether here the race of Man will end* : P. L. XI. 785.

Unforbid, *adj.* not prohibited, allowed, permitted : P. L. VII. 94.

Unforeknown, *adj.* not known beforehand : P. L. III. 119.

Unforeseen, adj. not seen beforehand, unexpected : P. L. II. 821.

Unforeskinned, adj. circumcised : S. A. 1100.

Unforewarned, adj. not put on one's guard beforehand : P. L. v. 245.

Unformed, adj. without form or shape ; thus God the Heaven created, thus the Earth, matter unformed : P. L. VII. 233.

Unfortunate, adj. (a) not favoured by fortune, unsuccessful ; I am that Spirit unfortunate : P. R. I. 358 ; his lot unfortunate in nuptial choices : S. A. 1743.

(b) causing ill-fortune, disastrous ; my words ... so unfortunate: P. L. x. 970 ; misdeed : S. A. 747.

Unfound, adj. undiscovered : P. L. VI. 500.

Unfounded, adj. having no base or foundation, bottomless ; with lonely steps to tread the unfounded Deep : P. L. II. 829.

Unfrequented, adj. seldom resorted to, rarely visited : S. A. 17 ; unfrequented left his righteous altar : P. L. I. 433.

Unfriended, adj. lacking friends : P. R. II. 413.

Unfulfilled, adj. unsatisfied ; fierce desire ... still unfulfilled: P. L. IV. 511.

Unfumed, adj. not extracted by fumigating or vaporizing, undistilled : P. L. v. 349.

Unfurl, vb. tr. to unroll, spread out, unfold : P. L. I. 535.

Ungodly, adj. godless, wicked, sinful ; ungodly deeds : S. A. 898 ; Soph. 2.

absol. those who are wicked : P. L. VII. 185.

Ungoverned, adj. not restrained, uncontrolled : P. L. XI. 517.

Ungraceful, adj. lacking in ease and elegance of speech ; nor are thy lips ungraceful : P. L. VIII. 218.

Ungratefully, adv. with ingratitude: V. Ex. 78.

Unguarded, adj. not defended, unprotected : P. L. x. 419 ; the throne of God unguarded : P. L. VI. 133 ; your fair side all unguarded : C. 283.

Unhallowed, adj. unholy, profane, impure ; fruit ... unhallowed : P. L. IX. 931 ; this unhallowed air : C. 757.

Unhappily, adv. unfortunately, miserably : P. L. x. 917.

Unhappy, adj. (a) not happy, miserable, wretched : C. 511.

(b) marked by ill-fortune, disastrous, calamitous ; this unhappy morn : P. L. IX. 1136.

(c) causing misery and unrest, pernicious; this unhappy mansion: P. L. I. 268.

Unharboured, adj. not yielding a harbour, not affording shelter ; unharboured heaths : C. 423.

Unhardy, adj. not bold, timorous : P. R. III. 243.

Unharmonious, adj. inharmonious, incongruous; those ... elements, that know no gross, no unharmonious mixture foul : P. L. XI. 51.

Unhazarded, adj. not exposed to chance or danger : S. A. 809.

Unheard, adj. (a) not perceived by the ear : P. L. I. 395 ; III. 645.

(b) not known to fame ; nor was his name unheard : P. L. I. 738.

Unheeded, adj. not heeded, unnoticed : P. L. IV. 350.

Unheedy, adj. unheeding, careless ; some unheedy swain : M.W. 38.

Unhide-bound, adj. having the skin not drawn tightly but hanging loosely; used of Death; this vast unhide-bound corpse : P. L. x. 601.

Unhoard, vb. tr. to take away from a hoard, steal : P. L. IV. 188.

Unholy, adj. not holy, wicked, profane ; sights unholy : L'A. 4.

absol. one who is sinful : P. L. XI. 106.

Unhoped, adj. not hoped or looked for, unexpected : P. L. x. 348.

Unhouse, vb. tr. to take away from a home or habitation ; fig. unhoused thy virgin soul from her fair biding-place : D. F. I. 21.

Unhumbled, adj. not meek or submissive : P. R. III. 429.

Unhurt, adj. not harmed, free from injury ; while we can preserve unhurt our minds : P. L. VI. 444.

Unimaginable (únimágináble), adj. not capable of being imagined, inconceivable ; P. L. VII. 54.

Unimmortal, adj. subject to death ; to destroy, or unimmortal make all kinds : P. L. x. 611.

Unimplored, adj. not asked or prayed for, unsolicited : P. L. III. 231 ; IX. 22.

Uninformed, *adj.* not instructed, untaught ; *not uninformed of nuptial sanctity* : P. L. VIII. 486.

Uninjured, *adj.* having suffered no harm, unhurt : C. 403.

Uninterrupted, *adj.* not broken off, unceasing ; *uninterrupted joy* : P. L. III. 68.

Uninvented, *adj.* not found out, undiscovered : P. L. VI. 470.

Union (trisyl. únión), *sb.* (*a*) the state of being united, junction ; *spirits embrace ... union of pure with pure desiring* : P. L. VIII. 627 ; *canst raise thy creature to what highth thou wilt of union or communion* : P. L. VIII. 431 ; in marriage : P. L. IX. 966.

(*b*) agreement, harmony, concord ; *union of mind* : P. L. VIII. 604 ; *Earth be changed to Heaven, and Heaven to Earth ... joy and union without end* : P. L. VII. 161 ; *hold all Heaven and Earth in happier union* : N. O. 108.

(*c*) coalition, combination, alliance : P. L. II. 36 ; Ps. LXXXIII. 20 ; *Him who disobeys me disobeys, breaks union* : P. L. V. 612 ; *in mighty quadrate joined of union irresistible* : P. L. VI. 63.

Unison, *adj.* unisonous, sounding alone ; *with voice choral or unison* : P. L. VII. 599.

Unite, *vb.* (1) *tr.* (*a*) to combine so as to form one : P. L. IV. 230 ; *murmuring waters ... unite their streams* : P. L. IV. 263 ; to combine in allegiance to the government of one ; *under his great vicegerent reign abide, united* : P. L. V. 610 ; *under one head more near united* : P. L. V. 831 ; to make act as a whole ; *to fear thy name my heart unite* : Ps. LXXXVI. 39.

(*b*) to join, combine, link together : P. L. IX. 608 ; *though in thee be united what of perfection can in Man be found* : P. R. III. 229 ; *to his celestial consort us unite* : S. M. 27 ; *themselves against thee they unite* : Ps. LXXXIII. 19 ; *such fatal consequence unites us three* : P. L. X. 364 ; *unite with secret amity things of like kind* : P. L. X. 247.

(*c*) *absol.* to add (?), to gather up and concentrate (?) ; *would utmost vigour raise, and raised unite* : P. L. IX. 314.

(2) *intr.* to become one ; *so*

God with Man unites : P. L. XII. 382.

part. adj. **united** ; (*a*) combined ; *united force* : P. L. I. 560, 629 ; *powers* : S. A. 1110.

(*b*) agreeing, harmonious ; *united thoughts and counsels* : P. L. I. 88.

Unity, *sb.* the state of being one, oneness : P. L. VIII. 425 ; *Trinal Unity*, the Trinity : N.·O. 11.

Universal, *adj.* (1) of the universe ; *the hollow universal orb* : P. L. VII. 257 ; *this universal frame* : P. L. v. 154.

(*b*) of the universe or of all created beings ; *universal King, Maker, Lord, Dame* : P. L. III. 317, 676 ; v. 205 ; VIII. 376 ; IX. 612.

(*c*) embracing or ruling all things ; *universal Pan* : P. L. IV. 266.

(2) pertaining to all mankind ; *God's universal law* : S. A. 1053.

(3) whole, entire, all ; *the universal host* : P. L. I. 541 ; *the bare Earth ... her universal face* : P. L. VII. 316 ; *universal nature* : L. 60.

(4) pertaining to or coming from all or the whole ; *universal peace* : N. O. 52 ; *reproach* : P. L. VI. 34 ; *ruin, wrack* : P. L. VI. 797 ; XI. 821 ; *hubbub, shout, hiss, groan* : P. L. II. 951 ; X. 505, 508 ; S. A. 1511 ; *a universal blank of Nature works* : P. L. III. 48.

Universally, *adv.* so as to embrace all, without exception : P. L. IX. 542 ; S. A. 175.

Universe, *sb.* (*a*) the whole creation, the world ; *the Universe* : P. L. III. 584 ; *this Universe* : P. L. III. 721 ; VII. 227 ; VIII. 360 ; IX. 684 ; P. R. I. 49.

(*b*) *fig.* the body as a microcosm ; *man's less universe* : P. R. IV. 459.

(*c*) the totality of things considered ; *a universe of death* : P. L. II. 622.

Unjointed, *adj.* disconnected ; *the sound of words ; their sense the air dissolves unjointed ere it reach my ear* : S. A. 177.

Unjust, *adj.* (*a*) not acting according to right and justice, unrighteous ; *an unjust and wicked king* : Seneca 3 ; *some blood more precious must be paid for Man, just for unjust* : P. L. XII. 294.

(*b*) not conforming or conformable to right and justice, wrongful ;

nor the law unjust : P. L. II. 200;
unjust tribunals : S. A. 695; *force* :
C. 590 ; *their power unjust* : P. R.
II. 45 ; *suffering death unjust* : P.
R. III. 98.

(*c*) not rendering what is due ;
*unjust, thou say'st, ... to bind with
laws the free* : P. L. v. 818 ; *grant
it thee unjust that equal over equals
monarch reign* : P. L. v. 831.

absol. one acting contrary to
right and justice, an unrighteous
person : S. A. 703 ; *the unjust* :
P. L. III. 215 ; XI. 455 ; Ps. VII.
45.

Unjustly, *adv.* in an unjust manner,
wrongfully : P. L. VI. 174 ; S. A.
889.

Unkindly, (1) *adj.* unfavourable,
malignant; *unkindly fog* : C. 269;
sleep bred of unkindly fumes : P.
L. IX. 1050.

(2) *adv.* in a manner contrary
to nature ; *the...works of Nature's
hand...unkindly mixed* : P. L. III.
456.

Unkindness, *sb.* the want of love and
tenderness : P. L. IX. 271.

Unknown (únknown : P. L. II. 443,
444), *adj.* (*a*) not known, not
become an object of knowledge :
P. L. III. 496 ; VII. 75 ; IX. 905 ;
*many are the trees of God...yet
unknown* : P. L. IX. 619 ; *a small
unsightly root...unknown* : C. 634 ;
nor unknown the serpent : P. L.
VII. 494 ; *regions, land* : P. L. II.
443 ; XII. 134 ; *neighbours* : S. A.
180 ; *words* : P. L. XII. 55 ;
dangers, evil, good : P. L. II. 444;
VI. 262 ; IX. 756, 757, 864 ; C.
361 ; *to me is not unknown what
hath been done* : P. R. II. 444.

(*b*) not publicly known, obscure,
nameless, inglorious : P. R. I. 25 ;
II. 413 ; *not to know me argues
yourself unknown* : P. L. IV. 830.

Unlaid (únlaid), *adj.* not exorcised ;
unlaid ghost : C. 434.

Unless (únless : P. L. VIII. 186 ; P.
R. III. 352), *conj.* if it be not that,
if...not ; introducing a clause
containing the subj. : P. L. II.
915 ; III. 210 ; *unless an age too
late...damp my intended wing* : P.
L. IX. 44 ; *unless be meant whom
I conjecture* : P. L. x. 1032; *unless
thou endeavour* : P. R. III. 352 ;
unless there be : S. A. 295 ; *unless
he feel* : S. A. 663 ; the vb. in the
plural and hence the mood in-

determinable : P. L. II. 236 ; VIII.
186 ; the vb. omitted : P. L. IX.
125 ; P. R. IV. 351 ; C. 267, 417.

Unlettered, *adj.* unlearned, ignorant:
C. 174.

Unlibidinous, *adj.* not lewd or lascivious : P. L. v. 449.

Unlicensed, *adj.* without permission,
not having leave : P. L. IV. 909.

Unlightsome, *adj.* without light,
dark ; *the Sun, a mighty sphere he
framed, unlightsome first* : P. L.
VII. 355.

Unlike, *adj.* not like, different from ;
how unlike the place : P. L. I. 75 ;
unlike the former shout : S. A.
1510 ; *be not unlike all others* : S.
A. 815 ; *with to ; how unlike to
that first naked glory* : P. L. IX.
1114 ; the sb. understood ; *nor
hath this Earth entrails unlike* : P.
L. VI. 517.

Unlimited, *adj.* not restrained, unrestricted : P. L. IV. 435.

Unlock, *vb. tr.* (*a*) to unfasten, un-
bolt ; *forbidden to unlock these
adamantine gates* : P. L. II. 852.

(*b*) to open ; *unlocked my lips* :
C. 756.

(*c*) to loosen; *she can unlock the
clasping charm* : C. 852.

(*d*) to reveal ; with *acc.* and
dat. ; unlocked her all my heart :
S. A. 407.

Unlooked, *adj.* unexpected, not
anticipated; with *for* ; *what relapse unlooked for* : P. R. II. 31.

Unmake, *vb. tr.* to deprive of being,
annihilate ; *wilt thou...unmake...
what for thy glory thou hast made?*:
P. L. III. 163.

Unmanly, *adj.* unworthy of a man,
cowardly : S. A. 417.

Unmarked, *adj.* not noted, unobserved : P. L. x. 441 ; P. R. I.
25.

Unmeasured-out, *adj.* not distributed
by measure, hence boundless : P.
L. v. 399.

Unmeditated, *adj.* unpremeditated,
not thought out beforehand ; *in
fit strains pronounced, or sung
unmeditated* : P. L. v. 149.

Unmeet, *adj.* not suited or adapted ;
fellowship...unmeet for thee : P.
L. VIII. 442.

Unmerited, *adj.* not deserved : P.
L. XII. 278.

Unminded, *adj.* not taken notice of;
he...unminded slunk into the wood:
P. L. x. 332.

Unmindful, *adj.* regardless, heedless, negligent; *unmindful of their Maker*: P. L. XI. 611; *of the crown*: C. 9; *of flattering gales*: Hor. O. 12; with *prep. inf.; nor stood unmindful Abdiel to annoy*: P. L. VI. 369.

Unmixed, *adj.* having no foreign admixture, pure; *fig., praise unmixed*: P. R. III. 48; *thy Saints, unmixed, and from the impure far separate*: P. L. VI. 742.

Unmould, *vb. tr.* to turn into another shape or form; *unmoulding reason's mintage charactered in the face*: C. 529.

Unmoved, *adj.* (*a*) not changed in position; *waters ... spread into a liquid plain; then stood unmoved*: P. L. IV. 455.

(*b*) not changed in purpose, firm, unshaken: P. L. II. 429; v. 898; P. R. III. 386; IV. 109; *unmoved with fear*: P. L. IV. 822; *unmoved with dread of death to flight*: P. L. I. 554.

(*c*) not having the passions or feelings excited, calm: P. L. VIII. 532; XI. 192.

Unmuffle, *vb. intr.* to throw off coverings, reveal oneself; *unmuffle, ye faint stars*: C. 331.

Unnamed, *adj.* (*a*) not having received a name: P. L. XII. 140.

(*b*) not spoken of, unmentioned; *Evil ... unnamed in Heaven*: P. L. VI. 263; or having no fame or reputation: P. L. X. 595.

Unnumbered, *adj.* innumerable: P. L. VII. 432; *unnumbered as the sands of Barca or Cyrene's torrid soil*: P. L. II. 903.

Unobeyed, *adj.* not obeyed; *leave ... unobeyed, the Throne supreme*: P. L. V. 670.

Unobnoxious, *adj.* not liable, not subject; *unobnoxious to be pained by wound*: P. L. VI. 404.

Unobscured, *adj.* not hidden, not rendered less bright; *his glory unobscured*: P. L. II. 265.

Unobserved, *adj.* not noticed, not regarded: P. L. IV. 130; P. R. IV. 638.

Unopposed, *adj.* unresisted: P. L. VI. 132.

Unoriginal, *adj.* having no origin or beginning; *in the womb of unoriginal Night and Chaos*: P. L. X. 477.

Unowned, *adj.* unclaimed, and hence unprotected; *our unowned sister*: C. 407.

Unpaid, *adj.* not discharged; *knee-tribute yet unpaid*: P. L. V. 782.

Unpained, *adj.* incapable of feeling pain: P. L. VI. 455.

Unparalleled, *adj.* unequalled, unmatched; *since man on earth, unparalleled*: S. A. 165; *a deity so unparalleled*: A. 25.

Unpeopled, *adj.* deprived of inhabitants, depopulated: P. L. III. 497.

Unperceived, *adj.* (*a*) not found out or discovered; *so spake the false dissembler unperceived*: P. L. III. 681.

(*b*) not seen; *he ... not unperceived of Adam*: P. L. XI. 224.

Unpierced (*trisyl.* unpiercèd), *adj.* not penetrated; *the unpierced shade*: P. L. IV. 245.

Unpillowed, *adj.* having no pillow; *her unpillowed head*: C. 355.

Unpitied, *adj.* not regarded with sympathetic sorrow: P. L. II. 185; IV. 375; P. R. I. 414.

Unplausible, *adj.* not apparently worthy of acceptance; *reasons not unplausible*: C. 162.

Unpolluted, *adj.* not defiled, pure; *our great Enemy ... would on his throne sit unpolluted*: P. L. II. 139; *the unpolluted temple of the mind*: C. 461.

Unpossessed, *adj.* not occupied; *room in Nature unpossessed*: P. L. VIII. 153.

Unpractised, *adj.* not having experience, unskilful: P. L. VIII. 197.

Unpraised, *adj.* not commended or extolled: P. L. IX. 232; *the deed becomes unpraised*: P. R. III. 103; *the All-giver ... would be unpraised*: C. 723.

Unpredict, *vb. intr.* to revoke prediction; *prediction else will unpredict, and fail me of the throne*: P. R. III. 395.

Unpremeditated, *adj.* not previously thought over: P. L. IX. 24.

Unprepared, *adj.* not made ready: P. L. VIII. 197.

Unprevented, *adj.* not anticipated, not preceded by prayer; *Grace ... to all comes unprevented*: P. L. III. 231.

Unprincipled, *adj.* not grounded in principles: C. 367.

Unproclaimed, *adj.* not made known or proclaimed by public declaration: P. L. XI. 220.

Unpronounced, *adj.* not uttered articulately : V. Ex. 4.

Unpropt, *adj.* not supported : S. A. 119.

Unpurged (*trisyl.* unpurgèd), *adj.* unpurified ; *unpurged vapours not yet into her* (the moon's) *substance turned* : P. L. v. 419 ; not rendered fine and sensitive ; *gross unpurged ear* : A. 73.

Unpursued, *adj.* not followed (by an enemy) : P. L. vi. 1.

Unquenchable, *adj.* incapable of being extinguished : P. L. vi. 877 ; *fig.* incapable of being quieted or restrained ; *the people, on their holy-days, impetuous, insolent, unquenchable* : S. A. 1422.

Unquiet, *adj.* restless, agitated, disturbed : P. L. v. 11 ; x. 975.

Unrazored, *adj.* unshaved, not having yet known the razor : C. 290.

Unreal (únreal), *adj.* having no actual and fixed existence ; *the unreal, vast, unbounded Deep* : P. L. x. 471.

Unrecorded, *adj.* not related, untold : P. R. i. 16.

Unreformed, *adj.* not restored to former goodness, not freed from sin : P. R. iii. 429.

Unreined, *adj.* not restrained by reins or bridle : P. L. vii. 17.

Unremoved, *adj.* not to be removed, firm, unshaken ; *Satan .. stood, like Teneriff or Atlas, unremoved* : P. L. iv. 987.

Unrepentant, *adj.* not penitent, not contrite for sin : P. R. iii. 429.

Unrepented, *adj.* not repented of : S. A. 1376.

Unreprieved, *adj.* not given temporary suspension of punishment : P. L. ii. 185.

Unreproved (*tetrasyl.* unreprovèd : L'A. 40), *adj.* not to be reproved, blameless ; *our general mother... with eyes of conjugal attraction unreproved* : P. L. iv. 493 ; *in unreproved pleasures* : L'A. 40.

Unrespited, *adj.* allowed no temporary intermission of suffering : P. L. ii. 185.

Unrest, *sb.* the lack of rest in bed, a sleepless or unquiet night : P. L. ix. 1052 ; xi. 174.

Unrevoked, *adj.* not annulled : P. L. v. 602.

Unrighteous, *adj.* unjust, evil, wicked : P. L. iii. 292.

Unrivalled, *adj.* matchless, un-

equalled ; *unrivalled love* : P. L. iii. 68.

Unsafe, *adj.* not free from danger, exposed to peril : P. L. vi. 309.

Unsavoury, *adj.* (*a*) having a disagreeable taste : P. L. v. 401.

(*b*) *fig.* lacking pleasure or delight : C. 742.

Unsay, *vb. tr.* to deny or recall (something said) ; *not a period shall be unsaid for me* : C. 586 ; *how soon unsay what feigned submission swore* : P. L. iv. 95 ; absol. ; *say and unsay* : P. R. i. 474 ; *say and straight unsay* : P. L. iv. 947.

Unsearchable, *adj.* incapable of being discovered or understood, inscrutable ; P. L. viii. 10 ; *the unsearchable dispose of Highest Wisdom* : S. A. 1746.

Unsearched, *adj.* not carefully examined, unexplored : P. L. iv. 789.

Unseasonable, *adj.* not suited to the time or occasion, untimely ; *something not unseasonable to ask* : P. L. viii. 201.

Unseduced, *adj.* not enticed into evil : P. L. v. 899.

Unseemly, *adj.* not fit, unbecoming, improper : S. A. 690, 1451 ; *her gifts ... unseemly to bear rule* : P. L. x. 155 ; *sup., the parts of each ... unseemliest seen* : P. L. ix. 1094.

Unseen (únseen : Il P. 154), *adj.* (*a*) not seen, not perceived or discovered : P. L. ii. 659 ; iv. 130 ; L'A. 57 ; Il P. 65 ; *the subtle Fiend had stolen entrance unseen* : P. L. x. 21 ; *Eve, who unseen yet all had heard* : P. L. xi. 265 ; *at his birth a star, unseen before in heaven* : P. L. xii. 361.

(*b*) that cannot be seen, invisible : P. L. iii. 585 ; x. 448 ; xi. 671 ; *led by her Heavenly Maker, though unseen* : P. L. viii. 485 ; *God, who oft descends to visit men unseen* : P. L. xii. 49 ; *millions of spiritual creatures walk the Earth unseen* : P. L. iv. 678 ; *thou and Death ... unseen* : P. L. ii. 841 ; *the unseen Genius of the wood* : Il P. 154 ; *sweet Echo...that liv'st unseen* : C. 230.

Unsettled, *adj.* not fixed, vacillating in mind or character : P. R. iv. 326.

Unshaken, *adj.* not moved in resolution, firm, steady : P. L. iv. 64 ;

v. 899 ; P. R. IV. 421 ; *thy firm unshaken virtue* : S. XV. 5.

Unshared, *adj.* not enjoyed in common : P. L. IX. 880.

Unshed, *adj.* not caused to flow from the animal body ; *to blood unshed the rivers must be turned* : P. L. XII. 176.

Unshorn, *adj.* (*a*) not cut or clipped ; *these locks unshorn* : S. A. 1143.

(*b*) with uncut hair ; the Greek youths wore their hair uncut until they reached manhood, hence here, ever-young : V. Ex. 37.

Unshowered, *adj.* not watered by showers ; *the unshowered grass* : N. O. 215.

Unsightly, *adj.* displeasing to the eye : P. L. IV. 631 ; *the bare Earth ... unsightly* : P. L. VII. 314 ; *a small unsightly root* : C. 629 ; *such unsightly sufferings* : P. L. XI. 510.

Unskilful, *adj.* wanting knowledge : P. L. XI. 32.

Unsleeping, *adj.* ever wakeful ; *the unsleeping eyes of God* : P. L. V. 647.

Unsmooth, *adj.* not even, rough : P. L. IV. 631.

Unsought (únsought : C. 732), *adj.* (*a*) not sought after, not searched for : P. R. II. 59 ; *the unsought diamonds* : C. 732 ; *trial will come unsought* : P. L. IX. 366 ; *trial unsought* : P. L. IX. 370 ; *duty erewhile appeared unsought* : P. L. X. 106.

(*b*) unasked for, unsolicited ; *she ... that would be wooed and not unsought be won* : P. L. VIII. 503 ; *Grace ... comes ... unsought* : P. L. II. 231.

Unsound, *adj.* not founded on truth, erroneous ; *whose reason I have tried unsound* : P. L. VI. 121.

Unspared, *adj.* not saved from death or destruction : P. L. X. 606.

Unsparing, *adj.* liberal, bountiful : P. L. V. 344.

Unspeakable, *adj.* that cannot be uttered or adequately described, unutterable, inexpressible ; *Thyself how wondrous then! Unspeakable* : P. L. V. 156 ; *fight unspeakable* : P. L. VI. 297 ; *desire* : P. L. III. 662.

Unsphere, *vb. tr.* to bring back from the sphere or invisible world (where he now dwells); *unsphere the spirit of Plato* : Il P. 88.

Unspied, *adj.* not narrowly searched, unexplored : P. L. IV. 529.

Unspoiled, *adj.* not dispoiled, not plundered ; *yet unspoiled Guiana* : P. L. XI. 409.

Unspotted, *adj.* free from moral stain, pure, spotless : C. 1009 ; *my unspotted soul* : P. L. III. 248.

Unstable, *adj.* not to be relied upon, irresolute : Ps. v. 25.

Unstained, *adj.* (*a*) not soiled, unspotted : N. O. 57.

(*b*) not dishonoured, unpolluted : S. X. 3.

Unsteady, *adj.* changeable, variable; *keep unsteady Nature to her law* : A. 70.

Unsubstantial, *adj.* not having substance, unreal ; *daylight .. Night ... unsubstantial both* : P. R. IV. 399.

Unsucceeded, *adj.* that has no successor, everlasting ; *with unsucceeded power* : P. L. V. 821.

Unsuccessful, *adj.* not successful, meeting with failure : P. L. X. 35.

Unsucked, *adj.* not drawn from or drained by the mouth ; *teats ... unsucked of lamb or kid* : P. L. IX. 583.

Unsufferable (unsúfferáble), *adj.* intolerable ; *the unsufferable noise* : P. L. VI. 867 ; *that light unsufferable* : N. O. 8.

Unsuitable, *adj.* unbecoming, unfit : P. R. III. 132.

Unsung, *adj.* not related or celebrated in song : P. L. I. 442 ; *the first Day even and morn ; nor passed uncelebrated, nor unsung* : P. L. VII. 253 ; in verse : P. L. VII. 21 ; P. R. I. 17 ; *heroic martyrdom unsung* : P. L. IX. 33.

Unsunned, *adj.* not exposed to the sun, hidden : C. 398.

Unsuperfluous, *adj.* not more than is needed : C. 773.

Unsupported, *adj.* not upheld, unassisted, unaided : P. L. IX. 432.

Unsuspect, *adj.* not to be suspected, not to be looked upon as likely to do an evil act : P. L. IX. 771.

Unsuspected, *adj.* not imagined to exist, not surmised : P. L. IX. 69.

Unsuspicious, *adj.* unsuspecting, not imagining evil : S. A. 1635.

Unsustained, *adj.* not upheld or supported : P. L. IX. 430.

Untamed, *adj.* not brought under control, unsubdued ; *untamed re-*

luctance, and revenge : P. L. II. 337.

Untaught, *adj.* not having learned by experience ; *by success untaught* : P. L. II. 9.

Unterrified, *adj.* not frightened, undaunted : P. L. II. 708 ; v. 899.

Unthanked, *adj.* not repaid with acknowledgments for kindness bestowed; *the All-giver would be unthanked* : C. 723.

Unthought-of, *adj.* not conceived or imagined : P. L. II. 821.

Unthread, *vb. tr.* to relax the ligaments of, loosen ; *he with his bare wand can unthread thy joints* : C. 614.

Unthrone, *vb. tr.* to remove from supreme authority, dethrone : P. L. II. 231.

Until, *conj.* up to the time that : N. O. 76 ; U. C. II. 6.

***Unto** (untó : P. L. x. 206 ; P. R. III. 166 ; N. O. 27 ; V. Ex. 9), *prep.* (*a*) ; of motion toward a person, place, or goal ; *till thou return unto the ground* : P. L. x. 206 ; *my life ... unto the grave draws nigh* : Ps. LXXXVIII. 12 ; *unto Heaven aspire* : D. F. I. 63 ; *he indeed retired unto the Desert* : P. R. III. 166 ; *I cried unto Jehovah* : Ps. III. 11 ; *unto thee I pray* : Ps. v. 4 ; *unto thy servant give thy strength* : Ps. LXXXVI. 59; *small loss it is that thence can come unto thee* : V. Ex. 9 ; *unto my supplication, Lord, give ear* : Ps. LXXXVI. 17.

(*b*) by way of addition to ; *join thy voice unto the Angel Quire* : N. O. 27.

Untold, *adj.* not related : A. 41.

Untouched, *adj.* ungathered ; *store of fruit untouched* : P. L. IX. 621.

Untractable, *adj.* difficult to pass **over or through,** rough, stormy ; *to ride the untractable Abyss* : P. L. x. 476.

Untrained, *adj.* not trained, undisciplined : P. L. XII. 222.

Untried, *adj.* (*a*) not felt or known by experience: P. L. IX. 860; *danger by himself untried* : P. L. IV. 934.

(*b*) not tested, unproved ; *ventures his filial virtue, though untried* : P. R. I. 177 ; *thou untried*: Hor. O. 13.

Untrod, *adj.* not walked on or passed over, unfrequented : P. L. III. 497 ; *a pathless desert ... by*

human steps untrod : P. R. I. 298 ; *the heaven, by the Sun's team untrod* : N. O. 19.

Untroubled, *adj.* not agitated, undisturbed, tranquil : P. L. VIII. 289 ; P. R. IV. 401.

Untwist, *vb. tr.* to untie, disentangle; *untwisting all the chains that tie the hidden soul of harmony* : L'A. 143.

Unused, *adj.* not accustomed ; *can my ears unused hear these dishonours* : S. A. 1231.

Unusual, *adj.* not customary, uncommon, strange : P. L. I. 227 ; *an unusual stop of sudden silence* : C. 552.

Unutterable (unútteráble), *adj.* incapable of being uttered, inexpressible : P. L. XI. 6.

Unvalued, *adj.* not to be valued, inestimable ; *thy unvalued book* : W. S. 11.

Unvanquished, *adj.* not overcome, unconquered : P. L. VI. 286.

Unveil, *vb. tr.* to disclose to view, reveal : P. L. IV. 608.

Unviolated, *adj.* unbroken, not transgressed ; *my unviolated vow*: S. A. 1144.

Unvisited, *adj.* not shone upon ; *not unvisited of Heaven's fair light* : P. L. II. 398.

Unvoyageable (unvóyageáble), *adj.* not to be crossed, impassable : P. L. x. 366.

Unwakened, *adj.* not roused from sleep : P. L. v. 9.

Unware, *adv.* while not on one's guard ; *not wilfully misdoing, but unware misled* : P. R. I. 225.

Unwares, *adv.* undesignedly, inadvertently: D. F. I. 20.

Unwary, *adj.* not vigilant against danger, unguarded, heedless : P. L. IX. 614 ; x. 947 ; S. A. 930 ; *the unwary breast* : P. L. VI. 695; *the unwary sense* : C. 538.

Unwearied, *adj.* not fatigued ; *in fight they* (angels) *stood unwearied* : P. L. VI. 404 ; *the Creator from his work desisting, though unwearied* : P. L. VII. 552.

Unweeting, *adj.* unwitting, not knowing, unconscious, ignorant : P. L. x. 335 ; *them that pass unweeting by the way* : C. 539 ; *Apollo, with unweeting hand* : D. F. I. 23 ; or *adv.* unwittingly ; *and unweeting have offended* : P. L. x. 916 ; *unweeting he fulfilled the purposed counsel* : P. R. I. 126.

Unweetingly, *adv.* without knowing, unconsciously : S. A. 1680.

Unwelcome, *adj.* not welcome, unpleasing ; *the unwelcome news* : P. L. x. 21.

Unwept, *adj.* not lamented, unmourned : L. 13.

Unwholesome, *adj.* unfavourable to health, insalubrious : S. A. 9.

Unwieldy, *adj.* moving with difficulty because of size or shape ; *the unwieldy elephant* : P. L. iv. 345 ; or *adv.* in an awkward manner ; *part, huge of bulk, wallowing unwieldy* : P. L. vii. 411 ; difficult to use or manage ; *what is strength without a double share of wisdom? Vast, unwieldy* : S. A. 54.

Unwilling, *adj.* not willing, disinclined, reluctant : P. L. xii. 617.

Unwillingly, *adv.* against one's will, reluctantly : S. A. 14.

Unwise, *adj.* lacking wisdom or judgement : P. R. iii. 115 ; S. xx. 14 ; *comp.* less wise (than Prometheus) : P. L. iv. 716.

absol. one who lacks wisdom ; *to serve the unwise* : P. L. vi. 179.

Unwithdrawing, *adj.* withholding nothing, continually liberal : C. 711.

Unwonted, *adj.* unusual ; *storms unwonted* : Hor. O. 8.

Unworshipped, *adj.* not adored ; *leave unworshipped ... the Throne supreme* : P. L. v. 670.

Unworthy, *adj.* (*a*) not worthy, undeserving : P. L. x. 1059 ; xii. 622.

(*b*) lacking worth or merit, unfit, worthless, base ; *permits within himself unworthy powers to reign* : P. L. xii. 91 ; *the rest ... will far be found unworthy to compare with Sion's songs* : P. R. iv. 346 ; *comp., the unworthier they* : S. A. 1216.

(*c*) unsuitable, unbecoming ; *of me expect to hear nothing ... unworthy* : S. A. 1424.

Unwounded, *adj.* not injured by external violence, unhurt : P. L. vi. 466 ; S. A. 1582.

*****Up,** I. *adv.* (1) in or on a higher place, aloft ; *up in the broad fields of the sky* : C. 979 ; *to serve their Lord high up in Heaven* : P. L. iv. 944.

(2) to or toward a higher place :

P. L. ii. 76, 393, 635 ; iv. 1004 ; vii. 553 ; P. R. ii. 14 ; *the way ... that out of Hell leads up to Light* : P. L. ii. 433 ; *my way ... up to light* : P. L. ii. 974 ; *drawn up to Heaven* : P. L. iii. 517 ; *from the Earth up hither flew* : P. L. iii. 445 ; *up to the clouds ... I flew* : P. L. v. 86 ; *look up* : P. L. iv. 1010 ; *call up him* : Il P. 109 ; *up and down* : P. L. ii. 841 ; iii. 441 ; x. 287 ; *up or down* : P. L. iii. 574.

(*b*) to a place considered higher because north ; *up beyond the river Ob* : P. L. ix. 78 ; in the sky north of the equator ; *up to the Tropic Crab* : P. L. x. 675.

(*c*) so that the under side is uppermost ; *up they turned wide the celestial soil* : P. L. vi. 509 ; *the ... Abyss ... up from the bottom turned* : P. L. vii. 213.

(3) in or to an erect position ; (*a*) not kneeling, lying, or sitting : P. L. i. 331 ; iv. 819 ; *stood up* : P. L. ii. 44 ; v. 807 ; *up rose* : P. L. ii. 108 ; vi. 525 ; *up I sprung* : P. L. viii. 259 ; *up he starts* : P. L. iv. 813.

(*b*) so as to keep from falling ; *to bear up Heaven* : S. A. 150.

(4) out of the ground or away from a place of attachment ; *rend up both rocks and hills* : P. L. ii. 540 ; *tore ... up by the roots Thessalian pines* : P. L. ii. 544 ; *oaks ... torn up sheer* : P. R. iv. 419 : *pulled up ... the gates of Azza* : S. A. 146.

(5) to or toward a higher degree or rank : P. L. iv. 49 ; *growing up to Godhead* : P. L. ix. 877 ; *till body up to spirit work* : P. L. v. 478.

(6) to a point of equal extent, as great as ; *till men grow up to their provision* : P. L. ix. 623 ; as far as ; *matters now are strained up to the highth* : S. A. 1349.

(7) to a greater size ; *desires, blown up with high conceits* : P. L. iv. 809.

(8) in or into existence, activity, or operation : *the ... roar was up amidst the wood* : C. 549 ; *whom thrift keeps up about his country gear* : C. 167 ; *no strife can grow up there* : P. L. ii. 31 ; *build up here a growing empire* : P. L. ii. 314 ; *to set up his tabernacle* : P.

L. XII. 247 ; *take up a weeping* :
P. 51; *who out of Darkness called
up Light* : P. L. v. 179 ; *by stirring up Sin* : P. L. XII. 288; *bring
up thy van* : S. A. 1234 ; *to keep
up a frail ... being* : C. 8; *merriment ... stirs up* : C. 174 ; *whose
guile, stirred up* : P. L. I. 35;
with blending of (4) or (2) ; *up
stood the corny reed* : P. L. VII.
321 ; *a dewy mist went up* : P. L.
VII. 334.

(9) to complete existence or
maturity ; *flowers ... which I bred
up* : P. L. XI. 276 ; *his strength
again to grow up with his hair* :
S. A. 1496 ; *to manhood* : C. 58 ;
I grew up : S. A. 637 ; *bred up in
poverty* : P. R. II. 415 ; *bred up
in idol-worship* : P. L. XII. 115.

(10) into a place of confinement;
shut up from outward light : S. A.
160 ; *close up the stars* : C. 197 ;
*if your influence be quite dammed
up* : C. 336.

(b) into a place of safe-keeping:
S. A. 1485 ; *I pursed it up* : C.
642 ; *sayings laid up* : P. R. II.
104.

(11) in a state of readiness;
feast served up in hall : P. L. IX.
38 ; *the daintiest dishes shall be
served up last* : V. Ex. 14.

(12) out of control, keeping, or
possession : P. L. XI. 623 : P. R.
I. 369, 442 ; S. A. 1209 ; *given up*:
P. L. X. 488 ; *yielded up* : P. L.
X. 628 ; *resigns him up* : P. L. XI.
66 ; *to resign them ... up to a better
covenant* : P. L. XII. 302 ; *rendering up* : P. L. XI. 551.

(13) to the uttermost point,
wholly, completely ; *swallowed
up* ; P. L. I. 142 ; II. 149 ; IX.
642 ; *filled up* : P. L. VIII. 468 ;
seal up : P. L. X. 637 ; *summed
up* : P. L. VIII. 473 ; IX. 113 ;
*the birds ... cleared up their choicest
notes* : P. R. IV. 437 ; *to lick up
the draff* : P. L. X. 630 ; *make up
full consort* : N. O. 132.

(14) elliptically ; (go or rise) up:
P. L. X. 503.

II. *prep.* toward the top of :
P. L. VIII. 302 ; *up the trees climbing* : P. L. X. 558 ; *up the hill of
heavenly Truth* : S. IX. 4.

Upbear, *vb.* (*pret.* upbore and *past
part.* upborne) *tr.* to bear, carry,
raise, or sustain aloft: P. R. IV.
584 ; *upborne with indefatigable

wings : P. L. II. 408 ; *the passive
air upbore their nimble tread* : P.
L. VI. 72 ; *one short sigh of human
breath, upborne even to the seat of
God* : P. L. XI. 147.

Upbraid, *vb. tr.* (a) to reproach ; *me
... with his good upbraided none* :
P. L. IV. 45.

(b) to make the subject of or
reason for reproach ; *dar'st our
ministering upbraid* : P. L. VI.
182.

(c) to accuse of something regarded as a ground for reproach ;
am I now upbraided : P. L. IX.
1168 ; *her own transgressions, to
upbraid me mine* : S. A. 820.

Up-call, *vb. tr.* to cause to appear ;
up-called a pitchy cloud of locusts:
P. L. I. 340.

Up-draw, *vb.* (*pret.* up-drew ; *past
part.* up-drawn) *tr.* to cause to
rise to a higher position ; *the huge
portcullis high up-drew* : P. L. II.
874 ; *to the surface of the earth ;
the rapid current ... through veins
of porous earth ... up-drawn* : P.
L. IV. 228.

Up-grow, *vb.* (*pret.* up-grew ; *past
part.* upgrown) *intr.* (a) to increase
in size as plants ; *up-grew ... cedar,
and pine, and fir* : P. L. IV. 137.

(b) to arrive at a state of manhood : P. R. I. 140.

(c) to rise up : P. L. IX. 677.

Uphang, *vb.* (*past part.* uphung) *tr.*
to suspend on some support : N.
O. 55.

Upheave, *vb. tr.* to raise with effort ;
behemoth ... upheaved his vastness:
P. L. VII. 471 ; *the mountains ...
their broad bare backs upheave
into the clouds* : P. L. VII. 286.

Up-hill, *adv.* up an ascent : P. L. IV.
777.

Uphold, *vb.* (*pret.* and *past part.* upheld) *tr.* to keep from overthrow
or loss, support, sustain, maintain : P. L. I. 133 ; III. 178, 180;
his throne, upheld by old repute :
P. L. I. 639 ; *men conspiring to
uphold their state* : S. A. 892 ;
how war may best, upheld : S.
XVII. 7 ; *fainting spirits uphold* :
S. A. 666 ; *taste after taste upheld
with kindliest change* : P. L. V. 336.

Upland, *adj.* of the higher country ;
the upland hamlets : L'A. 92.

Uplift, *vb. tr.* (a) to lift or bear up,
raise : P. L. II. 929 ; VI. 317 ; P.
R. IV. 558 ; *the seated hills ... by

their shaggy tops uplifting: P. L.
VI. 646 ; *on the wings of Cherubim
uplifted* : P. L. VII. 219 ; *the
floating vessel swum uplifted* : P.
L. XI. 746.

(*b*) to exalt, elevate ; *from despair thus high uplifted beyond
hope* : P. L. II. 7.
part. adj. **uplifted**, raised ; *the
uplifted spear* : P. L. I. 347 ;
hands : P. L. XI. 863 ; *angel-
trumpets* : S. M. 11 ; **uplift** ; *with
head uplift* : P. L. I. 193.

Up-lock, *vb. tr.* to make inactive ;
*though grief my feeble hands up-
lock* : P. 45.

*Upon (úpon : P. L. II. 995), *prep.*
(1) above and in contact with or
supported by : P. L. III. 418 ; C.
936 ; *to sit upon thy Father
David's throne* : P. R. III. 153 ;
to sit upon the nine infolded spheres:
A. 64 ; *danced upon the hearth* :
V. Ex. 60 ; *far upon the eastern
road* : N. O. 22 ; *pillows his chin
upon an orient wave* : N. O. 231 ;
fig.: P. L. XII. 489 ; *sets upon
their tongues a various spirit* : P.
L. XII. 53 ; *to live upon their
tongues* : P. R. III. 55 ; *mine own
that bide upon me* : P. L. X. 738.

(*b*) of the surface touched ;
*God had not yet rained upon the
Earth* : P. L. VII. 332 ; *thrice
upon thy finger's tip* : C. 914.

(*c*) of the supporting part of
the body ; *upon the wing* : P. L.
I. 332 ; II. 529 ; *upon thy belly* :
P. L. X. 177.

(*d*) of an axis ; *Earth now rests
upon her centre poised* : P. L. V.
579.

(2) within the limits or bounds
of ; *to bring twilight upon the
Earth* : P. L. IX. 50 ; *peace upon
the earth* : N. O. 63 ; *whose seed
is in herself upon the Earth* : P.L.
VII. 312.

(3) above, over ; *his garden-
mould, high raised upon the rapid
current* : P. L. IV. 227 ; and perhaps, in contact with ; *hovering
upon the waters* : P. L. X. 285 ;
*winds, blowing adverse upon the
Cronian sea* : P. L. X. 290.

(4) in a position at or near ;
*I upon my frontiers here keep
residence* ; P. L. II. 998.

(5) in ; *the innocence which is
upon me* : Ps. VII. 34.

(6) of cumulative addition ;

ruin upon ruin : P. L. II. 995 ;
repulse upon repulse : P. R. IV.
21 ; *Confusion heaped upon confusion* : P. L. VI. 669.

(7) in a direction towards ; *look
so near upon her foul deformities* :
N. O. 44 ; *gazed upon his clustering locks* : C. 54 ; *to gaze upon the
sun* : C. 736.

(8) of the person or thing to
which action is directed ; *come
upon him his deserts* : S. A. 205 ;
*the brand of infamy upon my
name* : S. A. 968 ; *power and rule
conferred upon us* : P. L. IV. 430 ;
upon him shower his benediction :
P. L. XII. 124 ; *force upon free
will hath here no place* : P. L. IX.
1174 ; *avenged upon his enemies* :
P. L. VI. 677 ; *strife pollution
brings upon the temple* : P. L. XII.
356 ; *we shall call upon thy Name*:
Ps. LXXX. 76 ; *his guileful act ...
seconded upon her husband* : P. L.
X. 336 ; *upon our, his, or my head*:
P. L. II. 178 ; III. 86, 220 ; P. R.
I. 55, 267.

(*b*) in regard to, concerning ;
to gloss upon : S. A. 948.

(9) of the business of action ;
us he sends upon his high behests :
P. L. VIII. 238 ; *stand upon our
guard* : C. 487.

(10) towards or against with
hostile intent ; *to set upon them* :
S. A. 255 ; *lest I run upon thee* :
S. A. 1237.

(11) of the object of mental
activity ; *think'st upon him* : Ps.
VIII. 13.

Upper, *adj.* higher : P. L. I. 346 ;
the upper World : P. L. X. 422 ;
at the upper end : P. L. X. 446.

Upraise, *vb. tr.* (*a*) to lift up : P.L.
X. 946.

(*b*) to increase ; *our joy upraise*:
P. L. II. 372.

Uprear, *vb. tr.* to lift up, raise : P.
L. I. 532.

Upright (upright : P. L. I. 221 ; IV.
837 ; VI. 270, 627 ; VII. 509, 632 ;
VIII. 260 ; P. R. IV. 551 ; Ps. VII.
29, 42) (1) *adj.* (*a*) in a vertical
position, erect : P. L. VI. 82.

(*b*) erect on one's feet, as a
human being ; *upright with front
serene* : P. L. VII. 509 ; *lost his
upright shape* : C. 52.

(*c*) flying upward or in an
ascending direction ; *with upright
wing* : P. L. II. 72.

(d) morally right, righteous, pure : P. L. VII. 632 ; *the upright heart* : P. L. I. 18 ; *upright and pure* : P. L. IV. 837 ; *upright and faithful* : P. L. VI. 270 ; *the upright way* : Ps. I. 15.

    absol. one who is just and honest; *the upright of heart* : Ps. VII. 42.

    (2) *adv.* (a) vertically : P. L. I. 221 ; *upright stood on his feet* : P. L. VIII. 260 ; P. R. IV. 551 ; *our foes walk not upright* : P. L. VI. 627.

    (b) justly ; *Jehovah judgeth most upright* : Ps. VII. 29.

Uprightness, *sb.* integrity, righteousness : P. L. III. 693.

Uprise, *vb. intr.* to ascend above the horizon : P. L. V. 139.

Uproar (upróar) *sb.* a great tumult, violent disturbance and noise ; *Chaos ... with clamorous uproar* : P. L. X. 479 ; *Hell scarce holds the wild uproar* : P. L. II. 541 ; *war seemed a civil game to this uproar* : P. L. VI. 668 ; *personified ; wild Uproar stood ruled* : P. L. III. 710.

Uproll, *vb. tr.* to cause to flow together into one place : P. L. VII. 291.

Uprooted, *part. adj.* torn up by the roots ; *the uprooted hills* : P. L. VI. 781.

Up-send, *vb. tr.* to cause to rise ; *the universal host up-sent a shout* : P. L. I. 541.

Upspring, *vb.* (*pret.* upsprung) *intr.* to spring or rise up ; *the .. wall of Paradise upsprung* : P. L. IV. 143 ; with blending of, to come into being ; *the cattle in the fields ... upsprung* : P. L. VII. 462.

Upstand, *vb.* (*pret.* upstood) *intr.* (a) to rise on the feet ; *next upstood Nisroch* : P. L. VI. 446.

    (b) to rise in opposition or rebellion ; *the kings of the earth upstand with power* : Ps. II. 22.

Upstart, *adj.* suddenly rising or being raised to power ; *a race of upstart creatures* : P. L. II. 834; *fig.*, *upstart passions catch the government from Reason* : P. L. XII. 88.

Upstay, *vb. tr.* to sustain, support : P. L. IX. 430 ; to hold in an upright position : P. L. VI. 195.

Uptear, *vb.* (*pret.* uptore) *tr.* to rend out of their places ; *the neighbouring hills uptore* : P. L. VI. 663.

Upturn, *vb. tr.* (a) to turn or lift up : P. L. X. 279.

    (b) to tear up : Ps. LXXX. 54.

    (c) to cause violent commotion in ; *Thrascias rend the woods, and seas upturn ; with adverse blast upturns them ... Notus and Afer* : P. L. X. 700, 701.

Upward, (1) *adj.* directed toward a higher place ; *the slope sun his upward beam shoots* : C. 98.

    (2) *adv.* (a) toward a higher place, in an ascending direction : P. L. II. 1013 ; III. 618, 717 ; Ps. LXXX. 47 ; *the bottom of the mountains upward turned* : P. L. VI. 649.

    (b) in the upper parts ; *upward man and downward fish* : P. L. I. 426.

Upwhirl, *vb. tr.* to raise upward with a whirling motion : P. L. III. 493.

Ur, *sb.* the place from which Abraham started to go into the Land of Canaan. Its location has not been certainly determined : P. L. XII. 130.

Urania, *sb.* the Heavenly One ; in Greek mythology, the Muse of astronomy ; here, the divine spirit of poetry : P. L. VII. 1, 31.

Urchin, *sb. attrib.* of mischievous elves : C. 845.

Urge, *vb.* (1) *tr.* (a) to press, drive, impel, incite : P. L. VI. 864 ; *urged them on with mad desire* : S. A. 1677.

    (b) to hasten, press forward ; *urged the marriage on* : S. A. 223.

    (c) to follow up, keep to, carry out ; *the sad sentence rigorously urged* : P. L. XI. 109.

    (d) to press or ply hard with argument or entreaty : P. R. I. 469 ; S. A. 852 ; *how far urged his patience bears* : S. A. 755.

    (e) to press earnestly the consideration or acceptance of, insist on : P. L. II. 120 ; VIII. 114; used quibblingly with double meaning of (a) and (e) : *terms of weight ... and full of force urged home* : P. L. VI. 622.

    (f) to press the will of, impel, constrain : P. L. IX. 588.

    (g) to quicken the desire of, impel to ; *short retirement urges sweet return* : P. L. IX. 250.

(2) *intr.* to drive, press : P. L.
I. 68 ; *my foes that urge like fire* :
Ps. VII. 21.

Uriel, *sb.* the archangel : P. L. VI.
363 ; *one of the seven who in God's
presence ... stand ready at command* : P. L. III. 648 ; *thou of
those seven Spirits ... the first* : P.
L. III. 654 ; as ruling over the
sun : P. L. IV. 125, 555, 589 ;
Uriel, Regent of the Sun : P. L. III.
690 ; IX. 60 ; *Uriel, no wonder if
thy perfect sight ... see far and
wide* : P. L. IV. 577.

Urim, *sb.* (*a*) *Urim and Thummim,*
the objects within the 'breast-
plate of judgment' by which the
will of Jehovah was ascertained :
P. R. III. 14.

(*b*) precious stones ; *in celestial
panoply all armed of radiant
Urim* : P. L. VI. 761.

Urn, *sb.* (*a*) a water-jar ; *other stars
... in their golden urns draw light* :
P. L. VII. 365.

(*b*) the vessel in which the
ashes of the dead were kept : N.
O. 192 ; *fig.* the grave : L. 20.

Us. *See* **We.**

Usage, *sb.* treatment : S. A. 1108 ;
gentle usage and soft delicacy : C.
681.

Use, I. *sb.* (*a*) the act of employing
or the state of being employed,
employment, application : P. L.
VIII. 29 ; IX. 750 ; *perverts best
things ... to their meanest use* : P.
L. IV. 204 ; *use of strongest wines* :
S. A. 553 ; *ripe for use* : P. L. V.
323 ; *the rest ordained for uses to
his Lord best known* : P. L. VIII.
106 ; *all things to Man's delightful
use* : P. L. IV. 692.

(*b*) that property of a thing
which renders it suitable for a
purpose, availability, serviceable-
ness, utility, service ; *two great
Lights, great for their use to Man* :
P. L. VII. 346 ; *what is of use to
know* : P. R. III. 7 ; *bade me keep
it as of sovran use* : C. 639.

(*c*) ordinary experience ; *to
know at large of things remote
from use* : P. L. VIII. 192.

II. *vb.* (*pres. 2d sing.* usest :
P. L. VII. 616) (1) *tr.* (*a*) to employ
for the accomplishment of a purpose, make use of : P. L. IV. 199,
200, 346 ; VIII. 525 ; X. 1078 ; P.
R. II. 380 ; III. 356 ; S. A. 1139 ;
V. Ex. 8, 30 ; C. 821 ; S. II. 13 ;

light after light well used : P. L.
III. 196 ; *the holy salutation used
... to blest Mary* : P. L. V. 386 ;
his evil thou usest : P. L. VII. 616 ;
freedom used : P. L. VIII. 434 ;
that advantage use on our belief :
P. L. IX. 718 ; *the bait of Eve used
by the Tempter* : P. L. X. 552 ;
means I must use : P. R. III. 394 ;
I used hostility : S. A. 1203 ; *to
use him further yet in some great
service* : S. A. 1499 ; *used no ambition to commend my deeds* : S. A.
247 ; *absol.* to have or hold it as
a custom : P. L. IV. 762.

(*b*) *past part.* **used,** accustomed ;
thy compeers, used to his yoke : P.
L. IV. 975 ; *used to such disport* :
P. L. IX. 519.

(*c*) to act toward, treat : S. A.
941.

(2) *intr.* (*a*) to do a thing cus-
tomarily, be accustomed, be in
the habit : L. 67 ; *God ... with
Man ... familiar used to sit* : P. L.
IX. 2.

(*b*) to be accustomed to go,
haunt ; *where the mild whispers
use* : L. 136.

Useful, *adj.* serving a use or purpose, profitable, helpful : P. L. II.
259 ; VIII. 200 ; *to what can I be
useful* : S. A. 564.

Useless, *adj.* not serving or capable
of serving a valuable purpose, not
helpful, unserviceable, unprofitable : P. L. VIII. 25 ; S. A. 1282 ;
*when Will and Reason ... useless
and vain* : P. L. III. 109 ; *useless
the forgery of brazen shield* : S. A.
131 ; *so great a gift useless* : S. A.
1501 ; *that one talent ... lodged
with me useless* : S. XIX. 4.

Usher, *vb. tr.* to serve as a harbinger of, announce the approach,
forerun ; *the stars that usher evening rose* : P. L. IV. 355 ; *Morn ...
ushered with a shower still* : Il P.
127 ; *gentle airs ... usher in the
evening cool* : P. L. X. 94.

See **Near-ushering.**

Usual, *adv.* in common use, customary : P. L. IV. 316.

Usurp (*disyl.* usurpèd : N. O. 170)
vb. (1) *tr.* to seize and hold in
possession without right or by
force, appropriate or assume unlawfully : P. L. XII. 66 ; *David's
throne usurped* : P. R. III. 169 ;
*the kingdoms of the world ... by
thee usurped* : P. R. IV. 183 ; *the*

realm itself of Satan, long usurped:
P. L. x. 189 ; *Death over him no
power shall long usurp* : P. L. XII.
421.

(2) *intr.* (*a*) to seize and hold
regal power without right ; *Jove
usurping reigned* : P. L. I. 514 ;
*sensual Appetite ... usurping over
sovran Reason* : P. L. IX. 1130.

(*b*) to encroach ; *the ocean to
usurp beyond his bounds* : P. L. XI.
827.

part. adj. (1) **usurping**, encroaching ; *black usurping mists* :
C. 337.

(2) **usurped**, unlawfully obtained ; *his usurped sway* : N. O.
170.

Usurpation, *sb.* the act of seizing
the power or place of another
without right, illegal occupation :
P. L. II. 983 ; *female usurpation* :
S. A. 1060.

Usurper, *sb.* one who seizes power
without right : P. L. XII. 72.

Utensil (útensíl), *sb.* implement,
instrument ; *utensils of war* : P.
R. III. 336.

Uther, *sb.* Uther Pendragon, king
of England and father of King
Arthur : P. L. I. 580.

Utmost, (1) *adj.* (*a*) being at the
farthest limit or the most distant
point, extreme : P. L. II. 361 ;
C. 136 ; *utmost pole* : P. L. I. 74 ;
the utmost Orb of this frail World :
P. L. II. 1029 ; *Earth's utmost
bounds* : Ps. II. 19 ; *Ethiop's
utmost ends* : Ps. LXXXVII. 15 ;
the stream of utmost Arnon : P. L.
I. 399 ; *the utmost Isles* : P. L. I.
521 ; *utmost Indian isle Taprobane* : P. R. IV. 75 ; *utmost port
Ercoco* : P. L. XI. 397 ; *Hell* : P.
L. x. 437 ; *longitude* : P. L. IV.
539 ; *end of misery* : P. L. x.
1020 ; *skirts of glory* : P. L. XI.
332 ; *edge of hazard* : P. R. I.
94 ; *destruction at the utmost
point* : S. A. 1514 ; at the extreme
north of England ; *utmost Tweed* :
V. Ex. 92.

(*b*) being in the highest degree
or quantity : P. L. v. 517 ; IX.
591 ; *utmost power, force, vigour,
vigilance* : P. L. I. 103 ; VI. 293 ;
IX. 314 ; x. 30 ; *subtlety* : P. R. I.
144 ; *aid* : P. R. II. 148 ; *shifts* :
C. 617 ; *ire, hope* : P. L. II. 95 ;
XII. 376.

(2) *sb.* or *absol.* the greatest

possible limit, extent, or power ;
the utmost of mere man : P. R. IV.
535 ; *the utmost of his godhead* ;
S. A. 1153 ; *their utmost of revenge* : S. A. 484.

Utter, *adj.* (*a*) beyond given limits,
outer ; *utter darkness* : P. L. I.
72 ; v. 614 ; *through utter and
through middle Darkness* : P. L.
III. 16 ; *drive them out from all
Heaven's bounds into the utter
Deep* : P. L. VI. 716.

(*b*) total, absolute ; *utter woe* :
P. L. II. 87 ; *dissolution, loss* : P.
L. II. 127 ; III. 308 ; IX. 131 ; *loss
of being* : P. L. II. 440.

Utter, *vb.* (*pret. 2d sing.* utter'dst :
P. L. XI. 762) *tr.* (*a*) to give out
or send forth ; *he uttered thus his
voice* : P. L. x. 33, 615.

(*b*) to give expression to in
words, pronounce, speak : P. L.
III. 143 ; v. 683 ; P. R. I. 320 ;
IV. 172 ; S. A. 1556, 1566 ; C.
786 ; *this dire change, hateful to
utter* : P. L. I. 626 ; *the multitude
of Angels ... uttering joy* : P. L.
III. 347 ; *utter odious truths* : P.
L. XI. 704 ; *utter'dst thus thy
plaint* : P. L. XI. 762 ; *this
uttered* : S. A. 1646.

Utterance, *sb.* (*a*) expression in
words ; *beatitude past utterance* :
P. L. III. 62 ; *Eve ... at length
gave utterance to these words* :
P. L. IX. 1066 ; *thy words to thy
large heart give utterance* : P. R.
III. 10. *See* **Give**.

(*b*) something expressed in
words ; *turned him all ear to hear
new utterance* : P. L. IV. 410.

Uttermost, *adj.* (*a*) being at the
farthest limit : P. L. VII. 266.

(*b*) being in the highest degree,
greatest : P. L. x. 920.

Uxorious, *adj.* servilely devoted to
a wife : P. L. I. 444 ; *I must live
uxurious to thy will in perfect
thraldom* : S. A. 945.

Uzzean, *adj.* of the land of Uz : P.
R. I. 369.

Uzziel, *sb.* a cherub : P. L. IV. 782.

V

Vacant, *adj.* (*a*) empty, void ; *that
no corner may be vacant of her
plenty* : C. 718.

(*b*) unoccupied, unfilled ; *vacant
room, possession* : P. L. II. 835 ;
VII. 190 ; XI. 103.

(c) at leisure, unoccupied; transferred epithet (?) ; *the Moon...hid in her vacant interlunar cave*: S. A. 89; or free from company, alone : P. R. II. 116; *free from other lovers* : Hor. O. 10.

Vacation, *sb.* a time in which there is an intermission of a stated employment: U. C. II. 14.

Vacuity, *sb.* unfilled space: P. L. II. 932.

Vacuous, *adj.* void, empty, unfilled: P. L. VII. 169.

Vagabond, *adv.* aimlessly about or to and fro; *by envious winds blown vagabond* : P. L. XI. 16.

Vagary, *sb.* an action arising from a wild fancy or whim: P. L. VI. 614.

Vain, (1) *adj.* (a) having no real value or importance, worthless, unsubstantial, empty, trivial : P. L. III. 446, 448 ; T. 5 ; Ps. IV. 12; *hatching vain empires* : P. L. II. 378 ; *wisdom* : P. L. II. 565; *the world's vain mask* : S. XXII. 13; or in sense (b) ; *what not in man deceivable and vain* : S. A. 350 ; *vain monument of strength* : S. A. 570.

(b) producing no desired effect, destitute of force, fruitless, ineffectual, unavailing, useless, futile : P. L. II. 191, 234 ; IV. 466 ; X. 50 ; P. R. III. 387 ; C. 513 ; *to strive or fly he held it vain* : P. L. IV. 860 ; *how vain against the Omnipotent to rise in arms* : P. L. VI. 135 ; *Will and Reason ... useless and vain*: P. L. III. 109; *vain attempt, war, exploit, design*, etc.: P. L. I. 44 ; II. 9 : III. 465, 467 ; V. 737 ; IX. 1189 ; *battery, importunity, reasoning* : P. R. IV. 20, 24 ; S. A. 322 ; *evasions, denial* : P. L. X. 829 ; L. 18 ; *covering, covertures* : P. L. IX. 1113 ; X. 337 ; *circumcision* : P. R. III. 425 ; *powerless* ; *pennons vain* : P. L. II. 933.

(c) unwise, foolish : P. L. VII. 610 ; P. R. IV. 307 ; S. A. 1504 ; *that boast so vain* : P. L. IV. 87 ; *vain hopes, vain aims* : P. L. IV. 808 ; *their thoughts proved fond and vain* : P. L. VI. 90 ; *wandering thoughts, and notions vain* : P. L. VIII. 187 ; *his heart I know how variable and vain* : P. L. XI. 92 ; *vain deluding Joys* : Il P. 1 ; *the Gentiles ... muse a vain thing* : Ps. II. 2.

(d) proud, conceited, arrogant; *cam'st thou for this, vain boaster* : S. A. 1227.

(e) craving the admiration of others, greedy of praise: P. R. III. 105.

(2) *sb. in vain*, to no purpose, without effect : P. L. III. 23, 457, 601 ; IV. 675, 833 ; V. 43 ; IX. 296 ; X. 515 ; XI. 726 ; XII. 377 ; P. R. I. 459 ; II. 24, 388 ; IV. 407, 498 ; S. A. 841, 914 ; N. O. 204, 208, 219 ; S. XV. 13.

Vain-glorious, *adj.* vain to excess of one's own attainments : P. L. VI. 384.

Vainly, *adv.* proudly, arrogantly : P. L. II. 811.

Valdarno, *sb.* the valley of the river Arno in Italy : P. L. I. 290.

Vale, *sb.* a valley : L. 134 ; *on mountain or in vale* : P. L. XI. 567 ; *on hill ... in shady vale* : P. R. I. 304 ; *the vales redoubled to the hills* : S. XVIII. 9 ; *flowery vales* : P. L. III. 569 ; *violet-embroidered* : C. 233 ; *the Pythian vale* : P. L. X. 530 ; *the vale of Aialon* : P. L. XII. 266 ; *the vale of Sorec* : S. A. 229 ; *Zora's fruitful vale* : S. A. 181; *Baca's thirsty vale* : Ps. LXXXIV. 31 ; *in heaven*; *nor obvious hill, nor straitening vale* : P. L. VI. 70 ; *the vales of Heaven* : P. L. I. 321 ; *in hell* ; *through many a dark and dreary vale* : P. L. II. 618.

fig. applied to hell; *this infernal vale* : P. L. II. 742 ; *to the lake of hell* ; *the flames driven backward ... leave i' the midst a horrid vale* : P. L. I. 224.

Valiant, *adj.* (a) brave, courageous: P. R. IV. 143 ; S. A. 1738.

(b) bravely done, heroic; *valiant acts* : S. A. 1101.

Valid, *adj.* strong, powerful, efficient ; *valid arms* : P. L. VI. 438.

Valley, *sb.* level or low land lying between hills : P. L. VII. 327 ; P. R. III. 332 ; C. 282 ; Ariosto I. 2 ; *in valley or in plain* : P. L. XI. 349 ; *in valley or green meadow* : P. R. II. 185 ; *hill and valley* : P. L. II. 495 ; IX. 116 ; *hill or valley* : P. L. V. 203 ; *flowery* : P. R. IV. 586 ; *irriguous* : P. L. IV. 255 ; *the pleasant valley of Hinnom* : P. L. I. 404 ; in direct address : L. 136 ; *in heaven* : *hill and valley* : P. L. VI. 784 ; in

hell; *a silent valley*: P. L. II.
547.

Vallombrosa, *sb.* the valley about
eighteen miles east of Florence:
P. L. I. 303.

Valour, *sb.* bravery, courage: P. L.
I. 554; *for contemplation he and
valour formed*: P. L. IV. 297;
valour or strength: P. L. VI. 457;
valour and heroic virtue: P. L.
XI. 690; *virtue, wisdom, valour*:
S. A. 1010; *matchless*: S. A.
1740; personified; *in vain doth
Valour bleed*: S. XV. 13.

(*b*) *concr.* a valiant person; *while
virtue, valour, wisdom sit in want*:
P. R. II. 431; *no worthy match
for valour to assail*: S. A. 1165.

Value, *vb.* (*pres. 2d sing.* valuest:
P. R. IV. 156) *tr.* (*a*) to consider
with respect to worth or importance, regard: P. L. IV. 202; P.
R. IV. 156; S. A. 1029; *absol.* to
estimate or appraise both; *weigh
with her thyself; then value*: P. L.
VIII. 571.

(*b*) to take into account, care
for, consider as important; *created
thing naught valued he*: P. L. II.
679.

Van, *sb.* a wing; *his sail-broad vans
he spreads for flight*: P. L. II.
927; *their plumy vans*: P. R. IV.
583.

Van, *sb.* the front rank of an army
on the march or in line of battle:
P. L. II. 535; *'twixt van and rear*:
P. L. V. 589; *before the cloudy van*:
P. L. VI. 107; *fig.*: S. A. 1234.

Vane, *sb.* Sir Henry Vane the
younger: S. XVII. 1.

Vanguard, *sb.* the van of an army:
P. L. VI. 558.

Vanish, *vb. intr.* (*a*) to disappear
from sight: P. R. II. 402; *from
before her* (Morn) *vanished Night*:
P. L. VI. 14.

(*b*) to pass away, be no more;
these delights will vanish: P. L.
IV. 368.

Vanity, *sb.* that which is empty or
worthless; *with vanity had filled
the works of men*: P. L. III. 447;
still to love vanity: Ps. IV. 10;
*unsatisfying pleasure; in the joys
of vanity*: Ps. LXXXIV. 35; *pride
and wandering vanity*: P. L. X.
875; *triumph, that insulting
vanity*: P. R. IV. 138; *speckled*:
N. O. 136; *he travails big with
vanity*: Ps. VII. 51.

Vanquish, *vb. tr.* (*a*) to defeat in
battle: P. L. VI. 365; *he, with his
horrid crew, lay vanquished*: P.
L. I. 52; *the gods whom he had
vanquished*: P. L. I. 476.

(*b*) to overcome; *under his*
(death's) *gloomy power I shall not
long lie vanquished*: P. L. III.
243; *to vanquish by wisdom hellish
wiles*: P. R. I. 175; *vanquished
with a peal of words*: S. A. 235;
effeminately: S. A. 562; *vanquishing temptation*: P. R. IV.
607.

part. adj. **vanquished,** conquered: S. A. 281; *absol.* one
who is conquered; *both retired,
victor and vanquished*: P. L. VI.
410.

Vanquisher, *sb.* one who conquers;
applied to death: P. L. III. 251.

Vant-brace, *sb.* armour for the arm:
S. A. 1121.

Vapour, *sb.* (*a*) moisture in the air:
P. L. X. 694; *the hills to their
supply vapour ... sent up amain*:
P. L. XI. 741; *wrapped in mist of
midnight vapour*: P. L. IX. 159;
*a wandering fire, compact of unc-
tuous vapour*: P. L. IX. 635;
*pl.; unpurged vapours not yet into
her* (the moon's) *substance turned*:
P. L. V. 420; *when vapours fired
impress the air*: P. L. IV. 557;
*the rank vapours of this sin-worn
mould*: C. 17; *aerial*: P. L. III.
445; *blasting*: A. 49.

(*b*) an emanation or efflux in
the human body; *his sleep was
aery light, from pure digestion bred,
and temperate vapours bland*: P.
L. V. 5; *the force of that fallacious
fruit, that with exhilarating vapour
bland about their spirits played*:
P. L. IX. 1047.

(*c*) heat: P. L. II. 216; *with
torrid heat, and vapour as the
Libyan air adust*: P. L. XII. 635.

Variable, *adj.* liable to change, inconstant: P. L. XI. 92.

Variance, *sb.* dissension; *at variance, into a state of enmity or
conflict; brought him so soon at
variance with himself*: S. A. 1585.

Variety, *sb.* (*a*) a collection of different things, varied assortment:
P. L. VII. 542.

(*b*) kind; *Earth hath this variety
... of pleasure*: P. L. VI. 640.

Various, *adj.* (*a*) different in character or quality, diverse: P. L.

I. 375; III. 582, 717; VI. 84; VIII. 609; P. R. II. 240; IV. 68; S. A. 71; C. 22; L. 188; *Discord with a thousand various mouths*: P. L. II. 967; *call up unbound in various shapes old Proteus*: P. L. III. 604; *various forms, various degrees of substance*: P. L. V. 473; *kindly heat of various influence*: P. L. IV. 669; *other Stars...dance about him various rounds*: P. L. VIII. 125; *various living creatures*: P. L. VIII. 370; *tents of various hue*: P. L. XI. 557; *colours*: P. L. VII. 318; *names*: P. L. I. 374; *fruit, fruits, trees*: P. L. IV. 423; V. 390; IX. 619; *laws*: P. L. XII. 282; *style*: P. L. V. 146.

(*b*) having a diversity of forms or aspects; *within the ground a various mould*: P. L. I. 706; *sets upon their tongues a various spirit*: P. L. XII. 53; *sad discourse and various plaint*: P. L. X. 343; *a happy rural seat of various view*: P. L. IV. 247; *a prospect wide and various*: P. L. V. 89; *the sky with various face*: P. L. X. 1064; *in the various bustle of resort*: C. 379; exercising or manifesting itself in a diversity of ways; *with hand so various*: S. A. 668; waged under different conditions; *wide was spread that war, and various*: P. L. VI. 242.

Variously, *adv.* in different ways: P. L. VIII. 610.

Various-measured, *adj.* having a variety of metres: P. R. IV. 256.

Varnish, (1) *sb.* that which is laid on as varnish to give a fair appearance; *thick-laid as varnish on a harlot's cheek*: P. R. IV. 344.

(2) *vb. tr.* to cover with something that gives a fair external appearance; *close ambition varnished o'er with zeal*: P. L. II. 485.

part. adj. **varnished,** laid on as varnish; *fig.*, *these false pretexts and varnished colours*: S. A. 901.

Vary, *vb.* (1) *tr.* (*a*) to diversify: *God hath here varied his bounty*: P. L. V. 431.

(*b*) to express variously; *let your ceaseless change vary to our great Maker still new praise*: P. L. V. 184.

(2) *intr.* to change position: P. L. IX. 516.

Vassal, *sb.* one who is subject to the

power of another, subject; *that people ... made vassal*: P. R. IV. 133; a slave; *the vassals of his anger*: P. L. II. 90.

Vassalage, *sb.* servitude, subjection, slavery: P. L. II. 252.

Vast, I. *adj.* (1) very large or spacious, boundless, immense: P. L. VIII. 24, 153; *a vast vacuity*: P. L. II. 932; *vast Infinitude*: P. L. III. 711; *this vast sublunar vault*: P. L. IV. 777; *ethereal Sky*: P. L. V. 267; *regions*: Il P. 90; applied to chaos; *the vast Abyss*: P. L. I. 21; *the vast immeasurable Abyss*: P. L. VII. 211; *the unreal, vast, unbounded Deep*: P. L. II. 471; *the vast and boundless Deep*: P. L. I. 177; *Abrupt*: P. L. II. 409; *profundity*: P. L. VII. 229; applied to the cosmos: P. L. II. 832; to hell; *this vast recess*: P. L. II. 254.

(*b*) very great in size: P. R. III. 286; S. A. 54, 1238; *his ample shield, a vast circumference*: P. L. VI. 256; *Satan, with vast and haughty strides*: P. L. VI. 109; *a scaly fold, voluminous and vast*: P. L. II. 652; *this vast unhide-bound corpse*: P. L. X. 601.

(2) very great in degree; *vast Typhœan rage*: P. L. II. 539; *force*: P. R. I. 153; *excess*: C. 771; *increase*: Ps. IV. 36.

II. *sb.* boundless space; *through the vast of Heaven it sounded*: P. L. VI. 203.

Vastness, *sb. concr.* a vast body; *Behemoth ... upheaved his vastness*: P. L. VII. 472.

Vault, (1) *sb.* an arched roof; used of the sky; *the vault of Heaven*: P. L. I. 669; *this vast sublunar vault*: P. L. IV. 777.

(2) *vb. tr.* to form with an arched roof: S. A. 1606.

fig. to cover in the form of an arch; *the torrid clime ... vaulted with fire*: P. L. I. 298; *fiery darts ... vaulted either host with fire*: P. L. VI. 214.

See **Charnel-vault, Deep-vaulted, Empty-vaulted.**

Vaunt, I. *sb.* a boastful assertion: P. L. IV. 84.

II. *vb.* (1) *intr.* to talk with vain ostentation, boast, brag: P. L. I. 126; *he...vaunts of his great cunning*: P. R. I. 145.

(2) *tr.* to speak of boastfully, brag of; *vaunting my strength* : S. A. 1360.

part. adj. (*a*) **vaunting**, boasting : P. L. VI. 363.

(*b*) **vaunted**, boasted of, gloried in ; *his vaunted spoil* : P. L. III. 251; *that same vaunted name, Virginity* : C. 738.

Veer, *vb. intr.* to shift, change direction : P. L. IX. 515.

Vegetable (végetáble), *adj.* having the characteristics of a plant; *fruit of vegetable gold* : P. L. IV. 220.

Vehemence, *sb.* (*a*) violent ardour, fervour, passion ; *a flame of sacred vehemence* : C. 795.

(*b*) impetuous force accompanying energetic action, violence, fury; *a universal hubbub...assaults his ear with loudest vehemence* : P. L. II. 954.

Vehement, *adj.* very eager, ardent, passionate : P. L. VIII. 526 ; *despair* : P. L. X. 1007.

Veil, (1) *sb.* a piece of cloth, or other material, worn to protect or conceal the face or body : P. L. IV. 304 ; V. 383; IX. 1054; *silken* : S. A. 730 ; *virgin* : S. A. 1035.

(*b*) *fig.* of snow ; *the saintly veil of maiden white* : N. O. 42 ; of night ; *Night comes not there in darker veil* : P. L. V. 646.

(2) *vb. tr.* to cover with a veil : S. XXIII. 10.

(*b*) *fig.* to cover, envelop, conceal : P. L. III. 26 ; *Eve ... veiled in a cloud of fragrance* : P. L. IX. 425 ; *he...veiled with his gorgeous wings* : P. L. V. 250 ; *with both wings veil their eyes* : P. L. III. 382 ; *yonder blazing cloud that veils the hill* : P. L. XI. 229 ; *Darkness ... veil the heaven* : P. L. VI. 11 ; *Night's hemisphere had veiled the horizon* : P. L. IX. 52.

See **Dark-veiled.**

Vein, *sb.* (*a*) a blood-vessel : P. L. IX. 891.

(*b*) the ore filling a fissure in a rock, a lode; *part hidden veins digged up* : P. L. VI. 516 ; *fig. veins of liquid fire sluiced from the lake* : P. L. I. 701.

(*c*) a fissure, cleft, or cavity in the earth's surface : P. L. XI. 568 ; *through veins of porous earth ...rose a fresh fountain* : P. L. IV. 227.

(*d*) manner of speech, strain, style; *in pleasant vein* : P. L. VI. 628.

(*e*) humour, mood, temper : N. O. 15.

Velvet, *adj.* resembling velvet in softness and smoothness; *the cowslip's velvet head* : C. 898.

Venereal, *adj.* pertaining to venery or sexual intercourse : S. A. 533.

Vengeance, *sb.* (*a*) the infliction of a deserved penalty, by God as the person injured : P. L. VI. 279, 808 ; C. 218 ; *his ministers of vengeance* : P. L. I. 170 ; *on himself ... vengeance poured* : P. L. I. 220 ; *to execute fierce vengeance on his foes* : P. L. III. 399 ; *vengeance to the wicked* : P. L. XII. 541 ; *should intermitted vengeance arm again his red right hand* : P. L. II. 173.

(*b*) *with a vengeance,* vehemently, furiously : P. L. IV. 170.

Vengeful, *adj.* revengeful, retributive ; *vengeful ire* : P. L. I. 148 ; X. 1023 ; *justice* : Cir. 24.

Venial, *adj.* pardonable, permissible, harmless : P. L. IX. 5.

Venom, *sb.* the poisonous fluid secreted by animals : P. L. IV. 804 ; A. 53.

Venomed, *part. adj.* covered or infected as with venom; *this marble venomed seat* : C. 916.

Vent, (1) *sb.* (*a*) a small hole or opening : P. L. VI. 583.

(*b*) a means of relief, outlet ; *the vent of words* : P. L. XII. 374.

(2) *vb. tr.* to give utterance to ; *to vent more lies* : P. R. I. 433 ; *vented much policy* : P. R. III. 391 ; *to vent his rage* : P. R. IV. 445.

Venture, *vb.* (1) *intr.* to undertake that which incurs risk, have courage to go or come, dare ; *to venture down the dark descent* : P. L. III. 19 ; *one ... hath ventured from the Deep* : P. L. IV. 574 ; *boldly venture to whatever place* : P. L. IV. 891 ; *by venturing higher than my lot* : P. L. IX. 690 ; with *prep. inf.* : S. A. 1373.

(2) *tr.* (*a*) to expose to hazard, stake, risk : P. R. I. 177.

(*b*) to have courage to make, run the hazard of ; *such noise ... I'll venture* : C. 228.

Venturous, *adj.* daring, bold, fearless : P. L. II. 205; V. 64 ; C. 609.

Venus, *sb.* Aphrodite, the goddess of beauty and love : C. 124 ; *to enamour, as the zone of Venus:* P. R. II. 214 ; as the mother of the Graces : L'A. 14.

Verbal, *adj.* consisting of words : P. R. III. 104.

Verdant, *adj.* green ; *burnished neck of verdant gold :* P. L. IX. 501 ; of vegetation ; *verdant grass, leaf:* P. L. VII. 310 ; C. 622 ; green because composed of or covered with vegetation : P. R. III. 253 ; *wall :* P. L. IV. 697 ; *roof:* P. L. IX. 1038 ; *isles :* P. L. VIII. 631.

Verdit, *sb.* verdict, decision, judgement : S. A. 324, 1228.

Verdure, *sb.* fresh growing foliage or vegetation : P. L. VII. 315 ; XI. 832.

Verdurous, *adj.* covered with verdure : P. L. IV. 143.

Verge, *sb.* (*a*) brink ; *themselves they threw down from the verge of Heaven :* P. L. VI. 865.

(*b*) border ; *a flowery verge to bind the fluid skirts of that...cloud:* P. L. XI. 881.

(*c*) boundary, limit ; *Nature first begins her farthest verge :* P. L. II. 1038.

Verify, *vb. tr.* (*a*) to fulfil : P. L. X. 182 ; *to verify that solemn message:* P. R. I. 133.

(*b*) to confirm the truthfulness of, prove to have spoken truth ; *verify, the Prophets old:* P. R. III. 177.

Vermeil-tinctured, *adj.* tinged with the colour of vermilion : C. 752.

Vermin, *sb. collect.* noxious insects : S. A. 574.

Vernal, *adj.* belonging to or coming with the spring ; *vernal bloom, flowers :* P. L. III. 43 ; L. 141 ; *shower :* M. W. 40 ; *airs :* P. L. IV. 264 ; *breath of vernal air :* S. A. 628 ; *delight:* P. L. IV. 155.

Vernant, *adj.* vernal ; *vernant flowers :* P. L. X. 679.

Verse, *sb.* metrical composition, poetry ; *prose or numerous verse :* P. L. V. 150 ; *various-measured :* P. R. IV. 256 ; *unpremeditated :* P. L. IX. 24 ; *immortal :* L'A. 137 ; C. 516 ; *adjuring :* C. 859 ; *plaining :* P. 47 ; *roving:* P. 22 ; *Verse must lend her wing to honour thee :* S. XIII. 9 ; personified; *sisters, Voice and Verse :* S. M. 2.

(*b*) a poem : N. O. 17.

See **Deep-versed.**

Vertumnus, *sb.* the god of the changing seasons and the lover of Pomona : P. L. IX. 395.

Very, (1) *adj.* real, actual ; used for emphasis ; *my very soul :* P. R. II. 90 ; *for very spite :* P. R. IV. 12 ; *where very desolation dwells :* C. 428 ; *the very lime-twigs of his spell :* C. 646.

(2) *adv.* exceedingly : Ps. VI. 4.

Vessel, *sb.* (1) a hollow dish or other utensil for holding things : P. L. V. 348 ; *a potter's vessel :* Ps. II. 21.

(*b*) *fig.* applied to man ; *my fill of knowledge, what this vessel can contain :* P. L. XII. 559 ; to the serpent ; *the Serpent ... his final sentence chose fit vessel :* P. L. IX. 89.

(2) a ship : P. L. II. 1043 ; the ark : P. L. XI. 729, 745 ; *fig.* of life ; *who, like a foolish pilot, have shipwracked my vessel trusted to me from above :* S. A. 199.

Vest, (1) *sb.* an outer garment ; *a military vest of purple :* P. L. XI. 241.

(2) *vb. tr.* to clothe, robe : S. XXIII. 9.

part. adj. **vested,** clothed in sacerdotal robes ; *the vested priest :* P. R. I. 257.

See **Sable-vested.**

Vesta, *sb.* the goddess of the hearth and the mother of Melancholy by Saturn : Il P. 23.

Vesture, *sb.* a garment, robe : A. 83.

Vex, *vb. tr.* (*a*) to annoy, plague, torment : C. 666 ; *far less abhorred than these vexed Scylla:* P. L. II. 660 ; *with conscious terrors vex me round :* P. L. II. 801.

(*b*) to throw into physical commotion, agitate, disturb ; *Orion armed hath vexed the Red-Sea coast:* P. L. I. 306 ; *air less vexed with tempest loud :* P. L. III. 429.

part. adj. **vexed,** thrown into commotion, greatly disturbed ; *the vexed Abyss :* P. L. X. 314 ; *the vexed wilderness:* P. R. IV. 416.

Vialed, *part. adj.* preserved in vials : C. 847.

Viand, *sb. pl.* food, victuals : P. L. V. 434 ; P. R. II. 370.

Vice, *sb.* the habitual deviation from moral rectitude ; esp. the indulgence of degrading appetites and passions: P. L. I. 492; II. 116; S. A. 269; *the vices of their deities*: P. R. IV. 340; *brutish*: P. L. XI. 518; P. R. III. 86; personified; *I hate when vice can bolt her arguments*: C. 760.

Vicegerent, *adj.* acting in the place of another, having delegated power; used of Christ; *thee, vicegerent Son*: P. L. X. 56; *his great vicegerent reign*: P. L. V. 609.

Vicious, *adj.* habitually violating moral law, depraved, wicked: P. L. XII. 104.

Vicissitude, *sb.* alternate succession, regular change: P. L. VI. 8; *grateful vicissitude, like day and night*: P. L. VI. 8; *the Stars ... rule the day in their vicissitude, and rule the night*: P. L. VII. 351.

Victor, *sb.* (*a*) one who overcomes an antagonist in a contest or an enemy in battle: P. L. VI. 124, 410, 609; one who conquers and subdues a nation: P. R. IV. 337; *that people, victor once*: P. R. IV. 132; applied to God or Christ: P. L. II. 199; P. R. IV. 571; *the potent Victor*: P. L. I. 95; *the angry*: P. L. I. 169; *the Almighty*: P. L. II. 144; *sole victor...Messiah*: P. L. VI. 880; *there let him still victor sway*: P. L. X. 376; *they ... our Saviour meek, sung victor*: P. R. IV. 637; applied to Satan: P. L. XII. 433; *what stroke shall bruise the Victor's heel*: P. L. XII. 385.

(*b*) one who conquers circumstances; *victor over all that tyranny or fortune can inflict*: S. A. 1290.

attrib. victorious; *the victor host*: P. L. VI. 590; *victor Angels*: P. L. VI. 525.

Victorious, *adj.* (*a*) having overcome an antagonist or enemy, conquering: S. A. 1663; *Heaven-gates poured out ... victorious bands*: P. L. II. 997; applied to Christ: P. L. VII. 136; *I shall rise victorious* (over death): P. L. III. 250; *victorious King*: P. L. VI. 886; *at one sling of thy victorious arm*: P. L. X. 634; applied *fig.* to heaven; *the ethereal mould ... purge off the baser fire, victorious*: P. L. II. 142.

(*b*) pertaining to victory, bringing victory: P. R. I. 215.

(*c*) being the scene of victory; *his victorious field*: P. R. I. 9.

(*d*) emblematic of or celebrating victory; *victorious palms, dance*: S. M. 14; C. 974.

Victor-people, *sb.* people who have conquered their enemies: P. R. IV. 102.

Victory, *sb.* (*a*) the overcoming of an antagonist in a contest or an enemy in battle: P. L. II. 105; VI. 201, 630; S. XV. 6; *that ... victory at Chæronea*: S. X. 6; *to our Almighty Foe clear victory*: P. L. II. 770; *to the Heaven of Heavens he shall ascend with victory*: P. L. XII. 452; *in his arm the moment lay of victory*: P. L. VI. 240; personified; *at his right hand Victory sat eagle-winged*: P. L. VI. 762.

(*b*) the overcoming in a moral or spiritual struggle; *suffering for Truth's sake is fortitude to highest victory*: P. L. XII. 570; *Peace hath her victories no less renowned than War*: S. XVI. 10; *his* (Christ's) *victory over temptation*: P. R. IV. 594; *victory ... to the Son of God*: P. R. I. 173.

View, I. *sb.* (1) the act or fact of seeing or beholding, sight, survey, inspection; *fiery steeds...first met his view*: P. L. VI. 18; *nearer view*: P. L. VI. 81; P. R. IV. 514; S. A. 723; *to have a view of*: P. R. III. 298; *to our weaker view*: Il P. 15; *to outward view*: S. XXII. 2; of God: P. L. II. 190; *Heaven hides nothing from thy view*: P. L. I. 27.

(*b*) *in view*, within the limit of sight or range of vision: P. L. I. 563; VI. 603; VII. 618; XI. 761; P. R. II. 287; *in Ephraim's view*: Ps. LXXX. 9; *in view of those bright confines*: P. L. II. 394; *in sudden view*: P. L. II. 890; *in his view*: P. R. IV. 27.

(2) a sight presented to the eye, scene; *the sudden view of all this World*: P. L. III. 542; *a woody theatre of stateliest view*: P. L. IV. 142; *a happy rural seat of various view*: P. L. IV. 247.

(3) mental survey: P. L. X. 1030.

II. *vb.* (*pres. 2d sing.* view'st: P. L. X. 355) (1) *tr.* (*a*) to see, behold: P. R. II. 198; III. 233; S. A. 1491; *thyself in me thy perfect image viewing*: P. L. II. 764.

(b) to look at more or less scrutinizingly ; sometimes, to examine
attentively or inspect : P. L. I.
59, 569 ; II. 617 ; P. R. II. 131,
297 ; IV. 250 ; *the moon ... the
Tuscan artist views* : P. L. I. 288 ;
he views ... Nature's whole wealth :
P. L. IV. 205 ; *nearer to view his
prey* : P. L. IV. 399 ; *each the
other viewing* : P. L. IX. 1052 ;
each other viewing : P. L. X. 235 ;
of God or Christ : P. L. III. 59 ;
VII. 211 ; *whose eye views all things
at one view* : P. L. II. 190 ; *all
that he had made viewed* : P. L.
VII. 548.

(c) to look at and consider ;
which thou view'st as not thine own :
P. L. X. 355.

(2) *intr.* to look, make an
examination ; *I view far round* :
P. L. IX. 482 ; *from pole to pole he
views* : P. L. III. 561.

Viewless, *adj.* not perceived or
capable of being perceived by the
eye, invisible : P. L. III. 518 ; *I
must be viewless now* : C. 92 ; *on
viewless wing* : P. 50.

Vigil, *sb. pl.* evening devotions ;
*they in Heaven their odes and
vigils tuned* : P. R. I. 182.

Vigilance, *sb.* (a) watchfulness, wariness : P. L. IX. 157 ; X. 30.

(b) *concr.* a guard or watch ;
none pass the vigilance here placed :
P. L. IV. 580.

Vigorous, *adj.* having vitality, exerting force, powerful : S. A. 1704 ;
C. 628.

Vigour, *sb.* (a) active strength, force
of body or mind : P. L. I. 140 ;
IX. 314 ; X. 405 ; *by native vigour
healed* : P. L. VI. 436 ; *of their
wonted vigour left them drained* :
P. L. VI. 851 ; *celestial* : S. A.
1280 ; *immortal* : P. L. II. 13 ;
divine : P. L. VI. 158 ; *lively* : P.
L. VIII. 269.

(b) energy, efficacy, potency :
P. L. VIII. 97.

Vile, (1) *adj.* (a) low, base, despicable ; *prostration vile* : P. L. V.
782.

(b) morally base, depraved,
wicked : P. L. X. 971 ; P. R. IV.
132 ; *unblessed enchanter vile* : C.
907 ; *that vile rout that tore the
Thracian bard* : P. L. VII. 34.

(c) arising from depravity or
wickedness : P. L. XII. 510 ;
vaunting my strength ... how vile :

S. A. 1361 ; *if aught seem vile, as
vile hath been my folly* : S. A. 376.
sup. absol. one held in least
esteem, the basest : S. A. 74 ; *the
vilest ... of man or worm* : S. A.
73.

(2) *adv.* in a low or base condition ; *shall we, then, live thus
vile* : P. L. II. 194.

Vilified, *vb. refl.* to make vile, debase, degrade : P. L. XI. 516.

Village, *sb.* a collection of houses
larger than a hamlet and smaller
than a town : P. L. IX. 448 ; *town
or village* : P. R. I. 332.

attrib. belonging to a village ;
village cock count the night-watches :
C. 346.

Villager, *sb.* one who lives in a
village ; *neighbour villager* : C.
576 ; *harmless, gentle* : C. 166,
304.

Villatic, *adj.* of or pertaining to a
farm : S. A. 1695.

Vindicate, *vb. tr.* to defend against
an enemy ; *vindicate thy glory* :
P. R. II. 47 ; *to vindicate the glory
of his name* : S. A. 475.

Vine, *sb.* a climbing plant ; probably
always the grape-vine : L' A. 47 ;
the clustering vine : P. L. VII.
320 ; *the gadding* : L. 40 ; *a green
mantling* : C. 294 ; *the flowery dale
of Sibma clad with vines* : P. L. I.
410 ; *the mantling vine lays forth
her purple grape* : P. L. IV. 258 ;
they led the vine to wed her elm :
P. L. V. 215 ; *the vine curls her
tendrils* : P. L. IV. 307 ; a similar
plant in Heaven ; *in Heaven ...
vines yield nectar* : P. L. V. 427 ;
nectar ... fruit of delicious vines :
P. L. V. 635.

Vintage-time, *sb.* the grape-harvest :
P. R. IV. 15.

Viol, *sb.* the stringed musical instrument played with a bow ; *lute or
viol* : P. 28.

Violate, *vb. tr.* (a) to do violence to,
outrage : S. A. 893.

(b) to break in upon, interrupt,
disturb ; *violate sleep, bliss* : P. L.
IV. 883 ; x. 109.

(c) to treat irreverently, desecrate, profane ; *to violate the
sacred fruit* : P. L. IX. 903 ; *they
violated the temple* : P. R. III.
160.

(d) to set at naught, transgress, be false to ; *to violate the
sacred trust of silence* : S. A. 428.

Violence, *sb.* (*a*) vehemence, intensity, fury : P. L. IV. 995.

(*b*) violent or unjust exercise of power, force, outrage, injury : P. L. V. 905 ; VI. 35 ; IX. 282 ; XI. 671, 812 ; P. R. I. 389 ; III. 90, 191 ; S. XV. 11 ; *who filled with lust and violence the house of God* : P. L. I. 496 ; *of violence against ourselves* : P. L. X. 1041 ; *when violence was ceased and war on Earth* : P. L. XI. 780 ; *the whole Earth filled with violence* : P. L. XI. 888 ; *did* or *do ... violence* : S. A. 1191 ; C. 392 ; *his ill trade of violence* : Ps. VII. 59 ; *violence and stripes* : P. R. IV. 388 ; *violence or harm* : P. L. IV. 901 ; *violence and war* : P. L. VI. 274 ; *brute* : P. R. I. 219 ; C. 451 ; *rudest* : Ps. LXXX. 52 ; *by violence* : P. L. V. 242 ; VI. 405 ; or *concr.* attack, assault ; *the violence of Ramiel* : P. L. VI. 371.

See **Self-violence.**

Violent, *adj.* (*a*) proceeding from or marked by great physical force, forcible, furious ; *a violent cross wind* : P. L. III. 487 ; *death* : P. R. III. 87 ; *stroke* : P. L. XI. 471 ; capable of producing great effects, powerful ; *weapons more violent* : P. L. VI. 439.

(*b*) made or produced by force ; *breaking violent way* : P. L. II. 782.

(*c*) acting with or marked by unjust or unlawful exercise of force ; *violent deeds, hands* : P. L. XI. 428, 669.

(*d*) vehement, passionate, fierce, furious : P. L. IX. 324 ; *violent lords, men* : P. L. XII. 93 ; S. A. 1273 ; Ps. LXXXVI. 50.

(*e*) due to force, compulsory ; *vows made in pain, as violent* : P. L. IV. 97.

Violet, *sb.* the plant *Viola* : P. L. IV. 700 ; IX. 1040 ; *blue, glowing* : L'A. 21 ; L. 145.

Violet-embroidered, *adj.* adorned or variegated with violets : C. 233.

Viper, *sb.* the animal *Vipera* ; as a symbol of treachery : S. A. 1001.

Virgin, *sb.* (1) a woman who has had no carnal knowledge of man, maiden : S. A. 1741 ; C. 148 ; *Sidonian virgins* : P. L. I. 441 ; *wise Minerva ... unconquered virgin* : C. 448 ; *fair* : P. L. IX. 452 ; *wise and pure* : S. IX. 14 ; *sad* : Il P. 103 ; applied to the

Lady in Comus : C. 582, 856 ; *true* : C. 905 ; *fair* : C. 689 ; *hapless* : C. 350 ; to Sabrina ; *a virgin pure* : C. 826 ; *Virgin, daughter of Locrine* : C. 922 ; to Mary, the mother of Christ : P. L. XII. 368 ; P. R. I. 138, 239 ; *the Virgin pure* : P. R. I. 134 ; *the Virgin blest* : N. O. 237.

(*b*) yet virgin of, not yet the mother of : P. L. IX. 396.

(2) the zodiacal constellation Virgo : P. L. X. 676.

attrib. or *adj.* (*a*) who is a maiden : N. O. 3 ; *Virgin Mother* : P. L. XII. 379 ; *my virgin Lady* : C. 507.

(*b*) composed of maidens : M. W. 17 ; H. B. 6.

(*c*) of, pertaining to, or befitting, a virgin : S. A. 1035 ; *virgin seed* : P. L. III. 284 ; *modesty, majesty, purity* : P. L. VIII. 501 ; IX. 270 ; P. R. II. 159 ; C. 427 ; *fig.*, *Nature ... played at will her virgin fancies* : P. L. V. 296.

(*d*) pure, chaste ; *thy virgin soul* : D. F. I. 21.

Virgin-born, *adj.* born of a virgin : P. R. IV. 500.

Virginity, *sb.* the state of being a virgin, chastity : C. 437, 738 ; *the sage and serious doctrine of Virginity* : C. 787.

Virtual, *adj.* (*a*) being in essence or effect, but not actually : P. L. VIII. 617.

(*b*) having peculiar efficacy : P. L. XI. 338.

Virtue, *sb.* (1) strength, valour, courage, bravery : P. L. X. 372 ; S. A. 1697 ; S. XV. 5 ; *repose your wearied virtue* : P. L. I. 320 ; *his fiery virtue roused* : S. A. 1690 ; *dauntless* : P. L. IX. 694 ; *heroic* : P. L. XI. 690 ; possibly personified ; *complain that Fate free Virtue should enthrall to Force or Chance* : P. L. II. 551.

(2) moral excellence, uprightness, rectitude ; sometimes with blending of senses (1) or (4) : P. L. VI. 117 ; VIII. 502 ; IX. 317 ; 374 ; XI. 798 ; P. R. I. 68 ; II. 248, 464 ; III. 348 ; S. A. 173, 756, 870, 1010, 1039, 1050 ; S. IX. 7 ; *add virtue, patience, temperance* : P. L. XII. 583 ; *neither do the Spirits damned lose all their virtue* : P. L. II. 483 ; *what is faith, love, virtue, unassayed* :

P. L. IX. 335 ; *bare of all their virtue* : P. L. IX. 1063 ; *yield up all their virtue* : P. L. XI. 623 ; *nations will decline so low from virtue, which is reason* : P. L. XII. 98 ; *in themselves seek virtue* : P. R. IV. 314 ; *virtue may be assailed, but never hurt* : C. 589 ; *so unprincipled in virtue's book* : C. 367 ; *solid* : P. L. X. 884 ; *true* : P. L. XI. 790 ; *consummate* : P. R. I. 165 ; *filial* : P. R. I. 177 ; *sacred* : P. R. I. 231 ; *moral* : P. R. IV. 351.

(*b*) more or less definitely personified ; *seated as on the top of Virtue's hill* : P. R. II. 217 ; fem. gender : C. 1019, 1022 ; *saw Virtue in her shape how lovely* : P. L. IV. 848 ; *most men admire Virtue who follow not her lore* : P. R. I. 483 ; *to slacken virtue and abate her edge* : P. R. II. 455 ; *the crown that Virtue gives ... to her true servants* : C. 9 ; *Virtue could see to do what Virtue would by her own radiant light* : C. 373 ; *virtue has no tongue to check her pride* : C. 761.

(*c*) *concr.* an upright person : P. R. II. 431.

(**3**) with reference to the usage of Greek philosophers ; excellence in general, physical, mental, and moral : P. R. IV. 298 ; *others in virtue placed felicity* : P. R. IV. 297 ; *philosophic pride, by him called virtue* : P. R. IV. 301.

(**4**) any admirable quality or excellence : M. W. 4 ; *receive access in every virtue* : P. L. IX. 310 ; *these godlike virtues* : P. R. III. 21 ; *endued with regal virtues* : P. R. IV. 98 ; *his noble virtues* : S. X. 12.

(**5**) inherent power or strength, potency, force, efficacy, influence ; *vital virtue* : P. L. VII. 236 ; *the virtue of that magic dust* : C. 165 ; the efficacy of the forbidden fruit : P. L. IV. 198 ; IX. 649, 973 ; *the virtue of that fruit* : P. L. IX. 616 ; *of virtue to make wise* : P. L. IX. 778 ; or in sense (**4**) ; *great or thy virtues* : P. L. IX. 745.

(*b*) the power of God or Christ ; *whether such virtue ... failed more Angels to create* : P. L. IX. 145 ; *into thee such virtue ... I have transfused* : P. L. VI. 703.

(*c*) the force or influence of heavenly bodies : P. L. IX. 110 ; *the Sun ... his attractive virtue* : P. L. VIII. 124 ; *the Sun ... whose virtue on itself works no effect* : P. L. VIII. 95 ; (the sun) *shoots invisible virtue even to the Deep* : P. L. III. 586 ; *shed down their stellar virtue* : P. L. IV. 671.

(**6**) the fifth of the nine orders of angels, or a member of this order : P. L. II. 311 ; *Thrones, Dominations, Princedoms, Virtues, Powers* : P. L. V. 601, 773, 840 ; X. 460 ; *Potentates, and Thrones, and Virtues* : P. L. VII. 199 ; applied to Raphael ; *the angelic Virtue* : P. L. V. 371 ; or the meaning may be sense (**1**) ; *celestial Virtues* : P. L. II. 15.

Virtue-proof, *adj.* proof against all attacks upon virtue : P. L. V. 384.

Virtuous, *adj.* (*a*) being in conformity with the moral law, morally good, upright ; *virtuous man* : P. R. II. 468 ; *who finds one* (woman) *virtuous* : S. A. 1047 ; *Lawrence, of virtuous father virtuous son* : S. XX. 1 ; *youth* : S. IX. 1 ; *mind* : C. 211 ; *name* : M. W. 60 ; *sup., what she wills to do or say seems ... virtuousest* : P. L. VIII. 550.

(*b*) efficacious by inherent qualities, potent ; *with one virtuous touch, the arch-chemic Sun* : P. L. III. 608 ; *the virtuous ring* : Il P. 113 ; *every virtuous plant* : C. 621 ; *virtuous, precious of all trees in Paradise* : P. L. IX. 795 ; *this virtuous tree* : P. L. IX. 1033.

(*c*) possessing virtue (*see* Virtue (**3**)) : P. R. IV. 301.

absol. integrity, uprightness : P. R. I. 382.

Visage, *sb.* face, countenance, look : P. L. X. 511 ; *whose pleasing poison the visage quite transforms* : C. 527 ; *radiant, saintly* : P. L. III. 646 ; Il P. 13 ; *incomposed, inflamed* : P. L. II. 989 ; VI. 261 ; *gory* : L. 62 ; *borrowed* : P. L. IV. 116 ; *pl., their visages and stature as of gods* : P. L. I. 570 ; *sadness did not spare ... celestial visages* : P. L. X. 24.

(*b*) *fig.* of the moon ; *thy pale visage* : C. 333 ; *her visage round* : P. L. V. 419.

See **Fourfold-visaged.**

Viscount, *sb.* one holding the title of nobility next in rank below that of earl; here, Lord Viscount Savage: M. W. 3.

Visible, *adj.* (*a*) perceivable by the eye; *the visible Diurnal Sphere*: P. L. VII. 22; *all things visible in Heaven*: P. L. IX. 604; *darkness visible*: P. L. I. 63; of God: P. L. III. 386; XI. 321.

(*b*) apparent, manifest, known: P. L. VI. 145.

Visibly, *adv.* in a manner perceivable by the eye: P. L. VI. 682; C. 216; *in his face divine compassion visibly appeared*: P. L. III. 141; *his lustre visibly impaired*: P. L. IV. 850.

Vision, *sb.* (*a*) the faculty of seeing; *by what strange parallax, or optic skill of vision*: P. R. IV. 41.

(*b*) the act of seeing; here, the direct sight of God, the seeing God face to face; *vision beatific*: P. L. I. 684; *cast out from God and blessed vision*: P. L. V. 513.

(*c*) a supernatural or prophetic appearance or revelation: P. L. XI. 599, 736; *Ezekiel ... by the vision led*: P. L. I. 455; *both ascend in the visions of God*: P. L. XI. 377; *to call by vision*: P. L. XII. 121; *Anna, warned by vision*: P. R. I. 256; *holy, solemn*: P. 41; C. 457; *faery*: C. 298; *the Heavenly Vision, the Vision,* God as appearing to man: P. L. VIII. 356, 367; *the great Vision of the guarded mount,* an apparition of St. Michael: L. 161.

Visit, *vb.* (*pres. 2d sing.* visit'st): P. L. VII. 29; L. 158; Ps. VIII. 14) *tr.* (1) to go or come to for the purpose of kindness, friendship, or love: P. L. V. 375; S. A. 182; D. F. I. 52; *shall Grace not ... visit all thy creatures*: P. L. III. 230; *to visit oft those happy tribes ... his Angels ... passed*: P. L. III. 532; *God will deign to visit oft the dwellings of just men*: P. L. VII. 570.

(*b*) to go or come to, to look after or care for; *she ... visits the herds*: C. 844; *visit every sprout with puissant words*: A. 59.

(*c*) to come to in order to honour; *my tomb with odours visited and annual flowers*: S. A. 987; *visit his tomb with flowers*: S. A. 1742.

(*d*) to comfort, bless; *what is man ... that him thou visit'st*: Ps. VIII. 14; *visit this Vine*: Ps. LXXX. 60, 61.

(2) to go or come to: L. 158; with more or less blending of the idea of (1); *Sion ... nightly I visit*: P. L. III. 32; *the crisped brooks ... visiting each plant*: P. L. IV. 240; *thou visit'st my slumbers nightly*: P. L. VII. 29; *some gentle taper ... visit us*: C. 339.

(3) to go for the purpose of inspection, examine, survey; *as his* (God's) *eye to visit oft this new Creation*: P. L. III. 661; *God ... descends to visit men unseen*: P. L. XII. 48; with clause; *to visit how they prospered*: P. L. VIII. 45.

(4) to inflict punishment; *upon my head all might be visited*: P. L. X. 955.

Visitant, *sb.* one who goes or comes to see another: P. L. XI. 225; S. A. 567.

Visitation, *sb.* (*a*) a visit; *my celestial Patroness, who deigns her nightly visitation*: P. L. IX. 22.

(*b*) the object of a visit; *O flowers ... my early visitation*: P. L. XI. 275.

Visored, *part. adj.* hidden by a mask; *fig.*, *vizored falsehood*: C. 698.

Visual, *adj.* pertaining to sight; (*a*) optic; *visual nerve*: P. L. XI. 415.

(*b*) giving the power of seeing: *visual beam*: S. A. 163; *visual ray*: P. L. III. 620. *See* **Ray.**

Vital, *adj.* (*a*) containing life, living; *Spirits, that live throughout vital in every part*: P. L. VI. 345; *flowers ... to vital spirits aspire*: P. L. V. 484.

(*b*) necessary to life, giving life: P. L. III. 22; VII. 236.

(*c*) that severs life; *the vital shears*: A. 65.

Vitiate, *vb. tr.* to render vicious, corrupt, pollute: P. L. X. 169; *spousal embraces, vitiated with gold*: S. A. 389.

Vocal, *adj.* (*a*) uttered by the voice, oral: P. L. IX. 198.

(*b*) having voice or resounding with voices, endowed with utterance; *hill or valley ... made vocal by my song*: P. L. V. 204; *air*: P. L. IX. 530; C. 247; *reeds*: L. 86.

Voice, *sb.* (1) the sound produced by the vocal organs of living creatures; (*a*) of Man : P. L. VII. 513; C. 492, 563; Ps. LXXXVI. 12; *to counterfeit Man's voice* : P. L. IX. 1069; *Man's voice commanding* : P. L. XII. 265; *a voice of weeping* : N. O. 183; *the voice of my complaining* : Ps. V. 3; *the voice of my weeping* : Ps. VI. 17; *loudest* : P. R. I. 275; *with voice mild* : P. L. V. 15; *enchanting* : S. A. 1065; *dread, awful* : L. 132; P. R. I. 18; *early* : Ps. V. 5.

(*b*) of God or Christ : P. L. IV. 467; VI. 782; X. 97, 116, 119, 615; XI. 321; P. R. II. 85, 314; IV. 512, 539; *guided by his voice* : P. L. VIII. 486; *confusion heard his voice* : P. L. III. 710; *a voice from midst a golden cloud* : P. L. VI. 27; *that command sole daughter of his voice* : P. L. IX. 653; *in thunder uttered thus his voice* : P. L. X. 33; *O voice, once heard delightfully* : P. L. X. 729; *the Father's voice from Heaven* : P. R. I. 31; *my Father's voice, audibly heard from Heaven* : P. R. I. 283; *the terror of his voice* : P. R. IV. 627; *his dreadful voice no more would thunder in my ears* : P. L. X. 779; *the voice of God to mortal ear is dreadful* : P. L. XII. 235; *divine, sovran* : P. R. I. 35, 84.

as inspiring to prophetic speech; *vouchsafed his voice to Balaam* : P. R. I. 490.

(*c*) of angels or other supernatural beings : P. L. I. 274; II. 474, 952; VII. 100; *to their General's voice they soon obeyed* : P. L. I. 337; *by harald's voice explained* : P. L. II. 518; *O for that warning voice* : P. L. IV. 1; *with no friendly voice* : P. L. IV. 36; *with gentle voice* : P. L. V. 37; *so charming left his voice* : P. L. VIII. 2; of Urania; *whose voice divine following, above the Olympian hill I soar* : P. L. VII. 2; of an oracle : N. O. 174.

(*d*) of animals; *join voices, all ye living Souls. Ye birds* : P. L. V. 197; *at the voice* (of the serpent) *much marvelling* : P. L. IX. 551.

(*e*) *fig.* of inanimate objects : P. R. IV. 482.

(*f*) of the above (*a*) (*b*) or (*c*) as used in singing : P. L. III. 347; 370; N. O. 27; *both harp and voice* : P. L. VII. 37; *voice choral or unison* : P. L. VII. 598; *the hand sung with the voice* : P. R. I. 172; *numbers hit by voice or hand* : P. R. IV. 256; *if my inferior hand or voice could hit inimitable sounds* : A. 77; *artful* : S. XX. 11; *melting* : L'A. 142; *divinely-warbled* : N. O. 96; *celestial* : P. L. IV. 682; *undiscording* : S. M. 17; *sweet* : P. L. I. 712; personified : S. M. 2.

fig. of composing poetry; *I sing with mortal voice* : P. L. VII. 24.

(2) the power of vocal utterance : P. L. IX. 561; *creatures wanting voice* : P. L. IX. 199; *endued with human voice* : P. L. IX. 871.

(3) choice expressed, opinion : P. L. II. 188.

(4) wish, command, injunction : P. L. V. 705; combining the meaning in sense (1) : Ps. LXXXI. 46; *because thou hast hearkened to the voice of thy wife* : P. L. X. 198; *her thou didst obey before his voice* : P. L. X. 146; *at the voice of God* : P. L. III. 9; *Chaos heard his voice* : P. L. VII. 221; prayer; *Jehovah ... will hear my voice* : Ps. IV. 18.

(5) used for the person; of God; *so spake the Sovran Voice* : P. L. VI. 56; *this answer from the gracious Voice Divine* : P. L. VIII. 436.

See **Full-voiced.**

Void, (1) *adj.* (*a*) lacking content or substance; *the void and formless Infinite* : P. L. III. 12; *matter unformed and void* : P. L. VII. 233.

(*b*) unoccupied : H. B. 10.

(*c*) being without, lacking; with *of* : S. A. 616; *void of light* : P. L. I. 181; *of works* : P. L. XII. 427; *of pain, rest, honour, etc.* : P. L. II. 219; VI. 415; IX. 1074; XI. 790; P. R. IV. 189.

(*d*) not producing any effect, null, useless : P. L. X. 50; *that made void all his wiles* : P. R. III. 442; *vows made in pain, as violent and void* : P. L. IV. 97.

(2) *sb.* empty or matterless space; *the void profound of unessential Night* : P. L. II. 438;

*the unfounded Deep ... the void
immense* : P. L. II. 829.
Volant, *adj.* light and quick, nimble,
rapid : P. L. XI. 561.
Volatile, *adj.* evaporating rapidly ;
with double reference to Hermes,
the winged god (*L.* volare), and
to mercury or quicksilver : P. L.
III. 603.
Volley, *sb.* a flight of many missiles
simultaneously discharged ; *fiery
darts in flaming volleys flew* : P.
L. VI. 213.
See **Mid-volley.**
Volleyed, *part. adj.* discharged with
a sudden burst ; *the blasting volleyed thunder* : P. L. IV. 928.
Voluble (spelled and accented
volúbil : P. L. IV. 594), *adj.* (*a*)
rotating or revolving ; *this less
volubil Earth* : P. L. IV. 594.
  (*b*) rolling, moving as a serpent :
P. L. IX. 436.
  (*c*) fluent ; *his message will be
short and voluble* : S. A. 1307.
Volume, *sb.* book : S. XXI. 3.
Voluminous, *adj.* (*a*) consisting of
coils or convolutions : P. L. II.
652.
  (*b*) in volumes or books collectively ; *fig.*, *the stars voluminous* :
P. R. IV. 384.
Voluntary, (1) *adj.* acting or rendered with free will or unrestricted choice ; *Redeemer voluntary* : P. L. X. 61 ; *our voluntary
service* : P. L. V. 529.
  (2) *adv.* voluntarily, spontane-
ously, freely : P. R. II. 394 ;
*thoughts that voluntary move har-
monious numbers* : P. L. III. 37.
Voluptuous, (1) *adj.* (*a*) of or pertaining to the indulgence in sensual
pleasure ; *voluptuous hope* : P. R.
II. 165.
  (*b*) passed or spent in luxury or
sensuality : S. A. 534.
  (2) *adv.* in a voluptuous manner,
luxuriously : P. L. II. 869.
Vomit, *vb. tr.* to eject, throw out ;
*like the sons of Vulcan, vomit
smoke* : C. 655.
Votarist, *sb.* one who is engaged in
the fulfilment of a vow, votary :
C. 189.
Vote, (1) *sb.* a formal expression of
will in regard to some question
submitted for decision : P. L. II.
313 ; P. R. II. 129.
  (2) *vb. intr.* to express formally
the will or choice : P. L. II. 389.

Vouch, *vb. tr.* to support, confirm,
put beyond doubt ; *such bold
words vouched with a deed so bold* :
P. L. V. 66.
Vouchsafe (usually spelled voutsafe ;
pres. 2d sing. voutsaf'st : P. L.
XI. 170), *vb. tr.* to grant, permit,
or bestow, usually with implied
condescension : P. L. VIII. 8, 581 ;
P. R. II. 210 ; Ps. LXXX. 14, 30,
78 ; *nor other strife with them do I
voutsafe* : P. L. VI. 823 ; *terms of
peace yet none voutsafed* : P. L.
II. 332 ; *grace in me freely voutsafed* : P. L. III. 175 ; *where he
voutsafed Presence Divine* : P. L.
XI. 318 ; *such favour I unworthy
am voutsafed* : P. L. XII. 622 ;
vouchsafed his voice to Balaam :
P. R. I. 490 ; *those indulgent laws
will not be now voutsafed* : P. L.
V. 884.
  (*b*) to condescend, deign ; with
prep. inf. : P. L. V. 312, 463 ;
VII. 80 ; XI. 877 ; XII. 246 ; *voutsafe with us ... to rest* : P. L. V.
365 ; *to entitle me voutsaf'st* : P. L.
XI. 170 ; *him God the Most High
voutsafes to call* : P. L. XII. 120.
Vow, I. *sb.* (*a*) a solemn promise or
engagement : P. L. IV. 97 ; S. A.
520, 750 ; A. 6 ; *Sidonian virgins
paid their vows* : P. L. I. 441 ;
Death ... oft invoked with vows : P.
L. XI. 493 ; *his vow of strictest
purity* : S. A. 319 ; *under pledge
of vow* : S. A. 379 ; *the pledge of
my unviolated vow* : S. A. 1144 ;
my vow of Nazarite : S. A. 1386 ;
our moist vows : L. 159.
  (*b*) a solemn asseveration : F. of
C. 2.
  II. *vb.* (1) *tr.* to maintain solemnly, asseverate, swear ; with
clause : U. C. II. 19.
  (2) *intr.* to make a solemn
promise : P. R. I. 490.
part. adj. **vowed** ; (*a*) devoted,
consecrated ; *vowed priests* : C.
136 ; *temples vowed* : H. B. 6.
  (*b*) given in consequence of a
vow ; *my vowed picture* : Hor. O.
13.
Voyage, (1) *sb.* a journey ; through
the air : P. R. I. 103 ; *so steers
the prudent crane her annual
voyage* : P. L. VII. 431 ; through
chaos : P. L. VIII. 230 ; Satan's
journey from hell to the earth : P.
L. II. 919 ; *the dreadful voyage* :
P. L. II. 426.

(2) *vb. tr.* to pass over or through, traverse ; *voyaged the... unbounded Deep* : P. L. x. 471.

Vulcan, *sb.* the god of fire and of the arts of forging and smelting, and also a skilful craftsman : C. 655. *See* **Mulciber.**

Vulgar, *adj.* (*a*) common, ordinary ; *the vulgar constellations* : P. L. iii. 577.

(*b*) low, mean, base : P. R. iii. 51.

absol. the common people ; *the vulgar only scaped* : S. A. 1659.

Vulture, *sb.* the bird of prey : P. L. iii. 431.

W

Wade, *vb. intr.* to walk through a substance that yields to the feet like water : P. L. ii. 950.

Waft, *vb.* (1) *tr.* to bear gently on or through a buoyant medium : P. L. iii. 521 ; P. R. i. 104 ; to bear over the sea ; *ye dolphins, waft the hapless youth* : L. 164.

(2) *intr.* to be borne or conveyed on or through such a medium ; *Satan...wafts on the calmer wave* : P. L. ii. 1042.

vbl. sb. **wafting,** the action of bearing ; *a gentle wafting to immortal life* : P. L. xii. 435.

Wage, *vb. tr.* to engage in, carry on : P. L. i. 121 ; *war appears waged in the troubled sky* : P. L. ii. 534.

Waggon, *sb.* (*a*) a vehicle designed for the transportation of heavy loads : P. R. iii. 336.

(*b*) a light cart or carriage ; *Chineses drive ... their cany waggons light* : P. L. iii. 439.

Wail, *vb. tr.* to bewail, grieve over : S. A. 66 ; *wailing thy absence* : S. A. 806 ; *nothing is here ... to wail* : S. A. 1721.

Wain, *sb.* (*a*) chariot ; *Phœbus' wain* : C. 190.

(*b*) used punningly with the double meaning of wagon and wane, the periodic decrease of the moon's visible illuminated surface from full to new moon : U. C. ii. 32.

Waist, *sb.* the small part of the human body between the thorax and hips : P. L. ii. 650 ; *down cloven to the waist* : P. L. vi. 361; *the middle pair girt like a starry zone his waist* : P. L. v. 281 ;

slender : P. L. iv. 304 ; including the body to the legs : P. L. ix. 1113.

Wait, I. *sb.* ambush ; *lay in wait* : P. L. ix. 1173 ; *sat'st ... in wait* : P. L. iv. 825.

II. *vb.* (1) *intr.* (*a*) to watch, lie in wait ; *hellish foes ... for his destruction wait* : P. L. ii. 505 ; *such ambush ... waited ... to intercept thy way* : P. L. ix. 409.

(*b*) to rest patiently in expectation : P. R. ii. 49, 102 ; *what change worth waiting* : P. L. ii. 223 ; *they also serve who only stand and wait* : S. xix. 14.

(*c*) to be ready to serve ; *to wait in Amphitrite's bower* : C. 921.

(*d*) **wait on,** to be in the service of, attend as a servant : A. 107 ; to accompany, escort : P. L. v. 354 ; *fig., on her as Queen a pomp of winning graces waited* : P. L. viii. 61 ; *Authority and Reason on her wait* : P. L. viii. 554.

(2) *tr.* (*a*) to await, watch for ; *Saint Peter ... seems to wait them* : P. L. iii. 485 ; *Adam ... waiting desirous her return* : P. L. ix. 839 ; *pride waiting revenge* : P. L. i. 604 ; to be in readiness for ; *death that waits him near* : Ps. vii. 48.

(*b*) to delay departure or action until the coming of : P. L. ii. 55 ; ix. 191 ; P. R. i. 269 ; iii. 173.

Wake, I. *sb.* originally a festival, preceded by a night vigil, in commemoration of the completion and dedication of a parish church ; hence as here, a night-watch : C. 121.

II. *vb.* (*pres. 2d sing.* wak'st : P. L. xi. 368 ; *pret.* and *past part.* waked) (1) *intr.* (*a*) to be or remain awake : P. L. v. 121, 678 ; *when we wake, and when we sleep* : P. L. iv. 678 ; *when we wake, and when we seek ...thy gift of sleep* : P. L. iv. 734 ; *waking or asleep* : P. L. v. 14 ; *sleeping ... nor waking* : P. R. i. 311 ; *though Wisdom wake, Suspicion sleeps* : P. L. iii. 686 ; or, possibly, to keep watch : P. L. v. 657 ; *fig., Heaven wakes with all his eyes* : P. L. v. 44 ; to watch, or in sense (*b*) ; *rise Jehovah ... wake for me* : P. L. vii. 22.

(b) to be roused from sleep, cease to sleep : P. L. III. 515 ; V. 3, 92 ; VIII. 309, 478 ; IX. 1061 ; XII. 608 ; P. R. II. 284 ; Il P. 151 ; S. XXIII. 14 ; Ps. III. 13 ; *Venus now wakes, and wakens Love* : C. 124 ; *Leucothea waked* : P. L. XI. 135.

(c) to be aroused from inaction ; *while thou to foresight wak'st* : P. L. XI. 368 ; *mimic Fancy wakes* : P. L. V. 110 ; *gentle airs ... to fan the Earth now waked* : P. L. X. 94 ; *fig.* to begin, come : *I shall know ere morrow wake* : C. 317.

(2) *tr.* (a) to rouse from sleep : P. L. V. 26 ; *fig., Morn, waked by the circling Hours* : P. L. VI. 3.

(b) to arouse, excite ; *fierce remembrance wake my sudden rage* : S. A. 952 ; *conscience wakes despair ... wakes the bitter memory* : P. L. IV. 23, 24 ; *the hour of noon ... waked an eager appetite* : P. L. IX. 739.

(c) to bring to life again, resurrect ; *waked in the renovation of the just* : P. L. XI. 65.

part. adj. **waking**, experienced while awake : C. 263.

See **New-waked**.

Wakeful, *adj.* (a) remaining awake ; *the wakeful bird, nightingale* : P. L. III. 38 ; IV. 602.

(b) rousing from the sleep of death ; *the wakeful trump of doom* : N. O. 156.

(c) watchful, vigilant : P. L. XI. 131 ; *a wakeful foe* : P. L. II. 463 ; *custody* : P. L. II. 946.

Waken, *vb. tr.* (a) to rouse from sleep : P. L. XII. 594 ; C. 124.

(b) to call forth or excite ; *waken raptures high* : P. L. III. 369.

Walk, I. *sb.* (a) the act of walking : P. L. IV. 655 ; *the Son communed in silent walk* : P. R. II. 261.

(b) a place laid out or set apart for walking, or resorted to by those who walk : P. L. VIII. 305, 528 ; IX. 434 ; P. R. II. 293 ; *the circuit of these walks* : P. L. IV. 586 ; *yonder alleys green, our walk* : P. L. IV. 627 ; *echoing walks between* : P. L. IX. 1107 ; *pleasant, happy* : P. L. XI. 179, 270 ; *studious walks and shades* : P. R. IV. 243 ; *arched walks of twilight groves* : Il P. 133; *my daily walks* : C. 314.

(c) way, course, path ; *I directed then my walk* : P. L. V. 49 ; *his walk the fiery serpent fled* : P. R. I. 311 ; *set women ... in his walk* : P. R. II. 153 ; *if that way be your walk* : P. L. II. 1007.

II. *vb.* (*pres. 2d sing.* walk'st : H. B. 2) (1) *intr.* (a) to advance slowly by alternate steps : P. L. VII. 459 ; *walked or flew* : P. L. VIII. 264 ; *while one might walk to Mile-End Green* : S. XI. 7. *walk with*, to use in walking : P. L. I. 295.

(b) oftener the meaning is simply, to go or move about on the feet : P. L. III. 430 ; IV. 685 ; V. 351 ; IX. 246 ; P. R. I. 189 ; *walk'st on the rolling sphere* : H. B. 2 ; *others on ground walked* : P. L. VII. 443 ; *upon the ... globe ... Satan alighted walks* : P. L. III. 422 ; *they on the plain...walked* : P. L. XI. 581 ; *walking on a sunny hill* : P. R. IV. 447 ; *like a petty god I walked about* : S. A. 530 ; *the Fiend walked up and down* : P. L. III. 441 ; *I must walk round this garden* : P. L. IV. 528 ; *God ... now walking in the garden* : P. L. X. 98 ; *God ... through their habitations walks* : P. L. XII. 49. for pleasure or recreation : P. L. V. 36 ; IX. 114 ; L'A. 57 ; Il P. 65.

used quibblingly in both a physical and moral sense : P. L. VI. 627.

(c) to go or move ; nearly in meaning, to be : C. 384 ; *that thou shouldst ... walk invisible* : V. Ex. 66 ; *the virtuous mind, that ever walks attended by...Conscience* : C. 211.

(d) to be abroad, go about ; *the only evil that walks invisible* : P. L. III. 683 ; *no evil thing that walks by night* : C. 432 ; *walked about, was current* : S. A. 1089.

(e) to live or act in any particular manner, pursue any course of life : Ps. I. 1 ; LXXXII. 18 ; *to walk with God* : P. L. XI. 707 ; *to walk as in his presence* : P. L. XII. 562 ; *they walk obscure* : S. A. 296.

(2) *tr.* (a) to move over or upon by walking : Il P. 156 ; *ye that walk the earth* : P. L. V. 200 ; *Earth, by ... beast ... was walked* : P. L. VII. 503 ; *walked their streets* : S. A. 343 ; *Him that walked the*

waves: L. 173; with cognate object; *he ... walk his way*: S. A. 1530.

(*b*) to go or move about; *millions of spiritual creatures walk the Earth*: P. L. IV. 677; *fig.* to be current in: S. XI. 3.

(*c*) to live in accordance with; with cognate object; *to walk my righteous ways*: Ps. LXXXI. 56; *hard are the ways of truth, and rough to walk*: P. R. I. 478.

See **Sheep-walk.**

Wall, I. *sb.* (1) a continuous structure serving to enclose and defend a place: P. L. XI. 657; *the floods ...like walls of glass*: Ps. CXXXVI. 49; *Nineveh, of length within her wall*: P. R. III. 275; *Troy wall*: P. L. IX. 16; *walls of Cambalu*: P. L. XI. 387; of *Babylon*: P. L. XII. 342; of *Athens*: P. R. IV. 250; *the Athenian walls*: S. VIII. 14; in hell; *the walls of Pandemonium*: P. L. X. 423.

(*b*) enclosing heaven: P. L. II. 343, 1035; III. 71, 427, 503; *the crystal wall of Heaven*: P. L. VI. 860; enclosing Olympus; *the wall of sheeny Heaven*: D. F. I. 47; enclosing the garden of Eden: P. L. IV. 146, 182; *the verdurous wall of Paradise*: P. L. IV. 143.

(*c*) enclosing a dwelling; *the sacred wall*: Hor. O. 14; *each odorous bushy shrub, fenced up the verdant wall*: P. L. IV. 697.

(2) something resembling a wall; of water; *crystal wall, walls*: P. L. VII. 293; XII. 197; the solid shell enclosing the universe; *the wall immovable of this ... World*: P. L. X. 302.

II. *vb. tr.* to enclose with a wall: P. R. II. 22; as with a wall; *the rest in circuit walls this Universe*: P. L. III. 721.

Wallow, *vb. intr.* to roll the body about in water: P. L. VII. 411.

Wan, *adj.* (*a*) pale; *with praise enough for Envy to look wan*: S. XIII. 6.

(*b*) lacking intensity or depth of colour; *faded splendour wan*: P. L. IV. 870; *the blasted stars looked wan*: P. L. X. 412; *cowslips wan*: L. 147.

Wand, *sb.* (1) a slender stick; *his spear—to equal which the tallest pine ... were but a wand*: P. L. I. 294.

(2) a rod; (*a*) probably to indicate authority; *held before his decent steps a silver wand*: P. L. III. 644.

(*b*) used by a conjurer: C. 653, 659, 815; *he with his bare wand can unthread thy joints*: C. 614; of the rod of Peace, with allusion to the conjurer's wand; *waving wide her myrtle wand, she strikes a universal peace*: N. O. 51.

Wander, *vb.* (1) *intr.* (*a*) to travel, go, or move from place to place without any certain course; roam; stray: P. L. II. 523; III. 499, 667; VII. 20; XII. 133; P. R. II. 313; C. 351; D. F. I. 17; *wandering o'er the earth*: P. L. I. 365; *not the more cease I to wander where the Muses haunt*: P. L. III. 27; *wander, with delight*: P. L. VII. 330; *all the unaccomplished works of Nature's hand ... wander here*: P. L. III. 458; *wandering loose about*: S. A. 675; *whither wander down into a lower world*: P. L. XI. 282; *wander forth*: P. L. I. 501; *the clouded ark of God, till then in tents wandering*: P. L. XII. 334; *thoughts that wander through eternity*: P. L. II. 148; to flow; *the watery throng ... with serpent error wandering*: P. L. VII. 302.

(*b*) to go astray; *to all that wander in that perilous flood*: L. 185.

(2) *tr.* to travel over without a certain course; *wandering this darksome desert*: P. L. II. 973; *wandering that watery desert*: P. L. XI. 779; *wandered this barren waste*: P. R. I. 354; *this woody maze*: P. R. II. 246; *the wilderness*: P. R. IV. 600; to flow through; *four main streams ... wandering many a famous realm*: P. L. IV. 234.

part. adj. **wandering;** (1) having or pursuing no fixed course or way; *wandering gods*: P. L. I. 481; *Spirit*: P. L. IV. 531; *feet, steps*: P. L. II. 404; XII. 648; C. 193; *a wandering fire*: P. L. IX. 634; *the wandering Moon*: Il P. 67; of stars; *ye five other wandering Fires*: P. L. V. 177.

(*b*) apparently having no fixed plan or arrangement; *fig., in wandering mazes lost*: P. L. II. 561.

(*c*) not keeping to a subject; *my wandering Muse*: V. Ex. 53;

going astray from the proper subject; *wandering thoughts, thought*: P. L. VIII. 187 ; S. A. 302 ; *mind* : Ps. LXXXI. 50.

(*d*) involving much wandering; *her wandering labours long* : C. 1006; *quest, flight, course* : P. L. II. 830 ; III. 631 ; VIII. 126.·

(*e*) leading to wandering; *wandering vanity* : P. L. X. 875.

(*f*) who has gone astray or lost the way ; *wandering passenger* : C. 39.

(2) variable, changeable : P. L. VII. 50.

vbl. sb. **wandering**, the act of one who wanders: P. L.' VIII. 312; of one who strays away from home or protection ; *desire, will of wandering* : P. L. IX. 1136, 1146.

See **Long-wandered.**

Wanderer, *sb.* traveller : C. 524.
See **Night-wanderer.**

Wannish, *adj.* dull in colour, greyish ; *a wannish white* : P. 35.

Want, I. *sb.* (*a*) the state of not having, lack or absence of something necessary or desirable : P. L. IX. 755 ; with *of* : P. L. II. 806; *want of words* : S. A. 905 ; *of light* : C. 369 ; *for want of well pronouncing Shibboleth* : S. A. 289.

(*b*) the lack of the necessaries of life, poverty, indigence ; *pines with want* : C. 768 ; *sit in want* : P. R. II. 431; *with want oppressed* : P. R. II. 331 ; *constrained by want* : P. R. I. 331.

II. *vb.* (1) *tr.* (*a*) to be without, be destitute of : P. L. I. 556 ; V. 147 ; IX. 601 ; XII. 396 ; S. A. 315, 1484 ; *nor want we skill* : P. L. II. 272 ; *those happy places thou hast deigned a while to want* : P. L. V. 365 ; *can we want obedience* : P. L. V. 514 ; *creatures wanting voice* : P. L. IX. 199 ; *other senses want not their delights*: S. A. 916 ; *this desert soil wants not her hidden lustre* : P. L. II. 271 ; *Heaven would want spectators* : P. L. IV. 676 ; with *prep. inf. ; the great Light of Day yet wants to run much of his race* : P. L. VII. 98 ; or *intr.* to be absent ; *nor wanted clouds of foot, nor ... cuirassiers* : P. R. III. 327.

(*b*) to need, have occasion for : P. L. VIII. 355 ; *timely rest have wanted* : C. 689 ; *thy abundance wants partakers* : P. L. IV. 730 ; *thy mansion wants thee* : P. L. VIII. 296.

(2) *intr.* to be absent, lacking, or deficient : P. L. I. 715 ; IV. 989 ; X. 869 ; *nor will occasion want* : P. L. II. 341 ; *nor endearing smiles wanted* : P. L. IV. 338 ; *there wanted yet the master-work* : P. L. VII. 505 ; *what wants in female sex* : P. L. IX. 821 ; with dat., *nor these to hold wants her fit vessels* : P. L. V. 348.

part. adj. **wanting**,˙ lacking, deficient, missing ; *what in me seems wanting* : P. R. II. 450 ; *nor shall I ... be wanting* : P. L. X. 271.

Wanton, I. *adj.* (1) wild, disordered ; *in wanton dance* : C. 176 ; not bound, loose ; *in wanton ringlets* : P. L. IV. 306.

(*b*) without plan or order ; *the grove with ... wanton windings* : A. 47.

(*c*) roving at will : *wanton winds* : L. 137.

(2) heedless, careless ; *with wanton heed and giddy cunning* : L'A. 141.

(3) playful, frolicsome : P. L. IX. 517 ; *wanton wiles* : L'A. 27.

(4) rank, luxuriant ; *wanton growth* : P. L. IV. 629 ; IX. 211.

(5) full of lust ; *wanton gods* : D. F. I. 14 ; marked by or inviting to lust, lascivious, lustful ; *wanton eyes* : P. R. II. 180 ; *dress* : P. L. XI. 583; *mask* : P. L. IV. 768 ; *rites, passions* : P. L. I. 414, 454.

II. *vb. intr.* to revel unrestrainedly, frolic, sport ; *fig., Nature here wantoned* : P. L. V. 295 ; *Nature ... to wanton with the Sun* : N. O. 36.

Wantonly, *adv.* lasciviously : P. L. IX. 1015.

Wantonness, *sb.* the state of unrestrained indulgence of the natural appetites : P. L. XI. 795.

War, I. *sb.* (1) a contest between powers or parties carried on by force of arms : P. L. IV. 817 ; VI. 506 ; IX. 28 ; XI. 780, 784 ; XII. 31, 218 ; P. R. III. 90 ; N. O. 53 ; S. XV. 10 ; XVI. 11 ; *how war may best ... move by her two main nerves, iron and gold* : S. XVII. 7 ; *the brazen throat of war* : P. L. XI. 713 ; *the array of war* : P. R. III. 17 ; *with utensils of war* :

P. R. III. 336 ; *much instrument
of war* : P. R. III. 388; *cumbersome
luggage of war* : P. R. III. 401 ;
feats of war : S. A. 1278 ; *levy
wars* : P. L. II. 501 ; *who ... had
levied war* : P. L. XI. 219 ; *fierce
faces threatening war* : P. L. XI.
641 ; *enslaved by war* : P. L. XI.
797 ; *devouring* : V. Ex. 86 ; *war
appears waged in the troubled
sky* : P. L. II. 533 ; *a comet ...
from his horrid hair shakes...war* :
P. L. II. 711.

(*b*) the contest between God
and Satan as waged in heaven or
planned in hell : P. L. I. 129,
645 : II. 121, 160, 230, 283, 329,
330, 767 ; VI. 19, 242, 274, 695,
897 ; X. 374 ; *war so near the
peace of God in bliss* : P. L. VII.
55 ; *impious war in Heaven* : P.
L. I. 43 ; *rain war with Heaven* :
P. L. II. 9 ; *intestine war in
Heaven* : P. L. VI. 259 ; *war
seemed a civil game to this uproar* :
P. L. VI. 667 ; *din of war* : P. L.
I. 668 ; VI. 408 ; *the files of war* :
P. L. VI. 339 ; *acts of war* : P. L.
VI. 377 ; *his thralls by right of
war* : P. L. I. 150 ; *war, then,
war open or understood* : P. L. I.
661 ; *eternal war* : P. L. I. 121 ;
glorious, grim, great : P. L. II.
179 ; VI. 236, 702 ; *open* : P. L.
II. 41, 51, 119, 187.

(*c*) the conflict between the
elements in chaos ; *the noise of
endless wars* : P. L. II. 897.

(*d*) a conflict among the stars ;
*if ... among the constellations war
were sprung* : P. L. VI. 312.

(2) warlike forces, an army ;
P. L. XII. 214.

(3) instruments of war, weapons :
P. L. VI. 712.

II. *vb. intr.* to carry on war,
fight : P. L. VI. 225 ; *me ...
warring in Heaven* : P. L. IV. 41 ;
that Angel should with Angel war :
P. L. VI. 92 ; *to disenthrone the
King of Heaven we war* : P. L. II.
230 ; *that warred on Jove* : P.
L. I. 198 ; *that small infantry
warred on by cranes* : P. L. I. 576.

(*b*) to struggle, fight ; *beast now
with beast 'gan war* : P. L. X. 710.

part. adj. **warring**, fighting ;
Angels, Spirits : P. L. III. 396 ;
V. 566 ; *fig.* of the wind : P. L.
II. 905.

See **Heaven-warring**.

Warble, *vb.* (*pres. 2d sing.* warblest :
S. I. 2) (1) *intr.* (*a*) to sing with
trills and turns as a bird : P. L.
VIII. 265 ; *nor then the solemn
nightingale ceased warbling* : P. L.
VII. 436 ; *O Nightingale ... that
warblest* : S. I. 2.

(*b*) to give forth a liquid murmuring sound ; *the flowery brooks
... warbling flow* : P. L. III. 31.

(2) *tr.* (*a*) to sing as a bird ;
fig., *Shakespeare ... warble his
native wood-notes wild* : L'A. 134.

(*b*) to sing ; *artful voice warble
immortal notes* : S. XX. 12 ; *warbling his Doric lay* : L. 189 ; *notes
... warbled to the string* : Il P.
106.

(*c*) to give forth melodiously :
P. L. V. 196 ; *ye, that warble, as
ye flow, melodious murmurs* : P.
L. V. 195.

(*d*) to celebrate in song : Ps.
CXXXVI. 89.

part. adj. (1) **warbling**, consisting of song ; *warbling charms* :
S. A. 934.

(2) **warbled** ; (*a*) sung melodiously : P. L. II. 242 ; C. 854.

(*b*) caused to vibrate (?), accompanied by singing (?) ; *the warbled
string* : A. 87.

See **Divinely-warbled, Thick-
warbled, Night-warbling**.

Ward, *sb.* the projection inside a
lock or the corresponding notch
in the bit of a key, or simply,
a bolt : P. L. II. 877.

Wardrobe, *sb.* (*a*) a place where
clothes are kept ; *fig.* of lan-
guages : V. Ex. 18.

(*b*) apparel ; *fig.*, *flowers that
their gay wardrobe wear* : L. 47.

Ware, *adj.* (*a*) aware, conscious : C.
558.

(*b*) on one's guard, cautious :
P. L. IX. 353.

Warfare, *sb.* (*a*) the waging of
war, armed conflict : P. L. VI.
803.

(*b*) the spiritual conflict between Christ and Satan : P. R. I.
158.

Warlike, *adj.* (*a*) of or pertaining
to war ; *warlike parade, muster* :
P. L. IV. 780 ; P. R. III. 380 ;
sound, toil, tools : P. L. I. 531 ;
VI. 257 ; S. A. 137.

(*b*) disposed to engage in war,
prepared for war ; *the warlike
Angel* : P. L. IV. 902.

Warm, (1) *adj.* (*a*) having a moderate degree of heat : P. L. VII. 279 ; VIII. 466.

(*b*) marked by the ardour of affection or passion : M. M. 6.

(2) *vb. tr.* to heat in a moderate degree, raise the temperature of ; *to warm him wet returned from field at eve* : P. R. I. 318 ; of the sun, the stars, the power of God : P. L. IV. 669 ; S. VIII. 8 ; *his magnetic beam, that gently warms the Universe* : P. L. III. 583 ; *the mounted Sun ... to warm Earth's inmost womb* : P. L. V. 301 ; *this fair Earth ... warmed by the Sun* : P. L. IX. 721 ; *land, sea, and air ... fomented by his* (God's) *virtual power and warmed* : P. L. XI. 338.

Warmly, *adv.* with moderate heat : P. L. IV. 244.

Warmth, *sb.* (*a*) moderate heat : P. L. V. 302 ; *the Spirit of God ... infused ... vital warmth* : P. L. VII. 236 ; *the sedentary Earth ... her warmth and light* : P. L. VIII. 37 ; the heat of the body, or perhaps, the warm body ; *to starve in ice their soft ethereal warmth* : P. L. II. 601.

(*b*) a means of protection from the cold : P. L. X. 1068 ; *a stable was our warmth* : P. R. II. 74.

Warn, *vb. tr.* (*a*) to give notice to of approaching danger or of something to be guarded against, put on guard : P. L. IV. 6, 125 ; VI. 547 ; IX. 363, 371, 1171 ; XI. 195, 777 ; P. R. IV. 483 ; *to warn proud cities* : P. L. II. 533 ; *warned by oft experience* : S. A. 382 ; *warn thy weaker* : P. L. VI. 908 ; *the mind or fancy ... warned* : P. L. VIII. 190 ; *to warn all creatures from thee* : P. L. X. 871 ; with double object ; *remember what I warn thee* : P. L. VIII. 327 ; *what hath been warned us* : P. L. IX. 253 ; *the rest ... oft be warned their sinful state* : P. L. III. 185 ; *warn him to beware he swerve not* : P. L. V. 237.

(*b*) to summon or bid to go ; *fig., the stars ... Lucifer that often warned them thence* : N. O. 74.

(*c*) to make aware, apprise, inform previously : P. L. IV. 467 ; P. R. I. 26, 255.

part. adj. **warning,** admonishing : P. L. IV. 1.

Warp, *vb. intr.* to fly with a bending or swerving motion ; *locusts, warping on the eastern wind* : P. L. I. 341.

Warrant, *vb. tr.* (*a*) to safeguard, protect : C. 327.

(*b*) to declare with assurance ; *the last of me or no I cannot warrant* : S. A. 1426.

Warrior, *sb.* a soldier : P. L. I. 565 ; XI. 662 ; *old warriors turned their plated backs* : S. A. 139 ; *famous, noble* : S. A. 542, 1166 ; used of angels : P. L. VI. 233, 537 ; *Warriors, the Flower of Heaven* : P. L. I. 316 ; *flaming, winged* : P. L. XI. 101 ; Cir. 1 ; Gabriel ; *the winged Warrior* : P. L. IV. 576.

Warrior-Angel, *sb.* an angel who is a warrior ; of Gabriel : P. L. IV. 946.

Wary, *adj.* (*a*) cautious, carefully watching : P. L. II. 917.

(*b*) characterized by caution, guarded ; *his wary speech* : P. L. V. 459.

Wash, *vb. tr.* (*a*) to cleanse by ablution ; *as when he washed his servants' feet* : P. L. X. 215.

(*b*) to cleanse from sin, purify ; *washing them from guilt of sin* : P. L. XII. 443 ; to cleanse both physically and morally : S. XXIII. 5.

(*c*) to wet, moisten : P. 35 ; *fresh-blown roses washed in dew* : L'A. 22.

(*d*) to remove by ablution ; *wash off the clotted gore* : S. A. 1727 ; *in the consecrated stream pretends to wash off sin* : P. R. I. 73.

(*e*) to sweep over or dash against : used of water : P. L. III. 31 ; *another plain ... washed by the southern sea* : P. R. IV. 28.

(*f*) to sweep over and carry along ; *washed by stream from underground* : P. L. XI. 569 ; *thee the ... sounding seas wash far away* : L. 155.

vbl. sb. **washing,** the act of cleansing with water, ablution : S. A. 1107.

Washy, *adj.* watery, moist ; *the washy ooze* : P. L. VII. 303.

Wassailer, *sb.* one who participates in a wassail or drinking-bout : C. 179.

Waste, (1) *adj.* (*a*) desert, desolate, dreary, barren : P. L. I. 60 ; III.

424; *this waste wild*: P. R. IV.
523; *the waste Wilderness*: P. R.
I. 7; *the waste wide anarchy of
Chaos*: P. L. X. 282.

(*b*) destroyed, ruined, devastated; *leaves all waste beyond the
realm of Aladule*: P. L. X. 434;
Jerusalem laid waste: P. R. III.
283.

(*c*) of no significance, idle, vain;
a waste or needless sound: C.
942.

(*d*) exuberant, over-abundant;
waste fertility: C. 729.

(**2**) *sb.* (*a*) a wild uncultivated
region, desert: P. L. IV. 538;
this wild surrounding waste: C.
403; *Eliah ... wandered this barren
waste*: P. R. I. 354.

(*b*) unoccupied space, the void
of chaos; *the emptier waste, resembling air*: P. L. II. 1045.

(*c*) destruction, devastation;
done much waste: P. L. XI. 791.

(*d*) unnecessary or useless expenditure; *waste of wealth*: S.
XII. 14; *of time*: P. R. IV. 123.

(**3**) *vb. tr.* (*a*) to desolate, devastate, ruin, destroy: P. L. XI.
567; *with Hell-fire to waste his
whole creation*: P. L. II. 365;
wars wasting the earth: P. L. II.
502; *to waste and havoc yonder
World*: P. L. X. 617; *whose incursions wild have wasted Sogdiana*: P. R. III. 302; *absol.*: P.
L. XI. 784.

(*b*) to spend; *to waste eternal
days in woe*: P. L. II. 695; *by the
fire help waste a sullen day*: S.
XX. 4.

(*c*) to expend unnecessarily,
squander, dissipate: P. L. X. 820.
part. adj. **wasted**, devastated,
desolated: P. R. III. 102.

vbl. sb. **wasting**, wearing away,
consumption; *this body's wasting*:
P. R. II. 256.

See **Wide-wasting.**

Wasteful, *adj.* (*a*) destructive, devastating: P. R. IV. 461; *these
dogs of Hell ... these wasteful furies*:
P. L. X. 620.

(*b*) waste, desolate; of chaos;
the wasteful Deep: P. L. II. 961;
VI. 862; *dark, wasteful, wild*: P.
L. VII. 212.

Watch, I. *sb.* (*a*) precaution against
surprise or attack, vigilance,
attention; *intermit no watch
against a wakeful foe*: P. L. II.

462; *coast the south with strictest
watch*: P. L. IV. 783; *diverted
from continual watch our great
Forbidder*: P. L. IX. 814; *careful*: P. L. X. 438; *couchant*:
P. L. IV. 406; *mountain*: C. 89;
keeping watch: P. L. IX. 363.

(*b*) one or more persons set for
a guard, sentry, sentinel; *the
towers of Heaven are filled with
armed watch*: P. L. II. 130;
*placed in guard their watches
round*: P. L. VI. 412; *cherubic*:
P. L. IX. 68; XI. 120; or in sense
(*c*); *sat watch*: P. L. X. 594.

(*c*) the duty of acting as a
guard or sentinel; *to thee thy
course by lot hath given ... strict
watch*: P. L. IV. 562; *under
watch*: P. L. V. 288: keep, *keeping, or kept watch*: P. L. IV. 685;
IX. 62; X. 427; XII. 365; N. O.
2. *See* **Keep.**

II. *vb.* (**1**) *intr.* (*a*) to be or
remain awake; *Sleep listening to
thee will watch*: P. L. VII. 106.

(*b*) to be vigilant, be on the
lookout (to do evil or against the
attack of an enemy); P. L. IV.
826; IX. 257; C. 543; *shepherds
watching at their folds by night*:
P. R. I. 244; *at his head the
Tempter watched*: P. R. IV. 408;
a prowling wolf ... watching: P.
L. IV. 185.

(*c*) to do duty as a guard, act
as sentinel: P. L. I. 332.

(*d*) to seek opportunity; *watching to oppress Israel's oppressors*:
S. A. 232.

(*e*) to wait expectantly: Ps.
v. 8.

(**2**) *tr.* (*a*) to observe narrowly,
keep in view: P. R. IV. 522.

(*b*) to lie in wait for; *under
rocks their food in jointed armour
watch*: P. L. VII. 409.

(*c*) to have in keeping, guard;
*Angel-wings ... to watch and tend
their earthy charge*: P. L. IX.
156.

See **Dragon-watch, Morning-watch, Night-watch, Over-watch.**

Watchful, *adj.* keeping watch, being
on guard, vigilant: P. L. IX. 311;
watchful shepherds' ears: Cir.
3; *fig.*, *the five watchful senses*:
P. L. V. 104; *zeal and duty ... on
Occasion's forelock watchful wait*:
P. R. III. 173; *the spheres of
watchful fire*: V. Ex. 40.

(b) serving as a guard; *the cohort bright of watchful Cherubim* : P. L. XI. 128.

(c) being the place in which they keep watch ; *the starry quire ...in their nightly watchful spheres* : C. 113.

Watch-tower, *sb.* a tower upon which a sentinel is stationed ; *fig.*, *the dull night, from his watchtower in the skies* : L'A. 43.

Water, I. *sb.* (1) the colourless limpid liquid ; (a) in hell ; *of itself the water flies all taste of living wight* : P. L. II. 612.

(b) as falling in rain ; *water with fire in ruin reconciled* : P. R. IV. 412.

(c) as one of the four elements which form the universe : P. R. II. 124.

(d) as distinguished from air or land ; *Water ... by ... fish ... was swum* ; P. L. VII. 502.

(2) a body of water, stream, river, lake, sea ; *pl.*; sometimes with blending of (2) (c) : P. L. VI. 196 ; VII. 393, 397, 446 ; VIII. 301 ; S. A. 1647 ; C. 896 ; *bed of waters* : P. L. VII. 290 ; *the great receptacle of congregated waters he called Seas* : P. L. VII. 308 ; *ye that in waters glide* : P. L. V. 200; *let the waters generate reptile* : P. L. VII. 387 ; *the sound of waters deep* : P. L. V. 872 ; *murmuring* : P. L. IV. 260 ; Il P. 144 ; *murmuring sound of waters* : P. L. IV. 454 ; *smoothly the waters kissed* : N. O. 65 ; in heaven : P. L. VI. 645.

(b) a fountain or spring ; *the water steep of Meribah* : Ps. LXXXI. 31 ; in heaven ; *fountain or spring, by the waters of life* : P. L. XI. 79.

(c) as encompassing the earth or the universe : P. L. VII. 263, 268, 283 ; *Chaos ... the waters* : P. L. X. 285 ; *the rising World of waters* : P. L. III. 11 ; *let there be firmament amid the waters* : P. L. VII. 262 ; *the World built on circumfluous waters* : P. L. VII. 270; *the Earth ... in the womb as yet of waters* : P. L. VII. 277.

(d) the water of the great flood : P. L. XI. 749.

(e) as a place of baptism ; *on him, rising out of the water* : P. R. I. 81.

II. *vb. tr.* (a) to wet ; *with tears watering the ground* : P. L. X. 1090, 1102 ; *my bed I water with my tears* : Ps. VI. 13.

(b) to irrigate ; *many a rill watered the garden* : P. L. IV. 230 ; *watered all the ground* : P. L. VII. 334 ; *Iris ... waters the odorous banks* : C. 993 ; *absol.* : P. L. XI. 279 ; *fig., from whose mouth issued ... streams, that watered all the schools of Academics* : P. R. IV. 277.

See **Wide-watered.**

Water-nymph, *sb.* the tutelary spirit of a river : C. 833.

Watery, *adj.* (a) abounding in water, well-watered : Ps. LXXXIV. 23 ; *Rabba and her watery plain* : P. L. I. 397 ; covered with or caused by the waters ; *that watery desert* : P. L. XI. 779.

(b) consisting of water; *Lethe ... her watery labyrinth* : P. L. II. 584 ; *the watery throng* : P. L. VII. 297 ; *streams, plain* : Ps. I. 8 ; CXXXVI. 22 ; that is the water ; *fish within their watery residence* : P. L. VIII. 346 ; *his watery bier* : L. 12.

(c) of or pertaining to the water ; *watery gleam, calm, glass, floor* : P. L. IV. 461 ; VII. 234 ; XI. 844 ; L. 167.

(d) full of water ; *that same watery cloud* : P. L. XI. 882.

(e) seen in or reflected by the water ; *watery image* : P. L. IV. 480.

Wattled, *part. adj.* surrounded by a fence formed of plaited twigs : C. 344.

Wave, I. *sb.* (1) a ridge or swell of water : P. L. XI. 747, 830 ; XII. 213 ; L. 91 ; Ps. LXXXVIII. 68 ; *the ocean wave* : P. L. III. 539 ; *the Red Sea ... whose waves* : P. L. I. 306 ; *Neptune ... mustering all his waves* : V. Ex. 44 ; *wave rolling after wave* : P. L. VII. 298 ; *Him that walked the waves* : L. 173 ; *surging* : P. L. VII. 214 ; P. R. IV. 18 ; *weltering, headlong, brimmed* : N. O. 124 ; C. 887, 924 ; *green, orient, translucent, ruddy* : P. L. VII. 402 ; N. O. 231 ; C. 861 ; Ps. CXXXVI. 45 ; *fresh* : P. L. XI. 845 ; *indignant, charmed, barking* : P. L. X. 311 ; N. O. 68 ; C. 258.

(b) of the waters of chaos : P. L. II. 1042 ; *Silence, ye troubled waves* : P. L. VII. 216.

(c) of the lake or river of fire in hell; *fiery waves*: P. L. I. 184 ; *head uplift above the wave* : P. L. I. 193 ; *Phelegeton, whose waves of torrent fire* : P. L. II. 581.

(d) *fig.* of wrath: Ps. LXXXVIII. 31, 32.

(2) the wave-like motion of a serpent's body : P. L. IX. 496.

II. *vb.* (1) *intr.* (a) to move or sway to and fro ; *a field of Ceres ...waving*: P. L. IV. 981 ; *banners ...waving*: P. L. I. 546; *streamers*: S. A. 718.

(b) to be brandished or flourished; *the uplifted spear waving ...to direct their course* : P. L. I. 348; *a flaming sword... waves*: P. L. XII. 593.

(c) to float or move with wave-like motion (?) ; *some mysterious dream wave at his wings* : Il P. 148.

(d) to have an undulating surface : S. A. 1493 ; *his locks ... lay waving round* : P. L. III. 628.

(2) *tr.* (a) to cause to move to and fro in the air : P. L. V. 194, 687; *waves his purple wings*: P. L. IV. 764 ; *waved their limber fans*: P. L. VII. 476 ; *wave your tops, ye Pines* : P. L. V. 193.

(b) to brandish, flourish : P. L. I. 340 ; N. O. 51 ; *waved over by that flaming brand* : P. L. XII. 643 ; *waved their fiery swords*: P. L. VI. 304 ; *a reed stood waving*: P. L. VI. 580 ; *if I but wave this wand* : C. 659.

(c) to form with an undulating surface ; *ringlets waved*: P. L. IV. 306.

part. adj. (1) **waving**, moving to and fro ; *waving woods*: C. 88 ; flaming : P. L. VI. 413.

(2) **waved**, formed so as to show a changeable play of light ; *fish... their waved coats dropt with gold*: P. L. VII. 406.

See **Wide-waving**.

Waver, *vb. intr.* to be irresolute, vacillate : S. A. 456.

part. adj. **wavering** ; (a) swaying ; *to the moon in wavering morrice move* : C. 116.

(b) vacillating : S. A. 732.

Wax, *vb.* (*pret.* not used ; *past part.* waxen) *intr.* to grow, become : C.

1000 ; *waxing more in rage* : P. L. IV. 969 ; *mine eye ... is waxen old* : Ps. VI. 14.

Waxen, *adj.* made of wax : P. L. VII. 491.

Way, *sb.* (1) a course leading from one place to another, path, road ; sometimes difficult to distinguish from (3) : P. L. V. 50 ; VII. 302 ; IX. 626, 640 ; XI. 223 ; P. R. I. 297 ; C. 36, 539 ; *readiest way* : P. L. XII. 216 ; C. 305 ; *dark and desert ways* : P. L. III. 544 ; *wave rolling after wave, where way they found*: P. L. VII. 298 ; *over heaps of slaughtered walk his way*?: S. A. 1530 ; *the way she took* : P. L. IX. 847 ; *through Eden took their solitary way* : P. L. XII. 649 ; *over Hellespont bridging his way* : P. L. X. 310 ; *the imagined way beyond Petsora* : P. L. X. 291 ; *give way* (*see* Give): P. L. V. 252; street, road ; *the ways being foul*: U. C. I. 3 ; *now that the ... ways are mire* : S. XX. 2 ; *some flowers ... to strew the ways*: M. W. 58 ; *adv.* by the road or path ; *return the way thou cam'st* : S. A. 1332.

(b) in heaven ; *before him Power Divine his way prepared* : P. L. VI. 780 ; *led to God's eternal house direct the way* : P. L. VII. 576.

(c) in hell : P. L. II. 683 ; *each his several way pursues* : P. L. II. 523.

(d) the course leading from hell to the world : P. L. II. 71, 973 ; X. 262 ; *I shall not ... err the way*: P. L. X. 267 ; *their way to Earth* : P. L. X. 325 ; *through the palpable obscure find out his uncouth way* : P. L. II. 407 ; *long is the way and hard, that out of Hell leads up to Light* : P. L. II. 432 ; *Sin and Death ... paved after him a broad and beaten way* : P. L. II. 1026 ; *by Sin and Death a broad way now is paved* : P. L. X. 473 ; *he wings his way* : P. L. III. 87 ; *from the earth to heaven* : P. L. VII. 158 ; *to Heaven their prayers flew up, nor missed the way* : P. L. XI. 15; from the outer shell of the universe to heaven, hell, or earth ; *three several ways ... to each of these three places* : S. A. 323 ; from the sun to the earth : P. L. III. 735 ; *adv.* ; *whose eye pursued him down the way he went* : P. L. IV. 126.

(e) of the sky; *through heaven's wide pathless way*: Il P. 70; *milky way*, the Galaxy: P. L. VII. 579.

(f) *fig.* usually of a course of action; *who was to come before Messiah, and his way prepare*: P. R. I. 272; *Love ... is both the way and guide*: P. L. VIII. 613; *Wisdom's way*: P. L. IX. 809; *nor to evil unknown opening the way*: P. L. IX. 865; *the ways that lead to his* (Death's) *grim cave*: P. L. XI. 468; *hard are the ways of truth*: P. R. I. 478; *to guide nations in the way of truth*: P. R. II. 473; *his way to peace is smooth*: S. A. 1049; *to peace ... thy glorious way hast ploughed*: S. XVI. 4; *the broad way*: S. IX. 2; *I have trod thy ways*: Ps. LXXXVI. 6; *walk my righteous ways*: Ps. LXXXI. 56; *adv.*; *what leads the nearest way*: S. XXI. 10.

(2) the line along which motion takes place or by means of which direction is indicated; always adverbially = in or by (some) direction: P. L. II. 1007; IV. 73, 177; X. 610; XI. 203, 646; S. A. 713, 1072, 1301, 1541; N. O. 71; C. 170; *which way the wind sways them*: P. L. IV. 982; *many feet steering this way*: S. A. 111; *feet hasting this way*: P. L. IV. 867; *bend four ways their flying march*: P. L. II. 574; *which way the nearest coast of darkness lies*: P. L. II. 958; *which way I fly is Hell*: P. L. IV. 75; *this way ... right down to Paradise*: P. L. X. 397; *the other way ... to Hell-gate*: P. L. X. 414; *whence no way round shadow from body opaque can fall*: P. L. III. 618; sing. for pl.; *where the shadow both way falls*: P. R. IV. 70.

(b) *fig.* the direction of thought or speech; *expectation calls thee now another way*: V. Ex. 54.

(3) passage or movement along some particular course: P. L. II. 949; IX. 410; *waters forcing way*: P. L. VI. 196; *wedge their way*: P. L. VII. 426; *addressed his way*: P. L. IX. 496; *sidelong he works his way*: P. L. IX. 512; *held his way*: P. L. VI. 2; *he bent his way*: P. R. II. 291; *winds ... his oblique way amongst innumerable stars*: P. L. III. 564; *o'er Heaven's*

high towers to force resistless way: P. L. II. 62; *wins his way*: P. L. II. 1016; *could we break our way*: P. L. II. 134; *breaking violent way*: P. L. II. 782; *in his way*: P. L. III. 437; *I descried his way*: P. L. IV. 567.

(b) *fig.*, *in his way to virtue*: S. A. 1039.

(4) length of space, distance; *long way*: C. 183; *adv.*: P. L. V. 904.

(5) a course of conduct or action, the manner or means of obtaining or accomplishing something: P. L. XI. 462, 527; P. R. IV. 470; S. A. 781, 797, 823, 838, 1091; *many ways to die*: P. L. X. 1005; *some other way to generate Mankind*: P. L. X. 894; *by what best way*: P. L. II. 40; *some worse way his wrath may find*: P. L. II. 83; *Grace ... finds her way*: P. L. III. 228; *a dreadful way ... to thy revenge*: S. A. 1591; *the way which to her ruin now I tend*: P. L. IX. 493; with blending of (1); *through ways of danger*: P. L. IV. 934; *the way found prosperous*: P. R. I. 104; *well hast thou taught the way*: P. L. V. 508.

(b) used adverbially; in (some) manner, by (some) means; *which way first publish his godlike office*: P. R. I. 187; *what other way I see not*: P. R. I. 338; *his virtue or weakness which way to assail*: S. A. 756; *God can satisfy that need some other way*: P. R. II. 254; *which way ... dost thou aspire to greatness*: P. R. II. 417; *stir them up some way or other ... to afflict thee*: S. A. 1252; *and not every way ... secure thy safety*: P. R. III. 348; *trial hath indamaged thee no way*: P. R. IV. 206; *my pardon no way secured*: S. A. 739; to (some) cause; *which way soever men refer it*: S. A. 1015.

(6) habitual manner of doing or acting: P. L. VIII. 373; *in their* (beasts') *ways complacence find*: P. L. VIII. 433; *the ways of highest agents*: P. L. IX. 682; *all flesh corrupting each their way*: P. L. XI. 889.

(7) mode, style, wise; *adv. taught to live the easiest way*: P. L. VIII. 183.

(8) the purposes and ordinances of God, his manner of dealing

with men : P. L. I. 26 ; *wise are all his ways* : P. L. III. 680 ; *to remove his ways from human sense* : P. L. VIII. 119 ; *the ways of God with Man* : P. L. VIII. 226 ; *just are thy ways* : P. L. X. 643 ; *just are the ways of God* : S. A. 293 ; *his ways not just* : S. A. 300 ; *thy eternal ways* : P. L. VIII. 413.

(9) a course of thought, feeling, and action prescribed and approved by God : S. XVIII. 13 ; Ps. V. 24 ; LXXXIV. 20 ; LXXXVI. 37.

(10) a course of life or the acts of a life : P. L. IV. 620 ; Ps. I. 2, 15, 16 ; LXXXIV. 44 ; *mutable are all the ways of men* : S. A. 1407 ; *my way must lie through many a hard assay* : P. R. I. 263 ; *testified against their ways* : P. L. XI. 721 ; *their wicked ways* : P. L. XI. 812 ; *their own polluted ways* : P. L. XII. 110 ; *to ways of sin and shame* : Ps. LXXX. 74.

(b) active life or the activities of life ; *from the cheerful ways of men cut off* : P. L. III. 46.

In combination with other words ; (a) **bring on one's way,** to accompany in setting out : P. R. IV. 638.

(b) **find way,** to discover a means of entrance, exit, or escape : P. L. X. 844 ; *finding way, break loose from Hell* : P. L. IV. 889 ; *he ...found unsuspected way* : P. L. IX. 69 ; *sighs found out their way* : P. L. I. 621 ; a path by which one may advance ; *further way found none* : P. L. IV. 174.

(c) **in the way,** on the road while going or proceeding ; *fig.* : Ps. II. 26.

(d) **make way into** or **to,** to reach : P. L. IX. 550 ; to obtain a hearing with : S. A. 481.

See **Half-way, Mid-way.**

Waylay, *vb. tr.* to lie in wait for in order to accost or seize : P. R. II. 185.

*****We,** *pers. pron. (dat.* and *acc.* us) (1) referring to the person speaking and those associated with him or her : P. L. I. 120 ; VI. 289 ; VIII. 246 ; *hath lost us Heaven* : P. L. I. 136 ; *let us ... rise* : P. L. V. 125 ; *it now concerns us* : P. L. V. 721 ; *to work us woe* : P. L. IX. 255 ; *descent and fall to us is adverse* : P. L. II. 77 ; *wherefore let we then our faithful friends* : P.

L. I. 264 ; *This deep world of darkness do we dread ?* : P. L. II. 263 ; *nor want we skill* : P. L. II. 272 ; *not to Earth confined ... as we* : P. L. V. 79 ; *ethereal, as we* : P. L. V. 499 ; *we ourselves* : P. L. VIII. 186 ; *to be created like to us* : P. L. II. 349 ; *seek deliverance for us all* : P. L. II. 465 ; *from us two a race* : P. L. IV. 732 ; *us three* : P. L. X. 364 ; followed by an *adj.; whereof we wretched seldom taste* : P. R. I. 345.

referring to the human race ; *for us frail dust* : Cir. 19 ; *till one greater Man restore us* : P. L. I. 5 ; *work us a perpetual peace* : N. O. 7 ; *the arch-chemic Sun, so far from us remote* : P. L. III. 609 ; *we on Earth* : S. M. 17 ; referring to the English nation ; *to ride us with a Classic Hierarchy* : F. of C. 7 ; to the Gentile nations : Ps. II. 6 ; to the Hebrew nation ; *Greece from us these arts derived* : P. R. IV. 338.

(b) the antecedent of a rel. pron. ; *we ... who dwell this wild* : P. R. I. 331 ; *we, that are of purer fire* : C. 111.

(c) in absolute construction with a part. ; *us dispossessed* : P. L. VII. 142 ; *we not endued single with like defense* : P. L. IX. 324 ; the part. omitted ; *us asunder* : P. L. IX. 258.

(d) *pl.* for *sing.,* the royal we : P. L. V. 684 ; VI. 433 ; the authorial we : M. M. 9 ; L'A. 117.

(2) our territory or realm ; *such an enemy is risen to invade us* : P. R. II. 127.

Weak, *adj.* (1) lacking in physical power or strength : V. Ex. 1 ; *comp.; to our weaker view* : Il P. 15 ; *sup.; wherefore should not strength and might...weakest prove* : P. L. VI. 117 ; or in sense (2) or (4), or combining these ideas : Ps. LXXXVIII. 15.

(b) feeble, infirm : Ps. VI. 4.

(c) unable to defend oneself ; *how weak if thou resist* : P. L. IV. 1012 ; *wicked, and thence weak* : P. L. IV. 856.

(2) lacking in moral strength or firmness : P. L. VIII. 532.

(3) lacking courage, resolution, and fortitude ; *to be weak is miserable* : P. L. I. 157.

(4) lacking mental power; *weak minds* : P. R. II. 221.

(5) wanting effective power; *those shadowy expiations weak* : P. L. XII. 291 ; *weak arguing* : P. R. III. 4 ; *such weak witness of thy name* : W. S. 6; *by things deemed weak* : P. L. XII. 567 ; *sup. ; weakest subtleties* : S. A. 56.

(6) resulting from lack of judgement and firmness : P. L. IX. 1186.

absol. (a) one lacking bodily or mental strength or both ; *regard the weak* : Ps. LXXXII. 9 ; *comp.; the weaker seek* : P. L. IX. 383 ; *thy weaker* : P. L. VI. 909.

(b) a condition of feebleness : P. L. XI. 540.

Weaken, *vb. tr.* to reduce the strength or power of ; *weakening the sceptre of old Night* : P. L. II. 1002.

Weakly, *adv.* in a weak manner morally : S. A. 50, 499.

Weakness, *sb.* **(1)** the want of strength or inherent power ; *human weakness* : P. R. III. 402; *the unarmed weakness of one virgin* : C. 582; referring to the human nature of Christ ; *his weakness shall o'er-come Satanic strength* : P. R. I. 161; referring the limitation of God's power ; *which to God himself impossible is held, as argument of weakness* : P. L. X. 801.

(b) the assailable or vulnerable part : P. L. II. 357.

(2) the want of moral strength : S. A. 756, 785, 829, 830, 831, 843, 1722; *all wickedness is weakness* : S. A. 834 ; *O weakness!* : S. A. 235 ; rather, a weak or foolish act ; *it was a weakness in me* : S. A. 773 ; *was it not weakness also to make known* : S. A. 778.

Weal, *sb.* well-being, prosperity, happiness ; *weal or woe* : P. L. VIII. 638 ; IX. 133.

Wealth, *sb.* (a) valuable material possessions, riches : P. L. XII. 133, 332 ; P. R. II. 433; IV. 82, 141, 368 ; S. XII. 14 ; Petr. 4; *Egypt with Assyria strove in wealth* : P. L. I. 722 ; *the wealth of Ormus and of Ind* : P. L. II. 2; *the fleecy wealth that doth enrich these downs* : C. 504 ; *grown in wealth and multitude* : P. L. XII. 352 ; *full of honour, wealth* : P. R. II. 202 ; *thrive in wealth* : P. R. II. 430 ; *in highth of all their flowing wealth* : P. R. II. 436 ; *contemning all wealth* : P. R. IV. 305; *a penurious niggard of his wealth* : C. 726 ; *get or seek wealth* : P. R. II. 427 ; III. 44 ; *fig., Nature's whole wealth* : P. L. IV. 207.

(b) the state of displaying great riches : P. L. XI. 788.

Wealthy, *adj.* having great riches : Dante 3.

Weanling, *adj.* newly weaned : L. 46.

Weapon, *sb.* an instrument of offense : C. 612; used by an angel: P. L. VI. 439 ; *with mountains, as with weapons armed* : P. L. VI. 697 ; *down their idle weapons dropped* : P. L. VI. 839 ; *the jaw of an ass used by Samson; trivial weapon* : S. A. 142, 263.

Weaponless, *adj.* having no weapon, unarmed : S. A. 130.

Wear, *vb.* (*pret.* wore ; *past part.* worn) *tr.* **(1)** to carry, bear, or have on the body as a garment or an ornament : C. 722 ; *a military vest of purple ... worn by kings* : P. L. XI. 243 ; *these troublesome disguises which we wear* : P. L. IV. 740.

(b) of parts of the body ; *wings he wore* : P. L. III. 641 ; serving for a covering ; *six wings he wore, to shade his lineaments divine* : P. L. V. 277 ; *her .. golden tresses wore* : P. L. IV. 305.

(c) of that which serves as a sign of power or victory ; to bear on the head ; *him who wears the regal diadem* : P. R. II. 461 ; *wear their sapphire crowns* : C. 26 ; to carry in the hand ; *those just Spirits that wear victorious palms* : S. M. 14.

(d) of weapons ; *arms ... in battle worn* : S. A. 1131 ; *that ... Gorgon shield that wise Minerva wore* : C. 448.

(e) *fig., like glories wearing, Mercy will sit between* : N. O. 143 ; *those pearls of dew she wears* : M. W. 43; *flowers that their gay wardrobe wear* : L. 47; *every flower that sad embroidery wears* : L. 148.

(2) to exhaust ; *worn with famine* : P. L. X. 573.

(3) to cause by constant attrition ; *on the washy ooze deep channels wore* : P. L. VII. 303.

(4) *wear out*, to spend tediously ; *wear out miserable days* : S. A. 762 ; *intr.* to pass tediously ; *thus wore out night* : P. R. II. 279.

See **O'er-worn, Sin-worn.**

Wearer, *sb.* one who wears clothing on the body : P. L. III. 490.

Wearisome, *adj.* tiresome ; *how wearisome eternity so spent* : P. L. II. 247 ; *many books are wearisome* : P. R. IV. 322.

Weary, I. *adj.* (*a*) fatigued physically, tired : C. 64 ; *they left me weary* : C. 280 ; weak, feeble ; *may at last my weary age* : Il P. 167.

(*b*) discontented or vexed by the continued endurance *of* : V. Ex. 25 ; *Nature within me seems ... weary of herself* : S. A. 596.

II. *vb. tr.* (**1**) to fatigue, tire : P. L. IX. 1045 ; P. R. IV. 591 ; Ps. VI. 11 ; *wearied with slaughter* : S. A. 1583 ; *with sorrow and heart's distress wearied* : P. L. XII. 614 ; *weary human sense* : P. L. XII. 10.

(*b*) *fig.* of war ; *war wearied hath performed what war can do* : P. L. VI. 695.

(*c*) *weary out*, to fatigue to exhaustion : S. A. 405 ; C. 182.

(**2**) to tire the patience of : P. L. XI. 310 ; *God ... wearied with their iniquities* : P. L. XII. 107.

part. adj. **wearied,** tired, exhausted : P. L. I. 320 ; *with wearied wings* : P. L. III. 73.

See **O'er-weary.**

Weather-beaten, *adj.* injured by exposure to severe weather : P. L. II. 1043.

Weave, *vb.* (*pret.* wove ; *past. part.* wove : P. L. IX. 839 ; A. 47 ; woven : S. XI. 2) *tr.* (*a*) to interweave, interlace : A. 47 ; *the serpent sly ... wove ... his braided train* : P. L. IV. 348.

(*b*) to form by interlacing threads or other pliable material : *spinning worms ... weave the smooth-haired silk* : C. 716 ; *wove ... a garland* : P. L. IX. 839.

fig. of the contents of a book : S. XI. 2.

See **Thick-woven, Well-woven.**

Weaver, *sb.* one who weaves cloth : S. A. 1122.

Wed, *vb.* (**1**) *tr.* (*a*) to take for wife, marry : P. L. IX. 1030 ; D. F. I.

11 ; *thou shouldst wed Philistian women* : S. A. 216 ; *I sought to wed the daughter of an infidel* : S. A. 220 ; *fig.*, *led the vine to wed her elm* : P. L. v. 216.

(*b*) to unite in wedlock ; *Adam wedded to another Eve* : P. L. IX. 828.

(*c*) to unite closely or inseparably : S. M. 3.

part. adj. **wedded** ; (*a*) married ; *wedded pair, maid* : P. L. VIII. 605 ; N. O. 3.

(*b*) pertaining to marriage ; *wedded love* : P. L. IV. 750.

See **Seven-times-wedded.**

Wedge, (**1**) *sb.* a wedge-shaped line of battle : P. R. III. 309.

(**2**) *vb. tr.* to make (a way) by forming or moving in a wedge-shaped body : P. L. VII. 426.

Wedlock, *sb.* marriage : S. A. 353.

attrib. entered into at the time of marriage ; *wedlock bands* : S. A. 986.

Wedlock-bound, *adj.* bound in wedlock : P. L. X. 905.

Wedlock-treachery, *sb.* the violation of faith plighted in wedlock, traitorous conduct of a wife toward her husband : S. A. 1009.

Weed, *sb.* a garment ; *palmer's weed* : C. 189 ; *pl.* : Hor. O. 15 ; *the weeds of Dominic* : P. L. III. 479 ; *an aged man in rural weeds* : P. R. I. 314 ; *the weeds and likeness of a swain* : C. 84 ; *rob a hermit of his weeds* : C. 390 ; *ill-fitted* : S. A. 122 ; *pure ambrosial* : C. 16 ; *in weeds of peace* : L'A. 120.

fig. the body ; *having clad thyself in human weed* : D. F. I. 58.

See **Sea-weed.**

Weekly, *adj.* occurring each week : U. C. I. 10.

Ween, *vb.* (**1**) *intr.* to be of opinion, think : P. L. IV. 741.

(**2**) *tr.* to expect, hope ; *they weened ... to win the Mount of God* : P. L. VI. 86 ; *weening to prosper* : P. L. VI. 795.

Weep, *vb.* (*pret.* and *past part.* wept ; weept : M. W. 56) (**1**) *tr.* (*a*) to shed ; *tears such as angels weep* : P. L. I. 620 ; *sad drops wept at completing of the mortal Sin* : P. L. XII. 1003 ; *for which ... a world of tears must weep* : P. L. XI. 627 ; *seas wept from our deep sorrow* : Cir. 9.

(b) *fig.* to write or compose with sorrow or tears : M. W. 56.

(c) *fig.* to let fall in drops ; *trees wept odorous gums* : P. L. IV. 248.

(2) *intr.* to shed tears : P. L. IX. 1121 ; X. 937 ; XI. 495 ; S. A. 728 ; L. 182 ; Ps. LXXXVIII. 3 ; *for joy tenderly wept* : P. L. IX. 991 ; *Scylla wept* : C. 257 ; *weep no more, woeful shepherds, weep no more* : L. 165 ; *wept that he had lived so long inglorious* : P. R. III. 41.

vbl. sb. **weeping,** wailing, lamentation ; *the voice of my weeping* : Ps. VI. 17 ; *a voice of weeping* : N. O. 183 ; *take up a weeping* : P. 51.

Weigh, *vb.* (*pres. 2d sing.* weigh'st : P. R. II. 173) *tr.* (*a*) to balance in order to determine the weight of ; *all things created first he weighed* : P. L. IV. 999.

(b) to estimate the worth or power of : P. R. III. 51 ; *weighed the strength he was to cope with* : P. R. IV. 8 ; with definite *figurative* reference to (a) ; *where thou art weighed* : P. L. IV. 1012 ; *weigh with her thyself* : P. L. VIII. 570 ; *in much uneven scale thou weigh'st all others by thyself* : P. R. II. 173 ; *if it be weighed by itself* : S. A. 768.

(c) to keep steady, balance, poise ; *Satan ... weighs his spread wings* : P. L. II. 1046.

(d) to equal in amount ; *that crystalline sphere whose balance weighs the trepidation talked* : P. L. III. 482.

(e) to consider, regard ; *my meditation weigh* : Ps. V. 2.

(*f*) *weigh ... down,* to burden, oppress : P. L. XI. 545.

Weight, *sb.* (*a*) the downward pressure of a body, heaviness, ponderosity : U. C. II. 26 ; *the weight of mountains* : P. L. VI. 652 ; *the dusky air that felt unusual weight* : P. L. I. 227 ; *the timely dew of sleep, now falling with soft slumberous weight* : P. L. IV. 615 ; (Nature) *would be quite surcharged with her own weight* : C. 728.

(b) a body of determinate mass used in weighing-machines as a standard ; *in these he* (God) *put two weights* : P. L. IV. 1002 ; used as a counterpoise or to exert

pressure ; *an engine moved with wheel and weight* : U. C. II. 9.

(c) a load or burden of care or responsibility : P. L. II. 416 ; *the weight of mightiest monarchies* : P. L. II. 307 ; *for the public all this weight he bears* : P. R. II. 465 ; *a kingdom's weight* : P. R. IV. 282 ; *the World ... under her own weight groaning* : P. L. XII. 539 ; *of sin* ; *mankind, whose sins' full weight must be transferred upon my head* : P. R. I. 267.

(d) importance, consequence P. L. X. 968 ; used punningly with the double meaning of heaviness and importance : P. L. VI. 621.

Welcome, (1) *adj.* gladly received, grateful, agreeable : P. L. XI. 140 ; *O welcome hour* : P. L. X. 771 ; *the welcome end of all my pains* : S. A. 576 ; *me ... a welcome prey* : S. A. 260.

absol. as a salutation ; *O, welcome, pure-eyed Faith* : C. 213.

(2) *vb. tr.* to salute or receive with gladness : M. M. 10 ; *to welcome him to this his new abode* : N. O. 18 ; to begin gladly ; *welcome joy and feast* : C. 102.

See **New-welcome.**

Welkin, *sb.* the vault of the sky ; *the bowed welkin* : C. 1015 ; *the welkin burns* : P. L. II. 538.

Well, *sb.* a spring of water, fountain ; *the sacred well that from beneath the seat of Jove doth spring* : L. 15 ; in heaven ; *the well of life* : P. L. XI. 416.

*****Well,** I. *adv.* (1) in a good or excellent manner, worthily, rightly : P. L. III. 196 ; IV. 200 ; V. 335 ; VIII. 573 ; XI. 451 ; S. A. 289 ; S. XX. 11 ; *well hast thou fought the better fight* : P. L. VI. 29 ; *let each his adamantine coat gird well* : P. L. VI. 542 ; *govern well thy appetite* : P. L. VII. 546 ; *well aimed* : P. L. IX. 173 ; *not well conceived of God* : P. L. IX. 945 ; *live well* : P. L. XI. 554, 629 ; *their ... race well run* : P. L. XII. 505 ; *conquered well* : P. R. IV. 134 ; *the bearing well of all calamities* : S. A. 655.

(b) rightly, correctly ; *as well as I may guess* : C. 201.

(c) skilfully ; *so well he feigned* : P. L. III. 639 ; *love well feigned* : P. L. IX. 492.

(2) agreeably to one's wishes, gratifyingly, satisfactorily; *well have we speeded* : P. R. III. 267 ; *all would have then gone well* : P. L. XI. 781.

(3) suitably to circumstances or the nature of things, advantageously, conveniently, fittingly : P. L. III. 555 ; VII. 128 ; VIII. 388 ; XI. 257 ; P. R. I. 301 ; S. A. 204, 1258 ; *well may we afford our givers their own gifts* : P. L. V. 316 ; *well thou com'st before thy fellows* : P. L. VI. 159 ; *well may we labour still to dress this Garden* : P. L. IX. 205 ; *so well I have disposed my aery microscope* : P. R. IV. 56 ; *these thoughts may startle well* : C. 210 ; *he comes well* : C. 488.

(4) to a great extent or degree, thoroughly, fully, amply, completely, adequately : P. L. VIII. 540, 548 ; IX. 184 ; P. R. II. 97 ; *ere well awake* : P. L. I. 334 ; *well thou know'st* : P. L. IV. 426, 926 ; *well known* : P. L. IV. 581 ; *now know I well thy favour* : P. L. V. 461 ; *well understand* : P. L. VI. 625 ; *worthy well thy cherishing* : P. L. VIII. 568 ; *well pleased* : P. L. III. 241 ; IV. 164 ; V. 617 ; X. 71 ; *well skilled* : C. 620 ; *he loved me well* : C. 623 ; *too well* : P. L. I. 134 ; S. A. 878.

(b) *well nigh*, very nearly, almost : P. L. IX. 141.

II. *adj.* (a) agreeable to desire; *such as under government well seemed* : P. L. X. 154 ; *nothing is here for tears ... nothing but well and fair* : S. A. 1723 ; *this may be well* : P. L. IX. 826 ; elliptical for, it would be or is well : P. L. X. 725, 887.

(b) sound in body ; *waxing well of his deep wound* : C. 1000.

Well-attired, *adj.* suitably or becomingly dressed or adorned ; *fig.*, *the well-attired woodbine* : L. 146.

Well-balanced, *adj.* rightly or properly adjusted ; *the well-balanced world* : N. O. 122.

Well-being, *sb.* welfare : P. L. VIII. 361.

Well-couched, *adj.* skilfully concealed ; *well-couched fraud* : P. R. I. 97.

Well-dispensed, *adj.* distributed in the right manner : C. 772.

Well-feasted, *adj.* having eaten sumptuously : S. A. 1419.

Well-governed, *adj.* rightly regulated : C. 705.

Well-lighted, *adj.* clearly or brightly burning; *a well-lighted flame* : M. W. 20.

Well-measured, *adj.* rightly divided into measures, rhythmical : S. XIII. 1.

Well-placed, *adj.* skilfully ordered or arranged ; *well-placed words* : C. 161.

Well-pleasing, *adj.* giving great pleasure ; *well-pleasing Son* : P. L. X. 634.

Well-practised, *adj.* having skill, experienced ; *well-practised feet* : C. 310.

Well-trod, *adj.* having skilful actors ; *the well-trod stage* : L'A. 131.

Well-woven, *adj.* skilfully contrived; *well-woven snares* : P. R. I. 97.

Welter, *vb. intr.* to roll or tumble about in a fluid : P. L. I. 78 ; *he must not ... welter to the parching wind* : L. 13.

part. adj. **weltering,** rolling; *the weltering waves* : N. O. 124.

West, (1) *adv.* to or toward the west : P. L. IV. 784 ; *west from Orontes to the ocean barred at Darien* : P. L. IX. 80 ; *Indus east, Euphrates west* : P. R. III. 272 ; *due west it rises* : C. 306.

(2) *sb.* (a) the portion of the horizon or the sky near the place of the sun's setting : P. L. VII. 376 ; *she* (the earth) *from west her silent course advance* : P. L. VIII. 163 ; *the low Sun ... not known or east or west* : P. L. X. 685 ; *more to west* : P. R. IV. 71 ; with *def. art.* : P. L. XII. 40 ; H. B. 7.

(b) a country lying toward the west ; *the British west* : P. R. IV. 77.

(c) the western side : P. R. IV. 448.

(3) *adj.* (a) situated toward the west ; *India East or West* : P. L. V. 339.

(b) coming from the west ; *west winds* : C. 989.

See **South-west.**

Westering, *part. adj.* moving toward the west ; *the star ... had sloped his westering wheel* : L. 31.

Western, *adj.* being or lying in or toward the west : P. L. IV. 862 ; P. R. IV. 25 ; Ps. LXXX. 45 ;

clouds that on his western throne attend : P. L. IV. 597 ; the sun in western cadence : P. L. X. 92 ; yon western cloud : P. L. XI. 205 ; the great western sea : P. L. XII. 141 ; the western bay : L. 191.

Westward, adv. toward the west : P. R. IV. 237.

Wet, (1) adj. (a) moist or saturated with water : Ps. LXXX. 24 ; to warm him wet : P. R. I. 318 ; me worse than wet : P. R. IV. 486.

(b) composed of water ; the wet sea-paths : Ps. VIII. 21.

(c) rainy ; wet October's torrent flood : C. 930.

(2) sb. rain, moisture ; dried the wet from drooping plant : P. R. IV. 433.

(3) vb. tr. to make wet, moisten ; wet the thirsty earth with falling showers : P. L. V. 190 ; tears ... wetting the borders of her silken veil : S. A. 730.

Wether, sb. a castrated ram : S. A. 538 ; C. 499.

Whale, sb. the marine mammal : P. L. VII. 391.

*__What,__ I. pron. (1) interrog. inquiring for some specification concerning things or persons referred to ; (a) in direct questions ; referring to things : S. XXII. 9 ; What can it then avail : P. L. I. 153 ; What can be worse : P. L. II. 85 ; What fear we then ? : P. L. II. 94 ; what transports thee so ? : P. L. VIII. 567 ; what shall we do : S. A. 1520 ; referring to persons ; what are these ? : P. L. XI. 675 ; whence and what art thou (Death) : P. L. II. 681 ; what is Man : S. A. 667 ; = who ; What are you ? : C. 490.

in elliptical clause : P. L. II. 165, 553 ; What though the field be lost : P. L. I. 105 ; what if, what will or would happen if : P. L. I. 143 ; II. 170, 174, 344 ; IX. 826 ; X. 760.

(b) in dependent questions : P. L. IV. 452 ; to know what passes there : P. L. VIII. 173 ; she what was honour knew : P. L. VIII. 508.

adj. inquiring as to the character or nature of things or persons qualified by it ; (a) in direct questions ; referring to things ; what power of mind : P. L. I. 626 ; what place can be for us : P. L. II. 235 ; for what peace will be given to us : P. L. II. 332 ; what strength,

what art : P. L. II. 410 ; wha proof could they have given : P. L III. 103 ; what food will he convey up thither : P. L. XII. 74 ; referring to persons ; what God : P. L. IX. 102.

in elliptical clause ; what matter : P. L. I. 256 ; what wonder : P. L. III. 606 ; VI. 219.

(b) in dependent questions ; I know of thee what thing thou art : P. L. II. 741 ; see what life the gods live there : P. L. V. 80 ; say first what cause : P. L. I. 28 ; tell him ... what enemy : P. L. V. 239 ; learn what creatures : P. L. II. 355.

(c) emphatically : P. L. II. 80 ; in exclamations ; What ! : C. 814 ; what folly then : P. L. IV. 1007 ; yet what compare ! : P. L. V. 467 ; with what delight : P. L. IX. 114 ; what abyss of fears : P. L. X. 842 ; what love sincere : P. L. X. 915 ; what a multitude : P. R. I. 196 ; what a disguise ! : P. 19.

(2) rel. (a) that which : P. L. I. 95, 647, 698 ; II. 20, 340 ; what in me is dark illumine : P. L. I. 22 ; He ... can dispose and bid what shall be right : P. L. I. 247 ; if what was urged : P. L. II. 120 ; what seemed both spear and shield : P. L. IV. 990.

(b) referring to persons and nearly or quite equivalent to, the one who ; and what I should be : P. L. I. 257 ; with regard of what we are : P. L. II. 282 ; like to what ye are : P. L. II. 391 ; the bitter memory of what he was, what is : P. L. IV. 25 ; what there thou seest ... is thyself : P. L. IV. 465 ; what stood recoiled : P. L. VI. 391 ; what by Deity I am : P. L. VI. 682 ; to what I was in Heaven : P. L. IX. 488.

(c) whatever : P. L. IV. 694 ; P. R. IV. 108 ; maugre what might hap : P. L. IX. 56 ; what she did : P. L. X. 141 ; what they met : P. L. X. 285 ; or = that ; all what we affirm or what deny : P. L. V. 107 ; all what thou command'st : P. L. IX. 570.

adj. (a) that ... which ; referring to things ; I seek, what readiest path : P. L. II. 976 ; from what state I fell : P. L. IV. 38 ; to what highth thou wilt : P. L. VIII. 430 ; referring to persons ; behold ...

what glorious Shape comes : P. L.
v. 309.

(*b*) such ... as ; *what day* or *time*:
P. L. IV. 712 ; C. 291 ; L. 28.

(*c*) any which, whatever ; *in
what shape they choose* : P. L. I.
428 ; *awaiting what command* : P.
L. I. 566 ; *in what bower* : P. L.
v. 230 ; *what trivial weapon* : S.
A. 142.

(3) *indef.* anything ; *nor had
what to reply* : P. R. IV. 2.

II. *adv.* (*a*) in what respect? :
P. L. VI. 456 ; *What can your
knowledge hurt him* : P. L. IX. 727.

(*b*) why? : W. S. 1, 6 ; C. 362 ;
*what doubt we to incense his utmost
ire?* : P. L. II. 94 ; *What sit we
then projecting peace and war?* :
P. L. II. 329.

What-d'ye-call, *sb.* used in place of
a proper name : F. of C. 12.

Whatever (contracted to whate'er :
P. L. I. 150 ; II. 733 ; IV. 425 ;
VIII. 273 ; P. R. I. 83, 149, 178 ;
S. A. 1034, 1156 ; A. 79) (1) *pron.*
the whole that, anything which,
no matter what ; (*a*) followed by
the indicative : P. L. II. 733 ; v.
414 ; VI. 489 ; IX. 898 ; x. 245 ; P.
R. I. 83, 178 ; A. 79; *whatever
creeps the ground* : P. L. VII. 475 ;
whatever pure thou...enjoy'st : P. L.
VIII. 622 ; *whate'er Death is* : P. L.
IV. 425 ; *whate'er I saw* : P. L.
VIII. 273 ; *whate'er his cruel malice
could invent* : P. R. I. 149.

(*b*) followed by the subjunctive ;
whate'er his business be : P. L. I.
150 ; *whate'er it* or *he be* : S. A.
1034, 1156 ; *whatever be her cause* :
S. A. 904.

(*c*) the clause elliptical : P. L.
IV. 744 ; v. 338 ; x. 141 ; *then
should have been refused those terms
whatever* : P. L. x. 757 ; *my error
was my error...whatever* : P. R. III.
213 ; *whatever doing* : P. L. II. 162.

(2) *adj.* of what kind or sort it
may be : P. L. II. 442, 955 ; IV.
891 ; IX. 92 ; x. 11, 605 ; *whatever
thing is good* : Ps. LXXXV. 50 ;
whatever thing Death be : P. L.
IX. 695 ; *whatever place, clime* :
P. R. IV. 600 ; S. VIII. 8.

Whatsoever, *adj.* whatever : P. L.
. IV. 587 ; *in what place soe'er* : P.
L. II. 260. *See* **Soe'er**.

Wheat, *sb.* the edible product of the
plant *Triticum vulgare* : Ps. LXXXI.
66.

Wheel, I. *sb.* (1) a circular frame
or solid disk turning on an axis :
Ps. LXXXIII. 49 ; forming part of
a machine ; *an engine moved with
wheel and weight* : U. C. II. 9 ;
forming part of a chariot ; *the
chariot of Paternal Deity ... wheel
within wheel* : P. L. VI. 751 ; pl. ;
shun the goal with rapid wheels :
P. L. II. 532 ; *the madding wheels
of brazen chariots* : P. L. VI. 210;
*the rapid wheels that shake
Heaven's basis* : P. L. VI. 711 ;
rushing : P. 36; *burning, living,
fervid, fiery* : P. L. VI. 832, 846 ;
VII. 224 ; P. R. II. 16 ; *the wheels
of beryl* : P. L. VI. 755 ; forming
part of a gun-carriage : P. L. VI.
753.

(*b*) *pl. fig.* put for the whole
chariot ; *draw'st his triumphant
wheels* : P. L. IV. 975.

(*c*) *fig.* with reference to a
heavenly body ; *the hindmost
wheels of Phœbus' wain* : C. 190 ;
or probably put for the whole
chariot ; *the Sun ..with wheels yet
hovering o'er the ocean-brim* : P. L.
v. 140 ; *the star ... had sloped his
westering wheel* : L. 31.

(*d*) *fig.* that which has the
shape and motion of a wheel ; *the
wheel of Day and Night* : P. L.
VIII. 135. *See* **Rhomb**.

(2) a circular course or motion :
P. L. VI. 326 ; *throws his steep
flight in many an aery wheel* : P.
L. III. 741 ; revolution ; *yonder
starry sphere ... in all her wheels* :
P. L. v. 621.

II. *vb.* (1) *tr.* (*a*) to give a circular direction to ; *the Moon ...
wheels her pale course* : P. L. I.
786 ; *as the great First Mover's
hand first wheeled their course* : P.
L. VII. 501.

(*b*) to change direction toward,
turn about to ; *these other wheel
the north* : P. L. IV. 783.

(2) *intr.* (*a*) to change direction
or course : P. R. III. 323 ; *half
wheeling to the shield* : P. L. IV.
785.

(*b*) to move in a circuitous course,
or to advance by rolling onward ;
*hail mixed with fire, must...wheel
on the earth* : P. L. XII. 183.

part. adj. **wheeling**, rotating :
V. Ex. 34.

See **Chariot - wheel**, **Fiery-
wheeled**.

Whelm, *vb. tr.* (*a*) to engulf, submerge ; *whelmed thy legions under darkness* : P. L. VI. 141.

(*b*) to throw over so as to cover and destroy : P. L. VI. 651.

part. adj. **whelming,** engulfing: L. 157.

Whelp, *vb. intr.* to bring forth young: P. L. XI. 751.

******When,** I. *adv.* (1) *interrog.* at what time? ; (*a*) in direct questions : P. L. VIII. 57.

(*b*) in dependent questions ; *say where and when their fight* : P. L. XII. 384 ; *expectation when to see in triumph issuing forth their glorious Chief* : P. L. X. 539.

(2) *rel.* (*a*) at the time that ; *battle, when it raged* : P. L. I. 271 ; *when the priest turns atheist* : P. L. I. 494 ; *when Charlemain fell* : P. L. I. 586 ; *then ... when* : P. L. V. 109, 624 ; VI. 145 ; *then verified when Jesus ... saw Satan fall* : P. L. X. 183 ; *then due by sentence when thou didst transgress*: P. L. XI. 253 ; *such ... as when* : P. L. I. 230 ; *as when* : P. L. I. 338, 675 ; II. 636.

(*b*) as soon as : P. L. II. 299 ; III. 284 ; IV. 179 ; *when sin with vanity had filled the works of men*: P. L. III. 446 ; *when in orbs ... they stood* : P. L. V. 594 ; *when ... then*: P. L. I. 499.

(*c*) at what or which time : P. L. II. 64 ; IV. 356, 781 ; V. 3 ; *when Adam thus to Eve*: P. L. IV. 610 ; *when the Sun with Taurus rides* : P. L. I. 769.

in elliptical and exclamatory clause ; *when, lo !* : P. L. XI. 733 ; or in sense (*f*) : P. L. III. 486 ; X. 1050.

(*d*) in or on which ; *that day ... when from sleep I first awaked* : P. L. IV. 449 ; *Time may come when Men with Angels may participate* : P. L. V. 493 ; *We know no time when we were not as now* : P. L. V. 859.

(*e*) = the time that ; *I saw when ... the formless mass ... came to a heap* : P. L. III. 708 ; *Who saw when this creation was ?* : P. L. V. 856 ; *attending when that fatal wound shall be inflicted* : P. R. I. 52 ; the situation in which (or elliptical) ; *I hate when vice can bolt her arguments* : C. 760.

(*f*) during the time that ; *when we wake, and when we sleep* : P. L. IV. 678 ; *when sleep hath shut all eyes* : P. L. IV. 658 ; *save when they journey* : P. L. XII. 258.

(*g*) as long as ; *when I was yet a child* : P. R. I. 201.

(*h*) at the very time that, whereas, although : P. L. III. 302 ; *Earth sitting still, when she alone receives the benefit* : P. L. VIII. 89.

(*i*) inasmuch as, since : P. L. II. 124 ; III. 608 ; VI. 219 ; S. A. 555 ; *What could it less when Spirits immortal sing ?* : P. L. II. 553 ; *when Will and Reason ... had served Necessity* : P. L. III. 108 ; *when on his shoulders each man's burden lies* : P. R. II. 462.

(*j*) if : P. L. VI. 177.

II. *sb.* the time (in which) ; *the when and how is nowhere told* : P. R. IV. 472.

Whenas, *adv.* at the time that : P. L. IX. 192 ; as soon as : T. 9.

*****Whence,** *adv.* I. *interrog.* (1) from what place ? ; (*a*) in direct questions : P. L. II. 681.

(*b*) in dependent questions ; *wondering ... whence thither brought*: P. L. IV. 452 ; *witness whence I am* : P. R. III. 107 ; *whence thou return'st I know* : P. L. XII. 610.

(2) from what source ? ; (*a*) in direct questions : P. R. II. 418 ; *yet evil whence* : P. L. V. 99 ; *whence hast thou then thy truth* : P. R. I. 446.

(*b*) in dependent questions ; *we would know whence learned* : P. L. V. 856 ; *desire of wandering ... I know not whence possessed thee* : P. L. XII. 610 ; *to acknowledge whence his good descends* : P. L. VII. 512.

(3) from what cause ? wherefore ? ; *But whence to thee this zeal ?* : P. R. III. 407.

II. *rel.* (1) from what or which place : P. L. II. 395, 639 ; IV. 158 ; XI. 558 ; *fly thither, whence thou fledd'st* : P. L. IV. 963 ; *the ground whence he was taken* : P. L. XI. 98 ; *from whence* : P. L. I. 75 ; II. 267, 1006 ; VI. 27, 477 ; X. 88 ; XI. 343 ; P. R. I. 281.

(*b*) = to the place from which ; *repaired her mural breach, returning whence it rolled* : P. L. VI. 879.

(2) from what or which source: P. L. IV. 295; VIII. 200; IX. 1078.

(3) for which cause or reason, wherefore: P. L. VI. 678, 693; XI. 158; XII. 167, 531; S. A. 1216, 1752; or in which case: P. L. II. 213.

Whenever, *rel. adv.* at whatever time: P. L. II. 809; *O welcome hour whenever!*: P. L. X. 771.

*****Where**, *adv.* (1) *interrog.* at or in what place?; (*a*) in direct questions: P. L. IX. 617; XI. 328; P. R. I. 470; II. 95; C. 179.

(*b*) in dependent questions; *to learn ... where their weakness*: P. L. II. 357; *sought where to lie hid*: P. L. IX. 76; *to find where Adam sheltered*: P. L. XI. 223.

(2) *rel.* (*a*) at or in what or which place, at or in the place in which: P. L. VIII. 41; *thither haste where stood their great Commander*: P. L. I. 357; *where ... there*: P. L. II. 30; XI. 292.

(*b*) in which state or condition; *to better life shall yield him, where*: P. L. XI. 42; *those ill-mated marriages ... where good with bad were matched*: P. L. XI. 685.

(*c*) to the place at or in which: P. L. I. 379; IV. 213; V. 375; *what readiest path leads where your gloomy bounds confine*: P. L. II. 976; *I will bring thee where no shadow stays*: P. L. IV. 470; *chance may lead where I may meet*: P. L. IV. 530.

(*d*) of the place in which: P. L. II. 3; from the place in which: P. R. IV. 70.

(*e*) the or a place in which: P. L. IV. 790; XI. 653; *from where I first drew air*: P. L. VIII. 284.

(*f*) at, in, or on which; *brightness where thou sitt'st throned*: P. L. III. 376; *a seat where gods might dwell*: P. L. VII. 329; *there was a place ... where Tigris*: P. L. IX. 71; *the land where flows Ganges*: P. L. IX. 81; *the altar where an offering burned*: S. A. 26; *such where*: V. Ex. 33.

(*g*) at the time at which; *manhood where youth ended*: P. L. XI. 246.

(*h*) except in those cases in which: P. L. XII. 222.

(*i*) whereas, since, seeing that: P. L. III. 105; S. A. 916.

(*j*) wherever; *wave rolling after wave, where way they found*: P. L. VI. 298; *hail mixed with fire ... devouring where it rolls*: P. L. XII. 183; *where passing fair allured them*: P. L. XI. 717; *almost = if*; *where the heart joins not, outward acts defile not*: S. A. 1368; *where an equal poise of hope and fear does arbitrate the event*: C. 410.

Whereat (whéreat: P. L. VI. 202), *rel. adv.* at which: P. L. I. 616; II. 389; V. 851; VI. 202; VIII. 309; XI. 444, 868; XII. 636.

Whereby, *rel. adv.* by which: P. L. III. 621; V. 411; VIII. 579; P. R. I. 396.

Where'er. *See* **Wherever**.

Wherefore, *interrog. adv.* for what reason or cause? why?: P. L. I. 264; II. 159, 450; IV. 657, 917, 960; VI. 116; IX. 331; X. 762; P. R. III. 21, 23; S. A. 23, 356, 1441; C. 710; *Ah, wherefore?*: P. L. IV. 42.

Wherein (whérein: P. L. IX. 725; S. A. 564), *adv.* (1) *interrog.* in what?: P. L. IX. 725; S. A. 564.

(2) *rel.* in which or what; (*a*) referring to place, thing, position, etc.: P. L. III. 78, 262, 335; IV. 999; VIII. 68; XI. 479, 608, 901; XII. 41; S. A. 780; C. 135; *looks downcast ... yet such wherein appeared*: P. L. I. 523; *delight, wherein the brute cannot be human consort*: P. L. VIII. 391; *passion ... wherein true Love consists not*: P. L. VIII. 589; *good wherein consists ... honour*: P. L. XI. 616; *bliss wherein he sat*: P. L. III. 408; *the place wherein God set thee above her*: P. L. X. 149; referring to action; *fields were fought ... wherein*: P. L. II. 768.

(*b*) referring to time: S. X. 10; *hours ... wherein*: P. R. I. 58; *days ... wherein thou may'st repent*: P. L. XI. 255; *the happy morn, wherein*: N. O. 2; *the night wherein*: N. O. 62.

Whereof (whéreof: P. L. IV. 235, 419), *rel. adv.* of which or what; referring to place, thing, condition, etc.: P. L. I. 650; II. 584; IV. 119, 937; VI. 518; VII. 64; VIII. 342; IX. 967; P. R. I. 345; III. 345; IV. 481; *at top whereof*: P. L. III. 504; *a famous realm and country whereof*: P. L. IV.

235 ; *the tree whereof*: P. L. x.
123 ; *the strength whereof*: P. R.
ii. 276 ; *in confidence whereof*: S.
A. 1174 ; referring to action ;
*great deeds ... whereof all Hell had
rung*: P. L. ii. 723 ; *nor can perform aught whereof*: P. L. iv.
419 ; or to a person = of Ẁhom :
P. L. xii. 150.

Whereon (whéreon : P. L. iii. 510)
rel. adv. on which or what ; (*a*)
referring to place or thing : P. L.
i. 474 ; iii. 519 ; v. 510, 764 ; vi.
473, 758 ; ix. 526 ; xi. 382, 556,
858, 897 ; P. R. ii. 228 ; P. 34 ;
a field ... whereon were sheaves: P.
L. xi. 430 ; *the stairs were such as
whereon Jacob saw*: P. L. iii. 510;
*O fair foundation laid whereon to
build* : P. L. iv. 521 ; *bereave me
not whereon I live, thy gentle looks*:
P. L. x. 919.

　　(*b*) referring to time ; *the day
whereon* : Ps. lxxxi. 11.

Whereso, *rel. adv.* wheresoever : P.
L. xi. 722.

Wheresoe'er, *rel. adv.* in what place
soever, wherever : P. R. iii. 79.

Whereto, *rel. adv.* to which ; referring to a preceding speech : P. L.
i. 156 ; vi. 469 ; viii. 398 ; xii.
63.

Wherever (contracted to where'er :
P. L. xi. 79, 177 ; D. F. I. 38 ; L.
155 ; Ps. iv. 40), *rel. adv.* in or at
whatsoever place : P. L. vii. 535;
viii. 170 ; ix. 325 ; P. R. iv. 404 ;
S. A. 547 ; *wherever chanced, I
used hostility* : S. A. 1202 ; *salvation ... to the sons of Abraham's
faith wherever through the world* :
P. L. xii. 449.

　　(*b*) whatever place in which ;
*his eye might there command
wherever stood city of old* : P. L.
xi. 385.

Wherewith, *adv.* (1) *interrog.* with
what ?: P. R. ii. 411.

　　(2) *rel.* with which : P. L. iii.
148; ix. 1011; S. A. 585; N. O.
10 ; P. 2; C. 443, 449, 881 ; Ps.
lxxx. 24.

Wherewithal, *sb.* the necessary means
or resources ; *had they wherewithal* : P. L. iii. 468.

Whet, *vb. tr.* to make sharp, sharpen ;
the mower whets his scythe : L'A.
66 ; *fig.*, *his sword he* (God) *whets* :
Ps. vii. 46.

*****Whether**, (1) *interrog. adv.* intro-
ducing dependent questions ; *who*

*knows ... whether our angry Foe
can give it, or will ever?* : P. L. ii.
152 ; *know whether I be dextrous
... or be found the worst* : P. L. v.
741 ; *a question ... whether he durst
accept the offer or not*: S. A. 1255;
*in doubt whether to hold them wise
or not* : P. L. iv. 907 ; *full of
doubt .. whether I should repent
me ... or rejoice* : P. L. xii. 474 ;
*doubtful whether God be Lord or
Dagon* : S. A. 477 ; the second
member omitted : P. L. v. 867 ;
xi. 786 ; P. R. iv. 198.

　　(2) *conj.* the co-ordinating particle introducing an alternative ;
the second member introduced by
or : P. L. v. 14 ; ix. 237, 788 ;
xii. 47 ; *whether in Heaven, or
Earth, or Hell*: P. L. x. 57 ;
*whether upheld by strength, or
chance, or fate* : P. L. i. 132 ;
*whether scorn or satiate fury yield
it* : P. L. i. 178 ; *whether thou
reign or reign not* : P. R. iii. 214 ;
*whether to withdraw ... or to dis-
turb* : P. L. ix. 261 ; *whether to
settle ... or to unfold* : S. xvii. 5 ;
whether to dare ... or aggravate :
P. L. iii. 523 ; *whether to deck ..
or wet* : P. L. v. 189 ; *whether to
wind ... or direct* : P. L. ix. 215 ;
the second member introduced by
or whether : P. L. xi. 566 ; L.
159 ; *whether thus these things, or
whether not* : P. L. viii. 159 ;
whether omitted before the first
member : L'A. 17.

*****Which**, *pron.* I. *interrog.* what one
of a certain class or number ; (*a*)
in direct questions : P. L. iv.
823 ; vi. 472 ; *which of ye will be
mortal* : P. L. iii. 214 ; *which
shall I first bewail* : S. A. 151.

　　(*b*) in dependent questions ; *tell
in which of all these* : P. L. iii.
668; *which of them ... should prove
tempestuous* : P. L. x. 663 ; *to try
with me in battle which the stronger
proves* : P. L. vi. 819 ; *choose
which thou wilt* : P. R. iii. 370.

　　adj. (*a*) in direct questions ;
*which way shall I fly ... infinite
despair?* : P. L. iv. 73 ; *Which
way ... dost thou aspire to greatness?* : P. R. ii. 417.

　　(*b*) in dependent questions ; *to
ask which way the nearest coast* :
P. L. ii. 958 ; *musing ... which way
first publish* : P. R. i. 187.

　　II. *rel.* (1) introducing a subordinate clause descriptive of the antecedent; (*a*) referring to a place, thing, etc. : P. L. I. 201; II. 1, 25, 286; III. 547; IV. 144; VI. 54; *the evil plight in which they were* : P. L. I. 336; *wisdom, which alone is truly fair* : P. L. IV. 491; *which uttering* : P. L. III. 143; *which having passed* : P. L. V. 754; *in both which we . participate* : S. A. 1507; *and which* : P. L II. 914; *conjugal love...than which perhaps no bliss ... excites his envy more* : P. L. IX. 263; = it; *he gave it me, which I as freely give* : P. L. IV. 381.

(*b*) referring to a person; = who; *our descent ... which must be born to certain woe* : P. L. X. 980; *Latona's twin-born progeny, which after held the Sun and Moon* : S. XII. 7; *I am the Lord thy God, which brought thee* : Ps. LXXXI. 41.

(*c*) referring to a phrase, clause, or sentence : P. L. I. 166, 414; II. 105; IV. 271, 439; V. 111; *at which the universal host up-sent* : P. L. I. 541; *live content—which is the calmest life* : P. L. VI. 461; *I feel I hunger; which declares* : P. R. II. 252; *the antecedent a clause introduced by what; yet what thou canst attain, which best may serve* : P. L. VII. 115.

adj. referring to the one indicated by the antecedent; *at which time* : P. L. II. 774; *from which evil* : P. L. VI. 455; *which two great sexes* : P. L. VIII. 151; *in which fight they most excel* : P. R. III. 307; *by which means* : S. A. 562.

(2) introducing a subordinate clause restricting the antecedent = this or that : P. L. III. 353; V. 14; *the high repute which he... must earn* : P. L. II. 473; *that little which is left* : P. L. II. 1000; *these troublesome disguises which we wear* : P. L. IV. 740; *that same fruit ... which he had plucked* : P. L. V. 84; *this Heaven which we behold* : P. L. VII. 88; *the creatures which I made* : P. L. VIII. 409; *to do aught which else free-will would not admit* : P. L. VIII. 636; *a land which he will show him* : P. L. XII. 123.

(*b*) *that* or *this* as antecedent; *to know that which before us lies* :

P. L. VIII. 193; *not that which justly gives* : P. L. IX. 40; *what is this which thou hast done?* : P. L. X. 158; *those which* : P. L. XI. 28; *which these he breathed*, probably = *these which* : P. L. XII. 374.

adj. whatever; *which way I fly is Hell* : P. L. IV. 75; *which way the wind sways them* : P. L. IV. 982.

*While, (1) *sb.* a short space of time; in adv. phrase; (*a*) *a while, for a time* : P. L. II. 567, 918; III. 280; V. 364, 395; VI. 556, 634; VIII. 2; IX. 744; X. 504; P. R. I. 37; III. 2; S. A. 1632, 1636; S. XI. 3; *gazed a while the ample sky* : P. L. VIII. 258; *down a while he sat* : P. L. X. 447; *softly a while* : S. A. 115; *listened them a while* : C. 551.

(*b*) *the while*, in the mean time : P. L. II. 731; VII. 249; P. R. II. 109; III. 180; S. A. 1728; *mindless the while herself* : P. L. IX. 431; *Adam the while...had wove* : P. L. IX. 838; *all the while* : P. R. II. 362.

(*c*) = time; *one while ... then* : P. R. I. 216.

(2) *conj.* (*a*) during or in the time that : P. L. I. 15, 308; II. 54; III. 135, 187, 395; IV. 685; *while thus he spake* : P. L. II. 309; *thus while he spake* : P. L. IV. 114; *while day arises* : P. L. V. 170; *while time was* : P. L. IV. 6; *while now* : P. L. V. 300.

(*b*) as long as; *while night invests the sea* : P. L. I. 207; *while here shall be our home* : P. L. II. 458; *while they feel vigour* : P. L. VI. 157; *live while ye may* : P. L. IV. 533; *while we can preserve unhurt our minds* : P. L. VI. 443; *while I preserved these locks unshorn* : S. A. 1143.

(*c*) at the same time that : P. L. I. 215, 380; II. 243; VI. 580; VII. 611; VIII. 32; *while they adore me ... the lower still I fall* : P. L. IV. 89; *while I to Hell am thrust* : P. L. IV. 508; *thou where choice leads thee...while I in yonder spring of roses* : P. L. IX. 217; *pitying while he judged* : P. L. X. 1059.

Whilere, *adv.* a short time ago : Cir. 10.

Whilom, *adv.* once, formerly : D. F. I. 24; C. 827.

Whilst, *conj.* (*a*) during the time that : W. S. 9 ; L'A. 70 ; C. 896 ; *whilst yet there was no fear of Jove* : Il P. 30.

(*b*) as long as ; *whilst they stood in first obedience* : S. M. 23.

(*c*) at the same time that : M. W. 61 ; L. 154.

Whip, *sb.* an instrument for flagellation ; *with a whip of scorpions* : P. L. II. 701.

Whirl, *vb. tr.* to bear rapidly away with revolving motion : P. 37.

Whirlpool, *sb.* a vortex of water ; here Scylla ; *shunned Charybis, and by the other Whirlpool steered* : P. L. II. 1020. *See* **Scylla.**

Whirlwind, *sb.* a violent tempest : Ps. LXXXIII. 57 ; in hell ; with more or less clear suggestion of the whirling motion of the air ; *others ... ride the air in whirlwind* : P. L. II. 541 ; *perpetual storms of whirlwind and dire hail* : P. L. II. 589.

fig. of fire ; *whirlwinds of tempestuous fire* : P. L. I. 77 ; *the sport ... of racking whirlwinds* : P. L. II. 182.

attrib. resembling that of a whirlwind ; *with whirlwind sound* : P. L. VI. 749.

Whisper, I. *sb.* a low rustling sound ; *the mild whispers ... of shades, and ... winds, and ... brooks* : L. 136.

II. *vb.* (1) *intr.* (*a*) to speak without uttering voice : P. L. V. 17.

(*b*) to make a low rustling sound ; *a tuft of shade ... whispering soft* : P. L. IV. 326 ; *winds ... whispering play* : P. R. II. 26.

(2) *tr.* to utter in whispers ; *gentle airs whispered it to the woods* : P. L. VIII. 516 ; *the winds ... whispering new joys* : N. O. 66 ; *gentle gales ... whisper whence they stole those balmy spoils* : P. L. IV. 158.

part. adj. **whispering,** making a low rustling sound ; *whispering stream, winds* : P. R. IV. 250 ; L'A. 116.

vbl. sb. **whispering,** whispered talk : P. L. V. 26.

Whist, *past part.* hushed ; *the winds, with wonder whist* : N. O. 64.

Whistle, (1) *sb.* the shrill musical sound produced by forcing the breath through the contracted lips : C. 346.

(2) *vb. intr.* to make this sound ;

the ploughman ... whistles o'er the furrowed land : L'A. 64.

Whit, *sb.* the smallest particle ; *no whit,* not in the least : C. 774.

White, (1) *adj.* (*a*) of the colour, or approaching the colour, of snow : P. R. IV. 76 ; *the white pink* : L. 144 ; *locks white as down* : S. A. 327 ; *her white wings* : P. L. VII. 439 ; *wings, one black, the other white* : S. A. 974.

(*b*) characterized by a white garb : P. L. III. 475.

(2) *sb.* the colour of snow ; *yon western cloud, that draws o'er the blue firmament a radiant white* : P. L. XI. 206 ; *vested all in white* : S. XXIII. 9 ; *my tears have washed a wannish white* : P. 35 ; used of snow ; *the saintly veil of maiden white* : N. O. 42.

Whited, *past part.* made white ; *his own house ... sees his foul inside through his whited skin* : **Hor.** Epist. 6.

White-handed, *adj.* having clean hands, unspotted ; *white-handed Hope* : C. 213.

White-robed (robèd, *disyl.*), *adj.* clothed in white garments ; *white-robed Truth* : D. F. I. 54.

White-thorn, *sb.* the hawthorn : L. 48.

Whither, *adv.* (1) *interrog.* to what place ? ; (*a*) in direct questions : P. L. IX. 473 ; X. 922 ; XI. 282 ; P. R. II. 39 ; S. A. 1541 ; C. 351.

(*b*) in dependent questions : P. L. III. 272 ; VI. 531 ; *I ... strayed I knew not whither* : P. L. VIII. 283 ; *whither* (thou) *went'st I know* : P. L. XII. 610.

(2) *rel.* to which place ; *Go whither ... fate leads thee* : P. L. X. 265 ; *the ford of Jordan, whither all flocked* : P. R. IV. 510.

*Who, *pron.* (*gen.* whose ; *dat.* and *acc.* whom) I. *interrog.* what person ? ; (*a*) in direct questions : P. L. I. 33, 95 ; IV. 748 ; V. 794 ; VI. 297 ; VII. 608 ; VIII. 251 ; IX. 138 ; *whom shall we send* : P. L. II. 402 ; *Whose fault ? Whose but his own ?* : P. L. III. 96.

(*b*) in dependent questions ; *to find who might direct* : P. L. III. 631 ; *Say ... who first* : P. L. I. 376 ; *awaiting who appeared* : P. L. II. 418 ; *who dwelt happy there he staid not to inquire* : P. L. III. 570 ; *to try who is our equal* : P.

L. V. 866 ; *who I was ... knew not* :
P. L. VIII. 270 ; *Who this is we
must learn* : P. R. I. 91.

II. *rel.* (1) introducing a subordinate clause descriptive of the
antecedent : P. L. V. 366 ; VII.
515 ; X. 191 ; XI. 170 ; XII. 134 ;
S. A. 115 ; *his Saints, who silent
stood* : P. L. VI. 882 ; *my celestial.
Patroness, who deigns* : P. L. IX.
21 ; *gen.* whose : P. L. I. 38, 782 ;
III. 385 ; IV. 125, 189 ; *whom* following *than* : P. L. V. 805 ; *than
whom a Spirit more lewd* : P. L.
I. 490 ; *than whom ... none higher
sat* : P. L. II. 299.

(*b*) =him or her ; in introducing speeches where the antecedent is remote : P. L. IV. 576,
634, 834 ; V. 544 ; VI. 149 ; VIII.
618 ; X. 863.

(*c*) the antecedent a beast or
bird ; *a prowling wolf, whom
hunger drives* : P. L. IV. 184 ;
beasts, whom God ... created : P.
L. IX. 556 ; *the birds, who all
things now behold* : P. R. IV.
435.

(*d*) *gen.* whose ; the antecedent
a thing=of which : P. L. I. 233,
670 ; II. 581 ; III. 8, 432, 482 ; IV.
34, 135, 590 ; V. 598 ; VIII. 293 ;
*that forbidden tree whose mortal
taste* : P. L. I. 2 ; *the moon, whose
orb* : P. L. I. 287 ; *the Red-Sea
coast, whose waves* : P. L. I. 306 ;
Heaven, whose high walls : P. L.
II. 343 ; *the dark Abyss, whose
boiling gulf* : P. L. II. 1027 ; *this
round World, whose first convex* :
P. L. III. 419 ; *that globe, whose
hither side* : P. L. III. 722 ;
*eternity, whose end no eye can
reach* : P. L. XII. 556.

(2) introducing a subordinate
clause restricting the antecedent
=that ; *that shepherd who first
taught* : P. L. I. 8 ; *him who next
provokes my anger* : P. L. IX. 174 ;
*deify his power who ... doubted his
empire* : P. L. I. 113 ; *He who
now is sovran* : P. L. I. 246 ; *they
stood who stood* : P. L. III. 102 ;
they only lived who fled : S. A.
264 ; *he whom* : P. L. I. 87 ; *his
high will whom we resist* : P. L. I.
162 ; correlative with *such ; such
a foe is rising, who intends* : P. L.
V. 725 ; *gen.* whose ; *none whose
portion is so small* : P. L. II. 33 ;
Son in whose face : P. L. VI. 681 ;

Him whose just avenging ire : P.
L. VII. 184.

(3) referring to various things
with more or less personification ;
to Appetite : P. L. IX. 1129 ; XI.
518 ; Conscience : P. L. III. 195 ;
the deep : P. L. XI. 848 ; Faith :
S. XIV. 9 ; Nature : C. 728 ; May :
M. M. 3 ; Morning : P. R. IV.
428 ; the ocean : N. O. 67 ; the
stars : C. 113 ; the sun : P. L. V.
139 ; with no personification ;
*among them he a spirit of phrensy
sent, who hurt their minds* : S. A.
1676 ; or the pronoun may=you
whom ; *your dauntless virtue, whom
the pain of death denounced ... de-
terred not* : P. L. IX. 694.

(4) he or they who or that : P.
L. I. 519 ; II. 27 ; III. 520 ; *there
be who faith prefer* : P. L. VI. 143 ;
met who to meet him came : P. L.
X. 349 ; *as huge as whom the fables
name* : P. L. I. 197 ; *worship paid
to whom we hate* : P. L. II. 249 ;
to find who might direct : P. L.
III. 63 ; *except whom God and good
Angels guard* : P. L. II. 1032 ; *the
story of ... who* : Il P. 112 ; *him
whose* ; *sent from whose sovran
goodness I adore* : P. L. VIII. 647 ;
they whose ; *happy whose strength
in thee doth bide* : Ps. LXXXIV. 19.

(5) whoever ; *who overcomes by
force* : P. L. I. 648 ; *whereof who
drinks* : P. L. II. 584 ; *saved who
will* : P. L. III. 173 ; *Who seeks
to lessen thee* : P. L. VII. 613 ;
Who aspires : P. L. IX. 168 ; *Who
can advise may speak* : P. L. III.
42 ; whomever : P. R. II. 395 ;
IV. 164.

Whoever, *pron.* any person whatever, no matter who : P. L. X.
14, 73 ; S. A. 995 ; C. 52.

Whole, (1) *adj.* (*a*) entire, complete :
P. L. VII. 273 ; S. A. 1059, 1651 ;
Heaven's whole circumference : P.
L. II. 353 ; *creation, world, Earth* :
P. L. II. 365 ; XI. 874, 888 ;
Nature's whole wealth : P. L. IV.
207 ; *my whole inheritance* : S. A.
1476 ; *a whole day's journey* : P.
L. IV. 284 ; *success, delight* : P. L.
II. 123 ; VI. 727 ; P. R. I. 208.

(*b*) being every part or unit of
the aggregate, all ; *the whole battalion* : P. L. I. 569 ; *legions, host,
united powers* : P. L. VI. 655 ; S.
A. 262, 1110 ; *race, posterity,
tribe,* etc. : P. L. III. 161, 209,

280 ; IX. 416 ; XII. 269 ; S. A.
265, 1512 ; Hor. Epist. 5 ; following the word it qualifies ; *armies
whole* : P. L. II. 594 ; *them whole,*
all of them : P. L. VI. 875.

(2) *adv.* wholly, entirely : S. A.
809.

Wholesome, *adj.* (*a*) tending to promote health : P. L. X. 847 ;
wholesome thirst : P. L. IV. 330 ;
*harmless, if not wholesome, as a
sneeze* : P. R. IV. 458.

(*b*) favourable to virtue, salutary : F. of C. 16.

Wholly, *adv.* entirely : P. L. IX.
786 ; P. R. II. 207.

Whom. *See* **Who.**

Whore, *sb.* a prostitute ; *fig., the
widowed whore Plurality* : F. of
C. 3 ; of the church : Petr. 3.

Whose. *See* **Who.**

Whoso, *pron.* whoever : P. L. IX.
724 ; *to exempt whomso it pleases
him* : S. A. 311.

Whosoever, *pron.* whatever person ;
of whomsoever taught : P. L. IX.
1068.

*****Why,** *adv.* (**1**) *interrog.* for what
cause, purpose, or reason? ; (*a*)
in direct questions : P. L. V. 38 ;
VI. 424, 609 ; IX. 699, 1155 ; X.
235 ; *Yet why not?* : P. L. IV. 61 ;
*Why should their Lord envy them
that?* : P. L. IV. 516.

(*b*) in dependent questions :
P. L. II. 741 ; XII. 378 ; D. F. I.
42 ; C. 191 ; *I oft have heard men
wonder why thou shouldst wed* :
S. A. 216 ; *listen why* : C. 43.

(**2**) *rel.* for which ; *thy reason
why they should be sought* : P. R.
II. 485 ; *yet hadst no reason why* :
S. I. 12.

Wicked, *adj.* (*a*) evil in principle
and practice, immoral, sinful ; of
persons : P. R. IV. 95 ; Seneca 3 ;
one whole world of wicked sons :
P. L. XI. 875 ; of the fallen
angels : P. L. VI. 277 ; *against
thee* (Satan) *wicked* : P. L. IV.
856 ; of the acts of men ; *wicked
ways, deed* : P. L. XI. 812 ; S. A.
826.

(*b*) being the home or abode of
immorality ; *this wicked earth* :
Ps. LXXXII. 26 ; *tents* : P. L. V.
890.

absol. those who are sinful ;
the wicked : P. L. XII. 541 ; S. A.
1285 ; Ps. I. 2, 11, 12 ; LXXXII.
7.

Wickedness, *sb.* immorality, sinfulness, crime : Ps. V. 10 ; VII. 8,
35 ; *all wickedness is weakness* : S.
A. 834 ; *the tents of wickedness* :
P. L. XI. 608.

Wicker, *adj.* covered with plaited
twigs : C. 338.

Wicket, *sb.* a small gate or door ;
Heaven's wicket : P. L. III. 484.

Wide, (**1**) *adj.* (*a*) having relatively
great extent from side to side :
P. L. I. 762 ; III. 528, 538 ; VII.
301 ; P. R. IV. 27 ; *rivers, river
wide* : L'A. 76 ; Ps. LXXX. 47 ;
wide was the wound : P. L. VIII.
467 ; *his nostril wide* : P. L. X.
280 ; *comp.* : P. L. III. 529 ; *sup.* :
P. L. IV. 382.

(*b*) extended far in every direction, ample, spacious, vast : P. L.
II. 1047 ; V. 88 ; XI. 844 ; P. R.
III. 337 : Il. P. 70 ; C. 945 ; S.
XIX. 2 ; *the wide womb of uncreated Night* : P. L. II. 150 ; *the
waste wide anarchy of Chaos* : P.
L. X. 283 ; *Heaven's wide cham-
pagne, circuit, bounds* : P. L. VI.
2 ; VIII. 100 ; XI. 68 ; *Earth's
wide bounds* : P. L. XII. 371 ; *this
wide World* : P. R. I. 44 ; *province, realm, territory,* etc. : P. L.
VI. 77 ; VII. 148 ; XI. 638 ; XII.
224 ; P. R. I. 118 ; II. 359 ; IV.
81 ; *the wide Ethiopian* : P. L. II.
641 ; *ocean* : P. L. VII. 270 ; H.
B. 7 ; *in wide landskip* : P. L. V.
142 ; *circuit wide* : P. L. V. 287 ;
VIII. 304 ; P. R. III. 254 ; *air* :
P. L. VIII. 141 ; V. Ex. 41.

(*c*) distant from the desired
end ; *their quaint opinions wide* :
P. L. VIII. 78.

(*d*) expanded, fully open ; *wide
... mouths* : P. L. II. 655.

(**2**) *adv.* (*a*) to a great distance :
P. L. I. 724 ; V. 648 ; VII. 89 ;
IX. 203, 245 ; *wide was spread
that war* : P. L. VI. 241 ; *to discover wide that dismal world* : P.
L. II. 571 ; *wide remote* : P. L. IV.
284 ; *waving wide her myrtle
wand* : N. O. 51 ; *that destruction
wide may range* : P. L. IX. 134 ;
far and wide : P. L. II. 133, 519,
1003 ; III. 614 ; IV. 579 ; VI. 773 ;
P. R. III. 72 ; *comp.* : P. L. V.
648.

(*b*) so as to have a large space
from one side to the other, or to
form a large, or the largest possible, opening : P. L. II. 755, 888,

961; III. 84; IV. 77; VI. 577, 860; VII. 575; X. 232; N. O. 148; *the gates wide open stood*: P. L. II. 884; *the gate self-opened wide*: P. L. V. 254; *the gate, wide open*: P. L. X. 419; *Heaven opened wide her ... gates*: P. L. VII. 205; *Tartarus...opens wide his fiery chaos*: P. L. VI. 54; *up they turned wide the celestial soil*: P. L. VI. 510; *comp.*: P. L. XI. 381.

Wide-encroaching, *adj.* entering or intruding widely upon the possessions or rights of another: P. L. X. 581.

Wide-gaping, *adj.* exhibiting a wide chasm, yawning widely: P. L. II. 440.

Wide-hovering, *adj.* hovering over a great extent of territory; *the South-wind ... with black wings wide-hovering*: P. L. XI. 739.

Wide-wasting, *adj.* carrying great or extensive injury, ruin, or destruction: P. L. VI. 253; XI. 487.

Wide-watered, *adj.* bordered by a broad sheet of water: Il P. 75.

Wide-waving, *adj.* moving to and fro over a relatively large circuit: P. L. XI. 121.

Widowed, *part. adj.* bereaved of a husband; *my widowed bed*: S. A. 806; *fig., the widowed whore Plurality*: F. of C. 3.

Widowhood, *sb.* the state of being a widow: S. A. 958.

Wield, *vb. tr.* (*a*) to have power over, sway; *whose resistless eloquence wielded at will that fierce democraty*: P. R. IV. 269; to use in governing; *wield their little tridents*: C. 27.

(*b*) to use, handle; *part wield their arms*: P. L. XI. 643; *wield these elements*: P. L. VI. 221.

(*c*) to deal with or handle with the mind; *how will they wield the mighty frame* (of heaven): P. L. VIII. 80.

Wife, *sb.* (*pl.* wives) a woman joined to a man in wedlock: P. L. VIII. 498; IX. 267; XI. 737; S. A. 957; *the gods of his* (Solomon's) *wives*: P. R. II. 171; *who had Canace to wife*: Il P. 112; *the wife of Thone,* Polydamna: C. 675; *the honoured wife of Winchester*: M. W. 2; of Eve: P. L. X. 198; *man and wife*: P. L. X. 101;

Adam by his wife's allurement fell: P. R. II. 134; of Dalilah; S. A. 724, 725, 885, 1193; *the next I took to wife*: S. A. 227.

Wight, *sb.* a being, person; *living, human, mortal*: P. L. II. 613; D. F. I. 41; P. 14.

Wild, I. *adj.* (1) stormy, turbulent, furious, violent; *wild ·winter, winds*: N. O. 29; C. 87; *uproar, hubbub, work*: P. L. II. 541, 951; III. 710; VI. 698; uncontrolled; *sorrows wild*: D. F. I. 73.

(*b*) filled with stormy and furiously contending elements or forces; used of chaos: P. L. II. 910, 917, 1014; V. 577; VI. 873; VII. 212; X. 477.

(*c*) carried away by passion; *that wild rout that tore the Thracian bard*: P. L. VII. 34.

(2) bold, daring; *incursions wild*; P. R. III. 301.

(3) wanting order and regularity, extravagant, fantastic, disordered; *with thicket overgrown, grotesque and wild*: P. L. IV. 136; *a dance ... extravagant and wild*: P. L. VI. 616; *wild aery flight*: S. A. 974; *Fancy ... misjoining shapes, wild work produces*: P. L. V. 112.

(4) bewildered, distracted, mad; *wild amazement*: C. 356.

(5) not tame or domesticated, feral; *wild beast, beasts*: P. L. IV. 341; VII. 457; P. R. I. 310, 502; S. A. 127, 1403; Ps. LXXX. 55; *wild boars*: S. A. 1138.

(6) savage, uncivilized: P. L. IX. 1117.

(7) growing without culture; *with wild thyme*: L. 40.

(8) produced in a state of nature, not due to training or culture: L'A. 134.

(9) uninhabited, uncultivated, desert: P. L. XI. 284; *this wild surrounding waste*: C. 403; *forest, woods, desert,* etc.: P. L. VII. 458; IX. 910; XII. 216; P. R. I. 193; II. 109, 232, 304; P. 51; C. 312; used of the garden of Eden; *this enclosure wild*: P. L. IX. 543; of hell; *the dismal situation waste and wild*: P. L. I. 60; *yon dreary plain, forlorn and wild*: P. L. I, 180; *a frozen continent ... wild*: P. L. II. 588; of the outside of the universe; *a boundless continent ... wild*: P. L. III. 424.

II. *sb.* (*a*) an uninhabited tract or uncultivated region, a wilderness : P. R. I. 331; IV. 523; *sandy perilous wilds* : C. 424; *the wild of southmost Abarim* : P. L. I. 407.

(*b*) wildness, a state of growing too luxuriantly and without restraint : P. L. IX. 912.

III. *adv.* extravagantly, prodigally : P. L. V. 297.

Wilderness, *sb.* (1) an uninhabited and barren or uncultivated region, desert : P. L. II. 943; IV. 342; *steep, desert* : P. L. IV. 135; C. 209; where the Israelites wandered ; *wide, wasteful* : P. L. XII. 224; Ps. CXXXVI. 58; where Christ was tempted by Satan : P. L. XI. 383; P. R. I. 156, 291; II. 307, 384; IV. 372, 395, 543, 600; *wild, savage, vexed* : P. R. II. 232; III. 23; IV. 416.

(*b*) applied *fig.* to the world or to life in the world ; *bring back through the world's wilderness long-wandered Man* : P. L. XII. 313; *Eden raised in the waste Wilderness* : P. R. I. 7.

(2) a confused and bewildering growth ; *cassia, nard, and balm, a wilderness of sweets* : P. L. V. 294.

(3) the state of being covered by a disorderly and too luxuriant growth of vegetation ; *these paths and bowers...keep from wilderness* : P. L. IX. 245.

Wile, *sb.* (*a*) a means of practising deceit, trick, stratagem ; *the wile of unblessed enchanter* : C. 906; *pl.* : P. L. II. 51; P. R. III. 442; S. A. 402; *all our plots and wiles* : P. L. II. 193; *wiles of foe or seeming friend* : P. L. X. 11; *which ... might serve his wiles* : P. L. IX. 85; *the Tempter foiled in all his wiles* : P. R. I. 6; *subtle, snaky, hellish, serpent* : P. L. IX. 184; P. R. I. 120, 175; III. 5; *circling* : S. A. 871.

(*b*) with no evil import ; *wanton wiles*, playful tricks : L'A. 27.

Wilful, *adj.* resulting from the exercise of one's own will, voluntary, intentional, deliberate ; *wilful barrenness, crime* : P. L. X. 1042; XII. 619.

Wilfully, *adv.* voluntarily, intentionally, deliberately : P. L. V. 244; P. R. I. 225.

*Will, I. *sb.* (1) the faculty of the mind by which it chooses and purposes : P. L. V. 539, 549; IX. 350, 355, 1127; X. 825; P. R. I. 469; *the unconquerable will* : P. L. I. 106; *reasoned high of ... Will, and Fate* : P. L. II. 559; *Will and Reason ... made passive both* : P. L. III. 108; *as if Predestination overruled their will* : P. L. III. 115; *thy will chose freely* : P. L. IV. 71; *his will though free* : P. L. V. 236; *thy will by nature free* : P. L. V. 526; *God left free the Will* : P. L. IX. 351; *my will concurred not to my being* : P. L. X. 746; *thy husband's will* : P. L. X. 195; *lets her* (woman's) *will rule* : P. L. IX. 1184; God's will ; *to incline his will* : P. L. XI. 145.

free will : P. L. II. 560; IV. 66; V. 236; IX. 1174; X. 9, 46; *free-will* : P. L. VIII. 636.

(2) an act of willing, volition ; *saved...not of will in him, but grace in me* : P. L. III. 174; of God ; *as the will of God ordained* : P. L. IX. 343; of Jove ; *if Jove's will have linked that amorous power to thy soft lay* : S. I. 7.

(3) what one wishes or determines shall be done, wish, choice, desire : S. A. 1450; *will of wandering* : P. L. IX. 1145; *thinking to terrify me to thy will* : P. R. IV. 497; *uxorious to thy will* : S. A. 945; *then did I leave them to their will* : Ps. LXXXI. 49.

(*b*) what God wills to be done or to come to pass ; God's purpose, design, command, or determination : P. L. I. 211; II. 1025; IV. 897; VI. 816; X. 549; *omnipotent decree, the Victor's will* : P. L. II. 199; *so was His will pronounced* : P. L. II. 351; *such was heard declared the Almighty's will* : P. L. VII. 181; *he attends the will of his great Father* : P. L. III. 270; *to do thy will* : P. L. X. 69; *to do my Father's will* : P. R. II. 259; *the contrary to His high will* : P. L. I. 161; *his great authentic will ... to bring* : P. L. III. 656; *to subdue us to his will* : P. L. VI. 427; *by his permissive will* : P. L. III. 685; *declar'st thy will fulfilled* : P. L. VI. 728.

(*c*) God's purpose, decree, or command regarding man : P. L. III. 184; IX. 728; XI. 308; XII.

237; C. 600; S. ii. 12; *the Almighty thus pronounced his sovran will*: P. L. xi. 83; *transgress his will for one restraint*: P. L. i. 31; *observe immutably his sovran will*: P. L. vii. 79; *men obedient to his will*: P. L. xii. 246; *teach his final will*: P. R. i. 461; *I argue not against Heaven's hand or will*: S. xxii. 7; *I must not quarrel with the will of highest dispensation*: S. A. 60.

(4) free disposal, discretion; *thy punishment, then, justly is at his will*: P. L. x. 768.

(b) *at will*, at pleasure, as one chooses: P. L. ix. 855; P. R. ii. 167, 383; iv. 269; S. A. 97; H. B. 1; *ruled in manner at our will the affairs of Earth*: P. R. i. 50; *Nature...played at will her virgin fancies*: P. L. v. 295; *have at will*, to have at one's free disposal; *these mid-hours ... I have at will*: P. L. v. 377.

II. *vb.* (*pres. part.* willing; *ind. 3d sing.* wills) (1) to make an object of choice or purpose; *hearts ...willing or no, who will but what they must*: P. L. v. 533; *to will the same with me*: P. L. x. 826; *what she wills to do or say*: P. L. viii. 549; *absol.; saved who will*: P. L. iii. 173.

(2) to decree; *as Nature wills, Night bids us rest*: P. L. iv. 633.

part. adj. **willing**; (a) ready, inclined; *some other able, and as willing*: P. L. iii. 211; *willing feet*: P. L. iii. 73.

as *adv.* gladly, voluntarily; *whether they serve willing or no*: P. L. v. 533; *the willinger I go*: P. L. ix. 382.

(b) cheerfully given or borne; *willing hearts*: P. R. i. 222; *chains*: V. Ex. 52.

III. *vb.* (*pres. 2d sing.* wilt: P. L. ii. 866; iii. 162; iv. 896, etc.; *3d sing.* will; *pret.* would; *2d sing.* wouldst: P. L. iv. 890; ix. 300, etc.; contracted to *I'll* with the preceding pronoun: U. C. ii. 18; C. 228, 513, 606; *'twill*; C. 690) as auxiliary with simple infinitive; (1) in the principal clause; (a) denoting desire, preference, or consent: P. L. viii. 401; S. A. 1353; *Will ye submit your necks*: P. L. v. 787; *they know not, nor will understand*: Ps. LXXXII.

17; *if you the truth will have*: Ariosto ii. 3.

(b) denoting determination; *I will not argue that*: P. R. ii. 94; *I will not come*: S. A. 1332.

(c) denoting a promise: P. L. x. 179; *I will renew his lapsed powers*: P. L. iii. 175; *I for his sake will leave thy bosom*: P. L. iii. 238; *I will bring thee*: P. L. iv. 470.

(d) denoting simple futurity; in 1st person: P. L. iv. 112; in the 2d and 3d persons: P. L. iv. 853; v. 312; ix. 939; in direct question; *will God incense his ire*: P. L. ix. 692; *whom will he next?*: P. L. ix. 950; *What woman will you find*: P. R. ii. 208; nearer in meaning to certainty or inevitability as regards the future; *trial will come unsought*: P. L. ix. 366; *thou wilt bring me*: P. L. ii. 866; *there will be room*: P. L. iv. 383.

(e) denoting customary action; C. 750; *what will not ... revenge descend to?*: P. L. ix. 168; *yet this will prayer*: P. L. xi. 146; *sometimes nations will decline*: P. L. xii. 97; *the wisest...will be ever timorous*: P. R. iii. 240; *when they list, would creep*: P. L. ii. 656; *he on the tender grass would sit*: C. 625.

(2) in dependent clauses; (a) *will* in sb. adj. or adv. clause: P. L. ii. 393; x. 1025; *his wrath, which one day will destroy ye both*: P. L. ii. 734; *saved who will*: P. L. iii. 173; *when all these delights will vanish*: P. L. iv. 368; *forbid who will*: P. L. v. 62; *flowers that never will in other climate grow*: P. L. xi. 274; *would* in similar clause: P. L. iii. 106; iv. 51; v. 856; P. R. iv. 453; S. A. 66; *her worth, that would be wooed*: P. L. viii. 503.

(b) in conditional clause; *will* in the protasis; the apodosis containing *shall*: P. L. iii. 195; containing *will*: Il P. 77; containing the imper.; *there stand, if thou wilt stand*: P. R. iv. 551; *would* in the protasis; the apodosis containing *can*: P. R. iv. 331; containing the imper.: P. L. ix. 367; P. R. ii. 426; the apodosis ellipt.: P. L. x. 725; S. A. 1214. *would* in the apodosis, the protasis containing the ind.: P.

L. VI. 602 ; P. R. III. 18 ; containing the subj. : P. L. III. 468 ; VIII. 582 ; IX. 978 ; P. R. II. 321 ; C. 219, 702 ; containing *could* : P. L. X. 954 ; containing *should* : P. L. IX. 913 ; P. R. II. 216 ; III. 13 ; C. 723 ; containing *could* and *should* : P. L. II. 138 ; the protasis omitted or ellipt. : P. L. II. 186, 370 ; III. 726 ; IV. 96 ; VI. 500, 868 ; IX. 102, 123 ; X. 821.

(*c*) in an exclamation containing a wish ; *would thou hadst hearkened to my words* : P. L. IX. 1134 ; *how gladly would I meet mortality* : P. L. X. 775.

(*d*) in dependent question : P. L. XI. 786 ; *to draw what further would be learned* : P. L. IV. 533 ; *foretold...what would come to pass* : P. L. X. 38.

See **Good-will.**

Willingly, *adv.* of one's own choice, voluntarily, freely, gladly : P. L. V. 466 ; IX. 1167 ; XI. 885 ; P. R. I. 45 ; III. 216 ; S. A. 258, 1477, 1665.

Willow, *sb.* the plant *Salix* : C. 891 ; L. 42.

Wily, *adj.* (*a*) subtle, cunning, crafty ; *the wily snake* : P. L. IX. 91 ; *the wily Adder* : P. L. IX. 625 ; *my wily trains* : C. 151.

(*b*) executed with cunning, skill, or art (?) ; *the nymphs ... dance ... with wily glance* : C. 884.

Win, *vb.* (*pret.* and *past part.* won) I. *tr.* (1) to gain against difficulties or competitors : S. XX. 4 ; *winning cheap the high repute* : P. L. II. 472 ; *more glory will be won* : P. L. IV. 853 ; *rest from labour won* : P. L. XI. 375 ; *opinion wins the cause* : Hor. Epist. 4.

(2) to gain or secure by victory, take possession of : P. L. VI. 160 ; XII. 262 ; P. R. III. 156, 297 ; IV. 469 ; *to win the Mount of God* : P. L. VI. 88 ; *this fair empire won of Earth and Air* : P. R. I. 63 ; *the son of Macedonian Philip ...won Asia* : P. R. III. 33 ; *who thus shall Canaan win* : P. L. XII. 269 ; *these boasted trophies won on me* : S. A. 470 ; *glory, honour ... won* : S. A. 1099, 1102 ; *to win the fairest of her sex, Angelica* : P.R. III. 340.

(*b*) used of Christ in conflict with Satan : P. R. I. 154.

(*c*) to take as victor ; used of

God : P. L. II. 978 ; *the rising World of waters ... won from the void and formless Infinite!* : P. L. III. 12.

(3) to gain by persuasion or other influence : P. L. IX. 674 ; X. 372 ; P. R. IV. 530 ; S. A. 1012 ; L'A. 124 ; *his words ... too easy entrance won* : P. L. IX. 734 ; *with hand silence ... won* : P. L. X. 459 ; *won so much on Eve* : P. R. IV. 5 ; *to win from me my capital secret* : S. A. 393.

(*b*) to persuade, influence, or prevail on (a person) : P. L. IX. 131, 991 ; P. R. IV. 530 ; with *acc.* and *prep. inf.* : P. L. XII. 502 ; S. A. 1411 ; L'A. 148 ; *that won who saw to wish her stay* : P. L. VIII. 43 ; *won to think her part was done* : N. O. 104 ; with *inf.* omitted : P. R. I. 279.

(4) to be victorious in : P. R. III. 73 ; or the sense may be (1) : P. L. VI. 290.

(5) to make or accomplish by effort : *Satan ... wins his way* : P. L. II. 1016.

(6) to gain the respect, esteem or love of : P. L. II. 762 ; VIII 503.

II. *intr.* to gain the victory, be successful : P. L. II. 122, 123 ; in a moral sense : P. R. I. 426.

part. adj. **winning,** charming, attractive : P. L. IV. 479 ; *graces, words, charms* : P. L. VIII. 81 ; P. R. I. 222 ; II. 213.

Winchester, *sb.* John Paulet, fifth Marquis of Winchester : M. W. 2.

Wind, *sb.* (1) a current of air : P. L. I. 235 ; II. 717 ; III. 439 ; IV. 982 ; VII. 431 ; X. 1074 ; XI. 312 ; P. R. II. 26 ; IV. 429 ; S. A. 719, 961, 1062, 1070, 1647 ; N. O. 64 ; C. 49 : *to the winds they set their corners* : P. L. X. 664 ; *nor slept the winds within their stony caves* : P. R. IV. 413 ; *winds under ground* : P. L. VI. 196 ; *a meteor streaming in the wind* : P. L. I. 537 ; *the sport of winds* : P. L. III. 493 : *where the wind veers oft* : P. L. IX. 514 ; *fear of death deliver to the winds* : P. L. IX. 989 ; *his praise, ye Winds ... breath soft or loud* : P. L. V. 192 ; *a violent cross wind* : P. L. III. 487 ; *subterranean* : P. L. I. 231 ; *equinoctial* : P. L. II. 637 ; *fierce, blustering,* *warring*, etc.: P. L. I. 305 ; II. 286, 905 ; IV. 560 ; VII. 213 ; C. 87 ; L. 13 ; Hor. O. 7 ; *moist and keen* : P. L. X. 1065 ; P. R. I. 317 ; *noisome* : A. 49 ; *cool, soft* : P. L. V. 655 ; X. 98 ; *frolic, whispering, rocking* : L'A. 18, 116 ; Il P. 126 ; *envious, felon, wanton* : P. L. XI. 15 ; L. 91, 137 ; *fig.* : L. 126.

(*b*) as bearing odours ; *winds... odours fanned from their soft wings* : P. R. II. 363.

(*c*) with an adjective indicating direction ; *eastern* : P. L. I. 341 ; *north-east* : P. L. IV. 161 ; *west* : C. 989 ; *Ponent* : P. L. X. 704 ; *polar* : P. L. V. 269 ; X. 289.

(*d*) *fig.* that which is light as wind ; *with wind of airy threats* : P. L. VI. 282.

(*e*) *fig.* the excitement of passion ; *not only tears ... but high winds worse within began to rise* : P. L. IX. 1122.

(*f*) *within the wind of*, near, close to : P. L. VI. 309.

(2) one of the four points of the compass ; *nations besides from all the quartered winds* : P. R. IV. 202 ; *toward the four winds* : P.L. II. 516 ; *from all winds ... the cited dead ... shall hasten* : P. L. III. 326.

(3) air in motion by artificial means : P. L. I. 708.

(4) flatulence : P. L. VII. 130.

See **North-wind, South-wind.**

Wind, *vb.* (*pret.* and *past part.* wound) I. *intr.* to rise or go in a devious course : P. L. IV. 545 ; *wind out of*, to extricate oneself from by turning and twisting about : P. L. VI. 659.

II. *tr.* (1) to take in a devious course ; *winds with ease ... his oblique way* : P. L. III. 563.

(2) to cause to pass spirally round a fixed centre : *the adamantine spindle ... on which the fate of gods and men is wound* : A. 67 ; to twine, wreathe ; *to wind the woodbine* : P. L. IX. 215.

(*b*) *refl.* to twine the body round and round and so ascend as a serpent : *about the mossy trunk I wound me soon* : P. L. IX. 589.

(3) *refl.* to worm ; *wind me into the easy-hearted man* : C. 163.

part. adj. winding ; (*a*) devious : P. R. III. 256 ; used of music ; *many a winding bout of linked sweetness* : L'A. 139.

(*b*) **spiral** ; *Triton's winding shell* : C. 873.

vbl. sb. **winding,** a path that turns and bends (?) : A. 47.

Wind, *vb. tr.* to blow ; *fig., the grey-fly winds her sultry horn* : L. 28.

Window, *sb.* an opening in the wall of a building for the admission of light and air : P. L. IV. 191 ; L'A. 46 ; *storied windows richly dight* : Il P. 159 ; *fig.* of the clouds as letting out the rain ; *heaven his windows shut* : P. L. XI. 849.

Windy, *adj.* (*a*) tempestuous, stormy : P. L. III. 440.

(*b*) fleeting, unsubstantial, empty : S. A. 1574.

Wine, *sb.* the fermented juice of the grape : P. L. I. 502 ; IX. 793 ; S. A. 443, 541 ; C. 106 ; S. XX. 10 ; *drunk with wine* : S. A. 1670 ; *lords are lordliest in their wine* : S. A. 1418 ; *mirth, high cheer, and wine* : S. A. 1613 ; *the sweet poison of misused wine* : C. 47 ; *wine, that fragrant smell diffused* : P. R. II. 350 ; *wines of Setia* : P. R. IV. 117 ; *strongest* : S. A. 543 ; *new* : P. L. IX. 1008 ; possibly the unfermented juice of the grape ; *their corn and wine abounds* : Ps. IV. 36 ; *corn, wine, and oil* : P. L. XII. 19 ; *corn ... oil, and wine* : P. R. III. 259.

Wine-offering, *sb.* wine offered in sacrifice : P. L. XII. 21.

Wine-press, *sb.* a press for squeezing the juice from grapes : P. R. IV. 16.

Wing, I. *sb.* (1) the limb of an animal adapted for flight : P. L. VII. 389, 477 ; VIII. 351 ; *the swan ... her white wings* : P. L. VII. 439 ; *their painted wings* : P. L. VII. 434 ; *Ye Birds ... bear on your wings ... his praise* : P. L. V. 199 ; *some of serpent kind ... added wings* : P. L. VII. 484 ; *fig., their serpent wings* : S. XV. 8 ; *sing.* for *pl.* : P. L. VII. 429 ; of the spirit of God as a bird ; *his brooding wings the Spirit of God outspread* : P. L. VII. 235.

(*b*) the analogous part of an angel : P. L. II. 949 ; III. 627 ; IV. 974 ; N. O. 114 ; Il P. 52 ; *veiled with his gorgeous wings* : P. L. V. 250 ; *six wings he wore, to shade his lineaments divine* : P. L. V. 277 ; *with both wings veil their*

eyes: P. L. III. 382; *wings ...
sprinkled with gold*: P. L. III.
641; *mighty, indefatigable*: P. L.
I. 20; II. 408; *expanded, spread*:
P. L. I. 225, 1046; *rustling*: P.
L. I. 768; *wearied*: P. L. III. 73;
sing. for *pl.*: P. L. II. 72; of the
four cherubic shapes: P. L. VI.
755, 771; *their starry wings*:
P. L. VI. 827; probably also:
P. L. VII. 218; of the figures on
the ark of the covenant: Ps.
LXXX. 6; *between the wings of two
bright Cherubim*: P. L. XII. 253;
of Adam and Eve imagining themselves becoming divine: P. L. IX.
1010; of Sin: P. L. X. 244.

(c) the analogous part of a
mythical or personified being: S.
XIV. 11; *harpies' wings*: P. R. II.
403; *wing of hippogrif*: P. R. IV.
541; *Night with her sullen wing*:
P. R. I. 500; *Darkness spreads his
jealous wings*: L'A. 6; *the wings
of silence*: C. 249; *Wisdom's self
...lets grow her wings*: C. 378;
Love...waves his purple wings:
P. L. IV. 764; *Fame... his wings*:
S. A. 973; *Sleep*: Il P. 148;
*white-handed Hope... with golden
wings*: C. 214; *sing.* for *pl.*: S.
II. 2; *the flight of Pegasean wing*:
P. L. VII. 4; *the meek-eyed Peace
...with turtle wing*: N. O. 50;
Verse must send her wing: S.
XIII. 9.

(d) as an emblem of swiftness;
to thy speed add wings: P. L. II.
700.

(e) used *fig.* of the wind: P. L.
II. 906; *with black wings*: P. L.
XI. 738; *gust of wings*, winged
gust: L. 93; as bearing or dis-
pensing perfume: P. L. IV. 157;
VIII. 516; P. R. II. 365; *west
winds with musky wing*: C. 989.

(2) the act or manner of flying,
flight: P. L. II. 132; *with steady
wing*: P. L. V. 268; *shaves with
level wing the deep*: P. L. II. 634;
first lighted from his wing: P. L.
X. 316; *swiftest wing*, swiftest in
flight: P. L. VI. 535; in various
phrases; *on* or *upon wing* or *the
wing*, in flight, flying: P. L. I.
332, 345; II. 529; VI. 74; *joy is
ever on the wing*: P. 5; *on main
wing*: P. L. VI. 243; *puts on swift
wings*: P. L. II. 631; *on full sail
of wing*: P. R. IV. 582; *hurried
on viewless wing*: P. 50.

(b) *fig.* of poetic flight; *with
prosperous wing full summed*: P.
R. I. 14; *thee I revisit now with
bolder wing*: P. L. III. 13; *damp
my intended wing*: P. L. IX. 45.

(c) *of wing*, having the power
of flight: P. L. VII. 394.

(3) one of the two outside divisions of an army: P. L. I. 617;
II. 885; VI. 362, 778; P. R. III.
309; IV. 66.

II. *vb.* (*part. disyl.* winged except: P. L. VII. 199; C. 730) *tr.*
(a) to furnish with wings: P. L.
v. 55, 498; *a Seraph winged*: P.
L. v. 277; *winged with speed*, in
swift flight: P. L. I. 674.
  fig., sighs ... winged for Heaven:
P. L. XI. 7; *time ... with swiftest
minutes winged*: P. L. X. 91;
vengeance, winged from God: P.
L. VI. 279.

(b) to traverse in flight: P. L.
II. 842; *to wing the desolate Abyss*:
P. L. IV. 936; *wing the region*: P.
L. VII. 425.

(c) to make or accomplish by
flying; *he wings his way*: P. L.
III. 87.

(d) to feather an arrow; *fig.,
the thunder, winged with red
lightning*: P. L. I. 175.
  part. adj. **winged**; (a) having
or furnished with wings; *winged
Warrior, Saint*, etc.: P. L. IV.
576; v. 247, 468; VII. 199; Cir.
1; *heralds, messenger*: P. L. I.
752; III. 229; VII. 572; *chariots,
steeds*: P. L. VII. 199; XI. 706.

(b) accomplished by flying: P.
L. II. 944; or with the swiftness
of flight; *winged speed, expedition*: P. L. IV. 788; v. 744; S. A.
1283.

(c) abounding with wings, swarming with birds; *winged air*: C.
730.

See **Angel-wing, Eagle-winged,
Golden-winged.**

Wink, *vb. intr.* to close the eyes so
as not to see; *fig., bid me hope
Danger will wink on Opportunity*:
C. 401.

Winnow, *vb. tr.* to separate (grain)
from husks; here *fig.* probably
with the meaning to part and
pass through; *with quick fan
winnows the buxom air*: P. L. v.
270.

Winter, *sb.* the cold season of the
year: P. R. I. 317; *winter wild*:

N. O. 29; *winter's frost, nip* : S.
A. 1577 ; M. W. 36 ; *decrepit* : P.
L. x. 655 ; personified : D. F. I.
4, 28.

Wipe, *vb. tr.* to remove by gently
rubbing : P. L. v. 131 ; xii. 645 ;
L. 181 ; *wipe away,* to remove,
efface : D. F. I. 12.

Wire, *sb.* the string of a musical
instrument ; *golden wire, wires* :
P. L. vii. 597 ; V. Ex. 38 ; S. M.
13.

Wisdom, *sb.* (1) the power of forming
the fittest and truest judgements;
(*a*) the wisdom of God as evidenced in forming and executing
his designs : P. L. iii. 706 ; *by his
wisdom did create the painted
heavens* : Ps. cxxxvi. 17 ; *whose
wisdom had ordained good out of
evil to create* : P. L. vii. 187 ;
highest Wisdom, God ·himself : P.
L. vii. 83 ; S. A. 1747.

the expression of the wisdom of
God in the personality of Christ ;
*Son who art alone my word, my
wisdom* : P. L. iii. 170.

personified as the regulating
principle present with God before
and during the creation of the
world : P. L. vii. 9, 10.

(*b*) of Christ on earth, knowledge and sagacity : P. R. i. 68 ;
iv. 222, 528 ; spiritual sagacity ;
to vanquish by wisdom hellish wiles :
P. R. i. 175.

concr. the expression of wisdom,
wise words ; *to hear attent thy
wisdom* : P. R. i. 386 ; *we have
heard ... his wisdom full of grace
and truth* : P. R. ii. 34.

(*c*) of Satan : P. L. iv. 914 ;
*thy wisdom ... gained what war
hath lost* : P. L. x. 873.

(*d*) of men : P. L. iv. 293; vii.
130 ; xi. 636 ; xii. 154 ; P. R.
iii. 91 ; S. A. 57, 207, 1010 ; *what
is strength without a double share
of wisdom ?* : S. A. 54 ; *how beauty
is excelled by manly grace and
wisdom* : P. L. iv. 491 ; *true
wisdom* : P. R. iv. 319 ; (Solomon)
for wealth and wisdom famed : P.
L. xii. 332.

concr. a wise person : P. R. ii.
431 ; an act or choice showing
wisdom ; *not to know at large of
things remote...is the prime wisdom*:
P. L. viii. 194.

(*e*) *adder's wisdom,* the cunning
of an adder : S. A. 936.

(*f*) personified : P. L. viii.
552, 563 ; *though Wisdom wake,
Suspicion sleeps at Wisdom's gate*:
P. L. iii. 686, 687 ; *Wisdom's self
oft seeks to sweet retired solitude* :
C. 375 ; *black, staid Wisdom's hue*:
Il P. 16.

(2) knowledge gained through
the senses : P. L. iii. 50; shown in
philosophical discussion ; P. L. ii.
565 ; knowledge of things human
and divine : P. L. xii. 576 ; the
knowledge of all things such as
God possesses : P. L. ix. 725 ;
perhaps personified ; *thou open'st
Wisdom's way ... though secret she
retire* : P. L. ix. 809.

Wisdom-giving, *adj.* conferring the
power of knowing all things ; *O...
wisdom-giving Plant* : P. L. ix.
679.

Wise, I. *adj.* (1) having the power
of discerning and judging rightly ;
possessed of knowledge, discernment, discretion, and judgement;
(*a*) of God : P. L. ii. 155 ; P. R.
i. 486 ; *the Maker wise* : P. L. ix.
338 ; *Creator wise* : P. L. ix. 938;
x. 889 ; *in all things wise and just*:
P. L. x. 7 ; *just and wise* : Ps.
vii. 41 ; nearer to the meaning
skilful ; *wise to frustrate all our
plots* : P. L. ii. 193.

(*b*) of angels : P. L. ii. 202 ;
iv. 907.

(*c*) of man : P. L. viii. 578 ; x.
881 ; P. R. ii. 468 ; iv. 302, 322 ;
wise and good : S. xii. 12 ; *more
wise* : P. L. ix. 311 ; *wise or unwise* : P. R. iii. 115 ; *wise and
valiant* : P. R. iv. 143 ; *riches ...
the wise man's cumbrance* : P. R.
ii. 454 ; *Virgin wise and pure* : S.
ix. 14 ; *the wise Latona* : A. 20 ;
wise Ulysses : C. 637 ; *Oh that my
people would be wise* : Ps. lxxxi.
53 ; *be wise at length* : Ps. ii. 22 ;
be wise : C. 813 ; or *adv.* (?) : S.
A. 212 ; of Christ on earth ; *to the
utmost of mere man both wise and
good* : P. R. iv. 535.

comp. *wiser far than Solomon* :
P. R. ii. 205.

sup. *wisest men* : S. A. 210, 867,
1034 ; *wisest and best men* : S. A.
759 ; *the wisest heart of Solomon* :
P. L. i. 400 ; *the heart of wisest
Solomon* : P. R. ii. 170 ; *wisest
Fate* : N. O. 149.

(*d*) of nature ; *Nature, wise and
frugal* : P. L. viii. 26.

(*e*) of animals : P. L. VII. 425 ; *the Serpent wise* : P. L. IX. 867.

(2) suited to a man of wisdom, sage, grave, serious : P. L. XI. 666.

(3) marked, dictated, or guided by wisdom : P. L. IV. 910 ; S. XXI. 12 ; *a wise appetite* : C. 705 ; *wise are all his ways* : P. L. III. 680 ; *pretending first wise to fly pain* : P. L. IV. 948 ; *sup., what she wills to do ... seems wisest* : P. L. VIII. 550.

(4) possessing knowledge ; *be lowly wise* : P. L. VIII. 173 ; *sup.* a blending of (1) and (3) : P. R. IV. 276, 293.

(*b*) possessing such knowledge as God possesses, esp. the knowledge of good and evil : P. L. IX. 683, 759, 778 ; said of the forbidden tree : P. L. IX. 679.

(*c*) possessing supreme knowledge and discernment ; *wise Minerva* : C. 448.

(*d*) possessed of great astrological learning ; *the wise men ... from the East* : P. R. I. 250.

(*e*) skilled in the art of music : V. Ex. 48.

absol. a person possessed of knowledge or right judgement ; *the wise* : P. R. III. 58 ; S. A. 652 ; *sup.* : P. R. III. 240.

II. *sb.* wisdom : P. L. IV. 886, 904 ; P. R. III. 11.

See **Worldly-wise.**

‾**Wisely,** *adv.* (*a*) with sound judgement, prudently, judiciously : D. F. I. 73 ; S. IX. 2 ; of God : P. L. VIII. 73 ; *comp., God hath wislier armed his vengeful ire* : P. L. X. **1023.**

(*b*) knowingly, with skill ; *far events full wisely could presage* : V. Ex. 70.

‾**Wish, I.** *sb.* (*a*) desire ; *when to his wish* : P. L. IX. 423 ; *to our wish* : S. A. 1539 ; *to whom ... our wishes bend* : A. 6 ; *effect shall end our wish* : P. L. VI. 493 ; the desire expressed in words ; *O that I never had! fond wish too late!* : S. A. 228 ; *so might the wrath! fond wish!* : P. L. X. 834.

(*b*) something desired : P. L. VI. 818 ; *to find his wish* : P. L. IX. 258 ; *thy wish exactly to thy heart's desire* : P. L. VIII. 451 ; *to give his enemies their wish* : P. L. II. 157.

II. *vb.* (*disyl.* wishèd : P. L. I.

208 ; VI. 150 ; C. 574, 950) (1) *intr.* to have or express a desire : P. L. XI. 181.

(2) *tr.* to desire, long for : P. L. VIII. 43 ; X. 454, 901 ; *your company along I will not wish* : S. A. 1414 ; *I should have forced thee soon wish other arms* : S. A. 1096 ; *death to be wished* : P. L. IX. 714 ; with clause : P. L. VI. 842 ; IX. 1025 ; P. R. IV. 376 ; C. 558 ; *wished his hap might find Eve separate* : P. L. IX. 421 ; *yet wish it had not been* : S. A. 1077 ; *absol.* : P. L. IX. 422 ; with elliptical phrase, the construction probably *acc.* and *inf.* : P. L. VIII. 63 ; S. A. 1127 ; *wish thee long* : M. M. 10 ; with *prep. inf.* : P. L. II. 606 ; *wish to die* : W. S. 16.

part. adj. **wishèd,** longed for, earnestly desired : C. 574, 950 ; *morn, hour* : P. L. I. 208 ; VI. 150.

Wit, *sb.* (*a*) judgement, understanding, imagination ; *virtue, wisdom, valour, wit* : S. A. 1010 ; rather cleverness of mind ; *enjoy your dear wit, and gay rhetoric* : C. 790.

(*b*) ingenuity, skill ; *judge the prize of wit or arms* : L'A. 123.

(*c*) cunning, craftiness ; *the wily snake ... his wit and native subtlety* : P. L. IX. 93.

(*d*) *pl.* men of genius and learning ; *Greece ... native to famous wits* : P. R. IV. 241 ; *deepest spirits and choicest wits* : V. Ex. 22.

Witch, *sb.* a person who practices sorcery ; *Lapland witches* : P. L. II. 665.

Witchery, *sb.* sorcery, enchantment : C. 523.

*****With,** *prep.* (1) of opposition ; against ; *when Egypt with Assyria strove* : P. L. I. 721 ; *to pursue vain war with Heaven* : P. L. II. 9 ; *to contend with Spirits of Heaven* : P. L. II. 687 ; *with the Mightiest raised me to contend* : P. L. I. 99 ; *decrees and degrees jar not with liberty* : P. L. V. 793.

(2) of association or connection ; with many shades of meaning in noting the relations of words ; (*a*) of accompaniment : P. L. I. 419 ; *he with his rebellious rout* : P. L. I. 749 ; *they ... with thousands trooping came* : P. L. I. 760 ; *Evil go with thee along* : P. L. VI. 275.

superfluous; *without more train accompanied than with his own complete perfections* : P. L. v. 352.

(*b*) of identity of place; *would thou hadst ... stayed with me* : P. L. IX. 1135; *with the serpent meeting* : P. L. X. 879.

by the side of; *with him enthroned sat* : P. L. II. 961; *sat him down with his great Father* : P. L. VII. 588; *while I sit with thee* : P. L. VIII. 210.

(*c*) of junction, etc.; *where Heaven with Earth and Ocean meets* : P. L. IV. 546; *your gloomy bounds confine with Heaven* : P. L. II. 977; *Europe with Asia joined* : P. L. X. 311; of union; *his end with mine involved* : P. L. II. 807; of combination; *Earth with Hell to mingle* : P. L. II. 383; *flesh to mix with flesh* : P. L. VIII. 629; *with the centre mix the pole* : P. L. VII. 215; *affliction and dismay mixed with obdurate pride* : P. L. I. 58; *words interwove with sighs* : P. L. I. 621; *his throne itself mixed with Tartarean sulphur* : P. L. II. 69.

(*d*) of addition : P. L. II. 20; *all our woe, with loss of Eden* : P. L. I. 4; *thou silent Night, with this her solemn bird* : P. L. IV. 655; *his three sons, with their three wives* : P. L. XI. 737; *empire with revenge enlarged* : P. L. IV. 390.

(*e*) of simultaneousness : P. R. II. 401; S. A. 331; *with that thy gentle hand seized mine* : P. L. IV. 488; *with that care lost went all his fear* : P. L. II. 48; *a grove ... sprung up with this their change* : P. L. X. 548; at the same time as; *with the setting sun dropt* : P. L. I. 744; *with the year seasons return* : P. L. III. 40; *the gates I entered with sun-rise* : S. A. 1597.

(*f*) of alliance, fellowship, intercourse, etc.; *he whom mutual league ... joined with me* : P. L. I. 90; *devil with devil damned firm concord holds* : P. L. II. 496; *to share with us their part* : P. L. I. 267; *as friend with friend converse with Adam* : P. L. v. 230; *such joy thou took'st with me* : P. L. II. 766; *there to converse with everlasting groans* : P. L. II. 184.

of union in marriage; *his marriage with the ... maid* : P. L. v. 223.

(*g*) in the class of, among; *named with these* : P. L. I. 574; *reckon'st thou thyself with Spirits of Heaven* : P. L. II. 696; *with the first I knew* : P. R. IV. 504; *to number thee with those* : S. A. 1295.

(*h*) of comparison : P. L. II. 46; *equal with gods* : P. L. IV. 526; *to compare great things with small* : P. L. II. 922; *two equalled with me in fate* : P. L. III. 33; *weigh with her thyself* : P. L. VIII. 570.

(3) of accompanying condition, manner, or result; *my adventurous song, that with no middle flight intends to soar* : P. L. I. 14; *with mighty wings outspread ... sat'st* : P. L. I. 20; *with vain attempt* : P. L. I. 44; *sue for grace with suppliant knee* : P. L. I. 112; *came ... with looks downcast* : P. L. I. 522; *with what ... laborious flight we sunk* : P. L. II. 80; *with a vengeance sent* : P. L. IV. 170; *with care sought lost Eliah* : P. R. II. 18; *I to wait with patience am inured* : P. R. II. 102; *with joy they haste* : P. R. III. 437; *nor with less dread the loud ethereal trumpet from on high gan blow* : P. L. VI. 59; *the thunder when to roll with terror* : P. L. X. 666.

(4) of one's feeling or judgement; *what can force or guile with him* : P. L. II. 189; *such with him finds no acceptance* : P. L. v. 530; *nor example with him wrought* : P. L. v. 901; *how little weight my words with thee can find* : P. L. X. 968; *with me ... hath so prevailed* : P. L. IX. 872.

(5) in the care of; *trusting all his wealth with God* : P. L. XII. 134.

(6) as regards, in relation to; *will they not deal worse with his followers* : P. L. XII. 484; *the ways of God with Man* : P. L. VIII. 226; *what had passed with Man recounted* : P. L. X. 227; *how with Mankind I proceed* : P. L. X. 69; *the strife with me hath end* : S. A. 461.

(7) having, possessing, or characterized by; *Astarte ... with crescent horns* : P. L. I. 439; *the gorgeous East with richest hand* : P. L. II. 3; *with regard of* : P. L. II. 281.

(8) of means; *fed with ever-burning sulphur*: P. L. I. 69; *o'erwhelmed with flood*: P. L. I. 77; *he with his thunder*: P. L. I. 93; *with rallied arms to try*: P. L. I. 269; *pressed her matron lip with kisses*: P. L. IV. 502; *lured with the smell of infant blood*: P. L. II. 664; *ransomed with his own dear life*: P. L. III. 297.

(9) of cause; *stirred up with envy and revenge*: P. L. I. 35; *racked with deep despair*: P. L. I. 126; *unmoved with dread of death*: P. L. I. 555; *wearied with their iniquities*: P. L. XII. 107.

(10) of material, content, etc.; *with gems ... emblazed*: P. L. I. 538; *impaled with circling fire*: P. L. II. 647; *involved with stench and smoke*: P. L. I. 237; *with heaven's artillery fraught*: P. L. II. 715; *filled with pasture*: P. L. IV. 351; *filled with lust*: P. L. I. 496.

(11) of separation; *nor what I part with*: P. R. IV. 161.

(12) for; *to change torment with ease*: P. L. IV. 893.

Withal, *adv.* in addition, moreover, likewise: P. L. V. 238; XII. 82; P. R. IV. 128; S. A. 58.

Withdraw, *vb.* (*pret.* withdrew; *past part.* not used) *tr.* to take away, remove: P. L. VII. 612; IX. 386; S. A. 192; *to withdraw our fealty from God*: P. L. IX. 261; *God ... withdraw his presence from among them*: P. L. XII. 107; *Night her shadowy cloud withdraws*: P. L. V. 686.

refl. he *will not fail, nor will withdraw him now*: P. R. II. 55.

Wither, *vb.* (1) *tr.* to cause to decline or perish; *their glory withered*: P. L. I. 612; *that withered all their strength*: P. L. VI. 850.

(2) *intr.* to lose native freshness, fade; *like a neglected rose it* (beauty) *withers on the stock*: C. 744.

part. adj. **withered,** dry; *withered sticks*: P. R. I. 316.

part. absol. a condition wanting the freshness of youth: P. L. XI. 540.

Withhold, *vb.* (*pret.* and *past part.* withheld) *tr.* (*a*) to keep from action, restrain, check, hinder; *who withholds my power*: P. R. II. 380; *no man withholds thee*:

S. A. 1233; *the Sun himself withheld his wonted speed*: N. O. 79; *withhold me from*, keep me from reaching: S. A. 1125.

(*b*) to keep back, not to give or grant: P. L. V. 62; X. 903; *no good from them shall be withheld*: Ps. LXXXIV. 43; *what thou canst attain ... shall not be withheld thy hearing*: P. L. VII. 117.

*****Within** (within: P. L. VII. 120), I. *adv.* (*a*) in the inner part, on the inside: P. L. I. 725, 792; II. 659; IV. 182; VIII. 242; IX. 836; XI. 470.

(*b*) in the mind or heart: P. L. VIII. 642; IX. 333, 1122; X. 717; XII. 523; P. R. II. 471; S. A. 663; *while I consider what from within I feel*: P. R. I. 198; *from within ... to all temptations armed*: P. L. IV. 64; said of the serpent; *diabolic power active within*: P. L. IX. 96.

(*c*) in the house, indoors: P. L. V. 303; S. VIII. 4.

II. *prep.* (1) in the inner part of, in the space enclosed by, inside of: P. L. I. 388; P. R. III. 275; IV. 414; *orb within orb*: P. L. V. 596; *wheel within wheel*: P. L. VI. 751; *prison within prison*: S. A. 153; *cause light again within thy eyes to spring*: S. A. 584; *within thick clouds*: P. R. I. 41; *within the ground*: P. L. I. 705; *no deep within her gulf*: P. L. II. 12; *within the watery gleam*: P. L. IV. 461; *fish within their watery residence*: P. L. VIII. 346; *from within the golden lamps*: P. L. V. 713.

(*b*) used of the mind or heart; *within our thoughts*: P. L. VI. 581; *within my heart I feel*: P. L. IX. 955; *within her breast*: P. R. II. 63.

(*c*) in the mind or heart of; *within them, him, me*, etc.: P. L. II. 295; III. 194; IV. 20; V. 554; VIII. 440; IX. 315, 348; XII. 91, 587.

(*d*) in the whole body or being of: P. L. V. 410; *while they feel vigour divine within them*: P. L. VI. 158; *I feel new strength within me rise*: P. L. X. 243.

(*e*) in all the parts of; *within them* (chariots) *Spirit lived*: P. L. VII. 204.

(*f*) *within doors*, in the house: S. A. 77.

(2) in the reach, compass, or limits of ; *within Heaven's bound* : P. L. II. 236 ; *within the circuit of these walks* : P. L. IV. 586 ; *within ken* : P. L. III. 622 ; *within soar of towering eagles* : P. L. V. 270 ; *within the wind of such commotion* : P. L. VI. 309. (3) in the reach or scope of ; *within his power* : P. L. IX. 349 ; *within his care* : Ps. LXXXVII. 8 ; *within the grasp of*, controlled by or suffering from : C. 357.

*Without (without : P. L. I. 67 ; II. 89, 870, 975, etc.), I. *adv.* (a) outside of the house : S. A. 1659.

(b) externally to the person ; opposed to *Within*, I. *b* ; *from without* : P. L. IV. 65 ; X. 714 ; XII. 93 ; P. R. I. 199.

II. *prep.* (1) on the outside of ; *within Eden, or without* : P. L. VII. 65.

(b) out of (the house) ; *within doors or without* ; S. A. 77.

(2) out of the reach of, beyond ; *without number* : P. L. I. 791 ; III. 346 ; *without fear* : P. R. IV. 617 ; *secure without all doubt* : C. 409 ; *without recall* : P. L. V. 885.

(3) not having or employing, destitute or independent of, lacking, wanting : P. L. II. 892 ; III. 75 ; IV. 265 ; V. 798 ; VIII. 621 ; IX. 791 ; X. 118, 893 ; XI. 586 ; P. R. III. 90 ; *How can I live without thee?* : P. L. IX. 908 ; *without whom* : P. L. IV. 442 ; *day without night* : P. L. V. 162 ; *sea without shore* : P. L. XI. 750 ; *bulk without spirit* : S. A. 1238 ; *without leave asked of thee* : P. L. II. 685 ; *without defence* : P. L. III. 166 ; *without longer pause* : P. L. III. 561 ; *without hope of end* : P. L. II. 89 ; *without redemption* : P. L. III. 222 ; *without my opening* : P. L. II. 777 ; *without end* (*see* End) : P. L. I. 67 ; II. 870 ; III. 142 ; V. 165, 615 ; VI. 137 ; VII. 161.

Withstand, *vb.* (*pret.* and *past part.* withstood) *tr.* to oppose, resist : P. L. V. 242 ; VI. 253 ; S. A. 127; *nor withstood them rock or hill* : P. L. VII. 300 ; *in fight withstand me* : S. A. 1111 ; *how best their opposition to withstand* : P. R. III. 250 ; *absol. but Fate withstands* : P. L. II. 610.

Witness, I. *sb.* (a) testimony, attestation : P. R. I. 29 ; *whose witness ... wins the cause* : Hor. Epist. 4 ; *I bear thee witness* : S. A. 239 ; *He ... hath in place bore witness gloriously* : S. A. 1752 ; *the Baptist ... witness bore* : P. R. I. 26 ; rather the power or the act of judging and deciding (?) : L. 82.

(b) one who or that which bears testimony or furnishes proof : W. S. 6 ; *for me, be witness all the host of Heaven* : P. L. I. 635 ; or the meaning may be one who is present and looks on at an act : P. L. IX. 317 ; *favour from Heaven, our witness* : P. L. IX. 334.

II. *vb.* (1) *intr.* (a) to bear testimony : P. L. XII. 101 ; *witness when I was worried with thy peals* : S. A. 906 ; *witness the streets of Sodom* : P. L. I. 503 ; *witness this new-made World* : P. L. VII. 617 ; *witness those ancient empires of the earth* : P. R. II. 435.

(b) to take notice, observe ; *witness Heaven! Heaven, witness thou anon* : P. L. VI. 563, 564.

(2) *tr.* (a) to bear testimony to : P. L. I. 57 ; X. 914 ; with clause ; *witness if I be silent* : P. L. V. 202 ; *witness whence I am* : P. R. III. 107.

(b) to see by personal presence ; *to witness with thine eyes* : P. L. III. 700.

See Eye-witness.

Wizard, *sb.* (a) a wise man ; here *pl.* the Magi : N. O. 23.

(b) a sorcerer : C. 571.

(c) one who has the power to foretell future events ; *the Carpathian Wizard's hook* : C. 872.

attrib. or *adj.* having the power of divination ; *Deva spreads her wizard stream* : L. 55.

Woe, *sb.* (a) overwhelming sorrow, dire misery, grief, calamity : P. L. I. 3 ; II. 225, 872 ; III. 633 ; IV. 368, 369 ; V. 543 ; VI. 907 ; IX. 255, 645, 916 ; X. 935, 961 ; XI. 60 ; P. R. I. 399 ; S. A. 813 ; P. 32 ; Ps. LXXXV. 6 ; *sights of woe* : P. L. I. 64 ; *the house of woe* : P. L. X. 465 ; *a world of woe* : P. L. IX. 11 ; *a world of woe and sorrow* : P. L. VIII. 333 ; *to lose ... all pain and woe* : P. L. II. 608 ; *eternal days in woe and pain* : P. L. II. 695 ; *the house of woe and pain* : P. L. VI. 877 ; *the weal or*

woe in thee is placed: P. L. VIII.
638 ; *to him linked in weal or woe*:
P. L. IX. 133 ; *share with me in
bliss or woe*: P. L. IX. 831;
Nature ... gave signs of woe: P. L.
IX. 783 ; *to work them further woe
or shame*: P. L. X. 555; *misery
and woe*: P. R. I. 398 ; *which cost
them woe*: P. L. I. 414; *utter*:
P. L. II. 87 ; *saddest*: P. 9 ; *eternal, certain*: P. L. II. 161 ; IV.
70 ; X. 980 ; *Man's woe*: P.L. IX.
632.

pl.: P. L. IV. 535; Ps. LXXXVIII.
9 ; *piteous of her woes*: C. 836 ;
lasting, endless: P. L. X. 742,
754.

in an exclamation ; *Woe to the
inhabitants on Earth!*: P. L. IV.
5.

(*b*) a source of sorrow or misery :
S. A. 351 ; S. XVIII. 14.

(*c*) words or characters indicating sorrow ; *that sanguine
flower inscribed with woe*: L. 106.
Woeful, *adj.* burdened with sorrow
or misery, sorrowful, wretched :
P. L. X. 984 ; L. 165.
Wolf, *sb.* (*a*) the animal *Canis lupus*:
C. 70 ; *prowling, pilfering*: P. L.
IV. 183 ; C. 504; *stabled*: C. 534.

(*b*) a cruel or rapacious person ;
*wolves shall succeed for teachers,
grievous wolves*: P. L. XII. 508;
hireling wolves, the Presbyterian
clergy : S. XVI. 14 ; *the grim wolf*,
popish priest collectively (?): L.
128.
Woman, *sb.* (**1**) an adult female of
the human race : P. R. I. 65 ; II.
71, 153, 169, 204, 208 ; S. A. 844,
903 ; S. XXII. 6 ; *first of women,
Eve* : P. L. IV. 409 ; *Adam ... not
of woman born* : P. L. XI. 496;
the one (Sin) *seemed woman to the
waist* : P. L. II. 650 ; *a bevy of
fair women* : P. L. XI. 582 ; *bad* :
S. A. 211 ; *every woman false
like thee* : S. A. 749 ; *among women
blest* : P. R. II. 68 ; *among illustrious women* : S. A. 957 ; *the
famousest of women* : S. A. 983 ;
Philistian women : S. A. 216 ;
Dalilah : S. A. 50, 236, 379,
1114 ; *a deceitful woman* : S. A.
202.

(*b*) Eve ; *the Woman*: P. L. IX.
481 ; X. 179, 192 ; *this Woman* :
P. L. X. 137 ; *that bad Woman* :
P. L. X. 837 ; in direct address ;
O Woman: P. L. IX. 343 ; *say*,

Woman: P. L. X. 158 ; *as representing the female race ; the
Woman's Seed* : P. L. XII. 543,
601 ; P. R. I. 64; *intermix my
covenant in the Woman's seed* : P.
L. XI. 116 ; *the Woman's Seed to
thee foretold* : P. L. XII. 327 ; *our
great Expectation should be called
the Seed of Woman* : P. L. XII.
379.

(*c*) women individually and collectively, the female sex : P. L.
IV. 638 ; IX. 233 ; S. A. 1012 ;
woman's domestic honour : P. L.
XI. 617 ; *nor should'st thou have
trusted to woman's frailty* : S. A.
783 ; *Man's woe ... from Woman
to begin* : P. L. XI. 633 ; pl.; *to
worth in women overtrusting* : P.
L. IX. 1183.

(**2**) the name given to Eve ;
Woman is her name : P. L. VIII.
496.

See **Bond-woman**.
Womankind, *sb.* the female sex,
women in general : P. R. II. 175.
Womb, *sb.* (*a*) stomach ; used *fig.* of
time ; *glut thyself with what thy
womb devours* : T. 4.

(*b*) the uterus of the female :
S. A. 634 ; M. W. 33 ; *trouble he
hath conceived of old as in a womb* :
Ps. VII. 53; *that of Eve* : P. L. X.
1053 ; *whose fruitful womb shall
fill the world* : P. L. V. 388 ; *of*
the Virgin Mary ; *from thy womb
the Son of God Most High* : P. L.
XII. 381 ; *of Sin* : P. L. II. 657,
778 ; *my womb conceived a growing burden* : P. L. II. 766 ; *into
the womb that bred them they return* : P. L. II. 798.

(*c*) applied *fig.* to various things
that resemble the uterus in producing or containing something ;
Earth's inmost womb : P. L. V.
302 ; *the Earth ... opening her fertile womb* : P. L. VII. 454 ; *earth's
dark womb* : D. F. I. 30 ; *in his*
(a hill's) *womb was hid metallic
ore* : P. L. I. 673 ; *this wild Abyss,
the womb of Nature* : P. L. II.
911 ; *Air, and ye Elements, the
eldest birth of Nature's womb* :
P. L. V. 181; *Earth ... in the
womb as yet of waters* : P. L. VII.
276 ; *the dragon womb of Stygian
darkness* : C. 131 ; *swallowed up
and lost in the wide womb of uncreated Night* : P. L. II. 150 ;
plunged in the womb of unoriginal

Night : P. L. x. 476 ; (the
phœnix) *from out her ashy womb* :
S. A. 1703.
Won, *vb. intr.* to dwell, abide ; *the
wild beast, where he wons in forest
wild* : P. L. VII. 457. *See* **Wont.**
Wonder, I. *sb.* (1) a strange thing,
that which causes surprise or
astonishment : P. L. IX. 566 ; XI.
733 ; S. A. 753 ; *great things, and
full of wonder in our ears* : P. L.
VII. 70 ; *no wonder* : P. L. I. 282;
IV. 577 ; P. R. III. 229 ; Ps. VII.
4 ; or in sense (*b*) ; *what wonder,
why is it a wonderful thing, or
why is there any surprise* : P. L.
III. 606 ; VI. 219 ; IX. 221 ; P. R.
I. 481.

(*b*) a marvel, prodigy, miracle:
P. L. I. 777 ; Ps. VII. 4 ; LXXXVI.
33 ; CXIV. 5 ; *Wilt thou do wonders
on the dead ?* : Ps. LXXXVIII. 41 ;
*what ... wonders move the obdurate
to relent ?* : P. L. VI. 790 ; *the
wonders of his* (God's) *might* : P.
L. VII. 223 ; *to have wrought such
wonders with an ass's jaw* : S. A.
1095.

(*c*) a person who arouses surprise and admiration ; *thou canst
who art sole wonder* : P. L. IX.
533 ; *what woman...though of this
age the wonder* : P. R. II. 209 ;
Hail, foreign wonder : C. 265 ; a
place ; *Babylon, the wonder of all
tongues* : P. R. III. 280.

(2) a feeling of mingled surprise
and curiosity excited by something extraordinary : P. L. III.
552 ; v. 9 ; x. 487 ; *wherefore
deprive all Earth her wonder at thy
acts* : P. R. III. 24 ; *with* or *without wonder* : P. L. IV. 205; VIII. 11;
P. R. I. 38 ; S. A. 1642; *looks
down with wonder* : P. L. III. 542;
*whom my thoughts pursue with
wonder* : P. L. IV. 363 ; *our Sire,
replete with joy and wonder* : P. L.
XII. 468 ; *the winds, with wonder
whist* : N. O. 64 ; *in our wonder* :
W. S. 7.

II. *vb.* (1) *intr.* to be astonished,
marvel : P. L. I. 693 ; v. 54, 439;
x. 509 ; *wonder not* : P. L. v. 491;
IX. 532 ; with *at* : P. L. v. 89;
IX. 856 ; x. 510 ; A. 43 ; C. 747.

(2) *tr.* to be filled with surprise
and curiosity in regard to ; with
clause; *wonder that the Son of God
... so long should abide* : P. R. II.
303.

(*b*) to wish to know ; with
clause; *what this might mean ...
wondering* : P. L. III. 273 ; *much
wondering where and what I was* :
P. L. IV. 451 ; *wondering how the
subtle Fiend* : P. L. x. 20 ; *men
wonder why thou should'st wed* :
S. A. 215.

part. adj. **wondering,** expressing
astonishment ; *my wondering eyes* :
P. L. VIII. 257.
Wonderful, *adj.* of a nature to excite
wonder, surprising, marvellous,
strange : P. L. III. 702 ; IX. 862 ;
x. 482 ; XII. 471.
Wondrous, (1) *adj.* wonderful, marvellous, astonishing : P. L. III.
663, 665 ; VI. 377 ; VII. 483 ; IX.
650 ; x. 348 ; XII. 200, 500 ; P.
R. III. 434 ; S. A. 589, 1440 ; Ps.
LXXXVIII. 50 ; *a wondrous ark* :
P. L. XI. 819 ; *the wondrous horse
of brass* : Il P. 114 ; *a bridge of
wondrous length* : P. L. II. 1028 ;
made flesh ... by wondrous birth :
P. L. III. 285; *the top of wondrous
glory* : S. A. 167 ; *with* or *by
wondrous art* : P. L. I. 703 ; x.
312 ; *his wondrous works* : P. L.
VIII. 68 ; *four faces each had wondrous* : P. L. VI. 754.

(2) *adv.* marvellously ; *wondrous
fair, great* : P. L. v. 155 ; Ps.
VIII. 1, 23 ; very, exceedingly ;
wondrous harsh : S. A. 1461.
Wondrously, *adv.* in a marvellous
manner : P. L. III. 587.
Wont, *vb.* (*pres. 2d sing.* wont'st :
C. 332 ; *pret.* wont ; *past part.*
wont and when *adj.* wonted ;
originally *pret.* of won and hence
not inflected in *3d pers. sing.*)
intr. to be accustomed ; with simple
inf. ; *where champions bold wont
ride* : P. L. I. 764; with *prep.
inf.* : P. L. I. 332 ; v. 123 ; VI.
93 ; x. 103 ; N. O. 10 ; C. 332.

past part. accustomed ; in the
predicate with *be ; as I oft am
wont* : P. L. v. 32 ; with *prep.
inf.* : P. L. III. 656 ; v. 677 ; S. A.
1487 ; *I am wont to sit* : S. A. 4 ;
*fathers are wont to lay up for their
sons* : S. A. 1485 ; *as she was wont
... to hunt* : Il P. 123 ; *as appetite
is wont to dream* : P. R. II. 264 ;
the *inf.* understood : P. L. IX.
842 ; P. R. I. 12.

part. adj. **wonted,** customary :
S. A. 748 ; N. O. 196 ; *wonted
ornaments, shape, speed,* etc. : P.

L. IX. 1076; P. R. IV. 449; N. O. 79; II P. 37; C. 549; *pride, calm, vigour, favour*: P. L. I. 527; v. 210; VI. 851; VIII. 202; *signal*: P. L. v. 705; *Heaven his wonted face renewed*: P. L. v. 783; **wont**, customary; *as is wont*: Ps. LXXXI. 9; *as to superior Spirits is wont*: P. L. III. 737.

Woo, *vb. tr.* (*a*) to solicit in love: P. L. VIII. 503.

(*b*) to seek to influence, persuade, or win; *thee chauntress, ... I woo, to hear thy even-song*: II P. 64; *his Casella, whom he wooed to sing*: S. XIII. 13; *she woos the gentle air to hide her guilty front*: N. O. 38.

Wood, *sb.* (*a*) a large and thick collection of growing trees, a forest: P. L. X. 333; A. 32; *the unseen Genius of the wood*: II P. 154; *in wood or mountain*: P. L. VI. 575; *in wood or grove*: P. R. II. 184; *wood or wilderness*: P. L. IV. 342; *through wood, through waste*: P. L. IV. 538; *nor wood, nor stream*: P. L. VI. 70; *thick, high, fair, tall*: P. R. IV. 448; L'A. 56; A. 45; C. 270; *tangled*: C. 181; *drear, ominous, wild, hideous*: C. 37, 61, 312, 520; pl.: P. L. VI. 645; VII. 35, 434; VIII. 516; X. 700; XI. 567; II P. 63; C. 150, 549; S. I. 2; *Dian ... was queen of the woods*: C. 446; *the beast that reigns in woods*: P. L. XI. 187; *wild beasts came forth the woods to roam*: P. R. I. 502; *rivers, woods, and plains*: P. L. IX. 116; *woods, and springs*: P. R. II. 374; *woods and groves*: M. W. 7; *woods or valleys*: P. R. III. 332; *the woods and desert caves*: L. 39; *O woods, O fountains, hillocks, dales, and bowers!* P. L. X. 860; *ye rivers, woods, and plains*: P. L. VIII. 275; *high, highest*: P. L. VII. 326; IX. 1086; *shady, wild*: P. L. VIII. 262; IX. 910; *waving*: C. 88; *fresh*: L. 193; *hospitable*: C. 187; *in the Arabian woods*: S. A. 1700.

(*b*) the hard substance of trees: P. L. XI. 440; *to worship their own work in wood and stone for gods*: P. L. XII. 119.

Woodbine (woodbíne: L. 146), *sb.* the honeysuckle: P. L. IX. 216; *the well-attired woodbine*: L. 146.

Wood-god, *sb.* a god of the forest: P. R. II. 297.

Woodman, *sb.* a dweller in the forest (?), a huntsman (?): C. 484.

Wood-note, *sb.* a simple natural song, as characteristic as is that of a wild bird; *Shakespeare ... warble his native wood-notes wild*: L'A. 134.

Wood-nymph, *sb.* a goddess of the forest, a Dryad or Oread: P. L. v. 381; P. R. II. 297; C. 120; *like a wood-nymph light, Oread or Dryad, or of Delia's train*: P. L. IX. 386.

Woody, *adj.* (*a*) abounding in or covered with trees; *woody mountains, shores*: P. L. VIII. 303; IX. 1118; *a woody scene*: P. R. II. 294; *woody Ida's inmost grove*: II P. 29; *a woody theatre*: P. L. IV. 141.

(*b*) determined by the growth of trees, or leading through the forest; *wandering this woody maze*: P. R. II. 246.

See **Over-woody**.

Woof, *sb.* the cross threads of a woven fabric; *my sky-robes, spun out Iris' woof*: C. 83; *Iris had dipt the woof*: P. L. XI. 244.

Wool, *sb.* the fine soft hair growing on sheep, used in the manufacture of clothing: C. 751.

Worcester, *sb.* the battle of Worcester, fought Sept. 3, 1651: S. XVI. 9.

Word, *sb.* (*a*) a vocal sound or combination of sounds used as the sign of an idea: P. L. VIII. 223; S. A. 905; *submission; and that word disdain forbids me*: P. L. IV. 81; *imperfect words with childish trips, half unpronounced*: V. Ex. 3; *visit every sprout with puissant words*: A. 60; *to span words with just note and accent*: S. XIII. 3; *a jangling noise of words unknown*: P. L. XII. 55.

(*b*) a vocable considered merely as sound; *a peal of words*: S. A. 235; *I hear the sound of words*: S. A. 176.

(*c*) a combination of printed letters; *what a word on a title-page is this*: S. XI. 5.

(*d*) speech, language, talk, discourse; *sing.*: P. L. IV. 401; *in word mightier than they in arms*: P. L. VI. 32; *pl.*: P. L. I. 663; II. 735, 737; III. 266; v. 113, 544, 616, 810, 873; VI. 496; VII. 113; VIII. 57, 215, 248, 602; IX.

550, 733, 920, 1066, 1144 ; x. 459, 608 ; xi. 32 ; xii. 609 ; P. R. i. 106, 228, 320 ; ii. 34, 301, 337, 405 ; iii. 9, 346 ; S. A. 277, 729, 947, 1351 ; C. 801 ; S. x. 12 ; Ps. v. 1 ; Soph. 2 ; *new train of words* : P. R. iii. 266 ; *words interwoven with sighs* : P. L. i. 621 ; *words clothed in reason's garb* : P. L. ii. 226 ; *thy words at random* : P. L. iv. 930 ; *let not my words offend thee* : P. L. viii. 379 ; *these words thereafter spake* : P. L. ii. 50 ; *how little weight my words with thee can find* : P. L. x. 968 ; *the vent of words* : P. L. xii. 374 ; *thy actions to thy words accord* : P. R. iii. 9 ; *these words I as a prophecy receive* : S. A. 472 ; *in words deceiving* : N. O. 175 ; *bold, high, contemptuous* : P. L. i. 82, 528 ; v. 66 ; C. 781 ; *healing, persuasive, bland, soft, peaceful*, etc. : P. L. ix. 290, 737, 855 ; x. 865, 946 ; xi. 140, 295 ; P. R. i. 222 ; iii. 6 ; S. A. 184, 605, 1066 ; C. 161 ; *ambiguous* : P. L. v. 703 : vi. 568 ; *reasoning* : P. L. ix. 379 ; *speedy* : P. L. i. 156.

(*e*) *pl.* a poem : L. 20.

(*f*) the power of speech ; *scarce recovering words* : P. L. xi. 499.

(*g*) a decree, order, mandate ; *Father, thy word is passed* : P. L. iii. 227 ; *at his word* : P. L. iii. 708 ; *by thy commanding word* : Ps. viii. 19 ; *thou great Word, "Let there be light, and light was over all"* : S. A. 83 ; perhaps with blending of sense (*i*) ; *each word proceeding from the mouth of God* : P. R. i. 349.

(*h*) an injunction, admonition ; *would thou hadst hearkened to my words* : P. L. ix. 1134.

(*i*) an affirmation, a declaration or promise : P. L. iii. 144 ; Ps. v. 26 ; *thou hast fulfilled thy words* : P. L. viii. 492 ; *Shepherd, I take thy word* : C. 321 ; *Shall Truth fail to keep her word* : P. L. x. 856.

(*j*) a request, entreaty : S. A. 200.

(*k*) the Logos, the Divine Reason as expressed in the personality of Christ : P. L. vii. 208 ; *Son who art alone my word, my wisdom* : P. L. iii. 170 ; *begotten Son, by whom as by his Word, the mighty Father made all things* :

P. L. v. 836 ; *my Word, begotten Son, by thee this I perform* : P. L. vii. 163 ; *his Word, the Filial Godhead* : P. L. vii. 175 ; *said then the omnific Word* : P. L. vii. 217 ; *his Word all things produced* : P. R. iii. 122.

Work, I. *sb.* (1) exertion or activity directed to the accomplishment of some purpose, labour, toil : P. L. ix. 224 ; S. A. 1260 ; *man's work* : S. xix. 10 ; *the bee .. that at his flowery work doth sing* : Il P. 143 ; *fig.* to be played upon ; *the harp had work* : P. L. vii. 595.

(*b*) applied to the creative activity of God ; *by work divine* : P. L. v. 255 ; *the Creator, from his work desisting* : P. L. vii. 551 ; *from work now resting* : P. L. vii. 591 ; *resting on that day from all his work* : P. L. vii. 593.

(2) that upon which labour is expended, undertaking, task, employment : P. L. iv. 726 ; v. 853 ; vi. 507 ; ix. 202, 230 ; x. 270 ; *our day's work* : P. L. xi. 177 ; *Man hath his daily work of body or mind appointed* : P. L. iv. 618 ; *to their morning's rural work they haste* : P. L. v. 211 ; *the work under our labour grows* : P. L. ix. 208 ; *make persuasion do the work of fear* : P. R. i. 223 ; *adventurous* : P. L. x. 255 ; *glorious* : P. L. x. 391 ; pl. *laborious works* : S. A. 14.

(*b*) applied to battle : P. L. vi. 453 ; *number to this day's work is not ordained* : P. L. vi. 809.

(*c*) applied to the mission of Christ in coming to earth : P. R. ii. 112 ; *thy glorious work* : P. R. iv. 634 ; *how best the mighty work he might begin* : P. R. i. 186 ; applied to the mission of Samson : S. A. 680 ; *the work to which I was divinely called* : S. A. 226 ; *the work from Heaven imposed* : S. A. 565 ; *the work for which thou wast foretold* : S. A. 1662 ; to the mission of Cromwell : S. xvi. 6.

(*d*) applied to the creation as that upon which God expends labour ; *from his work returned magnificent, his six days' work, a World* : P. L. vii. 567, 568 ; or in sense (1) : P. L. vii. 93 ; *the work ordained* : P. L. vii. 590 ; *while God was in his work* : P. L. viii. 234.

(3) that which is produced by labour, something made or created; to worship their own work in wood ...for gods: P. L. XII. 119; the flourishing works of peace destroy: P. R. III. 80 ; Fancy ... wild work produces : P. L. V. 112.

(b) that which is created by God, or probably in some instances rather an act or deed of God : P. L. I. 201; III. 59, 277 ; IV. 380, 679 ; VI. 761; VII. 97, 516, 629 ; IX. 897; XI. 578; XII. 579 ; Ps. VIII. 17; LXXXVI. 26, 28 ; with repenting hand abolish his own works: P. L. II. 370; his wondrous works, but chiefly Man : P. L. III. 663 ; the Almighty's works, and chiefly Man : P. L. IV. 566 ; to know the works of God : P. L. III. 695 ; praised God and his works : P. L. VII. 259 ; God saw, surveying his great work : P. L. VII. 353 ; Great are thy works, Jehovah!: P. L. VII. 602; Heaven ... wherein to read his wondrous works : P. L. VIII. 68 ; us ... set over all his works : P. L. IX. 941 ; thy decrees on all thy works: P. L. X. 644 ; merciful over all his works : P. L. XII. 565 ; Light, the prime work of God : S. A. 70; wondrous, wonderful, etc. : P. L. III. 665, 702 ; V. 153 ; VII. 112 ; lowest: P. L. V. 158.

(c) that which is produced by nature : P. R. II. 295 ; works of Nature's hand : P. L. III. 455; Nature from her seat, sighing through all her works : P. L. IX. 783 ; Nature's works : P. L. III. 49 ; IV. 314 ; XII. 578.

(d) a product ; metallic ore, the work of sulphur : P. L. I. 674.

(e) a structure built : P. L. I. 731 ; X. 312; the works of Memphian kings : P. L. I. 694; the work as of a kingly palace-gate : P. I . III. 505 ; the work Confusion named : P. L. XII. 62 ; towns, and rural works : P. L. XI. 639 ; a fortification : P. L. II. 1039.

(f) design, pattern ; carved work : P. R. IV. 59.

(4) an act, deed, achievement : P. L. VI. 698 ; XI. 34 ; works of love : P. L. I. 431 ; works of violence and war : P. L. VI. 274 ; Satan ... his works in thee and in thy seed : P. L. XII. 394 ; good, pious : P. L. IX. 234 ; S. A. 955 ;

or in sense (3) ; P. L. III. 59 ; when sin with vanity had filled the works of men : P. L. III. 447 ; works of day past : P. L. V. 33.

(5) pl. a course of conduct demanded by and agreeing with the Mosaic law : P. L. XII. 306, 410 ; modelled according to the standard set by Christ : S. XIV. 5; by faith not void of works : P. L. XII. 427; prompted and guided by faith in God : P. L. XII. 306; works of Faith rarely be found : P. L. XII. 536 ; refined by faith and faithful works : P. L. XI. 64.

II. vb. (pret. and past part. wrought) (1) intr. (a) to labour, toil ; to work with slaves : S. A. 367 ; here in the heart of Hell to work in fire : P. L. I. 151 ; set to work millions of spinning worms : C. 715.

(b) work up to, to attain to by effort ; till body up to spirit work : P. L. V. 478.

(c) to act, operate, be effective : P. L. II. 295 ; soon as the potion works : C. 68 ; it was not gold ... that wrought with me : S. A. 850 ; nor example with him wrought : P. L. V. 901 ; sin ... hath wrought insensibly : P. L. VI. 691 ; nature ... wrought in her so : P. L. VIII. 507 ; the law of faith working through love : P. L. XII. 489.

(2) tr. (a) to make, form, fashion : P. L. IV. 699 ; VI. 761 ; XI. 572 ; wrought on, extended by labour : P. L. X. 300.

(b) to bring about, cause, produce, effect, do, accomplish : P. L. I. 642, 646 ; VIII. 95, 525 ; IX. 1080 ; XI. 424 ; P. R. II. 215 ; S. A. 813, 1095, 1532 ; Ps. VII. 9 ; in Adam wrought commiseration : P. L. X. 939 ; his good ... wrought but malice : P. L. IV. 49 ; Sin ... first wrought the change : P. L. IX. 70 ; to what may work his utter loss : P. L. IX. 131 ; dissolution wrought by sin : P. L. XI. 55 ; work redemption for mankind : P. R. I. 266 ; they who wrought their own captivity : P. R. III. 415 ; all ye that work iniquity : Ps. VI. 16 ; with acc. and dat. : P. L. X. 555 ; Ps. LXXXV. 6 ; work him danger : P. L. III. 635 ; wrought them pain : P. L. VI. 657 ; work us woe : P. L. IX. 255.

(c) to effect or gain gradually and by effort ; *he works his way*: P. L. IX. 512 ; *to work his liberty*: S. A. 1454 ; *work ease out of pain*: P. L. II. 261 ; with *acc.* and *dat.*; *work us a perpetual peace*: N. O. 7.

(d) to cause one to have, confer upon one ; *the tree which tasted works knowledge of good and evil*: P. L. VII. 543 ; *their taste no knowledge works*: P. R. II. 371.

(e) to direct the movements of, guide; *a ship, by skilful steersman wrought*: P. L. IX. 513.

(f) to induce, persuade ; *work my flattered fancy to believe*: P. 31.

part. adj. **working**, given up to labour, devoted to toil ; *the working day*: S. A. 1299.

See **Master-work**.

Worker, *sb.* a doer: Ps. v. 13.

Workmanship, *sb.* the skill of a workman: C. 747.

Work-master, *sb.* an author, a creator ; of God: P. L. III. 696.

World, *sb.* (Because of the confusion of cosmological and theological ideas the exact meaning in many instances cannot be certainly determined) (1) the starry universe: P. L. II. 347 ; III. 74, 334, 494, 543, 554, 562, 567, 709 ; IV. 107 ; v. 188, 577; VII. 71, 231, 568, 636; VIII. 123, 151 ; IX. 153 ; x. 322, 372, 392, 422, 489, 500, 836 ; XII. 459, 467; P. R. I. 392 ; IV. 203, 223, 311 ; *space may produce new Worlds*: P. L. I. 650; *to create more worlds*: P. L. II. 916; *the rising World of waters*: P. L. III. 11 ; *this World of heaven and earth*: P. L. VII. 62 ; *this World, of Heaven and Earth consisting*: P. L. VIII. 15 ; *he the World built on circumfluous waters calm*: P. L. VIII. 269 ; *stars...seemed other worlds*: P. L. III. 566 ; *new*: P. L. II. 403, 867 ; IV. 34, 113, 391 ; x. 257, 377, 721 ; *new-created, new-made*: P. L. III. 89 ; IV. 937; VII. 554, 617; x. 481 ; Ps. CXXXVI. 26; *round, ample, great, orbicular,* etc.: P. L. III. 419 ; IV. 413 ; v. 171 ; x. 318, 381, 467 ; P. R. I. 44 ; *frail, fenceless, perverted, transient*: P. L. II. 1030; x. 303; XII. 547, 554 ; *unborn*: P. L. VII. 220 ; *pendent*: P. L. II. 1052; *fair*: P. L. IX. 568 ; *yonder*: P.

L. x. 617; pl. for sing. ; *coming to create new worlds*: P. L. VII. 209.

(b) perhaps rather the earth as the centre of the universe and as the abode of man ; *brought death into the World*: P. L. I. 3; *brought into this World a world of woe*: P. L. IX. 11.

(c) as a measure of distance; *distant from thee worlds between*: P. L. x. 362.

(2) the terraqueous globe, the earth: P. R. I. 34; *the four hinges of the world*: P. R. IV. 415; *the riches of this world*: P. L. XII. 580 ; more definitely as the abode of man: P. L. I. 32 ; IV. 272 ; XII. 449, 646 ; P. R. I. 461 ; II. 443 ; IV. 105 ; N. O. 54 ; Cir. 11 ; *fill the World...with men as Angels*: P. L. x. 892; *whose fruitful womb shall fill the world... with thy sons*: P. L. v. 389; *the kingdoms of the or this world*: P. R. IV. 89, 163, 182, 210 ; *all monarchies besides throughout the world*: P. R. IV. 150; *the world inhabited*: P. L. x. 689 ; *this cursed world*: P. L. x. 984 ; *this dark world*: S. XIX. 2; *the world's wilderness*: P. L. XII. 313.

(b) or the meaning may be sense (1): P. L. VIII. 472 ; XI. 134; N. O. 82 ; *the world's last end*: D. F. I. 77; *the well-balanced World on hinges hung*: N. O. 122; *the low world in measured motion draw*: A. 71 ; *the world's foundation*: Ps. VII. 30 ; *when fair Morning first smiles on the world*: P. L. v. 124.

(c) both *Worlds*, heaven and earth : P. R. IV. 633.

(d) as a place of sin, or the meaning may be (5) (b) : D. F. I. 63 ; *talking like this world's brood*: Ps. IV. 27 ; *his weakness shall o'ercome ... all the world*: P. R. I. 162.

(e) the earth and all created things in it, as overwhelmed by the great flood: P. L. XI. 821, 894 ; XII. 3.

(3) any place or sphere of existence or habitation likened to the earth or the universe ; *in a moment will create another world*: P. L. VII. 155 ; *Heaven and Earth, another world*: P. L. II. 1004 ; *our great author, thrives in other worlds*: P. L. x. 237 ; *expecting*

... their great Adventurer from the search of foreign worlds: P. L. x. 441 ; *into whatever world, or unknown region*: P. L. ii. 442; *what worlds or what vast regions hold the immortal mind*: II P. 90; applied to heaven the abode of God ; *the secrets of another world*: P. L. v. 569; applied to hell : P. R. iv. 203; *hail, Infernal World!*: P. L. i. 251 ; *this deep world of darkness*: P. L. ii. 262; *that dismal world*: P. L. ii. 572.

(4) a particular part of the earth or of its inhabitants considered as an independent whole : P. L. viii. 332; *yonder nether world*: P. L. xi. 328; *a lower world*: P. L. xi. 283; *the Heathen World*: P. L. i. 375; *the ancient world*: P. L. iii. 464; applied to the ocean ; *the bottom of the monstrous world*: L. 158.

(5) the inhabitants of the earth, the human race : P. L. xi. 877; D. F. I. 32, 56; M. W. 51; C. 720; L. 80; *thou hast seen one world begin and end*: P. L. xii. 6; *at the world's last session*: N. O. 163.

(*b*) as prone to or lost in sin : P. L. xi. 627; xii. 105; *a world perverse*: P. L. xi. 701; *to save a world from utter loss*: P. L. iii. 308; *one whole world of wicked sons*: P. L. xi. 874; *so shall the World go on, to good malignant*: P. L. xii. 537.

(*c*) rather the nations of the earth : P. R. iii. 18, 225; iv. 379; H. B. 14; *Rome was to sway the world*: P. L. xi. 406; *achieved thereby fame in the world*: P. L. xi. 793; *Great Julius, whom now all the world admires*: P. R. iii. 39; *Great Alexander to subdue the world*: P. R. iv. 252.

(6) any celestial body : P. L. v. 268 ; as resembling the earth in habitability : P. L. viii. 175 ; *on whom the great Creator hath bestowed Worlds*: P. L. iii. 674; *every star perhaps a world of destined habitation*: P. L. vii. 621.

(7) organized human society, the customs and usages of men ; *the world thou hast not seen*: P. R. iii. 236; *the world's vain mask*: S. xxii. 13.

(8) society, the people among whom one lives; *policy...plausible to the world*: P. R. iii. 393; *a world offended*: P. L. xi. 810.

(9) life among men as opposed to a solitary existence : P. R. iv. 372.

(10) a vast number of persons ; *though worlds judged thee perverse*: P. L. vi. 36.

(11) a vast quantity or amount of something ; *a world of woe*: P. L. ix. 11 ; *of tears*: P. L. xi. 627.

(12) the sphere of physical perception or of experience: P. L. v. 455.

(13) the sphere of power or authority : P. L. vi. 146.

(14) an æon : P. L. vii. 191.

Worldly, *adj.* (*a*) of or pertaining to this world, earthly; *a worldly crown*: P. R. iv. 213.

(*b*) devoted to the things of this world ; *to live secure, worldly or dissolute*: P. L. xi. 803.

Worldly-strong, *adj.* strong in the strength which this world affords: P. L. xii. 568.

Worldly-wise, *adj.* wise in the wisdom of this world: P. L. xii. 568.

Worm, *sb.* (*a*) any small vermiform animal : P. L. iv. 704; vii. 476; S. A. 74 ; *noxious, hurtful*: P. R. i. 312; A. 53; *spinning worms,* silkworms : C. 715.

(*b*) the serpent; *in evil hour thou didst give ear to that false Worm*: P. L. ix. 1068.

(*c*) *fig.* punishment in hell after death ; *the undying worm*: P. L. vi. 739.

See **Taint-worm.**

Wormy, *adj.* infested with worms; *wormy bed*, the grave : D. F. I. 31.

Worry, *vb. tr.* to trouble, harass : A. 906.

Worse, (1) *adj.* (*comp.* of bad, evil, or ill) (*a*) bad or evil in a greater degree : P. R. iii. 419; S. A. 433 ; *rape, deeds*: P. L. i. 505 ; iv. 26 ; *relapse*: P. L. iv. 100; *reason, ambition*: P. L. ii. 113; iv. 40; *way*: P. L. ii. 83; *by worse than hostile deeds*: S. A. 893 ; *your plots ... worse than those of Trent*: F. of C. 14.

(*b*) more to be feared; more dreadful, terrible, severe, painful, or grievous: P. L. ii. 626; vi. 863; xi. 601; P. R. iv. 320; S. A. 485 ; *high winds worse within* :

P. L. IX. 1122 ; stroke, worse than
of Death ! : P. L. XI. 268 ; that
blindness worse than this : S. A.
418 ; worse sufferings : P. L. IV.
26 ; in the predicate with be :
P. L. II. 85, 169, 186 ; IX. 123 ;
S. A. 399 ; idleness had been worse :
P. L. X. 1055 ; the vb. understood : P. L. II. 163 ; III. 9 ; P.
R. III. 205.
(c) less favourably situated as
to means or circumstances : P. L.
I. 119 ; P. R. IV. 486.
absol. (a) a more evil state; tend
from bad to worse : P. L. XII. 106.
(b) a person or thing of less
excellence : P. L. IX. 102 ; see
her gained by a far worse : P. L.
X. 903.
(c) a thing more to be dreaded :
P. L. II. 196 ; IX. 715 ; S. A. 68 ;
of God, or Hell, or worse, he
recked not : P. L. II. 49 ; or this,
or worse : P. L. IX. 265 ; more intense pain, grief, or misery : P.
L. IX. 128 ; X. 717 ; P. R. III.
207 ; P. 11 ; the expectation more
of worse : P. R. III. 208 ; no fear
of worse : P. L. X. 780.
(d) defeat : S. A. 904. See **Go.**
(2) adv. (a) in a manner more
evil, severe, or dreadful : P. L.
VIII. 397 ; Ps. LXXXV. 12 ; fear to
be worse destroyed : P. L. II. 85 ;
will they not deal worse : P. L. XII.
484.
(b) in a less adequate manner :
P. L. VIII. 397 ; by argument, not
worse than by his shield and spear :
defended Israel : S. A. 284.
(c) less easy, harder : P. L. VI.
34.
(d) in a greater degree ; confusion worse confounded : P. L. II.
996 ; they dreaded worse : P. L.
II. 293 ; they worse abhorred : P.
L. VI. 607 ; hated not learning
worse : S. XI. 13.
(3) vb. tr. to put to disadvantage ; worse our foes : P. L. VI.
440.

Worship, (1) sb. adoration paid to
God : P. L. XI. 318 ; eternity so
spent in worship : P. L. II. 248 ;
in the worship persevere of Spirit
and Truth : P. L. XII. 532 ; every
Plant, in sign of worship wave :
P. L. V. 194 ; vocal : P. L. IX.
198 ; and also to idols ; God with
idols in their worship joined : P.R.
III. 426.

(2) vb. tr. |to adore (God) : P.
L. VII. 515, 628 ; XI. 578 ; P. R.
II. 475 ; Thou shalt worship the
Lord thy God : P. R. IV. 176 ; I
... will towards thy holy temple
worship low : Ps. V. 20 ; to adore
(gods, idols, the Devil) : P. L.
XII. 119 ; H. B. 5 ; to worship
calves : P. R. III. 416 ; stocks and
stones : S. XVIII. 4 ; Him (Moloch)
the Ammonite worshipped in
Rabba : P. L. I. 397 ; worship me,
thee : P. R. IV. 167, 179, 192 ; to
pay divine honours to (people as
superior beings or as gods) : P. L.
IX. 611 ; C. 302 ; worshipped with
temple, priest, and sacrifice ? : P.
R. III. 83.
part. adj. **worshipped,** adored ;
his worshiped ark : N. O. 220.
See **All-worshipped, Idor-wor-
ship.**
Worshipper, sb. one who pays homage ; to God : P. L. VII. 613, 630 ;
IX. 705 ; to Dagon : P. L. I. 461 ;
S. A. 471.
Worst, adj. (sup. of bad, evil, or ill)
dreadful, severe, or grievous in
the highest degree ; for ill not
worst : P. L. II. 224 ; extremes,
abuse, imprisonment : P. L. I.
276 ; IV. 204 ; S. A. 155 ; is this
then worst : P. L. II. 163.
(b) at worst, in the most evil or
undesirable state : P. L. II. 100 ;
on the most unlikely or undesirable supposition : C. 484.
absol. (a) that which is bad,
evil, or dreadful in the highest
degree ; worst of other evils : S.
A. 105 ; with def. art. : P. R. III.
223 ; S. A. 195, 1264, 1570, 1571 ;
with her the worst endures : P. L.
IX. 269 ; I would sustain alone the
worst : P. L. IX. 979 ; the worst on
me must light : P. L. X. 73 ; I
would be at the worst ; worst is my
port : P. R. III. 209 : I have
thither packed the worst : V. Ex.
12 ; the worst of evils : P. L. VI.
462 ; the worst of all indignities :
S. A. 1341.
(b) one who has the least power ;
or be found the worst in Heaven :
P. L. V. 742.
Worth, (1) adj. deserving, meriting : P. L. V. 308 ; P. R. III.
51, 393 ; IV. 86, 514, 539 ; S.
A. 250 ; to reign is worth ambition : P. L. I. 262 ; what change
worth waiting : P. L. II. 223 ; if

this be worth attempting : P. L. II.
376; worth your laughter : P. L.
X. 488; not worth the seeking : P.
R. III. 151; worth a sponge : P.
R. IV. 329; worth a thought : C.
505.

(2) sb. (a) those qualities in a
character that make it deserving
of esteem, trust, or honour : P. L.
I. 378; V. Ex. 79; A. 80; S.
XIII. 5; his (God's) mighty majesty
and worth : Ps. CXXXVI. 90; the
conscience of her worth : P. L. VIII.
502; to worth in women overtrusting : P. L. IX. 1183; highest, high:
P. L. II. 429; P. R. I. 370; A. 8;
true : P. R. I. 231.

(b) value, importance, excellence ; words that bore semblance
of worth : P. L. I. 529; objects ...
such as have more show of worth :
P. R. II. 227; the .. worth of this
pure cause : C. 793.

Worthily, adv. deservedly, justly :
P. L. XI. 524.

Worthless, adj. destitute of excellence or virtue : S. A. 1020.

Worthy, adj. (1) having such qualities as to be deserving of esteem,
trust, praise, or honour : P. L.
IV. 291; the worthy bidden guest :
L. 118; worthy deeds : P. L. XII.
161; comp., thou ... worthier canst
not be : P. L. V. 76; things : P. R.
II. 195; sup., when he who rules is
worthiest : P. L. VI. 177; thou,
who worthiest art : P. R. III. 226;
deed : S. A. 276, 369.

(2) having such qualities as to
be deserving of, or suitable for,
some specified place or thing ; no
worthy match for valour : S. A.
1164.

(b) with prep. inf. : P. L. VIII.
584; IX. 746; worthy to have not
remained : P. R. I. 17; sup.;
such music worthiest were to blaze :
A. 74; worthiest to be so : P. L.
III. 310; to be all had in remembrance : P. L. III. 703; to be
obeyed : P. L. VI. 185; to be heir :
P. L. VI. 707; to reign : P. L.
VI. 888.

(c) with acc.; worthy well thy
cherishing : P. L. VIII. 568; with
clause ; worthy that thou shouldst :
C. 788.

(d) worthy of; fit for, suited to,
equal in excellence : P. L. IV.
241; to show him worthy of his
birth : P. R. I. 141; comp., seat

worthier of gods : P. L. IX. 100;
meriting, deserving : P. R. II.
445; men not worthy of fame :
P. R. III. 70; worthy of sacred
silence : P. L. V. 557; found
worthy not of liberty alone : P. L.
VI. 420.

absol. (a) pl. eminent persons ;
what do these worthies : P. R. III.
74.

(b) comp. his worthier, one more
deserving of honour than himself :
P. L. VI. 180; P. R. I. 27.

(c) sup. the most esteemed or
honoured persons ; the worthiest :
P. L. I. 759.

See **Ill-worthy.**

Wound, (1) sb. (a) a hurt or injury
caused by external violence, a
breach of the flesh and skin : P.
L. II. 168; VI. 405, 435; wide
was the wound : P. L. VIII. 467;
the local wounds of head or heel :
P. L. XII. 387; exempt from
wound : P. L. IX. 486; the body's
wounds and sores : S. A. 607;
gave Samson his death's wound :
S. A. 1581; Adonis ... waxing well
of his deep wound : C. 1000;
Thammuz ... whose annual wound
in Lebanon : P. L. I. 447; festered,
immedicable : S. A. 186, 620; mortal, ghastly : P. L. VI. 348, 368;
discontinuous : P. L. VI. 329.

(b) in various figurative senses ;
with ten wounds the river-dragon
(Pharaoh) tamed at length : P. L.
XII. 190; Death his death's wound
shall then receive : P. L. III. 252;
Earth felt the wound : P. L. IX.
782; wounds of deadly hate : P.
L. IV. 99; of the final overthrow
of Satan ; fatal, long-threatened,
deadliest : P. R. I. 53, 59; IV.
622; of sin; thy death's wound :
P. L. XII. 392.

(c) an opening in the earth's
crust ; opened into the hill a
spacious wound : P. L. I. 689.

(2) vb. tr. (a) to hurt by violence; Thammuz yearly wounded :
P. L. I. 452.

(b) to hurt the feelings of,
grieve, pain : P. L. XI. 299; P.
R. I. 404.

part. adj. (1) **wounding,** causing
pain ; wounding smart : Cir. 25.
(2) **wounded,** mortally hurt ;
wounded Thammuz : N. O. 204.

Wrack, sb. destruction, ruin ; a
world devote to universal wrack :

P. L. XI. 821 ; *all Heaven had gone to wrack* : P. L. VI. 670 ; *the Elements ... had gone to wrack* : P. L. IV. 994 ; the tumult of a storm bringing ruin ; *I heard the wrack* : P. R. IV. 452.

Wrap, *vb.* (*pret.* not used ; *past part.* wrapt) (*a*) to envelop or enfold with something thrown or wound around ; *the ... child ... wrapt in a rude manger lies* : N. O. 31 ; *wrapt in chains* : P. L. II. 183.

(*b*) to envelop so as to conceal ; *wrapt in mist of midnight vapour* : P. L. IX. 158.

(*c*) wholly to engross ; *wrapt in a pleasing fit of melancholy* : C. 546.

Wrath, *sb.* (*a*) deep, determined, and lasting anger ; *the wrath of stern Achilles* : P. L. IX. 14 ; *the wrath of Jove* : C. 803.

(*b*) that in God which is opposed to sin and manifests itself in punishing the same : P. L. I. 110, 220 ; II. 734 ; III. 264 ; IV. 912 ; V. 890 ; VI. 826 ; X. 95, 340, 795, 834 ; Cir. 23 ; Ps. II. 10 ; *some worse way his wrath may find to our destruction* : P. L. II. 83 ; *his wrath, which He calls justice* : P. L. II. 733 ; *flames, the sign of wrath awaked* : P. L. VI. 59 ; *eternal wrath burnt after them* : P. L. VI. 865 ; *if once his wrath take fire* : Ps. II. 27 ; *to appease thy wrath* : P. L. III. 406 ; *over wrath grace shall abound* : P. L. XII. 478 ; *wrath without end on Man* : P. L. X. 797 ; *ill able to sustain his full wrath* : P. L. X. 951 ; *to slake his wrath* : D. F. I. 66 ; *smoking, fierce* : Ps. LXXX. 19 ; LXXXV. 11 ; rather the just punishment of sin by God ; *his doom reserved him to more wrath* : P. L. I. 54 ; *which way shall I fly infinite wrath* : P. L. IV. 74 ; *denouncing wrath to come* : P. L. XI. 815 ; the expression of God's anger ; *without wrath or reviling* : P. L. X. 1048 ; *into* or *under wrath*, under the just condemnation of God : P. L. III. 275 ; S. A. 1683.

(*c*) uncontrolled passion, rage : P. L. II. 688.

Wrathful, *adj.* angry, raging : Ps. CXXXVI. 10.

Wreak, *vb. tr.* (*a*) to take vengeance

for, revenge ; *to wreak on ... Man his loss* : P. L. IV. 11.

(*b*) to execute or inflict as a revenge ; *on me let Death wreak all his rage* : P. L. III. 241.

Wreath, *sb.* (*a*) a twisted band ; *for whom bind'st thou in wreaths thy golden hair* : Hor. O. 4 ; of flowers : C. 850 ; a chaplet ; *a crown ... is but a wreath of thorns* : P. R. II. 459 ; fig., *Worcester's laureate wreath* : S. XVI. 9.

(*b*) something resembling a twisted band ; *smoke to roll in dusky wreaths* : P. L. VI. 58 ; (the serpent) *curled many a wanton wreath* : P. L. IX. 517.

Wreathe (wreathèd, *disyl.* : L'A. 28), *vb. tr.* (*a*) to form into a circular band ; *the garland wreathed for Eve* : P. L. IX. 892.

(*b*) to surround with a wreath of ; *his ... locks, with ivy berries wreathed* : C. 55 ; with that which is twisted as a wreath ; *faces with ... turbants wreathed* : P. R. IV. 76.

(*c*) to twist, intertwine : P. L. IV. 346.

part. adj. **wreathed,** that curve or twist the lines of the face (?) ; *wreathed smiles* : L'A. 28.

Wreck, *vb. intr.* (*a*) to suffer shipwreck : S. A. 1044.

(*b*) *fig.* to suffer moral ruin : P. R. II. 228.

Wrench, *vb. tr.* to twist from the proper intent or use, pervert : S. XXI. 4.

Wrest, *vb. tr.* to take away by violence ; *Why is life given to be thus wrested from us ?* : P. L. XI. 503.

with *from* = to compel one to part with ; *the secret wrested from me* : S. A. 384 ; to compel one to do or perform ; *doings which not will, but misery, have wrested from me* : P. R. I. 470.

Wrestler, *sb.* one who wrestles as a professional athlete : S. A. 1324.

Wretched, *adj.* (*a*) suffering from or characterized by extreme misery or distress : P. R. I. 345 ; *life, state* : P. L. X. 985 ; XI. 501 ; probably with the added idea of despicable : P. L. XII. 74.

(*b*) poor, worthless, mean : L. 124.

Wring, *vb. tr.* to extort ; *to wring from me ... my secret* : S. A. 1199

Wrinkle, *vb. tr.* to contract into furrows and ridges ; *wrinkled the face of deluge* : P. L. XI. 843.

part. adj. **wrinkled**, marked with wrinkles ; *Nereus' wrinkled look* : C. 871 : *wrinkled Care* : L'A. 31.

Wrist, *sb.* the part of the arm immediately adjoining the hand : C. 834.

Writ, *sb.* that which is written ; *Holy Writ*, the New Testament Scriptures : P. R. II. 8 ; *Prophetic Writ*, the Old Testament Scriptures : P. R. III. 184.

Write, *vb.* (*pret.* wrote ; *past part.* written : P. L. XII. 506, 513 ; P. R. I. 347 ; IV. 175, 556, 560 ; writ : P. L. I. 260 ; S. A. 657 ; S. XI. 1 ; XIII. 7 ; F. of C. 20), (1) *tr.* (*a*) to set down or inscribe on a surface by means of letters ; *the Lord shall write it in a scroll* : Ps. LXXXVII. 21 ; *new Presbyter is but old Priest writ large* : F. of C. 20.

(*b*) to express or communicate in writing ; *their story written left* : P. L. XII. 506 ; *what was writ concerning the Messiah* : P. R. I. 260 ; *what the Prophets wrote* : P. R. IV. 226 ; *Is it not written* : P. R. I. 347 ; *it is written* : P. R. IV. 175, 556, 560.

fig., *if ... heaven write aught of of fate* : P. R. IV. 383.

(*c*) to compose as an author : S. A. 657 ; *A Book was writ* : S. XI. 1.

(*d*) to style or entitle in writing ; *thou shalt be writ the man* : S. XIII. 7 ; with double object ; *that I should write thee sin or blame* : P. L. IV. 758.

(*e*) to impress durably ; *the law of faith ... upon their hearts shall write* : P. L. XII. 489.

(2) *intr.* (*a*) to trace or inscribe letters on a surface : P. 34.

(*b*) to express ideas in writing : P. R. IV. 227.

part. adj. **written**, set down in writing : P. L. XII. 513.

Writhe, *vb. tr.* to twist with violence as in agony : P. L. X. 569.

refl., *Satan ... writhed him to and fro* : P. L. VI. 328.

Wrong, (1) *adj.* violating the law of right and justice : Ps. LXXXII. 6.

(2) *sb.* (*a*) that which deviates

from justice and the moral law ; *to affect the wrong ?* : S. A. 1030 ; *spake much of right and wrong* : P. L. XI. 666.

(*b*) an act involving injustice to another, injury, harm : S. A. 76 ; *the offered wrong* : P. L. IX. 300 ; *indignation at his wrong* : P. L. IX. 666 ; *they to me never did wrong or violence* : P. R. I. 389 ; *the sparrow, freed from wrong* : Ps. LXXXIV. 9 ; *no wrong ... deprives them of their outward liberty* : P. L. XII. 98 ; pl. : P. R. III. 93 ; S. A. 105 ; P. 11.

(3) *vb. tr.* to inflict injustice or injury on : P. L. IV. 387.

Wroth, *adj.* moved by violent resentment and indignation, wrathful : N. O. 171.

X

Xerxes, *sb.* the King of Persia : P. L. X. 307.

Y

Yawn, *vb. intr.* to gape, open wide, be ready to engulf ; *Hell at last, yawning* : P. L. VI. 875.

part. adj. **yawning**, wide open and ready to engulf ; *yawning Grave* : P. L. X. 635.

Ychained : N. O. 155. *See* **Chain**, *vb.*

Yclept : L'A. 12. *See* **Clepe**.

*****Ye**, *pers. pron.* (*dat.* and *acc.* ye) (1) referring to the person addressed ; *sing.* : C. 438 ; *pl. nom.* : P. L. I. 322 ; II. 283 ; III. 341 ; IV. 366 ; *dat.* or *acc.* : P. L. IV. 368 ; V. 789 ; X. 40 ; P. R. II. 141 ; A. 81, 101 ; following a *prep.* ; *which of ye* : P. L. III. 214.

(*b*) interchanging with *you* in the context ; *ye ... you find* : P. L. I. 318 ; *Ye ... do as you have in charge* : P. L. VI. 565 ; *have you let the false enchanter scape ? O ye mistook* : C. 815.

(*d*) any person, as antecedent of *rel. pron.* : Ps. VI. 16.

(*c*) referring to various things with more, less, or no personification ; to Birds, etc. : P. L. IV. 197, 200 ; Death and Sin : P. L. II. 840 ; dolphins : L. 164 ; the Elements : P. L. V. 180 ; Faith, Hope, Chastity : C. 216 ; flowers :

P. L. XI. 277 ; gates : P. L. VII. 565 ; the Heavens : P. L. VII. 566 ; hills and dales : P. L. VIII. 275 ; laurels, myrtles : L. I. 2 ; Mists and Exhalations : P. L. V. 185 ; night and shades : C. 581 ; Pines, pines, cedars : P. L. V. 193 ; IX. 1088, 1089 ; Powers and Spirits of chaos : P. L. II. 968 ; rivers, woods : P. L. VIII. 275 ; shame and honour : P. L. IV. 315 ; the spheres : N. O. 125 ; stars : C. 331 ; stratagems : P. R. I. 180 ; thoughts : P. L. IX. 473 ; valleys : L. 136 ; waters : P. L. VII. 283 ; waves : P. L. VII. 216 ; Winds : P. L. V. 192.

(2) persons indefinitely ; without antecedent : P. L. III. 489 ; M. W. 22.

Yea, *adv.* used to intensify or amplify what has gone before : P. L. I. 387 ; IV. 207 ; P. R. I. 117 ; V. Ex. 87 ; C. 428, 591.

Yeanling, *sb. attrib.* that are the young of goats ; *yeanling kids* : P. L. III. 434.

Year, *sb.* (*a*) the period of the earth's revolution round the sun : P. L. III. 40 ; P. R. III. 234 ; S. XXII. 5 ; *hours, or days, or months, or years* : P. L. VIII. 69 ; *days, months, and years* : P. L. III. 581 ; *for seasons, and for days, and circling years* : P. L. VII. 342 ; *the months and years* : C. 114 ; *a year of glut* : Ps. IV. 33 ; *years of barrenness* : M. W. 64 ; *of mourning* : S. A. 1712 ; *seventy, twice six, twelve, two* : P. L. XII. 345 ; P. R. I. 210 ; II. 96 ; V. Ex. 6 ; *three years' day* : S. XXII. 1 ; *my three-and-twentieth year* : S. II. 2 ; *many* : P. L. XI. 534 ; P. R. II. 80 ; *the years of men,* the years as men reckon time : P. R. I. 48.

(*b*) a particular part of this period, season : *the mellowing year* : L. 5 ; *from year to year,* each spring : S. I. 11.

(*c*) a vast cycle ; *Heaven's great year* : P. L. V. 583.

(*d*) *pl.* time of life, age : P. R. I. 206 ; III. 40 ; *young in years* : S. XVII. 1 ; *thy years are ripe, ripe years* : P. R. III. 31, 37 ; *till length of years ... craze my limbs* : S. A. 570 ; *unless ... years, damp my intended wing* : P. L. IX. 45.

Yearly, *adv.* once a year, annually : P. L. I. 452 ; X. 575.

Yell, *vb. intr.* to cry out with a sharp loud noise : P. R. IV. 629 ; *hellish furies ... yelled* : P. R. IV. 423.

part. adj. **yelling** ; crying out with such a noise ; *these yelling monsters* : P. L. II. 795.

Yellow, *adj.* being of a colour resembling that of gold ; *the yellow sheaf* : P. L. XI. 435 ; *cowslip* : M. M. 4.

Yellow-skirted, *adj.* wearing yellow skirts : N. O. 235.

Yes, *adv.* the word expressing affirmation : C. 584.

Yesterday, *sb.* the day next preceding the present day : P. L. V. 675.

***Yet,** *adv.* (*a*) at the present time, now ; *as one whose drouth, yet scarce allayed* : P. L. VII. 67 ; *Shall I to him make known as yet my change* : P. L. IX. 818 ; superfluous ; *ere yet dim Night her shadowy cloud withdraws* : P. L. V. 685.

(*b*) still, now as formerly ; in continuance of a previous state ; P. L. I. 153 ; IV. 534 ; *the...crowd stood yet aloof* : P. L. I. 380 ; *princely counsel in his face yet shone* : P. L. II. 304 ; *if these magnific titles yet remain* : P. L. V. 773.

(*c*) up to this or the present time, thus far, hitherto ; *worse than fables yet have feigned* : P. L. II. 627 ; *sin ... yet hath wrought insensibly* : P. L. VI. 691 ; *the end of all yet done* : P. L. VII. 506 ; preceded by a negative : P. L. I. 16, 364 ; V. 420 ; VII. 536 ; followed by a negative : P. L. I. 591 ; V. 782 ; VI. 466 ; VII. 331 ; VIII. 206 ; *as yet* : P. L. V. 577 ; VII. 276 ; X. 951.

(*d*) in addition, besides, still : P. L. III. 83 ; *yet once more he shall stand* : P. L. III. 178 ; *is there yet no other way* : P. L. XI. 527 ; *Much thou hast yet to see* : P. L. XII. 8 ; with comparatives : P. L. IV. 142 ; VI. 602.

(*e*) after all, as matters stand, though the case be such ; *what may be yet regained in Heaven* : P. L. I. 269 ; *But yet all is not done* : P. L. III. 203 ; *which taught thee yet no better* : P. L. IV. 915.

(*f*) nevertheless, notwithstanding : P. L. I. 94, 415, 463, 493, 611 ; II. 137, 331 ; IV. 389 ; V. 116 ; *which, if not victory, is yet revenge* : *?*. L. II. 105 ; *his thoughts were low ... Yet he pleased the ear* : P. L. II. 117 ; *Firm they might have stood, yet fell* : P. L. VI. 912.

(*g*) however : P. L. IV. 61, 373 ; *yet from those flames no light* : P. L. I. 62 ; *saved who will ; yet not of will in him* : P. L. III. 174.

Yield, *vb.* I. *tr.* (1) to bear, produce : P. L. V. 401 ; VII. 541 ; *whatever Earth ... yields* : P. L. V. 338 ; *vines yield nectar* : P. L. V. 428 ; *herb yielding seed* : P. L. VII. 310 ; *fruit-tree yielding fruit* : P. L. VII. 311 ; *a tree ... to yield his fruit* : Ps. I. 9.

(*b*) to furnish, provide ; with *acc.* and *dat.*; *fruits, which the compliant boughs yielded them* : P. L. IV. 333..

(*c*) to emit ; *a row of starry lamps ... yielded light* : P. L. I. 729.

(2) to afford, give, grant, confer : P. L. II. 24 ; with *acc.* and *dat.* : Ps. LXXXIII. 59 ; *this rest their superstition yields me* : S. A. 15 ; *if any clime perhaps might yield them easier habitation* : P. L. II. 573.

(*b*) to be the cause of affording or allowing ; *whether scorn or satiate fury yield it* (the occasion) *from our Foe* : P. L. I. 179.

(3) to give up as to a superior power, relinquish, surrender : S. A. 259, 593 ; *till death ... to better life shall yield him* : P. L. XI. 42 ; *to realities yield all her shows* : P. L. VIII. 575 ; with *up* : P. L. X. 628 ; *that sober race of men ... shall yield up all their virtue* : P. L. XI. 623 ; with *acc.* and *dat.*; *these in their dark nativity the Deep shall yield us* : P. L. VI. 483.

(*b*) to quit possession of ; *this which yields or fills all space, the ambient Air* : P. L. VII. 88.

(4) to allow as a right : P. L. IV. 310 ; *subjection ... by her yielded* : P. L. IV. 309.

(*b*) to concede ; with two *acc.* ; *I yield it just* : P. L. XI. 526 ; with *acc.* and *dat.*; *I the praise yield thee* : P. L. IX. 1021.

II. *intr.* (1) to acknowledge the supremacy of another, surrender, give up : P. L. IV. 489 ; *courage never to submit or yield* : P. L. I. 108 ; *when everlasting Fate shall yield to fickle Chance* : P. L. II. 232 ; *now to Death I yield* : P. L. III. 245 ; *thy temperance ... for no allurement yields to appetite* : P. R. II. 409 ; *to the public good private respects must yield* : S. A. 868 ; to give place to ; *silence yields to the night-warbling bird* : P. L. V. 39.

(2) to consent, comply : S. A. 407, 848 ; *to short absence I could yield* : P. L. IX. 248 ; with *prep. inf.; how hast thou yielded to transgress* : P. L. IX. 902.

Yoke, (1) *sb.* (*a*) the curved piece of timber fitted with bows at each end to receive the necks of draftanimals ; always used *fig.* as an emblem of submission or slavery, either physical or moral, or both ; *free thy people from their yoke!* : P. R. II. 48 ; *the nations under yoke* : P. R. IV. 135 ; *overlay with bridges rivers proud, as with a yoke* : P. R. III. 334 ; *servile* : P. R. IV. 102 ; *the Roman yoke* : P. R. I. 217 ; *a province under Roman yoke* : P. R. III. 158 ; *Philistian yoke* : S. A. 39, 42 ; the submission or slavery being to God ; *thou with thy compeers used to the yoke* : P. L. IV. 975 ; *teach us to cast off this yoke!* : P. L. V. 786 ; *God and his just yoke* : P. L. X. 1045 ; *the easy yoke of servile pomp* : P. L. II. 256 ; *the yoke of God's Messiah* : P. L. V. 882 ; *mild* : S. XIX. 11.

(*b*) a pair of animals yoked together ; *Cynthia checks her dragon yoke* : Il P. 59.

(2) *vb. tr.* to bring into bondage, subdue, enslave : Ps. LXXXVII. 12 ; *Xerxes, the liberty of Greece to yoke* : P. L. X. 307 ; *effeminacy held me yoked* : S. A. 410.

Yon, (1) *adj.* yonder ; *yon lake* : P. L. I. 280 ; followed by another *adj.* : P. L. I. 180 ; IV. 1011 ; C. 295 ; S. I. 1 ; *yon boiling ocean* : P. L. II. 183 ; *flowery arbours* : P. L. IV. 626 ; *western cloud* : P. L. XI. 205 ; *princely shrine* : A. 36.

(2) *adv.* in that place, there ; *Him that yon soars on golden wing* : Il P. 52.

Yonder, *adj.* being at a distance and in the place indicated by word, gesture, or glance : P. L. II. 684 ; IV. 626 ; IX. 218 ; X. 617 ; XII. 142, 591 ; S. A. 3 ; followed by another adj. ; *yonder shady bower* : P. L. V. 367 ; *starry sphere* : P. L. V. 620 ; *blazing cloud* : P. L. XI. 229 ; *nether world* : P. L. XI. 328.

Yore, *sb.* long of yore, of old time, long ago : Il P. 23.

*****You,** *pers. pron.* (*dat.* and *acc.* you) (1) referring to the person addressed ; *sing.* : P. L. II. 1007 ; S. A. 1511 ; *pl. nom.* : P. L. I. 320 ; V. 537 ; VI. 566 ; *you two this way...descend* : P. L. X. 397 ; *dat. or acc.* : P. L. IV. 374, 829 ; V. 491 ; VI. 812 ; IX. 686 ; S. A. 1644 ; C. 43 ; *to entertain you two* : P. L. IV. 382.

(*b*) referring to personifications; to Mirth, Sport, etc. : L'A. 33 ; Joys : Il P. 3. *See* **Thou** and **Ye.**

Young, *adj.* (*a*) being in the early period of life, not yet arrived at maturity, not old : P. R. II. 18 ; C. 492, 498 ; *African* : P. R. III. 101 ; *young Adonis* : C. 999 ; *Bacchus* : P. L. IV. 279 ; *Hyacinth* : D. F. I. 25 ; *Pompey* : P. R. III. 35 ; *Scipio* : P. R. III. 34 ; *Daniel* : P. R. II. 329 ; *Lycidas, swain* : L. 9, 113 ; *Vane, young in years* : S. XVII. 1 ; *you are but young* : C. 755.

comp. : P. L. XII. 160 ; *Saturn* : P. L. I. 512 ; *hands* : P. L. IX. 246 ; hence, strong and active ; *your younger feet* : S. A. 336.

sup. : *Man...thy youngest son* : P. L. III. 151.

(*b*) being in the early stage of growth ; *the young branch* : Ps. LXXX. 63.

absol. (*a*) persons in the early part of life : P. L. XI. 668 ; L'A. 97.

(*b*) the offspring of birds collectively ; *to lay her young* : Ps. LXXXIV. 11 ; *forth disclosed their callow young* : P. L. VII. 420.

Youngest-teemed (teemèd, *disyl.*), *adj.* latest born ; *fig.*, *Heaven's youngest-teemed star* : N. O. 240.

*****Your,** *poss. pron.* of or belonging to you ; (1) referring to a person or persons ; with sb. ; *sing.* : P. L. II. 1007 ; IV. 954 ; V. 408 ; *pl.* : P. L. II. 19, 29 ; IV. 367 ; *will ye submit your necks* : P. L. V. 787 ;

your dauntless virtue : P. L. IX. 694 ; *your once gloried friend* : S. A. 334 ; *obj. gen.* : A. 100 ; without sb. ; *three fair branches of your own* : C. 969.

(2) referring to various things with more, less, or no personification ; to Air, Elements : P. L. V. 183 ; Birds : P. L. V. 199 ; Chaos and Night : P. L. II. 972 ; flowers : P. L. XI. 299 ; the Heavens : P. L. VII. 566 ; Joys : Il P. 4 ; laurels, myrtles : L. 3 ; Mists and Exhalations : P. L. V. 187 ; moon and stars : C. 336 ; Pines : P. L. V. 193 ; the Spheres : N. O. 128 ; valleys : L. 139 ; Voice and Verse : S. M. 3 ; Waves and the Deep : P. L. VII. 217 ; woods, fountains, etc. : P. L. X. 861.

Yours, *poss. pron.* that or those belonging to you ; referring to preceding sb. ; *Heaven — once yours* : P. L. I. 316 ; *our happy state hold, as you yours* : P. L. V. 537 ; *these numerous orbs, all yours* : P. L. X. 398 ; *to a following sb.* ; *yours be the advantage* : P. L. II. 987 ; *this quest of yours* : A. 34 ; *absol.* your power ; *Discourse is oftest yours* : P. L. V. 489.

Yourself, *pron.* (*pl.* yourselves) (1) emphatic ; *not to know me argues yourselves unknown* : P. L. IV. 830.

(2) *refl.* *if ye know yourselves* : P. L. V. 789 ; with a *prep.*, so *cruel to yourself* : C. 679.

Youth, *sb.* (1) the state or condition of being young, youthfulness : P. L. XI. 594 ; *in his face youth smiled* : P. L. III. 638 ; *the air of youth* : P. L. XI. 542 ; *his blithe youth* : C. 55 ; *thou must outlive thy youth* : P. L. XI. 539 ; personified : C. 1011.

(*b*) hence, innocence, purity ; *Heaven hath timely tried their youth* : C. 970.

(*c*) the feelings or emotions of the young ; *May, that dost inspire mirth, and youth* : M. M. 6.

(2) the period between childhood and manhood, adolescence ; *in manhood where youth ended* : P. L. XI. 246 ; *in his prime youth* : P. R. II. 200 ; *thy childhood, and thy youth* : P. R. IV. 508 ; *earliest* : S. IX. 1 ; *Time, the subtle thief of youth* : S. II. 1 ; or the meaning

may be (**1**) ; *his growth now to youth's full flower* : P. R. I. 67 ; *in my flower of youth* : S. A. 938.

(**3**) a young person : L'A. 95 ; *slender* : Hor. O. 1 ; *tall stripling youths* : P. R. II. 352 ; *that Pellean conqueror, a youth* : P. R. II. 197 ; applied to Lycidas : L. 164 ; to the Elder Brother : C. 609 ; to mercy (?) personified : D. F. I. 53.

(*b*) young persons collectively ; *the unarmed youth of Heaven* : P. L. IV. 552 ; *their choicest youth* : S. A. 264 ; *all the valiant youth* : S. A. 1738 ; applied *fig.* to bees ; *pour forth their populous youth* : P. L. I. 770.

Youthful, *adj.* (*a*) being in the early period of life ; *youthful poets* : L'A. 129.

(*b*) pertaining, belonging, or suitable to the early period of life ; · *youthful dalliance, jollity* : P. L. IV. 338 ; L'A. 26 ; *beauty, bloom* : P. L. IV. 845 ; C. 289 ; *courage, thoughts* : S. A. 524 ; C. 669 ; like those of youth ; *wherefore comes old Manoa...with youthful steps ?* : S. A. 1442.

(*c*) fresh, new ; *the snake, with youthful coat* : P. L. X. 218.

See **Star-ypointing.**

Z

Zalmunna, *sb.* one of the kings of Midian : Ps. LXXXIII. 43. *See* **Zeba.**

Zeal, *sb.* ardour for a cause or a person, enthusiastic devotion : P. L. V. 849, 900 ; P. R. III. 171, 175, 407 ; S. A. 895 ; *the well-feasted priest then soonest fired with zeal* : S. A. 1420 ; *a flame of zeal* : P. L. V. 807 ; *cooled in zeal* : P. L. XI. 801 ; *none with more zeal adored the Deity* : P. L. V. 805 ; *ambition varnished o'er with zeal* : P. L. II. 485 ; *his zeal of right* : P. L. IX. 676 ; *acts of zeal and love* : P. L. V. 593 ; *show of zeal and love to Man* : P. L. IX. 665 ;

zeal to Israel : P. R. III. 412 ; *blind* : P. L. III. 452.

Zealous, *adj.* filled with ardour, incited by an eager desire : P. L. IV. 565.

Zealously, *adv.* with ardour, fervently : S. IX. 9.

Zeb, *sb.* Zeeb, a prince of Midian ; spelled Zeb in Vulg. ; *as Zeb and Oreb evil sped* : Ps. LXXXIII. 41.

Zeba, *sb.* one of the two kings of Midian who appear to have commanded the invasion of Canaan, and who fell by the hand of Gideon ; *as Zeba and Zalmunna bled* : Ps. LXXXIII. 43.

Zenith, *sb.* the highest point in the celestial hemisphere : P. L. I. 745 ; the highest point in the universe or cosmos : P. L. X. 329.

Zephon, *sb.* a cherub : P. L. IV. 788, 834, 854, 868.

Zephyr, *sb.* Zephyrus ; *to recommend cool Zephyr* : P. L. IV. 329 ; *Eurus and Zephyr* : P. L. X. 705 ; personified ; *Zephyr with Aurora playing* : L'A. 19.

Zephyrus, *sb.* the west wind ; personified ; *Zephyrus on Flora breathes* : P. L. V. 16.

Zodiac, *sb.* the belt of twelve constellations encircling the heavens and extending about 8° on each side of the ecliptic : P. L. XI. 247 ; XII. 255.

Zone, *sb.* (*a*) a girdle worn as an article of dress ; *the zone of Venus* : P. R. II. 214 ; probably with reference to (*c*) ; *the middle pair* (of wings) *girt like a starry zone his waist* : P. L. V. 281.

(*b*) a surrounding band ; *the Galaxy ... as a circling zone thou seest* : P. L. VII. 580.

(*c*) the Zodiac ; *the Sun...begins his other half in the great zone of heaven* : P. L. V. 560.

(*d*) a region ; *in some wild zone dwell* : P. L. II. 397.

Zophiel, *sb.* a cherub : P. L. VI. 535.

Zora, *sb.* a town a short distance south of Eshtaol : S. A. 181. *See* **Eshtaol.**

ADDITIONS AND CORRECTIONS.

p. 11 under **Alcairo** for '*See* Memphis' read '*See* **Memphian.**'

p. 12 under **All-conquering** for 'P. L. x. 951' read 'P. L. x. 591.'

p. 20 under **Archangel** delete 'P. L. III. 445, 446.'

p. 28 under **Avail** (1) for 'P. R.' read 'P. L.'

p. 35 add '*See* **Sea-beast.**'

p. 41 under **Bind** (1) (a) add 'P. L. IX. 210.'

p. 46 for '**Thrice-bolted**' read '**Three-bolted.**'

p. 49 under **Break** (1) (a) add 'Ps. III. 23.'

p. 62 under **Change** II. (b) add 'with *acc.* and **with**: P. L. IV. 893.'

p. 75 under **Confidence** (b) delete 'P. L. VI. 651'; (a) add '*concr.* that in which trust is placed: P. L. VI. 651.'

p. 95 under **Deep** III. (2) add 'V. Ex. 33.'

p. 98 under **Dense** add 'here *absol.* matter that is compact.'

p. 115 under **Drouth** (a) instead of 'C. 298' read 'C. 928.'

p. 117 under **Early** (1) add '(d) acting without delay, timely: M. W. 23.'

p. 119 under **East** (3) for '**East India**' read '**India East.**'

p. 125 under **End** II. (2) (a) delete 'S. A. 1043' and add it to II. (1) (b).

p. 130 under **Estate** (a) add 'Ps. LXXXII. 15.'

p. 145 under **Favourable**, for ('fávoráble') read ('fávouráble').

p. 147 add '*See* **New-felt.**'

p. 157 under **Flower** II. add '*part. adj.* flowering, opening, unfolding (?); like that coming from flowers?: P. L. V. 293.'

p. 160 under **For** add '(o) in spite of, notwithstanding: D. F. I. 33.'

p. 164 under **Found** (d) add 'P. L. I. 427.'

p. 179 under **Go** (c) add 'Ps. LXXXII. 20.'

p. 180 under **Godhead** for 'P. L. VII. 125' read 'P. L. VII. 175.'

p. 183 under **Grain** add '(f) hue, colour: C. 750.'

p. 193 add '*See* **Timely-happy.**'

p. 200 under **Heaven** (4) delete 'P. L. VII. 215' and add it to (1) (b).

p. 201 under **Heaven** (8) add 'V. Ex. 48'; (9) for 'V. Ex. 44' read 'V. Ex. 33.'

p. 207 under **High** II. (b) add 'P. L. IV. 90.'

p. 243 under **King** (1) add 'Ps. II. 2.'

p. 251 under **Lay** (c) add 'Ps. LXXXIV. 11.'

p. 262 under **Lightning** add '(in original text spelled light'ning: P. L. V. 734).'

p. 263 under **Lineament** for 'P. L. VII. 277' read 'P. L. VII. 477.'

p. 285 under **May** for 'protasis' read 'apodosis' and for 'apodosis' read 'protasis'; in (f) for 'P. L. V. 493' read 'P. L. V. 499.'

p. 291 under **Mexico** for 'country' read 'city.'

p. 291 add '*See* **Sea-mew.**'

p. 313, 314 under **Need** II. (1) delete 'P. L. III. 340' and add it to II. (2).

p. 321 for '*See* **Wood-notes**' read '*See* **Wood-note.**'

p. 337 for '**Self-opened**' read '**Self-open.**'

p. 356 under **Peace** (5) for 'S. 16' read 'T. 16.'

p. 357 under **Pencil** for 'paint-brush' read 'drawing-pencil.'

p. 371 add '*See* **Re-possess.**'

p. 372 under **Power** (1) for 'P. L. I. 637' read 'P. L. I. 753.'

p. 373 under **Power** (3) add 'Ps. II. 3.'

p. 446 under **Seduce** add 'P. L. II. 368; VI. 901; IX. 307; *absol.*: P. L. I. 178.'

p. 450 under **Seem** change 'P. L. IV. 316' from *vbl. sb.* to *part. adj.*

p. 452 under **Send** (1) (b) add 'S. XIII. 9.'

p. 456 under **Set** (1) add 'Ps. LXXXV. 44.'

p. 483 under **Smell** add '*part. adj.* smelling, giving out an odour: P. L. VII. 321.'

p. 504 under **Spring-time** for 'P. L. I. 669' read 'P. L. I. 769.'

p. 535 add '**Taint-worm,** *sb.* a noxious worm: L. 46.'

p. 601 under **Upstand** (b) for 'Ps. II. 22' read 'Ps. II. 2.'

COMPOUND WORDS AS OCCURRING IN THE ORIGINAL TEXT.

Love-tale : P. L. I. 452.
low-brow'd : L'A. 8.
low-rooft : P. R. IV. 273 ; P. 18.
low-thoughted : C. 6.

Man-slaughter : P. L. XI. 689.
meek-eyd : N. O. 46.
Mercie-seat : P. L. XI. 2 ; XII. 258.
mid-course : P. L. XI. 204.
mid-day : P. L. VIII. 112 ; C. 384.
mid-hours : P. L. V. 376.
mid-night : C. 130.
mid-noon : P. L. V. 311.
Mile-End : S. XI. 7.
mis-becoming : C. 372.
mis-doing : P. R. I. 225.
mis-used : C. 47.
Moon-lov'd : N. O. 236.
Musk-rose : L. 146.

neat-handed : L'A. 86.
neer-ushering : C. 279.
never-ending : P. L. II. 221.
never-sear : L. 2.
new-arriv'd : P. L. X. 26.
new-baptiz'd : P. R. II. 1.
new-born : N. O. 116.
new-declar'd : P. R. I. 121.
new-entrusted : C. 36.
new-made : P. L. VII. 617 ; Ps.
   CXXXVI. 26.
night-founder'd : P. L. I. 204 ; C.
   483.
Night-Hag : P. L. II. 662.
night-Raven : L'A. 7.
Night-steed : N. O. 236.
Night-wanderer : P. L. IX. 640.
night-warbling : P. L. VI. 40.
Noon-tide : P. L. II. 309.
North-East : P. L. IV. 161.
North-winde : P. L. XI. 838.
Nut-brown : L'A. 100.

off-spring : P. L. II. 310 ; P. R. II.
   440 ; III. 375 ; IV. 399 ; D. F. I.
   76 ; C. 34.
oft-invocated : S. A. 575.
oft-times : P. R. I. 472.
oughly-headed : C. 695.
out-cast : P. L. IV. 106.
out-cries : S. A. 1124.
out-flew : P. L. I. 663.
out-go : V. Ex. 79.
out-lasted : D. F. I. 3.
out-law : C. 399.
out-living : P. 7.
out-pow'rd : S. A. 544.
out-side : P. L. VIII. 596.
out-spread : Ps. LXXX. 6.
out-stretch'd : U. C. II. 17.
out-watch : Il P. 87.

out-worn : S. A. 580 ; Ps. LXXXVII.
   22.
over-cloy : Ps. IV. 34.
over-exquisite : C. 359.
over-heard : P. L. IX. 276.
over-just : S. A. 514.
over-labour'd : S. A. 1327.
over-lay : P. R. III. 333.
over-match : P. R. IV. 7.
over-match'd : P. R. II. 146.
over-multitude : C. 731.
over-pass'd : P. R. II. 198.
over-potent : S. A. 427.
over-powr'd : S. A. 880.
over-reach : P. L. X. 879.
over-reacht : P. L. IX. 313 ; P. R.
   IV. 11.
over-ripe : P. R. III. 31.
over-rul'd : P. L. III. 114 ; V. 527 ;
   VI. 228.
over-shadowing : P. R. IV. 148.
over-spread : Ps. LXXX. 42.
over-strong : S. A. 1590.
over-sure : P. R. II. 142.
over-tir'd : S. A. 1632.
over-watch't : S. A. 405.
over-weening : P. R. I. 147.

Padan-Aram : P. L. III. 513.
pale-ey'd : N. O. 180.
Palm-tree : P. L. VIII. 212.
pin-fold : C. 7.
Planet-strook : P. L. X. 413.
pre-ordain'd : P. R. I. 127.
Primrose-season : C. 671.
prison-house : S. A. 922.
pure-ey'd : C. 213.

Rain-bow : N. O. 143.
Ramath-lechi : S. A. 145.
re-admit : S. A. 1173.
re-ascend : P. L. I. 633.
Red-Sea : P. L. I. 306.
re-edifie : P. L. XII. 350.
re-enter : P. L. II. 397.
re-inspire : S. XX. 6.
re-install : P. R. IV. 615.
re-visit : P. L. III. 13.
River-dragon : P. L. XII. 191.
root-bound : C. 662.
rosie-boosom'd : C. 986.
rushy-fringed : C. 890.

sable-stoled : N. O. 220.
Sable-vested : P. L. II. 962.
Sail-broad : P. L. II. 927.
saphire-colour'd : S. M. 7.
scarce-well-lighted : M. W. 20.
Sea-beast : P. L. I. 200.
sea-faring : P. L. II. 288.
Sea-girt : C. 21 ; H. B. 9.

Sea-Idol : S. A. 13.
Sew-mews : P. L. XI. 831.
Sea-monsters : P. L. XI. 747.
sea-paths : Ps. VIII. 22.
seaventimes-wedded : P. L. V. 223.
self-ballanc't : P. L. VII. 242.
self-begot : P. L. V. 857.
self-begott'n : S. A. 1669.
self-consumed : C. 597.
self-destruction : P. L. X. 1016.
self-delusion : C. 365.
self-deprav'd : P. L. III. 130.
self-esteem : P. L. VIII. 572.
self-fed : C. 597.
self-kill'd : S. A. 1664.
self-knowing : P. L. VII. 510.
self-left : P. L. XI. 93.
self-lost : P. L. VII. 154.
self-love : S. A. 1031.
self-offence : S. A. 514.
self-opend : P. L. V. 254.
self-preservation : S. A. 505.
self-rais'd : P. L. I. 634 ; V. 857.
self-rigorous : S. A. 513.
self-rowld : P. L. IX. 183.
self-same : P. L. XI. 203 ; L. 2.
self-satisfying : S. A. 306.
self-severe : S. A. 827.
self-tempted : P. L. III. 130.
self-violence : S. A. 1584.
seven-times-folded : S. A. 1122.
shallow-searching : A. 41.
shame-fac't : N. O. 111.
Sheep-cote : P. R. II. 287, 288.
Sheep-hook : L. 120.
sheep-walks : P. L. XI. 431.
side-board : P. R. II. 350.
side-long : P. L. IV. 333 ; IX. 512.
side-ways : M. W. 42.
silver-buskind : A. 33.
silver-shafted : C. 442.
Sin-born : P. L. X. 596.
Sin-bred : P. L. IV. 315.
Sin-worn : C. 17.
skie-tinctur'd : P. L. V. 285.
slow-endeavouring : W. S. 9.
slow-pac't : P. L. V. 963.
smooth-dittied : C. 86.
smooth-hair'd : C. 716.
smooth-shaven : Il P. 66.
smooth-sliding : L. 86.
snaky-headed : C. 447.
Snow-soft : D. F. I. 19.
soft-ebbing : P. L. VII. 300.
sooth-saying : C. 874.
sound-board : P. L. I. 709.
sphear-born : S. M. 2.
sphear-metal : U. C. II. 5.
stall-reader : S. XI. 5.
Starr-bright : P. L. X. 450.
Star-led : N. O. 23.

Starr-light : P. L. IV. 656 ; C. 308.
Star-pav'd : P. L. IV. 976.
Star-proof : A. 89.
Star-ypointing : W. S. 4.
Stears-mate : S. A. 1045.
store-house : P. R. II. 103.
Straw-built : P. L. I. 773.
Sun-bright : P. L. VI. 100.
Sun-clad : C. 782.
Sun-light : P. L. IX. 1087.
Sun-rise : S. A. 1597.
Sun-shine : P. L. III. 616 ; C. 959.
Sweet-Briar : L'A. 47.
sweet-smelling : P. L. IV. 709.
Swift-rushing : D. F. I. 67.
Sword-Law : P. L. XI. 668.
Sword-players : S. A. 1323.

Taint-worm : L. 46.
tel-tale : C. 141.
ten-fold : P. R. I. 41.
thick-rammed : P. L. VI. 485.
thick-warbl'd : P. R. IV. 246.
thick-wov'n : P. L. IX. 437.
thither-ward : P. L. III. 500.
thorough-fare : P. L. X. 393.
three-bolted : P. L. VI. 764.
thunder-clasping : Ps. CXXXVI. 37.
Thunder-struck : P. L. VI. 858 ; P. R. I. 36.
timely-happy : S. VII. (II.) 8.
tinsel-slipper'd : C. 877.
tongue-batteries : S. A. 403.
tongue-doubtie : S. A. 1181.
triple-colour'd : P. L. XI. 893.
triple-mounted : P. L. VI. 572.
triple-row : P. L. VI. 651.
Turchestan-born : P. L. XI. 396.
twin-born : S. XII. 6.
twise-batter'd : N. O. 199.
two-handed : P. L. VI. 251 ; L. 130.

unhide-bound : P. L. X. 601.
up-borne : P. L. XI. 147.
up-grown : P. R. I. 140.
up-land : L'A. 92.
up-lift : P. L. I. 193.
up-lifted : S. M. 11.
up-lock : P. 45.
up-turns : P. L. X. 701.

vaut-brass : S. A. 1121.
various-measur'd : P. R. IV. 256.
vermeil-tinctured : C. 752.
Vertue-proof : P. L. V. 384.
Vice-gerent : P. L. V. 609.
Virgin-born : P. R. IV. 500.

watch-towre : L'A. 43.
way-lay : P. R. II. 185.
weather-beaten : P. L. II. 1043.

For Reference

Not to be taken from this room